MILITARY HISTORY
FROM PRIMARY SOURCES

WAR IN ANCIENT GREECE

EDITED AND INTRODUCED
BY BOB CARRUTHERS

Pen & Sword
MILITARY

This edition published in 2013 by
Pen & Sword Military
An imprint of
Pen & Sword Books Ltd
47 Church Street
Barnsley
South Yorkshire
S70 2AS

First published in Great Britain in 2012 in digital format by
Coda Books Ltd.

ISBN 978 1 78159 217 5

A CIP catalogue record for this book is
available from the British Library

Printed and bound by CPI Group (UK) Ltd, Croydon, CR0 4YY

Pen & Sword Books Ltd incorporates the Imprints of Pen & Sword Aviation, Pen &
Sword Family History, Pen & Sword Maritime, Pen & Sword Military, Pen & Sword
Discovery, Pen & Sword Politics, Pen & Sword Atlas, Pen & Sword Archaeology,
Wharncliffe Local History, Wharncliffe True Crime, Wharncliffe Transport, Pen &
Sword Select, Pen & Sword Military Classics, Leo Cooper, The Praetorian Press, Clay-
more Press, Remember When, Seaforth Publishing and Frontline Publishing

For a complete list of Pen & Sword titles please contact
PEN & SWORD BOOKS LIMITED
47 Church Street, Barnsley, South Yorkshire, S70 2AS, England
E-mail: enquiries@pen-and-sword.co.uk
Website: www.pen-and-sword.co.uk

CONTENTS

INTRODUCTION 4

CHAPTER I 6

CHAPTER II 22

CHAPTER III 46

CHAPTER IV 61

CHAPTER V 77

CHAPTER VI 98

CHAPTER VII 127

CHAPTER VIII 144

CHAPTER IX 169

CHAPTER X 198

CHAPTER XI 220

CHAPTER XII 238

CHAPTER XIII 264

CHAPTER XIV 283

CHAPTER XV 319

CHAPTER XVI 335

CHAPTER XVII 372

CHAPTER XVIII 381

CHAPTER XIX 402

CHAPTER XX 421

CHAPTER XXI 450

CHAPTER XXII 476

CHAPTER XXIII 483

CHAPTER XXIV 509

CHAPTER XXV 533

CHAPTER XXVI 556

INTRODUCTION

ANCIENT GREECE was a civilization belonging to a period of Greek history that lasted from the Archaic period of the 8th to 6th centuries BC to the end of antiquity (ca. 600 AD). Immediately following this period was the beginning of the Early Middle Ages and the Byzantine era. Included in Ancient Greece is the period of Classical Greece, which flourished during the 5th to 4th centuries BC. Classical Greece began with the repelling of a Persian invasion by Athenian leadership. Because of conquests by Alexander the Great, Hellenistic civilization flourished from Central Asia to the western end of the Mediterranean Sea.

Classical Greek culture, especially philosophy, had a powerful influence on the Roman Empire, which carried a version of it to many parts of the Mediterranean region and Europe, for which reason Classical Greece is generally considered to be the seminal culture which provided the foundation of modern Western culture.

At least in the Archaic Period, the fragmentary nature of ancient Greece, with many competing city-states, increased the frequency of conflict, but conversely limited the scale of warfare. Unable to maintain professional armies, the city-states relied on their own citizens to fight. This inevitably reduced the potential duration of campaigns, as citizens would need to return to their own professions (especially in the case of, for example, farmers). Campaigns would therefore often be restricted to summer. When battles occurred, they were usually set piece and intended to be decisive. Casualties were slight compared to later battles, rarely amounting to more than 5% of the losing side, but the slain often included the most prominent citizens and generals who led from the front.

The scale and scope of warfare in ancient Greece changed dramatically as a result of the Greco-Persian Wars. To fight the enormous armies of the Achaemenid Empire was effectively beyond the capabilities of a single city-state. The eventual triumph of the Greeks was achieved by alliances of city-states (the exact composition changing over time), allowing the pooling of resources and division of labour. Although alliances between city-states occurred before this time, nothing on this scale had been seen before. The rise of Athens and Sparta as pre-eminent powers during this conflict led directly to the Peloponnesian War, which saw further development of the nature of warfare, strategy and tactics. Fought between leagues of cities dominated by Athens and Sparta, the increased manpower and financial resources increased the scale, and allowed the diversification of warfare. Set-piece battles during the Peloponnesian war proved indecisive and instead there was increased reliance on attritionary strategies, naval battle and blockades and sieges. These changes greatly increased the number of casualties and the disruption of Greek society. Athens owned one of the largest war fleets in ancient Greece. It had over 200 triremes each powered by 170 oarsmen who were seated in 3 rows on each side of the ship. The city could afford such a large fleet-it had over 34,000 oars men-because it owned a lot of silver mines that were worked by slaves.

CHAPTER I

*The State of Greece from the Earliest Times to the
Commencement of the Peloponnesian War*

Bust of Thucydides

THUCYDIDES, AN Athenian, wrote the history of the war between the Peloponnesians and the Athenians, beginning at the moment that it broke out, and believing that it would be a great war and more worthy of relation than any that had preceded it. This belief was not without its grounds. The preparations of both the combatants were in every department in the last state of perfection; and he could see the rest of the Hellenic race taking sides in the quarrel; those who delayed doing so at once having it in contemplation. Indeed this was the greatest movement yet known in history, not only of the Hellenes, but of a large part of the barbarian world - I had almost said of mankind.

For though the events of remote antiquity, and even those that more immediately preceded the war, could not from lapse of time be clearly ascertained, yet the evidences which an inquiry carried as far back as was practicable leads me to trust, all point to the conclusion that there was nothing on a great scale, either in war or in other matters.

For instance, it is evident that the country now called Hellas had in ancient times no settled population; on the contrary, migrations were of frequent occurrence, the several tribes readily abandoning their homes under the pressure of superior numbers. Without commerce, without freedom of communication either by land or sea, cultivating no more of their territory than the exigencies of life required, destitute of capital, never planting their land (for they could not tell when an invader might not come and take it all away, and when he did come they had no walls to stop him), thinking that the necessities of daily sustenance could be supplied at one place as well as another, they cared little for shifting their habitation, and consequently neither built large cities nor attained to any other form of greatness. The richest soils were always most subject to this change of masters; such as the district now called Thessaly, Boeotia, most of the Peloponnese, Arcadia excepted, and the most fertile parts of the rest of Hellas. The goodness of the land favoured the aggrandizement of particular individuals, and thus created faction which proved a fertile source of ruin. It also invited invasion. Accordingly Attica, from the poverty of its soil enjoying from a very remote period freedom from faction, never changed its inhabitants. And here is no inconsiderable exemplification of my assertion that the migrations were the cause of there being no correspondent growth in other parts. The most powerful victims of war or faction from the rest of Hellas took refuge with the Athenians as a safe retreat; and at an early period, becoming naturalized, swelled the already large population of the city to such a height that Attica became at last too small to hold them, and they had to send out colonies to Ionia.

There is also another circumstance that contributes not a little to my conviction of the weakness of ancient times. Before the Trojan war there is no indication of any common action in Hellas, nor indeed of the universal prevalence of the name; on the contrary, before the time of Hellen, son of Deucalion, no such appellation existed, but the country went by the names of the different tribes, in particular of the Pelasgian. It was not till Hellen and his sons grew strong in Phthiotis, and were invited as allies into the other cities, that one by one they gradually acquired from the connection the name of Hellenes; though a long time elapsed before that name could fasten itself upon all. The best proof of this is furnished by Homer. Born long after the Trojan War, he nowhere calls all of them by that name, nor indeed any of them except the followers of Achilles from Phthiotis, who were the original Hellenes: in his poems they are called Danaans, Argives, and Achaeans. He does not even use the term barbarian, probably because the Hellenes had not yet been marked off from the rest of the world by one distinctive appellation. It appears therefore that the several Hellenic communities, comprising not only those who first acquired the name, city by city, as they came to understand each other, but also those who assumed it afterwards as the name of the whole people, were before the Trojan war prevented by their want of strength and the absence of mutual intercourse from displaying any collective action.

Indeed, they could not unite for this expedition till they had gained increased familiarity with the sea. And the first person known to us by tradition as having established a navy is Minos. He made himself master of what is now called the Hellenic sea, and ruled over the Cyclades, into most of which he sent the first colonies, expelling the Carians and appointing his own sons governors; and thus did his best to put down piracy in those waters, a necessary step to secure the revenues for his own use.

For in early times the Hellenes and the barbarians of the coast and islands, as communication by sea became more common, were tempted to turn pirates, under the conduct of their most powerful men; the motives being to serve their own cupidity and to support the needy. They would fall upon a town unprotected by walls, and consisting of a mere collection of villages, and would plunder it; indeed, this came to be the main source of their livelihood, no disgrace being yet attached to such an achievement, but even some glory. An illustration of this is furnished by the honour with which some of the inhabitants of the continent still regard a successful marauder, and by the question we find the old poets everywhere representing the people as asking of voyagers - "Are they pirates?" - as if those who are asked the question would have no idea of disclaiming the imputation, or their interrogators of reproaching them for it. The same rapine prevailed also by land.

And even at the present day many of Hellas still follow the old fashion, the Ozolian Locrians for instance, the Aetolians, the Acarnanians, and that region of the continent; and the custom of carrying arms is still kept up among these continentals, from the old piratical habits. The whole of Hellas used once to carry arms, their habitations being unprotected and their communication with each other unsafe; indeed, to wear arms was as much a part of everyday life with them as with the barbarians. And the fact that the people in these parts of Hellas are still living in the old way points to a time when the same mode of life was once equally common to all. The Athenians were the first to lay aside their weapons, and to adopt an easier and more luxurious mode of life; indeed, it is only lately that their rich old men left off the luxury of wearing undergarments of linen, and fastening a knot of their hair with a tie of golden grasshoppers, a fashion which spread to their Ionian kindred and long prevailed among the old men there. On the contrary, a modest style of dressing, more in conformity with modern ideas, was first adopted by the Lacedaemonians, the rich doing their best to assimilate their way of life to that of the common people. They also set the example of contending naked, publicly stripping and anointing themselves with oil in their gymnastic exercises. Formerly, even in the Olympic contests, the athletes who contended wore belts across their middles; and it is but a few years since that the practice ceased. To this day among some of the barbarians, especially in Asia, when prizes for boxing and wrestling are offered, belts are worn by the combatants. And there are many other points in which a likeness might be shown between the life of the Hellenic world of old and the barbarian of to-day.

With respect to their towns, later on, at an era of increased facilities of navigation and a greater supply of capital, we find the shores becoming the site of walled towns, and the isthmuses being occupied for the purposes of commerce and defence against a neighbour. But the old towns, on account of the great prevalence of piracy, were built away from the sea, whether on the islands or the continent, and still remain in their old sites. For the pirates used to plunder one another, and indeed all coast populations, whether seafaring or not.

The islanders, too, were great pirates. These islanders were Carians and Phoenicians, by whom most of the islands were colonized, as was proved by the following fact. During the

Olympia in Ancient Greece.

purification of Delos by Athens in this war all the graves in the island were taken up, and it was found that above half their inmates were Carians: they were identified by the fashion of the arms buried with them, and by the method of interment, which was the same as the Carians still follow. But as soon as Minos had formed his navy, communication by sea became easier, as he colonized most of the islands, and thus expelled the malefactors. The coast population now began to apply themselves more closely to the acquisition of wealth, and their life became more settled; some even began to build themselves walls on the strength of their newly acquired riches. For the love of gain would reconcile the weaker to the dominion of the stronger, and the possession of capital enabled the more powerful to reduce the smaller towns to subjection. And it was at a somewhat later stage of this development that they went on the expedition against Troy.

What enabled Agamemnon to raise the armament was more, in my opinion, his superiority in strength, than the oaths of Tyndareus, which bound the suitors to follow him. Indeed, the account given by those Peloponnesians who have been the recipients of the most credible tradition is this. First of all Pelops, arriving among a needy population from Asia with vast wealth, acquired such power that, stranger though he was, the country was called after him; and this power fortune saw fit materially to increase in the hands of his descendants. Eurystheus had been killed in Attica by the Heraclids. Atreus was his mother's brother; and to the hands of his relation, who had left his father on account of the death of Chrysippus, Eurystheus, when he set out on his expedition, had committed Mycenae and the government. As time went on and Eurystheus did not return, Atreus complied with the wishes of the Mycenaeans, who were influenced by fear of the Heraclids - besides, his power seemed considerable, and he had not neglected to court the favour of the populace - and assumed the sceptre of Mycenae and the rest of the dominions of Eurystheus. And so the power of the descendants of Pelops came to be greater than that of the descendants of Perseus. To all this Agamemnon succeeded. He had also a navy far stronger than his contemporaries, so that, in my opinion, fear was quite as strong an element as love in the formation of the confederate expedition. The strength of his navy is shown by the fact that his own was the largest contingent, and that of the Arcadians was furnished by him; this at least is what Homer says, if his testimony is deemed sufficient. Besides, in his account of the transmission of the sceptre, he calls him of many an isle, and of all Argos king.

Now Agamemnon's was a continental power; and he could not have been master of any except the adjacent islands (and these would not be many), but through the possession of a fleet.

And from this expedition we may infer the character of earlier enterprises. Now Mycenae may have been a small place, and many of the towns of that age may appear comparatively insignificant, but no exact observer would therefore feel justified in rejecting the estimate given by the poets and by tradition of the magnitude of the armament. For I suppose if Lacedaemon were to become desolate, and the temples and the foundations of the public buildings were left, that as time went on there would be a strong disposition with posterity to refuse to accept her fame as a true exponent of her power. And yet they occupy two-fifths of Peloponnese and lead the whole, not to speak of their numerous allies without. Still, as the city is neither built in a compact form nor adorned with magnificent temples and public edifices, but composed of villages after the old fashion of Hellas, there would be an impression of inadequacy. Whereas, if Athens were to suffer the same misfortune, I suppose that any inference from the appearance presented to the eye would make her power to have been twice as great as it is. We have therefore no right to be sceptical, nor to content ourselves with an inspection of a town to the exclusion of a consideration of its power; but we may safely conclude that the armament in question surpassed all before it, as it fell short of modern efforts; if we can here also accept the testimony of Homer's poems, in which, without allowing for the exaggeration which a poet would feel himself licensed to employ, we can see that it was far from equalling ours. He has represented it as consisting of twelve hundred vessels; the Boeotian complement of each ship being a hundred and twenty men, that of the ships of Philoctetes fifty. By this, I conceive, he meant to convey the maximum and the minimum complement: at any rate, he does not specify the amount of any others in his catalogue of the ships. That they were all rowers as well as warriors we see from his account of the ships of Philoctetes, in which all the men at the oar are bowmen. Now it is improbable that many supernumeraries sailed, if we except the kings and high officers; especially as they had to cross the open sea with munitions of war, in ships, moreover, that had no decks, but were equipped in the old piratical fashion. So that if we strike the average of the largest and smallest ships, the number of those who sailed will appear inconsiderable, representing, as they did, the whole force of Hellas. And this was due not so much to scarcity of men as of money. Difficulty of subsistence made the invaders reduce the numbers of the army to a point at which it might live on the country during the prosecution of the war. Even after the victory they obtained on their arrival - and a victory there must have been, or the fortifications of the naval camp could never have been built - there is no indication of their whole force having been employed; on the contrary, they seem to have turned to cultivation of the Chersonese and to piracy from want of supplies. This was what really enabled the Trojans to keep the field for ten years against them; the dispersion of the enemy making them always a match for the detachment left behind. If they had brought plenty of supplies with them, and had persevered in the war without scattering for piracy and agriculture, they would have easily defeated the Trojans in the field, since they could hold their own against them with the division on service. In short, if they had stuck to the siege, the capture of Troy would have cost them less time and less trouble. But as want of money proved the weakness of earlier expeditions, so from the same cause even the one in question, more famous than its predecessors, may be pronounced on the evidence of what it effected to have been inferior to its renown and to the current opinion about it formed under the tuition of the poets.

Even after the Trojan War, Hellas was still engaged in removing and settling, and thus could not attain to the quiet which must precede growth. The late return of the Hellenes from Ilium caused many revolutions, and factions ensued almost everywhere; and it was the citizens thus driven into exile who founded the cities. Sixty years after the capture of Ilium, the modern Boeotians were driven out of Arne by the Thessalians, and settled in the present Boeotia, the former Cadmeis; though there was a division of them there before, some of whom joined the expedition to Ilium. Twenty years later, the Dorians and the Heraclids became masters of Peloponnese; so that much had to be done and many years had to elapse before Hellas could attain to a durable tranquillity undisturbed by removals, and could begin to send out colonies, as Athens did to Ionia and most of the islands, and the Peloponnesians to most of Italy and Sicily and some places in the rest of Hellas. All these places were founded subsequently to the war with Troy.

But as the power of Hellas grew, and the acquisition of wealth became more an object, the revenues of the states increasing, tyrannies were by their means established almost everywhere - the old form of government being hereditary monarchy with definite prerogatives - and Hellas began to fit out fleets and apply herself more closely to the sea. It is said that the Corinthians were the first to approach the modern style of naval architecture, and that Corinth was the first place in Hellas where galleys were built; and we have Ameinocles, a Corinthian shipwright, making four ships for the Samians. Dating from the end of this war, it is nearly three hundred years ago that Ameinocles went to Samos. Again, the earliest sea-fight in history was between the Corinthians and Corcyraeans; this was about two hundred and sixty years ago, dating from the same time. Planted on an isthmus, Corinth had from time out of mind been a commercial emporium; as formerly almost all communication between the Hellenes within and without Peloponnese was carried on overland, and the Corinthian territory was the highway through which it travelled. She had consequently great money resources, as is shown by the epithet "wealthy" bestowed by the old poets on the place, and this enabled her, when traffic by sea became more common, to procure her navy and put down piracy; and as she could offer a mart for both branches of the trade, she acquired for herself all the power which a large revenue affords. Subsequently the Ionians attained to great naval strength in the reign of Cyrus, the first king of the Persians, and of his son Cambyses, and while they were at war with the former commanded for a while the Ionian sea. Polycrates also, the tyrant of Samos, had a powerful navy in the reign of Cambyses, with which he reduced many of the islands, and among them Rhenea, which he consecrated to the Delian Apollo. About this time also the Phocaeans, while they were founding Marseilles, defeated the Carthaginians in a sea-fight. These were the most powerful navies. And even these, although so many generations had elapsed since the Trojan war, seem to have been principally composed of the old fifty-oars and long-boats, and to have counted few galleys among their ranks. Indeed it was only shortly the Persian war, and the death of Darius the successor of Cambyses, that the Sicilian tyrants and the Corcyraeans acquired any large number of galleys. For after these there were no navies of any account in Hellas till the expedition of Xerxes; Aegina, Athens, and others may have possessed a few vessels, but they were principally fifty-oars. It was quite at the end of this period that the war with Aegina and the prospect of the barbarian invasion enabled Themistocles to persuade the Athenians to build the fleet with which they fought at Salamis; and even these vessels had not complete decks.

The navies, then, of the Hellenes during the period we have traversed were what I have described. All their insignificance did

15

not prevent their being an element of the greatest power to those who cultivated them, alike in revenue and in dominion. They were the means by which the islands were reached and reduced, those of the smallest area falling the easiest prey. Wars by land there were none, none at least by which power was acquired; we have the usual border contests, but of distant expeditions with conquest for object we hear nothing among the Hellenes. There was no union of subject cities round a great state, no spontaneous combination of equals for confederate expeditions; what fighting there was consisted merely of local warfare between rival neighbours. The nearest approach to a coalition took place in the old war between Chalcis and Eretria; this was a quarrel in which the rest of the Hellenic name did to some extent take sides.

Various, too, were the obstacles which the national growth encountered in various localities. The power of the Ionians was advancing with rapid strides, when it came into collision with Persia, under King Cyrus, who, after having dethroned Croesus and overrun everything between the Halys and the sea, stopped not till he had reduced the cities of the coast; the islands being only left to be subdued by Darius and the Phoenician navy.

Again, wherever there were tyrants, their habit of providing simply for themselves, of looking solely to their personal comfort and family aggrandizement, made safety the great aim of their policy, and prevented anything great proceeding from them; though they would each have their affairs with their immediate neighbours. All this is only true of the mother country, for in Sicily they attained to very great power. Thus for a long time everywhere in Hellas do we find causes which make the states alike incapable of combination for great and national ends, or of any vigorous action of their own.

But at last a time came when the tyrants of Athens and the far older tyrannies of the rest of Hellas were, with the exception of those in Sicily, once and for all put down by Lacedaemon; for this city, though after the settlement of the Dorians, its present inhabitants, it suffered from factions for an unparalleled length of time, still at a very early period obtained good laws, and enjoyed a freedom from tyrants which was unbroken; it has possessed the same form of government for more than four hundred years, reckoning to the end of the late war, and has thus been in a position

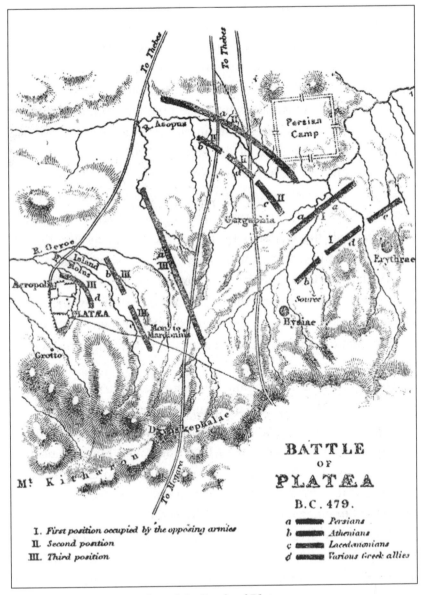

Plan of the Battle of Plataea.

to arrange the affairs of the other states. Not many years after the deposition of the tyrants, the battle of Marathon was fought between the Medes and the Athenians. Ten years afterwards, the barbarian returned with the armada for the subjugation of Hellas. In the face of this great danger, the command of the confederate Hellenes was assumed by the Lacedaemonians in virtue of their superior power; and the Athenians, having made up their minds to abandon their city, broke up their homes, threw themselves into their ships, and became a naval people. This coalition, after repulsing the barbarian, soon afterwards split into two sections, which included the Hellenes who had revolted from the King, as well as those who had aided him in the war. At the end of the one stood Athens, at the head of the other Lacedaemon, one the first naval, the other the first military power in Hellas. For a short time the league held together, till the Lacedaemonians and Athenians quarrelled and made war upon each other with their allies, a duel into which all the Hellenes sooner or later were drawn, though some might at first remain neutral. So that the whole period from the Median war to this, with some peaceful intervals, was spent by each power in war, either with its rival, or with its own revolted allies, and consequently afforded them constant practice in military matters, and that experience which is learnt in the school of danger.

The policy of Lacedaemon was not to exact tribute from her allies, but merely to secure their subservience to her interests by establishing oligarchies among them; Athens, on the contrary, had by degrees deprived hers of their ships, and imposed instead contributions in money on all except Chios and Lesbos. Both found their resources for this war separately to exceed the sum of their strength when the alliance flourished intact.

Having now given the result of my inquiries into early times, I grant that there will be a difficulty in believing every particular detail. The way that most men deal with traditions, even traditions of their own country, is to receive them all alike as they are delivered, without applying any critical test whatever. The general Athenian public fancy that Hipparchus was tyrant when he fell by the hands of Harmodius and Aristogiton, not knowing that Hippias, the eldest of the sons of Pisistratus, was really supreme, and that Hipparchus and Thessalus were his brothers; and that Harmodius and Aristogiton suspecting, on the very day, nay at the very moment fixed on for the deed, that information had been conveyed to Hippias by their accomplices, concluded that he had been warned, and did not attack him, yet, not liking to be apprehended and risk their lives for nothing, fell upon Hipparchus near the temple of the daughters of Leos, and slew him as he was arranging the Panathenaic procession.

There are many other unfounded ideas current among the rest of the Hellenes, even on matters of contemporary history, which have not been obscured by time. For instance, there is the notion that the Lacedaemonian kings have two votes each, the fact being that they have only one; and that there is a company of Pitane, there being simply no such thing. So little pains do the vulgar take in the investigation of truth, accepting readily the first story that comes to hand. On the whole, however, the conclusions I have drawn from the proofs quoted may, I believe, safely be relied on. Assuredly they will not be disturbed either by the lays of a poet displaying the exaggeration of his craft, or by the compositions of the chroniclers that are attractive at truth's expense; the subjects they treat of being out of the reach of evidence, and time having robbed most of them of historical value by enthroning them in the region of legend. Turning from these, we can rest satisfied with having proceeded upon the clearest data, and having arrived at conclusions as exact as can be expected in matters of such antiquity. To come to this war: despite the known disposition of the actors in a struggle to overrate its importance, and when it is over to return to their admiration of earlier events, yet an examination of the facts will show that it was much greater than the wars which preceded it.

With reference to the speeches in this history, some were delivered before the war began, others while it was going on; some I heard myself, others I got from various quarters; it was in all cases difficult to carry them word for word in one's memory, so my habit has been to make the speakers say what was in my opinion demanded of them by the various occasions, of course adhering as closely as possible to the general sense of what they really said. And with reference to the narrative of events, far from permitting myself to derive it from the first source that came to hand, I did not even trust my own impressions, but it rests partly on what I saw myself, partly on what others saw for me, the accuracy of the report being always tried by the most severe and detailed tests possible. My conclusions have cost me some labour from the want of coincidence between accounts of the same occurrences by different eye-witnesses, arising sometimes from imperfect memory, sometimes from undue partiality for one side or the other. The absence of romance in my history will, I fear, detract somewhat from its interest; but if it be judged useful by those inquirers who desire an exact knowledge of the past as an aid to the interpretation of the future, which in the course of human things must resemble if it does not reflect it, I shall be content. In fine, I have written my work, not as an essay which is to win the applause of the moment, but as a possession for all time.

The Median War, the greatest achievement of past times, yet found a speedy decision in two actions by sea and two by land. The Peloponnesian War was prolonged to an immense length, and, long as it was, it was short without parallel for the misfortunes that it brought upon Hellas. Never had so many cities been taken and laid desolate, here by the barbarians, here by the parties contending (the old inhabitants being sometimes removed to make room for others); never was there so much banishing and blood-shedding, now on the field of battle, now in the strife of faction. Old stories of occurrences handed down by tradition, but scantily confirmed by experience, suddenly ceased to be incredible; there were earthquakes of unparalleled extent and violence; eclipses of the sun occurred with a frequency unrecorded in previous history; there were great droughts in sundry places and consequent famines, and that most calamitous and awfully fatal visitation, the plague. All this came upon them with the late war, which was begun by the Athenians and Peloponnesians by the dissolution of the thirty years' truce made after the conquest of Euboea. To the question why they broke the treaty, I answer by placing first an account of their grounds of complaint and points of difference, that no one may ever have to ask the immediate cause which plunged the Hellenes into a war of such magnitude. The real cause I consider to be the one which was formally most kept out of sight. The growth of the power of Athens, and the alarm which this inspired in Lacedaemon, made war inevitable. Still it is well to give the grounds alleged by either side which led to the dissolution of the treaty and the breaking out of the war.

CHAPTER II

Causes of the War - The Affair of Epidamnus -
The Affair of Potidaea

THE CITY of Epidamnus stands on the right of the entrance of the Ionic Gulf. Its vicinity is inhabited by the Taulantians, an Illyrian people. The place is a colony from Corcyra, founded by Phalius, son of Eratocleides, of the family of the Heraclids, who had according to ancient usage been summoned for the purpose from Corinth, the mother country. The colonists were joined by some Corinthians, and others of the Dorian race. Now, as time went on, the city of Epidamnus became great and populous; but falling a prey to factions arising, it is said, from a war with her neighbours the barbarians, she became much enfeebled, and lost a considerable amount of her power. The last act before the war was the expulsion of the nobles by the people. The exiled party joined the barbarians, and proceeded to plunder those in the city by sea and land; and the Epidamnians, finding themselves hard pressed, sent ambassadors to Corcyra beseeching their mother country not to allow them to perish, but to make up matters between them and the exiles, and to rid them of the war with the barbarians. The ambassadors seated themselves in the temple of Hera as suppliants, and made the above requests to the Corcyraeans. But the Corcyraeans refused to accept their supplication, and they were dismissed without having effected anything.

When the Epidamnians found that no help could be expected from Corcyra, they were in a strait what to do next. So they sent to Delphi and inquired of the God whether they should deliver their city to the Corinthians and endeavour to obtain some assistance from their founders. The answer he gave them was to deliver the city and place themselves under Corinthian protection. So the Epidamnians went to Corinth and delivered over the colony in obedience to the commands of the oracle. They showed that their founder came from Corinth, and revealed the answer of the god; and they begged them not to allow them to perish, but to assist them. This the Corinthians consented to do. Believing the colony to belong as much to themselves as to the Corcyraeans, they felt it to be a kind of duty to undertake their protection. Besides, they hated the Corcyraeans for their contempt of the mother country. Instead of meeting with the usual honours accorded to the parent city by every other colony at public assemblies, such as precedence at sacrifices, Corinth found herself treated with contempt by a power which in point of wealth could stand comparison with any even of the richest communities in Hellas, which possessed great military strength, and which sometimes could not repress a pride in the high naval position of an island whose nautical renown dated from the days of its old inhabitants, the Phaeacians. This was one reason of the care that they lavished on their fleet, which became very efficient; indeed they began the war with a force of a hundred and twenty galleys.

All these grievances made Corinth eager to send the promised aid to Epidamnus. Advertisement was made for volunteer settlers, and a force of Ambraciots, Leucadians, and Corinthians was dispatched. They marched by land to Apollonia, a Corinthian colony, the route by sea being avoided from fear of Corcyraean interruption. When the Corcyraeans heard of the arrival of the settlers and troops in Epidamnus, and the surrender of the colony to Corinth, they took fire. Instantly putting to sea with five-and-twenty ships, which were quickly followed by others, they insolently commanded the Epidamnians to receive back the banished nobles - (it must be premised that the Epidamnian exiles had come to Corcyra and, pointing to the sepulchres of their ancestors, had appealed to their kindred to restore them) - and to dismiss the Corinthian garrison and settlers. But to all this the Epidamnians turned a deaf ear. Upon this the Corcyraeans commenced operations against them with a fleet of forty sail. They took with them the exiles, with a view to their restoration, and also secured the services of the Illyrians. Sitting down before the city, they issued a proclamation to the effect that any of the natives that chose, and the foreigners, might depart unharmed, with the alternative of being treated as enemies. On their refusal the Corcyraeans proceeded to besiege the city, which stands on an isthmus; and the Corinthians, receiving intelligence of the investment of Epidamnus, got together an armament and proclaimed a colony to Epidamnus, perfect political equality being guaranteed to all who chose to go. Any who were not prepared to sail at once might, by paying down the sum of fifty Corinthian drachmae, have a share in the colony without leaving Corinth. Great numbers took advantage of this proclamation, some being ready to start directly, others paying the requisite forfeit. In case of their passage being disputed by the Corcyraeans, several cities were asked to lend them a convoy. Megara prepared to accompany them with eight ships, Pale in Cephallonia with four; Epidaurus furnished five, Hermione one, Troezen two, Leucas ten, and Ambracia eight. The Thebans and Phliasians were asked for money, the Eleans for hulls as well; while Corinth herself furnished thirty ships and three thousand heavy infantry.

When the Corcyraeans heard of their preparations they came to Corinth with envoys from Lacedaemon and Sicyon, whom they persuaded to accompany them, and bade her recall the garrison and settlers, as she had nothing to do with Epidamnus. If, however, she had any claims to make, they were willing to submit the matter to the arbitration of such of the cities in Peloponnese as should be chosen by mutual agreement, and that the colony should remain with the city to whom the arbitrators might assign it. They were also willing to refer the matter to the oracle at Delphi. If, in defiance of their protestations, war was appealed to, they should be themselves compelled by this violence to seek friends in quarters where they had no desire to seek them, and to make even old ties give way to the necessity of assistance. The answer they got from Corinth was that, if they would withdraw their fleet and the barbarians from Epidamnus, negotiation might be possible; but, while the town was still being besieged, going before arbitrators was out of the question. The Corcyraeans retorted that if Corinth would withdraw her troops from Epidamnus they would withdraw theirs, or they were ready to let both parties remain in statu quo, an armistice being concluded till judgment could be given.

Turning a deaf ear to all these proposals, when their ships were manned and their allies had come in, the Corinthians sent a herald before them to declare war and, getting under way with seventy-five ships and two thousand heavy infantry, sailed for Epidamnus to give battle to the Corcyraeans. The fleet was under the command of Aristeus, son of Pellichas, Callicrates, son of Callias, and Timanor, son of Timanthes; the troops under that of Archetimus, son of Eurytimus, and Isarchidas, son of Isarchus. When they had reached Actium in the territory of Anactorium, at the mouth of the mouth of the Gulf of Ambracia, where the temple of Apollo stands, the Corcyraeans sent on a herald in a light boat to warn them not to sail against them. Meanwhile they proceeded to man their ships, all of which had been equipped for action, the old vessels being undergirded to make them seaworthy. On the return of the herald without any peaceful answer from the Corinthians, their ships being now manned, they put out to sea to meet the enemy with a fleet of eighty sail (forty were engaged in the siege of Epidamnus), formed line, and went into action, and gained a decisive victory, and destroyed fifteen of the Corinthian vessels. The same day had seen Epidamnus compelled by its besiegers to capitulate; the conditions being that the foreigners should be sold, and the Corinthians kept as prisoners of war, till their fate should be otherwise decided.

After the engagement the Corcyraeans set up a trophy on Leukimme, a headland of Corcyra, and slew all their captives except the Corinthians, whom they kept as prisoners of war. Defeated at sea, the Corinthians and their allies repaired home, and left the Corcyraeans masters of all the sea about those parts.

Sailing to Leucas, a Corinthian colony, they ravaged their territory, and burnt Cyllene, the harbour of the Eleans, because they had furnished ships and money to Corinth. For almost the whole of the period that followed the battle they remained masters of the sea, and the allies of Corinth were harassed by Corcyraean cruisers. At last Corinth, roused by the sufferings of her allies, sent out ships and troops in the fall of the summer, who formed an encampment at Actium and about Chimerium, in Thesprotis, for the protection of Leucas and the rest of the friendly cities. The Corcyraeans on their part formed a similar station on Leukimme. Neither party made any movement, but they remained confronting each other till the end of the summer, and winter was at hand before either of them returned home.

Corinth, exasperated by the war with the Corcyraeans, spent the whole of the year after the engagement and that succeeding it in building ships, and in straining every nerve to form an efficient fleet; rowers being drawn from Peloponnese and the rest of Hellas by the inducement of large bounties. The Corcyraeans, alarmed at the news of their preparations, being without a single ally in Hellas (for they had not enrolled themselves either in the Athenian or in the Lacedaemonian confederacy), decided to repair to Athens in order to enter into alliance and to endeavour to procure support from her. Corinth also, hearing of their intentions, sent an embassy to Athens to prevent the Corcyraean navy being joined by the Athenian, and her prospect of ordering the war according to her wishes being thus impeded. An assembly was convoked, and the rival advocates appeared: the Corcyraeans spoke as follows:

"Athenians! when a people that have not rendered any important service or support to their neighbours in times past, for which they might claim to be repaid, appear before them as we now appear before you to solicit their assistance, they may fairly be required to satisfy certain preliminary conditions. They should show, first, that it is expedient or at least safe to grant their request; next, that they will retain a lasting sense of the kindness.

But if they cannot clearly establish any of these points, they must not be annoyed if they meet with a rebuff. Now the Corcyraeans believe that with their petition for assistance they can also give you a satisfactory answer on these points, and they have therefore dispatched us hither. It has so happened that our policy as regards you with respect to this request, turns out to be inconsistent, and as regards our interests, to be at the present crisis inexpedient. We say inconsistent, because a power which has never in the whole of her past history been willing to ally herself with any of her neighbours, is now found asking them to ally themselves with her. And we say inexpedient, because in our present war with Corinth it has left us in a position of entire isolation, and what once seemed the wise precaution of refusing to involve ourselves in alliances with other powers, lest we should also involve ourselves in risks of their choosing, has now proved to be folly and weakness. It is true that in the late naval engagement we drove back the Corinthians from our shores single-handed. But they have now got together a still larger armament from Peloponnese and the rest of Hellas; and we, seeing our utter inability to cope with them without foreign aid, and the magnitude of the danger which subjection to them implies, find it necessary to ask help from you and from every other power. And we hope to be excused if we forswear our old principle of complete political isolation, a principle which was not adopted with any sinister intention, but was rather the consequence of an error in judgment.

"Now there are many reasons why in the event of your compliance you will congratulate yourselves on this request having been made to you. First, because your assistance will be rendered to a power which, herself inoffensive, is a victim to the injustice of others. Secondly, because all that we most value is at stake in the present contest, and your welcome of us under these circumstances will be a proof of goodwill which will ever keep alive the gratitude you will lay up in our hearts. Thirdly, yourselves excepted, we are the greatest naval power in Hellas.

Moreover, can you conceive a stroke of good fortune more rare in itself, or more disheartening to your enemies, than that the power whose adhesion you would have valued above much material and moral strength should present herself self-invited, should deliver herself into your hands without danger and without expense, and should lastly put you in the way of gaining a high character in the eyes of the world, the gratitude of those whom you shall assist, and a great accession of strength for yourselves? You may search all history without finding many instances of a people gaining all these advantages at once, or many instances of a power that comes in quest of assistance being in a position to give to the people whose alliance she solicits as much safety and honour as she will receive. But it will be urged that it is only in the case of a war that we shall be found useful. To this we answer that if any of you imagine that that war is far off, he is grievously mistaken, and is blind to the fact that Lacedaemon regards you with jealousy and desires war, and that Corinth is powerful there - the same, remember, that is your enemy, and is even now trying to subdue us as a preliminary to attacking you. And this she does to prevent our becoming united by a common enmity, and her having us both on her hands, and also to ensure getting the start of you in one of two ways, either by crippling our power or by making its strength her own. Now it is our policy to be beforehand with her - that is, for Corcyra to make an offer of alliance and for you to accept it; in fact, we ought to form plans against her instead of waiting to defeat the plans she forms against us.

"If she asserts that for you to receive a colony of hers into alliance is not right, let her know that every colony that is well treated honours its parent state, but becomes estranged from it by injustice. For colonists are not sent forth on the understanding that they are to be the slaves of those that remain behind, but that they are to be their equals. And that Corinth was injuring us is clear. Invited to refer the dispute about Epidamnus to arbitration, they chose to prosecute their complaints war rather than by a fair trial. And let their conduct towards us who are their kindred be a warning to you not to be misled by their deceit, nor to yield to their direct requests; concessions to adversaries only end in self-reproach, and the more strictly they are avoided the greater will be the chance of security.

"If it be urged that your reception of us will be a breach of the treaty existing between you and Lacedaemon, the answer is that we are a neutral state, and that one of the express provisions of that treaty is that it shall be competent for any Hellenic state that is neutral to join whichever side it pleases. And it is intolerable for Corinth to be allowed to obtain men for her navy not only from her allies, but also from the rest of Hellas, no small number being furnished by your own subjects; while we are to be excluded both from the alliance left open to us by treaty, and from any assistance that we might get from other quarters, and you are to be accused of political immorality if you comply with our request. On the other hand, we shall have much greater cause to complain of you, if you do not comply with it; if we, who are in peril and are no enemies of yours, meet with a repulse at your hands, while Corinth, who is the aggressor and your enemy, not only meets with no hindrance from you, but is even allowed to draw material for war from your dependencies. This ought not to be, but you should either forbid her enlisting men in your dominions, or you should lend us too what help you may think advisable.

"But your real policy is to afford us avowed countenance and support. The advantages of this course, as we premised in the beginning of our speech, are many. We mention one that is perhaps the chief. Could there be a clearer guarantee of our good faith than is offered by the fact that the power which is at enmity with you is also at enmity with us, and that that power is fully able to punish defection? And there is a wide difference between declining the alliance of an inland and of a maritime power. For your first endeavour should be to prevent, if possible, the existence of any naval power except your own; failing this, to secure the friendship of the strongest that does exist. And if any of you believe that what we urge is expedient, but fear to act upon this belief, lest it should lead to a breach of the treaty, you must remember that on the one hand, whatever your fears, your strength will be formidable to your antagonists; on the other, whatever the confidence you derive from refusing to receive us, your weakness will have no terrors for a strong enemy. You must also remember that your decision is for Athens no less than Corcyra, and that you are not making the best provision for her interests, if at a time when you are anxiously scanning the horizon that you may be in readiness for the breaking out of the war which is all but upon you, you hesitate to attach to your side a place whose adhesion or estrangement is alike pregnant with the most vital consequences. For it lies conveniently for the coast-navigation in the direction of Italy and Sicily, being able to bar the passage of naval reinforcements from thence to Peloponnese, and from Peloponnese thither; and it is in other respects a most desirable station. To sum up as shortly as possible, embracing both general and particular considerations, let this show you the folly of sacrificing us. Remember that there are but three considerable naval powers in Hellas - Athens, Corcyra, and Corinth - and that if you allow two of these three to become one, and Corinth to secure us for herself, you will have to hold the sea against the united fleets of Corcyra and Peloponnese. But if you receive us, you will have our ships to reinforce you in the struggle."

Such were the words of the Corcyraeans. After they had finished, the Corinthians spoke as follows:

"These Corcyraeans in the speech we have just heard do not confine themselves to the question of their reception into your alliance. They also talk of our being guilty of injustice, and their being the victims of an unjustifiable war. It becomes necessary for us to touch upon both these points before we proceed to the rest of what we have to say, that you may have a more correct idea of the grounds of our claim, and have good cause to reject their petition. According to them, their old policy of refusing all offers of alliance was a policy of moderation. It was in fact adopted for bad ends, not for good; indeed their conduct is such as to make them by no means desirous of having allies present to witness it, or of having the shame of asking their concurrence. Besides, their geographical situation makes them independent of others, and consequently the decision in cases where they injure any lies not with judges appointed by mutual agreement, but with themselves, because, while they seldom make voyages to their neighbours, they are constantly being visited by foreign vessels which are compelled to put in to Corcyra. In short, the object that they propose to themselves, in their specious policy of complete isolation, is not to avoid sharing in the crimes of others, but to secure monopoly of crime to themselves - the licence of outrage wherever they can compel, of fraud wherever they can elude, and the enjoyment of their gains without shame. And yet if they were the honest men they pretend to be, the less hold that others had upon them, the stronger would be the light in which they might have put their honesty by giving and taking what was just.

"But such has not been their conduct either towards others or towards us. The attitude of our colony towards us has always been one of estrangement and is now one of hostility; for, say they: 'We were not sent out to be ill-treated.' We rejoin that we did not found the colony to be insulted by them, but to be their head and to be regarded with a proper respect. At any rate our other colonies honour us, and we are much beloved by our colonists; and clearly, if the majority are satisfied with us, these can have no good reason for a dissatisfaction in which they stand alone, and we are not acting improperly in making war against them, nor are we making war against them without having received signal provocation. Besides, if we were in the wrong, it would be honourable in them to give way to our wishes, and disgraceful for us to trample on their moderation; but in the pride and licence of wealth they have sinned again and again against us, and never more deeply than when Epidamnus, our dependency, which they took no steps to claim in its distress upon our coming to relieve it, was by them seized, and is now held by force of arms.

"As to their allegation that they wished the question to be first submitted to arbitration, it is obvious that a challenge coming from the party who is safe in a commanding position cannot gain the credit due only to him who, before appealing to arms, in deeds as well as words, places himself on a level with his adversary. In their case, it was not before they laid siege to the place, but after they at length understood that we should not tamely suffer it, that they thought of the specious word arbitration. And not satisfied with their own misconduct there, they appear here now requiring you to join with them not in alliance but in crime, and to receive them in spite of their being at enmity with us. But it was when they stood firmest that they should have made overtures to you, and not at a time when we have been wronged and they are in peril; nor yet at a time when you will be admitting to a share in your protection those who never admitted you to a share in their power, and will be incurring an equal amount of blame from us with those in whose offences you had no hand. No, they should have shared their power with you before they asked you to share your fortunes with them.

"So then the reality of the grievances we come to complain of, and the violence and rapacity of our opponents, have both been proved. But that you cannot equitably receive them, this you have still to learn. It may be true that one of the provisions of the treaty is that it shall be competent for any state, whose name was not down on the list, to join whichever side it pleases. But this agreement is not meant for those whose object in joining is the injury of other powers, but for those whose need of support does not arise from the fact of defection, and whose adhesion will not bring to the power that is mad enough to receive them war instead of peace; which will be the case with you, if you refuse to listen to us. For you cannot become their auxiliary and remain our friend; if you join in their attack, you must share the punishment which the defenders inflict on them. And yet you have the best possible right to be neutral, or, failing this, you should on the contrary join us against them. Corinth is at least in treaty with you; with Corcyra you were never even in truce. But do not lay down the principle that defection is to be patronized. Did we on the defection of the Samians record our vote against you, when the rest of the Peloponnesian powers were equally divided on the question whether they should assist them? No, we told them to their face that every power has a right to punish its own allies. Why, if you make it your policy to receive and assist all offenders, you will find that just as many of your dependencies will come over to us, and the principle that you establish will press less heavily on us than on yourselves.

"This then is what Hellenic law entitles us to demand as a right. But we have also advice to offer and claims on your gratitude, which, since there is no danger of our injuring you, as we are not enemies, and since our friendship does not amount to very frequent intercourse, we say ought to be liquidated at the present juncture. When you were in want of ships of war for the war against the Aeginetans, before the Persian invasion, Corinth supplied you with twenty vessels. That good turn, and the line we took on the Samian question, when we were the cause of the Peloponnesians refusing to assist them, enabled you to conquer Aegina and to punish Samos. And we acted thus at crises when, if ever, men are wont in their efforts against their enemies to forget everything for the sake of victory, regarding him who assists them then as a friend, even if thus far he has been a foe, and him who opposes them then as a foe, even if he has thus far been a friend; indeed they allow their real interests to suffer from their absorbing preoccupation in the struggle.

"Weigh well these considerations, and let your youth learn what they are from their elders, and let them determine to do unto us as we have done unto you. And let them not acknowledge the justice of what we say, but dispute its wisdom in the contingency of war. Not only is the straightest path generally speaking the wisest; but the coming of the war, which the Corcyraeans have used as a bugbear to persuade you to do wrong, is still uncertain, and it is not worth while to be carried away by it into gaining the instant and declared enmity of Corinth. It were, rather, wise to try and counteract the unfavourable impression which your conduct to Megara has created. For kindness opportunely shown has a greater power of removing old grievances than the facts of the case may warrant. And do not be seduced by the prospect of a great naval alliance. Abstinence from all injustice to other first-rate powers is a greater tower of strength than anything that can be gained by the sacrifice of permanent tranquillity for an apparent temporary advantage. It is now our turn to benefit by the principle that we laid down at Lacedaemon, that every power has a right to punish her own allies. We now claim to receive the same from you, and protest against your rewarding us for benefiting you by our vote by injuring us by yours. On the contrary, return us like for like, remembering that this is that very crisis in which he who lends aid is most a friend, and he who opposes is most a foe. And for these Corcyraeans - neither receive them into alliance in our despite, nor be their abettors in crime. So do, and you will act as we have a right to expect of you, and at the same time best consult your own interests."

Such were the words of the Corinthians.

When the Athenians had heard both out, two assemblies were held. In the first there was a manifest disposition to listen to the representations of Corinth; in the second, public feeling had changed and an alliance with Corcyra was decided on, with certain reservations. It was to be a defensive, not an offensive alliance. It did not involve a breach of the treaty with Peloponnese: Athens could not be required to join Corcyra in any attack upon Corinth. But each of the contracting parties had a right to the other's assistance against invasion, whether of his own territory or that of an ally. For it began now to be felt that the coming of the Peloponnesian war was only a question of time, and no one was willing to see a naval power of such magnitude as Corcyra sacrificed to Corinth; though if they could let them weaken each other by mutual conflict, it would be no bad preparation for the struggle which Athens might one day have to wage with Corinth and the other naval powers. At the same time the island seemed to lie conveniently on the coasting passage to Italy and Sicily. With these views, Athens received Corcyra into alliance and, on the departure of the Corinthians not long afterwards, sent ten ships to their assistance. They were commanded by Lacedaemonius, the son of Cimon, Diotimus, the son of Strombichus, and Proteas, the son of Epicles. Their instructions were to avoid collision with the Corinthian fleet except under certain circumstances. If it sailed to Corcyra and threatened a landing on her coast, or in any of her possessions, they were to do their utmost to prevent it. These instructions were prompted by an anxiety to avoid a breach of the treaty.

Meanwhile the Corinthians completed their preparations, and sailed for Corcyra with a hundred and fifty ships. Of these Elis furnished ten, Megara twelve, Leucas ten, Ambracia twenty-seven, Anactorium one, and Corinth herself ninety. Each of these contingents had its own admiral, the Corinthian being under the command of Xenoclides, son of Euthycles, with four colleagues. Sailing from Leucas, they made land at the part of the continent opposite Corcyra. They anchored in the harbour of Chimerium, in the territory of Thesprotis, above which, at some distance from the sea, lies the city of Ephyre, in the Elean district. By this city the Acherusian lake pours its waters into the sea. It gets its name from the river Acheron, which flows through Thesprotis and falls into the lake. There also the river Thyamis flows, forming the boundary between Thesprotis and Kestrine; and between these rivers rises the point of Chimerium. In this part of the continent the Corinthians now came to anchor, and formed an encampment.

When the Corcyraeans saw them coming, they manned a hundred and ten ships, commanded by Meikiades, Aisimides, and Eurybatus, and stationed themselves at one of the Sybota isles; the ten Athenian ships being present. On Point Leukimme they posted their land forces, and a thousand heavy infantry who had come from Zacynthus to their assistance. Nor were the Corinthians on the mainland without their allies. The barbarians flocked in large numbers to their assistance, the inhabitants of this part of the continent being old allies of theirs.

When the Corinthian preparations were completed, they took three days' provisions and put out from Chimerium by night, ready for action. Sailing with the dawn, they sighted the Corcyraean fleet out at sea and coming towards them. When they perceived each other, both sides formed in order of battle. On the Corcyraean right wing lay the Athenian ships, the rest of the line being occupied by their own vessels formed in three squadrons, each of which was commanded by one of the three admirals. Such was the Corcyraean formation. The Corinthian was as follows: on the right wing lay the Megarian and Ambraciot ships, in the centre the rest of the allies in order. But the left was composed of the best sailers in the Corinthian navy, to encounter the Athenians and the right wing of the Corcyraeans. As soon as the signals were raised on either side, they joined battle. Both sides had a large number of heavy infantry on their decks, and a large number of archers and darters, the old imperfect armament still prevailing. The sea-fight was an obstinate one, though not remarkable for its science; indeed it was more like a battle by land. Whenever they charged each other, the multitude and crush of the vessels made it by no means easy to get loose; besides, their hopes of victory lay principally in the heavy infantry on the decks, who stood and fought in order, the ships remaining stationary. The manoeuvre of breaking the line was not tried; in short, strength and pluck had more share in the fight than science. Everywhere tumult reigned, the battle being one scene of confusion; meanwhile the Athenian ships, by coming up to the Corcyraeans whenever they were pressed, served to alarm the enemy, though their commanders could not join in the battle from fear of their instructions. The right wing of the Corinthians suffered most. The Corcyraeans routed it, and chased them in disorder to the continent with twenty ships, sailed up to their camp, and burnt the tents which they found empty, and plundered the stuff. So in this quarter the Corinthians and their allies were defeated, and the Corcyraeans were victorious. But where the Corinthians themselves were, on the left, they gained a decided success; the scanty forces of the Corcyraeans being further weakened by the want of the twenty ships absent on the pursuit. Seeing the Corcyraeans hard pressed, the Athenians began at length to assist them more unequivocally. At first, it is true, they refrained from charging any ships; but when the rout was becoming patent, and the Corinthians were pressing on, the time at last came when every one set to, and all distinction was laid aside, and it came to this point, that the Corinthians and Athenians raised their hands against each other.

After the rout, the Corinthians, instead of employing themselves in lashing fast and hauling after them the hulls of the vessels which they had disabled, turned their attention to the men, whom they butchered as they sailed through, not caring so much to make prisoners. Some even of their own friends were slain by them, by mistake, in their ignorance of the defeat of the right wing For the number of the ships on both sides, and the distance to which they covered the sea, made it difficult, after they had once joined, to distinguish between the conquering and the conquered; this battle proving far greater than any before it, any at least between Hellenes, for the number of vessels engaged. After the Corinthians had chased the Corcyraeans to the land, they turned to the wrecks and their dead, most of whom they succeeded in getting hold of and conveying to Sybota, the rendezvous of the land forces furnished by their barbarian allies. Sybota, it must be known, is a desert harbour of Thesprotis. This task over, they mustered anew, and sailed against the Corcyraeans, who on their part advanced to meet them with all their ships that were fit for service and remaining to them, accompanied by the Athenian vessels, fearing that they might attempt a landing in their territory. It was by this time getting late, and the paean had been sung for the attack, when the Corinthians suddenly began to back water. They had observed twenty Athenian ships sailing up, which had been sent out afterwards to reinforce the ten vessels by the Athenians, who feared, as it turned out justly, the defeat of the Corcyraeans and the inability of their handful of ships to protect them. These ships were thus seen by the Corinthians first. They suspected that they were from Athens, and that those which they saw were not all, but that there were more behind; they accordingly began to retire. The Corcyraeans meanwhile had not sighted them, as they were advancing from a point which they could not so well see, and were wondering why the Corinthians were backing water, when some caught sight of them, and cried out that there were ships in sight ahead. Upon this they also retired; for it was now getting dark, and the retreat of the Corinthians had suspended hostilities. Thus they parted from each other, and the battle ceased with night. The Corcyraeans were in their camp at Leukimme, when these twenty ships from Athens, under the command of Glaucon, the son of Leagrus, and Andocides, son of Leogoras, bore on through the corpses and the wrecks, and sailed up to the camp, not long after they were sighted. It was now night, and the Corcyraeans feared that they might be hostile vessels; but they soon knew them, and the ships came to anchor.

The next day the thirty Athenian vessels put out to sea, accompanied by all the Corcyraean ships that were seaworthy, and sailed to the harbour at Sybota, where the Corinthians lay, to see if they would engage. The Corinthians put out from the land and formed a line in the open sea, but beyond this made no further movement, having no intention of assuming the offensive. For they saw reinforcements arrived fresh from Athens, and themselves confronted by numerous difficulties, such as the necessity of guarding the prisoners whom they had on board and the want of all means of refitting their ships in a desert place. What they were thinking more about was how their voyage home was to be effected; they feared that the Athenians might consider that the treaty was dissolved by the collision which had occurred, and forbid their departure.

Accordingly they resolved to put some men on board a boat, and send them without a herald's wand to the Athenians, as an experiment. Having done so, they spoke as follows: "You do wrong, Athenians, to begin war and break the treaty. Engaged in chastising our enemies, we find you placing yourselves in our path in arms against us. Now if your intentions are to prevent us sailing to Corcyra, or anywhere else that we may wish, and if you are for breaking the treaty, first take us that are here and treat us as enemies." Such was what they said, and all the Corcyraean armament that were within hearing immediately called out to take them and kill them. But the Athenians answered as follows: "Neither are we beginning war, Peloponnesians, nor are we breaking the treaty; but these Corcyraeans are our allies, and we are come to help them. So if you want to sail anywhere else, we place no obstacle in your way; but if you are going to sail against Corcyra, or any of her possessions, we shall do our best to stop you."

Receiving this answer from the Athenians, the Corinthians commenced preparations for their voyage home, and set up a trophy in Sybota, on the continent; while the Corcyraeans took up the wrecks and dead that had been carried out to them by the current, and by a wind which rose in the night and scattered them in all directions, and set up their trophy in Sybota, on the island, as victors. The reasons each side had for claiming the victory were these. The Corinthians had been victorious in the sea-fight until night; and having thus been enabled to carry off most wrecks and dead, they were in possession of no fewer than a thousand prisoners of war, and had sunk close upon seventy vessels. The Corcyraeans had destroyed about thirty ships, and after the arrival of the Athenians had taken up the wrecks and dead on their side; they had besides seen the Corinthians retire before them, backing water on sight of the Athenian vessels, and upon the arrival of the Athenians refuse to sail out against them from Sybota. Thus both sides claimed the victory.

The Corinthians on the voyage home took Anactorium, which stands at the mouth of the Ambracian gulf. The place was taken by treachery, being common ground to the Corcyraeans and Corinthians. After establishing Corinthian settlers there, they retired home. Eight hundred of the Corcyraeans were slaves; these they sold; two hundred and fifty they retained in captivity, and treated with great attention, in the hope that they might bring over their country to Corinth on their return; most of them being, as it happened, men of very high position in Corcyra. In this way Corcyra maintained her political existence in the war with Corinth, and the Athenian vessels left the island. This was the first cause of the war that Corinth had against the Athenians, viz., that they had fought against them with the Corcyraeans in time of treaty.

Almost immediately after this, fresh differences arose between the Athenians and Peloponnesians, and contributed their share to the war. Corinth was forming schemes for retaliation, and Athens suspected her hostility. The Potidaeans, who inhabit the isthmus of Pallene, being a Corinthian colony, but tributary allies of Athens, were ordered to raze the wall looking towards Pallene, to give hostages, to dismiss the Corinthian magistrates, and in future not to receive the persons sent from Corinth annually to succeed them. It was feared that they might be persuaded by Perdiccas and the Corinthians to revolt, and might draw the rest of the allies in the direction of Thrace to revolt with them. These precautions against the Potidaeans were taken by the Athenians immediately after the battle at Corcyra. Not only was Corinth at length openly hostile, but Perdiccas, son of Alexander, king of the Macedonians, had from an old friend and ally been made an enemy. He had been made an enemy by the Athenians entering into alliance with his brother Philip and Derdas, who were in league against him. In his alarm he had sent to Lacedaemon to try and involve the Athenians in a war with the Peloponnesians, and was endeavouring to win over Corinth in order to bring about the revolt of Potidaea. He also made overtures to the Chalcidians in the direction of Thrace, and to the Bottiaeans, to persuade them to join in the revolt; for he thought that if these places on the border could be made his allies, it would be easier to carry on the war with their co-operation. Alive to all this, and wishing to anticipate the revolt of the cities, the Athenians acted as follows. They were just then sending off thirty ships and a thousand heavy infantry for his country under the command of Archestratus, son of Lycomedes, with four colleagues. They instructed the captains to take hostages of the Potidaeans, to raze the wall, and to be on their guard against the revolt of the neighbouring cities.

Meanwhile the Potidaeans sent envoys to Athens on the chance of persuading them to take no new steps in their matters; they also went to Lacedaemon with the Corinthians to secure support in case of need. Failing after prolonged negotiation to obtain anything satisfactory from the Athenians; being unable, for all they could say, to prevent the vessels that were destined for Macedonia from also sailing against them; and receiving from the Lacedaemonian government a promise to invade Attica, if the Athenians should attack Potidaea, the Potidaeans, thus favoured by the moment, at last entered into league with the Chalcidians and Bottiaeans, and revolted. And Perdiccas induced the Chalcidians to abandon and demolish their towns on the seaboard and, settling inland at Olynthus, to make that one city a strong place: meanwhile to those who followed his advice he gave a part of his territory in Mygdonia round Lake Bolbe as a place of abode while the war against the Athenians should last. They accordingly demolished their towns, removed inland and prepared for war. The thirty ships of the

Athenians, arriving before the Thracian places, found Potidaea and the rest in revolt. Their commanders, considering it to be quite impossible with their present force to carry on war with Perdiccas and with the confederate towns as well turned to Macedonia, their original destination, and, having established themselves there, carried on war in co-operation with Philip, and the brothers of Derdas, who had invaded the country from the interior.

Meanwhile the Corinthians, with Potidaea in revolt and the Athenian ships on the coast of Macedonia, alarmed for the safety of the place and thinking its danger theirs, sent volunteers from Corinth, and mercenaries from the rest of Peloponnese, to the number of sixteen hundred heavy infantry in all, and four hundred light troops. Aristeus, son of Adimantus, who was always a steady friend to the Potidaeans, took command of the expedition, and it was principally for love of him that most of the men from Corinth volunteered. They arrived in Thrace forty days after the revolt of Potidaea.

The Athenians also immediately received the news of the revolt of the cities. On being informed that Aristeus and his reinforcements were on their way, they sent two thousand heavy infantry of their own citizens and forty ships against the places in revolt, under the command of Callias, son of Calliades, and four colleagues. They arrived in Macedonia first, and found the force of a thousand men that had been first sent out, just become masters of Therme and besieging Pydna. Accordingly they also joined in the investment, and besieged Pydna for a while. Subsequently they came to terms and concluded a forced alliance with Perdiccas, hastened by the calls of Potidaea and by the arrival of Aristeus at that place. They withdrew from Macedonia, going to Beroea and thence to Strepsa, and, after a futile attempt on the latter place, they pursued by land their march to Potidaea with three thousand heavy infantry of their own citizens, besides a number of their allies, and six hundred Macedonian horsemen, the followers of Philip and Pausanias. With these sailed seventy ships along the coast. Advancing by short marches, on the third day they arrived at Gigonus, where they encamped.

Meanwhile the Potidaeans and the Peloponnesians with Aristeus were encamped on the side looking towards Olynthus on the isthmus, in expectation of the Athenians, and had established their market outside the city. The allies had chosen Aristeus general of all the infantry; while the command of the cavalry was given to Perdiccas, who had at once left the alliance of the Athenians and gone back to that of the Potidaeans, having deputed Iolaus as his general: The plan of Aristeus was to keep his own force on the isthmus, and await the attack of the Athenians; leaving the Chalcidians and the allies outside the isthmus, and the two hundred cavalry from Perdiccas in Olynthus to act upon the Athenian rear, on the occasion of their advancing against him; and thus to place the enemy between two fires. While Callias the Athenian general and his colleagues dispatched the Macedonian horse and a few of the allies to Olynthus, to prevent any movement being made from that quarter, the Athenians themselves broke up their camp and marched against Potidaea. After they had arrived at the isthmus, and saw the enemy preparing for battle, they formed against him, and soon afterwards engaged. The wing of Aristeus, with the Corinthians and other picked troops round him, routed the wing opposed to it, and followed for a considerable distance in pursuit. But the rest of the army of the Potidaeans and of the Peloponnesians was defeated by the Athenians, and took refuge within the fortifications. Returning from the pursuit, Aristeus perceived the defeat of the rest of the army. Being at a loss which of the two risks to choose, whether to go to Olynthus or to Potidaea, he at last determined to draw his men into as small a space as possible, and force his way with a run into Potidaea. Not without difficulty, through a storm of missiles, he passed along by the breakwater through the sea, and brought off most of his men safe, though a few were lost. Meanwhile the auxiliaries of the Potidaeans from Olynthus, which is about seven miles off and in sight of Potidaea, when the battle began and the signals were raised, advanced a little way to render assistance; and the Macedonian horse formed against them to prevent it. But on victory speedily declaring for the Athenians and the signals being taken down, they retired back within the wall; and the Macedonians returned to the Athenians. Thus there were no cavalry present on either side. After the battle the Athenians set up a trophy, and gave back their dead to the Potidaeans under truce. The Potidaeans and their allies had close upon three hundred killed; the Athenians a hundred and fifty of their own citizens, and Callias their general.

The wall on the side of the isthmus had now works at once raised against it, and manned by the Athenians. That on the side of Pallene had no works raised against it. They did not think themselves strong enough at once to keep a garrison in the isthmus and to cross over to Pallene and raise works there; they were afraid that the Potidaeans and their allies might take advantage of their division to attack them. Meanwhile the Athenians at home learning that there were no works at Pallene, some time afterwards sent off sixteen hundred heavy infantry of their own citizens under the command of Phormio, son of Asopius. Arrived at Pallene, he fixed his headquarters at Aphytis, and led his army against Potidaea by short marches, ravaging the country as he advanced. No one venturing to meet him in the field, he raised works against the wall on the side of Pallene. So at length Potidaea was strongly invested on either side, and from the sea by the ships co-operating in the blockade. Aristeus, seeing its investment complete, and having no hope of its salvation, except in the event of some movement from the Peloponnese, or of some other improbable contingency, advised all except five hundred to watch for a wind and sail out of the place, in order that their provisions might last the longer. He was willing to be himself one of those who remained. Unable to persuade them, and desirous of acting on the next alternative, and of having things outside in the best posture possible, he eluded the guardships of the Athenians and sailed out. Remaining among the Chalcidians, he continued to carry on the war; in particular he laid an ambuscade near the city of the Sermylians, and cut off many of them; he also communicated with Peloponnese, and tried to contrive some method by which help might be brought. Meanwhile, after the completion of the investment of Potidaea, Phormio next employed his sixteen hundred men in ravaging Chalcidice and Bottica: some of the towns also were taken by him.

CHAPTER III

Congress of the Peloponnesian Confederacy at Lacedaemon

T HE ATHENIANS and Peloponnesians had these antecedent grounds of complaint against each other: the complaint of Corinth was that her colony of Potidaea, and Corinthian and Peloponnesian citizens within it, were being besieged; that of Athens against the Peloponnesians that they had incited a town of hers, a member of her alliance and a contributor to her revenue, to revolt, and had come and were openly fighting against her on the side of the Potidaeans. For all this, war had not yet broken out: there was still truce for a while; for this was a private enterprise on the part of Corinth.

But the siege of Potidaea put an end to her inaction; she had men inside it: besides, she feared for the place. Immediately summoning the allies to Lacedaemon, she came and loudly accused Athens of breach of the treaty and aggression on the rights of Peloponnese. With her, the Aeginetans, formally unrepresented from fear of Athens, in secret proved not the least urgent of the advocates for war, asserting that they had not the independence guaranteed to them by the treaty. After extending the summons to any of their allies and others who might have complaints to make of Athenian aggression, the Lacedaemonians held their ordinary assembly, and invited them to speak. There were many who came forward and made their several accusations; among them the Megarians, in a long list of grievances, called special attention to the fact of their exclusion from the ports of the Athenian empire and the market of Athens, in defiance of the treaty. Last of all the Corinthians came forward, and having let those who preceded them inflame the Lacedaemonians, now followed with a speech to this effect:

"Lacedaemonians! the confidence which you feel in your constitution and social order, inclines you to receive any reflections of ours on other powers with a certain scepticism.

Hence springs your moderation, but hence also the rather limited knowledge which you betray in dealing with foreign politics. Time after time was our voice raised to warn you of the blows about to be dealt us by Athens, and time after time, instead of taking the trouble to ascertain the worth of our communications, you contented yourselves with suspecting the speakers of being inspired by private interest. And so, instead of calling these allies together before the blow fell, you have delayed to do so till we are smarting under it; allies among whom we have not the worst title to speak, as having the greatest complaints to make, complaints of Athenian outrage and Lacedaemonian neglect. Now if these assaults on the rights of Hellas had been made in the dark, you might be unacquainted with the facts, and it would be our duty to enlighten you. As it is, long speeches are not needed where you see servitude accomplished for some of us, meditated for others - in particular for our allies - and prolonged preparations in the aggressor against the hour of war. Or what, pray, is the meaning of their reception of Corcyra by fraud, and their holding it against us by force? what of the siege of Potidaea? - places one of which lies most conveniently for any action against the Thracian towns; while the other would have contributed a very large navy to the Peloponnesians?

"For all this you are responsible. You it was who first allowed them to fortify their city after the Median war, and afterwards to erect the long walls - you who, then and now, are always depriving of freedom not only those whom they have enslaved, but also those who have as yet been your allies. For the true author of the subjugation of a people is not so much the immediate agent, as the power which permits it having the means to prevent it; particularly if that power aspires to the glory of being the liberator of Hellas. We are at last assembled. It has not been easy to assemble, nor even now are our objects defined. We ought not to be still inquiring into the fact of our wrongs, but into the means of our defence. For the aggressors with matured plans to oppose to our indecision have cast threats aside and betaken themselves to action. And we know what are the paths by which Athenian aggression travels, and how insidious is its progress. A degree of confidence she may feel from the idea that your bluntness of perception prevents your noticing her; but it is nothing to the impulse which her advance will receive from the knowledge that you see, but do not care to interfere. You, Lacedaemonians, of all the Hellenes are alone inactive, and defend yourselves not by doing anything but by looking as if you would do something; you alone wait till the power of an enemy is becoming twice its original size, instead of crushing it in its infancy. And yet the world used to say that you were to be depended upon; but in your case, we fear, it said more than the truth. The Mede, we ourselves know, had time to come from the ends of the earth to Peloponnese, without any force of yours worthy of the name advancing to meet him. But this was a distant enemy. Well, Athens at all events is a near neighbour, and yet Athens you utterly disregard; against Athens you prefer to act on the defensive instead of on the offensive, and to make it an affair of chances by deferring the struggle till she has grown far stronger than at first. And yet you know that on the whole the rock on which the barbarian was wrecked was himself, and that if our present enemy Athens has not again and again annihilated us, we owe it more to her blunders than to your protection; Indeed, expectations from you have before now been the ruin of some, whose faith induced them to omit preparation.

"We hope that none of you will consider these words of remonstrance to be rather words of hostility; men remonstrate with friends who are in error, accusations they reserve for enemies who have wronged them. Besides, we consider that we have as good a right as any one to point out a neighbour's faults, particularly when we contemplate the great contrast between the two national characters; a contrast of which, as far as we can see, you have little perception, having never yet considered what sort of antagonists you will encounter in the Athenians, how widely, how absolutely different from yourselves. The Athenians are addicted to innovation, and their designs are characterized by swiftness alike in conception and execution; you have a genius for keeping what you have got, accompanied by a total want of invention, and when forced to act you never go far enough. Again, they are adventurous beyond their power, and daring beyond their judgment, and in danger they are sanguine; your wont is to attempt less than is justified by your power, to mistrust even what is sanctioned by your judgment, and to fancy that from danger there is no release. Further, there is promptitude on their side against procrastination on yours; they are never at home, you are never from it: for they hope by their absence to extend their acquisitions, you fear by your advance to endanger what you have left behind. They are swift to follow up a success, and slow to recoil from a reverse. Their bodies they spend ungrudgingly in their country's cause; their intellect they jealously husband to be employed in her service. A scheme unexecuted is with them a positive loss, a successful enterprise a comparative failure. The deficiency created by the miscarriage of an undertaking is soon filled up by fresh hopes; for they alone are enabled to call a thing hoped for a thing got, by the speed with which they act upon their resolutions. Thus they toil on in trouble and danger all the days of their life, with little opportunity for enjoying, being ever engaged in getting: their only idea of a holiday is to do what the occasion demands, and to them laborious occupation is less of a misfortune than the peace of a quiet life. To describe their character in a word, one might truly say that they were born into the world to take no rest themselves and to give none to others.

"Such is Athens, your antagonist. And yet, Lacedaemonians, you still delay, and fail to see that peace stays longest with those, who are not more careful to use their power justly than to show their determination not to submit to injustice. On the contrary, your ideal of fair dealing is based on the principle that, if you do not injure others, you need not risk your own fortunes in preventing others from injuring you. Now you could scarcely have succeeded in such a policy even with a neighbour like yourselves; but in the present instance, as we have just shown, your habits are old-fashioned as compared with theirs. It is the law as in art, so in politics, that improvements ever prevail; and though fixed usages may be best for undisturbed communities, constant necessities of action must be accompanied by the constant improvement of methods. Thus it happens that the vast experience of Athens has carried her further than you on the path of innovation.

"Here, at least, let your procrastination end. For the present, assist your allies and Potidaea in particular, as you promised, by a speedy invasion of Attica, and do not sacrifice friends and kindred to their bitterest enemies, and drive the rest of us in despair to some other alliance. Such a step would not be condemned either by the Gods who received our oaths, or by the men who witnessed them. The breach of a treaty cannot be laid to the people whom desertion compels to seek new relations, but to the power that fails to assist its confederate. But if you will only act, we will stand by you; it would be unnatural for us to change, and never should we meet with such a congenial ally. For these reasons choose the right course, and endeavour not to let Peloponnese under your supremacy degenerate from the prestige that it enjoyed under that of your ancestors."

Such were the words of the Corinthians. There happened to be Athenian envoys present at Lacedaemon on other business. On hearing the speeches they thought themselves called upon to come before the Lacedaemonians. Their intention was not to offer a defence on any of the charges which the cities brought against them, but to show on a comprehensive view that it was not a matter to be hastily decided on, but one that demanded further consideration. There was also a wish to call attention to the great power of Athens, and to refresh the memory of the old and enlighten the ignorance of the young, from a notion that their words might have the effect of inducing them to prefer tranquillity to war. So they came to the Lacedaemonians and said that they too, if there was no objection, wished to speak to their assembly. They replied by inviting them to come forward. The Athenians advanced, and spoke as follows:

"The object of our mission here was not to argue with your allies, but to attend to the matters on which our state dispatched us. However, the vehemence of the outcry that we hear against us has prevailed on us to come forward. It is not to combat the accusations of the cities (indeed you are not the judges before whom either we or they can plead), but to prevent your taking the wrong course on matters of great importance by yielding too readily to the persuasions of your allies. We also wish to show on a review of the whole indictment that we have a fair title to our possessions, and that our country has claims to consideration. We need not refer to remote antiquity: there we could appeal to the voice of tradition, but not to the experience of our audience. But to the Median War and contemporary history we must refer, although we are rather tired of continually bringing this subject forward. In our action during that war we ran great risk to obtain certain advantages: you had your share in the solid results, do not try to rob us of all share in the good that the glory may do us. However, the story shall be told not so much to deprecate hostility as to testify against it, and to show, if you are so ill advised as to enter into a struggle with Athens, what sort of an antagonist she is likely to prove. We assert that at Marathon we were at the front, and faced the barbarian single-handed. That when he came the second time, unable to cope with him by land we went on board our ships with all our people, and joined in the action at Salamis. This prevented his taking the Peloponnesian states in detail, and ravaging them with his fleet; when the multitude of his vessels would have made any combination for self-defence impossible. The best proof of this was furnished by the invader himself. Defeated at sea, he considered his power to be no longer what it had been, and retired as speedily as possible with the greater part of his army.

"Such, then, was the result of the matter, and it was clearly proved that it was on the fleet of Hellas that her cause depended. Well, to this result we contributed three very useful elements, viz., the largest number of ships, the ablest commander, and the most unhesitating patriotism. Our contingent of ships was little less than two-thirds of the whole four hundred; the commander was Themistocles, through whom chiefly it was that the battle took place in the straits, the acknowledged salvation of our cause. Indeed, this was the reason of your receiving him with honours such as had never been accorded to any foreign visitor. While for daring patriotism we had no competitors. Receiving no reinforcements from behind, seeing everything in front of us already subjugated, we had the spirit, after abandoning our city, after sacrificing our property (instead of deserting the remainder of the league or depriving them of our services by dispersing), to throw ourselves into our ships and meet the danger, without a thought of resenting your neglect to assist us. We assert, therefore, that we conferred on you quite as much as we received. For you had a stake to fight for; the cities which you had left were still filled with your homes, and

The Peloponnesian War

52

you had the prospect of enjoying them again; and your coming was prompted quite as much by fear for yourselves as for us; at all events, you never appeared till we had nothing left to lose. But we left behind us a city that was a city no longer, and staked our lives for a city that had an existence only in desperate hope, and so bore our full share in your deliverance and in ours. But if we had copied others, and allowed fears for our territory to make us give in our adhesion to the Mede before you came, or if we had suffered our ruin to break our spirit and prevent us embarking in our ships, your naval inferiority would have made a sea-fight unnecessary, and his objects would have been peaceably attained.

"Surely, Lacedaemonians, neither by the patriotism that we displayed at that crisis, nor by the wisdom of our counsels, do we merit our extreme unpopularity with the Hellenes, not at least unpopularity for our empire. That empire we acquired by no violent means, but because you were unwilling to prosecute to its conclusion the war against the barbarian, and because the allies attached themselves to us and spontaneously asked us to assume the command. And the nature of the case first compelled us to advance our empire to its present height; fear being our principal motive, though honour and interest afterwards came in. And at last, when almost all hated us, when some had already revolted and had been subdued, when you had ceased to be the friends that you once were, and had become objects of suspicion and dislike, it appeared no longer safe to give up our empire; especially as all who left us would fall to you. And no one can quarrel with a people for making, in matters of tremendous risk, the best provision that it can for its interest.

"You, at all events, Lacedaemonians, have used your supremacy to settle the states in Peloponnese as is agreeable to you. And if at the period of which we were speaking you had persevered to the end of the matter, and had incurred hatred in your command, we are sure that you would have made yourselves just as galling to the allies, and would have been forced to choose between a strong government and danger to yourselves. It follows that it was not a very wonderful action, or contrary to the common practice of mankind, if we did accept an empire that was offered to us, and refused to give it up under the pressure of three of the strongest motives, fear, honour, and interest. And it was not we who set the example, for it has always been law that the weaker should be subject to the stronger. Besides, we believed ourselves to be worthy of our position, and so you thought us till now, when calculations of interest have made you take up the cry of justice - a consideration which no one ever yet brought forward to hinder his ambition when he had a chance of gaining anything by might. And praise is due to all who, if not so superior to human nature as to refuse dominion, yet respect justice more than their position compels them to do.

"We imagine that our moderation would be best demonstrated by the conduct of others who should be placed in our position; but even our equity has very unreasonably subjected us to condemnation instead of approval. Our abatement of our rights in the contract trials with our allies, and our causing them to be decided by impartial laws at Athens, have gained us the character of being litigious. And none care to inquire why this reproach is not brought against other imperial powers, who treat their subjects with less moderation than we do; the secret being that where force can be used, law is not needed. But our subjects are so habituated to associate with us as equals that any defeat whatever that clashes with their notions of justice, whether it proceeds from a legal judgment or from the power which our empire gives us, makes them forget to be grateful for being allowed to retain most of their possessions, and more vexed at a part being taken, than if we had from the first cast law aside and openly gratified our covetousness. If we had done so, not even would they have disputed that the weaker must give way to the stronger. Men's indignation, it seems, is more excited by legal wrong than by violent wrong; the first looks like being cheated by an equal, the second like being compelled by a superior. At all events they contrived to put up with much worse treatment than this from the Mede, yet they think our rule severe, and this is to be expected, for the present always weighs heavy on the conquered. This at least is certain. If you were to succeed in overthrowing us and in taking our place, you would speedily lose the popularity with which fear of us has invested you, if your policy of to-day is at all to tally with the sample that you gave of it during the brief period of your command against the Mede. Not only is your life at home regulated by rules and institutions incompatible with those of others, but your citizens abroad act neither on these rules nor on those which are recognized by the rest of Hellas.

"Take time then in forming your resolution, as the matter is of great importance; and do not be persuaded by the opinions and complaints of others to bring trouble on yourselves, but consider the vast influence of accident in war, before you are engaged in it. As it continues, it generally becomes an affair of chances, chances from which neither of us is exempt, and whose event we must risk in the dark. It is a common mistake in going to war to begin at the wrong end, to act first, and wait for disaster to discuss the matter. But we are not yet by any means so misguided, nor, so far as we can see, are you; accordingly, while it is still open to us both to choose aright, we bid you not to dissolve the treaty, or to break your oaths, but to have our differences settled by arbitration according to our agreement. Or else we take the gods who heard the oaths to witness, and if you begin hostilities, whatever line of action you choose, we will try not to be behindhand in repelling you."

Such were the words of the Athenians. After the Lacedaemonians had heard the complaints of the allies against the Athenians, and the observations of the latter, they made all withdraw, and consulted by themselves on the question before them. The opinions of the majority all led to the same conclusion; the Athenians were open aggressors, and war must be declared at once. But Archidamus, the Lacedaemonian king, came forward, who had the reputation of being at once a wise and a moderate man, and made the following speech:

"I have not lived so long, Lacedaemonians, without having had the experience of many wars, and I see those among you of the same age as myself, who will not fall into the common misfortune of longing for war from inexperience or from a belief in its advantage and its safety. This, the war on which you are now debating, would be one of the greatest magnitude, on a sober consideration of the matter. In a struggle with Peloponnesians and neighbours our strength is of the same character, and it is possible to move swiftly on the different points. But a struggle with a people who live in a distant land, who have also an extraordinary familiarity with the sea, and who are in the highest state of preparation in every other department; with wealth private and public, with ships, and horses, and heavy infantry, and a population such as no one other Hellenic place can equal, and lastly a number of tributary allies - what can justify us in rashly beginning such a struggle? wherein is our trust that we should rush on it unprepared? Is it in our ships? There we are inferior; while if we are to practise and become a match for them, time must intervene. Is it in our money? There we have a far greater deficiency. We neither have it in our treasury, nor are we ready to contribute it from our private funds. Confidence might possibly be felt in our superiority in heavy infantry and population, which will enable us to invade and devastate their lands. But the Athenians have plenty of other land in their empire, and can import what they want by sea. Again, if we are to attempt an insurrection of their allies, these will have to be supported with a fleet, most of them being islanders. What then is to be our war? For unless we can either beat them at sea, or deprive them of the revenues which feed their navy, we shall meet with little but disaster. Meanwhile our honour will be pledged to keeping on, particularly if it be the opinion that we began the quarrel. For let us never be elated by the fatal hope of the war being quickly ended by the devastation of their lands. I fear rather that we may leave it as a legacy to our children; so improbable is it that the Athenian spirit will be the slave of their land, or Athenian experience be cowed by war.

"Not that I would bid you be so unfeeling as to suffer them to injure your allies, and to refrain from unmasking their intrigues; but I do bid you not to take up arms at once, but to send and remonstrate with them in a tone not too suggestive of war, nor again too suggestive of submission, and to employ the interval in perfecting our own preparations. The means will be, first, the acquisition of allies, Hellenic or barbarian it matters not, so long as they are an accession to our strength naval or pecuniary - I say Hellenic or barbarian, because the odium of such an accession to all who like us are the objects of the designs of the Athenians is taken away by the law of self-preservation - and secondly the development of our home resources. If they listen to our embassy, so much the better; but if not, after the lapse of two or three years our position will have become materially strengthened, and we can then attack them if we think proper. Perhaps by that time the sight of our preparations, backed by language equally significant, will have disposed them to submission, while their land is still untouched, and while their counsels may be directed to the retention of advantages as yet undestroyed. For the only light in which you can view their land is that of a hostage in your hands, a hostage the more valuable the better it is cultivated. This you ought to spare as long as possible, and not make them desperate, and so increase the difficulty of dealing with them. For if while still unprepared, hurried away by the complaints of our allies, we are induced to lay it waste, have a care that we do not bring deep disgrace and deep perplexity upon Peloponnese. Complaints, whether of communities or individuals, it is possible to adjust; but war undertaken by a coalition for sectional interests, whose progress there is no means of foreseeing, does not easily admit of creditable settlement.

"And none need think it cowardice for a number of confederates to pause before they attack a single city. The Athenians have allies as numerous as our own, and allies that pay tribute, and war is a matter not so much of arms as of money, which makes arms of use. And this is more than ever true in a struggle between a continental and a maritime power. First, then, let us provide money, and not allow ourselves to be carried away by the talk of our allies before we have done so: as we shall have the largest share of responsibility for the consequences be they good or bad, we have also a right to a tranquil inquiry respecting them.

"And the slowness and procrastination, the parts of our character that are most assailed by their criticism, need not make you blush. If we undertake the war without preparation, we should by hastening its commencement only delay its conclusion: further, a free and a famous city has through all time been ours. The quality which they condemn is really nothing but a wise moderation; thanks to its possession, we alone do not become insolent in success and give way less than others in misfortune; we are not carried away by the pleasure of hearing ourselves cheered on to risks which our judgment condemns; nor, if annoyed, are we any the more convinced by attempts to exasperate us by accusation. We are both warlike and wise, and it is our sense of order that makes us so. We are warlike, because self-control contains honour as a chief constituent, and honour bravery. And we are wise, because we are educated with too little learning to despise the laws, and with too severe a self-control to disobey them, and are brought up not to be too knowing in useless matters - such as the knowledge which can give a specious criticism of an enemy's plans in theory, but fails to assail them with equal success in practice - but are taught to consider that the schemes of our enemies are not dissimilar to our own, and that the freaks of chance are not determinable by calculation. In practice we always base our preparations against an enemy on the assumption that his plans are good; indeed, it is right to rest our hopes not on a belief in his blunders, but on the soundness of our provisions. Nor ought we to believe that there is much difference between man and man, but to think that the superiority lies with him who is reared in the severest school. These practices, then, which our ancestors have delivered to us, and by whose maintenance we have always profited, must not be given up. And we must not be hurried into deciding in a day's brief space a question which concerns many lives and fortunes and many cities, and in which honour is deeply involved - but we must decide calmly. This our strength peculiarly enables us to do. As for the Athenians, send to them on the matter of Potidaea, send on the matter of the alleged wrongs of the allies, particularly as they are prepared with legal satisfaction; and to proceed against one who offers arbitration as against a wrongdoer, law forbids. Meanwhile do not omit preparation for war. This decision will be the best for yourselves, the most terrible to your opponents."

Such were the words of Archidamus. Last came forward Sthenelaidas, one of the ephors for that year, and spoke to the Lacedaemonians as follows:

"The long speech of the Athenians I do not pretend to understand. They said a good deal in praise of themselves, but nowhere denied that they are injuring our allies and Peloponnese. And yet if they behaved well against the Mede then, but ill towards us now, they deserve double punishment for having ceased to be good and for having become bad. We meanwhile are the same then and now, and shall not, if we are wise, disregard the wrongs of our allies, or put off till to-morrow the duty of assisting those who must suffer to-day. Others have much money and ships and horses, but we have good allies whom we must not give up to the Athenians, nor by lawsuits and words decide the matter, as it is anything but in word that we are harmed, but render instant and powerful help. And let us not be told that it is fitting for us to deliberate under injustice; long deliberation is rather fitting for those who have injustice in contemplation. Vote therefore, Lacedaemonians, for war, as the honour of Sparta demands, and neither allow the further aggrandizement of Athens, nor betray our allies to ruin, but with the gods let us advance against the aggressors."

With these words he, as ephor, himself put the question to the assembly of the Lacedaemonians. He said that he could not determine which was the loudest acclamation (their mode of decision is by acclamation not by voting); the fact being that he wished to make them declare their opinion openly and thus to increase their ardour for war. Accordingly he said: "All Lacedaemonians who are of opinion that the treaty has been broken, and that Athens is guilty, leave your seats and go there," pointing out a certain place; "all who are of the opposite opinion, there." They accordingly stood up and divided; and those who held that the treaty had been broken were in a decided majority. Summoning the allies, they told them that their opinion was that Athens had been guilty of injustice, but that they wished to convoke all the allies and put it to the vote; in order that they might make war, if they decided to do so, on a common resolution. Having thus gained their point, the delegates returned home at once; the Athenian envoys a little later, when they had dispatched the objects of their mission. This decision of the assembly, judging that the treaty had been broken, was made in the fourteenth year of the thirty years' truce, which was entered into after the affair of Euboea.

The Lacedaemonians voted that the treaty had been broken, and that the war must be declared, not so much because they were persuaded by the arguments of the allies, as because they feared the growth of the power of the Athenians, seeing most of Hellas already subject to them.

CHAPTER IV

From the End of the Persian to the Beginning of the
Peloponnesian War - The Progress from Supremacy to Empire

The end of the Persian War.

THE WAY in which Athens came to be placed in the circumstances under which her power grew was this. After the Medes had returned from Europe, defeated by sea and land by the Hellenes, and after those of them who had fled with their ships to Mycale had been destroyed, Leotychides, king of the Lacedaemonians, the commander of the Hellenes at Mycale, departed home with the allies from Peloponnese. But the Athenians and the allies from Ionia and Hellespont, who had now revolted from the King, remained and laid siege to Sestos, which was still held by the Medes. After wintering before it, they became masters of the place on its evacuation by the barbarians; and after this they sailed away from Hellespont to their respective cities. Meanwhile the Athenian people, after the departure of the barbarian from their country, at once proceeded to carry over their children and wives, and such property as they had left, from the places where they had deposited them, and prepared to rebuild their city and their walls. For only isolated portions of the circumference had been left standing, and most of the houses were in ruins; though a few remained, in which the Persian grandees had taken up their quarters.

Perceiving what they were going to do, the Lacedaemonians sent an embassy to Athens. They would have themselves preferred to see neither her nor any other city in possession of a wall; though here they acted principally at the instigation of their allies, who were alarmed at the strength of her newly acquired navy and the valour which she had displayed in the war with the Medes. They begged her not only to abstain from building walls for herself, but also to join them in throwing down the walls that still held together of the ultra-Peloponnesian cities. The real meaning of their advice, the suspicion that it contained against the Athenians, was not proclaimed; it was urged that so the barbarian, in the event of a third invasion, would not have any strong place, such as he now had in Thebes, for his base of operations; and that Peloponnese would suffice for all as a base both for retreat and offence. After the Lacedaemonians had thus spoken, they were, on the advice of Themistocles, immediately dismissed by the Athenians, with the answer that ambassadors should be sent to Sparta to discuss the question. Themistocles told the Athenians to send him off with all speed to Lacedaemon, but not to dispatch his colleagues as soon as they had selected them, but to wait until they had raised their wall to the height from which defence was possible. Meanwhile the whole population in the city was to labour at the wall, the Athenians, their wives, and their children, sparing no edifice, private or public, which might be of any use to the work, but throwing all down. After giving these instructions, and adding that he would be responsible for all other matters there, he departed. Arrived at Lacedaemon he did not seek an audience with the authorities, but tried to gain time and made excuses. When any of the government asked him why he did not appear in the assembly, he would say that he was waiting for his colleagues, who had been detained in Athens by some engagement; however, that he expected their speedy arrival, and wondered that they were not yet there. At first the Lacedaemonians trusted the words of Themistocles, through their friendship for him; but when others arrived, all distinctly declaring that the work was going on and already attaining some elevation, they did not know how to disbelieve it. Aware of this, he told them that rumours are deceptive, and should not be trusted; they should send some reputable persons from Sparta to inspect, whose report might be trusted. They dispatched them accordingly. Concerning these Themistocles secretly sent word to the Athenians to detain them as far as possible without putting them under open constraint, and not to let them go until they had themselves returned. For his colleagues had now joined him, Abronichus, son of Lysicles, and Aristides, son of Lysimachus, with the news that the wall was sufficiently advanced; and he feared that when the Lacedaemonians heard the facts, they might refuse to let them go. So the Athenians detained the envoys according to his message, and Themistocles had an audience with the Lacedaemonians, and at last openly told them that Athens was now fortified sufficiently to protect its inhabitants; that any embassy which the Lacedaemonians or their allies might wish to send to them should in future proceed on the assumption that the people to whom they were going was able to distinguish both its own and the general interests. That when the Athenians thought fit to abandon their city and to embark in their ships, they ventured on that perilous step without consulting them; and that on the other hand, wherever they had deliberated with the Lacedaemonians, they had proved themselves to be in judgment second to none. That they now thought it fit that their city should have a wall, and that this would be more for the advantage of both the citizens of Athens and the Hellenic confederacy; for without equal military strength it was impossible to contribute equal or fair counsel to the common interest. It followed, he observed, either that all the members of the confederacy should be without walls, or that the present step should be considered a right one.

The Lacedaemonians did not betray any open signs of anger against the Athenians at what they heard. The embassy, it seems, was prompted not by a desire to obstruct, but to guide the counsels of their government: besides, Spartan feeling was at that time very friendly towards Athens on account of the patriotism which she had displayed in the struggle with the Mede. Still the defeat of their wishes could not but cause them secret annoyance. The envoys of each state departed home without complaint.

In this way the Athenians walled their city in a little while. To this day the building shows signs of the haste of its execution; the foundations are laid of stones of all kinds, and in some places not wrought or fitted, but placed just in the order in which they were brought by the different hands; and many columns, too, from tombs, and sculptured stones were put in with the rest. For the bounds of the city were extended at every point of the circumference; and so they laid hands on everything without exception in their haste. Themistocles also persuaded them to finish the walls of Piraeus, which had been begun before, in his year of office as archon; being influenced alike by the fineness of a locality that has three natural harbours, and by the great start which the Athenians would gain in the acquisition of power by becoming a naval people. For he first ventured to tell them to stick to the sea and forthwith began to lay the foundations of the empire. It was by his advice, too, that they built the walls of that thickness which can still be discerned round Piraeus, the stones being brought up by two wagons meeting each other. Between the walls thus formed there was neither rubble nor mortar, but great stones hewn square and fitted together, cramped to each other on the outside with iron and lead. About half the height that he intended was finished. His idea was by their size and thickness to keep off the attacks of an enemy; he thought that they might be adequately defended by a small garrison of invalids, and the rest be freed for service in the fleet. For the fleet claimed most of his attention. He saw, as I think, that the approach by sea was easier for the king's army than that by land: he also thought Piraeus more valuable than the upper city; indeed, he was always advising the Athenians, if a day should come when they were hard pressed by land, to go down into Piraeus, and defy the world with their fleet. Thus, therefore, the Athenians completed their wall, and commenced their other buildings immediately after the retreat of the Mede.

Meanwhile Pausanias, son of Cleombrotus, was sent out from Lacedaemon as commander-in-chief of the Hellenes, with twenty ships from Peloponnese. With him sailed the Athenians with thirty ships, and a number of the other allies. They made an expedition against Cyprus and subdued most of the island, and afterwards against Byzantium, which was in the hands of the Medes, and compelled it to surrender. This event took place while the Spartans were still supreme. But the violence of Pausanias had already begun to be disagreeable to the Hellenes, particularly to the Ionians and the newly liberated populations. These resorted to the Athenians and requested them as their kinsmen to become their leaders, and to stop any attempt at violence on the part of Pausanias. The Athenians accepted their overtures, and determined to put down any attempt of the kind and to settle everything else as their interests might seem to demand. In the meantime the Lacedaemonians recalled Pausanias for an investigation of the reports which had reached them. Manifold and grave accusations had been brought against him by Hellenes arriving in Sparta; and, to all appearance, there had been in him more of the mimicry of a despot than of the attitude of a general. As it happened, his recall came just at the time when the hatred which he had inspired had induced the allies to desert him, the soldiers from Peloponnese excepted, and to range themselves by the side of the Athenians. On his arrival at Lacedaemon, he was censured for his private acts of oppression, but was acquitted on the heaviest counts and pronounced not guilty; it must be known that the charge of

Medism formed one of the principal, and to all appearance one of the best founded, articles against him. The Lacedaemonians did not, however, restore him to his command, but sent out Dorkis and certain others with a small force; who found the allies no longer inclined to concede to them the supremacy. Perceiving this they departed, and the Lacedaemonians did not send out any to succeed them. They feared for those who went out a deterioration similar to that observable in Pausanias; besides, they desired to be rid of the Median War, and were satisfied of the competency of the Athenians for the position, and of their friendship at the time towards themselves.

The Athenians, having thus succeeded to the supremacy by the voluntary act of the allies through their hatred of Pausanias, fixed which cities were to contribute money against the barbarian, which ships; their professed object being to retaliate for their sufferings by ravaging the King's country. Now was the time that the office of "Treasurers for Hellas" was first instituted by the Athenians. These officers received the tribute, as the money contributed was called. The tribute was first fixed at four hundred and sixty talents. The common treasury was at Delos, and the congresses were held in the temple. Their supremacy commenced with independent allies who acted on the resolutions of a common congress. It was marked by the following undertakings in war and in administration during the interval between the Median and the present war, against the barbarian, against their own rebel allies, and against the Peloponnesian powers which would come in contact with them on various occasions. My excuse for relating these events, and for venturing on this digression, is that this passage of history has been omitted by all my predecessors, who have confined themselves either to Hellenic history before the Median War, or the Median War itself. Hellanicus, it is true, did touch on these events in his Athenian history; but he is somewhat concise and not accurate in his dates. Besides, the history of these events contains an explanation of the growth of the Athenian empire.

First the Athenians besieged and captured Eion on the Strymon from the Medes, and made slaves of the inhabitants, being under the command of Cimon, son of Miltiades. Next they enslaved Scyros, the island in the Aegean, containing a Dolopian population, and colonized it themselves. This was followed by a war against Carystus, in which the rest of Euboea remained neutral, and which was ended by surrender on conditions. After this Naxos left the confederacy, and a war ensued, and she had to return after a siege; this was the first instance of the engagement being broken by the subjugation of an allied city, a precedent which was followed by that of the rest in the order which circumstances prescribed. Of all the causes of defection, that connected with arrears of tribute and vessels, and with failure of service, was the chief; for the Athenians were very severe and exacting, and made themselves offensive by applying the screw of necessity to men who were not used to and in fact not disposed for any continuous labour. In some other respects the Athenians were not the old popular rulers they had been at first; and if they had more than their fair share of service, it was correspondingly easy for them to reduce any that tried to leave the confederacy. For this the allies had themselves to blame; the wish to get off service making most of them arrange to pay their share of the expense in money instead of in ships, and so to avoid having to leave their homes. Thus while Athens was increasing her navy with the funds which they contributed, a revolt always found them without resources or experience for war.

Next we come to the actions by land and by sea at the river Eurymedon, between the Athenians with their allies, and the Medes, when the Athenians won both battles on the same day under the conduct of Cimon, son of Miltiades, and captured and destroyed the whole Phoenician fleet, consisting of two hundred vessels. Some time afterwards occurred the defection of the Thasians, caused by disagreements about the marts on the opposite coast of Thrace, and about the mine in their possession. Sailing with a fleet to Thasos, the Athenians defeated them at sea and effected a landing on the island. About the same time they sent ten thousand settlers of their own citizens and the allies to settle the place then called Ennea Hodoi or Nine Ways, now Amphipolis. They succeeded in gaining possession of Ennea Hodoi from the Edonians, but on advancing into the interior of Thrace were cut off in Drabescus, a town of the Edonians, by the assembled Thracians, who regarded the settlement of the place Ennea Hodoi as an act of hostility. Meanwhile the Thasians being defeated in the field and suffering siege, appealed to Lacedaemon, and desired her to assist them by an invasion of Attica. Without informing Athens, she promised and intended to do so, but was prevented by the occurrence of the earthquake, accompanied by the secession of the Helots and the Thuriats and Aethaeans of the Perioeci to Ithome. Most of the Helots were the descendants of the old Messenians that were enslaved in the famous war; and so all of them came to be called Messenians. So the Lacedaemonians being engaged in a war with the rebels in Ithome, the Thasians in the third year of the siege obtained terms from the Athenians by razing their walls, delivering up their ships, and arranging to pay the moneys demanded at once, and tribute in future; giving up their possessions on the continent together with the mine.

The Lacedaemonians, meanwhile, finding the war against the rebels in Ithome likely to last, invoked the aid of their allies, and especially of the Athenians, who came in some force under the command of Cimon. The reason for this pressing summons lay in their reputed skill in siege operations; a long siege had taught the Lacedaemonians their own deficiency in this art, else they would have taken the place by assault. The first open quarrel between the Lacedaemonians and Athenians arose out of this expedition. The Lacedaemonians, when assault failed to take the place, apprehensive of the enterprising and revolutionary character of the Athenians, and further looking upon them as of alien extraction, began to fear that, if they remained, they might be tempted by the besieged in Ithome to attempt some political changes. They accordingly dismissed them alone of the allies, without declaring their suspicions, but merely saying that they had now no need of them. But the Athenians, aware that their dismissal did not proceed from the more honourable reason of the two, but from suspicions which had been conceived, went away deeply offended, and conscious of having done nothing to merit such treatment from the Lacedaemonians; and the instant that they returned home they broke off the alliance which had been made against the Mede, and allied themselves with Sparta's enemy Argos; each of the contracting parties taking the same oaths and making the same alliance with the Thessalians.

Meanwhile the rebels in Ithome, unable to prolong further a ten years' resistance, surrendered to Lacedaemon; the conditions being that they should depart from Peloponnese under safe conduct, and should never set foot in it again: any one who might hereafter be found there was to be the slave of his captor. It must be known that the Lacedaemonians had an old oracle from Delphi, to the effect that they should let go the suppliant of Zeus at Ithome. So they went forth with their children and their wives, and being received by Athens from the hatred that she now felt for the Lacedaemonians, were located at Naupactus, which she had lately taken from the Ozolian Locrians. The Athenians received another addition to their confederacy in the Megarians; who left the Lacedaemonian alliance, annoyed by a war about boundaries forced on them by Corinth. The Athenians occupied Megara and Pegae, and built the Megarians their long walls from the city to Nisaea, in which they placed an Athenian garrison. This was the principal cause of the Corinthians conceiving such a deadly hatred against Athens.

Meanwhile Inaros, son of Psammetichus, a Libyan king of the Libyans on the Egyptian border, having his headquarters at Marea, the town above Pharos, caused a revolt of almost the whole of Egypt from King Artaxerxes and, placing himself at its head, invited the Athenians to his assistance. Abandoning a Cyprian expedition upon which they happened to be engaged with two hundred ships of their own and their allies, they arrived in Egypt and sailed from the sea into the Nile, and making themselves masters of the river and two-thirds of Memphis, addressed themselves to the attack of the remaining third, which is called White Castle. Within it were Persians and Medes who had taken refuge there, and Egyptians who had not joined the rebellion.

Meanwhile the Athenians, making a descent from their fleet upon Haliae, were engaged by a force of Corinthians and Epidaurians; and the Corinthians were victorious. Afterwards the Athenians engaged the Peloponnesian fleet off Cecruphalia; and the Athenians were victorious. Subsequently war broke out between Aegina and Athens, and there was a great battle at sea off Aegina between the Athenians and Aeginetans, each being aided by their allies; in which victory remained with the Athenians, who took seventy of the enemy's ships, and landed in the country and commenced a siege under the command of Leocrates, son of Stroebus. Upon this the Peloponnesians, desirous of aiding the Aeginetans, threw into Aegina a force of three hundred heavy infantry, who had before been serving with the Corinthians and Epidaurians. Meanwhile the Corinthians and their allies occupied the heights of Geraneia, and marched down into the Megarid, in the belief that, with a large force absent in Aegina and Egypt, Athens would be unable to help the Megarians without raising the siege of Aegina. But the Athenians, instead of moving the army of Aegina, raised a force of the old and young men that had been left in the city, and marched into the Megarid under the command of Myronides. After a drawn battle with the Corinthians, the rival hosts parted, each with the impression that they had gained the victory. The Athenians, however, if anything, had rather the advantage, and on the departure of the Corinthians set up a trophy. Urged by the taunts of the elders in their city, the Corinthians made their preparations, and about twelve days afterwards came and set up their trophy as victors. Sallying out from Megara, the Athenians cut off the party that was employed in erecting the trophy, and engaged and defeated the rest. In the retreat of the vanquished army, a considerable division, pressed by the pursuers and mistaking the road, dashed into a field on some private property, with a deep trench all round it, and no way out. Being acquainted with the place, the Athenians hemmed their front with heavy infantry and, placing the light troops round in a circle, stoned all who had gone in. Corinth here suffered a severe blow. The bulk of her army continued its retreat home.

About this time the Athenians began to build the long walls to the sea, that towards Phalerum and that towards Piraeus. Meanwhile the Phocians made an expedition against Doris, the old home of the Lacedaemonians, containing the towns of Boeum, Kitinium, and Erineum. They had taken one of these towns, when the Lacedaemonians under Nicomedes, son of Cleombrotus, commanding for King Pleistoanax, son of Pausanias, who was still a minor, came to the aid of the Dorians with fifteen hundred heavy infantry of their own, and ten thousand of their allies. After compelling the Phocians to restore the town on conditions, they began their retreat. The route by sea, across the Crissaean Gulf, exposed them to the risk of being stopped by the Athenian fleet; that across Geraneia seemed scarcely safe, the Athenians holding Megara and Pegae. For the pass was a difficult one, and was always guarded by the Athenians; and, in the present instance, the Lacedaemonians had information that they meant to dispute their passage. So they resolved to remain in Boeotia, and to consider which would be the safest line of march. They had also another reason for this resolve. Secret encouragement had been given them by a party in Athens, who hoped to put an end to the reign of democracy and the building of the Long Walls. Meanwhile the Athenians marched against them with their whole levy and a thousand Argives and the respective contingents of the rest of their allies. Altogether they were fourteen thousand strong. The march was prompted by the notion that the Lacedaemonians were at a loss how to effect their passage, and also by suspicions of an attempt to overthrow the democracy. Some cavalry also joined the Athenians from their Thessalian allies; but these went over to the Lacedaemonians during the battle.

The battle was fought at Tanagra in Boeotia. After heavy loss on both sides, victory declared for the Lacedaemonians and their allies. After entering the Megarid and cutting down the fruit trees, the Lacedaemonians returned home across Geraneia and the isthmus. Sixty-two days after the battle the Athenians marched into Boeotia under the command of Myronides, defeated the Boeotians in battle at Oenophyta, and became masters of Boeotia and Phocis. They dismantled the walls of the Tanagraeans, took a hundred of the richest men of the Opuntian Locrians as hostages, and finished their own long walls. This was followed by the surrender of the Aeginetans to Athens on conditions; they pulled down their walls, gave up their ships, and agreed to pay tribute in future. The Athenians sailed round Peloponnese under Tolmides, son of Tolmaeus, burnt the arsenal of Lacedaemon, took Chalcis, a town of the Corinthians, and in a descent upon Sicyon defeated the Sicyonians in battle.

Meanwhile the Athenians in Egypt and their allies were still there, and encountered all the vicissitudes of war. First the Athenians were masters of Egypt, and the King sent Megabazus a Persian to Lacedaemon with money to bribe the Peloponnesians to invade Attica and so draw off the Athenians from Egypt. Finding that the matter made no progress, and that the money was only being wasted, he recalled Megabazus with the remainder of the money, and sent Megabuzus, son of Zopyrus, a Persian, with a large army to Egypt. Arriving by land he defeated the Egyptians and their allies in a battle, and drove the Hellenes out of Memphis, and at length shut them up in the island of Prosopitis, where he besieged them for a year and six months. At last, draining the canal of its waters, which he diverted into another channel, he left their ships high and dry and joined most of the island to the mainland,

and then marched over on foot and captured it. Thus the enterprise of the Hellenes came to ruin after six years of war. Of all that large host a few travelling through Libya reached Cyrene in safety, but most of them perished. And thus Egypt returned to its subjection to the King, except Amyrtaeus, the king in the marshes, whom they were unable to capture from the extent of the marsh; the marshmen being also the most warlike of the Egyptians. Inaros, the Libyan king, the sole author of the Egyptian revolt, was betrayed, taken, and crucified. Meanwhile a relieving squadron of fifty vessels had sailed from Athens and the rest of the confederacy for Egypt. They put in to shore at the Mendesian mouth of the Nile, in total ignorance of what had occurred. Attacked on the land side by the troops, and from the sea by the Phoenician navy, most of the ships were destroyed; the few remaining being saved by retreat. Such was the end of the great expedition of the Athenians and their allies to Egypt.

Meanwhile Orestes, son of Echecratidas, the Thessalian king, being an exile from Thessaly, persuaded the Athenians to restore him. Taking with them the Boeotians and Phocians their allies, the Athenians marched to Pharsalus in Thessaly. They became masters of the country, though only in the immediate vicinity of the camp; beyond which they could not go for fear of the Thessalian cavalry. But they failed to take the city or to attain any of the other objects of their expedition, and returned home with Orestes without having effected anything. Not long after this a thousand of the Athenians embarked in the vessels that were at Pegae (Pegae, it must be remembered, was now theirs), and sailed along the coast to Sicyon under the command of Pericles, son of Xanthippus. Landing in Sicyon and defeating the Sicyonians who engaged them, they immediately took with them the Achaeans and, sailing across, marched against and laid siege to Oeniadae in Acarnania. Failing however to take it, they returned home.

Three years afterwards a truce was made between the Peloponnesians and Athenians for five years. Released from

Hellenic war, the Athenians made an expedition to Cyprus with two hundred vessels of their own and their allies, under the command of Cimon. Sixty of these were detached to Egypt at the instance of Amyrtaeus, the king in the marshes; the rest laid siege to Kitium, from which, however, they were compelled to retire by the death of Cimon and by scarcity of provisions. Sailing off Salamis in Cyprus, they fought with the Phoenicians, Cyprians, and Cilicians by land and sea, and, being victorious on both elements departed home, and with them the returned squadron from Egypt. After this the Lacedaemonians marched out on a sacred war, and, becoming masters of the temple at Delphi, it in the hands of the Delphians. Immediately after their retreat, the Athenians marched out, became masters of the temple, and placed it in the hands of the Phocians.

Some time after this, Orchomenus, Chaeronea, and some other places in Boeotia being in the hands of the Boeotian exiles, the Athenians marched against the above-mentioned hostile places with a thousand Athenian heavy infantry and the allied contingents, under the command of Tolmides, son of Tolmaeus. They took Chaeronea, and made slaves of the inhabitants, and, leaving a garrison, commenced their return. On their road they were attacked at Coronea by the Boeotian exiles from Orchomenus, with some Locrians and Euboean exiles, and others who were of the same way of thinking, were defeated in battle, and some killed, others taken captive. The Athenians evacuated all Boeotia by a treaty providing for the recovery of the men; and the exiled Boeotians returned, and with all the rest regained their independence.

This was soon afterwards followed by the revolt of Euboea from Athens. Pericles had already crossed over with an army of Athenians to the island, when news was brought to him that Megara had revolted, that the Peloponnesians were on the point of invading Attica, and that the Athenian garrison had been cut off by the Megarians, with the exception of a few who had taken refuge in Nisaea. The Megarians had introduced the Corinthians, Sicyonians, and Epidaurians into the town before they revolted.

Meanwhile Pericles brought his army back in all haste from Euboea. After this the Peloponnesians marched into Attica as far as Eleusis and Thrius, ravaging the country under the conduct of King Pleistoanax, the son of Pausanias, and without advancing further returned home. The Athenians then crossed over again to Euboea under the command of Pericles, and subdued the whole of the island: all but Histiaea was settled by convention; the Histiaeans they expelled from their homes, and occupied their territory themselves.

Not long after their return from Euboea, they made a truce with the Lacedaemonians and their allies for thirty years, giving up the posts which they occupied in Peloponnese - Nisaea, Pegae, Troezen, and Achaia. In the sixth year of the truce, war broke out between the Samians and Milesians about Priene. Worsted in the war, the Milesians came to Athens with loud complaints against the Samians. In this they were joined by certain private persons from Samos itself, who wished to revolutionize the government. Accordingly the Athenians sailed to Samos with forty ships and set up a democracy; took hostages from the Samians, fifty boys and as many men, lodged them in Lemnos, and after leaving a garrison in the island returned home. But some of the Samians had not remained in the island, but had fled to the continent. Making an agreement with the most powerful of those in the city, and an alliance with Pissuthnes, son of Hystaspes, the then satrap of Sardis, they got together a force of seven hundred mercenaries, and under cover of night crossed over to Samos. Their first step was to rise on the commons, most of whom they secured; their next to steal their hostages from Lemnos; after which they revolted, gave up the Athenian garrison left with them and its commanders to Pissuthnes, and instantly prepared for an expedition against Miletus. The Byzantines also revolted with them.

As soon as the Athenians heard the news, they sailed with sixty ships against Samos. Sixteen of these went to Caria to look out for the Phoenician fleet, and to Chios and Lesbos carrying round orders for reinforcements, and so never engaged; but forty-four ships under the command of Pericles with nine colleagues gave battle, off the island of Tragia, to seventy Samian vessels, of which twenty were transports, as they were sailing from Miletus. Victory remained with the Athenians. Reinforced afterwards by forty ships from Athens, and twenty-five Chian and Lesbian vessels, the Athenians landed, and having the superiority by land invested the city with three walls; it was also invested from the sea. Meanwhile Pericles took sixty ships from the blockading squadron, and departed in haste for Caunus and Caria, intelligence having been brought in of the approach of the Phoenician fleet to the aid of the Samians; indeed Stesagoras and others had left the island with five ships to bring them. But in the meantime the Samians made a sudden sally, and fell on the camp, which they found unfortified. Destroying the look-out vessels, and engaging and defeating such as were being launched to meet them, they remained masters of their own seas for fourteen days, and carried in and carried out what they pleased. But on the arrival of Pericles, they were once more shut up. Fresh reinforcements afterwards arrived - forty ships from Athens with Thucydides, Hagnon, and Phormio; twenty with Tlepolemus and Anticles, and thirty vessels from Chios and Lesbos. After a brief attempt at fighting, the Samians, unable to hold out, were reduced after a nine months' siege and surrendered on conditions; they razed their walls, gave hostages, delivered up their ships, and arranged to pay the expenses of the war by instalments. The Byzantines also agreed to be subject as before.

CHAPTER V

Second Congress at Lacedaemon - Preparations for War and Diplomatic Skirmishes - Cylon - Pausanias - Themistocles

AFTER THIS, though not many years later, we at length come to what has been already related, the affairs of Corcyra and Potidaea, and the events that served as a pretext for the present war. All these actions of the Hellenes against each other and the barbarian occurred in the fifty years' interval between the retreat of Xerxes and the beginning of the present war. During this interval the Athenians succeeded in placing their empire on a firmer basis, and advanced their own home power to a very great height. The Lacedaemonians, though fully aware of it, opposed it only for a little while, but remained inactive during most of the period, being of old slow to go to war except under the pressure of necessity, and in the present instance being hampered by wars at home; until the growth of the Athenian power could be no longer ignored, and their own confederacy became the object of its encroachments. They then felt that they could endure it no longer, but that the time had come for them to throw themselves heart and soul upon the hostile power, and break it, if they could, by commencing the present war. And though the Lacedaemonians had made up their own minds on the fact of the breach of the treaty and the guilt of the Athenians, yet they sent to Delphi and inquired of the God whether it would be well with them if they went to war; and, as it is reported, received from him the answer that if they put their whole strength into the war, victory would be theirs, and the promise that he himself would be with them, whether invoked or uninvoked. Still they wished to summon their allies again, and to take their vote on the propriety of making war. After the ambassadors from the confederates had arrived and a congress had been convened, they all spoke their minds, most of them denouncing the Athenians and demanding that the war should begin. In particular the Corinthians. They had before on their own account canvassed the cities in detail to induce them to vote for the war, in the fear that it might come too late to save Potidaea; they were present also on this occasion, and came forward the last, and made the following speech:

"Fellow allies, we can no longer accuse the Lacedaemonians of having failed in their duty: they have not only voted for war themselves, but have assembled us here for that purpose. We say their duty, for supremacy has its duties. Besides equitably administering private interests, leaders are required to show a special care for the common welfare in return for the special honours accorded to them by all in other ways. For ourselves, all who have already had dealings with the Athenians require no warning to be on their guard against them. The states more inland and out of the highway of communication should understand that, if they omit to support the coast powers, the result will be to injure the transit of their produce for exportation and the reception in exchange of their imports from the sea; and they must not be careless judges of what is now said, as if it had nothing to do with them, but must expect that the sacrifice of the powers on the coast will one day be followed by the extension of the danger to the interior, and must recognize that their own interests are deeply involved in this discussion. For these reasons they should not hesitate to exchange peace for war. If wise men remain quiet, while they are not injured, brave men abandon peace for war when they are injured, returning to an understanding on a favourable opportunity: in fact, they are neither intoxicated by their success in war, nor disposed to take an injury for the sake of the delightful tranquillity of peace. Indeed, to falter for the sake of such delights is, if you remain inactive, the quickest way of losing the sweets of repose to which you cling; while to conceive extravagant pretensions from success in war is to forget how hollow is the confidence by which you are elated. For if many ill-conceived plans have succeeded through the still greater fatuity of an opponent, many more, apparently well laid, have on the contrary ended in disgrace. The confidence with which we form our schemes is never completely justified in their execution; speculation is carried on in safety, but, when it comes to action, fear causes failure.

"To apply these rules to ourselves, if we are now kindling war it is under the pressure of injury, with adequate grounds of complaint; and after we have chastised the Athenians we will in season desist. We have many reasons to expect success - first, superiority in numbers and in military experience, and secondly our general and unvarying obedience in the execution of orders. The naval strength which they possess shall be raised by us from our respective antecedent resources, and from the moneys at Olympia and Delphi. A loan from these enables us to seduce their foreign sailors by the offer of higher pay. For the power of Athens is more mercenary than national; while ours will not be exposed to the same risk, as its strength lies more in men than in money. A single defeat at sea is in all likelihood their ruin: should they hold out, in that case there will be the more time for us to exercise ourselves in naval matters; and as soon as we have arrived at an equality in science, we need scarcely ask whether we shall be their superiors in courage. For the advantages that we have by nature they cannot acquire by education; while their superiority in science must be removed by our practice. The money required for these objects shall be provided by our contributions: nothing indeed could be more monstrous than the suggestion that, while their allies never tire of contributing for their own servitude, we should refuse to spend for vengeance and self-preservation the treasure which by such refusal we shall forfeit to Athenian rapacity and see employed for our own ruin.

"We have also other ways of carrying on the war, such as revolt of their allies, the surest method of depriving them of their revenues, which are the source of their strength, and establishment of fortified positions in their country, and various operations which cannot be foreseen at present. For war of all things proceeds least upon definite rules, but draws principally upon itself for contrivances to meet an emergency; and in such cases the party who faces the struggle and keeps his temper best meets with most security, and he who loses his temper about it with correspondent disaster. Let us also reflect that if it was merely a number of disputes of territory between rival neighbours, it might be borne; but here we have an enemy in Athens that is a match for our whole coalition, and more than a match for any of its members; so that unless as a body and as individual nationalities and individual cities we make an unanimous stand against her, she will easily conquer us divided and in detail. That conquest, terrible as it may sound, would, it must be known, have no other end than slavery pure and simple; a word which Peloponnese cannot even hear whispered without disgrace, or without disgrace see so many states abused by one. Meanwhile the opinion would be either that we were justly so used, or that we put up with it from cowardice, and were proving degenerate sons in not even securing for ourselves the freedom which our fathers gave to Hellas; and in allowing the establishment in Hellas of a tyrant state, though in individual states we think it our duty to put down sole rulers. And we do not know how this conduct can be held free from three of the gravest failings, want of sense, of courage, or of vigilance. For we do not suppose that you have taken refuge in that contempt of an enemy which has proved so fatal in so many instances - a feeling which from the numbers that it has ruined has come to be called not contemptuous but contemptible.

"There is, however, no advantage in reflections on the past further than may be of service to the present. For the future we must provide by maintaining what the present gives us and redoubling our efforts; it is hereditary to us to win virtue as the fruit of labour, and you must not change the habit, even though you should have a slight advantage in wealth and resources; for it is not right that what was won in want should be lost in plenty; no, we must boldly advance to the war for many reasons; the god has commanded it and promised to be with us, and the rest of Hellas will all join in the struggle, part from fear, part from interest. You will be the first to break a treaty which the god, in advising us to go to war, judges to be violated already, but rather to support a treaty that has been outraged: indeed, treaties are broken not by resistance but by aggression.

"Your position, therefore, from whatever quarter you may view it, will amply justify you in going to war; and this step we recommend in the interests of all, bearing in mind that identity of interest is the surest of bonds, whether between states or individuals. Delay not, therefore, to assist Potidaea, a Dorian city besieged by Ionians, which is quite a reversal of the order of things; nor to assert the freedom of the rest. It is impossible for us to wait any longer when waiting can only mean immediate disaster for some of us, and, if it comes to be known that we have conferred but do not venture to protect ourselves, like disaster in the near future for the rest. Delay not, fellow allies, but, convinced of the necessity of the crisis and the wisdom of this counsel, vote for the war, undeterred by its immediate terrors, but looking beyond to the lasting peace by which it will be succeeded. Out of war peace gains fresh stability, but to refuse to abandon repose for war is not so sure a method of avoiding danger. We must believe that the tyrant city that has been established in Hellas has been established against all alike, with a programme of universal empire, part fulfilled, part in contemplation; let us then attack and reduce it, and win future security for ourselves and freedom for the Hellenes who are now enslaved."

Such were the words of the Corinthians. The Lacedaemonians, having now heard all, give their opinion, took the vote of all the allied states present in order, great and small alike; and the majority voted for war. This decided, it was still impossible for them to commence at once, from their want of preparation; but it was resolved that the means requisite were to be procured by the different states, and that there was to be no delay. And indeed,

81

in spite of the time occupied with the necessary arrangements, less than a year elapsed before Attica was invaded, and the war openly begun.

This interval was spent in sending embassies to Athens charged with complaints, in order to obtain as good a pretext for war as possible, in the event of her paying no attention to them. The first Lacedaemonian embassy was to order the Athenians to drive out the curse of the goddess; the history of which is as follows. In former generations there was an Athenian of the name of Cylon, a victor at the Olympic games, of good birth and powerful position, who had married a daughter of Theagenes, a Megarian, at that time tyrant of Megara. Now this Cylon was inquiring at Delphi; when he was told by the god to seize the Acropolis of Athens on the grand festival of Zeus. Accordingly, procuring a force from Theagenes and persuading his friends to join him, when the Olympic festival in Peloponnese came, he seized the Acropolis, with the intention of making himself tyrant, thinking that this was the grand festival of Zeus, and also an occasion appropriate for a victor at the Olympic games. Whether the grand festival that was meant was in Attica or elsewhere was a question which he never thought of, and which the oracle did not offer to solve. For the Athenians also have a festival which is called the grand festival of Zeus Meilichios or Gracious, viz., the Diasia. It is celebrated outside the city, and the whole people sacrifice not real victims but a number of bloodless offerings peculiar to the country. However, fancying he had chosen the right time, he made the attempt. As soon as the Athenians perceived it, they flocked in, one and all, from the country, and sat down, and laid siege to the citadel. But as time went on, weary of the labour of blockade, most of them departed; the responsibility of keeping guard being left to the nine archons, with plenary powers to arrange everything according to their good judgment. It must be known that at that time most political functions were discharged by the nine archons. Meanwhile Cylon and his besieged companions were distressed for want of food and water. Accordingly Cylon and his brother made their escape; but the rest being hard pressed, and some even dying of famine, seated themselves as suppliants at the altar in the Acropolis. The Athenians who were charged with the duty of keeping guard, when they saw them at the point of death in the temple, raised them up on the understanding that no harm should be done to them, led them out, and slew them. Some who as they passed by took refuge at the altars of the awful goddesses were dispatched on the spot. From this deed the men who killed them were called accursed and guilty against the goddess, they and their descendants. Accordingly these cursed ones were driven out by the Athenians, driven out again by Cleomenes of Lacedaemon and an Athenian faction; the living were driven out, and the bones of the dead were taken up; thus they were cast out. For all that, they came back afterwards, and their descendants are still in the city.

This, then was the curse that the Lacedaemonians ordered them to drive out. They were actuated primarily, as they pretended, by a care for the honour of the gods; but they also know that Pericles, son of Xanthippus, was connected with the curse on his mother's side, and they thought that his banishment would materially advance their designs on Athens. Not that they really hoped to succeed in procuring this; they rather thought to create a prejudice against him in the eyes of his countrymen from the feeling that the war would be partly caused by his misfortune. For being the most powerful man of his time, and the leading Athenian statesman, he opposed the Lacedaemonians in everything, and would have no concessions, but ever urged the Athenians on to war.

The Athenians retorted by ordering the Lacedaemonians to drive out the curse of Taenarus. The Lacedaemonians had once raised up some Helot suppliants from the temple of Poseidon at Taenarus, led them away and slain them; for which they believe the great earthquake at Sparta to have been a retribution. The Athenians also ordered them to drive out the curse of the goddess of the Brazen House; the history of which is as follows. After

Pausanias the Lacedaemonian had been recalled by the Spartans from his command in the Hellespont (this is his first recall), and had been tried by them and acquitted, not being again sent out in a public capacity, he took a galley of Hermione on his own responsibility, without the authority of the Lacedaemonians, and arrived as a private person in the Hellespont. He came ostensibly for the Hellenic war, really to carry on his intrigues with the King, which he had begun before his recall, being ambitious of reigning over Hellas. The circumstance which first enabled him to lay the King under an obligation, and to make a beginning of the whole design, was this. Some connections and kinsmen of the King had been taken in Byzantium, on its capture from the Medes, when he was first there, after the return from Cyprus. These captives he sent off to the King without the knowledge of the rest of the allies, the account being that they had escaped from him. He managed this with the help of Gongylus, an Eretrian, whom he had placed in charge of Byzantium and the prisoners. He also gave Gongylus a letter for the King, the contents of which were as follows, as was afterwards discovered: "Pausanias, the general of Sparta, anxious to do you a favour, sends you these his prisoners of war. I propose also, with your approval, to marry your daughter, and to make Sparta and the rest of Hellas subject to you. I may say that I think I am able to do this, with your co-operation. Accordingly if any of this please you, send a safe man to the sea through whom we may in future conduct our correspondence."

This was all that was revealed in the writing, and Xerxes was pleased with the letter. He sent off Artabazus, son of Pharnaces, to the sea with orders to supersede Megabates, the previous governor in the satrapy of Daskylion, and to send over as quickly as possible to Pausanias at Byzantium a letter which he entrusted to him; to show him the royal signet, and to execute any commission which he might receive from Pausanias on the King's matters with all care and fidelity. Artabazus on his arrival carried the King's orders into effect, and sent over the letter, which contained the following answer: "Thus saith King Xerxes to Pausanias. For the men whom you have saved for me across sea from Byzantium, an obligation is laid up for you in our house, recorded for ever; and with your proposals I am well pleased. Let neither night nor day stop you from diligently performing any of your promises to me; neither for cost of gold nor of silver let them be hindered, nor yet for number of troops, wherever it may be that their presence is needed; but with Artabazus, an honourable man whom I send you, boldly advance my objects and yours, as may be most for the honour and interest of us both."

Before held in high honour by the Hellenes as the hero of Plataea, Pausanias, after the receipt of this letter, became prouder than ever, and could no longer live in the usual style, but went out of Byzantium in a Median dress, was attended on his march through Thrace by a bodyguard of Medes and Egyptians, kept a Persian table, and was quite unable to contain his intentions, but betrayed by his conduct in trifles what his ambition looked one day to enact on a grander scale. He also made himself difficult of access, and displayed so violent a temper to every one without exception that no one could come near him. Indeed, this was the principal reason why the confederacy went over to the Athenians.

The above-mentioned conduct, coming to the ears of the Lacedaemonians, occasioned his first recall. And after his second voyage out in the ship of Hermione, without their orders, he gave proofs of similar behaviour. Besieged and expelled from Byzantium by the Athenians, he did not return to Sparta; but news came that he had settled at Colonae in the Troad, and was intriguing with the barbarians, and that his stay there was for no good purpose; and the ephors, now no longer hesitating, sent him a herald and a scytale with orders to accompany the herald or be declared a public enemy. Anxious above everything to avoid suspicion, and confident that he could quash the charge by means of money, he returned a second time to Sparta. At first thrown into prison by the ephors (whose powers enable them to do this to the King), soon

85

compromised the matter and came out again, and offered himself for trial to any who wished to institute an inquiry concerning him.

Now the Spartans had no tangible proof against him - neither his enemies nor the nation - of that indubitable kind required for the punishment of a member of the royal family, and at that moment in high office; he being regent for his first cousin King Pleistarchus, Leonidas's son, who was still a minor. But by his contempt of the laws and imitation of the barbarians, he gave grounds for much suspicion of his being discontented with things established; all the occasions on which he had in any way departed from the regular customs were passed in review, and it was remembered that he had taken upon himself to have inscribed on the tripod at Delphi, which was dedicated by the Hellenes as the first-fruits of the spoil of the Medes, the following couplet:The Mede defeated, great Pausanias raised this monument, that Phoebus might be praised.

At the time the Lacedaemonians had at once erased the couplet, and inscribed the names of the cities that had aided in the overthrow of the barbarian and dedicated the offering. Yet it was considered that Pausanias had here been guilty of a grave offence, which, interpreted by the light of the attitude which he had since assumed, gained a new significance, and seemed to be quite in keeping with his present schemes. Besides, they were informed that he was even intriguing with the Helots; and such indeed was the fact, for he promised them freedom and citizenship if they would join him in insurrection and would help him to carry out his plans to the end. Even now, mistrusting the evidence even of the Helots themselves, the ephors would not consent to take any decided step against him; in accordance with their regular custom towards themselves, namely, to be slow in taking any irrevocable resolve in the matter of a Spartan citizen without indisputable proof. At last, it is said, the person who was going to carry to Artabazus the last letter for the King, a man of Argilus, once the favourite and most trusty servant of Pausanias, turned informer. Alarmed by the reflection that none of the previous messengers had ever returned, having counterfeited the seal, in order that, if he found himself mistaken in his surmises, or if Pausanias should ask to make some correction, he might not be discovered, he undid the letter, and found the postscript that he had suspected, viz. an order to put him to death.

On being shown the letter, the ephors now felt more certain. Still, they wished to hear Pausanias commit himself with their own ears. Accordingly the man went by appointment to Taenarus as a suppliant, and there built himself a hut divided into two by a partition; within which he concealed some of the ephors and let them hear the whole matter plainly. For Pausanias came to him and asked him the reason of his suppliant position; and the man reproached him with the order that he had written concerning him, and one by one declared all the rest of the circumstances, how he who had never yet brought him into any danger, while employed as agent between him and the King, was yet just like the mass of his servants to be rewarded with death. Admitting all this, and telling him not to be angry about the matter, Pausanias gave him the pledge of raising him up from the temple, and begged him to set off as quickly as possible, and not to hinder the business in hand.

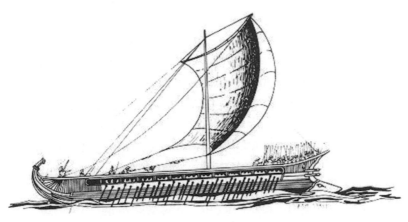

200 triremes each powered by 170 oarsmen

87

The ephors listened carefully, and then departed, taking no action for the moment, but, having at last attained to certainty, were preparing to arrest him in the city. It is reported that, as he was about to be arrested in the street, he saw from the face of one of the ephors what he was coming for; another, too, made him a secret signal, and betrayed it to him from kindness. Setting off with a run for the temple of the goddess of the Brazen House, the enclosure of which was near at hand, he succeeded in taking sanctuary before they took him, and entering into a small chamber, which formed part of the temple, to avoid being exposed to the weather, lay still there. The ephors, for the moment distanced in the pursuit, afterwards took off the roof of the chamber, and having made sure that he was inside, shut him in, barricaded the doors, and staying before the place, reduced him by starvation. When they found that he was on the point of expiring, just as he was, in the chamber, they brought him out of the temple, while the breath was still in him, and as soon as he was brought out he died. They were going to throw him into the Kaiadas, where they cast criminals, but finally decided to inter him somewhere near. But the god at Delphi afterwards ordered the Lacedaemonians to remove the tomb to the place of his death - where he now lies in the consecrated ground, as an inscription on a monument declares - and, as what had been done was a curse to them, to give back two bodies instead of one to the goddess of the Brazen House. So they had two brazen statues made, and dedicated them as a substitute for Pausanias. The Athenians retorted by telling the Lacedaemonians to drive out what the god himself had pronounced to be a curse.

To return to the Medism of Pausanias. Matter was found in the course of the inquiry to implicate Themistocles; and the Lacedaemonians accordingly sent envoys to the Athenians and required them to punish him as they had punished Pausanias. The Athenians consented to do so. But he had, as it happened, been ostracized, and, with a residence at Argos, was in the habit of visiting other parts of Peloponnese. So they sent with the Lacedaemonians, who were ready to join in the pursuit, persons with instructions to take him wherever they found him. But Themistocles got scent of their intentions, and fled from Peloponnese to Corcyra, which was under obligations towards him. But the Corcyraeans alleged that they could not venture to shelter him at the cost of offending Athens and Lacedaemon, and they conveyed him over to the continent opposite. Pursued by the officers who hung on the report of his movements, at a loss where to turn, he was compelled to stop at the house of Admetus, the Molossian king, though they were not on friendly terms. Admetus happened not to be indoors, but his wife, to whom he made himself a suppliant, instructed him to take their child in his arms and sit down by the hearth. Soon afterwards Admetus came in, and Themistocles told him who he was, and begged him not to revenge on Themistocles in exile any opposition which his requests might have experienced from Themistocles at Athens. Indeed, he was now far too low for his revenge; retaliation was only honourable between equals. Besides, his opposition to the king had only affected the success of a request, not the safety of his person; if the king were to give him up to the pursuers that he mentioned, and the fate which they intended for him, he would just be consigning him to certain death.

The King listened to him and raised him up with his son, as he was sitting with him in his arms after the most effectual method of supplication, and on the arrival of the Lacedaemonians not long afterwards, refused to give him up for anything they could say, but sent him off by land to the other sea to Pydna in Alexander's dominions, as he wished to go to the Persian king. There he met with a merchantman on the point of starting for Ionia. Going on board, he was carried by a storm to the Athenian squadron which was blockading Naxos. In his alarm - he was luckily unknown to the people in the vessel - he told the master who he was and what he was flying for, and said that, if he refused to save him, he would declare that he was taking him for a bribe. Meanwhile their safety consisted in letting no one leave the ship until a favourable time for sailing should arise. If he complied with his wishes, he promised him a proper recompense. The master acted as he desired, and, after lying to for a day and a night out of reach of the squadron, at length arrived at Ephesus.

After having rewarded him with a present of money, as soon as he received some from his friends at Athens and from his secret hoards at Argos, Themistocles started inland with one of the coast Persians, and sent a letter to King Artaxerxes, Xerxes's son, who had just come to the throne. Its contents were as follows: "I, Themistocles, am come to you, who did your house more harm than any of the Hellenes, when I was compelled to defend myself against your father's invasion - harm, however, far surpassed by the good that I did him during his retreat, which brought no danger for me but much for him. For the past, you are a good turn in my debt" - here he mentioned the warning sent to Xerxes from Salamis to retreat, as well as his finding the bridges unbroken, which, as he falsely pretended, was due to him - "for the present, able to do you great service, I am here, pursued by the Hellenes for my friendship for you. However, I desire a year's grace, when I shall be able to declare in person the objects of my coming."

It is said that the King approved his intention, and told him to do as he said. He employed the interval in making what progress he could in the study of the Persian tongue, and of the customs of the country. Arrived at court at the end of the year, he attained to very high consideration there, such as no Hellene has ever possessed before or since; partly from his splendid antecedents, partly from the hopes which he held out of effecting for him the subjugation of Hellas, but principally by the proof which experience daily gave of his capacity. For Themistocles was a man who exhibited the most indubitable signs of genius; indeed, in this particular he has a claim on our admiration quite extraordinary and unparalleled. By his own native capacity, alike unformed and unsupplemented by study, he was at once the best judge in those sudden crises which admit of little or of no deliberation, and the best prophet of the future, even to its most distant possibilities. An able theoretical expositor of all that came within the sphere of his practice, he was not without the power of passing an adequate judgment in matters in which he had no experience. He could also excellently divine the good and evil which lay hid in the unseen future. In fine, whether we consider the extent of his natural powers, or the slightness of his application, this extraordinary man must be allowed to have surpassed all others in the faculty of intuitively meeting an emergency. Disease was the real cause of his death; though there is a story of his having ended his life by poison, on finding himself unable to fulfil his promises to the king. However this may be, there is a monument to him in the marketplace of Asiatic Magnesia. He was governor of the district, the King having given him Magnesia, which brought in fifty talents a year, for bread, Lampsacus, which was considered to be the richest wine country, for wine, and Myos for other provisions. His bones, it is said, were conveyed home by his relatives in accordance with his wishes, and interred in Attic ground. This was done without the knowledge of the Athenians; as it is against the law to bury in Attica an outlaw for treason. So ends the history of Pausanias and Themistocles, the Lacedaemonian and the Athenian, the most famous men of their time in Hellas.

To return to the Lacedaemonians. The history of their first embassy, the injunctions which it conveyed, and the rejoinder which it provoked, concerning the expulsion of the accursed persons, have been related already. It was followed by a second, which ordered Athens to raise the siege of Potidaea, and to respect the independence of Aegina. Above all, it gave her most distinctly to understand that war might be prevented by the revocation of the Megara decree, excluding the Megarians from the use of Athenian harbours and of the market of Athens. But Athens was not inclined either to revoke the decree, or to entertain their other proposals; she accused the Megarians of pushing their cultivation into the consecrated ground and the unenclosed land on the border, and of harbouring her runaway slaves. At last an embassy arrived with the Lacedaemonian ultimatum. The ambassadors were Ramphias, Melesippus, and Agesander. Not a word was said on any of the old subjects; there was simply this: "Lacedaemon wishes the peace to continue, and there is no reason why it should not, if you would leave the Hellenes independent." Upon this the Athenians held an assembly, and laid the matter before their consideration. It was resolved to deliberate once for all on all their demands, and to give them an answer. There were many speakers who came forward and gave their support to one side or the other, urging the necessity of war, or the revocation of the decree and the folly of allowing it to stand in the way of peace. Among them came forward Pericles, son of Xanthippus, the first man of his time at Athens, ablest alike in counsel and in action, and gave the following advice:

"There is one principle, Athenians, which I hold to through everything, and that is the principle of no concession to the Peloponnesians. I know that the spirit which inspires men while they are being persuaded to make war is not always retained in action; that as circumstances change, resolutions change. Yet I see that now as before the same, almost literally the same, counsel is demanded of me; and I put it to those of you who are allowing yourselves to be persuaded, to support the national resolves even in the case of reverses, or to forfeit all credit for their wisdom in the event of success. For sometimes the course of things is as arbitrary as the plans of man; indeed this is why we usually blame chance for whatever does not happen as we expected. Now it was clear before that Lacedaemon entertained designs against us; it is still more clear now. The treaty provides that we shall mutually submit our differences to legal settlement, and that we shall meanwhile each keep what we have. Yet the Lacedaemonians never yet made us any such offer, never yet would accept from us any such offer; on the contrary, they wish complaints to be settled by war instead of by negotiation; and in the end we find them here dropping the tone of expostulation and adopting that of command. They order us to raise the siege of Potidaea, to let Aegina be independent, to revoke the Megara decree; and they conclude with an ultimatum warning us to leave the Hellenes independent. I hope that you will none of you think that we shall be going to war for a trifle if we refuse to revoke the Megara decree, which appears in front of their complaints, and the revocation of which is to save us from war, or let any feeling of self-reproach linger in your minds, as if you went to war for slight cause. Why, this trifle contains the whole seal and trial of your resolution. If you give way, you will instantly have to meet some greater demand, as having been frightened into obedience in the first instance; while a firm refusal will make them clearly understand that they must treat you more as equals. Make your decision therefore at once, either to submit before you are harmed, or if we are to go to war, as I for one think we ought, to do so without caring whether the ostensible cause be great or small, resolved against making concessions or consenting to a precarious tenure of our possessions. For all claims from an equal, urged upon a neighbour as commands before any attempt at legal settlement, be they great or be they small, have only one meaning, and that is slavery.

"As to the war and the resources of either party, a detailed comparison will not show you the inferiority of Athens. Personally engaged in the cultivation of their land, without funds either private or public, the Peloponnesians are also without experience in long wars across sea, from the strict limit which poverty imposes on their attacks upon each other. Powers of this description are quite incapable of often manning a fleet or often sending out an army: they cannot afford the absence from their homes, the expenditure from their own funds; and besides, they have not command of the sea. Capital, it must be remembered, maintains a war more than forced contributions. Farmers are a class of men that are always more ready to serve in person than in purse. Confident that the former will survive the dangers, they are by no means so sure that the latter will not be prematurely exhausted, especially if the war last longer than they expect, which it very likely will. In a single battle the Peloponnesians and their allies may be able to defy all Hellas, but they are incapacitated from carrying on a war against a power different in character from their own, by the want of the single council-chamber requisite to prompt and vigorous action, and the substitution of a diet composed of various races, in which every state possesses an equal vote, and each presses its own ends, a condition of things which generally results in no action at all. The great wish of some is to avenge themselves on some particular enemy, the great wish of others to save their own pocket. Slow in assembling, they devote a very small fraction of the time to the consideration of any public object, most of it to the prosecution of their own objects. Meanwhile each fancies that no harm will come of his neglect, that it is the business of somebody else to look after this or that for him; and so, by the same notion being entertained by all separately, the common cause imperceptibly decays.

"But the principal point is the hindrance that they will experience from want of money. The slowness with which it comes in will cause delay; but the opportunities of war wait for no man. Again, we need not be alarmed either at the possibility of their raising fortifications in Attica, or at their navy. It would be difficult for any system of fortifications to establish a rival city, even in time of peace, much more, surely, in an enemy's country, with Athens just as much fortified against it as it against Athens; while a mere post might be able to do some harm to the country by incursions and by the facilities which it would afford for desertion, but can never prevent our sailing into their country and raising fortifications there, and making reprisals with our powerful fleet. For our naval skill is of more use to us for service on land, than their military skill for service at sea. Familiarity with the sea they will not find an easy acquisition. If you who have been practising at it ever since the Median invasion have not yet brought it to perfection, is there any chance of anything considerable being effected by an agricultural, unseafaring population, who will besides be prevented from practising by the constant presence of strong squadrons of observation from Athens? With a small squadron they might hazard an engagement, encouraging their ignorance by numbers; but the restraint of a strong force will prevent their moving, and through want of practice they will grow more clumsy, and consequently more timid. It must be kept in mind that seamanship, just like anything else, is a matter of art, and will not admit of being taken up occasionally as an occupation for times of leisure; on the contrary, it is so exacting as to leave leisure for nothing else.

"Even if they were to touch the moneys at Olympia or Delphi, and try to seduce our foreign sailors by the temptation of higher pay, that would only be a serious danger if we could not still be a match for them by embarking our own citizens and the aliens resident among us. But in fact by this means we are always a match for them; and, best of all, we have a larger and higher class of native coxswains and sailors among our own citizens than all the rest of Hellas. And to say nothing of the danger of such a step, none of our foreign sailors would consent to become an outlaw from his country, and to take service with them and their hopes, for the sake of a few days' high pay.

"This, I think, is a tolerably fair account of the position of the Peloponnesians; that of Athens is free from the defects that I have criticized in them, and has other advantages of its own, which they can show nothing to equal. If they march against our country we will sail against theirs, and it will then be found that the desolation of the whole of Attica is not the same as that of even a fraction of Peloponnese; for they will not be able to supply the deficiency except by a battle, while we have plenty of land both on the islands and the continent. The rule of the sea is indeed a great matter. Consider for a moment. Suppose that we were islanders; can you conceive a more impregnable position? Well, this in future should, as far as possible, be our conception of our position. Dismissing all thought of our land and houses, we must vigilantly guard the sea and the city. No irritation that we may feel for the former must provoke us to a battle with the numerical superiority of the Peloponnesians. A victory would only be succeeded by another battle against the same superiority: a reverse involves the loss of our allies, the source of our strength, who will not remain quiet a day after we become unable to march against them. We must cry not over the loss of houses and land but of men's lives; since houses and land do not gain men, but men them. And if I had thought that I could persuade you, I would have bid you go out and lay them waste with your own hands, and show the Peloponnesians that this at any rate will not make you submit.

"I have many other reasons to hope for a favourable issue, if you can consent not to combine schemes of fresh conquest with the conduct of the war, and will abstain from wilfully involving yourselves in other dangers; indeed, I am more afraid of our own blunders than of the enemy's devices. But these matters shall be explained in another speech, as events require; for the present dismiss these men with the answer that we will allow Megara the use of our market and harbours, when the Lacedaemonians suspend their alien acts in favour of us and our allies, there being nothing in the treaty to prevent either one or the other: that we will leave the cities independent, if independent we found them when we made the treaty, and when the Lacedaemonians grant to their cities an independence not involving subservience to Lacedaemonian interests, but such as each severally may desire: that we are willing to give the legal satisfaction which our agreements specify, and that we shall not commence hostilities, but shall resist those who do commence them. This is an answer agreeable at once to the rights and the dignity of Athens. It must be thoroughly understood that war is a necessity; but that the more readily we accept it, the less will be the ardour of our opponents, and that out of the greatest dangers communities and individuals acquire the greatest glory. Did not our fathers resist the Medes not only with resources far different from ours, but even when those resources had been abandoned; and more by wisdom than by fortune, more by daring than by strength, did not they beat off the barbarian and advance their affairs to their present height? We must not fall behind them, but must resist our enemies in any way and in every way, and attempt to hand down our power to our posterity unimpaired."

Such were the words of Pericles. The Athenians, persuaded of the wisdom of his advice, voted as he desired, and answered the Lacedaemonians as he recommended, both on the separate points and in the general; they would do nothing on dictation, but were ready to have the complaints settled in a fair and impartial manner by the legal method, which the terms of the truce prescribed. So the envoys departed home and did not return again.

These were the charges and differences existing between the rival powers before the war, arising immediately from the affair at Epidamnus and Corcyra. Still intercourse continued in spite of them, and mutual communication. It was carried on without heralds, but not without suspicion, as events were occurring which were equivalent to a breach of the treaty and matter for war.

CHAPTER VI

Beginning of the Peloponnesian War - First Invasion of Attica - Funeral Oration of Pericles

Funeral Oration of Pericles

T HE WAR between the Athenians and Peloponnesians and the allies on either side now really begins. For now all intercourse except through the medium of heralds ceased, and hostilities were commenced and prosecuted without intermission. The history follows the chronological order of events by summers and winters.

The thirty years' truce which was entered into after the conquest of Euboea lasted fourteen years. In the fifteenth, in the forty-eighth year of the priestess-ship of Chrysis at Argos, in the ephorate of Aenesias at Sparta, in the last month but two of the archonship of Pythodorus at Athens, and six months after the battle of Potidaea, just at the beginning of spring, a Theban force a little over three hundred strong, under the command of their Boeotarchs, Pythangelus, son of Phyleides, and Diemporus, son of Onetorides, about the first watch of the night, made an armed entry into Plataea, a town of Boeotia in alliance with Athens. The gates were opened to them by a Plataean called Naucleides, who, with his party, had invited them in, meaning to put to death the citizens of the opposite party, bring over the city to Thebes, and thus obtain power for themselves. This was arranged through Eurymachus, son of Leontiades, a person of great influence at Thebes. For Plataea had always been at variance with Thebes; and the latter, foreseeing that war was at hand, wished to surprise her old enemy in time of peace, before hostilities had actually broken out. Indeed this was how they got in so easily without being observed, as no guard had been posted. After the soldiers had grounded arms in the market-place, those who had invited them in wished them to set to work at once and go to their enemies' houses. This, however, the Thebans refused to do, but determined to make a conciliatory proclamation, and if possible to come to a friendly understanding with the citizens. Their herald accordingly invited any who wished to resume their old place in the confederacy of their countrymen to ground arms with them, for they thought that in this way the city would readily join them.

On becoming aware of the presence of the Thebans within their gates, and of the sudden occupation of the town, the Plataeans concluded in their alarm that more had entered than was really the case, the night preventing their seeing them. They accordingly came to terms and, accepting the proposal, made no movement; especially as the Thebans offered none of them any violence. But somehow or other, during the negotiations, they discovered the scanty numbers of the Thebans, and decided that they could easily attack and overpower them; the mass of the Plataeans being averse to revolting from Athens. At all events they resolved to attempt it. Digging through the party walls of the houses, they thus managed to join each other without being seen going through the streets, in which they placed wagons without the beasts in them, to serve as a barricade, and arranged everything else as seemed convenient for the occasion. When everything had been done that circumstances permitted, they watched their opportunity and went out of their houses against the enemy. It was still night, though daybreak was at hand: in daylight it was thought that their attack would be met by men full of courage and on equal terms with their assailants, while in darkness it would fall upon panic-stricken troops, who would also be at a disadvantage from their enemy's knowledge of the locality. So they made their assault at once, and came to close quarters as quickly as they could.

The Thebans, finding themselves outwitted, immediately closed up to repel all attacks made upon them. Twice or thrice they beat back their assailants. But the men shouted and charged them, the women and slaves screamed and yelled from the houses and pelted them with stones and tiles; besides, it had been raining hard all night; and so at last their courage gave way, and they turned and fled through the town. Most of the fugitives were quite ignorant of the right ways out, and this, with the mud, and the darkness caused by the moon being in her last quarter, and the fact that their pursuers knew their way about and could easily stop their escape, proved fatal to many. The only gate open was the one by which they had entered, and this was shut by one of the Plataeans driving the spike of a javelin into the bar instead of the bolt; so that even here there was no longer any means of exit. They were now chased all over the town. Some got on the wall and threw themselves over, in most cases with a fatal result. One party managed to find a deserted gate, and obtaining an axe from a woman, cut through the bar; but as they were soon observed only a few succeeded in getting out. Others were cut off in detail in different parts of the city. The most numerous and compact body rushed into a large building next to the city wall: the doors on the side of the street happened to be open, and the Thebans fancied that they were the gates of the town, and that there was a passage right through to the outside. The Plataeans, seeing their enemies in a trap, now consulted whether they should set fire to the building and burn them just as they were, or whether there was anything else that they could do with them; until at length these and the rest of the Theban survivors found wandering about the town agreed to an unconditional surrender of themselves and their arms to the Plataeans.

While such was the fate of the party in Plataea, the rest of the Thebans who were to have joined them with all their forces before daybreak, in case of anything miscarrying with the body that had entered, received the news of the affair on the road, and pressed forward to their succour. Now Plataea is nearly eight miles from Thebes, and their march delayed by the rain that had fallen in the night, for the river Asopus had risen and was not easy of passage; and so, having to march in the rain, and being hindered in crossing the river, they arrived too late, and found the whole party either slain or captive. When they learned what had happened, they at once formed a design against the Plataeans outside the city. As the attack had been made in time of peace, and was perfectly unexpected, there were of course men and stock in the fields; and the Thebans wished if possible to have some prisoners to exchange against their countrymen in the town, should any chance to have been taken alive. Such was their plan. But the Plataeans suspected their intention almost before it was formed, and becoming alarmed for their fellow citizens outside the town, sent a herald to the Thebans, reproaching them for their unscrupulous attempt to seize their city in time of peace, and warning them against any outrage on those outside. Should the warning be disregarded, they threatened to put to death the men they had in their hands, but added that, on the Thebans retiring from their territory, they would surrender the prisoners to their friends. This is the Theban account of the matter, and they say that they had an oath given them. The Plataeans, on the other hand, do not admit any promise of an immediate surrender, but make it contingent upon subsequent negotiation: the oath they deny altogether. Be this as it may, upon the Thebans retiring from their territory without committing any injury, the Plataeans hastily got in whatever they had in the country and immediately put the men to death. The prisoners were a hundred and eighty in number; Eurymachus, the person with whom the traitors had negotiated, being one.

This done, the Plataeans sent a messenger to Athens, gave back the dead to the Thebans under a truce, and arranged things in the city as seemed best to meet the present emergency. The Athenians meanwhile, having had word of the affair sent them immediately after its occurrence, had instantly seized all the Boeotians in Attica, and sent a herald to the Plataeans to forbid their proceeding to extremities with their Theban prisoners without instructions from Athens. The news of the men's death had of course not arrived; the first messenger having left Plataea just when the Thebans entered it, the second just after their defeat and capture; so there was no later news. Thus the Athenians sent orders in ignorance of the facts; and the herald on his arrival found the men slain. After this the Athenians marched to Plataea and brought in provisions, and left a garrison in the place, also taking away the women and children and such of the men as were least efficient.

After the affair at Plataea, the treaty had been broken by an overt act, and Athens at once prepared for war, as did also Lacedaemon and her allies. They resolved to send embassies to the King and to such other of the barbarian powers as either party could look to for assistance, and tried to ally themselves with the independent states at home. Lacedaemon, in addition to the existing marine, gave orders to the states that had declared for her in Italy and Sicily to build vessels up to a grand total of five hundred, the quota of each city being determined by its size, and also to provide a specified sum of money. Till these were ready they were to remain neutral and to admit single Athenian ships into their harbours. Athens on her part reviewed her existing confederacy, and sent embassies to the places more immediately round Peloponnese - Corcyra,

Cephallenia, Acarnania, and Zacynthus - perceiving that if these could be relied on she could carry the war all round Peloponnese.

And if both sides nourished the boldest hopes and put forth their utmost strength for the war, this was only natural. Zeal is always at its height at the commencement of an undertaking; and on this particular occasion Peloponnese and Athens were both full of young men whose inexperience made them eager to take up arms, while the rest of Hellas stood straining with excitement at the conflict of its leading cities. Everywhere predictions were being recited and oracles being chanted by such persons as collect them, and this not only in the contending cities. Further, some while before this, there was an earthquake at Delos, for the first time in the memory of the Hellenes. This was said and thought to be ominous of the events impending; indeed, nothing of the kind that happened was allowed to pass without remark. The good wishes of men made greatly for the Lacedaemonians, especially as they proclaimed themselves the liberators of Hellas. No private or public effort that could help them in speech or action was omitted; each thinking that the cause suffered wherever he could not himself see to it. So general was the indignation felt against Athens, whether by those who wished to escape from her empire, or were apprehensive of being absorbed by it. Such were the preparations and such the feelings with which the contest opened.

The allies of the two belligerents were the following. These were the allies of Lacedaemon: all the Peloponnesians within the Isthmus except the Argives and Achaeans, who were neutral; Pellene being the only Achaean city that first joined in the war, though her example was afterwards followed by the rest. Outside Peloponnese the Megarians, Locrians, Boeotians, Phocians, Ambraciots, Leucadians, and Anactorians. Of these, ships were furnished by the Corinthians, Megarians, Sicyonians, Pellenians, Eleans, Ambraciots, and Leucadians; and cavalry by the Boeotians, Phocians, and Locrians. The other states sent infantry. This was the Lacedaemonian confederacy. That of Athens comprised the

Chians, Lesbians, Plataeans, the Messenians in Naupactus, most of the Acarnanians, the Corcyraeans, Zacynthians, and some tributary cities in the following countries, viz., Caria upon the sea with her Dorian neighbours, Ionia, the Hellespont, the Thracian towns, the islands lying between Peloponnese and Crete towards the east, and all the Cyclades except Melos and Thera. Of these, ships were furnished by Chios, Lesbos, and Corcyra, infantry and money by the rest. Such were the allies of either party and their resources for the war.

Immediately after the affair at Plataea, Lacedaemon sent round orders to the cities in Peloponnese and the rest of her confederacy to prepare troops and the provisions requisite for a foreign campaign, in order to invade Attica. The several states were ready at the time appointed and assembled at the Isthmus: the contingent of each city being two-thirds of its whole force. After the whole army had mustered, the Lacedaemonian king, Archidamus, the leader of the expedition, called together the generals of all the states and the principal persons and officers, and exhorted them as follows:

"Peloponnesians and allies, our fathers made many campaigns both within and without Peloponnese, and the elder men among us here are not without experience in war. Yet we have never set out with a larger force than the present; and if our numbers and efficiency are remarkable, so also is the power of the state against which we march. We ought not then to show ourselves inferior to our ancestors, or unequal to our own reputation. For the hopes and attention of all Hellas are bent upon the present effort, and its sympathy is with the enemy of the hated Athens. Therefore, numerous as the invading army may appear to be, and certain as some may think it that our adversary will not meet us in the field, this is no sort of justification for the least negligence upon the march; but the officers and men of each particular city should always be prepared for the advent of danger in their own quarters. The course of war cannot be foreseen, and its attacks are generally dictated by the impulse of the moment; and where overweening self-confidence has despised preparation, a wise apprehension often been able to make head against superior numbers. Not that confidence is out of place in an army of invasion, but in an enemy's country it should also be accompanied by the precautions of apprehension: troops will by this combination be best inspired for dealing a blow, and best secured against receiving one. In the present instance, the city against which we are going, far from being so impotent for defence, is on the contrary most excellently equipped at all points; so that we have every reason to expect that they will take the field against us, and that if they have not set out already before we are there, they will certainly do so when they see us in their territory wasting and destroying their property. For men are always exasperated at suffering injuries to which they are not accustomed, and on seeing them inflicted before their very eyes; and where least inclined for reflection, rush with the greatest heat to action. The Athenians are the very people of all others to do this, as they aspire to rule the rest of the world, and are more in the habit of invading and ravaging their neighbours' territory, than of seeing their own treated in the like fashion. Considering, therefore, the power of the state against which we are marching, and the greatness of the reputation which, according to the event, we shall win or lose for our ancestors and ourselves, remember as you follow where you may be led to regard discipline and vigilance as of the first importance, and to obey with alacrity the orders transmitted to you; as nothing contributes so much to the credit and safety of an army as the union of large bodies by a single discipline."

With this brief speech dismissing the assembly, Archidamus first sent off Melesippus, son of Diacritus, a Spartan, to Athens, in case she should be more inclined to submit on seeing the Peloponnesians actually on the march. But the Athenians did not admit into the city or to their assembly, Pericles having already carried a motion against admitting either herald or embassy from the Lacedaemonians after they had once marched out.

The herald was accordingly sent away without an audience, and ordered to be beyond the frontier that same day; in future, if those who sent him had a proposition to make, they must retire to their own territory before they dispatched embassies to Athens. An escort was sent with Melesippus to prevent his holding communication with any one. When he reached the frontier and was just going to be dismissed, he departed with these words: "This day will be the beginning of great misfortunes to the Hellenes." As soon as he arrived at the camp, and Archidamus learnt that the Athenians had still no thoughts of submitting, he at length began his march, and advanced with his army into their territory. Meanwhile the Boeotians, sending their contingent and cavalry to join the Peloponnesian expedition, went to Plataea with the remainder and laid waste the country.

While the Peloponnesians were still mustering at the Isthmus, or on the march before they invaded Attica, Pericles, son of Xanthippus, one of the ten generals of the Athenians, finding that the invasion was to take place, conceived the idea that Archidamus, who happened to be his friend, might possibly pass by his estate without ravaging it. This he might do, either from a personal wish to oblige him, or acting under instructions from Lacedaemon for the purpose of creating a prejudice against him, as had been before attempted in the demand for the expulsion of the accursed family. He accordingly took the precaution of announcing to the Athenians in the assembly that, although Archidamus was his friend, yet this friendship should not extend to the detriment of the state, and that in case the enemy should make his houses and lands an exception to the rest and not pillage them, he at once gave them up to be public property, so that they should not bring him into suspicion. He also gave the citizens some advice on their present affairs in the same strain as before. They were to prepare for the war, and to carry in their property from the country. They were not to go out to battle, but to come into the city and guard it, and get ready their fleet, in which their real strength lay. They were also to keep a tight rein on their allies - the strength of Athens being derived from the money brought in by their payments, and success in war depending principally upon conduct and capital, had no reason to despond. Apart from other sources of income, an average revenue of six hundred talents of silver was drawn from the tribute of the allies; and there were still six thousand talents of coined silver in the Acropolis, out of nine thousand seven hundred that had once been there, from which the money had been taken for the porch of the Acropolis, the other public buildings, and for Potidaea. This did not include the uncoined gold and silver in public and private offerings, the sacred vessels for the processions and games, the Median spoils, and similar resources to the amount of five hundred talents. To this he added the treasures of the other temples. These were by no means inconsiderable, and might fairly be used. Nay, if they were ever absolutely driven to it, they might take even the gold ornaments of Athene herself; for the statue contained forty talents of pure gold and it was all removable. This might be used for self-preservation, and must every penny of it be restored. Such was their financial position - surely a satisfactory one. Then they had an army of thirteen thousand heavy infantry, besides sixteen thousand more in the garrisons and on home duty at Athens. This was at first the number of men on guard in the event of an invasion: it was composed of the oldest and youngest levies and the resident aliens who had heavy armour. The Phaleric wall ran for four miles, before it joined that round the city; and of this last nearly five had a guard, although part of it was left without one, viz., that between the Long Wall and the Phaleric. Then there were the Long Walls to Piraeus, a distance of some four miles and a half, the outer of which was manned. Lastly, the circumference of Piraeus with Munychia was nearly seven miles and a half; only half of this, however, was guarded. Pericles also showed them that they had twelve hundred horse including mounted archers, with sixteen hundred archers unmounted, and three hundred galleys fit for service. Such were the resources of Athens in the different departments when the Peloponnesian invasion was impending and hostilities were being commenced. Pericles also urged his usual arguments for expecting a favourable issue to the war.

The Athenians listened to his advice, and began to carry in their wives and children from the country, and all their household furniture, even to the woodwork of their houses which they took down. Their sheep and cattle they sent over to Euboea and the adjacent islands. But they found it hard to move, as most of them had been always used to live in the country.

From very early times this had been more the case with the Athenians than with others. Under Cecrops and the first kings, down to the reign of Theseus, Attica had always consisted of a number of independent townships, each with its own town hall and magistrates. Except in times of danger the king at Athens was not consulted; in ordinary seasons they carried on their government and settled their affairs without his interference; sometimes even they waged war against him, as in the case of the Eleusinians with Eumolpus against Erechtheus. In Theseus, however, they had a king of equal intelligence and power; and one of the chief features

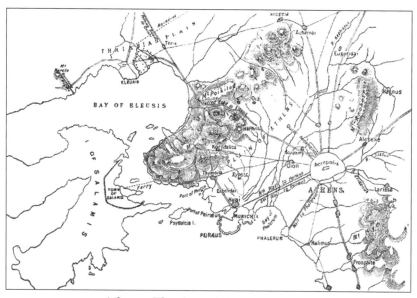

Athens - The city and its surroundings.

in his organization of the country was to abolish the council-chambers and magistrates of the petty cities, and to merge them in the single council-chamber and town hall of the present capital. Individuals might still enjoy their private property just as before, but they were henceforth compelled to have only one political centre, viz., Athens; which thus counted all the inhabitants of Attica among her citizens, so that when Theseus died he left a great state behind him. Indeed, from him dates the Synoecia, or Feast of Union; which is paid for by the state, and which the Athenians still keep in honour of the goddess. Before this the city consisted of the present citadel and the district beneath it looking rather towards the south. This is shown by the fact that the temples of the other deities, besides that of Athene, are in the citadel; and even those that are outside it are mostly situated in this quarter of the city, as that of the Olympian Zeus, of the Pythian Apollo, of Earth, and of Dionysus in the Marshes, the same in whose honour the older Dionysia are to this day celebrated in the month of Anthesterion not only by the Athenians but also by their Ionian descendants. There are also other ancient temples in this quarter. The fountain too, which, since the alteration made by the tyrants, has been called Enneacrounos, or Nine Pipes, but which, when the spring was open, went by the name of Callirhoe, or Fairwater, was in those days, from being so near, used for the most important offices. Indeed, the old fashion of using the water before marriage and for other sacred purposes is still kept up. Again, from their old residence in that quarter, the citadel is still known among Athenians as the city.

The Athenians thus long lived scattered over Attica in independent townships. Even after the centralization of Theseus, old habit still prevailed; and from the early times down to the present war most Athenians still lived in the country with their families and households, and were consequently not at all inclined to move now, especially as they had only just restored their establishments after the Median invasion. Deep was their trouble and discontent at abandoning their houses and the hereditary temples of the ancient constitution, and at having to change their habits of life and to bid farewell to what each regarded as his native city.

When they arrived at Athens, though a few had houses of their own to go to, or could find an asylum with friends or relatives, by far the greater number had to take up their dwelling in the parts of the city that were not built over and in the temples and chapels of the heroes, except the Acropolis and the temple of the Eleusinian Demeter and such other Places as were always kept closed. The occupation of the plot of ground lying below the citadel called the Pelasgian had been forbidden by a curse; and there was also an ominous fragment of a Pythian oracle which said:

Leave the Pelasgian parcel desolate, Woe worth the day that men inhabit it!

Yet this too was now built over in the necessity of the moment. And in my opinion, if the oracle proved true, it was in the opposite sense to what was expected. For the misfortunes of the state did not arise from the unlawful occupation, but the necessity of the occupation from the war; and though the god did not mention this, he foresaw that it would be an evil day for Athens in which the plot came to be inhabited. Many also took up their quarters in the towers of the walls or wherever else they could. For when they were all come in, the city proved too small to hold them; though afterwards they divided the Long Walls and a great part of Piraeus into lots and settled there. All this while great attention was being given to the war; the allies were being mustered, and an armament of a hundred ships equipped for Peloponnese. Such was the state of preparation at Athens.

Meanwhile the army of the Peloponnesians was advancing. The first town they came to in Attica was Oenoe, where they to enter the country. Sitting down before it, they prepared to assault the wall with engines and otherwise. Oenoe, standing upon the Athenian and Boeotian border, was of course a walled town, and was used as a fortress by the Athenians in time of war. So the Peloponnesians prepared for their assault, and wasted some valuable time before the place. This delay brought the gravest censure upon Archidamus. Even during the levying of the war he had credit for weakness and Athenian sympathies by the half measures he had advocated; and after the army had assembled he had further injured himself in public estimation by his loitering at the Isthmus and the slowness with which the rest of the march had been conducted. But all this was as nothing to the delay at Oenoe. During this interval the Athenians were carrying in their property; and it was the belief of the Peloponnesians that a quick advance would have found everything still out, had it not been for his procrastination. Such was the feeling of the army towards Archidamus during the siege. But he, it is said, expected that the Athenians would shrink from letting their land be wasted, and would make their submission while it was still uninjured; and this was why he waited.

But after he had assaulted Oenoe, and every possible attempt to take it had failed, as no herald came from Athens, he at last broke up his camp and invaded Attica. This was about eighty days after the Theban attempt upon Plataea, just in the middle of summer, when the corn was ripe, and Archidamus, son of Zeuxis, king of Lacedaemon, was in command. Encamping in Eleusis and the Thriasian plain, they began their ravages, and putting to flight some Athenian horse at a place called Rheiti, or the Brooks, they then advanced, keeping Mount Aegaleus on their right, through Cropia, until they reached Acharnae, the largest of the Athenian demes or townships. Sitting down before it, they formed a camp there, and continued their ravages for a long while.

The reason why Archidamus remained in order of battle at Acharnae during this incursion, instead of descending into the plain, is said to have been this. He hoped that the Athenians might possibly be tempted by the multitude of their youth and the unprecedented efficiency of their service to come out to battle and attempt to stop the devastation of their lands. Accordingly, as they had met him at Eleusis or the Thriasian plain, he tried if they could be provoked to a sally by the spectacle of a camp at Acharnae. He thought the place itself a good position for encamping; and it seemed likely that such an important part of the state as the three thousand heavy infantry of the Acharnians would refuse to submit to the ruin of their property, and would force a battle on the rest of the citizens. On the other hand, should the Athenians not take the field during this incursion, he could then fearlessly ravage the plain in future invasions, and extend his advance up to the very walls of Athens. After the Acharnians had lost their own property they would be less willing to risk themselves for that of their neighbours; and so there would be division in the Athenian counsels. These were the motives of Archidamus for remaining at Acharnae.

In the meanwhile, as long as the army was at Eleusis and the Thriasian plain, hopes were still entertained of its not advancing any nearer. It was remembered that Pleistoanax, son of Pausanias, king of Lacedaemon, had invaded Attica with a Peloponnesian army fourteen years before, but had retreated without advancing farther than Eleusis and Thria, which indeed proved the cause of his exile from Sparta, as it was thought he had been bribed to retreat. But when they saw the army at Acharnae, barely seven miles from Athens, they lost all patience. The territory of Athens was being ravaged before the very eyes of the Athenians, a sight which the young men had never seen before and the old only in the Median wars; and it was naturally thought a grievous insult, and the determination was universal, especially among the young men, to sally forth and stop it. Knots were formed in the streets and engaged in hot discussion; for if the proposed sally was warmly recommended, it was also in some cases opposed. Oracles of the most various import were recited by the collectors, and found eager listeners in one or other of the disputants. Foremost in pressing for the sally were the Acharnians, as constituting no small part of the army of the state, and as it was their land that was being ravaged. In short, the whole city was in a most excited state; Pericles was the object of general indignation; his previous counsels were totally forgotten; he was abused for not leading out the army which he commanded, and was made responsible for the whole of the public suffering.

He, meanwhile, seeing anger and infatuation just now in the ascendant, and of his wisdom in refusing a sally, would not call either assembly or meeting of the people, fearing the fatal results of a debate inspired by passion and not by prudence. Accordingly he addressed himself to the defence of the city, and kept it as quiet as possible, though he constantly sent out cavalry to prevent raids on the lands near the city from flying parties of the enemy. There was a trifling affair at Phrygia between a squadron of the Athenian horse with the Thessalians and the Boeotian cavalry; in which the former had rather the best of it, until the heavy infantry advanced to the support of the Boeotians, when the Thessalians and Athenians were routed and lost a few men, whose bodies, however, were recovered the same day without a truce. The next day the Peloponnesians set up a trophy. Ancient alliance brought the Thessalians to the aid of Athens; those who came being the Larisaeans, Pharsalians, Cranonians, Pyrasians, Gyrtonians, and Pheraeans. The Larisaean commanders were Polymedes and Aristonus, two party leaders in Larisa; the Pharsalian general was Menon; each of the other cities had also its own commander.

In the meantime the Peloponnesians, as the Athenians did not come out to engage them, broke up from Acharnae and ravaged some of the demes between Mount Parnes and Brilessus. While they were in Attica the Athenians sent off the hundred ships which they had been preparing round Peloponnese, with a thousand heavy infantry and four hundred archers on board, under the command of Carcinus, son of Xenotimus, Proteas, son of Epicles, and Socrates, son of Antigenes. This armament weighed anchor and started on its cruise, and the Peloponnesians, after remaining in Attica as long as their provisions lasted, retired through Boeotia by a different road to that by which they had entered. As they passed Oropus they ravaged the territory of Graea, which is held by the Oropians from Athens, and reaching Peloponnese broke up to their respective cities.

After they had retired the Athenians set guards by land and sea at the points at which they intended to have regular stations during the war. They also resolved to set apart a special fund of a thousand talents from the moneys in the Acropolis. This was not to be spent, but the current expenses of the war were to be otherwise provided for. If any one should move or put to the vote a proposition for using the money for any purpose whatever except that of defending the city in the event of the enemy bringing a fleet to make an attack by sea, it should be a capital offence. With this sum of money they also set aside a special fleet of one hundred galleys, the best ships of each year, with their captains. None of these were to be used except with the money and against the same peril, should such peril arise.

Meanwhile the Athenians in the hundred ships round Peloponnese, reinforced by a Corcyraean squadron of fifty vessels and some others of the allies in those parts, cruised about the coasts and ravaged the country. Among other places they landed in Laconia and made an assault upon Methone; there being no garrison in the place, and the wall being weak. But it so happened that Brasidas, son of Tellis, a Spartan, was in command of a guard for the defence of the district. Hearing of the attack, he hurried with a hundred heavy infantry to the assistance of the besieged, and dashing through the army of the Athenians, which was scattered over the country and had its attention turned to the wall, threw himself into Methone. He lost a few men in making good his entrance, but saved the place and won the thanks of Sparta by his exploit, being thus the first officer who obtained this notice during the war. The Athenians at once weighed anchor and continued their cruise. Touching at Pheia in Elis, they ravaged the country for two days and defeated a picked force of three hundred men that had come from the vale of Elis and the immediate neighbourhood to the rescue. But a stiff squall came down upon them, and, not liking to face it in a place where there was no harbour, most of them got on board their ships, and doubling Point Ichthys sailed into the port of Pheia. In the meantime the Messenians, and some others who could not get on board, marched over by land and took Pheia. The fleet afterwards sailed round and picked them up and then put to sea; Pheia being evacuated, as the main army of the Eleans had now come up. The Athenians continued their cruise, and ravaged other places on the coast.

About the same time the Athenians sent thirty ships to cruise round Locris and also to guard Euboea; Cleopompus, son of Clinias, being in command. Making descents from the fleet he ravaged certain places on the sea-coast, and captured Thronium and took hostages from it. He also defeated at Alope the Locrians that had assembled to resist him.

During the summer the Athenians also expelled the Aeginetans with their wives and children from Aegina, on the ground of their having been the chief agents in bringing the war upon them. Besides, Aegina lies so near Peloponnese that it seemed safer to send colonists of their own to hold it, and shortly afterwards the settlers were sent out. The banished Aeginetans found an asylum in Thyrea, which was given to them by Lacedaemon, not only on account of her quarrel with Athens, but also because the Aeginetans had laid her under obligations at the time of the earthquake and the revolt of the Helots. The territory of Thyrea is on the frontier of Argolis and Laconia, reaching down to the sea. Those of the Aeginetans who did not settle here were scattered over the rest of Hellas.

The same summer, at the beginning of a new lunar month, the only time by the way at which it appears possible, the sun was eclipsed after noon. After it had assumed the form of a crescent and some of the stars had come out, it returned to its natural shape.

During the same summer Nymphodorus, son of Pythes, an Abderite, whose sister Sitalces had married, was made their proxenus by the Athenians and sent for to Athens. They had hitherto considered him their enemy; but he had great influence with Sitalces, and they wished this prince to become their ally. Sitalces was the son of Teres and King of the Thracians. Teres, the father of Sitalces, was the first to establish the great kingdom of the Odrysians on a scale quite unknown to the rest of Thrace, a large portion of the Thracians being independent. This Teres is in no way related to Tereus who married Pandion's daughter Procne from Athens; nor indeed did they belong to the same part of Thrace. Tereus lived in Daulis, part of what is now called Phocis, but which at that time was inhabited by Thracians. It was in this land that the women perpetrated the outrage upon Itys; and many of the poets when they mention the nightingale call it the Daulian bird. Besides, Pandion in contracting an alliance for his daughter would consider the advantages of mutual assistance, and would naturally prefer a match at the above moderate distance to the journey of many days which separates Athens from the Odrysians. Again the names are different; and this Teres was king of the Odrysians, the first by the way who attained to any power. Sitalces, his son, was now sought as an ally by the Athenians, who desired his aid in the reduction of the Thracian towns and of Perdiccas. Coming to Athens, Nymphodorus concluded the alliance with Sitalces and made his son Sadocus an Athenian citizen, and promised to finish the war in Thrace by persuading Sitalces to send the Athenians a force of Thracian horse and targeteers. He also reconciled them with Perdiccas, and induced them to restore Therme to him; upon which Perdiccas at once joined the Athenians and Phormio in an expedition against the Chalcidians. Thus Sitalces, son of Teres, King of the Thracians, and Perdiccas, son of Alexander, King of the Macedonians, became allies of Athens.

Meanwhile the Athenians in the hundred vessels were still cruising round Peloponnese. After taking Sollium, a town belonging to Corinth, and presenting the city and territory to the Acarnanians of Palaira, they stormed Astacus, expelled its tyrant Evarchus, and gained the place for their confederacy. Next they sailed to the island of Cephallenia and brought it over without using force. Cephallenia lies off Acarnania and Leucas, and consists of four states, the Paleans, Cranians, Samaeans, and Pronaeans. Not long afterwards the fleet returned to Athens. Towards the autumn of this year the Athenians invaded the Megarid with their whole levy, resident aliens included, under the command of Pericles, son of Xanthippus. The Athenians in the hundred ships round Peloponnese on their journey home had just reached Aegina, and hearing that the citizens at home were in full force at Megara, now sailed over and joined them. This was without doubt the largest army of Athenians ever assembled, the state being still in the flower of her strength and yet unvisited by the plague. Full ten thousand heavy infantry were in the field, all Athenian citizens, besides the three thousand before Potidaea. Then the resident aliens who joined in the incursion were at least three thousand strong; besides which there was a multitude of light troops. They ravaged the greater part of the territory, and then retired. Other incursions into the Megarid were afterwards made by the Athenians annually during the war, sometimes only with cavalry, sometimes with all their forces. This went on until the capture of Nisaea. Atalanta also, the desert island off the Opuntian coast, was towards the end of this summer converted into a fortified post by the Athenians, in order to prevent privateers issuing from Opus and the rest of Locris and plundering Euboea. Such were the events of this summer after the return of the Peloponnesians from Attica.

In the ensuing winter the Acarnanian Evarchus, wishing to return to Astacus, persuaded the Corinthians to sail over with forty ships and fifteen hundred heavy infantry and restore him; himself also hiring some mercenaries. In command of the force were Euphamidas, son of Aristonymus, Timoxenus, son of Timocrates, and Eumachus, son of Chrysis, who sailed over and restored him and, after failing in an attempt on some places on the Acarnanian coast which they were desirous of gaining, began their voyage home. Coasting along shore they touched at Cephallenia and made a descent on the Cranian territory, and losing some men by the treachery of the Cranians, who fell suddenly upon them after having agreed to treat, put to sea somewhat hurriedly and returned home.

In the same winter the Athenians gave a funeral at the public cost to those who had first fallen in this war. It was a custom of their ancestors, and the manner of it is as follows. Three days before the ceremony, the bones of the dead are laid out in a tent which has been erected; and their friends bring to their relatives such offerings as they please. In the funeral procession cypress coffins are borne in cars, one for each tribe; the bones of the deceased being placed in the coffin of their tribe. Among these is carried one empty bier decked for the missing, that is, for those whose bodies could not be recovered. Any citizen or stranger who pleases, joins in the procession: and the female relatives are there to wail at the burial. The dead are laid in the public sepulchre in the Beautiful suburb of the city, in which those who fall in war are always buried; with the exception of those slain at Marathon, who for their singular and extraordinary valour were interred on the spot where they fell. After the bodies have been laid in the earth, a man chosen by the state, of approved wisdom and eminent reputation, pronounces over them an appropriate panegyric; after which all retire. Such is the manner of the burying; and throughout the whole of the war, whenever the occasion arose, the established custom was observed. Meanwhile these were the first that had fallen, and Pericles, son of Xanthippus, was chosen to pronounce their eulogium. When the proper time arrived, he advanced from the sepulchre to an elevated platform in order to be heard by as many of the crowd as possible, and spoke as follows:

"Most of my predecessors in this place have commended him who made this speech part of the law, telling us that it is well that it should be delivered at the burial of those who fall in battle. For myself, I should have thought that the worth which had displayed itself in deeds would be sufficiently rewarded by honours also shown by deeds; such as you now see in this funeral prepared at the people's cost. And I could have wished that the reputations of many brave men were not to be imperilled in the mouth of a single individual, to stand or fall according as he spoke well or ill. For it is hard to speak properly upon a subject where it is even difficult to convince your hearers that you are speaking the truth. On the one hand, the friend who is familiar with every fact of the story may think that some point has not been set forth with that fullness which he wishes and knows it to deserve; on the other, he who is a stranger to the matter may be led by envy to suspect exaggeration if he hears anything above his own nature. For men can endure to hear others praised only so long as they can severally persuade themselves of their own ability to equal the actions recounted: when this point is passed, envy comes in and with it incredulity. However, since our ancestors have stamped this custom with their approval, it becomes my duty to obey the law and to try to satisfy your several wishes and opinions as best I may.

"I shall begin with our ancestors: it is both just and proper that they should have the honour of the first mention on an occasion like the present. They dwelt in the country without break in the succession from generation to generation, and handed it down free to the present time by their valour. And if our more remote ancestors deserve praise, much more do our own fathers, who added to their inheritance the empire which we now possess, and spared no pains to be able to leave their acquisitions to us of the present generation. Lastly, there are few parts of our dominions that have not been augmented by those of us here, who are still more or less in the vigour of life; while the mother country has been furnished by us with everything that can enable her to depend on her own resources whether for war or for peace. That part of our history which tells of the military achievements which gave us our several possessions, or of the ready valour with which either we or our fathers stemmed the tide of Hellenic or foreign aggression, is a theme too familiar to my hearers for me to dilate on, and I shall therefore pass it by. But what was the road by which we reached our position, what the form of government under which our greatness grew, what the national habits out of which it sprang; these are questions which I may try to solve before I proceed to my panegyric upon these men; since I think this to be a subject upon which on the present occasion a speaker may properly dwell, and to which the whole assemblage, whether citizens or foreigners, may listen with advantage.

"Our constitution does not copy the laws of neighbouring states; we are rather a pattern to others than imitators ourselves. Its administration favours the many instead of the few; this is why it is called a democracy. If we look to the laws, they afford equal justice to all in their private differences; if no social standing, advancement in public life falls to reputation for capacity, class considerations not being allowed to interfere with merit; nor again does poverty bar the way, if a man is able to serve the state, he is not hindered by the obscurity of his condition. The freedom which we enjoy in our government extends also to our ordinary life. There, far from exercising a jealous surveillance over each other, we do not feel called upon to be angry with our neighbour for doing what he likes, or even to indulge in those injurious looks which cannot fail to be offensive, although they inflict no positive penalty. But all this ease in our private relations does not make us lawless as citizens. Against this fear is our chief safeguard, teaching us to obey the magistrates and the laws, particularly such as regard the protection of the injured, whether they are actually on the statute book, or belong to that code which, although unwritten, yet cannot be broken without acknowledged disgrace.

"Further, we provide plenty of means for the mind to refresh itself from business. We celebrate games and sacrifices all the year round, and the elegance of our private establishments forms a daily source of pleasure and helps to banish the spleen; while the magnitude of our city draws the produce of the world into our harbour, so that to the Athenian the fruits of other countries are as familiar a luxury as those of his own.

"If we turn to our military policy, there also we differ from our antagonists. We throw open our city to the world, and never by alien acts exclude foreigners from any opportunity of learning or observing, although the eyes of an enemy may occasionally profit by our liberality; trusting less in system and policy than to the native spirit of our citizens; while in education, where our rivals from their very cradles by a painful discipline seek after manliness, at Athens we live exactly as we please, and yet are just as ready to encounter every legitimate danger. In proof of this it may be noticed that the Lacedaemonians do not invade our country alone, but bring with them all their confederates; while we Athenians advance unsupported into the territory of a neighbour, and fighting upon a foreign soil usually vanquish with ease men who are defending their homes. Our united force was never yet encountered by any enemy, because we have at once to attend to our marine and to dispatch our citizens by land upon a hundred different services; so that, wherever they engage with some such fraction of our strength, a success against a detachment is magnified into a victory over the nation, and a defeat into a reverse suffered at the hands of our entire people. And yet if with habits not of labour but of ease, and courage not of art but of nature, we are still willing to encounter danger, we have the double advantage of escaping the experience of hardships in anticipation and of facing them in the hour of need as fearlessly as those who are never free from them.

"Nor are these the only points in which our city is worthy of admiration. We cultivate refinement without extravagance and knowledge without effeminacy; wealth we employ more for use than for show, and place the real disgrace of poverty not in owning to the fact but in declining the struggle against it. Our public men have, besides politics, their private affairs to attend to, and our ordinary citizens, though occupied with the pursuits of industry, are still fair judges of public matters; for, unlike any other nation, regarding him who takes no part in these duties not as unambitious but as useless, we Athenians are able to judge at all events if we cannot originate, and, instead of looking on discussion as a stumbling-block in the way of action, we think it an indispensable preliminary to any wise action at all. Again, in our enterprises we present the singular spectacle of daring and deliberation, each carried to its highest point, and both united in the same persons; although usually decision is the fruit of ignorance, hesitation of reflection. But the palm of courage will surely be adjudged most justly to those, who best know the difference between hardship and pleasure and yet are never tempted to shrink from danger. In generosity we are equally singular, acquiring our friends by conferring, not by receiving, favours. Yet, of course, the doer of the favour is the firmer friend of the two, in order by continued kindness to keep the recipient in his debt; while the debtor feels less keenly from the very consciousness that the return he makes will be a payment, not a free gift. And it is only the Athenians, who, fearless of consequences, confer their benefits not from calculations of expediency, but in the confidence of liberality.

"In short, I say that as a city we are the school of Hellas, while I doubt if the world can produce a man who, where he has only himself to depend upon, is equal to so many emergencies, and graced by so happy a versatility, as the Athenian. And that this is no mere boast thrown out for the occasion, but plain matter of fact, the power of the state acquired by these habits proves. For Athens alone of her contemporaries is found when tested to be greater than her reputation, and alone gives no occasion to her assailants to blush at the antagonist by whom they have been worsted, or to her subjects to question her title by merit to rule. Rather, the admiration of the present and succeeding ages will be ours, since we have not left our power without witness, but have shown it by mighty proofs; and far from needing a Homer for our panegyrist, or other of his craft whose verses might charm for the moment only for the impression which they gave to melt at the touch of fact, we have forced every sea and land to be the highway of our daring, and everywhere, whether for evil or for good, have left imperishable monuments behind us. Such is the Athens for which these men, in the assertion of their resolve not to lose her, nobly fought and died; and well may every one of their survivors be ready to suffer in her cause.

"Indeed if I have dwelt at some length upon the character of our country, it has been to show that our stake in the struggle is not the same as theirs who have no such blessings to lose, and also that the panegyric of the men over whom I am now speaking might be by definite proofs established. That panegyric is now in a great measure complete; for the Athens that I have celebrated is only what the heroism of these and their like have made her, men whose fame, unlike that of most Hellenes, will be found to be only commensurate with their deserts. And if a test of worth be wanted, it is to be found in their closing scene, and this not only in cases in which it set the final seal upon their merit, but also in those in which it gave the first intimation of their having any. For there is justice in the claim that steadfastness in his country's battles should be as a cloak to cover a man's other imperfections; since the good action has blotted out the bad, and his merit as a citizen more than outweighed his demerits as an individual. But none of these allowed either wealth with its prospect of future enjoyment to unnerve his spirit, or poverty with its hope of a day of freedom and riches to tempt him to shrink from danger. No, holding that vengeance upon their enemies was more to be desired than any personal blessings, and reckoning this to be the most glorious of hazards, they joyfully determined to accept the risk, to make sure of their vengeance, and to let their wishes wait; and while committing to hope the uncertainty of final success, in the business before them they thought fit to act boldly and trust in themselves. Thus choosing to die resisting, rather than to live submitting, they fled only from dishonour, but met danger face to face, and after one brief moment, while at the summit of their fortune, escaped, not from their fear, but from their glory.

"So died these men as became Athenians. You, their survivors, must determine to have as unfaltering a resolution in the field, though you may pray that it may have a happier issue. And not contented with ideas derived only from words of the advantages which are bound up with the defence of your country, though these would furnish a valuable text to a speaker even before an audience so alive to them as the present, you must yourselves realize the power of Athens, and feed your eyes upon her from day to day, till love of her fills your hearts; and then, when all her greatness shall break upon you, you must reflect that it was by courage, sense of duty, and a keen feeling of honour in action that men were enabled to win all this, and that no personal failure in an enterprise could make them consent to deprive their country of their valour, but they laid it at her feet as the most glorious contribution that they could offer. For this offering of their lives made in common by them all they each of them individually received that renown which never grows old, and for a sepulchre, not so much that in which their bones have been deposited, but that noblest of shrines wherein their glory is laid up to be eternally remembered upon every occasion on which deed or story shall call for its commemoration. For heroes have the whole earth for their tomb; and in lands far from their own, where the column with its epitaph declares it, there is enshrined in every breast a record unwritten with no tablet to preserve it, except that of the heart. These take as your model and, judging happiness to be the fruit of freedom and freedom of valour, never decline the dangers of war. For it is not the miserable that would most justly be unsparing of their lives; these have nothing to hope for: it is rather they to whom continued life may bring reverses as yet unknown, and to whom a fall, if it came, would be most tremendous in its consequences. And surely, to a man of spirit, the degradation of cowardice must be immeasurably more grievous than the unfelt death which strikes him in the midst of his strength and patriotism!

"Comfort, therefore, not condolence, is what I have to offer to the parents of the dead who may be here. Numberless are the chances to which, as they know, the life of man is subject; but fortunate indeed are they who draw for their lot a death so glorious as that which has caused your mourning, and to whom life has been so exactly measured as to terminate in the happiness in which it has been passed. Still I know that this is a hard saying, especially when those are in question of whom you will constantly be reminded by seeing in the homes of others blessings of which once you also boasted: for grief is felt not so much for the want of what we have never known, as for the loss of that to which we have been long accustomed. Yet you who are still of an age to beget children must bear up in the hope of having others in their stead; not only will they help you to forget those whom you have lost, but will be to the state at once a reinforcement and a security; for never can a fair or just policy be expected of the citizen who does not, like his fellows, bring to the decision the interests and apprehensions of a father. While those of you who have passed your prime must congratulate yourselves with the thought that the best part of your life was fortunate, and that the brief span that remains will be cheered by the fame of the departed. For it is only the love of honour that never grows old; and honour it is, not gain, as some would have it, that rejoices the heart of age and helplessness.

"Turning to the sons or brothers of the dead, I see an arduous struggle before you. When a man is gone, all are wont to praise him, and should your merit be ever so transcendent, you will still find it difficult not merely to overtake, but even to approach their renown. The living have envy to contend with, while those who are no longer in our path are honoured with a goodwill into which rivalry does not enter. On the other hand, if I must say anything on the subject of female excellence to those of you who will now be in widowhood, it will be all comprised in this brief exhortation. Great will be your glory in not falling short of your natural character; and greatest will be hers who is least talked of among the men, whether for good or for bad.

"My task is now finished. I have performed it to the best of my ability, and in word, at least, the requirements of the law are now satisfied. If deeds be in question, those who are here interred have received part of their honours already, and for the rest, their children will be brought up till manhood at the public expense: the state thus offers a valuable prize, as the garland of victory in this race of valour, for the reward both of those who have fallen and their survivors. And where the rewards for merit are greatest, there are found the best citizens.

"And now that you have brought to a close your lamentations for your relatives, you may depart."

CHAPTER VII

*Second Year of the War - The Plague of Athens -
Position and Policy of Pericles - Fall of Potidaea*

The plague of Athens.

S UCH WAS the funeral that took place during this winter, with which the first year of the war came to an end. In the first days of summer the Lacedaemonians and their allies, with two-thirds of their forces as before, invaded Attica, under the command of Archidamus, son of Zeuxidamus, King of Lacedaemon, and sat down and laid waste the country. Not many days after their arrival in Attica the plague first began to show itself among the Athenians. It was said that it had broken out in many places previously in the neighbourhood of Lemnos and elsewhere; but a pestilence of such extent and mortality was nowhere remembered. Neither were the physicians at first of any service, ignorant as they were of the proper way to treat it, but they died themselves the most thickly, as they visited the sick most often; nor did any human art succeed any better. Supplications in the temples, divinations, and so forth were found equally futile, till the overwhelming nature of the disaster at last put a stop to them altogether.

It first began, it is said, in the parts of Ethiopia above Egypt, and thence descended into Egypt and Libya and into most of the King's country. Suddenly falling upon Athens, it first attacked the population in Piraeus - which was the occasion of their saying that the Peloponnesians had poisoned the reservoirs, there being as yet no wells there - and afterwards appeared in the upper city, when the deaths became much more frequent. All speculation as to its origin and its causes, if causes can be found adequate to produce so great a disturbance, I leave to other writers, whether lay or professional; for myself, I shall simply set down its nature, and explain the symptoms by which perhaps it may be recognized by the student, if it should ever break out again. This I can the better do, as I had the disease myself, and watched its operation in the case of others.

That year then is admitted to have been otherwise unprecedentedly free from sickness; and such few cases as occurred all determined in this. As a rule, however, there was no ostensible cause; but people in good health were all of a sudden attacked by violent heats in the head, and redness and inflammation in the eyes, the inward parts, such as the throat or tongue, becoming bloody and emitting an unnatural and fetid breath. These symptoms were followed by sneezing and hoarseness, after which the pain soon reached the chest, and produced a hard cough. When it fixed in the stomach, it upset it; and discharges of bile of every kind named by physicians ensued, accompanied by very great distress. In most cases also an ineffectual retching followed, producing violent spasms, which in some cases ceased soon after, in others much later. Externally the body was not very hot to the touch, nor pale in its appearance, but reddish, livid, and breaking out into small pustules and ulcers. But internally it burned so that the patient could not bear to have on him clothing or linen even of the very lightest description; or indeed to be otherwise than stark naked. What they would have liked best would have been to throw themselves into cold water; as indeed was done by some of the neglected sick, who plunged into the rain-tanks in their agonies of unquenchable thirst; though it made no difference whether they drank little or much. Besides this, the miserable feeling of not being able to rest or sleep never ceased to torment them. The body meanwhile did not waste away so long as the distemper was at its height, but held out to a marvel against its ravages; so that when they succumbed, as in most cases, on the seventh or eighth day to the internal inflammation, they had still some strength in them. But if they passed this stage, and the disease descended further into the bowels, inducing a violent ulceration there accompanied by severe diarrhoea, this brought on a weakness which was generally fatal. For the disorder first settled in the head, ran its course from thence through the whole of the body, and, even where it did not prove mortal, it still left its mark on the extremities; for it settled in the privy parts, the fingers and the toes, and many escaped with the loss of these, some too with that of their eyes. Others again were seized with an entire loss of memory on their first recovery, and did not know either themselves or their friends.

But while the nature of the distemper was such as to baffle all description, and its attacks almost too grievous for human nature to endure, it was still in the following circumstance that its difference from all ordinary disorders was most clearly shown. All the birds and beasts that prey upon human bodies, either abstained from touching them (though there were many lying unburied), or died after tasting them. In proof of this, it was noticed that birds of this kind actually disappeared; they were not about the bodies, or indeed to be seen at all. But of course the effects which I have mentioned could best be studied in a domestic animal like the dog.

Such then, if we pass over the varieties of particular cases which were many and peculiar, were the general features of the distemper. Meanwhile the town enjoyed an immunity from all the ordinary disorders; or if any case occurred, it ended in this. Some died in neglect, others in the midst of every attention. No remedy was found that could be used as a specific; for what did good in one case, did harm in another. Strong and weak constitutions proved equally incapable of resistance, all alike being swept away, although dieted with the utmost precaution. By far the most terrible feature in the malady was the dejection which ensued when any one felt himself sickening, for the despair into which they instantly fell took away their power of resistance, and left them a much easier prey to the disorder; besides which, there was the awful spectacle of men dying like sheep, through having caught the infection in nursing each other. This caused the greatest mortality. On the one hand, if they were afraid to visit each other, they perished from neglect; indeed many houses were emptied of their inmates for want of a nurse: on the other, if they ventured to do so, death was the consequence. This was especially the case with such as made any pretensions to goodness: honour made them unsparing of themselves in their attendance in their friends' houses, where even the members of the family were at last worn out by the moans of the dying, and succumbed to the force of the disaster. Yet it was with those who had recovered from the disease that the sick and the dying found most compassion. These knew what it was from experience, and had now no fear for themselves; for the same man was never attacked twice - never at least fatally. And such persons not only received the congratulations of others, but themselves also, in the elation of the moment, half entertained the vain hope that they were for the future safe from any disease whatsoever.

An aggravation of the existing calamity was the influx from the country into the city, and this was especially felt by the new arrivals. As there were no houses to receive them, they had to be lodged at the hot season of the year in stifling cabins, where the mortality raged without restraint. The bodies of dying men lay one upon another, and half-dead creatures reeled about the streets and gathered round all the fountains in their longing for water. The sacred places also in which they had quartered themselves were full of corpses of persons that had died there, just as they were; for as the disaster passed all bounds, men, not knowing what was to become of them, became utterly careless of everything, whether sacred or profane. All the burial rites before in use were entirely upset, and they buried the bodies as best they could. Many from want of the proper appliances, through so many of their friends having died already, had recourse to the most shameless sepultures: sometimes getting the start of those who had raised a pile, they threw their own dead body upon the stranger's pyre and ignited it; sometimes they tossed the corpse which they were carrying on the top of another that was burning, and so went off.

Nor was this the only form of lawless extravagance which owed its origin to the plague. Men now coolly ventured on what they had formerly done in a corner, and not just as they pleased, seeing the rapid transitions produced by persons in prosperity suddenly dying and those who before had nothing succeeding to their property. So they resolved to spend quickly and enjoy themselves, regarding their lives and riches as alike things of a day. Perseverance in what men called honour was popular with none, it was so uncertain whether they would be spared to attain the object; but it was settled that present enjoyment, and all that contributed to it, was both honourable and useful. Fear of gods or law of man there was none to restrain them. As for the first, they judged it to be just the same whether they worshipped them or not, as they saw all alike perishing; and for the last, no one expected to live to be brought to trial for his offences, but each felt that a far severer sentence had been already passed upon them all and hung ever over their heads, and before this fell it was only reasonable to enjoy life a little.

Such was the nature of the calamity, and heavily did it weigh on the Athenians; death raging within the city and devastation without. Among other things which they remembered in their distress was, very naturally, the following verse which the old men said had long ago been uttered:

A Dorian war shall come and with it death.

So a dispute arose as to whether dearth and not death had not been the word in the verse; but at the present juncture, it was of course decided in favour of the latter; for the people made their recollection fit in with their sufferings. I fancy, however, that if another Dorian war should ever afterwards come upon us, and a dearth should happen to accompany it, the verse will probably be read accordingly. The oracle also which had been given to the Lacedaemonians was now remembered by those who knew of it. When the god was asked whether they should go to war, he answered that if they put their might into it, victory would be theirs, and that he would himself be with them. With this oracle events were supposed to tally. For the plague broke out as soon as the Peloponnesians invaded Attica, and never entering Peloponnese (not at least to an extent worth noticing), committed its worst ravages at Athens, and next to Athens, at the most populous of the other towns. Such was the history of the plague.

After ravaging the plain, the Peloponnesians advanced into the Paralian region as far as Laurium, where the Athenian silver mines are, and first laid waste the side looking towards Peloponnese, next that which faces Euboea and Andros. But Pericles, who was still general, held the same opinion as in the former invasion, and would not let the Athenians march out against them.

However, while they were still in the plain, and had not yet entered the Paralian land, he had prepared an armament of a hundred ships for Peloponnese, and when all was ready put out to sea. On board the ships he took four thousand Athenian heavy infantry, and three hundred cavalry in horse transports, and then for the first time made out of old galleys; fifty Chian and Lesbian vessels also joining in the expedition. When this Athenian armament put out to sea, they left the Peloponnesians in Attica in the Paralian region. Arriving at Epidaurus in Peloponnese they ravaged most of the territory, and even had hopes of taking the town by an assault: in this however they were not successful. Putting out from Epidaurus, they laid waste the territory of Troezen, Halieis, and Hermione, all towns on the coast of Peloponnese, and thence sailing to Prasiai, a maritime town in Laconia, ravaged part of its territory, and took and sacked the place itself; after which they returned home, but found the Peloponnesians gone and no longer in Attica.

During the whole time that the Peloponnesians were in Attica and the Athenians on the expedition in their ships, men kept dying of the plague both in the armament and in Athens. Indeed it was actually asserted that the departure of the Peloponnesians was hastened by fear of the disorder; as they heard from deserters that it was in the city, and also could see the burials going on. Yet in this invasion they remained longer than in any other, and ravaged the whole country, for they were about forty days in Attica.

The same summer Hagnon, son of Nicias, and Cleopompus, son of Clinias, the colleagues of Pericles, took the armament of which he had lately made use, and went off upon an expedition against the Chalcidians in the direction of Thrace and Potidaea, which was still under siege. As soon as they arrived, they brought up their engines against Potidaea and tried every means of taking it, but did not succeed either in capturing the city or in doing anything else worthy of their preparations. For the plague attacked them here also, and committed such havoc as to cripple them completely, even the previously healthy soldiers of the former expedition catching the infection from Hagnon's troops; while Phormio and the sixteen hundred men whom he commanded only escaped by being no longer in the neighbourhood of the Chalcidians. The end of it was that Hagnon returned with his ships to Athens, having lost one thousand and fifty out of four thousand heavy infantry in about forty days; though the soldiers stationed there before remained in the country and carried on the siege of Potidaea.

After the second invasion of the Peloponnesians a change came over the spirit of the Athenians. Their land had now been twice laid waste; and war and pestilence at once pressed heavy upon them. They began to find fault with Pericles, as the author of the war and the cause of all their misfortunes, and became eager to come to terms with Lacedaemon, and actually sent ambassadors thither, who did not however succeed in their mission. Their despair was now complete and all vented itself upon Pericles. When he saw them exasperated at the present turn of affairs and acting exactly as he had anticipated, he called an assembly, being (it must be remembered) still general, with the double object of restoring confidence and of leading them from these angry feelings to a calmer and more hopeful state of mind. He accordingly came forward and spoke as follows:

"I was not unprepared for the indignation of which I have been the object, as I know its causes; and I have called an assembly for the purpose of reminding you upon certain points, and of protesting against your being unreasonably irritated with me, or cowed by your sufferings. I am of opinion that national greatness is more for the advantage of private citizens, than any individual well-being coupled with public humiliation. A man may be personally ever so well off, and yet if his country be ruined he must be ruined with it; whereas a flourishing commonwealth always affords chances of salvation to unfortunate individuals. Since then a state can support the misfortunes of private citizens, while they cannot support hers, it is surely the duty of every one to be forward in her defence, and not like you to be so confounded with your domestic afflictions as to give up all thoughts of the common safety, and to blame me for having counselled war and yourselves for having voted it. And yet if you are angry with me, it is with one who, as I believe, is second to no man either in knowledge of the proper policy, or in the ability to expound it, and who is moreover not only a patriot but an honest one. A man possessing that knowledge without that faculty of exposition might as well have no idea at all on the matter: if he had both these gifts, but no love for his country, he would be but a cold advocate for her interests; while were his patriotism not proof against bribery, everything would go for a price. So that if you thought that I was even moderately distinguished for these qualities when you took my advice and went to war, there is certainly no reason now why I should be charged with having done wrong.

"For those of course who have a free choice in the matter and whose fortunes are not at stake, war is the greatest of follies. But if the only choice was between submission with loss of independence, and danger with the hope of preserving that independence, in such a case it is he who will not accept the risk that deserves blame, not he who will. I am the same man and do not alter, it is you who change, since in fact you took my advice while unhurt, and waited for misfortune to repent of it; and the apparent error of my policy lies in the infirmity of your resolution, since the suffering that it entails is being felt by every one among you, while its advantage is still remote and obscure to all, and a great and sudden reverse having befallen you, your mind is too much depressed to persevere in your resolves. For before what is sudden, unexpected, and least within calculation, the spirit quails; and putting all else aside, the plague has certainly been an emergency of this kind. Born, however, as you are, citizens of a great state, and brought up, as you have been, with habits equal to your birth, you should be ready to face the greatest disasters and still to keep unimpaired the lustre of your name. For the judgment of mankind is as relentless to the weakness that falls short of a recognized renown, as it is jealous of the arrogance that aspires higher than its due. Cease then to grieve for your private afflictions, and address yourselves instead to the safety of the commonwealth.

"If you shrink before the exertions which the war makes necessary, and fear that after all they may not have a happy result, you know the reasons by which I have often demonstrated to you the groundlessness of your apprehensions. If those are not enough, I will now reveal an advantage arising from the greatness of your dominion, which I think has never yet suggested itself to you, which I never mentioned in my previous speeches, and which has so bold a sound that I should scarce adventure it now, were it not for the unnatural depression which I see around me. You perhaps think that your empire extends only over your allies; I will declare to you the truth. The visible field of action has two parts, land and sea. In the whole of one of these you are completely supreme, not merely as far as you use it at present, but also to what further extent you may think fit: in fine, your naval resources are such that your vessels may go where they please, without the King or any other nation on earth being able to stop them. So that although you may think it a great privation to lose the use of your land and houses, still you must see that this power is something widely different; and instead of fretting on their account, you should really regard them in the light of the gardens and other accessories that embellish a great fortune, and as, in comparison, of little moment. You should know too that liberty preserved by your efforts will easily recover for us what we have lost, while, the knee once bowed, even what you have will pass from you. Your fathers receiving these possessions not from others, but from themselves, did not let slip what their labour had acquired, but delivered them safe to you; and in this respect at least you must prove yourselves their equals, remembering that to lose what one has got is more disgraceful than to be balked in getting, and you must confront your enemies not merely with spirit but with disdain. Confidence indeed a blissful ignorance can impart, ay, even to a coward's breast, but disdain is the privilege of those who, like us, have been assured by reflection of their superiority to their adversary. And where the chances are the same, knowledge fortifies courage by the contempt which is its consequence, its trust being placed, not in hope, which is the prop of the desperate, but in a judgment grounded upon existing resources, whose anticipations are more to be depended upon.

"Again, your country has a right to your services in sustaining the glories of her position. These are a common source of pride to you all, and you cannot decline the burdens of empire and still expect to share its honours. You should remember also that what you are fighting against is not merely slavery as an exchange for independence, but also loss of empire and danger from the animosities incurred in its exercise. Besides, to recede is no longer possible, if indeed any of you in the alarm of the moment has become enamoured of the honesty of such an unambitious part. For what you hold is, to speak somewhat plainly, a tyranny; to take it perhaps was wrong, but to let it go is unsafe. And men of these retiring views, making converts of others, would quickly ruin a state; indeed the result would be the same if they could live independent by themselves; for the retiring and unambitious are never secure without vigorous protectors at their side; in fine, such qualities are useless to an imperial city, though they may help a dependency to an unmolested servitude.

"But you must not be seduced by citizens like these or angry with me - who, if I voted for war, only did as you did yourselves - in spite of the enemy having invaded your country and done what you could be certain that he would do, if you refused to comply with his demands; and although besides what we counted for, the plague has come upon us - the only point indeed at which our calculation has been at fault. It is this, I know, that has had a large share in making me more unpopular than I should otherwise have been - quite undeservedly, unless you are also prepared to give me the credit of any success with which chance may present you. Besides, the hand of heaven must be borne with resignation, that of the enemy with fortitude; this was the old way at Athens, and do not you prevent it being so still. Remember, too, that if your country has the greatest name in all the world, it is because she never bent before disaster; because she has expended more life and effort in war than any other city, and has won for herself a power greater than any hitherto known, the memory of which will descend to the latest posterity; even if now, in obedience to the general law of decay, we should ever be forced to yield, still it will be remembered that we held rule over more Hellenes than any other Hellenic state, that we sustained the greatest wars against their united or separate powers, and inhabited a city unrivalled by any other in resources or magnitude. These glories may incur the censure of the slow and unambitious; but in the breast of energy they will awake emulation, and in those who must remain without them an envious regret. Hatred and unpopularity at the moment have fallen to the lot of all who have aspired to rule others; but where odium must be incurred, true wisdom incurs it for the highest objects. Hatred also is short-lived; but that which makes the splendour of the present and the glory of the future remains for ever unforgotten. Make your decision, therefore, for glory then and honour now, and attain both objects by instant and zealous effort: do not send heralds to Lacedaemon, and do not betray any sign of being oppressed by your present sufferings, since they whose minds are least sensitive to calamity, and whose hands are most quick to meet it, are the greatest men and the greatest communities."

Such were the arguments by which Pericles tried to cure the Athenians of their anger against him and to divert their thoughts from their immediate afflictions. As a community he succeeded in convincing them; they not only gave up all idea of sending to Lacedaemon, but applied themselves with increased energy to the war; still as private individuals they could not help smarting under their sufferings, the common people having been deprived of the little that they were possessed, while the higher orders had lost fine properties with costly establishments and buildings in the country, and, worst of all, had war instead of peace. In fact, the public feeling against him did not subside until he had been fined. Not long afterwards, however, according to the way of the multitude, they again elected him general and committed all their affairs to his hands, having now become less sensitive to their private and domestic afflictions, and understanding that he was the best man of all for the public necessities. For as long as he was at the head of the state during the peace, he pursued a moderate and conservative policy; and in his time its greatness was at its height. When the war broke out, here also he seems to have rightly gauged the power of his country. He outlived its commencement two years and six months, and the correctness of his previsions respecting it became better known by his death. He told them to wait quietly, to pay attention to their marine, to attempt no new conquests, and to expose the city to no hazards during the war, and doing this, promised them a favourable result. What they did was the very contrary, allowing private ambitions and private interests, in matters apparently quite foreign to the war, to lead them into projects unjust both to themselves and to their allies - projects whose success would only conduce to the honour and advantage of private persons, and whose failure entailed certain disaster on the country in the war. The causes of this are not far to seek. Pericles indeed, by his rank, ability, and known integrity, was enabled to exercise an independent control over the multitude - in short, to lead them instead of being led by them; for as he never sought power by improper means, he was never compelled to flatter them, but, on the contrary, enjoyed so high an estimation that he could afford to anger them by contradiction. Whenever he saw them unseasonably and insolently elated, he would with a word reduce them to alarm; on the other hand, if they fell victims to a panic, he could at once restore them to confidence. In short, what was nominally a democracy became in his hands government by the first citizen. With his successors it was different. More on a level with one another, and each grasping at supremacy, they ended by committing even the conduct of state affairs to the whims of the multitude. This, as might have been expected in a great and sovereign state, produced a host of blunders, and amongst them the Sicilian expedition; though this failed not so much through a miscalculation of the power of those against whom it was sent, as through a fault in the senders in not taking the best measures afterwards to assist those who had gone out, but choosing rather to occupy themselves with private cabals for the leadership of the commons, by which they not only paralysed operations in the field, but also first introduced civil discord at home. Yet after losing most of their fleet besides other forces in Sicily, and with faction already dominant in the city, they could still for three years make head against their original adversaries, joined not only by the Sicilians, but also by their own allies nearly all in revolt, and at last by the King's son, Cyrus, who furnished the funds for the Peloponnesian navy. Nor did they finally succumb till they fell the victims of their own intestine disorders. So superfluously abundant were the resources from which the genius of Pericles foresaw an easy triumph in the war over the unaided forces of the Peloponnesians.

During the same summer the Lacedaemonians and their allies made an expedition with a hundred ships against Zacynthus, an island lying off the coast of Elis, peopled by a colony of Achaeans from Peloponnese, and in alliance with Athens. There were a thousand Lacedaemonian heavy infantry on board, and Cnemus, a Spartan, as admiral. They made a descent from their ships, and ravaged most of the country; but as the inhabitants would not submit, they sailed back home.

At the end of the same summer the Corinthian Aristeus, Aneristus, Nicolaus, and Stratodemus, envoys from Lacedaemon, Timagoras, a Tegean, and a private individual named Pollis from Argos, on their way to Asia to persuade the King to supply funds and join in the war, came to Sitalces, son of Teres in Thrace, with the idea of inducing him, if possible, to forsake the alliance of Athens and to march on Potidaea then besieged by an Athenian force, and also of getting conveyed by his means to their destination across the Hellespont to Pharnabazus, who was to send them up the country to the King. But there chanced to be with Sitalces some Athenian ambassadors - Learchus, son of Callimachus, and Ameiniades, son of Philemon - who persuaded Sitalces' son, Sadocus, the new Athenian citizen, to put the men into their hands and thus prevent their crossing over to the King and doing their part to injure the country of his choice. He accordingly had them seized, as they were travelling through Thrace to the vessel in which they were to cross the Hellespont, by a party whom he had sent on with Learchus and Ameiniades, and gave orders for their delivery to the Athenian ambassadors, by whom they were brought to Athens. On their arrival, the Athenians, afraid that Aristeus, who had been notably the prime mover in the previous affairs of Potidaea and their Thracian possessions, might live to do them still more mischief if he escaped, slew them all the same day, without giving them a trial or hearing the defence which they wished to offer, and cast their bodies into a pit; thinking themselves justified in using in retaliation the same mode of warfare which the Lacedaemonians had begun, when they slew and cast into pits all the Athenian and allied traders whom they caught on board the merchantmen round Peloponnese. Indeed, at the outset of the war, the Lacedaemonians butchered as enemies all whom they took on the sea, whether allies of Athens or neutrals.

About the same time towards the close of the summer, the Ambraciot forces, with a number of barbarians that they had raised, marched against the Amphilochian Argos and the rest of that country. The origin of their enmity against the Argives was this. This Argos and the rest of Amphilochia were colonized by Amphilochus, son of Amphiaraus. Dissatisfied with the state of affairs at home on his return thither after the Trojan War, he built this city in the Ambracian Gulf, and named it Argos after his own country. This was the largest town in Amphilochia, and its inhabitants the most powerful. Under the pressure of misfortune many generations afterwards, they called in the Ambraciots, their neighbours on the Amphilochian border, to join their colony; and it was by this union with the Ambraciots that they learnt their present Hellenic speech, the rest of the Amphilochians being barbarians. After a time the Ambraciots expelled the Argives and held the city themselves. Upon this the Amphilochians gave themselves over to the Acarnanians; and the two together called the Athenians, who sent them Phormio as general and thirty ships; upon whose arrival they took Argos by storm, and made slaves of the Ambraciots; and the Amphilochians and Acarnanians inhabited the town in common. After this began the alliance between the Athenians and Acarnanians. The enmity of the Ambraciots against the Argives thus commenced with the enslavement of their citizens; and afterwards during the war they collected this armament among themselves and the Chaonians, and other of the neighbouring barbarians. Arrived before Argos, they became masters of the country; but not being successful in their attacks upon the town, returned home and dispersed among their different peoples.

Such were the events of the summer. The ensuing winter the Athenians sent twenty ships round Peloponnese, under the command of Phormio, who stationed himself at Naupactus and kept watch against any one sailing in or out of Corinth and the Crissaean Gulf. Six others went to Caria and Lycia under Melesander, to collect tribute in those parts, and also to prevent the Peloponnesian privateers from taking up their station in those waters and molesting the passage of the merchantmen from Phaselis and Phoenicia and the adjoining continent. However, Melesander, going up the country into Lycia with a force of Athenians from the ships and the allies, was defeated and killed in battle, with the loss of a number of his troops.

The same winter the Potidaeans at length found themselves no longer able to hold out against their besiegers. The inroads of the Peloponnesians into Attica had not had the desired effect of making the Athenians raise the siege. Provisions there were none left; and so far had distress for food gone in Potidaea that, besides a number of other horrors, instances had even occurred of the people having eaten one another. In this extremity they at last made proposals for capitulating to the Athenian generals in command against them - Xenophon, son of Euripides, Hestiodorus, son of Aristocleides, and Phanomachus, son of Callimachus. The generals accepted their proposals, seeing the sufferings of the army in so exposed a position; besides which the state had already spent two thousand talents upon the siege. The terms of the capitulation were as follows: a free passage out for themselves, their children, wives and auxiliaries, with one garment apiece, the women with two, and a fixed sum of money for their journey. Under this treaty they went out to Chalcidice and other places, according as was their power. The Athenians, however, blamed the generals for granting terms without instructions from home, being of opinion that the place would have had to surrender at discretion. They afterwards sent settlers of their own to Potidaea, and colonized it. Such were the events of the winter, and so ended the second year of this war of which Thucydides was the historian.

CHAPTER VIII

Third Year of the War -
Investment of Plataea - Naval Victories of Phormio -
Thracian Irruption into Macedonia under Sitalces

Third year of the war.

THE NEXT summer the Peloponnesians and their allies, instead of invading Attica, marched against Plataea, under the command of Archidamus, son of Zeuxidamus, king of the Lacedaemonians. He had encamped his army and was about to lay waste the country, when the Plataeans hastened to send envoys to him, and spoke as follows: "Archidamus and Lacedaemonians, in invading the Plataean territory, you do what is wrong in itself, and worthy neither of yourselves nor of the fathers who begot you. Pausanias, son of Cleombrotus, your countryman, after freeing Hellas from the Medes with the help of those Hellenes who were willing to undertake the risk of the battle fought near our city, offered sacrifice to Zeus the Liberator in the marketplace of Plataea, and calling all the allies together restored to the Plataeans their city and territory, and declared it independent and inviolate against aggression or conquest. Should any such be attempted, the allies present were to help according to their power. Your fathers rewarded us thus for the courage and patriotism that we displayed at that perilous epoch; but you do just the contrary, coming with our bitterest enemies, the Thebans, to enslave us. We appeal, therefore, to the gods to whom the oaths were then made, to the gods of your ancestors, and lastly to those of our country, and call upon you to refrain from violating our territory or transgressing the oaths, and to let us live independent, as Pausanias decreed."

The Plataeans had got thus far when they were cut short by Archidamus saying: "There is justice, Plataeans, in what you say, if you act up to your words. According, to the grant of Pausanias, continue to be independent yourselves, and join in freeing those of your fellow countrymen who, after sharing in the perils of that period, joined in the oaths to you, and are now subject to the Athenians; for it is to free them and the rest that all this provision and war has been made. I could wish that you would share our labours and abide by the oaths yourselves; if this is impossible, do what we have already required of you - remain neutral, enjoying your own; join neither side, but receive both as friends, neither as allies for the war. With this we shall be satisfied." Such were the words of Archidamus. The Plataeans, after hearing what he had to say, went into the city and acquainted the people with what had passed, and presently returned for answer that it was impossible for them to do what he proposed without consulting the Athenians, with whom their children and wives now were; besides which they had their fears for the town. After his departure, what was to prevent the Athenians from coming and taking it out of their hands, or the Thebans, who would be included in the oaths, from taking advantage of the proposed neutrality to make a second attempt to seize the city? Upon these points he tried to reassure them by saying: "You have only to deliver over the city and houses to us Lacedaemonians, to point out the boundaries of your land, the number of your fruit-trees, and whatever else can be numerically stated, and yourselves to withdraw wherever you like as long as the war shall last. When it is over we will restore to you whatever we received, and in the interim hold it in trust and keep it in cultivation, paying you a sufficient allowance."

When they had heard what he had to say, they re-entered the city, and after consulting with the people said that they wished first to acquaint the Athenians with this proposal, and in the event of their approving to accede to it; in the meantime they asked him to grant them a truce and not to lay waste their territory. He accordingly granted a truce for the number of days requisite for the journey, and meanwhile abstained from ravaging their territory. The Plataean envoys went to Athens, and consulted with the Athenians, and returned with the following message to those in the city: "The Athenians say, Plataeans, that they never hitherto, since we became their allies, on any occasion abandoned us to an enemy, nor will they now neglect us, but will help us according to their ability; and they adjure you by the oaths which your fathers swore, to keep the alliance unaltered."

On the delivery of this message by the envoys, the Plataeans resolved not to be unfaithful to the Athenians but to endure, if it must be, seeing their lands laid waste and any other trials that might come to them, and not to send out again, but to answer from the wall that it was impossible for them to do as the Lacedaemonians proposed. As soon as he had received this answer, King Archidamus proceeded first to make a solemn appeal to the gods and heroes of the country in words following: "Ye gods and heroes of the Plataean territory, be my witnesses that not as aggressors originally, nor until these had first departed from the common oath, did we invade this land, in which our fathers offered you their prayers before defeating the Medes, and which you made auspicious to the Hellenic arms; nor shall we be aggressors in the measures to which we may now resort, since we have made many fair proposals but have not been successful. Graciously accord that those who were the first to offend may be punished for it, and that vengeance may be attained by those who would righteously inflict it."

After this appeal to the gods Archidamus put his army in motion. First he enclosed the town with a palisade formed of the fruit-trees which they cut down, to prevent further egress from Plataea; next they threw up a mound against the city, hoping that the largeness of the force employed would ensure the speedy reduction of the place. They accordingly cut down timber from Cithaeron, and built it up on either side, laying it like lattice-work to serve as a wall to keep the mound from spreading abroad, and carried to it wood and stones and earth and whatever other material might help to complete it. They continued to work at the mound for seventy days and nights without intermission, being divided into relief parties to allow of some being employed in carrying while others took sleep and refreshment; the Lacedaemonian officer attached to each contingent keeping the men to the work. But the Plataeans, observing the progress of the mound, constructed a wall of wood and fixed it upon that part of the city wall against which the mound was being erected, and built up bricks inside it which they took from the neighbouring houses. The timbers served to bind the building together, and to prevent its becoming weak as it advanced in height; it had also a covering of skins and hides, which protected the woodwork against the attacks of burning missiles and allowed the men to work in safety. Thus the wall was raised to a great height, and the mound opposite made no less rapid progress. The Plataeans also thought of another expedient; they pulled out part of the wall upon which the mound abutted, and carried the earth into the city.

Discovering this the Peloponnesians twisted up clay in wattles of reed and threw it into the breach formed in the mound, in order to give it consistency and prevent its being carried away like the soil. Stopped in this way the Plataeans changed their mode of operation, and digging a mine from the town calculated their way under the mound, and began to carry off its material as before. This went on for a long while without the enemy outside finding it out, so that for all they threw on the top their mound made no progress in proportion, being carried away from beneath and constantly settling down in the vacuum. But the Plataeans, fearing that even thus they might not be able to hold out against the superior numbers of the enemy, had yet another invention. They stopped working at the large building in front of the mound, and starting at either end of it inside from the old low wall, built a new one in the form of a crescent running in towards the town; in order that in the event of the great wall being taken this might remain, and the enemy have to throw up a fresh mound against it, and as they advanced within might not only have their trouble over again, but also be exposed to missiles on their flanks. While raising the mound the Peloponnesians also brought up engines against the city, one of which was brought up upon the mound against the great building and shook down a good piece of it, to the no small alarm of the Plataeans. Others were advanced against different parts of the wall but were lassoed and broken by the Plataeans; who also hung up great beams by long iron chains from either extremity of two poles laid on the wall and projecting over it, and drew them up at an angle whenever any point was threatened by the engine, and loosing their hold let the beam go with its chains slack, so that it fell with a run and snapped off the nose of the battering ram.

After this the Peloponnesians, finding that their engines effected nothing, and that their mound was met by the counterwork, concluded that their present means of offence were unequal to the taking of the city, and prepared for its circumvallation. First, however, they determined to try the effects of fire and see whether they could not, with the help of a wind, burn the town, as it was not a large one; indeed they thought of every possible expedient by which the place might be reduced without the expense of a blockade. They accordingly brought faggots of brushwood and threw them from the mound, first into the space between it and the wall; and this soon becoming full from the number of hands at work, they next heaped the faggots up as far into the town as they could reach from the top, and then lighted the wood by setting fire to it with sulphur and pitch. The consequence was a fire greater than any one had ever yet seen produced by human agency, though it could not of course be compared to the spontaneous conflagrations sometimes known to occur through the wind rubbing the branches of a mountain forest together. And this fire was not only remarkable for its magnitude, but was also, at the end of so many perils, within an ace of proving fatal to the Plataeans; a great part of the town became entirely inaccessible, and had a wind blown upon it, in accordance with the hopes of the enemy, nothing could have saved them. As it was, there is also a story of heavy rain and thunder having come on by which the fire was put out and the danger averted.

Failing in this last attempt the Peloponnesians left a portion of their forces on the spot, dismissing the rest, and built a wall of circumvallation round the town, dividing the ground among the various cities present; a ditch being made within and without the lines, from which they got their bricks. All being finished by about the rising of Arcturus, they left men enough to man half the wall, the rest being manned by the Boeotians, and drawing off their army dispersed to their several cities. The Plataeans had before sent off their wives and children and oldest men and the mass of the non-combatants to Athens; so that the number of the besieged left in the place comprised four hundred of their own citizens, eighty Athenians, and a hundred and ten women to bake their bread. This was the sum total at the commencement of the siege, and there was no one else within the walls, bond or free. Such were the arrangements made for the blockade of Plataea.

The same summer and simultaneously with the expedition against Plataea, the Athenians marched with two thousand heavy infantry and two hundred horse against the Chalcidians in the direction of Thrace and the Bottiaeans, just as the corn was getting ripe, under the command of Xenophon, son of Euripides, with two colleagues. Arriving before Spartolus in Bottiaea, they destroyed the corn and had some hopes of the city coming over through the intrigues of a faction within. But those of a different way of thinking had sent to Olynthus; and a garrison of heavy infantry and other troops arrived accordingly. These issuing from Spartolus were engaged by the Athenians in front of the town: the Chalcidian heavy infantry, and some auxiliaries with them, were beaten and retreated into Spartolus; but the Chalcidian horse and light troops defeated the horse and light troops of the Athenians. The Chalcidians had already a few targeteers from Crusis, and presently after the battle were joined by some others from Olynthus; upon seeing whom the light troops from Spartolus, emboldened by this accession and by their previous success, with the help of the Chalcidian horse and the reinforcement just arrived again attacked the Athenians, who retired upon the two divisions which they had left with their baggage. Whenever the Athenians advanced, their adversary gave way, pressing them with missiles the instant they began to retire. The Chalcidian horse also, riding up and charging them just as they pleased, at last caused a panic amongst them and routed and pursued them to a great distance. The Athenians took refuge in Potidaea, and afterwards recovered their dead under truce, and returned to Athens with the remnant of their army; four hundred and thirty men and all the generals having fallen. The Chalcidians and Bottiaeans set up a trophy, took up their dead, and dispersed to their several cities.

The same summer, not long after this, the Ambraciots and Chaonians, being desirous of reducing the whole of Acarnania and detaching it from Athens, persuaded the Lacedaemonians to equip a fleet from their confederacy and send a thousand heavy infantry to Acarnania, representing that, if a combined movement were made by land and sea, the coast Acarnanians would be unable to march, and the conquest of Zacynthus and Cephallenia easily following on the possession of Acarnania, the cruise round Peloponnese would be no longer so convenient for the Athenians. Besides which there was a hope of taking Naupactus. The Lacedaemonians accordingly at once sent off a few vessels with Cnemus, who was still high admiral, and the heavy infantry on board; and sent round orders for the fleet to equip as quickly as possible and sail to Leucas. The Corinthians were the most forward in the business; the Ambraciots being a colony of theirs. While the ships from Corinth, Sicyon, and the neighbourhood were getting ready, and those from Leucas, Anactorium, and Ambracia, which had arrived before, were waiting for them at Leucas, Cnemus and his thousand heavy infantry had run into the gulf, giving the slip to Phormio, the commander of the Athenian squadron stationed off Naupactus, and began at once to prepare for the land expedition. The Hellenic troops with him consisted of the Ambraciots, Leucadians, and Anactorians, and the thousand Peloponnesians with whom he came; the barbarian of a thousand Chaonians, who, belonging to a nation that has no king, were led by Photys and Nicanor, the two members of the royal family to whom the chieftainship for that year had been confided. With the Chaonians came also some Thesprotians, like them without a king, some Molossians and Atintanians led by Sabylinthus, the guardian of King Tharyps who was still a minor, and some Paravaeans, under their king Oroedus, accompanied by a thousand Orestians, subjects of King Antichus and placed by him under the command of Oroedus. There were also a thousand Macedonians sent by Perdiccas without the knowledge of the Athenians, but they arrived too late. With this force Cnemus set out, without waiting for the fleet from Corinth. Passing through the territory of Amphilochian Argos, and sacking the open village of Limnaea, they advanced to Stratus the Acarnanian capital; this once taken, the rest of the country, they felt convinced, would speedily follow.

The Acarnanians, finding themselves invaded by a large army by land, and from the sea threatened by a hostile fleet, made no combined attempt at resistance, but remained to defend their homes, and sent for help to Phormio, who replied that, when a fleet was on the point of sailing from Corinth, it was impossible for him to leave Naupactus unprotected. The Peloponnesians meanwhile and their allies advanced upon Stratus in three divisions, with the intention of encamping near it and attempting the wall by force if they failed to succeed by negotiation. The order of march was as follows: the centre was occupied by the Chaonians and the rest of the barbarians, with the Leucadians and Anactorians and their followers on the right, and Cnemus with the Peloponnesians and Ambraciots on the left; each division being a long way off from, and sometimes even out of sight of, the others. The Hellenes advanced in good order, keeping a look-out till they encamped in a good position; but the Chaonians, filled with self-confidence, and having the highest character for courage among the tribes of that part of the continent, without waiting to occupy their camp, rushed on with the rest of the barbarians, in the idea that they should take the town by assault and obtain the sole glory of the enterprise. While they were coming on, the Stratians, becoming aware how things stood, and thinking that the defeat of this division would considerably dishearten the Hellenes behind it, occupied the environs of the town with ambuscades, and as soon as they approached engaged them at close quarters from the city and the ambuscades. A panic seizing the Chaonians, great numbers of them were slain; and as soon as they were seen to give way the rest of the barbarians turned and fled. Owing to the distance by which their allies had preceded them, neither of the Hellenic divisions knew anything of the battle, but fancied they were hastening on to encamp. However, when the flying barbarians broke in upon them, they opened their ranks to receive them, brought their divisions together, and stopped quiet where they were for the day; the Stratians not offering to engage them, as the rest of the Acarnanians had not yet arrived, but contenting themselves with slinging at them from a distance, which distressed them greatly, as there was no stirring without their armour. The Acarnanians would seem to excel in this mode of warfare.

As soon as night fell, Cnemus hastily drew off his army to the river Anapus, about nine miles from Stratus, recovering his dead next day under truce, and being there joined by the friendly Oeniadae, fell back upon their city before the enemy's reinforcements came up. From hence each returned home; and the Stratians set up a trophy for the battle with the barbarians.

Meanwhile the fleet from Corinth and the rest of the confederates in the Crissaean Gulf, which was to have co-operated with Cnemus and prevented the coast Acarnanians from joining their countrymen in the interior, was disabled from doing so by being compelled about the same time as the battle at Stratus to fight with Phormio and the twenty Athenian vessels stationed at Naupactus. For they were watched, as they coasted along out of the gulf, by Phormio, who wished to attack in the open sea. But the Corinthians and allies had started for Acarnania without any idea of fighting at sea, and with vessels more like transports for carrying soldiers; besides which, they never dreamed of the twenty Athenian ships venturing to engage their forty-seven. However, while they were coasting along their own shore, there were the Athenians sailing along in line with them; and when they tried to cross over from Patrae in Achaea to the mainland on the other side, on their way to Acarnania, they saw them again coming out from Chalcis and the river Evenus to meet them. They slipped from their moorings in the night, but were observed, and were at length compelled to fight in mid passage. Each state that contributed to the armament had its own general; the Corinthian commanders were Machaon, Isocrates, and Agatharchidas. The

Peloponnesians ranged their vessels in as large a circle as possible without leaving an opening, with the prows outside and the sterns in; and placed within all the small craft in company, and their five best sailers to issue out at a moment's notice and strengthen any point threatened by the enemy.

The Athenians, formed in line, sailed round and round them, and forced them to contract their circle, by continually brushing past and making as though they would attack at once, having been previously cautioned by Phormio not to do so till he gave the signal. His hope was that the Peloponnesians would not retain their order like a force on shore, but that the ships would fall foul of one another and the small craft cause confusion; and if the wind should blow from the gulf (in expectation of which he kept sailing round them, and which usually rose towards morning), they would not, he felt sure, remain steady an instant. He also thought that it rested with him to attack when he pleased, as his ships were better sailers, and that an attack timed by the coming of the wind would tell best. When the wind came down, the enemy's ships were now in a narrow space, and what with the wind and the small

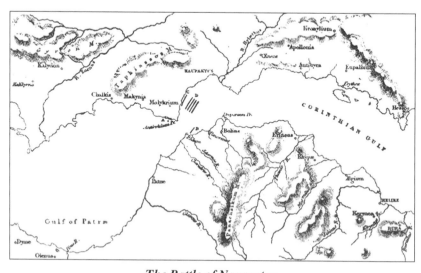

The Battle of Naupactus
A. Athenian Trophy   B. Peloponnesian Naval Base
C. Athenian Fleet   D. Peloponnesian Fleet

craft dashing against them, at once fell into confusion: ship fell foul of ship, while the crews were pushing them off with poles, and by their shouting, swearing, and struggling with one another, made captains' orders and boatswains' cries alike inaudible, and through being unable for want of practice to clear their oars in the rough water, prevented the vessels from obeying their helmsmen properly. At this moment Phormio gave the signal, and the Athenians attacked. Sinking first one of the admirals, they then disabled all they came across, so that no one thought of resistance for the confusion, but fled for Patrae and Dyme in Achaea. The Athenians gave chase and captured twelve ships, and taking most of the men out of them sailed to Molycrium, and after setting up a trophy on the promontory of Rhium and dedicating a ship to Poseidon, returned to Naupactus. As for the Peloponnesians, they at once sailed with their remaining ships along the coast from Dyme and Patrae to Cyllene, the Eleian arsenal; where Cnemus, and the ships from Leucas that were to have joined them, also arrived after the battle at Stratus.

The Lacedaemonians now sent to the fleet to Cnemus three commissioners - Timocrates, Bradidas, and Lycophron - with orders to prepare to engage again with better fortune, and not to be driven from the sea by a few vessels; for they could not at all account for their discomfiture, the less so as it was their first attempt at sea; and they fancied that it was not that their marine was so inferior, but that there had been misconduct somewhere, not considering the long experience of the Athenians as compared with the little practice which they had had themselves. The commissioners were accordingly sent in anger. As soon as they arrived they set to work with Cnemus to order ships from the different states, and to put those which they already had in fighting order. Meanwhile Phormio sent word to Athens of their preparations and his own victory, and desired as many ships as possible to be speedily sent to him, as he stood in daily expectation of a battle. Twenty were accordingly sent, but instructions were given to their commander to go first to Crete. For Nicias, a Cretan of Gortys, who was proxenus of the Athenians, had persuaded them to sail against Cydonia, promising to procure the reduction of that hostile town; his real wish being to oblige the Polichnitans, neighbours of the Cydonians. He accordingly went with the ships to Crete, and, accompanied by the Polichnitans, laid waste the lands of the Cydonians; and, what with adverse winds and stress of weather wasted no little time there.

While the Athenians were thus detained in Crete, the Peloponnesians in Cyllene got ready for battle, and coasted along to Panormus in Achaea, where their land army had come to support them. Phormio also coasted along to Molycrian Rhium, and anchored outside it with twenty ships, the same as he had fought with before. This Rhium was friendly to the Athenians. The other, in Peloponnese, lies opposite to it; the sea between them is about three-quarters of a mile broad, and forms the mouth of the Crissaean gulf. At this, the Achaean Rhium, not far off Panormus, where their army lay, the Peloponnesians now cast anchor with seventy-seven ships, when they saw the Athenians do so. For six or seven days they remained opposite each other, practising and preparing for the battle; the one resolved not to sail out of the Rhia into the open sea, for fear of the disaster which had already happened to them, the other not to sail into the straits, thinking it advantageous to the enemy, to fight in the narrows. At last Cnemus and Brasidas and the rest of the Peloponnesian commanders, being desirous of bringing on a battle as soon as possible, before reinforcements should arrive from Athens, and noticing that the men were most of them cowed by the previous defeat and out of heart for the business, first called them together and encouraged them as follows:

"Peloponnesians, the late engagement, which may have made some of you afraid of the one now in prospect, really gives no just ground for apprehension. Preparation for it, as you know, there was little enough; and the object of our voyage was not so much to fight at sea as an expedition by land. Besides this, the chances of war were largely against us; and perhaps also inexperience had something to do with our failure in our first naval action. It was not, therefore, cowardice that produced our defeat, nor ought the determination which force has not quelled, but which still has a word to say with its adversary, to lose its edge from the result of an accident; but admitting the possibility of a chance miscarriage, we should know that brave hearts must be always brave, and while they remain so can never put forward inexperience as an excuse for misconduct. Nor are you so behind the enemy in experience as you are ahead of him in courage; and although the science of your opponents would, if valour accompanied it, have also the presence of mind to carry out at in emergency the lesson it has learnt, yet a faint heart will make all art powerless in the face of danger. For fear takes away presence of mind, and without valour art is useless. Against their superior experience set your superior daring, and against the fear induced by defeat the fact of your having been then unprepared; remember, too, that you have always the advantage of superior numbers, and of engaging off your own coast, supported by your heavy infantry; and as a rule, numbers and equipment give victory. At no point, therefore, is defeat likely; and as for our previous mistakes, the very fact of their occurrence will teach us better for the future. Steersmen and sailors may, therefore, confidently attend to their several duties, none quitting the station assigned to them: as for ourselves, we promise to prepare for the engagement at least as well as your previous commanders, and to give no excuse for any one misconducting himself. Should any insist on doing so, he shall meet with the punishment he deserves, while the brave shall be honoured with the appropriate rewards of valour."

The Peloponnesian commanders encouraged their men after this fashion. Phormio, meanwhile, being himself not without fears for the courage of his men, and noticing that they were forming in groups among themselves and were alarmed at the odds against them, desired to call them together and give them confidence and counsel in the present emergency. He had before continually told them, and had accustomed their minds to the idea, that there was no numerical superiority that they could not face; and the men themselves had long been persuaded that Athenians need never retire before any quantity of Peloponnesian vessels. At the moment, however, he saw that they were dispirited by the sight before them, and wishing to refresh their confidence, called them together and spoke as follows:

"I see, my men, that you are frightened by the number of the enemy, and I have accordingly called you together, not liking you to be afraid of what is not really terrible. In the first place, the Peloponnesians, already defeated, and not even themselves thinking that they are a match for us, have not ventured to meet us on equal terms, but have equipped this multitude of ships against us. Next, as to that upon which they most rely, the courage which they suppose constitutional to them, their confidence here only arises from the success which their experience in land service usually gives them, and which they fancy will do the same for them at sea. But this advantage will in all justice belong to us on this element, if to them on that; as they are not superior to us in courage, but we are each of us more confident, according to our experience in our particular department. Besides, as the Lacedaemonians use their supremacy over their allies to promote their own glory, they are most of them being brought into danger against their will, or they would never, after such a decided defeat, have ventured upon a fresh engagement. You need not, therefore, be afraid of their dash. You, on the contrary, inspire a much greater and better founded alarm, both because of your late victory and also of their belief that we should not face them unless about to do something worthy of a success so signal. An adversary numerically superior, like the one before us, comes into action trusting more to strength than to resolution; while he who voluntarily confronts tremendous odds must have very great internal resources to draw upon. For these reasons the Peloponnesians fear our irrational audacity more than they would ever have done a more commensurate preparation. Besides, many armaments have before now succumbed to an inferior through want of skill or sometimes of courage; neither of which defects certainly are ours. As to the battle, it shall not be, if I can help it, in the strait, nor will I sail in there at all; seeing that in a contest between a number of clumsily managed vessels and a small, fast, well-handled squadron, want of sea room is an undoubted disadvantage. One cannot run down an enemy properly without having a sight of him a good way off, nor can one retire at need when pressed; one can neither break the line nor return upon his rear, the proper tactics for a fast sailer; but the naval action necessarily becomes a land one, in which numbers must decide the matter. For all this I will provide as far as can be. Do you stay at your posts by your ships, and be sharp at catching the word of command, the more so as we are observing one another from so short a distance; and in action think order and silence all-important - qualities useful in war generally, and in naval engagements in particular; and behave before the enemy in a manner worthy of your past exploits. The issues you will fight for are great - to destroy the naval hopes of the Peloponnesians or to bring nearer to the Athenians their fears for the sea. And I may once more remind you that you have defeated most of them already; and beaten men do not face a danger twice with the same determination."

Such was the exhortation of Phormio. The Peloponnesians finding that the Athenians did not sail into the gulf and the narrows, in order to lead them in whether they wished it or not, put out at dawn, and forming four abreast, sailed inside the gulf in the direction of their own country, the right wing leading as they had lain at anchor. In this wing were placed twenty of their best sailers; so that in the event of Phormio thinking that their object was Naupactus, and coasting along thither to save the place, the Athenians might not be able to escape their onset by getting outside their wing, but might be cut off by the vessels in question.

As they expected, Phormio, in alarm for the place at that moment emptied of its garrison, as soon as he saw them put out, reluctantly and hurriedly embarked and sailed along shore; the Messenian land forces moving along also to support him. The Peloponnesians seeing him coasting along with his ships in single file, and by this inside the gulf and close inshore as they so much wished, at one signal tacked suddenly and bore down in line at their best speed on the Athenians, hoping to cut off the whole squadron. The eleven leading vessels, however, escaped the Peloponnesian wing and its sudden movement, and reached the more open water; but the rest were overtaken as they tried to run through, driven ashore and disabled; such of the crews being slain as had not swum out of them. Some of the ships the Peloponnesians lashed to their own, and towed off empty; one they took with the men in it; others were just being towed off, when they were saved by the Messenians dashing into the sea with their armour and fighting from the decks that they had boarded.

Thus far victory was with the Peloponnesians, and the Athenian fleet destroyed; the twenty ships in the right wing being meanwhile in chase of the eleven Athenian vessels that had escaped their sudden movement and reached the more open water. These, with the exception of one ship, all outsailed them and got safe into Naupactus, and forming close inshore opposite the temple of Apollo, with their prows facing the enemy, prepared to defend themselves in case the Peloponnesians should sail inshore against them. After a while the Peloponnesians came up, chanting the paean for their victory as they sailed on; the single Athenian ship remaining being chased by a Leucadian far ahead of the rest. But there happened to be a merchantman lying at anchor in the roadstead, which the Athenian ship found time to sail round, and struck the Leucadian in chase amidships and sank her. An exploit so sudden and unexpected produced a panic among the Peloponnesians; and having fallen out of order in the excitement of victory, some of them dropped their oars and stopped their way in order to let the main body come up - an unsafe thing to do considering how near they were to the enemy's prows; while others ran aground in the shallows, in their ignorance of the localities.

Elated at this incident, the Athenians at one word gave a cheer, and dashed at the enemy, who, embarrassed by his mistakes and the disorder in which he found himself, only stood for an instant, and then fled for Panormus, whence he had put out. The Athenians following on his heels took the six vessels nearest them, and recovered those of their own which had been disabled close inshore and taken in tow at the beginning of the action; they killed some of the crews and took some prisoners. On board the Leucadian which went down off the merchantman, was the Lacedaemonian Timocrates, who killed himself when the ship was sunk, and was cast up in the harbour of Naupactus. The Athenians on their return set up a trophy on the spot from which they had put out and turned the day, and picking up the wrecks and dead that were on their shore, gave back to the enemy their dead under truce. The Peloponnesians also set up a trophy as victors for the defeat inflicted upon the ships they had disabled in shore, and dedicated the vessel which they had taken at Achaean Rhium, side by side with the trophy. After this, apprehensive of the reinforcement expected from Athens, all except the Leucadians sailed into the Crissaean Gulf for Corinth. Not long after their retreat, the twenty Athenian ships, which were to have joined Phormio before the battle, arrived at Naupactus.

Thus the summer ended. Winter was now at hand; but dispersing the fleet, which had retired to Corinth and the Crissaean Gulf, Cnemus, Brasidas, and the other Peloponnesian captains allowed themselves to be persuaded by the Megarians to make an attempt upon Piraeus, the port of Athens, which from her decided superiority at sea had been naturally left unguarded and open. Their plan was as follows: The men were each to take their oar, cushion, and rowlock thong, and, going overland from Corinth to the sea on the Athenian side, to get to Megara as quickly as they could, and launching forty vessels, which happened to be in the docks at Nisaea, to sail at once to Piraeus. There was no fleet on the look-out in the harbour, and no one had the least idea of the enemy attempting a surprise; while an open attack would, it was thought, never be deliberately ventured on, or, if in contemplation, would be speedily known at Athens. Their plan formed, the next step was to put it in execution. Arriving by night and launching the vessels from Nisaea, they sailed, not to Piraeus as they had originally intended, being afraid of the risk, besides which there was some talk of a wind having stopped them, but to the point of Salamis that looks towards Megara; where there was a fort and a squadron of three ships to prevent anything sailing in or out of Megara. This fort they assaulted, and towed off the galleys empty, and surprising the inhabitants began to lay waste the rest of the island.

Meanwhile fire signals were raised to alarm Athens, and a panic ensued there as serious as any that occurred during the war. The idea in the city was that the enemy had already sailed into Piraeus: in Piraeus it was thought that they had taken Salamis and might at any moment arrive in the port; as indeed might easily have been done if their hearts had been a little firmer: certainly no wind would have prevented them. As soon as day broke, the Athenians assembled in full force, launched their ships, and embarking in haste and uproar went with the fleet to Salamis, while their soldiery mounted guard in Piraeus. The Peloponnesians, on becoming aware of the coming relief, after they had overrun most of Salamis, hastily sailed off with their plunder and captives and the three ships from Fort Budorum to Nisaea; the state of their ships also causing them some anxiety, as it was a long while since they had been launched, and they were not water-tight. Arrived at Megara, they returned back on foot to Corinth. The Athenians finding them no longer at Salamis, sailed back themselves; and after this made arrangements for guarding Piraeus more diligently in future, by closing the harbours, and by other suitable precautions.

About the same time, at the beginning of this winter, Sitalces, son of Teres, the Odrysian king of Thrace, made an expedition against Perdiccas, son of Alexander, king of Macedonia, and the Chalcidians in the neighbourhood of Thrace; his object being to enforce one promise and fulfil another. On the one hand Perdiccas had made him a promise, when hard pressed at the commencement of the war, upon condition that Sitalces should reconcile the Athenians to him and not attempt to restore his brother and enemy, the pretender Philip, but had not offered to fulfil his engagement; on the other he, Sitalces, on entering into alliance with the Athenians, had agreed to put an end to the Chalcidian war in Thrace. These were the two objects of his invasion. With him he brought Amyntas, the son of Philip, whom he destined for the throne of Macedonia, and some Athenian envoys then at his court on this business, and Hagnon as general; for the Athenians were to join him against the Chalcidians with a fleet and as many soldiers as they could get together.

Beginning with the Odrysians, he first called out the Thracian tribes subject to him between Mounts Haemus and Rhodope and the Euxine and Hellespont; next the Getae beyond Haemus, and the other hordes settled south of the Danube in the neighbourhood of the Euxine, who, like the Getae, border on the Scythians and are armed in the same manner, being all mounted archers. Besides these he summoned many of the hill Thracian independent swordsmen, called Dii and mostly inhabiting Mount Rhodope, some of whom came as mercenaries, others as volunteers; also the Agrianes and Laeaeans, and the rest of the Paeonian tribes in his empire, at the confines of which these lay, extending up to the Laeaean Paeonians and the river Strymon, which flows from Mount Scombrus through the country of the Agrianes and Laeaeans; there the empire of Sitalces ends and the territory of the independent Paeonians begins. Bordering on the Triballi, also independent, were the Treres and Tilataeans, who dwell to the north of Mount Scombrus and extend towards the setting sun as far as the river Oskius. This river rises in the same mountains as the Nestus and Hebrus, a wild and extensive range connected with Rhodope.

The empire of the Odrysians extended along the seaboard from Abdera to the mouth of the Danube in the Euxine. The navigation of this coast by the shortest route takes a merchantman four days and four nights with a wind astern the whole way: by land an active man, travelling by the shortest road, can get from Abdera to the Danube in eleven days. Such was the length of its coast line. Inland from Byzantium to the Laeaeans and the Strymon, the farthest limit of its extension into the interior, it is a journey of thirteen days for an active man. The tribute from all the barbarian districts and the Hellenic cities, taking what they brought in under Seuthes, the successor of Sitalces, who raised it to its greatest height, amounted to about four hundred talents in gold and silver. There were also presents in gold and silver to a no less amount, besides stuff, plain and embroidered, and other articles, made not only for the king, but also for the Odrysian lords and nobles. For there was here established a custom opposite to that prevailing in the Persian kingdom, namely, of taking rather than giving; more disgrace being attached to not giving when asked than to asking and being refused; and although this prevailed elsewhere in Thrace, it was practised most extensively among the powerful Odrysians, it being impossible to get anything done without a present. It was thus a very powerful kingdom; in revenue and general prosperity surpassing all in Europe between the Ionian Gulf and the Euxine, and in numbers and military resources coming decidedly next to the Scythians, with whom indeed no people in Europe can bear comparison, there not being even in Asia any nation singly a match for them if unanimous, though of course they are not on a level with other races in general intelligence and the arts of civilized life.

It was the master of this empire that now prepared to take the field. When everything was ready, he set out on his march for Macedonia, first through his own dominions, next over the desolate range of Cercine that divides the Sintians and Paeonians, crossing by a road which he had made by felling the timber on a former campaign against the latter people. Passing over these mountains, with the Paeonians on his right and the Sintians and Maedians on the left, he finally arrived at Doberus, in Paeonia, losing none of his army on the march, except perhaps by sickness, but receiving some augmentations, many of the independent Thracians volunteering to join him in the hope of plunder; so that the whole is said to have formed a grand total of a hundred and fifty thousand. Most of this was infantry, though there was about a third cavalry, furnished principally by the Odrysians themselves and next to them by the Getae. The most warlike of the infantry were the independent swordsmen who came down from Rhodope; the rest of the mixed multitude that followed him being chiefly formidable by their numbers.

Assembling in Doberus, they prepared for descending from the heights upon Lower Macedonia, where the dominions of Perdiccas lay; for the Lyncestae, Elimiots, and other tribes more inland, though Macedonians by blood, and allies and dependants of their kindred, still have their own separate governments. The country on the sea coast, now called Macedonia, was first acquired by Alexander, the father of Perdiccas, and his ancestors, originally Temenids from Argos. This was effected by the expulsion from Pieria of the Pierians, who afterwards inhabited Phagres and other places under Mount Pangaeus, beyond the Strymon (indeed the country between Pangaeus and the sea is still called the Pierian Gulf); of the Bottiaeans, at present neighbours of the Chalcidians, from Bottia, and by the acquisition in Paeonia of a narrow strip along the river Axius extending to Pella and the sea; the district of Mygdonia, between the Axius and the Strymon, being also added by the expulsion of the Edonians. From Eordia also were driven the Eordians, most of whom perished, though a few of them still live round Physca, and the Almopians from Almopia. These

Macedonians also conquered places belonging to the other tribes, which are still theirs - Anthemus, Crestonia, Bisaltia, and much of Macedonia proper. The whole is now called Macedonia, and at the time of the invasion of Sitalces, Perdiccas, Alexander's son, was the reigning king.

These Macedonians, unable to take the field against so numerous an invader, shut themselves up in such strong places and fortresses as the country possessed. Of these there was no great number, most of those now found in the country having been erected subsequently by Archelaus, the son of Perdiccas, on his accession, who also cut straight roads, and otherwise put the kingdom on a better footing as regards horses, heavy infantry, and other war material than had been done by all the eight kings that preceded him. Advancing from Doberus, the Thracian host first invaded what had been once Philip's government, and took Idomene by assault, Gortynia, Atalanta, and some other places by negotiation, these last coming over for love of Philip's son, Amyntas, then with Sitalces. Laying siege to Europus, and failing to take it, he next advanced into the rest of Macedonia to the left of Pella and Cyrrhus, not proceeding beyond this into Bottiaea and Pieria, but staying to lay waste Mygdonia, Crestonia, and Anthemus.

The Macedonians never even thought of meeting him with infantry; but the Thracian host was, as opportunity offered, attacked by handfuls of their horse, which had been reinforced from their allies in the interior. Armed with cuirasses, and excellent horsemen, wherever these charged they overthrew all before them, but ran considerable risk in entangling themselves in the masses of the enemy, and so finally desisted from these efforts, deciding that they were not strong enough to venture against numbers so superior.

Meanwhile Sitalces opened negotiations with Perdiccas on the objects of his expedition; and finding that the Athenians, not believing that he would come, did not appear with their fleet, though they sent presents and envoys, dispatched a large part of his army against the Chalcidians and Bottiaeans, and shutting them up inside their walls laid waste their country. While he remained in these parts, the people farther south, such as the Thessalians, Magnetes, and the other tribes subject to the Thessalians, and the Hellenes as far as Thermopylae, all feared that the army might advance against them, and prepared accordingly. These fears were shared by the Thracians beyond the Strymon to the north, who inhabited the plains, such as the Panaeans, the Odomanti, the Droi, and the Dersaeans, all of whom are independent. It was even matter of conversation among the Hellenes who were enemies of Athens whether he might not be invited by his ally to advance also against them. Meanwhile he held Chalcidice and Bottice and Macedonia, and was ravaging them all; but finding that he was not succeeding in any of the objects of his invasion, and that his army was without provisions and was suffering from the severity of the season, he listened to the advice of Seuthes, son of Spardacus, his nephew and highest officer, and decided to retreat without delay. This Seuthes had been secretly gained by Perdiccas by the promise of his sister in marriage with a rich dowry. In accordance with this advice, and after a stay of thirty days in all, eight of which were spent in Chalcidice, he retired home as quickly as he could; and Perdiccas afterwards gave his sister Stratonice to Seuthes as he had promised. Such was the history of the expedition of Sitalces.

In the course of this winter, after the dispersion of the Peloponnesian fleet, the Athenians in Naupactus, under Phormio, coasted along to Astacus and disembarked, and marched into the interior of Acarnania with four hundred Athenian heavy infantry and four hundred Messenians. After expelling some suspected persons from Stratus, Coronta, and other places, and restoring Cynes, son of Theolytus, to Coronta, they returned to their ships, deciding that it was impossible in the winter season to march against Oeniadae, a place which, unlike the rest of Acarnania, had been always hostile to them; for the river Achelous flowing from Mount Pindus through Dolopia and the country of the Agraeans and Amphilochians and the plain of Acarnania, past the town of Stratus in the upper part of its course, forms lakes where it falls into the sea round Oeniadae, and thus makes it impracticable for an army in winter by reason of the water. Opposite to Oeniadae lie most of the islands called Echinades, so close to the mouths of the Achelous that that powerful stream is constantly forming deposits against them, and has already joined some of the islands to the continent, and seems likely in no long while to do the same with the rest. For the current is strong, deep, and turbid, and the islands are so thick together that they serve to imprison the alluvial deposit and prevent its dispersing, lying, as they do, not in one line, but irregularly, so as to leave no direct passage for the water into the open sea. The islands in question are uninhabited and of no great size. There is also a story that Alcmaeon, son of Amphiraus, during his wanderings after the murder of his mother was bidden by Apollo to inhabit this spot, through an oracle which intimated that he would have no release from his terrors until he should find a country to dwell in which had not been seen by the sun, or existed as land at the time he slew his mother; all else being to him polluted ground. Perplexed at this, the story goes on to say, he at last observed this deposit of the Achelous, and considered that a place sufficient to support life upon, might have been thrown up during the long interval that had elapsed since the death of his mother and the beginning of his wanderings. Settling, therefore, in the district round Oeniadae, he founded a dominion, and left the country its name from his son Acarnan. Such is the story we have received concerning Alcmaeon.

The Athenians and Phormio putting back from Acarnania and arriving at Naupactus, sailed home to Athens in the spring, taking with them the ships that they had captured, and such of the prisoners made in the late actions as were freemen; who were exchanged, man for man. And so ended this winter, and the third year of this war, of which Thucydides was the historian.

CHAPTER IX

Fourth and Fifth Years of the War - Revolt of Mitylene

Greek soldiers.

THE NEXT summer, just as the corn was getting ripe, the Peloponnesians and their allies invaded Attica under the command of Archidamus, son of Zeuxidamus, king of the Lacedaemonians, and sat down and ravaged the land; the Athenian horse as usual attacking them, wherever it was practicable, and preventing the mass of the light troops from advancing from their camp and wasting the parts near the city. After staying the time for which they had taken provisions, the invaders retired and dispersed to their several cities.

Immediately after the invasion of the Peloponnesians all Lesbos, except Methymna, revolted from the Athenians. The Lesbians had wished to revolt even before the war, but the Lacedaemonians would not receive them; and yet now when they did revolt, they were compelled to do so sooner than they had intended. While they were waiting until the moles for their harbours and the ships and walls that they had in building should be finished, and for the arrival of archers and corn and other things that they were engaged in fetching from the Pontus, the Tenedians, with whom they were at enmity, and the Methymnians, and some factious persons in Mitylene itself, who were proxeni of Athens, informed the Athenians that the Mitylenians were forcibly uniting the island under their sovereignty, and that the preparations about which they were so active, were all concerted with the Boeotians their kindred and the Lacedaemonians with a view to a revolt, and that, unless they were immediately prevented, Athens would lose Lesbos.

However, the Athenians, distressed by the plague, and by the war that had recently broken out and was now raging, thought it a serious matter to add Lesbos with its fleet and untouched resources to the list of their enemies; and at first would not believe the charge, giving too much weight to their wish that it might not be true. But when an embassy which they sent had failed to persuade the Mitylenians to give up the union and preparations complained of, they became alarmed, and resolved to strike the first blow. They accordingly suddenly sent off forty ships that had been got ready to sail round Peloponnese, under the command of Cleippides, son of Deinias, and two others; word having been brought them of a festival in honour of the Malean Apollo outside the town, which is kept by the whole people of Mitylene, and at which, if haste were made, they might hope to take them by surprise. If this plan succeeded, well and good; if not, they were to order the Mitylenians to deliver up their ships and to pull down their walls, and if they did not obey, to declare war. The ships accordingly set out; the ten galleys, forming the contingent of the Mitylenians present with the fleet according to the terms of the alliance, being detained by the Athenians, and their crews placed in custody. However, the Mitylenians were informed of the expedition by a man who crossed from Athens to Euboea, and going overland to Geraestus, sailed from thence by a merchantman which he found on the point of putting to sea, and so arrived at Mitylene the third day after leaving Athens. The Mitylenians accordingly refrained from going out to the temple at Malea, and moreover barricaded and kept guard round the half-finished parts of their walls and harbours.

When the Athenians sailed in not long after and saw how things stood, the generals delivered their orders, and upon the Mitylenians refusing to obey, commenced hostilities. The Mitylenians, thus compelled to go to war without notice and unprepared, at first sailed out with their fleet and made some show of fighting, a little in front of the harbour; but being driven back by the Athenian ships, immediately offered to treat with the commanders, wishing, if possible, to get the ships away for the present upon any tolerable terms. The Athenian commanders accepted their offers, being themselves fearful that they might not be able to cope with the whole of Lesbos; and an armistice having been concluded, the Mitylenians sent to Athens one of the informers, already repentant of his conduct, and others with him, to try to persuade the Athenians of the innocence of their intentions and to get the fleet recalled. In the meantime, having no great hope of a favourable answer from Athens, they also sent off a galley with envoys to Lacedaemon, unobserved by the Athenian fleet which was anchored at Malea to the north of the town.

While these envoys, reaching Lacedaemon after a difficult journey across the open sea, were negotiating for succours being sent them, the ambassadors from Athens returned without having effected anything; and hostilities were at once begun by the Mitylenians and the rest of Lesbos, with the exception of the Methymnians, who came to the aid of the Athenians with the Imbrians and Lemnians and some few of the other allies. The Mitylenians made a sortie with all their forces against the Athenian camp; and a battle ensued, in which they gained some slight advantage, but retired notwithstanding, not feeling sufficient confidence in themselves to spend the night upon the field. After this they kept quiet, wishing to wait for the chance of reinforcements arriving from Peloponnese before making a second venture, being encouraged by the arrival of Meleas, a Laconian, and Hermaeondas, a Theban, who had been sent off before the insurrection but had been unable to reach Lesbos before the Athenian expedition, and who now stole in in a galley after the battle, and advised them to send another galley and envoys back with them, which the Mitylenians accordingly did.

Meanwhile the Athenians, greatly encouraged by the inaction

of the Mitylenians, summoned allies to their aid, who came in all the quicker from seeing so little vigour displayed by the Lesbians, and bringing round their ships to a new station to the south of the town, fortified two camps, one on each side of the city, and instituted a blockade of both the harbours. The sea was thus closed against the Mitylenians, who, however, commanded the whole country, with the rest of the Lesbians who had now joined them; the Athenians only holding a limited area round their camps, and using Malea more as the station for their ships and their market.

While the war went on in this way at Mitylene, the Athenians, about the same time in this summer, also sent thirty ships to Peloponnese under Asopius, son of Phormio; the Acarnanians insisting that the commander sent should be some son or relative of Phormio. As the ships coasted along shore they ravaged the seaboard of Laconia; after which Asopius sent most of the fleet home, and himself went on with twelve vessels to Naupactus, and afterwards raising the whole Acarnanian population made an expedition against Oeniadae, the fleet sailing along the Achelous, while the army laid waste the country. The inhabitants, however, showing no signs of submitting, he dismissed the land forces and himself sailed to Leucas, and making a descent upon Nericus was cut off during his retreat, and most of his troops with him, by the people in those parts aided by some coastguards; after which the Athenians sailed away, recovering their dead from the Leucadians under truce.

Meanwhile the envoys of the Mitylenians sent out in the first ship were told by the Lacedaemonians to come to Olympia, in order that the rest of the allies might hear them and decide upon their matter, and so they journeyed thither. It was the Olympiad in which the Rhodian Dorieus gained his second victory, and the envoys having been introduced to make their speech after the festival, spoke as follows:

"Lacedaemonians and allies, the rule established among the Hellenes is not unknown to us. Those who revolt in war and forsake their former confederacy are favourably regarded by those who receive them, in so far as they are of use to them, but otherwise are thought less well of, through being considered traitors to their former friends. Nor is this an unfair way of judging, where the rebels and the power from whom they secede are at one in policy and sympathy, and a match for each other in resources and power, and where no reasonable ground exists for the rebellion. But with us and the Athenians this was not the case; and no one need think the worse of us for revolting from them in danger, after having been honoured by them in time of peace.

"Justice and honesty will be the first topics of our speech, especially as we are asking for alliance; because we know that there can never be any solid friendship between individuals, or union between communities that is worth the name, unless the parties be persuaded of each other's honesty, and be generally congenial the one to the other; since from difference in feeling springs also difference in conduct. Between ourselves and the Athenians alliance began, when you withdrew from the Median War and they remained to finish the business. But we did not become allies of the Athenians for the subjugation of the Hellenes, but allies of the Hellenes for their liberation from the Mede; and as long as the Athenians led us fairly we followed them loyally; but when we saw them relax their hostility to the Mede, to try to compass the subjection of the allies, then our apprehensions began. Unable, however, to unite and defend themselves, on account of the number of confederates that had votes, all the allies were enslaved, except ourselves and the Chians, who continued to send our contingents as independent and nominally free. Trust in Athens as a leader, however, we could no longer feel, judging by the examples already given; it being unlikely that she would reduce our fellow confederates, and not do the same by us who were left, if ever she had the power.

"Had we all been still independent, we could have had more faith in their not attempting any change; but the greater number being their subjects, while they were treating us as equals, they would naturally chafe under this solitary instance of independence as contrasted with the submission of the majority; particularly as they daily grew more powerful, and we more destitute. Now the only sure basis of an alliance is for each party to be equally afraid of the other; he who would like to encroach is then deterred by the reflection that he will not have odds in his favour. Again, if we were left independent, it was only because they thought they saw their way to empire more clearly by specious language and by the paths of policy than by those of force. Not only were we useful as evidence that powers who had votes, like themselves, would not, surely, join them in their expeditions, against their will, without the party attacked being in the wrong; but the same system also enabled them to lead the stronger states against the weaker first, and so to leave the former to the last, stripped of their natural allies, and less capable of resistance. But if they had begun with us, while all the states still had their resources under their own control, and there was a centre to rally round, the work of subjugation would have been found less easy. Besides this, our navy gave them some apprehension: it was always possible that it might unite with you or with some other power, and become dangerous to Athens. The court which we paid to their commons and its leaders for the time being also helped us to maintain our independence. However, we did not expect to be able to do so much longer, if this war had not broken out, from the examples that we had had of their conduct to the rest.

"How then could we put our trust in such friendship or freedom as we had here? We accepted each other against our inclination; fear made them court us in war, and us them in peace; sympathy, the ordinary basis of confidence, had its place supplied by terror, fear having more share than friendship in detaining us in the alliance; and the first party that should be encouraged by the hope of impunity was certain to break faith with the other. So that to condemn us for being the first to break off, because they delay the blow that we dread, instead of ourselves delaying to know for certain whether it will be dealt or not, is to take a false view of the case. For if we were equally able with them to meet their plots and imitate their delay, we should be their equals and should be under no necessity of being their subjects; but the liberty of offence being always theirs, that of defence ought clearly to be ours.

"Such, Lacedaemonians and allies, are the grounds and the reasons of our revolt; clear enough to convince our hearers of the fairness of our conduct, and sufficient to alarm ourselves, and to make us turn to some means of safety. This we wished to do long ago, when we sent to you on the subject while the peace yet lasted, but were balked by your refusing to receive us; and now, upon the Boeotians inviting us, we at once responded to the call, and decided upon a twofold revolt, from the Hellenes and from the Athenians, not to aid the latter in harming the former, but to join in their liberation, and not to allow the Athenians in the end to destroy us, but to act in time against them. Our revolt, however, has taken place prematurely and without preparation - a fact which makes it all the more incumbent on you to receive us into alliance and to send us speedy relief, in order to show that you support your friends, and at the same time do harm to your enemies. You have an opportunity such as you never had before. Disease and expenditure have wasted the Athenians: their ships are either cruising round your coasts, or engaged in blockading us; and it is not probable that they will have any to spare, if you invade them a second time this summer by sea and land; but they will either offer no resistance to your vessels, or withdraw from both our shores. Nor must it be thought that this is a case of putting yourselves into danger for a country which is not yours. Lesbos may appear far off, but when help is wanted she will be found near enough. It is not in Attica that the war will be decided, as some imagine, but in the countries by which Attica is supported; and the Athenian revenue is drawn from the allies, and will become still larger if they reduce us; as not only will no other state revolt, but our resources will be added to theirs, and we shall be treated worse than those that were enslaved before. But if you will frankly support us, you will add to your side a state that has a large navy, which is your great want; you will smooth the way to the overthrow of the Athenians by depriving them of their allies, who will be greatly encouraged to come over; and you will free yourselves from the imputation made against you, of not supporting insurrection. In short, only show yourselves as liberators, and you may count upon having the advantage in the war.

"Respect, therefore, the hopes placed in you by the Hellenes, and that Olympian Zeus, in whose temple we stand as very suppliants; become the allies and defenders of the Mitylenians, and do not sacrifice us, who put our lives upon the hazard, in a cause in which general good will result to all from our success, and still more general harm if we fail through your refusing to help us; but be the men that the Hellenes think you, and our fears desire."

Such were the words of the Mitylenians. After hearing them out, the Lacedaemonians and confederates granted what they urged, and took the Lesbians into alliance, and deciding in favour of the invasion of Attica, told the allies present to march as quickly as possible to the Isthmus with two-thirds of their forces; and arriving there first themselves, got ready hauling machines to carry their ships across from Corinth to the sea on the side of Athens, in order to make their attack by sea and land at once. However, the zeal which they displayed was not imitated by the rest of the confederates, who came in but slowly, being engaged in harvesting their corn and sick of making expeditions.

Meanwhile the Athenians, aware that the preparations of the enemy were due to his conviction of their weakness, and wishing to show him that he was mistaken, and that they were able, without moving the Lesbian fleet, to repel with ease that with which they were menaced from Peloponnese, manned a hundred ships by embarking the citizens of Athens, except the knights and Pentacosiomedimni, and the resident aliens; and putting out to the Isthmus, displayed their power, and made descents upon Peloponnese wherever they pleased. A disappointment so signal made the Lacedaemonians think that the Lesbians had not spoken the truth; and embarrassed by the non-appearance of the confederates, coupled with the news that the thirty ships round Peloponnese were ravaging the lands near Sparta, they went back home. Afterwards, however, they got ready a fleet to send to Lesbos, and ordering a total of forty ships from the different cities in the league, appointed Alcidas to command the expedition in his capacity of high admiral. Meanwhile the Athenians in the hundred ships, upon seeing the Lacedaemonians go home, went home likewise.

If, at the time that this fleet was at sea, Athens had almost the largest number of first-rate ships in commission that she ever possessed at any one moment, she had as many or even more when the war began. At that time one hundred guarded Attica, Euboea, and Salamis; a hundred more were cruising round Peloponnese, besides those employed at Potidaea and in other places; making a grand total of two hundred and fifty vessels employed on active service in a single summer. It was this, with Potidaea, that most exhausted her revenues - Potidaea being blockaded by a force of heavy infantry (each drawing two drachmae a day, one for himself and another for his servant), which amounted to three thousand at first, and was kept at this number down to the end of the siege; besides sixteen hundred with Phormio who went away before it was over; and the ships being all paid at the same rate. In this way her money was wasted at first; and this was the largest number of ships ever manned by her.

About the same time that the Lacedaemonians were at the Isthmus, the Mitylenians marched by land with their mercenaries against Methymna, which they thought to gain by treachery. After assaulting the town, and not meeting with the success that they anticipated, they withdrew to Antissa, Pyrrha, and Eresus;

and taking measures for the better security of these towns and strengthening their walls, hastily returned home. After their departure the Methymnians marched against Antissa, but were defeated in a sortie by the Antissians and their mercenaries, and retreated in haste after losing many of their number. Word of this reaching Athens, and the Athenians learning that the Mitylenians were masters of the country and their own soldiers unable to hold them in check, they sent out about the beginning of autumn Paches, son of Epicurus, to take the command, and a thousand Athenian heavy infantry; who worked their own passage and, arriving at Mitylene, built a single wall all round it, forts being erected at some of the strongest points. Mitylene was thus blockaded strictly on both sides, by land and by sea; and winter now drew near.

The Athenians needing money for the siege, although they had for the first time raised a contribution of two hundred talents from their own citizens, now sent out twelve ships to levy subsidies from their allies, with Lysicles and four others in command. After cruising to different places and laying them under contribution, Lysicles went up the country from Myus, in Caria, across the plain of the Meander, as far as the hill of Sandius; and being attacked by the Carians and the people of Anaia, was slain with many of his soldiers.

The same winter the Plataeans, who were still being besieged by the Peloponnesians and Boeotians, distressed by the failure of their provisions, and seeing no hope of relief from Athens, nor any other means of safety, formed a scheme with the Athenians besieged with them for escaping, if possible, by forcing their way over the enemy's walls; the attempt having been suggested by Theaenetus, son of Tolmides, a soothsayer, and Eupompides, son of Daimachus, one of their generals. At first all were to join: afterwards, half hung back, thinking the risk great; about two hundred and twenty, however, voluntarily persevered in the attempt, which was carried out in the following way. Ladders were made to match the height of the enemy's wall, which they measured by the layers of bricks, the side turned towards them not being thoroughly whitewashed. These were counted by many persons at once; and though some might miss the right calculation, most would hit upon it, particularly as they counted over and over again, and were no great way from the wall, but could see it easily enough for their purpose. The length required for the ladders was thus obtained, being calculated from the breadth of the brick.

Now the wall of the Peloponnesians was constructed as follows. It consisted of two lines drawn round the place, one against the Plataeans, the other against any attack on the outside from Athens, about sixteen feet apart. The intermediate space of sixteen feet was occupied by huts portioned out among the soldiers on guard, and built in one block, so as to give the appearance of a single thick wall with battlements on either side. At intervals of every ten battlements were towers of considerable size, and the same breadth as the wall, reaching right across from its inner to its outer face, with no means of passing except through the middle. Accordingly on stormy and wet nights the battlements were deserted, and guard kept from the towers, which were not far apart and roofed in above.

Such being the structure of the wall by which the Plataeans were blockaded, when their preparations were completed, they waited for a stormy night of wind and rain and without any moon, and then set out, guided by the authors of the enterprise. Crossing first the ditch that ran round the town, they next gained the wall of the enemy unperceived by the sentinels, who did not see them in the darkness, or hear them, as the wind drowned with its roar the noise of their approach; besides which they kept a good way off from each other, that they might not be betrayed by the clash of their weapons. They were also lightly equipped, and had only the left foot shod to preserve them from slipping in the mire. They came up to the battlements at one of the intermediate spaces where they knew them to be unguarded: those who carried the ladders went first and planted them; next twelve light-armed soldiers with only a dagger and a breastplate mounted, led by Ammias, son of Coroebus, who was the first on the wall; his followers getting up after him and going six to each of the towers. After these came another party of light troops armed with spears, whose shields, that they might advance the easier, were carried by men behind, who were to hand them to them when they found themselves in presence of the enemy. After a good many had mounted they were discovered by the sentinels in the towers, by the noise made by a tile which was knocked down by one of the Plataeans as he was laying hold of the battlements. The alarm was instantly given, and the troops rushed to the wall, not knowing the nature of the danger, owing to the dark night and stormy weather; the Plataeans in the town having also chosen that moment to make a sortie against the wall of the Peloponnesians upon the side opposite to that on which their men were getting over, in order to divert the attention of the besiegers. Accordingly they remained distracted at their several posts, without any venturing to stir to give help from his own station, and at a loss to guess what was going on. Meanwhile the three hundred set aside for service on emergencies went outside the wall in the direction of the alarm. Fire-signals of an attack were also raised towards Thebes; but the Plataeans in the town at once displayed a number of others, prepared beforehand for this very purpose, in order to render the enemy's signals unintelligible, and to prevent his friends getting a true idea of what was passing and coming to his aid before their comrades who had gone out should have made good their escape and be in safety.

Meanwhile the first of the scaling party that had got up, after carrying both the towers and putting the sentinels to the sword, posted themselves inside to prevent any one coming through against them; and rearing ladders from the wall, sent several men up on the towers, and from their summit and base kept in check all of the enemy that came up, with their missiles, while their main body planted a number of ladders against the wall, and knocking down the battlements, passed over between the towers; each as soon as he had got over taking up his station at the edge of the ditch, and plying from thence with arrows and darts any who came along the wall to stop the passage of his comrades. When all were over, the party on the towers came down, the last of them not without difficulty, and proceeded to the ditch, just as the three hundred came up carrying torches. The Plataeans, standing on the edge of the ditch in the dark, had a good view of their opponents, and discharged their arrows and darts upon the unarmed parts of their bodies, while they themselves could not be so well seen in the obscurity for the torches; and thus even the last of them got over the ditch, though not without effort and difficulty; as ice had formed in it, not strong enough to walk upon, but of that watery kind which generally comes with a wind more east than north, and the snow which this wind had caused to fall during the night had made the water in the ditch rise, so that they could scarcely breast it as they crossed. However, it was mainly the violence of the storm that enabled them to effect their escape at all.

Starting from the ditch, the Plataeans went all together along the road leading to Thebes, keeping the chapel of the hero Androcrates upon their right; considering that the last road which the Peloponnesians would suspect them of having taken would be that towards their enemies' country. Indeed they could see them pursuing with torches upon the Athens road towards Cithaeron and Druoskephalai or Oakheads. After going for rather more than half a mile upon the road to Thebes, the Plataeans turned off and took that leading to the mountain, to Erythrae and Hysiae, and reaching the hills, made good their escape to Athens, two hundred and twelve men in all; some of their number having turned back into the town before getting over the wall, and one archer having been taken prisoner at the outer ditch. Meanwhile the Peloponnesians gave up the pursuit and returned to their posts; and the Plataeans in the town, knowing nothing of what had passed, and informed by those who had turned back that not a man had escaped, sent out a herald as soon as it was day to make a truce for the recovery of the dead bodies, and then, learning the truth, desisted. In this way the Plataean party got over and were saved.

Towards the close of the same winter, Salaethus, a Lacedaemonian, was sent out in a galley from Lacedaemon to Mitylene. Going by sea to Pyrrha, and from thence overland, he passed along the bed of a torrent, where the line of circumvallation was passable, and thus entering unperceived into Mitylene told the magistrates that Attica would certainly be invaded, and the forty ships destined to relieve them arrive, and that he had been sent on to announce this and to superintend matters generally. The Mitylenians upon this took courage, and laid aside the idea of treating with the Athenians; and now this winter ended, and with it ended the fourth year of the war of which Thucydides was the historian.

The next summer the Peloponnesians sent off the forty-two ships for Mitylene, under Alcidas, their high admiral, and themselves and their allies invaded Attica, their object being to distract the Athenians by a double movement, and thus to make it less easy for them to act against the fleet sailing to Mitylene. The commander in this invasion was Cleomenes, in the place of King

Pausanias, son of Pleistoanax, his nephew, who was still a minor. Not content with laying waste whatever had shot up in the parts which they had before devastated, the invaders now extended their ravages to lands passed over in their previous incursions; so that this invasion was more severely felt by the Athenians than any except the second; the enemy staying on and on until they had overrun most of the country, in the expectation of hearing from Lesbos of something having been achieved by their fleet, which they thought must now have got over. However, as they did not obtain any of the results expected, and their provisions began to run short, they retreated and dispersed to their different cities.

In the meantime the Mitylenians, finding their provisions failing, while the fleet from Peloponnese was loitering on the way instead of appearing at Mitylene, were compelled to come to terms with the Athenians in the following manner. Salaethus having himself ceased to expect the fleet to arrive, now armed the commons with heavy armour, which they had not before possessed, with the intention of making a sortie against the Athenians. The commons, however, no sooner found themselves possessed of arms than they refused any longer to obey their officers; and forming in knots together, told the authorities to bring out in public the provisions and divide them amongst them all, or they would themselves come to terms with the Athenians and deliver up the city.

The government, aware of their inability to prevent this, and of the danger they would be in, if left out of the capitulation, publicly agreed with Paches and the army to surrender Mitylene at discretion and to admit the troops into the town; upon the understanding that the Mitylenians should be allowed to send an embassy to Athens to plead their cause, and that Paches should not imprison, make slaves of, or put to death any of the citizens until its return. Such were the terms of the capitulation; in spite of which the chief authors of the negotiation with Lacedaemon were so completely overcome by terror when the army entered that they went and seated themselves by the altars, from which they were raised up by Paches under promise that he would do them no wrong, and lodged by him in Tenedos, until he should learn the pleasure of the Athenians concerning them. Paches also sent some galleys and seized Antissa, and took such other military measures as he thought advisable.

Meanwhile the Peloponnesians in the forty ships, who ought to have made all haste to relieve Mitylene, lost time in coming round Peloponnese itself, and proceeding leisurely on the remainder of the voyage, made Delos without having been seen by the Athenians at Athens, and from thence arriving at Icarus and Myconus, there first heard of the fall of Mitylene. Wishing to know the truth, they put into Embatum, in the Erythraeid, about seven days after the capture of the town. Here they learned the truth, and began to consider what they were to do; and Teutiaplus, an Elean, addressed them as follows:

"Alcidas and Peloponnesians who share with me the command of this armament, my advice is to sail just as we are to Mitylene, before we have been heard of. We may expect to find the Athenians as much off their guard as men generally are who have just taken a city: this will certainly be so by sea, where they have no idea of any enemy attacking them, and where our strength, as it happens, mainly lies; while even their land forces are probably scattered about the houses in the carelessness of victory. If therefore we were to fall upon them suddenly and in the night, I have hopes, with the help of the well-wishers that we may have left inside the town, that we shall become masters of the place. Let us not shrink from the risk, but let us remember that this is just the occasion for one of the baseless panics common in war: and that to be able to guard against these in one's own case, and to detect the moment when an attack will find an enemy at this disadvantage, is what makes a successful general."

These words of Teutiaplus failing to move Alcidas, some of the Ionian exiles and the Lesbians with the expedition began to urge him, since this seemed too dangerous, to seize one of the Ionian cities or the Aeolic town of Cyme, to use as a base for effecting the revolt of Ionia. This was by no means a hopeless enterprise, as their coming was welcome everywhere; their object would be by this move to deprive Athens of her chief source of revenue, and at the same time to saddle her with expense, if she chose to blockade them; and they would probably induce Pissuthnes to join them in the war. However, Alcidas gave this proposal as bad a reception as the other, being eager, since he had come too late for Mitylene, to find himself back in Peloponnese as soon as possible.

Accordingly he put out from Embatum and proceeded along shore; and touching at the Teian town, Myonnesus, there butchered most of the prisoners that he had taken on his passage. Upon his coming to anchor at Ephesus, envoys came to him from the Samians at Anaia, and told him that he was not going the right way to free Hellas in massacring men who had never raised a hand against him, and who were not enemies of his, but allies of Athens against their will, and that if he did not stop he would turn many more friends into enemies than enemies into friends. Alcidas agreed to this, and let go all the Chians still in his hands and some of the others that he had taken; the inhabitants, instead of flying at the sight of his vessels, rather coming up to them, taking them for Athenian, having no sort of expectation that while the Athenians commanded the sea Peloponnesian ships would venture over to Ionia.

From Ephesus Alcidas set sail in haste and fled. He had been seen by the Salaminian and Paralian galleys, which happened to be sailing from Athens, while still at anchor off Clarus; and fearing pursuit he now made across the open sea, fully determined to touch nowhere, if he could help it, until he got to Peloponnese. Meanwhile news of him had come in to Paches from the Erythraeid, and indeed from all quarters. As Ionia was unfortified, great fears were felt that the Peloponnesians coasting along shore, even if they did not intend to stay, might make descents in passing and plunder the towns; and now the Paralian and Salaminian, having seen him at Clarus, themselves brought intelligence of the fact. Paches accordingly gave hot chase, and continued the pursuit as far as the isle of Patmos, and then finding that Alcidas had got on too far to be overtaken, came back again. Meanwhile he thought it fortunate that, as he had not fallen in with them out at sea, he had not overtaken them anywhere where they would have been forced to encamp, and so give him the trouble of blockading them.

On his return along shore he touched, among other places, at Notium, the port of Colophon, where the Colophonians had settled after the capture of the upper town by Itamenes and the barbarians, who had been called in by certain individuals in a party quarrel. The capture of the town took place about the time of the second Peloponnesian invasion of Attica. However, the refugees, after settling at Notium, again split up into factions, one of which called in Arcadian and barbarian mercenaries from Pissuthnes and, entrenching these in a quarter apart, formed a new community with the Median party of the Colophonians who joined them from the upper town. Their opponents had retired into exile, and now called in Paches, who invited Hippias, the commander of the Arcadians in the fortified quarter, to a parley, upon condition that, if they could not agree, he was to be put back safe and sound in the fortification. However, upon his coming out to him, he put him into custody, though not in chains, and attacked suddenly and took by surprise the fortification, and putting the Arcadians and the barbarians found in it to the sword, afterwards took Hippias into it as he had promised, and, as soon as he was inside, seized him and shot him down. Paches then gave up Notium to the Colophonians not of the Median party; and settlers were afterwards sent out from Athens, and the place colonized according to Athenian laws, after collecting all the Colophonians found in any of the cities.

Arrived at Mitylene, Paches reduced Pyrrha and Eresus; and finding the Lacedaemonian, Salaethus, in hiding in the town, sent him off to Athens, together with the Mitylenians that he had placed in Tenedos, and any other persons that he thought concerned in the revolt. He also sent back the greater part of his forces, remaining with the rest to settle Mitylene and the rest of Lesbos as he thought best.

Upon the arrival of the prisoners with Salaethus, the Athenians at once put the latter to death, although he offered, among other things, to procure the withdrawal of the Peloponnesians from Plataea, which was still under siege; and after deliberating as to what they should do with the former, in the fury of the moment determined to put to death not only the prisoners at Athens, but the whole adult male population of Mitylene, and to make slaves of the women and children. It was remarked that Mitylene had revolted without being, like the rest, subjected to the empire; and what above all swelled the wrath of the Athenians was the fact of the Peloponnesian fleet having ventured over to Ionia to her support, a fact which was held to argue a long meditated rebellion. They accordingly sent a galley to communicate the decree to Paches, commanding him to lose no time in dispatching the Mitylenians. The morrow brought repentance with it and reflection on the horrid cruelty of a decree, which condemned a whole city to the fate merited only by the guilty. This was no sooner perceived by the Mitylenian ambassadors at Athens and their Athenian supporters, than they moved the authorities to put the question again to the vote; which they the more easily consented to do, as they themselves plainly saw that most of the citizens wished some one to give them an opportunity for reconsidering the matter. An assembly was therefore at once called, and after much expression of opinion upon both sides, Cleon, son of Cleaenetus, the same who had carried the former motion of putting the Mitylenians to death, the most violent man at Athens, and at that time by far the most powerful with the commons, came forward again and spoke as follows:

"I have often before now been convinced that a democracy is incapable of empire, and never more so than by your present change of mind in the matter of Mitylene. Fears or plots being unknown to you in your daily relations with each other, you feel just the same with regard to your allies, and never reflect that the mistakes into which you may be led by listening to their appeals, or by giving way to your own compassion, are full of danger to yourselves, and bring you no thanks for your weakness from your allies; entirely forgetting that your empire is a despotism and your subjects disaffected conspirators, whose obedience is ensured not by your suicidal concessions, but by the superiority given you by your own strength and not their loyalty. The most alarming feature in the case is the constant change of measures with which we appear to be threatened, and our seeming ignorance of the fact that bad laws which are never changed are better for a city than good ones that have no authority; that unlearned loyalty is more serviceable than quick-witted insubordination; and that ordinary men usually manage public affairs better than their more gifted fellows. The latter are always wanting to appear wiser than the laws, and to overrule every proposition brought forward, thinking that they cannot show their wit in more important matters, and by such behaviour too often ruin their country; while those who mistrust their own cleverness are content to be less learned than the laws, and less able to pick holes in the speech of a good speaker; and being fair judges rather than rival athletes, generally conduct affairs successfully. These we ought to imitate, instead of being led on by cleverness and intellectual rivalry to advise your people against our real opinions.

"For myself, I adhere to my former opinion, and wonder at those who have proposed to reopen the case of the Mitylenians, and who are thus causing a delay which is all in favour of the guilty, by making the sufferer proceed against the offender with the edge of his anger blunted; although where vengeance follows most closely upon the wrong, it best equals it and most amply requites it. I wonder also who will be the man who will maintain the contrary, and will pretend to show that the crimes of the Mitylenians are of service to us, and our misfortunes injurious to the allies. Such a man must plainly either have such confidence in his rhetoric as to adventure to prove that what has been once for all decided is still undetermined, or be bribed to try to delude us by elaborate sophisms. In such contests the state gives the rewards to others, and takes the dangers for herself. The persons to blame are you who are so foolish as to institute these contests; who go to see an oration as you would to see a sight, take your facts on hearsay, judge of the practicability of a project by the wit of its advocates, and trust for the truth as to past events not to the fact which you saw more than to the clever strictures which you heard; the easy victims of new-fangled arguments, unwilling to follow received conclusions; slaves to every new paradox, despisers of the commonplace; the first wish of every man being that he could speak himself, the next to rival those who can speak by seeming to be quite up with their ideas by applauding every hit almost before it is made, and by being as quick in catching an argument as you are slow in foreseeing its consequences; asking, if I may so say, for something different from the conditions under which we live, and yet comprehending inadequately those very conditions; very slaves to the pleasure of the ear, and more like the audience of a rhetorician than the council of a city.

"In order to keep you from this, I proceed to show that no one state has ever injured you as much as Mitylene. I can make allowance for those who revolt because they cannot bear our empire, or who have been forced to do so by the enemy. But for those who possessed an island with fortifications; who could fear our enemies only by sea, and there had their own force of galleys to protect them; who were independent and held in the highest honour by you - to act as these have done, this is not revolt - revolt implies oppression; it is deliberate and wanton aggression; an attempt to ruin us by siding with our bitterest enemies; a worse offence than a war undertaken on their own account in the acquisition of power. The fate of those of their neighbours who had already rebelled and had been subdued was no lesson to them; their own prosperity could not dissuade them from affronting danger; but blindly confident in the future, and full of hopes beyond their power though not beyond their ambition, they declared war and made their decision to prefer might to right, their attack being determined not by provocation but by the moment which seemed propitious. The truth is that great good fortune coming suddenly and unexpectedly tends to make a people insolent; in most cases it is safer for mankind to have success in reason than out of reason; and it is easier for them, one may say, to stave off adversity than to preserve prosperity. Our mistake has been to distinguish the Mitylenians as we have done: had they been long ago treated like the rest, they never would have so far forgotten themselves, human nature being as surely made arrogant by consideration as it is awed by firmness. Let them now therefore be punished as their crime requires, and do not, while you condemn the aristocracy, absolve the people. This is certain, that all attacked you without distinction, although they might have come over to us and been now again in possession of their city. But no, they thought it safer to throw in their lot with the aristocracy and so joined their rebellion! Consider therefore: if you subject to the same punishment the ally who is forced to rebel by the enemy, and him who does so by his own free choice, which of them, think you, is there that will not rebel upon the slightest pretext; when the reward of success is freedom, and the penalty of failure nothing so very terrible? We meanwhile shall have to risk our money and our lives against one state after another; and if successful, shall receive a ruined town from which we can no longer draw the revenue upon which our strength depends; while if unsuccessful, we shall have an enemy the more upon our hands, and shall spend the time that might be employed in combating our existing foes in warring with our own allies.

"No hope, therefore, that rhetoric may instil or money purchase, of the mercy due to human infirmity must be held out to the Mitylenians. Their offence was not involuntary, but of malice and deliberate; and mercy is only for unwilling offenders.

I therefore, now as before, persist against your reversing your first decision, or giving way to the three failings most fatal to empire - pity, sentiment, and indulgence. Compassion is due to those who can reciprocate the feeling, not to those who will never pity us in return, but are our natural and necessary foes: the orators who charm us with sentiment may find other less important arenas for their talents, in the place of one where the city pays a heavy penalty for a momentary pleasure, themselves receiving fine acknowledgments for their fine phrases; while indulgence should be shown towards those who will be our friends in future, instead of towards men who will remain just what they were, and as much our enemies as before. To sum up shortly, I say that if you follow my advice you will do what is just towards the Mitylenians, and at the same time expedient; while by a different decision you will not oblige them so much as pass sentence upon yourselves. For if they were right in rebelling, you must be wrong in ruling. However, if, right or wrong, you determine to rule, you must carry out your principle and punish the Mitylenians as your interest requires; or else you must give up your empire and cultivate honesty without danger. Make up your minds, therefore, to give them like for like; and do not let the victims who escaped the plot be more insensible than the conspirators who hatched it; but reflect what they would have done if victorious over you, especially they were the aggressors. It is they who wrong their neighbour without a cause, that pursue their victim to the death, on account of the danger which they foresee in letting their enemy survive; since the object of a wanton wrong is more dangerous, if he escape, than an enemy who has not this to complain of. Do not, therefore, be traitors to yourselves, but recall as nearly as possible the moment of suffering and the supreme importance which you then attached to their reduction; and now pay them back in their turn, without yielding to present weakness or forgetting the peril that once hung over you. Punish them as they deserve, and teach your other allies by a striking example that the penalty of rebellion is death. Let them once understand this and you will not have so often to neglect your enemies while you are fighting with your own confederates."

Such were the words of Cleon. After him Diodotus, son of Eucrates, who had also in the previous assembly spoken most strongly against putting the Mitylenians to death, came forward and spoke as follows:

"I do not blame the persons who have reopened the case of the Mitylenians, nor do I approve the protests which we have heard against important questions being frequently debated. I think the two things most opposed to good counsel are haste and passion; haste usually goes hand in hand with folly, passion with coarseness and narrowness of mind. As for the argument that speech ought not to be the exponent of action, the man who uses it must be either senseless or interested: senseless if he believes it possible to treat of the uncertain future through any other medium; interested if, wishing to carry a disgraceful measure and doubting his ability to speak well in a bad cause, he thinks to frighten opponents and hearers by well-aimed calumny. What is still more intolerable is to accuse a speaker of making a display in order to be paid for it. If ignorance only were imputed, an unsuccessful speaker might retire with a reputation for honesty, if not for wisdom; while the charge of dishonesty makes him suspected, if successful, and thought, if defeated, not only a fool but a rogue. The city is no gainer by such a system, since fear deprives it of its advisers; although in truth, if our speakers are to make such assertions, it would be better for the country if they could not speak at all, as we should then make fewer blunders. The good citizen ought to triumph not by frightening his opponents but by beating them fairly in argument; and a wise city, without over-distinguishing its best advisers, will nevertheless not deprive them of their due, and, far from punishing an unlucky counsellor, will not even regard him as disgraced. In this way successful orators would be least tempted to sacrifice their convictions to popularity, in the hope of still higher honours, and unsuccessful speakers to resort to the same popular arts in order to win over the multitude.

"This is not our way; and, besides, the moment that a man is suspected of giving advice, however good, from corrupt motives, we feel such a grudge against him for the gain which after all we are not certain he will receive, that we deprive the city of its certain benefit. Plain good advice has thus come to be no less suspected than bad; and the advocate of the most monstrous measures is not more obliged to use deceit to gain the people, than the best counsellor is to lie in order to be believed. The city and the city only, owing to these refinements, can never be served openly and without disguise; he who does serve it openly being always suspected of serving himself in some secret way in return. Still, considering the magnitude of the interests involved, and the position of affairs, we orators must make it our business to look a little farther than you who judge offhand; especially as we, your advisers, are responsible, while you, our audience, are not so. For if those who gave the advice, and those who took it, suffered equally, you would judge more calmly; as it is, you visit the disasters into which the whim of the moment may have led you upon the single person of your adviser, not upon yourselves, his numerous companions in error.

"However, I have not come forward either to oppose or to accuse in the matter of Mitylene; indeed, the question before us as sensible men is not their guilt, but our interests. Though I prove them ever so guilty, I shall not, therefore, advise their death, unless it be expedient; nor though they should have claims to indulgence, shall I recommend it, unless it be dearly for the good of the country. I consider that we are deliberating for the future more than for the present; and where Cleon is so positive as to the useful deterrent effects that will follow from making rebellion capital, I, who consider the interests of the future quite as much as he, as positively maintain the contrary. And I require you not to reject my useful considerations for his specious ones: his speech may have the attraction of seeming the more just in your present temper against Mitylene; but we are not in a court of justice, but in a political assembly; and the question is not justice, but how to make the Mitylenians useful to Athens.

"Now of course communities have enacted the penalty of death for many offences far lighter than this: still hope leads men to venture, and no one ever yet put himself in peril without the inward conviction that he would succeed in his design. Again, was there ever city rebelling that did not believe that it possessed either in itself or in its alliances resources adequate to the enterprise? All, states and individuals, are alike prone to err, and there is no law that will prevent them; or why should men have exhausted the list of punishments in search of enactments to protect them from evildoers? It is probable that in early times the penalties for the greatest offences were less severe, and that, as these were disregarded, the penalty of death has been by degrees in most cases arrived at, which is itself disregarded in like manner. Either then some means of terror more terrible than this must be discovered, or it must be owned that this restraint is useless; and that as long as poverty gives men the courage of necessity, or plenty fills them with the ambition which belongs to insolence and pride, and the other conditions of life remain each under the thraldom of some fatal and master passion, so long will the impulse never be wanting to drive men into danger. Hope also and cupidity, the one leading and the other following, the one conceiving the attempt, the other suggesting the facility of succeeding, cause the widest ruin, and, although invisible agents, are far stronger than the dangers that are seen. Fortune, too, powerfully helps the delusion and, by the unexpected aid that she sometimes lends, tempts men to venture with inferior means; and this is especially the case with communities, because the stakes played for are the highest, freedom or empire, and, when all are acting together, each man irrationally magnifies his own capacity. In fine, it is impossible to prevent, and only great simplicity can hope to prevent, human nature doing what it has once set its mind upon, by force of law or by any other deterrent force whatsoever.

"We must not, therefore, commit ourselves to a false policy through a belief in the efficacy of the punishment of death, or exclude rebels from the hope of repentance and an early atonement of their error. Consider a moment. At present, if a city that has already revolted perceive that it cannot succeed, it will come to terms while it is still able to refund expenses, and pay tribute afterwards. In the other case, what city, think you, would not prepare better than is now done, and hold out to the last against its besiegers, if it is all one whether it surrender late or soon? And how can it be otherwise than hurtful to us to be put to the expense of a siege, because surrender is out of the question; and if we take the city, to receive a ruined town from which we can no longer draw the revenue which forms our real strength against the enemy? We must not, therefore, sit as strict judges of the offenders to our own prejudice, but rather see how by moderate chastisements we may be enabled to benefit in future by the revenue-producing powers of our dependencies; and we must make up our minds to look for our protection not to legal terrors but to careful administration. At present we do exactly the opposite. When a free community, held in subjection by force, rises, as is only natural, and asserts its independence, it is no sooner reduced than we fancy ourselves obliged to punish it severely; although the right course with freemen is not to chastise them rigorously when they do rise, but rigorously to watch them before they rise, and to prevent their ever entertaining the idea, and, the insurrection suppressed, to make as few responsible for it as possible.

"Only consider what a blunder you would commit in doing as Cleon recommends. As things are at present, in all the cities the people is your friend, and either does not revolt with the oligarchy, or, if forced to do so, becomes at once the enemy of the insurgents; so that in the war with the hostile city you have the masses on your side. But if you butcher the people of Mitylene, who had nothing to do with the revolt, and who, as soon as they got arms, of their own motion surrendered the town, first you will commit the crime of killing your benefactors; and next you will play directly into the hands of the higher classes, who when they induce their cities to rise, will immediately have the people on their side, through your having announced in advance the same punishment for those who are guilty and for those who are not. On the contrary, even if they were guilty, you ought to seem not to notice it, in order to avoid alienating the only class still friendly to us. In short, I consider it far more useful for the preservation of our empire voluntarily to put up with injustice, than to put to death, however justly, those whom it is our interest to keep alive. As for Cleon's idea that in punishment the claims of justice and expediency can both be satisfied, facts do not confirm the possibility of such a combination.

"Confess, therefore, that this is the wisest course, and without conceding too much either to pity or to indulgence, by neither of which motives do I any more than Cleon wish you to be influenced, upon the plain merits of the case before you, be persuaded by me to try calmly those of the Mitylenians whom Paches sent off as guilty, and to leave the rest undisturbed. This is at once best for the future, and most terrible to your enemies at the present moment; inasmuch as good policy against an adversary is superior to the blind attacks of brute force."

Such were the words of Diodotus. The two opinions thus expressed were the ones that most directly contradicted each other; and the Athenians, notwithstanding their change of feeling, now proceeded to a division, in which the show of hands was almost equal, although the motion of Diodotus carried the day. Another galley was at once sent off in haste, for fear that the first might reach Lesbos in the interval, and the city be found destroyed; the first ship having about a day and a night's start. Wine and barley-cakes were provided for the vessel by the Mitylenian ambassadors, and great promises made if they arrived in time; which caused the men to use such diligence upon the voyage that they took their meals of barley-cakes kneaded with oil and wine as they rowed, and only slept by turns while the others were at the oar. Luckily they met with no contrary wind, and the first ship making no haste upon so horrid an errand, while the second pressed on in the manner described, the first arrived so little before them, that Paches had only just had time to read the decree, and to prepare to execute the sentence, when the second put into port and prevented the massacre. The danger of Mitylene had indeed been great.

The other party whom Paches had sent off as the prime movers in the rebellion, were upon Cleon's motion put to death by the Athenians, the number being rather more than a thousand. The Athenians also demolished the walls of the Mitylenians, and took possession of their ships. Afterwards tribute was not imposed upon the Lesbians; but all their land, except that of the Methymnians, was divided into three thousand allotments, three hundred of which were reserved as sacred for the gods, and the rest assigned by lot to Athenian shareholders, who were sent out to the island. With these the Lesbians agreed to pay a rent of two minae a year for each allotment, and cultivated the land themselves. The Athenians also took possession of the towns on the continent belonging to the Mitylenians, which thus became for the future subject to Athens. Such were the events that took place at Lesbos.

CHAPTER X

*Fifth Year of the War - Trial and Execution of the Plataeans -
Corcyraean Revolution*

D
URING THE same summer, after the reduction of
Lesbos, the Athenians under Nicias, son of Niceratus,
made an expedition against the island of Minoa,
which lies off Megara and was used as a fortified post by the
Megarians, who had built a tower upon it. Nicias wished to enable
the Athenians to maintain their blockade from this nearer station
instead of from Budorum and Salamis; to stop the Peloponnesian
galleys and privateers sailing out unobserved from the island, as
they had been in the habit of doing; and at the same time prevent
anything from coming into Megara. Accordingly, after taking
two towers projecting on the side of Nisaea, by engines from the
sea, and clearing the entrance into the channel between the island
and the shore, he next proceeded to cut off all communication
by building a wall on the mainland at the point where a bridge
across a morass enabled succours to be thrown into the island,
which was not far off from the continent. A few days sufficing to
accomplish this, he afterwards raised some works in the island
also, and leaving a garrison there, departed with his forces.

About the same time in this summer, the Plataeans, being now
without provisions and unable to support the siege, surrendered to
the Peloponnesians in the following manner. An assault had been
made upon the wall, which the Plataeans were unable to repel. The
Lacedaemonian commander, perceiving their weakness, wished to
avoid taking the place by storm; his instructions from Lacedaemon
having been so conceived, in order that if at any future time peace
should be made with Athens, and they should agree each to restore
the places that they had taken in the war, Plataea might be held
to have come over voluntarily, and not be included in the list.
He accordingly sent a herald to them to ask if they were willing

voluntarily to surrender the town to the Lacedaemonians, and accept them as their judges, upon the understanding that the guilty should be punished, but no one without form of law. The Plataeans were now in the last state of weakness, and the herald had no sooner delivered his message than they surrendered the town. The Peloponnesians fed them for some days until the judges from Lacedaemon, who were five in number, arrived. Upon their arrival no charge was preferred; they simply called up the Plataeans, and asked them whether they had done the Lacedaemonians and allies any service in the war then raging. The Plataeans asked leave to speak at greater length, and deputed two of their number to represent them: Astymachus, son of Asopolaus, and Lacon, son of Aeimnestus, proxenus of the Lacedaemonians, who came forward and spoke as follows:

"Lacedaemonians, when we surrendered our city we trusted in you, and looked forward to a trial more agreeable to the forms of law than the present, to which we had no idea of being subjected; the judges also in whose hands we consented to place ourselves were you, and you only (from whom we thought we were most likely to obtain justice), and not other persons, as is now the case. As matters stand, we are afraid that we have been doubly deceived. We have good reason to suspect, not only that the issue to be tried is the most terrible of all, but that you will not prove impartial; if we may argue from the fact that no accusation was first brought forward for us to answer, but we had ourselves to ask leave to speak, and from the question being put so shortly, that a true answer to it tells against us, while a false one can be contradicted. In this dilemma, our safest, and indeed our only course, seems to be to say something at all risks: placed as we are, we could scarcely be silent without being tormented by the damning thought that speaking might have saved us. Another difficulty that we have to encounter is the difficulty of convincing you. Were we unknown to each other we might profit by bringing forward new matter with which you were unacquainted: as it is, we can tell you nothing that you do not know already, and we fear, not that you have condemned us in your own minds of having failed in our duty towards you, and make this our crime, but that to please a third party we have to submit to a trial the result of which is already decided. Nevertheless, we will place before you what we can justly urge, not only on the question of the quarrel which the Thebans have against us, but also as addressing you and the rest of the Hellenes; and we will remind you of our good services, and endeavour to prevail with you.

"To your short question, whether we have done the Lacedaemonians and allies any service in this war, we say, if you ask us as enemies, that to refrain from serving you was not to do you injury; if as friends, that you are more in fault for having marched against us. During the peace, and against the Mede, we acted well: we have not now been the first to break the peace, and we were the only Boeotians who then joined in defending against the Mede the liberty of Hellas. Although an inland people, we were present at the action at Artemisium; in the battle that took place in our territory we fought by the side of yourselves and Pausanias; and in all the other Hellenic exploits of the time we took a part quite out of proportion to our strength. Besides, you, as Lacedaemonians, ought not to forget that at the time of the great panic at Sparta, after the earthquake, caused by the secession of the Helots to Ithome, we sent the third part of our citizens to assist you.

"On these great and historical occasions such was the part that we chose, although afterwards we became your enemies. For this you were to blame. When we asked for your alliance against our Theban oppressors, you rejected our petition, and told us to go to the Athenians who were our neighbours, as you lived too far off. In the war we never have done to you, and never should have done to you, anything unreasonable. If we refused to desert the Athenians when you asked us, we did no wrong; they had helped us against the Thebans when you drew back, and we could no longer give them up with honour; especially as we had obtained their alliance and had been admitted to their citizenship at our own request, and after receiving benefits at their hands; but it was plainly our duty loyally to obey their orders. Besides, the faults that either of you may commit in your supremacy must be laid, not upon the followers, but on the chiefs that lead them astray.

"With regard to the Thebans, they have wronged us repeatedly, and their last aggression, which has been the means of bringing us into our present position, is within your own knowledge. In seizing our city in time of peace, and what is more at a holy time in the month, they justly encountered our vengeance, in accordance with the universal law which sanctions resistance to an invader; and it cannot now be right that we should suffer on their account. By taking your own immediate interest and their animosity as the test of justice, you will prove yourselves to be rather waiters on expediency than judges of right; although if they seem useful to you now, we and the rest of the Hellenes gave you much more valuable help at a time of greater need. Now you are the assailants, and others fear you; but at the crisis to which we allude, when the barbarian threatened all with slavery, the Thebans were on his side. It is just, therefore, to put our patriotism then against our error now, if error there has been; and you will find the merit outweighing the fault, and displayed at a juncture when there were few Hellenes who would set their valour against the strength of Xerxes, and when greater praise was theirs who preferred the dangerous path of honour to the safe course of consulting their own interest with respect to the invasion. To these few we belonged, and highly were we honoured for it; and yet we now fear to perish by having again acted on the same principles, and chosen to act well with Athens sooner than wisely with Sparta. Yet in justice the same cases should be decided in the same way, and policy should not mean anything else than lasting gratitude for the service of good ally combined with a proper attention to one's own immediate interest.

"Consider also that at present the Hellenes generally regard you as a pattern of worth and honour; and if you pass an unjust sentence upon us in this which is no obscure cause, but one in which you, the judges, are as illustrious as we, the prisoners, are blameless, take care that displeasure be not felt at an unworthy decision in the matter of honourable men made by men yet more honourable than they, and at the consecration in the national temples of spoils taken from the Plataeans, the benefactors of Hellas. Shocking indeed will it seem for Lacedaemonians to destroy Plataea, and for the city whose name your fathers inscribed upon the tripod at Delphi for its good service, to be by you blotted out from the map of Hellas, to please the Thebans. To such a depth of misfortune have we fallen that, while the Medes' success had been our ruin, Thebans now supplant us in your once fond regards; and we have been subjected to two dangers, the greatest of any - that of dying of starvation then, if we had not surrendered our town, and now of being tried for our lives. So that we Plataeans, after exertions beyond our power in the cause of the Hellenes, are rejected by all, forsaken and unassisted; helped by none of our allies, and reduced to doubt the stability of our only hope, yourselves.

"Still, in the name of the gods who once presided over our confederacy, and of our own good service in the Hellenic cause, we adjure you to relent; to recall the decision which we fear that the Thebans may have obtained from you; to ask back the gift that you have given them, that they disgrace not you by slaying us; to gain a pure instead of a guilty gratitude, and not to gratify others to be yourselves rewarded with shame. Our lives may be quickly taken, but it will be a heavy task to wipe away the infamy of the deed; as we are no enemies whom you might justly punish, but friends forced into taking arms against you. To grant us our lives would be, therefore, a righteous judgment; if you consider also that we are prisoners who surrendered of their own accord, stretching out our hands for quarter, whose slaughter Hellenic law forbids, and who besides were always your benefactors. Look at the sepulchres of your fathers, slain by the Medes and buried in our country, whom year by year we honoured with garments and all other dues, and the first-fruits of all that our land produced in their season, as friends from a friendly country and allies to our old companions in arms. Should you not decide aright, your conduct would be the very opposite to ours. Consider only: Pausanias buried them thinking that he was laying them in friendly ground and among men as friendly; but you, if you kill us and make the Plataean territory Theban, will leave your fathers and kinsmen in a hostile soil and among their murderers, deprived of the honours which they now enjoy. What is more, you will enslave the land in which the freedom of the Hellenes was won, make desolate the temples of the gods to whom they prayed before they overcame the Medes, and take away your ancestral sacrifices from those who founded and instituted them.

"It were not to your glory, Lacedaemonians, either to offend in this way against the common law of the Hellenes and against your own ancestors, or to kill us your benefactors to gratify another's hatred without having been wronged yourselves: it were more so to spare us and to yield to the impressions of a reasonable compassion; reflecting not merely on the awful fate in store for us, but also on the character of the sufferers, and on the impossibility of predicting how soon misfortune may fall even upon those who deserve it not. We, as we have a right to do and as our need impels us, entreat you, calling aloud upon the gods at whose common altar all the Hellenes worship, to hear our request, to be not unmindful of the oaths which your fathers swore, and which we now plead - we supplicate you by the tombs of your fathers, and appeal to those that are gone to save us from falling into the hands of the Thebans and their dearest friends from being given up to their most detested foes. We also remind you of that day on which we did the most glorious deeds, by your fathers' sides, we who now on this are like to suffer the most dreadful fate. Finally, to do what is necessary and yet most difficult for men in our situation - that is, to make an end of speaking, since with that ending the peril of our lives draws near - in conclusion we say that we did not surrender our city to the Thebans (to that we would have preferred inglorious starvation), but trusted in and capitulated to you; and it would be just, if we fail to persuade you, to put us back in the same position and let us take the chance that falls to us. And at the same time we adjure you not to give us up - your suppliants, Lacedaemonians, out of your hands and faith, Plataeans foremost of the Hellenic patriots, to Thebans, our most hated enemies - but to be our saviours, and not, while you free the rest of the Hellenes, to bring us to destruction."

Such were the words of the Plataeans. The Thebans, afraid that the Lacedaemonians might be moved by what they had heard, came forward and said that they too desired to address them, since the Plataeans had, against their wish, been allowed to speak at length instead of being confined to a simple answer to the question. Leave being granted, the Thebans spoke as follows:

"We should never have asked to make this speech if the Plataeans on their side had contented themselves with shortly answering the question, and had not turned round and made charges against us, coupled with a long defence of themselves upon matters outside the present inquiry and not even the subject of accusation, and with praise of what no one finds fault with. However, since they have done so, we must answer their charges and refute their self-praise, in order that neither our bad name nor their good may help them, but that you may hear the real truth on both points, and so decide.

"The origin of our quarrel was this. We settled Plataea some time after the rest of Boeotia, together with other places out of which we had driven the mixed population. The Plataeans not choosing to recognize our supremacy, as had been first arranged, but separating themselves from the rest of the Boeotians, and proving traitors to their nationality, we used compulsion; upon which they went over to the Athenians, and with them did as much harm, for which we retaliated.

"Next, when the barbarian invaded Hellas, they say that they were the only Boeotians who did not Medize; and this is where they most glorify themselves and abuse us. We say that if they did not Medize, it was because the Athenians did not do so either; just as afterwards when the Athenians attacked the Hellenes they, the Plataeans, were again the only Boeotians who Atticized. And yet consider the forms of our respective governments when we so acted. Our city at that juncture had neither an oligarchical constitution in which all the nobles enjoyed equal rights, nor a democracy, but that which is most opposed to law and good government and nearest a tyranny - the rule of a close cabal. These, hoping to strengthen their individual power by the success of the Mede, kept down by force the people, and brought him into the town. The city as a whole was not its own mistress when it so acted, and ought not to be reproached for the errors that it committed while deprived of its constitution. Examine only how we acted after the departure of the Mede and the recovery of the constitution; when the Athenians attacked the rest of Hellas and endeavoured to subjugate our country, of the greater part of which faction had already made them masters. Did not we fight and conquer at Coronea and liberate Boeotia, and do we not now actively contribute to the liberation of the rest, providing horses to the cause and a force unequalled by that of any other state in the confederacy?

"Let this suffice to excuse us for our Medism. We will now endeavour to show that you have injured the Hellenes more than we, and are more deserving of condign punishment. It was in defence against us, say you, that you became allies and citizens of Athens. If so, you ought only to have called in the Athenians against us, instead of joining them in attacking others: it was open to you to do this if you ever felt that they were leading you where you did not wish to follow, as Lacedaemon was already your ally against the Mede, as you so much insist; and this was surely sufficient to keep us off, and above all to allow you to deliberate in security. Nevertheless, of your own choice and without compulsion you chose to throw your lot in with Athens. And you say that it had been base for you to betray your benefactors; but it was surely far baser and more iniquitous to sacrifice the whole body of the Hellenes, your fellow confederates, who were liberating Hellas, than the Athenians only, who were enslaving it. The return that you made them was therefore neither equal nor honourable, since you called them in, as you say, because you were being oppressed yourselves, and then became their accomplices in oppressing others; although baseness rather consists in not returning like for like than in not returning what is justly due but must be unjustly paid.

"Meanwhile, after thus plainly showing that it was not for the sake of the Hellenes that you alone then did not Medize, but because the Athenians did not do so either, and you wished to side with them and to be against the rest; you now claim the benefit of good deeds done to please your neighbours. This cannot be admitted: you chose the Athenians, and with them you must stand or fall. Nor can you plead the league then made and claim that it should now protect you. You abandoned that league, and offended against it by helping instead of hindering the subjugation of the Aeginetans and others of its members, and that not under compulsion, but while in enjoyment of the same institutions that you enjoy to the present hour, and no one forcing you as in our case. Lastly, an invitation was addressed to you before you were blockaded to be neutral and join neither party: this you did not accept. Who then merit the detestation of the Hellenes more justly than you, you who sought their ruin under the mask of honour? The former virtues that you allege you now show not to be proper to your character; the real bent of your nature has been at length damningly proved: when the Athenians took the path of injustice you followed them.

"Of our unwilling Medism and your wilful Atticizing this then is our explanation. The last wrong wrong of which you complain consists in our having, as you say, lawlessly invaded your town in time of peace and festival. Here again we cannot think that we were more in fault than yourselves. If of our own proper motion we made an armed attack upon your city and ravaged your territory, we are guilty; but if the first men among you in estate and family, wishing to put an end to the foreign connection and to restore you to the common Boeotian country, of their own free will invited us, wherein is our crime? Where wrong is done, those who lead, as you say, are more to blame than those who follow. Not that, in our judgment, wrong was done either by them or by us. Citizens like yourselves, and with more at stake than you, they opened their own walls and introduced us into their own city, not as foes but as friends, to prevent the bad among you from becoming worse; to give honest men their due; to reform principles without attacking persons, since you were not to be banished from your city, but brought home to your kindred, nor to be made enemies to any, but friends alike to all.

"That our intention was not hostile is proved by our behaviour. We did no harm to any one, but publicly invited those who wished to live under a national, Boeotian government to come over to us; which as first you gladly did, and made an agreement with us and remained tranquil, until you became aware of the smallness of our numbers. Now it is possible that there may have been something not quite fair in our entering without the consent of your commons. At any rate you did not repay us in kind. Instead of refraining, as we had done, from violence, and inducing us to retire by negotiation, you fell upon us in violation of your agreement, and slew some of us in fight, of which we do not so much complain, for in that there was a certain justice; but others who held out their hands and received quarter, and whose lives you subsequently promised us, you lawlessly butchered. If this was not abominable, what is? And after these three crimes committed one after the other - the violation of your agreement, the murder of the men afterwards, and the lying breach of your promise not to kill them, if we refrained from injuring your property in the country - you still affirm that we are the criminals and yourselves pretend to escape justice. Not so, if these your judges decide aright, but you will be punished for all together.

"Such, Lacedaemonians, are the facts. We have gone into them at some length both on your account and on our own, that you may fed that you will justly condemn the prisoners, and we, that we have given an additional sanction to our vengeance. We would also prevent you from being melted by hearing of their past virtues, if any such they had: these may be fairly appealed to by the victims of injustice, but only aggravate the guilt of criminals, since they offend against their better nature. Nor let them gain anything by crying and wailing, by calling upon your fathers' tombs and their own desolate condition. Against this we point to the far more dreadful fate of our youth, butchered at their hands; the fathers of whom either fell at Coronea, bringing Boeotia over to you, or seated, forlorn old men by desolate hearths, with far more reason implore your justice upon the prisoners. The pity which they appeal to is rather due to men who suffer unworthily; those who suffer justly as they do are on the contrary subjects for triumph. For their

present desolate condition they have themselves to blame, since they wilfully rejected the better alliance. Their lawless act was not provoked by any action of ours: hate, not justice, inspired their decision; and even now the satisfaction which they afford us is not adequate; they will suffer by a legal sentence, not as they pretend as suppliants asking for quarter in battle, but as prisoners who have surrendered upon agreement to take their trial. Vindicate, therefore, Lacedaemonians, the Hellenic law which they have broken; and to us, the victims of its violation, grant the reward merited by our zeal. Nor let us be supplanted in your favour by their harangues, but offer an example to the Hellenes, that the contests to which you invite them are of deeds, not words: good deeds can be shortly stated, but where wrong is done a wealth of language is needed to veil its deformity. However, if leading powers were to do what you are now doing, and putting one short question to all alike were to decide accordingly, men would be less tempted to seek fine phrases to cover bad actions."

Such were the words of the Thebans. The Lacedaemonian judges decided that the question whether they had received any service from the Plataeans in the war, was a fair one for them to put; as they had always invited them to be neutral, agreeably to the original covenant of Pausanias after the defeat of the Mede, and had again definitely offered them the same conditions before the blockade. This offer having been refused, they were now, they conceived, by the loyalty of their intention released from their covenant; and having, as they considered, suffered evil at the hands of the Plataeans, they brought them in again one by one and asked each of them the same question, that is to say, whether they had done the Lacedaemonians and allies any service in the war; and upon their saying that they had not, took them out and slew them, all without exception. The number of Plataeans thus massacred was not less than two hundred, with twenty-five Athenians who had shared in the siege. The women were taken as slaves. The city the Thebans gave for about a year to some political emigrants from Megara and to the surviving Plataeans of their own party to inhabit, and afterwards razed it to the ground from the very foundations, and built on to the precinct of Hera an inn two hundred feet square, with rooms all round above and below, making use for this purpose of the roofs and doors of the Plataeans: of the rest of the materials in the wall, the brass and the iron, they made couches which they dedicated to Hera, for whom they also built a stone chapel of a hundred feet square. The land they confiscated and let out on a ten years' lease to Theban occupiers. The adverse attitude of the Lacedaemonians in the whole Plataean affair was mainly adopted to please the Thebans, who were thought to be useful in the war at that moment raging. Such was the end of Plataea, in the ninety-third year after she became the ally of Athens.

Meanwhile, the forty ships of the Peloponnesians that had gone to the relief of the Lesbians, and which we left flying across the open sea, pursued by the Athenians, were caught in a storm off Crete, and scattering from thence made their way to Peloponnese, where they found at Cyllene thirteen Leucadian and Ambraciot galleys, with Brasidas, son of Tellis, lately arrived as counsellor to Alcidas; the Lacedaemonians, upon the failure of the Lesbian expedition, having resolved to strengthen their fleet and sail to Corcyra, where a revolution had broken out, so as to arrive there before the twelve Athenian ships at Naupactus could be reinforced from Athens. Brasidas and Alcidas began to prepare accordingly.

The Corcyraean revolution began with the return of the prisoners taken in the sea-fights off Epidamnus. These the Corinthians had released, nominally upon the security of eight hundred talents given by their proxeni, but in reality upon their engagement to bring over Corcyra to Corinth. These men proceeded to canvass each of the citizens, and to intrigue with the view of detaching the city from Athens. Upon the arrival of an Athenian and a Corinthian vessel, with envoys on board, a conference was held in which the Corcyraeans voted to remain allies of the Athenians according to their agreement, but to be friends of the Peloponnesians as they had been formerly. Meanwhile, the returned prisoners brought Peithias, a volunteer proxenus of the Athenians and leader of the commons, to trial, upon the charge of enslaving Corcyra to Athens. He, being acquitted, retorted by accusing five of the richest of their number of cutting stakes in the ground sacred to Zeus and Alcinous; the legal penalty being a stater for each stake. Upon their conviction, the amount of the penalty being very large, they seated themselves as suppliants in the temples to be allowed to pay it by instalments; but Peithias, who was one of the senate, prevailed upon that body to enforce the law; upon which the accused, rendered desperate by the law, and also learning that Peithias had the intention, while still a member of the senate, to persuade the people to conclude a defensive and offensive alliance with Athens, banded together armed with daggers, and suddenly bursting into the senate killed Peithias and sixty others, senators and private persons; some few only of the party of Peithias taking refuge in the Athenian galley, which had not yet departed.

After this outrage, the conspirators summoned the Corcyraeans to an assembly, and said that this would turn out for the best, and would save them from being enslaved by Athens: for the future, they moved to receive neither party unless they came peacefully in a single ship, treating any larger number as enemies. This motion made, they compelled it to be adopted, and instantly sent off envoys to Athens to justify what had been done and to dissuade the refugees there from any hostile proceedings which might lead to a reaction.

Upon the arrival of the embassy, the Athenians arrested the envoys and all who listened to them, as revolutionists, and lodged them in Aegina. Meanwhile a Corinthian galley arriving in the island with Lacedaemonian envoys, the dominant Corcyraean party attacked the commons and defeated them in battle. Night coming on, the commons took refuge in the Acropolis and the higher parts of the city, and concentrated themselves there, having also possession of the Hyllaic harbour; their adversaries occupying the market-place, where most of them lived, and the harbour adjoining, looking towards the mainland.

The next day passed in skirmishes of little importance, each party sending into the country to offer freedom to the slaves and to invite them to join them. The mass of the slaves answered the appeal of the commons; their antagonists being reinforced by eight hundred mercenaries from the continent.

After a day's interval hostilities recommenced, victory remaining with the commons, who had the advantage in numbers and position, the women also valiantly assisting them, pelting with tiles from the houses, and supporting the melee with a fortitude beyond their sex. Towards dusk, the oligarchs in full rout, fearing that the victorious commons might assault and carry the arsenal and put them to the sword, fired the houses round the marketplace and the lodging-houses, in order to bar their advance; sparing neither their own, nor those of their neighbours; by which much stuff of the merchants was consumed and the city risked total destruction, if a wind had come to help the flame by blowing on it. Hostilities now ceasing, both sides kept quiet, passing the night on guard, while the Corinthian ship stole out to sea upon the victory of the commons, and most of the mercenaries passed over secretly to the continent.

The next day the Athenian general, Nicostratus, son of Diitrephes, came up from Naupactus with twelve ships and five hundred Messenian heavy infantry. He at once endeavoured to bring about a settlement, and persuaded the two parties to agree together to bring to trial ten of the ringleaders, who presently fled, while the rest were to live in peace, making terms with each other, and entering into a defensive and offensive alliance with the Athenians. This arranged, he was about to sail away, when the leaders of the commons induced him to leave them five of his ships to make their adversaries less disposed to move, while they manned and sent with him an equal number of their own. He had no sooner consented, than they began to enroll their enemies for the ships; and these, fearing that they might be sent off to Athens, seated themselves as suppliants in the temple of the Dioscuri. An attempt on the part of Nicostratus to reassure them and to persuade them to rise proving unsuccessful, the commons armed upon this pretext, alleging the refusal of their adversaries to sail with them as a proof of the hollowness of their intentions, and took their arms out of their houses, and would have dispatched some whom they fell in with, if Nicostratus had not prevented it. The rest of the party, seeing what was going on, seated themselves as suppliants in the temple of Hera, being not less than four hundred in number; until the commons, fearing that they might adopt some desperate resolution, induced them to rise, and conveyed them over to the island in front of the temple, where provisions were sent across to them.

At this stage in the revolution, on the fourth or fifth day after the removal of the men to the island, the Peloponnesian ships arrived from Cyllene where they had been stationed since their return from Ionia, fifty-three in number, still under the command of Alcidas, but with Brasidas also on board as his adviser; and dropping anchor at Sybota, a harbour on the mainland, at daybreak made sail for Corcyra.

The Corcyraeans in great confusion and alarm at the state of things in the city and at the approach of the invader, at once proceeded to equip sixty vessels, which they sent out, as fast as they were manned, against the enemy, in spite of the Athenians recommending them to let them sail out first, and to follow themselves afterwards with all their ships together. Upon their vessels coming up to the enemy in this straggling fashion, two immediately deserted: in others the crews were fighting among themselves, and there was no order in anything that was done; so that the Peloponnesians, seeing their confusion, placed twenty ships to oppose the Corcyraeans, and ranged the rest against the twelve Athenian ships, amongst which were the two vessels Salaminia and Paralus.

While the Corcyraeans, attacking without judgment and in small detachments, were already crippled by their own misconduct, the Athenians, afraid of the numbers of the enemy and of being surrounded, did not venture to attack the main body or even the centre of the division opposed to them, but fell upon its wing and sank one vessel; after which the Peloponnesians formed in a circle, and the Athenians rowed round them and tried to throw them into disorder. Perceiving this, the division opposed to the Corcyraeans, fearing a repetition of the disaster of Naupactus, came to support their friends, and the whole fleet now bore down, united, upon the Athenians, who retired before it, backing water, retiring as leisurely as possible in order to give the Corcyraeans time to escape, while the enemy was thus kept occupied. Such was the character of this sea-fight, which lasted until sunset.

The Corcyraeans now feared that the enemy would follow up their victory and sail against the town and rescue the men in the island, or strike some other blow equally decisive, and accordingly carried the men over again to the temple of Hera, and kept guard over the city. The Peloponnesians, however, although victorious in the sea-fight, did not venture to attack the town, but took the thirteen Corcyraean vessels which they had captured, and with them sailed back to the continent from whence they had put out. The next day equally they refrained from attacking the city, although the disorder and panic were at their height, and though Brasidas, it is said, urged Alcidas, his superior officer, to do so, but they landed upon the promontory of Leukimme and laid waste the country.

Meanwhile the commons in Corcyra, being still in great fear of the fleet attacking them, came to a parley with the suppliants and their friends, in order to save the town; and prevailed upon some of them to go on board the ships, of which they still manned thirty, against the expected attack. But the Peloponnesians after ravaging the country until midday sailed away, and towards nightfall were informed by beacon signals of the approach of sixty Athenian vessels from Leucas, under the command of Eurymedon, son of Thucles; which had been sent off by the Athenians upon the news of the revolution and of the fleet with Alcidas being about to sail for Corcyra.

The Peloponnesians accordingly at once set off in haste by night for home, coasting along shore; and hauling their ships across the Isthmus of Leucas, in order not to be seen doubling it, so departed. The Corcyraeans, made aware of the approach of the Athenian fleet and of the departure of the enemy, brought the Messenians from outside the walls into the town, and ordered the fleet which they had manned to sail round into the Hyllaic harbour; and while it was so doing, slew such of their enemies as they laid hands on, dispatching afterwards, as they landed them, those whom they had persuaded to go on board the ships. Next they went to the sanctuary of Hera and persuaded about fifty men to take their trial, and condemned them all to death. The mass of the suppliants who had refused to do so, on seeing what was taking place, slew each other there in the consecrated ground; while some hanged themselves upon the trees, and others destroyed themselves as they were severally able. During seven days that Eurymedon stayed with his sixty ships, the Corcyraeans were engaged in butchering those of their fellow citizens whom they regarded as their enemies: and although the crime imputed was that of attempting to put down the democracy, some were slain also for private hatred, others by their debtors because of the moneys owed to them. Death thus raged in every shape; and, as usually happens at such times, there was no length to which violence did not go; sons were killed by their fathers, and suppliants dragged from the altar or slain upon it; while some were even walled up in the temple of Dionysus and died there.

So bloody was the march of the revolution, and the impression which it made was the greater as it was one of the first to occur. Later on, one may say, the whole Hellenic world was convulsed; struggles being every, where made by the popular chiefs to bring in the

215

Athenians, and by the oligarchs to introduce the Lacedaemonians. In peace there would have been neither the pretext nor the wish to make such an invitation; but in war, with an alliance always at the command of either faction for the hurt of their adversaries and their own corresponding advantage, opportunities for bringing in the foreigner were never wanting to the revolutionary parties. The sufferings which revolution entailed upon the cities were many and terrible, such as have occurred and always will occur, as long as the nature of mankind remains the same; though in a severer or milder form, and varying in their symptoms, according to the variety of the particular cases. In peace and prosperity, states and individuals have better sentiments, because they do not find themselves suddenly confronted with imperious necessities; but war takes away the easy supply of daily wants, and so proves a rough master, that brings most men's characters to a level with their fortunes. Revolution thus ran its course from city to city, and the places which it arrived at last, from having heard what had been done before, carried to a still greater excess the refinement of their inventions, as manifested in the cunning of their enterprises and the atrocity of their reprisals. Words had to change their ordinary meaning and to take that which was now given them. Reckless audacity came to be considered the courage of a loyal ally; prudent hesitation, specious cowardice; moderation was held to be a cloak for unmanliness; ability to see all sides of a question, inaptness to act on any. Frantic violence became the attribute of manliness; cautious plotting, a justifiable means of self-defence. The advocate of extreme measures was always trustworthy; his opponent a man to be suspected. To succeed in a plot was to have a shrewd head, to divine a plot a still shrewder; but to try to provide against having to do either was to break up your party and to be afraid of your adversaries. In fine, to forestall an intending criminal, or to suggest the idea of a crime where it was wanting, was equally commended until even blood became a weaker tie than party, from the superior readiness of those united by the latter to dare everything without reserve; for such associations had not in view the blessings derivable from established institutions but were formed by ambition for their overthrow; and the confidence of their members in each other rested less on any religious sanction than upon complicity in crime. The fair proposals of an adversary were met with jealous precautions by the stronger of the two, and not with a generous confidence. Revenge also was held of more account than self-preservation. Oaths of reconciliation, being only proffered on either side to meet an immediate difficulty, only held good so long as no other weapon was at hand; but when opportunity offered, he who first ventured to seize it and to take his enemy off his guard, thought this perfidious vengeance sweeter than an open one, since, considerations of safety apart, success by treachery won him the palm of superior intelligence. Indeed it is generally the case that men are readier to call rogues clever than simpletons honest, and are as ashamed of being the second as they are proud of being the first. The cause of all these evils was the lust for power arising from greed and ambition; and from these passions proceeded the violence of parties once engaged in contention. The leaders in the cities, each provided with the fairest professions, on the one side with the cry of political equality of the people, on the other of a moderate aristocracy, sought prizes for themselves in those public interests which they pretended to cherish, and, recoiling from no means in their struggles for ascendancy engaged in the direst excesses; in their acts of vengeance they went to even greater lengths, not stopping at what justice or the good of the state demanded, but making the party caprice of the moment their only standard, and invoking with equal readiness the condemnation of an unjust verdict or the authority of the strong arm to glut the animosities of the hour. Thus religion was in honour with neither party; but the use of fair phrases to arrive at guilty ends was in high reputation. Meanwhile the moderate part of the citizens perished between the two, either for not joining in the quarrel, or because envy would not suffer them to escape.

Thus every form of iniquity took root in the Hellenic countries by reason of the troubles. The ancient simplicity into which honour so largely entered was laughed down and disappeared; and society became divided into camps in which no man trusted his fellow. To put an end to this, there was neither promise to be depended upon, nor oath that could command respect; but all parties dwelling rather in their calculation upon the hopelessness of a permanent state of things, were more intent upon self-defence than capable of confidence. In this contest the blunter wits were most successful. Apprehensive of their own deficiencies and of the cleverness of their antagonists, they feared to be worsted in debate and to be surprised by the combinations of their more versatile opponents, and so at once boldly had recourse to action: while their adversaries, arrogantly thinking that they should know in time, and that it was unnecessary to secure by action what policy afforded, often fell victims to their want of precaution.

Meanwhile Corcyra gave the first example of most of the crimes alluded to; of the reprisals exacted by the governed who had never experienced equitable treatment or indeed aught but insolence from their rulers - when their hour came; of the iniquitous resolves of those who desired to get rid of their accustomed poverty, and ardently coveted their neighbours' goods; and lastly, of the savage and pitiless excesses into which men who had begun the struggle, not in a class but in a party spirit, were hurried by their ungovernable passions. In the confusion into which life was now thrown in the cities, human nature, always rebelling against the law and now its master, gladly showed itself ungoverned in passion, above respect for justice, and the enemy of all superiority; since revenge would not have been set above religion, and gain above justice, had it not been for the fatal power of envy. Indeed men too often take upon themselves in the prosecution of their revenge to set the example of doing away with those general laws to which all alike can look for salvation in adversity, instead of allowing them to subsist against the day of danger when their aid may be required.

While the revolutionary passions thus for the first time displayed themselves in the factions of Corcyra, Eurymedon and the Athenian fleet sailed away; after which some five hundred Corcyraean exiles who had succeeded in escaping, took some forts on the mainland, and becoming masters of the Corcyraean territory over the water, made this their base to Plunder their countrymen in the island, and did so much damage as to cause a severe famine in the town. They also sent envoys to Lacedaemon and Corinth to negotiate their restoration; but meeting with no success, afterwards got together boats and mercenaries and crossed over to the island, being about six hundred in all; and burning their boats so as to have no hope except in becoming masters of the country, went up to Mount Istone, and fortifying themselves there, began to annoy those in the city and obtained command of the country.

At the close of the same summer the Athenians sent twenty ships under the command of Laches, son of Melanopus, and Charoeades, son of Euphiletus, to Sicily, where the Syracusans and Leontines were at war. The Syracusans had for allies all the Dorian cities except Camarina - these had been included in the Lacedaemonian confederacy from the commencement of the war, though they had not taken any active part in it - the Leontines had Camarina and the Chalcidian cities. In Italy the Locrians were for the Syracusans, the Rhegians for their Leontine kinsmen. The allies of the Leontines now sent to Athens and appealed to their ancient alliance and to their Ionian origin, to persuade the Athenians to send them a fleet, as the Syracusans were blockading them by land and sea. The Athenians sent it upon the plea of their common descent, but in reality to prevent the exportation of Sicilian corn to Peloponnese and to test the possibility of bringing Sicily into subjection. Accordingly they established themselves at Rhegium in Italy, and from thence carried on the war in concert with their allies.

CHAPTER XI

Year of the War - Campaigns of Demosthenes in Western Greece - Ruin of Ambracia

SUMMER WAS now over. The winter following, the plague a second time attacked the Athenians; for although it had never entirely left them, still there had been a notable abatement in its ravages. The second visit lasted no less than a year, the first having lasted two; and nothing distressed the Athenians and reduced their power more than this. No less than four thousand four hundred heavy infantry in the ranks died of it and three hundred cavalry, besides a number of the multitude that was never ascertained. At the same time took place the numerous earthquakes in Athens, Euboea, and Boeotia, particularly at Orchomenus in the last-named country.

The same winter the Athenians in Sicily and the Rhegians, with thirty ships, made an expedition against the islands of Aeolus; it being impossible to invade them in summer, owing to the want of water. These islands are occupied by the Liparaeans, a Cnidian colony, who live in one of them of no great size called Lipara; and from this as their headquarters cultivate the rest, Didyme, Strongyle, and Hiera. In Hiera the people in those parts believe that Hephaestus has his forge, from the quantity of flame which they see it send out by night, and of smoke by day. These islands lie off the coast of the Sicels and Messinese, and were allies of the Syracusans. The Athenians laid waste their land, and as the inhabitants did not submit, sailed back to Rhegium. Thus the winter ended, and with it ended the fifth year of this war, of which Thucydides was the historian.

The next summer the Peloponnesians and their allies set out to invade Attica under the command of Agis, son of Archidamus, and went as far as the Isthmus, but numerous earthquakes occurring, turned back again without the invasion taking place. About the same time that these earthquakes were so common, the sea at Orobiae, in Euboea, retiring from the then line of coast, returned in a huge wave and invaded a great part of the town, and retreated leaving some of it still under water; so that what was once land is now sea; such of the inhabitants perishing as could not run up to the higher ground in time. A similar inundation also occurred at Atalanta, the island off the Opuntian Locrian coast, carrying away part of the Athenian fort and wrecking one of two ships which were drawn up on the beach. At Peparethus also the sea retreated a little, without however any inundation following; and an earthquake threw down part of the wall, the town hall, and a few other buildings. The cause, in my opinion, of this phenomenon must be sought in the earthquake. At the point where its shock has been the most violent, the sea is driven back and, suddenly recoiling with redoubled force, causes the inundation. Without an earthquake I do not see how such an accident could happen.

During the same summer different operations were carried on by the different belligerents in Sicily; by the Siceliots themselves against each other, and by the Athenians and their allies: I shall however confine myself to the actions in which the Athenians took part, choosing the most important. The death of the Athenian general Charoeades, killed by the Syracusans in battle, left Laches in the sole command of the fleet, which he now directed in concert with the allies against Mylae, a place belonging to the Messinese. Two Messinese battalions in garrison at Mylae laid an ambush for the party landing from the ships, but were routed with great slaughter by the Athenians and their allies, who thereupon assaulted the fortification and compelled them to surrender the Acropolis and to march with them upon Messina. This town afterwards also submitted upon the approach of the Athenians and their allies, and gave hostages and all other securities required.

The same summer the Athenians sent thirty ships round Peloponnese under Demosthenes, son of Alcisthenes, and Procles, son of Theodorus, and sixty others, with two thousand heavy infantry, against Melos, under Nicias, son of Niceratus; wishing to reduce the Melians, who, although islanders, refused to be subjects of Athens or even to join her confederacy. The devastation of their land not procuring their submission, the fleet, weighing from Melos, sailed to Oropus in the territory of Graea, and landing at nightfall, the heavy infantry started at once from the ships by land for Tanagra in Boeotia, where they were met by the whole levy from Athens, agreeably to a concerted signal, under the command of Hipponicus, son of Callias, and Eurymedon, son of Thucles. They encamped, and passing that day in ravaging the Tanagraean territory, remained there for the night; and next day, after defeating those of the Tanagraeans who sailed out against them and some Thebans who had come up to help the Tanagraeans, took some arms, set up a trophy, and retired, the troops to the city and the others to the ships. Nicias with his sixty ships coasted alongshore and ravaged the Locrian seaboard, and so returned home.

About this time the Lacedaemonians founded their colony of Heraclea in Trachis, their object being the following: the Malians form in all three tribes, the Paralians, the Hiereans, and the Trachinians. The last of these having suffered severely in a war with their neighbours the Oetaeans, at first intended to give themselves up to Athens; but afterwards fearing not to find in her the security that they sought, sent to Lacedaemon, having chosen Tisamenus for their ambassador. In this embassy joined also the Dorians from the mother country of the Lacedaemonians, with the same request, as they themselves also suffered from the same enemy. After hearing them, the Lacedaemonians determined to send out the colony, wishing to assist the Trachinians and Dorians, and also because they thought that the proposed town would lie conveniently for the purposes of the war against the Athenians. A fleet might be got ready there against Euboea, with the advantage of a short passage to the island; and the town would also be useful as a station on the road to Thrace. In short, everything made the Lacedaemonians eager to found the place. After first consulting the god at Delphi and receiving a favourable answer, they sent off the colonists, Spartans, and Perioeci, inviting also any of the rest of the Hellenes who might wish to accompany them, except Ionians, Achaeans, and certain other nationalities; three Lacedaemonians leading as founders of the colony, Leon, Alcidas, and Damagon. The settlement effected, they fortified anew the city, now called Heraclea, distant about four miles and a half from Thermopylae and two miles and a quarter from the sea, and commenced building docks, closing the side towards Thermopylae just by the pass itself, in order that they might be easily defended.

The foundation of this town, evidently meant to annoy Euboea (the passage across to Cenaeum in that island being a short one), at first caused some alarm at Athens, which the event however did nothing to justify, the town never giving them any trouble. The reason of this was as follows. The Thessalians, who were sovereign in those parts, and whose territory was menaced by its foundation, were afraid that it might prove a very powerful neighbour, and accordingly continually harassed and made war upon the new settlers, until they at last wore them out in spite of their originally considerable numbers, people flocking from all quarters to a place founded by the Lacedaemonians, and thus thought secure of prosperity. On the other hand the Lacedaemonians themselves, in the persons of their governors, did their full share towards ruining its prosperity and reducing its population, as they frightened away the greater part of the inhabitants by governing harshly and in some cases not fairly, and thus made it easier for their neighbours to prevail against them.

The same summer, about the same time that the Athenians were detained at Melos, their fellow citizens in the thirty ships cruising round Peloponnese, after cutting off some guards in an ambush at Ellomenus in Leucadia, subsequently went against Leucas itself with a large armament, having been reinforced by the whole levy of the Acarnanians except Oeniadae, and by the Zacynthians and Cephallenians and fifteen ships from Corcyra. While the

Leucadians witnessed the devastation of their land, without and within the isthmus upon which the town of Leucas and the temple of Apollo stand, without making any movement on account of the overwhelming numbers of the enemy, the Acarnanians urged Demosthenes, the Athenian general, to build a wall so as to cut off the town from the continent, a measure which they were convinced would secure its capture and rid them once and for all of a most troublesome enemy.

Demosthenes however had in the meanwhile been persuaded by the Messenians that it was a fine opportunity for him, having so large an army assembled, to attack the Aetolians, who were not only the enemies of Naupactus, but whose reduction would further make it easy to gain the rest of that part of the continent for the Athenians. The Aetolian nation, although numerous and warlike, yet dwelt in unwalled villages scattered far apart, and had nothing but light armour, and might, according to the Messenians, be subdued without much difficulty before succours could arrive. The plan which they recommended was to attack first the Apodotians, next the Ophionians, and after these the Eurytanians, who are the largest tribe in Aetolia, and speak, as is said, a language exceedingly difficult to understand, and eat their flesh raw. These once subdued, the rest would easily come in.

To this plan Demosthenes consented, not only to please the Messenians, but also in the belief that by adding the Aetolians to his other continental allies he would be able, without aid from home, to march against the Boeotians by way of Ozolian Locris to Kytinium in Doris, keeping Parnassus on his right until he descended to the Phocians, whom he could force to join him if their ancient friendship for Athens did not, as he anticipated, at once decide them to do so. Arrived in Phocis he was already upon the frontier of Boeotia. He accordingly weighed from Leucas, against the wish of the Acarnanians, and with his whole armament sailed along the coast to Sollium, where he communicated to them his intention; and upon their refusing to agree to it on account of the non-investment of Leucas, himself with the rest of the forces, the Cephallenians, the Messenians, and Zacynthians, and three hundred Athenian marines from his own ships (the fifteen Corcyraean vessels having departed), started on his expedition against the Aetolians. His base he established at Oeneon in Locris, as the Ozolian Locrians were allies of Athens and were to meet him with all their forces in the interior. Being neighbours of the Aetolians and armed in the same way, it was thought that they would be of great service upon the expedition, from their acquaintance with the localities and the warfare of the inhabitants.

After bivouacking with the army in the precinct of Nemean Zeus, in which the poet Hesiod is said to have been killed by the people of the country, according to an oracle which had foretold that he should die in Nemea, Demosthenes set out at daybreak to invade Aetolia. The first day he took Potidania, the next Krokyle, and the third Tichium, where he halted and sent back the booty to Eupalium in Locris, having determined to pursue his conquests as far as the Ophionians, and, in the event of their refusing to submit, to return to Naupactus and make them the objects of a second expedition. Meanwhile the Aetolians had been aware of his design from the moment of its formation, and as soon as the army invaded their country came up in great force with all their tribes; even the most remote Ophionians, the Bomiensians, and Calliensians, who extend towards the Malian Gulf, being among the number.

The Messenians, however, adhered to their original advice. Assuring Demosthenes that the Aetolians were an easy conquest, they urged him to push on as rapidly as possible, and to try to take the villages as fast as he came up to them, without waiting until the whole nation should be in arms against him. Led on by his advisers and trusting in his fortune, as he had met with no opposition, without waiting for his Locrian reinforcements, who were to have supplied him with the light-armed darters in which he was most deficient, he advanced and stormed Aegitium, the inhabitants flying before him and posting themselves upon the hills above the town, which stood on high ground about nine miles from the sea. Meanwhile the Aetolians had gathered to the rescue, and now attacked the Athenians and their allies, running down from the hills on every side and darting their javelins, falling back when the Athenian army advanced, and coming on as it retired; and for a long while the battle was of this character, alternate advance and retreat, in both which operations the Athenians had the worst.

Still as long as their archers had arrows left and were able to use them, they held out, the light-armed Aetolians retiring before the arrows; but after the captain of the archers had been killed and his men scattered, the soldiers, wearied out with the constant repetition of the same exertions and hard pressed by the Aetolians with their javelins, at last turned and fled, and falling into pathless gullies and places that they were unacquainted with, thus perished, the Messenian Chromon, their guide, having also unfortunately been killed. A great many were overtaken in the pursuit by the swift-footed and light-armed Aetolians, and fell beneath their javelins; the greater number however missed their road and rushed into the wood, which had no ways out, and which was soon fired and burnt round them by the enemy. Indeed the Athenian army fell victims to death in every form, and suffered all the vicissitudes of flight; the survivors escaped with difficulty to the sea and Oeneon in Locris, whence they had set out. Many of the allies were killed, and about one hundred and twenty Athenian heavy infantry, not a man less, and all in the prime of life. These were by far the best men in the city of Athens that fell during this war. Among the slain was also Procles, the colleague of Demosthenes. Meanwhile the Athenians took up their dead under truce from the Aetolians, and retired to Naupactus, and from thence went in their ships to Athens; Demosthenes staying behind in Naupactus and in the neighbourhood, being afraid to face the Athenians after the disaster.

About the same time the Athenians on the coast of Sicily sailed to Locris, and in a descent which they made from the ships defeated the Locrians who came against them, and took a fort upon the river Halex.

The same summer the Aetolians, who before the Athenian expedition had sent an embassy to Corinth and Lacedaemon, composed of Tolophus, an Ophionian, Boriades, an Eurytanian, and Tisander, an Apodotian, obtained that an army should be sent them against Naupactus, which had invited the Athenian invasion. The Lacedaemonians accordingly sent off towards autumn three thousand heavy infantry of the allies, five hundred of whom were from Heraclea, the newly founded city in Trachis, under the command of Eurylochus, a Spartan, accompanied by Macarius and Menedaius, also Spartans.

The army having assembled at Delphi, Eurylochus sent a herald to the Ozolian Locrians; the road to Naupactus lying through their territory, and he having besides conceived the idea of detaching them from Athens. His chief abettors in Locris were the Amphissians, who were alarmed at the hostility of the Phocians. These first gave hostages themselves, and induced the rest to do the same for fear of the invading army; first, their neighbours the Myonians, who held the most difficult of the passes, and after them the Ipnians, Messapians, Tritaeans, Chalaeans, Tolophonians, Hessians, and Oeanthians, all of whom joined in the expedition; the Olpaeans contenting themselves with giving hostages, without accompanying the invasion; and the Hyaeans refusing to do either, until the capture of Polis, one of their villages.

His preparations completed, Eurylochus lodged the hostages in Kytinium, in Doris, and advanced upon Naupactus through the country of the Locrians, taking upon his way Oeneon and Eupalium, two of their towns that refused to join him. Arrived in the Naupactian territory, and having been now joined by the Aetolians, the army laid waste the land and took the suburb of the town, which was unfortified; and after this Molycrium also, a Corinthian colony subject to Athens. Meanwhile the Athenian Demosthenes, who since the affair in Aetolia had remained near

Naupactus, having had notice of the army and fearing for the town, went and persuaded the Acarnanians, although not without difficulty because of his departure from Leucas, to go to the relief of Naupactus. They accordingly sent with him on board his ships a thousand heavy infantry, who threw themselves into the place and saved it; the extent of its wall and the small number of its defenders otherwise placing it in the greatest danger. Meanwhile Eurylochus and his companions, finding that this force had entered and that it was impossible to storm the town, withdrew, not to Peloponnese, but to the country once called Aeolis, and now Calydon and Pleuron, and to the places in that neighbourhood, and Proschium in Aetolia; the Ambraciots having come and urged them to combine with them in attacking Amphilochian Argos and the rest of Amphilochia and Acarnania; affirming that the conquest of these countries would bring all the continent into alliance with Lacedaemon. To this Eurylochus consented, and dismissing the Aetolians, now remained quiet with his army in those parts, until the time should come for the Ambraciots to take the field, and for him to join them before Argos.

Summer was now over. The winter ensuing, the Athenians in Sicily with their Hellenic allies, and such of the Sicel subjects or allies of Syracuse as had revolted from her and joined their army, marched against the Sicel town Inessa, the acropolis of which was held by the Syracusans, and after attacking it without being able to take it, retired. In the retreat, the allies retreating after the Athenians were attacked by the Syracusans from the fort, and a large part of their army routed with great slaughter. After this, Laches and the Athenians from the ships made some descents in Locris, and defeating the Locrians, who came against them with Proxenus, son of Capaton, upon the river Caicinus, took some arms and departed.

The same winter the Athenians purified Delos, in compliance, it appears, with a certain oracle. It had been purified before by Pisistratus the tyrant; not indeed the whole island, but as much of it as could be seen from the temple. All of it was, however, now purified in the following way. All the sepulchres of those that had died in Delos were taken up, and for the future it was commanded that no one should be allowed either to die or to give birth to a child in the island; but that they should be carried over to Rhenea, which is so near to Delos that Polycrates, tyrant of Samos, having added Rhenea to his other island conquests during his period of naval ascendancy, dedicated it to the Delian Apollo by binding it to Delos with a chain.

The Athenians, after the purification, celebrated, for the first time, the quinquennial festival of the Delian games. Once upon a time, indeed, there was a great assemblage of the Ionians and the neighbouring islanders at Delos, who used to come to the festival, as the Ionians now do to that of Ephesus, and athletic and poetical contests took place there, and the cities brought choirs of dancers. Nothing can be clearer on this point than the following verses of Homer, taken from a hymn to Apollo:

Phoebus, wherever thou strayest, far or near,
Delos was still of all thy haunts most dear.
Thither the robed Ionians take their way
With wife and child to keep thy holiday,
Invoke thy favour on each manly game,
And dance and sing in honour of thy name.

That there was also a poetical contest in which the Ionians went to contend, again is shown by the following, taken from the same hymn. After celebrating the Delian dance of the women, he ends his song of praise with these verses, in which he also alludes to himself:

Well, may Apollo keep you all! and so,
Sweethearts, good-bye - yet tell me not I go
Out from your hearts; and if in after hours
Some other wanderer in this world of ours
Touch at your shores, and ask your maidens here
Who sings the songs the sweetest to your ear,

Think of me then, and answer with a smile,

'A blind old man of Scio's rocky isle.'

Homer thus attests that there was anciently a great assembly and festival at Delos. In later times, although the islanders and the Athenians continued to send the choirs of dancers with sacrifices, the contests and most of the ceremonies were abolished, probably through adversity, until the Athenians celebrated the games upon this occasion with the novelty of horse-races.

The same winter the Ambraciots, as they had promised Eurylochus when they retained his army, marched out against Amphilochian Argos with three thousand heavy infantry, and invading the Argive territory occupied Olpae, a stronghold on a hill near the sea, which had been formerly fortified by the Acarnanians and used as the place of assizes for their nation, and which is about two miles and three-quarters from the city of Argos upon the sea-coast. Meanwhile the Acarnanians went with a part of their forces to the relief of Argos, and with the rest encamped in Amphilochia at the place called Crenae, or the Wells, to watch for Eurylochus and his Peloponnesians, and to prevent their passing through and effecting their junction with the Ambraciots; while they also sent for Demosthenes, the commander of the Aetolian expedition, to be their leader, and for the twenty Athenian ships that were cruising off Peloponnese under the command of Aristotle, son of Timocrates, and Hierophon, son of Antimnestus. On their part, the Ambraciots at Olpae sent a messenger to their own city, to beg them to come with their whole levy to their assistance, fearing that the army of Eurylochus might not be able to pass through the Acarnanians, and that they might themselves be obliged to fight single-handed, or be unable to retreat, if they wished it, without danger.

Meanwhile Eurylochus and his Peloponnesians, learning that the Ambraciots at Olpae had arrived, set out from Proschium with all haste to join them, and crossing the Achelous advanced through Acarnania, which they found deserted by its population, who had gone to the relief of Argos; keeping on their right the city of the Stratians and its garrison, and on their left the rest of Acarnania. Traversing the territory of the Stratians, they advanced through Phytia, next, skirting Medeon, through Limnaea; after which they left Acarnania behind them and entered a friendly country, that of the Agraeans. From thence they reached and crossed Mount Thymaus, which belongs to the Agraeans, and descended into the Argive territory after nightfall, and passing between the city of Argos and the Acarnanian posts at Crenae, joined the Ambraciots at Olpae.

Uniting here at daybreak, they sat down at the place called Metropolis, and encamped. Not long afterwards the Athenians in the twenty ships came into the Ambracian Gulf to support the Argives, with Demosthenes and two hundred Messenian heavy infantry, and sixty Athenian archers. While the fleet off Olpae blockaded the hill from the sea, the Acarnanians and a few of the Amphilochians, most of whom were kept back by force by the Ambraciots, had already arrived at Argos, and were preparing to give battle to the enemy, having chosen Demosthenes to command the whole of the allied army in concert with their own generals. Demosthenes led them near to Olpae and encamped, a great ravine separating the two armies. During five days they remained inactive; on the sixth both sides formed in order of battle. The army of the Peloponnesians was the largest and outflanked their opponents; and Demosthenes fearing that his right might be surrounded, placed in ambush in a hollow way overgrown with bushes some four hundred heavy infantry and light troops, who were to rise up at the moment of the onset behind the projecting left wing of the enemy, and to take them in the rear. When both sides were ready they joined battle; Demosthenes being on the right wing with the Messenians and a few Athenians, while the rest of the line was made up of the different divisions of the Acarnanians, and of the Amphilochian carters. The Peloponnesians and Ambraciots were drawn up pell-mell together, with the exception of the Mantineans, who were massed on the left, without however reaching to the extremity of the wing, where Eurylochus and his men confronted the Messenians and Demosthenes.

The Peloponnesians were now well engaged and with their outflanking wing were upon the point of turning their enemy's right; when the Acarnanians from the ambuscade set upon them from behind, and broke them at the first attack, without their staying to resist; while the panic into which they fell caused the flight of most of their army, terrified beyond measure at seeing the division of Eurylochus and their best troops cut to pieces. Most of the work was done by Demosthenes and his Messenians, who were posted in this part of the field. Meanwhile the Ambraciots (who are the best soldiers in those countries) and the troops upon the right wing, defeated the division opposed to them and pursued it to Argos. Returning from the pursuit, they found their main body defeated; and hard pressed by the Acarnanians, with difficulty made good their passage to Olpae, suffering heavy loss on the way, as they dashed on without discipline or order, the Mantineans excepted, who kept their ranks best of any in the army during the retreat.

The battle did not end until the evening. The next day Menedaius, who on the death of Eurylochus and Macarius had succeeded to the sole command, being at a loss after so signal a defeat how to stay and sustain a siege, cut off as he was by land and by the Athenian fleet by sea, and equally so how to retreat in safety, opened a parley with Demosthenes and the Acarnanian generals for a truce and permission to retreat, and at the same time for the recovery of the dead. The dead they gave back to him, and setting up a trophy took up their own also to the number of about three hundred. The retreat demanded they refused publicly to the army; but permission to depart without delay was secretly granted to the Mantineans and to Menedaius and the other commanders and principal men of the Peloponnesians by Demosthenes and his Acarnanian colleagues; who desired to strip the Ambraciots and the mercenary host of foreigners of their supporters; and, above all, to discredit the Lacedaemonians and Peloponnesians with the Hellenes in those parts, as traitors and self-seekers.

While the enemy was taking up his dead and hastily burying them as he could, and those who obtained permission were secretly planning their retreat, word was brought to Demosthenes and the Acarnanians that the Ambraciots from the city, in compliance with the first message from Olpae, were on the march with their whole levy through Amphilochia to join their countrymen at Olpae, knowing nothing of what had occurred. Demosthenes prepared to march with his army against them, and meanwhile sent on at once a strong division to beset the roads and occupy the strong positions. In the meantime the Mantineans and others included in the agreement went out under the pretence of gathering herbs and firewood, and stole off by twos and threes, picking on the way the things which they professed to have come out for, until they had gone some distance from Olpae, when they quickened their pace. The Ambraciots and such of the rest as had accompanied them in larger parties, seeing them going on, pushed on in their turn, and began running in order to catch them up. The Acarnanians at first thought that all alike were departing without permission, and began to pursue the Peloponnesians; and believing that they were being betrayed, even threw a dart or two at some of their generals who tried to stop them and told them that leave had been given. Eventually, however, they let pass the Mantineans and Peloponnesians, and slew only the Ambraciots, there being much dispute and difficulty in distinguishing whether a man was an Ambraciot or a Peloponnesian. The number thus slain was about two hundred; the rest escaped into the bordering territory of Agraea, and found refuge with Salynthius, the friendly king of the Agraeans.

Meanwhile the Ambraciots from the city arrived at Idomene. Idomene consists of two lofty hills, the higher of which the troops sent on by Demosthenes succeeded in occupying after nightfall, unobserved by the Ambraciots, who had meanwhile ascended the smaller and bivouacked under it. After supper Demosthenes set out with the rest of the army, as soon as it was evening; himself with half his force making for the pass, and the remainder going by the Amphilochian hills. At dawn he fell upon the Ambraciots while they were still abed, ignorant of what had passed, and fully thinking that it was their own countrymen - Demosthenes having purposely put the Messenians in front with orders to address them in the Doric dialect, and thus to inspire confidence in the sentinels, who would not be able to see them as it was still night. In this way he routed their army as soon as he attacked it, slaying most of them where they were, the rest breaking away in flight over the hills. The roads, however, were already occupied, and while the Amphilochians knew their own country, the Ambraciots were ignorant of it and could not tell which way to turn, and had also heavy armour as against a light-armed enemy, and so fell into ravines and into the ambushes which had been set for them, and perished there. In their manifold efforts to escape some even turned to the sea, which was not far off, and seeing the Athenian ships coasting alongshore just while the action was going on, swam off to them, thinking it better in the panic they were in, to perish, if perish they must, by the hands of the Athenians, than by those of the barbarous and detested Amphilochians. Of the large Ambraciot force destroyed in this manner, a few only reached the city in safety; while the Acarnanians, after stripping the dead and setting up a trophy, returned to Argos.

The next day arrived a herald from the Ambraciots who had fled from Olpae to the Agraeans, to ask leave to take up the dead that had fallen after the first engagement, when they left the camp with the Mantineans and their companions, without, like them, having had permission to do so. At the sight of the arms of the Ambraciots from the city, the herald was astonished at their number, knowing nothing of the disaster and fancying that they were those of their own party. Some one asked him what he was so astonished at, and how many of them had been killed, fancying in his turn that this was the herald from the troops at Idomene. He replied: "About two hundred"; upon which his interrogator took him up, saying: "Why, the arms you see here are of more than a thousand." The herald replied: "Then they are not the arms of those who fought with us?" The other answered: "Yes, they are, if at least you fought at Idomene yesterday." "But we fought with no one yesterday; but the day before in the retreat." "However that may be, we fought yesterday with those who came to reinforce you from the city of the Ambraciots." When the herald heard this and knew that the reinforcement from the city had been destroyed, he broke into wailing and, stunned at the magnitude of the present evils, went away at once without having performed his errand, or again asking for the dead bodies. Indeed, this was by far the greatest disaster that befell any one Hellenic city in an equal number of days during this war; and I have not set down the number of the dead, because the amount stated seems so out of proportion to the size of the city as to be incredible. In any case I know that if the Acarnanians and Amphilochians had wished to take Ambracia as the Athenians and Demosthenes advised, they would have done so without a blow; as it was, they feared that if the Athenians had it they would be worse neighbours to them than the present.

After this the Acarnanians allotted a third of the spoils to the Athenians, and divided the rest among their own different towns. The share of the Athenians was captured on the voyage home; the arms now deposited in the Attic temples are three hundred panoplies, which the Acarnanians set apart for Demosthenes, and which he brought to Athens in person, his return to his country after the Aetolian disaster being rendered less hazardous by this exploit. The Athenians in the twenty ships also went off to Naupactus. The Acarnanians and Amphilochians, after the departure of Demosthenes and the Athenians, granted the Ambraciots and Peloponnesians who had taken refuge with Salynthius and the Agraeans a free retreat from Oeniadae, to which place they had removed from the country of Salynthius, and for the future concluded with the Ambraciots a treaty and alliance for one hundred years, upon the terms following. It was to be a defensive, not an offensive alliance; the Ambraciots could not be required to march with the Acarnanians against the Peloponnesians, nor the Acarnanians with the Ambraciots against the Athenians; for the rest the Ambraciots were to give up the places and hostages that they held of the Amphilochians, and not to give help to Anactorium, which was at enmity with the Acarnanians. With this arrangement they put an end to the war. After this the Corinthians sent a garrison of their own citizens to Ambracia, composed of three hundred heavy infantry, under the command of Xenocleides, son of Euthycles, who reached their destination after a difficult journey across the continent. Such was the history of the affair of Ambracia.

The same winter the Athenians in Sicily made a descent from their ships upon the territory of Himera, in concert with the Sicels, who had invaded its borders from the interior, and also sailed to the islands of Aeolus. Upon their return to Rhegium they found the Athenian general, Pythodorus, son of Isolochus, come to supersede Laches in the command of the fleet. The allies in Sicily had sailed to Athens and induced the Athenians to send out more vessels to their assistance, pointing out that the Syracusans who already commanded their land were making efforts to get together a navy, to avoid being any longer excluded from the sea by a few vessels. The Athenians proceeded to man forty ships to send to them, thinking that the war in Sicily would thus be the sooner ended, and also wishing to exercise their navy. One of the generals, Pythodorus, was accordingly sent out with a few ships; Sophocles, son of Sostratides, and Eurymedon, son of Thucles, being destined to follow with the main body. Meanwhile Pythodorus had taken the command of Laches' ships, and towards the end of winter sailed against the Locrian fort, which Laches had formerly taken, and returned after being defeated in battle by the Locrians.

In the first days of this spring, the stream of fire issued from Etna, as on former occasions, and destroyed some land of the Catanians, who live upon Mount Etna, which is the largest mountain in Sicily. Fifty years, it is said, had elapsed since the last eruption, there having been three in all since the Hellenes have inhabited Sicily. Such were the events of this winter; and with it ended the sixth year of this war, of which Thucydides was the historian.

CHAPTER XII

Seventh Year of the War - Occupation of Pylos -
Surrender of the Spartan Army in Sphacteria

NEXT SUMMER, about the time of the corn's coming into ear, ten Syracusan and as many Locrian vessels sailed to Messina, in Sicily, and occupied the town upon the invitation of the inhabitants; and Messina revolted from the Athenians. The Syracusans contrived this chiefly because they saw that the place afforded an approach to Sicily, and feared that the Athenians might hereafter use it as a base for attacking them with a larger force; the Locrians because they wished to carry on hostilities from both sides of the strait and to reduce their enemies, the people of Rhegium. Meanwhile, the Locrians had invaded the Rhegian territory with all their forces, to prevent their succouring Messina, and also at the instance of some exiles from Rhegium who were with them; the long factions by which that town had been torn rendering it for the moment incapable of resistance, and thus furnishing an additional temptation to the invaders. After devastating the country the Locrian land forces retired, their ships remaining to guard Messina, while others were being manned for the same destination to carry on the war from thence.

About the same time in the spring, before the corn was ripe, the Peloponnesians and their allies invaded Attica under Agis, the son of Archidamus, king of the Lacedaemonians, and sat down and laid waste the country. Meanwhile the Athenians sent off the forty ships which they had been preparing to Sicily, with the remaining generals Eurymedon and Sophocles; their colleague Pythodorus having already preceded them thither. These had also instructions as they sailed by to look to the Corcyraeans in the town, who were being plundered by the exiles in the mountain. To support these exiles sixty Peloponnesian vessels had lately sailed, it being thought that the famine raging in the city would make it easy for them to reduce it. Demosthenes also, who had remained without employment since his return from Acarnania, applied and obtained permission to use the fleet, if he wished it, upon the coast of Peloponnese.

Off Laconia they heard that the Peloponnesian ships were already at Corcyra, upon which Eurymedon and Sophocles wished to hasten to the island, but Demosthenes required them first to touch at Pylos and do what was wanted there, before continuing their voyage. While they were making objections, a squall chanced to come on and carried the fleet into Pylos. Demosthenes at once urged them to fortify the place, it being for this that he had come on the voyage, and made them observe there was plenty of stone and timber on the spot, and that the place was strong by nature, and together with much of the country round unoccupied; Pylos, or Coryphasium, as the Lacedaemonians call it, being about forty-five miles distant from Sparta, and situated in the old country of the Messenians. The commanders told him that there was no lack of desert headlands in Peloponnese if he wished to put the city to expense by occupying them. He, however, thought that this place was distinguished from others of the kind by having a harbour close by; while the Messenians, the old natives of the country, speaking the same dialect as the Lacedaemonians, could do them the greatest mischief by their incursions from it, and would at the same time be a trusty garrison.

After speaking to the captains of companies on the subject, and failing to persuade either the generals or the soldiers, he remained inactive with the rest from stress of weather; until the soldiers themselves wanting occupation were seized with a sudden impulse to go round and fortify the place. Accordingly they set to work in earnest, and having no iron tools, picked up stones, and put them together as they happened to fit, and where mortar was needed, carried it on their backs for want of hods, stooping down to make it stay on, and clasping their hands together behind to prevent it falling off; sparing no effort to be able to complete the most

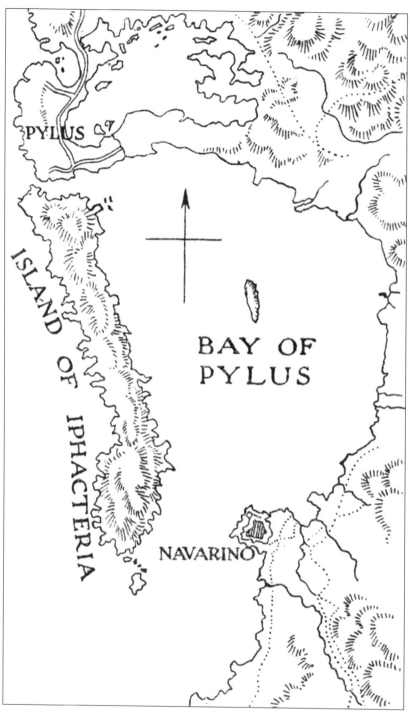

Pylos in Laconia

vulnerable points before the arrival of the Lacedaemonians, most of the place being sufficiently strong by nature without further fortifications.

Meanwhile the Lacedaemonians were celebrating a festival, and also at first made light of the news, in the idea that whenever they chose to take the field the place would be immediately evacuated by the enemy or easily taken by force; the absence of their army before Athens having also something to do with their delay. The Athenians fortified the place on the land side, and where it most required it, in six days, and leaving Demosthenes with five ships to garrison it, with the main body of the fleet hastened on their voyage to Corcyra and Sicily.

As soon as the Peloponnesians in Attica heard of the occupation of Pylos, they hurried back home; the Lacedaemonians and their king Agis thinking that the matter touched them nearly. Besides having made their invasion early in the season, and while the corn was still green, most of their troops were short of provisions: the weather also was unusually bad for the time of year, and greatly distressed their army. Many reasons thus combined to hasten their departure and to make this invasion a very short one; indeed they only stayed fifteen days in Attica.

About the same time the Athenian general Simonides getting together a few Athenians from the garrisons, and a number of the allies in those parts, took Eion in Thrace, a Mendaean colony and hostile to Athens, by treachery, but had no sooner done so than the Chalcidians and Bottiaeans came up and beat him out of it, with the loss of many of his soldiers.

On the return of the Peloponnesians from Attica, the Spartans themselves and the nearest of the Perioeci at once set out for Pylos, the other Lacedaemonians following more slowly, as they had just come in from another campaign. Word was also sent round Peloponnese to come up as quickly as possible to Pylos; while the sixty Peloponnesian ships were sent for from Corcyra, and being dragged by their crews across the isthmus of Leucas, passed unperceived by the Athenian squadron at Zacynthus, and reached Pylos, where the land forces had arrived before them. Before the Peloponnesian fleet sailed in, Demosthenes found time to send out unobserved two ships to inform Eurymedon and the Athenians on board the fleet at Zacynthus of the danger of Pylos and to summon them to his assistance. While the ships hastened on their voyage in obedience to the orders of Demosthenes, the Lacedaemonians prepared to assault the fort by land and sea, hoping to capture with ease a work constructed in haste, and held by a feeble garrison. Meanwhile, as they expected the Athenian ships to arrive from Zacynthus, they intended, if they failed to take the place before, to block up the entrances of the harbour to prevent their being able to anchor inside it. For the island of Sphacteria, stretching along in a line close in front of the harbour, at once makes it safe and narrows its entrances, leaving a passage for two ships on the side nearest Pylos and the Athenian fortifications, and for eight or nine on that next the rest of the mainland: for the rest, the island was entirely covered with wood, and without paths through not being inhabited, and about one mile and five furlongs in length. The inlets the Lacedaemonians meant to close with a line of ships placed close together, with their prows turned towards the sea, and, meanwhile, fearing that the enemy might make use of the island to operate against them, carried over some heavy infantry thither, stationing others along the coast. By this means the island and the continent would be alike hostile to the Athenians, as they would be unable to land on either; and the shore of Pylos itself outside the inlet towards the open sea having no harbour, and, therefore, presenting no point which they could use as a base to relieve their countrymen, they, the Lacedaemonians, without sea-fight or risk would in all probability become masters of the place, occupied as it had been on the spur of the moment, and unfurnished with provisions. This being determined, they carried over to the island the heavy infantry, drafted by lot from all the companies. Some others had crossed over before in relief parties, but these last who were left there were four hundred and twenty in number, with their Helot attendants, commanded by Epitadas, son of Molobrus.

Meanwhile Demosthenes, seeing the Lacedaemonians about to attack him by sea and land at once, himself was not idle. He drew up under the fortification and enclosed in a stockade the galleys remaining to him of those which had been left him, arming the sailors taken out of them with poor shields made most of them of osier, it being impossible to procure arms in such a desert place, and even these having been obtained from a thirty-oared Messenian privateer and a boat belonging to some Messenians who happened to have come to them. Among these Messenians were forty heavy infantry, whom he made use of with the rest. Posting most of his men, unarmed and armed, upon the best fortified and strong points of the place towards the interior, with orders to repel any attack of the land forces, he picked sixty heavy infantry and a few archers from his whole force, and with these went outside the wall down to the sea, where he thought that the enemy would most likely attempt to land. Although the ground was difficult and rocky, looking towards the open sea, the fact that this was the weakest part of the wall would, he thought, encourage their ardour, as the Athenians, confident in their naval superiority, had here paid little attention to their defences, and the enemy if he could force a landing might feel secure of taking the place. At this point, accordingly, going down to the water's edge, he posted his heavy infantry to prevent, if possible, a landing, and encouraged them in the following terms:

"Soldiers and comrades in this adventure, I hope that none of you in our present strait will think to show his wit by exactly calculating all the perils that encompass us, but that you will rather hasten to close with the enemy, without staying to count the odds, seeing in this your best chance of safety. In emergencies like ours calculation is out of place; the sooner the danger is faced the better. To my mind also most of the chances are for us, if we will only stand fast and not throw away our advantages, overawed by the numbers of the enemy. One of the points in our favour is the awkwardness of the landing. This, however, only helps us if we stand our ground. If we give way it will be practicable enough, in spite of its natural difficulty, without a defender; and the enemy will instantly become more formidable from the difficulty he will have in retreating, supposing that we succeed in repulsing him, which we shall find it easier to do, while he is on board his ships, than after he has landed and meets us on equal terms. As to his numbers, these need not too much alarm you. Large as they may be he can only engage in small detachments, from the impossibility of bringing to. Besides, the numerical superiority that we have to meet is not that of an army on land with everything else equal, but of troops on board ship, upon an element where many favourable accidents are required to act with effect. I therefore consider that his difficulties may be fairly set against our numerical deficiencies, and at the same time I charge you, as Athenians who know by experience what landing from ships on a hostile territory means, and how impossible it is to drive back an enemy determined enough to stand his ground and not to be frightened away by the surf and the terrors of the ships sailing in, to stand fast in the present emergency, beat back the enemy at the water's edge, and save yourselves and the place."

Thus encouraged by Demosthenes, the Athenians felt more confident, and went down to meet the enemy, posting themselves along the edge of the sea. The Lacedaemonians now put themselves in movement and simultaneously assaulted the fortification with their land forces and with their ships, forty-three in number, under their admiral, Thrasymelidas, son of Cratesicles, a Spartan, who made his attack just where Demosthenes expected. The Athenians had thus to defend themselves on both sides, from the land and from the sea; the enemy rowing up in small detachments, the one relieving the other - it being impossible for many to bring to at once - and showing great ardour and cheering each other on, in the endeavour to force a passage and to take the fortification. He who most distinguished himself was Brasidas. Captain of a galley, and seeing that the captains and steersmen, impressed by the difficulty of the position, hung back even where a landing might have seemed possible, for fear of wrecking their vessels, he shouted out to them, that they must never allow the enemy to fortify himself in their country for the sake of saving timber, but must shiver their vessels and force a landing; and bade the allies, instead of hesitating in such a moment to sacrifice their ships for Lacedaemon in return for her many benefits, to run them boldly aground, land in one way or another, and make themselves masters of the place and its garrison.

Not content with this exhortation, he forced his own steersman to run his ship ashore, and stepping on to the gangway, was endeavouring to land, when he was cut down by the Athenians, and after receiving many wounds fainted away. Falling into the bows, his shield slipped off his arm into the sea, and being thrown ashore was picked up by the Athenians, and afterwards used for the trophy which they set up for this attack. The rest also did their best, but were not able to land, owing to the difficulty of the ground and the unflinching tenacity of the Athenians. It was a strange reversal of the order of things for Athenians to be fighting from the land, and from Laconian land too, against Lacedaemonians coming from the sea; while Lacedaemonians were trying to land from shipboard in their own country, now become hostile, to attack Athenians, although the former were chiefly famous at the time as an inland people and superior by land, the latter as a maritime people with a navy that had no equal.

After continuing their attacks during that day and most of the next, the Peloponnesians desisted, and the day after sent some of their ships to Asine for timber to make engines, hoping to take by their aid, in spite of its height, the wall opposite the harbour, where the landing was easiest. At this moment the Athenian fleet from Zacynthus arrived, now numbering fifty sail, having been reinforced by some of the ships on guard at Naupactus and by four Chian vessels. Seeing the coast and the island both crowded with heavy infantry, and the hostile ships in harbour showing no signs of sailing out, at a loss where to anchor, they sailed for the moment to the desert island of Prote, not far off, where they passed the night. The next day they got under way in readiness to engage in the open sea if the enemy chose to put out to meet them, being determined in the event of his not doing so to sail in and attack him. The Lacedaemonians did not put out to sea, and having omitted to close the inlets as they had intended, remained quiet on shore, engaged in manning their ships and getting ready, in the case of any one sailing in, to fight in the harbour, which is a fairly large one.

Perceiving this, the Athenians advanced against them by each inlet, and falling on the enemy's fleet, most of which was by this time afloat and in line, at once put it to flight, and giving chase as far as the short distance allowed, disabled a good many vessels and took five, one with its crew on board; dashing in at the rest that had taken refuge on shore, and battering some that were still being manned, before they could put out, and lashing on to their own ships and towing off empty others whose crews had fled. At this sight the Lacedaemonians, maddened by a disaster which cut off their men on the island, rushed to the rescue, and going into the sea with their heavy armour, laid hold of the ships and tried to drag them back, each man thinking that success depended on his individual exertions. Great was the melee, and quite in contradiction to the naval tactics usual to the two combatants; the Lacedaemonians in their excitement and dismay being actually engaged in a sea-fight on land, while the victorious Athenians, in their eagerness to push their success as far as possible, were carrying on a land-fight from their ships. After great exertions and numerous wounds on both sides they separated, the Lacedaemonians saving their empty ships, except those first taken; and both parties returning to their camp, the Athenians set up a trophy, gave back the dead, secured the wrecks, and at once began to cruise round and jealously watch the island, with its intercepted garrison, while the Peloponnesians on the mainland, whose contingents had now all come up, stayed where they were before Pylos.

When the news of what had happened at Pylos reached Sparta, the disaster was thought so serious that the Lacedaemonians resolved that the authorities should go down to the camp, and decide on the spot what was best to be done. There, seeing that it was impossible to help their men, and not wishing to risk their being reduced by hunger or overpowered by numbers, they determined, with the consent of the Athenian generals, to conclude an armistice at Pylos and send envoys to Athens to obtain a convention, and to endeavour to get back their men as quickly as possible.

The generals accepting their offers, an armistice was concluded upon the terms following:

That the Lacedaemonians should bring to Pylos and deliver up to the Athenians the ships that had fought in the late engagement, and all in Laconia that were vessels of war, and should make no attack on the fortification either by land or by sea.

That the Athenians should allow the Lacedaemonians on the mainland to send to the men in the island a certain fixed quantity of corn ready kneaded, that is to say, two quarts of barley meal, one pint of wine, and a piece of meat for each man, and half the same quantity for a servant.

That this allowance should be sent in under the eyes of the Athenians, and that no boat should sail to the island except openly.

That the Athenians should continue to the island same as before, without however landing upon it, and should refrain from attacking the Peloponnesian troops either by land or by sea.

That if either party should infringe any of these terms in the slightest particular, the armistice should be at once void.

That the armistice should hold good until the return of the Lacedaemonian envoys from Athens - the Athenians sending them thither in a galley and bringing them back again - and upon the arrival of the envoys should be at an end, and the ships be restored by the Athenians in the same state as they received them.

Such were the terms of the armistice, and the ships were delivered over to the number of sixty, and the envoys sent off accordingly. Arrived at Athens they spoke as follows:

"Athenians, the Lacedaemonians sent us to try to find some way of settling the affair of our men on the island, that shall be at once satisfactory to our interests, and as consistent with our dignity in our misfortune as circumstances permit. We can venture to speak at some length without any departure from the habit of our country. Men of few words where many are not wanted, we can be less brief when there is a matter of importance to be illustrated and an end to be served by its illustration. Meanwhile we beg you to take what we may say, not in a hostile spirit, nor as if we thought you ignorant and wished to lecture you, but rather as a suggestion on the best course to be taken, addressed to intelligent judges. You can now, if you choose, employ your present success to advantage, so as to keep what you have got and gain honour and reputation besides, and you can avoid the mistake of those who meet with an extraordinary piece of good fortune, and are led on by hope to grasp continually at something further, through having already succeeded without expecting it. While those who have known most vicissitudes of good and bad, have also justly least faith in their prosperity; and to teach your city and ours this lesson experience has not been wanting.

"To be convinced of this you have only to look at our present misfortune. What power in Hellas stood higher than we did? and yet we are come to you, although we formerly thought ourselves more able to grant what we are now here to ask. Nevertheless, we have not been brought to this by any decay in our power, or through having our heads turned by aggrandizement; no, our resources are what they have always been, and our error has been an error of judgment, to which all are equally liable. Accordingly, the prosperity which your city now enjoys, and the accession that it has lately received, must not make you fancy that fortune will be always with you. Indeed sensible men are prudent enough to treat their gains as precarious, just as they would also keep a clear head in adversity, and think that war, so far from staying within the limit to which a combatant may wish to confine it, will run the course that its chances prescribe; and thus, not being puffed up by confidence in military success, they are less likely to come to grief, and most ready to make peace, if they can, while their fortune lasts. This, Athenians, you have a good opportunity to do now with us, and thus to escape the possible disasters which may follow upon your refusal, and the consequent imputation of having owed to accident even your present advantages, when you might have left behind you a reputation for power and wisdom which nothing could endanger.

"The Lacedaemonians accordingly invite you to make a treaty and to end the war, and offer peace and alliance and the most friendly and intimate relations in every way and on every occasion between us; and in return ask for the men on the island, thinking it better for both parties not to stand out to the end, on the chance of some favourable accident enabling the men to force their way out, or of their being compelled to succumb under the pressure of blockade. Indeed if great enmities are ever to be really settled, we think it will be, not by the system of revenge and military success, and by forcing an opponent to swear to a treaty to his disadvantage, but when the more fortunate combatant waives these his privileges, to be guided by gentler feelings conquers his rival in generosity, and accords peace on more moderate conditions than he expected. From that moment, instead of the debt of revenge which violence must entail, his adversary owes a debt of generosity to be paid in kind, and is inclined by honour to stand to his agreement. And men oftener act in this manner towards their greatest enemies than where the quarrel is of less importance; they are also by nature as glad to give way to those who first yield to them, as they are apt to be provoked by arrogance to risks condemned by their own judgment.

"To apply this to ourselves: if peace was ever desirable for both parties, it is surely so at the present moment, before anything irremediable befall us and force us to hate you eternally, personally as well as politically, and you to miss the advantages that we now offer you. While the issue is still in doubt, and you have reputation and our friendship in prospect, and we the compromise of our misfortune before anything fatal occur, let us be reconciled, and for ourselves choose peace instead of war, and grant to the rest of the Hellenes a remission from their sufferings, for which be sure they will think they have chiefly you to thank. The war that they labour under they know not which began, but the peace that concludes it, as it depends on your decision, will by their gratitude be laid to your door. By such a decision you can become firm friends with the Lacedaemonians at their own invitation, which you do not force from them, but oblige them by accepting. And from this friendship consider the advantages that are likely to follow: when Attica and Sparta are at one, the rest of Hellas, be sure, will remain in respectful inferiority before its heads."

Such were the words of the Lacedaemonians, their idea being that the Athenians, already desirous of a truce and only kept back by their opposition, would joyfully accept a peace freely offered, and give back the men. The Athenians, however, having the men on the island, thought that the treaty would be ready for them whenever they chose to make it, and grasped at something further. Foremost to encourage them in this policy was Cleon, son of Cleaenetus, a popular leader of the time and very powerful with the multitude, who persuaded them to answer as follows: First, the men in the island must surrender themselves and their arms and be brought to Athens. Next, the Lacedaemonians must restore Nisaea, Pegae, Troezen, and Achaia, all places acquired not by arms, but by the previous convention, under which they had been ceded by Athens herself at a moment of disaster, when a truce was more necessary to her than at present. This done they might take back their men, and make a truce for as long as both parties might agree.

To this answer the envoys made no reply, but asked that commissioners might be chosen with whom they might confer on each point, and quietly talk the matter over and try to come to some agreement. Hereupon Cleon violently assailed them, saying that he knew from the first that they had no right intentions, and that it was clear enough now by their refusing to speak before the people, and wanting to confer in secret with a committee of two or three. No, if they meant anything honest let them say it out before all. The Lacedaemonians, however, seeing that whatever concessions they might be prepared to make in their misfortune, it was impossible for them to speak before the multitude and lose credit with their allies for a negotiation which might after all miscarry, and on the other hand, that the Athenians would never grant what they asked upon moderate terms, returned from Athens without having effected anything.

Their arrival at once put an end to the armistice at Pylos, and the Lacedaemonians asked back their ships according to the convention. The Athenians, however, alleged an attack on the fort in contravention of the truce, and other grievances seemingly not worth mentioning, and refused to give them back, insisting upon the clause by which the slightest infringement made the armistice void. The Lacedaemonians, after denying the contravention and protesting against their bad faith in the matter of the ships, went away and earnestly addressed themselves to the war. Hostilities were now carried on at Pylos upon both sides with vigour. The Athenians cruised round the island all day with two ships going different ways; and by night, except on the seaward side in windy weather, anchored round it with their whole fleet, which, having been reinforced by twenty ships from Athens come to aid in the blockade, now numbered seventy sail; while the Peloponnesians remained encamped on the continent, making attacks on the fort, and on the look-out for any opportunity which might offer itself for the deliverance of their men.

Meanwhile the Syracusans and their allies in Sicily had brought up to the squadron guarding Messina the reinforcement which we left them preparing, and carried on the war from thence, incited chiefly by the Locrians from hatred of the Rhegians, whose territory they had invaded with all their forces. The Syracusans also wished to try their fortune at sea, seeing that the Athenians had only a few ships actually at Rhegium, and hearing that the main fleet destined to join them was engaged in blockading the island. A naval victory, they thought, would enable them to blockade Rhegium by sea and land, and easily to reduce it; a success which would at once place their affairs upon a solid basis, the promontory of Rhegium in Italy and Messina in Sicily being so near each other that it would be impossible for the Athenians to cruise against them and command the strait. The strait in question consists of the sea between Rhegium and Messina, at the point where Sicily approaches nearest to the continent, and is the Charybdis through which the story makes Ulysses sail; and the narrowness of the passage and the strength of the current that pours in from the vast Tyrrhenian and Sicilian mains, have rightly given it a bad reputation.

In this strait the Syracusans and their allies were compelled to fight, late in the day, about the passage of a boat, putting out with rather more than thirty ships against sixteen Athenian and eight Rhegian vessels. Defeated by the Athenians they hastily set off, each for himself, to their own stations at Messina and Rhegium, with the loss of one ship; night coming on before the battle was finished. After this the Locrians retired from the Rhegian territory, and the ships of the Syracusans and their allies united and came to anchor at Cape Pelorus, in the territory of Messina, where their land forces joined them. Here the Athenians and Rhegians sailed up, and seeing the ships unmanned, made an attack, in which they in their turn lost one vessel, which was caught by a grappling iron, the crew saving themselves by swimming. After this the Syracusans got on board their ships, and while they were being towed alongshore to Messina, were again attacked by the Athenians, but suddenly got out to sea and became the assailants, and caused them to lose another vessel. After thus holding their own in the voyage alongshore and in the engagement as above described, the Syracusans sailed on into the harbour of Messina.

Meanwhile the Athenians, having received warning that Camarina was about to be betrayed to the Syracusans by Archias and his party, sailed thither; and the Messinese took this opportunity to attack by sea and land with all their forces their Chalcidian neighbour, Naxos. The first day they forced the Naxians to keep their walls, and laid waste their country; the next they sailed round with their ships, and laid waste their land on the river Akesines, while their land forces menaced the city. Meanwhile the Sicels came down from the high country in great numbers, to aid against the Messinese; and the Naxians, elated at the sight, and animated by a belief that the Leontines and their other Hellenic allies were coming to their support, suddenly sallied out from the town, and attacked and routed the Messinese, killing more than a thousand of them; while the remainder suffered severely in their retreat home, being attacked by the barbarians on the road, and most of them cut off. The ships put in to Messina, and afterwards dispersed for their different homes. The Leontines and their allies, with the Athenians, upon this at once turned their arms against the now weakened Messina, and attacked, the Athenians with their ships on the side of the harbour, and the land forces on that of the town. The Messinese, however, sallying out with Demoteles and some Locrians who had been left to garrison the city after the disaster, suddenly attacked and routed most of the Leontine army, killing a great number; upon seeing which the Athenians landed from their ships, and falling on the Messinese in disorder chased them back into the town, and setting up a trophy retired to Rhegium. After this the Hellenes in Sicily continued to make war on each other by land, without the Athenians.

Meanwhile the Athenians at Pylos were still besieging the Lacedaemonians in the island, the Peloponnesian forces on the continent remaining where they were. The blockade was very laborious for the Athenians from want of food and water; there was no spring except one in the citadel of Pylos itself, and that not a large one, and most of them were obliged to grub up the shingle on the sea beach and drink such water as they could find. They also suffered from want of room, being encamped in a narrow space; and as there was no anchorage for the ships, some took their meals on shore in their turn, while the others were anchored out at sea. But their greatest discouragement arose from the unexpectedly long time which it took to reduce a body of men shut up in a desert island, with only brackish water to drink, a matter which they had imagined would take them only a few days. The fact was that the Lacedaemonians had made advertisement for volunteers to carry into the island ground corn, wine, cheese, and any other food useful in a siege; high prices being offered, and freedom promised to any of the Helots who should succeed in doing so. The Helots accordingly were most forward to engage in this risky traffic, putting off from this or that part of Peloponnese, and running in by night on the seaward side of the island. They were best pleased, however, when they could catch a wind to carry them in. It was more easy to elude the look-out of the galleys, when it blew from the seaward, as it became impossible for them to anchor round the island; while the Helots had their boats rated at their value in money, and ran them ashore, without caring how they landed, being sure to find the soldiers waiting for them at the landing-places. But all who risked it in fair weather were taken. Divers also swam in under water from the harbour, dragging by a cord in skins poppyseed mixed with honey, and bruised linseed; these at first escaped notice, but afterwards a look-out was kept for them. In short, both sides tried every possible contrivance, the one to throw in provisions, and the other to prevent their introduction.

At Athens, meanwhile, the news that the army was in great distress, and that corn found its way in to the men in the island, caused no small perplexity; and the Athenians began to fear that winter might come on and find them still engaged in the blockade. They saw that the convoying of provisions round Peloponnese would be then impossible. The country offered no resources in itself, and even in summer they could not send round enough. The blockade of a place without harbours could no longer be kept up; and the men would either escape by the siege being abandoned, or would watch for bad weather and sail out in the boats that brought in their corn. What caused still more alarm was the attitude of the Lacedaemonians, who must, it was thought by the Athenians, feel themselves on strong ground not to send them any more envoys; and they began to repent having rejected the treaty. Cleon, perceiving the disfavour with which he was regarded for having stood in the way of the convention, now said that their informants did not speak the truth; and upon the messengers recommending them, if they did not believe them, to send some commissioners to see, Cleon himself and Theagenes were chosen by the Athenians as commissioners. Aware that he would now be obliged either to say what had been already said by the men whom he was slandering, or be proved a liar if he said the contrary, he told the Athenians, whom he saw to be not altogether disinclined for a fresh expedition, that instead of sending and wasting their time and opportunities, if they believed what was told them, they ought to sail against the men. And pointing at Nicias, son of Niceratus, then general, whom he hated, he tauntingly said that it would be easy, if they had men for generals, to sail with a force and take those in the island, and that if he had himself been in command, he would have done it.

Nicias, seeing the Athenians murmuring against Cleon for not sailing now if it seemed to him so easy, and further seeing himself the object of attack, told him that for all that the generals cared, he might take what force he chose and make the attempt. At first Cleon fancied that this resignation was merely a figure of speech, and was ready to go, but finding that it was seriously meant, he drew back, and said that Nicias, not he, was general, being now frightened, and having never supposed that Nicias would go so far as to retire in his favour. Nicias, however, repeated his offer, and resigned the command against Pylos, and called the Athenians to witness that he did so. And as the multitude is wont to do, the more Cleon shrank from the expedition and tried to back out of what he had said, the more they encouraged Nicias to hand over his command, and clamoured at Cleon to go. At last, not knowing how to get out of his words, he undertook the expedition, and came forward and said that he was not afraid of the Lacedaemonians, but would sail without taking any one from the city with him, except the Lemnians and Imbrians that were at Athens, with some targeteers that had come up from Aenus, and four hundred archers from other quarters. With these and the soldiers at Pylos, he would within twenty days either bring the Lacedaemonians alive,

or kill them on the spot. The Athenians could not help laughing at his fatuity, while sensible men comforted themselves with the reflection that they must gain in either circumstance; either they would be rid of Cleon, which they rather hoped, or if disappointed in this expectation, would reduce the Lacedaemonians.

After he had settled everything in the assembly, and the Athenians had voted him the command of the expedition, he chose as his colleague Demosthenes, one of the generals at Pylos, and pushed forward the preparations for his voyage. His choice fell upon Demosthenes because he heard that he was contemplating a descent on the island; the soldiers distressed by the difficulties of the position, and rather besieged than besiegers, being eager to fight it out, while the firing of the island had increased the confidence of the general. He had been at first afraid, because the island having never been inhabited was almost entirely covered with wood and without paths, thinking this to be in the enemy's favour, as he might land with a large force, and yet might suffer loss by an attack from an unseen position. The mistakes and forces of the enemy the wood would in a great measure conceal from him, while every blunder of his own troops would be at once detected, and they would be thus able to fall upon him unexpectedly just where they pleased, the attack being always in their power. If, on the other hand, he should force them to engage in the thicket, the smaller number who knew the country would, he thought, have the advantage over the larger who were ignorant of it, while his own army might be cut off imperceptibly, in spite of its numbers, as the men would not be able to see where to succour each other.

The Aetolian disaster, which had been mainly caused by the wood, had not a little to do with these reflections. Meanwhile, one of the soldiers who were compelled by want of room to land on the extremities of the island and take their dinners, with outposts fixed to prevent a surprise, set fire to a little of the wood without meaning to do so; and as it came on to blow soon afterwards, almost the whole was consumed before they were aware of it.

Demosthenes was now able for the first time to see how numerous the Lacedaemonians really were, having up to this moment been under the impression that they took in provisions for a smaller number; he also saw that the Athenians thought success important and were anxious about it, and that it was now easier to land on the island, and accordingly got ready for the attempt, sent for troops from the allies in the neighbourhood, and pushed forward his other preparations. At this moment Cleon arrived at Pylos with the troops which he had asked for, having sent on word to say that he was coming. The first step taken by the two generals after their meeting was to send a herald to the camp on the mainland, to ask if they were disposed to avoid all risk and to order the men on the island to surrender themselves and their arms, to be kept in gentle custody until some general convention should be concluded.

On the rejection of this proposition the generals let one day pass, and the next, embarking all their heavy infantry on board a few ships, put out by night, and a little before dawn landed on both sides of the island from the open sea and from the harbour, being about eight hundred strong, and advanced with a run against the first post in the island.

The enemy had distributed his force as follows: In this first post there were about thirty heavy infantry; the centre and most level part, where the water was, was held by the main body, and by Epitadas their commander; while a small party guarded the very end of the island, towards Pylos, which was precipitous on the sea-side and very difficult to attack from the land, and where there was also a sort of old fort of stones rudely put together, which they thought might be useful to them, in case they should be forced to retreat. Such was their disposition.

The advanced post thus attacked by the Athenians was at once put to the sword, the men being scarcely out of bed and still arming, the landing having taken them by surprise, as they fancied the ships were only sailing as usual to their stations for the night. As soon as day broke, the rest of the army landed, that is to say, all the crews of rather more than seventy ships, except the lowest rank of oars, with the arms they carried, eight hundred archers, and as many targeteers, the Messenian reinforcements, and all the other troops on duty round Pylos, except the garrison on the fort. The tactics of Demosthenes had divided them into companies of two hundred, more or less, and made them occupy the highest points in order to paralyse the enemy by surrounding him on every side and thus leaving him without any tangible adversary, exposed to the cross-fire of their host; plied by those in his rear if he attacked in front, and by those on one flank if he moved against those on the other. In short, wherever he went he would have the assailants behind him, and these light-armed assailants, the most awkward of all; arrows, darts, stones, and slings making them formidable at a distance, and there being no means of getting at them at close quarters, as they could conquer flying, and the moment their pursuer turned they were upon him. Such was the idea that inspired Demosthenes in his conception of the descent, and presided over its execution.

Meanwhile the main body of the troops in the island (that under Epitadas), seeing their outpost cut off and an army advancing against them, serried their ranks and pressed forward to close with the Athenian heavy infantry in front of them, the light troops being upon their flanks and rear. However, they were not able to engage or to profit by their superior skill, the light troops keeping them in check on either side with their missiles, and the heavy infantry remaining stationary instead of advancing to meet them; and although they routed the light troops wherever they ran up and approached too closely, yet they retreated fighting, being lightly equipped, and easily getting the start in their flight, from the difficult and rugged nature of the ground, in an island hitherto desert, over which the Lacedaemonians could not pursue them with their heavy armour.

After this skirmishing had lasted some little while, the Lacedaemonians became unable to dash out with the same rapidity as before upon the points attacked, and the light troops finding that they now fought with less vigour, became more confident. They could see with their own eyes that they were many times more numerous than the enemy; they were now more familiar with his aspect and found him less terrible, the result not having justified the apprehensions which they had suffered, when they first landed in slavish dismay at the idea of attacking Lacedaemonians; and accordingly their fear changing to disdain, they now rushed all together with loud shouts upon them, and pelted them with stones, darts, and arrows, whichever came first to hand. The shouting accompanying their onset confounded the Lacedaemonians, unaccustomed to this mode of fighting; dust rose from the newly burnt wood, and it was impossible to see in front of one with the arrows and stones flying through clouds of dust from the hands of numerous assailants. The Lacedaemonians had now to sustain a rude conflict; their caps would not keep out the arrows, darts had broken off in the armour of the wounded, while they themselves were helpless for offence, being prevented from using their eyes to see what was before them, and unable to hear the words of command for the hubbub raised by the enemy; danger encompassed them on every side, and there was no hope of any means of defence or safety.

At last, after many had been already wounded in the confined space in which they were fighting, they formed in close order and retired on the fort at the end of the island, which was not far off, and to their friends who held it. The moment they gave way, the light troops became bolder and pressed upon them, shouting louder than ever, and killed as many as they came up with in their retreat, but most of the Lacedaemonians made good their escape to the fort, and with the garrison in it ranged themselves all along its whole extent to repulse the enemy wherever it was assailable. The Athenians pursuing, unable to surround and hem them in, owing to the strength of the ground, attacked them in front and tried to storm the position. For a long time, indeed for most of the day, both sides held out against all the torments of the battle, thirst, and sun, the one endeavouring to drive the enemy from the high ground, the other to maintain himself upon it, it being now more easy for the Lacedaemonians to defend themselves than before, as they could not be surrounded on the flanks.

The struggle began to seem endless, when the commander of the Messenians came to Cleon and Demosthenes, and told them that they were losing their labour: but if they would give him some archers and light troops to go round on the enemy's rear by a way he would undertake to find, he thought he could force the approach. Upon receiving what he asked for, he started from a point out of sight in order not to be seen by the enemy, and creeping on wherever the precipices of the island permitted, and where the Lacedaemonians, trusting to the strength of the ground, kept no guard, succeeded after the greatest difficulty in getting round without their seeing him, and suddenly appeared on the high ground in their rear, to the dismay of the surprised enemy and the still greater joy of his expectant friends. The Lacedaemonians thus placed between two fires, and in the same dilemma, to compare small things with great, as at Thermopylae, where the defenders were cut off through the Persians getting round by the path, being now attacked in front and behind, began to give way, and overcome by the odds against them and exhausted from want of food, retreated.

The Athenians were already masters of the approaches when Cleon and Demosthenes perceiving that, if the enemy gave way a single step further, they would be destroyed by their soldiery, put a stop to the battle and held their men back; wishing to take the Lacedaemonians alive to Athens, and hoping that their stubbornness might relax on hearing the offer of terms, and that they might surrender and yield to the present overwhelming danger. Proclamation was accordingly made, to know if they would surrender themselves and their arms to the Athenians to be dealt at their discretion.

The Lacedaemonians hearing this offer, most of them lowered their shields and waved their hands to show that they accepted it. Hostilities now ceased, and a parley was held between Cleon and Demosthenes and Styphon, son of Pharax, on the other side; since Epitadas, the first of the previous commanders, had been killed, and Hippagretas, the next in command, left for dead among the slain, though still alive, and thus the command had devolved upon Styphon according to the law, in case of anything happening to his superiors. Styphon and his companions said they wished to send a herald to the Lacedaemonians on the mainland, to know what they were to do. The Athenians would not let any of them go, but themselves called for heralds from the mainland, and after questions had been carried backwards and forwards two or three times, the last man that passed over from the Lacedaemonians on the continent brought this message: "The Lacedaemonians bid you to decide for yourselves so long as you do nothing dishonourable"; upon which after consulting together they surrendered themselves and their arms. The Athenians, after guarding them that day and night, the next morning set up a trophy in the island, and got ready to sail, giving their prisoners in batches to be guarded by the captains of the galleys; and the Lacedaemonians sent a herald and took up their dead. The number of the killed and prisoners taken in the island was as follows: four hundred and twenty heavy infantry had passed over; three hundred all but eight were taken alive to Athens; the rest were killed. About a hundred and twenty of the prisoners were Spartans. The Athenian loss was small, the battle not having been fought at close quarters.

The blockade in all, counting from the fight at sea to the battle in the island, had lasted seventy-two days. For twenty of these, during the absence of the envoys sent to treat for peace, the men had provisions given them, for the rest they were fed by the smugglers. Corn and other victual was found in the island; the commander Epitadas having kept the men upon half rations. The Athenians and Peloponnesians now each withdrew their forces

from Pylos, and went home, and crazy as Cleon's promise was, he fulfilled it, by bringing the men to Athens within the twenty days as he had pledged himself to do.

Nothing that happened in the war surprised the Hellenes so much as this. It was the opinion that no force or famine could make the Lacedaemonians give up their arms, but that they would fight on as they could, and die with them in their hands: indeed people could scarcely believe that those who had surrendered were of the same stuff as the fallen; and an Athenian ally, who some time after insultingly asked one of the prisoners from the island if those that had fallen were men of honour, received for answer that the atraktos - that is, the arrow - would be worth a great deal if it could tell men of honour from the rest; in allusion to the fact that the killed were those whom the stones and the arrows happened to hit.

Upon the arrival of the men the Athenians determined to keep them in prison until the peace, and if the Peloponnesians invaded their country in the interval, to bring them out and put them to death. Meanwhile the defence of Pylos was not forgotten; the Messenians from Naupactus sent to their old country, to which Pylos formerly belonged, some of the likeliest of their number, and began a series of incursions into Laconia, which their common dialect rendered most destructive. The Lacedaemonians, hitherto without experience of incursions or a warfare of the kind, finding the Helots deserting, and fearing the march of revolution in their country, began to be seriously uneasy, and in spite of their unwillingness to betray this to the Athenians began to send envoys to Athens, and tried to recover Pylos and the prisoners. The Athenians, however, kept grasping at more, and dismissed envoy after envoy without their having effected anything. Such was the history of the affair of Pylos.

CHAPTER XIII

Seventh and Eighth Years of the War - End of Corcyraean Revolution - Peace of Gela - Capture of Nisaea

THE SAME summer, directly after these events, the Athenians made an expedition against the territory of Corinth with eighty ships and two thousand Athenian heavy infantry, and two hundred cavalry on board horse transports, accompanied by the Milesians, Andrians, and Carystians from the allies, under the command of Nicias, son of Niceratus, with two colleagues. Putting out to sea they made land at daybreak between Chersonese and Rheitus, at the beach of the country underneath the Solygian hill, upon which the Dorians in old times established themselves and carried on war against the Aeolian inhabitants of Corinth, and where a village now stands called Solygia. The beach where the fleet came to is about a mile and a half from the village, seven miles from Corinth, and two and a quarter from the Isthmus. The Corinthians had heard from Argos of the coming of the Athenian armament, and had all come up to the Isthmus long before, with the exception of those who lived beyond it, and also of five hundred who were away in garrison in Ambracia and Leucadia; and they were there in full force watching for the Athenians to land. These last, however, gave them the slip by coming in the dark; and being informed by signals of the fact the Corinthians left half their number at Cenchreae, in case the Athenians should go against Crommyon, and marched in all haste to the rescue.

Battus, one of the two generals present at the action, went with a company to defend the village of Solygia, which was unfortified; Lycophron remaining to give battle with the rest. The Corinthians first attacked the right wing of the Athenians, which had just landed in front of Chersonese, and afterwards the rest of the army. The battle was an obstinate one, and fought throughout hand to hand.

The right wing of the Athenians and Carystians, who had been placed at the end of the line, received and with some difficulty repulsed the Corinthians, who thereupon retreated to a wall upon the rising ground behind, and throwing down the stones upon them, came on again singing the paean, and being received by the Athenians, were again engaged at close quarters. At this moment a Corinthian company having come to the relief of the left wing, routed and pursued the Athenian right to the sea, whence they were in their turn driven back by the Athenians and Carystians from the ships. Meanwhile the rest of the army on either side fought on tenaciously, especially the right wing of the Corinthians, where Lycophron sustained the attack of the Athenian left, which it was feared might attempt the village of Solygia.

After holding on for a long while without either giving way, the Athenians aided by their horse, of which the enemy had none, at length routed the Corinthians, who retired to the hill and, halting, remained quiet there, without coming down again. It was in this rout of the right wing that they had the most killed, Lycophron their general being among the number. The rest of the army, broken and put to flight in this way without being seriously pursued or hurried, retired to the high ground and there took up its position. The Athenians, finding that the enemy no longer offered to engage them, stripped his dead and took up their own and immediately set up a trophy. Meanwhile, the half of the Corinthians left at Cenchreae to guard against the Athenians sailing on Crommyon, although unable to see the battle for Mount Oneion, found out what was going on by the dust, and hurried up to the rescue; as did also the older Corinthians from the town, upon discovering what had occurred. The Athenians seeing them all coming against them, and thinking that they were reinforcements arriving from the neighbouring Peloponnesians, withdrew in haste to their ships with their spoils and their own dead, except two that they left behind, not being able to find them, and going on board crossed over to the islands opposite, and from thence sent a herald, and took up under truce the bodies which they had left behind. Two hundred and twelve Corinthians fell in the battle, and rather less than fifty Athenians.

Weighing from the islands, the Athenians sailed the same day to Crommyon in the Corinthian territory, about thirteen miles from the city, and coming to anchor laid waste the country, and passed the night there. The next day, after first coasting along to the territory of Epidaurus and making a descent there, they came to Methana between Epidaurus and Troezen, and drew a wall across and fortified the isthmus of the peninsula, and left a post there from which incursions were henceforth made upon the country of Troezen, Haliae, and Epidaurus. After walling off this spot, the fleet sailed off home.

While these events were going on, Eurymedon and Sophocles had put to sea with the Athenian fleet from Pylos on their way to Sicily and, arriving at Corcyra, joined the townsmen in an expedition against the party established on Mount Istone, who had crossed over, as I have mentioned, after the revolution and become masters of the country, to the great hurt of the inhabitants. Their stronghold having been taken by an attack, the garrison took refuge in a body upon some high ground and there capitulated, agreeing to give up their mercenary auxiliaries, lay down their arms, and commit themselves to the discretion of the Athenian people. The generals carried them across under truce to the island of Ptychia, to be kept in custody until they could be sent to Athens, upon the understanding that, if any were caught running away, all would lose the benefit of the treaty. Meanwhile the leaders of the Corcyraean commons, afraid that the Athenians might spare the lives of the prisoners, had recourse to the following stratagem. They gained over some few men on the island by secretly sending friends with instructions to provide them with a boat, and to tell them, as if for their own sakes, that they had best escape as quickly as possible, as the Athenian generals were going to give them up to the Corcyraean people.

These representations succeeding, it was so arranged that the men were caught sailing out in the boat that was provided, and the treaty became void accordingly, and the whole body were given up to the Corcyraeans. For this result the Athenian generals were in a great measure responsible; their evident disinclination to sail for Sicily, and thus to leave to others the honour of conducting the men to Athens, encouraged the intriguers in their design and seemed to affirm the truth of their representations. The prisoners thus handed over were shut up by the Corcyraeans in a large building, and afterwards taken out by twenties and led past two lines of heavy infantry, one on each side, being bound together, and beaten and stabbed by the men in the lines whenever any saw pass a personal enemy; while men carrying whips went by their side and hastened on the road those that walked too slowly.

As many as sixty men were taken out and killed in this way without the knowledge of their friends in the building, who fancied they were merely being moved from one prison to another. At last, however, someone opened their eyes to the truth, upon which they called upon the Athenians to kill them themselves, if such was their pleasure, and refused any longer to go out of the building, and said they would do all they could to prevent any one coming in. The Corcyraeans, not liking themselves to force a passage by the doors, got up on the top of the building, and breaking through the roof, threw down the tiles and let fly arrows at them, from which the prisoners sheltered themselves as well as they could. Most of their number, meanwhile, were engaged in dispatching themselves by thrusting into their throats the arrows shot by the enemy, and hanging themselves with the cords taken from some beds that happened to be there, and with strips made from their clothing; adopting, in short, every possible means of self-destruction, and also falling victims to the missiles of their enemies on the roof. Night came on while these horrors were enacting, and most of it had passed before they were concluded. When it was day the Corcyraeans threw them in layers upon wagons and carried them out of the city. All the women taken in the stronghold were sold as slaves. In this way the Corcyraeans of the mountain were destroyed by the commons; and so after terrible excesses the party strife came to an end, at least as far as the period of this war is concerned, for of one party there was practically nothing left. Meanwhile the Athenians sailed off to Sicily, their primary destination, and carried on the war with their allies there.

At the close of the summer, the Athenians at Naupactus and the Acarnanians made an expedition against Anactorium, the Corinthian town lying at the mouth of the Ambracian Gulf, and took it by treachery; and the Acarnanians themselves, sending settlers from all parts of Acarnania, occupied the place.

Summer was now over. During the winter ensuing, Aristides, son of Archippus, one of the commanders of the Athenian ships sent to collect money from the allies, arrested at Eion, on the Strymon, Artaphernes, a Persian, on his way from the King to Lacedaemon. He was conducted to Athens, where the Athenians got his dispatches translated from the Assyrian character and read them. With numerous references to other subjects, they in substance told the Lacedaemonians that the King did not know what they wanted, as of the many ambassadors they had sent him no two ever told the same story; if however they were prepared to speak plainly they might send him some envoys with this Persian. The Athenians afterwards sent back Artaphernes in a galley to Ephesus, and ambassadors with him, who heard there of the death of King Artaxerxes, son of Xerxes, which took place about that time, and so returned home.

The same winter the Chians pulled down their new wall at the command of the Athenians, who suspected them of meditating an insurrection, after first however obtaining pledges from the Athenians, and security as far as this was possible for their continuing to treat them as before. Thus the winter ended, and with it ended the seventh year of this war of which Thucydides is the historian.

In first days of the next summer there was an eclipse of the sun at the time of new moon, and in the early part of the same month an earthquake. Meanwhile, the Mitylenian and other Lesbian exiles set out, for the most part from the continent, with mercenaries hired in Peloponnese, and others levied on the spot, and took Rhoeteum, but restored it without injury on the receipt of two thousand Phocaean staters. After this they marched against Antandrus and took the town by treachery, their plan being to free Antandrus and the rest of the Actaean towns, formerly owned by Mitylene but now held by the Athenians. Once fortified there, they would have every facility for ship-building from the vicinity of Ida and the consequent abundance of timber, and plenty of other supplies, and might from this base easily ravage Lesbos, which was not far off, and make themselves masters of the Aeolian towns on the continent.

While these were the schemes of the exiles, the Athenians in the same summer made an expedition with sixty ships, two thousand heavy infantry, a few cavalry, and some allied troops from Miletus and other parts, against Cythera, under the command of Nicias, son of Niceratus, Nicostratus, son of Diotrephes, and Autocles, son of Tolmaeus. Cythera is an island lying off Laconia, opposite Malea; the inhabitants are Lacedaemonians of the class of the Perioeci; and an officer called the judge of Cythera went over to the place annually from Sparta. A garrison of heavy infantry was also regularly sent there, and great attention paid to the island, as it was the landing-place for the merchantmen from Egypt and Libya, and at the same time secured Laconia from the attacks of privateers from the sea, at the only point where it is assailable, as the whole coast rises abruptly towards the Sicilian and Cretan seas.

Coming to land here with their armament, the Athenians with ten ships and two thousand Milesian heavy infantry took the town of Scandea, on the sea; and with the rest of their forces landing on the side of the island looking towards Malea, went against the lower town of Cythera, where they found all the inhabitants encamped. A battle ensuing, the Cytherians held their ground for some little while, and then turned and fled into the upper town, where they soon afterwards capitulated to Nicias and his colleagues, agreeing to leave their fate to the decision of the Athenians, their lives only being safe. A correspondence had previously been going on between Nicias and certain of the inhabitants, which caused the surrender to be effected more speedily, and upon terms more advantageous, present and future, for the Cytherians; who would otherwise have been expelled by the Athenians on account of their being Lacedaemonians and their island being so near to Laconia. After the capitulation, the Athenians occupied the town of Scandea near the harbour, and appointing a garrison for Cythera, sailed to Asine, Helus, and most of the places on the sea, and making descents and passing the night on shore at such spots as were convenient, continued ravaging the country for about seven days.

The Lacedaemonians seeing the Athenians masters of Cythera, and expecting descents of the kind upon their coasts, nowhere opposed them in force, but sent garrisons here and there through the country, consisting of as many heavy infantry as the points menaced seemed to require, and generally stood very much upon the defensive. After the severe and unexpected blow that had befallen them in the island, the occupation of Pylos and Cythera, and the apparition on every side of a war whose rapidity defied precaution, they lived in constant fear of internal revolution, and now took the unusual step of raising four hundred horse and a force of archers, and became more timid than ever in military matters, finding themselves involved in a maritime struggle, which their organization had never contemplated, and that against Athenians, with whom an enterprise unattempted was always looked upon as a success sacrificed. Besides this, their late numerous reverses of fortune, coming close one upon another without any reason, had thoroughly unnerved them, and they were always afraid of a second disaster like that on the island, and thus scarcely dared to take the field, but fancied that they could not stir without a blunder, for being new to the experience of adversity they had lost all confidence in themselves.

Accordingly they now allowed the Athenians to ravage their seaboard, without making any movement, the garrisons in whose neighbourhood the descents were made always thinking their numbers insufficient, and sharing the general feeling. A single garrison which ventured to resist, near Cotyrta and Aphrodisia, struck terror by its charge into the scattered mob of light troops, but retreated, upon being received by the heavy infantry, with the loss of a few men and some arms, for which the Athenians set up a trophy, and then sailed off to Cythera. From thence they sailed round to Epidaurus Limera, ravaged part of the country, and so came to Thyrea in the Cynurian territory, upon the Argive and Laconian border. This district had been given by its Lacedaemonian owners to the expelled Aeginetans to inhabit, in return for their good offices at the time of the earthquake and the rising of the Helots; and also because, although subjects of Athens, they had always sided with Lacedaemon.

While the Athenians were still at sea, the Aeginetans evacuated a fort which they were building upon the coast, and retreated into the upper town where they lived, rather more than a mile from the sea. One of the Lacedaemonian district garrisons which was helping them in the work, refused to enter here with them at their entreaty, thinking it dangerous to shut themselves up within the wall, and retiring to the high ground remained quiet, not considering themselves a match for the enemy. Meanwhile the Athenians landed, and instantly advanced with all their forces and took Thyrea. The town they burnt, pillaging what was in it; the Aeginetans who were not slain in action they took with them to Athens, with Tantalus, son of Patrocles, their Lacedaemonian commander, who had been wounded and taken prisoner. They also took with them a few men from Cythera whom they thought it safest to remove. These the Athenians determined to lodge in the islands: the rest of the Cytherians were to retain their lands and pay four talents tribute; the Aeginetans captured to be all put to death, on account of the old inveterate feud; and Tantalus to share the imprisonment of the Lacedaemonians taken on the island.

The same summer, the inhabitants of Camarina and Gela in Sicily first made an armistice with each other, after which embassies from all the other Sicilian cities assembled at Gela to try to bring about a pacification. After many expressions of opinion on one side and the other, according to the griefs and pretensions of the different parties complaining, Hermocrates, son of Hermon, a Syracusan, the most influential man among them, addressed the following words to the assembly:

"If I now address you, Sicilians, it is not because my city is the least in Sicily or the greatest sufferer by the war, but in order to state publicly what appears to me to be the best policy for the whole island. That war is an evil is a proposition so familiar to every one that it would be tedious to develop it. No one is forced to engage in it by ignorance, or kept out of it by fear, if he fancies there is anything to be gained by it. To the former the gain appears greater than the danger, while the latter would rather stand the risk than put up with any immediate sacrifice. But if both should happen to have chosen the wrong moment for acting in this way, advice to make peace would not be unserviceable; and this, if we did but see it, is just what we stand most in need of at the present juncture.

"I suppose that no one will dispute that we went to war at first in order to serve our own several interests, that we are now, in view of the same interests, debating how we can make peace; and that if we separate without having as we think our rights, we shall go to war again. And yet, as men of sense, we ought to see that our separate interests are not alone at stake in the present congress: there is also the question whether we have still time to save Sicily, the whole of which in my opinion is menaced by Athenian ambition; and we ought to find in the name of that people more imperious arguments for peace than any which I can advance, when we see the first power in Hellas watching our mistakes with the few ships that she has at present in our waters, and under the fair name of alliance speciously seeking to turn to account the natural hostility that exists between us. If we go to war, and call in to help us a people that are ready enough to carry their arms even where they are not invited; and if we injure ourselves at our own expense, and at the same time serve as the pioneers of their dominion, we may expect, when they see us worn out, that they will one day come with a larger armament, and seek to bring all of us into subjection.

"And yet as sensible men, if we call in allies and court danger, it should be in order to enrich our different countries with new acquisitions, and not to ruin what they possess already; and we should understand that the intestine discords which are so fatal to communities generally, will be equally so to Sicily, if we, its inhabitants, absorbed in our local quarrels, neglect the common enemy. These considerations should reconcile individual with individual, and city with city, and unite us in a common effort to save the whole of Sicily. Nor should any one imagine that the Dorians only are enemies of Athens, while the Chalcidian race is secured by its Ionian blood; the attack in question is not inspired by hatred of one of two nationalities, but by a desire for the good things in Sicily, the common property of us all. This is proved by the Athenian reception of the Chalcidian invitation: an ally who has never given them any assistance whatever, at once receives from them almost more than the treaty entitles him to. That the Athenians should cherish this ambition and practise this policy is very excusable; and I do not blame those who wish to rule, but those who are over-ready to serve. It is just as much in men's nature to rule those who submit to them, as it is to resist those who molest them; one is not less invariable than the other. Meanwhile all who see these dangers and refuse to provide for them properly, or who have come here without having made up their minds that our first duty is to unite to get rid of the common peril, are mistaken. The quickest way to be rid of it is to make peace with each other; since the Athenians menace us not from their own country, but from that of those who invited them here. In this way instead of war issuing in war, peace quietly ends our quarrels; and the guests who come hither under fair pretences for bad ends, will have good reason for going away without having attained them.

"So far as regards the Athenians, such are the great advantages proved inherent in a wise policy. Independently of this, in the face of the universal consent, that peace is the first of blessings, how can we refuse to make it amongst ourselves; or do you not think that the good which you have, and the ills that you complain of, would be better preserved and cured by quiet than by war; that peace has its honours and splendours of a less perilous kind, not to mention the numerous other blessings that one might dilate on, with the not less numerous miseries of war? These considerations should teach you not to disregard my words, but rather to look in them every one for his own safety. If there be any here who feels certain either by right or might to effect his object, let not this surprise be to him too severe a disappointment. Let him remember that many before now have tried to chastise a wrongdoer, and failing to punish their enemy have not even saved themselves; while many who have trusted in force to gain an advantage, instead of gaining anything more, have been doomed to lose what they had. Vengeance is not necessarily successful because wrong has been done, or strength sure because it is confident; but the incalculable element in the future exercises the widest influence, and is the most treacherous, and yet in fact the most useful of all things, as it frightens us all equally, and thus makes us consider before attacking each other.

"Let us therefore now allow the undefined fear of this unknown future, and the immediate terror of the Athenians' presence, to produce their natural impression, and let us consider any failure to carry out the programmes that we may each have sketched out for ourselves as sufficiently accounted for by these obstacles, and send away the intruder from the country; and if everlasting peace be impossible between us, let us at all events make a treaty for as long a term as possible, and put off our private differences to another day. In fine, let us recognize that the adoption of my advice will leave us each citizens of a free state, and as such arbiters of our own destiny, able to return good or bad offices with equal effect; while its rejection will make us dependent on others, and thus not only impotent to repel an insult, but on the most favourable supposition, friends to our direst enemies, and at feud with our natural friends.

"For myself, though, as I said at first, the representative of a great city, and able to think less of defending myself than of attacking others, I am prepared to concede something in prevision of these dangers. I am not inclined to ruin myself for the sake of hurting my enemies, or so blinded by animosity as to think myself equally master of my own plans and of fortune which I cannot command; but I am ready to give up anything in reason. I call upon the rest of you to imitate my conduct of your own free will, without being forced to do so by the enemy. There is no disgrace in connections giving way to one another, a Dorian to a Dorian, or a Chalcidian to his brethren; above and beyond this we are neighbours, live in the same country, are girt by the same sea, and go by the same name of Sicilians. We shall go to war again, I suppose, when the time comes, and again make peace among ourselves by means of future congresses; but the foreign invader, if we are wise, will always find us united against him, since the hurt of one is the danger of all; and we shall never, in future, invite into the island either allies or mediators. By so acting we shall at the present moment do for Sicily a double service, ridding her at once of the Athenians, and of civil war, and in future shall live in freedom at home, and be less menaced from abroad."

Such were the words of Hermocrates. The Sicilians took his advice, and came to an understanding among themselves to end the war, each keeping what they had - the Camarinaeans taking

275

Morgantina at a price fixed to be paid to the Syracusans - and the allies of the Athenians called the officers in command, and told them that they were going to make peace and that they would be included in the treaty. The generals assenting, the peace was concluded, and the Athenian fleet afterwards sailed away from Sicily. Upon their arrival at Athens, the Athenians banished Pythodorus and Sophocles, and fined Eurymedon for having taken bribes to depart when they might have subdued Sicily. So thoroughly had the present prosperity persuaded the citizens that nothing could withstand them, and that they could achieve what was possible and impracticable alike, with means ample or inadequate it mattered not. The secret of this was their general extraordinary success, which made them confuse their strength with their hopes.

The same summer the Megarians in the city, pressed by the hostilities of the Athenians, who invaded their country twice every year with all their forces, and harassed by the incursions of their own exiles at Pegae, who had been expelled in a revolution by the popular party, began to ask each other whether it would not be better to receive back their exiles, and free the town from one of its two scourges. The friends of the emigrants, perceiving the agitation, now more openly than before demanded the adoption of this proposition; and the leaders of the commons, seeing that the sufferings of the times had tired out the constancy of their supporters, entered in their alarm into correspondence with the Athenian generals, Hippocrates, son of Ariphron, and Demosthenes, son of Alcisthenes, and resolved to betray the town, thinking this less dangerous to themselves than the return of the party which they had banished. It was accordingly arranged that the Athenians should first take the long walls extending for nearly a mile from the city to the port of Nisaea, to prevent the Peloponnesians coming to the rescue from that place, where they formed the sole garrison to secure the fidelity of Megara; and that after this the attempt should be made to put into their hands the upper town, which it was thought would then come over with less difficulty.

The Athenians, after plans had been arranged between themselves and their correspondents both as to words and actions, sailed by night to Minoa, the island off Megara, with six hundred heavy infantry under the command of Hippocrates, and took post in a quarry not far off, out of which bricks used to be taken for the walls; while Demosthenes, the other commander, with a detachment of Plataean light troops and another of Peripoli, placed himself in ambush in the precinct of Enyalius, which was still nearer. No one knew of it, except those whose business it was to know that night. A little before daybreak, the traitors in Megara began to act. Every night for a long time back, under pretence of marauding, in order to have a means of opening the gates, they had been used, with the consent of the officer in command, to carry by night a sculling boat upon a cart along the ditch to the sea, and so to sail out, bringing it back again before day upon the cart, and taking it within the wall through the gates, in order, as they pretended, to baffle the Athenian blockade at Minoa, there being no boat to be seen in the harbour. On the present occasion the cart was already at the gates, which had been opened in the usual way for the boat, when the Athenians, with whom this had been concerted, saw it, and ran at the top of their speed from the ambush in order to reach the gates before they were shut again, and while the cart was still there to prevent their being closed; their Megarian accomplices at the same moment killing the guard at the gates. The first to run in was Demosthenes with his Plataeans and Peripoli, just where the trophy now stands; and he was no sooner within the gates than the Plataeans engaged and defeated the nearest party of Peloponnesians who had taken the alarm and come to the rescue, and secured the gates for the approaching Athenian heavy infantry.

After this, each of the Athenians as fast as they entered went against the wall. A few of the Peloponnesian garrison stood their ground at first, and tried to repel the assault, and some of them were killed; but the main body took fright and fled; the night attack and the sight of the Megarian traitors in arms against them making them think that all Megara had gone over to the enemy. It so happened also that the Athenian herald of his own idea called out and invited any of the Megarians that wished, to join the Athenian ranks; and this was no sooner heard by the garrison than they gave way, and, convinced that they were the victims of a concerted attack, took refuge in Nisaea. By daybreak, the walls being now taken and the Megarians in the city in great agitation, the persons who had negotiated with the Athenians, supported by the rest of the popular party which was privy to the plot, said that they ought to open the gates and march out to battle. It had been concerted between them that the Athenians should rush in, the moment that the gates were opened, while the conspirators were to be distinguished from the rest by being anointed with oil, and so to avoid being hurt. They could open the gates with more security, as four thousand Athenian heavy infantry from Eleusis, and six hundred horse, had marched all night, according to agreement, and were now close at hand. The conspirators were all ready anointed and at their posts by the gates, when one of their accomplices denounced the plot to the opposite party, who gathered together and came in a body, and roundly said that they must not march out - a thing they had never yet ventured on even when in greater force than at present - or wantonly compromise the safety of the town, and that if what they said was not attended to, the battle would have to be fought in Megara. For the rest, they gave no signs of their knowledge of the intrigue, but stoutly maintained that their advice was the best, and meanwhile kept close by and watched the gates, making it impossible for the conspirators to effect their purpose.

The Athenian generals seeing that some obstacle had arisen, and that the capture of the town by force was no longer practicable, at once proceeded to invest Nisaea, thinking that, if they could take it before relief arrived, the surrender of Megara would soon follow. Iron, stone-masons, and everything else required quickly coming up from Athens, the Athenians started from the wall which they occupied, and from this point built a cross wall looking towards Megara down to the sea on either side of Nisaea; the ditch and the walls being divided among the army, stones and bricks taken from the suburb, and the fruit-trees and timber cut down to make a palisade wherever this seemed necessary; the houses also in the suburb with the addition of battlements sometimes entering into the fortification. The whole of this day the work continued, and by the afternoon of the next the wall was all but completed, when the garrison in Nisaea, alarmed by the absolute want of provisions, which they used to take in for the day from the upper town, not anticipating any speedy relief from the Peloponnesians, and supposing Megara to be hostile, capitulated to the Athenians on condition that they should give up their arms, and should each be ransomed for a stipulated sum; their Lacedaemonian commander, and any others of his countrymen in the place, being left to the discretion of the Athenians. On these conditions they surrendered and came out, and the Athenians broke down the long walls at their point of junction with Megara, took possession of Nisaea, and went on with their other preparations.

Just at this time the Lacedaemonian Brasidas, son of Tellis, happened to be in the neighbourhood of Sicyon and Corinth, getting ready an army for Thrace. As soon as he heard of the capture of the walls, fearing for the Peloponnesians in Nisaea and the safety of Megara, he sent to the Boeotians to meet him as quickly as possible at Tripodiscus, a village so called of the Megarid, under Mount Geraneia, and went himself, with two thousand seven hundred Corinthian heavy infantry, four hundred Phliasians, six hundred Sicyonians, and such troops of his own as he had already levied, expecting to find Nisaea not yet taken. Hearing of its fall (he had marched out by night to Tripodiscus), he took three hundred picked men from the army, without waiting till his coming should be known, and came up to Megara unobserved by the Athenians, who were down by the sea, ostensibly, and really if possible, to attempt Nisaea, but above all to get into Megara and secure the town. He accordingly invited the townspeople to admit his party, saying that he had hopes of recovering Nisaea.

However, one of the Megarian factions feared that he might expel them and restore the exiles; the other that the commons, apprehensive of this very danger, might set upon them, and the city be thus destroyed by a battle within its gates under the eyes of the ambushed Athenians. He was accordingly refused admittance, both parties electing to remain quiet and await the event; each expecting a battle between the Athenians and the relieving army, and thinking it safer to see their friends victorious before declaring in their favour.

Unable to carry his point, Brasidas went back to the rest of the army. At daybreak the Boeotians joined him. Having determined to relieve Megara, whose danger they considered their own, even before hearing from Brasidas, they were already in full force at Plataea, when his messenger arrived to add spurs to their resolution; and they at once sent on to him two thousand two hundred heavy infantry, and six hundred horse, returning home with the main body. The whole army thus assembled numbered six thousand heavy infantry. The Athenian heavy infantry were drawn up by Nisaea and the sea; but the light troops being scattered over the plain were attacked by the Boeotian horse and driven to the sea, being taken entirely by surprise, as on previous occasions no relief had ever come to the Megarians from any quarter. Here the Boeotians were in their turn charged and engaged by the Athenian horse, and a cavalry action ensued which lasted a long time, and in which both parties claimed the victory. The Athenians killed and stripped the leader of the Boeotian horse and some few of his comrades who had charged right up to Nisaea, and remaining masters of the bodies gave them back under truce, and set up a trophy; but regarding the action as a whole the forces separated without either side having gained a decisive advantage, the Boeotians returning to their army and the Athenians to Nisaea.

After this Brasidas and the army came nearer to the sea and to Megara, and taking up a convenient position, remained quiet in order of battle, expecting to be attacked by the Athenians and knowing that the Megarians were waiting to see which would be the victor. This attitude seemed to present two advantages. Without taking the offensive or willingly provoking the hazards of a battle, they openly showed their readiness to fight, and thus without bearing the burden of the day would fairly reap its honours; while at the same time they effectually served their interests at Megara. For if they had failed to show themselves they would not have had a chance, but would have certainly been considered vanquished, and have lost the town. As it was, the Athenians might possibly not be inclined to accept their challenge, and their object would be attained without fighting. And so it turned out. The Athenians formed outside the long walls and, the enemy not attacking, there remained motionless; their generals having decided that the risk was too unequal. In fact most of their objects had been already attained; and they would have to begin a battle against superior numbers, and if victorious could only gain Megara, while a defeat would destroy the flower of their heavy soldiery. For the enemy it was different; as even the states actually represented in his army risked each only a part of its entire force, he might well be more audacious. Accordingly, after waiting for some time without either side attacking, the Athenians withdrew to Nisaea, and the Peloponnesians after them to the point from which they had set out. The friends of the Megarian exiles now threw aside their hesitation, and opened the gates to Brasidas and the commanders from the different states - looking upon him as the victor and upon the Athenians as having declined the battle - and receiving them into the town proceeded to discuss matters with them; the party in correspondence with the Athenians being paralysed by the turn things had taken.

Afterwards Brasidas let the allies go home, and himself went back to Corinth, to prepare for his expedition to Thrace, his original destination. The Athenians also returning home, the Megarians in the city most implicated in the Athenian negotiation, knowing that they had been detected, presently disappeared; while the rest conferred with the friends of the exiles, and restored the party at Pegae, after binding them under solemn oaths to take no vengeance for the past, and only to consult the real interests of the town. However, as soon as they were in office, they held a review of the heavy infantry, and separating the battalions, picked out about a hundred of their enemies, and of those who were thought to be most involved in the correspondence with the Athenians, brought them before the people, and compelling the vote to be given openly, had them condemned and executed, and established a close oligarchy in the town - a revolution which lasted a very long while, although effected by a very few partisans.

CHAPTER XIV

Eighth and Ninth Years of the War - Invasion of Boeotia - Fall of Amphipolis - Brilliant Successes of Brasidas

THE SAME summer the Mitylenians were about to fortify Antandrus, as they had intended, when Demodocus and Aristides, the commanders of the Athenian squadron engaged in levying subsidies, heard on the Hellespont of what was being done to the place (Lamachus their colleague having sailed with ten ships into the Pontus) and conceived fears of its becoming a second Anaia-the place in which the Samian exiles had established themselves to annoy Samos, helping the Peloponnesians by sending pilots to their navy, and keeping the city in agitation and receiving all its outlaws. They accordingly got together a force from the allies and set sail, defeated in battle the troops that met them from Antandrus, and retook the place. Not long after, Lamachus, who had sailed into the Pontus, lost his ships at anchor in the river Calex, in the territory of Heraclea, rain having fallen in the interior and the flood coming suddenly down upon them; and himself and his troops passed by land through the Bithynian Thracians on the Asiatic side, and arrived at Chalcedon, the Megarian colony at the mouth of the Pontus.

The same summer the Athenian general, Demosthenes, arrived at Naupactus with forty ships immediately after the return from the Megarid. Hippocrates and himself had had overtures made to them by certain men in the cities in Boeotia, who wished to change the constitution and introduce a democracy as at Athens; Ptoeodorus, a Theban exile, being the chief mover in this intrigue. The seaport town of Siphae, in the bay of Crisae, in the Thespian territory, was to be betrayed to them by one party; Chaeronea (a dependency of what was formerly called the Minyan, now the Boeotian, Orchomenus) to be put into their hands by another from that town, whose exiles were very active in the business, hiring men in Peloponnese. Some Phocians also were in the plot, Chaeronea being the frontier town of Boeotia and close to Phanotis in Phocia. Meanwhile the Athenians were to seize Delium, the sanctuary of Apollo, in the territory of Tanagra looking towards Euboea; and all these events were to take place simultaneously upon a day appointed, in order that the Boeotians might be unable to unite to oppose them at Delium, being everywhere detained by disturbances at home. Should the enterprise succeed, and Delium be fortified, its authors confidently expected that even if no revolution should immediately follow in Boeotia, yet with these places in their hands, and the country being harassed by incursions, and a refuge in each instance near for the partisans engaged in them, things would not remain as they were, but that the rebels being supported by the Athenians and the forces of the oligarchs divided, it would be possible after a while to settle matters according to their wishes.

Such was the plot in contemplation. Hippocrates with a force raised at home awaited the proper moment to take the field against the Boeotians; while he sent on Demosthenes with the forty ships above mentioned to Naupactus, to raise in those parts an army of Acarnanians and of the other allies, and sail and receive Siphae from the conspirators; a day having been agreed on for the simultaneous execution of both these operations. Demosthenes on his arrival found Oeniadae already compelled by the united Acarnanians to join the Athenian confederacy, and himself raising all the allies in those countries marched against and subdued Salynthius and the Agraeans; after which he devoted himself to the preparations necessary to enable him to be at Siphae by the time appointed.

About the same time in the summer, Brasidas set out on his march for the Thracian places with seventeen hundred heavy infantry, and arriving at Heraclea in Trachis, from thence sent on a messenger to his friends at Pharsalus, to ask them to conduct himself and his army through the country. Accordingly there came to Melitia in Achaia Panaerus, Dorus, Hippolochidas, Torylaus, and Strophacus, the Chalcidian proxenus, under whose escort he resumed his march, being accompanied also by other Thessalians, among whom was Niconidas from Larissa, a friend of Perdiccas. It was never very easy to traverse Thessaly without an escort; and throughout all Hellas for an armed force to pass without leave through a neighbour's country was a delicate step to take. Besides this the Thessalian people had always sympathized with the Athenians. Indeed if instead of the customary close oligarchy there had been a constitutional government in Thessaly, he would never have been able to proceed; since even as it was, he was met on his march at the river Enipeus by certain of the opposite party who forbade his further progress, and complained of his making the attempt without the consent of the nation. To this his escort answered that they had no intention of taking him through against their will; they were only friends in attendance on an unexpected visitor. Brasidas himself added that he came as a friend to Thessaly and its inhabitants, his arms not being directed against them but against the Athenians, with whom he was at war, and that although he knew of no quarrel between the Thessalians and Lacedaemonians to prevent the two nations having access to each other's territory, he neither would nor could proceed against their wishes; he could only beg them not to stop him. With this answer they went away, and he took the advice of his escort, and pushed on without halting, before a greater force might gather to prevent him. Thus in the day that he set out from Melitia he performed the whole distance to Pharsalus, and encamped on the river Apidanus; and so to Phacium and from thence to Perrhaebia. Here his Thessalian escort went back, and the Perrhaebians, who are subjects of Thessaly, set him down at Dium in the dominions of Perdiccas, a Macedonian town under Mount Olympus, looking towards Thessaly.

In this way Brasidas hurried through Thessaly before any one could be got ready to stop him, and reached Perdiccas and

Chalcidice. The departure of the army from Peloponnese had been procured by the Thracian towns in revolt against Athens and by Perdiccas, alarmed at the successes of the Athenians. The Chalcidians thought that they would be the first objects of an Athenian expedition, not that the neighbouring towns which had not yet revolted did not also secretly join in the invitation; and Perdiccas also had his apprehensions on account of his old quarrels with the Athenians, although not openly at war with them, and above all wished to reduce Arrhabaeus, king of the Lyncestians. It had been less difficult for them to get an army to leave Peloponnese, because of the ill fortune of the Lacedaemonians at the present moment. The attacks of the Athenians upon Peloponnese, and in particular upon Laconia, might, it was hoped, be diverted most effectually by annoying them in return, and by sending an army to their allies, especially as they were willing to maintain it and asked for it to aid them in revolting. The Lacedaemonians were also glad to have an excuse for sending some of the Helots out of the country, for fear that the present aspect of affairs and the occupation of Pylos might encourage them to move. Indeed fear of their numbers and obstinacy even persuaded the Lacedaemonians to the action which I shall now relate, their policy at all times having been governed by the necessity of taking precautions against them. The Helots were invited by a proclamation to pick out those of their number who claimed to have most distinguished themselves against the enemy, in order that they might receive their freedom; the object being to test them, as it was thought that the first to claim their freedom would be the most high-spirited and the most apt to rebel. As many as two thousand were selected accordingly, who crowned themselves and went round the temples, rejoicing in their new freedom. The Spartans, however, soon afterwards did away with them, and no one ever knew how each of them perished. The Spartans now therefore gladly sent seven hundred as heavy infantry with Brasidas, who recruited the rest of his force by means of money in Peloponnese.

Brasidas himself was sent out by the Lacedaemonians mainly at his own desire, although the Chalcidians also were eager to have a man so thorough as he had shown himself whenever there was anything to be done at Sparta, and whose after-service abroad proved of the utmost use to his country. At the present moment his just and moderate conduct towards the towns generally succeeded in procuring their revolt, besides the places which he managed to take by treachery; and thus when the Lacedaemonians desired to treat, as they ultimately did, they had places to offer in exchange, and the burden of war meanwhile shifted from Peloponnese. Later on in the war, after the events in Sicily, the present valour and conduct of Brasidas, known by experience to some, by hearsay to others, was what mainly created in the allies of Athens a feeling for the Lacedaemonians. He was the first who went out and showed himself so good a man at all points as to leave behind him the conviction that the rest were like him.

Meanwhile his arrival in the Thracian country no sooner became known to the Athenians than they declared war against Perdiccas, whom they regarded as the author of the expedition, and kept a closer watch on their allies in that quarter.

Upon the arrival of Brasidas and his army, Perdiccas immediately started with them and with his own forces against Arrhabaeus, son of Bromerus, king of the Lyncestian Macedonians, his neighbour, with whom he had a quarrel and whom he wished to subdue. However, when he arrived with his army and Brasidas at the pass leading into Lyncus, Brasidas told him that before commencing hostilities he wished to go and try to persuade Arrhabaeus to become the ally of Lacedaemon, this latter having already made overtures intimating his willingness to make Brasidas arbitrator between them, and the Chalcidian envoys accompanying him having warned him not to remove the apprehensions of Perdiccas, in order to ensure his greater zeal in their cause. Besides, the envoys of Perdiccas had talked at Lacedaemon about his bringing many of the places round him into alliance with them; and thus Brasidas thought he might take a larger view of the question of Arrhabaeus. Perdiccas however retorted that he had not brought him with him to arbitrate in their quarrel, but to put down the enemies whom he might point out to him; and that while he, Perdiccas, maintained half his army it was a breach of faith for Brasidas to parley with Arrhabaeus. Nevertheless Brasidas disregarded the wishes of Perdiccas and held the parley in spite of him, and suffered himself to be persuaded to lead off the army without invading the country of Arrhabaeus; after which Perdiccas, holding that faith had not been kept with him, contributed only a third instead of half of the support of the army.

The same summer, without loss of time, Brasidas marched with the Chalcidians against Acanthus, a colony of the Andrians, a little before vintage. The inhabitants were divided into two parties on the question of receiving him; those who had joined the Chalcidians in inviting him, and the popular party. However, fear for their fruit, which was still out, enabled Brasidas to persuade the multitude to admit him alone, and to hear what he had to say before making a decision; and he was admitted accordingly and appeared before the people, and not being a bad speaker for a Lacedaemonian, addressed them as follows:

"Acanthians, the Lacedaemonians have sent out me and my army to make good the reason that we gave for the war when we began it, viz., that we were going to war with the Athenians in order to free Hellas. Our delay in coming has been caused by mistaken expectations as to the war at home, which led us to hope, by our own unassisted efforts and without your risking anything, to effect the speedy downfall of the Athenians; and you must not blame us for this, as we are now come the moment that we were able, prepared with your aid to do our best to subdue them. Meanwhile I am astonished at finding your gates shut against me, and at not meeting with a better welcome. We Lacedaemonians thought of you as allies eager to have us, to whom we should come in spirit even before we were with you in body; and in this expectation undertook all the risks of a march of many days through a strange country, so far did our zeal carry us. It will be a terrible thing if after this you have other intentions, and mean to stand in the way of your own and Hellenic freedom. It is not merely that you oppose me yourselves; but wherever I may go people will be less inclined to join me, on the score that you, to whom I first came - an important town like Acanthus, and prudent men like the Acanthians - refused to admit me. I shall have nothing to prove that the reason which I advance is the true one; it will be said either that there is something unfair in the freedom which I offer, or that I am in insufficient force and unable to protect you against an attack from Athens. Yet when I went with the army which I now have to the relief of Nisaea, the Athenians did not venture to engage me although in greater force than I; and it is not likely they will ever send across sea against you an army as numerous as they had at Nisaea. And for myself, I have come here not to hurt but to free the Hellenes, witness the solemn oaths by which I have bound my government that the allies that I may bring over shall be independent; and besides my object in coming is not by force or fraud to obtain your alliance, but to offer you mine to help you against your Athenian masters. I protest, therefore, against any suspicions of my intentions after the guarantees which I offer, and equally so against doubts of my ability to protect you, and I invite you to join me without hesitation.

"Some of you may hang back because they have private enemies, and fear that I may put the city into the hands of a party: none need be more tranquil than they. I am not come here to help this party or that; and I do not consider that I should be bringing you freedom in any real sense, if I should disregard your constitution, and enslave the many to the few or the few to the many. This would be heavier than a foreign yoke; and we Lacedaemonians, instead of being thanked for our pains, should get neither honour nor glory, but, contrariwise, reproaches. The charges which strengthen our hands in the war against the Athenians would on our own showing be merited by ourselves, and more hateful in us than in those who make no pretensions to honesty; as it is more disgraceful for persons of character to take what they covet by fair-seeming fraud than by open force; the one aggression having for its justification the might which fortune gives, the other being simply a piece of clever roguery. A matter which concerns us thus nearly we naturally look to most jealously; and over and above the oaths that I have mentioned, what stronger assurance can you have, when you see that our words, compared with the actual facts, produce the necessary conviction that it is our interest to act as we say?

"If to these considerations of mine you put in the plea of inability, and claim that your friendly feeling should save you from being hurt by your refusal; if you say that freedom, in your opinion, is not without its dangers, and that it is right to offer it to those who can accept it, but not to force it on any against their will, then I shall take the gods and heroes of your country to witness that I came for your good and was rejected, and shall do my best to compel you by laying waste your land. I shall do so without scruple, being justified by the necessity which constrains me, first, to prevent the Lacedaemonians from being damaged by you, their friends, in the event of your nonadhesion, through the moneys that you pay to the Athenians; and secondly, to prevent the Hellenes from being hindered by you in shaking off their servitude. Otherwise indeed we should have no right to act as we propose; except in the name of some public interest, what call should we Lacedaemonians have to free those who do not wish it? Empire we do not aspire to: it is what we are labouring to put down; and we should wrong the greater number if we allowed you to stand in the way of the independence that we offer to all. Endeavour, therefore, to decide wisely, and strive to begin the work of liberation for the Hellenes, and lay up for yourselves endless renown, while you escape private loss, and cover your commonwealth with glory."

Such were the words of Brasidas. The Acanthians, after much had been said on both sides of the question, gave their votes in secret, and the majority, influenced by the seductive arguments of Brasidas and by fear for their fruit, decided to revolt from Athens; not however admitting the army until they had taken his personal security for the oaths sworn by his government before they sent him out, assuring the independence of the allies whom he might bring over. Not long after, Stagirus, a colony of the Andrians, followed their example and revolted.

Such were the events of this summer. It was in the first days of the winter following that the places in Boeotia were to be put into the hands of the Athenian generals, Hippocrates and Demosthenes, the latter of whom was to go with his ships to Siphae, the former to Delium. A mistake, however, was made in the days on which they were each to start; and Demosthenes, sailing first to Siphae, with the Acarnanians and many of the allies from those parts on board, failed to effect anything, through the plot having been betrayed by Nicomachus, a Phocian from Phanotis, who told the Lacedaemonians, and they the Boeotians. Succours accordingly flocked in from all parts of Boeotia, Hippocrates not being yet there to make his diversion, and Siphae and Chaeronea were promptly secured, and the conspirators, informed of the mistake, did not venture on any movement in the towns.

Meanwhile Hippocrates made a levy in mass of the citizens, resident aliens, and foreigners in Athens, and arrived at his destination after the Boeotians had already come back from Siphae, and encamping his army began to fortify Delium, the sanctuary of Apollo, in the following manner. A trench was dug all round the temple and the consecrated ground, and the earth thrown up from the excavation was made to do duty as a wall, in which stakes were also planted, the vines round the sanctuary being cut down and thrown in, together with stones and bricks pulled down from the houses near; every means, in short, being used to run up the rampart. Wooden towers were also erected where they were wanted, and where there was no part of the temple buildings left standing, as on the side where the gallery once existing had fallen in. The work was begun on the third day after leaving home, and continued during the fourth, and till dinnertime on the fifth, when most of it being now finished the army removed from Delium about a mile and a quarter on its way home. From this point most of the light troops went straight on, while the heavy infantry halted and remained where they were; Hippocrates having stayed behind at Delium to arrange the posts, and to give directions for the completion of such part of the outworks as had been left unfinished.

During the days thus employed the Boeotians were mustering at Tanagra, and by the time that they had come in from all the towns, found the Athenians already on their way home. The rest of the eleven Boeotarchs were against giving battle, as the enemy was no longer in Boeotia, the Athenians being just over the Oropian border, when they halted; but Pagondas, son of Aeolidas, one of the Boeotarchs of Thebes (Arianthides, son of Lysimachidas, being the other), and then commander-in-chief, thought it best to hazard a battle. He accordingly called the men to him, company after company, to prevent their all leaving their arms at once, and urged them to attack the Athenians, and stand the issue of a battle, speaking as follows:

"Boeotians, the idea that we ought not to give battle to the Athenians, unless we came up with them in Boeotia, is one which should never have entered into the head of any of us, your generals. It was to annoy Boeotia that they crossed the frontier and built a fort in our country; and they are therefore, I imagine, our enemies wherever we may come up with them, and from wheresoever they may have come to act as enemies do. And if any one has taken up with the idea in question for reasons of safety, it is high time for him to change his mind. The party attacked, whose own country is in danger, can scarcely discuss what is prudent with the calmness of men who are in full enjoyment of what they have got, and are thinking of attacking a neighbour in order to get more. It is your national habit, in your country or out of it, to oppose the same resistance to a foreign invader; and when that invader is Athenian, and lives upon your frontier besides, it is doubly imperative to do so. As between neighbours generally, freedom means simply a determination to hold one's own; and with neighbours like these, who are trying to enslave near and far alike, there is nothing for it but to fight it out to the last. Look at the condition of the Euboeans and of most of the rest of Hellas, and be convinced that others have to fight with their neighbours for this frontier or that, but that for us conquest means one frontier for the whole country, about which no dispute can be made, for they will simply come and take by force what we have. So much more have we to fear from this neighbour than from another. Besides, people who, like the Athenians in the present instance, are tempted by pride of strength to attack their neighbours, usually march most confidently against those who keep still, and only defend themselves in their own country, but think twice before they grapple with those who meet them outside their frontier and strike the first blow if opportunity offers. The Athenians have shown us this themselves; the defeat which we inflicted upon them at Coronea, at the time when our quarrels had allowed them to occupy the country, has given great security to Boeotia until the present day. Remembering this, the old must equal their ancient exploits, and the young, the sons of the heroes of that time, must endeavour not to disgrace their native valour; and trusting in the help of the god whose temple has been sacrilegiously fortified, and in the victims which in our sacrifices have proved propitious, we must march against the enemy, and teach him that he must go and get what he wants by attacking someone who will not resist him, but that men whose glory it is to be always ready to give battle for the liberty of their own country, and never unjustly to enslave that of others, will not let him go without a struggle."

By these arguments Pagondas persuaded the Boeotians to attack the Athenians, and quickly breaking up his camp led his army forward, it being now late in the day. On nearing the enemy, he halted in a position where a hill intervening prevented the two armies from seeing each other, and then formed and prepared for action. Meanwhile Hippocrates at Delium, informed of the approach of the Boeotians, sent orders to his troops to throw themselves into line, and himself joined them not long afterwards, leaving about three hundred horse behind him at Delium, at once to guard the place in case of attack, and to watch their opportunity and fall upon the Boeotians during the battle. The Boeotians placed a detachment to deal with these, and when everything was arranged to their satisfaction appeared over the hill, and halted in the order which they had determined on, to the number of seven thousand heavy infantry, more than ten thousand light troops, one thousand horse, and five hundred targeteers. On their right were the Thebans and those of their province, in the centre the Haliartians, Coronaeans, Copaeans, and the other people around the lake, and on the left the Thespians, Tanagraeans, and Orchomenians, the cavalry and the light troops being at the extremity of each wing. The Thebans formed twenty-five shields deep, the rest as they pleased. Such was the strength and disposition of the Boeotian army.

On the side of the Athenians, the heavy infantry throughout the whole army formed eight deep, being in numbers equal to the enemy, with the cavalry upon the two wings. Light troops regularly armed there were none in the army, nor had there ever been any at Athens. Those who had joined in the invasion, though many times more numerous than those of the enemy, had mostly followed unarmed, as part of the levy in mass of the citizens and foreigners at Athens, and having started first on their way home were not present in any number. The armies being now in line and upon the point of engaging, Hippocrates, the general, passed along the Athenian ranks, and encouraged them as follows:

"Athenians, I shall only say a few words to you, but brave men require no more, and they are addressed more to your understanding than to your courage. None of you must fancy that we are going out of our way to run this risk in the country of another. Fought in their territory the battle will be for ours: if we conquer, the Peloponnesians will never invade your country without the Boeotian horse, and in one battle you will win Boeotia and in a manner free Attica. Advance to meet them then like citizens of a country in which you all glory as the first in Hellas, and like sons of the fathers who beat them at Oenophyta with Myronides and thus gained possession of Boeotia."

Hippocrates had got half through the army with his exhortation, when the Boeotians, after a few more hasty words from Pagondas, struck up the paean, and came against them from the hill; the Athenians advancing to meet them, and closing at a run. The extreme wing of neither army came into action, one like the other being stopped by the water-courses in the way; the rest engaged with the utmost obstinacy, shield against shield. The Boeotian left, as far as the centre, was worsted by the Athenians. The Thespians in that part of the field suffered most severely. The troops alongside them having given way, they were surrounded in a narrow space and cut down fighting hand to hand; some of the Athenians also fell into confusion in surrounding the enemy and mistook and so killed each other. In this part of the field the Boeotians were beaten, and retreated upon the troops still fighting; but the right, where the Thebans were, got the better of the Athenians and shoved them further and further back, though gradually at first. It so happened also that Pagondas, seeing the distress of his left, had sent two squadrons of horse, where they could not be seen, round the hill, and their sudden appearance struck a panic into the victorious wing of the Athenians, who thought that it was another army coming against them. At length in both parts of the field, disturbed by this panic, and with their line broken by the advancing Thebans, the whole Athenian army took to flight. Some made for Delium and the sea, some for Oropus, others for Mount Parnes, or wherever they had hopes of safety, pursued and cut down by the Boeotians, and in particular by the cavalry, composed partly of

Boeotians and partly of Locrians, who had come up just as the rout began. Night however coming on to interrupt the pursuit, the mass of the fugitives escaped more easily than they would otherwise have done. The next day the troops at Oropus and Delium returned home by sea, after leaving a garrison in the latter place, which they continued to hold notwithstanding the defeat.

The Boeotians set up a trophy, took up their own dead, and stripped those of the enemy, and leaving a guard over them retired to Tanagra, there to take measures for attacking Delium. Meanwhile a herald came from the Athenians to ask for the dead, but was met and turned back by a Boeotian herald, who told him that he would effect nothing until the return of himself the Boeotian herald, and who then went on to the Athenians, and told them on the part of the Boeotians that they had done wrong in transgressing the law of the Hellenes. Of what use was the universal custom protecting the temples in an invaded country, if the Athenians were to fortify Delium and live there, acting exactly as if they were on unconsecrated ground, and drawing and using for their purposes the water which they, the Boeotians, never touched except for sacred uses? Accordingly for the god as well as for themselves, in the name of the deities concerned, and of Apollo, the Boeotians invited them first to evacuate the temple, if they wished to take up the dead that belonged to them.

After these words from the herald, the Athenians sent their own herald to the Boeotians to say that they had not done any wrong to the temple, and for the future would do it no more harm than they could help; not having occupied it originally in any such design, but to defend themselves from it against those who were really wronging them. The law of the Hellenes was that conquest of a country, whether more or less extensive, carried with it possession of the temples in that country, with the obligation to keep up the usual ceremonies, at least as far as possible. The Boeotians and most other people who had turned out the owners of a country, and put themselves in their places by force, now held as of right the temples which they originally entered as usurpers. If the Athenians could have conquered more of Boeotia this would have been the case with them: as things stood, the piece of it which they had got they should treat as their own, and not quit unless obliged. The water they had disturbed under the impulsion of a necessity which they had not wantonly incurred, having been forced to use it in defending themselves against the Boeotians who first invaded Attica. Besides, anything done under the pressure of war and danger might reasonably claim indulgence even in the eye of the god; or why, pray, were the altars the asylum for involuntary offences? Transgression also was a term applied to presumptuous offenders, not to the victims of adverse circumstances. In short, which were most impious - the Boeotians who wished to barter dead bodies for holy places, or the Athenians who refused to give up holy places to obtain what was theirs by right? The condition of evacuating Boeotia must therefore be withdrawn. They were no longer in Boeotia. They stood where they stood by the right of the sword. All that the Boeotians had to do was to tell them to take up their dead under a truce according to the national custom.

The Boeotians replied that if they were in Boeotia, they must evacuate that country before taking up their dead; if they were in their own territory, they could do as they pleased: for they knew that, although the Oropid where the bodies as it chanced were lying (the battle having been fought on the borders) was subject to Athens, yet the Athenians could not get them without their leave. Besides, why should they grant a truce for Athenian ground? And what could be fairer than to tell them to evacuate Boeotia if they wished to get what they asked? The Athenian herald accordingly returned with this answer, without having accomplished his object.

Meanwhile the Boeotians at once sent for darters and slingers from the Malian Gulf, and with two thousand Corinthian heavy infantry who had joined them after the battle, the Peloponnesian garrison which had evacuated Nisaea, and some Megarians with them, marched against Delium, and attacked the fort, and after divers efforts finally succeeded in taking it by an engine of the following description. They sawed in two and scooped out a great beam from end to end, and fitting it nicely together again like a pipe, hung by chains a cauldron at one extremity, with which communicated an iron tube projecting from the beam, which was itself in great part plated with iron. This they brought up from a distance upon carts to the part of the wall principally composed of vines and timber, and when it was near, inserted huge bellows into their end of the beam and blew with them. The blast passing closely confined into the cauldron, which was filled with lighted coals, sulphur and pitch, made a great blaze, and set fire to the wall, which soon became untenable for its defenders, who left it and fled; and in this way the fort was taken. Of the garrison some were killed and two hundred made prisoners; most of the rest got on board their ships and returned home.

Soon after the fall of Delium, which took place seventeen days after the battle, the Athenian herald, without knowing what had happened, came again for the dead, which were now restored by the Boeotians, who no longer answered as at first. Not quite five hundred Boeotians fell in the battle, and nearly one thousand Athenians, including Hippocrates the general, besides a great number of light troops and camp followers.

Soon after this battle Demosthenes, after the failure of his voyage to Siphae and of the plot on the town, availed himself of the Acarnanian and Agraean troops and of the four hundred Athenian heavy infantry which he had on board, to make a descent on the Sicyonian coast. Before however all his ships had come to shore, the Sicyonians came up and routed and chased to their ships those that had landed, killing some and taking others prisoners; after which they set up a trophy, and gave back the dead under truce.

About the same time with the affair of Delium took place the death of Sitalces, king of the Odrysians, who was defeated in battle, in a campaign against the Triballi; Seuthes, son of Sparadocus, his nephew, succeeding to the kingdom of the Odrysians, and of the rest of Thrace ruled by Sitalces.

The same winter Brasidas, with his allies in the Thracian places, marched against Amphipolis, the Athenian colony on the river Strymon. A settlement upon the spot on which the city now stands was before attempted by Aristagoras, the Milesian (when he fled from King Darius), who was however dislodged by the Edonians; and thirty-two years later by the Athenians, who sent thither ten thousand settlers of their own citizens, and whoever else chose to go. These were cut off at Drabescus by the Thracians. Twenty-nine years after, the Athenians returned (Hagnon, son of Nicias, being sent out as leader of the colony) and drove out the Edonians, and founded a town on the spot, formerly called Ennea Hodoi or Nine Ways. The base from which they started was Eion, their commercial seaport at the mouth of the river, not more than three miles from the present town, which Hagnon named Amphipolis, because the Strymon flows round it on two sides, and he built it so as to be conspicuous from the sea and land alike, running a long wall across from river to river, to complete the circumference.

Brasidas now marched against this town, starting from Arne in Chalcidice. Arriving about dusk at Aulon and Bromiscus, where the lake of Bolbe runs into the sea, he supped there, and went on during the night. The weather was stormy and it was snowing a little, which encouraged him to hurry on, in order, if possible, to take every one at Amphipolis by surprise, except the party who were to betray it. The plot was carried on by some natives of Argilus, an Andrian colony, residing in Amphipolis, where they had also other accomplices gained over by Perdiccas or the Chalcidians. But the most active in the matter were the inhabitants of Argilus itself, which is close by, who had always been suspected by the Athenians, and had had designs on the place. These men now saw their opportunity arrive with Brasidas, and having for some time been in correspondence with their countrymen in Amphipolis for the betrayal of the town, at once received him into Argilus, and revolted from the Athenians, and that same night took him on to the bridge over the river; where he found only a small guard to oppose him, the town being at some distance from the passage, and the walls not reaching down to it as at present. This guard he easily drove in, partly through there being treason in their ranks, partly from the stormy state of the weather and the suddenness of his attack, and so got across the bridge, and immediately became master of all the property outside; the Amphipolitans having houses all over the quarter.

The passage of Brasidas was a complete surprise to the people in the town; and the capture of many of those outside, and the flight of the rest within the wall, combined to produce great confusion among the citizens; especially as they did not trust one another. It is even said that if Brasidas, instead of stopping to pillage, had advanced straight against the town, he would probably have taken it. In fact, however, he established himself where he was and overran the country outside, and for the present remained inactive, vainly awaiting a demonstration on the part of his friends within. Meanwhile the party opposed to the traitors proved numerous enough to prevent the gates being immediately thrown open, and in concert with Eucles, the general, who had come from Athens to defend the place, sent to the other commander in Thrace, Thucydides, son of Olorus, the author of this history, who was at the isle of Thasos, a Parian colony, half a day's sail from Amphipolis, to tell him to come to their relief. On receipt of this message he at once set sail with seven ships which he had with him, in order, if possible, to reach Amphipolis in time to prevent its capitulation, or in any case to save Eion.

Meanwhile Brasidas, afraid of succours arriving by sea from Thasos, and learning that Thucydides possessed the right of working the gold mines in that part of Thrace, and had thus great influence with the inhabitants of the continent, hastened to gain the town, if possible, before the people of Amphipolis should be encouraged by his arrival to hope that he could save them by getting together a force of allies from the sea and from Thrace, and so refuse to surrender. He accordingly offered moderate terms, proclaiming that any of the Amphipolitans and Athenians who chose, might continue to enjoy their property with full rights of citizenship; while those who did not wish to stay had five days to depart, taking their property with them.

The bulk of the inhabitants, upon hearing this, began to change their minds, especially as only a small number of the citizens were Athenians, the majority having come from different quarters, and many of the prisoners outside had relations within the walls. They found the proclamation a fair one in comparison of what their fear had suggested; the Athenians being glad to go out, as they thought they ran more risk than the rest, and further, did not expect any speedy relief, and the multitude generally being content at being left in possession of their civic rights, and at such an unexpected reprieve from danger. The partisans of Brasidas now openly advocated this course, seeing that the feeling of the people had changed, and that they no longer gave ear to the Athenian general present; and thus the surrender was made and Brasidas was admitted by them on the terms of his proclamation. In this way they gave up the city, and late in the same day Thucydides and his ships entered the harbour of Eion, Brasidas having just got hold of Amphipolis, and having been within a night of taking Eion: had the ships been less prompt in relieving it, in the morning it would have been his.

After this Thucydides put all in order at Eion to secure it against any present or future attack of Brasidas, and received such as had elected to come there from the interior according to the terms agreed on. Meanwhile Brasidas suddenly sailed with a number of boats down the river to Eion to see if he could not seize the point running out from the wall, and so command the entrance; at the same time he attempted it by land, but was beaten off on both sides and had to content himself with arranging matters at Amphipolis and in the neighbourhood. Myrcinus, an Edonian town, also came over to him; the Edonian king Pittacus having been killed by the sons of Goaxis and his own wife Brauro; and Galepsus and Oesime, which are Thasian colonies, not long after followed its example. Perdiccas too came up immediately after the capture and joined in these arrangements.

The news that Amphipolis was in the hands of the enemy caused great alarm at Athens. Not only was the town valuable for the timber it afforded for shipbuilding, and the money that it brought in; but also, although the escort of the Thessalians gave the Lacedaemonians a means of reaching the allies of Athens as far as the Strymon, yet as long as they were not masters of the bridge but were watched on the side of Eion by the Athenian galleys, and on the land side impeded by a large and extensive lake formed by the waters of the river, it was impossible for them to go any further. Now, on the contrary, the path seemed open. There was also the fear of the allies revolting, owing to the moderation displayed by Brasidas in all his conduct, and to the declarations which he was everywhere making that he sent out to free Hellas. The towns subject to the Athenians, hearing of the capture of Amphipolis and of the terms accorded to it, and of the gentleness of Brasidas, felt most strongly encouraged to change their condition, and sent secret messages to him, begging him to come on to them; each wishing to be the first to revolt. Indeed there seemed to be no danger in so doing; their mistake in their estimate of the Athenian power was as great as that power afterwards turned out to be, and their judgment was based more upon blind wishing than upon any sound prevision; for it is a habit of mankind to entrust to careless hope what they long for, and to use sovereign reason to thrust aside what they do not fancy. Besides the late severe blow which the Athenians had met with in Boeotia, joined to the seductive, though untrue, statements of Brasidas, about the Athenians not having ventured to engage his single army at Nisaea, made the allies confident, and caused them to believe that no Athenian force would be sent against them. Above all the wish to do what was agreeable at the moment, and the likelihood that they should find the Lacedaemonians full of zeal at starting, made them eager to venture. Observing this, the Athenians sent garrisons to the different towns, as far as was possible at such short notice and in winter; while Brasidas sent dispatches to Lacedaemon asking for reinforcements, and himself made preparations for building galleys in the Strymon. The Lacedaemonians however did not send him any, partly through envy on the part of their chief men, partly because they were more bent on recovering the prisoners of the island and ending the war.

The same winter the Megarians took and razed to the foundations the long walls which had been occupied by the Athenians; and Brasidas after the capture of Amphipolis marched with his allies against Acte, a promontory running out from the King's dike with an inward curve, and ending in Athos, a lofty mountain looking towards the Aegean Sea. In it are various towns, Sane, an Andrian colony, close to the canal, and facing the sea in the direction of Euboea; the others being Thyssus, Cleone, Acrothoi, Olophyxus, and Dium, inhabited by mixed barbarian races speaking the two languages. There is also a small Chalcidian element; but the greater number are Tyrrheno-Pelasgians once settled in Lemnos and Athens, and Bisaltians, Crestonians, and Edonians; the towns being all small ones. Most of these came over to Brasidas; but Sane and Dium held out and saw their land ravaged by him and his army.

Upon their not submitting, he at once marched against Torone in Chalcidice, which was held by an Athenian garrison, having been invited by a few persons who were prepared to hand over the town. Arriving in the dark a little before daybreak, he sat down with his army near the temple of the Dioscuri, rather more than a quarter of a mile from the city. The rest of the town of Torone and the Athenians in garrison did not perceive his approach; but his partisans knowing that he was coming (a few of them had secretly gone out to meet him) were on the watch for his arrival, and were no sooner aware of it than they took it to them seven light-armed men with daggers, who alone of twenty men ordered on this service dared to enter, commanded by Lysistratus an Olynthian. These passed through the sea wall, and without being seen went up and put to the sword the garrison of the highest post in the town, which stands on a hill, and broke open the postern on the side of Canastraeum.

Brasidas meanwhile came a little nearer and then halted with his main body, sending on one hundred targeteers to be ready to rush in first, the moment that a gate should be thrown open and the beacon lighted as agreed. After some time passed in waiting and wondering at the delay, the targeteers by degrees got up close to the town. The Toronaeans inside at work with the party that had entered had by this time broken down the postern and opened the gates leading to the market-place by cutting through the bar, and first brought some men round and let them in by the postern, in order to strike a panic into the surprised townsmen by suddenly attacking them from behind and on both sides at once; after which they raised the fire-signal as had been agreed, and took in by the market gates the rest of the targeteers.

Brasidas seeing the signal told the troops to rise, and dashed forward amid the loud hurrahs of his men, which carried dismay among the astonished townspeople. Some burst in straight by the gate, others over some square pieces of timber placed against the wall (which has fallen down and was being rebuilt) to draw up stones; Brasidas and the greater number making straight uphill for the higher part of the town, in order to take it from top to bottom, and once for all, while the rest of the multitude spread in all directions.

The capture of the town was effected before the great body of the Toronaeans had recovered from their surprise and confusion; but the conspirators and the citizens of their party at once joined the invaders. About fifty of the Athenian heavy infantry happened to be sleeping in the market-place when the alarm reached them. A few of these were killed fighting; the rest escaped, some by land, others to the two ships on the station, and took refuge in Lecythus, a fort garrisoned by their own men in the corner of the town running out into the sea and cut off by a narrow isthmus; where they were joined by the Toronaeans of their party.

Day now arrived, and the town being secured, Brasidas made a proclamation to the Toronaeans who had taken refuge with the Athenians, to come out, as many as chose, to their homes without fearing for their rights or persons, and sent a herald to invite the Athenians to accept a truce, and to evacuate Lecythus with their property, as being Chalcidian ground. The Athenians refused this offer, but asked for a truce for a day to take up their dead. Brasidas granted it for two days, which he employed in fortifying the houses near, and the Athenians in doing the same to their positions. Meanwhile he called a meeting of the Toronaeans, and said very much what he had said at Acanthus, namely, that they must not look upon those who had negotiated with him for the capture of the town as bad men or as traitors, as they had not acted as they had done from corrupt motives or in order to enslave the city, but for the good and freedom of Torone; nor again must those who had not shared in the enterprise fancy that they would not equally reap its fruits, as he had not come to destroy either city or individual. This was the reason of his proclamation to those that had fled for refuge to the Athenians: he thought none the worse of them for their friendship for the Athenians; he believed that they had only to make trial of the Lacedaemonians to like them as well, or even much better, as acting much more justly: it was for want of such a trial that they were now afraid of them. Meanwhile he warned all of them to prepare to be staunch allies, and for being held responsible for all faults in future: for the past, they had not wronged the Lacedaemonians but had been wronged by others who were too strong for them, and any opposition that they might have offered him could be excused.

Having encouraged them with this address, as soon as the truce expired he made his attack upon Lecythus; the Athenians defending themselves from a poor wall and from some houses with parapets. One day they beat him off; the next the enemy were preparing to bring up an engine against them from which they meant to throw fire upon the wooden defences, and the troops were already coming up to the point where they fancied they could best bring up the engine, and where place was most assailable; meanwhile the Athenians put a wooden tower upon a house opposite, and carried up a quantity of jars and casks of water and big stones, and a large number of men also climbed up. The house thus laden too heavily suddenly broke down with a loud crash; at which the men who were near and saw it were more vexed than frightened; but those not so near, and still more those furthest off, thought that the place was already taken at that point, and fled in haste to the sea and the ships.

Brasidas, perceiving that they were deserting the parapet, and seeing what was going on, dashed forward with his troops, and immediately took the fort, and put to the sword all whom he found in it. In this way the place was evacuated by the Athenians, who went across in their boats and ships to Pallene. Now there is a temple of Athene in Lecythus, and Brasidas had proclaimed in the moment of making the assault that he would give thirty silver minae to the man first on the wall. Being now of opinion that the capture was scarcely due to human means, he gave the thirty minae to the goddess for her temple, and razed and cleared Lecythus, and made the whole of it consecrated ground. The rest of the winter he spent in settling the places in his hands, and in making designs upon the rest; and with the expiration of the winter the eighth year of this war ended.

In the spring of the summer following, the Lacedaemonians and Athenians made an armistice for a year; the Athenians thinking that they would thus have full leisure to take their precautions before Brasidas could procure the revolt of any more of their towns, and might also, if it suited them, conclude a general peace; the Lacedaemonians divining the actual fears of the Athenians, and thinking that after once tasting a respite from trouble and misery they would be more disposed to consent to a reconciliation, and to give back the prisoners, and make a treaty for the longer period. The great idea of the Lacedaemonians was to get back their men while Brasidas's good fortune lasted: further successes might make the struggle a less unequal one in Chalcidice, but would leave them still deprived of their men, and even in Chalcidice not more than a match for the Athenians and by no means certain of victory. An armistice was accordingly concluded by Lacedaemon and her allies upon the terms following:

1. As to the temple and oracle of the Pythian Apollo, we are agreed that whosoever will shall have access to it, without fraud or fear, according to the usages of his forefathers. The Lacedaemonians and the allies present agree to this, and promise to send heralds to the Boeotians and Phocians, and to do their best to persuade them to agree likewise.

2. As to the treasure of the god, we agree to exert ourselves to detect all malversators, truly and honestly following the customs of our forefathers, we and you and all others willing to do so, all following the customs of our forefathers. As to these points the Lacedaemonians and the other allies are agreed as has been said.

3. As to what follows, the Lacedaemonians and the other allies agree, if the Athenians conclude a treaty, to remain, each of us in our own territory, retaining our respective acquisitions: the garrison in Coryphasium keeping within Buphras and Tomeus: that in Cythera attempting no communication with the Peloponnesian confederacy, neither we with them, nor they with us: that in Nisaea and Minoa not crossing the road leading from the gates of the temple of Nisus to that of Poseidon and from thence straight to the bridge at Minoa: the Megarians and the allies being equally bound not to cross this road, and the Athenians retaining the island they have taken, without any communication on either side: as to Troezen, each side retaining what it has, and as was arranged with the Athenians.

4. As to the use of the sea, so far as refers to their own coast and to that of their confederacy, that the Lacedaemonians and their allies may voyage upon it in any vessel rowed by oars and of not more than five hundred talents tonnage, not a vessel of war.

5. That all heralds and embassies, with as many attendants as they please, for concluding the war and adjusting claims, shall have free passage, going and coming, to Peloponnese or Athens by land and by sea.

6. That during the truce, deserters whether bond or free shall be received neither by you, nor by us.

7. Further, that satisfaction shall be given by you to us and by us to you according to the public law of our several countries, all disputes being settled by law without recourse to hostilities.

The Lacedaemonians and allies agree to these articles; but if you have anything fairer or juster to suggest, come to Lacedaemon and let us know: whatever shall be just will meet with no objection either from the Lacedaemonians or from the allies. Only let those who come come with full powers, as you desire us. The truce shall be for one year.

Approved by the people.

The tribe of Acamantis had the prytany, Phoenippus was secretary, Niciades chairman. Laches moved, in the name of the good luck of the Athenians, that they should conclude the armistice upon the terms agreed upon by the Lacedaemonians and the allies. It was agreed accordingly in the popular assembly that the armistice should be for one year, beginning that very day, the fourteenth of the month of Elaphebolion; during which time ambassadors and heralds should go and come between the two countries to discuss the bases of a pacification. That the generals and prytanes should call an assembly of the people, in which the Athenians should first consult on the peace, and on the mode in which the embassy for putting an end to the war should be admitted. That the embassy now present should at once take the engagement before the people to keep well and truly this truce for one year.

On these terms the Lacedaemonians concluded with the Athenians and their allies on the twelfth day of the Spartan month Gerastius; the allies also taking the oaths. Those who concluded and poured the libation were Taurus, son of Echetimides, Athenaeus, son of Pericleidas, and Philocharidas, son of Eryxidaidas, Lacedaemonians; Aeneas, son of Ocytus, and Euphamidas, son of Aristonymus, Corinthians; Damotimus, son of Naucrates, and Onasimus, son of Megacles, Sicyonians; Nicasus, son of Cecalus, and Menecrates, son of Amphidorus, Megarians; and Amphias, son of Eupaidas, an Epidaurian; and the Athenian generals Nicostratus, son of Diitrephes, Nicias, son of Niceratus, and Autocles, son of Tolmaeus. Such was the armistice, and during the whole of it conferences went on on the subject of a pacification.

In the days in which they were going backwards and forwards to these conferences, Scione, a town in Pallene, revolted from Athens, and went over to Brasidas. The Scionaeans say that they are Pallenians from Peloponnese, and that their first founders on their voyage from Troy were carried in to this spot by the storm which the Achaeans were caught in, and there settled. The Scionaeans had no sooner revolted than Brasidas crossed over by night to Scione, with a friendly galley ahead and himself in a small boat some way behind; his idea being that if he fell in with a vessel larger than the boat he would have the galley to defend him, while a ship that was a match for the galley would probably neglect the small vessel to attack the large one, and thus leave him time to escape. His passage effected, he called a meeting of the Scionaeans and spoke to the same effect as at Acanthus and Torone, adding that they merited the utmost commendation, in that, in spite of Pallene within the isthmus being cut off by the Athenian occupation of Potidaea and of their own practically insular position, they had of their own free will gone forward to meet their liberty instead of timorously waiting until they had been by force compelled to their own manifest good. This was a sign that they would valiantly undergo any trial, however great;

and if he should order affairs as he intended, he should count them among the truest and sincerest friends of the Lacedaemonians, and would in every other way honour them.

The Scionaeans were elated by his language, and even those who had at first disapproved of what was being done catching the general confidence, they determined on a vigorous conduct of the war, and welcomed Brasidas with all possible honours, publicly crowning him with a crown of gold as the liberator of Hellas; while private persons crowded round him and decked him with garlands as though he had been an athlete. Meanwhile Brasidas left them a small garrison for the present and crossed back again, and not long afterwards sent over a larger force, intending with the help of the Scionaeans to attempt Mende and Potidaea before the Athenians should arrive; Scione, he felt, being too like an island for them not to relieve it. He had besides intelligence in the above towns about their betrayal.

In the midst of his designs upon the towns in question, a galley arrived with the commissioners carrying round the news of the armistice, Aristonymus for the Athenians and Athenaeus for the Lacedaemonians. The troops now crossed back to Torone, and the commissioners gave Brasidas notice of the convention. All the Lacedaemonian allies in Thrace accepted what had been done; and Aristonymus made no difficulty about the rest, but finding, on counting the days, that the Scionaeans had revolted after the date of the convention, refused to include them in it. To this Brasidas earnestly objected, asserting that the revolt took place before, and would not give up the town. Upon Aristonymus reporting the case to Athens, the people at once prepared to send an expedition to Scione. Upon this, envoys arrived from Lacedaemon, alleging that this would be a breach of the truce, and laying claim to the town upon the faith of the assertion of Brasidas, and meanwhile offering to submit the question to arbitration. Arbitration, however, was what the Athenians did not choose to risk; being determined to send troops at once to the place, and furious at the idea of even the islanders now daring to revolt, in a vain reliance upon the power of the Lacedaemonians by land. Besides the facts of the revolt were rather as the Athenians contended, the Scionaeans having revolted two days after the convention. Cleon accordingly succeeded in carrying a decree to reduce and put to death the Scionaeans; and the Athenians employed the leisure which they now enjoyed in preparing for the expedition.

Meanwhile Mende revolted, a town in Pallene and a colony of the Eretrians, and was received without scruple by Brasidas, in spite of its having evidently come over during the armistice, on account of certain infringements of the truce alleged by him against the Athenians. This audacity of Mende was partly caused by seeing Brasidas forward in the matter and by the conclusions drawn from his refusal to betray Scione; and besides, the conspirators in Mende were few, and, as I have already intimated, had carried on their practices too long not to fear detection for themselves, and not to wish to force the inclination of the multitude. This news made the Athenians more furious than ever, and they at once prepared against both towns. Brasidas, expecting their arrival, conveyed away to Olynthus in Chalcidice the women and children of the Scionaeans and Mendaeans, and sent over to them five hundred Peloponnesian heavy infantry and three hundred Chalcidian targeteers, all under the command of Polydamidas.

Leaving these two towns to prepare together against the speedy arrival of the Athenians, Brasidas and Perdiccas started on a second joint expedition into Lyncus against Arrhabaeus; the latter with the forces of his Macedonian subjects, and a corps of heavy infantry composed of Hellenes domiciled in the country; the former with the Peloponnesians whom he still had with him and the Chalcidians, Acanthians, and the rest in such force as they were able. In all there were about three thousand Hellenic heavy infantry, accompanied by all the Macedonian cavalry with the Chalcidians, near one thousand strong, besides an immense crowd of barbarians. On entering the country of Arrhabaeus, they found the Lyncestians encamped awaiting them, and themselves took up a position opposite. The infantry on either side were upon a hill, with a plain between them, into which the horse of both armies first galloped down and engaged a cavalry action. After this the Lyncestian heavy infantry advanced from their hill to join their cavalry and offered battle; upon which Brasidas and Perdiccas also came down to meet them, and engaged and routed them with heavy loss; the survivors taking refuge upon the heights and there remaining inactive. The victors now set up a trophy and waited two or three days for the Illyrian mercenaries who were to join Perdiccas. Perdiccas then wished to go on and attack the villages of Arrhabaeus, and to sit still no longer; but Brasidas, afraid that the Athenians might sail up during his absence, and of something happening to Mende, and seeing besides that the Illyrians did not appear, far from seconding this wish was anxious to return.

While they were thus disputing, the news arrived that the Illyrians had actually betrayed Perdiccas and had joined Arrhabaeus; and the fear inspired by their warlike character made both parties now think it best to retreat. However, owing to the dispute, nothing had been settled as to when they should start; and night coming on, the Macedonians and the barbarian crowd took fright in a moment in one of those mysterious panics to which great armies are liable; and persuaded that an army many times more numerous than that which had really arrived was advancing and all but upon them, suddenly broke and fled in the direction of home, and thus compelled Perdiccas, who at first did not perceive what had occurred, to depart without seeing Brasidas, the two armies being encamped at a considerable distance from each other. At daybreak Brasidas, perceiving that the Macedonians had gone on, and that the Illyrians and Arrhabaeus were on the point of attacking him, formed his heavy infantry into a square, with the light troops in the centre, and himself also prepared to retreat. Posting his youngest soldiers to dash out wherever the enemy should attack them, he himself with three hundred picked men in the rear intended to face about during the retreat and beat off the most forward of their assailants, Meanwhile, before the enemy approached, he sought to sustain the courage of his soldiers with the following hasty exhortation:

"Peloponnesians, if I did not suspect you of being dismayed at being left alone to sustain the attack of a numerous and barbarian enemy, I should just have said a few words to you as usual without further explanation. As it is, in the face of the desertion of our friends and the numbers of the enemy, I have some advice and information to offer, which, brief as they must be, will, I hope, suffice for the more important points. The bravery that you habitually display in war does not depend on your having allies at your side in this or that encounter, but on your native courage; nor have numbers any terrors for citizens of states like yours, in which the many do not rule the few, but rather the few the many, owing their position to nothing else than to superiority in the field. Inexperience now makes you afraid of barbarians; and yet the trial of strength which you had with the Macedonians among them, and my own judgment, confirmed by what I hear from others, should be enough to satisfy you that they will not prove formidable. Where an enemy seems strong but is really weak, a true knowledge of the facts makes his adversary the bolder, just as a serious antagonist is encountered most confidently by those who do not know him. Thus the present enemy might terrify an inexperienced imagination; they are formidable in outward bulk, their loud yelling is unbearable, and the brandishing of their weapons in the air has a threatening appearance. But when it comes to real fighting with an opponent who stands his ground, they are not what they seemed; they have no regular order that they should be ashamed of deserting their positions when hard pressed; flight and attack are with them equally honourable, and afford no test of courage; their independent mode of fighting never leaving any one who wants to run away without a fair excuse for so doing. In short, they think frightening you at a secure distance a surer game than

313

meeting you hand to hand; otherwise they would have done the one and not the other. You can thus plainly see that the terrors with which they were at first invested are in fact trifling enough, though to the eye and ear very prominent. Stand your ground therefore when they advance, and again wait your opportunity to retire in good order, and you will reach a place of safety all the sooner, and will know for ever afterwards that rabble such as these, to those who sustain their first attack, do but show off their courage by threats of the terrible things that they are going to do, at a distance, but with those who give way to them are quick enough to display their heroism in pursuit when they can do so without danger."

With this brief address Brasidas began to lead off his army. Seeing this, the barbarians came on with much shouting and hubbub, thinking that he was flying and that they would overtake him and cut him off. But wherever they charged they found the young men ready to dash out against them, while Brasidas with his picked company sustained their onset. Thus the Peloponnesians withstood the first attack, to the surprise of the enemy, and afterwards received and repulsed them as fast as they came on, retiring as soon as their opponents became quiet. The main body of the barbarians ceased therefore to molest the Hellenes with Brasidas in the open country, and leaving behind a certain number to harass their march, the rest went on after the flying Macedonians, slaying those with whom they came up, and so arrived in time to occupy the narrow pass between two hills that leads into the country of Arrhabaeus. They knew that this was the only way by which Brasidas could retreat, and now proceeded to surround him just as he entered the most impracticable part of the road, in order to cut him off.

Brasidas, perceiving their intention, told his three hundred to run on without order, each as quickly as he could, to the hill which seemed easiest to take, and to try to dislodge the barbarians already there, before they should be joined by the main body closing round him. These attacked and overpowered the party upon the hill, and the main army of the Hellenes now advanced with less difficulty towards it - the barbarians being terrified at seeing their men on that side driven from the height and no longer following the main body, who, they considered, had gained the frontier and made good their escape. The heights once gained, Brasidas now proceeded more securely, and the same day arrived at Arnisa, the first town in the dominions of Perdiccas. The soldiers, enraged at the desertion of the Macedonians, vented their rage on all their yokes of oxen which they found on the road, and on any baggage which had tumbled off (as might easily happen in the panic of a night retreat), by unyoking and cutting down the cattle and taking the baggage for themselves. From this moment Perdiccas began to regard Brasidas as an enemy and to feel against the Peloponnesians a hatred which could not be congenial to the adversary of the Athenians. However, he departed from his natural interests and made it his endeavour to come to terms with the latter and to get rid of the former.

On his return from Macedonia to Torone, Brasidas found the Athenians already masters of Mende, and remained quiet where he was, thinking it now out of his power to cross over into Pallene and assist the Mendaeans, but he kept good watch over Torone. For about the same time as the campaign in Lyncus, the Athenians sailed upon the expedition which we left them preparing against Mende and Scione, with fifty ships, ten of which were Chians, one thousand Athenian heavy infantry and six hundred archers, one hundred Thracian mercenaries and some targeteers drawn from their allies in the neighbourhood, under the command of Nicias, son of Niceratus, and Nicostratus, son of Diitrephes. Weighing from Potidaea, the fleet came to land opposite the temple of Poseidon, and proceeded against Mende; the men of which town, reinforced by three hundred Scionaeans, with their Peloponnesian auxiliaries, seven hundred heavy infantry in all, under Polydamidas, they found encamped upon a strong hill outside the city. These Nicias, with one hundred and twenty light-armed Methonaeans, sixty picked men from the Athenian heavy infantry, and all the archers, tried to reach by a path running up the hill, but received a wound and found himself unable to force the position; while Nicostratus, with all the rest of the army, advancing upon the hill, which was naturally difficult, by a different approach further off, was thrown into utter disorder; and the whole Athenian army narrowly escaped being defeated. For that day, as the Mendaeans and their allies showed no signs of yielding, the Athenians retreated and encamped, and the Mendaeans at nightfall returned into the town.

The next day the Athenians sailed round to the Scione side, and took the suburb, and all day plundered the country, without any one coming out against them, partly because of intestine disturbances in the town; and the following night the three hundred Scionaeans returned home. On the morrow Nicias advanced with half the army to the frontier of Scione and laid waste the country; while Nicostratus with the remainder sat down before the town near the upper gate on the road to Potidaea. The arms of the Mendaeans and of their Peloponnesian auxiliaries within the wall happened to be piled in that quarter, where Polydamidas accordingly began to draw them up for battle, encouraging the Mendaeans to make a sortie. At this moment one of the popular party answered him factiously that they would not go out and did not want a war, and for thus answering was dragged by the arm and knocked about by Polydamidas. Hereupon the infuriated commons at once seized their arms and rushed at the Peloponnesians and at their allies of the opposite faction. The troops thus assaulted were at once routed, partly from the suddenness of the conflict and partly through fear of the gates being opened to the Athenians, with whom they imagined that the attack had been concerted. As many as were not killed on the spot took refuge in the citadel, which they had held from the first; and the whole, Athenian army, Nicias having by this time returned and being close to the city, now burst into Mende, which had opened its gates without any convention, and sacked it just as if they had taken it by storm, the generals even finding some difficulty in restraining them from also massacring the inhabitants. After this the Athenians told the Mendaeans that they might retain their civil rights, and themselves judge the supposed authors of the revolt; and cut off the party in the citadel by a wall built down to the sea on either side, appointing troops to maintain the blockade. Having thus secured Mende, they proceeded against Scione.

The Scionaeans and Peloponnesians marched out against them, occupying a strong hill in front of the town, which had to be captured by the enemy before they could invest the place. The Athenians stormed the hill, defeated and dislodged its occupants, and, having encamped and set up a trophy, prepared for the work of circumvallation. Not long after they had begun their operations, the auxiliaries besieged in the citadel of Mende forced the guard by the sea-side and arrived by night at Scione, into which most of them succeeded in entering, passing through the besieging army.

While the investment of Scione was in progress, Perdiccas sent a herald to the Athenian generals and made peace with the Athenians, through spite against Brasidas for the retreat from Lyncus, from which moment indeed he had begun to negotiate. The Lacedaemonian Ischagoras was just then upon the point of starting with an army overland to join Brasidas; and Perdiccas, being now required by Nicias to give some proof of the sincerity of his reconciliation to the Athenians, and being himself no longer disposed to let the Peloponnesians into his country, put in motion his friends in Thessaly, with whose chief men he always took care to have relations, and so effectually stopped the army and its preparation that they did not even try the Thessalians. Ischagoras himself, however, with Ameinias and Aristeus, succeeded in reaching Brasidas; they had been commissioned by the Lacedaemonians to inspect the state of affairs, and brought out from Sparta (in violation of all precedent) some of their young men to put in command of the towns, to guard against their being entrusted to the persons upon the spot. Brasidas accordingly placed

Clearidas, son of Cleonymus, in Amphipolis, and Pasitelidas, son of Hegesander, in Torone.

The same summer the Thebans dismantled the wall of the Thespians on the charge of Atticism, having always wished to do so, and now finding it an easy matter, as the flower of the Thespian youth had perished in the battle with the Athenians. The same summer also the temple of Hera at Argos was burnt down, through Chrysis, the priestess, placing a lighted torch near the garlands and then falling asleep, so that they all caught fire and were in a blaze before she observed it. Chrysis that very night fled to Phlius for fear of the Argives, who, agreeably to the law in such a case, appointed another priestess named Phaeinis. Chrysis at the time of her flight had been priestess for eight years of the present war and half the ninth. At the close of the summer the investment of Scione was completed, and the Athenians, leaving a detachment to maintain the blockade, returned with the rest of their army.

During the winter following, the Athenians and Lacedaemonians were kept quiet by the armistice; but the Mantineans and Tegeans, and their respective allies, fought a battle at Laodicium, in the Oresthid. The victory remained doubtful, as each side routed one of the wings opposed to them, and both set up trophies and sent spoils to Delphi. After heavy loss on both sides the battle was undecided, and night interrupted the action; yet the Tegeans passed the night on the field and set up a trophy at once, while the Mantineans withdrew to Bucolion and set up theirs afterwards.

At the close of the same winter, in fact almost in spring, Brasidas made an attempt upon Potidaea. He arrived by night, and succeeded in planting a ladder against the wall without being discovered, the ladder being planted just in the interval between the passing round of the bell and the return of the man who brought it back. Upon the garrison, however, taking the alarm immediately afterwards, before his men came up, he quickly led off his troops, without waiting until it was day. So ended the winter and the ninth year of this war of which Thucydides is the historian.

CHAPTER XV

Tenth Year of the War - Death of Cleon and Brasidas - Peace of Nicias

THE NEXT summer the truce for a year ended, after lasting until the Pythian games. During the armistice the Athenians expelled the Delians from Delos, concluding that they must have been polluted by some old offence at the time of their consecration, and that this had been the omission in the previous purification of the island, which, as I have related, had been thought to have been duly accomplished by the removal of the graves of the dead. The Delians had Atramyttium in Asia given them by Pharnaces, and settled there as they removed from Delos.

Meanwhile Cleon prevailed on the Athenians to let him set sail at the expiration of the armistice for the towns in the direction of Thrace with twelve hundred heavy infantry and three hundred horse from Athens, a large force of the allies, and thirty ships. First touching at the still besieged Scione, and taking some heavy infantry from the army there, he next sailed into Cophos, a harbour in the territory of Torone, which is not far from the town. From thence, having learnt from deserters that Brasidas was not in Torone, and that its garrison was not strong enough to give him battle, he advanced with his army against the town, sending ten ships to sail round into the harbour. He first came to the fortification lately thrown up in front of the town by Brasidas in order to take in the suburb, to do which he had pulled down part of the original wall and made it all one city. To this point Pasitelidas, the Lacedaemonian commander, with such garrison as there was in the place, hurried to repel the Athenian assault; but finding himself hard pressed, and seeing the ships that had been sent round sailing into the harbour, Pasitelidas began to be afraid that they might get up to the city before its defenders were there and, the fortification being also carried, he might be taken prisoner, and so abandoned the outwork and ran into the town. But the Athenians from the ships had already taken Torone, and their land forces following at his heels burst in with him with a rush over the part of the old wall that had been pulled down, killing some of the Peloponnesians and Toronaeans in the melee, and making prisoners of the rest, and Pasitelidas their commander amongst them. Brasidas meanwhile had advanced to relieve Torone, and had only about four miles more to go when he heard of its fall on the road, and turned back again. Cleon and the Athenians set up two trophies, one by the harbour, the other by the fortification and, making slaves of the wives and children of the Toronaeans, sent the men with the Peloponnesians and any Chalcidians that were there, to the number of seven hundred, to Athens; whence, however, they all came home afterwards, the Peloponnesians on the conclusion of peace, and the rest by being exchanged against other prisoners with the Olynthians. About the same time Panactum, a fortress on the Athenian border, was taken by treachery by the Boeotians. Meanwhile Cleon, after placing a garrison in Torone, weighed anchor and sailed around Athos on his way to Amphipolis.

About the same time Phaeax, son of Erasistratus, set sail with two colleagues as ambassador from Athens to Italy and Sicily. The Leontines, upon the departure of the Athenians from Sicily after the pacification, had placed a number of new citizens upon the roll, and the commons had a design for redividing the land; but the upper classes, aware of their intention, called in the Syracusans and expelled the commons. These last were scattered in various directions; but the upper classes came to an agreement with the Syracusans, abandoned and laid waste their city, and went and lived at Syracuse, where they were made citizens. Afterwards some of them were dissatisfied, and leaving Syracuse occupied Phocaeae, a quarter of the town of Leontini, and Bricinniae, a strong place in the Leontine country, and being there joined by most of the exiled commons carried on war from the fortifications. The Athenians hearing this, sent Phaeax to see if they could not by some means so convince their allies there and the rest of the Sicilians of the ambitious designs of Syracuse as to induce them to form a general coalition against her, and thus save the commons of Leontini. Arrived in Sicily, Phaeax succeeded at Camarina and Agrigentum, but meeting with a repulse at Gela did not go on to the rest, as he saw that he should not succeed with them, but returned through the country of the Sicels to Catana, and after visiting Bricinniae as he passed, and encouraging its inhabitants, sailed back to Athens.

During his voyage along the coast to and from Sicily, he treated with some cities in Italy on the subject of friendship with Athens, and also fell in with some Locrian settlers exiled from Messina, who had been sent thither when the Locrians were called in by one of the factions that divided Messina after the pacification of Sicily, and Messina came for a time into the hands of the Locrians. These being met by Phaeax on their return home received no injury at his hands, as the Locrians had agreed with him for a treaty with Athens. They were the only people of the allies who, when the reconciliation between the Sicilians took place, had not made peace with her; nor indeed would they have done so now, if they had not been pressed by a war with the Hipponians and Medmaeans who lived on their border, and were colonists of theirs. Phaeax meanwhile proceeded on his voyage, and at length arrived at Athens.

Cleon, whom we left on his voyage from Torone to Amphipolis, made Eion his base, and after an unsuccessful assault upon the Andrian colony of Stagirus, took Galepsus, a colony of Thasos, by storm. He now sent envoys to Perdiccas to command his attendance with an army, as provided by the alliance; and others to Thrace, to Polles, king of the Odomantians, who was to bring as many Thracian mercenaries as possible; and himself remained inactive in Eion, awaiting their arrival. Informed of this, Brasidas on his part took up a position of observation upon Cerdylium, a place situated in the Argilian country on high ground across the river, not far from Amphipolis, and commanding a view on all sides, and thus made it impossible for Cleon's army to move without his seeing it; for he fully expected that Cleon, despising the scanty numbers of his opponent, would march against Amphipolis with the force that he had got with him. At the same time Brasidas made his preparations, calling to his standard fifteen hundred Thracian mercenaries and all the Edonians, horse and targeteers; he also had a thousand Myrcinian and Chalcidian targeteers, besides those in Amphipolis, and a force of heavy infantry numbering altogether about two thousand, and three hundred Hellenic horse. Fifteen hundred of these he had with him upon Cerdylium; the rest were stationed with Clearidas in Amphipolis.

After remaining quiet for some time, Cleon was at length obliged to do as Brasidas expected. His soldiers, tired of their inactivity, began also seriously to reflect on the weakness and incompetence of their commander, and the skill and valour that would be opposed to him, and on their own original unwillingness to accompany him. These murmurs coming to the ears of Cleon, he resolved not to disgust the army by keeping it in the same place, and broke up his camp and advanced. The temper of the general was what it had been at Pylos, his success on that occasion having given him confidence in his capacity. He never dreamed of any one coming out to fight him, but said that he was rather going up to view the place; and if he waited for his reinforcements, it was not in order to make victory secure in case he should be compelled to engage, but to be enabled to surround and storm the city. He accordingly came and posted his army upon a strong hill in front of Amphipolis, and proceeded to examine the lake formed by the Strymon, and how the town lay on the side of Thrace. He thought to retire at pleasure without fighting, as there was no one to be seen upon the wall or coming out of the gates, all of which were shut. Indeed, it seemed a mistake not to have brought down engines with him; he could then have taken the town, there being no one to defend it.

As soon as Brasidas saw the Athenians in motion he descended himself from Cerdylium and entered Amphipolis. He did not venture to go out in regular order against the Athenians: he mistrusted his strength, and thought it inadequate to the attempt; not in numbers - these were not so unequal - but in quality, the flower of the Athenian army being in the field, with the best of the Lemnians and Imbrians. He therefore prepared to assail them by stratagem. By showing the enemy the number of his troops, and the shifts which he had been put to to to arm them, he thought that he should have less chance of beating him than by not letting him have a sight of them, and thus learn how good a right he had to despise them. He accordingly picked out a hundred and fifty heavy infantry and, putting the rest under Clearidas, determined to attack suddenly before the Athenians retired; thinking that he should not have again such a chance of catching them alone, if their reinforcements were once allowed to come up; and so calling all his soldiers together in order to encourage them and explain his intention, spoke as follows:

"Peloponnesians, the character of the country from which we have come, one which has always owed its freedom to valour, and the fact that you are Dorians and the enemy you are about to fight Ionians, whom you are accustomed to beat, are things that do not need further comment. But the plan of attack that I propose to pursue, this it is as well to explain, in order that the fact of our adventuring with a part instead of with the whole of our forces may not damp your courage by the apparent disadvantage at which it places you. I imagine it is the poor opinion that he has of us, and the fact that he has no idea of any one coming out to engage him, that has made the enemy march up to the place and carelessly look about him as he is doing, without noticing us. But the most successful soldier will always be the man who most happily detects a blunder like this, and who carefully consulting his own means makes his attack not so much by open and regular approaches, as by seizing the opportunity of the moment; and these stratagems, which do the greatest service to our friends by most completely deceiving our enemies, have the most brilliant name in war. Therefore, while their careless confidence continues, and they are still thinking, as in my judgment they are now doing, more of retreat than of maintaining their position, while their spirit is slack and not high-strung with expectation, I with the men under my command will, if possible, take them by surprise and fall with a run upon their centre; and do you, Clearidas, afterwards, when you see me already upon them, and, as is likely, dealing terror among them, take with you the Amphipolitans, and the rest of the allies, and suddenly open the gates and dash at them, and hasten to engage as quickly as you can. That is our best chance of establishing a panic among them, as a fresh assailant has always more terrors for an enemy than the one he is immediately engaged with. Show yourself a brave man, as a Spartan should; and do you, allies, follow him like men, and remember that zeal, honour, and obedience mark the good soldier, and that this day will make you either free men and allies of Lacedaemon, or slaves of Athens; even if you escape without personal loss of liberty or life, your bondage will be on harsher terms than before, and you will also hinder the liberation of the rest of the Hellenes. No cowardice then on your part, seeing the greatness of the issues at stake, and I will show that what I preach to others I can practise myself."

After this brief speech Brasidas himself prepared for the sally, and placed the rest with Clearidas at the Thracian gates to support him as had been agreed. Meanwhile he had been seen coming down from Cerdylium and then in the city, which is overlooked from the outside, sacrificing near the temple of Athene; in short, all his movements had been observed, and word was brought to Cleon, who had at the moment gone on to look about him, that the whole of the enemy's force could be seen in the town, and that the feet of horses and men in great numbers were visible under the gates, as if a sally were intended. Upon hearing this he went up to look, and having done so, being unwilling to venture upon the decisive step of a battle before his reinforcements came up, and fancying that he would have time to retire, bid the retreat be sounded and sent orders to the men to effect it by moving on the left wing in the direction of Eion, which was indeed the only way practicable. This however not being quick enough for him, he joined the retreat in person and made the right wing wheel round, thus turning its unarmed side to the enemy. It was then that Brasidas, seeing the Athenian force in motion and his opportunity come, said to the men with him and the rest: "Those fellows will never stand before us, one can see that by the way their spears and heads are going. Troops which do as they do seldom stand a charge. Quick, someone, and open the gates I spoke of, and let us be out and at them with no fears for the result." Accordingly issuing out by the palisade gate and by the first in the long wall then existing, he ran at the top of his speed along the straight road, where the trophy now stands as you go by the steepest part of the hill, and fell upon and routed the centre of the Athenians, panic-stricken by their own disorder and astounded at his audacity. At the same moment Clearidas in execution of his orders issued out from the Thracian gates to support him, and also attacked the enemy. The result was that the Athenians, suddenly and unexpectedly attacked on both sides, fell into confusion; and their left towards Eion, which had already got on some distance, at once broke and fled. Just as it was in full retreat and Brasidas was passing on to attack the right, he received a wound; but his fall was not perceived by the Athenians, as he was taken up by those near him and carried off the field. The Athenian right made a better stand, and though Cleon, who from the first had no thought of fighting, at once fled and was overtaken and slain by a Myrcinian targeteer, his infantry forming in close order upon the hill twice or thrice repulsed the attacks of Clearidas, and did not finally give way until they were surrounded and routed by the missiles of the Myrcinian and Chalcidian horse and the targeteers. Thus the Athenian army was all now in flight; and such as escaped being killed in the battle, or by the Chalcidian horse and the targeteers, dispersed among the hills, and with difficulty made their way to Eion. The men who had taken up and rescued Brasidas, brought him into the town with the breath still in him: he lived to hear of the victory of his troops, and not long after expired. The rest of the army returning with Clearidas from the pursuit stripped the dead and set up a trophy.

After this all the allies attended in arms and buried Brasidas at the public expense in the city, in front of what is now the marketplace, and the Amphipolitans, having enclosed his tomb, ever afterwards sacrifice to him as a hero and have given to him the honour of games and annual offerings. They constituted him the founder of their colony, and pulled down the Hagnonic erections, and obliterated everything that could be interpreted as a memorial of his having founded the place; for they considered that Brasidas had been their preserver, and courting as they did the alliance of Lacedaemon for fear of Athens, in their present hostile relations with the latter they could no longer with the same advantage or satisfaction pay Hagnon his honours. They also gave the Athenians back their dead. About six hundred of the latter had fallen and only seven of the enemy, owing to there having been no regular engagement, but the affair of accident and panic that I have described. After taking up their dead the Athenians sailed off home, while Clearidas and his troops remained to arrange matters at Amphipolis.

About the same time three Lacedaemonians - Ramphias, Autocharidas, and Epicydidas - led a reinforcement of nine hundred heavy infantry to the towns in the direction of Thrace, and arriving at Heraclea in Trachis reformed matters there as seemed good to them. While they delayed there, this battle took place and so the summer ended.

With the beginning of the winter following, Ramphias and his companions penetrated as far as Pierium in Thessaly; but as the Thessalians opposed their further advance, and Brasidas whom they came to reinforce was dead, they turned back home, thinking that the moment had gone by, the Athenians being defeated and gone, and themselves not equal to the execution of Brasidas's designs. The main cause however of their return was because they knew that when they set out Lacedaemonian opinion was really in favour of peace.

Indeed it so happened that directly after the battle of Amphipolis and the retreat of Ramphias from Thessaly, both sides ceased to prosecute the war and turned their attention to peace. Athens had suffered severely at Delium, and again shortly afterwards at Amphipolis, and had no longer that confidence in her strength which had made her before refuse to treat, in the belief of ultimate victory which her success at the moment had inspired; besides, she was afraid of her allies being tempted by her reverses to rebel more generally, and repented having let go the splendid opportunity for peace which the affair of Pylos had offered. Lacedaemon, on the other hand, found the event of the war to falsify her notion that a few years would suffice for the overthrow of the power of the Athenians by the devastation of their land. She had suffered on the island a disaster hitherto unknown at Sparta; she saw her country plundered from Pylos and Cythera; the Helots were deserting, and she was in constant apprehension that those who remained in Peloponnese would rely upon those outside and take advantage of the situation to renew their old attempts at revolution. Besides this, as chance would have it, her thirty years' truce with the Argives was upon the point of expiring; and they refused to renew it unless Cynuria were restored to them; so that it seemed impossible to fight Argos and Athens at once. She also suspected some of the cities in Peloponnese of intending to go over to the enemy and that was indeed the case.

These considerations made both sides disposed for an accommodation; the Lacedaemonians being probably the most eager, as they ardently desired to recover the men taken upon the island, the Spartans among whom belonged to the first families and were accordingly related to the governing body in Lacedaemon.

Negotiations had been begun directly after their capture, but the Athenians in their hour of triumph would not consent to any reasonable terms; though after their defeat at Delium, Lacedaemon, knowing that they would be now more inclined to listen, at once concluded the armistice for a year, during which they were to confer together and see if a longer period could not be agreed upon.

Now, however, after the Athenian defeat at Amphipolis, and the death of Cleon and Brasidas, who had been the two principal opponents of peace on either side - the latter from the success and honour which war gave him, the former because he thought that, if tranquillity were restored, his crimes would be more open to detection and his slanders less credited - the foremost candidates for power in either city, Pleistoanax, son of Pausanias, king of Lacedaemon, and Nicias, son of Niceratus, the most fortunate general of his time, each desired peace more ardently than ever. Nicias, while still happy and honoured, wished to secure his good fortune, to obtain a present release from trouble for himself and his countrymen, and hand down to posterity a name as an ever-successful statesman, and thought the way to do this was to keep out of danger and commit himself as little as possible to fortune, and that peace alone made this keeping out of danger possible. Pleistoanax, again, was assailed by his enemies for his restoration, and regularly held up by them to the prejudice of his countrymen, upon every reverse that befell them, as though his unjust restoration were the cause; the accusation being that he and his brother Aristocles had bribed the prophetess of Delphi to tell the Lacedaemonian deputations which successively arrived at the temple to bring home the seed of the demigod son of Zeus from abroad, else they would have to plough with a silver share. In this way, it was insisted, in time he had induced the Lacedaemonians in the nineteenth year of his exile to Lycaeum (whither he had gone when banished on suspicion of having been bribed to retreat from Attica, and had built half his house within the consecrated precinct of Zeus for fear of the Lacedaemonians), to restore him with the same dances and sacrifices with which they had instituted their kings upon the first settlement of Lacedaemon. The smart of this accusation, and the reflection that in peace no disaster could occur, and that when Lacedaemon had recovered her men there would be nothing for his enemies to take hold of (whereas, while war lasted, the highest station must always bear the scandal of everything that went wrong), made him ardently desire a settlement. Accordingly this winter was employed in conferences; and as spring rapidly approached, the Lacedaemonians sent round orders to the cities to prepare for a fortified occupation of Attica, and held this as a sword over the heads of the Athenians to induce them to listen to their overtures; and at last, after many claims had been urged on either side at the conferences a peace was agreed on upon the following basis. Each party was to restore its conquests, but Athens was to keep Nisaea; her demand for Plataea being met by the Thebans asserting that they had acquired the place not by force or treachery, but by the voluntary adhesion upon agreement of its citizens; and the same, according to the Athenian account, being the history of her acquisition of Nisaea. This arranged, the Lacedaemonians summoned their allies, and all voting for peace except the Boeotians, Corinthians, Eleans, and Megarians, who did not approve of these proceedings, they concluded the treaty and made peace, each of the contracting parties swearing to the following articles:

The Athenians and Lacedaemonians and their allies made a treaty, and swore to it, city by city, as follows;

1. Touching the national temples, there shall be a free passage by land and by sea to all who wish it, to sacrifice, travel, consult, and attend the oracle or games, according to the customs of their countries.

2. The temple and shrine of Apollo at Delphi and the Delphians shall be governed by their own laws, taxed by their own state, and judged by their own judges, the land and the people, according to the custom of their country.

3. The treaty shall be binding for fifty years upon the Athenians and the allies of the Athenians, and upon the Lacedaemonians and the allies of the Lacedaemonians, without fraud or hurt by land or by sea.

4. It shall not be lawful to take up arms, with intent to do hurt, either for the Lacedaemonians and their allies against the Athenians and their allies, or for the Athenians and their allies against the Lacedaemonians and their allies, in any way or means whatsoever. But should any difference arise between them they are to have recourse to law and oaths, according as may be agreed between the parties.

5. The Lacedaemonians and their allies shall give back Amphipolis to the Athenians. Nevertheless, in the case of cities given up by the Lacedaemonians to the Athenians, the inhabitants shall be allowed to go where they please and to take their property with them: and the cities shall be independent, paying only the tribute of Aristides. And it shall not be lawful for the Athenians or their allies to carry on war against them after the treaty has been concluded, so long as the tribute is paid. The cities referred to are Argilus, Stagirus, Acanthus, Scolus, Olynthus, and Spartolus. These cities shall be neutral, allies neither of the Lacedaemonians nor of the Athenians: but if the cities consent, it shall be lawful for the Athenians to make them their allies, provided always that the cities wish it. The Mecybernaeans, Sanaeans, and Singaeans shall inhabit their own cities, as also the Olynthians and Acanthians: but the Lacedaemonians and their allies shall give back Panactum to the Athenians.

6. The Athenians shall give back Coryphasium, Cythera, Methana, Lacedaemonians that are in the prison at Athens or elsewhere in the Athenian dominions, and shall let go the Peloponnesians besieged in Scione, and all others in Scione that are allies of the Lacedaemonians, and all whom Brasidas sent in there, and any others of the allies of the Lacedaemonians that may be in the prison at Athens or elsewhere in the Athenian dominions.

7. The Lacedaemonians and their allies shall in like manner give back any of the Athenians or their allies that they may have in their hands.

8. In the case of Scione, Torone, and Sermylium, and any other cities that the Athenians may have, the Athenians may adopt such measures as they please.

9. The Athenians shall take an oath to the Lacedaemonians and their allies, city by city. Every man shall swear by the most binding oath of his country, seventeen from each city. The oath shall be as follows; "I will abide by this agreement and treaty honestly and without deceit." In the same way an oath shall be taken by the Lacedaemonians and their allies to the Athenians: and the oath shall be renewed annually by both parties. Pillars shall be erected at Olympia, Pythia, the Isthmus, at Athens in the Acropolis, and at Lacedaemon in the temple at Amyclae.

10. If anything be forgotten, whatever it be, and on whatever point, it shall be consistent with their oath for both parties, the Athenians and Lacedaemonians, to alter it, according to their discretion.

The treaty begins from the ephoralty of Pleistolas in Lacedaemon, on the 27th day of the month of Artemisium, and from the archonship, of Alcaeus at Athens, on the 25th day of the month of Elaphebolion. Those who took the oath and poured the libations for the Lacedaemonians were Pleistoanax, Agis, Pleistolas, Damagetis, Chionis, Metagenes, Acanthus, Daithus, Ischagoras, Philocharidas, Zeuxidas, Antippus, Tellis, Alcinadas, Empedias, Menas, and Laphilus: for the Athenians, Lampon, Isthmonicus, Nicias, Laches, Euthydemus, Procles, Pythodorus, Hagnon, Myrtilus, Thrasycles, Theagenes, Aristocrates, Iolcius, Timocrates, Leon, Lamachus, and Demosthenes.

This treaty was made in the spring, just at the end of winter, directly after the city festival of Dionysus, just ten years, with the difference of a few days, from the first invasion of Attica and the commencement of this war. This must be calculated by the seasons rather than by trusting to the enumeration of the names of the several magistrates or offices of honour that are used to mark past events. Accuracy is impossible where an event may have occurred in the beginning, or middle, or at any period in their tenure of office. But by computing by summers and winters, the method adopted in this history, it will be found that, each of these amounting to half a year, there were ten summers and as many winters contained in this first war.

Meanwhile the Lacedaemonians, to whose lot it fell to begin the work of restitution, immediately set free all the prisoners of war in their possession, and sent Ischagoras, Menas, and Philocharidas as envoys to the towns in the direction of Thrace, to order Clearidas to hand over Amphipolis to the Athenians, and the rest of their allies each to accept the treaty as it affected them. They, however, did not like its terms, and refused to accept it; Clearidas also, willing to oblige the Chalcidians, would not hand over the town, averring his inability to do so against their will. Meanwhile he hastened in person to Lacedaemon with envoys from the place, to defend his disobedience against the possible accusations of Ischagoras and his companions, and also to see whether it was too late for the agreement to be altered; and on finding the Lacedaemonians were bound, quickly set out back again with instructions from them to hand over the place, if possible, or at all events to bring out the Peloponnesians that were in it.

The allies happened to be present in person at Lacedaemon, and those who had not accepted the treaty were now asked by the Lacedaemonians to adopt it. This, however, they refused to do, for the same reasons as before, unless a fairer one than the present were agreed upon; and remaining firm in their determination were dismissed by the Lacedaemonians, who now decided on forming an alliance with the Athenians, thinking that Argos, who had refused the application of Ampelidas and Lichas for a renewal of the treaty, would without Athens be no longer formidable, and that the rest of the Peloponnese would be most likely to keep quiet, if the coveted alliance of Athens were shut against them. Accordingly, after conference with the Athenian ambassadors, an alliance was agreed upon and oaths were exchanged, upon the terms following:

1. The Lacedaemonians shall be allies of the Athenians for fifty years.

2. Should any enemy invade the territory of Lacedaemon and injure the Lacedaemonians, the Athenians shall help in such way as they most effectively can, according to their power. But if the invader be gone after plundering the country, that city shall be the enemy of Lacedaemon and Athens, and shall be chastised by both, and one shall not make peace without the other. This to be honestly, loyally, and without fraud.

3. Should any enemy invade the territory of Athens and injure the Athenians, the Lacedaemonians shall help them in such way as they most effectively can, according to their power. But if the invader be gone after plundering the country, that city shall be the enemy of Lacedaemon and Athens, and shall be chastised by both, and one shall not make peace without the other. This to be honestly, loyally, and without fraud.

4. Should the slave population rise, the Athenians shall help the Lacedaemonians with all their might, according to their power.

5. This treaty shall be sworn to by the same persons on either side that swore to the other. It shall be renewed annually by the Lacedaemonians going to Athens for the Dionysia, and the Athenians to Lacedaemon for the Hyacinthia, and a pillar shall be set up by either party: at Lacedaemon near the statue of Apollo at Amyclae, and at Athens on the Acropolis near the statue of Athene. Should the Lacedaemonians and Athenians see to add to or take away from the alliance in any particular, it shall be consistent with their oaths for both parties to do so, according to their discretion.

Those who took the oath for the Lacedaemonians were Pleistoanax, Agis, Pleistolas, Damagetus, Chionis, Metagenes, Acanthus, Daithus, Ischagoras, Philocharidas, Zeuxidas,

Antippus, Alcinadas, Tellis, Empedias, Menas, and Laphilus; for the Athenians, Lampon, Isthmionicus, Laches, Nicias, Euthydemus, Procles, Pythodorus, Hagnon, Myrtilus, Thrasycles, Theagenes, Aristocrates, Iolcius, Timocrates, Leon, Lamachus, and Demosthenes.

This alliance was made not long after the treaty; and the Athenians gave back the men from the island to the Lacedaemonians, and the summer of the eleventh year began. This completes the history of the first war, which occupied the whole of the ten years previously.

CHAPTER XVI

Feeling against Sparta in Peloponnese - League of the Mantineans, Eleans, Argives, and Athenians - Battle of Mantinea and Breaking up of the League

AFTER THE treaty and the alliance between the Lacedaemonians and Athenians, concluded after the ten years' war, in the ephorate of Pleistolas at Lacedaemon, and the archonship of Alcaeus at Athens, the states which had accepted them were at peace; but the Corinthians and some of the cities in Peloponnese trying to disturb the settlement, a fresh agitation was instantly commenced by the allies against Lacedaemon. Further, the Lacedaemonians, as time went on, became suspected by the Athenians through their not performing some of the provisions in the treaty; and though for six years and ten months they abstained from invasion of each other's territory, yet abroad an unstable armistice did not prevent either party doing the other the most effectual injury, until they were finally obliged to break the treaty made after the ten years' war and to have recourse to open hostilities.

The history of this period has been also written by the same Thucydides, an Athenian, in the chronological order of events by summers and winters, to the time when the Lacedaemonians and their allies put an end to the Athenian empire, and took the Long Walls and Piraeus. The war had then lasted for twenty-seven years in all. Only a mistaken judgment can object to including the interval of treaty in the war. Looked at by the light of facts it cannot, it will be found, be rationally considered a state of peace, where neither party either gave or got back all that they had agreed, apart from the violations of it which occurred on both sides in the Mantinean and Epidaurian wars and other instances, and the fact that the allies in the direction of Thrace were in as open hostility as ever, while the Boeotians had only a truce renewed every ten days. So that the first ten years' war, the treacherous armistice that followed it, and the subsequent war will, calculating by the seasons, be found to make up the number of years which I have mentioned, with the difference of a few days, and to afford an instance of faith in oracles being for once justified by the event. I certainly all along remember from the beginning to the end of the war its being commonly declared that it would last thrice nine years. I lived through the whole of it, being of an age to comprehend events, and giving my attention to them in order to know the exact truth about them. It was also my fate to be an exile from my country for twenty years after my command at Amphipolis; and being present with both parties, and more especially with the Peloponnesians by reason of my exile, I had leisure to observe affairs somewhat particularly. I will accordingly now relate the differences that arose after the ten years' war, the breach of the treaty, and the hostilities that followed.

After the conclusion of the fifty years' truce and of the subsequent alliance, the embassies from Peloponnese which had been summoned for this business returned from Lacedaemon. The rest went straight home, but the Corinthians first turned aside to Argos and opened negotiations with some of the men in office there, pointing out that Lacedaemon could have no good end in view, but only the subjugation of Peloponnese, or she would never have entered into treaty and alliance with the once detested Athenians, and that the duty of consulting for the safety of Peloponnese had now fallen upon Argos, who should immediately pass a decree inviting any Hellenic state that chose, such state being independent and accustomed to meet fellow powers upon the fair and equal ground of law and justice, to make a defensive alliance with the Argives; appointing a few individuals with plenipotentiary powers, instead of making the people the medium of negotiation, in order that, in the case of an applicant being rejected, the fact of his overtures might not be made public. They said that many would come over from hatred of the Lacedaemonians. After this explanation of their views, the Corinthians returned home.

The persons with whom they had communicated reported the proposal to their government and people, and the Argives passed the decree and chose twelve men to negotiate an alliance for any Hellenic state that wished it, except Athens and Lacedaemon, neither of which should be able to join without reference to the Argive people. Argos came into the plan the more readily because she saw that war with Lacedaemon was inevitable, the truce being on the point of expiring; and also because she hoped to gain the supremacy of Peloponnese. For at this time Lacedaemon had sunk very low in public estimation because of her disasters, while the Argives were in a most flourishing condition, having taken no part in the Attic war, but having on the contrary profited largely by their neutrality. The Argives accordingly prepared to receive into alliance any of the Hellenes that desired it.

The Mantineans and their allies were the first to come over through fear of the Lacedaemonians. Having taken advantage of the war against Athens to reduce a large part of Arcadia into subjection, they thought that Lacedaemon would not leave them undisturbed in their conquests, now that she had leisure to interfere, and consequently gladly turned to a powerful city like Argos, the historical enemy of the Lacedaemonians, and a sister democracy. Upon the defection of Mantinea, the rest of Peloponnese at once began to agitate the propriety of following her example, conceiving that the Mantineans not have changed sides without good reason; besides which they were angry with Lacedaemon among other reasons for having inserted in the treaty with Athens that it should be consistent with their oaths for both parties, Lacedaemonians and Athenians, to add to or take away from it according to their discretion. It was this clause that was the real origin of the panic in Peloponnese, by exciting suspicions of a Lacedaemonian and Athenian combination against their liberties: any alteration should properly have been made conditional upon the consent of the whole body of the allies. With these apprehensions there was a very general desire in each state to place itself in alliance with Argos.

In the meantime the Lacedaemonians perceiving the agitation going on in Peloponnese, and that Corinth was the author of it and was herself about to enter into alliance with the Argives, sent ambassadors thither in the hope of preventing what was in contemplation. They accused her of having brought it all about, and told her that she could not desert Lacedaemon and become the ally of Argos, without adding violation of her oaths to the crime which she had already committed in not accepting the treaty with Athens, when it had been expressly agreed that the decision of the majority of the allies should be binding, unless the gods or heroes stood in the way. Corinth in her answer, delivered before those of her allies who had like her refused to accept the treaty, and whom she had previously invited to attend, refrained from openly stating the injuries she complained of, such as the non-recovery of Sollium or Anactorium from the Athenians, or any other point in which she thought she had been prejudiced, but took shelter under the pretext that she could not give up her Thracian allies, to whom her separate individual security had been given, when they first rebelled with Potidaea, as well as upon subsequent occasions. She denied, therefore, that she committed any violation of her oaths to the allies in not entering into the treaty with Athens; having sworn upon the faith of the gods to her Thracian friends, she could not honestly give them up. Besides, the expression was, "unless the gods or heroes stand in the way." Now here, as it appeared to her, the gods stood in the way. This was what she said on the subject of her former oaths. As to the Argive alliance, she would confer with her friends and do whatever was right. The Lacedaemonian envoys returning home, some Argive ambassadors who happened to be in Corinth pressed her to conclude the alliance without further delay, but were told to attend at the next congress to be held at Corinth.

Immediately afterwards an Elean embassy arrived, and first

making an alliance with Corinth went on from thence to Argos, according to their instructions, and became allies of the Argives, their country being just then at enmity with Lacedaemon and Lepreum. Some time back there had been a war between the Lepreans and some of the Arcadians; and the Eleans being called in by the former with the offer of half their lands, had put an end to the war, and leaving the land in the hands of its Leprean occupiers had imposed upon them the tribute of a talent to the Olympian Zeus. Till the Attic war this tribute was paid by the Lepreans, who then took the war as an excuse for no longer doing so, and upon the Eleans using force appealed to Lacedaemon. The case was thus submitted to her arbitrament; but the Eleans, suspecting the fairness of the tribunal, renounced the reference and laid waste the Leprean territory. The Lacedaemonians nevertheless decided that the Lepreans were independent and the Eleans aggressors, and as the latter did not abide by the arbitration, sent a garrison of heavy infantry into Lepreum. Upon this the Eleans, holding that Lacedaemon had received one of their rebel subjects, put forward the convention providing that each confederate should come out of the Attic war in possession of what he had when he went into it, and considering that justice had not been done them went over to the Argives, and now made the alliance through their ambassadors, who had been instructed for that purpose. Immediately after them the Corinthians and the Thracian Chalcidians became allies of Argos. Meanwhile the Boeotians and Megarians, who acted together, remained quiet, being left to do as they pleased by Lacedaemon, and thinking that the Argive democracy would not suit so well with their aristocratic government as the Lacedaemonian constitution.

About the same time in this summer Athens succeeded in reducing Scione, put the adult males to death, and, making slaves of the women and children, gave the land for the Plataeans to live in. She also brought back the Delians to Delos, moved by her misfortunes in the field and by the commands of the god at Delphi. Meanwhile the Phocians and Locrians commenced hostilities. The

Corinthians and Argives, being now in alliance, went to Tegea to bring about its defection from Lacedaemon, seeing that, if so considerable a state could be persuaded to join, all Peloponnese would be with them. But when the Tegeans said that they would do nothing against Lacedaemon, the hitherto zealous Corinthians relaxed their activity, and began to fear that none of the rest would now come over. Still they went to the Boeotians and tried to persuade them to alliance and a common action generally with Argos and themselves, and also begged them to go with them to Athens and obtain for them a ten days' truce similar to that made between the Athenians and Boeotians not long after the fifty years' treaty, and, in the event of the Athenians refusing, to throw up the armistice, and not make any truce in future without Corinth. These were the requests of the Corinthians. The Boeotians stopped them on the subject of the Argive alliance, but went with them to Athens, where however they failed to obtain the ten days' truce; the Athenian answer being that the Corinthians had truce already, as being allies of Lacedaemon. Nevertheless the Boeotians did not throw up their ten days' truce, in spite of the prayers and reproaches of the Corinthians for their breach of faith; and these last had to content themselves with a de facto armistice with Athens.

The same summer the Lacedaemonians marched into Arcadia with their whole levy under Pleistoanax, son of Pausanias, king of Lacedaemon, against the Parrhasians, who were subjects of Mantinea, and a faction of whom had invited their aid. They also meant to demolish, if possible, the fort of Cypsela which the Mantineans had built and garrisoned in the Parrhasian territory, to annoy the district of Sciritis in Laconia. The Lacedaemonians accordingly laid waste the Parrhasian country, and the Mantineans, placing their town in the hands of an Argive garrison, addressed themselves to the defence of their confederacy, but being unable to save Cypsela or the Parrhasian towns went back to Mantinea. Meanwhile the Lacedaemonians made the Parrhasians independent, razed the fortress, and returned home.

The same summer the soldiers from Thrace who had gone out with Brasidas came back, having been brought from thence after the treaty by Clearidas; and the Lacedaemonians decreed that the Helots who had fought with Brasidas should be free and allowed to live where they liked, and not long afterwards settled them with the Neodamodes at Lepreum, which is situated on the Laconian and Elean border; Lacedaemon being at this time at enmity with Elis. Those however of the Spartans who had been taken prisoners on the island and had surrendered their arms might, it was feared, suppose that they were to be subjected to some degradation in consequence of their misfortune, and so make some attempt at revolution, if left in possession of their franchise. These were therefore at once disfranchised, although some of them were in office at the time, and thus placed under a disability to take office, or buy and sell anything. After some time, however, the franchise was restored to them.

The same summer the Dians took Thyssus, a town on Acte by Athos in alliance with Athens. During the whole of this summer intercourse between the Athenians and Peloponnesians continued, although each party began to suspect the other directly after the treaty, because of the places specified in it not being restored. Lacedaemon, to whose lot it had fallen to begin by restoring Amphipolis and the other towns, had not done so. She had equally failed to get the treaty accepted by her Thracian allies, or by the Boeotians or the Corinthians; although she was continually promising to unite with Athens in compelling their compliance, if it were longer refused. She also kept fixing a time at which those who still refused to come in were to be declared enemies to both parties, but took care not to bind herself by any written agreement. Meanwhile the Athenians, seeing none of these professions performed in fact, began to suspect the honesty of her intentions, and consequently not only refused to comply with her demands for Pylos, but also repented having given up the prisoners from the island, and kept tight hold of the other places, until Lacedaemon's part of the treaty should be fulfilled. Lacedaemon, on the other hand, said she had done what she could, having given up the Athenian prisoners of war in her possession, evacuated Thrace, and performed everything else in her power. Amphipolis it was out of her ability to restore; but she would endeavour to bring the Boeotians and Corinthians into the treaty, to recover Panactum, and send home all the Athenian prisoners of war in Boeotia. Meanwhile she required that Pylos should be restored, or at all events that the Messenians and Helots should be withdrawn, as her troops had been from Thrace, and the place garrisoned, if necessary, by the Athenians themselves. After a number of different conferences held during the summer, she succeeded in persuading Athens to withdraw from Pylos the Messenians and the rest of the Helots and deserters from Laconia, who were accordingly settled by her at Cranii in Cephallenia. Thus during this summer there was peace and intercourse between the two peoples.

Next winter, however, the ephors under whom the treaty had been made were no longer in office, and some of their successors were directly opposed to it. Embassies now arrived from the Lacedaemonian confederacy, and the Athenians, Boeotians, and Corinthians also presented themselves at Lacedaemon, and after much discussion and no agreement between them, separated for their several homes; when Cleobulus and Xenares, the two ephors who were the most anxious to break off the treaty, took advantage of this opportunity to communicate privately with the Boeotians and Corinthians, and, advising them to act as much as possible together, instructed the former first to enter into alliance with Argos, and then try and bring themselves and the Argives into alliance with Lacedaemon. The Boeotians would so be least likely to be compelled to come into the Attic treaty; and the Lacedaemonians would prefer gaining the friendship and alliance of Argos even at the price of the hostility of Athens and the rupture of the treaty. The Boeotians knew that an honourable friendship with Argos had been long the desire of Lacedaemon; for the Lacedaemonians believed that this would considerably facilitate the conduct of the war outside Peloponnese. Meanwhile they begged the Boeotians to place Panactum in her hands in order that she might, if possible, obtain Pylos in exchange for it, and so be more in a position to resume hostilities with Athens.

After receiving these instructions for their governments from Xenares and Cleobulus and their friends at Lacedaemon, the Boeotians and Corinthians departed. On their way home they were joined by two persons high in office at Argos, who had waited for them on the road, and who now sounded them upon the possibility of the Boeotians joining the Corinthians, Eleans, and Mantineans in becoming the allies of Argos, in the idea that if this could be effected they would be able, thus united, to make peace or war as they pleased either against Lacedaemon or any other power. The Boeotian envoys were were pleased at thus hearing themselves accidentally asked to do what their friends at Lacedaemon had told them; and the two Argives perceiving that their proposal was agreeable, departed with a promise to send ambassadors to the Boeotians. On their arrival the Boeotians reported to the Boeotarchs what had been said to them at Lacedaemon and also by the Argives who had met them, and the Boeotarchs, pleased with the idea, embraced it with the more eagerness from the lucky coincidence of Argos soliciting the very thing wanted by their friends at Lacedaemon. Shortly afterwards ambassadors appeared from Argos with the proposals indicated; and the Boeotarchs approved of the terms and dismissed the ambassadors with a promise to send envoys to Argos to negotiate the alliance.

In the meantime it was decided by the Boeotarchs, the Corinthians, the Megarians, and the envoys from Thrace first to interchange oaths together to give help to each other whenever it was required and not to make war or peace except in common; after which the Boeotians and Megarians, who acted together, should make the alliance with Argos. But before the oaths were taken the Boeotarchs communicated these proposals to the four councils of the Boeotians, in whom the supreme power resides, and advised them to interchange oaths with all such cities as should be willing to enter into a defensive league with the Boeotians. But the members of the Boeotian councils refused their assent to the proposal, being afraid of offending Lacedaemon by entering into a league with the deserter Corinth; the Boeotarchs not having acquainted them with what had passed at Lacedaemon and with the advice given by Cleobulus and Xenares and the Boeotian partisans there, namely, that they should become allies of Corinth and Argos as a preliminary to a junction with Lacedaemon; fancying that, even if they should say nothing about this, the councils would not vote against what had been decided and advised by the Boeotarchs. This difficulty arising, the Corinthians and the envoys from Thrace departed without anything having been concluded; and the Boeotarchs, who had previously intended after carrying this to try and effect the alliance with Argos, now omitted to bring the Argive question before the councils, or to send to Argos the envoys whom they had promised; and a general coldness and delay ensued in the matter.

In this same winter Mecyberna was assaulted and taken by the Olynthians, having an Athenian garrison inside it.

All this while negotiations had been going on between the Athenians and Lacedaemonians about the conquests still retained by each, and Lacedaemon, hoping that if Athens were to get back Panactum from the Boeotians she might herself recover Pylos, now sent an embassy to the Boeotians, and begged them to place Panactum and their Athenian prisoners in her hands, in order that she might exchange them for Pylos. This the Boeotians refused to do, unless Lacedaemon made a separate alliance with them as she had done with Athens. Lacedaemon knew that this would be a breach of faith to Athens, as it had been agreed that neither of them should make peace or war without the other; yet wishing to obtain Panactum which she hoped to exchange for Pylos, and the party who pressed for the dissolution of the treaty strongly affecting the

Boeotian connection, she at length concluded the alliance just as winter gave way to spring; and Panactum was instantly razed. And so the eleventh year of the war ended.

In the first days of the summer following, the Argives, seeing that the promised ambassadors from Boeotia did not arrive, and that Panactum was being demolished, and that a separate alliance had been concluded between the Boeotians and Lacedaemonians, began to be afraid that Argos might be left alone, and all the confederacy go over to Lacedaemon. They fancied that the Boeotians had been persuaded by the Lacedaemonians to raze Panactum and to enter into the treaty with the Athenians, and that Athens was privy to this arrangement, and even her alliance, therefore, no longer open to them - a resource which they had always counted upon, by reason of the dissensions existing, in the event of the noncontinuance of their treaty with Lacedaemon. In this strait the Argives, afraid that, as the result of refusing to renew the treaty with Lacedaemon and of aspiring to the supremacy in Peloponnese, they would have the Lacedaemonians, Tegeans, Boeotians, and Athenians on their hands all at once, now hastily sent off Eustrophus and Aeson, who seemed the persons most likely to be acceptable, as envoys to Lacedaemon, with the view of making as good a treaty as they could with the Lacedaemonians, upon such terms as could be got, and being left in peace.

Having reached Lacedaemon, their ambassadors proceeded to negotiate the terms of the proposed treaty. What the Argives first demanded was that they might be allowed to refer to the arbitration of some state or private person the question of the Cynurian land, a piece of frontier territory about which they have always been disputing, and which contains the towns of Thyrea and Anthene, and is occupied by the Lacedaemonians. The Lacedaemonians at first said that they could not allow this point to be discussed, but were ready to conclude upon the old terms. Eventually, however, the Argive ambassadors succeeded in obtaining from them this concession: For the present there was to be a truce for fifty years, but it should be competent for either party, there being neither plague nor war in Lacedaemon or Argos, to give a formal challenge and decide the question of this territory by battle, as on a former occasion, when both sides claimed the victory; pursuit not being allowed beyond the frontier of Argos or Lacedaemon. The Lacedaemonians at first thought this mere folly; but at last, anxious at any cost to have the friendship of Argos they agreed to the terms demanded, and reduced them to writing. However, before any of this should become binding, the ambassadors were to return to Argos and communicate with their people and, in the event of their approval, to come at the feast of the Hyacinthia and take the oaths.

The envoys returned accordingly. In the meantime, while the Argives were engaged in these negotiations, the Lacedaemonian ambassadors - Andromedes, Phaedimus, and Antimenidas - who were to receive the prisoners from the Boeotians and restore them and Panactum to the Athenians, found that the Boeotians had themselves razed Panactum, upon the plea that oaths had been anciently exchanged between their people and the Athenians, after a dispute on the subject to the effect that neither should inhabit the place, but that they should graze it in common. As for the Athenian prisoners of war in the hands of the Boeotians, these were delivered over to Andromedes and his colleagues, and by them conveyed to Athens and given back. The envoys at the same time announced the razing of Panactum, which to them seemed as good as its restitution, as it would no longer lodge an enemy of Athens. This announcement was received with great indignation by the Athenians, who thought that the Lacedaemonians had played them false, both in the matter of the demolition of Panactum, which ought to have been restored to them standing, and in having, as they now heard, made a separate alliance with the Boeotians, in spite of their previous promise to join Athens in compelling the adhesion of those who refused to accede to the treaty. The Athenians also considered the other points in which

Lacedaemon had failed in her compact, and thinking that they had been overreached, gave an angry answer to the ambassadors and sent them away.

The breach between the Lacedaemonians and Athenians having gone thus far, the party at Athens, also, who wished to cancel the treaty, immediately put themselves in motion. Foremost amongst these was Alcibiades, son of Clinias, a man yet young in years for any other Hellenic city, but distinguished by the splendour of his ancestry. Alcibiades thought the Argive alliance really preferable, not that personal pique had not also a great deal to do with his opposition; he being offended with the Lacedaemonians for having negotiated the treaty through Nicias and Laches, and having overlooked him on account of his youth, and also for not having shown him the respect due to the ancient connection of his family with them as their proxeni, which, renounced by his grandfather, he had lately himself thought to renew by his attentions to their prisoners taken in the island. Being thus, as he thought, slighted on all hands, he had in the first instance spoken against the treaty, saying that the Lacedaemonians were not to be trusted, but that they only treated, in order to be enabled by this means to crush Argos, and afterwards to attack Athens alone; and now, immediately upon the above occurring, he sent privately to the Argives, telling them to come as quickly as possible to Athens, accompanied by the Mantineans and Eleans, with proposals of alliance; as the moment was propitious and he himself would do all he could to help them.

Upon receiving this message and discovering that the Athenians, far from being privy to the Boeotian alliance, were involved in a serious quarrel with the Lacedaemonians, the Argives paid no further attention to the embassy which they had just sent to Lacedaemon on the subject of the treaty, and began to incline rather towards the Athenians, reflecting that, in the event of war, they would thus have on their side a city that was not only an ancient ally of Argos, but a sister democracy and very powerful at sea. They accordingly at once sent ambassadors to Athens to treat for an alliance, accompanied by others from Elis and Mantinea.

At the same time arrived in haste from Lacedaemon an embassy consisting of persons reputed well disposed towards the Athenians - Philocharidas, Leon, and Endius - for fear that the Athenians in their irritation might conclude alliance with the Argives, and also to ask back Pylos in exchange for Panactum, and in defence of the alliance with the Boeotians to plead that it had not been made to hurt the Athenians. Upon the envoys speaking in the senate upon these points, and stating that they had come with full powers to settle all others at issue between them, Alcibiades became afraid that, if they were to repeat these statements to the popular assembly, they might gain the multitude, and the Argive alliance might be rejected, and accordingly had recourse to the following stratagem. He persuaded the Lacedaemonians by a solemn assurance that if they would say nothing of their full powers in the assembly, he would give back Pylos to them (himself, the present opponent of its restitution, engaging to obtain this from the Athenians), and would settle the other points at issue. His plan was to detach them from Nicias and to disgrace them before the people, as being without sincerity in their intentions, or even common consistency in their language, and so to get the Argives, Eleans, and Mantineans taken into alliance. This plan proved successful. When the envoys appeared before the people, and upon the question being put to them, did not say as they had said in the senate, that they had come with full powers, the Athenians lost all patience, and carried away by Alcibiades, who thundered more loudly than ever against the Lacedaemonians, were ready instantly to introduce the Argives and their companions and to take them into alliance. An earthquake, however, occurring, before anything definite had been done, this assembly was adjourned.

In the assembly held the next day, Nicias, in spite of the Lacedaemonians having been deceived themselves, and having allowed him to be deceived also in not admitting that they had come with full powers, still maintained that it was best to be friends with the Lacedaemonians, and, letting the Argive proposals stand over, to send once more to Lacedaemon and learn her intentions. The adjournment of the war could only increase their own prestige and injure that of their rivals; the excellent state of their affairs making it their interest to preserve this prosperity as long as possible, while those of Lacedaemon were so desperate that the sooner she could try her fortune again the better. He succeeded accordingly in persuading them to send ambassadors, himself being among the number, to invite the Lacedaemonians, if they were really sincere, to restore Panactum intact with Amphipolis, and to abandon their alliance with the Boeotians (unless they consented to accede to the treaty), agreeably to the stipulation which forbade either to treat without the other. The ambassadors were also directed to say that the Athenians, had they wished to play false, might already have made alliance with the Argives, who were indeed come to Athens for that very purpose, and went off furnished with instructions as to any other complaints that the Athenians had to make. Having reached Lacedaemon, they communicated their instructions, and concluded by telling the Lacedaemonians that unless they gave up their alliance with the Boeotians, in the event of their not acceding to the treaty, the Athenians for their part would ally themselves with the Argives and their friends. The Lacedaemonians, however, refused to give up the Boeotian alliance - the party of Xenares the ephor, and such as shared their view, carrying the day upon this point - but renewed the oaths at the request of Nicias, who feared to return without having accomplished anything and to be disgraced; as was indeed his fate, he being held the author of the treaty with Lacedaemon. When he returned, and the Athenians heard that nothing had been done at Lacedaemon, they flew into a passion, and deciding that faith had not been kept with them, took advantage of the presence of the Argives and their allies, who had been introduced by Alcibiades, and made a treaty and alliance with them upon the terms following:

The Athenians, Argives, Mantineans, and Eleans, acting for themselves and the allies in their respective empires, made a treaty for a hundred years, to be without fraud or hurt by land and by sea.

1. It shall not be lawful to carry on war, either for the Argives, Eleans, Mantineans, and their allies, against the Athenians, or the allies in the Athenian empire: or for the Athenians and their allies against the Argives, Eleans, Mantineans, or their allies, in any way or means whatsoever.

The Athenians, Argives, Eleans, and Mantineans shall be allies for a hundred years upon the terms following:

2. If an enemy invade the country of the Athenians, the Argives, Eleans, and Mantineans shall go to the relief of Athens, according as the Athenians may require by message, in such way as they most effectually can, to the best of their power. But if the invader be gone after plundering the territory, the offending state shall be the enemy of the Argives, Mantineans, Eleans, and Athenians, and war shall be made against it by all these cities: and no one of the cities shall be able to make peace with that state, except all the above cities agree to do so.

3. Likewise the Athenians shall go to the relief of Argos, Mantinea, and Elis, if an enemy invade the country of Elis, Mantinea, or Argos, according as the above cities may require by message, in such way as they most effectually can, to the best of their power. But if the invader be gone after plundering the territory, the state offending shall be the enemy of the Athenians, Argives, Mantineans, and Eleans, and war shall be made against it by all these cities, and peace may not be made with that state except all the above cities agree to it.

4. No armed force shall be allowed to pass for hostile purposes through the country of the powers contracting, or of the allies in their respective empires, or to go by sea, except all the cities - that is to say, Athens, Argos, Mantinea, and Elis - vote for such passage.

5. The relieving troops shall be maintained by the city sending

them for thirty days from their arrival in the city that has required them, and upon their return in the same way: if their services be desired for a longer period, the city that sent for them shall maintain them, at the rate of three Aeginetan obols per day for a heavy-armed soldier, archer, or light soldier, and an Aeginetan drachma for a trooper.

6. The city sending for the troops shall have the command when the war is in its own country: but in case of the cities resolving upon a joint expedition the command shall be equally divided among all the cities.

7. The treaty shall be sworn to by the Athenians for themselves and their allies, by the Argives, Mantineans, Eleans, and their allies, by each state individually. Each shall swear the oath most binding in his country over full-grown victims: the oath being as follows:

"I STAND BY THE ALLIANCE AND ITS ARTICLES, JUSTLY, INNOCENTLY, AND SINCERELY, AND I WILL NOT TRANSGRESS THE SAME IN ANY WAY OR MEANS WHATSOEVER."

The oath shall be taken at Athens by the Senate and the magistrates, the Prytanes administering it: at Argos by the Senate, the Eighty, and the Artynae, the Eighty administering it: at Mantinea by the Demiurgi, the Senate, and the other magistrates, the Theori and Polemarchs administering it: at Elis by the Demiurgi, the magistrates, and the Six Hundred, the Demiurgi and the Thesmophylaces administering it. The oaths shall be renewed by the Athenians going to Elis, Mantinea, and Argos thirty days before the Olympic games: by the Argives, Mantineans, and Eleans going to Athens ten days before the great feast of the Panathenaea. The articles of the treaty, the oaths, and the alliance shall be inscribed on a stone pillar by the Athenians in the citadel, by the Argives in the market-place, in the temple of Apollo: by the Mantineans in the temple of Zeus, in the market-place: and a brazen pillar shall be erected jointly by them at the Olympic games now at hand. Should the above cities see good to make any addition in these articles, whatever all the above cities shall agree upon, after consulting together, shall be binding.

Although the treaty and alliances were thus concluded, still the treaty between the Lacedaemonians and Athenians was not renounced by either party. Meanwhile Corinth, although the ally of the Argives, did not accede to the new treaty, any more than she had done to the alliance, defensive and offensive, formed before this between the Eleans, Argives, and Mantineans, when she declared herself content with the first alliance, which was defensive only, and which bound them to help each other, but not to join in attacking any. The Corinthians thus stood aloof from their allies, and again turned their thoughts towards Lacedaemon.

At the Olympic games which were held this summer, and in which the Arcadian Androsthenes was victor the first time in the wrestling and boxing, the Lacedaemonians were excluded from the temple by the Eleans, and thus prevented from sacrificing or contending, for having refused to pay the fine specified in the Olympic law imposed upon them by the Eleans, who alleged that they had attacked Fort Phyrcus, and sent heavy infantry of theirs into Lepreum during the Olympic truce. The amount of the fine was two thousand minae, two for each heavy-armed soldier, as the law prescribes. The Lacedaemonians sent envoys, and pleaded that the imposition was unjust; saying that the truce had not yet been proclaimed at Lacedaemon when the heavy infantry were sent off. But the Eleans affirmed that the armistice with them had already begun (they proclaim it first among themselves), and that the aggression of the Lacedaemonians had taken them by surprise while they were living quietly as in time of peace, and not expecting anything. Upon this the Lacedaemonians submitted, that if the Eleans really believed that they had committed an aggression, it was useless after that to proclaim the truce at Lacedaemon; but they had proclaimed it notwithstanding, as believing nothing of the kind, and from that moment the Lacedaemonians had made no attack upon their country. Nevertheless the Eleans adhered to what they had said, that nothing would persuade them that an aggression had not been committed; if, however, the Lacedaemonians would restore Lepreum, they would give up their own share of the money and pay that of the god for them.

As this proposal was not accepted, the Eleans tried a second. Instead of restoring Lepreum, if this was objected to, the Lacedaemonians should ascend the altar of the Olympian Zeus, as they were so anxious to have access to the temple, and swear before the Hellenes that they would surely pay the fine at a later day. This being also refused, the Lacedaemonians were excluded from the temple, the sacrifice, and the games, and sacrificed at home; the Lepreans being the only other Hellenes who did not attend. Still the Eleans were afraid of the Lacedaemonians sacrificing by force, and kept guard with a heavy-armed company of their young men; being also joined by a thousand Argives, the same number of Mantineans, and by some Athenian cavalry who stayed at Harpina during the feast. Great fears were felt in the assembly of the Lacedaemonians coming in arms, especially after Lichas, son of Arcesilaus, a Lacedaemonian, had been scourged on the course by the umpires; because, upon his horses being the winners, and the Boeotian people being proclaimed the victor on account of his having no right to enter, he came forward on the course and crowned the charioteer, in order to show that the chariot was his. After this incident all were more afraid than ever, and firmly looked for a disturbance: the Lacedaemonians, however, kept quiet, and let the feast pass by, as we have seen. After the Olympic games, the Argives and the allies repaired to Corinth to invite her to come over to them. There they found some Lacedaemonian envoys; and a long discussion ensued, which after all ended in nothing, as an earthquake occurred, and they dispersed to their different homes.

Summer was now over. The winter following a battle took place between the Heracleots in Trachinia and the Aenianians, Dolopians, Malians, and certain of the Thessalians, all tribes bordering on and hostile to the town, which directly menaced their country. Accordingly, after having opposed and harassed it from its very foundation by every means in their power, they now in this battle defeated the Heracleots, Xenares, son of Cnidis, their Lacedaemonian commander, being among the slain. Thus the winter ended and the twelfth year of this war ended also. After the battle, Heraclea was so terribly reduced that in the first days of the summer following the Boeotians occupied the place and sent away the Lacedaemonian Agesippidas for misgovernment, fearing that the town might be taken by the Athenians while the Lacedaemonians were distracted with the affairs of Peloponnese. The Lacedaemonians, nevertheless, were offended with them for what they had done.

The same summer Alcibiades, son of Clinias, now one of the generals at Athens, in concert with the Argives and the allies, went into Peloponnese with a few Athenian heavy infantry and archers and some of the allies in those parts whom he took up as he passed, and with this army marched here and there through Peloponnese, and settled various matters connected with the alliance, and among other things induced the Patrians to carry their walls down to the sea, intending himself also to build a fort near the Achaean Rhium. However, the Corinthians and Sicyonians, and all others who would have suffered by its being built, came up and hindered him.

The same summer war broke out between the Epidaurians and Argives. The pretext was that the Epidaurians did not send an offering for their pasture-land to Apollo Pythaeus, as they were bound to do, the Argives having the chief management of the temple; but, apart from this pretext, Alcibiades and the Argives were determined, if possible, to gain possession of Epidaurus, and thus to ensure the neutrality of Corinth and give the Athenians a shorter passage for their reinforcements from Aegina than if they had to sail round Scyllaeum. The Argives accordingly prepared to invade Epidaurus by themselves, to exact the offering.

About the same time the Lacedaemonians marched out with

all their people to Leuctra upon their frontier, opposite to Mount Lycaeum, under the command of Agis, son of Archidamus, without any one knowing their destination, not even the cities that sent the contingents. The sacrifices, however, for crossing the frontier not proving propitious, the Lacedaemonians returned home themselves, and sent word to the allies to be ready to march after the month ensuing, which happened to be the month of Carneus, a holy time for the Dorians. Upon the retreat of the Lacedaemonians the Argives marched out on the last day but three of the month before Carneus, and keeping this as the day during the whole time that they were out, invaded and plundered Epidaurus. The Epidaurians summoned their allies to their aid, some of whom pleaded the month as an excuse; others came as far as the frontier of Epidaurus and there remained inactive.

While the Argives were in Epidaurus embassies from the cities assembled at Mantinea, upon the invitation of the Athenians. The conference having begun, the Corinthian Euphamidas said that their actions did not agree with their words; while they were sitting deliberating about peace, the Epidaurians and their allies and the Argives were arrayed against each other in arms; deputies from each party should first go and separate the armies, and then the talk about peace might be resumed. In compliance with this suggestion, they went and brought back the Argives from Epidaurus, and afterwards reassembled, but without succeeding any better in coming to a conclusion; and the Argives a second time invaded Epidaurus and plundered the country. The Lacedaemonians also marched out to Caryae; but the frontier sacrifices again proving unfavourable, they went back again, and the Argives, after ravaging about a third of the Epidaurian territory, returned home. Meanwhile a thousand Athenian heavy infantry had come to their aid under the command of Alcibiades, but finding that the Lacedaemonian expedition was at an end, and that they were no longer wanted, went back again.

So passed the summer. The next winter the Lacedaemonians managed to elude the vigilance of the Athenians, and sent in a garrison of three hundred men to Epidaurus, under the command of Agesippidas. Upon this the Argives went to the Athenians and complained of their having allowed an enemy to pass by sea, in spite of the clause in the treaty by which the allies were not to allow an enemy to pass through their country. Unless, therefore, they now put the Messenians and Helots in Pylos to annoy the Lacedaemonians, they, the Argives, should consider that faith had not been kept with them. The Athenians were persuaded by Alcibiades to inscribe at the bottom of the Laconian pillar that the Lacedaemonians had not kept their oaths, and to convey the Helots at Cranii to Pylos to plunder the country; but for the rest they remained quiet as before. During this winter hostilities went on between the Argives and Epidaurians, without any pitched battle taking place, but only forays and ambuscades, in which the losses were small and fell now on one side and now on the other. At the close of the winter, towards the beginning of spring, the Argives went with scaling ladders to Epidaurus, expecting to find it left unguarded on account of the war and to be able to take it by assault, but returned unsuccessful. And the winter ended, and with it the thirteenth year of the war ended also.

In the middle of the next summer the Lacedaemonians, seeing the Epidaurians, their allies, in distress, and the rest of Peloponnese either in revolt or disaffected, concluded that it was high time for them to interfere if they wished to stop the progress of the evil, and accordingly with their full force, the Helots included, took the field against Argos, under the command of Agis, son of Archidamus, king of the Lacedaemonians. The Tegeans and the other Arcadian allies of Lacedaemon joined in the expedition. The allies from the rest of Peloponnese and from outside mustered at Phlius; the Boeotians with five thousand heavy infantry and as many light troops, and five hundred horse and the same number of dismounted troopers; the Corinthians with two thousand heavy infantry; the rest more or less as might happen; and the Phliasians with all their forces, the army being in their country.

The preparations of the Lacedaemonians from the first had been known to the Argives, who did not, however, take the field until the enemy was on his road to join the rest at Phlius. Reinforced by the Mantineans with their allies, and by three thousand Elean heavy infantry, they advanced and fell in with the Lacedaemonians at Methydrium in Arcadia. Each party took up its position upon a hill, and the Argives prepared to engage the Lacedaemonians while they were alone; but Agis eluded them by breaking up his camp in the night, and proceeded to join the rest of the allies at Phlius. The Argives discovering this at daybreak, marched first to Argos and then to the Nemean road, by which they expected the Lacedaemonians and their allies would come down. However, Agis, instead of taking this road as they expected, gave the Lacedaemonians, Arcadians, and Epidaurians their orders, and went along another difficult road, and descended into the plain of Argos. The Corinthians, Pellenians, and Phliasians marched by another steep road; while the Boeotians, Megarians, and Sicyonians had instructions to come down by the Nemean road where the Argives were posted, in order that, if the enemy advanced into the plain against the troops of Agis, they might fall upon his rear with their cavalry. These dispositions concluded, Agis invaded the plain and began to ravage Saminthus and other places.

Discovering this, the Argives came up from Nemea, day having now dawned. On their way they fell in with the troops of the Phliasians and Corinthians, and killed a few of the Phliasians and had perhaps a few more of their own men killed by the Corinthians. Meanwhile the Boeotians, Megarians, and Sicyonians, advancing upon Nemea according to their instructions, found the Argives no longer there, as they had gone down on seeing their property ravaged, and were now forming for battle, the Lacedaemonians imitating their example. The Argives were now completely surrounded; from the plain the Lacedaemonians and their allies shut them off from their city; above them were the Corinthians, Phliasians, and Pellenians; and on the side of Nemea the Boeotians,

Sicyonians, and Megarians. Meanwhile their army was without cavalry, the Athenians alone among the allies not having yet arrived. Now the bulk of the Argives and their allies did not see the danger of their position, but thought that they could not have a fairer field, having intercepted the Lacedaemonians in their own country and close to the city. Two men, however, in the Argive army, Thrasylus, one of the five generals, and Alciphron, the Lacedaemonian proxenus, just as the armies were upon the point of engaging, went and held a parley with Agis and urged him not to bring on a battle, as the Argives were ready to refer to fair and equal arbitration whatever complaints the Lacedaemonians might have against them, and to make a treaty and live in peace in future.

The Argives who made these statements did so upon their own authority, not by order of the people, and Agis on his accepted their proposals, and without himself either consulting the majority, simply communicated the matter to a single individual, one of the high officers accompanying the expedition, and granted the Argives a truce for four months, in which to fulfil their promises; after which he immediately led off the army without giving any explanation to any of the other allies. The Lacedaemonians and allies followed their general out of respect for the law, but amongst themselves loudly blamed Agis for going away from so fair a field (the enemy being hemmed in on every side by infantry and cavalry) without having done anything worthy of their strength. Indeed this was by far the finest Hellenic army ever yet brought together; and it should have been seen while it was still united at Nemea, with the Lacedaemonians in full force, the Arcadians, Boeotians, Corinthians, Sicyonians, Pellenians, Phliasians and Megarians, and all these the flower of their respective populations, thinking themselves a match not merely for the Argive confederacy, but for another such added to it. The army thus retired blaming Agis, and returned every man to his home. The Argives however blamed still more loudly the persons who had concluded the truce without consulting the people, themselves thinking that they had let escape with the Lacedaemonians an opportunity such as they should never see again; as the struggle would have been under the walls of their city, and by the side of many and brave allies. On their return accordingly they began to stone Thrasylus in the bed of the Charadrus, where they try all military causes before entering the city. Thrasylus fled to the altar, and so saved his life; his property however they confiscated.

After this arrived a thousand Athenian heavy infantry and three hundred horse, under the command of Laches and Nicostratus; whom the Argives, being nevertheless loath to break the truce with the Lacedaemonians, begged to depart, and refused to bring before the people, to whom they had a communication to make, until compelled to do so by the entreaties of the Mantineans and Eleans, who were still at Argos. The Athenians, by the mouth of Alcibiades their ambassador there present, told the Argives and the allies that they had no right to make a truce at all without the consent of their fellow confederates, and now that the Athenians had arrived so opportunely the war ought to be resumed. These arguments proving successful with the allies, they immediately marched upon Orchomenos, all except the Argives, who, although they had consented like the rest, stayed behind at first, but eventually joined the others. They now all sat down and besieged Orchomenos, and made assaults upon it; one of their reasons for desiring to gain this place being that hostages from Arcadia had been lodged there by the Lacedaemonians. The Orchomenians, alarmed at the weakness of their wall and the numbers of the enemy, and at the risk they ran of perishing before relief arrived, capitulated upon condition of joining the league, of giving hostages of their own to the Mantineans, and giving up those lodged with them by the Lacedaemonians. Orchomenos thus secured, the allies now consulted as to which of the remaining places they should attack next. The Eleans were urgent for Lepreum; the Mantineans for Tegea; and the Argives and Athenians giving their support to the Mantineans, the Eleans went home in a rage at their not having voted for Lepreum; while the rest of the allies made ready at Mantinea for going against Tegea, which a party inside had arranged to put into their hands.

Meanwhile the Lacedaemonians, upon their return from Argos after concluding the four months' truce, vehemently blamed Agis for not having subdued Argos, after an opportunity such as they thought they had never had before; for it was no easy matter to bring so many and so good allies together. But when the news arrived of the capture of Orchomenos, they became more angry than ever, and, departing from all precedent, in the heat of the moment had almost decided to raze his house, and to fine him ten thousand drachmae. Agis however entreated them to do none of these things, promising to atone for his fault by good service in the field, failing which they might then do to him whatever they pleased; and they accordingly abstained from razing his house or fining him as they had threatened to do, and now made a law, hitherto unknown at Lacedaemon, attaching to him ten Spartans as counsellors, without whose consent he should have no power to lead an army out of the city.

At this juncture arrived word from their friends in Tegea that, unless they speedily appeared, Tegea would go over from them to the Argives and their allies, if it had not gone over already. Upon this news a force marched out from Lacedaemon, of the Spartans and Helots and all their people, and that instantly and upon a scale never before witnessed. Advancing to Orestheum in Maenalia, they directed the Arcadians in their league to follow close after them to Tegea, and, going on themselves as far as Orestheum, from thence sent back the sixth part of the Spartans, consisting of the oldest and youngest men, to guard their homes, and with the rest of their army arrived at Tegea; where their Arcadian allies soon after joined them. Meanwhile they sent to Corinth, to the Boeotians, the Phocians, and Locrians, with orders to come up as quickly as possible to Mantinea. These had but short notice; and it was not easy except all together, and after waiting for each other, to pass through the enemy's country, which lay right across and blocked up the line of communication. Nevertheless they made what haste they could. Meanwhile the Lacedaemonians with the Arcadian allies that had joined them, entered the territory of Mantinea, and encamping near the temple of Heracles began to plunder the country.

Here they were seen by the Argives and their allies, who immediately took up a strong and difficult position, and formed in order of battle. The Lacedaemonians at once advanced against them, and came on within a stone's throw or javelin's cast, when one of the older men, seeing the enemy's position to be a strong one, hallooed to Agis that he was minded to cure one evil with another; meaning that he wished to make amends for his retreat, which had been so much blamed, from Argos, by his present untimely precipitation. Meanwhile Agis, whether in consequence of this halloo or of some sudden new idea of his own, quickly led back his army without engaging, and entering the Tegean territory, began to turn off into that of Mantinea the water about which the Mantineans and Tegeans are always fighting, on account of the extensive damage it does to whichever of the two countries it falls into. His object in this was to make the Argives and their allies come down from the hill, to resist the diversion of the water, as they would be sure to do when they knew of it, and thus to fight the battle in the plain. He accordingly stayed that day where he was, engaged in turning off the water. The Argives and their allies were at first amazed at the sudden retreat of the enemy after advancing so near, and did not know what to make of it; but when he had gone away and disappeared, without their having stirred to pursue him, they began anew to find fault with their generals, who had not only let the Lacedaemonians get off before, when they were so happily intercepted before Argos, but who now again allowed them to run away, without any one pursuing them, and to escape at their leisure while the Argive army was leisurely betrayed. The generals, half-stunned for the moment, afterwards led them down from the hill, and went forward and encamped in the plain, with the intention of attacking the enemy.

The next day the Argives and their allies formed in the order in which they meant to fight, if they chanced to encounter the enemy; and the Lacedaemonians returning from the water to their old encampment by the temple of Heracles, suddenly saw their adversaries close in front of them, all in complete order, and advanced from the hill. A shock like that of the present moment the Lacedaemonians do not ever remember to have experienced: there was scant time for preparation, as they instantly and hastily fell into their ranks, Agis, their king, directing everything, agreeably to the law. For when a king is in the field all commands proceed from him: he gives the word to the Polemarchs; they to the Lochages; these to the Pentecostyes; these again to the Enomotarchs, and these last to the Enomoties. In short all orders required pass in the same way and quickly reach the troops; as almost the whole Lacedaemonian army, save for a small part, consists of officers under officers, and the care of what is to be done falls upon many.

In this battle the left wing was composed of the Sciritae, who in a Lacedaemonian army have always that post to themselves alone; next to these were the soldiers of Brasidas from Thrace, and the Neodamodes with them; then came the Lacedaemonians themselves, company after company, with the Arcadians of Heraea at their side. After these were the Maenalians, and on the right wing the Tegeans with a few of the Lacedaemonians at the extremity; their cavalry being posted upon the two wings. Such was the Lacedaemonian formation. That of their opponents was as follows: On the right were the Mantineans, the action taking place in their country; next to them the allies from Arcadia; after whom came the thousand picked men of the Argives, to whom the state had given a long course of military training at the public expense; next to them the rest of the Argives, and after them their allies, the Cleonaeans and Orneans, and lastly the Athenians on the extreme

362

left, and lastly the Athenians on the extreme left, and their own cavalry with them.

Such were the order and the forces of the two combatants. The Lacedaemonian army looked the largest; though as to putting down the numbers of either host, or of the contingents composing it, I could not do so with any accuracy. Owing to the secrecy of their government the number of the Lacedaemonians was not known, and men are so apt to brag about the forces of their country that the estimate of their opponents was not trusted. The following calculation, however, makes it possible to estimate the numbers of the Lacedaemonians present upon this occasion. There were seven companies in the field without counting the Sciritae, who numbered six hundred men: in each company there were four Pentecostyes, and in the Pentecosty four Enomoties. The first rank of the Enomoty was composed of four soldiers: as to the depth, although they had not been all drawn up alike, but as each captain chose, they were generally ranged eight deep; the first rank along the whole line, exclusive of the Sciritae, consisted of four hundred and forty-eight men.

The armies being now on the eve of engaging, each contingent received some words of encouragement from its own commander. The Mantineans were, reminded that they were going to fight for their country and to avoid returning to the experience of servitude after having tasted that of empire; the Argives, that they would contend for their ancient supremacy, to regain their once equal share of Peloponnese of which they had been so long deprived, and to punish an enemy and a neighbour for a thousand wrongs; the Athenians, of the glory of gaining the honours of the day with so many and brave allies in arms, and that a victory over the Lacedaemonians in Peloponnese would cement and extend their empire, and would besides preserve Attica from all invasions in future. These were the incitements addressed to the Argives and their allies. The Lacedaemonians meanwhile, man to man, and with their war-songs in the ranks, exhorted each brave comrade to remember what he had learnt before; well aware that the long training of action was of more saving virtue than any brief verbal exhortation, though never so well delivered.

After this they joined battle, the Argives and their allies advancing with haste and fury, the Lacedaemonians slowly and to the music of many flute-players - a standing institution in their army, that has nothing to do with religion, but is meant to make them advance evenly, stepping in time, without break their order, as large armies are apt to do in the moment of engaging.

Just before the battle joined, King Agis resolved upon the following manoeuvre. All armies are alike in this: on going into action they get forced out rather on their right wing, and one and the other overlap with this adversary's left; because fear makes each man do his best to shelter his unarmed side with the shield of the man next him on the right, thinking that the closer the shields are locked together the better will he be protected. The man primarily responsible for this is the first upon the right wing, who is always striving to withdraw from the enemy his unarmed side; and the same apprehension makes the rest follow him. On the present occasion the Mantineans reached with their wing far beyond the Sciritae, and the Lacedaemonians and Tegeans still farther beyond the Athenians, as their army was the largest. Agis, afraid of his left being surrounded, and thinking that the Mantineans outflanked it too far, ordered the Sciritae and Brasideans to move out from their place in the ranks and make the line even with the Mantineans, and told the Polemarchs Hipponoidas and Aristocles to fill up the gap thus formed, by throwing themselves into it with two companies taken from the right wing; thinking that his right would still be strong enough and to spare, and that the line fronting the Mantineans would gain in solidity.

However, as he gave these orders in the moment of the onset, and at short notice, it so happened that Aristocles and Hipponoidas would not move over, for which offence they were afterwards banished from Sparta, as having been guilty of cowardice; and the enemy meanwhile closed before the Sciritae (whom Agis on seeing that the two companies did not move over ordered to return to their place) had time to fill up the breach in question. Now it was, however, that the Lacedaemonians, utterly worsted in respect of skill, showed themselves as superior in point of courage. As soon as they came to close quarters with the enemy, the Mantinean right broke their Sciritae and Brasideans, and, bursting in with their allies and the thousand picked Argives into the unclosed breach in their line, cut up and surrounded the Lacedaemonians, and drove them in full rout to the wagons, slaying some of the older men on guard there. But the Lacedaemonians, worsted in this part of the field, with the rest of their army, and especially the centre, where the three hundred knights, as they are called, fought round King Agis, fell on the older men of the Argives and the five companies so named, and on the Cleonaeans, the Orneans, and the Athenians next them, and instantly routed them; the greater number not even waiting to strike a blow, but giving way the moment that they came on, some even being trodden under foot, in their fear of being overtaken by their assailants.

The army of the Argives and their allies, having given way in this quarter, was now completely cut in two, and the Lacedaemonian and Tegean right simultaneously closing round the Athenians with the troops that outflanked them, these last found themselves placed between two fires, being surrounded on one side and already defeated on the other. Indeed they would have suffered more severely than any other part of the army, but for the services of the cavalry which they had with them. Agis also on perceiving the distress of his left opposed to the Mantineans and the thousand Argives, ordered all the army to advance to the support of the defeated wing; and while this took place, as the enemy moved past and slanted away from them, the Athenians escaped at their leisure, and with them the beaten Argive division. Meanwhile the Mantineans and their allies and the picked body of the Argives ceased to press the enemy, and seeing their friends defeated and the

Lacedaemonians in full advance upon them, took to flight. Many of the Mantineans perished; but the bulk of the picked body of the Argives made good their escape. The flight and retreat, however, were neither hurried nor long; the Lacedaemonians fighting long and stubbornly until the rout of their enemy, but that once effected, pursuing for a short time and not far.

Such was the battle, as nearly as possible as I have described it; the greatest that had occurred for a very long while among the Hellenes, and joined by the most considerable states. The Lacedaemonians took up a position in front of the enemy's dead, and immediately set up a trophy and stripped the slain; they took up their own dead and carried them back to Tegea, where they buried them, and restored those of the enemy under truce. The Argives, Orneans, and Cleonaeans had seven hundred killed; the Mantineans two hundred, and the Athenians and Aeginetans also two hundred, with both their generals. On the side of the Lacedaemonians, the allies did not suffer any loss worth speaking of: as to the Lacedaemonians themselves it was difficult to learn the truth; it is said, however, that there were slain about three hundred of them.

While the battle was impending, Pleistoanax, the other king, set out with a reinforcement composed of the oldest and youngest men, and got as far as Tegea, where he heard of the victory and went back again. The Lacedaemonians also sent and turned back the allies from Corinth and from beyond the Isthmus, and returning themselves dismissed their allies, and kept the Carnean holidays, which happened to be at that time. The imputations cast upon them by the Hellenes at the time, whether of cowardice on account of the disaster in the island, or of mismanagement and slowness generally, were all wiped out by this single action: fortune, it was thought, might have humbled them, but the men themselves were the same as ever.

The day before this battle, the Epidaurians with all their forces invaded the deserted Argive territory, and cut off many of the guards left there in the absence of the Argive army. After the battle three thousand Elean heavy infantry arriving to aid the Mantineans, and a reinforcement of one thousand Athenians, all these allies marched at once against Epidaurus, while the Lacedaemonians were keeping the Carnea, and dividing the work among them began to build a wall round the city. The rest left off; but the Athenians finished at once the part assigned to them round Cape Heraeum; and having all joined in leaving a garrison in the fortification in question, they returned to their respective cities.

Summer now came to an end. In the first days of the next winter, when the Carnean holidays were over, the Lacedaemonians took the field, and arriving at Tegea sent on to Argos proposals of accommodation. They had before had a party in the town desirous of overthrowing the democracy; and after the battle that had been fought, these were now far more in a position to persuade the people to listen to terms. Their plan was first to make a treaty with the Lacedaemonians, to be followed by an alliance, and after this to fall upon the commons. Lichas, son of Arcesilaus, the Argive proxenus, accordingly arrived at Argos with two proposals from Lacedaemon, to regulate the conditions of war or peace, according as they preferred the one or the other. After much discussion, Alcibiades happening to be in the town, the Lacedaemonian party, who now ventured to act openly, persuaded the Argives to accept the proposal for accommodation; which ran as follows:

The assembly of the Lacedaemonians agrees to treat with the Argives upon the terms following:

1. The Argives shall restore to the Orchomenians their children, and to the Maenalians their men, and shall restore the men they have in Mantinea to the Lacedaemonians.

2. They shall evacuate Epidaurus, and raze the fortification there. If the Athenians refuse to withdraw from Epidaurus, they shall be declared enemies of the Argives and of the Lacedaemonians, and of the allies of the Lacedaemonians and the allies of the Argives.

3. If the Lacedaemonians have any children in their custody, they shall restore them every one to his city.

4. As to the offering to the god, the Argives, if they wish, shall impose an oath upon the Epidaurians, but, if not, they shall swear it themselves.

5. All the cities in Peloponnese, both small and great, shall be independent according to the customs of their country.

6. If any of the powers outside Peloponnese invade Peloponnesian territory, the parties contracting shall unite to repel them, on such terms as they may agree upon, as being most fair for the Peloponnesians.

7. All allies of the Lacedaemonians outside Peloponnese shall be on the same footing as the Lacedaemonians, and the allies of the Argives shall be on the same footing as the Argives, being left in enjoyment of their own possessions.

8. This treaty shall be shown to the allies, and shall be concluded, if they approve; if the allies think fit, they may send the treaty to be considered at home.

The Argives began by accepting this proposal, and the Lacedaemonian army returned home from Tegea. After this intercourse was renewed between them, and not long afterwards the same party contrived that the Argives should give up the league with the Mantineans, Eleans, and Athenians, and should make a treaty and alliance with the Lacedaemonians; which was consequently done upon the terms following:

The Lacedaemonians and Argives agree to a treaty and alliance for fifty years upon the terms following:

1. All disputes shall be decided by fair and impartial arbitration, agreeably to the customs of the two countries.

2. The rest of the cities in Peloponnese may be included in this treaty and alliance, as independent and sovereign, in full enjoyment of what they possess, all disputes being decided by fair and impartial arbitration, agreeably to the customs of the said cities.

3. All allies of the Lacedaemonians outside Peloponnese shall be upon the same footing as the Lacedaemonians themselves, and the allies of the Argives shall be upon the same footing as the Argives themselves, continuing to enjoy what they possess.

4. If it shall be anywhere necessary to make an expedition in common, the Lacedaemonians and Argives shall consult upon it and decide, as may be most fair for the allies.

5. If any of the cities, whether inside or outside Peloponnese, have a question whether of frontiers or otherwise, it must be settled, but if one allied city should have a quarrel with another allied city, it must be referred to some third city thought impartial by both parties. Private citizens shall have their disputes decided according to the laws of their several countries.

The treaty and above alliance concluded, each party at once released everything whether acquired by war or otherwise, and thenceforth acting in common voted to receive neither herald nor embassy from the Athenians unless they evacuated their forts and withdrew from Peloponnese, and also to make neither peace nor war with any, except jointly. Zeal was not wanting: both parties sent envoys to the Thracian places and to Perdiccas, and persuaded the latter to join their league. Still he did not at once break off from Athens, although minded to do so upon seeing the way shown him by Argos, the original home of his family. They also renewed their old oaths with the Chalcidians and took new ones: the Argives, besides, sent ambassadors to the Athenians, bidding them evacuate the fort at Epidaurus. The Athenians, seeing their own men outnumbered by the rest of the garrison, sent Demosthenes to bring them out. This general, under colour of a gymnastic contest which he arranged on his arrival, got the rest of the garrison out of the place, and shut the gates behind them. Afterwards the Athenians renewed their treaty with the Epidaurians, and by themselves gave up the fortress.

After the defection of Argos from the league, the Mantineans, though they held out at first, in the end finding themselves powerless without the Argives, themselves too came to terms with Lacedaemon, and gave up their sovereignty over the towns. The Lacedaemonians and Argives, each a thousand strong, now took the field together, and the former first went by themselves to Sicyon and made the government there more oligarchical than before, and then both, uniting, put down the democracy at Argos and set up an oligarchy favourable to Lacedaemon. These events occurred at the close of the winter, just before spring; and the fourteenth year of the war ended. The next summer the people of Dium, in Athos, revolted from the Athenians to the Chalcidians, and the Lacedaemonians settled affairs in Achaea in a way more agreeable to the interests of their country. Meanwhile the popular party at Argos little by little gathered new consistency and courage, and waited for the moment of the Gymnopaedic festival at Lacedaemon, and then fell upon the oligarchs. After a fight in the city, victory declared for the commons, who slew some of their opponents and banished others. The Lacedaemonians for a long while let the messages of their friends at Argos remain without effect. At last they put off the Gymnopaediae and marched to their succour, but learning at Tegea the defeat of the oligarchs, refused to go any further in spite of the entreaties of those who had escaped, and returned home and kept the festival. Later on, envoys arrived with messages from the Argives in the town and from the exiles, when the allies were also at Sparta; and after much had been said on both sides, the Lacedaemonians decided that the party in the town had done wrong, and resolved to march against Argos, but kept delaying and putting off the matter. Meanwhile the commons at Argos, in fear of the Lacedaemonians, began again to court the Athenian alliance, which they were convinced would be of the greatest service to them; and accordingly proceeded to build long walls to the sea, in order that in case of a blockade by land; with the help of the Athenians they might have the advantage of importing what they wanted by sea. Some of the cities in Peloponnese were also privy to the building of these walls; and the Argives with all their people, women and slaves not excepted, addressed themselves to the work, while carpenters and masons came to them from Athens.

Summer was now over. The winter following the Lacedaemonians, hearing of the walls that were building, marched against Argos with their allies, the Corinthians excepted, being also not without intelligence in the city itself; Agis, son of Archidamus, their king, was in command. The intelligence which they counted upon within the town came to nothing; they however took and razed the walls which were being built, and after capturing the Argive town Hysiae and killing all the freemen that fell into their hands, went back and dispersed every man to his city. After this the Argives marched into Phlius and plundered it for harbouring their exiles, most of whom had settled there, and so returned home. The same winter the Athenians blockaded Macedonia, on the score of the league entered into by Perdiccas with the Argives and Lacedaemonians, and also of his breach of his engagements on the occasion of the expedition prepared by Athens against the Chalcidians in the direction of Thrace and against Amphipolis, under the command of Nicias, son of Niceratus, which had to be broken up mainly because of his desertion. He was therefore proclaimed an enemy. And thus the winter ended, and the fifteenth year of the war ended with it.

CHAPTER XVII

Sixteenth Year of the War - The Melian Conference - Fate of Melos

THE NEXT summer Alcibiades sailed with twenty ships to Argos and seized the suspected persons still left of the Lacedaemonian faction to the number of three hundred, whom the Athenians forthwith lodged in the neighbouring islands of their empire. The Athenians also made an expedition against the isle of Melos with thirty ships of their own, six Chian, and two Lesbian vessels, sixteen hundred heavy infantry, three hundred archers, and twenty mounted archers from Athens, and about fifteen hundred heavy infantry from the allies and the islanders. The Melians are a colony of Lacedaemon that would not submit to the Athenians like the other islanders, and at first remained neutral and took no part in the struggle, but afterwards upon the Athenians using violence and plundering their territory, assumed an attitude of open hostility. Cleomedes, son of Lycomedes, and Tisias, son of Tisimachus, the generals, encamping in their territory with the above armament, before doing any harm to their land, sent envoys to negotiate. These the Melians did not bring before the people, but bade them state the object of their mission to the magistrates and the few; upon which the Athenian envoys spoke as follows:

Athenians. Since the negotiations are not to go on before the people, in order that we may not be able to speak straight on without interruption, and deceive the ears of the multitude by seductive arguments which would pass without refutation (for we know that this is the meaning of our being brought before the few), what if you who sit there were to pursue a method more cautious still? Make no set speech yourselves, but take us up at whatever you do not like, and settle that before going any farther. And first tell us if this proposition of ours suits you.

The Melian commissioners answered:

Melians. To the fairness of quietly instructing each other as you propose there is nothing to object; but your military preparations are too far advanced to agree with what you say, as we see you are come to be judges in your own cause, and that all we can reasonably expect from this negotiation is war, if we prove to have right on our side and refuse to submit, and in the contrary case, slavery.

Athenians. If you have met to reason about presentiments of the future, or for anything else than to consult for the safety of your state upon the facts that you see before you, we will give over; otherwise we will go on.

Melians. It is natural and excusable for men in our position to turn more ways than one both in thought and utterance. However, the question in this conference is, as you say, the safety of our country; and the discussion, if you please, can proceed in the way which you propose.

Athenians. For ourselves, we shall not trouble you with specious pretences - either of how we have a right to our empire because we overthrew the Mede, or are now attacking you because of wrong that you have done us - and make a long speech which would not be believed; and in return we hope that you, instead of thinking to influence us by saying that you did not join the Lacedaemonians, although their colonists, or that you have done us no wrong, will aim at what is feasible, holding in view the real sentiments of us both; since you know as well as we do that right, as the world goes, is only in question between equals in power, while the strong do what they can and the weak suffer what they must.

Melians. As we think, at any rate, it is expedient - we speak as we are obliged, since you enjoin us to let right alone and talk only of interest - that you should not destroy what is our common protection, the privilege of being allowed in danger to invoke what is fair and right, and even to profit by arguments not strictly valid if they can be got to pass current. And you are as much interested in this as any, as your fall would be a signal for the heaviest vengeance and an example for the world to meditate upon.

Athenians. The end of our empire, if end it should, does not frighten us: a rival empire like Lacedaemon, even if Lacedaemon was our real antagonist, is not so terrible to the vanquished as subjects who by themselves attack and overpower their rulers. This, however, is a risk that we are content to take. We will now proceed to show you that we are come here in the interest of our empire, and that we shall say what we are now going to say, for the preservation of your country; as we would fain exercise that empire over you without trouble, and see you preserved for the good of us both.

Melians. And how, pray, could it turn out as good for us to serve as for you to rule?

Athenians. Because you would have the advantage of submitting before suffering the worst, and we should gain by not destroying you.

Melians. So that you would not consent to our being neutral, friends instead of enemies, but allies of neither side.

Athenians. No; for your hostility cannot so much hurt us as your friendship will be an argument to our subjects of our weakness, and your enmity of our power.

Melians. Is that your subjects' idea of equity, to put those who have nothing to do with you in the same category with peoples that are most of them your own colonists, and some conquered rebels?

Athenians. As far as right goes they think one has as much of it as the other, and that if any maintain their independence it is because they are strong, and that if we do not molest them it is because we are afraid; so that besides extending our empire we should gain in security by your subjection; the fact that you are islanders and weaker than others rendering it all the more important that you should not succeed in baffling the masters of the sea.

Melians. But do you consider that there is no security in the policy which we indicate? For here again if you debar us from talking about justice and invite us to obey your interest, we also must explain ours, and try to persuade you, if the two happen to coincide. How can you avoid making enemies of all existing neutrals who shall look at case from it that one day or another you will attack them? And what is this but to make greater the enemies that you have already, and to force others to become so who would otherwise have never thought of it?

Athenians. Why, the fact is that continentals generally give us but little alarm; the liberty which they enjoy will long prevent their taking precautions against us; it is rather islanders like yourselves, outside our empire, and subjects smarting under the yoke, who would be the most likely to take a rash step and lead themselves and us into obvious danger.

Melians. Well then, if you risk so much to retain your empire, and your subjects to get rid of it, it were surely great baseness and cowardice in us who are still free not to try everything that can be tried, before submitting to your yoke.

Athenians. Not if you are well advised, the contest not being an equal one, with honour as the prize and shame as the penalty, but a question of self-preservation and of not resisting those who are far stronger than you are.

Melians. But we know that the fortune of war is sometimes more impartial than the disproportion of numbers might lead one to suppose; to submit is to give ourselves over to despair, while action still preserves for us a hope that we may stand erect.

Athenians. Hope, danger's comforter, may be indulged in by those who have abundant resources, if not without loss at all events without ruin; but its nature is to be extravagant, and those who go so far as to put their all upon the venture see it in its true colours only when they are ruined; but so long as the discovery would enable them to guard against it, it is never found wanting. Let not this be the case with you, who are weak and hang on a single turn of the scale; nor be like the vulgar, who, abandoning such security as human means may still afford, when visible hopes fail them in extremity, turn to invisible, to prophecies and oracles, and other such inventions that delude men with hopes to their destruction.

Melians. You may be sure that we are as well aware as you of the difficulty of contending against your power and fortune, unless the terms be equal. But we trust that the gods may grant us fortune as good as yours, since we are just men fighting against unjust, and that what we want in power will be made up by the alliance of the Lacedaemonians, who are bound, if only for very shame, to come to the aid of their kindred. Our confidence, therefore, after all is not so utterly irrational.

Athenians. When you speak of the favour of the gods, we may as fairly hope for that as yourselves; neither our pretensions nor our conduct being in any way contrary to what men believe of the gods, or practise among themselves. Of the gods we believe, and of men we know, that by a necessary law of their nature they rule wherever they can. And it is not as if we were the first to make this law, or to act upon it when made: we found it existing before us, and shall leave it to exist for ever after us; all we do is to make use of it, knowing that you and everybody else, having the same power as we have, would do the same as we do. Thus, as far as the gods are concerned, we have no fear and no reason to fear that we shall be at a disadvantage. But when we come to your notion about the Lacedaemonians, which leads you to believe that shame will make them help you, here we bless your simplicity but do not envy your folly. The Lacedaemonians, when their own interests or their country's laws are in question, are the worthiest men alive; of their conduct towards others much might be said, but no clearer idea of it could be given than by shortly saying that of all the men we know they are most conspicuous in considering what is agreeable honourable, and what is expedient just. Such a way of thinking does not promise much for the safety which you now unreasonably count upon.

Melians. But it is for this very reason that we now trust to their respect for expediency to prevent them from betraying the

Melians, their colonists, and thereby losing the confidence of their friends in Hellas and helping their enemies.

Athenians. Then you do not adopt the view that expediency goes with security, while justice and honour cannot be followed without danger; and danger the Lacedaemonians generally court as little as possible.

Melians. But we believe that they would be more likely to face even danger for our sake, and with more confidence than for others, as our nearness to Peloponnese makes it easier for them to act, and our common blood ensures our fidelity.

Athenians. Yes, but what an intending ally trusts to is not the goodwill of those who ask his aid, but a decided superiority of power for action; and the Lacedaemonians look to this even more than others. At least, such is their distrust of their home resources that it is only with numerous allies that they attack a neighbour; now is it likely that while we are masters of the sea they will cross over to an island?

Melians. But they would have others to send. The Cretan Sea is a wide one, and it is more difficult for those who command it to intercept others, than for those who wish to elude them to do so safely. And should the Lacedaemonians miscarry in this, they would fall upon your land, and upon those left of your allies whom Brasidas did not reach; and instead of places which are not yours, you will have to fight for your own country and your own confederacy.

Athenians. Some diversion of the kind you speak of you may one day experience, only to learn, as others have done, that the Athenians never once yet withdrew from a siege for fear of any. But we are struck by the fact that, after saying you would consult for the safety of your country, in all this discussion you have mentioned nothing which men might trust in and think to be saved by. Your strongest arguments depend upon hope and the future, and your actual resources are too scanty, as compared with those arrayed against you, for you to come out victorious.

You will therefore show great blindness of judgment, unless, after allowing us to retire, you can find some counsel more prudent than this. You will surely not be caught by that idea of disgrace, which in dangers that are disgraceful, and at the same time too plain to be mistaken, proves so fatal to mankind; since in too many cases the very men that have their eyes perfectly open to what they are rushing into, let the thing called disgrace, by the mere influence of a seductive name, lead them on to a point at which they become so enslaved by the phrase as in fact to fall wilfully into hopeless disaster, and incur disgrace more disgraceful as the companion of error, than when it comes as the result of misfortune. This, if you are well advised, you will guard against; and you will not think it dishonourable to submit to the greatest city in Hellas, when it makes you the moderate offer of becoming its tributary ally, without ceasing to enjoy the country that belongs to you; nor when you have the choice given you between war and security, will you be so blinded as to choose the worse. And it is certain that those who do not yield to their equals, who keep terms with their superiors, and are moderate towards their inferiors, on the whole succeed best. Think over the matter, therefore, after our withdrawal, and reflect once and again that it is for your country that you are consulting, that you have not more than one, and that upon this one deliberation depends its prosperity or ruin.

The Athenians now withdrew from the conference; and the Melians, left to themselves, came to a decision corresponding with what they had maintained in the discussion, and answered: "Our resolution, Athenians, is the same as it was at first. We will not in a moment deprive of freedom a city that has been inhabited these seven hundred years; but we put our trust in the fortune by which the gods have preserved it until now, and in the help of men, that is, of the Lacedaemonians; and so we will try and save ourselves. Meanwhile we invite you to allow us to be friends to you and foes to neither party, and to retire from our country after making such a treaty as shall seem fit to us both."

Such was the answer of the Melians. The Athenians now departing from the conference said: "Well, you alone, as it seems to us, judging from these resolutions, regard what is future as more certain than what is before your eyes, and what is out of sight, in your eagerness, as already coming to pass; and as you have staked most on, and trusted most in, the Lacedaemonians, your fortune, and your hopes, so will you be most completely deceived."

The Athenian envoys now returned to the army; and the Melians showing no signs of yielding, the generals at once betook themselves to hostilities, and drew a line of circumvallation round the Melians, dividing the work among the different states. Subsequently the Athenians returned with most of their army, leaving behind them a certain number of their own citizens and of the allies to keep guard by land and sea. The force thus left stayed on and besieged the place.

About the same time the Argives invaded the territory of Phlius and lost eighty men cut off in an ambush by the Phliasians and Argive exiles. Meanwhile the Athenians at Pylos took so much plunder from the Lacedaemonians that the latter, although they still refrained from breaking off the treaty and going to war with Athens, yet proclaimed that any of their people that chose might plunder the Athenians. The Corinthians also commenced hostilities with the Athenians for private quarrels of their own; but the rest of the Peloponnesians stayed quiet. Meanwhile the Melians attacked by night and took the part of the Athenian lines over against the market, and killed some of the men, and brought in corn and all else that they could find useful to them, and so returned and kept quiet, while the Athenians took measures to keep better guard in future.

Summer was now over. The next winter the Lacedaemonians intended to invade the Argive territory, but arriving at the frontier found the sacrifices for crossing unfavourable, and went back again. This intention of theirs gave the Argives suspicions of certain of their fellow citizens, some of whom they arrested; others, however, escaped them. About the same time the Melians again took another part of the Athenian lines which were but feebly garrisoned. Reinforcements afterwards arriving from Athens in consequence, under the command of Philocrates, son of Demeas, the siege was now pressed vigorously; and some treachery taking place inside, the Melians surrendered at discretion to the Athenians, who put to death all the grown men whom they took, and sold the women and children for slaves, and subsequently sent out five hundred colonists and inhabited the place themselves.

CHAPTER XVIII

Seventeenth Year of the War - The Sicilian Campaign -
Affair of the Hermae - Departure of the Expedition

T HE SAME winter the Athenians resolved to sail again to Sicily, with a greater armament than that under Laches and Eurymedon, and, if possible, to conquer the island; most of them being ignorant of its size and of the number of its inhabitants, Hellenic and barbarian, and of the fact that they were undertaking a war not much inferior to that against the Peloponnesians. For the voyage round Sicily in a merchantman is not far short of eight days; and yet, large as the island is, there are only two miles of sea to prevent its being mainland.

It was settled originally as follows, and the peoples that occupied it are these. The earliest inhabitants spoken of in any part of the country are the Cyclopes and Laestrygones; but I cannot tell of what race they were, or whence they came or whither they went, and must leave my readers to what the poets have said of them and to what may be generally known concerning them. The Sicanians appear to have been the next settlers, although they pretend to have been the first of all and aborigines; but the facts show that they were Iberians, driven by the Ligurians from the river Sicanus in Iberia. It was from them that the island, before called Trinacria, took its name of Sicania, and to the present day they inhabit the west of Sicily. On the fall of Ilium, some of the Trojans escaped from the Achaeans, came in ships to Sicily, and settled next to the Sicanians under the general name of Elymi; their towns being called Eryx and Egesta. With them settled some of the Phocians carried on their way from Troy by a storm, first to Libya, and afterwards from thence to Sicily. The Sicels crossed over to Sicily from their first home Italy, flying from the Opicans, as tradition says and as seems not unlikely, upon rafts, having watched till the wind set down the strait to effect the passage; although perhaps they may have sailed over in some other way. Even at the present day there are still Sicels in Italy; and the country got its name of Italy from Italus, a king of the Sicels, so called. These went with a great host to Sicily, defeated the Sicanians in battle and forced them to remove to the south and west of the island, which thus came to be called Sicily instead of Sicania, and after they crossed over continued to enjoy the richest parts of the country for near three hundred years before any Hellenes came to Sicily; indeed they still hold the centre and north of the island. There were also Phoenicians living all round Sicily, who had occupied promontories upon the sea coasts and the islets adjacent for the purpose of trading with the Sicels. But when the Hellenes began to arrive in considerable numbers by sea, the Phoenicians abandoned most of their stations, and drawing together took up their abode in Motye, Soloeis, and Panormus, near the Elymi, partly because they confided in their alliance, and also because these are the nearest points for the voyage between Carthage and Sicily.

These were the barbarians in Sicily, settled as I have said. Of the Hellenes, the first to arrive were Chalcidians from Euboea

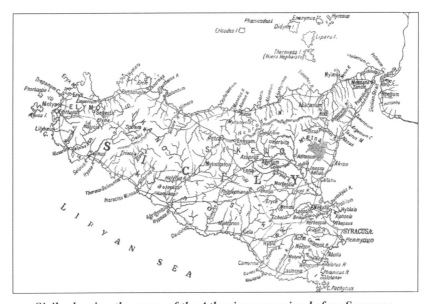

Sicily showing the scene of the Athenian campaign before Syracuse.

382

with Thucles, their founder. They founded Naxos and built the altar to Apollo Archegetes, which now stands outside the town, and upon which the deputies for the games sacrifice before sailing from Sicily. Syracuse was founded the year afterwards by Archias, one of the Heraclids from Corinth, who began by driving out the Sicels from the island upon which the inner city now stands, though it is no longer surrounded by water: in process of time the outer town also was taken within the walls and became populous. Meanwhile Thucles and the Chalcidians set out from Naxos in the fifth year after the foundation of Syracuse, and drove out the Sicels by arms and founded Leontini and afterwards Catana; the Catanians themselves choosing Evarchus as their founder.

About the same time Lamis arrived in Sicily with a colony from Megara, and after founding a place called Trotilus beyond the river Pantacyas, and afterwards leaving it and for a short while joining the Chalcidians at Leontini, was driven out by them and founded Thapsus. After his death his companions were driven out of Thapsus, and founded a place called the Hyblaean Megara; Hyblon, a Sicel king, having given up the place and inviting them thither. Here they lived two hundred and forty-five years; after which they were expelled from the city and the country by the Syracusan tyrant Gelo. Before their expulsion, however, a hundred years after they had settled there, they sent out Pamillus and founded Selinus; he having come from their mother country Megara to join them in its foundation. Gela was founded by Antiphemus from Rhodes and Entimus from Crete, who joined in leading a colony thither, in the forty-fifth year after the foundation of Syracuse. The town took its name from the river Gelas, the place where the citadel now stands, and which was first fortified, being called Lindii. The institutions which they adopted were Dorian. Near one hundred and eight years after the foundation of Gela, the Geloans founded Acragas (Agrigentum), so called from the river of that name, and made Aristonous and Pystilus their founders; giving their own institutions to the colony. Zancle was originally founded by pirates from Cuma, the Chalcidian town in the country of the Opicans: afterwards, however, large numbers came from Chalcis and the rest of Euboea, and helped to people the place; the founders being Perieres and Crataemenes from Cuma and Chalcis respectively. It first had the name of Zancle given it by the Sicels, because the place is shaped like a sickle, which the Sicels call zanclon; but upon the original settlers being afterwards expelled by some Samians and other Ionians who landed in Sicily flying from the Medes, and the Samians in their turn not long afterwards by Anaxilas, tyrant of Rhegium, the town was by him colonized with a mixed population, and its name changed to Messina, after his old country.

Himera was founded from Zancle by Euclides, Simus, and Sacon, most of those who went to the colony being Chalcidians; though they were joined by some exiles from Syracuse, defeated in a civil war, called the Myletidae. The language was a mixture of Chalcidian and Doric, but the institutions which prevailed were the Chalcidian. Acrae and Casmenae were founded by the Syracusans; Acrae seventy years after Syracuse, Casmenae nearly twenty after Acrae. Camarina was first founded by the Syracusans, close upon a hundred and thirty-five years after the building of Syracuse; its founders being Daxon and Menecolus. But the Camarinaeans being expelled by arms by the Syracusans for having revolted, Hippocrates, tyrant of Gela, some time later receiving their land in ransom for some Syracusan prisoners, resettled Camarina, himself acting as its founder. Lastly, it was again depopulated by Gelo, and settled once more for the third time by the Geloans.

Such is the list of the peoples, Hellenic and barbarian, inhabiting Sicily, and such the magnitude of the island which the Athenians were now bent upon invading; being ambitious in real truth of conquering the whole, although they had also the specious design of succouring their kindred and other allies in the island. But they were especially incited by envoys from Egesta, who had come to Athens and invoked their aid more urgently than ever. The Egestaeans had gone to war with their neighbours the

Selinuntines upon questions of marriage and disputed territory, and the Selinuntines had procured the alliance of the Syracusans, and pressed Egesta hard by land and sea. The Egestaeans now reminded the Athenians of the alliance made in the time of Laches, during the former Leontine war, and begged them to send a fleet to their aid, and among a number of other considerations urged as a capital argument that if the Syracusans were allowed to go unpunished for their depopulation of Leontini, to ruin the allies still left to Athens in Sicily, and to get the whole power of the island into their hands, there would be a danger of their one day coming with a large force, as Dorians, to the aid of their Dorian brethren, and as colonists, to the aid of the Peloponnesians who had sent them out, and joining these in pulling down the Athenian empire. The Athenians would, therefore, do well to unite with the allies still left to them, and to make a stand against the Syracusans; especially as they, the Egestaeans, were prepared to furnish money sufficient for the war. The Athenians, hearing these arguments constantly repeated in their assemblies by the Egestaeans and their supporters, voted first to send envoys to Egesta, to see if there was really the money that they talked of in the treasury and temples, and at the same time to ascertain in what posture was the war with the Selinuntines.

The envoys of the Athenians were accordingly dispatched to Sicily. The same winter the Lacedaemonians and their allies, the Corinthians excepted, marched into the Argive territory, and ravaged a small part of the land, and took some yokes of oxen and carried off some corn. They also settled the Argive exiles at Orneae, and left them a few soldiers taken from the rest of the army; and after making a truce for a certain while, according to which neither Orneatae nor Argives were to injure each other's territory, returned home with the army. Not long afterwards the Athenians came with thirty ships and six hundred heavy infantry, and the Argives joining them with all their forces, marched out and besieged the men in Orneae for one day; but the garrison escaped by night, the besiegers having bivouacked some way off. The next day the Argives, discovering it, razed Orneae to the ground, and went back again; after which the Athenians went home in their ships. Meanwhile the Athenians took by sea to Methone on the Macedonian border some cavalry of their own and the Macedonian exiles that were at Athens, and plundered the country of Perdiccas. Upon this the Lacedaemonians sent to the Thracian Chalcidians, who had a truce with Athens from one ten days to another, urging them to join Perdiccas in the war, which they refused to do. And the winter ended, and with it ended the sixteenth year of this war of which Thucydides is the historian.

Early in the spring of the following summer the Athenian envoys arrived from Sicily, and the Egestaeans with them, bringing sixty talents of uncoined silver, as a month's pay for sixty ships, which they were to ask to have sent them. The Athenians held an assembly and, after hearing from the Egestaeans and their own envoys a report, as attractive as it was untrue, upon the state of affairs generally, and in particular as to the money, of which, it was said, there was abundance in the temples and the treasury, voted to send sixty ships to Sicily, under the command of Alcibiades, son of Clinias, Nicias, son of Niceratus, and Lamachus, son of Xenophanes, who were appointed with full powers; they were to help the Egestaeans against the Selinuntines, to restore Leontini upon gaining any advantage in the war, and to order all other matters in Sicily as they should deem best for the interests of Athens. Five days after this a second assembly was held, to consider the speediest means of equipping the ships, and to vote whatever else might be required by the generals for the expedition; and Nicias, who had been chosen to the command against his will, and who thought that the state was not well advised, but upon a slight aid specious pretext was aspiring to the conquest of the whole of Sicily, a great matter to achieve, came forward in the hope of diverting the Athenians from the enterprise, and gave them the following counsel:

"Although this assembly was convened to consider the preparations to be made for sailing to Sicily, I think, notwithstanding, that we have still this question to examine, whether it be better to send out the ships at all, and that we ought not to give so little consideration to a matter of such moment, or let ourselves be persuaded by foreigners into undertaking a war with which we have nothing to do. And yet, individually, I gain in honour by such a course, and fear as little as other men for my person - not that I think a man need be any the worse citizen for taking some thought for his person and estate; on the contrary, such a man would for his own sake desire the prosperity of his country more than others - nevertheless, as I have never spoken against my convictions to gain honour, I shall not begin to do so now, but shall say what I think best. Against your character any words of mine would be weak enough, if I were to advise your keeping what you have got and not risking what is actually yours for advantages which are dubious in themselves, and which you may or may not attain. I will, therefore, content myself with showing that your ardour is out of season, and your ambition not easy of accomplishment.

"I affirm, then, that you leave many enemies behind you here to go yonder and bring more back with you. You imagine, perhaps, that the treaty which you have made can be trusted; a treaty that will continue to exist nominally, as long as you keep quiet - for nominal it has become, owing to the practices of certain men here and at Sparta - but which in the event of a serious reverse in any quarter would not delay our enemies a moment in attacking us; first, because the convention was forced upon them by disaster and was less honourable to them than to us; and secondly, because in this very convention there are many points that are still disputed. Again, some of the most powerful states have never yet accepted the arrangement at all. Some of these are at open war with us; others (as the Lacedaemonians do not yet move) are restrained by truces renewed every ten days, and it is only too probable that if they found our power divided, as we are hurrying to divide it, they would attack us vigorously with the Siceliots, whose alliance they would have in the past valued as they would that of few others. A man ought, therefore, to consider these points, and not to think of running risks with a country placed so critically, or of grasping at another empire before we have secured the one we have already; for in fact the Thracian Chalcidians have been all these years in revolt from us without being yet subdued, and others on the continents yield us but a doubtful obedience. Meanwhile the Egestaeans, our allies, have been wronged, and we run to help them, while the rebels who have so long wronged us still wait for punishment.

"And yet the latter, if brought under, might be kept under; while the Sicilians, even if conquered, are too far off and too numerous to be ruled without difficulty. Now it is folly to go against men who could not be kept under even if conquered, while failure would leave us in a very different position from that which we occupied before the enterprise. The Siceliots, again, to take them as they are at present, in the event of a Syracusan conquest (the favourite bugbear of the Egestaeans), would to my thinking be even less dangerous to us than before. At present they might possibly come here as separate states for love of Lacedaemon; in the other case one empire would scarcely attack another; for after joining the Peloponnesians to overthrow ours, they could only expect to see the same hands overthrow their own in the same way. The Hellenes in Sicily would fear us most if we never went there at all, and next to this, if after displaying our power we went away again as soon as possible. We all know that that which is farthest off, and the reputation of which can least be tested, is the object of admiration; at the least reverse they would at once begin to look down upon us, and would join our enemies here against us. You have yourselves experienced this with regard to the Lacedaemonians and their allies, whom your unexpected success, as compared with what you feared at first, has made you suddenly despise, tempting you further to aspire to the conquest of Sicily. Instead, however, of being puffed up by the misfortunes of your adversaries, you ought to think of breaking their spirit before giving yourselves up to confidence, and to understand that the one thought awakened in the Lacedaemonians by their disgrace is how they may even now, if possible, overthrow us and repair their dishonour; inasmuch as military reputation is their oldest and chiefest study. Our struggle, therefore, if we are wise, will not be for the barbarian Egestaeans in Sicily, but how to defend ourselves most effectually against the oligarchical machinations of Lacedaemon.

"We should also remember that we are but now enjoying some respite from a great pestilence and from war, to the no small benefit of our estates and persons, and that it is right to employ these at home on our own behalf, instead of using them on behalf of these exiles whose interest it is to lie as fairly as they can, who do nothing but talk themselves and leave the danger to others, and who if they succeed will show no proper gratitude, and if they fail will drag down their friends with them. And if there be any man here, overjoyed at being chosen to command, who urges you to make the expedition, merely for ends of his own - specially if he be still too young to command - who seeks to be admired for his stud of horses, but on account of its heavy expenses hopes for some profit from his appointment, do not allow such a one to maintain his private splendour at his country's risk, but remember that such persons injure the public fortune while they squander their own, and that this is a matter of importance, and not for a young man to decide or hastily to take in hand.

"When I see such persons now sitting here at the side of that same individual and summoned by him, alarm seizes me; and I, in my turn, summon any of the older men that may have such a person sitting next him not to let himself be shamed down, for fear of being thought a coward if he do not vote for war, but, remembering how rarely success is got by wishing and how often by forecast, to leave to them the mad dream of conquest, and as a true lover of his country, now threatened by the greatest danger in its history, to hold up his hand on the other side; to vote that the Siceliots be left in the limits now existing between us, limits of which no one can complain (the Ionian sea for the coasting voyage, and the Sicilian across the open main), to enjoy their own possessions and to settle their own quarrels; that the Egestaeans, for their part, be told to end by themselves with the Selinuntines the war which they began without consulting the Athenians; and that for the future we do not enter into alliance, as we have been used to do, with people whom we must help in their need, and who can never help us in ours.

"And you, Prytanis, if you think it your duty to care for the commonwealth, and if you wish to show yourself a good citizen, put the question to the vote, and take a second time the opinions of the Athenians. If you are afraid to move the question again, consider that a violation of the law cannot carry any prejudice with so many abettors, that you will be the physician of your misguided city, and that the virtue of men in office is briefly this, to do their country as much good as they can, or in any case no harm that they can avoid."

Such were the words of Nicias. Most of the Athenians that came forward spoke in favour of the expedition, and of not annulling what had been voted, although some spoke on the other side. By far the warmest advocate of the expedition was, however, Alcibiades, son of Clinias, who wished to thwart Nicias both as his political opponent and also because of the attack he had made upon him in his speech, and who was, besides, exceedingly ambitious of a command by which he hoped to reduce Sicily and Carthage, and personally to gain in wealth and reputation by means of his successes. For the position he held among the citizens led him to indulge his tastes beyond what his real means would bear, both in keeping horses and in the rest of his expenditure; and this later on had not a little to do with the ruin of the Athenian state. Alarmed at the greatness of his licence in his own life and habits, and of the ambition which he showed in all things soever that he undertook, the mass of the people set him down as a pretender to the tyranny, and became his enemies; and although publicly his conduct of the war was as good as could be desired, individually, his habits gave offence to every one, and caused them to commit affairs to other hands, and thus before long to ruin the city. Meanwhile he now came forward and gave the following advice to the Athenians:

"Athenians, I have a better right to command than others - I must begin with this as Nicias has attacked me - and at the same time I believe myself to be worthy of it. The things for which I am abused, bring fame to my ancestors and to myself, and to the country profit besides. The Hellenes, after expecting to see our city ruined by the war, concluded it to be even greater than it really is, by reason of the magnificence with which I represented it at the Olympic games, when I sent into the lists seven chariots, a number never before entered by any private person, and won the first prize, and was second and fourth, and took care to have everything else in a style worthy of my victory. Custom regards such displays as honourable, and they cannot be made without leaving behind them an impression of power. Again, any splendour that I may have exhibited at home in providing choruses or otherwise, is naturally envied by my fellow citizens, but in the eyes of foreigners has an air of strength as in the other instance. And this is no useless folly, when a man at his own private cost benefits not himself only, but his city: nor is it unfair that he who prides himself on his position should refuse to be upon an equality with the rest. He who is badly off has his misfortunes all to himself, and as we do not see men courted in adversity, on the like principle a man ought to accept the insolence of prosperity; or else, let him first mete out equal measure to all, and then demand to have it meted out to him. What I know is that persons of this kind and all others that have attained to any distinction, although they may be unpopular in their lifetime in their relations with their fellow-men and especially with their equals, leave to posterity the desire of claiming connection with them even without any ground, and are vaunted by the country to which they belonged, not as strangers or ill-doers, but as fellow-countrymen and heroes. Such are my aspirations, and however I am abused for them in private, the question is whether any one manages public affairs better than I do. Having united the most powerful states of Peloponnese, without great danger or expense to you, I compelled the Lacedaemonians to stake their all upon the issue of a single day at Mantinea; and although victorious in the battle, they have never since fully recovered confidence.

"Thus did my youth and so-called monstrous folly find fitting arguments to deal with the power of the Peloponnesians, and by its ardour win their confidence and prevail. And do not be afraid of my youth now, but while I am still in its flower, and Nicias appears fortunate, avail yourselves to the utmost of the services of us both. Neither rescind your resolution to sail to Sicily, on the ground that you would be going to attack a great power. The cities in Sicily are peopled by motley rabbles, and easily change their institutions and adopt new ones in their stead; and consequently the inhabitants, being without any feeling of patriotism, are not provided with arms for their persons, and have not regularly established themselves on the land; every man thinks that either by fair words or by party strife he can obtain something at the public expense, and then in the event of a catastrophe settle in some other country, and makes his preparations accordingly. From a mob like this you need not look for either unanimity in counsel or concert in action; but they will probably one by one come in as they get a fair offer, especially if they are torn by civil strife as we are told. Moreover, the Siceliots have not so many heavy infantry as they boast; just as the Hellenes generally did not prove so numerous as each state reckoned itself, but Hellas greatly over-estimated their numbers, and has hardly had an adequate force of heavy infantry throughout this war. The states in Sicily, therefore, from all that I can hear, will be found as I say, and I have not pointed out all our advantages, for we shall have the help of many barbarians, who from their hatred of the Syracusans will join us in attacking them; nor will the powers at home prove any hindrance, if you judge rightly. Our fathers with these very adversaries, which it is said we shall now leave behind us when we sail, and the Mede as their enemy as well, were able to win the empire, depending solely on their superiority at sea. The Peloponnesians had never so little hope against us as at present; and let them be ever so sanguine, although strong enough to invade our country even if we stay at home, they can never hurt us with their navy, as we leave one of our own behind us that is a match for them.

"In this state of things what reason can we give to ourselves for holding back, or what excuse can we offer to our allies in Sicily for not helping them? They are our confederates, and we are bound to assist them, without objecting that they have not assisted us. We did not take them into alliance to have them to help us in Hellas, but that they might so annoy our enemies in Sicily as to prevent them from coming over here and attacking us. It is thus that empire has been won, both by us and by all others that have held it, by a constant readiness to support all, whether barbarians or Hellenes, that invite assistance; since if all were to keep quiet or to pick and choose whom they ought to assist, we should make but few new conquests, and should imperil those we have already won. Men do not rest content with parrying the attacks of a superior, but often strike the first blow to prevent the attack being made. And we cannot fix the exact point at which our empire shall stop; we have reached a position in which we must not be content with retaining but must scheme to extend it, for, if we cease to rule others, we are in danger of being ruled ourselves. Nor can you look at inaction from the same point of view as others, unless you are prepared to change your habits and make them like theirs.

"Be convinced, then, that we shall augment our power at home by this adventure abroad, and let us make the expedition, and so humble the pride of the Peloponnesians by sailing off to Sicily, and letting them see how little we care for the peace that we are now enjoying; and at the same time we shall either become masters, as we very easily may, of the whole of Hellas through the accession of the Sicilian Hellenes, or in any case ruin the Syracusans, to the no small advantage of ourselves and our allies. The faculty of staying if successful, or of returning, will be secured to us by our navy, as we shall be superior at sea to all the Siceliots put together. And do not let the do-nothing policy which Nicias advocates, or his setting of the young against the old, turn you from your purpose, but in the good old fashion by which our fathers, old and young together, by their united counsels brought our affairs to their present height, do you endeavour still to advance them; understanding that neither youth nor old age can do anything the one without the other, but that levity, sobriety, and deliberate judgment are strongest when united, and that, by sinking into inaction, the city, like everything else, will wear itself out, and its skill in everything decay; while each fresh struggle will give it fresh experience, and make it more used to defend itself not in word but in deed. In short, my conviction is that a city not inactive by nature could not choose a quicker way to ruin itself than by suddenly adopting such a policy, and that the safest rule of life is to take one's character and institutions for better and for worse, and to live up to them as closely as one can."

Such were the words of Alcibiades. After hearing him and the Egestaeans and some Leontine exiles, who came forward reminding them of their oaths and imploring their assistance, the Athenians became more eager for the expedition than before. Nicias, perceiving that it would be now useless to try to deter them by the old line of argument, but thinking that he might perhaps alter their resolution by the extravagance of his estimates, came forward a second time and spoke as follows:

"I see, Athenians, that you are thoroughly bent upon the expedition, and therefore hope that all will turn out as we wish, and proceed to give you my opinion at the present juncture. From all that I hear we are going against cities that are great and not subject to one another, or in need of change, so as to be glad to pass from enforced servitude to an easier condition, or in the least likely to accept our rule in exchange for freedom; and, to take only the Hellenic towns, they are very numerous for one island. Besides Naxos and Catana, which I expect to join us from their connection with Leontini, there are seven others armed at all points just like our own power, particularly Selinus and Syracuse, the chief objects of our expedition. These are full of heavy infantry, archers, and darters, have galleys in abundance and crowds to man them; they have also money, partly in the hands of private persons, partly in the temples at Selinus, and at Syracuse first-fruits from some of the barbarians as well. But their chief advantage over us lies in the number of their horses, and in the fact that they grow their corn at home instead of importing it.

"Against a power of this kind it will not do to have merely a weak naval armament, but we shall want also a large land army to sail with us, if we are to do anything worthy of our ambition, and are not to be shut out from the country by a numerous cavalry; especially if the cities should take alarm and combine, and we should be left without friends (except the Egestaeans) to furnish us with horse to defend ourselves with. It would be disgraceful to have to retire under compulsion, or to send back for reinforcements, owing to want of reflection at first: we must therefore start from home with a competent force, seeing that we are going to sail far from our country, and upon an expedition not like any which you may undertaken undertaken the quality of allies, among your subject states here in Hellas, where any additional supplies needed were easily drawn from the friendly territory; but we are cutting ourselves off, and going to a land entirely strange, from which during four months in winter it is not even easy for a messenger get to Athens.

"I think, therefore, that we ought to take great numbers of heavy infantry, both from Athens and from our allies, and not merely from our subjects, but also any we may be able to get for love or for money in Peloponnese, and great numbers also of archers and slingers, to make head against the Sicilian horse. Meanwhile we must have an overwhelming superiority at sea, to enable us the more easily to carry in what we want; and we must take our own corn in merchant vessels, that is to say, wheat and parched barley, and bakers from the mills compelled to serve for pay in the proper proportion; in order that in case of our being weather-bound the armament may not want provisions, as it is not every city that will be able to entertain numbers like ours. We must also provide ourselves with everything else as far as we can, so as not to be dependent upon others; and above all we must take with us from home as much money as possible, as the sums talked of as ready at Egesta are readier, you may be sure, in talk than in any other way.

"Indeed, even if we leave Athens with a force not only equal to that of the enemy except in the number of heavy infantry in the field, but even at all points superior to him, we shall still find it difficult to conquer Sicily or save ourselves. We must not disguise from ourselves that we go to found a city among strangers and enemies, and that he who undertakes such an enterprise should be prepared to become master of the country the first day he lands, or failing in this to find everything hostile to him. Fearing this, and knowing that we shall have need of much good counsel and more good fortune - a hard matter for mortal man to aspire to - I wish as far as may be to make myself independent of fortune before sailing, and when I do sail, to be as safe as a strong force can make me. This I believe to be surest for the country at large, and safest for us who are to go on the expedition. If any one thinks differently I resign to him my command."

With this Nicias concluded, thinking that he should either disgust the Athenians by the magnitude of the undertaking, or, if obliged to sail on the expedition, would thus do so in the safest way possible. The Athenians, however, far from having their taste for the voyage taken away by the burdensomeness of the preparations, became more eager for it than ever; and just the contrary took place of what Nicias had thought, as it was held that he had given good advice, and that the expedition would be the safest in the world. All alike fell in love with the enterprise. The older men thought that they would either subdue the places against which they were to sail, or at all events, with so large a force, meet with no disaster; those in the prime of life felt a longing for foreign sights and spectacles, and had no doubt that they should come safe home again; while the idea of the common people and the soldiery was to earn wages at the moment, and make conquests that would supply a never-ending fund of pay for the future. With this enthusiasm of the majority, the few that liked it not, feared to appear unpatriotic by holding up their hands against it, and so kept quiet.

At last one of the Athenians came forward and called upon Nicias and told him that he ought not to make excuses or put them off, but say at once before them all what forces the Athenians should vote him. Upon this he said, not without reluctance, that he would advise upon that matter more at leisure with his colleagues; as far however as he could see at present, they must sail with at least one hundred galleys - the Athenians providing as many transports as they might determine, and sending for others from the allies - not less than five thousand heavy infantry in all, Athenian and allied, and if possible more; and the rest of the armament in proportion; archers from home and from Crete, and slingers, and whatever else might seem desirable, being got ready by the generals and taken with them.

Upon hearing this the Athenians at once voted that the generals should have full powers in the matter of the numbers of the army and of the expedition generally, to do as they judged best for the interests of Athens. After this the preparations began; messages being sent to the allies and the rolls drawn up at home. And as the city had just recovered from the plague and the long war, and a number of young men had grown up and capital had accumulated by reason of the truce, everything was the more easily provided.

In the midst of these preparations all the stone Hermae in

the city of Athens, that is to say the customary square figures, so common in the doorways of private houses and temples, had in one night most of them their fares mutilated. No one knew who had done it, but large public rewards were offered to find the authors; and it was further voted that any one who knew of any other act of impiety having been committed should come and give information without fear of consequences, whether he were citizen, alien, or slave. The matter was taken up the more seriously, as it was thought to be ominous for the expedition, and part of a conspiracy to bring about a revolution and to upset the democracy.

Information was given accordingly by some resident aliens and body servants, not about the Hermae but about some previous mutilations of other images perpetrated by young men in a drunken frolic, and of mock celebrations of the mysteries, averred to take place in private houses. Alcibiades being implicated in this charge, it was taken hold of by those who could least endure him, because he stood in the way of their obtaining the undisturbed direction of the people, and who thought that if he were once removed the first place would be theirs. These accordingly magnified the matter and loudly proclaimed that the affair of the mysteries and the mutilation of the Hermae were part and parcel of a scheme to overthrow the democracy, and that nothing of all this had been done without Alcibiades; the proofs alleged being the general and undemocratic licence of his life and habits.

Alcibiades repelled on the spot the charges in question, and also before going on the expedition, the preparations for which were now complete, offered to stand his trial, that it might be seen whether he was guilty of the acts imputed to him; desiring to be punished if found guilty, but, if acquitted, to take the command. Meanwhile he protested against their receiving slanders against him in his absence, and begged them rather to put him to death at once if he were guilty, and pointed out the imprudence of sending him out at the head of so large an army, with so serious a charge still undecided. But his enemies feared that he would have the army for him if he were tried immediately, and that the people might relent in favour of the man whom they already caressed as the cause of the Argives and some of the Mantineans joining in the expedition, and did their utmost to get this proposition rejected, putting forward other orators who said that he ought at present to sail and not delay the departure of the army, and be tried on his return within a fixed number of days; their plan being to have him sent for and brought home for trial upon some graver charge, which they would the more easily get up in his absence. Accordingly it was decreed that he should sail.

After this the departure for Sicily took place, it being now about midsummer. Most of the allies, with the corn transports and the smaller craft and the rest of the expedition, had already received orders to muster at Corcyra, to cross the Ionian Sea from thence in a body to the Iapygian promontory. But the Athenians themselves, and such of their allies as happened to be with them, went down to Piraeus upon a day appointed at daybreak, and began to man the ships for putting out to sea. With them also went down the whole population, one may say, of the city, both citizens and foreigners; the inhabitants of the country each escorting those that belonged to them, their friends, their relatives, or their sons, with hope and lamentation upon their way, as they thought of the conquests which they hoped to make; or of the friends whom they might never see again, considering the long voyage which they were going to make from their country. Indeed, at this moment, when they were now upon the point of parting from one another, the danger came more home to them than when they voted for the expedition; although the strength of the armament, and the profuse provision which they remarked in every department, was a sight that could not but comfort them. As for the foreigners and the rest of the crowd, they simply went to see a sight worth looking at and passing all belief.

Indeed this armament that first sailed out was by far the most costly and splendid Hellenic force that had ever been sent out by a single city up to that time. In mere number of ships and heavy infantry that against Epidaurus under Pericles, and the same when going against Potidaea under Hagnon, was not inferior; containing as it did four thousand Athenian heavy infantry, three hundred horse, and one hundred galleys accompanied by fifty Lesbian and Chian vessels and many allies besides. But these were sent upon a short voyage and with a scanty equipment. The present expedition was formed in contemplation of a long term of service by land and sea alike, and was furnished with ships and troops so as to be ready for either as required. The fleet had been elaborately equipped at great cost to the captains and the state; the treasury giving a drachma a day to each seaman, and providing empty ships, sixty men-of-war and forty transports, and manning these with the best crews obtainable; while the captains gave a bounty in addition to the pay from the treasury to the thranitae and crews generally, besides spending lavishly upon figure-heads and equipments, and one and all making the utmost exertions to enable their own ships to excel in beauty and fast sailing. Meanwhile the land forces had been picked from the best muster-rolls, and vied with each other in paying great attention to their arms and personal accoutrements. From this resulted not only a rivalry among themselves in their different departments, but an idea among the rest of the Hellenes that it was more a display of power and resources than an armament against an enemy. For if any one had counted up the public expenditure of the state, and the private outlay of individuals - that is to say, the sums which the state had already spent upon the expedition and was sending out in the hands of the generals, and those which individuals had expended upon their personal outfit, or as captains of galleys had laid out and were still to lay out upon their vessels; and if he had added to this the journey money which each was likely to have provided himself with, independently of the pay from the treasury, for a voyage of such length, and what the soldiers or traders took with them for the purpose of exchange - it would have been found that many talents in all were being taken out of the city. Indeed the expedition became not less famous for its wonderful boldness and for the splendour of its appearance, than for its overwhelming strength as compared with the peoples against whom it was directed, and for the fact that this was the longest passage from home hitherto attempted, and the most ambitious in its objects considering the resources of those who undertook it.

The ships being now manned, and everything put on board with which they meant to sail, the trumpet commanded silence, and the prayers customary before putting out to sea were offered, not in each ship by itself, but by all together to the voice of a herald; and bowls of wine were mixed through all the armament, and libations made by the soldiers and their officers in gold and silver goblets. In their prayers joined also the crowds on shore, the citizens and all others that wished them well. The hymn sung and the libations finished, they put out to sea, and first out in column then raced each other as far as Aegina, and so hastened to reach Corcyra, where the rest of the allied forces were also assembling.

CHAPTER XIX

Seventeenth Year of the War - Parties at Syracuse -
Story of Harmodius and Aristogiton - Disgrace of Alcibiades

MEANWHILE AT Syracuse news came in from many quarters of the expedition, but for a long while met with no credence whatever. Indeed, an assembly was held in which speeches, as will be seen, were delivered by different orators, believing or contradicting the report of the Athenian expedition; among whom Hermocrates, son of Hermon, came forward, being persuaded that he knew the truth of the matter, and gave the following counsel:

"Although I shall perhaps be no better believed than others have been when I speak upon the reality of the expedition, and although I know that those who either make or repeat statements thought not worthy of belief not only gain no converts but are thought fools for their pains, I shall certainly not be frightened into holding my tongue when the state is in danger, and when I am persuaded that I can speak with more authority on the matter than other persons. Much as you wonder at it, the Athenians nevertheless have set out against us with a large force, naval and military, professedly to help the Egestaeans and to restore Leontini, but really to conquer Sicily, and above all our city, which once gained, the rest, they think, will easily follow. Make up your minds, therefore, to see them speedily here, and see how you can best repel them with the means under your hand, and do be taken off your guard through despising the news, or neglect the common weal through disbelieving it. Meanwhile those who believe me need not be dismayed at the force or daring of the enemy. They will not be able to do us more hurt than we shall do them; nor is the greatness of their armament altogether without advantage to us. Indeed, the greater it is the better, with regard to the rest of the Siceliots, whom dismay will make more ready to join us; and if we defeat or drive them away, disappointed of the objects of their ambition (for I do not fear for a moment that they will get what they want), it will be a most glorious exploit for us, and in my judgment by no means an unlikely one. Few indeed have been the large armaments, either Hellenic or barbarian, that have gone far from home and been successful. They cannot be more numerous than the people of the country and their neighbours, all of whom fear leagues together; and if they miscarry for want of supplies in a foreign land, to those against whom their plans were laid none the less they leave renown, although they may themselves have been the main cause of their own discomfort. Thus these very Athenians rose by the defeat of the Mede, in a great measure due to accidental causes, from the mere fact that Athens had been the object of his attack; and this may very well be the case with us also.

"Let us, therefore, confidently begin preparations here; let us send and confirm some of the Sicels, and obtain the friendship and alliance of others, and dispatch envoys to the rest of Sicily to show that the danger is common to all, and to Italy to get them to become our allies, or at all events to refuse to receive the Athenians. I also think that it would be best to send to Carthage as well; they are by no means there without apprehension, but it is their constant fear that the Athenians may one day attack their city, and they may perhaps think that they might themselves suffer by letting Sicily be sacrificed, and be willing to help us secretly if not openly, in one way if not in another. They are the best able to do so, if they will, of any of the present day, as they possess most gold and silver, by which war, like everything else, flourishes. Let us also send to Lacedaemon and Corinth, and ask them to come here and help us as soon as possible, and to keep alive the war in Hellas. But the true thing of all others, in my opinion, to do at the present moment, is what you, with your constitutional love of quiet, will be slow to see, and what I must nevertheless mention. If we Siceliots, all together, or at least as many as possible besides ourselves, would only launch the whole of our actual navy with two months' provisions, and meet the Athenians at Tarentum and the Iapygian promontory, and show them that before fighting for Sicily they must first fight for their passage across the Ionian Sea, we should strike dismay into their army, and set them on thinking that we have a base for our defensive - for Tarentum is ready to receive us - while they have a wide sea to cross with all their armament, which could with difficulty keep its order through so long a voyage, and would be easy for us to attack as it came on slowly and in small detachments. On the other hand, if they were to lighten their vessels, and draw together their fast sailers and with these attack us, we could either fall upon them when they were wearied with rowing, or if we did not choose to do so, we could retire to Tarentum; while they, having crossed with few provisions just to give battle, would be hard put to it in desolate places, and would either have to remain and be blockaded, or to try to sail along the coast, abandoning the rest of their armament, and being further discouraged by not knowing for certain whether the cities would receive them. In my opinion this consideration alone would be sufficient to deter them from putting out from Corcyra; and what with deliberating and reconnoitring our numbers and whereabouts, they would let the season go on until winter was upon them, or, confounded by so unexpected a circumstance, would break up the expedition, especially as their most experienced general has, as I hear, taken the command against his will, and would grasp at the first excuse offered by any serious demonstration of ours. We should also be reported, I am certain, as more numerous than we really are, and men's minds are affected by what they hear, and besides the first to attack, or to show that they mean to defend themselves against an attack, inspire greater fear because men see that they are ready for the emergency. This would just be the case with the Athenians at present. They are now attacking us in the belief that we shall not resist, having a right to judge us severely because we did not help the Lacedaemonians in crushing them;

but if they were to see us showing a courage for which they are not prepared, they would be more dismayed by the surprise than they could ever be by our actual power. I could wish to persuade you to show this courage; but if this cannot be, at all events lose not a moment in preparing generally for the war; and remember all of you that contempt for an assailant is best shown by bravery in action, but that for the present the best course is to accept the preparations which fear inspires as giving the surest promise of safety, and to act as if the danger was real. That the Athenians are coming to attack us, and are already upon the voyage, and all but here - this is what I am sure of."

Thus far spoke Hermocrates. Meanwhile the people of Syracuse were at great strife among themselves; some contending that the Athenians had no idea of coming and that there was no truth in what he said; some asking if they did come what harm they could do that would not be repaid them tenfold in return; while others made light of the whole affair and turned it into ridicule. In short, there were few that believed Hermocrates and feared for the future. Meanwhile Athenagoras, the leader of the people and very

Naval battle in the harbor of Syracuse where Sparta defeated the Athenians.

405

powerful at that time with the masses, came forward and spoke as follows:

"For the Athenians, he who does not wish that they may be as misguided as they are supposed to be, and that they may come here to become our subjects, is either a coward or a traitor to his country; while as for those who carry such tidings and fill you with so much alarm, I wonder less at their audacity than at their folly if they flatter themselves that we do not see through them. The fact is that they have their private reasons to be afraid, and wish to throw the city into consternation to have their own terrors cast into the shade by the public alarm. In short, this is what these reports are worth; they do not arise of themselves, but are concocted by men who are always causing agitation here in Sicily. However, if you are well advised, you will not be guided in your calculation of probabilities by what these persons tell you, but by what shrewd men and of large experience, as I esteem the Athenians to be, would be likely to do. Now it is not likely that they would leave the Peloponnesians behind them, and before they have well ended the war in Hellas wantonly come in quest of a new war quite as arduous in Sicily; indeed, in my judgment, they are only too glad that we do not go and attack them, being so many and so great cities as we are.

"However, if they should come as is reported, I consider Sicily better able to go through with the war than Peloponnese, as being at all points better prepared, and our city by itself far more than a match for this pretended army of invasion, even were it twice as large again. I know that they will not have horses with them, or get any here, except a few perhaps from the Egestaeans; or be able to bring a force of heavy infantry equal in number to our own, in ships which will already have enough to do to come all this distance, however lightly laden, not to speak of the transport of the other stores required against a city of this magnitude, which will be no slight quantity. In fact, so strong is my opinion upon the subject, that I do not well see how they could avoid annihilation if they brought with them another city as large as Syracuse, and settled down and carried on war from our frontier; much less can they hope to succeed with all Sicily hostile to them, as all Sicily will be, and with only a camp pitched from the ships, and composed of tents and bare necessaries, from which they would not be able to stir far for fear of our cavalry.

"But the Athenians see this as I tell you, and as I have reason to know are looking after their possessions at home, while persons here invent stories that neither are true nor ever will be. Nor is this the first time that I see these persons, when they cannot resort to deeds, trying by such stories and by others even more abominable to frighten your people and get into their hands the government: it is what I see always. And I cannot help fearing that trying so often they may one day succeed, and that we, as long as we do not feel the smart, may prove too weak for the task of prevention, or, when the offenders are known, of pursuit. The result is that our city is rarely at rest, but is subject to constant troubles and to contests as frequent against herself as against the enemy, not to speak of occasional tyrannies and infamous cabals. However, I will try, if you will support me, to let nothing of this happen in our time, by gaining you, the many, and by chastising the authors of such machinations, not merely when they are caught in the act - a difficult feat to accomplish - but also for what they have the wish though not the power to do; as it is necessary to punish an enemy not only for what he does, but also beforehand for what he intends to do, if the first to relax precaution would not be also the first to suffer. I shall also reprove, watch, and on occasion warn the few - the most effectual way, in my opinion, of turning them from their evil courses. And after all, as I have often asked, what would you have, young men? Would you hold office at once? The law forbids it, a law enacted rather because you are not competent than to disgrace you when competent. Meanwhile you would not be on a legal equality with the many! But how can it be right that citizens of the same state should be held unworthy of the same privileges?

"It will be said, perhaps, that democracy is neither wise nor equitable, but that the holders of property are also the best fitted to rule. I say, on the contrary, first, that the word demos, or people, includes the whole state, oligarchy only a part; next, that if the best guardians of property are the rich, and the best counsellors the wise, none can hear and decide so well as the many; and that all these talents, severally and collectively, have their just place in a democracy. But an oligarchy gives the many their share of the danger, and not content with the largest part takes and keeps the whole of the profit; and this is what the powerful and young among you aspire to, but in a great city cannot possibly obtain.

"But even now, foolish men, most senseless of all the Hellenes that I know, if you have no sense of the wickedness of your designs, or most criminal if you have that sense and still dare to pursue them - even now, if it is not a case for repentance, you may still learn wisdom, and thus advance the interest of the country, the common interest of us all. Reflect that in the country's prosperity the men of merit in your ranks will have a share and a larger share than the great mass of your fellow countrymen, but that if you have other designs you run a risk of being deprived of all; and desist from reports like these, as the people know your object and will not put up with it. If the Athenians arrive, this city will repulse them in a manner worthy of itself; we have moreover, generals who will see to this matter. And if nothing of this be true, as I incline to believe, the city will not be thrown into a panic by your intelligence, or impose upon itself a self-chosen servitude by choosing you for its rulers; the city itself will look into the matter, and will judge your words as if they were acts, and, instead of allowing itself to be deprived of its liberty by listening to you, will strive to preserve that liberty, by taking care to have always at hand the means of making itself respected."

Such were the words of Athenagoras. One of the generals now stood up and stopped any other speakers coming forward, adding these words of his own with reference to the matter in hand: "It is not well for speakers to utter calumnies against one another, or for their hearers to entertain them; we ought rather to look to the intelligence that we have received, and see how each man by himself and the city as a whole may best prepare to repel the invaders. Even if there be no need, there is no harm in the state being furnished with horses and arms and all other insignia of war; and we will undertake to see to and order this, and to send round to the cities to reconnoitre and do all else that may appear desirable. Part of this we have seen to already, and whatever we discover shall be laid before you." After these words from the general, the Syracusans departed from the assembly.

In the meantime the Athenians with all their allies had now arrived at Corcyra. Here the generals began by again reviewing the armament, and made arrangements as to the order in which they were to anchor and encamp, and dividing the whole fleet into three divisions, allotted one to each of their number, to avoid sailing all together and being thus embarrassed for water, harbourage, or provisions at the stations which they might touch at, and at the same time to be generally better ordered and easier to handle, by each squadron having its own commander. Next they sent on three ships to Italy and Sicily to find out which of the cities would receive them, with instructions to meet them on the way and let them know before they put in to land.

After this the Athenians weighed from Corcyra, and proceeded to cross to Sicily with an armament now consisting of one hundred and thirty-four galleys in all (besides two Rhodian fifty-oars), of which one hundred were Athenian vessels - sixty men-of-war, and forty troopships - and the remainder from Chios and the other allies; five thousand and one hundred heavy infantry in all, that is to say, fifteen hundred Athenian citizens from the rolls at Athens and seven hundred Thetes shipped as marines, and the rest allied troops, some of them Athenian subjects, and besides these five hundred Argives, and two hundred and fifty Mantineans serving for hire; four hundred and eighty archers in all, eighty of whom were Cretans, seven hundred slingers from Rhodes, one hundred and twenty light-armed exiles from Megara, and one horse-transport carrying thirty horses.

Such was the strength of the first armament that sailed over for the war. The supplies for this force were carried by thirty ships of burden laden with corn, which conveyed the bakers, stone-masons, and carpenters, and the tools for raising fortifications, accompanied by one hundred boats, like the former pressed into the service, besides many other boats and ships of burden which followed the armament voluntarily for purposes of trade; all of which now left Corcyra and struck across the Ionian Sea together. The whole force making land at the Iapygian promontory and Tarentum, with more or less good fortune, coasted along the shores of Italy, the cities shutting their markets and gates against them, and according them nothing but water and liberty to anchor, and Tarentum and Locri not even that, until they arrived at Rhegium, the extreme point of Italy. Here at length they reunited, and not gaining admission within the walls pitched a camp outside the city in the precinct of Artemis, where a market was also provided for them, and drew their ships on shore and kept quiet. Meanwhile they opened negotiations with the Rhegians, and called upon them as Chalcidians to assist their Leontine kinsmen; to which the Rhegians replied that they would not side with either party, but should await the decision of the rest of the Italiots, and do as they did. Upon this the Athenians now began to consider what would be the best action to take in the affairs of Sicily, and meanwhile waited for the ships sent on to come back from Egesta, in order to know whether there was really there the money mentioned by the messengers at Athens.

In the meantime came in from all quarters to the Syracusans, as well as from their own officers sent to reconnoitre, the positive tidings that the fleet was at Rhegium; upon which they laid aside their incredulity and threw themselves heart and soul into the work of preparation. Guards or envoys, as the case might be, were sent round to the Sicels, garrisons put into the posts of the Peripoli in the country, horses and arms reviewed in the city to see that nothing was wanting, and all other steps taken to prepare for a war which might be upon them at any moment.

Meanwhile the three ships that had been sent on came from Egesta to the Athenians at Rhegium, with the news that so far from there being the sums promised, all that could be produced was thirty talents. The generals were not a little disheartened at being thus disappointed at the outset, and by the refusal to join in the expedition of the Rhegians, the people they had first tried to gain and had had had most reason to count upon, from their relationship to the Leontines and constant friendship for Athens. If Nicias was prepared for the news from Egesta, his two colleagues were taken completely by surprise. The Egestaeans had had recourse to the following stratagem, when the first envoys from Athens came to inspect their resources. They took the envoys in question to the temple of Aphrodite at Eryx and showed them the treasures deposited there: bowls, wine-ladles, censers, and a large number of other pieces of plate, which from being in silver gave an impression of wealth quite out of proportion to their really small value. They also privately entertained the ships' crews, and collected all the cups of gold and silver that they could find in Egesta itself or could borrow in the neighbouring Phoenician and Hellenic towns, and each brought them to the banquets as their own; and as all used pretty nearly the same, and everywhere a great quantity of plate was shown, the effect was most dazzling upon the Athenian sailors, and made them talk loudly of the riches they had seen when they got back to Athens. The dupes in question - who had in their turn persuaded the rest - when the news got abroad that there was not the money supposed at Egesta, were much blamed by the soldiers.

Meanwhile the generals consulted upon what was to be done. The opinion of Nicias was to sail with all the armament to Selinus, the main object of the expedition, and if the Egestaeans could provide money for the whole force, to advise accordingly; but if they could not, to require them to supply provisions for the sixty ships that they had asked for, to stay and settle matters between them and the Selinuntines either by force or by agreement, and then to coast past the other cities, and after displaying the power of Athens and proving their zeal for their friends and allies, to sail home again (unless they should have some sudden and unexpected opportunity of serving the Leontines, or of bringing over some of the other cities), and not to endanger the state by wasting its home resources.

Alcibiades said that a great expedition like the present must not disgrace itself by going away without having done anything; heralds must be sent to all the cities except Selinus and Syracuse, and efforts be made to make some of the Sicels revolt from the Syracusans, and to obtain the friendship of others, in order to have corn and troops; and first of all to gain the Messinese, who lay right in the passage and entrance to Sicily, and would afford an excellent harbour and base for the army. Thus, after bringing over the towns and knowing who would be their allies in the war, they might at length attack Syracuse and Selinus; unless the latter came to terms with Egesta and the former ceased to oppose the restoration of Leontini.

Lamachus, on the other hand, said that they ought to sail straight to Syracuse, and fight their battle at once under the walls of the town while the people were still unprepared, and the panic at its height. Every armament was most terrible at first; if it allowed time to run on without showing itself, men's courage revived, and they saw it appear at last almost with indifference. By attacking suddenly, while Syracuse still trembled at their coming, they would have the best chance of gaining a victory for themselves and of striking a complete panic into the enemy by the aspect of their numbers - which would never appear so considerable as at present - by the anticipation of coming disaster, and above all by the immediate danger of the engagement. They might also count upon surprising many in the fields outside, incredulous of their coming; and at the moment that the enemy was carrying in his property the army would not want for booty if it sat down in force before the city. The rest of the Siceliots would thus be immediately less disposed to enter into alliance with the Syracusans, and would join the Athenians, without waiting to see which were the strongest. They must make Megara their naval station as a place to retreat to and a base from which to attack: it was an uninhabited place at no great distance from Syracuse either by land or by sea.

After speaking to this effect, Lamachus nevertheless gave his support to the opinion of Alcibiades. After this Alcibiades sailed in his own vessel across to Messina with proposals of alliance, but met with no success, the inhabitants answering that they could not receive him within their walls, though they would provide him with a market outside. Upon this he sailed back to Rhegium. Immediately upon his return the generals manned and victualled sixty ships out of the whole fleet and coasted along to Naxos, leaving the rest of the armament behind them at Rhegium with one of their number. Received by the Naxians, they then coasted on to Catana, and being refused admittance by the inhabitants, there being a Syracusan party in the town, went on to the river Terias. Here they bivouacked, and the next day sailed in single file to Syracuse with all their ships except ten which they sent on in front to sail into the great harbour and see if there was any fleet launched, and to proclaim by herald from shipboard that the Athenians were come to restore the Leontines to their country, as being their allies and kinsmen, and that such of them, therefore, as were in Syracuse should leave it without fear and join their friends and benefactors the Athenians. After making this proclamation and reconnoitring the city and the harbours, and the features of the country which they would have to make their base of operations in the war, they sailed back to Catana.

An assembly being held here, the inhabitants refused to receive the armament, but invited the generals to come in and say what

413

they desired; and while Alcibiades was speaking and the citizens were intent on the assembly, the soldiers broke down an ill-walled-up postern gate without being observed, and getting inside the town, flocked into the marketplace. The Syracusan party in the town no sooner saw the army inside than they became frightened and withdrew, not being at all numerous; while the rest voted for an alliance with the Athenians and invited them to fetch the rest of their forces from Rhegium. After this the Athenians sailed to Rhegium, and put off, this time with all the armament, for Catana, and fell to work at their camp immediately upon their arrival.

Meanwhile word was brought them from Camarina that if they went there the town would go over to them, and also that the Syracusans were manning a fleet. The Athenians accordingly sailed alongshore with all their armament, first to Syracuse, where they found no fleet manning, and so always along the coast to Camarina, where they brought to at the beach, and sent a herald to the people, who, however, refused to receive them, saying that their oaths bound them to receive the Athenians only with a single vessel, unless they themselves sent for more. Disappointed here, the Athenians now sailed back again, and after landing and plundering on Syracusan territory and losing some stragglers from their light infantry through the coming up of the Syracusan horse, so got back to Catana.

There they found the Salaminia come from Athens for Alcibiades, with orders for him to sail home to answer the charges which the state brought against him, and for certain others of the soldiers who with him were accused of sacrilege in the matter of the mysteries and of the Hermae. For the Athenians, after the departure of the expedition, had continued as active as ever in investigating the facts of the mysteries and of the Hermae, and, instead of testing the informers, in their suspicious temper welcomed all indifferently, arresting and imprisoning the best citizens upon the evidence of rascals, and preferring to sift the matter to the bottom sooner than to let an accused person of good character pass unquestioned, owing to the rascality of the informer. The commons had heard how oppressive the tyranny of Pisistratus and his sons had become before it ended, and further that that had been put down at last, not by themselves and Harmodius, but by the Lacedaemonians, and so were always in fear and took everything suspiciously.

Indeed, the daring action of Aristogiton and Harmodius was undertaken in consequence of a love affair, which I shall relate at some length, to show that the Athenians are not more accurate than the rest of the world in their accounts of their own tyrants and of the facts of their own history. Pisistratus dying at an advanced age in possession of the tyranny, was succeeded by his eldest son, Hippias, and not Hipparchus, as is vulgarly believed. Harmodius was then in the flower of youthful beauty, and Aristogiton, a citizen in the middle rank of life, was his lover and possessed him. Solicited without success by Hipparchus, son of Pisistratus, Harmodius told Aristogiton, and the enraged lover, afraid that the powerful Hipparchus might take Harmodius by force, immediately formed a design, such as his condition in life permitted, for overthrowing the tyranny. In the meantime Hipparchus, after a second solicitation of Harmodius, attended with no better success, unwilling to use violence, arranged to insult him in some covert way. Indeed, generally their government was not grievous to the multitude, or in any way odious in practice; and these tyrants cultivated wisdom and virtue as much as any, and without exacting from the Athenians more than a twentieth of their income, splendidly adorned their city, and carried on their wars, and provided sacrifices for the temples. For the rest, the city was left in full enjoyment of its existing laws, except that care was always taken to have the offices in the hands of some one of the family. Among those of them that held the yearly archonship at Athens was Pisistratus, son of the tyrant Hippias, and named after his grandfather, who dedicated during his term of office the altar to the twelve gods in the market-place, and that of Apollo in the Pythian precinct. The Athenian people afterwards built on to and lengthened the altar in the market-place, and obliterated the inscription; but that in the Pythian precinct can still be seen, though in faded letters, and is to the following effect:

Pisistratus, the son of Hippias, Sent up this record of his archonship In precinct of Apollo Pythias.

That Hippias was the eldest son and succeeded to the government, is what I positively assert as a fact upon which I have had more exact accounts than others, and may be also ascertained by the following circumstance. He is the only one of the legitimate brothers that appears to have had children; as the altar shows, and the pillar placed in the Athenian Acropolis, commemorating the crime of the tyrants, which mentions no child of Thessalus or of Hipparchus, but five of Hippias, which he had by Myrrhine, daughter of Callias, son of Hyperechides; and naturally the eldest would have married first. Again, his name comes first on the pillar after that of his father; and this too is quite natural, as he was the eldest after him, and the reigning tyrant. Nor can I ever believe that Hippias would have obtained the tyranny so easily, if Hipparchus had been in power when he was killed, and he, Hippias, had had to establish himself upon the same day; but he had no doubt been long accustomed to overawe the citizens, and to be obeyed by his mercenaries, and thus not only conquered, but conquered with ease, without experiencing any of the embarrassment of a younger brother unused to the exercise of authority. It was the sad fate which made Hipparchus famous that got him also the credit with posterity of having been tyrant.

To return to Harmodius; Hipparchus having been repulsed in his solicitations insulted him as he had resolved, by first inviting a sister of his, a young girl, to come and bear a basket in a certain procession, and then rejecting her, on the plea that she had never been invited at all owing to her unworthiness. If Harmodius was indignant at this, Aristogiton for his sake now became more exasperated than ever; and having arranged everything with those who were to join them in the enterprise, they only waited for the great feast of the Panathenaea, the sole day upon which the citizens forming part of the procession could meet together in arms without suspicion. Aristogiton and Harmodius were to begin, but were to be supported immediately by their accomplices against the bodyguard. The conspirators were not many, for better security, besides which they hoped that those not in the plot would be carried away by the example of a few daring spirits, and use the arms in their hands to recover their liberty.

At last the festival arrived; and Hippias with his bodyguard was outside the city in the Ceramicus, arranging how the different parts of the procession were to proceed. Harmodius and Aristogiton had already their daggers and were getting ready to act, when seeing one of their accomplices talking familiarly with Hippias, who was easy of access to every one, they took fright, and concluded that they were discovered and on the point of being taken; and eager if possible to be revenged first upon the man who had wronged them and for whom they had undertaken all this risk, they rushed, as they were, within the gates, and meeting with Hipparchus by the Leocorium recklessly fell upon him at once, infuriated, Aristogiton by love, and Harmodius by insult, and smote him and slew him. Aristogiton escaped the guards at the moment, through the crowd running up, but was afterwards taken and dispatched in no merciful way: Harmodius was killed on the spot.

When the news was brought to Hippias in the Ceramicus, he at once proceeded not to the scene of action, but to the armed men in the procession, before they, being some distance away, knew anything of the matter, and composing his features for the occasion, so as not to betray himself, pointed to a certain spot, and bade them repair thither without their arms. They withdrew accordingly, fancying he had something to say; upon which he told the mercenaries to remove the arms, and there and then picked out the men he thought guilty and all found with daggers, the shield and spear being the usual weapons for a procession.

In this way offended love first led Harmodius and Aristogiton to conspire, and the alarm of the moment to commit the rash action recounted. After this the tyranny pressed harder on the Athenians, and Hippias, now grown more fearful, put to death many of the citizens, and at the same time began to turn his eyes abroad for a refuge in case of revolution. Thus, although an Athenian, he gave his daughter, Archedice, to a Lampsacene, Aeantides, son of the tyrant of Lampsacus, seeing that they had great influence with Darius. And there is her tomb in Lampsacus with this inscription:

Archedice lies buried in this earth, Hippias her sire, and Athens gave her birth; Unto her bosom pride was never known, Though daughter, wife, and sister to the throne.

Hippias, after reigning three years longer over the Athenians, was deposed in the fourth by the Lacedaemonians and the banished Alcmaeonidae, and went with a safe conduct to Sigeum, and to Aeantides at Lampsacus, and from thence to King Darius; from whose court he set out twenty years after, in his old age, and came with the Medes to Marathon.

With these events in their minds, and recalling everything they knew by hearsay on the subject, the Athenian people grow difficult of humour and suspicious of the persons charged in the affair of the mysteries, and persuaded that all that had taken place was part of an oligarchical and monarchical conspiracy. In the state of irritation thus produced, many persons of consideration had been already thrown into prison, and far from showing any signs of abating, public feeling grew daily more savage, and more arrests were made; until at last one of those in custody, thought to be the most guilty of all, was induced by a fellow prisoner to make a revelation, whether true or not is a matter on which there are two opinions, no one having been able, either then or since, to say for certain who did the deed. However this may be, the other found arguments to persuade him, that even if he had not done it, he ought to save himself by gaining a promise of impunity, and free the state of its present suspicions; as he would be surer of safety if he confessed after promise of impunity than if he denied and were brought to trial. He accordingly made a revelation, affecting himself and others in the affair of the Hermae; and the Athenian people, glad at last, as they supposed, to get at the truth, and furious until then at not being able to discover those who had conspired against the commons, at once let go the informer and all the rest whom he had not denounced, and bringing the accused to trial executed as many as were apprehended, and condemned to death such as had fled and set a price upon their heads. In this it was, after all, not clear whether the sufferers had been punished unjustly, while in any case the rest of the city received immediate and manifest relief.

To return to Alcibiades: public feeling was very hostile to him, being worked on by the same enemies who had attacked him before he went out; and now that the Athenians fancied that they had got at the truth of the matter of the Hermae, they believed more firmly than ever that the affair of the mysteries also, in which he was implicated, had been contrived by him in the same intention and was connected with the plot against the democracy. Meanwhile it so happened that, just at the time of this agitation, a small force of Lacedaemonians had advanced as far as the Isthmus, in pursuance of some scheme with the Boeotians. It was now thought that this had come by appointment, at his instigation, and not on account of the Boeotians, and that, if the citizens had not acted on the information received, and forestalled them by arresting the prisoners, the city would have been betrayed. The citizens went so far as to sleep one night armed in the temple of Theseus within the walls. The friends also of Alcibiades at Argos were just at this time suspected of a design to attack the commons; and the Argive hostages deposited in the islands were given up by the Athenians to the Argive people to be put to death upon that account: in short, everywhere something was found to create suspicion against Alcibiades. It was therefore decided to bring him to trial and execute him, and the Salaminia was sent to Sicily for him and the others named in the information, with instructions to order him to come and answer the charges against him, but not to arrest him, because they wished to avoid causing any agitation in the army or among the enemy in Sicily, and above all to retain the services of the Mantineans and Argives, who, it was thought, had been induced to join by his influence. Alcibiades, with his own ship and his fellow accused, accordingly sailed off with the Salaminia from Sicily, as though to return to Athens, and went with her as far as Thurii, and there they left the ship and disappeared, being afraid to go home for trial with such a prejudice existing against them. The crew of the Salaminia stayed some time looking for Alcibiades and his companions, and at length, as they were nowhere to be found, set sail and departed. Alcibiades, now an outlaw, crossed in a boat not long after from Thurii to Peloponnese; and the Athenians passed sentence of death by default upon him and those in his company.

CHAPTER XX

*Seventeenth and Eighteenth Years of the War - Inaction of the
Athenian Army - Alcibiades at Sparta - Investment of Syracuse*

THE ATHENIAN generals left in Sicily now divided the
armament into two parts, and, each taking one by lot,
sailed with the whole for Selinus and Egesta, wishing to
know whether the Egestaeans would give the money, and to look
into the question of Selinus and ascertain the state of the quarrel
between her and Egesta. Coasting along Sicily, with the shore
on their left, on the side towards the Tyrrhene Gulf they touched
at Himera, the only Hellenic city in that part of the island, and
being refused admission resumed their voyage. On their way they
took Hyccara, a petty Sicanian seaport, nevertheless at war with
Egesta, and making slaves of the inhabitants gave up the town
to the Egestaeans, some of whose horse had joined them; after
which the army proceeded through the territory of the Sicels until
it reached Catana, while the fleet sailed along the coast with the
slaves on board. Meanwhile Nicias sailed straight from Hyccara
along the coast and went to Egesta and, after transacting his other
business and receiving thirty talents, rejoined the forces. They now
sold their slaves for the sum of one hundred and twenty talents,
and sailed round to their Sicel allies to urge them to send troops;
and meanwhile went with half their own force to the hostile town
of Hybla in the territory of Gela, but did not succeed in taking it.

Summer was now over. The winter following, the Athenians at
once began to prepare for moving on Syracuse, and the Syracusans
on their side for marching against them. From the moment when
the Athenians failed to attack them instantly as they at first feared
and expected, every day that passed did something to revive their
courage; and when they saw them sailing far away from them on
the other side of Sicily, and going to Hybla only to fail in their
attempts to storm it, they thought less of them than ever, and called

upon their generals, as the multitude is apt to do in its moments of confidence, to lead them to Catana, since the enemy would not come to them. Parties also of the Syracusan horse employed in reconnoitring constantly rode up to the Athenian armament, and among other insults asked them whether they had not really come to settle with the Syracusans in a foreign country rather than to resettle the Leontines in their own.

Aware of this, the Athenian generals determined to draw them out in mass as far as possible from the city, and themselves in the meantime to sail by night alongshore, and take up at their leisure a convenient position. This they knew they could not so well do, if they had to disembark from their ships in front of a force prepared for them, or to go by land openly. The numerous cavalry of the Syracusans (a force which they were themselves without) would then be able to do the greatest mischief to their light troops and the crowd that followed them; but this plan would enable them to take up a position in which the horse could do them no hurt worth speaking of, some Syracusan exiles with the army having told them of the spot near the Olympieum, which they afterwards occupied. In pursuance of their idea, the generals imagined the following stratagem. They sent to Syracuse a man devoted to them, and by the Syracusan generals thought to be no less in their interest; he was a native of Catana, and said he came from persons in that place, whose names the Syracusan generals were acquainted with, and whom they knew to be among the members of their party still left in the city. He told them that the Athenians passed the night in the town, at some distance from their arms, and that if the Syracusans would name a day and come with all their people at daybreak to attack the armament, they, their friends, would close the gates upon the troops in the city, and set fire to the vessels, while the Syracusans would easily take the camp by an attack upon the stockade. In this they would be aided by many of the Catanians, who were already prepared to act, and from whom he himself came.

The generals of the Syracusans, who did not want confidence, and who had intended even without this to march on Catana, believed the man without any sufficient inquiry, fixed at once a day upon which they would be there, and dismissed him, and the Selinuntines and others of their allies having now arrived, gave orders for all the Syracusans to march out in mass. Their preparations completed, and the time fixed for their arrival being at hand, they set out for Catana, and passed the night upon the river Symaethus, in the Leontine territory. Meanwhile the Athenians no sooner knew of their approach than they took all their forces and such of the Sicels or others as had joined them, put them on board their ships and boats, and sailed by night to Syracuse. Thus, when morning broke the Athenians were landing opposite the Olympieum ready to seize their camping ground, and the Syracusan horse having ridden up first to Catana and found that all the armament had put to sea, turned back and told the infantry, and then all turned back together, and went to the relief of the city.

In the meantime, as the march before the Syracusans was a long one, the Athenians quietly sat down their army in a convenient position, where they could begin an engagement when they pleased, and where the Syracusan cavalry would have least opportunity of annoying them, either before or during the action, being fenced off on one side by walls, houses, trees, and by a marsh, and on the other by cliffs. They also felled the neighbouring trees and carried them down to the sea, and formed a palisade alongside of their ships, and with stones which they picked up and wood hastily raised a fort at Daskon, the most vulnerable point of their position, and broke down the bridge over the Anapus. These preparations were allowed to go on without any interruption from the city, the first hostile force to appear being the Syracusan cavalry, followed afterwards by all the foot together. At first they came close up to the Athenian army, and then, finding that they did not offer to engage, crossed the Helorine road and encamped for the night.

The next day the Athenians and their allies prepared for battle, their dispositions being as follows: Their right wing was occupied by the Argives and Mantineans, the centre by the Athenians, and the rest of the field by the other allies. Half their army was drawn up eight deep in advance, half close to their tents in a hollow square, formed also eight deep, which had orders to look out and be ready to go to the support of the troops hardest pressed. The camp followers were placed inside this reserve. The Syracusans, meanwhile, formed their heavy infantry sixteen deep, consisting of the mass levy of their own people, and such allies as had joined them, the strongest contingent being that of the Selinuntines; next to them the cavalry of the Geloans, numbering two hundred in all, with about twenty horse and fifty archers from Camarina. The cavalry was posted on their right, full twelve hundred strong, and next to it the darters. As the Athenians were about to begin the attack, Nicias went along the lines, and addressed these words of encouragement to the army and the nations composing it:

"Soldiers, a long exhortation is little needed by men like ourselves, who are here to fight in the same battle, the force itself being, to my thinking, more fit to inspire confidence than a fine speech with a weak army. Where we have Argives, Mantineans, Athenians, and the first of the islanders in the ranks together, it were strange indeed, with so many and so brave companions in arms, if we did not feel confident of victory; especially when we have mass levies opposed to our picked troops, and what is more, Siceliots, who may disdain us but will not stand against us, their skill not being at all commensurate to their rashness. You may also remember that we are far from home and have no friendly land near, except what your own swords shall win you; and here I put before you a motive just the reverse of that which the enemy are appealing to; their cry being that they shall fight for their country, mine that we shall fight for a country that is not ours, where we must conquer or hardly get away, as we shall have their horse upon us in great numbers. Remember, therefore, your renown, and go boldly against the enemy, thinking the present strait and necessity more terrible than they."

After this address Nicias at once led on the army. The Syracusans were not at that moment expecting an immediate engagement, and some had even gone away to the town, which was close by; these now ran up as hard as they could and, though behind time, took their places here or there in the main body as fast as they joined it. Want of zeal or daring was certainly not the fault of the Syracusans, either in this or the other battles, but although not inferior in courage, so far as their military science might carry them, when this failed them they were compelled to give up their resolution also. On the present occasion, although they had not supposed that the Athenians would begin the attack, and although constrained to stand upon their defence at short notice, they at once took up their arms and advanced to meet them. First, the stone-throwers, slingers, and archers of either army began skirmishing, and routed or were routed by one another, as might be expected between light troops; next, soothsayers brought forward the usual victims, and trumpeters urged on the heavy infantry to the charge; and thus they advanced, the Syracusans to fight for their country, and each individual for his safety that day and liberty hereafter; in the enemy's army, the Athenians to make another's country theirs and to save their own from suffering by their defeat; the Argives and independent allies to help them in getting what they came for, and to earn by victory another sight of the country they had left behind; while the subject allies owed most of their ardour to the desire of self-preservation, which they could only hope for if victorious; next to which, as a secondary motive, came the chance of serving on easier terms, after helping the Athenians to a fresh conquest.

The armies now came to close quarters, and for a long while fought without either giving ground. Meanwhile there occurred some claps of thunder with lightning and heavy rain, which did not fail to add to the fears of the party fighting for the first time, and very little acquainted with war; while to their more experienced adversaries these phenomena appeared to be produced by the time of year, and much more alarm was felt at the continued resistance of the enemy. At last the Argives drove in the Syracusan left, and after them the Athenians routed the troops opposed to them, and the Syracusan army was thus cut in two and betook itself to flight. The Athenians did not pursue far, being held in check by the numerous and undefeated Syracusan horse, who attacked and drove back any of their heavy infantry whom they saw pursuing in advance of the rest; in spite of which the victors followed so far as was safe in a body, and then went back and set up a trophy. Meanwhile the Syracusans rallied at the Helorine road, where they re-formed as well as they could under the circumstances, and even sent a garrison of their own citizens to the Olympieum, fearing that the Athenians might lay hands on some of the treasures there. The rest returned to the town.

The Athenians, however, did not go to the temple, but collected their dead and laid them upon a pyre, and passed the night upon the field. The next day they gave the enemy back their dead under truce, to the number of about two hundred and sixty, Syracusans and allies, and gathered together the bones of their own, some fifty, Athenians and allies, and taking the spoils of the enemy, sailed back to Catana. It was now winter; and it did not seem possible for the moment to carry on the war before Syracuse, until horse should have been sent for from Athens and levied among the allies in Sicily - to do away with their utter inferiority in cavalry - and money should have been collected in the country and received from Athens, and until some of the cities, which they hoped would be now more disposed to listen to them after the battle, should have been brought over, and corn and all other necessaries provided, for a campaign in the spring against Syracuse.

With this intention they sailed off to Naxos and Catana for the winter. Meanwhile the Syracusans burned their dead and then held an assembly, in which Hermocrates, son of Hermon, a man

426

who with a general ability of the first order had given proofs of military capacity and brilliant courage in the war, came forward and encouraged them, and told them not to let what had occurred make them give way, since their spirit had not been conquered, but their want of discipline had done the mischief. Still they had not been beaten by so much as might have been expected, especially as they were, one might say, novices in the art of war, an army of artisans opposed to the most practised soldiers in Hellas. What had also done great mischief was the number of the generals (there were fifteen of them) and the quantity of orders given, combined with the disorder and insubordination of the troops. But if they were to have a few skilful generals, and used this winter in preparing their heavy infantry, finding arms for such as had not got any, so as to make them as numerous as possible, and forcing them to attend to their training generally, they would have every chance of beating their adversaries, courage being already theirs and discipline in the field having thus been added to it. Indeed, both these qualities would improve, since danger would exercise them in discipline, while their courage would be led to surpass itself by the confidence which skill inspires. The generals should be few and elected with full powers, and an oath should be taken to leave them entire discretion in their command: if they adopted this plan, their secrets would be better kept, all preparations would be properly made, and there would be no room for excuses.

The Syracusans heard him, and voted everything as he advised, and elected three generals, Hermocrates himself, Heraclides, son of Lysimachus, and Sicanus, son of Execestes. They also sent envoys to Corinth and Lacedaemon to procure a force of allies to join them, and to induce the Lacedaemonians for their sakes openly to address themselves in real earnest to the war against the Athenians, that they might either have to leave Sicily or be less able to send reinforcements to their army there.

The Athenian forces at Catana now at once sailed against Messina, in the expectation of its being betrayed to them. The intrigue, however, after all came to nothing: Alcibiades, who was in the secret, when he left his command upon the summons from home, foreseeing that he would be outlawed, gave information of the plot to the friends of the Syracusans in Messina, who had at once put to death its authors, and now rose in arms against the opposite faction with those of their way of thinking, and succeeded in preventing the admission of the Athenians. The latter waited for thirteen days, and then, as they were exposed to the weather and without provisions, and met with no success, went back to Naxos, where they made places for their ships to lie in, erected a palisade round their camp, and retired into winter quarters; meanwhile they sent a galley to Athens for money and cavalry to join them in the spring. During the winter the Syracusans built a wall on to the city, so as to take in the statue of Apollo Temenites, all along the side looking towards Epipolae, to make the task of circumvallation longer and more difficult, in case of their being defeated, and also erected a fort at Megara and another in the Olympieum, and stuck palisades along the sea wherever there was a landing Place. Meanwhile, as they knew that the Athenians were wintering at Naxos, they marched with all their people to Catana, and ravaged the land and set fire to the tents and encampment of the Athenians, and so returned home. Learning also that the Athenians were sending an embassy to Camarina, on the strength of the alliance concluded in the time of Laches, to gain, if possible, that city, they sent another from Syracuse to oppose them. They had a shrewd suspicion that the Camarinaeans had not sent what they did send for the first battle very willingly; and they now feared that they would refuse to assist them at all in future, after seeing the success of the Athenians in the action, and would join the latter on the strength of their old friendship. Hermocrates, with some others, accordingly arrived at Camarina from Syracuse, and Euphemus and others from the Athenians; and an assembly of the Camarinaeans having been convened, Hermocrates spoke as follows, in the hope of prejudicing them against the Athenians:

"Camarinaeans, we did not come on this embassy because we were afraid of your being frightened by the actual forces of the Athenians, but rather of your being gained by what they would say to you before you heard anything from us. They are come to Sicily with the pretext that you know, and the intention which we all suspect, in my opinion less to restore the Leontines to their homes than to oust us from ours; as it is out of all reason that they should restore in Sicily the cities that they lay waste in Hellas, or should cherish the Leontine Chalcidians because of their Ionian blood and keep in servitude the Euboean Chalcidians, of whom the Leontines are a colony. No; but the same policy which has proved so successful in Hellas is now being tried in Sicily. After being chosen as the leaders of the Ionians and of the other allies of Athenian origin, to punish the Mede, the Athenians accused some of failure in military service, some of fighting against each other, and others, as the case might be, upon any colourable pretext that could be found, until they thus subdued them all. In fine, in the struggle against the Medes, the Athenians did not fight for the liberty of the Hellenes, or the Hellenes for their own liberty, but the former to make their countrymen serve them instead of him, the latter to change one master for another, wiser indeed than the first, but wiser for evil.

"But we are not now come to declare to an audience familiar with them the misdeeds of a state so open to accusation as is the Athenian, but much rather to blame ourselves, who, with the warnings we possess in the Hellenes in those parts that have been enslaved through not supporting each other, and seeing the same sophisms being now tried upon ourselves - such as restorations of Leontine kinsfolk and support of Egestaean allies - do not stand together and resolutely show them that here are no Ionians, or Hellespontines, or islanders, who change continually, but always serve a master, sometimes the Mede and sometimes some other, but free Dorians from independent Peloponnese, dwelling in Sicily. Or, are we waiting until we be taken in detail, one city after another; knowing as we do that in no other way can we be conquered, and seeing that they turn to this plan, so as to divide some of us by words, to draw some by the bait of an alliance into open war with each other, and to ruin others by such flattery as different circumstances may render acceptable? And do we fancy when destruction first overtakes a distant fellow countryman that the danger will not come to each of us also, or that he who suffers before us will suffer in himself alone?

"As for the Camarinaean who says that it is the Syracusan, not he, that is the enemy of the Athenian, and who thinks it hard to have to encounter risk in behalf of my country, I would have him bear in mind that he will fight in my country, not more for mine than for his own, and by so much the more safely in that he will enter on the struggle not alone, after the way has been cleared by my ruin, but with me as his ally, and that the object of the Athenian is not so much to punish the enmity of the Syracusan as to use me as a blind to secure the friendship of the Camarinaean. As for him who envies or even fears us (and envied and feared great powers must always be), and who on this account wishes Syracuse to be humbled to teach us a lesson, but would still have her survive, in the interest of his own security the wish that he indulges is not humanly possible. A man can control his own desires, but he cannot likewise control circumstances; and in the event of his calculations proving mistaken, he may live to bewail his own misfortune, and wish to be again envying my prosperity. An idle wish, if he now sacrifice us and refuse to take his share of perils which are the same, in reality though not in name, for him as for us; what is nominally the preservation of our power being really his own salvation. It was to be expected that you, of all people in the world, Camarinaeans, being our immediate neighbours and the next in danger, would have foreseen this, and instead of supporting us in the lukewarm way that you are now doing, would rather come to us of your own accord, and be now offering at Syracuse the aid which you would have asked for at Camarina, if to Camarina the Athenians had first come, to encourage us to resist the invader. Neither you, however, nor the rest have as yet bestirred yourselves in this direction.

"Fear perhaps will make you study to do right both by us and by the invaders, and plead that you have an alliance with the Athenians. But you made that alliance, not against your friends, but against the enemies that might attack you, and to help the Athenians when they were wronged by others, not when as now they are wronging their neighbours. Even the Rhegians, Chalcidians though they be, refuse to help to restore the Chalcidian Leontines; and it would be strange if, while they suspect the gist of this fine pretence and are wise without reason, you, with every reason on your side, should yet choose to assist your natural enemies, and should join with their direst foes in undoing those whom nature has made your own kinsfolk. This is not to do right; but you should help us without fear of their armament, which has no terrors if we hold together, but only if we let them succeed in their endeavours to separate us; since even after attacking us by ourselves and being victorious in battle, they had to go off without effecting their purpose.

"United, therefore, we have no cause to despair, but rather new encouragement to league together; especially as succour will come to us from the Peloponnesians, in military matters the undoubted superiors of the Athenians. And you need not think that your prudent policy of taking sides with neither, because allies of both, is either safe for you or fair to us. Practically it is not as fair as it pretends to be. If the vanquished be defeated, and the victor conquer, through your refusing to join, what is the effect of your abstention but to leave the former to perish unaided, and to allow the latter to offend unhindered? And yet it were more honourable to join those who are not only the injured party, but your own kindred, and by so doing to defend the common interests of Sicily and save your friends the Athenians from doing wrong.

"In conclusion, we Syracusans say that it is useless for us to demonstrate either to you or to the rest what you know already as

431

well as we do; but we entreat, and if our entreaty fail, we protest that we are menaced by our eternal enemies the Ionians, and are betrayed by you our fellow Dorians. If the Athenians reduce us, they will owe their victory to your decision, but in their own name will reap the honour, and will receive as the prize of their triumph the very men who enabled them to gain it. On the other hand, if we are the conquerors, you will have to pay for having been the cause of our danger. Consider, therefore; and now make your choice between the security which present servitude offers and the prospect of conquering with us and so escaping disgraceful submission to an Athenian master and avoiding the lasting enmity of Syracuse."

Such were the words of Hermocrates; after whom Euphemus, the Athenian ambassador, spoke as follows:

"Although we came here only to renew the former alliance, the attack of the Syracusans compels us to speak of our empire and of the good right we have to it. The best proof of this the speaker himself furnished, when he called the Ionians eternal enemies of the Dorians. It is the fact; and the Peloponnesian Dorians being our superiors in numbers and next neighbours, we Ionians looked out for the best means of escaping their domination. After the Median War we had a fleet, and so got rid of the empire and supremacy of the Lacedaemonians, who had no right to give orders to us more than we to them, except that of being the strongest at that moment; and being appointed leaders of the King's former subjects, we continue to be so, thinking that we are least likely to fall under the dominion of the Peloponnesians, if we have a force to defend ourselves with, and in strict truth having done nothing unfair in reducing to subjection the Ionians and islanders, the kinsfolk whom the Syracusans say we have enslaved. They, our kinsfolk, came against their mother country, that is to say against us, together with the Mede, and, instead of having the courage to revolt and sacrifice their property as we did when we abandoned our city, chose to be slaves themselves, and to try to make us so.

"We, therefore, deserve to rule because we placed the largest fleet and an unflinching patriotism at the service of the Hellenes, and because these, our subjects, did us mischief by their ready subservience to the Medes; and, desert apart, we seek to strengthen ourselves against the Peloponnesians. We make no fine profession of having a right to rule because we overthrew the barbarian single-handed, or because we risked what we did risk for the freedom of the subjects in question any more than for that of all, and for our own: no one can be quarrelled with for providing for his proper safety. If we are now here in Sicily, it is equally in the interest of our security, with which we perceive that your interest also coincides. We prove this from the conduct which the Syracusans cast against us and which you somewhat too timorously suspect; knowing that those whom fear has made suspicious may be carried away by the charm of eloquence for the moment, but when they come to act follow their interests.

"Now, as we have said, fear makes us hold our empire in Hellas, and fear makes us now come, with the help of our friends, to order safely matters in Sicily, and not to enslave any but rather to prevent any from being enslaved. Meanwhile, let no one imagine that we are interesting ourselves in you without your having anything to do with us, seeing that, if you are preserved and able to make head against the Syracusans, they will be less likely to harm us by sending troops to the Peloponnesians. In this way you have everything to do with us, and on this account it is perfectly reasonable for us to restore the Leontines, and to make them, not subjects like their kinsmen in Euboea, but as powerful as possible, to help us by annoying the Syracusans from their frontier. In Hellas we are alone a match for our enemies; and as for the assertion that it is out of all reason that we should free the Sicilian, while we enslave the Chalcidian, the fact is that the latter is useful to us by being without arms and contributing money only; while the former, the Leontines and our other friends, cannot be too independent.

"Besides, for tyrants and imperial cities nothing is unreasonable if expedient, no one a kinsman unless sure; but friendship or enmity is everywhere an affair of time and circumstance. Here, in Sicily, our interest is not to weaken our friends, but by means of their strength to cripple our enemies. Why doubt this? In Hellas we treat our allies as we find them useful. The Chians and Methymnians govern themselves and furnish ships; most of the rest have harder terms and pay tribute in money; while others, although islanders and easy for us to take, are free altogether, because they occupy convenient positions round Peloponnese. In our settlement of the states here in Sicily, we should therefore; naturally be guided by our interest, and by fear, as we say, of the Syracusans. Their ambition is to rule you, their object to use the suspicions that we excite to unite you, and then, when we have gone away without effecting anything, by force or through your isolation, to become the masters of Sicily. And masters they must become, if you unite with them; as a force of that magnitude would be no longer easy for us to deal with united, and they would be more than a match for you as soon as we were away.

"Any other view of the case is condemned by the facts. When you first asked us over, the fear which you held out was that of danger to Athens if we let you come under the dominion of Syracuse; and it is not right now to mistrust the very same argument by which you claimed to convince us, or to give way to suspicion because we are come with a larger force against the power of that city. Those whom you should really distrust are the Syracusans. We are not able to stay here without you, and if we proved perfidious enough to bring you into subjection, we should be unable to keep you in bondage, owing to the length of the voyage and the difficulty of guarding large, and in a military sense continental, towns: they, the Syracusans, live close to you, not in a camp, but in a city greater than the force we have with us, plot always against you, never let slip an opportunity once offered, as they have shown in the case of the Leontines and others, and now have the face, just as if you were fools, to invite you to aid them against the power that hinders this, and that has thus far maintained Sicily independent. We, as against them, invite you to a much more real safety, when we beg you not to betray that common safety which we each have in the other, and to reflect that they, even without allies, will, by their numbers, have always the way open to you, while you will not often have the opportunity of defending yourselves with such numerous auxiliaries; if, through your suspicions, you once let these go away unsuccessful or defeated, you will wish to see if only a handful of them back again, when the day is past in which their presence could do anything for you.

"But we hope, Camarinaeans, that the calumnies of the Syracusans will not be allowed to succeed either with you or with the rest: we have told you the whole truth upon the things we are suspected of, and will now briefly recapitulate, in the hope of convincing you. We assert that we are rulers in Hellas in order not to be subjects; liberators in Sicily that we may not be harmed by the Sicilians; that we are compelled to interfere in many things, because we have many things to guard against; and that now, as before, we are come as allies to those of you who suffer wrong in this island, not without invitation but upon invitation. Accordingly, instead of making yourselves judges or censors of our conduct, and trying to turn us, which it were now difficult to do, so far as there is anything in our interfering policy or in our character that chimes in with your interest, this take and make use of; and be sure that, far from being injurious to all alike, to most of the Hellenes that policy is even beneficial. Thanks to it, all men in all places, even where we are not, who either apprehend or meditate aggression, from the near prospect before them, in the one case, of obtaining our intervention in their favour, in the other, of our arrival making the venture dangerous, find themselves constrained, respectively, to be moderate against their will, and to be preserved without trouble of their own. Do not you reject this security that is open to all who desire it, and is now offered to you; but do like others, and

435

instead of being always on the defensive against the Syracusans, unite with us, and in your turn at last threaten them."

Such were the words of Euphemus. What the Camarinaeans felt was this. Sympathizing with the Athenians, except in so far as they might be afraid of their subjugating Sicily, they had always been at enmity with their neighbour Syracuse. From the very fact, however, that they were their neighbours, they feared the Syracusans most of the two, and being apprehensive of their conquering even without them, both sent them in the first instance the few horsemen mentioned, and for the future determined to support them most in fact, although as sparingly as possible; but for the moment in order not to seem to slight the Athenians, especially as they had been successful in the engagement, to answer both alike. Agreeably to this resolution they answered that as both the contending parties happened to be allies of theirs, they thought it most consistent with their oaths at present to side with neither; with which answer the ambassadors of either party departed.

In the meantime, while Syracuse pursued her preparations for war, the Athenians were encamped at Naxos, and tried by negotiation to gain as many of the Sicels as possible. Those more in the low lands, and subjects of Syracuse, mostly held aloof; but the peoples of the interior who had never been otherwise than independent, with few exceptions, at once joined the Athenians, and brought down corn to the army, and in some cases even money. The Athenians marched against those who refused to join, and forced some of them to do so; in the case of others they were stopped by the Syracusans sending garrisons and reinforcements. Meanwhile the Athenians moved their winter quarters from Naxos to Catana, and reconstructed the camp burnt by the Syracusans, and stayed there the rest of the winter. They also sent a galley to Carthage, with proffers of friendship, on the chance of obtaining assistance, and another to Tyrrhenia; some of the cities there having spontaneously offered to join them in the war. They also sent round to the Sicels and to Egesta, desiring them to send them as many horses as possible, and meanwhile prepared bricks, iron, and all other things necessary for the work of circumvallation, intending by the spring to begin hostilities.

In the meantime the Syracusan envoys dispatched to Corinth and Lacedaemon tried as they passed along the coast to persuade the Italiots to interfere with the proceedings of the Athenians, which threatened Italy quite as much as Syracuse, and having arrived at Corinth made a speech calling on the Corinthians to assist them on the ground of their common origin. The Corinthians voted at once to aid them heart and soul themselves, and then sent on envoys with them to Lacedaemon, to help them to persuade her also to prosecute the war with the Athenians more openly at home and to send succours to Sicily. The envoys from Corinth having reached Lacedaemon found there Alcibiades with his fellow refugees, who had at once crossed over in a trading vessel from Thurii, first to Cyllene in Elis, and afterwards from thence to Lacedaemon; upon the Lacedaemonians' own invitation, after first obtaining a safe conduct, as he feared them for the part he had taken in the affair of Mantinea. The result was that the Corinthians, Syracusans, and Alcibiades, pressing all the same request in the assembly of the Lacedaemonians, succeeded in persuading them; but as the ephors and the authorities, although resolved to send envoys to Syracuse to prevent their surrendering to the Athenians, showed no disposition to send them any assistance, Alcibiades now came forward and inflamed and stirred the Lacedaemonians by speaking as follows:

"I am forced first to speak to you of the prejudice with which I am regarded, in order that suspicion may not make you disinclined to listen to me upon public matters. The connection, with you as your proxeni, which the ancestors of our family by reason of some discontent renounced, I personally tried to renew by my good offices towards you, in particular upon the occasion of the disaster at Pylos. But although I maintained this friendly attitude, you yet chose to negotiate the peace with the Athenians through my enemies, and thus to strengthen them and to discredit me. You had therefore no right to complain if I turned to the Mantineans and Argives, and seized other occasions of thwarting and injuring you; and the time has now come when those among you, who in the bitterness of the moment may have been then unfairly angry with me, should look at the matter in its true light, and take a different view. Those again who judged me unfavourably, because I leaned rather to the side of the commons, must not think that their dislike is any better founded. We have always been hostile to tyrants, and all who oppose arbitrary power are called commons; hence we continued to act as leaders of the multitude; besides which, as democracy was the government of the city, it was necessary in most things to conform to established conditions. However, we endeavoured to be more moderate than the licentious temper of the times; and while there were others, formerly as now, who tried to lead the multitude astray - the same who banished me - our party was that of the whole people, our creed being to do our part in preserving the form of government under which the city enjoyed the utmost greatness and freedom, and which we had found existing. As for democracy, the men of sense among us knew what it was, and I perhaps as well as any, as I have the more cause to complain of it; but there is nothing new to be said of a patent absurdity; meanwhile we did not think it safe to alter it under the pressure of your hostility.

"So much then for the prejudices with which I am regarded: I now can call your attention to the questions you must consider, and upon which superior knowledge perhaps permits me to speak. We sailed to Sicily first to conquer, if possible, the Siceliots, and after them the Italiots also, and finally to assail the empire and city of Carthage. In the event of all or most of these schemes succeeding, we were then to attack Peloponnese, bringing with us the entire force of the Hellenes lately acquired in those parts, and taking a number of barbarians into our pay, such as the Iberians and others in those countries, confessedly the most warlike known, and building numerous galleys in addition to those which we had already, timber being plentiful in Italy; and with this fleet blockading Peloponnese from the sea and assailing it with our armies by land, taking some of the cities by storm, drawing works of circumvallation round others, we hoped without difficulty to effect its reduction, and after this to rule the whole of the Hellenic name. Money and corn meanwhile for the better execution of these plans were to be supplied in sufficient quantities by the newly acquired places in those countries, independently of our revenues here at home.

"You have thus heard the history of the present expedition from the man who most exactly knows what our objects were; and the remaining generals will, if they can, carry these out just the same. But that the states in Sicily must succumb if you do not help them, I will now show. Although the Siceliots, with all their inexperience, might even now be saved if their forces were united, the Syracusans alone, beaten already in one battle with all their people and blockaded from the sea, will be unable to withstand the Athenian armament that is now there. But if Syracuse falls, all Sicily falls also, and Italy immediately afterwards; and the danger which I just now spoke of from that quarter will before long be upon you. None need therefore fancy that Sicily only is in question; Peloponnese will be so also, unless you speedily do as I tell you, and send on board ship to Syracuse troops that shall able to row their ships themselves, and serve as heavy infantry the moment that they land; and what I consider even more important than the troops, a Spartan as commanding officer to discipline the forces already on foot and to compel recusants to serve. The friends that you have already will thus become more confident, and the waverers will be encouraged to join you. Meanwhile you must carry on the war here more openly, that the Syracusans, seeing that you do not forget them, may put heart into their resistance, and that the Athenians may be less able to reinforce their armament. You must fortify Decelea in Attica, the blow of which the Athenians are always most afraid and the only one that they think they have not experienced in the present war; the surest method of harming an enemy being to find out what he most fears, and to choose this means of attacking him, since every one naturally knows best his own weak points and fears accordingly. The fortification in question, while it benefits you, will create difficulties for your adversaries, of which I shall pass over many, and shall only mention the chief. Whatever property there is in the country will most of it become yours, either by capture or surrender; and the Athenians will at once be deprived of their revenues from the silver mines at Laurium, of their present gains from their land and from the law courts, and above all of the revenue from their allies, which will be paid less regularly, as they lose their awe of Athens and see you addressing yourselves with vigour to the war. The zeal and speed with which all this shall be done depends, Lacedaemonians, upon yourselves; as to its possibility, I am quite confident, and I have little fear of being mistaken.

"Meanwhile I hope that none of you will think any the worse of me if, after having hitherto passed as a lover of my country, I now actively join its worst enemies in attacking it, or will suspect what I say as the fruit of an outlaw's enthusiasm. I am an outlaw from the iniquity of those who drove me forth, not, if you will be guided by me, from your service; my worst enemies are not you who only harmed your foes, but they who forced their friends to become enemies; and love of country is what I do not feel when I am wronged, but what I felt when secure in my rights as a citizen. Indeed I do not consider that I am now attacking a country that is still mine; I am rather trying to recover one that is mine no longer; and the true lover of his country is not he who consents to lose it unjustly rather than attack it, but he who longs for it so much that he will go all lengths to recover it. For myself, therefore, Lacedaemonians, I beg you to use me without scruple for danger and trouble of every kind, and to remember the argument in every one's mouth, that if I did you great harm as an enemy, I could likewise do you good service as a friend, inasmuch as I know the plans of the Athenians, while I only guessed yours. For yourselves I entreat you to believe that your most capital interests are now under deliberation; and I urge you to send without hesitation the expeditions to Sicily and Attica; by the presence of a small part of your forces you will save important cities in that island, and you will destroy the power of Athens both present and prospective; after this you will dwell in security and enjoy the supremacy over all Hellas, resting not on force but upon consent and affection."

Such were the words of Alcibiades. The Lacedaemonians, who had themselves before intended to march against Athens, but were still waiting and looking about them, at once became much more in earnest when they received this particular information from Alcibiades, and considered that they had heard it from the man who best knew the truth of the matter. Accordingly they now turned their attention to the fortifying of Decelea and sending immediate aid to the Sicilians; and naming Gylippus, son of Cleandridas, to the command of the Syracusans, bade him consult with that people and with the Corinthians and arrange for succours reaching the island, in the best and speediest way possible under the circumstances. Gylippus desired the Corinthians to send him at once two ships to Asine, and to prepare the rest that they intended to send, and to have them ready to sail at the proper time. Having settled this, the envoys departed from Lacedaemon.

In the meantime arrived the Athenian galley from Sicily sent by the generals for money and cavalry; and the Athenians, after hearing what they wanted, voted to send the supplies for the armament and the cavalry. And the winter ended, and with it ended the seventeenth year of the present war of which Thucydides is the historian.

The next summer, at the very beginning of the season, the Athenians in Sicily put out from Catana, and sailed along shore to Megara in Sicily, from which, as I have mentioned above, the Syracusans expelled the inhabitants in the time of their tyrant

Gelo, themselves occupying the territory. Here the Athenians landed and laid waste the country, and after an unsuccessful attack upon a fort of the Syracusans, went on with the fleet and army to the river Terias, and advancing inland laid waste the plain and set fire to the corn; and after killing some of a small Syracusan party which they encountered, and setting up a trophy, went back again to their ships. They now sailed to Catana and took in provisions there, and going with their whole force against Centoripa, a town of the Sicels, acquired it by capitulation, and departed, after also burning the corn of the Inessaeans and Hybleans. Upon their return to Catana they found the horsemen arrived from Athens, to the number of two hundred and fifty (with their equipments, but without their horses which were to be procured upon the spot), and thirty mounted archers and three hundred talents of silver.

The same spring the Lacedaemonians marched against Argos, and went as far as Cleonae, when an earthquake occurred and caused them to return. After this the Argives invaded the Thyreatid, which is on their border, and took much booty from the Lacedaemonians, which was sold for no less than twenty-five talents. The same summer, not long after, the Thespian commons made an attack upon the party in office, which was not successful, but succours arrived from Thebes, and some were caught, while others took refuge at Athens.

The same summer the Syracusans learned that the Athenians had been joined by their cavalry, and were on the point of marching against them; and seeing that without becoming masters of Epipolae, a precipitous spot situated exactly over the town, the Athenians could not, even if victorious in battle, easily invest them, they determined to guard its approaches, in order that the enemy might not ascend unobserved by this, the sole way by which ascent was possible, as the remainder is lofty ground, and falls right down to the city, and can all be seen from inside; and as it lies above the rest the place is called by the Syracusans Epipolae or Overtown. They accordingly went out in mass at daybreak into the meadow along the river Anapus, their new generals, Hermocrates and his colleagues, having just come into office, and held a review of their heavy infantry, from whom they first selected a picked body of six hundred, under the command of Diomilus, an exile from Andros, to guard Epipolae, and to be ready to muster at a moment's notice to help wherever help should be required.

Meanwhile the Athenians, the very same morning, were holding a review, having already made land unobserved with all the armament from Catana, opposite a place called Leon, not much more than half a mile from Epipolae, where they disembarked their army, bringing the fleet to anchor at Thapsus, a peninsula running out into the sea, with a narrow isthmus, and not far from the city of Syracuse either by land or water. While the naval force of the Athenians threw a stockade across the isthmus and remained quiet at Thapsus, the land army immediately went on at a run to Epipolae, and succeeded in getting up by Euryelus before the Syracusans perceived them, or could come up from the meadow and the review. Diomilus with his six hundred and the rest advanced as quickly as they could, but they had nearly three miles to go from the meadow before reaching them. Attacking in this way in considerable disorder, the Syracusans were defeated in battle at Epipolae and retired to the town, with a loss of about three hundred killed, and Diomilus among the number. After this the Athenians set up a trophy and restored to the Syracusans their dead under truce, and next day descended to Syracuse itself; and no one coming out to meet them, reascended and built a fort at Labdalum, upon the edge of the cliffs of Epipolae, looking towards Megara, to serve as a magazine for their baggage and money, whenever they advanced to battle or to work at the lines.

Not long afterwards three hundred cavalry came to them from Egesta, and about a hundred from the Sicels, Naxians, and others; and thus, with the two hundred and fifty from Athens, for whom they had got horses from the Egestaeans and Catanians, besides others that they bought, they now mustered six hundred and fifty

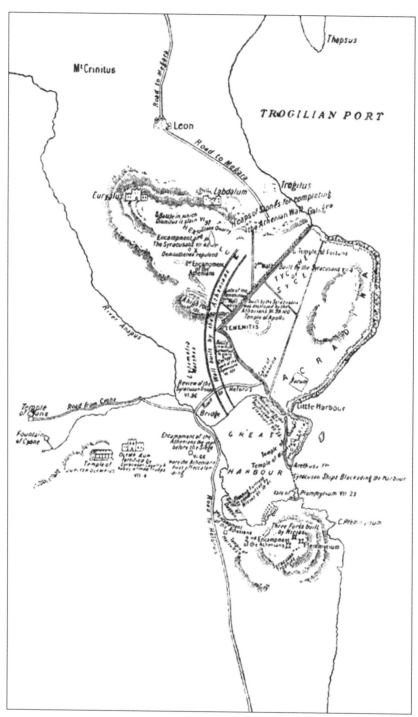

Plan of Syracuse - the harbours and the Athenian position.

444

cavalry in all. After posting a garrison in Labdalum, they advanced to Syca, where they sat down and quickly built the Circle or centre of their wall of circumvallation. The Syracusans, appalled at the rapidity with which the work advanced, determined to go out against them and give battle and interrupt it; and the two armies were already in battle array, when the Syracusan generals observed that their troops found such difficulty in getting into line, and were in such disorder, that they led them back into the town, except part of the cavalry. These remained and hindered the Athenians from carrying stones or dispersing to any great distance, until a tribe of the Athenian heavy infantry, with all the cavalry, charged and routed the Syracusan horse with some loss; after which they set up a trophy for the cavalry action.

The next day the Athenians began building the wall to the north of the Circle, at the same time collecting stone and timber, which they kept laying down towards Trogilus along the shortest line for their works from the great harbour to the sea; while the Syracusans, guided by their generals, and above all by Hermocrates, instead of risking any more general engagements, determined to build a counterwork in the direction in which the Athenians were going to carry their wall. If this could be completed in time, the enemy's lines would be cut; and meanwhile, if he were to attempt to interrupt them by an attack, they would send a part of their forces against him, and would secure the approaches beforehand with their stockade, while the Athenians would have to leave off working with their whole force in order to attend to them. They accordingly sallied forth and began to build, starting from their city, running a cross wall below the Athenian Circle, cutting down the olives and erecting wooden towers. As the Athenian fleet had not yet sailed round into the great harbour, the Syracusans still commanded the seacoast, and the Athenians brought their provisions by land from Thapsus.

The Syracusans now thought the stockades and stonework of their counterwall sufficiently far advanced; and as the Athenians,

445

afraid of being divided and so fighting at a disadvantage, and intent upon their own wall, did not come out to interrupt them, they left one tribe to guard the new work and went back into the city. Meanwhile the Athenians destroyed their pipes of drinking-water carried underground into the city; and watching until the rest of the Syracusans were in their tents at midday, and some even gone away into the city, and those in the stockade keeping but indifferent guard, appointed three hundred picked men of their own, and some men picked from the light troops and armed for the purpose, to run suddenly as fast as they could to the counterwork, while the rest of the army advanced in two divisions, the one with one of the generals to the city in case of a sortie, the other with the other general to the stockade by the postern gate. The three hundred attacked and took the stockade, abandoned by its garrison, who took refuge in the outworks round the statue of Apollo Temenites. Here the pursuers burst in with them, and after getting in were beaten out by the Syracusans, and some few of the Argives and Athenians slain; after which the whole army retired, and having demolished the counterwork and pulled up the stockade, carried away the stakes to their own lines, and set up a trophy.

The next day the Athenians from the Circle proceeded to fortify the cliff above the marsh which on this side of Epipolae looks towards the great harbour; this being also the shortest line for their work to go down across the plain and the marsh to the harbour. Meanwhile the Syracusans marched out and began a second stockade, starting from the city, across the middle of the marsh, digging a trench alongside to make it impossible for the Athenians to carry their wall down to the sea. As soon as the Athenians had finished their work at the cliff they again attacked the stockade and ditch of the Syracusans. Ordering the fleet to sail round from Thapsus into the great harbour of Syracuse, they descended at about dawn from Epipolae into the plain, and laying doors and planks over the marsh, where it was muddy and firmest, crossed over on these, and by daybreak took the ditch and the stockade, except a small portion which they captured afterwards. A battle now ensued, in which the Athenians were victorious, the right wing of the Syracusans flying to the town and the left to the river. The three hundred picked Athenians, wishing to cut off their passage, pressed on at a run to the bridge, when the alarmed Syracusans, who had with them most of their cavalry, closed and routed them, hurling them back upon the Athenian right wing, the first tribe of which was thrown into a panic by the shock. Seeing this, Lamachus came to their aid from the Athenian left with a few archers and with the Argives, and crossing a ditch, was left alone with a few that had crossed with him, and was killed with five or six of his men. These the Syracusans managed immediately to snatch up in haste and get across the river into a place of security, themselves retreating as the rest of the Athenian army now came up.

Meanwhile those who had at first fled for refuge to the city, seeing the turn affairs were taking, now rallied from the town and formed against the Athenians in front of them, sending also a part of their number to the Circle on Epipolae, which they hoped to take while denuded of its defenders. These took and destroyed the Athenian outwork of a thousand feet, the Circle itself being saved by Nicias, who happened to have been left in it through illness, and who now ordered the servants to set fire to the engines and timber thrown down before the wall; want of men, as he was aware, rendering all other means of escape impossible. This step was justified by the result, the Syracusans not coming any further on account of the fire, but retreating. Meanwhile succours were coming up from the Athenians below, who had put to flight the troops opposed to them; and the fleet also, according to orders, was sailing from Thapsus into the great harbour. Seeing this, the troops on the heights retired in haste, and the whole army of the Syracusans re-entered the city, thinking that with their present force they would no longer be able to hinder the wall reaching the sea.

After this the Athenians set up a trophy and restored to the Syracusans their dead under truce, receiving in return Lamachus and those who had fallen with him. The whole of their forces, naval and military, being now with them, they began from Epipolae and the cliffs and enclosed the Syracusans with a double wall down to the sea. Provisions were now brought in for the armament from all parts of Italy; and many of the Sicels, who had hitherto been looking to see how things went, came as allies to the Athenians: there also arrived three ships of fifty oars from Tyrrhenia. Meanwhile everything else progressed favourably for their hopes. The Syracusans began to despair of finding safety in arms, no relief having reached them from Peloponnese, and were now proposing terms of capitulation among themselves and to Nicias, who after the death of Lamachus was left sole commander. No decision was come to, but, as was natural with men in difficulties and besieged more straitly than before, there was much discussion with Nicias and still more in the town. Their present misfortunes had also made them suspicious of one another; and the blame of their disasters was thrown upon the ill-fortune or treachery of the generals under whose command they had happened; and these were deposed and others, Heraclides, Eucles, and Tellias, elected in their stead.

Meanwhile the Lacedaemonian, Gylippus, and the ships from Corinth were now off Leucas, intent upon going with all haste to the relief of Sicily. The reports that reached them being of an alarming kind, and all agreeing in the falsehood that Syracuse was already completely invested, Gylippus abandoned all hope of Sicily, and wishing to save Italy, rapidly crossed the Ionian Sea to Tarentum with the Corinthian, Pythen, two Laconian, and two Corinthian vessels, leaving the Corinthians to follow him after manning, in addition to their own ten, two Leucadian and two Ambraciot ships. From Tarentum Gylippus first went on an embassy to Thurii, and claimed anew the rights of citizenship which his father had enjoyed; failing to bring over the townspeople, he weighed anchor and coasted along Italy. Opposite the Terinaean Gulf he was caught by the wind which blows violently and steadily from the north in that quarter, and was carried out to sea; and after experiencing very rough weather, remade Tarentum, where he hauled ashore and refitted such of his ships as had suffered most from the tempest. Nicias heard of his approach, but, like the Thurians, despised the scanty number of his ships, and set down piracy as the only probable object of the voyage, and so took no precautions for the present.

About the same time in this summer, the Lacedaemonians invaded Argos with their allies, and laid waste most of the country. The Athenians went with thirty ships to the relief of the Argives, thus breaking their treaty with the Lacedaemonians in the most overt manner. Up to this time incursions from Pylos, descents on the coast of the rest of Peloponnese, instead of on the Laconian, had been the extent of their co-operation with the Argives and Mantineans; and although the Argives had often begged them to land, if only for a moment, with their heavy infantry in Laconia, lay waste ever so little of it with them, and depart, they had always refused to do so. Now, however, under the command of Phytodorus, Laespodius, and Demaratus, they landed at Epidaurus Limera, Prasiae, and other places, and plundered the country; and thus furnished the Lacedaemonians with a better pretext for hostilities against Athens. After the Athenians had retired from Argos with their fleet, and the Lacedaemonians also, the Argives made an incursion into the Phlisaid, and returned home after ravaging their land and killing some of the inhabitants.

CHAPTER XXI

Eighteenth and Nineteenth Years of the War -
Arrival of Gylippus at Syracuse - Fortification of Decelea -
Successes of the Syracusans

A FTER REFITTING their ships, Gylippus and Pythen coasted along from Tarentum to Epizephyrian Locris. They now received the more correct information that Syracuse was not yet completely invested, but that it was still possible for an army arriving at Epipolae to effect an entrance; and they consulted, accordingly, whether they should keep Sicily on their right and risk sailing in by sea, or, leaving it on their left, should first sail to Himera and, taking with them the Himeraeans and any others that might agree to join them, go to Syracuse by land. Finally they determined to sail for Himera, especially as the four Athenian ships which Nicias had at length sent off, on hearing that they were at Locris, had not yet arrived at Rhegium. Accordingly, before these reached their post, the Peloponnesians crossed the strait and, after touching at Rhegium and Messina, came to Himera. Arrived there, they persuaded the Himeraeans to join in the war, and not only to go with them themselves but to provide arms for the seamen from their vessels which they had drawn ashore at Himera; and they sent and appointed a place for the Selinuntines to meet them with all their forces. A few troops were also promised by the Geloans and some of the Sicels, who were now ready to join them with much greater alacrity, owing to the recent death of Archonidas, a powerful Sicel king in that neighbourhood and friendly to Athens, and owing also to the vigour shown by Gylippus in coming from Lacedaemon. Gylippus now took with him about seven hundred of his sailors and marines, that number only having arms, a thousand heavy infantry and light troops from Himera with a body of a hundred horse, some light troops and cavalry from Selinus, a few Geloans, and Sicels numbering a thousand in all, and set out on his march for Syracuse.

Meanwhile the Corinthian fleet from Leucas made all haste to arrive; and one of their commanders, Gongylus, starting last with a single ship, was the first to reach Syracuse, a little before Gylippus. Gongylus found the Syracusans on the point of holding an assembly to consider whether they should put an end to the war. This he prevented, and reassured them by telling them that more vessels were still to arrive, and that Gylippus, son of Cleandridas, had been dispatched by the Lacedaemonians to take the command. Upon this the Syracusans took courage, and immediately marched out with all their forces to meet Gylippus, who they found was now close at hand. Meanwhile Gylippus, after taking Ietae, a fort of the Sicels, on his way, formed his army in order of battle, and so arrived at Epipolae, and ascending by Euryelus, as the Athenians had done at first, now advanced with the Syracusans against the Athenian lines. His arrival chanced at a critical moment. The Athenians had already finished a double wall of six or seven furlongs to the great harbour, with the exception of a small portion next the sea, which they were still engaged upon; and in the remainder of the circle towards Trogilus on the other sea, stones had been laid ready for building for the greater part of the distance, and some points had been left half finished, while others were entirely completed. The danger of Syracuse had indeed been great.

Meanwhile the Athenians, recovering from the confusion into which they had been first thrown by the sudden approach of Gylippus and the Syracusans, formed in order of battle. Gylippus halted at a short distance off and sent on a herald to tell them that, if they would evacuate Sicily with bag and baggage within five days' time, he was willing to make a truce accordingly. The Athenians treated this proposition with contempt, and dismissed the herald without an answer. After this both sides began to prepare for action. Gylippus, observing that the Syracusans were in disorder and did not easily fall into line, drew off his troops more into the open ground, while Nicias did not lead on the Athenians but lay still by his own wall. When Gylippus saw that they did not come on, he led off his army to the citadel of the quarter of Apollo Temenites, and passed the night there. On the following day he led out the main body of his army, and, drawing them up in order of battle before the walls of the Athenians to prevent their going to the relief of any other quarter, dispatched a strong force against Fort Labdalum, and took it, and put all whom he found in it to the sword, the place not being within sight of the Athenians. On the same day an Athenian galley that lay moored off the harbour was captured by the Syracusans.

After this the Syracusans and their allies began to carry a single wall, starting from the city, in a slanting direction up Epipolae, in order that the Athenians, unless they could hinder the work, might be no longer able to invest them. Meanwhile the Athenians, having now finished their wall down to the sea, had come up to the heights; and part of their wall being weak, Gylippus drew out his army by night and attacked it. However, the Athenians who happened to be bivouacking outside took the alarm and came out to meet him, upon seeing which he quickly led his men back again. The Athenians now built their wall higher, and in future kept guard at this point themselves, disposing their confederates along the remainder of the works, at the stations assigned to them. Nicias also determined to fortify Plemmyrium, a promontory over against the city, which juts out and narrows the mouth of the Great Harbour. He thought that the fortification of this place would make it easier to bring in supplies, as they would be able to carry on their blockade from a less distance, near to the port occupied by the Syracusans; instead of being obliged, upon every movement of the enemy's navy, to put out against them from the bottom of the great harbour. Besides this, he now began to pay more attention to the war by sea, seeing that the coming of Gylippus had diminished their hopes by land. Accordingly, he conveyed over his ships and some troops, and built three forts in which he placed most of his baggage, and moored there for the future the larger craft and men-of-war. This was the first and chief occasion of the losses which the crews experienced. The water which they used was scarce and had to be fetched from far, and the sailors could not go out for firewood without being cut off by the Syracusan horse, who were masters of the country; a third of the enemy's cavalry being stationed at the little town of Olympieum, to prevent plundering incursions on the part of the Athenians at Plemmyrium. Meanwhile Nicias learned that the rest of the Corinthian fleet was approaching, and sent twenty ships to watch for them, with orders to be on the look-out for them about Locris and Rhegium and the approach to Sicily.

Gylippus, meanwhile, went on with the wall across Epipolae, using the stones which the Athenians had laid down for their own wall, and at the same time constantly led out the Syracusans and their allies, and formed them in order of battle in front of the lines, the Athenians forming against him. At last he thought that the moment was come, and began the attack; and a hand-to-hand fight ensued between the lines, where the Syracusan cavalry could be of no use; and the Syracusans and their allies were defeated and took up their dead under truce, while the Athenians erected a trophy. After this Gylippus called the soldiers together, and said that the fault was not theirs but his; he had kept their lines too much within the works, and had thus deprived them of the services of their cavalry and darters. He would now, therefore, lead them on a second time. He begged them to remember that in material force they would be fully a match for their opponents, while, with respect to moral advantages, it were intolerable if Peloponnesians and Dorians should not feel confident of overcoming Ionians and islanders with the motley rabble that accompanied them, and of driving them out of the country.

After this he embraced the first opportunity that offered of again leading them against the enemy. Now Nicias and the Athenians held the opinion that even if the Syracusans should not wish to offer battle, it was necessary for them to prevent the building of the cross wall, as it already almost overlapped the extreme point of their own, and if it went any further it would from that moment make no difference whether they fought ever so many successful actions, or never fought at all. They accordingly came out to meet the Syracusans. Gylippus led out his heavy infantry further from the fortifications than on the former occasion, and so joined battle; posting his horse and darters upon the flank of the Athenians in the open space, where the works of the two walls terminated. During the engagement the cavalry attacked and routed the left wing of the Athenians, which was opposed to them; and the rest of the Athenian army was in consequence defeated by the Syracusans and driven headlong within their lines. The night following the Syracusans carried their wall up to the Athenian works and passed them, thus putting it out of their power any longer to stop them, and depriving them, even if victorious in the field, of all chance of investing the city for the future.

After this the remaining twelve vessels of the Corinthians, Ambraciots, and Leucadians sailed into the harbour under the command of Erasinides, a Corinthian, having eluded the Athenian ships on guard, and helped the Syracusans in completing the remainder of the cross wall. Meanwhile Gylippus went into the rest of Sicily to raise land and naval forces, and also to bring over any of the cities that either were lukewarm in the cause or had hitherto kept out of the war altogether. Syracusan and Corinthian envoys were also dispatched to Lacedaemon and Corinth to get a fresh force sent over, in any way that might offer, either in merchant vessels or transports, or in any other manner likely to prove successful, as the Athenians too were sending for reinforcements; while the Syracusans proceeded to man a fleet and to exercise, meaning to try their fortune in this way also, and generally became exceedingly confident.

Nicias perceiving this, and seeing the strength of the enemy and his own difficulties daily increasing, himself also sent to Athens. He had before sent frequent reports of events as they occurred, and felt it especially incumbent upon him to do so now, as he thought that they were in a critical position, and that, unless speedily recalled or strongly reinforced from home, they had no hope of safety. He feared, however, that the messengers, either through inability to speak, or through failure of memory, or from a wish to please the multitude, might not report the truth, and so thought it best to write a letter, to ensure that the Athenians should know his own opinion without its being lost in transmission, and be able to decide upon the real facts of the case.

His emissaries, accordingly, departed with the letter and the requisite verbal instructions; and he attended to the affairs of the army, making it his aim now to keep on the defensive and to avoid any unnecessary danger.

At the close of the same summer the Athenian general Euetion marched in concert with Perdiccas with a large body of Thracians against Amphipolis, and failing to take it brought some galleys round into the Strymon, and blockaded the town from the river, having his base at Himeraeum.

Summer was now over. The winter ensuing, the persons sent by Nicias, reaching Athens, gave the verbal messages which had been entrusted to them, and answered any questions that were asked them, and delivered the letter. The clerk of the city now came forward and read out to the Athenians the letter, which was as follows:

"Our past operations, Athenians, have been made known to you by many other letters; it is now time for you to become equally familiar with our present condition, and to take your measures accordingly. We had defeated in most of our engagements with them the Syracusans, against whom we were sent, and we had built the works which we now occupy, when Gylippus arrived from Lacedaemon with an army obtained from Peloponnese and from some of the cities in Sicily. In our first battle with him we were victorious; in the battle on the following day we were overpowered by a multitude of cavalry and darters, and compelled to retire within our lines. We have now, therefore, been forced by the numbers of those opposed to us to discontinue the work of circumvallation, and to remain inactive; being unable to make use even of all the force we have, since a large portion of our heavy infantry is absorbed in the defence of our lines. Meanwhile the enemy have carried a single wall past our lines, thus making it impossible for us to invest them in future, until this cross wall be attacked by a strong force and captured. So that the besieger in name has become, at least from the land side, the besieged in reality; as we are prevented by their cavalry from even going for any distance into the country.

"Besides this, an embassy has been dispatched to Peloponnese to procure reinforcements, and Gylippus has gone to the cities in Sicily, partly in the hope of inducing those that are at present neutral to join him in the war, partly of bringing from his allies additional contingents for the land forces and material for the navy. For I understand that they contemplate a combined attack, upon our lines with their land forces and with their fleet by sea. You must none of you be surprised that I say by sea also. They have discovered that the length of the time we have now been in commission has rotted our ships and wasted our crews, and that with the entireness of our crews and the soundness of our ships the pristine efficiency of our navy has departed. For it is impossible for us to haul our ships ashore and careen them, because, the enemy's vessels being as many or more than our own, we are constantly anticipating an attack. Indeed, they may be seen exercising, and it lies with them to take the initiative; and not having to maintain a blockade, they have greater facilities for drying their ships.

"This we should scarcely be able to do, even if we had plenty of ships to spare, and were freed from our present necessity of exhausting all our strength upon the blockade. For it is already difficult to carry in supplies past Syracuse; and were we to relax our vigilance in the slightest degree it would become impossible. The losses which our crews have suffered and still continue to suffer arise from the following causes. Expeditions for fuel and for forage, and the distance from which water has to be fetched, cause our sailors to be cut off by the Syracusan cavalry; the loss of our previous superiority emboldens our slaves to desert; our foreign seamen are impressed by the unexpected appearance of a navy against us, and the strength of the enemy's resistance; such of them as were pressed into the service take the first opportunity of departing to their respective cities; such as were originally seduced by the temptation of high pay, and expected little fighting and large gains, leave us either by desertion to the enemy or by availing themselves of one or other of the various facilities of escape which the magnitude of Sicily affords them. Some even engage in trade themselves and prevail upon the captains to take Hyccaric slaves on board in their place; thus they have ruined the efficiency of our navy.

"Now I need not remind you that the time during which a crew is in its prime is short, and that the number of sailors who can start a ship on her way and keep the rowing in time is small. But by far my greatest trouble is, that holding the post which I do, I am prevented by the natural indocility of the Athenian seaman from putting a stop to these evils; and that meanwhile we have no source from which to recruit our crews, which the enemy can do from many quarters, but are compelled to depend both for supplying the crews in service and for making good our losses upon the men whom we brought with us. For our present confederates, Naxos and Catana, are incapable of supplying us. There is only one thing more wanting to our opponents, I mean the defection of our Italian markets. If they were to see you neglect to relieve us from our present condition, and were to go over to the enemy, famine would compel us to evacuate, and Syracuse would finish the war without a blow.

"I might, it is true, have written to you something different and more agreeable than this, but nothing certainly more useful, if it is desirable for you to know the real state of things here before taking your measures. Besides I know that it is your nature to love to be told the best side of things, and then to blame the teller if the expectations which he has raised in your minds are not answered by the result; and I therefore thought it safest to declare to you the truth.

"Now you are not to think that either your generals or your soldiers have ceased to be a match for the forces originally opposed to them. But you are to reflect that a general Sicilian coalition is being formed against us; that a fresh army is expected from Peloponnese, while the force we have here is unable to cope even with our present antagonists; and you must promptly decide either to recall us or to send out to us another fleet and army as numerous again, with a large sum of money, and someone to succeed me, as a disease in the kidneys unfits me for retaining my post. I have, I think, some claim on your indulgence, as while I was in my prime I did you much good service in my commands. But whatever you mean to do, do it at the commencement of spring and without delay, as the enemy will obtain his Sicilian reinforcements shortly, those from Peloponnese after a longer interval; and unless you attend to the matter the former will be here before you, while the latter will elude you as they have done before."

Such were the contents of Nicias's letter. When the Athenians had heard it they refused to accept his resignation, but chose him two colleagues, naming Menander and Euthydemus, two of the officers at the seat of war, to fill their places until their arrival, that Nicias might not be left alone in his sickness to bear the whole weight of affairs. They also voted to send out another army and navy, drawn partly from the Athenians on the muster-roll, partly from the allies. The colleagues chosen for Nicias were Demosthenes, son of Alcisthenes, and Eurymedon, son of Thucles. Eurymedon was sent off at once, about the time of the winter solstice, with ten ships, a hundred and twenty talents of silver, and instructions to tell the army that reinforcements would arrive, and that care would be taken of them; but Demosthenes stayed behind to organize the expedition, meaning to start as soon as it was spring, and sent for troops to the allies, and meanwhile got together money, ships, and heavy infantry at home.

The Athenians also sent twenty vessels round Peloponnese to prevent any one crossing over to Sicily from Corinth or Peloponnese. For the Corinthians, filled with confidence by the favourable alteration in Sicilian affairs which had been reported by the envoys upon their arrival, and convinced that the fleet which they had before sent out had not been without its use, were now preparing to dispatch a force of heavy infantry in merchant vessels to Sicily, while the Lacedaemonians did the like for the rest of Peloponnese. The Corinthians also manned a fleet of twenty-five vessels, intending to try the result of a battle with the squadron on guard at Naupactus, and meanwhile to make it less easy for the Athenians there to hinder the departure of their merchantmen, by obliging them to keep an eye upon the galleys thus arrayed against them.

In the meantime the Lacedaemonians prepared for their invasion of Attica, in accordance with their own previous resolve, and at the instigation of the Syracusans and Corinthians, who wished for an invasion to arrest the reinforcements which they heard that Athens was about to send to Sicily. Alcibiades also urgently advised the fortification of Decelea, and a vigorous prosecution of the war. But the Lacedaemonians derived most encouragement from the belief that Athens, with two wars on her hands, against themselves and against the Siceliots, would be more easy to subdue, and from the conviction that she had been the first to infringe the truce. In the former war, they considered, the offence had been more on their own side, both on account of the entrance of the Thebans into Plataea in time of peace, and also of their own refusal to listen to the Athenian offer of arbitration, in spite of the clause in the former treaty that where arbitration should be offered there should be no appeal to arms. For this reason they thought that they deserved their misfortunes, and took to heart seriously the disaster at Pylos and whatever else had befallen them. But when, besides the ravages from Pylos, which went on without any intermission, the thirty Athenian ships came out from Argos and wasted part of Epidaurus, Prasiae, and other places; when upon every dispute that arose as to the interpretation of any doubtful point in the treaty, their own offers of arbitration were always rejected by the Athenians, the Lacedaemonians at length decided that Athens had now committed the very same offence as they had before done, and had become the guilty party; and they began to be full of ardour for the war. They spent this winter in sending round to their allies for iron, and in getting ready the other implements for building their fort; and meanwhile began raising at home, and also by forced requisitions in the rest of Peloponnese, a force to be sent out in the merchantmen to their allies in Sicily. Winter thus ended, and with it the eighteenth year of this war of which Thucydides is the historian.

In the first days of the spring following, at an earlier period than usual, the Lacedaemonians and their allies invaded Attica, under the command of Agis, son of Archidamus, king of the Lacedaemonians. They began by devastating the parts bordering upon the plain, and next proceeded to fortify Decelea, dividing the work among the different cities. Decelea is about thirteen or fourteen miles from the city of Athens, and the same distance or not much further from Boeotia; and the fort was meant to annoy the plain and the richest parts of the country, being in sight of Athens. While the Peloponnesians and their allies in Attica were engaged in the work of fortification, their countrymen at home sent off, at about the same time, the heavy infantry in the merchant vessels to Sicily; the Lacedaemonians furnishing a picked force of Helots and Neodamodes (or freedmen), six hundred heavy infantry in all, under the command of Eccritus, a Spartan; and the Boeotians three hundred heavy infantry, commanded by two Thebans, Xenon and Nicon, and by Hegesander, a Thespian. These were among the first to put out into the open sea, starting from

Taenarus in Laconia. Not long after their departure the Corinthians sent off a force of five hundred heavy infantry, consisting partly of men from Corinth itself, and partly of Arcadian mercenaries, placed under the command of Alexarchus, a Corinthian. The Sicyonians also sent off two hundred heavy infantry at same time as the Corinthians, under the command of Sargeus, a Sicyonian. Meantime the five-and-twenty vessels manned by Corinth during the winter lay confronting the twenty Athenian ships at Naupactus until the heavy infantry in the merchantmen were fairly on their way from Peloponnese; thus fulfilling the object for which they had been manned originally, which was to divert the attention of the Athenians from the merchantmen to the galleys.

During this time the Athenians were not idle. Simultaneously with the fortification of Decelea, at the very beginning of spring, they sent thirty ships round Peloponnese, under Charicles, son of Apollodorus, with instructions to call at Argos and demand a force of their heavy infantry for the fleet, agreeably to the alliance. At the same time they dispatched Demosthenes to Sicily, as they had intended, with sixty Athenian and five Chian vessels, twelve hundred Athenian heavy infantry from the muster-roll, and as many of the islanders as could be raised in the different quarters, drawing upon the other subject allies for whatever they could supply that would be of use for the war. Demosthenes was instructed first to sail round with Charicles and to operate with him upon the coasts of Laconia, and accordingly sailed to Aegina and there waited for the remainder of his armament, and for Charicles to fetch the Argive troops.

In Sicily, about the same time in this spring, Gylippus came to Syracuse with as many troops as he could bring from the cities which he had persuaded to join. Calling the Syracusans together, he told them that they must man as many ships as possible, and try their hand at a sea-fight, by which he hoped to achieve an advantage in the war not unworthy of the risk. With him Hermocrates actively joined in trying to encourage his countrymen to attack the Athenians at sea, saying that the latter had not inherited their naval prowess nor would they retain it for ever; they had been landsmen even to a greater degree than the Syracusans, and had only become a maritime power when obliged by the Mede. Besides, to daring spirits like the Athenians, a daring adversary would seem the most formidable; and the Athenian plan of paralysing by the boldness of their attack a neighbour often not their inferior in strength could now be used against them with as good effect by the Syracusans. He was convinced also that the unlooked-for spectacle of Syracusans daring to face the Athenian navy would cause a terror to the enemy, the advantages of which would far outweigh any loss that Athenian science might inflict upon their inexperience. He accordingly urged them to throw aside their fears and to try their fortune at sea; and the Syracusans, under the influence of Gylippus and Hermocrates, and perhaps some others, made up their minds for the sea-fight and began to man their vessels.

When the fleet was ready, Gylippus led out the whole army by night; his plan being to assault in person the forts on Plemmyrium by land, while thirty-five Syracusan galleys sailed according to appointment against the enemy from the great harbour, and the forty-five remaining came round from the lesser harbour, where they had their arsenal, in order to effect a junction with those inside and simultaneously to attack Plemmyrium, and thus to distract the Athenians by assaulting them on two sides at once. The Athenians quickly manned sixty ships, and with twenty-five of these engaged the thirty-five of the Syracusans in the great harbour, sending the rest to meet those sailing round from the arsenal; and an action now ensued directly in front of the mouth of the great harbour, maintained with equal tenacity on both sides; the one wishing to force the passage, the other to prevent them.

In the meantime, while the Athenians in Plemmyrium were down at the sea, attending to the engagement, Gylippus made a sudden attack on the forts in the early morning and took the largest first, and afterwards the two smaller, whose garrisons did not wait for him, seeing the largest so easily taken. At the fall of the first fort, the men from it who succeeded in taking refuge in their boats and merchantmen, found great difficulty in reaching the camp, as the Syracusans were having the best of it in the engagement in the great harbour, and sent a fast-sailing galley to pursue them. But when the two others fell, the Syracusans were now being defeated; and the fugitives from these sailed alongshore with more ease. The Syracusan ships fighting off the mouth of the harbour forced their way through the Athenian vessels and sailing in without any order fell foul of one another, and transferred the victory to the Athenians; who not only routed the squadron in question, but also that by which they were at first being defeated in the harbour, sinking eleven of the Syracusan vessels and killing most of the men, except the crews of three ships whom they made prisoners. Their own loss was confined to three vessels; and after hauling ashore the Syracusan wrecks and setting up a trophy upon the islet in front of Plemmyrium, they retired to their own camp.

Unsuccessful at sea, the Syracusans had nevertheless the forts in Plemmyrium, for which they set up three trophies. One of the two last taken they razed, but put in order and garrisoned the two others. In the capture of the forts a great many men were killed and made prisoners, and a great quantity of property was taken in all. As the Athenians had used them as a magazine, there was a large stock of goods and corn of the merchants inside, and also a large stock belonging to the captains; the masts and other furniture of forty galleys being taken, besides three galleys which had been drawn up on shore. Indeed the first and chiefest cause of the ruin of the Athenian army was the capture of Plemmyrium; even the entrance of the harbour being now no longer safe for carrying in provisions, as the Syracusan vessels were stationed there to prevent it, and nothing could be brought in without fighting; besides the general impression of dismay and discouragement produced upon the army.

After this the Syracusans sent out twelve ships under the command of Agatharchus, a Syracusan. One of these went to Peloponnese with ambassadors to describe the hopeful state of their affairs, and to incite the Peloponnesians to prosecute the war there even more actively than they were now doing, while the eleven others sailed to Italy, hearing that vessels laden with stores were on their way to the Athenians. After falling in with and destroying most of the vessels in question, and burning in the Caulonian territory a quantity of timber for shipbuilding, which had been got ready for the Athenians, the Syracusan squadron went to Locri, and one of the merchantmen from Peloponnese coming in, while they were at anchor there, carrying Thespian heavy infantry, took these on board and sailed alongshore towards home. The Athenians were on the look-out for them with twenty ships at Megara, but were only able to take one vessel with its crew; the rest getting clear off to Syracuse. There was also some skirmishing in the harbour about the piles which the Syracusans had driven in the sea in front of the old docks, to allow their ships to lie at anchor inside, without being hurt by the Athenians sailing up and running them down. The Athenians brought up to them a ship of ten thousand talents burden furnished with wooden turrets and screens, and fastened ropes round the piles from their boats, wrenched them up and broke them, or dived down and sawed them in two. Meanwhile the Syracusans plied them with missiles from the docks, to which they replied from their large vessel; until at last most of the piles were removed by the Athenians. But the most awkward part of the stockade was the part out of sight: some of the piles which had been driven in did not appear above water, so that it was dangerous to sail up, for fear of running the ships upon them, just as upon a reef, through not seeing them. However divers went down and sawed off even these for reward; although the Syracusans drove in others. Indeed there was no end to the contrivances to which they resorted against each other, as might be expected between two hostile armies confronting each other at such a short distance: and skirmishes and all kinds of other attempts were of constant occurrence. Meanwhile the Syracusans sent embassies to the cities, composed of Corinthians, Ambraciots, and Lacedaemonians, to tell them of the capture of Plemmyrium, and that their defeat in the sea-fight was due less to the strength of the enemy than to their own disorder; and generally, to let them know that they were full of hope, and to desire them to come to their help with ships and troops, as the Athenians were expected with a fresh army, and if the one already there could be destroyed before the other arrived, the war would be at an end.

While the contending parties in Sicily were thus engaged, Demosthenes, having now got together the armament with which he was to go to the island, put out from Aegina, and making sail for Peloponnese, joined Charicles and the thirty ships of the Athenians. Taking on board the heavy infantry from Argos they sailed to Laconia, and, after first plundering part of Epidaurus Limera, landed on the coast of Laconia, opposite Cythera, where the temple of Apollo stands, and, laying waste part of the country, fortified a sort of isthmus, to which the Helots of the Lacedaemonians might desert, and from whence plundering incursions might be made as from Pylos. Demosthenes helped to occupy this place, and then immediately sailed on to Corcyra to take up some of the allies in that island, and so to proceed without delay to Sicily; while Charicles waited until he had completed the fortification of the place and, leaving a garrison there, returned home subsequently with his thirty ships and the Argives also.

This same summer arrived at Athens thirteen hundred targeteers, Thracian swordsmen of the tribe of the Dii, who were to have sailed to Sicily with Demosthenes. Since they had come too late, the Athenians determined to send them back to Thrace, whence they had come; to keep them for the Decelean war appearing too expensive, as the pay of each man was a drachma a day. Indeed since Decelea had been first fortified by the whole Peloponnesian army during this summer, and then occupied for the annoyance of the country by the garrisons from the cities relieving each other at stated intervals, it had been doing great mischief to the Athenians; in fact this occupation, by the destruction of property and loss of men which resulted from it, was one of the principal causes of their ruin. Previously the invasions were short, and did not prevent their enjoying their land during the rest of the time: the enemy was now permanently fixed in Attica; at one time it was an attack in force, at another it was the regular garrison overrunning the country and making forays for its subsistence, and the Lacedaemonian king, Agis, was in the field and diligently prosecuting the war; great mischief was therefore done to the Athenians. They were deprived of their whole country: more than twenty thousand slaves had deserted, a great part of them artisans, and all their sheep and beasts of burden were lost; and as the cavalry rode out daily upon excursions to Decelea and to guard the country, their horses were either lamed by being constantly worked upon rocky ground, or wounded by the enemy.

Besides, the transport of provisions from Euboea, which had before been carried on so much more quickly overland by Decelea from Oropus, was now effected at great cost by sea round Sunium; everything the city required had to be imported from abroad, and instead of a city it became a fortress. Summer and winter the Athenians were worn out by having to keep guard on the fortifications, during the day by turns, by night all together, the cavalry excepted, at the different military posts or upon the wall. But what most oppressed them was that they had two wars at once, and had thus reached a pitch of frenzy which no one would have believed possible if he had heard of it before it had come to pass. For could any one have imagined that even when besieged by the Peloponnesians entrenched in Attica, they would still, instead of withdrawing from Sicily, stay on there besieging in like manner Syracuse, a town (taken as a town) in no way inferior to Athens, or would so thoroughly upset the Hellenic estimate of their strength and audacity, as to give the spectacle of a people which, at the beginning of the war, some thought might hold out one year, some two, none more than three, if the Peloponnesians invaded their country, now seventeen years after the first invasion, after having already suffered from all the evils of war, going to Sicily and undertaking a new war nothing inferior to that which they already had with the Peloponnesians? These causes, the great losses from Decelea, and the other heavy charges that fell upon them, produced their financial embarrassment; and it was at this time that they imposed upon their subjects, instead of the tribute, the tax of a twentieth upon all imports and exports by sea, which they thought would bring them in more money; their expenditure being now not the same as at first, but having grown with the war while their revenues decayed.

Accordingly, not wishing to incur expense in their present want of money, they sent back at once the Thracians who came too late for Demosthenes, under the conduct of Diitrephes, who was instructed, as they were to pass through the Euripus, to make use of them if possible in the voyage alongshore to injure the enemy. Diitrephes first landed them at Tanagra and hastily snatched some booty; he then sailed across the Euripus in the evening from Chalcis in Euboea and disembarking in Boeotia led them against Mycalessus. The night he passed unobserved near the temple of Hermes, not quite two miles from Mycalessus, and at daybreak assaulted and took the town, which is not a large one; the inhabitants being off their guard and not expecting that any one would ever come up so far from the sea to molest them, the wall too being weak, and in some places having tumbled down, while in others it had not been built to any height, and the gates also being left open through their feeling of security. The Thracians bursting into Mycalessus sacked the houses and temples, and butchered the inhabitants, sparing neither youth nor age, but killing all they fell in with, one after the other, children and women, and even beasts of burden, and whatever other living creatures they saw; the Thracian race, like the bloodiest of the barbarians, being even more so when it has nothing to fear. Everywhere confusion reigned and death in all its shapes; and in particular they attacked a boys' school, the largest that there was in the place, into which the children had just gone, and massacred them all. In short, the disaster falling upon the whole town was unsurpassed in magnitude, and unapproached by any in suddenness and in horror.

Meanwhile the Thebans heard of it and marched to the rescue, and overtaking the Thracians before they had gone far, recovered the plunder and drove them in panic to the Euripus and the sea, where the vessels which brought them were lying. The greatest slaughter took place while they were embarking, as they did not know how to swim, and those in the vessels on seeing what was going on on on shore moored them out of bowshot: in the rest of the retreat the Thracians made a very respectable defence against the Theban horse, by which they were first attacked, dashing out and closing their ranks according to the tactics of their country, and lost only a few men in that part of the affair. A good number who were after plunder were actually caught in the town and put to death. Altogether the Thracians had two hundred and fifty killed out of thirteen hundred, the Thebans and the rest who came to the rescue about twenty, troopers and heavy infantry, with Scirphondas, one of the Boeotarchs. The Mycalessians lost a large proportion of their population.

While Mycalessus thus experienced a calamity for its extent as lamentable as any that happened in the war, Demosthenes, whom we left sailing to Corcyra, after the building of the fort in Laconia, found a merchantman lying at Phea in Elis, in which the Corinthian heavy infantry were to cross to Sicily. The ship he destroyed, but the men escaped, and subsequently got another in which they pursued their voyage. After this, arriving at Zacynthus and Cephallenia, he took a body of heavy infantry on board, and sending for some of the Messenians from Naupactus, crossed over to the opposite coast of Acarnania, to Alyzia, and to Anactorium which was held by the Athenians. While he was in these parts he was met by Eurymedon returning from Sicily, where he had been sent, as has been mentioned, during the winter, with the money for the army, who told him the news, and also that he had heard, while at sea, that the Syracusans had taken Plemmyrium. Here, also, Conon came to them, the commander at Naupactus, with news that the twenty-five Corinthian ships stationed opposite to him, far from giving over the war, were meditating an engagement; and he therefore begged them to send him some ships, as his own eighteen were not a match for the enemy's twenty-five. Demosthenes and Eurymedon, accordingly, sent ten of their best sailers with Conon to reinforce the squadron at Naupactus, and meanwhile prepared for the muster of their forces; Eurymedon, who was now the colleague of Demosthenes, and had turned back in consequence of his appointment, sailing to Corcyra to tell them to man fifteen ships and to enlist heavy infantry; while Demosthenes raised slingers and darters from the parts about Acarnania.

Meanwhile the envoys, already mentioned, who had gone from Syracuse to the cities after the capture of Plemmyrium, had succeeded in their mission, and were about to bring the army that they had collected, when Nicias got scent of it, and sent to the Centoripae and Alicyaeans and other of the friendly Sicels, who held the passes, not to let the enemy through, but to combine to prevent their passing, there being no other way by which they could even attempt it, as the Agrigentines would not give them a passage through their country. Agreeably to this request the Sicels laid a triple ambuscade for the Siceliots upon their march, and attacking them suddenly, while off their guard, killed about eight hundred of them and all the envoys, the Corinthian only excepted, by whom fifteen hundred who escaped were conducted to Syracuse.

About the same time the Camarinaeans also came to the assistance of Syracuse with five hundred heavy infantry, three hundred darters, and as many archers, while the Geloans sent crews for five ships, four hundred darters, and two hundred horse. Indeed almost the whole of Sicily, except the Agrigentines, who were neutral, now ceased merely to watch events as it had hitherto done, and actively joined Syracuse against the Athenians.

While the Syracusans after the Sicel disaster put off any immediate attack upon the Athenians, Demosthenes and Eurymedon, whose forces from Corcyra and the continent were now ready, crossed the Ionian Gulf with all their armament to the Iapygian promontory, and starting from thence touched at the Choerades Isles lying off Iapygia, where they took on board a hundred and fifty Iapygian darters of the Messapian tribe, and after renewing an old friendship with Artas the chief, who had furnished them with the darters, arrived at Metapontium in Italy. Here they persuaded their allies the Metapontines to send with them three hundred darters and two galleys, and with this reinforcement coasted on to Thurii, where they found the party hostile to Athens recently expelled by a revolution, and accordingly remained there to muster and review the whole army, to see if any had been left behind, and to prevail upon the Thurians resolutely to join them in their expedition, and in the circumstances in which they found themselves to conclude a defensive and offensive alliance with the Athenians.

About the same time the Peloponnesians in the twenty-five ships stationed opposite to the squadron at Naupactus to protect the passage of the transports to Sicily had got ready for engaging, and manning some additional vessels, so as to be numerically little inferior to the Athenians, anchored off Erineus in Achaia in the Rhypic country. The place off which they lay being in the form of a crescent, the land forces furnished by the Corinthians and their allies on the spot came up and ranged themselves upon the projecting headlands on either side, while the fleet, under the command of Polyanthes, a Corinthian, held the intervening space and blocked up the entrance. The Athenians under Diphilus now sailed out against them with thirty-three ships from Naupactus, and the Corinthians, at first not moving, at length thought they saw their opportunity, raised the signal, and advanced and engaged the Athenians. After an obstinate struggle, the Corinthians lost three ships, and without sinking any altogether, disabled seven of the enemy, which were struck prow to prow and had their foreships stove in by the Corinthian vessels, whose cheeks had been strengthened for this very purpose. After an action of this even character, in which either party could claim the victory (although the Athenians became masters of the wrecks through the wind driving them out to sea, the Corinthians not putting out again to meet them), the two combatants parted. No pursuit took place, and no prisoners were made on either side; the Corinthians and Peloponnesians who were fighting near the shore escaping with ease, and none of the Athenian vessels having been sunk. The Athenians now sailed back to Naupactus, and the Corinthians immediately set up a trophy as victors, because they had disabled a greater number of the enemy's ships. Moreover they held that they had not been worsted, for the very same reason that their opponent held that he had not been victorious; the Corinthians considering that they were conquerors, if not decidedly conquered, and the Athenians thinking themselves vanquished, because not decidedly victorious. However, when the Peloponnesians sailed off and their land forces had dispersed, the Athenians also set up a trophy as victors in Achaia, about two miles and a quarter from Erineus, the Corinthian station.

This was the termination of the action at Naupactus. To return to Demosthenes and Eurymedon: the Thurians having now got ready to join in the expedition with seven hundred heavy infantry and three hundred darters, the two generals ordered the ships to sail along the coast to the Crotonian territory, and meanwhile held a review of all the land forces upon the river Sybaris, and then led them through the Thurian country. Arrived at the river Hylias, they here received a message from the Crotonians, saying that they would not allow the army to pass through their country; upon which the Athenians descended towards the shore, and bivouacked near the sea and the mouth of the Hylias, where the fleet also met them, and the next day embarked and sailed along the coast touching at all the cities except Locri, until they came to Petra in the Rhegian territory.

Meanwhile the Syracusans hearing of their approach resolved to make a second attempt with their fleet and their other forces on shore, which they had been collecting for this very purpose in order to do something before their arrival. In addition to other improvements suggested by the former sea-fight which they now adopted in the equipment of their navy, they cut down their prows to a smaller compass to make them more solid and made their cheeks stouter, and from these let stays into the vessels' sides for a length of six cubits within and without, in the same way as the Corinthians had altered their prows before engaging the squadron at Naupactus. The Syracusans thought that they would thus have an advantage over the Athenian vessels, which were not constructed with equal strength, but were slight in the bows, from their being more used to sail round and charge the enemy's side than to meet him prow to prow, and that the battle being in the great harbour, with a great many ships in not much room, was also a fact in their favour. Charging prow to prow, they would stave in the enemy's bows, by striking with solid and stout beaks against hollow and weak ones; and secondly, the Athenians for want of room would be unable to use their favourite manoeuvre of breaking the line or of sailing round, as the Syracusans would do their best not to let them do the one, and want of room would prevent their doing the other. This charging prow to prow, which had hitherto been thought want of skill in a helmsman, would be the Syracusans' chief manoeuvre, as being that which they should find most useful, since the Athenians, if repulsed, would not be able to back water in any direction except towards the shore, and that only for a little way, and in the little space in front of their own camp. The rest of the harbour would be commanded by the Syracusans; and the Athenians, if hard pressed, by crowding together in a small space and all to the same point, would run foul of one another and fall into disorder, which was, in fact, the thing that did the Athenians most harm in all the sea-fights, they not having, like the Syracusans, the whole harbour to retreat over. As to their sailing round into the open sea, this would be impossible, with the Syracusans in possession of the way out and in, especially as Plemmyrium would be hostile to them, and the mouth of the harbour was not large.

With these contrivances to suit their skill and ability, and now more confident after the previous sea-fight, the Syracusans attacked by land and sea at once. The town force Gylippus led out a little the first and brought them up to the wall of the Athenians, where it looked towards the city, while the force from the Olympieum, that is to say, the heavy infantry that were there with the horse and the light troops of the Syracusans, advanced against the wall from the opposite side; the ships of the Syracusans and allies sailing out immediately afterwards. The Athenians at first fancied that they were to be attacked by land only, and it was not without alarm that they saw the fleet suddenly approaching as well; and while some were forming upon the walls and in front of them against the advancing enemy, and some marching out in haste against the numbers of horse and darters coming from the Olympieum and from outside, others manned the ships or rushed down to the beach to oppose the enemy, and when the ships were manned put out with seventy-five sail against about eighty of the Syracusans.

After spending a great part of the day in advancing and retreating and skirmishing with each other, without either being able to gain any advantage worth speaking of, except that the Syracusans sank one or two of the Athenian vessels, they parted, the land force at the same time retiring from the lines. The next day the Syracusans remained quiet, and gave no signs of what they were going to do; but Nicias, seeing that the battle had been a drawn one, and expecting that they would attack again, compelled the captains to refit any of the ships that had suffered, and moored merchant vessels before the stockade which they had driven into the sea in front of their ships, to serve instead of an enclosed harbour, at about two hundred feet from each other, in order that any ship that was hard pressed might be able to retreat in safety and sail out again at leisure. These preparations occupied the Athenians all day until nightfall.

The next day the Syracusans began operations at an earlier hour, but with the same plan of attack by land and sea. A great part of the day the rivals spent as before, confronting and skirmishing with each other; until at last Ariston, son of Pyrrhicus, a Corinthian, the ablest helmsman in the Syracusan service, persuaded their naval commanders to send to the officials in the city, and tell them to move the sale market as quickly as they could down to the sea, and oblige every one to bring whatever eatables he had and sell them there, thus enabling the commanders to land the crews and dine at once close to the ships, and shortly afterwards, the selfsame day, to attack the Athenians again when they were not expecting it.

In compliance with this advice a messenger was sent and the market got ready, upon which the Syracusans suddenly backed water and withdrew to the town, and at once landed and took their dinner upon the spot; while the Athenians, supposing that they had returned to the town because they felt they were beaten, disembarked at their leisure and set about getting their dinners and about their other occupations, under the idea that they done with fighting for that day. Suddenly the Syracusans had manned their ships and again sailed against them; and the Athenians, in great confusion and most of them fasting, got on board, and with great difficulty put out to meet them. For some time both parties remained on the defensive without engaging, until the Athenians at last resolved not to let themselves be worn out by waiting where they were, but to attack without delay, and giving a cheer, went into action. The Syracusans received them, and charging prow to prow as they had intended, stove in a great part of the Athenian foreships by the strength of their beaks; the darters on the decks also did great damage to the Athenians, but still greater damage was done by the Syracusans who went about in small boats, ran in upon the oars of the Athenian galleys, and sailed against their sides, and discharged from thence their darts upon the sailors.

At last, fighting hard in this fashion, the Syracusans gained the victory, and the Athenians turned and fled between the merchantmen to their own station. The Syracusan ships pursued them as far as the merchantmen, where they were stopped by the beams armed with dolphins suspended from those vessels over the passage. Two of the Syracusan vessels went too near in the excitement of victory and were destroyed, one of them being taken with its crew. After sinking seven of the Athenian vessels and disabling many, and taking most of the men prisoners and killing others, the Syracusans retired and set up trophies for both the engagements, being now confident of having a decided superiority by sea, and by no means despairing of equal success by land.

CHAPTER XXII

Nineteenth Year of the War - Arrival of Demosthenes - Defeat of the Athenians at Epipolae - Folly and Obstinancy of Nicias

I N THE meantime, while the Syracusans were preparing for a second attack upon both elements, Demosthenes and Eurymedon arrived with the succours from Athens, consisting of about seventy-three ships, including the foreigners; nearly five thousand heavy infantry, Athenian and allied; a large number of darters, Hellenic and barbarian, and slingers and archers and everything else upon a corresponding scale. The Syracusans and their allies were for the moment not a little dismayed at the idea that there was to be no term or ending to their dangers, seeing, in spite of the fortification of Decelea, a new army arrive nearly equal to the former, and the power of Athens proving so great in every quarter. On the other hand, the first Athenian armament regained a certain confidence in the midst of its misfortunes. Demosthenes, seeing how matters stood, felt that he could not drag on and fare as Nicias had done, who by wintering in Catana instead of at once attacking Syracuse had allowed the terror of his first arrival to evaporate in contempt, and had given time to Gylippus to arrive with a force from Peloponnese, which the Syracusans would never have sent for if he had attacked immediately; for they fancied that they were a match for him by themselves, and would not have discovered their inferiority until they were already invested, and even if they then sent for succours, they would no longer have been equally able to profit by their arrival. Recollecting this, and well aware that it was now on the first day after his arrival that he like Nicias was most formidable to the enemy, Demosthenes determined to lose no time in drawing the utmost profit from the consternation at the moment inspired by his army; and seeing that the counterwall of the Syracusans, which hindered the Athenians from investing them, was a single one, and that he who should become master of the way up to Epipolae, and afterwards of the camp there, would find no difficulty in taking it, as no one would even wait for his attack, made all haste to attempt the enterprise. This he took to be the shortest way of ending the war, as he would either succeed and take Syracuse, or would lead back the armament instead of frittering away the lives of the Athenians engaged in the expedition and the resources of the country at large.

First therefore the Athenians went out and laid waste the lands of the Syracusans about the Anapus and carried all before them as at first by land and by sea, the Syracusans not offering to oppose them upon either element, unless it were with their cavalry and darters from the Olympieum. Next Demosthenes resolved to attempt the counterwall first by means of engines. As however the engines that he brought up were burnt by the enemy fighting from the wall, and the rest of the forces repulsed after attacking at many different points, he determined to delay no longer, and having obtained the consent of Nicias and his fellow commanders, proceeded to put in execution his plan of attacking Epipolae. As by day it seemed impossible to approach and get up without being observed, he ordered provisions for five days, took all the masons and carpenters, and other things, such as arrows, and everything else that they could want for the work of fortification if successful, and, after the first watch, set out with Eurymedon and Menander and the whole army for Epipolae, Nicias being left behind in the lines. Having come up by the hill of Euryelus (where the former army had ascended at first) unobserved by the enemy's guards, they went up to the fort which the Syracusans had there, and took it, and put to the sword part of the garrison. The greater number, however, escaped at once and gave the alarm to the camps, of which there were three upon Epipolae, defended by outworks, one of the Syracusans, one of the other Siceliots, and one of the allies; and also to the six hundred Syracusans forming the original garrison for this part of Epipolae. These at once advanced against the assailants and, falling in with Demosthenes and the

Athenians, were routed by them after a sharp resistance, the victors immediately pushing on, eager to achieve the objects of the attack without giving time for their ardour to cool; meanwhile others from the very beginning were taking the counterwall of the Syracusans, which was abandoned by its garrison, and pulling down the battlements. The Syracusans and the allies, and Gylippus with the troops under his command, advanced to the rescue from the outworks, but engaged in some consternation (a night attack being a piece of audacity which they had never expected), and were at first compelled to retreat. But while the Athenians, flushed with their victory, now advanced with less order, wishing to make their way as quickly as possible through the whole force of the enemy not yet engaged, without relaxing their attack or giving them time to rally, the Boeotians made the first stand against them, attacked them, routed them, and put them to flight.

The Athenians now fell into great disorder and perplexity, so that it was not easy to get from one side or the other any detailed account of the affair. By day certainly the combatants have a clearer notion, though even then by no means of all that takes place, no one knowing much of anything that does not go on in his own immediate neighbourhood; but in a night engagement (and this was the only one that occurred between great armies during the war) how could any one know anything for certain? Although there was a bright moon they saw each other only as men do by moonlight, that is to say, they could distinguish the form of the body, but could not tell for certain whether it was a friend or an enemy. Both had great numbers of heavy infantry moving about in a small space. Some of the Athenians were already defeated, while others were coming up yet unconquered for their first attack. A large part also of the rest of their forces either had only just got up, or were still ascending, so that they did not know which way to march. Owing to the rout that had taken place all in front was now in confusion, and the noise made it difficult to distinguish anything. The victorious Syracusans and allies were cheering each other on with loud cries, by night the only possible means of communication, and meanwhile receiving all who came against them; while the Athenians were seeking for one another, taking all in front of them for enemies, even although they might be some of their now flying friends; and by constantly asking for the watchword, which was their only means of recognition, not only caused great confusion among themselves by asking all at once, but also made it known to the enemy, whose own they did not so readily discover, as the Syracusans were victorious and not scattered, and thus less easily mistaken. The result was that if the Athenians fell in with a party of the enemy that was weaker than they, it escaped them through knowing their watchword; while if they themselves failed to answer they were put to the sword. But what hurt them as much, or indeed more than anything else, was the singing of the paean, from the perplexity which it caused by being nearly the same on either side; the Argives and Corcyraeans and any other Dorian peoples in the army, struck terror into the Athenians whenever they raised their paean, no less than did the enemy. Thus, after being once thrown into disorder, they ended by coming into collision with each other in many parts of the field, friends with friends, and citizens with citizens, and not only terrified one another, but even came to blows and could only be parted with difficulty. In the pursuit many perished by throwing themselves down the cliffs, the way down from Epipolae being narrow; and of those who got down safely into the plain, although many, especially those who belonged to the first armament, escaped through their better acquaintance with the locality, some of the newcomers lost their way and wandered over the country, and were cut off in the morning by the Syracusan cavalry and killed.

The next day the Syracusans set up two trophies, one upon Epipolae where the ascent had been made, and the other on the spot where the first check was given by the Boeotians; and the Athenians took back their dead under truce. A great many of the

Athenians and allies were killed, although still more arms were taken than could be accounted for by the number of the dead, as some of those who were obliged to leap down from the cliffs without their shields escaped with their lives and did not perish like the rest.

After this the Syracusans, recovering their old confidence at such an unexpected stroke of good fortune, dispatched Sicanus with fifteen ships to Agrigentum where there was a revolution, to induce if possible the city to join them; while Gylippus again went by land into the rest of Sicily to bring up reinforcements, being now in hope of taking the Athenian lines by storm, after the result of the affair on Epipolae.

In the meantime the Athenian generals consulted upon the disaster which had happened, and upon the general weakness of the army. They saw themselves unsuccessful in their enterprises, and the soldiers disgusted with their stay; disease being rife among them owing to its being the sickly season of the year, and to the marshy and unhealthy nature of the spot in which they were encamped; and the state of their affairs generally being thought desperate. Accordingly, Demosthenes was of opinion that they ought not to stay any longer; but agreeably to his original idea in risking the attempt upon Epipolae, now that this had failed, he gave his vote for going away without further loss of time, while the sea might yet be crossed, and their late reinforcement might give them the superiority at all events on that element. He also said that it would be more profitable for the state to carry on the war against those who were building fortifications in Attica, than against the Syracusans whom it was no longer easy to subdue; besides which it was not right to squander large sums of money to no purpose by going on with the siege.

This was the opinion of Demosthenes. Nicias, without denying the bad state of their affairs, was unwilling to avow their weakness, or to have it reported to the enemy that the Athenians in full council were openly voting for retreat; for in that case they would be much less likely to effect it when they wanted without discovery. Moreover, his own particular information still gave him reason to hope that the affairs of the enemy would soon be in a worse state than their own, if the Athenians persevered in the siege; as they would wear out the Syracusans by want of money, especially with the more extensive command of the sea now given them by their present navy. Besides this, there was a party in Syracuse who wished to betray the city to the Athenians, and kept sending him messages and telling him not to raise the siege. Accordingly, knowing this and really waiting because he hesitated between the two courses and wished to see his way more clearly, in his public speech on this occasion he refused to lead off the army, saying he was sure the Athenians would never approve of their returning without a vote of theirs. Those who would vote upon their conduct, instead of judging the facts as eye-witnesses like themselves and not from what they might hear from hostile critics, would simply be guided by the calumnies of the first clever speaker; while many, indeed most, of the soldiers on the spot, who now so loudly proclaimed the danger of their position, when they reached Athens would proclaim just as loudly the opposite, and would say that their generals had been bribed to betray them and return. For himself, therefore, who knew the Athenian temper, sooner than perish under a dishonourable charge and by an unjust sentence at the hands of the Athenians, he would rather take his chance and die, if die he must, a soldier's death at the hand of the enemy. Besides, after all, the Syracusans were in a worse case than themselves. What with paying mercenaries, spending upon fortified posts, and now for a full year maintaining a large navy, they were already at a loss and would soon be at a standstill: they had already spent two thousand talents and incurred heavy debts besides, and could not lose even ever so small a fraction of their present force through not paying it, without ruin to their cause; depending as they did more upon mercenaries than upon soldiers obliged to serve, like their own. He therefore said that they ought to stay and carry on the siege, and not depart defeated in point of money, in which they were much superior.

Nicias spoke positively because he had exact information of the financial distress at Syracuse, and also because of the strength of the Athenian party there which kept sending him messages not to raise the siege; besides which he had more confidence than before in his fleet, and felt sure at least of its success. Demosthenes, however, would not hear for a moment of continuing the siege, but said that if they could not lead off the army without a decree from Athens, and if they were obliged to stay on, they ought to remove to Thapsus or Catana; where their land forces would have a wide extent of country to overrun, and could live by plundering the enemy, and would thus do them damage; while the fleet would have the open sea to fight in, that is to say, instead of a narrow space which was all in the enemy's favour, a wide sea-room where their science would be of use, and where they could retreat or advance without being confined or circumscribed either when they put out or put in. In any case he was altogether opposed to their staying on where they were, and insisted on removing at once, as quickly and with as little delay as possible; and in this judgment Eurymedon agreed. Nicias however still objecting, a certain diffidence and hesitation came over them, with a suspicion that Nicias might have some further information to make him so positive.

CHAPTER XXIII

Nineteenth Year of the War - Battles in the Great Harbour -
Retreat and Annihilation of the Athenian Army

WHILE THE Athenians lingered on in this way without moving from where they were, Gylippus and Sicanus now arrived at Syracuse. Sicanus had failed to gain Agrigentum, the party friendly to the Syracusans having been driven out while he was still at Gela; but Gylippus was accompanied not only by a large number of troops raised in Sicily, but by the heavy infantry sent off in the spring from Peloponnese in the merchantmen, who had arrived at Selinus from Libya. They had been carried to Libya by a storm, and having obtained two galleys and pilots from the Cyrenians, on their voyage alongshore had taken sides with the Euesperitae and had defeated the Libyans who were besieging them, and from thence coasting on to Neapolis, a Carthaginian mart, and the nearest point to Sicily, from which it is only two days' and a night's voyage, there crossed over and came to Selinus. Immediately upon their arrival the Syracusans prepared to attack the Athenians again by land and sea at once. The Athenian generals seeing a fresh army come to the aid of the enemy, and that their own circumstances, far from improving, were becoming daily worse, and above all distressed by the sickness of the soldiers, now began to repent of not having removed before; and Nicias no longer offering the same opposition, except by urging that there should be no open voting, they gave orders as secretly as possible for all to be prepared to sail out from the camp at a given signal. All was at last ready, and they were on the point of sailing away, when an eclipse of the moon, which was then at the full, took place. Most of the Athenians, deeply impressed by this occurrence, now urged the generals to wait; and Nicias, who was somewhat over-addicted to divination and practices of that kind, refused from that moment even to take the question of departure into consideration, until they had waited the thrice nine days prescribed by the soothsayers.

The besiegers were thus condemned to stay in the country; and the Syracusans, getting wind of what had happened, became more eager than ever to press the Athenians, who had now themselves acknowledged that they were no longer their superiors either by sea or by land, as otherwise they would never have planned to sail away. Besides which the Syracusans did not wish them to settle in any other part of Sicily, where they would be more difficult to deal with, but desired to force them to fight at sea as quickly as possible, in a position favourable to themselves. Accordingly they manned their ships and practised for as many days as they thought sufficient. When the moment arrived they assaulted on the first day the Athenian lines, and upon a small force of heavy infantry and horse sallying out against them by certain gates, cut off some of the former and routed and pursued them to the lines, where, as the entrance was narrow, the Athenians lost seventy horses and some few of the heavy infantry.

Drawing off their troops for this day, on the next the Syracusans went out with a fleet of seventy-six sail, and at the same time advanced with their land forces against the lines. The Athenians put out to meet them with eighty-six ships, came to close quarters, and engaged. The Syracusans and their allies first defeated the Athenian centre, and then caught Eurymedon, the commander of the right wing, who was sailing out from the line more towards the land in order to surround the enemy, in the hollow and recess of the harbour, and killed him and destroyed the ships accompanying him; after which they now chased the whole Athenian fleet before them and drove them ashore.

Gylippus seeing the enemy's fleet defeated and carried ashore beyond their stockades and camp, ran down to the breakwater with some of his troops, in order to cut off the men as they landed and make it easier for the Syracusans to tow off the vessels by the shore being friendly ground. The Tyrrhenians who guarded this point for the Athenians, seeing them come on in disorder, advanced out against them and attacked and routed their van, hurling it into the marsh of Lysimeleia. Afterwards the Syracusan and allied troops arrived in greater numbers, and the Athenians fearing for their ships came up also to the rescue and engaged them, and defeated and pursued them to some distance and killed a few of their heavy infantry. They succeeded in rescuing most of their ships and brought them down by their camp; eighteen however were taken by the Syracusans and their allies, and all the men killed. The rest the enemy tried to burn by means of an old merchantman which they filled with faggots and pine-wood, set on fire, and let drift down the wind which blew full on the Athenians. The Athenians, however, alarmed for their ships, contrived means for stopping it and putting it out, and checking the flames and the nearer approach of the merchantman, thus escaped the danger.

After this the Syracusans set up a trophy for the sea-fight and for the heavy infantry whom they had cut off up at the lines, where they took the horses; and the Athenians for the rout of the foot driven by the Tyrrhenians into the marsh, and for their own victory with the rest of the army.

The Syracusans had now gained a decisive victory at sea, where until now they had feared the reinforcement brought by Demosthenes, and deep, in consequence, was the despondency of the Athenians, and great their disappointment, and greater still their regret for having come on the expedition. These were the only cities that they had yet encountered, similar to their own in character, under democracies like themselves, which had ships and horses, and were of considerable magnitude. They had been unable to divide and bring them over by holding out the prospect of changes in their governments, or to crush them by their great superiority in force, but had failed in most of their attempts, and being already in perplexity, had now been defeated at sea, where defeat could never have been expected, and were thus plunged deeper in embarrassment than ever.

Meanwhile the Syracusans immediately began to sail freely along the harbour, and determined to close up its mouth, so that the Athenians might not be able to steal out in future, even if they wished. Indeed, the Syracusans no longer thought only of saving themselves, but also how to hinder the escape of the enemy; thinking, and thinking rightly, that they were now much the stronger, and that to conquer the Athenians and their allies by land and sea would win them great glory in Hellas. The rest of the Hellenes would thus immediately be either freed or released from apprehension, as the remaining forces of Athens would be henceforth unable to sustain the war that would be waged against her; while they, the Syracusans, would be regarded as the authors of this deliverance, and would be held in high admiration, not only with all men now living but also with posterity. Nor were these the only considerations that gave dignity to the struggle. They would thus conquer not only the Athenians but also their numerous allies, and conquer not alone, but with their companions in arms, commanding side by side with the Corinthians and Lacedaemonians, having offered their city to stand in the van of danger, and having been in a great measure the pioneers of naval success.

Indeed, there were never so many peoples assembled before a single city, if we except the grand total gathered together in this war under Athens and Lacedaemon. The following were the states on either side who came to Syracuse to fight for or against Sicily, to help to conquer or defend the island. Right or community of blood was not the bond of union between them, so much as interest or compulsion as the case might be. The Athenians themselves being Ionians went against the Dorians of Syracuse of their own free will; and the peoples still speaking Attic and using the Athenian laws, the Lemnians, Imbrians, and Aeginetans, that is to say the then occupants of Aegina, being their colonists, went with them. To these must be also added the Hestiaeans dwelling at Hestiaea in Euboea. Of the rest some joined in the expedition as subjects of the Athenians, others as independent allies, others as mercenaries. To the number of the subjects paying tribute belonged the Eretrians, Chalcidians, Styrians, and Carystians from Euboea; the Ceans, Andrians, and Tenians from the islands; and the Milesians, Samians, and Chians from Ionia. The Chians, however, joined as independent allies, paying no tribute, but furnishing ships. Most of these were Ionians and descended from the Athenians, except the Carystians, who are Dryopes, and although subjects and obliged to serve, were still Ionians fighting against Dorians. Besides these there were men of Aeolic race, the Methymnians, subjects who provided ships, not tribute, and the Tenedians and Aenians who paid tribute. These Aeolians fought against their Aeolian founders, the Boeotians in the Syracusan army, because they were obliged, while the Plataeans, the only native Boeotians opposed to Boeotians, did so upon a just quarrel. Of the Rhodians and Cytherians, both Dorians, the latter, Lacedaemonian colonists, fought in the Athenian ranks against their Lacedaemonian countrymen with Gylippus; while the Rhodians, Argives by race, were compelled to bear arms against the Dorian Syracusans and their own colonists, the Geloans, serving with the Syracusans. Of the islanders round Peloponnese, the Cephallenians and Zacynthians accompanied the Athenians as independent allies, although their insular position really left them little choice in the matter, owing to the maritime supremacy of Athens, while the Corcyraeans, who were not only Dorians but Corinthians, were openly serving against Corinthians and Syracusans, although colonists of the former and of the same race as the latter, under colour of compulsion, but really out of free will through hatred of Corinth. The Messenians, as they are now called in Naupactus and from Pylos, then held by the Athenians, were taken with them to the war. There were also a few Megarian exiles, whose fate it was to be now fighting against the Megarian Selinuntines.

The engagement of the rest was more of a voluntary nature. It was less the league than hatred of the Lacedaemonians and the immediate private advantage of each individual that persuaded the Dorian Argives to join the Ionian Athenians in a war against Dorians; while the Mantineans and other Arcadian mercenaries, accustomed to go against the enemy pointed out to them at the moment, were led by interest to regard the Arcadians serving with the Corinthians as just as much their enemies as any others. The Cretans and Aetolians also served for hire, and the Cretans who had joined the Rhodians in founding Gela, thus came to consent to fight for pay against, instead of for, their colonists. There were also some Acarnanians paid to serve, although they came chiefly for love of Demosthenes and out of goodwill to the Athenians whose allies they were. These all lived on the Hellenic side of the Ionian Gulf. Of the Italiots, there were the Thurians and Metapontines, dragged into the quarrel by the stern necessities of a time of revolution; of the Siceliots, the Naxians and the Catanians; and of the barbarians, the Egestaeans, who called in the Athenians, most of the Sicels, and outside Sicily some Tyrrhenian enemies of Syracuse and Iapygian mercenaries.

Such were the peoples serving with the Athenians. Against these the Syracusans had the Camarinaeans their neighbours, the Geloans who live next to them; then passing over the neutral Agrigentines, the Selinuntines settled on the farther side of the island. These inhabit the part of Sicily looking towards Libya; the Himeraeans came from the side towards the Tyrrhenian Sea, being the only Hellenic inhabitants in that quarter, and the only people that came from thence to the aid of the Syracusans. Of the Hellenes in Sicily the above peoples joined in the war, all Dorians and independent, and of the barbarians the Sicels only, that is to say, such as did not go over to the Athenians. Of the Hellenes outside Sicily there were the Lacedaemonians, who provided a Spartan to take the command, and a force of Neodamodes or Freedmen, and of Helots; the Corinthians, who alone joined with naval and land forces, with their Leucadian and Ambraciot kinsmen; some mercenaries sent by Corinth from Arcadia; some Sicyonians forced to serve, and from outside Peloponnese the Boeotians. In comparison, however, with these foreign auxiliaries, the great Siceliot cities furnished more in every department - numbers of heavy infantry, ships, and horses, and an immense multitude besides having been brought together; while in comparison, again, one may say, with all the rest put together, more was provided by the Syracusans themselves, both from the greatness of the city and from the fact that they were in the greatest danger.

Such were the auxiliaries brought together on either side, all of which had by this time joined, neither party experiencing any subsequent accession. It was no wonder, therefore, if the Syracusans and their allies thought that it would win them great glory if they could follow up their recent victory in the sea-fight by the capture of the whole Athenian armada, without letting it escape either by sea or by land. They began at once to close up the Great Harbour by means of boats, merchant vessels, and galleys moored broadside across its mouth, which is nearly a mile wide, and made all their other arrangements for the event of the Athenians again venturing to fight at sea. There was, in fact, nothing little either in their plans or their ideas.

The Athenians, seeing them closing up the harbour and informed of their further designs, called a council of war. The generals and colonels assembled and discussed the difficulties of the situation; the point which pressed most being that they no longer had provisions for immediate use (having sent on to Catana to tell them not to send any, in the belief that they were going away), and that they would not have any in future unless they could command the sea. They therefore determined to evacuate their upper lines, to enclose with a cross wall and garrison a small space close to the ships, only just sufficient to hold their stores and sick, and manning all the ships, seaworthy or not, with every man that could be spared from the rest of their land forces, to fight it out at sea, and, if victorious, to go to Catana, if not, to burn their vessels, form in close order, and retreat by land for the nearest friendly place they could reach, Hellenic or barbarian. This was no sooner settled than carried into effect; they descended gradually from the upper lines and manned all their vessels, compelling all to go on board who were of age to be in any way of use. They thus succeeded in manning about one hundred and ten ships in all, on board of which they embarked a number of archers and darters taken from the Acarnanians and from the other foreigners, making all other provisions allowed by the nature of their plan and by the necessities which imposed it. All was now nearly ready, and Nicias, seeing the soldiery disheartened by their unprecedented and decided defeat at sea, and by reason of the scarcity of provisions eager to fight it out as soon as possible, called them all together, and first addressed them, speaking as follows:

"Soldiers of the Athenians and of the allies, we have all an equal interest in the coming struggle, in which life and country are at stake for us quite as much as they can be for the enemy; since if our fleet wins the day, each can see his native city again, wherever that city may be. You must not lose heart, or be like men without any experience, who fail in a first essay and ever afterwards fearfully forebode a future as disastrous. But let the Athenians among you who have already had experience of many wars, and the allies who have joined us in so many expeditions, remember the surprises of war, and with the hope that fortune will not be always against us, prepare to fight again in a manner worthy of the number which you see yourselves to be.

"Now, whatever we thought would be of service against the crush of vessels in such a narrow harbour, and against the force upon the decks of the enemy, from which we suffered before, has all been considered with the helmsmen, and, as far as our means allowed, provided. A number of archers and darters will go on board, and a multitude that we should not have employed in an action in the open sea, where our science would be crippled by the weight of the vessels; but in the present land-fight that we are forced to make from shipboard all this will be useful. We have also discovered the changes in construction that we must make to meet theirs; and against the thickness of their cheeks, which did us the greatest mischief, we have provided grappling-irons, which will prevent an assailant backing water after charging, if the soldiers on deck here do their duty; since we are absolutely compelled to fight a land battle from the fleet, and it seems to be our interest neither to back water ourselves, nor to let the enemy do so, especially as the shore, except so much of it as may be held by our troops, is hostile ground.

"You must remember this and fight on as long as you can, and must not let yourselves be driven ashore, but once alongside must make up your minds not to part company until you have swept the heavy infantry from the enemy's deck. I say this more for the heavy infantry than for the seamen, as it is more the business of the men on deck; and our land forces are even now on the whole the strongest. The sailors I advise, and at the same time implore, not to be too much daunted by their misfortunes, now that we have our decks better armed and greater number of vessels. Bear in mind how well worth preserving is the pleasure felt by those of you who through your knowledge of our language and imitation of our manners were always considered Athenians, even though not so in reality, and as such were honoured throughout Hellas, and had your full share of the advantages of our empire, and more than your share in the respect of our subjects and in protection from ill treatment. You, therefore, with whom alone we freely share our empire, we now justly require not to betray that empire in its extremity, and in scorn of Corinthians, whom you have often conquered, and of Siceliots, none of whom so much as presumed to stand against us when our navy was in its prime, we ask you to repel them, and to show that even in sickness and disaster your skill is more than a match for the fortune and vigour of any other.

"For the Athenians among you I add once more this reflection: You left behind you no more such ships in your docks as these, no more heavy infantry in their flower; if you do aught but conquer, our enemies here will immediately sail thither, and those that are left of us at Athens will become unable to repel their home assailants, reinforced by these new allies. Here you will fall at once into the hands of the Syracusans - I need not remind you of the intentions with which you attacked them - and your countrymen at home will fall into those of the Lacedaemonians. Since the fate of both thus hangs upon this single battle, now, if ever, stand firm, and remember, each and all, that you who are now going on board are the army and navy of the Athenians, and all that is left of the state and the great name of Athens, in whose defence if any man has any advantage in skill or courage, now is the time for him to show it, and thus serve himself and save all."

After this address Nicias at once gave orders to man the ships. Meanwhile Gylippus and the Syracusans could perceive by the preparations which they saw going on that the Athenians meant to fight at sea. They had also notice of the grappling-irons, against which they specially provided by stretching hides over the prows and much of the upper part of their vessels, in order that the irons when thrown might slip off without taking hold. All being now ready, the generals and Gylippus addressed them in the following terms:

"Syracusans and allies, the glorious character of our past achievements and the no less glorious results at issue in the coming battle are, we think, understood by most of you, or you would never have thrown yourselves with such ardour into the struggle; and if there be any one not as fully aware of the facts as he ought to be, we will declare them to him. The Athenians came to this country first to effect the conquest of Sicily, and after that, if successful, of Peloponnese and the rest of Hellas, possessing already the greatest empire yet known, of present or former times, among the Hellenes. Here for the first time they found in you men who faced their navy which made them masters everywhere; you have already defeated them in the previous sea-fights, and will in all likelihood defeat them again now. When men are once checked in what they consider their special excellence, their whole opinion of themselves suffers more than if they had not at first believed in their superiority, the unexpected shock to their pride causing them to give way more than their real strength warrants; and this is probably now the case with the Athenians.

"With us it is different. The original estimate of ourselves which gave us courage in the days of our unskilfulness has been strengthened, while the conviction superadded to it that we must be the best seamen of the time, if we have conquered the best, has given a double measure of hope to every man among us; and, for the most part, where there is the greatest hope, there is also the greatest ardour for action. The means to combat us which they have tried to find in copying our armament are familiar to our warfare, and will be met by proper provisions; while they will never be able to have a number of heavy infantry on their decks, contrary to their custom, and a number of darters (born landsmen, one may say, Acarnanians and others, embarked afloat, who will not know how to discharge their weapons when they have to keep still), without hampering their vessels and falling all into confusion among themselves through fighting not according to their own tactics. For they will gain nothing by the number of their ships - I say this to those of you who may be alarmed by having to fight against odds - as a quantity of ships in a confined space will only be slower in executing the movements required, and most exposed to injury from our means of offence. Indeed, if you would know the plain truth, as we are credibly informed, the excess of their sufferings and the necessities of their present distress have made them desperate; they have no confidence in their force, but wish to try their fortune in the only way they can, and either to force their passage and sail out, or after this to retreat by land, it being impossible for them to be worse off than they are.

"The fortune of our greatest enemies having thus betrayed itself, and their disorder being what I have described, let us engage in anger, convinced that, as between adversaries, nothing is more legitimate than to claim to sate the whole wrath of one's soul in punishing the aggressor, and nothing more sweet, as the proverb has it, than the vengeance upon an enemy, which it will now be ours to take. That enemies they are and mortal enemies you all know, since they came here to enslave our country, and if successful had in reserve for our men all that is most dreadful, and for our children and wives all that is most dishonourable, and for the whole city the name which conveys the greatest reproach. None should therefore relent or think it gain if they go away without further danger to us. This they will do just the same, even if they get the victory; while if we succeed, as we may expect, in chastising them, and in handing down to all Sicily her ancient freedom strengthened and confirmed, we shall have achieved no mean triumph. And the rarest dangers are those in which failure brings little loss and success the greatest advantage."

After the above address to the soldiers on their side, the Syracusan generals and Gylippus now perceived that the Athenians were manning their ships, and immediately proceeded to man their own also. Meanwhile Nicias, appalled by the position of affairs, realizing the greatness and the nearness of the danger now that they were on the point of putting out from shore, and thinking, as men are apt to think in great crises, that when all has been done they have still something left to do, and when all has been said that they have not yet said enough, again called on the captains one by one, addressing each by his father's name and by his own, and by that of his tribe, and adjured them not to belie their own personal renown, or to obscure the hereditary virtues for which their ancestors were illustrious: he reminded them of their country, the freest of the free, and of the unfettered discretion allowed in it to all to live as they pleased; and added other arguments such as men would use at such a crisis, and which, with little alteration, are made to serve on all occasions alike - appeals to wives, children, and national gods - without caring whether they are thought commonplace, but loudly invoking them in the belief that they will be of use in the consternation of the moment. Having thus admonished them, not, he felt, as he would, but as he could, Nicias withdrew and led the troops to the sea, and ranged them in as long a line as he was able, in order to aid as far as possible in sustaining the courage of the men afloat; while Demosthenes, Menander, and Euthydemus, who took the command on board, put out from their own camp and sailed straight to the barrier across the mouth of the harbour and to the passage left open, to try to force their way out.

The Syracusans and their allies had already put out with about the same number of ships as before, a part of which kept guard at the outlet, and the remainder all round the rest of the harbour, in order to attack the Athenians on all sides at once; while the land forces held themselves in readiness at the points at which the vessels might put into the shore. The Syracusan fleet was commanded by Sicanus and Agatharchus, who had each a wing of the whole force, with Pythen and the Corinthians in the centre. When the rest of the Athenians came up to the barrier, with the first shock of their charge they overpowered the ships stationed there, and tried to undo the fastenings; after this, as the Syracusans and allies bore down upon them from all quarters, the action spread from the barrier over the whole harbour, and was more obstinately disputed than any of the preceding ones. On either side the rowers showed great zeal in bringing up their vessels at the boatswains' orders, and the helmsmen great skill in manoeuvring, and great emulation one with another; while the ships once alongside, the soldiers on board did their best not to let the service on deck be outdone by the others; in short, every man strove to prove himself the first in his particular department. And as many ships were engaged in a small compass (for these were the largest fleets fighting in the narrowest space ever known, being together little short of two hundred), the regular attacks with the beak were few, there being no opportunity of backing water or of breaking the line; while the collisions caused by one ship chancing to run foul of another, either in flying from or attacking a third, were more frequent. So long as a vessel was coming up to the charge the men on the decks rained darts and arrows and stones upon her; but once alongside, the heavy infantry tried to board each other's vessel, fighting hand to hand. In many quarters it happened, by reason of the narrow room, that a vessel was charging an enemy on one side and being charged herself on another, and that two or sometimes more ships had perforce got entangled round one, obliging the helmsmen to attend to defence here, offence there, not to one thing at once, but to many on all sides; while the huge din caused by the number of ships crashing together not only spread terror, but made the orders of the boatswains inaudible. The boatswains on either side in the discharge of their duty and in the heat of the conflict shouted incessantly orders and appeals to their men; the Athenians they urged to force the passage out, and now if ever to show their mettle and lay hold of a safe return to their country; to the Syracusans and their allies they cried that it would be glorious to prevent the escape of the enemy, and, conquering, to exalt the countries that were theirs. The generals, moreover, on either side, if they saw any in any part of the battle backing ashore without being forced to do so, called out to the captain by name and asked him - the Athenians, whether they were retreating because they thought the thrice hostile shore more their own than that sea which had cost them so much labour to win; the Syracusans, whether they were flying from the flying Athenians, whom they well knew to be eager to escape in whatever way they could.

Meanwhile the two armies on shore, while victory hung in the balance, were a prey to the most agonizing and conflicting emotions; the natives thirsting for more glory than they had already won, while the invaders feared to find themselves in even worse plight than before. The all of the Athenians being set upon their fleet, their fear for the event was like nothing they had ever felt; while their view of the struggle was necessarily as chequered as the battle itself. Close to the scene of action and not all looking at the same point at once, some saw their friends victorious and took courage and fell to calling upon heaven not to deprive them of salvation, while others who had their eyes turned upon the losers, wailed and cried aloud, and, although spectators, were more overcome than the actual combatants. Others, again, were gazing at some spot where the battle was evenly disputed; as the strife was protracted without decision, their swaying bodies reflected the agitation of their minds, and they suffered the worst agony of all, ever just within reach of safety or just on the point of destruction. In short, in that one Athenian army as long as the sea-fight remained doubtful there was every sound to be heard at once, shrieks, cheers, "We win," "We lose," and all the other manifold exclamations that a great host would necessarily utter in great peril; and with the men in the fleet it was nearly the same; until at last the Syracusans and their allies, after the battle had lasted a long while, put the Athenians to flight, and with much shouting and cheering chased them in open rout to the shore. The naval force, one one way, one another, as many as were not taken afloat now ran ashore and rushed from on board their ships to their camp; while the army, no more divided, but carried away by one impulse, all with shrieks and groans deplored the event, and ran down, some to help the ships, others to guard what was left of their wall, while the remaining and most numerous part already began to consider how they should save themselves. Indeed, the panic of the present moment had never been surpassed. They now suffered very nearly what they had inflicted at Pylos; as then the Lacedaemonians with the loss of their fleet lost also the men who had crossed over to the island, so now the Athenians had no hope of escaping by land, without the help of some extraordinary accident.

The sea-fight having been a severe one, and many ships and lives having been lost on both sides, the victorious Syracusans and their allies now picked up their wrecks and dead, and sailed off to the city and set up a trophy. The Athenians, overwhelmed by their misfortune, never even thought of asking leave to take up their dead or wrecks, but wished to retreat that very night. Demosthenes, however, went to Nicias and gave it as his opinion that they should man the ships they had left and make another effort to force their passage out next morning; saying that they had still left more ships fit for service than the enemy, the Athenians having about sixty remaining as against less than fifty of their opponents. Nicias was quite of his mind; but when they wished to man the vessels, the sailors refused to go on board, being so utterly overcome by their defeat as no longer to believe in the possibility of success.

Accordingly they all now made up their minds to retreat by land. Meanwhile the Syracusan Hermocrates - suspecting their intention, and impressed by the danger of allowing a force of that magnitude to retire by land, establish itself in some other part of Sicily, and from thence renew the war - went and stated his views to the authorities, and pointed out to them that they ought not to let the enemy get away by night, but that all the Syracusans and their allies should at once march out and block up the roads and seize and guard the passes. The authorities were entirely of his opinion, and thought that it ought to be done, but on the other hand felt sure that the people, who had given themselves over to rejoicing, and were taking their ease after a great battle at sea, would not be easily brought to obey; besides, they were celebrating a festival, having on that day a sacrifice to Heracles, and most of them in their rapture at the victory had fallen to drinking at the festival, and would probably consent to anything sooner than to take up their arms and march out at that moment. For these reasons the thing appeared impracticable to the magistrates; and Hermocrates, finding himself unable to do anything further with them, had now recourse to the following stratagem of his own. What he feared was that the Athenians might quietly get the start of them by passing the most difficult places during the night; and he therefore sent, as soon as it was dusk, some friends of his own to the camp with some horsemen who rode up within earshot and called out to some of the men, as though they were well-wishers of the Athenians, and told them to tell Nicias (who had in fact some correspondents who informed him of what went on inside the town) not to lead off the army by night as the Syracusans were guarding the roads, but to make his preparations at his leisure and to retreat by day. After saying this they departed; and their hearers informed the Athenian generals, who put off going for that night on the strength of this message, not doubting its sincerity.

Since after all they had not set out at once, they now determined to stay also the following day to give time to the soldiers to pack up as well as they could the most useful articles, and, leaving everything else behind, to start only with what was strictly necessary for their personal subsistence. Meanwhile the Syracusans and Gylippus marched out and blocked up the roads through the country by which the Athenians were likely to pass, and kept guard at the fords of the streams and rivers, posting themselves so as to receive them and stop the army where they thought best; while their fleet sailed up to the beach and towed off the ships of the Athenians. Some few were burned by the Athenians themselves as they had intended; the rest the Syracusans lashed on to their own at their leisure as they had been thrown up on shore, without any one trying to stop them, and conveyed to the town.

After this, Nicias and Demosthenes now thinking that enough had been done in the way of preparation, the removal of the army took place upon the second day after the sea-fight. It was a lamentable scene, not merely from the single circumstance that they were retreating after having lost all their ships, their great hopes gone, and themselves and the state in peril; but also in leaving the camp there were things most grievous for every eye and heart to contemplate. The dead lay unburied, and each man as he recognized a friend among them shuddered with grief and horror; while the living whom they were leaving behind, wounded or sick, were to the living far more shocking than the dead, and more to be pitied than those who had perished. These fell to entreating and bewailing until their friends knew not what to do, begging them to take them and loudly calling to each individual comrade or relative whom they could see, hanging upon the necks of their tent-fellows in the act of departure, and following as far as they could, and, when their bodily strength failed them, calling again and again upon heaven and shrieking aloud as they were left behind. So that the whole army being filled with tears and distracted after this fashion found it not easy to go, even from an enemy's land, where they had already suffered evils too great for tears and in the unknown future before them feared to suffer more. Dejection and self-condemnation were also rife among them. Indeed they could only be compared to a starved-out town, and that no small one, escaping; the whole multitude upon the march being not less than forty thousand men. All carried anything they could which might be of use, and the heavy infantry and troopers, contrary to their wont, while under arms carried their own victuals, in some cases for want of servants, in others through not trusting them; as they had long been deserting and now did so in greater numbers than ever. Yet even thus they did not carry enough, as there was no longer food in the camp. Moreover their disgrace generally, and the universality of their sufferings, however to a certain extent alleviated by being borne in company, were still felt at the moment a heavy burden, especially when they contrasted the splendour and glory of their setting out with the humiliation in which it had ended. For this was by far the greatest reverse that ever befell an Hellenic army. They had come to enslave others, and were departing in fear of being enslaved themselves: they had sailed out with prayer and paeans, and now started to go back with omens directly contrary; travelling by land instead of by sea, and trusting not in their fleet but in their heavy infantry. Nevertheless the greatness of the danger still impending made all this appear tolerable.

Nicias seeing the army dejected and greatly altered, passed along the ranks and encouraged and comforted them as far as was possible under the circumstances, raising his voice still higher and higher as he went from one company to another in his earnestness, and in his anxiety that the benefit of his words might reach as many as possible:

"Athenians and allies, even in our present position we must still hope on, since men have ere now been saved from worse straits than this; and you must not condemn yourselves too severely either because of your disasters or because of your present unmerited sufferings. I myself who am not superior to any of you in strength - indeed you see how I am in my sickness - and who in the gifts of fortune am, I think, whether in private life or otherwise, the equal of any, am now exposed to the same danger as the meanest among you; and yet my life has been one of much devotion toward the gods, and of much justice and without offence toward men. I have, therefore, still a strong hope for the future, and our misfortunes do not terrify me as much as they might. Indeed we may hope that they will be lightened: our enemies have had good fortune enough; and if any of the gods was offended at our expedition, we have been already amply punished. Others before us have attacked their neighbours and have done what men will do without suffering more than they could bear; and we may now justly expect to find the gods more kind, for we have become fitter objects for their pity than their jealousy. And then look at yourselves, mark the numbers and efficiency of the heavy infantry marching in your ranks, and do not give way too much to despondency, but reflect that you are yourselves at once a city wherever you sit down, and that there is no other in Sicily that could easily resist your attack, or expel you when once established. The safety and order of the march is for yourselves to look to; the one thought of each man being that the spot on which he may be forced to fight must be conquered and held as his country and stronghold. Meanwhile we shall hasten on our way night and day alike, as our provisions are scanty; and if we can reach some friendly place of the Sicels, whom fear of the Syracusans still keeps true to us, you may forthwith consider yourselves safe. A message has been sent on to

501

them with directions to meet us with supplies of food. To sum up, be convinced, soldiers, that you must be brave, as there is no place near for your cowardice to take refuge in, and that if you now escape from the enemy, you may all see again what your hearts desire, while those of you who are Athenians will raise up again the great power of the state, fallen though it be. Men make the city and not walls or ships without men in them."

As he made this address, Nicias went along the ranks, and brought back to their place any of the troops that he saw straggling out of the line; while Demosthenes did as much for his part of the army, addressing them in words very similar. The army marched in a hollow square, the division under Nicias leading, and that of Demosthenes following, the heavy infantry being outside and the baggage-carriers and the bulk of the army in the middle. When they arrived at the ford of the river Anapus there they found drawn up a body of the Syracusans and allies, and routing these, made good their passage and pushed on, harassed by the charges of the Syracusan horse and by the missiles of their light troops. On that day they advanced about four miles and a half, halting for the night upon a certain hill. On the next they started early and got on about two miles further, and descended into a place in the plain and there encamped, in order to procure some eatables from the houses, as the place was inhabited, and to carry on with them water from thence, as for many furlongs in front, in the direction in which they were going, it was not plentiful. The Syracusans meanwhile went on and fortified the pass in front, where there was a steep hill with a rocky ravine on each side of it, called the Acraean cliff. The next day the Athenians advancing found themselves impeded by the missiles and charges of the horse and darters, both very numerous, of the Syracusans and allies; and after fighting for a long while, at length retired to the same camp, where they had no longer provisions as before, it being impossible to leave their position by reason of the cavalry.

Early next morning they started afresh and forced their way to the hill, which had been fortified, where they found before them the enemy's infantry drawn up many shields deep to defend the fortification, the pass being narrow. The Athenians assaulted the work, but were greeted by a storm of missiles from the hill, which told with the greater effect through its being a steep one, and unable to force the passage, retreated again and rested. Meanwhile occurred some claps of thunder and rain, as often happens towards autumn, which still further disheartened the Athenians, who thought all these things to be omens of their approaching ruin. While they were resting, Gylippus and the Syracusans sent a part of their army to throw up works in their rear on the way by which they had advanced; however, the Athenians immediately sent some of their men and prevented them; after which they retreated more towards the plain and halted for the night. When they advanced the next day the Syracusans surrounded and attacked them on every side, and disabled many of them, falling back if the Athenians advanced and coming on if they retired, and in particular assaulting their rear, in the hope of routing them in detail, and thus striking a panic into the whole army. For a long while the Athenians persevered in this fashion, but after advancing for four or five furlongs halted to rest in the plain, the Syracusans also withdrawing to their own camp.

During the night Nicias and Demosthenes, seeing the wretched condition of their troops, now in want of every kind of necessary, and numbers of them disabled in the numerous attacks of the enemy, determined to light as many fires as possible, and to lead off the army, no longer by the same route as they had intended, but towards the sea in the opposite direction to that guarded by the Syracusans. The whole of this route was leading the army not to Catana but to the other side of Sicily, towards Camarina, Gela, and the other Hellenic and barbarian towns in that quarter. They accordingly lit a number of fires and set out by night. Now all armies, and the greatest most of all, are liable to fears and alarms, especially when they are marching by night through an enemy's country and with the enemy near; and the Athenians falling into one of these panics, the leading division, that of Nicias, kept together and got on a good way in front, while that of Demosthenes, comprising rather more than half the army, got separated and marched on in some disorder. By morning, however, they reached the sea, and getting into the Helorine road, pushed on in order to reach the river Cacyparis, and to follow the stream up through the interior, where they hoped to be met by the Sicels whom they had sent for. Arrived at the river, they found there also a Syracusan party engaged in barring the passage of the ford with a wall and a palisade, and forcing this guard, crossed the river and went on to another called the Erineus, according to the advice of their guides.

Meanwhile, when day came and the Syracusans and allies found that the Athenians were gone, most of them accused Gylippus of having let them escape on purpose, and hastily pursuing by the road which they had no difficulty in finding that they had taken, overtook them about dinner-time. They first came up with the troops under Demosthenes, who were behind and marching somewhat slowly and in disorder, owing to the night panic above referred to, and at once attacked and engaged them, the Syracusan horse surrounding them with more ease now that they were separated from the rest and hemming them in on one spot. The division of Nicias was five or six miles on in front, as he led them more rapidly, thinking that under the circumstances their safety lay not in staying and fighting, unless obliged, but in retreating as fast as possible, and only fighting when forced to do so. On the other hand, Demosthenes was, generally speaking, harassed more incessantly, as his post in the rear left him the first exposed to the attacks of the enemy; and now, finding that the Syracusans were in pursuit, he omitted to push on, in order to form his men for battle, and so lingered until he was surrounded by his pursuers and himself and the Athenians with him placed in the most distressing position, being huddled into an enclosure with a wall all round it, a road on this side and on that, and olive-trees in great number, where missiles were showered in upon them from every quarter. This mode of attack the Syracusans had with good reason adopted in preference to fighting at close quarters, as to risk a struggle with desperate men was now more for the advantage of the Athenians than for their own; besides, their success had now become so certain that they began to spare themselves a little in order not to be cut off in the moment of victory, thinking too that, as it was, they would be able in this way to subdue and capture the enemy.

In fact, after plying the Athenians and allies all day long from every side with missiles, they at length saw that they were worn out with their wounds and other sufferings; and Gylippus and the Syracusans and their allies made a proclamation, offering their liberty to any of the islanders who chose to come over to them; and some few cities went over. Afterwards a capitulation was agreed upon for all the rest with Demosthenes, to lay down their arms on condition that no one was to be put to death either by violence or imprisonment or want of the necessaries of life. Upon this they surrendered to the number of six thousand in all, laying down all the money in their possession, which filled the hollows of four shields, and were immediately conveyed by the Syracusans to the town.

Meanwhile Nicias with his division arrived that day at the river Erineus, crossed over, and posted his army upon some high ground upon the other side. The next day the Syracusans overtook him and told him that the troops under Demosthenes had surrendered, and invited him to follow their example. Incredulous of the fact, Nicias asked for a truce to send a horseman to see, and upon the return of the messenger with the tidings that they had surrendered, sent a herald to Gylippus and the Syracusans, saying that he was ready to agree with them on behalf of the Athenians to repay whatever money the Syracusans had spent upon the war if they would let his army go; and offered until the money was paid to give Athenians as hostages, one for every talent. The Syracusans and Gylippus rejected this proposition, and attacked this division as they had the other, standing all round and plying them with missiles until the evening. Food and necessaries were as miserably wanting to the troops of Nicias as they had been to their comrades; nevertheless they watched for the quiet of the night to resume their march. But as they were taking up their arms the Syracusans perceived it and raised their paean, upon which the Athenians, finding that they were discovered, laid them down again, except about three hundred men who forced their way through the guards and went on during the night as they were able.

As soon as it was day Nicias put his army in motion, pressed, as before, by the Syracusans and their allies, pelted from every side by their missiles, and struck down by their javelins. The Athenians pushed on for the Assinarus, impelled by the attacks made upon them from every side by a numerous cavalry and the swarm of other arms, fancying that they should breathe more freely if once across the river, and driven on also by their exhaustion and craving for water. Once there they rushed in, and all order was at an end, each man wanting to cross first, and the attacks of the enemy making it difficult to cross at all; forced to huddle together, they fell against and trod down one another, some dying immediately upon the javelins, others getting entangled together and stumbling over the articles of baggage, without being able to rise again. Meanwhile the opposite bank, which was steep, was lined by the Syracusans, who showered missiles down upon the Athenians, most of them drinking greedily and heaped together in disorder in the hollow bed of the river. The Peloponnesians also came down and butchered them, especially those in the water, which was thus immediately spoiled, but which they went on drinking just the same, mud and all, bloody as it was, most even fighting to have it.

At last, when many dead now lay piled one upon another in the stream, and part of the army had been destroyed at the river, and the few that escaped from thence cut off by the cavalry, Nicias surrendered himself to Gylippus, whom he trusted more than he did the Syracusans, and told him and the Lacedaemonians to do what they liked with him, but to stop the slaughter of the soldiers. Gylippus, after this, immediately gave orders to make prisoners; upon which the rest were brought together alive, except a large number secreted by the soldiery, and a party was sent in pursuit of the three hundred who had got through the guard during the night, and who were now taken with the rest. The number of the enemy collected as public property was not considerable; but that secreted was very large, and all Sicily was filled with them, no convention having been made in their case as for those taken with Demosthenes. Besides this, a large portion were killed outright, the carnage being very great, and not exceeded by any in this Sicilian war. In the numerous other encounters upon the march, not a few also had fallen. Nevertheless many escaped, some at the moment, others served as slaves, and then ran away subsequently. These found refuge at Catana.

The Syracusans and their allies now mustered and took up the spoils and as many prisoners as they could, and went back to the city. The rest of their Athenian and allied captives were deposited in the quarries, this seeming the safest way of keeping them; but Nicias and Demosthenes were butchered, against the will of Gylippus, who thought that it would be the crown of his triumph if he could take the enemy's generals to Lacedaemon. One of them, as it happened, Demosthenes, was one of her greatest enemies, on account of the affair of the island and of Pylos; while the other, Nicias, was for the same reasons one of her greatest friends, owing to his exertions to procure the release of the prisoners by persuading the Athenians to make peace. For these reasons the Lacedaemonians felt kindly towards him; and it was in this that Nicias himself mainly confided when he surrendered to Gylippus. But some of the Syracusans who had been in correspondence with him were afraid, it was said, of his being put to the torture and troubling their success by his revelations; others, especially the Corinthians, of his escaping, as he was wealthy, by means of bribes, and living to do them further mischief; and these persuaded the allies and put him to death. This or the like was the cause of the death of a man who, of all the Hellenes in my time, least deserved such a fate, seeing that the whole course of his life had been regulated with strict attention to virtue.

The prisoners in the quarries were at first hardly treated by the Syracusans. Crowded in a narrow hole, without any roof to cover them, the heat of the sun and the stifling closeness of the air tormented them during the day, and then the nights, which came on autumnal and chilly, made them ill by the violence of the change; besides, as they had to do everything in the same place for want of room, and the bodies of those who died of their wounds or from the variation in the temperature, or from similar causes, were left heaped together one upon another, intolerable stenches arose; while hunger and thirst never ceased to afflict them, each man during eight months having only half a pint of water and a pint of corn given him daily. In short, no single suffering to be apprehended by men thrust into such a place was spared them. For some seventy days they thus lived all together, after which all, except the Athenians and any Siceliots or Italiots who had joined in the expedition, were sold. The total number of prisoners taken it would be difficult to state exactly, but it could not have been less than seven thousand.

This was the greatest Hellenic achievement of any in thig war, or, in my opinion, in Hellenic history; at once most glorious to the victors, and most calamitous to the conquered. They were beaten at all points and altogether; all that they suffered was great; they were destroyed, as the saying is, with a total destruction, their fleet, their army, everything was destroyed, and few out of many returned home. Such were the events in Sicily.

CHAPTER XXIV

Nineteenth and Twentieth Years of the War - Revolt of Ionia -
Intervention of Persia - The War in Ionia

WHEN THE news was brought to Athens, for a long while they disbelieved even the most respectable of the soldiers who had themselves escaped from the scene of action and clearly reported the matter, a destruction so complete not being thought credible. When the conviction was forced upon them, they were angry with the orators who had joined in promoting the expedition, just as if they had not themselves voted it, and were enraged also with the reciters of oracles and soothsayers, and all other omen-mongers of the time who had encouraged them to hope that they should conquer Sicily. Already distressed at all points and in all quarters, after what had now happened, they were seized by a fear and consternation quite without example. It was grievous enough for the state and for every man in his proper person to lose so many heavy infantry, cavalry, and able-bodied troops, and to see none left to replace them; but when they saw, also, that they had not sufficient ships in their docks, or money in the treasury, or crews for the ships, they began to despair of salvation. They thought that their enemies in Sicily would immediately sail with their fleet against Piraeus, inflamed by so signal a victory; while their adversaries at home, redoubling all their preparations, would vigorously attack them by sea and land at once, aided by their own revolted confederates. Nevertheless, with such means as they had, it was determined to resist to the last, and to provide timber and money, and to equip a fleet as they best could, to take steps to secure their confederates and above all Euboea, to reform things in the city upon a more economical footing, and to elect a board of elders to advise upon the state of affairs as occasion should arise. In short, as is the way of a democracy, in the panic of the moment they were ready to be as prudent as possible.

These resolves were at once carried into effect. Summer was now over. The winter ensuing saw all Hellas stirring under the impression of the great Athenian disaster in Sicily. Neutrals now felt that even if uninvited they ought no longer to stand aloof from the war, but should volunteer to march against the Athenians, who, as they severally reflected, would probably have come against them if the Sicilian campaign had succeeded. Besides, they considered that the war would now be short, and that it would be creditable for them to take part in it. Meanwhile the allies of the Lacedaemonians felt all more anxious than ever to see a speedy end to their heavy labours. But above all, the subjects of the Athenians showed a readiness to revolt even beyond their ability, judging the circumstances with passion, and refusing even to hear of the Athenians being able to last out the coming summer. Beyond all this, Lacedaemon was encouraged by the near prospect of being joined in great force in the spring by her allies in Sicily, lately forced by events to acquire their navy. With these reasons for confidence in every quarter, the Lacedaemonians now resolved to throw themselves without reserve into the war, considering that, once it was happily terminated, they would be finally delivered from such dangers as that which would have threatened them from Athens, if she had become mistress of Sicily, and that the overthrow of the Athenians would leave them in quiet enjoyment of the supremacy over all Hellas.

Their king, Agis, accordingly set out at once during this winter with some troops from Decelea, and levied from the allies contributions for the fleet, and turning towards the Malian Gulf exacted a sum of money from the Oetaeans by carrying off most of their cattle in reprisal for their old hostility, and, in spite of the protests and opposition of the Thessalians, forced the Achaeans of Phthiotis and the other subjects of the Thessalians in those parts to give him money and hostages, and deposited the hostages at

Corinth, and tried to bring their countrymen into the confederacy. The Lacedaemonians now issued a requisition to the cities for building a hundred ships, fixing their own quota and that of the Boeotians at twenty-five each; that of the Phocians and Locrians together at fifteen; that of the Corinthians at fifteen; that of the Arcadians, Pellenians, and Sicyonians together at ten; and that of the Megarians, Troezenians, Epidaurians, and Hermionians together at ten also; and meanwhile made every other preparation for commencing hostilities by the spring.

In the meantime the Athenians were not idle. During this same winter, as they had determined, they contributed timber and pushed on their ship-building, and fortified Sunium to enable their corn-ships to round it in safety, and evacuated the fort in Laconia which they had built on their way to Sicily; while they also, for economy, cut down any other expenses that seemed unnecessary, and above all kept a careful look-out against the revolt of their confederates.

While both parties were thus engaged, and were as intent upon preparing for the war as they had been at the outset, the Euboeans first of all sent envoys during this winter to Agis to treat of their revolting from Athens. Agis accepted their proposals, and sent for Alcamenes, son of Sthenelaidas, and Melanthus from Lacedaemon, to take the command in Euboea. These accordingly arrived with some three hundred Neodamodes, and Agis began to arrange for their crossing over. But in the meanwhile arrived some Lesbians, who also wished to revolt; and these being supported by the Boeotians, Agis was persuaded to defer acting in the matter of Euboea, and made arrangements for the revolt of the Lesbians, giving them Alcamenes, who was to have sailed to Euboea, as governor, and himself promising them ten ships, and the Boeotians the same number. All this was done without instructions from home, as Agis while at Decelea with the army that he commanded had power to send troops to whatever quarter he pleased, and to levy men and money. During this period, one might say, the allies obeyed him much more than they did the

Lacedaemonians in the city, as the force he had with him made him feared at once wherever he went. While Agis was engaged with the Lesbians, the Chians and Erythraeans, who were also ready to revolt, applied, not to him but at Lacedaemon; where they arrived accompanied by an ambassador from Tissaphernes, the commander of King Darius, son of Artaxerxes, in the maritime districts, who invited the Peloponnesians to come over, and promised to maintain their army. The King had lately called upon him for the tribute from his government, for which he was in arrears, being unable to raise it from the Hellenic towns by reason of the Athenians; and he therefore calculated that by weakening the Athenians he should get the tribute better paid, and should also draw the Lacedaemonians into alliance with the King; and by this means, as the King had commanded him, take alive or dead Amorges, the bastard son of Pissuthnes, who was in rebellion on the coast of Caria.

While the Chians and Tissaphernes thus joined to effect the same object, about the same time Calligeitus, son of Laophon, a Megarian, and Timagoras, son of Athenagoras, a Cyzicene, both of them exiles from their country and living at the court of Pharnabazus, son of Pharnaces, arrived at Lacedaemon upon a mission from Pharnabazus, to procure a fleet for the Hellespont; by means of which, if possible, he might himself effect the object of Tissaphernes' ambition and cause the cities in his government to revolt from the Athenians, and so get the tribute, and by his own agency obtain for the King the alliance of the Lacedaemonians.

The emissaries of Pharnabazus and Tissaphernes treating apart, a keen competition now ensued at Lacedaemon as to whether a fleet and army should be sent first to Ionia and Chios, or to the Hellespont. The Lacedaemonians, however, decidedly favoured the Chians and Tissaphernes, who were seconded by Alcibiades, the family friend of Endius, one of the ephors for that year. Indeed, this is how their house got its Laconic name, Alcibiades being the family name of Endius. Nevertheless the Lacedaemonians first sent to Chios Phrynis, one of the Perioeci, to see whether they had as many ships as they said, and whether their city generally was as great as was reported; and upon his bringing word that they had been told the truth, immediately entered into alliance with the Chians and Erythraeans, and voted to send them forty ships, there being already, according to the statement of the Chians, not less than sixty in the island. At first the Lacedaemonians meant to send ten of these forty themselves, with Melanchridas their admiral; but afterwards, an earthquake having occurred, they sent Chalcideus instead of Melanchridas, and instead of the ten ships equipped only five in Laconia. And the winter ended, and with it ended also the nineteenth year of this war of which Thucydides is the historian.

At the beginning of the next summer the Chians were urging that the fleet should be sent off, being afraid that the Athenians, from whom all these embassies were kept a secret, might find out what was going on, and the Lacedaemonians at once sent three Spartans to Corinth to haul the ships as quickly as possible across the Isthmus from the other sea to that on the side of Athens, and to order them all to sail to Chios, those which Agis was equipping for Lesbos not excepted. The number of ships from the allied states was thirty-nine in all.

Meanwhile Calligeitus and Timagoras did not join on behalf of Pharnabazus in the expedition to Chios or give the money - twenty-five talents - which they had brought with them to help in dispatching a force, but determined to sail afterwards with another force by themselves. Agis, on the other hand, seeing the Lacedaemonians bent upon going to Chios first, himself came in to their views; and the allies assembled at Corinth and held a council, in which they decided to sail first to Chios under the command of Chalcideus, who was equipping the five vessels in Laconia, then to Lesbos, under the command of Alcamenes, the same whom Agis had fixed upon, and lastly to go to the Hellespont, where the command was given to Clearchus, son of Ramphias. Meanwhile they would take only half the ships across the Isthmus first, and let those sail off at once, in order that the Athenians might attend less to the departing squadron than to those to be taken across afterwards, as no care had been taken to keep this voyage secret through contempt of the impotence of the Athenians, who had as yet no fleet of any account upon the sea. Agreeably to this determination, twenty-one vessels were at once conveyed across the Isthmus.

They were now impatient to set sail, but the Corinthians were not willing to accompany them until they had celebrated the Isthmian festival, which fell at that time. Upon this Agis proposed to them to save their scruples about breaking the Isthmian truce by taking the expedition upon himself. The Corinthians not consenting to this, a delay ensued, during which the Athenians conceived suspicions of what was preparing at Chios, and sent Aristocrates, one of their generals, and charged them with the fact, and, upon the denial of the Chians, ordered them to send with them a contingent of ships, as faithful confederates. Seven were sent accordingly. The reason of the dispatch of the ships lay in the fact that the mass of the Chians were not privy to the negotiations, while the few who were in the secret did not wish to break with the multitude until they had something positive to lean upon, and no longer expected the Peloponnesians to arrive by reason of their delay.

In the meantime the Isthmian games took place, and the Athenians, who had been also invited, went to attend them, and now seeing more clearly into the designs of the Chians, as soon as they returned to Athens took measures to prevent the fleet putting out from Cenchreae without their knowledge. After the festival the Peloponnesians set sail with twenty-one ships for Chios, under the command of Alcamenes. The Athenians first sailed against them with an equal number, drawing off towards the open sea. The enemy, however, turning back before he had followed them far, the Athenians returned also, not trusting the seven Chian ships

514

which formed part of their number, and afterwards manned thirty-seven vessels in all and chased him on his passage alongshore into Spiraeum, a desert Corinthian port on the edge of the Epidaurian frontier. After losing one ship out at sea, the Peloponnesians got the rest together and brought them to anchor. The Athenians now attacked not only from the sea with their fleet, but also disembarked upon the coast; and a melee ensued of the most confused and violent kind, in which the Athenians disabled most of the enemy's vessels and killed Alcamenes their commander, losing also a few of their own men.

After this they separated, and the Athenians, detaching a sufficient number of ships to blockade those of the enemy, anchored with the rest at the islet adjacent, upon which they proceeded to encamp, and sent to Athens for reinforcements; the Peloponnesians having been joined on the day after the battle by the Corinthians, who came to help the ships, and by the other inhabitants in the vicinity not long afterwards. These saw the difficulty of keeping guard in a desert place, and in their perplexity at first thought of burning the ships, but finally resolved to haul them up on shore and sit down and guard them with their land forces until a convenient opportunity for escaping should present itself. Agis also, on being informed of the disaster, sent them a Spartan of the name of Thermon. The Lacedaemonians first received the news of the fleet having put out from the Isthmus, Alcamenes having been ordered by the ephors to send off a horseman when this took place, and immediately resolved to dispatch their own five vessels under Chalcideus, and Alcibiades with him. But while they were full of this resolution came the second news of the fleet having taken refuge in Spiraeum; and disheartened at their first step in the Ionian war proving a failure, they laid aside the idea of sending the ships from their own country, and even wished to recall some that had already sailed.

Perceiving this, Alcibiades again persuaded Endius and the other ephors to persevere in the expedition, saying that the voyage would be made before the Chians heard of the fleet's misfortune, and that as soon as he set foot in Ionia, he should, by assuring them of the weakness of the Athenians and the zeal of Lacedaemon, have no difficulty in persuading the cities to revolt, as they would readily believe his testimony. He also represented to Endius himself in private that it would be glorious for him to be the means of making Ionia revolt and the King become the ally of Lacedaemon, instead of that honour being left to Agis (Agis, it must be remembered, was the enemy of Alcibiades); and Endius and his colleagues thus persuaded, he put to sea with the five ships and the Lacedaemonian Chalcideus, and made all haste upon the voyage.

About this time the sixteen Peloponnesian ships from Sicily, which had served through the war with Gylippus, were caught on their return off Leucadia and roughly handled by the twenty-seven Athenian vessels under Hippocles, son of Menippus, on the lookout for the ships from Sicily. After losing one of their number, the rest escaped from the Athenians and sailed into Corinth.

Meanwhile Chalcideus and Alcibiades seized all they met with on their voyage, to prevent news of their coming, and let them go at Corycus, the first point which they touched at in the continent. Here they were visited by some of their Chian correspondents and, being urged by them to sail up to the town without announcing their coming, arrived suddenly before Chios. The many were amazed and confounded, while the few had so arranged that the council should be sitting at the time; and after speeches from Chalcideus and Alcibiades stating that many more ships were sailing up, but saying nothing of the fleet being blockaded in Spiraeum, the Chians revolted from the Athenians, and the Erythraeans immediately afterwards. After this three vessels sailed over to Clazomenae, and made that city revolt also; and the Clazomenians immediately crossed over to the mainland and began to fortify Polichna, in order to retreat there, in case of necessity, from the island where they dwelt.

While the revolted places were all engaged in fortifying and preparing for the war, news of Chios speedily reached Athens. The Athenians thought the danger by which they were now menaced great and unmistakable, and that the rest of their allies would not consent to keep quiet after the secession of the greatest of their number. In the consternation of the moment they at once took off the penalty attaching to whoever proposed or put to the vote a proposal for using the thousand talents which they had jealously avoided touching throughout the whole war, and voted to employ them to man a large number of ships, and to send off at once under Strombichides, son of Diotimus, the eight vessels, forming part of the blockading fleet at Spiraeum, which had left the blockade and had returned after pursuing and failing to overtake the vessels with Chalcideus. These were to be followed shortly afterwards by twelve more under Thrasycles, also taken from the blockade. They also recalled the seven Chian vessels, forming part of their squadron blockading the fleet in Spiraeum, and giving the slaves on board their liberty, put the freemen in confinement, and speedily manned and sent out ten fresh ships to blockade the Peloponnesians in the place of all those that had departed, and decided to man thirty more. Zeal was not wanting, and no effort was spared to send relief to Chios.

In the meantime Strombichides with his eight ships arrived at Samos, and, taking one Samian vessel, sailed to Teos and required them to remain quiet. Chalcideus also set sail with twenty-three ships for Teos from Chios, the land forces of the Clazomenians and Erythraeans moving alongshore to support him. Informed of this in time, Strombichides put out from Teos before their arrival, and while out at sea, seeing the number of the ships from Chios, fled towards Samos, chased by the enemy. The Teians at first would not receive the land forces, but upon the flight of the Athenians took them into the town. There they waited for some time for Chalcideus to return from the pursuit, and as time went on without his appearing, began themselves to demolish the wall which the Athenians had built on the land side of the city of the Teians, being assisted by a few of the barbarians who had come up under the command of Stages, the lieutenant of Tissaphernes.

Meanwhile Chalcideus and Alcibiades, after chasing Strombichides into Samos, armed the crews of the ships from Peloponnese and left them at Chios, and filling their places with substitutes from Chios and manning twenty others, sailed off to effect the revolt of Miletus. The wish of Alcibiades, who had friends among the leading men of the Milesians, was to bring over the town before the arrival of the ships from Peloponnese, and thus, by causing the revolt of as many cities as possible with the help of the Chian power and of Chalcideus, to secure the honour for the Chians and himself and Chalcideus, and, as he had promised, for Endius who had sent them out. Not discovered until their voyage was nearly completed, they arrived a little before Strombichides and Thrasycles (who had just come with twelve ships from Athens, and had joined Strombichides in pursuing them), and occasioned the revolt of Miletus. The Athenians sailing up close on their heels with nineteen ships found Miletus closed against them, and took up their station at the adjacent island of Lade. The first alliance between the King and the Lacedaemonians was now concluded immediately upon the revolt of the Milesians, by Tissaphernes and Chalcideus, and was as follows:

The Lacedaemonians and their allies made a treaty with the King and Tissaphernes upon the terms following:

1. Whatever country or cities the King has, or the King's ancestors had, shall be the king's: and whatever came in to the Athenians from these cities, either money or any other thing, the King and the Lacedaemonians and their allies shall jointly hinder the Athenians from receiving either money or any other thing.

2. The war with the Athenians shall be carried on jointly by the King and by the Lacedaemonians and their allies: and it shall not be lawful to make peace with the Athenians except both agree, the King on his side and the Lacedaemonians and their allies on theirs.

3. If any revolt from the King, they shall be the enemies of the Lacedaemonians and their allies. And if any revolt from the Lacedaemonians and their allies, they shall be the enemies of the King in like manner.

This was the alliance. After this the Chians immediately manned ten more vessels and sailed for Anaia, in order to gain intelligence of those in Miletus, and also to make the cities revolt. A message, however, reaching them from Chalcideus to tell them to go back again, and that Amorges was at hand with an army by land, they sailed to the temple of Zeus, and there sighting ten more ships sailing up with which Diomedon had started from Athens after Thrasycles, fled, one ship to Ephesus, the rest to Teos. The Athenians took four of their ships empty, the men finding time to escape ashore; the rest took refuge in the city of the Teians; after which the Athenians sailed off to Samos, while the Chians put to sea with their remaining vessels, accompanied by the land forces, and caused Lebedos to revolt, and after it Erae. After this they both returned home, the fleet and the army.

About the same time the twenty ships of the Peloponnesians in Spiraeum, which we left chased to land and blockaded by an equal number of Athenians, suddenly sallied out and defeated the blockading squadron, took four of their ships, and, sailing back to Cenchreae, prepared again for the voyage to Chios and Ionia. Here they were joined by Astyochus as high admiral from Lacedaemon, henceforth invested with the supreme command at sea. The land forces now withdrawing from Teos, Tissaphernes repaired thither in person with an army and completed the demolition of anything that was left of the wall, and so departed. Not long after his departure Diomedon arrived with ten Athenian ships, and, having made a convention by which the Teians admitted him as they had the enemy, coasted along to Erae, and, failing in an attempt upon the town, sailed back again.

About this time took place the rising of the commons at Samos against the upper classes, in concert with some Athenians, who were there in three vessels. The Samian commons put to death some two hundred in all of the upper classes, and banished four hundred more, and themselves took their land and houses; after which the Athenians decreed their independence, being now sure of their fidelity, and the commons henceforth governed the city, excluding the landholders from all share in affairs, and forbidding any of the commons to give his daughter in marriage to them or to take a wife from them in future.

After this, during the same summer, the Chians, whose zeal continued as active as ever, and who even without the Peloponnesians found themselves in sufficient force to effect the revolt of the cities and also wished to have as many companions in peril as possible, made an expedition with thirteen ships of their own to Lesbos; the instructions from Lacedaemon being to go to that island next, and from thence to the Hellespont. Meanwhile the land forces of the Peloponnesians who were with the Chians and of the allies on the spot, moved alongshore for Clazomenae and Cuma, under the command of Eualas, a Spartan; while the fleet under Diniadas, one of the Perioeci, first sailed up to Methymna and caused it to revolt, and, leaving four ships there, with the rest procured the revolt of Mitylene.

In the meantime Astyochus, the Lacedaemonian admiral, set sail from Cenchreae with four ships, as he had intended, and arrived at Chios. On the third day after his arrival, the Athenian ships, twenty-five in number, sailed to Lesbos under Diomedon and Leon, who had lately arrived with a reinforcement of ten ships from Athens. Late in the same day Astyochus put to sea, and taking one Chian vessel with him sailed to Lesbos to render what assistance he could. Arrived at Pyrrha, and from thence the next day at Eresus, he there learned that Mitylene had been taken, almost without a blow, by the Athenians, who had sailed up and unexpectedly put into the harbour, had beaten the Chian ships, and landing and defeating the troops opposed to them had become masters of the city. Informed of this by the Eresians and the Chian ships, which had been left with Eubulus at Methymna, and had fled upon the capture of Mitylene, and three of which he now fell in with, one having been taken by the Athenians, Astyochus did not go on to Mitylene, but raised and armed Eresus, and, sending the heavy infantry from his own ships by land under Eteonicus to Antissa and Methymna, himself proceeded alongshore thither with the ships which he had with him and with the three Chians, in the hope that the Methymnians upon seeing them would be encouraged to persevere in their revolt. As, however, everything went against him in Lesbos, he took up his own force and sailed back to Chios; the land forces on board, which were to have gone to the Hellespont, being also conveyed back to their different cities. After this six of the allied Peloponnesian ships at Cenchreae joined the forces at Chios. The Athenians, after restoring matters to their old state in Lesbos, set sail from thence and took Polichna, the place that the Clazomenians were fortifying on the continent, and carried the inhabitants back to their town upon the island, except the authors of the revolt, who withdrew to Daphnus; and thus Clazomenae became once more Athenian.

The same summer the Athenians in the twenty ships at Lade, blockading Miletus, made a descent at Panormus in the Milesian territory, and killed Chalcideus the Lacedaemonian commander, who had come with a few men against them, and the third day after sailed over and set up a trophy, which, as they were not masters of the country, was however pulled down by the Milesians. Meanwhile Leon and Diomedon with the Athenian fleet from Lesbos issuing from the Oenussae, the isles off Chios, and from their forts of Sidussa and Pteleum in the Erythraeid, and from Lesbos, carried on the war against the Chians from the ships, having on board heavy infantry from the rolls pressed to serve as marines. Landing in Cardamyle and in Bolissus they defeated with heavy loss the Chians that took the field against them and, laying desolate the places in that neighbourhood, defeated the Chians again in another battle at Phanae, and in a third at Leuconium. After this the Chians ceased to meet them in the field, while the Athenians devastated the country, which was beautifully stocked and had remained uninjured ever since the Median wars. Indeed, after the Lacedaemonians, the Chians are the only people that I have known who knew how to be wise in prosperity, and who ordered their city the more securely the greater it grew. Nor was this revolt, in which they might seem to have erred on the side of rashness, ventured upon until they had numerous and gallant allies to share the danger with them, and until they perceived the Athenians after the Sicilian disaster themselves no longer denying the thoroughly desperate state of their affairs. And if they were thrown out by one of the surprises which upset human calculations, they found out their mistake in company with many others who believed, like them, in the speedy collapse of the Athenian power. While they were thus blockaded from the sea and plundered by land, some of the citizens undertook to bring the city over to the Athenians. Apprised of this the authorities took no action themselves, but brought Astyochus, the admiral, from Erythrae, with four ships that he had with him, and considered how they could most quietly, either by taking hostages or by some other means, put an end to the conspiracy.

While the Chians were thus engaged, a thousand Athenian heavy infantry and fifteen hundred Argives (five hundred of whom were light troops furnished with armour by the Athenians), and one thousand of the allies, towards the close of the same summer sailed from Athens in forty-eight ships, some of which were transports, under the command of Phrynichus, Onomacles, and Scironides, and putting into Samos crossed over and encamped at Miletus. Upon this the Milesians came out to the number of eight hundred heavy infantry, with the Peloponnesians who had come with Chalcideus, and some foreign mercenaries of Tissaphernes, Tissaphernes himself and his cavalry, and engaged the Athenians and their allies. While the Argives rushed forward on their own wing with the careless disdain of men advancing against Ionians who would never stand their charge, and were defeated by the Milesians with a loss little short of three hundred men, the Athenians first defeated the Peloponnesians, and driving before them the barbarians and the ruck of the army, without engaging the Milesians, who after the rout of the Argives retreated into the town upon seeing their comrades worsted, crowned their victory by grounding their arms under the very walls of Miletus. Thus, in this battle, the Ionians on both sides overcame the Dorians, the Athenians defeating the Peloponnesians opposed to them, and the Milesians the Argives. After setting up a trophy, the Athenians prepared to draw a wall round the place, which stood upon an isthmus; thinking that, if they could gain Miletus, the other towns also would easily come over to them.

Meanwhile about dusk tidings reached them that the fifty-five ships from Peloponnese and Sicily might be instantly expected. Of these the Siceliots, urged principally by the Syracusan Hermocrates to join in giving the finishing blow to the power of Athens, furnished twenty-two - twenty from Syracuse, and two from Silenus; and the ships that we left preparing in Peloponnese being now ready, both squadrons had been entrusted to Therimenes, a Lacedaemonian, to take to Astyochus, the admiral. They now put in first at Leros the island off Miletus, and from thence, discovering that the Athenians were before the town, sailed into the Iasic Gulf, in order to learn how matters stood at Miletus. Meanwhile Alcibiades came on horseback to Teichiussa in the Milesian territory, the point of the gulf at which they had put in for the night, and told them of the battle in which he had fought in person by the side of the Milesians and Tissaphernes, and advised them, if they did not wish to sacrifice Ionia and their cause, to fly to the relief of Miletus and hinder its investment.

Accordingly they resolved to relieve it the next morning. Meanwhile Phrynichus, the Athenian commander, had received precise intelligence of the fleet from Leros, and when his colleagues expressed a wish to keep the sea and fight it out, flatly refused either to stay himself or to let them or any one else do so if he could help it. Where they could hereafter contend, after full and undisturbed preparation, with an exact knowledge of the number of the enemy's fleet and of the force which they could oppose to him, he would never allow the reproach of disgrace to drive him into a risk that was unreasonable. It was no disgrace for an Athenian fleet to retreat when it suited them: put it as they would, it would be more disgraceful to be beaten, and to expose the city not only to disgrace, but to the most serious danger. After its late misfortunes it could hardly be justified in voluntarily taking the offensive even with the strongest force, except in a case of absolute necessity: much less then without compulsion could it rush upon peril of its own seeking. He told them to take up their wounded as quickly as they could and the troops and stores which they had brought with them, and leaving behind what they had taken from the enemy's country, in order to lighten the ships, to sail off to Samos, and there concentrating all their ships to attack as opportunity served. As he spoke so he acted; and thus not now more than afterwards, nor in this alone but in all that he had to do with, did Phrynichus show himself a man of sense. In this way that very evening the Athenians broke up from before Miletus, leaving their victory unfinished, and the Argives, mortified at their disaster, promptly sailed off home from Samos.

As soon as it was morning the Peloponnesians weighed from Teichiussa and put into Miletus after the departure of the Athenians; they stayed one day, and on the next took with them the Chian vessels originally chased into port with Chalcideus, and resolved to sail back for the tackle which they had put on shore at Teichiussa. Upon their arrival Tissaphernes came to them with his land forces and induced them to sail to Iasus, which was held by his enemy Amorges. Accordingly they suddenly attacked and took Iasus, whose inhabitants never imagined that the ships could be other than Athenian. The Syracusans distinguished themselves most in the action. Amorges, a bastard of Pissuthnes and a rebel from the King, was taken alive and handed over to Tissaphernes, to carry to the King, if he chose, according to his orders: Iasus was sacked by the army, who found a very great booty there, the place being wealthy from ancient date. The mercenaries serving with Amorges the Peloponnesians received and enrolled in their army without doing them any harm, since most of them came from Peloponnese, and handed over the town to Tissaphernes with all the captives, bond or free, at the stipulated price of one Doric stater a head; after which they returned to Miletus. Pedaritus, son of Leon, who had been sent by the Lacedaemonians to take the command at Chios, they dispatched by land as far as Erythrae with the mercenaries taken from Amorges; appointing Philip to remain as governor of Miletus.

Summer was now over. The winter following, Tissaphernes put Iasus in a state of defence, and passing on to Miletus distributed a month's pay to all the ships as he had promised at Lacedaemon, at the rate of an Attic drachma a day for each man. In future, however, he was resolved not to give more than three obols, until he had consulted the King; when if the King should so order he would give, he said, the full drachma. However, upon the protest of the Syracusan general Hermocrates (for as Therimenes was not admiral, but only accompanied them in order to hand over the ships to Astyochus, he made little difficulty about the pay), it was agreed that the amount of five ships' pay should be given over and above the three obols a day for each man; Tissaphernes paying thirty talents a month for fifty-five ships, and to the rest, for as many ships as they had beyond that number, at the same rate.

The same winter the Athenians in Samos, having been joined by thirty-five more vessels from home under Charminus, Strombichides, and Euctemon, called in their squadron at Chios and all the rest, intending to blockade Miletus with their navy, and to send a fleet and an army against Chios; drawing lots for the respective services. This intention they carried into effect; Strombichides, Onamacles, and Euctemon sailing against Chios, which fell to their lot, with thirty ships and a part of the thousand heavy infantry, who had been to Miletus, in transports; while the rest remained masters of the sea with seventy-four ships at Samos, and advanced upon Miletus.

Meanwhile Astyochus, whom we left at Chios collecting the hostages required in consequence of the conspiracy, stopped upon learning that the fleet with Therimenes had arrived, and that the affairs of the league were in a more flourishing condition, and putting out to sea with ten Peloponnesian and as many Chian vessels, after a futile attack upon Pteleum, coasted on to Clazomenae, and ordered the Athenian party to remove inland to Daphnus, and to join the Peloponnesians, an order in which also joined Tamos the king's lieutenant in Ionia. This order being disregarded, Astyochus made an attack upon the town, which was unwalled, and having failed to take it was himself carried off by a strong gale to Phocaea and Cuma, while the rest of the ships put in at the islands adjacent to Clazomenae - Marathussa, Pele, and Drymussa. Here they were detained eight days by the winds, and, plundering and consuming all the property of the Clazomenians there deposited, put the rest on shipboard and sailed off to Phocaea and Cuma to join Astyochus.

While he was there, envoys arrived from the Lesbians who wished to revolt again. With Astyochus they were successful; but the Corinthians and the other allies being averse to it by reason of their former failure, he weighed anchor and set sail for Chios, where they eventually arrived from different quarters, the fleet having been scattered by a storm. After this Pedaritus, whom we left marching along the coast from Miletus, arrived at Erythrae, and thence crossed over with his army to Chios, where he found also about five hundred soldiers who had been left there by Chalcideus from the five ships with their arms. Meanwhile some Lesbians making offers to revolt, Astyochus urged upon Pedaritus and the Chians that they ought to go with their ships and effect the revolt of Lesbos, and so increase the number of their allies, or, if not successful, at all events harm the Athenians. The Chians, however, turned a deaf ear to this, and Pedaritus flatly refused to give up to him the Chian vessels.

Upon this Astyochus took five Corinthian and one Megarian vessel, with another from Hermione, and the ships which had come with him from Laconia, and set sail for Miletus to assume his command as admiral; after telling the Chians with many threats that he would certainly not come and help them if they should be in need. At Corycus in the Erythraeid he brought to for the night; the Athenian armament sailing from Samos against Chios being only separated from him by a hill, upon the other side of which it brought to; so that neither perceived the other. But a letter arriving in the night from Pedaritus to say that some liberated Erythraean prisoners had come from Samos to betray Erythrae, Astyochus at once put back to Erythrae, and so just escaped falling in with the Athenians. Here Pedaritus sailed over to join him; and after inquiry into the pretended treachery, finding that the whole story had been made up to procure the escape of the men from Samos, they acquitted them of the charge, and sailed away, Pedaritus to Chios and Astyochus to Miletus as he had intended.

Meanwhile the Athenian armament sailing round Corycus fell in with three Chian men-of-war off Arginus, and gave immediate chase. A great storm coming on, the Chians with difficulty took refuge in the harbour; the three Athenian vessels most forward in the pursuit being wrecked and thrown up near the city of Chios, and the crews slain or taken prisoners. The rest of the Athenian fleet took refuge in the harbour called Phoenicus, under Mount Mimas, and from thence afterwards put into Lesbos and prepared for the work of fortification.

The same winter the Lacedaemonian Hippocrates sailed out from Peloponnese with ten Thurian ships under the command of Dorieus, son of Diagoras, and two colleagues, one Laconian and one Syracusan vessel, and arrived at Cnidus, which had already revolted at the instigation of Tissaphernes. When their arrival was known at Miletus, orders came to them to leave half their squadron to guard Cnidus, and with the rest to cruise round Triopium and seize all the merchantmen arriving from Egypt. Triopium is a promontory of Cnidus and sacred to Apollo. This coming to the knowledge of the Athenians, they sailed from Samos and captured the six ships on the watch at Triopium, the crews escaping out of them. After this the Athenians sailed into Cnidus and made an assault upon the town, which was unfortified, and all but took it; and the next day assaulted it again, but with less effect, as the inhabitants had improved their defences during the night, and had been reinforced by the crews escaped from the ships at Triopium. The Athenians now withdrew, and after plundering the Cnidian territory sailed back to Samos.

About the same time Astyochus came to the fleet at Miletus. The Peloponnesian camp was still plentifully supplied, being in receipt of sufficient pay, and the soldiers having still in hand the large booty taken at Iasus. The Milesians also showed great ardour for the war. Nevertheless the Peloponnesians thought the first convention with Tissaphernes, made with Chalcideus, defective, and more advantageous to him than to them, and consequently while Therimenes was still there concluded another, which was as follows:

The convention of the Lacedaemonians and the allies with King Darius and the sons of the King, and with Tissaphernes for a treaty and friendship, as follows:

1. Neither the Lacedaemonians nor the allies of the Lacedaemonians shall make war against or otherwise injure any country or cities that belong to King Darius or did belong to his father or to his ancestors; neither shall the Lacedaemonians nor the allies of the Lacedaemonians exact tribute from such cities. Neither shall King Darius nor any of the subjects of the King make war against or otherwise injure the Lacedaemonians or their allies.

2. If the Lacedaemonians or their allies should require any

assistance from the King, or the King from the Lacedaemonians or their allies, whatever they both agree upon they shall be right in doing.

3. Both shall carry on jointly the war against the Athenians and their allies: and if they make peace, both shall do so jointly.

4. The expense of all troops in the King's country, sent for by the King, shall be borne by the King.

5. If any of the states comprised in this convention with the King attack the King's country, the rest shall stop them and aid the King to the best of their power. And if any in the King's country or in the countries under the King's rule attack the country of the Lacedaemonians or their allies, the King shall stop it and help them to the best of his power.

After this convention Therimenes handed over the fleet to Astyochus, sailed off in a small boat, and was lost. The Athenian armament had now crossed over from Lesbos to Chios, and being master by sea and land began to fortify Delphinium, a place naturally strong on the land side, provided with more than one harbour, and also not far from the city of Chios. Meanwhile the Chians remained inactive. Already defeated in so many battles, they were now also at discord among themselves; the execution of the party of Tydeus, son of Ion, by Pedaritus upon the charge of Atticism, followed by the forcible imposition of an oligarchy upon the rest of the city, having made them suspicious of one another; and they therefore thought neither themselves not the mercenaries under Pedaritus a match for the enemy. They sent, however, to Miletus to beg Astyochus to assist them, which he refused to do, and was accordingly denounced at Lacedaemon by Pedaritus as a traitor. Such was the state of the Athenian affairs at Chios; while their fleet at Samos kept sailing out against the enemy in Miletus, until they found that he would not accept their challenge, and then retired again to Samos and remained quiet.

In the same winter the twenty-seven ships equipped by the Lacedaemonians for Pharnabazus through the agency of the

Megarian Calligeitus, and the Cyzicene Timagoras, put out from Peloponnese and sailed for Ionia about the time of the solstice, under the command of Antisthenes, a Spartan. With them the Lacedaemonians also sent eleven Spartans as advisers to Astyochus; Lichas, son of Arcesilaus, being among the number. Arrived at Miletus, their orders were to aid in generally superintending the good conduct of the war; to send off the above ships or a greater or less number to the Hellespont to Pharnabazus, if they thought proper, appointing Clearchus, son of Ramphias, who sailed with them, to the command; and further, if they thought proper, to make Antisthenes admiral, dismissing Astyochus, whom the letters of Pedaritus had caused to be regarded with suspicion. Sailing accordingly from Malea across the open sea, the squadron touched at Melos and there fell in with ten Athenian ships, three of which they took empty and burned. After this, being afraid that the Athenian vessels escaped from Melos might, as they in fact did, give information of their approach to the Athenians at Samos, they sailed to Crete, and having lengthened their voyage by way of precaution made land at Caunus in Asia, from whence considering themselves in safety they sent a message to the fleet at Miletus for a convoy along the coast.

Meanwhile the Chians and Pedaritus, undeterred by the backwardness of Astyochus, went on sending messengers pressing him to come with all the fleet to assist them against their besiegers, and not to leave the greatest of the allied states in Ionia to be shut up by sea and overrun and pillaged by land. There were more slaves at Chios than in any one other city except Lacedaemon, and being also by reason of their numbers punished more rigorously when they offended, most of them, when they saw the Athenian armament firmly established in the island with a fortified position, immediately deserted to the enemy, and through their knowledge of the country did the greatest mischief. The Chians therefore urged upon Astyochus that it was his duty to assist them, while there was still a hope and a possibility of stopping the enemy's progress, while Delphinium was still in process of fortification and unfinished, and before the completion of a higher rampart which was being added to protect the camp and fleet of their besiegers. Astyochus now saw that the allies also wished it and prepared to go, in spite of his intention to the contrary owing to the threat already referred to.

In the meantime news came from Caunus of the arrival of the twenty-seven ships with the Lacedaemonian commissioners; and Astyochus, postponing everything to the duty of convoying a fleet of that importance, in order to be more able to command the sea, and to the safe conduct of the Lacedaemonians sent as spies over his behaviour, at once gave up going to Chios and set sail for Caunus. As he coasted along he landed at the Meropid Cos and sacked the city, which was unfortified and had been lately laid in ruins by an earthquake, by far the greatest in living memory, and, as the inhabitants had fled to the mountains, overran the country and made booty of all it contained, letting go, however, the free men. From Cos arriving in the night at Cnidus he was constrained by the representations of the Cnidians not to disembark the sailors, but to sail as he was straight against the twenty Athenian vessels, which with Charminus, one of the commanders at Samos, were on the watch for the very twenty-seven ships from Peloponnese which Astyochus was himself sailing to join; the Athenians in Samos having heard from Melos of their approach, and Charminus being on the look-out off Syme, Chalce, Rhodes, and Lycia, as he now heard that they were at Caunus.

Astyochus accordingly sailed as he was to Syme, before he was heard of, in the hope of catching the enemy somewhere out at sea. Rain, however, and foggy weather encountered him, and caused his ships to straggle and get into disorder in the dark. In the morning his fleet had parted company and was most of it still straggling round the island, and the left wing only in sight of Charminus and the Athenians, who took it for the squadron which they were watching for from Caunus, and hastily put out against it with part only of their twenty vessels, and attacking immediately sank three ships and disabled others, and had the advantage in the action until the main body of the fleet unexpectedly hove in sight, when they were surrounded on every side. Upon this they took to flight, and after losing six ships with the rest escaped to Teutlussa or Beet Island, and from thence to Halicarnassus. After this the Peloponnesians put into Cnidus and, being joined by the twenty-seven ships from Caunus, sailed all together and set up a trophy in Syme, and then returned to anchor at Cnidus.

As soon as the Athenians knew of the sea-fight, they sailed with all the ships at Samos to Syme, and, without attacking or being attacked by the fleet at Cnidus, took the ships' tackle left at Syme, and touching at Lorymi on the mainland sailed back to Samos. Meanwhile the Peloponnesian ships, being now all at Cnidus, underwent such repairs as were needed; while the eleven Lacedaemonian commissioners conferred with Tissaphernes, who had come to meet them, upon the points which did not satisfy them in the past transactions, and upon the best and mutually most advantageous manner of conducting the war in future. The severest critic of the present proceedings was Lichas, who said that neither of the treaties could stand, neither that of Chalcideus, nor that of Therimenes; it being monstrous that the King should at this date pretend to the possession of all the country formerly ruled by himself or by his ancestors - a pretension which implicitly put back under the yoke all the islands - Thessaly, Locris, and everything as far as Boeotia - and made the Lacedaemonians give to the Hellenes instead of liberty a Median master. He therefore invited Tissaphernes to conclude another and a better treaty, as they certainly would not recognize those existing and did not want any of his pay upon such conditions. This offended Tissaphernes so much that he went away in a rage without settling anything.

CHAPTER XXV

*Twentieth and Twenty-first Years of the War - Intrigues of
Alcibiades - Withdrawal of the Persian Subsidies - Oligarchical
Coup d'Etat at Athens - Patriotism of the Army at Samos*

THE PELOPONNESIANS now determined to sail to Rhodes, upon the invitation of some of the principal men there, hoping to gain an island powerful by the number of its seamen and by its land forces, and also thinking that they would be able to maintain their fleet from their own confederacy, without having to ask for money from Tissaphernes. They accordingly at once set sail that same winter from Cnidus, and first put in with ninety-four ships at Camirus in the Rhodian country, to the great alarm of the mass of the inhabitants, who were not privy to the intrigue, and who consequently fled, especially as the town was unfortified. They were afterwards, however, assembled by the Lacedaemonians together with the inhabitants of the two other towns of Lindus and Ialysus; and the Rhodians were persuaded to revolt from the Athenians and the island went over to the Peloponnesians. Meanwhile the Athenians had received the alarm and set sail with the fleet from Samos to forestall them, and came within sight of the island, but being a little too late sailed off for the moment to Chalce, and from thence to Samos, and subsequently waged war against Rhodes, issuing from Chalce, Cos, and Samos.

The Peloponnesians now levied a contribution of thirty-two talents from the Rhodians, after which they hauled their ships ashore and for eighty days remained inactive. During this time, and even earlier, before they removed to Rhodes, the following intrigues took place. After the death of Chalcideus and the battle at Miletus, Alcibiades began to be suspected by the Peloponnesians; and Astyochus received from Lacedaemon an order from them to put him to death, he being the personal enemy of Agis, and in other respects thought unworthy of confidence. Alcibiades in his alarm first withdrew to Tissaphernes, and immediately began to do all he could with him to injure the Peloponnesian cause. Henceforth becoming his adviser in everything, he cut down the pay from an Attic drachma to three obols a day, and even this not paid too regularly; and told Tissaphernes to say to the Peloponnesians that the Athenians, whose maritime experience was of an older date than their own, only gave their men three obols, not so much from poverty as to prevent their seamen being corrupted by being too well off, and injuring their condition by spending money upon enervating indulgences, and also paid their crews irregularly in order to have a security against their deserting in the arrears which they would leave behind them. He also told Tissaphernes to bribe the captains and generals of the cities, and so to obtain their connivance - an expedient which succeeded with all except the Syracusans, Hermocrates alone opposing him on behalf of the whole confederacy. Meanwhile the cities asking for money Alcibiades sent off, by roundly telling them in the name of Tissaphernes that it was great impudence in the Chians, the richest people in Hellas, not content with being defended by a foreign force, to expect others to risk not only their lives but their money as well in behalf of their freedom; while the other cities, he said, had had to pay largely to Athens before their rebellion, and could not justly refuse to contribute as much or even more now for their own selves. He also pointed out that Tissaphernes was at present carrying on the war at his own charges, and had good cause for economy, but that as soon as he received remittances from the king he would give them their pay in full and do what was reasonable for the cities.

Alcibiades further advised Tissaphernes not to be in too great a hurry to end the war, or to let himself be persuaded to bring up the Phoenician fleet which he was equipping, or to provide pay for more Hellenes, and thus put the power by land and sea into the same hands; but to leave each of the contending parties in possession of one element, thus enabling the king when he found one troublesome to call in the other. For if the command of the sea and land were united in one hand, he would not know where to turn for help to overthrow the dominant power; unless he at last chose to stand up himself, and go through with the struggle at great expense and hazard. The cheapest plan was to let the Hellenes wear each other out, at a small share of the expense and without risk to himself. Besides, he would find the Athenians the most convenient partners in empire as they did not aim at conquests on shore, and carried on the war upon principles and with a practice most advantageous to the King; being prepared to combine to conquer the sea for Athens, and for the King all the Hellenes inhabiting his country, whom the Peloponnesians, on the contrary, had come to liberate. Now it was not likely that the Lacedaemonians would free the Hellenes from the Hellenic Athenians, without freeing them also from the barbarian Mede, unless overthrown by him in the meanwhile. Alcibiades therefore urged him to wear them both out at first, and, after docking the Athenian power as much as he could, forthwith to rid the country of the Peloponnesians. In the main Tissaphernes approved of this policy, so far at least as could be conjectured from his behaviour; since he now gave his confidence to Alcibiades in recognition of his good advice, and kept the Peloponnesians short of money, and would not let them fight at sea, but ruined their cause by pretending that the Phoenician fleet would arrive, and that they would thus be enabled to contend with the odds in their favour, and so made their navy lose its efficiency, which had been very remarkable, and generally betrayed a coolness in the war that was too plain to be mistaken.

Alcibiades gave this advice to Tissaphernes and the King, with whom he then was, not merely because he thought it really the best, but because he was studying means to effect his restoration to his country, well knowing that if he did not destroy it he might one day hope to persuade the Athenians to recall him, and thinking that his best chance of persuading them lay in letting them see that he possessed the favour of Tissaphernes. The event proved him to be right. When the Athenians at Samos found that he had influence with Tissaphernes, principally of their own motion (though partly also through Alcibiades himself sending word to their chief men to tell the best men in the army that, if there were only an oligarchy in the place of the rascally democracy that had banished him, he would be glad to return to his country and to make Tissaphernes their friend), the captains and chief men in the armament at once embraced the idea of subverting the democracy.

The design was first mooted in the camp, and afterwards from thence reached the city. Some persons crossed over from Samos and had an interview with Alcibiades, who immediately offered to make first Tissaphernes, and afterwards the King, their friend, if they would give up the democracy and make it possible for the King to trust them. The higher class, who also suffered most severely from the war, now conceived great hopes of getting the government into their own hands, and of triumphing over the enemy. Upon their return to Samos the emissaries formed their partisans into a club, and openly told the mass of the armament that the King would be their friend, and would provide them with money, if Alcibiades were restored and the democracy abolished. The multitude, if at first irritated by these intrigues, were nevertheless kept quiet by the advantageous prospect of the pay from the King; and the oligarchical conspirators, after making this communication to the people, now re-examined the proposals of Alcibiades among themselves, with most of their associates. Unlike the rest, who thought them advantageous and trustworthy, Phrynichus, who was still general, by no means approved of the proposals. Alcibiades, he rightly thought, cared no more for an oligarchy than for a democracy, and only sought to change the institutions of his country in order to get himself recalled by his associates; while for themselves their one object should be to avoid civil discord. It was not the King's interest, when the Peloponnesians were now their equals at sea, and in possession of some of the chief cities in his empire, to go out of his way to side with the Athenians whom he did not trust, when he might make friends of the Peloponnesians who had never injured him. And as for the allied states to whom oligarchy was now offered, because the democracy was to be put down at Athens, he well knew that this would not make the rebels come in any the sooner, or confirm the loyal in their allegiance; as the allies would never prefer servitude with an oligarchy or democracy to freedom with the constitution which they actually enjoyed, to whichever type it belonged. Besides, the cities thought that the so-called better classes would prove just as oppressive as the commons, as being those who originated, proposed, and for the most part benefited from the acts of the commons injurious to the confederates. Indeed, if it depended on the better classes, the confederates would be put to death without trial and with violence; while the commons were their refuge and the chastiser of these men. This he positively knew that the cities had learned by experience, and that such was their opinion. The propositions of Alcibiades, and the intrigues now in progress, could therefore never meet with his approval.

However, the members of the club assembled, agreeably to their original determination, accepted what was proposed, and prepared to send Pisander and others on an embassy to Athens to treat for the restoration of Alcibiades and the abolition of the democracy in the city, and thus to make Tissaphernes the friend of the Athenians.

Phrynichus now saw that there would be a proposal to restore Alcibiades, and that the Athenians would consent to it; and fearing after what he had said against it that Alcibiades, if restored, would revenge himself upon him for his opposition, had recourse to the following expedient. He sent a secret letter to the Lacedaemonian admiral Astyochus, who was still in the neighbourhood of Miletus, to tell him that Alcibiades was ruining their cause by making Tissaphernes the friend of the Athenians, and containing an express revelation of the rest of the intrigue, desiring to be excused if he sought to harm his enemy even at the expense of the interests of his country. However, Astyochus, instead of thinking of punishing Alcibiades, who, besides, no longer ventured within his reach as formerly, went up to him and Tissaphernes at Magnesia, communicated to them the letter from Samos, and turned informer, and, if report may be trusted, became the paid creature of Tissaphernes, undertaking to inform him as to this and all other matters; which was also the reason why he did not remonstrate more strongly against the pay not being given in full. Upon this Alcibiades instantly sent to the authorities at Samos a letter against Phrynichus, stating what he had done, and requiring that he should be put to death. Phrynichus distracted, and placed in the utmost peril by the denunciation, sent again to Astyochus, reproaching him with having so ill kept the secret of his previous letter, and saying that he was now prepared to give them an opportunity of destroying the whole Athenian armament at Samos; giving a detailed account of the means which he should employ, Samos being unfortified, and pleading that, being in danger of his life on their account, he could not now be blamed for doing this or anything else to escape being destroyed by his mortal enemies. This also Astyochus revealed to Alcibiades.

Meanwhile Phrynichus having had timely notice that he was playing him false, and that a letter on the subject was on the point of arriving from Alcibiades, himself anticipated the news, and told the army that the enemy, seeing that Samos was unfortified and the fleet not all stationed within the harbour, meant to attack the camp, that he could be certain of this intelligence, and that they must fortify Samos as quickly as possible, and generally look to their defences. It will be remembered that he was general, and had himself authority to carry out these measures. Accordingly they addressed themselves to the work of fortification, and Samos was thus fortified sooner than it would otherwise have been. Not long afterwards came the letter from Alcibiades, saying that the army was betrayed by Phrynichus, and the enemy about to attack it. Alcibiades, however, gained no credit, it being thought that he was in the secret of the enemy's designs, and had tried to fasten them upon Phrynichus, and to make out that he was their accomplice, out of hatred; and consequently far from hurting him he rather bore witness to what he had said by this intelligence.

After this Alcibiades set to work to persuade Tissaphernes to become the friend of the Athenians. Tissaphernes, although afraid of the Peloponnesians because they had more ships in Asia than the Athenians, was yet disposed to be persuaded if he could, especially after his quarrel with the Peloponnesians at Cnidus about the treaty of Therimenes. The quarrel had already taken place, as the Peloponnesians were by this time actually at Rhodes; and in it the original argument of Alcibiades touching the liberation of all the towns by the Lacedaemonians had been verified by the declaration of Lichas that it was impossible to submit to a convention which made the King master of all the states at any former time ruled by himself or by his fathers.

While Alcibiades was besieging the favour of Tissaphernes with an earnestness proportioned to the greatness of the issue, the Athenian envoys who had been dispatched from Samos with Pisander arrived at Athens, and made a speech before the people, giving a brief summary of their views, and particularly insisting that, if Alcibiades were recalled and the democratic constitution changed, they could have the King as their ally, and would be able to overcome the Peloponnesians. A number of speakers opposed them on the question of the democracy, the enemies of Alcibiades cried out against the scandal of a restoration to be effected by a violation of the constitution, and the Eumolpidae and Ceryces protested in behalf of the mysteries, the cause of his banishment, and called upon the gods to avert his recall; when Pisander, in the midst of much opposition and abuse, came forward, and taking each of his opponents aside asked him the following question: In the face of the fact that the Peloponnesians had as many ships as their own confronting them at sea, more cities in alliance with them, and the King and Tissaphernes to supply them with money, of which the Athenians had none left, had he any hope of saving the state, unless someone could induce the King to come over to their side? Upon their replying that they had not, he then plainly said to them: "This we cannot have unless we have a more moderate form of government, and put the offices into fewer hands, and so gain the King's confidence, and forthwith restore Alcibiades, who is the only man living that can bring this about. The safety of the state, not the form of its government, is for the moment the most pressing question, as we can always change afterwards whatever we do not like."

The people were at first highly irritated at the mention of an oligarchy, but upon understanding clearly from Pisander that this was the only resource left, they took counsel of their fears, and promised themselves some day to change the government again, and gave way. They accordingly voted that Pisander should sail with ten others and make the best arrangement that they could with Tissaphernes and Alcibiades. At the same time the people, upon a false accusation of Pisander, dismissed Phrynichus from his post together with his colleague Scironides, sending Diomedon and Leon to replace them in the command of the fleet. The accusation was that Phrynichus had betrayed Iasus and Amorges; and Pisander brought it because he thought him a man unfit for the business now in hand with Alcibiades. Pisander also went the round of all the clubs already existing in the city for help in lawsuits and elections, and urged them to draw together and to unite their efforts for the overthrow of the democracy; and after taking all other measures required by the circumstances, so that no time might be lost, set off with his ten companions on his voyage to Tissaphernes.

In the same winter Leon and Diomedon, who had by this time joined the fleet, made an attack upon Rhodes. The ships of the Peloponnesians they found hauled up on shore, and, after making a descent upon the coast and defeating the Rhodians who appeared in the field against them, withdrew to Chalce and made that place their base of operations instead of Cos, as they could better observe from thence if the Peloponnesian fleet put out to sea. Meanwhile Xenophantes, a Laconian, came to Rhodes from Pedaritus at Chios, with the news that the fortification of the Athenians was now finished, and that, unless the whole Peloponnesian fleet came to the rescue, the cause in Chios must be lost. Upon this they resolved to go to his relief. In the meantime Pedaritus, with the mercenaries that he had with him and the whole force of the Chians, made an assault upon the work round the Athenian ships and took a portion of it, and got possession of some vessels that were hauled up on shore, when the Athenians sallied out to the rescue, and first routing the Chians, next defeated the remainder of the force round Pedaritus, who was himself killed, with many of the Chians, a great number of arms being also taken.

After this the Chians were besieged even more straitly than before by land and sea, and the famine in the place was great. Meanwhile the Athenian envoys with Pisander arrived at the court of Tissaphernes, and conferred with him about the proposed agreement. However, Alcibiades, not being altogether sure of Tissaphernes (who feared the Peloponnesians more than the Athenians, and besides wished to wear out both parties, as Alcibiades himself had recommended), had recourse to the following stratagem to make the treaty between the Athenians and Tissaphernes miscarry by reason of the magnitude of his demands. In my opinion Tissaphernes desired this result, fear being his motive; while Alcibiades, who now saw that Tissaphernes was determined not to treat on any terms, wished the Athenians to think, not that he was unable to persuade Tissaphernes, but that after the latter had been persuaded and was willing to join them, they had not conceded enough to him. For the demands of Alcibiades, speaking for Tissaphernes, who was present, were so extravagant that the Athenians, although for a long while they agreed to whatever he asked, yet had to bear the blame of failure: he required the cession of the whole of Ionia, next of the islands adjacent, besides other concessions, and these passed without opposition; at last, in the third interview, Alcibiades, who now feared a complete discovery of his inability, required them to allow the King to build ships and sail along his own coast wherever and with as many as he pleased. Upon this the Athenians would yield no further, and concluding that there was nothing to be done, but that they had been deceived by Alcibiades, went away in a passion and proceeded to Samos.

Tissaphernes immediately after this, in the same winter, proceeded along shore to Caunus, desiring to bring the Peloponnesian fleet back to Miletus, and to supply them with pay, making a fresh convention upon such terms as he could get, in order not to bring matters to an absolute breach between them. He was afraid that if many of their ships were left without pay they would be compelled to engage and be defeated, or that their vessels being left without hands the Athenians would attain their objects without his assistance. Still more he feared that the Peloponnesians might ravage the continent in search of supplies. Having calculated and considered all this, agreeably to his plan of keeping the two sides equal, he now sent for the Peloponnesians and gave them pay, and concluded with them a third treaty in words following:

In the thirteenth year of the reign of Darius, while Alexippidas was ephor at Lacedaemon, a convention was concluded in the plain of the Maeander by the Lacedaemonians and their allies with Tissaphernes, Hieramenes, and the sons of Pharnaces, concerning the affairs of the King and of the Lacedaemonians and their allies.

1. The country of the King in Asia shall be the King's, and the King shall treat his own country as he pleases.

2. The Lacedaemonians and their allies shall not invade or injure the King's country: neither shall the King invade or injure that of the Lacedaemonians or of their allies. If any of the Lacedaemonians or of their allies invade or injure the King's country, the Lacedaemonians and their allies shall prevent it: and if any from the King's country invade or injure the country of the Lacedaemonians or of their allies, the King shall prevent it.

3. Tissaphernes shall provide pay for the ships now present, according to the agreement, until the arrival of the King's vessels: but after the arrival of the King's vessels the Lacedaemonians and their allies may pay their own ships if they wish it. If, however, they choose to receive the pay from Tissaphernes, Tissaphernes shall furnish it: and the Lacedaemonians and their allies shall repay him at the end of the war such moneys as they shall have received.

4. After the vessels have arrived, the ships of the Lacedaemonians and of their allies and those of the King shall carry on the war jointly, according as Tissaphernes and the Lacedaemonians and their allies shall think best. If they wish to make peace with the Athenians, they shall make peace also jointly.

This was the treaty. After this Tissaphernes prepared to bring up the Phoenician fleet according to agreement, and to make good his other promises, or at all events wished to make it appear that he was so preparing.

Winter was now drawing towards its close, when the Boeotians took Oropus by treachery, though held by an Athenian garrison. Their accomplices in this were some of the Eretrians and of the Oropians themselves, who were plotting the revolt of Euboea, as the place was exactly opposite Eretria, and while in Athenian hands was necessarily a source of great annoyance to Eretria and the rest of Euboea. Oropus being in their hands, the Eretrians now came to Rhodes to invite the Peloponnesians into Euboea. The latter, however, were rather bent on the relief of the distressed Chians, and accordingly put out to sea and sailed with all their ships from Rhodes. Off Triopium they sighted the Athenian fleet out at sea sailing from Chalce, and, neither attacking the other, arrived, the latter at Samos, the Peloponnesians at Miletus, seeing that it was no longer possible to relieve Chios without a battle. And this winter ended, and with it ended the twentieth year of this war of which Thucydides is the historian.

Early in the spring of the summer following, Dercyllidas, a

Spartan, was sent with a small force by land to the Hellespont to effect the revolt of Abydos, which is a Milesian colony; and the Chians, while Astyochus was at a loss how to help them, were compelled to fight at sea by the pressure of the siege. While Astyochus was still at Rhodes they had received from Miletus, as their commander after the death of Pedaritus, a Spartan named Leon, who had come out with Antisthenes, and twelve vessels which had been on guard at Miletus, five of which were Thurian, four Syracusans, one from Anaia, one Milesian, and one Leon's own. Accordingly the Chians marched out in mass and took up a strong position, while thirty-six of their ships put out and engaged thirty-two of the Athenians; and after a tough fight, in which the Chians and their allies had rather the best of it, as it was now late, retired to their city.

Immediately after this Dercyllidas arrived by land from Miletus; and Abydos in the Hellespont revolted to him and Pharnabazus, and Lampsacus two days later. Upon receipt of this news Strombichides hastily sailed from Chios with twenty-four Athenian ships, some transports carrying heavy infantry being of the number, and defeating the Lampsacenes who came out against him, took Lampsacus, which was unfortified, at the first assault, and making prize of the slaves and goods restored the freemen to their homes, and went on to Abydos. The inhabitants, however, refusing to capitulate, and his assaults failing to take the place, he sailed over to the coast opposite, and appointed Sestos, the town in the Chersonese held by the Medes at a former period in this history, as the centre for the defence of the whole Hellespont.

In the meantime the Chians commanded the sea more than before; and the Peloponnesians at Miletus and Astyochus, hearing of the sea-fight and of the departure of the squadron with Strombichides, took fresh courage. Coasting along with two vessels to Chios, Astyochus took the ships from that place, and now moved with the whole fleet upon Samos, from whence, however, he sailed back to Miletus, as the Athenians did not put out against him, owing to their suspicions of one another. For it was about this time, or even before, that the democracy was put down at Athens. When Pisander and the envoys returned from Tissaphernes to Samos they at once strengthened still further their interest in the army itself, and instigated the upper class in Samos to join them in establishing an oligarchy, the very form of government which a party of them had lately risen to avoid. At the same time the Athenians at Samos, after a consultation among themselves, determined to let Alcibiades alone, since he refused to join them, and besides was not the man for an oligarchy; and now that they were once embarked, to see for themselves how they could best prevent the ruin of their cause, and meanwhile to sustain the war, and to contribute without stint money and all else that might be required from their own private estates, as they would henceforth labour for themselves alone.

After encouraging each other in these resolutions, they now at once sent off half the envoys and Pisander to do what was necessary at Athens (with instructions to establish oligarchies on their way in all the subject cities which they might touch at), and dispatched the other half in different directions to the other dependencies. Diitrephes also, who was in the neighbourhood of Chios, and had been elected to the command of the Thracian towns, was sent off to his government, and arriving at Thasos abolished the democracy there. Two months, however, had not elapsed after his departure before the Thasians began to fortify their town, being already tired of an aristocracy with Athens, and in daily expectation of freedom from Lacedaemon. Indeed there was a party of them (whom the Athenians had banished), with the Peloponnesians, who with their friends in the town were already making every exertion to bring a squadron, and to effect the revolt of Thasos; and this party thus saw exactly what they most wanted done, that is to say, the reformation of the government without risk, and the abolition of the democracy which would have opposed them. Things at Thasos thus turned out just the contrary to what the oligarchical conspirators at Athens expected; and the same in my opinion was the case in many of the other dependencies; as the cities no sooner got a moderate government and liberty of action, than they went on to absolute freedom without being at all seduced by the show of reform offered by the Athenians.

Pisander and his colleagues on their voyage alongshore abolished, as had been determined, the democracies in the cities, and also took some heavy infantry from certain places as their allies, and so came to Athens. Here they found most of the work already done by their associates. Some of the younger men had banded together, and secretly assassinated one Androcles, the chief leader of the commons, and mainly responsible for the banishment of Alcibiades; Androcles being singled out both because he was a popular leader and because they sought by his death to recommend themselves to Alcibiades, who was, as they supposed, to be recalled, and to make Tissaphernes their friend. There were also some other obnoxious persons whom they secretly did away with in the same manner. Meanwhile their cry in public was that no pay should be given except to persons serving in the war, and that not more than five thousand should share in the government, and those such as were most able to serve the state in person and in purse.

But this was a mere catchword for the multitude, as the authors of the revolution were really to govern. However, the Assembly and the Council of the Bean still met notwithstanding, although they discussed nothing that was not approved of by the conspirators, who both supplied the speakers and reviewed in advance what they were to say. Fear, and the sight of the numbers of the conspirators, closed the mouths of the rest; or if any ventured to rise in opposition, he was presently put to death in some convenient way, and there was neither search for the murderers nor justice to be had against them if suspected; but the people remained motionless, being so thoroughly cowed that men thought themselves lucky to escape violence, even when they held their tongues. An exaggerated belief in the numbers of the conspirators also demoralized the people, rendered helpless by the magnitude of the city, and by their want of intelligence with each other, and being without means of finding out what those numbers really were. For the same reason it was impossible for any one to open his grief to a neighbour and to concert measures to defend himself, as he would have had to speak either to one whom he did not know, or whom he knew but did not trust. Indeed all the popular party approached each other with suspicion, each thinking his neighbour concerned in what was going on, the conspirators having in their ranks persons whom no one could ever have believed capable of joining an oligarchy; and these it was who made the many so suspicious, and so helped to procure impunity for the few, by confirming the commons in their mistrust of one another.

At this juncture arrived Pisander and his colleagues, who lost no time in doing the rest. First they assembled the people, and moved to elect ten commissioners with full powers to frame a constitution, and that when this was done they should on an appointed day lay before the people their opinion as to the best mode of governing the city. Afterwards, when the day arrived, the conspirators enclosed the assembly in Colonus, a temple of Poseidon, a little more than a mile outside the city; when the commissioners simply brought forward this single motion, that any Athenian might propose with impunity whatever measure he pleased, heavy penalties being imposed upon any who should indict for illegality, or otherwise molest him for so doing. The way thus cleared, it was now plainly declared that all tenure of office and receipt of pay under the existing institutions were at an end, and that five men must be elected as presidents, who should in their turn elect one hundred, and each of the hundred three apiece; and that this body thus made up to four hundred should enter the council chamber with full powers and govern as they judged best, and should convene the five thousand whenever they pleased.

The man who moved this resolution was Pisander, who

was throughout the chief ostensible agent in putting down the democracy. But he who concerted the whole affair, and prepared the way for the catastrophe, and who had given the greatest thought to the matter, was Antiphon, one of the best men of his day in Athens; who, with a head to contrive measures and a tongue to recommend them, did not willingly come forward in the assembly or upon any public scene, being ill looked upon by the multitude owing to his reputation for talent; and who yet was the one man best able to aid in the courts, or before the assembly, the suitors who required his opinion. Indeed, when he was afterwards himself tried for his life on the charge of having been concerned in setting up this very government, when the Four Hundred were overthrown and hardly dealt with by the commons, he made what would seem to be the best defence of any known up to my time. Phrynichus also went beyond all others in his zeal for the oligarchy. Afraid of Alcibiades, and assured that he was no stranger to his intrigues with Astyochus at Samos, he held that no oligarchy was ever likely to restore him, and once embarked in the enterprise, proved, where danger was to be faced, by far the staunchest of them all. Theramenes, son of Hagnon, was also one of the foremost of the subverters of the democracy - a man as able in council as in debate. Conducted by so many and by such sagacious heads, the enterprise, great as it was, not unnaturally went forward; although it was no light matter to deprive the Athenian people of its freedom, almost a hundred years after the deposition of the tyrants, when it had been not only not subject to any during the whole of that period, but accustomed during more than half of it to rule over subjects of its own.

The assembly ratified the proposed constitution, without a single opposing voice, and was then dissolved; after which the Four Hundred were brought into the council chamber in the following way. On account of the enemy at Decelea, all the Athenians were constantly on the wall or in the ranks at the various military posts. On that day the persons not in the secret were allowed to go home as usual, while orders were given to the accomplices of the conspirators to hang about, without making any demonstration, at some little distance from the posts, and in case of any opposition to what was being done, to seize the arms and put it down. There were also some Andrians and Tenians, three hundred Carystians, and some of the settlers in Aegina come with their own arms for this very purpose, who had received similar instructions. These dispositions completed, the Four Hundred went, each with a dagger concealed about his person, accompanied by one hundred and twenty Hellenic youths, whom they employed wherever violence was needed, and appeared before the Councillors of the Bean in the council chamber, and told them to take their pay and be gone; themselves bringing it for the whole of the residue of their term of office, and giving it to them as they went out.

Upon the Council withdrawing in this way without venturing any objection, and the rest of the citizens making no movement, the Four Hundred entered the council chamber, and for the present contented themselves with drawing lots for their Prytanes, and making their prayers and sacrifices to the gods upon entering office, but afterwards departed widely from the democratic system of government, and except that on account of Alcibiades they did not recall the exiles, ruled the city by force; putting to death some men, though not many, whom they thought it convenient to remove, and imprisoning and banishing others. They also sent to Agis, the Lacedaemonian king, at Decelea, to say that they desired to make peace, and that he might reasonably be more disposed to treat now that he had them to deal with instead of the inconstant commons.

Agis, however, did not believe in the tranquillity of the city, or that the commons would thus in a moment give up their ancient liberty, but thought that the sight of a large Lacedaemonian force would be sufficient to excite them if they were not already in commotion, of which he was by no means certain. He accordingly gave to the envoys of the Four Hundred an answer which held out no hopes of an accommodation, and sending for large reinforcements from Peloponnese, not long afterwards, with these and his garrison from Decelea, descended to the very walls of Athens; hoping either that civil disturbances might help to subdue them to his terms, or that, in the confusion to be expected within and without the city, they might even surrender without a blow being struck; at all events he thought he would succeed in seizing the Long Walls, bared of their defenders. However, the Athenians saw him come close up, without making the least disturbance within the city; and sending out their cavalry, and a number of their heavy infantry, light troops, and archers, shot down some of his soldiers who approached too near, and got possession of some arms and dead. Upon this Agis, at last convinced, led his army back again and, remaining with his own troops in the old position at Decelea, sent the reinforcement back home, after a few days' stay in Attica. After this the Four Hundred persevering sent another embassy to Agis, and now meeting with a better reception, at his suggestion dispatched envoys to Lacedaemon to negotiate a treaty, being desirous of making peace.

They also sent ten men to Samos to reassure the army, and to explain that the oligarchy was not established for the hurt of the city or the citizens, but for the salvation of the country at large; and that there were five thousand, not four hundred only, concerned; although, what with their expeditions and employments abroad, the Athenians had never yet assembled to discuss a question important enough to bring five thousand of them together. The emissaries were also told what to say upon all other points, and were so sent off immediately after the establishment of the new government, which feared, as it turned out justly, that the mass of seamen would not be willing to remain under the oligarchical constitution, and, the evil beginning there, might be the means of their overthrow.

Indeed at Samos the question of the oligarchy had already entered upon a new phase, the following events having taken place just at the time that the Four Hundred were conspiring. That part of the Samian population which has been mentioned as rising against the upper class, and as being the democratic party, had now turned round, and yielding to the solicitations of Pisander during his visit, and of the Athenians in the conspiracy at Samos, had bound themselves by oaths to the number of three hundred, and were about to fall upon the rest of their fellow citizens, whom they now in their turn regarded as the democratic party. Meanwhile they put to death one Hyperbolus, an Athenian, a pestilent fellow that had been ostracized, not from fear of his influence or position, but because he was a rascal and a disgrace to the city; being aided in this by Charminus, one of the generals, and by some of the Athenians with them, to whom they had sworn friendship, and with whom they perpetrated other acts of the kind, and now determined to attack the people. The latter got wind of what was coming, and told two of the generals, Leon and Diomedon, who, on account of the credit which they enjoyed with the commons, were unwilling supporters of the oligarchy; and also Thrasybulus and Thrasyllus, the former a captain of a galley, the latter serving with the heavy infantry, besides certain others who had ever been thought most opposed to the conspirators, entreating them not to look on and see them destroyed, and Samos, the sole remaining stay of their empire, lost to the Athenians. Upon hearing this, the persons whom they addressed now went round the soldiers one by one, and urged them to resist, especially the crew of the Paralus, which was made up entirely of Athenians and freemen, and had from time out of mind been enemies of oligarchy, even when there was no such thing existing; and Leon and Diomedon left behind some ships for their protection in case of their sailing away anywhere themselves. Accordingly, when the Three Hundred attacked the people, all these came to the rescue, and foremost of all the crew of the Paralus; and the Samian commons gained the victory, and putting to death some thirty of the Three Hundred, and banishing three others of the ringleaders, accorded an amnesty to the rest, and lived together under a democratic government for the future.

The ship Paralus, with Chaereas, son of Archestratus, on board, an Athenian who had taken an active part in the revolution, was now without loss of time sent off by the Samians and the army to Athens to report what had occurred; the fact that the Four Hundred were in power not being yet known. When they sailed into harbour the Four Hundred immediately arrested two or three of the Parali and, taking the vessel from the rest, shifted them into a troopship and set them to keep guard round Euboea. Chaereas, however, managed to secrete himself as soon as he saw how things stood, and returning to Samos, drew a picture to the soldiers of the horrors enacting at Athens, in which everything was exaggerated; saying that all were punished with stripes, that no one could say a word against the holders of power, that the soldiers' wives and children were outraged, and that it was intended to seize and shut up the relatives of all in the army at Samos who were not of the government's way of thinking, to be put to death in case of their disobedience; besides a host of other injurious inventions.

On hearing this the first thought of the army was to fall upon the chief authors of the oligarchy and upon all the rest concerned. Eventually, however, they desisted from this idea upon the men of moderate views opposing it and warning them against ruining their cause, with the enemy close at hand and ready for battle. After this, Thrasybulus, son of Lycus, and Thrasyllus, the chief leaders in the revolution, now wishing in the most public manner to change the government at Samos to a democracy, bound all the soldiers by the most tremendous oaths, and those of the oligarchical party more than any, to accept a democratic government, to be united, to prosecute actively the war with the Peloponnesians, and to be enemies of the Four Hundred, and to hold no communication with them. The same oath was also taken by all the Samians of full age; and the soldiers associated the Samians in all their affairs and in the fruits of their dangers, having the conviction that there was no way of escape for themselves or for them, but that the success of the Four Hundred or of the enemy at Miletus must be their ruin.

The struggle now was between the army trying to force a democracy upon the city, and the Four Hundred an oligarchy upon the camp. Meanwhile the soldiers forthwith held an assembly, in which they deposed the former generals and any of the captains whom they suspected, and chose new captains and generals to replace them, besides Thrasybulus and Thrasyllus, whom they had already. They also stood up and encouraged one another, and among other things urged that they ought not to lose heart because the city had revolted from them, as the party seceding was smaller and in every way poorer in resources than themselves. They had the whole fleet with which to compel the other cities in their empire to give them money just as if they had their base in the capital, having a city in Samos which, so far from wanting strength, had when at war been within an ace of depriving the Athenians of the command of the sea, while as far as the enemy was concerned they had the same base of operations as before. Indeed, with the fleet in their hands, they were better able to provide themselves with supplies than the government at home. It was their advanced position at Samos which had throughout enabled the home authorities to command the entrance into Piraeus; and if they refused to give them back the constitution, they would now find that the army was more in a position to exclude them from the sea than they were to exclude the army. Besides, the city was of little or no use towards enabling them to overcome the enemy; and they had lost nothing in losing those who had no longer either money to send them (the soldiers having to find this for themselves), or good counsel, which entitles cities to direct armies. On the contrary, even in this the home government had done wrong in abolishing the institutions of their ancestors, while the army maintained the said institutions, and would try to force the home government to do so likewise. So that even in point of good counsel the camp had as good counsellors as the city. Moreover, they had but to grant him security for his person and his recall, and Alcibiades would be only too glad to procure them the alliance of the King. And above all if they failed altogether, with the navy which they possessed, they had numbers of places to retire to in which they would find cities and lands.

Debating together and comforting themselves after this manner, they pushed on their war measures as actively as ever; and the ten envoys sent to Samos by the Four Hundred, learning how matters stood while they were still at Delos, stayed quiet there. About this time a cry arose a Peloponnesian fleet at Miletus that Astyochus and Tissaphernes were ruining their cause. Astyochus had not been willing to fight at sea - either before, while they were still in full vigour and the fleet of the Athenians small, or now, when the enemy was, as they were informed, in a state of sedition and his ships not yet united - but kept them waiting for the Phoenician fleet from Tissaphernes, which had only a nominal existence, at the risk of wasting away in inactivity. While Tissaphernes not only did not bring up the fleet in question, but was ruining their navy by payments made irregularly, and even then not made in full. They must therefore, they insisted, delay no longer, but fight a decisive naval engagement. The Syracusans were the most urgent of any. The confederates and Astyochus, aware of these murmurs, had already decided in council to fight a decisive battle; and when the news reached them of the disturbance at Samos, they put to sea with all their ships, one hundred and ten in number, and, ordering the Milesians to move by land upon Mycale, set sail thither. The Athenians with the eighty-two ships from Samos were at the moment lying at Glauce in Mycale, a point where Samos approaches near to the continent; and, seeing the Peloponnesian fleet sailing against them, retired into Samos, not thinking themselves numerically strong enough to stake their all upon a battle. Besides, they had notice from Miletus of the wish of the enemy to engage, and were expecting to be joined from the Hellespont by Strombichides, to whom a messenger had been already dispatched, with the ships that had gone from Chios to Abydos. The Athenians accordingly withdrew to Samos, and the

Peloponnesians put in at Mycale, and encamped with the land forces of the Milesians and the people of the neighbourhood. The next day they were about to sail against Samos, when tidings reached them of the arrival of Strombichides with the squadron from the Hellespont, upon which they immediately sailed back to Miletus. The Athenians, thus reinforced, now in their turn sailed against Miletus with a hundred and eight ships, wishing to fight a decisive battle, but, as no one put out to meet them, sailed back to Samos.

CHAPTER XXVI

Twenty-first Year of the War - Recall of Alcibiades to Samos -
Revolt of Euboea and Downfall of the Four Hundred -
Battle of Cynossema

I N THE same summer, immediately after this, the
Peloponnesians having refused to fight with their fleet
united, through not thinking themselves a match for the
enemy, and being at a loss where to look for money for such a
number of ships, especially as Tissaphernes proved so bad a
paymaster, sent off Clearchus, son of Ramphias, with forty
ships to Pharnabazus, agreeably to the original instructions from
Peloponnese; Pharnabazus inviting them and being prepared to
furnish pay, and Byzantium besides sending offers to revolt to
them. These Peloponnesian ships accordingly put out into the open
sea, in order to escape the observation of the Athenians, and being
overtaken by a storm, the majority with Clearchus got into Delos,
and afterwards returned to Miletus, whence Clearchus proceeded
by land to the Hellespont to take the command: ten, however,
of their number, under the Megarian Helixus, made good their
passage to the Hellespont, and effected the revolt of Byzantium.
After this, the commanders at Samos were informed of it, and sent
a squadron against them to guard the Hellespont; and an encounter
took place before Byzantium between eight vessels on either side.

Meanwhile the chiefs at Samos, and especially Thrasybulus,
who from the moment that he had changed the government
had remained firmly resolved to recall Alcibiades, at last in an
assembly brought over the mass of the soldiery, and upon their
voting for his recall and amnesty, sailed over to Tissaphernes and
brought Alcibiades to Samos, being convinced that their only
chance of salvation lay in his bringing over Tissaphernes from the
Peloponnesians to themselves. An assembly was then held in which
Alcibiades complained of and deplored his private misfortune in

having been banished, and speaking at great length upon public affairs, highly incited their hopes for the future, and extravagantly magnified his own influence with Tissaphernes. His object in this was to make the oligarchical government at Athens afraid of him, to hasten the dissolution of the clubs, to increase his credit with the army at Samos and heighten their own confidence, and lastly to prejudice the enemy as strongly as possible against Tissaphernes, and blast the hopes which they entertained. Alcibiades accordingly held out to the army such extravagant promises as the following: that Tissaphernes had solemnly assured him that if he could only trust the Athenians they should never want for supplies while he had anything left, no, not even if he should have to coin his own silver couch, and that he would bring the Phoenician fleet now at Aspendus to the Athenians instead of to the Peloponnesians; but that he could only trust the Athenians if Alcibiades were recalled to be his security for them.

Upon hearing this and much more besides, the Athenians at once elected him general together with the former ones, and put all their affairs into his hands. There was now not a man in the army who would have exchanged his present hopes of safety and vengeance upon the Four Hundred for any consideration whatever; and after what they had been told they were now inclined to disdain the enemy before them, and to sail at once for Piraeus. To the plan of sailing for Piraeus, leaving their more immediate enemies behind them, Alcibiades opposed the most positive refusal, in spite of the numbers that insisted upon it, saying that now that he had been elected general he would first sail to Tissaphernes and concert with him measures for carrying on the war. Accordingly, upon leaving this assembly, he immediately took his departure in order to have it thought that there was an entire confidence between them, and also wishing to increase his consideration with Tissaphernes, and to show that he had now been elected general and was in a position to do him good or evil as he chose; thus managing to frighten the Athenians with Tissaphernes and Tissaphernes with the Athenians.

Meanwhile the Peloponnesians at Miletus heard of the recall of Alcibiades and, already distrustful of Tissaphernes, now became far more disgusted with him than ever. Indeed after their refusal to go out and give battle to the Athenians when they appeared before Miletus, Tissaphernes had grown slacker than ever in his payments; and even before this, on account of Alcibiades, his unpopularity had been on the increase. Gathering together, just as before, the soldiers and some persons of consideration besides the soldiery began to reckon up how they had never yet received their pay in full; that what they did receive was small in quantity, and even that paid irregularly, and that unless they fought a decisive battle or removed to some station where they could get supplies, the ships' crews would desert; and that it was all the fault of Astyochus, who humoured Tissaphernes for his own private advantage.

The army was engaged in these reflections, when the following disturbance took place about the person of Astyochus. Most of the Syracusan and Thurian sailors were freemen, and these the freest crews in the armament were likewise the boldest in setting upon Astyochus and demanding their pay. The latter answered somewhat stiffly and threatened them, and when Dorieus spoke up

Socrates seeking Alcibiades in the house of Aspasia, Jean-Léon Gérôme, 1861

for his own sailors even went so far as to lift his baton against him; upon seeing which the mass of men, in sailor fashion, rushed in a fury to strike Astyochus. He, however, saw them in time and fled for refuge to an altar; and they were thus parted without his being struck. Meanwhile the fort built by Tissaphernes in Miletus was surprised and taken by the Milesians, and the garrison in it turned out - an act which met with the approval of the rest of the allies, and in particular of the Syracusans, but which found no favour with Lichas, who said moreover that the Milesians and the rest in the King's country ought to show a reasonable submission to Tissaphernes and to pay him court, until the war should be happily settled. The Milesians were angry with him for this and for other things of the kind, and upon his afterwards dying of sickness, would not allow him to be buried where the Lacedaemonians with the army desired.

The discontent of the army with Astyochus and Tissaphernes had reached this pitch, when Mindarus arrived from Lacedaemon to succeed Astyochus as admiral, and assumed the command. Astyochus now set sail for home; and Tissaphernes sent with him one of his confidants, Gaulites, a Carian, who spoke the two languages, to complain of the Milesians for the affair of the fort, and at the same time to defend himself against the Milesians, who were, as he was aware, on their way to Sparta chiefly to denounce his conduct, and had with them Hermocrates, who was to accuse Tissaphernes of joining with Alcibiades to ruin the Peloponnesian cause and of playing a double game. Indeed Hermocrates had always been at enmity with him about the pay not being restored in full; and eventually when he was banished from Syracuse, and new commanders - Potamis, Myscon, and Demarchus - had come out to Miletus to the ships of the Syracusans, Tissaphernes, pressed harder than ever upon him in his exile, and among other charges against him accused him of having once asked him for money, and then given himself out as his enemy because he failed to obtain it.

While Astyochus and the Milesians and Hermocrates made

sail for Lacedaemon, Alcibiades had now crossed back from Tissaphernes to Samos. After his return the envoys of the Four Hundred sent, as has been mentioned above, to pacify and explain matters to the forces at Samos, arrived from Delos; and an assembly was held in which they attempted to speak. The soldiers at first would not hear them, and cried out to put to death the subverters of the democracy, but at last, after some difficulty, calmed down and gave them a hearing. Upon this the envoys proceeded to inform them that the recent change had been made to save the city, and not to ruin it or to deliver it over to the enemy, for they had already had an opportunity of doing this when he invaded the country during their government; that all the Five Thousand would have their proper share in the government; and that their hearers' relatives had neither outrage, as Chaereas had slanderously reported, nor other ill treatment to complain of, but were all in undisturbed enjoyment of their property just as they had left them. Besides these they made a number of other statements which had no better success with their angry auditors; and amid a host of different opinions the one which found most favour was that of sailing to Piraeus. Now it was that Alcibiades for the first time did the state a service, and one of the most signal kind. For when the Athenians at Samos were bent upon sailing against their countrymen, in which case Ionia and the Hellespont would most certainly at once have passed into possession of the enemy, Alcibiades it was who prevented them. At that moment, when no other man would have been able to hold back the multitude, he put a stop to the intended expedition, and rebuked and turned aside the resentment felt, on personal grounds, against the envoys; he dismissed them with an answer from himself, to the effect that he did not object to the government of the Five Thousand, but insisted that the Four Hundred should be deposed and the Council of Five Hundred reinstated in power: meanwhile any retrenchments for economy, by which pay might be better found for the armament, met with his entire approval. Generally, he bade them hold out and show a bold face to the enemy, since if the city were saved there was good hope that the two parties might some day be reconciled, whereas if either were once destroyed, that at Samos, or that at Athens, there would no longer be any one to be reconciled to. Meanwhile arrived envoys from the Argives, with offers of support to the Athenian commons at Samos: these were thanked by Alcibiades, and dismissed with a request to come when called upon. The Argives were accompanied by the crew of the Paralus, whom we left placed in a troopship by the Four Hundred with orders to cruise round Euboea, and who being employed to carry to Lacedaemon some Athenian envoys sent by the Four Hundred - Laespodias, Aristophon, and Melesias - as they sailed by Argos laid hands upon the envoys, and delivering them over to the Argives as the chief subverters of the democracy, themselves, instead of returning to Athens, took the Argive envoys on board, and came to Samos in the galley which had been confided to them.

The same summer at the time that the return of Alcibiades coupled with the general conduct of Tissaphernes had carried to its height the discontent of the Peloponnesians, who no longer entertained any doubt of his having joined the Athenians, Tissaphernes wishing, it would seem, to clear himself to them of these charges, prepared to go after the Phoenician fleet to Aspendus, and invited Lichas to go with him; saying that he would appoint Tamos as his lieutenant to provide pay for the armament during his own absence. Accounts differ, and it is not easy to ascertain with what intention he went to Aspendus, and did not bring the fleet after all. That one hundred and forty-seven Phoenician ships came as far as Aspendus is certain; but why they did not come on has been variously accounted for. Some think that he went away in pursuance of his plan of wasting the Peloponnesian resources, since at any rate Tamos, his lieutenant, far from being any better, proved a worse paymaster than himself: others that he brought the Phoenicians to Aspendus to exact money from them for their discharge, having never intended to employ them: others again that it was in view of the outcry against him at

Lacedaemon, in order that it might be said that he was not in fault, but that the ships were really manned and that he had certainly gone to fetch them. To myself it seems only too evident that he did not bring up the fleet because he wished to wear out and paralyse the Hellenic forces, that is, to waste their strength by the time lost during his journey to Aspendus, and to keep them evenly balanced by not throwing his weight into either scale. Had he wished to finish the war, he could have done so, assuming of course that he made his appearance in a way which left no room for doubt; as by bringing up the fleet he would in all probability have given the victory to the Lacedaemonians, whose navy, even as it was, faced the Athenian more as an equal than as an inferior. But what convicts him most clearly, is the excuse which he put forward for not bringing the ships. He said that the number assembled was less than the King had ordered; but surely it would only have enhanced his credit if he spent little of the King's money and effected the same end at less cost. In any case, whatever was his intention, Tissaphernes went to Aspendus and saw the Phoenicians; and the Peloponnesians at his desire sent a Lacedaemonian called Philip with two galleys to fetch the fleet.

Alcibiades finding that Tissaphernes had gone to Aspendus, himself sailed thither with thirteen ships, promising to do a great and certain service to the Athenians at Samos, as he would either bring the Phoenician fleet to the Athenians, or at all events prevent its joining the Peloponnesians. In all probability he had long known that Tissaphernes never meant to bring the fleet at all, and wished to compromise him as much as possible in the eyes of the Peloponnesians through his apparent friendship for himself and the Athenians, and thus in a manner to oblige him to join their side.

While Alcibiades weighed anchor and sailed eastward straight for Phaselis and Caunus, the envoys sent by the Four Hundred to Samos arrived at Athens. Upon their delivering the message from Alcibiades, telling them to hold out and to show a firm front to the enemy, and saying that he had great hopes of reconciling them with the army and of overcoming the Peloponnesians, the majority of the members of the oligarchy, who were already discontented and only too much inclined to be quit of the business in any safe way that they could, were at once greatly strengthened in their resolve. These now banded together and strongly criticized the administration, their leaders being some of the principal generals and men in office under the oligarchy, such as Theramenes, son of Hagnon, Aristocrates, son of Scellias, and others; who, although among the most prominent members of the government (being afraid, as they said, of the army at Samos, and most especially of Alcibiades, and also lest the envoys whom they had sent to Lacedaemon might do the state some harm without the authority of the people), without insisting on objections to the excessive concentration of power in a few hands, yet urged that the Five Thousand must be shown to exist not merely in name but in reality, and the constitution placed upon a fairer basis. But this was merely their political cry; most of them being driven by private ambition into the line of conduct so surely fatal to oligarchies that arise out of democracies. For all at once pretend to be not only equals but each the chief and master of his fellows; while under a democracy a disappointed candidate accepts his defeat more easily, because he has not the humiliation of being beaten by his equals. But what most clearly encouraged the malcontents was the power of Alcibiades at Samos, and their own disbelief in the stability of the oligarchy; and it was now a race between them as to which should first become the leader of the commons.

Meanwhile the leaders and members of the Four Hundred most opposed to a democratic form of government - Phrynichus who had had the quarrel with Alcibiades during his command at Samos, Aristarchus the bitter and inveterate enemy of the commons, and Pisander and Antiphon and others of the chiefs who already as soon as they entered upon power, and again when the army at Samos seceded from them and declared for a democracy, had sent envoys from their own body to Lacedaemon and made every effort for peace, and had built the wall in Eetionia - now redoubled their exertions when their envoys returned from Samos, and they saw not only the people but their own most trusted associates turning against them. Alarmed at the state of things at Athens as at Samos, they now sent off in haste Antiphon and Phrynichus and ten others with injunctions to make peace with Lacedaemon upon any terms, no matter what, that should be at all tolerable. Meanwhile they pushed on more actively than ever with the wall in Eetionia. Now the meaning of this wall, according to Theramenes and his supporters, was not so much to keep out the army of Samos, in case of its trying to force its way into Piraeus, as to be able to let in, at pleasure, the fleet and army of the enemy. For Eetionia is a mole of Piraeus, close alongside of the entrance of the harbour, and was now fortified in connection with the wall already existing on the land side, so that a few men placed in it might be able to command the entrance; the old wall on the land side and the new one now being built within on the side of the sea, both ending in one of the two towers standing at the narrow mouth of the harbour. They also walled off the largest porch in Piraeus which was in immediate connection with this wall, and kept it in their own hands, compelling all to unload there the corn that came into the harbour, and what they had in stock, and to take it out from thence when they sold it.

These measures had long provoked the murmurs of Theramenes, and when the envoys returned from Lacedaemon without having effected any general pacification, he affirmed that this wall was like to prove the ruin of the state. At this moment forty-two ships from Peloponnese, including some Siceliot and Italiot vessels from Locri and Tarentum, had been invited over by the Euboeans and were already riding off Las in Laconia preparing for the voyage to Euboea, under the command of Agesandridas, son of Agesander, a Spartan. Theramenes now affirmed that this squadron was destined not so much to aid Euboea as the party fortifying Eetionia, and that unless precautions were speedily taken the city would be surprised and lost. This was no mere calumny, there being really some such plan entertained by the accused. Their first wish was to have the oligarchy without giving up the empire; failing this to keep their ships and walls and be independent; while, if this also were denied them, sooner than be the first victims of the restored democracy, they were resolved to call in the enemy and make peace, give up their walls and ships, and at all costs retain possession of the government, if their lives were only assured to them.

For this reason they pushed forward the construction of their work with posterns and entrances and means of introducing the enemy, being eager to have it finished in time. Meanwhile the murmurs against them were at first confined to a few persons and went on in secret, until Phrynichus, after his return from the embassy to Lacedaemon, was laid wait for and stabbed in full market by one of the Peripoli, falling down dead before he had gone far from the council chamber. The assassin escaped; but his accomplice, an Argive, was taken and put to the torture by the Four Hundred, without their being able to extract from him the name of his employer, or anything further than that he knew of many men who used to assemble at the house of the commander of the Peripoli and at other houses. Here the matter was allowed to drop. This so emboldened Theramenes and Aristocrates and the rest of their partisans in the Four Hundred and out of doors, that they now resolved to act. For by this time the ships had sailed round from Las, and anchoring at Epidaurus had overrun Aegina; and Theramenes asserted that, being bound for Euboea, they would never have sailed in to Aegina and come back to anchor at Epidaurus, unless they had been invited to come to aid in the designs of which he had always accused the government. Further inaction had therefore now become impossible. In the end, after a great many seditious harangues and suspicions, they set to work in real earnest. The heavy infantry in Piraeus building the wall in Eetionia, among whom was Aristocrates, a colonel, with his own tribe, laid hands upon Alexicles, a general under the oligarchy and the devoted adherent of the cabal, and took him into a house and confined him there. In this they were assisted by one Hermon, commander of the Peripoli in Munychia, and others, and above all had with them the great bulk of the heavy infantry. As soon as the news reached the Four Hundred, who happened to be sitting in the council chamber, all except the disaffected wished at once to go to the posts where the arms were, and menaced Theramenes and his party. Theramenes defended himself, and said that he was ready immediately to go and help to rescue Alexicles; and taking with him one of the generals belonging to his party, went down to Piraeus, followed by Aristarchus and some young men of the cavalry. All was now panic and confusion. Those in the city imagined that Piraeus was already taken and the prisoner put to death, while those in Piraeus expected every moment to be attacked by the party in the city. The older men, however, stopped the persons running up and down the town and making for the stands of arms; and Thucydides the Pharsalian, proxenus of the city, came forward and threw himself in the way of the rival factions, and appealed to them not to ruin the state, while the enemy was still at hand waiting for his opportunity, and so at length succeeded in quieting them and in keeping their hands off each other. Meanwhile Theramenes came down to Piraeus, being himself one of the generals, and raged and stormed against the heavy infantry, while Aristarchus and the adversaries of the people were angry in right earnest. Most of the heavy infantry, however, went on with the business without faltering, and asked Theramenes if he thought the wall had been constructed for any good purpose, and whether it would not be better that it should be pulled down. To this he answered that if they thought it best to pull it down, he for his part agreed with them. Upon this the heavy infantry and a number of the people in Piraeus immediately got up on the fortification and began to demolish it. Now their cry to the multitude was that all should join in the work who wished the Five Thousand to govern instead of the Four Hundred. For instead of saying in so many words "all who wished the commons to govern," they still disguised themselves under the name of the Five Thousand; being afraid that these might really exist, and that they might be speaking to one of their number and get into trouble through ignorance. Indeed this was why the Four Hundred neither wished the Five Thousand to exist, nor to have it known that they did not exist; being of opinion that to give themselves so many partners in empire would be downright democracy, while the mystery in question would make the people afraid of one another.

The next day the Four Hundred, although alarmed, nevertheless assembled in the council chamber, while the heavy infantry in Piraeus, after having released their prisoner Alexicles and pulled down the fortification, went with their arms to the theatre of Dionysus, close to Munychia, and there held an assembly in which they decided to march into the city, and setting forth accordingly halted in the Anaceum. Here they were joined by some delegates from the Four Hundred, who reasoned with them one by one, and persuaded those whom they saw to be the most moderate to remain quiet themselves, and to keep in the rest; saying that they would make known the Five Thousand, and have the Four Hundred chosen from them in rotation, as should be decided by the Five Thousand, and meanwhile entreated them not to ruin the state or drive it into the arms of the enemy. After a great many had spoken and had been spoken to, the whole body of heavy infantry became calmer than before, absorbed by their fears for the country at large, and now agreed to hold upon an appointed day an assembly in the theatre of Dionysus for the restoration of concord.

When the day came for the assembly in the theatre, and they were upon the point of assembling, news arrived that the forty-two ships under Agesandridas were sailing from Megara along the coast of Salamis. The people to a man now thought that it was just what Theramenes and his party had so often said, that the ships were sailing to the fortification, and concluded that they had done well to demolish it. But though it may possibly have been by appointment that Agesandridas hovered about Epidaurus and the neighbourhood, he would also naturally be kept there by the hope of an opportunity arising out of the troubles in the town. In any case the Athenians, on receipt of the news immediately ran down in mass to Piraeus, seeing themselves threatened by the enemy with a worse war than their war among themselves, not at a distance, but close to the harbour of Athens. Some went on board the ships already afloat, while others launched fresh vessels, or ran to defend the walls and the mouth of the harbour.

Meanwhile the Peloponnesian vessels sailed by, and rounding Sunium anchored between Thoricus and Prasiae, and afterwards arrived at Oropus. The Athenians, with revolution in the city, and unwilling to lose a moment in going to the relief of their most important possession (for Euboea was everything to them now that they were shut out from Attica), were compelled to put to sea in haste and with untrained crews, and sent Thymochares with some vessels to Eretria. These upon their arrival, with the ships already in Euboea, made up a total of thirty-six vessels, and were immediately forced to engage. For Agesandridas, after his crews had dined, put out from Oropus, which is about seven miles from Eretria by sea; and the Athenians, seeing him sailing up, immediately began to man their vessels. The sailors, however, instead of being by their ships, as they supposed, were gone away to purchase provisions for their dinner in the houses in the outskirts of the town; the Eretrians having so arranged that there should be nothing on sale in the marketplace, in order that the Athenians might be a long time in manning their ships, and, the enemy's attack taking them by surprise, might be compelled to put to sea just as they were. A signal also was raised in Eretria to give them notice in Oropus when to put to sea. The Athenians, forced to put out so poorly prepared, engaged off the harbour of Eretria, and after holding their own for some little while notwithstanding, were at length put to flight and chased to the shore. Such of their number as took refuge in Eretria, which they presumed to be friendly to them, found their fate in that city, being butchered by the inhabitants; while those who fled to the Athenian fort in the Eretrian territory, and the vessels which got to Chalcis, were saved. The Peloponnesians, after taking twenty-two Athenian ships, and killing or making prisoners of the crews, set up a trophy, and not long afterwards effected the revolt of the whole of Euboea (except Oreus, which was held by the Athenians themselves), and made a general settlement of the affairs of the island.

When the news of what had happened in Euboea reached Athens, a panic ensued such as they had never before known. Neither the disaster in Sicily, great as it seemed at the time, nor any other had ever so much alarmed them. The camp at Samos was in revolt; they had no more ships or men to man them; they were at discord among themselves and might at any moment come to blows; and a disaster of this magnitude coming on the top of all, by which they lost their fleet, and worst of all Euboea, which was of more value to them than Attica, could not occur without throwing them into the deepest despondency. Meanwhile their greatest and most immediate trouble was the possibility that the enemy, emboldened by his victory, might make straight for them and sail against Piraeus, which they had no longer ships to defend; and every moment they expected him to arrive. This, with a little more courage, he might easily have done, in which case he would either have increased the dissensions of the city by his presence, or, if he had stayed to besiege it, have compelled the fleet from Ionia, although the enemy of the oligarchy, to come to the rescue of their country and of their relatives, and in the meantime would have become master of the Hellespont, Ionia, the islands, and of everything as far as Euboea, or, to speak roundly, of the whole Athenian empire. But here, as on so many other occasions, the Lacedaemonians proved the most convenient people in the world for the Athenians to be at war with. The wide difference between the two characters, the slowness and want of energy of the Lacedaemonians as contrasted with the dash and enterprise of their opponents, proved of the greatest service, especially to a maritime empire like Athens. Indeed this was shown by the Syracusans, who were most like the Athenians in character, and also most successful in combating them.

Nevertheless, upon receipt of the news, the Athenians manned twenty ships and called immediately a first assembly in the Pnyx, where they had been used to meet formerly, and deposed the Four Hundred and voted to hand over the government to the Five Thousand, of which body all who furnished a suit of armour were to be members, decreeing also that no one should receive pay for the discharge of any office, or if he did should be held accursed. Many other assemblies were held afterwards, in which law-makers were elected and all other measures taken to form a constitution. It was during the first period of this constitution that the Athenians appear to have enjoyed the best government that they ever did, at least in my time. For the fusion of the high and the low was effected with judgment, and this was what first enabled the state to raise up her head after her manifold disasters. They also voted for the recall of Alcibiades and of other exiles, and sent to him and to the camp at Samos, and urged them to devote themselves vigorously to the war.

Upon this revolution taking place, the party of Pisander and Alexicles and the chiefs of the oligarchs immediately withdrew to Decelea, with the single exception of Aristarchus, one of the generals, who hastily took some of the most barbarian of the archers and marched to Oenoe. This was a fort of the Athenians upon the Boeotian border, at that moment besieged by the Corinthians, irritated by the loss of a party returning from Decelea, who had been cut off by the garrison. The Corinthians had volunteered for this service, and had called upon the Boeotians to assist them. After communicating with them, Aristarchus deceived the garrison in Oenoe by telling them that their countrymen in the city had compounded with the Lacedaemonians, and that one of the terms of the capitulation was that they must surrender the place to the Boeotians. The garrison believed him as he was general, and besides knew nothing of what had occurred owing to the siege, and so evacuated the fort under truce. In this way the Boeotians gained possession of Oenoe, and the oligarchy and the troubles at Athens ended.

To return to the Peloponnesians in Miletus. No pay was forthcoming from any of the agents deputed by Tissaphernes for that purpose upon his departure for Aspendus; neither the Phoenician fleet nor Tissaphernes showed any signs of appearing, and Philip, who had been sent with him, and another Spartan, Hippocrates, who was at Phaselis, wrote word to Mindarus, the admiral, that the ships were not coming at all, and that they were being grossly abused by Tissaphernes. Meanwhile Pharnabazus was inviting them to come, and making every effort to get the fleet and, like Tissaphernes, to cause the revolt of the cities in his government still subject to Athens, founding great hopes on his success; until at length, at about the period of the summer which we have now reached, Mindarus yielded to his importunities, and, with great order and at a moment's notice, in order to elude the enemy at Samos, weighed anchor with seventy-three ships from Miletus and set sail for the Hellespont. Thither sixteen vessels had already preceded him in the same summer, and had overrun part of the Chersonese. Being caught in a storm, Mindarus was compelled to run in to Icarus and, after being detained five or six days there by stress of weather, arrived at Chios.

Meanwhile Thrasyllus had heard of his having put out from Miletus, and immediately set sail with fifty-five ships from Samos, in haste to arrive before him in the Hellespont. But learning that he was at Chios, and expecting that he would stay there, he posted scouts in Lesbos and on the continent opposite to prevent the fleet moving without his knowing it, and himself coasted along to Methymna, and gave orders to prepare meal and other necessaries, in order to attack them from Lesbos in the event of their remaining for any length of time at Chios. Meanwhile he resolved to sail against Eresus, a town in Lesbos which had revolted, and, if he could, to take it. For some of the principal Methymnian exiles had carried over about fifty heavy infantry, their sworn associates, from Cuma, and hiring others from the continent, so as to make up three hundred in all, chose Anaxander, a Theban, to command them, on account of the community of blood existing between the Thebans and the Lesbians, and first attacked Methymna. Balked in this attempt by the advance of the Athenian guards from Mitylene, and repulsed a second time in a battle outside the city, they then crossed the mountain and effected the revolt of Eresus. Thrasyllus accordingly determined to go there with all his ships and to attack the place. Meanwhile Thrasybulus had preceded him thither with five ships from Samos, as soon as he heard that the exiles had crossed over, and coming too late to save Eresus, went on and anchored before the town. Here they were joined also by two vessels on their way home from the Hellespont, and by the ships of the Methymnians, making a grand total of sixty-seven vessels; and the forces on board now made ready with engines and every other means available to do their utmost to storm Eresus.

In the meantime Mindarus and the Peloponnesian fleet at Chios, after taking provisions for two days and receiving three Chian pieces of money for each man from the Chians, on the third day put out in haste from the island; in order to avoid falling in with the ships at Eresus, they did not make for the open sea, but keeping Lesbos on their left, sailed for the continent. After touching at the port of Carteria, in the Phocaeid, and dining, they went on along the Cumaean coast and supped at Arginusae, on the continent over against Mitylene. From thence they continued their voyage along the coast, although it was late in the night, and arriving at Harmatus on the continent opposite Methymna, dined there; and swiftly passing Lectum, Larisa, Hamaxitus, and the neighbouring towns, arrived a little before midnight at Rhoeteum. Here they were now in the Hellespont. Some of the ships also put in at Sigeum and at other places in the neighbourhood.

Meanwhile the warnings of the fire signals and the sudden increase in the number of fires on the enemy's shore informed the eighteen Athenian ships at Sestos of the approach of the Peloponnesian fleet. That very night they set sail in haste just as they were, and, hugging the shore of the Chersonese, coasted along to Elaeus, in order to sail out into the open sea away from the fleet of the enemy.

After passing unobserved the sixteen ships at Abydos, which had nevertheless been warned by their approaching friends to be on the alert to prevent their sailing out, at dawn they sighted the fleet of Mindarus, which immediately gave chase. All had not time to get away; the greater number however escaped to Imbros and Lemnos, while four of the hindmost were overtaken off Elaeus. One of these was stranded opposite to the temple of Protesilaus and taken with its crew, two others without their crews; the fourth was abandoned on the shore of Imbros and burned by the enemy.

After this the Peloponnesians were joined by the squadron from Abydos, which made up their fleet to a grand total of eighty-six vessels; they spent the day in unsuccessfully besieging Elaeus, and then sailed back to Abydos. Meanwhile the Athenians, deceived by their scouts, and never dreaming of the enemy's fleet getting by undetected, were tranquilly besieging Eresus. As soon as they heard the news they instantly abandoned Eresus, and made with all speed for the Hellespont, and after taking two of the Peloponnesian ships which had been carried out too far into the open sea in the ardour of the pursuit and now fell in their way, the next day dropped anchor at Elaeus, and, bringing back the ships that had taken refuge at Imbros, during five days prepared for the coming engagement.

After this they engaged in the following way. The Athenians formed in column and sailed close alongshore to Sestos; upon perceiving which the Peloponnesians put out from Abydos to meet them. Realizing that a battle was now imminent, both combatants extended their flank; the Athenians along the Chersonese from

Idacus to Arrhiani with seventy-six ships; the Peloponnesians from Abydos to Dardanus with eighty-six. The Peloponnesian right wing was occupied by the Syracusans, their left by Mindarus in person with the best sailers in the navy; the Athenian left by Thrasyllus, their right by Thrasybulus, the other commanders being in different parts of the fleet. The Peloponnesians hastened to engage first, and outflanking with their left the Athenian right sought to cut them off, if possible, from sailing out of the straits, and to drive their centre upon the shore, which was not far off. The Athenians perceiving their intention extended their own wing and outsailed them, while their left had by this time passed the point of Cynossema. This, however, obliged them to thin and weaken their centre, especially as they had fewer ships than the enemy, and as the coast round Point Cynossema formed a sharp angle which prevented their seeing what was going on on the other side of it.

The Peloponnesians now attacked their centre and drove ashore the ships of the Athenians, and disembarked to follow up their victory. No help could be given to the centre either by the squadron of Thrasybulus on the right, on account of the number of ships attacking him, or by that of Thrasyllus on the left, from whom the point of Cynossema hid what was going on, and who was also hindered by his Syracusan and other opponents, whose numbers were fully equal to his own. At length, however, the Peloponnesians in the confidence of victory began to scatter in pursuit of the ships of the enemy, and allowed a considerable part of their fleet to get into disorder. On seeing this the squadron of Thrasybulus discontinued their lateral movement and, facing about, attacked and routed the ships opposed to them, and next fell roughly upon the scattered vessels of the victorious Peloponnesian division, and put most of them to flight without a blow. The Syracusans also had by this time given way before the squadron of Thrasyllus, and now openly took to flight upon seeing the flight of their comrades.

The rout was now complete. Most of the Peloponnesians fled for refuge first to the river Midius, and afterwards to Abydos.

Only a few ships were taken by the Athenians; as owing to the narrowness of the Hellespont the enemy had not far to go to be in safety. Nevertheless nothing could have been more opportune for them than this victory. Up to this time they had feared the Peloponnesian fleet, owing to a number of petty losses and to the disaster in Sicily; but they now ceased to mistrust themselves or any longer to think their enemies good for anything at sea. Meanwhile they took from the enemy eight Chian vessels, five Corinthian, two Ambraciot, two Boeotian, one Leucadian, Lacedaemonian, Syracusan, and Pellenian, losing fifteen of their own. After setting up a trophy upon Point Cynossema, securing the wrecks, and restoring to the enemy his dead under truce, they sent off a galley to Athens with the news of their victory. The arrival of this vessel with its unhoped-for good news, after the recent disasters of Euboea, and in the revolution at Athens, gave fresh courage to the Athenians, and caused them to believe that if they put their shoulders to the wheel their cause might yet prevail.

On the fourth day after the sea-fight the Athenians in Sestos having hastily refitted their ships sailed against Cyzicus, which had revolted. Off Harpagium and Priapus they sighted at anchor the eight vessels from Byzantium, and, sailing up and routing the troops on shore, took the ships, and then went on and recovered the town of Cyzicus, which was unfortified, and levied money from the citizens. In the meantime the Peloponnesians sailed from Abydos to Elaeus, and recovered such of their captured galleys as were still uninjured, the rest having been burned by the Elaeusians, and sent Hippocrates and Epicles to Euboea to fetch the squadron from that island.

About the same time Alcibiades returned with his thirteen ships from Caunus and Phaselis to Samos, bringing word that he had prevented the Phoenician fleet from joining the Peloponnesians, and had made Tissaphernes more friendly to the Athenians than before. Alcibiades now manned nine more ships, and levied large sums of money from the Halicarnassians, and fortified Cos.

After doing this and placing a governor in Cos, he sailed back to Samos, autumn being now at hand. Meanwhile Tissaphernes, upon hearing that the Peloponnesian fleet had sailed from Miletus to the Hellespont, set off again back from Aspendus, and made all sail for Ionia. While the Peloponnesians were in the Hellespont, the Antandrians, a people of Aeolic extraction, conveyed by land across Mount Ida some heavy infantry from Abydos, and introduced them into the town; having been ill-treated by Arsaces, the Persian lieutenant of Tissaphernes. This same Arsaces had, upon pretence of a secret quarrel, invited the chief men of the Delians to undertake military service (these were Delians who had settled at Atramyttium after having been driven from their homes by the Athenians for the sake of purifying Delos); and after drawing them out from their town as his friends and allies, had laid wait for them at dinner, and surrounded them and caused them to be shot down by his soldiers. This deed made the Antandrians fear that he might some day do them some mischief; and as he also laid upon them burdens too heavy for them to bear, they expelled his garrison from their citadel.

Tissaphernes, upon hearing of this act of the Peloponnesians in addition to what had occurred at Miletus and Cnidus, where his garrisons had been also expelled, now saw that the breach between them was serious; and fearing further injury from them, and being also vexed to think that Pharnabazus should receive them, and in less time and at less cost perhaps succeed better against Athens than he had done, determined to rejoin them in the Hellespont, in order to complain of the events at Antandros and excuse himself as best he could in the matter of the Phoenician fleet and of the other charges against him. Accordingly he went first to Ephesus and offered sacrifice to Artemis…

[When the winter after this summer is over the twenty-first year of this war will be completed.]

THE END

The Perception
of People
and Events

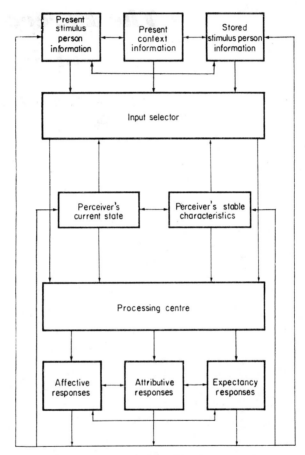

Schematic representation of person perception

The Perception of People and Events

PETER B. WARR

Department of Psychology, University of Sheffield, England

CHRISTOPHER KNAPPER

*Division of Social Sciences, University of Saskatchewan
Regina Campus*

John Wiley & Sons   London · New York · Sydney

/

Library of Congress catalog card No. 68–25509

SBN 471 92109 2

Printed in Great Britain by
ROBERT MACLEHOSE AND CO. LTD
The University Press, Glasgow

PREFACE

The impetus for *The Perception of People and Events* came in a rather unlikely way when we were challenged by some of our academic colleagues to offer our views on the accuracy of the British press. For years it has been a grumble of those people (among them psychologists) who are occasionally called upon to speak or debate in public that their all-important pronouncements have been grossly distorted at the hands of the local newspaper reporter. What light, we were asked, could social psychology shed upon this problem? To answer this and related questions we embarked in the autumn of 1963 upon a three-year research project with a grant from the Nuffield Foundation to study the "Accuracy of Communication to the Public".

Most studies of newspaper accuracy have been concerned with trivia such as the misspelling of names or discrepancies between estimates of crowd sizes. There have been some more valuable achievements, notably those investigating the role of editorial bias, but these have not yielded many generalizable conclusions. We started by working in this area — trying to delimit the factors operative as information becomes filtered and modified on its way onto the newspaper page.

We quickly saw, however, that it was not the content of a newspaper item so much as the reader's impression based upon that item that was of greatest importance. Two reports might appear to be different, yet convey effectively the same impression. Or one of two reports might generate an impression much more akin to that obtained by people present at the actual event, and as such it might be thought to be more accurate. It was this kind of notion which led us to abandon content analysis and to concentrate instead on measuring readers' impressions or perceptions.

The majority of news items concern people, and specifically people who are part of an event of some kind. So our interest in newspaper accuracy fused at that point with our interest in interpersonal judgment to give rise to the ideas and investigations described in this book. First of all we spent some time satisfying ourselves that we could validly and reliably measure personal impressions, and our efforts in this sphere culminated in Chapter 2. Confident of our measurement techniques we moved on to study the way different stimulus information yielded different perceptions of a person or event. Typically we examined news stories or photographs, but we were quickly led to stimulus material which could more readily be controlled. Finally our interest broadened considerably and we became engrossed in the whole area of person perception. We studied the way characteristics of the perceiver affect his judgments, how he processes the information available to him, how a general affective reaction colours his judgment. All this became part of a research programme around a model of person perception which could not have been foreseen when we started to look at newspaper accuracy.

But we believe that the programme is still very relevant to our original aim. This aim ensured that we kept before us the need for realistic stimulus material and experimental conditions, and it made very clear the fact that what we have come to call "indirect" perception was of tremendous importance. These two themes permeate several chapters of the book.

As the title indicates, our major focus is now on the way people and events are judged. We describe some forty empirical studies of our own. (The true number is somewhat less than forty, since we have occasionally found it most convenient to describe different portions of the same experiment in different chapters. This is always indicated in the text.) These studies range widely over the whole area of person perception, and in most cases derive from earlier work in this field. In consequence we have a fairly coherent pattern of research to describe.

But in describing this research we have become very conscious of the lack of a comprehensive textbook on person perception. Studies of the process are accumulating very rapidly, but at the time of writing there is available no book which reviews in detail the previous work and which tries to set this within a single framework. So this volume is much more than an original research report. It is also an attempt to bring together research data and conceptualizations from a variety of sources. In discussing each topic and our own approach to it we have provided a great deal of contextual information which otherwise could be obtained only after lengthy searches of the journals and the dissertation libraries.

We have thought of a modal reader who is not an expert in the field. Our goal is not only to communicate with those who already are *au fait* with the issues we raise. We want also to interest others so that they will move on to become experts themselves. This means that we have aimed our writing at an intelligent student of any branch of psychology, sociology or journalism. We have been careful to introduce terms which are commonplace to the social psychologist in a manner which keeps other specialists and even non-specialists abreast of the argument. The expert in person perception may sometimes feel the need to skip over a page quickly, but we hope that in doing so he will bear with us in our concern for the less knowledgeable.

In summary, this book is an account of many people's work on person perception as well as a presentation of our own peculiar approach to the subject. We have drawn upon ideas from experimental psychology, mass media research, philosophy and other disciplines in addition to our own speciality, social psychology. Our interest in psychometric considerations has resulted in a particularly comprehensive review of work on the semantic differential. This measuring instrument is at present extremely popular but no thorough account of its operational characteristics has been published since 1957. In Chapter 2 we have tried to fill this gap, and the discussion there will perhaps be of value to students of other types of judgment as well as to those concerned only with person perception.

A final happy task is to acknowledge our debt to all those people who contributed advice, criticism and even material assistance. Firstly our thanks to the Nuffield Foundation for providing financial support for the enterprise and for remaining unperturbed when our research took an unexpected turn. Our colleagues at the Psychology Department at Sheffield University were always on hand to offer their help: Professor Harry Kay initially sponsored the project and gave us his encouragement and support throughout, Dr. Godfrey Harrison was extremely patient in helping us develop computing procedures and most other members of the department assisted at one time or another. A number of people read parts of the manuscript and made valuable comments. Amongst these we should thank S. E. Asch, T. L. Coffman, H. M. Schroder, R. T. Talbot, H. C. Triandis and most of the Sheffield Psychology Department, not to mention anonymous publishers' reviewers. Still others helped by allowing us to cite their unpublished research results; we are particularly grateful to Dr. Jay Blumler whose work on political judgment is described in Chapter 2.

A major debt of gratitude is owed to the men of the media —

editors, subeditors, reporters and compositors — who by giving fully of their time provided us with a good deal of our stimulus material. The staffs of two newspapers even went as far as to provide us with editions containing material prepared and printed especially for our experimental use; this entailed considerable reorganization of press runs and often meant that staffs had to work late into the early morning after the normal editions had been "put to bed". Our sincere thanks to the *Sheffield Telegraph*'s editor Michael Finley, production editor Jack Westwood and chief photographer David Vaughan; also to Harry Myers, Peter Clowes and Jeff Brereton — editor, deputy editor and night editor of the northern *Daily Mail*. All those listed above — and many more who remain unnamed — helped us to modify our own judgments. If these are still not of the clearest we have only ourselves to blame.

CHRISTOPHER KNAPPER
PETER B. WARR

Regina, Saskatchewan and
Sheffield, England, November 1967

CONTENTS

Chapter 1   An Introduction to Person Perception . . 1

BASIC CHARACTERISTICS OF THE PROCESS . . . 5
The Attributive Component 7
The Expectancy Component 13
The Affective Component 15
A SCHEMATIC MODEL OF PERSON PERCEPTION . 16
DIRECT AND INDIRECT PERCEPTION 26
THE PERCEPTION OF PERSONS AND OBJECTS . . 31
TWO TRENDS IN PERSON PERCEPTION RESEARCH . 46
THE ORGANIZATION OF THIS BOOK 49

Chapter 2   The Problem of Measurement . . . 52

THE NATURE OF THE SEMANTIC DIFFERENTIAL . 56
CORRELATIONS BETWEEN SCALES 63
Experiment 1 70
THE RELIABILITY OF THE SEMANTIC DIFFERENTIAL . 74
Stability over Time 75
Experiment 2 78
Experiment 3 80
Internal Consistency 83
Between-forms Reliability 84
Experiment 4 86
THE VALIDITY OF THE SEMANTIC DIFFERENTIAL . 88
Face Validity 89
Intrinsic Validity 89
Predictive Validity 90
Content Validity 93
Concurrent Validity 95
Experiment 5 100
Experiment 6 105
Construct Validity 107

FACTORS AFFECTING THE USE OF SCALES . . . 109
   Number of Scale Units 109
   Experiment 7 109
   Experiment 8 111
   Order of Concepts 112
   Experiment 9 113
CONCLUDING REMARKS 114

Chapter 3   The Processing Centre 117

CORRELATIONS BETWEEN PERSONAL CHARACTERISTICS. 118
   Experiments 10 and 11 126
   Experiments 12 and 13 131
OTHER TECHNIQUES TO STUDY IMPLICIT PERSONALITY
   THEORIES 132
   Experiment 14 136
A LOGICAL MODEL OF TRAIT IMPLICATION . . . 140
THE PHENOMENA OF COJUDGMENT 146
FACTORS AFFECTING IMPLICIT PERSONALITY THEORIES 152
COMBINATION RULES 163
RECAPITULATION 172

Chapter 4   Individual Differences in Person Perception . 174

STORED INFORMATION ABOUT THE STIMULUS PERSON . 174
   Experiment 15 177
   Other Studies of Conceptual Expectancy 179
   Experiment 18 180
   Experiments 19 and 20 183
SEX DIFFERENCES 185
   Experiment 21 193
PERSONALITY DIFFERENCES 195
   Self-perceptions on the semantic differential 202
   Self-perceptions on the Adjective Check List 203
   A note on ethnocentrism 205
OTHER STABLE CHARACTERISTICS . . . . · 206
   Experiment 22 218
   Recapitulation 221

THE PERCEIVER'S CURRENT STATE 222
Experiment 23 225
Experiment 24 228
ATTRACTION AND JUDGMENTS OF OTHERS . . . 231
SUMMARY 238

Chapter 5   The Direct Perception of People . . . 241

JUDGMENTS WITHOUT INTERPERSONAL INTERACTION . 242
JUDGMENTS BASED UPON INTERACTION 245
RECAPITULATION 253

Chapter 6   The Communication Variable in Indirect
Perception 255

FORMING IMPRESSIONS FROM NEWSPAPER REPORTS . 258
Experiment 25 260
READING MORE THAN ONE REPORT...PRIMACY AND
    RECENCY EFFECTS 264
Previous Research on Order Effects 265
Experiments 26, 27, 28 269
Methods of Measuring Order Effects 270
Order Effects and the Difference Score Measure . . . 271
Order Effects and Multiple Correlation Analysis . . . 273
Experiment 29 278
Order Effects and Story Content: A General Discussion of
    Experiments 26 to 29 and their Implications 282

Chapter 7   Variations within a Communication . . 289

THE INFLUENCE OF HEADLINES UPON PERCEPTION . 289
Experiment 30 292
Experiment 31 294
PERSON PERCEPTION THROUGH PHOTOGRAPHS . . 296
Experiment 32 302

Experiment *33*   303
Experiment *34*   305
Experiment *35*   308
Experiment *36*   310
Concluding Remarks on the Effects of Visual Material   .   .   . 316
TYPOGRAPHY AND PAGE MAKEUP   319
Experiment *37*   320
NEWSPAPERS AS A COMMUNICATION SOURCE.   .   . 324
Experiment *38*   326
CONCLUDING REMARKS   328

Chapter 8   Constancy Phenomena in Person Perception . 330

THE NATURE OF CONSTANCY   330
SOME GENERALIZATIONS ABOUT CONSTANCY.   .   . 334
Experiment *39*   339
Experiment *40*   344
FURTHER COMMENTS ON CONSTANCY IN PERSON
PERCEPTION   346

Chapter 9   A Partial Integration   349

DIAGRAMMATIC REPRESENTATION OF PERSON
PERCEPTION   351
COMPONENTS OF THE INFORMATION PROCESSING
SYSTEM 353
Present Stimulus Person Information 353
Present Context Information   356
Stored Stimulus Person Information 357
The Input Selector 359
The Perceiver's Stable Characteristics and Current State   .   . 361
The Processing Centre   362
The Output Components 363
The System in Operation   365

The Simulation of Person Perception . . . 366
   The Input 369
   The Processing Centre and Output 372
   The Perceiver 375
   Conclusions 379
Thoughts on Future Research 387
References 390
Author Index 429
Subject Index 439

1
AN INTRODUCTION TO PERSON PERCEPTION

IF psychologists were able to define completely the terms central to their study, their work would be much duller than it is at present. At the moment they can generate tests of intelligence which have strikingly low intercorrelations yet need bow to no arbitration over which is the correct one. They can carry out studies of personality with measures that vary only slightly, but which lead to a puzzlingly wide range of results and interpretations. They can investigate learning in the operant conditioning laboratory without having to heed the findings about apparently the same process taking place in the classroom, the paired-associates laboratory, the neonatal clinic or the physiological research centre. In their inability to provide complete and accepted definitions of important concepts psychologists have shown a very clear ability to produce widely varying sets of ideas and techniques.

And yet at the present time this state of affairs is surely a happy one. It signifies our communal unwillingness to follow one investigator down a possibly blind alley of definition. If a single measure of, say, cognitive complexity received universal acclaim at this stage, we should become less aware of the danger that this may not be the best way to conceptualize cognitive processes and of the possibility that other measures may ultimately prove more valuable. In fact then, although there is undoubtedly scope to tighten up many of our definitions, overemphasis on definitional precision is a danger to be

1

avoided. It is better that we should allow comprehensive definitions to emerge slowly from investigations and analyses conducted on a broad front than that we should close the door to potentially more fertile concepts by premature specification.

So it is far from disconcerting that books on perception cannot open with a complete definition of this concept. The nature of perception has been pondered by psychologists and philosophers for centuries, and yet we are still without a formally accepted definition. The broad lines of specification have, of course, long been sketched in, but about the finer details there is still much uncertainty. It is clear that in some sense perception involves an interaction or transaction between an individual and his environment; he receives information from the external world which in some way modifies his experience and behaviour. But beyond statements of this order of generality there are few formulations which are universally accepted. Writers with different backgrounds and objectives tend to emphasize different aspects of the process, so that various approaches are reflected in varying definitions.

All this is to the good. And as it applies to perception in the wider sense so also does it apply to that aspect of the process which has become known as person perception. The definition of person perception is far from clear. There is general agreement that the term should denote something about our understanding and knowledge of other people, and that the process is somehow concerned with the way we use the information we receive about other people and groups. In fact it is only recently that the term itself has become widely accepted; interpersonal perception, social cognition and person cognition are all titles that have been assigned to the activity which is designated here as "person perception". The uncertainty about labels arises mainly from a feeling that we do not *perceive* people in the same way that objects are perceived, so that we should perhaps strive for an expression which is not analogous with "object perception". We do not share this feeling, and believe instead that the correspondence between person perception and object perception is a very close one. This point is considered in detail later in the chapter.

We shall consequently use person perception to refer to the processes involved in knowing the external and internal states of other people. The term "social perception" will be reserved for discussions of the influence of social factors on the way objects or persons are perceived. This usage is now becoming fairly orthodox (e.g. Brown, 1965;

Secord and Backman, 1964a; Tagiuri, 1968; Tagiuri and Petrullo, 1958). Person perception not only involves the judgments we make about people as objects (tall, bald, wearing brown shoes, etc.) but is primarily concerned with the impressions we form of people as people (impulsive, religious, tired, happy, anxious and so on). A distinction by Brunswik (e.g. 1956) is most helpful here. He draws attention to the fact that in perceiving we draw conclusions about "covert distal variables" as well as "overt distal variables". "Distal" variables are those located in the stimulus in contrast to the "proximal" variables which impinge directly upon our sense organs. And *overt* distal variables in person perception are those which are directly observable (size, hair, colour of shoes), whilst the class of *covert* distal variables includes personality characteristics, intentions, needs, habits, values and so on.

In practice this distinction between covert and overt variables is usually easy to apply. As with most dichotomies, however, there are occasional doubts about the label to be attached to a particular characteristic. To judge that Mr. Jones is a bank manager may be to make a judgment about a fairly overt characteristic (he may be sitting in an office bearing the sign "Manager" and deciding whether to grant you a loan); or this characteristic may be covert, one which is inferred from his discussion of economic problems at a cocktail party. Despite this type of classificatory problem, the terms <u>overt</u> and <u>covert</u> are useful ones which we shall adopt in subsequent discussions.

Studies of person perception need to deal with both types of distal variable, and indeed the stimulus characteristics which have in the past been investigated include a tremendous variety of both. But although the stimulus attributes presented to subjects have been typically both covert and overt ones, the perceptual judgments requested have usually been only about covert variables. Research has been predominantly concerned with judgments about the personality of a stimulus person, and investigations of judgments about overt distal variables are lacking (cf. Ittelson, 1960, Chapter 10; Ittelson and Slack, 1958).

This concentration upon judgments about covert variables means that many investigations might appear to concern *attitudes* rather than perceptions. Many of the judgments we make about other people and groups do indeed have complexity, consistency and content similar to those usually attributed to attitudinal structures. The line between perception and attitude is clearly a blurred one, and it is probably fruitless at present to attempt to distinguish them in a definitive manner. But three points of difference are clear. In the first place attitudes are generally taken to be relatively permanent structures which are in most instances fairly resistant to change. Perceptions, on the other hand, are more transitory and flexible. Secondly, attitudes may have as their objects more general or abstract entities than do perceptions. One may hold an attitude concerning, say, communism, or academic freedom, but one cannot be said to perceive these in anything other than a very loose sense. A third difference between attitude and perception is more fundamental: it is implicit in the (as yet incomplete) definition of perception that this only occurs *in the presence of a stimulus*. Yet the more permanent, generalized nature of an attitude allows it to persist when no stimulus is present.

There is clearly an interplay between attitude and perception. Perception is influenced by attitude; and change and development of attitude is dependent upon the way a source person and his message are perceived. Yet the two concepts are separate. We are in this book only infrequently concerned with attitudes. But we are often interested in judgments about someone when he is not present (your current impression of the British Prime Minister for instance). It may be that impressions without a stimulus being present are very similar to attitudes, but we can well avoid possible confusion by refraining from employing "attitude" in this sense. So we shall use as synonymous general terms "judgment" and "impression". Judgments may be made in the presence of a stimulus, or in his absence. To distinguish these two kinds of judgment we shall employ the ideas of "perception" and "conception". Judgments or impressions of a person when he is not serving as a stimulus will be referred to as conceptions and those judgments in his presence will be treated as perceptions. (The "presence" of a stimulus needs to be interpreted very broadly; we discuss this later.) There are obvious similarities between a conception and an attitude in that both extend over time; and the correspondence between a perception and a conception is also clear since both have the same object and a related content. It has long been stressed that perception and remembering are closely interwoven (cf. Bartlett, 1932), and the notion of conception serves to emphasize the importance of the perceiver's stored information and earlier reactions to a stimulus person.

In a summary then, we shall use "judgment" and "impression" as generic terms and shall distinguish between "perception" and "conception" according to whether or not a stimulus is at the time present.* This distinction works well in practice and generates a number of methodological implications which will be outlined later. Yet despite its semantic virtues it does leave us with one inconsistency: the expression "person perception" is customarily employed to embrace both perception and conception in the sense of "judgment of others". This expression is now in common usage and is rather more elegant than phrases involving "judgment"; we shall consequently employ it in its usual unspecific meaning to refer to an area of study. Otherwise the distinction between conception and perception will be adhered to.

Just as investigations of person perception clearly impinge upon studies of attitude and of remembering, so also is an understanding of this topic relevant to our knowledge of interpersonal relationships. The way individuals behave in relation to each other is clearly in part determined by the manner in which they perceive each other. And the way people *learn* to relate to others is presumably affected by their ability to learn to perceive them accurately (Hammond, Wilkins and Todd, 1966). The nature of the interaction between person perception and interpersonal behaviour is complex and as yet incompletely known (cf. Gage and Exline, 1953; Smith, Jaffe and Livingston, 1955; Steiner, 1955, 1959; Taft, 1955; Tagiuri, 1968), but the existence of some interaction is beyond question. It seems then that our knowledge of intragroup processes will expand as our knowledge of person perception expands.

A similar point may be made about behaviour *between* groups. That there are many similarities between judgments (conceptions *and* perceptions) of people and of groups of people has often been noted (cf. Asch, 1952, Chapter 8; Jahoda, 1966; Levy and Richter, 1963), and renewed interest has latterly been shown in the impressions which groups have of each other (cf. Form and Sauer, 1960; Schroder, Driver and Streufert, 1967; Sherif and coauthors, 1961; Tanaka, 1962). Students of person perception may thus hope to say something about intergroup relationships as well as about relationships within groups.

BASIC CHARACTERISTICS OF THE PROCESS

We opened this chapter by lamenting—rather cheerfully—the absence

* For stylistic and grammatical reasons variants like "perceptual judgment", 'perceptual response" and so on will from time to time be used.

of an agreed definition of perception and pointing out that person perception was similarly without a universally accepted specification. Yet if we are to study and to interpret the activities involved in forming impressions of others we must be able to point out at least the essentials of these processes. In this section we shall consider some views that have been put forward about the nature of person perception and attempt to integrate these into a usable framework.

Several writers have found it helpful to conceptualize the process of judging others in terms derived from orthodox information or communication theory. There is clearly a sense in which a stimulus person is a source from which information is transmitted to a receiver. The intervening communication channel may be seen to have certain specifiable characteristics, and various types of "noise" will exist which distort the signals being transmitted. Concepts of this kind found their way into psychology from mathematical and statistical models developed by communications engineers, and each concept has been endowed by these engineers with its own clear operational definition. The concepts themselves might fruitfully be applied to social relationships and judgments (cf. Bieri and coauthors, 1966; Osgood and Sebeok, 1965), but it is clear that many of the operational indices cannot be used in this very different context without considerable modification. Hence, although notions like "input", "output", "encoding" and "decoding" are useful in drawing attention to and in describing some facets of person perception, it is doubtful whether they can be treated as more than loose analogies with the concepts given these labels by students of communication systems.

But there is another reason for doubting that information theory language is completely sufficient for an understanding of person perception. In forming impressions of others we certainly process information received from them and their environment, but we do more than this. We respond by deriving expectancies about the other people and their relationships to us. And our responses also have a component with a strongly affective nature: attraction, anxiety, love, hate, happiness, despair can all be involved in person perception. It is not clear that these expectancy and affective components of judgment can be woven into the texture of information theory.

We believe then that the process of judging others (conceiving and perceiving them) is too complex to be subsumed under this theory, and shall rest content merely to use some of the very convenient analogies it supplies. Let us start with the output of a system of judging. As hinted in the last paragraph it is helpful to see this as having three different components. These may be termed the attributive, the expectancy and the affective components. They undoubtedly interact with each other in a complex fashion and may ultimately be resolved into a single idea. However, let us first consider each component separately.

The Attributive Component

An essential part of forming an impression of another person is to attribute to him certain characteristics. Indeed most studies of person perception have been restricted to this aspect of the process. The work reviewed throughout this book is in the main concerned with how perceivers attribute overt and covert characteristics to other people. Judgments might concern a stimulus person's size, shape, facial characteristics, clothes, what he says and does or what he eats and drinks. They are certain also to include inferences from these characteristics about what other attributes he possesses. We shall deal in some detail with examples of these inferences later; for the present we wish to take a careful look at the general nature of the attributive component.

In so far as we "know" another person we are able to say that he is careful, alert, intelligent, enthusiastic, irritable, capable of driving a bus, keen to become chairman of the company and so on. An information-processing system with outputs of this kind is one which is capable of ordering its inputs along dimensions or of placing them into categories. In some cases the input might in fact coincide with an output (thus a stimulus person *himself* might say "I am keen to become chairman of the company"), but on most occasions the input information will be very different from outputs of the kind suggested above. The incoming information has to be transposed and combined in several ways; we shall later consider the rules built into the system according to which the output is decided. For the present we simply point out that the attributive component of judgment involves classifying and comparing sets of inputs.

This aspect of judging objects and people has been stressed by a number of workers. Bruner and his colleagues (e.g., Bruner, 1957; Bruner, Goodnow and Austin, 1956) have based their theoretical position upon the notion that perception always involves an act of categorization. They have argued that what is perceived derives its meaning from the category in which it is placed and from the way this category is distinguished from other categories. This same idea — that judgment involves a selective placing in one category of identity rather than another — has also interested Sarbin, Taft and Bailey (1960). They prefer the term "instantiation" to "categorization", "classification" and so on; this is used to convey that an input is treated as an instance of a class.

In related work Bieri and colleagues (1966) examine in some detail the way perceivers discriminate between possible stimuli. They point out that each stimulus can be defined in terms of the number of dimensions on which it falls (alertness, intelligence, etc.) and in terms of its postion on each dimension (very alert, fairly alert, etc.). A similar analysis from a rather different standpoint is provided by Sherif and Hovland (1961), who emphasize that an attributive judgment always involves a comparison between two or more stimuli (e.g. "loud" is always in relation to other intensities, and "intelligent" is always a relative term). They suggest — and produce evidence to support the suggestion — that we are continually forming frames of reference which include dimensions relevant to each class of stimulus and within which judgments are made.

This conceptualization is particularly attractive in that parallels between the perception of objects and of social stimuli have been brought out. All these writers draw freely upon findings from studies of psychophysical judgments, and all see the possibility of construing a wide range of judgmental phenomena within a single context. Thus we might hope ultimately to interpret judgments of size and those about a patient's mental state in terms of the same set of principles. A start in this direction has also been made by Helson and his associates (e.g. Helson, 1948, 1959, 1964). It might prove possible to view the other two components of judgment — the expectancy and affective ones — in the same light, but progress here will not be easy.

Attributive judgments themselves may be fruitfully placed into one of two categories. In this book we shall refer to them as "episodic" judgments and "dispositional" judgments.* Episodic judgments are those made about someone's state during a particular sequence or episode of behaviour. We might judge that a person is bored, or that he is trying to persuade us to accept his viewpoint. These judgments are to do with a temporary state of the person. They are quite different

---

* The terms "episodic" and "dispositional" are drawn from the philosophical work by Ryle (1949).

from dispositional judgments, which are those about permanent characteristics and which are relatively independent of a particular episode. To attribute intelligence or arrogance, a certain height or a particular shape to someone is to make a dispositional judgment about him. We are saying that he has this characteristic without limiting the situations in which he is alleged to possess it.

Let us look further at these two forms of judgment. We can use Brunswik's idea of overt and covert variables to subdivide each of the categories suggested here. We have four kinds of judgment:

1 *Episodic Judgments*
   (*a*) judgments of overt fact
   (*b*) judgments of covert fact

2 *Dispositional Judgments*
   (*a*) judgments of overt characteristics
   (*b*) judgments of covert characteristics

Consider first episodic judgments of overt fact. This is the most simple type of attributive judgment — "he said 'good morning' ", "he is driving a bus", "he is smoking a cigarette", "he is smiling", "he is wearing brown shoes". Although inferences may be made on the basis of these judgments, they themselves are relatively straightforward replicates of the stimulus situation. They are episodic judgments in that they concern only specific episodes of behaviour. A judgment of overt fact may be described as a judgment that an observable occurrence is taking place or has taken place; this judgment is specific to a particular stimulus situation and is not concerned with covert variables. It comes close to being an output which has not been processed within the perceptual system so that the input is virtually unaltered. And yet a judgment of this kind is in fact a brief summary of a very varied set of inputs about a stimulus person and his environment — his sequence of bodily movements and activities. To perceive that someone is driving a bus is to achieve a very considerable economy: a large set of inputs has been discriminated and classified.

The second form of episodic judgment is one of covert fact. A judgment in this category also summarizes a set of inputs about a stimulus person and his environment at one point in time, but in this case the summary is in terms of his covert state. In this way, "he is enjoying driving the bus" is an episodic judgment of covert fact, since it concerns the covert state of the stimulus person during one episode of bus-driving. Other examples are "he is arguing intelligently", "he is being arrogant", "he is afraid", "he is pretending to be sympathetic to my point of view" and "he wants to get away before the pubs shut". These judgments are more complex than those of overt fact, and are more obviously derived by means of a process of inference. The way in which an input is processed to generate a judgment of covert fact is a topic to which we shall devote a lot of attention later.

To recapitulate, episodic judgments are judgments about a person's activities during a particular episode or occurrence, and they may be about overt or covert behaviour. In either case they represent a summary of input information. Turning now to dispositional judgments we can see that these are also summaries, but with much greater generality. They are judgments about characteristics, tendencies, capacities, liabilities and pronenesses which are independent of a particular episode. A dispositional judgment may summarize behaviour over a wide range of situations ("he is adaptable", "he is cheerful" and so on) or it may seem to concern specific segments of behaviour ("he is a tennis player", "he is a university professor", "he is a grandfather"), but as we shall emphasize shortly these judgments do not stand in isolation from other impressions. Each one may play a part in generating inferences which are relatively free of situational restrictions.

What of the two varieties of dispositional judgment noted above? Consider first dispositional judgments of overt characteristics. Examples of this type of judgmental output are "he is likely to say 'good morning' when I meet him", "he never wears a tie" and "he is a habitual smoker". These are generalizations reached inductively through one or more episodic judgments of overt fact. The manner in which they are attained seems to be fairly straightforward; of greater interest may be the question of *which* overt characteristics are typically generalized in this way. There seems to be little work on this topic. The judgment most commonly investigated by students of person perception is the fourth type in our classification — the dispositional judgment of covert characteristics. "He is intelligent", "he is arrogant", "he is a nervous person" are all examples of this type of judgment, as are "he enjoys smoking", "he is good at bridge" and "he likes a glass of beer every evening". These judgments — and the similar ones of overt characteristics — subsume judgments about one or more episodes or occurrences. The dispositional judgment "he is a habitual smoker" could not be made unless some episodic judgment of the kind "he is smoking now" were possible; neither could "he is arrogant" be concluded unless judgments like "he is behaving arrogantly" had been made. But it is important to notice that the episode(s) from which a dispositional judgment is derived need not palpably concern the same characteristic as the latter does. For example, the dispositional judgment "he is intelligent" need not arise from one or more episodic judgments "he is behaving intelligently". It may derive from the judge's inference from another episodic or dispositional judgment — "he is just completing *The Times* crossword", "he is a university student" or even "he has a long nose".

It is clear that to possess a dispositional attribute need not imply that one is in a particular state all the time. As Ryle (1949) points out, to say that glass is brittle is not to say that it is actually breaking, but is rather to say that it would break under certain conditions. In effect then a dispositional judgment summarizes certain tendencies and potentialities of a person or object. And, as we pointed out earlier, episodic judgment also represents a synopsis or abstract — but this time summarizing inputs in terms of a situation-specific state. Both the major forms of attributive judgment can thus be seen to carry out one of the main functions of perception stressed by Bruner (1958) and other writers: they achieve a recoding into a simpler form of the diversity of data encountered by a perceiver. Not only does this result in economy in actual perceiving but also in organizing the material within one's memory.

If both forms of attributive judgment fulfil the same purpose why then do we need to distinguish them? In practice, when we perceive someone we may make episodic judgments (about his current state) or dispositional ones (about his more permanent characteristics) and in many cases our perception will comprise both types of response. But in studying and understanding person perception we should notice several methodological and theoretical reasons why they need to be differentiated. Firstly, most investigators have been concerned with dispositional judgments; their possibly unwitting lack of interest in episodic judgment has prevented research into certain important areas. For instance the study of constancy in perception is in practice a study of the relationships between several episodic judgments and a dispositional judgment about the same stimulus. And the development of dispositional judgments as a function of episodic ones might be an interesting topic of investigation. Secondly, it might be the case that certain processes are carried out differently in different forms of attributive judgment. Accuracy in episodic judgment (perceiving emotions or the reactions of others in a discussion group, for example) may be unrelated to accuracy in dispositional judgment; and certain personality characteristics of the perceiver might have different consequences for the two types of judgment. Again, the typical *content* of the two sorts of judgment warrants separate study, as does their relative frequency of occurrence in perceptual situations of different kinds.

We also need to separate episodic judgments from dispositional ones if we are to study the way *events* are perceived, for we are concerned in this book with the perception of events as well as of people. In referring to an event we are dealing with an occasion in which people may or may not participate.* Thus a football match, an examination, a political meeting, an earthquake or a nuclear explosion are all events. Judgments of an event can clearly be of the first type we have outlined above; episodic judgments of overt fact are very relevant to the perception of events. Episodic judgments of *covert* fact can only be made about events if people (or possibly animals) are involved. We can conclude that a football match is an ill-tempered one or that a political meeting was an enthusiastic one, but only in so far as these judgments somehow refer to the participants in the event.

Yet the important point here is that dispositional judgments can never be made about particular events, since "an event" does not have extension in space and time in the way "a person" does.† Indeed, an event is the same as an episode or an occurrence, which form the defining basis of non-dispositional judgments. The way in which specific events are perceived may therefore be similar to the perception of people, but the two processes cannot overlap completely.

On the other hand, we always perceive a person as part of an event. Perception only occurs in the presence of a stimulus person (without which it becomes conception), and persons are always in a behavioural, social or physical context. In other words the perception of people always goes along with the perception of some aspects of the event in

---

* Attention here will mainly be limited to events with human participants.

† An "annual event" is of course different each year, rather as each Prime Minister is different. Notice, however, that dispositional judgments can of course be made about *classes* of events just as they can be made about people in general.

which they are participating. It is to emphasize this straightforward fact that we have coupled two sorts of stimulus in the title of this book. Person perception always takes place against a background of events; we need then to study the background as well as the person.

To recapitulate this discussion of the attributive component of perceptual and conceptual judgments, let us note that this always involves summarizing some aspects of the stimulus person. Episodic judgments are concerned with the covert or overt state of a person within the framework of a specific event, and dispositional judgments attribute characteristics to him which are relatively independent of particular occurrences. Although most investigators have been interested in dispositional judgments of covert characteristics, the other facets of the attributive component deserve rather more close attention.

The Expectancy Component

Let us turn now to the second judgmental component which we have isolated. The perception of people does not simply involve judgments that a person falls into certain categories or is placed along certain dimensions. It includes a range of expectancies related to these attributive responses (G. A. Kelly, 1955). In most cases of course the expectancies are not conscious ones; we may notice their existence, however, because of the surprise we feel when they are disconfirmed (cf. R. Brown, 1965, p. 614). There is a sense in which these expectancies are determinants of the *input* into the system, rather than being aspects of the output as we here describe them. Bruner (1951, 1957, 1958) has, for example, analysed the role of perceptual expectancy in interesting detail, and many of his insights are very relevant to this discussion. But he has tended to emphasize the role of expectancy or perceptual readiness as an input selector rather than as part of the output of the perceptual process. In the model of the processing system to be presented shortly expectancy will be shown as both an output and an input variable, but at this stage we are dealing with it only as an output component.

Output expectancies may, for the purpose of discussion, be placed into two separate categories which parallel the two types of attributive judgments reviewed above — episodic and the dispositional judgments. Consider the second of these. As we have seen, dispositional judgments may be of overt characteristics or of covert characteristics ("he is a habitual smoker" or "he is intelligent", for example). But they have similar logical properties, in that all dispositional judgments are rather like scientific laws. As Ryle (1949) has suggested, they resemble season tickets which allow us to make inferences, predictions and retrodictions whenever we want to use them. It can be seen that an attributive judgment of dispositional characteristics carries with it an array of potential predictions or expectancies. To say that glass is brittle is to say that *if* certain conditions obtain *then* it will break. In a similar manner, to attribute to someone intelligence, arrogance, cheerfulness, a particular occupation, a religious belief, or other dispositional characteristics is to say that *if* certain conditions obtain *then* he will behave in certain ways.

These expectancies are not haphazardly organized. They can be shown to interweave in a coherent manner, so that making one attributive judgment leads us to make a predictable range of other ones. This process is one which we shall consider in detail in later chapters. For the moment it should be noted that as soon as a perceiver attributes dispositional characteristics to a stimulus person he assumes a set of expectancies about that person. And these expectancies "feed back" to influence the input information which he processes in later judgments.

What of the expectancies associated with episodic judgments of overt and covert fact? The expectancies accompanying "he is driving a bus" and "he is arguing intelligently" are a little different from those attached to dispositional judgments. They appear to be of two kinds. Firstly, we assume that a person's behaviour is fairly consistent so that unless circumstances change markedly he will continue to behave in the same way for the rest of the event or episode. We are surprised if a person's behaviour varies widely in the course of one episode: the judgment "he is arguing intelligently" leads us to assume that the rest of his argument will be cogent and insightful. One form of expectancy deriving from episodic judgments of other people is thus an extrapolation from these judgments. An aspect of this is the expectancy generated by the placement of a stimulus person in a *role* category. To see that someone is taking on a position corresponding to a certain role is to expect him in that situation to behave in certain ways. And behaviour which is "out-of-role" then becomes particularly noteworthy (Jones, Davis and Gergen, 1961).

But the second sort of expectancy based upon an episodic judgment is of greater consequence. Perceivers are extremely willing (as studies reviewed later show) to translate an episodic judgment into a dispositional one which relates also to other occasions. On the basis of limited information about what a person does in one situation we are prone to attribute to him dispositional characteristics which he is supposed to possess in an almost unrestricted range of situations. It is as if we use our one-way inference ticket (the limited one provided by the episodic judgment) as a season ticket of unlimited validity.

Although these expectancies from episodic judgments can be similar to those accompanying dispositional judgments, the ways in which they are reached are not the same. A dispositional judgment *by its very nature* carries with it expectancies which are independent of a particular episode. Episodic judgments do not do this, and only yield their season tickets when we have inductively arrived at a dispositional judgment. This process is analogous to the scientist's activities in propounding hypotheses which have more universal application than the factual observations on which they are based (cf. Sarbin, Taft and Bailey, 1960).

In summary, attributive judgments of disposition contain within themselves expectancies, so that in so far as the output of a perceptual system involves attributing characteristics to a stimulus so also does it involve expectancies about it. Episodic judgments are slightly different, but our demonstrable keenness to turn these into dispositional judgments means that they too tend to be associated with expectancies which extend outside the particular event in question.

A final, less philosophical point should perhaps be made. A very important set of expectancies in person perception concerns our predictions about the way the stimulus person may influence us. In many perceptual situations (especially those which we shall later define as "direct"), the perceiver selects information about the stimulus person's goals and intentions (e.g. Heider, 1958; Pepitone, 1958) and about the way the other might wish him to respond (e.g. Goffman, 1956). The expectancies generated by this type of input are likely to be particularly central to the way he is perceived (Jones and Davis, 1965).

The Affective Component

This is the final aspect of the perceptual output to be considered. When judging another person we do not only classify him and make predictions about him; we also respond to him in certain emotional ways. Indeed, as we shall argue in Chapter 4, this affective response is of outstanding importance and one which enters strongly into every interpersonal relationship.

The third component may involve responses of attraction, liking, interest, respect, sympathy and so on, which strongly influence the other types of judgment and the way we interact with the stimulus person. Or they may be responses of fear, anxiety, hostility, disapproval, animosity, resentment, malice or repulsion. There is evidence from many studies reviewed later that even simple, apparently non-affective inputs give rise to affective responses of this kind. It is as though our evaluation of a stimulus provides a necessary organizing framework into which the wide range of other judgments are set. Our attributive judgments are not derived solely on the basis of logical interconnected- ness, but they emerge partly from evaluations placed upon specific aspects of the stimulus person. If a person judges that a stimulus has an attribute or set of attributes which he finds attractive, he is likely to form other impressions which fit into this judgmental framework. Another perceiver may make the same attributive judgments but experience a different evaluation; his subsequent impressions will not parallel those of the first judge. The affective component of person perception is in this way not only an aspect of the output, but it is also important in determining the selection and processing of later inputs. We shall return to this issue shortly.

Some justification is perhaps needed for distinguishing this affective component from attributive judgments. It does not seem to be reducible to a set of attributive responses — that the stimulus person has "like- able" or "unattractive" characteristics — since the evaluations are so clearly part of the perceiver rather than of the other person. Neverthe- less, the attributive judgments we make about someone are undoubtedly associated with the affective reactions he produces; and both of these are clearly related to our expectancies about him. Although for the present the three components may be treated as conceptually distinct, it may eventually happen that new words and new ways of viewing this question will allow us to combine them into a single output.

A SCHEMATIC MODEL OF PERSON PERCEPTION

In our formulation of the activities undertaken in perceiving other people we have so far dealt only with the output — the perceptual response itself. We have looked rather closely at three components of this output, but have as yet said little about the earlier parts of a system of perception. In the present section this deficiency will be remedied by an attempt to represent the input and processing stages in relation

of the book. For the moment it might be helpful to represent these interacting components schematically and in so doing to introduce additional parts into the system. We have attempted this in Figure 1.

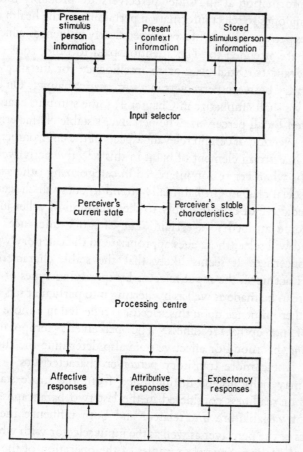

Figure 1　Schematic representation of person perception

In this diagram information is represented as in general flowing from top to bottom. The uppermost boxes correspond to the types of input which we have already discussed, and in the three lowest boxes are registered the output components of perception. It must be emphasized, however, that a simple top-to-bottom representation of complex processes like person perception is not entirely possible. A diagram like Figure 1 does not represent the flow of information successively through a sequence of individual components one by one; rather it indicates a

to the types of output we have specified. This task is made more difficult by the sequential, on-going nature of person perception. Except perhaps for the occasions when we form an impression of someone through a still photograph or picture we always take in information successively (cf. Heider, 1958, 1967; Tagiuri, 1968). Our judgments are therefore in part dependent upon what has gone before as well as upon current stimulation. This not only presents methodological problems for the would-be investigator, it also makes it very difficult to represent the process of person perception in a brief verbal or diagrammatic account. It is likely then that in the discussion which follows we shall oversimplify the dynamic aspects of the process.

It is manifest that in making judgments of our physical or social environment we do not process all of the information available to us. Indeed we probably *learn* to select only certain aspects of other people in the same way that acquiring a psycho-motor skill (car driving for instance) involves learning to discard less relevant stimulus information. A model of person perception requires some form of *input selector* which governs the information which is in fact processed. Let us consider the variables which act upon this selector.

Firstly we must consider the stimulus person himself. It is logically necessary that in person perception *some* information about a stimulus person is selected. One group of factors operating upon the input selector* is clearly to do with the stimulus. Some aspects of the stimulus will be sufficiently salient to warrant selection, whereas others (the shape of his ears perhaps) will not be noticed. Apart from the characteristics of the stimulus person himself there are two related types of variables which also operate upon the selector. We shall refer to these as "*present context information*" and "*stored stimulus person information*".

The first of these terms refers to the social, physical or behavioural context within which the person is perceived. Aspects of this context are selected and are placed in juxtaposition with selected aspects of the stimulus. Visitors to another country are particularly liable to notice the nationality of other people; in the context of a foreign country, nationality becomes much more salient. Less obvious perhaps is the fact that the framework provided by another person can influence per-

---

* Notice that "the input selector" in this discussion refers to a hypothesized component of a perceptual system. The term "the selector" does not refer to a person ("the perceiver") but rather to a component. This component is nevertheless in some sense part of a person.

ception so that a stimulus person is judged in relation to other people in the situation (e.g. M. G. Cline, 1956; Holmes and Berkowitz, 1961). And episodic judgments of emotional expression might be based upon information from the situation itself (e.g. Munn, 1940; Sherman, 1927a, 1927b). In a variety of ways the present context acts upon the input selector.

What we have termed "*stored stimulus person information*" is in a sense a form of context. By this phrase we refer to the information about the stimulus person which is within the perceiver's memory, being available as the basis of a conceptual judgment. Stored information about what the person has done on other occasions, about what other people have said about him, and information in the form of earlier dispositional judgments together with their expectancy and affective components — these are all aspects of stored stimulus person information. It is clear that this type of material will influence the selector to a very marked extent.* It is available in many instances of perception, whenever the perceiver has been previously acquainted with the stimulus person. On other occasions this form of input is not available.

So far we have pointed out that in perceiving other people we select only certain aspects of the person and of the situation in which he is placed. A model of person perception consequently requires a component to represent an input selector, and we have discussed how this selector may be influenced by the characteristics and behaviour of the stimulus person by the context within which he is perceived, and often by the judge's store of information about him. We now turn to a further set of variables which operate upon the selector — the characteristics of the perceiver himself. It is convenient to distinguish between his relatively stable and permanent characteristics and those of a more transitory nature. Both these aspects can influence the input selector and also what we shall later term the processing centre. Here we are dealing only with the input selector.

The *stable characteristics* likely to affect the selector are personality attributes, cognitive styles, age, sex, attitudes, religious affiliations, social class, and other variables of this type. These relatively stable attributes

* Stored information specific to a single particular stimulus person is here being distinguished from other material stored by a perceiver. Information about people in general, about particular stimulus characteristics, and the perceiver's previous experience in similar situations all influence the selector. But it is helpful to separate these latter types of information under different headings. They are discussed in the following paragraphs.

can be seen partly to determine the kind of environmental cues which are utilized (see Chapter 4). Some perceivers may always notice eye colour, length of nose and eyelashes, whereas others do not select this kind of information at all. Older perceivers are probably more likely than young ones to select information pertaining to the health or age of a stimulus person. The sex of a perceiver clearly influences which aspects of others are attended to. The attention paid to other sorts of cue — those relevant to social class or to intelligence for instance — is also likely to vary between perceivers in a systematic manner. On the other hand (as we shall emphasize in Chapter 4) some stimulus characteristics are selected by all perceivers. The perceiver's stable characteristics only affect the selection of certain relevant aspects of the environment.

There is a strong element of habit in this selective activity. A person who is for whatever reason interested in categorizing others according to their social class might habitually attend to cues which seem to him to be predictive of class (possibly to the exclusion of other inputs). He will become attuned to a certain "cue-category inference" (Bruner, 1957) and will select those cues appropriate to the category with which he is concerned. It seems likely that the stable characteristics of a perceiver act upon the input selector by specifying types of judgment which are to be made as well as by alerting it to particular sets of cues.

A further influence upon this selector is reflected in a more transitory form of perceptual readiness. The perceiver's temporary set or *Einstellung*, his mood or affective state also determine the cues that are noticed. These more transitory perceiver characteristics — his *current state* — may helpfully be distinguished from the more stable determinants of readiness considered in the last two paragraphs. The two classes of variable are interrelated, and both influence the *processing* activities of the perceiver as well as the input selector with which we are at present dealing. Several examples of the operation of the two types of characteristic are discussed in Chapter 4.

We have so far isolated six parts of the perceptual system which appears to operate when we make judgments of other people. In addition to an input selector, five components operating upon it have been considered — present stimulus person information, present context information and stored stimulus person information; and relatively stable and relatively transitory characteristics of the perceiver. As is no doubt obvious we have not reviewed the operation of these components in much detail. This is our task in later chapters

dynamic, to-and-fro interaction of activities which may seem instantaneous (as with tachistoscopic presentation of a photograph) or which may be extended over time (as during a conversation, a television programme or a film). Figure 1 is merely a beginning attempt to summarize a complex, dynamic, sequential but extremely rapid set of activities in a two-dimensional picture which is necessarily independent of time.

The one component of this perceptual system to which allusion has yet to be made is the *processing centre*. This can be viewed as a set of "decision rules" developed by the perceiver. It is useful to distinguish between two types of decision rule; let us refer to "inference rules" and "combination rules". Inference rules are concerned only with a single input. For example a perceiver with certain personality characteristics and in a particular state who receives the piece of information that a stimulus person is smiling might apply the inference rules "from *smiling* infer *friendly*". It appears to be logically necessary that a perceiver has a large ensemble of inference rules available to him, each indicating what is to be inferred from a single input item.

But input items do not usually come in singly. They are customarily available in groups — *laughing*, *fat*, *drinking whisky*, *aged 40*, *stockbroker* and so on. We take it that although there may be inference rules relevant to each of these inputs, there are also combination rules based upon the others which determine the output from the input as a whole. Combination rules are seen as prescriptions about inference from compound sets of individual inputs. The nature of combination rules is more complex than at first sight it may appear. We shall later review work suggesting that they are likely to involve more than simply adding or averaging the information from separate inputs. A perceiver does not apply one discrete rule after another until he reaches his judgment: the several inputs which are selected somehow fuse to create a unified set of stimulus material. The judge seems to apply decision rules within a framework which generates a type of Gestalt which arises from the patterning of inputs — "under a sustained interest in the structure of the other personality" (G. W. Allport, 1961, p. 546). There is no reason why these Gestalten should not be understood via an understanding of individual inference and combination rules, but it is manifest that we are as yet a long way from this happy state. In Chapter 3 some possible approaches will be examined.

A further aspect of decision rules needs to be introduced at this point.

They may well prescribe probabilistic inferences: "very likely to be intelligent", "probably a temperamental person", "could well be an imposter". The existence of this form of inference complicates the study of person perception still further. Sarbin, Taft and Bailey (1960) have suggested a useful approach to the question, and some ways to measure probabilistic inference are also dealt with in Chapter 3. In passing it should be noted that the perception of objects also involves probabilistic judgments in large measure. Brunswik (1956), for example, has stressed that a perceptual system has to operate as an "intuitive statistician" as the probable nature of distal objects is decided upon. And Reichenbach (1938) has thought in terms of the perceiver laying bets on the most likely outcomes (see Postman and Tolman, 1959).

Return now to Figure 1. The lines into the processing centre from the two boxes which stand for the perceiver's stable characteristics and his current state indicate that the nature of the inference rule which is applied to a particular input can vary between perceivers of different personalities, and even between different judgments by the same perceiver. And, as we have already suggested, the same influences operate on the input selector; we indicate these by the other two lines leading to the selector. The complex interaction between the three types of input information and that between the three output components is similarly represented in Figure 1 by interconnections. Other important aspects of the process are the feedback loops, for example those from the output to stimulus person store and to the perceiver's current state. The first of these indicates that the material in this store consists of previous episodic or dispositional judgments together with their expectancy and affective components. In other words when information from this store reenters the system it has already been processed. A second feedback loop — to the perceiver's current state — provides some sign of the changing sequential nature of the perception of others.

It is unquestionable that our schematic model needs to be more complicated than we have made it. For instance, we need ideally to say something about inputs to the perceiver's personality and to his current state. And the relatively static nature of the account also means that we have not considered the way the processing centre itself develops; we have treated it as containing certain programmed rules without looking at how these get written.

Yet, despite these deficiencies, it appears that the scheme meaningfully relates the various complicated activities that go together to constitute person perception. As such it comes close to being a form of definition. We are almost defining "person perception" in terms of what *happens* instead of in terms of what it *is*. A quasi-operational definition at this level of generality may ultimately prove more acceptable than either a short semantic definition or a closely specified set of operational measures. The model presented in Figure 1 will certainly be bettered, and as a definition it is incomplete, but it provides a useful framework within which to set later chapters.

With this in mind let us consider a few further points. The discussion so far has perhaps given the impression that we regard these activities as conscious, verbalized ones. If so, this is the wrong impression. The inference and combination rules are rarely applied in any self-conscious way, the input is of course not parcelled out into separate groupings, and the three components of the output need not all be known to the perceiver. The perceptual scheme suggested here picks out the *logical* components which seem to be necessary for the system to function in the way it appears to function. We have yet to explore the psychological representations of these components.

This raises a methodological point. When we try to observe the activities of particular components, how do we set about measuring them? How for example do we assess the influence of current state on input selection? We shall have to take a measure which in fact is an *output* measure of some kind. All our knowledge of componental activities has to derive from observations of the output components. This clearly requires a high degree of subtlety on the part of the investigator. It also presents him with a related uncertainty. When he tries to measure person perception, can he actually obtain indices of the whole of each of the three output components? This seems to be a task of the utmost difficulty, especially since the perceiver himself may not be able to give expression to them all. The investigator's aim is to induce the subject to put into words as much of the attributive, expectancy and affective components as can be contrived without interfering too grossly with the perceptual process itself. Little wonder that different investigators settle upon very different measuring instruments.*

It is of interest to look at the way the present model applies to activities other than person perception. What about the perception of objects for instance? Later in this chapter we shall review the relation-

* The question of measurement is discussed at some length in Chapter 2.

ship between object perception and person perception. To anticipate our conclusion, there appears to be no qualitative difference between these two processes. Consequently the model outlined here should apply equally to object perception. At present we can see no reason why it does not. Another related process to which we have already drawn attention is the conception of people. The only difference between perception and conception is that the stimulus is not present in the latter. A representation of the process of conception is therefore achieved by removing one or both of the two top left-hand boxes from Figure 1 (i.e. present stimulus information and possibly present context information).

Finally, the model presented here points out several research problems which will be considered later in the book. It makes clear for instance that what may be loosely termed "perceiver variables" affect a perceptual output by influencing the input selector or the processing centre or both of these. Attempts to separate these two influences might be valuable; or again, the interaction between the variables operating on the input selector itself has yet to be closely studied. Individual variables of this group (especially stored stimulus person characteristics) could themselves be rewarding topics of study, as of course could the other subsystems of the model. Again, the interaction between the three output components has still to be understood. Recent work on the structure of attitudes (e.g. Feldman, 1966; Fishbein, 1967; Rosenberg and coworkers, 1960) may shed light ont he similar interactions in person perception.

This rather molecular, analytic approach also serves to draw attention to the several separate guises in which "expectancy" may enter into perception. We have earlier stressed the importance of an expectancy output component, but its relevance elsewhere is clear (cf. Bruner, 1957; G. A. Kelly, 1955). Generalized expectancies about groups of individuals (Irishmen, Londoners, professors or pop singers) may be treated as attitudinal structures within the perceiver's stable characteristics; in addition his current state can be seen to generate a series of more transitory expectancies. These will be mediated by earlier judgments in a perceptual sequence which also feed back to the component we have labelled "stored stimulus person information". Thus a perceiver might make a dispositional judgment (which feeds back into the store) that a stimulus person is humorous, and from this expect him to exhibit joking behaviour. The perceiver will now be alerted to humorous aspects of his behaviour which another person may not notice. Similarly, episodic judgments may be retained as stored stimulus person information and thereby function as temporary expectancies. If a perceiver judges that another person is trying to belittle him, he will be attuned to facets of his behaviour which may otherwise pass unnoticed. A different form of perceptual expectancy is provided by the decision rules within the processing centre. As we shall discuss in Chapter 3 these make up a set of expected relationships between personal characteristics which naturally plays a major role in judgment.

So "expectancy" can be seen to be operative in all the components of the perceptual system. Each component will be considered individually in the course of the book, and we shall lead up to a more detailed examination of the interaction between components in the final chapter. At that point we shall assay a rudimentary computer simulation based upon the schema set out in Figure 1. Before moving on, however, a summary of the argument so far is in order. We began by noting the difficulty of defining "perception", and pointed out certain notions which are nevertheless central to this concept. Related ideas such as conceptions and attitudes were then introduced before we moved on to describe the components which appear necessary to a perceptual system. The complexities of the output from such a system were first considered and it was concluded that attributive responses, expectancy responses and affective responses all needed to be accounted for. Attributive responses were classed as either episodic judgments or dispositional judgments, and the logical nature of these judgment types was discussed.

Turning to the input to the system we have emphasized the importance of the context in which a person is perceived and the stored information about him which is available. The more stable and the more transitory characteristics of the perceiver were seen to influence each other and to influence both the input selector and the processing centre. A short consideration of the decision rules incorporated in this processing centre was then presented, and the whole system was represented diagrammatically in Figure 1. We have pointed out that a process specification of this type may prove to be the most satisfactory way of approaching the problem of defining complex activities and have drawn attention to several consequences of this kind of definition.

DIRECT AND INDIRECT PERCEPTION

As Figure 1 clearly points out, the input to person perception is of three kinds. As well as information about the present behaviour and characteristics of the stimulus person himself, information about the current context and stored material about the stimulus also enter into the judgmental process. How successful have researchers been in specifying these major input variables?

They have on the whole stressed present stimulus person information to the exclusion of the other two components. Most experiments have left aside *stored* stimulus person information by concentrating on imaginary or unknown stimuli. This is of course valid in that many objects of judgment are not previously familiar to us so that no stimulus person information can at the outset be in store. But investigations of these stimuli clearly do not tell us the whole story. Experimenters have also sought to achieve control over conditions by severely restricting present context information. In many cases this has meant that a list of traits or a written description of a person has constituted the stimulus material. Moving pictures have sometimes been used, as have transcripts of interviews or statements by people supposedly acquainted with the stimulus person. Still photographs of a person's face have also been much studied, occasionally with some limited verbal information about the name or ethnic background of the stimulus.

These procedures are useful ones in that investigators can gain quite a lot of control over their material. But the value of findings based upon them has been questioned by several writers (e.g. Asch, 1952, pp. 205–222; Bruner and Tagiuri, 1954; Lambert and Lambert, 1964, p. 33; Luchins, 1948). It has been argued that the stimulus material available in real life is much more complex than these techniques allow, and that we need to study the way people perceive each other in face-to-face interactions. It sometimes seems to be implied that face-to-face interaction characterizes all forms of impression formation. Clearly in this case studies of the type described above are only of small value.

Yet this argument is not wholly satisfactory. Although it is true that we form many impressions of others on the basis of face-to-face contacts, a great deal of person perception in real-life conditions is very different. One of the first people many of us perceive each morning is the leader of our national government. We perceive his behaviour at a recent meeting by reading a newspaper account or by listening to the radio although most of us have never encountered him face-to-face. Similarly we perceive lesser-known figures without ever meeting them in person. A colleague may tell us about Professor X, or we might read some of his work; in both cases we make judgments about him. There have been occasions when we have perceived prominent businessmen, film stars, television announcers and many other people, and yet have not interacted with them at all. Nor are people perceived in this way always "public figures". We have read in the newspapers about Mrs. Jones and her Siamese cat, Caroline Roberts who wants to be an artist, Henry Goodwin whose house is in the way of a new road, Dorothy Blackler who fell off a ship, and thousands of other people who have attracted journalistic attention for only brief periods.

What this means is that a great deal of our day-to-day perceptual activity involves impoverished stimulus material which is presented without any face-to-face interaction at all.* This suggests two prescriptions. First we should not be too concerned if research workers do not always deal with perceptions derived from interaction with a stimulus person. And secondly, we ought to study as of interest in their own right the perceptual situations cited in the previous paragraph. Their common characteristic is that they all involve a communication medium of some kind. This form of perception may conveniently be termed "indirect" and distinguished from "direct perception" which takes place in contact (and possibly interaction) with a stimulus (Warr and Knapper, 1966a, 1966b).† Both direct person perception and indirect person perception deserve investigation, and we need not always attempt to relate studies of one to our knowledge of the other.

Turning back to the types of present stimulus information in which experimenters have been interested, it can now be seen that many studies have in effect been of *indirect* perception. A list of traits is similar to many newspaper reports (a fact we exploit later in this book) or to

* We have previously categorized judgments as either perceptions or conceptions, and have suggested that conceptions take place when no stimulus is present. In judging people through newspaper reports we are *perceiving* them in that we are still processing information from an external stimulus. In this way when we read about the Prime Minister we are perceiving him, whereas a sudden judgment of him made as we daydream our way through a dull symphony concert is a conception.

† The distinction between direct and indirect perception has been made in a rather different context and with different terminology by McKellar (1963), who was interested in imagery and creativity. Referring to primary and secondary perception, he pointed out that many famous writers, for example, have provided vivid and realistic descriptions of environments they have never perceived in the primary sense.

assessments by teachers or managers. Photographs form the basis of many an indirect judgment of another person, and short statements by someone else regularly generate quite clear impressions. The psychological literature is consequently full of studies of indirect person perception. These are of value in themselves, not only as aids to learning about direct perception.

We have defined these two types of perception in terms of the presence or absence of an intervening communication medium. Most instances of perception can readily be assigned to one of the categories. Judgments arising from radio or television communications, those based upon newspaper reports, films, books, photographs and so on are obviously examples of indirect perception. Judgments based upon what another person has written — letters, books, examinations — are also indirect. Direct perception occurs at committee meetings, social gatherings, interviews, lectures and other events of this kind. The definition does, however, result in occasional difficulties of classification. Is perception of someone reflected in a mirror direct or indirect (cf. Ayer, 1963, p. 72)? Other slight anomalies ensue. For instance we have to categorize impressions formed on the basis of a telephone conversation as indirect, despite the fact that there might be considerable involvement and interaction. Rare cases arise in which perception seems both direct and indirect. Statesmen of different nationalities may form indirect impressions through the information provided by their interpreter and make direct judgments on the basis of facial cues, tone of voice and gestures. But in the vast majority of cases it is a straightforward decision whether perception is direct or indirect. We shall consider many more instances in the course of this book.

In all forms of person perception the stimulus person can to some extent limit the information he transmits. In indirect perception this limitation is quite severe, and differs in that it is usually imposed by *another* person or instrument. A raconteur selects those aspects of a person which he will talk about, the staff of a newspaper edit and control what information about an individual is printed, a television producer edits his camera shots and controls what the narrator says. Similar transmission restriction is present even in the case of telephone conversations, but here the editor is entirely mechanical. In a few cases, such as communications written by the stimulus person, this limitation is at the discretion of the stimulus himself rather than of any third party. There are various processes which are peculiar to either direct or indirect perception and we outline some of the unique features of each in Chapters 5, 6 and 7. For instance visual interaction occurs only in direct perception, whereas indirect perception involves a host of communication variables such as newspaper headlines and photographs. It is worth pointing out at this stage that the additional restriction of information in indirect perceptual situations gives rise to several important consequences.

First, those aspects of the stimulus person which are selected for presentation become more salient. This is of course because the perceiver almost certainly has fewer inputs than if he perceived the stimulus directly.*

The phrase "selected for presentation" provides us with a clue to the second consequence. Although the indirect perceiver is still at liberty to select inputs from the material presented, this material has already been preselected — by some human or mechanical editor — before it reaches him. In other words the increased input salience which is present in indirect perception is often a function of the communication channel rather than the stimulus or the perceiver. While drawing attention to the importance of the channel we should not, however, lose sight of the fact that factors within the perceiver himself may well become of more importance in indirect perception. The rationale here is the same as that underlying projective testing techniques: that when the input from the stimulus is restricted, certain perceiver characteristics have more scope to exert themselves. This point is pursued in Chapter 6 (p. 260), where we report a comparison between direct and indirect perception of the same event.

In both direct and indirect perception the judgments made can be either episodic or dispositional (see p. 8). But while direct perception must be of a current event — one taking place at the time of perception — we can indirectly perceive both current events and events which took place earlier in time. In fact some of the most common examples of indirect perception — reading a newspaper report, viewing a film, looking at a photograph — always involve retrospective judgments of this kind. In these circumstances interaction between the stimulus person and the perceiver is completely precluded, and even in live television and radio broadcasts which provide opportunities for indirect perception of a current event, interaction is impossible. In contrast,

* This in spite of the fact that in indirect perception inputs are sometimes available which he may not have selected if he had perceived the stimulus directly.

although there are some events (lectures, sports meetings, etc.) where we perceive directly without interaction,* by and large direct perception is characterized by face-to-face stimulus–perceiver interaction. Although we have specified these two types of perception in terms of the presence or absence of an intervening medium of communication, it is in general the case that direct perception involves interaction while indirect does not.

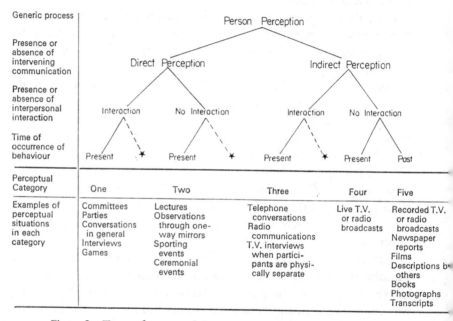

Figure 2   Types of perceptual situations organized in terms of three characteristics (direct/indirect, interaction/no interaction, present/past behaviour)

This is illustrated in Figure 2 which compares and contrasts the types of perception in terms of interpersonal interaction and the time of occurrence of the event. Category one on the diagram shows the supposed "paradigm case" of person perception according to most researches in this field. It is interesting to note, however, that there are no less than four further categories of person perception. Although it is

* It is not strictly true to say that no interaction takes place in these events. An audience influences a lecturer in so far as he picks up cues about their interest and comprehension. And cheers, applause and encouragement may well have some influence on a sporting event. In fact there is a dimension of low interaction–high interaction and we have here given examples of events at the low end of the scale.

not true to say that these categories have been ignored by psychologists, they have been regarded as worthy of attention only in so far as they provide an aid to our understanding of category one. There would seem to be no reason why these remaining categories do not warrant study in their own right.

One of our aims in this book is to give greater emphasis to indirect perception than it has hitherto been accorded. Many of our judgments of others are indirect, and it is unreasonable to strive only to understand those that are direct. Of course, in many respects direct and indirect perception are similar: these similarities, as well as the differences, will be considered in later chapters.

THE PERCEPTION OF PERSONS AND OF OBJECTS

Nearly everything we have said about direct and indirect person perception applies to the judgments we make of objects. Buildings, furniture, machines and living environments may all be perceived both directly and indirectly. Indirect judgments may be based upon visual communications (photographs or films) or on written or spoken accounts, and the intervening media restrict the stimulus information entering the perceptual system just as they do in person perception. Furthermore the categorization of perception summarized in Figure 2 turns out to apply also to object perception. Category two is often seen as the "paradigm case" of object perception — direct judgments when stimulus and perceiver do not interact — and this group of perceptual situations is clearly an important one. Nor is there difficulty in accepting the existence of object judgments in categories four and five — indirect perception of present and of past behaviour without interaction. But categories one and three, which involve interaction, are to many people not immediately relevant to object perception. It is therefore interesting to ponder examples of these two categories.

Interaction occurs whenever there is some sort of reciprocal influence: whenever A influences B, and B influences A. In all cases of perception the stimulus obviously influences the perceiver. But for interaction to occur, the perceiver has to influence the stimulus. If we treat this as a question of the perceiver influencing what information the stimulus presents, then interaction is clearly present in many cases of object perception. Judgments made as we pick up an object and move it around belong in category one, as do perceptions of a building as we move towards it. Less frequent are indirect judgments of this kind (those in category three), but examples can be found. Judgments made as a television set is adjusted, or perceptual impressions of industrial workers as they adjust instruments to sample the state of the manufacturing process are in this group. It seems then that the classificatory system set out in Figure 2 applies to object perception as well as to judgments of people.

The question may now be raised: is person perception intrinsically different from the perception of objects? Those students of person perception who have considered its relation to object perception have generally accepted that the two processes are in effect the same, but no detailed statement of the points of similarity seems to have been attempted. Amongst those writers who state or imply that the processes of object perception and person perception are closely related are F. H. Allport (1955), Bruner and Postman (1948), Brunswik (1934, 1956), Heider (1958), Hochberg (1964), Krech, Crutchfield and Ballachey (1962), Rommetweit (1960), Sarbin, Taft and Bailey (1960) and P. E. Vernon (1964). Equal emphasis is given to the similarities and the differences by G. W. Allport (1961), Argyle (1957), and by Tagiuri (1958a).

We accept as a working hypothesis (and at the moment it is no more than that) the tenet that the same set of principles applies to *all* kinds of perception. The perceptual system described earlier in this chapter is thus taken to apply to object perception as well as to the perception of people, and at present we can see no respect in which it is inappropriate. To take two examples, the distinction between episodic and dispositional judgments is quite relevant to object perception ("this cricket ball is moving towards me" and "this cricket ball is red"); and the importance of the stable characteristics and current state of the perceiver in object perception has repeatedly been demonstrated in research.

A considerable understanding of object perception has been acquired by experimental psychologists. Social psychological research into the way people are perceived has often been conducted without apparent awareness of this body of knowledge. In this section we shall look at some aspects of the relationship between the two processes. There are no great obstacles to our believing that judgments of the *overt* characteristics of people involve the same activities as those taking place in object perception (cf. Ittelson, 1960, Chapter 10; Ittelson and Slack, 1958). We perceive height, texture of skin, colour of clothes and so on in just the same way as we perceive the size, texture and colour of cardboard shapes in the experimental psychologist's laboratory. The perception of speech is admittedly rather more complex (e.g. Miller, 1951, Chapter 3), but this also seems to be based on principles not intrinsically different from those governing object perception (e.g. Osgood and Sebeok, 1965, pp. 50–60). But what of judgments about *covert* characteristics of other people? These might appear to present a special problem, for the gap here between object and person perception seems potentially greater. Our working hypothesis of no difference between the processes assumes that judgments of covert characteristics of people are ultimately explicable by the same set of principles that will explain object perception. We are of course some way from a complete understanding of either of these activities, so that conclusive evidence for the hypothesis is not yet available. But as a start it might be possible to consider some of the generalizations which have been established about object perception to see how far these are relevant to what is known about judgments of people's covert characteristics. In the next few pages we shall review some of these generalizations — as well as some of the methods used by students of object perception — to suggest points of contact between the two fields of study.

A fashionable and intriguing beginning is to look at the research which has been concerned with illusions. An illusory perception occurs when the perceiver experiences a situation which fails to correspond with the situation as objectively measured; an illusion might in this way be described as a false perception. In fact nearly all the investigations by experimental psychologists of perception are by this definition concerned with illusions, since these cases easily generate differences between perceivers which can be studied. So we should include the proviso that the false perception has to be *strikingly* false before it is considered an illusion.

Visual illusions are apparently caused by some cues being sufficiently important to change the perceived shape, size etc., of other variables in the situation so that a false perception results. Analogous studies of the perception of people suffer from the disadvantage that since the stimulus cannot always be objectively measured assessment of truth or falsity is difficult. But there have been many demonstrations that changes even in some apparently minor cues can alter the way in which a person is perceived. The most striking of these (and therefore the ones most appropriately termed illusions) concern the inclusion of a single particular trait in a list of stimulus characteristics. It has frequently been shown (e.g. Asch, 1946; Wishner, 1960; Chapter 3 of this volume) that changes in one item (*warm* for *cold*, say) in a list of characteristics result in widespread alterations in the way the stimulus person is perceived. These changes are analogous to changes in one part of a visual stimulus array (the slope of a line or the angle of a corner) which can generate illusory perceptions of a startling kind. The comparable alterations in person perception are observed not only in judgments logically related to the altered trait (*kind–unkind*, for example) but also in unrelated perceptions (*imaginative–unimaginative*, for instance). It is likely that illusory perceptions of people occur frequently, but we have less opportunity to be surprised than we have in the case of illusory object perception since in real life we are rarely able to compare our percept directly with the true nature of the stimulus person.

We might then expect generalizations about illusions in object perception to apply to studies like those of Asch in which an isolated personal characteristic is varied. For example, it has long been known that the approach adopted by an observer can radically affect the magnitude of a visual illusion.* Subjects adopting a "whole-perceiving" attitude are more susceptible to the Müller–Lyer illusion than those with a "part-isolating" approach. Similar differences might be observed in experiments on person perception using Asch's design. And several investigators have noted that practice can markedly reduce the magnitude of some illusions; perhaps this would also be found in the case of the "illusions" in person perception.

The perception of objects is not a passive process in which we merely become aware of the manner in which our sense organs are being stimulated. The perceiver organizes the material to which he is exposed and selects only certain aspects of it; we do not perceive an object as a simple aggregate of stimuli, but rather we impose our own organization on the material. The principles by which we carry out this organization are in part determined by the material itself. All psychology textbooks include examples of the way stimuli are grouped according to

---

* The findings from experimental studies of object perception to which we shall refer in this section are very well established and documented. We shall not trouble to cite primary references for each example. Further details are to be found in a number of standard textbooks. In preparing this section we have drawn on the useful accounts provided by Beardslee and Wertheimer (1958), Hochberg (1964), Osgood (1953), M. D. Vernon (1962), Woodworth and Schlosberg (1954), and by several other writers.

proximity, continuation, symmetry, good form, closure and so on; we have a general tendency to perceive objects with the maximum degree of simplicity, regularity and symmetry. The same process occurs when we perceive other people. Subjects who are given only a limited, incomplete set of information about a person (a list of characteristics or a photograph) impose their own organization upon this material so that they form an impression of the person which is detailed, ordered and self-consistent. Inference and combination rules which generate these phenomena have previously been alluded to; we shall look at the rules and the phenomena themselves in detail in later chapters.

A lot of the research stimulated by Gestalt psychology was intended to discover what stimulus factors make a pattern look like a figure. It was common to present patterns of dots in an attempt to isolate natural groupings. This methodological approach is of limited relevance to the study of person perception since it is usually obvious what pattern of stimulation constitutes an individual. But it might be rewarding to study what patterns of traits seem to go together to make up a person. A start has been made on this (e.g. Bruner, Shapiro and Tagiuri, 1958; Jackson, 1962; Chapter 3 of this volume) but so far no use has been made of procedures employed by Gestalt psychologists. For example, we might present subjects with a list of characteristics (*tolerant, ambitious, discreet, good, cruel, high-spirited, moody, thoughtful* and so on) and ask them to assign each of these to one of, say, two individuals about whom no further information is provided. In this way we could study the way in which people are "constructed", rather as experimental psychologists have asked subjects to "construct" figures from sets of physical characteristics.

In a similar manner it would be interesting to translate experimental psychologists' work on concealed figures into the field of person perception. Much effort has been expended to understand how figures can be concealed amongst other material; the aim of this is to learn more about the important factors affecting the way configurations are perceived. Comparable studies could be carried out with lists of personal characteristics in which subjects might be asked (on analogy with Boring's famous figure) to find the hidden mother-in-law or the hidden wife. By varying the stimulus material according to hypotheses about perceptual organization interesting results should emerge.

Related to the question of how material is organized into configurations is the figure–ground phenomenon. We do not perceive stimulus material as of uniform prominence; a part of it tends to appear as a figure and to be differentiated from the rest of the material which acts as a background. A figure has form and meaningfulness, and is readily attended to as a whole. But the ground seems to be less organized, and is less clearly perceived and remembered. A lot of work has been reported on figure–ground experiences in object perception and we can readily apply these concepts and the principles concerning them to the study of person perception (cf. Rudin and Stagner, 1958). There is no doubt that figure–ground phenomena occur in the perception of a group of people; the characteristics of a single person readily become a "figure" against which the others are less clearly-differentiated "ground". One factor accentuating figure–ground differences in object perception is the sharpness of the contours in a visual array. This will also be relevant to person perception. A contour is a sudden change in brightness, colour or other characteristics, and in this sense "contours" surround each person in a group. But just as sharper contours in a visual array generate more certain figure–ground experiences, so do greater differences in important characteristics between the members of a group make figure–ground perception more likely. And just as objects can be camouflaged by minimizing the sharpness of contours, so can a person make himself inconspicuous by minimizing the physical and behavioural differences between himself and other people.

Implicit in this discussion is the well-established principle that the context or background against which a physical stimulus is placed influences the way it is perceived. In the case of the visual illusions specific patterns of contextual cues are responsible for false perception, and background factors like colour, evenness of material and so on clearly influence figure–ground experiences. Principles about context effects in object perception are surely applicable to the perception of people. The importance of context in this latter type of perception was emphasized in the second section of this chapter. Its role has also been stressed by Berkowitz (1960a), Brunswik (1956), Heider (1958, 1967), Icheiser (1949) and Peak (1958). M. G. Cline (1956), Holmes and Berkowitz (1961) and Levy (1960) have also provided experimental demonstrations of context effects in impression formation. Investigations by Munn (1940), Sherman (1927a, 1927b) and many other workers have shown the importance of background information in judgments of emotional expression; these are reviewed in Chapter 7.

In studies of the way the behaviour of moving shapes is interpreted Heider and Simmel (1944) and Tagiuri (1960) have emphasized that contextual stimuli partly determine subjects' responses.

All these writers have been particularly interested in the context effects which occur when the stimulus and its background are presented simultaneously. Similar phenomena over a range of stimuli presented successively are often noticed in studies of the way objects are judged. Sequential context effects can be clearly demonstrated in laboratory studies of psychophysical judgments. A stimulus may be judged to be "very heavy" if it is presented after a series of light-weight ones, but appear much less heavy when presented after another set of stimuli. Much information is now available about this kind of effect, and valuable theoretical insights are accumulating (e.g. Helson, 1948; 1959; 1964). Figural after-effects constitute another example of the way immediately previous stimulation can influence later perception of objects.

How easily can these phenomena be observed in successive judgments of non-physical stimuli? Schilling (cited by Berkowitz, 1960a) and Anderson and Lampel (1965) have reported similar findings in studies of the way personality traits are judged, and Levy (1961) has observed adaptation effects in a series of judgments of people. The generalizations which have been established about context effects in the perception of objects are likely to be relevant to this type of study, and in several later chapters we shall discuss experiments of our own which bear upon the topic.

Students of object perception have been very interested in how subjects' expectancies influence the way they perceive physical stimuli. It can readily be shown that we perceive the relations between cues to be in accordance with our expectancy. In experiments where subjects are presented with playing cards with the colours of the suits reversed, judgments are often based upon expectations about suit–colour relationships rather than on the actual stimuli. Startling demonstrations of the way expected relationships determine perception are also provided by Ames' distorted room and rotating trapezoidal window.

There can be no doubt that our episodic and dispositional perceptions of people are similarly determined by expectations about the way characteristics are related to each other (cf. Luchins, 1957). We have broached this topic in an earlier section and shall consider relevant research evidence in Chapters 3, 4, and 6. The techniques used to investigate intertrait relationships are usually very different from those used in studies of object perception, and there is probably scope for interchange of methods here. For instance, would it be possible to construct an analogue of the Ames's room — an Ames's person, perhaps — in which the relations between traits are distorted from expectancy in various ways but in which a plausible combination is achieved? The confidence trickster and the charlatan are extreme examples of this type of person encountered in real-life situations.

Expectancy about what is to be presented can be manipulated by assigning names to objects exposed on a tachistoscope. It has long been known that by attaching names to ambiguous figures subjects can be made to perceive objects similar to the one suggested. Exactly the same phenomenon occurs in person perception: if names are attached to an incomplete set of stimulus material, perception is dramatically affected. Razran (1950) showed this clearly with ethnic labels attached to photographs, and Lambert and coworkers (1960) have reported similar effects with voices as the stimulus material. Investigations into this topic are considered in Chapter 7.

Another aspect of this phenomenon concerns the way an experimenter can manipulate a subject's set to perceive certain attributes of the situation. Subjects might be asked in advance to attend particularly to one characteristic of the stimulus array (number of items, items of a certain colour, the bottom items and so on). In these circumstances they will perceive markedly less about other characteristics of the array. A similar study could be made of the way people are perceived. If judges are asked in advance to look specifically at attributes related to, say, the Potency factor (see Chapter 2), would they be able to make adequate judgments of Activity? There is no doubt that set (an instance of what we have referred to as the perceiver's current state) is of paramount importance in person perception, and we shall review relevant work in Chapter 4. But more interaction between experimental psychologists and social psychologists on the meaning and functions of set would help to clarify the way its importance varies between situations.

Expectancy and set are partly determined by motivational factors, and many attempts have been made to show that motivational differences (in degree of hunger, for example) are related to differences in the way unclear stimuli are perceived. There is still controversy over the interpretation of many findings (e.g. Beach, 1951; Saugstad, 1966), but it does seem that on the whole food deprivation influences the way in which objects potentially related to food are perceived. Similar phenomena in person perception are likely to occur. It is not too fanciful to believe that people who have for some time been deprived of pleasant company see people in a different light from the way "satiated" observers see them. Indeed, studies of isolated working groups (scientists working in the Antarctic, for instance) have revealed systematic changes in emotional reactions to others (e.g. Gunderson and Nelson, 1963). And even the three-spined stickleback will respond to "suboptimal" models of a mate when the reproductive drive is high (Tinbergen, 1951)!

Interests and values influence the way we perceive people, just as they affect our perception of physical stimuli. Evaluations of Negroes, Jews and other classes of people are related to how they are perceived (e.g. Lindzey and Rogolsky, 1950; Secord, Bevan and Katz, 1956; Seeleman, 1940). In addition, Fensterheim and Tresselt (1953) and Tajfel and Wilkes (1964) have reported that characteristics which are particularly important to a person are noticed in others in a manner different from the way other attributes are perceived.

Brunswik (1934; 1956), Heider (1958), Icheiser (1949) and others have drawn attention to the likelihood that constancy phenomena occur in both types of perception. In perceiving the size, shape, brightness or colour of objects we tend to adjust our perception to minimize variability. As we move about, the tremendous changes in the cues presented by an object are largely ignored. As we walk towards a telephone kiosk it does not appear to double in size with every few steps; and as we walk past a motor car its circular headlights continue to appear circular despite changes in retinal stimulation which "ought to" make them appear elliptical. If we move a piece of black paper or a lump of coal from a dark corner of a room into direct sunlight, the intensity of the light reflecting from it increases greatly. But its "blackness" does not appear to alter very much. In a similar way we see the colour of an object to be fairly constant despite changes in the colour of the illumination falling upon it.

Laboratory measurement of these constancy phenomena has reached a stage of considerable sophistication, and a great deal is known about them. Subjects have usually been asked to match the apparent size, colour, shape or brightness with a variable standard, and comparison with the real stimulus can then be made. What is perceived in these conditions usually represents a compromise between actual stimulation and the nature of the object. Several generalizations about factors determining how much subjects will compromise are well supported and are reviewed in Chapter 8. It is very tempting to try to apply these generalizations to the perception of people. However, there is one great difficulty: we cannot readily obtain all the sets of measurements which are required. The judgment made by a perceiver represents a "perceptual compromise" (Brunswik, 1928) or a "regression to the real object" (Thouless, 1931a), and degree of constancy in object perception is calculated from indices of the real object, of the stimuli reaching the perceiver, and of the object as it is perceived. In studies of person perception we can probably measure the last of these — the impression the perceiver forms of a person. But the stimuli reaching him are not measureable in every case, and the "real object" is always extremely difficult to quantify.

There is a way around this difficulty which appears fruitful and which we shall consider when the measurement of constancy in person perception is discussed in Chapter 8; for the present it suffices to say that we report there close parallels between the operation of constancy in both types of perception.

Experimental psychologists have worked on many other aspects of the way we perceive objects. Their findings and explanations seem to be in large measure applicable to judgments of other people. Consider as a further example the research which has been concerned with the perception of differences in physical stimuli. It is generally acknowledged that it is easier to perceive differences between stimuli than it is to identify absolute levels of stimulation. Perhaps this notion should be applied to studies of person perception. In everyday life our judgments about others very often involve comparisons between people or between ourselves and others. Yet although many experiments on object perception require subjects to identify differences between one or more sets of stimuli, this is rarely done in studies of person perception (cf. Tajfel and Wilkes, 1964). It does, however, seem likely that by constructing appropriate sets of personal descriptions we could study threshold phenomena. How much do two lists of characteristics have to differ before they are seen to refer to two separate individuals? A version of Weber's law — that the change in intensity needed for a just noticeable difference is proportional to the absolute intensity of the illumination — might even be found to hold in person perception. To test this we might qualify the characteristics which are presented ("very", "somewhat", etc.; see Cliff, 1959) and see how subjects' ability to discriminate varies with degree of qualification. It might be anticipated that the more neutral attributes need to be changed more before discrimination is possible. But whether or not this is observed, we can certainly expect investigations of differences between people and between others and oneself to yield interesting findings.

Another methodological point is relevant here. Studies of object perception often involve stimuli which have to be matched with other stimuli. As P. E. Vernon (1936; 1964) has suggested, students of person perception might do well to see how these techniques are applicable to their own experimental situations. Similarly, techniques to study the amount of redundancy in a stimulus array (Attneave, 1954; Hochberg and McAlister, 1953) are likely to be useful in investigations of person perception; certainly redundancy seems to have the same effects on speed and variability of perception in both cases.

The perception of mechanical causality has been extensively studied in the laboratory. When two moving shapes come into contact with each other at an appropriate speed, subjects report that one shape appears to cause the other to move away. This seems to be a spontaneous, intuitive judgment. When subjects are asked to interpret the moving shapes as persons, judgments of causality which are similar but more complex are observed (Heider and Simmel, 1944; Tagiuri, 1960). This process might be termed the perception of social causality; and many phenomena of mechanical causality seem likely to be replicated in social situations (Heider, 1944; Strickland, 1958; Thibaut and Riecken, 1955).

Another aspect of object perception and person perception which could fruitfully be studied from the same standpoint is the way perception varies between different cultures. There is a fairly substantial body of evidence that cultural factors influence the way shapes, colours, illusions, and so on are perceived (e.g. Segall, Campbell and Herskovits, 1966). Cross-cultural studies of person perception are less common, but it is known that the way in which bodily characteristics are evaluated varies between cultures (Dennis, 1951). It is very likely that differences will be observed in the way people from different cultures select input material or in the inference and combination rules they employ. The development of perception in children is another topic which is likely to be studied more intensively in the future (cf. Gollin, 1958; Solley and Murphy, 1960; Tagiuri, 1967; Wohlwill, 1960). Investigations so far have been more concerned with the way the *physical* world is interpreted by children, but the same principles of learning are likely to be relevant to the perception of people and of social relationships. Both cultural and age differences in person perception will be examined in Chapter 4.

To summarize this discussion of the ways in which perception has been analysed and investigated: there are very marked similarities between many processes taking place in object perception and in person perception, and adopting the postulate that both will eventually be explicable by the same set of principles seems likely to lead to valuable methodological and theoretical advances. Nevertheless, several arguments have been levelled against this idea that both processes are essentially the same. We shall consider these objections, and attempt to show that none of them invalidates our working hypothesis.

First, it is sometimes felt that forming impressions of people involves so much inference and interpretation that it cannot really be the same as the "fairly simple" process of object perception. This issue has been raised by Jones and Thibaut (1958), and Taft (1960). Jones and Thibaut, for example, suggest that the processes of impression formation of greatest interest are "primarily those of inference, induction and deduction, rather than isomorphic reflections of social reality, as the word perception somehow suggests" (p. 153).

This argument rests upon a misstatement of the nature of object perception. As the previous discussion shows, we do not perceive objects in a passive manner so that the perceived world is a simple, isomorphic representation of our environment. There is rarely a direct relationship between the impression we form of a stimulus field and the objective characteristics of this field. Perception involves selection, organization, adjustment and accentuation, and this is the case with object perception as with the perception of people. Although the inferences and adjustments involved in judging people may well be more complicated than those in object perception, there is no reason to believe that the two processes are qualitatively distinct; Figure 1 applies to judgments of objects as to judgments of people.

A second type of argument that person perception is intrinsically different from object perception concerns the wide differences between individuals in the impressions they form of others. There are undoubtedly great individual differences in judgments of a particular stimulus person, and there is clearly a sense in which the perceiver contributes a great deal to his perception of others. (This point is developed in Chapters 3, 4 and 8.) But it is sometimes argued that systematic differences among perceivers are much less common in the field of object perception (e.g. Taft, 1960), and that it is therefore inadvisable to treat the two processes as the same.

The apparent lack of individual differences in the perception of objects which can be related to other variables — attitude, personality, background, age, sex and so on — is partly due to the fact that relatively few experiments have been designed to look for these differences; indeed between-subject variations are often treated as an undesirable aspect of research results (Eysenck, 1966). But there are in fact several studies of individual differences in the perception of objects, and these differences are now sufficiently well understood to justify a forecast that they operate in much the same manner in all kinds of perception. Variations between subjects' judgments of constancy have been systematized by Jenkin (1958), Thouless (1932) and others; and perceptual styles have been shown to influence the perception of illusions and causality by Brunswik (1956) and Gemelli and Cappellini (1958). There is now abundant evidence that different categories of mentally ill patients perceive the physical world in different ways (e.g. Angyal, 1948; Davis and Cullen, 1958; Hamilton, 1960; Johansson, Dureman and Sälde, 1955; Weckowicz and Witney, 1960). Klein (1951) has emphasized differences between "sharpeners" and "levellers", and Witkin and his colleagues (1954) have made fruitful studies of "field dependence". Successful attempts to isolate individual differences in object perception have been made on a wider scale by Gardner and coworkers (1959) and by Thurstone (1944). Clearly then, individual differences in object perception are both common and worthy of study. It is now necessary to investigate whether the style in which a person perceives the physical environment is related to his characteristic manner of judging others; studies of this are uncommon (cf. Bieri and Blacker, 1956; Bieri, Bradburn and Galinski, 1958).

Another difference between the two perceptual processes which has been emphasized is related to the social interaction which takes place between perceiver and perceived in person perception. Tagiuri (1958a) points out that this interaction ensures that another person is a source of cues in a manner very different to the way in which an inanimate object such as a rock is a source of cues. But as we have emphasized in the previous section, many instances of person perception involve no interaction between perceiver and perceived. Tagiuri's argument is of course inapplicable to these cases, where there are in fact surprisingly many similarities between a person and a rock. The many instances of comparable phenomena cited earlier do suggest too that person perception based upon interaction is not intrinsically different from the perception of objects. In both cases we organize and adjust our perceptions. Also we predict the future behaviour of objects (a rock thrown in our direction, for example) and modify our actions accordingly in just the same way as we react to our predictions about other people when we are interacting with them.

Related to this point is a fourth argument. The importance of sequential patterning of stimulus material in person perception is clear. We tend to sample sequences of input information, and our perceptual response is often based upon such sequences rather than on the input arising in the last second or two. It could appear that in object perception we do not need to sample such large sequences of information; our perception of the size of an object is fairly immediate for example. And yet we do depend considerably upon the sequential nature of inputs in many cases of object perception. The movements of a motor car, the frames of a cine-film, the sounds from a tape recorder are all sampled sequentially in making a judgment. The static nature of the stimulus material in psychological studies of object perception is perhaps responsible for the feeling that sequential sampling is less important here than in person perception; but it surely occurs in both cases.

A fifth point is more cogent. It has been suggested (e.g. Tagiuri, 1958a) that the way in which people are attracted to each other influences the impressions they form of each other in ways which cannot be relevant to object perception. The notion of "congruency" (Tagiuri, 1958b) is a good example of this: we tend to perceive another person's feelings for us as congruent with our feelings for him. Such a two-way process clearly cannot be at work when we perceive inanimate objects. This is indeed a valid comment, but it does not compel the conclusion that the two processes are intrinsically different. In the first place, attraction to an *object* also determines to a great extent the way in which the object is perceived. Secondly, in making judgments about objects we regularly take account of the way other people evaluate those objects. Our notion of someone's evaluation of, say, his car is not qualitatively different from our perception of how attracted he is to us, and our reaction both to him and to his car will be affected by how we perceive his evaluation of us and of the car.

Finally, it has been pointed out (e.g. Newcomb, 1958; Taft, 1960; Tagiuri, 1958a) that the similarity between the perceiver and perceived is greater in person perception than in any other instance of perception. This means that the perceiver can use himself as a frame of reference to a greater extent and can anticipate the feelings of the other on the basis of what he might feel in a similar situation. This is of course also true, but it does not point to a conceptual gap between person perception and object perception. We rely very much on frames of reference in our perception of the physical world just as we do in making judgments about other people. In all cases we build up these frames of reference through our past experience — of other people and objects as well as of ourselves.

We believe then that these six arguments against the idea that object perception and person perception are essentially the same are not sufficient to require that the idea be abandoned. The benefits which are likely to accrue from the acceptance of this working hypothesis seem to be considerable, and we have drawn attention to possible lines of investigation which are based on it. It should be emphasized that we do not regard this section as demonstrating that the two processes are in fact essentially the same. Rather, we have set up the working hypothesis that they are so and have looked at some methodological and theoretical implications of this assumption. In doing this we have attempted a slightly different demonstration — that arguments *against* the working hypothesis are not sufficiently strong for its rejection.

A final word about the differences between the two processes is, however, called for. When we assume that the two processes are essentially the same we do not mean that they involve precisely the same set of activities: in this case the two processes would be but one. We mean that the higher-order principles which will explain the processes are of the same kind in both cases. Although there are differences in the activities and stimuli involved, the arguments described above do not imply that the processes of object perception and person perception will not prove to be explicable by the same set of principles. Indeed, some differences are clearly present, and different ancillary principles will undoubtedly be required for the two processes. Just as an understanding of congruency and the importance of similarity between perceiver and perceived will not help explain the way in which we judge the size or shape of physical objects, neither will an understanding of sound localization, colour-blindness, retinal after-images and the physiological changes involved in dark adaptation tell us much about person perception. But, as we have argued, this point does not mean that there exists a qualitative difference between the two processes.

TWO TRENDS IN PERSON PERCEPTION RESEARCH

Two main lines of development of research into person perception itself may readily be isolated. Just as experimental psychologists' studies of object perception have been mainly concerned with determining how accurate are our judgments in varying circumstances, so have students of person perception also looked at length into the question of accuracy. This is the first trend to be noted. A good deal of research has been to do with a particularly interesting form of episodic judgment — perception of the emotions that another person is experiencing. Interest in the identification of emotions has been particularly strong because this topic is closely associated with the very nature of emotion and of emotional experience — areas studied intensively since the days of Darwin, James, Titchener and Wundt. There has, for example, been much work on the problem of how emotions may best be categorized. The development of this problem and of techniques to tackle it are well reviewed by Woodworth and Schlosberg (1954, Chapter 5). Research into the recognition of emotions in other people has typically required subjects to make episodic judgments based upon photographs or tape recordings in which specified emotions are simulated. Recent summaries of these studies are provided by Davitz (1964), Honkavaara (1961), and Tagiuri (1968). We touch upon the topic again in Chapter 7.

A related class of investigations deals with the accuracy of dispositional judgments. This question was tackled frequently in the early 1950s. A basic design required perceivers to make predictions about specified characteristics of a stimulus person. Accuracy of perception was assessed by comparing the perceiver's predictions with the other's self-description. For instance, Dymond (1949) used five-point scales representing six characteristics (self-confidence, selfishness, friendliness, etc.) as the basis of an "empathy test". The smaller the disparity between predictions and self-ratings, the more accurate was the perceiver said to be. This type of measure of accuracy was used by Bender and Hastorf (1950), Chowdhry and Newcomb (1952), Crockett and Meidinger (1956), Dymond (1950), Hastorf and Bender (1952), Nagle (1954), Notcutt and Silva (1951), Scodel and Friedman (1956), Scodel and Mussen (1953), and by several other investigators.

One major trend in research into person perception is thus concerned with accuracy — accuracy of episodic judgments of emotion, and accuracy of other (usually dispositional) judgments. Related studies have dealt with the validity of clinical and personnel interview techniques (e.g. Ulrich and Trumbo, 1965; Wedell and Smith, 1951). Recent developments have emphasized the potential artefacts and the methodological difficulties inherent in the study of perceptual accuracy. Important papers in this area have been published by Campbell (1955), Cronbach (1955), Cronbach and Gleser (1953), Gage and Cronbach (1955) and Hastorf, Bender and Weintraub (1955). Attempts to circumvent the obstacles revealed by these writers have been made by Bronfenbrenner, Harding and Gallwey (1958), Cline and Richards (1960), Cronbach (1958), Crow and Hammond (1957), Gage, Leavitt and Stone (1956), Hatch (1962), Smith (1966), and by others. But despite this intensive flurry of activity, a wholly satisfactory technique to measure accuracy in person perception has yet to be developed (cf. V. B. Cline, 1964; Tagiuri, 1968).

What are these difficulties that have so plagued research and have occupied so many able investigators? At this point we wish to identify trends in research rather than to cover each problem in depth. So we shall refer interested readers to those chapters by Cline and Tagiuri mentioned above, and shall merely summarize the main themes. Broadly speaking there are three areas of difficulty — the perceiver's judgment, the criterion against which this is assessed, and the relationships between perceiver and stimulus. The first problem — what judgments should perceivers make — is in effect the problem of what constitutes a satisfactory measure of person perception.* As we shall show in the next chapter, such a measure is not easy to come by. In the present context difficulties attach to the fact that different measures yield varying assessments of a person's judging ability. Studies using six five-point scales (in Dymond's measure cited above), predicted F-scale responses (e.g. Scodel and Mussen, 1953), or predicted attitude scale

---

* This problem does not so clearly beset those dealing with emotional recognition, since it is often possible to specify all alternative responses.

responses (e.g. Nagle, 1954) are unlikely to yield the same results.

Similarly, we are uncertain how to assess the criterion against which to check perceivers' predictions. In object perception this is relatively easy — size, shape and colour can be determined fairly objectively — but in the case of person perception the uncertainties are marked. Firstly, we do not know what aspect of an individual to study (this is the point made in the last paragraph), and even when a decision about this has been taken we do not know how accurate our index in fact is. Results may for example hinge on whether perceivers judge the "real nature" of the other person or what he *says* he is like (Steiner and Dodge, 1957). Or in the case of judgments of emotions being experienced by others we may have to rely upon posed facial expressions or vocal intonation which simulates an affective state. Indices of accuracy arise here from the skill and subtlety of the actor as well as from the perceiver's ability.* Generally speaking, the criterion in studies of dispositional judgments is some form of self-rating, and it is here that we face all the problems of response set and response style which beset those workers engaged in attempts to measure personality.

But the most subtle difficulties concern the way the perception and the criterion are placed together. Many early studies used global difference scores between these two measures. Cronbach (e.g. 1955) showed that behind this dyadic measure lurk several separate indices. He isolated four components of difference scores, the most relevant of which are "differential accuracy" and "stereotype accuracy". The first of these is an indication of a perceiver's ability to predict *differences between* stimulus persons, whereas stereotype accuracy (termed by Bronfenbrenner "sensitivity to the generalized other") is accuracy in judging "others in general". Scores on one component may not relate to scores on the others. Recent work (e.g. V. B. Cline, 1964) allows us to be more confident about what a given score represents, but we still have some way to go before the best measure or set of measures is determined.

Another possible artefact consists in the similarity of the perceiver and the stimulus he is asked to judge. There is ample evidence (e.g. Hastorf and Bender, 1952) that projection occurs regularly when subjects take part in an investigation of this kind. Perceivers tend to

---

* An interesting method of avoiding this difficulty has been reported by Leventhal and Sharp (1965) who recorded facial expressions of women in the labour ward of a maternity hospital.

project their own acknowledged characteristics onto others, assuming that others are similar to themselves. If a subject's response is in fact one of "assumed similarity", then the validity of this response is more dependent upon the stimulus person than on the subject himself. This is because the subject's judgment is likely to be much the same irrespective of the characteristics of the stimulus, and it will appear to be accurate when the stimulus is in fact similar to him. Unless we can control actual similarity between perceiver and perceived, accuracy estimates when projection is involved will be artefactual.

There are clearly difficulties attached to the measurement of accuracy in person perception. We touch upon these difficulties here to exemplify a major trend in research into the judgments we make of others. A great deal of work has involved the accuracy of episodic judgments (e.g. of emotions) and of dispositional judgments (e.g. in Dymond's "empathy test"). It is important to recognize, however, that studies need not necessarily deal with accuracy at all. We might investigate the way in which judgments are made and the factors which affect them, without being concerned with whether or not the judgments are correct. This would be similar to the many studies of attitude change which have been unconcerned with the propriety of the final attitude. In short, we might study "the process' rather than the accuracy of person perception.

The second major research strategy is to do just this — to concentrate upon the process itself. Fiedler (1958, 1964) has, for example, been interested in the concomitants and nature of judgments of assumed similarity without being at all concerned with the accuracy of these judgments. In general this emphasis on "process" is fairly recent. Its appeal is partly due to the recognition that to study accuracy is very difficult, and also to the advocacy of several authors in the influential volume *Person Perception and Interpersonal Behavior* (Tagiuri and Petrullo, 1958). A certain amount of hot air has been generated about which of these two approaches — concentrating on accuracy or on process — is more fruitful (e.g. G. W. Allport, 1961, p. 512). Yet it seems now to be accepted that they are not mutually exclusive, and research is progressing both into the question of perceptual accuracy and also into the nature of the process (e.g. Tagiuri, 1967).

THE ORGANIZATION OF THIS BOOK

As the layout of this first chapter has no doubt suggested, our emphasis is on the side of process studies. This book aims to increase understanding of the nature of person perception and the many factors which affect it. The importance of research into accuracy is beyond question, and major developments in this area are likely in the near future. But we deal with this topic only infrequently and in passing.

To learn about the process of judging others we have collated research findings, developed some new concepts and have carried out several experiments ourselves. In the coming chapters we bring together the resulting aggregate of ideas. Our experiments have ranged widely over the area and are described in relation to previous studies of each question. We have in most cases attempted a fairly thorough review of these earlier studies in the hope that the information brought together can summarize the present position and might suggest lines of advance.

Before the organization of later chapters is described, a brief review of the main ideas in the first chapter would assist someone dipping into the book at this point. We have suggested that it is more sensible to define person perception in terms of what *happens* than to attempt a simple verbal equivalent of the expression. An outline schema of the process has accordingly been suggested, and the relationships between major components sketched in (see Figure 1, p. 20). We have employed "judgment" or "impression" as generic terms embracing perceptions and conceptions, a conception taking place when a judgment is made in the absence of a stimulus person (see p. 4). All forms of judgment may be "dispositional" or "episodic" (see p. 8). A dispositional judgment is about the relatively permanent nature of another person (intelligent, irritable, a professor, a good tennis player, and so on), whereas episodic judgments are those made about a person's state during a specific sequence of behaviour (angry with me, enjoying his pipe, trying to get away).

A further distinction between "direct" and "indirect" perception has been suggested. This is based upon the absence or presence of a mediating communication, and five categories of perceptual situation have been listed (see Figure 2, p. 30). We have stressed that, although social psychologists' discussions have concentrated upon one of these categories, the other four should be studied in their own right. A working hypothesis that there is no qualitative difference between the

2

THE PROBLEM OF MEASUREMENT

How can we measure person perception? What are the requirements of a suitable measuring instrument and what factors have to be taken into consideration in selecting such an instrument? This chapter sets out to answer these questions by considering in detail one particular measuring technique and the rationale behind it, its validity and reliability, its limitations and general area of application. This is not a chapter concerned as such with empirical findings about judgments of others: instead it deals with the methods by which these findings may be obtained.

In Chapter 1 we drew attention to a number of ways in which perceptual activities might be classified. We said that perception could be direct or indirect, could be episodic or dispositional, could take the form of an attributive judgment, an expectancy or an affective state, and could concern both overt and covert variables. These many ways of looking at person perception present us with a special problem of measurement. For we have to decide whether we desire an instrument to measure all aspects of the process, or whether we should use a number of different instruments according to what aspect we are currently interested in.

There is another reason why we should carefully consider whether to use one general measure or a number of specific devices. This has to do with the fact that different classes of perceivers in different situations ɪerception of objects and of persons has been followed up, and reseɑ ɪnd methodological evidence bearing upon it has been examined. have noted that studies of person perception have typically aimed ɑ to assess the accuracy of judgment *or* to understand the factors uɪ lying this judgment, and we have observed that these two lin study are of course not mutually exclusive.

These themes recur throughout the book. Later chapters aim t some flesh on the skeleton of the model presented here. We shal at each component of the schema in Figure 1 and shall review ʋ known about its operation. In many cases additional research will be placed within the context of such a review. The decisio said to make up the processing centre are discussed in Chapter attributes of the perceiver (his stable characteristics and currer are stressed in Chapter 4. Chapter 5 deals specifically with feɑ direct perception, and Chapters 6 and 7 report work which oriented towards indirect perceptual situations. An effort is ɪ Chapter 8 to replicate findings about the perception of objects i of person perception. In that chapter some generalizatioɪ perceptual constancy are applied to judgments of others.

Chapter 9 is an attempt to integrate many of the ideas in sections. In that final chapter we look again at each of the co of the schema and at how these may interact in ongoing ɪ activities. Many of the points raised in this first chapter arɛ again there, and a general examination of the value of person perception is presented. Possibilities in the field of simulation and of experimental design are developed. ɪ moving on to these matters we need to spend some time how person perception may adequately be measured. This i of Chapter 2.

c

might need to be studied within different frameworks. Junior managers perceive others in an industrial setting in terms of the authority they hold, whereas female clerks are more concerned with how the same people rank as "eligible bachelors" (Triandis, 1959a); children's impressions of each other include estimates of how well they get along with their parents (Dornbusch and coworkers, 1965); members of T-groups judge other members in terms of the extent to which they openly express their feelings (Harrison and Lubin, 1965); impressions of gastric functioning might loom large in person perception in a doctor's surgery, and tailors may note features of a person's clothes which pass unnoticed by other perceivers.

Do we need to develop separate instruments to measure person perception in these different situations, or should we strive to find a technique of general applicability? Whichever we do we shall have a less-than-perfect measure. By taking *ad hoc* measures we meet grave practical difficulties, we are not able to compare outcomes with studies in other situations, and we may miss general themes relevant to all conditions. On the other hand a measure which is not bound to particular situations and subject groups is likely to ignore some of the more subtle aspects of person perception. Research workers have grasped this dilemma by both horns, and interesting measures of each type have been devised. Our personal bent is to studies of wide generality, and in our research we have settled for a non-specific instrument. This results in some loss of information about idiosyncratic aspects of judgment, but it does allow greater flexibility. Our choice of this type of measure is, however, accompanied by a recognition that more idiographic techniques can sometimes be of greater value.

What about the several categorizations of person perception we have noted above? Can a measure of dispositional judgment adequately deal with episodic perceptions? To measure the latter we need a device which will tap perceptions of a stimulus person's intentions and aspirations at one point in time. These perceptions will be more transient and possibly more subtle than those involved in dispositional judgments, and it may be difficult to develop a measure applicable to both. Such a general measure would clearly be valuable. It would also have to cope with all three aspects of the perceptual output suggested in Figure 1 (p. 20). In measuring the attributive aspect we are likely to cover the expectancy component, but additional steps may have to be taken to assess affective reactions. To measure both direct and indirect perception with a single instrument is not difficult, and studies of this are reported later.

A final point concerns whether we should try to deal with both covert and overt distal variables. As we pointed out previously, students of person perception have tended to avoid the measurement of overt variables and have concentrated on more covert ones. A disproportionately small body of knowledge about the perception of overt characteristics has been acquired, and we shall perforce deal mainly with the others. We are therefore more concerned to find a measure of the way covert distal variables are perceived. The distinction between judgments of overt and covert personal characteristics has much in common with the division between denotative and connotative meaning as applied to language. Denotative meaning is concerned with the referent of a word, what the word refers to or denotes. Connotative meaning on the other hand is concerned with the implications, associations or connotations of a word. The relationship between denotative and connotative meaning is not a straightforward one. Two denotatively distinct words may be connotatively similar; thus "Arctic" and "Antarctic" refer to different geographical locations, but both probably have very similar implications of temperature and terrain as far as most people are concerned. Furthermore a simple word like "book" has a fairly clear-cut denotative meaning, but it also has a connotative meaning that will vary from person to person and from culture to culture.

A specific person can also be said to have two meanings. A name might denote a person who is male, about six feet tall, has brown eyes and is wearing a green suit. Any index of denotative meaning should contain this sort of information. On the other hand the connotations of the name are of a very different kind: an index of connotative meaning might contain the notions of being unintelligent, pompous and unpleasant — ideas which are more subjective and hence more difficult to measure satisfactorily.

Thus when we ask about the "meaning" of a certain person we are concerned with two conceptually distinct notions. These notions coincide to a large extent with the two types of judgment involved in person perception. The denotative meaning of a person corresponds to those aspects which are overt while the connotative meaning of a person has to do with judgments of his covert characteristics. Since our main interest at present is in this latter kind of perceptual judgment, some measure of connotative meaning would obviously be of great help to us.

Osgood and his colleagues have developed just such an instrument to measure connotative meaning which appears to be of general utility. This instrument — the semantic differential — is one we have employed regularly in studies to be reported later. Throughout this book reviews and discussions of the present understanding of a topic are augmented with brief accounts of research we ourselves have conducted. Much of this research is based upon the use of the semantic differential. We originally approached this measure with caution and a certain amount of scepticism, and have spent considerable time investigating its suitability. We have gathered evidence which compels the conclusion that it is a very satisfactory measure which can fruitfully be used to measure a wide variety of aspects of person perception. Although the instrument is most fitted to tap judgments of covert characteristics, we believe it can cope effectively with both direct and indirect, episodic and dispositional perception, involving attributions and expectancies as well as some affective responses. Our evidence for this is set out in the present chapter. No up-to-date review of methodological work on this widely used instrument is available and we have accordingly brought together ideas and results from a diffuse variety of studies. This review may in consequence be of general value rather than being of interest only to students of person perception. Conversely, the issues raised are relevant to any techniques to measure impressions of others, and indeed we examine several other instruments in the course of the chapter.

One point will be emphasized frequently and we should like to draw attention to it at the outset. The semantic differential is a technique by which many different measures can be obtained rather than being in itself a single measuring device. We can perhaps draw a parallel between the semantic differential as used to measure meaning and the principle of expansion of various substances as used to measure temperature. Just as a temperature gauge or thermometer can be of many different types and contain different kinds of expanding substances to perform its measurements, so the semantic differential can vary in construction and comprise many different individual scales. The observation that one particular thermometer is a good instrument does not mean that all thermometers are equally efficient; similarly evidence for the validity of a particular combination of semantic differential scales cannot be generalized to all other combinations. Furthermore, just as certain thermometers, such as the clinical thermometer, are more suitable for certain tasks, so are some semantic differential forms more meaningful when used in one context than in another. Thus in reaching conclusions about the semantic differential or thermometers in general one must have regard to large numbers of individual instances of measurement, and make generalizations on the basis of these. If a number of studies suggest that measurement has been successful then we may conclude that the technique can be satisfactory. But we may still come across examples of bad semantic differential forms, and of inefficient thermometers.

There is of course now no doubt that the measurement of temperature by the principle of controlled expansion is usually a successful technique. In the following pages we aim to discover whether we can make similar claims for the measurement of person perception by the semantic differential.

THE NATURE OF THE SEMANTIC DIFFERENTIAL

As its name suggests, the semantic differential is a technique for specifying differences between concepts in terms of their meanings. The term "concept" is taken to cover all possible objects of judgment. Table, Father, This Red Patch, France, My Ideal Self, This Rorschach Card, Paper Clip and so on are all concepts whose connotative meaning may be ascertained by use of the semantic differential. We are most concerned with the way in which *people* are perceived, so that the concepts we have been most interested in are mainly persons. In this discussion we shall usually refer to "the perception (or conception) of a person", rather than to "the meaning of a concept", so that the Prime Minister is both a stimulus person and a concept, and "perception of the Prime Minister" is treated as equivalent to "connotative meaning of the Prime Minister".*

Early work on what was to become known as semantic differentiation is reported by Osgood (1952), Osgood and Stagner (1941), Osgood and Suci (1952) and Stagner and Osgood (1941, 1946), but the most detailed account of its rationale and use is provided in *The Measurement of Meaning* by Osgood, Suci and Tannenbaum (1957). More recently,

---

* That this omits consideration of some aspects of perception has of course been noted above.

considerable attention has been devoted to the use of the semantic differential in cross-linguistic studies (e.g. Jansen and Smolenaars, 1967; Osgood, 1962; Tanaka, 1962; Triandis, 1964b; Triandis and Osgood, 1958), and a number of striking intercultural similarities in meaning systems have been observed.

In the form in which it is administered the semantic differential typically contains a set of scales listed down a page, at the top of which the stimulus person is identified. Each individual scale comprises a number of gradations between an adjective and its opposite. These adjectives are usually referred to as "polar terms". A typical six-scale form might look like this:

President Johnson

False	:—:—:—:—:—:—:—:—:—:	True
Sharp	:—:—:—:—:—:—:—:—:—:	Dull
Delicate	:—:—:—:—:—:—:—:—:—:	Rugged
Worthless	:—:—:—:—:—:—:—:—:—:	Valuable
Fast	:—:—:—:—:—:—:—:—:—:	Slow
Tense	:—:—:—:—:—:—:—:—:—:	Relaxed

Subjects are asked to consider the stimulus person in terms of each of the scales on the form. They place a check mark in one of the divisions for each scale indicating how much they believe the particular scale is expressive of the meaning of the concept being rated. The closer the check mark is placed to one of the polar terms (the extremities of the scale) the more applicable is the particular term to the stimulus person as far as the subject is concerned. Most forms of the semantic differential employ scales which have an uneven number of response alternatives, so that a response placed in the central compartment indicates that the polar terms are seen as equally applicable to the stimulus person or that the subject has insufficient information on which to base a decision. It is possible to employ scales with an even number of response alternatives (e.g. Fiedler, 1958; Friedman and Gladden, 1964), but there are difficulties attached to this procedure when perceptions of relatively unknown people are being measured. In these cases subjects may feel they need a neutral point at which to respond.

Most research workers follow the example of Osgood and his colleagues and provide seven divisions along each scale. The choice of seven alternatives is based on early experience with different kinds of scale (see Osgood, Suci and Tannenbaum, 1957, p. 85). It was noted that fewer divisions irritated respondents and that if nine alternatives were used the distribution of responses was unsatisfactory. Related to the number of scale divisions used is the crucial point of whether verbal labels should be given to each scale point. In many studies an explicit label is attached to each of the possible responses; subjects might be instructed for instance to treat the outermost compartment as *extremely false* or *extremely rugged*, etc., the next response as *quite false* or *quite rugged*, and so on. If this procedure is adopted the number of alternatives that may usefully be offered is limited, since with a wide range of responses the small distinction between adjacent steps (e.g. between "somewhat" and "slightly") will become blurred. Wells and Smith (1960) have directly compared responses to (eight-point) scales with and without verbal labels, and they report that median scale responses are almost identical. However, it was found that when labels were available subjects made less extreme responses, and this might be an important consideration in some situations.

In the studies presented later we have not used verbal labels, apart from drawing subjects' attention to the middle alternative, but have merely requested that more extreme responses should be used to indicate greater applicability of a polar term. This form of instruction has worked very well with our subject samples and it has allowed us to use nine (and occasionally eleven) alternative responses for each scale. We believe that in research with relatively intelligent subjects the optimum number of divisions is nine, and we shall justify this claim when we discuss the results of Experiments 2, 7 and 8 later in this chapter. It may, however, be advisable to use fewer scale units in studies with less intelligent samples or with children (e.g., Donahoe, 1961; Maltz, 1963).

It is customary to ask subjects to work rapidly through the scales on each form without pausing for more than a few seconds on each response. After initial practice, subjects are able to respond at this speed without difficulty, so that one can expect a 12-scale form to be completed in less than a minute by subjects who have had previous experience. Such a rapid rate of response makes the semantic differential an attractive instrument both for the subject and for the investigator, but this ease of response also causes many people to be very suspicious about the reliability and validity of measurements so obtained. We shall consider reliability and validity in some detail later in this chapter, and pause here only to point out that the speed at which subjects work appears not to affect the stability of semantic differential responses. Evidence for this comes from an experiment by Miron (1961a) in which the stability coefficients of responses from two groups of subjects were compared. Subjects in one group had been instructed to respond rapidly by giving their first impressions, and the second group had been asked to work slowly and carefully through the scales and to give a considered judgment in each case. The responses of the rapidly-responding subjects were in fact more stable, although the differences between groups failed to reach significance. Miron observed that subjects prefer to work quickly, and we have also found this to be the case. In all the experiments we shall describe, subjects have been instructed to respond rapidly.

The raw data obtained with the semantic differential consist of checkmarks made against a number of bipolar scales. A numerical value may be attached to each individual response in order to make these data amenable to statistical treatment. We have numbered response alternatives from 1 to 9, specifying the positive polar term for each pair of adjectives as 9. With this range of alternatives, 5 is of course the mid-point. The responses of one subject to a set of scales can be represented diagrammatically by drawing a profile of these responses. Statistical analysis of responses by *a single subject* is sometimes required, especially in clinical studies, and several analytic procedures for use when $N=1$ have been developed (e.g. Osgood, Suci and Tannenbaum, 1957, Chapter 3). We have been more concerned to analyse the response patterns of *groups of subjects*; in this case the average response to each scale may be calculated.

Suppose for the moment that we wish to study the way in which the political beliefs of perceivers are related to differences in the way they judge the Prime Minister. We might obtain semantic differential profiles of the Prime Minister from two groups of subjects from two different political organizations. How can we say whether these profiles are significantly different? A commonly used measure is the generalized distance score (Cronbach and Gleser, 1953; Osgood and Suci, 1952). Such a score (D) indicates the *overall* distance between two profiles, and is defined as the square root of the sum of the squared differences between scores on each scale. ($D = \sqrt{\sum(X_1 - X_2)^2}$.) The calculation of D is fairly simple, and it is clear that a larger D indicates a greater difference between profiles. It is possible to test the significance of the value of a straightforward derivative from D (Horn, 1961) if certain assumptions about the data are made.

There are, however, several cogent arguments against the use of D-scores when assessing the difference between profiles. These have been clearly propounded by Cronbach (1958) and by Jackson (1962). The objections to D are based on the fact that the same D-score can be derived from a number of different relationships between profiles. Consider the following two pairs of profiles: P_1 and P_2; P_3 and P_4.

Scale	P_1	P_2	Scale	P_3	P_4
1	2	2	1	6	4
2	8	8	2	1	3
3	6	6	3	8	6
4	3	3	4	7	5
5	7	3	5	2	2

The D-score between P_1 and P_2 is the same as that between P_3 and P_4, despite the fact that there are differences on four scales between P_3 and P_4 but only on a single scale in the former comparison. A particular D-score tells us little about the nature of the relationship between a pair of profiles, and reliance on the D statistic may result in important differences on one or more scales being overlooked.

We prefer to study the differences between groups of subjects in greater detail, and have adopted the procedure of testing for significant differences between sets of responses *to each scale*. To carry further the discussion of our imaginary investigation into the way in which the Prime Minister is perceived: we should test for a significant difference in perceptions by studying the difference between average scores on *each* of the scales making up the profile. This is more laborious but it is a more rigorous procedure and one which is likely to lead to a more meaningful interpretation of a set of results.

An interesting issue in the analysis of semantic differential data has to do with the validity of using parametric statistics and significance tests. Can we for instance cite means and standard deviations, or should we deal in medians and semi-interquartile ranges? Are t-tests, F-tests and product–moment correlations to be forsaken for their non-parametric counterparts? Psychologists have been encouraged by Siegel (1956) and others to be very wary of violating assumptions behind the application of parametric procedures. How cautious need we be when studying responses to semantic differential scales?

It is commonly stipulated that for parametric methods to be applicable three main requirements have to be satisfied. Firstly, the variances of two samples need to be fairly similar if we are to use parametric tests. This condition should not trouble us unduly since the limited range of responses on a semantic differential scale usually guarantees it. Secondly it has been argued that scales need to have equal intervals; and finally there is the usual requirement that the response distributions should be approximately normal.

The degree to which a scale fulfils the second of these conditions — being an interval one — is often very difficult to establish. However, one study of semantic differential measurement has been published which is directly concerned with the question (Osgood, Suci and Tannenbaum, 1957, pp. 146–153; see also Messick, 1957). The results indicate that the deviations from equal intervals are small, and well within the error limits of the instrument. Certainly we would expect the errors introduced by the incorrect assumption of equal intervals to be extremely small: Messick reports that correlations between scaled and assumed values are of the order of 0·99.

So it would seem that the possibility of unequal scale intervals need not prevent us from using parametric techniques to analyse semantic differential responses. In fact it may be the case that the whole question of equal intervals has achieved a rather exaggerated importance. Certainly there are many practical instances where it is not necessary to meet the assumption that a particular scale is an interval one (e.g. Ghiselli, 1964, pp. 38–44). N. H. Anderson (1961) has forcefully denied that such a requirement is necessary. He cites Lord's (1953) observation that the statistical test we use can hardly be cognisant of the empirical meaning of the numbers with which it deals.

What of the third requirement — a normal distribution of responses? We may first wonder if semantic differential responses are likely to be markedly skewed. A very skewed distribution will arise if the average judgment of a group of subjects is located near the extremity of a scale. This might occur with concepts other than persons; consider the likely responses to Feather on the scale *light–heavy*. But in research on person perception the average response is normally less extreme, and we can conclude from study of the many sets of responses described in later chapters that it is not usual for the distribution of responses to be skewed. Furthermore Jenkins, Russell and Suci (1958) in a study of an extremely varied set of concepts observed a correlation between mean and median responses of 0·97; the distribution of responses from these subjects cannot have been skewed.

So far so good: semantic differential responses in studies of person perception are unlikely to be skewed. But non-normality can arise from another source. A distribution may have several peaks. A bimodal distribution in which the middle points of a scale are rarely used would, for example, present difficulties. We need not always strive for perfectly normal curves — rectangular distributions will suffice for product-moment correlations (Guilford 1965, p. 108) — but clearly bimodal ones would be unacceptable.

We have made many studies of the way responses are distributed, and in every instance except two a unimodal pattern has been found. This is particularly interesting since we have used nine-point scales instead of the more customary shorter ones. Mitchell (1965) has in fact shown that students' responses to politicians and to Self on eleven-point scales are also normally distributed. What about the two aberrant investigations to which we refer? These were the two studies in which we forsook a subject population of University students for the luxury of a nationally-representative sample (see Experiments 31 and 32). On these occasions our subjects tended to check the outermost positions (1 and 9) very frequently so that a bimodal distribution was generated. This difference between university subjects and less homogeneous samples can be viewed against a back-cloth of other research. Light, Zax and Gardiner (1965) studied schoolchildren's tendencies to make extreme responses. Outermost responses were very prevalent amongst younger and less intelligent subjects, but occurred significantly less frequently as age and I.Q. increased. Arthur (1966) observed variations in relation to psychiatric illness; frequency of extreme response was higher for psychotics than for neurotics. Similar findings have been reported by Neuringer (1963) and by Zax, Gardiner and Lowy (1964). Mogar (1960) observed that the tendency to employ extreme response categories was positively related to F-scale score.

These investigations — all using semantic differential instruments — yield a pattern of results into which our studies can be fitted. Subjects drawn from a university population are of high intelligence, are relatively normal, and tend to obtain fairly low F-scale scores. Their responses are likely to be normally distributed and to be amenable to parametric testing procedures, whereas the judgments made by other groups do not always allow this because they are bimodally distributed.

In nearly all the investigations reported later (those employing student subjects) we have used parametric procedures, and are confident about the validity of this strategy.

The dichotomy between parametric and non-parametric tests appears in fact to be breaking down. N. H. Anderson (1961) has argued that the type of measuring scale used has little relevance to whether parametric or non-parametric tests should be applied (p. 316). Characteristics common both to analysis of variance and to non-parametric tests have been pointed out by McHugh (1963), and Burke (1963) has raised a number of more general points about this issue. Boneau (1960) and Baker, Hardyck and Petrinovitch (1966) have studied the consequences of systematically violating assumptions said to underlie the t-test; they have provided startling indications of its robustness and by implication of the robustness of F-tests of analysis of variance. Boneau urges that psychologists feel free to use parametric procedures in many situations where "the current emphasis on non-parametric methods" would normally cause them to be apprehensive (p. 63). There are of course great benefits accruing from the use of parametric procedures. They tend to be more powerful, and we are able to make more use of the data at our disposal. Computer programmes are more readily available for data-processing assistance, and the whole range of factor-analytic techniques becomes appropriate.

The attraction of semantic differential scales lies partly in their amenability to parametric interpretation techniques. A particularly important contribution to the development of the instrument has been made by factor analysis, and we turn next to the part this has played.

CORRELATIONS BETWEEN SCALES

There have been many attempts to ascertain whether there is any correlation between responses to different scales, and thus evidence for clusters of scales which measure similar semantic connotations. If it were possible to show that responses to a wide range of scales always fell into a small number of independent groups, then (apart from the interesting theoretical implications of this) there might be a firm basis for selecting scales to be included in any semantic differential form. Suppose that factor analyses of scale responses always revealed three independent factors which accounted for nearly all the variance. This might suggest that if the scales included in a form were selected to cover each of these factors, then we could be sure that we had not missed out anything important in our measurement. If we could show by a series of analyses that people's responses to a wide range of concepts always generated three and only three independent factors, then we could predict that *only* these three factors needed to be measured in any future investigation. The practical value of this would obviously be enormous.

There have been many reports of factor-analytic studies of semantic differential data (e.g. Jenkins, Russell and Suci, 1958; Norman, 1959; Osgood, Suci and Tannenbaum, 1957; Osgood, 1962; Tanaka, Oyama and Osgood, 1963). Subjects are asked to give their judgments of a large number of concepts on a large number of scales, and the interrelationships between scales are analysed. The results of these studies have been remarkably consistent. Three factors appear to be dominant, and these three factors emerge in roughly the same order of magnitude from most analyses. They are usually termed the Evaluative, Potency and Activity factors. The Evaluative factor regularly appears first and accounts for up to three-quarters of the extractable variance. It appears that the most important component of the reaction to a concept is a general like-or-dislike, pro-or-con, approach-or-avoid response.* Examples of scales which are usually found to have a high loading on the Evaluative factor are *good–bad*, *beautiful–ugly*, *fair–unfair* and *honest–dishonest*. The second factor to appear in most analyses is a Potency factor which typically accounts for approximately half as much variance as the Evaluative factor. This second factor is concerned with power and related notions like size, weight and toughness. *Strong–weak*, *heavy–light*, *rugged–delicate* and *hard–soft* are all scales which normally have a high loading on the Potency factor. The third factor — Activity — is usually of similar magnitude to the Potency factor, and is exemplified by scales like *fast–slow*, *active–passive*, *tense–relaxed* and *excitable–calm*. It is sometimes found that the Potency and Activity factors collapse into a single Dynamism factor, but the consistency with which the three major factors are found is such that Osgood and his colleagues have felt able to use them as measures of the three dimensions of "semantic space". It

---

* Attempts have been made to prevent subjects from making this type of response, but they have not been successful (Krieger, 1964). One study (Komorita and Bass, 1967) has suggested that in some situations it may be helpful to view the general evaluative reaction as having several distinguishable components. The scales employed here were, however, not selected on the basis of prior analysis with the experimental subject and concept sample, and we should perhaps await further investigations before drawing a firm conclusion.

might appear then that if a research worker includes in a semantic differential form scales to represent each of these factors, he may be confident that he will obtain information about the major kinds of responses which people normally make.

However, let us look further into these factor-analytic studies before we accept this conclusion. Firstly, we should note that general statements which cover *all* concept-classes need to be treated with caution. For example, although the order of importance of factors is usually Evaluation, Potency and Activity, this is found to vary when certain classes of concepts are studied. Miron (1961b) found that the Potency factor (rather than the Evaluative one) was most salient in an analysis of responses to auditory stimuli. Tanaka, Oyama and Osgood (1963) observed that an Activity factor accounted for most variance in a study of the meaning of colours, and that Potency was most important in judging combinations of lines. These latter investigations did, however, note a relative dominance of the Evaluative factor in response to words. Elliott and Tannenbaum (1963) and Tanaka and Osgood (1965) have also studied colours and shapes, and they too have reported that the Evaluative factor is less important in judgments of these classes of concept.

It appears then that the factor structure for the meaning of non-linguistic concepts (sounds, colours, forms, etc.) may be slightly different from the meaning structure of linguistic concepts. Although the same factors are found, these may be in a different order of importance when we turn our attention away from the meaning of words, places, people, etc. In this book we are primarily concerned with the way in which people are perceived, and we shall henceforth restrict our discussion to concepts more similar to this class than the non-linguistic material investigated in the set of studies just referred to. For the present we shall merely note that our arguments probably need some revision when applied to non-linguistic concepts.

This leaves us with the question of how valid are the conclusions drawn from factor-analytic investigations of the meaning of people, places and words. A factor structure which emerges from any analysis is clearly dependent upon the scales, upon the subjects and upon the concepts which are studied. How confident can we be about the adequacy of the samples of scales, subjects and concepts which have been employed? Firstly, it is very important that the sample of scales chosen is a realistic one. If three-quarters of the scales admitted into the factor analysis are, say, evaluative items which have been unjustifiably selected, we could place little reliance on the finding that a large Evaluative factor emerges. We need to be confident that the scale sampling is unbiased.

In some of the earlier studies (e.g. Osgood, Suci and Tannenbaum, 1957), the scale sampling was somewhat unsatisfactory, and it might be argued that the results of the factor analysis are consequently suspect. Be that as it may, the techniques for scale sampling which have been developed more recently are of greater validity, and the factor structure which is observed is the same as that found in the previous research. One sophisticated method of sampling (e.g. Miron and Osgood, 1966) is based upon the spew hypothesis (Underwood and Schulz, 1960) — that the "availability" of words is directly related to the frequency with which the words have been experienced. The "availability" of words is assessed from responses to a word association task in which subjects give an adjectival associate to each of a comprehensive set of nouns (e.g. "The butterfly is . . ."). In studies by Osgood and his colleagues some 10,000 adjectives have been obtained by this technique, and these are assumed (via the spew hypothesis) to be those which subjects have experienced most frequently. A representative selection is then drawn from this population, and it is this latter sample of adjectives which is employed in the investigation of factor structure. Many samples of scales derived by this method have been analysed to reveal a factor structure essentially the same as that reported earlier.

It appears then that the Evaluative–Potency–Activity structure is fairly general across *scales*. To what extent does it depend on the subjects whose responses are analysed? There is a rapidly growing body of evidence that the same structure emerges from studies conducted with subjects of all kinds. Ware (1958) found (apparently to his surprise) that it did not vary with differences in the intelligence of his subjects, and Di Vesta (1966) observed a similar pattern of responses for children at every age from eight to twelve. Numerous studies of English-speaking subjects have indicated the prominence of these three factors, and a large-scale cross-cultural project (e.g. Osgood, 1962) is revealing the same structure in many different parts of the world. Other investigators who have not been directly concerned with establishing the "true" factorial structure of judgment have regularly noted that the structure present in their scales is unaffected by characteristics of the judge. For example, in Experiment 1 (reported on p. 70) factor structure was independent of perceivers' ethnocentrism. Triandis (1964a) reported broadly similar structures for different religious groups, and in a study of job perceptions (Triandis, 1960) he derived similar patterns of scale intercorrelations from managers and workers. Suci (1960) has reported a high degree of similarity between factors extracted from responses by different cultural groups in the United States. To a high degree then, factor structure is invariant across subjects.

An important issue concerns whether the emergent three-factor structure is an artefact arising from the way responses to a hetero-geneous collection of stimuli have been combined. Many of the supporting analyses have been based upon a summation of responses over concepts; in this way Jenkins, Russell and Suci (1958) and Norman (1959) analysed together subjects' responses to as many as 360 different concepts. It is possible that the factors they extracted would not have been observed if individual concepts had been studied separately. However, it appears from other investigations that we may rest satisfied on this point: the three major factors have also been extracted from analyses of judgments of single concepts (e.g. Osgood, 1962; Osgood, Suci and Tannenbaum, 1957). But it does seem likely that analyses of individual concepts will reveal differences in the nature and magnitude of factors beyond the third. We have for instance results of an analysis of judgments of a brand of cigarettes from which a small Situational factor emerges, related to whether the cigarettes are for special occasions or for everyday smoking. Such a factor is not likely to emerge from analysis of the way in which another concept (the Prime Minister, for example) is perceived.

In general then it looks as if the three major factors will be present in an analysis of responses to individual concepts, but that idiosyncratic factors will be of greater magnitude than in analysis of a miscellany of concepts (cf. Triandis, 1960). So it might appear that we could produce an all-purpose semantic differential form containing scales with high loadings on each of the three major factors, and that this could give us a virtually complete picture of the way in which any concept is judged. Such a form could perhaps be supplemented with a few scales which appear peculiarly relevant to a particular concept in which we are interested. The selection of scales in this way to cover all aspects of a concept's meaning would obviously be extremely convenient.

It would also enable us to deal with the three components of a perceptual response which were described in Chapter 1 — the attributive, expectancy and affective components. It is clear that semantic differential scales require subjects to make a series of attributive judgments. Expectancies are tapped in conjunction with these attributive judgments (see pp. 13 and 174) and at the same time we are also able to measure a strongly affective component by means of the Evaluative scales. Clearly we could with other measures be concerned with further affective reactions like fear or despondency, but the semantic differential does provide an index of one major aspect of emotional response which is seen to be of wide generality. The instrument is thus a technique embracing all three components of person perception.

But the actual selection of scales to cover all factors is not as easy as it might appear: although a similar set of factors may be observed in analyses of widely differing concepts, the identity of scales with high loadings on each factor varies considerably between concepts. Although *sociable–unsociable* may have a very high loading on the Evaluative factor for Concept *A*, the loading of this scale on the Evaluative factor for Concept *B* might be zero. Examples of this difficulty have been given by Osgood, Suci and Tannenbaum (1957, pp. 176 ff.). In one of their analyses they found that most of the 76 scales showed significant variation across concepts in the size (and sometimes even in the direction) of their correlations with other scales. For example, *graceful–awkward* was correlated +0·34 with *soft–hard* for the concept Family Life, but −0·26 with *soft–hard* for the concept Knife. These differences imply that the scales with highest loadings on a factor for one concept need not be the same scales as those with the highest loading on this factor for another concept. In fact, in the study by Osgood, Suci and Tannenbaum not one of the five scales with highest Evaluative factor loadings for Family Life appeared in the first five scales on this factor for Knife. We must conclude that an all-purpose semantic differential form could not validly be used for both of these two concepts.

It appears then that the meanings of individual scales and their correlation with each other may vary considerably from concept to concept. For example, *sharp* when applied to America has a dynamic, favourable meaning and is found to correlate highly with terms like *successful*, *intentional* and *progressive*. But when *sharp* is applied to Knife it has its ordinary denotative meaning and is found to correlate with scales like *angular* and *rough*. Instances of concept–scale interaction of this kind suggest that it may not be practicable to draw up a semantic differential form which adequately covers the three major factors and which is applicable to a wide range of concepts. If these factors are to be covered we may need a special form for each concept, and we may not know which polar terms to include until we have factor-analysed responses to a large number of scales previously applied to this concept. Such a procedure is impracticable, and if it were necessary much of the charm of semantic differential measurement would be lost.

We believe that the range of concepts employed by Osgood and his colleagues was in fact so wide that the evidence for concept–scale interaction was maximized. It may be possible to devise a single instrument which is applicable to a more restricted variety of concepts. Osgood's study was of concepts like America, Birth, Time, Snow, Me and Dawn. It is not surprising that the meaning of individual scales was found to vary over such a disparate selection. It may be the case that if the range of concepts in which we are interested is narrower it will be possible to construct an adequate semantic differential form which is applicable to all members of this concept class. Indeed there is a hint of this in two recent studies. Although Tanaka, Oyama and Osgood (1963) found that the meaning of a number of scales varied between applications to words and to shapes and colours, Tanaka and Osgood (1965) found little evidence for concept–scale interaction when scales were applied only to the two latter types of concept. Variations between concepts are clearly more limited in the later investigation. It is possible that variations between *persons* are also sufficiently limited for the meaning of a set of scales to be stable across this class of concepts. If this were so, when measuring person perception we could use a standard set of scales which had been selected from factor analysis of judgments of a fairly small number of people.*

To recapitulate the discussion so far: there is clear evidence that a similar factor structure emerges in the analysis of semantic differential responses to individual concepts, but that the meaning of scales, and hence their factor loading, varies between concepts. This implies that different scales might be required to cover each factor when we switch our attention from one concept to another. But it is likely that this concept–scale interaction will not be so marked across a restricted class of concepts. So, although the phenomenon raises difficulties for research workers wishing to measure the meaning of concepts of all kinds, the

* A recent paper by Mueller (1966) lends support to this suggestion.

effects of concept–scale interaction may not be as serious for those concerned only with judgment of persons.

We have tried to employ standard sets of scales in our studies of person perception. These scales were selected for their high loadings on the three major factors when applied to people. When a specific hypothesis about a set of results warranted it, we have supplemented these standard scales with others which appeared relevant. We have always indicated in the text when this supplementary procedure has been followed. The important point here is that the standard scales were selected quite independently of the predictions made about a particular experimental situation. This is a necessary precaution, since the unbiassed selection of scales *after* predictions have been made is not at all easy.

A standard form appears to have clear advantages. But before we can use this, one question has yet to be answered. Can we in fact show that the correlations between scales — and hence the factor structure — do not shift appreciably when the scales are applied to different concepts belonging to the same class, in this case the class of persons? If they do shift to a marked extent, as they did in the study by Osgood and his colleagues of a wide range of concepts, then our faith in the value of a standard set of scales for measuring the perception of people will be misplaced. We have investigated this question, and our findings are presented below.

Experiment 1

Ninety-seven undergraduate subjects indicated their judgments of eleven national leaders on a set of twelve semantic differential scales. The scales were selected to be representative of the Evaluative, Potency and Activity factors, and four scales from each factor were included in the forms. As in all the experiments to be reported later, the order of scale presentation and the direction of scale polarity were varied randomly to provide four versions of the instrument. At the time of the study all the stimulus persons were of international prominence. They were Castro, De Gaulle, Erhard, Johnson, Kenyatta, Makarios, Nasser, Nkrumah, Shastri, Tito and Wilson. The order in which these persons were judged was also varied randomly across subjects.

The scales employed were *good–bad, fair–unfair, true–false,* and *kind–cruel; hard–soft, rugged–delicate, strong–weak* and *bold–timid; emotional–unemotional, fast–slow, dangerous–safe* and *active–passive.* Responses to each stimulus person were factor analysed and the analyses submitted to varimax rotation.

Since we had begged the question of what is the "true" factor structure by using preselected groups of scales, these analyses naturally do not bear upon the conclusions reported earlier about the nature and relative importance of the factors which generally emerge. Suffice it to say that the three factors we had assumed to be present clearly were present, and that they accounted for 72% of the extractable variance, with no other single factor accounting for more than 3%. The assumptions about factor composition (i.e. about which scales represented which factor) were valid in every case except one: *dangerous–safe* turned out to be very heavily loaded on the Evaluative factor and not on the Activity factor. In retrospect, this is to be anticipated in the case of the stimulus persons studied.

What evidence for concept–scale interaction is there in the case of this more homogeneous class of concepts? Virtually none. The inter-correlations between scales were very similar for each of the eleven stimulus persons. The results may conveniently be summarized in terms of the agreement between the factor loadings of the twelve scales when applied to different stimuli. The degree to which each scale represents a factor (i.e. its loading) should be similar for each stimulus person. We can measure this similarity by means of the coefficient of concordance (W). In the case of each of the three factors we are studying W exceeds 0·80. It appears then that the meaning of scales is fairly stable within a class of people, and that Osgood's gloomy conclusions from a more variegated set of concepts need not apply to studies of person perception.

One other aspect of Experiment 1 may be mentioned at this point. It has already been noted (on p. 67) that factor structure appears to be consistent across different groups of subjects. We introduced a further test of this into the present study by obtaining subjects' responses to an ethnocentrism scale. Ethnocentrism might be considered a characteristic which is likely to affect perception of national leaders. And sure enough some differences in the judgments made by high and low E-scorers emerged (see Chapter 4). These differences could perhaps be interpreted in terms of different political ideologies (for E-score was significantly related to political belief), and we need not deal with them further at this stage. Of greater relevance is the question of whether variations in E-score are accompanied by differences in factor loadings. We looked

at this question by separately factor analysing the responses of high
E-scorers (the top 31 subjects) and of low E-scorers (the bottom 32
subjects). This time we summed the data across concepts in the more
orthodox manner. Similarity of factor structure was assessed by
calculating the rank correlation (*rho*) between the scale loadings of
high-E and low-E groups for each factor. The values of *rho* were $+0·91$
for the Evaluative factor, $+0·95$ for the Potency factor and $+0·86$ for
the Activity factor. It seems that this subject characteristic does not
influence the factor structure of responses, despite the fact that it can
affect the nature of the responses themselves.

Before moving on from factorial studies of semantic differential
responses one further point has to be made. Although it is important to
select scales to cover the three major factors, it does not follow from
this that responses are best analysed and interpreted only in terms of
factors. Quite a number of investigators have presented their results
merely in terms of factor scores (the weighted average score on the
scales representing a particular factor) and to do this they have factor
analysed their data first.

We are unhappy with this procedure in so far as it leads researchers
to cite and compare only the factor scores. Typically this involves
dealing with two or three values rather than the larger number which
was originally obtained. Instead of working in this way we prefer to
study and analyse findings scale by scale. Some justification for this
approach should be given. We believe firstly that factor scores suffer
from a disadvantage noted in connection with D-scores: that information might be lost in summation. This loss is of course smaller than
with a D-score since responses to the scales are by definition correlated,
but there seems no good reason to risk even this possible loss. As we
have already noted, most studies of person perception yield only
limited measures of the process, and there is no benefit in further
limiting the data available for interpretation.

Secondly, the factors which are quoted are often *ad hoc* constructs of
little general importance. This is because they are based on inadequate
samples of subjects, concepts and scales. To analyse the responses of an
experimental group to a concept on, say, ten scales is not to generate a
meaningful set of factors. There is little value in citing scores combined
in this way when we can cite all the ten scores which are available.

A third objection to a complete reliance on factor scores is that it
makes comparison between investigations almost impossible. A factor

which emerges from one set of results and is labelled "Potency" may have quite different components to another Potency factor extracted from another study in which other concepts, scales and subjects have been used. Attempts to compare factor scores across the two studies would be inappropriate. But if single scale scores were used it would be clear whether or not comparison across investigations was possible and fruitful. A similar point is that the factor score may be based upon a rather arbitrary selection decision. There is scope for disagreement about the size of a loading which is required before a scale can be said to be part of a factor. It follows that different investigators might cite quite discrepant factor scores from the same set of data. Fifthly, the picture is further confused by the fact that a number of different techniques for factoring and rotation are available, and we should therefore expect different analyses to generate different factor loadings for each scale. This implies that the components of a factor score can vary according to the analytic technique employed.

A final difficulty arises from the inevitable differences between respondents. Factor scores necessarily derive from an analysis of group data — the intercorrelations between scales which go into a factor analysis are summaries of the way scales are associated for the group as a whole. Yet the closeness of an association will vary between judges. Consider as an example a factor which is made up of two scales. (Such a small number is unlikely, but this is only an illustration.) These scales may be intercorrelated $+0.50$ for the group as a whole. Naturally there will be subjects in this group who treat the scales as unrelated (in effect as correlating less than $+0.20$) and others who treat them as very closely associated (effectively as correlating $+0.80$, say). The factor score which is derived for each subject does not take cognisance of this fact, and we have to assume that it is equally appropriate for all respondents. Yet it clearly is not appropriate for some of them (those who treat the scales as unrelated) and we are at this point dealing with a rather uncertain number. Worse still, we do not know for which subjects the score is appropriate and for which it is not, since we have no individual measures of interscale correlations. Phrasing this argument differently we might note that an Evaluative factor (for instance) may indeed exist for the group as a whole but that for some persons *wise–foolish* (say) will not be part of it. To collapse *wise–foolish* with other scales to provide a single score is to render an injustice to those subjects and to introduce unfortunate interpretative difficulties.

These arguments do not of course apply to the large-scale controlled studies cited earlier, in which attempts have been made to obtain general information about the dimensions of meaning. The value of factor analysis as a technique is beyond doubt, but we do question its *ad hoc* application to a limited set of semantic differential data unless this is required by a specific hypothesis which can be tested adequately with that set of data.

On the other hand it should be noted that scale-by-scale interpretation is not without its disadvantages. To compare average responses on, say, twelve scales necessarily introduces some redundancy since these scales will not be statistically independent. If each scale were closely related to *every one* of the others, this analysis would of course be positively misleading. But if the set of scales embraces three separate factors, the statistical clusters are by definition circumscribed so that we may place confidence on a pattern of results which includes many significant differences. In all cases, however, we must recognize that a few significant differences will emerge by chance, so that an isolated high value of *t* must be treated with caution.

We shall return from time to time to this type of question. Let us now pass on to discuss the reliability and validity of the semantic differential. Published work on these topics will be reviewed and several studies of our own will be presented.

THE RELIABILITY OF THE SEMANTIC DIFFERENTIAL

"Reliability" as applied to measuring instruments of all kinds can take on three meanings. These are:

(a) Consistency or *stability* of response *over time*. This characteristic is usually (though not always) measured by test–retest correlation techniques.

(b) *Internal consistency*. This is usually measured by means of an internal (e.g. split–half or odd–even) correlation.

(c) *Between-forms consistency*. This is usually measured by comparing forms of the instrument which there is reason to suppose are equivalent.

We shall consider in this section to what extent the semantic differential may be considered reliable in each of these three senses.

Stability over Time

Several investigations have been made of this kind of reliability, and Osgood, Suci and Tannenbaum (1957) quote a number of relevant studies. They argue (p. 127) that test–retest correlations (r_{tt}) are not appropriate as measures of stability, since subjects' responses have such a low variance: in making their judgment of a concept nearly all subjects give the same response so that stability coefficients become meaningless. Responses to Mother on *kind–cruel* are cited as an illustration of this possibility. The situation in which response variance is as low as this is undoubtedly very unusual, and appears to be one in which many statistical procedures (factor analyses, for example) are suspect. Fortunately, responses to the stimulus persons in which we have been interested are sufficiently evenly distributed to allow us to compute r_{tt} values. We favour this kind of stability measure, since it is in widespread use and comparisons between types of instruments are therefore possible. It is true that the maximum possible discrepancy with seven-point scales (or even with our nine-point scales) is not great, but it is worth noting that it is in the nature of a product–moment correlation that a small range of values will tend to generate a low correlation. This restricted spread of responses means therefore that the test–retest correlation provides a conservative estimate of semantic differential stability in relation to similar coefficients from instruments which generate a wider range of scores.

It is important to distinguish between two kinds of test–retest correlations which may be cited in discussions of the semantic differential. These are based (*a*) on the *mean* response values to each scale, and (*b*) on *individual* responses to each scale. Consider (*a*), in which the correlation between two samples of the *mean* scores on a set of scales is cited. If twelve scales are being employed the mean values of responses to these scales at time 1 will be correlated with the twelve mean values at time 2. There is a sense in which a correlation of this kind is a global measure of the stability of the particular semantic differential instrument being studied. Stability coefficients of this kind are usually found to be extremely high. Jenkins, Russell and Suci (1958) report a correlation of 0·97 between mean responses on 20 scales and Osgood, Suci and Tannenbaum (1957, pp. 127 and 191) cite similar coefficients of 0·85 and 0·91. An early analysis by Stagner and Osgood (1946) generated coefficients of 0·86 over 7 weeks and 0·75 over 59 weeks. We have correlated the mean scores on the scales and concepts shown in Tables 1 and 2 below, and in all cases r_{tt} exceeds 0·94.

But this is not a very sensitive measure of stability and is always likely to yield higher values than the second kind of measure referred to above. This latter index is drawn directly from individuals' responses. If twelve scales are being employed we may compute a value of r_{tt} for each of these scales. This provides more detailed information about the instrument and is likely to be more useful than the global measure.

We have made several studies of this kind of stability coefficient. A typical set of results is presented in Table 1. These values are from the

Table 1   Test–retest correlations over four weeks (nine-point scales; $N = 84$)

Scale	Stimulus person			
	Wilson	Brown	Home	Heath
1 True–false	0·62	0·46	0·56	0·45
2 Wise–foolish	0·60	0·51	0·46	0·44
3 Sweet–sour	0·32	0·53	0·51	0·51
4 Fair–unfair	0·49	0·48	0·52	0·56
5 Strong–weak	0·61	0·56	0·74	0·53
6 Hard–soft	0·51	0·51	0·31	0·50
7 Large–small	0·59	0·52	0·56	0·54
8 Rugged–delicate	0·44	0·55	0·38	0·56
9 Sharp–dull	0·61	0·58	0·61	0·44
10 Hot–cold	0·65	0·57	0·48	0·53
11 Active–passive	0·70	0·53	0·69	0·47
12 Fast–slow	0·50	0·70	0·58	0·31
Mean	0·55	0·54	0·53	0·49
Mean r_{tt} — 8 week interval	0·48	0·54	0·49	0·44

conceptions of four well-known British politcians given by 84 subjects. We have listed the scales in groups so that the first four represent the Evaluative factor, the middle four the Potency factor and the last four the Activity factor. Measurements were separated by a four-week interval, and were carried out during the period prior to the 1964 British General Election. Since subjects' attention was naturally directed at the behaviour of these politicians at this time, it is to be expected that their opinions of them might change somewhat during the long interval. Many of the r_{tt} values are nevertheless very satisfactory. We also obtained a third set of responses from the same subjects eight weeks after their original judgments. The stability characteristics of the scales over the eight-week period are summarized at the bottom of Table 1. We were pleasantly surprised by the small decline in r_{tt} which occurs over the additional four weeks.

The coefficients in Table 1 are based upon nine-point scales. It might be expected that the use of a larger number of alternative responses would lower the test–retest reliability of the instrument. It is often feared that the use of, say, eleven-point scales will lower the consistency of subjects' judgments. We have no results directly comparing the stability of nine-point and eleven-point scales, but we are satisfied that the stability of responses to eleven-point scales can be adequately high. Support for this conclusion comes from Mitchell's (1965) study. Some of his results are shown in Table 2. The r_{tt} values are based on judgments provided by 75 subjects over a period of one week. This period was also just prior to the 1964 General Election.

In this discussion of the second form of stability we have so far presented evidence to show that the stability of nine-point scales and of eleven-point scales can be satisfactory. What about the stability of

Table 2 Test–retest correlations over one week (eleven-point scales; $N = 75$)

	Stimulus person			
Scale	Wilson	Home	Grimond	Self
1 Good–bad	0·79	0·75	0·47	0·69
2 Progressive–regressive	0·83	0·67	0·58	0·65
3 True–false	0·72	0·76	0·65	0·76
4 Positive–negative	0·71	0·66	0·42	0·76
5 Believing–sceptical	0·63	0·48	0·45	0·82
6 Strong–weak	0·67	0·61	0·59	0·78
7 Active–passive	0·62	0·48	0·63	0·70
8 Hot–cold	0·71	0·63	0·53	0·62
9 Fast–slow	0·66	0·56	0·55	0·63
10 Stable–changeable	0·58	0·52	0·47	0·69
11 Rational–intuitive	0·72	0·65	0·63	0·74
12 Cautious–rash	0·83	0·47	0·39	0·70
Mean	0·71	0·60	0·53	0·71

responses to the more usual seven-point scales? Osgood, Suci and Tannenbaum (1957) argue that this is high, although (as we have seen) they place little emphasis on r_{tt}. However, a number of other researchers have quoted r_{tt} values to represent this type of reliability. Di Vesta and Dick (1966) have for example cited r_{tt} values using children's judgments. They quote stability coefficients based on an immediate retest of up to 0·86 and coefficients based on a 4 week test–retest interval up to 0·77. Norman (1959) quotes r_{tt} values obtained from measurements separated by 4 weeks, the median of which is 0·66.

Still other research workers have referred to a slightly different r_{tt} index, which is based on what we are describing as the second type of stability measure. The procedure involves averaging responses to scales which represent a single factor, so that a factor score of the kind mentioned on p. 72 is generated. In this way, if a form includes three scales representing the Potency factor, the responses to these three scales can be combined, and a stability coefficient for this single set of values can be calculated. The coefficients derived by this method from responses to seven-point scales usually indicate that stability is satisfactory. Norman (1959) quotes values based upon responses separated by 4 weeks; coefficients for the three major factors are all at least 0·75. Slightly lower coefficients of this kind are reported by Di Vesta and Dick (1966). It is typically found that r_{tt} values based on factor scores are higher than those derived from individual scales. This is of course to be expected from a homogeneous sample of scales, and the magnitude of r_{tt} based on factor scores is in part determined by the number of scales contributing to each factor score. We have already suggested reasons for preferring analyses of individual scales to those of groups of scales.

Studies of the type described above show that the stability of seven-point semantic differential scales can be very satisfactory. One point of great interest is whether nine-point scales are more or less reliable than the shorter scales. We have seen that nine-point scales can be adequately reliable, but it would be interesting to compare the stability of seven-point and nine-point scales holding constant the subjects, the scales and the concepts in one investigation.

Experiment 2

We have done this in a further study of judgments of well-known British politicians. Thirty-seven undergraduate students indicated their conception of Mr. Harold Wilson on seven-point scales, and a further 37 responded on nine-point versions of the same scales. Twelve scales were employed, these being the ones used in Experiment 1. To extend the generality of the findings, each subject also gave his judgment of the Conservative politician, Mr. Edward Heath. Judgments of the two stimuli were made on different lengths of scales, so that each subject used each type of scale and responded to each stimulus person. Order of presentation of scale type and of stimulus person was varied randomly.

One week after the original judgments were made, subjects were (without foreknowledge) required to respond on the same instruments. The stability of their responses was studied by calculating r_{tt} values for each scale. As in the investigations already reported, these values varied between scales. But their overall level was acceptably high. The findings are summarized in Table 3, from which it can be seen that the stability of seven-point scales is slightly higher than that of nine-point ones, but that this difference is far from significant. In the case of both stimulus persons five of the nine-point scales (out of twelve) yielded higher r_{tt} values than their seven-point counterparts.

Table 3   The stability of seven-point and nine-point semantic differential scales

Stimulus person	Seven-point scales		Nine-point scales	
	Mean r_{tt}	Mean deviation	Mean r_{tt}	Mean deviation
Wilson	0·63	0·17	0·57	0·19
Heath	0·60	0·16	0·52	0·24

We have also included in Table 3 the average deviation between mean scale values. This figure represents the average difference across the twelve scales between mean judgments on the two occasions. Subjects' conceptions of the stimulus persons were extremely similar over a week in all cases. And despite the greater opportunity for discrepancy on the nine-point scales, the average responses here are as similar over the interval as are those on seven-point scales. It may therefore be concluded that the stability of nine-point scales is as satisfactory as that of the more orthodox shorter ones.

A finding in all investigations of this kind is that r_{tt} varies widely between scales. Norman (1959) reports a range of from 0·38 to 0·77, Di Vesta and Dick (1966) find that values vary from 0·32 to 0·86 in their immediate retest condition, Mitchell (1965) observes a range of from 0·39 to 0·83, and a typical range of values in our own studies is from 0·31 to 0·74 (see Table 1, above). These variations are further reminders that we must be careful not to treat the semantic differential as a single instrument. It is meaningless to refer to the test–retest reliability of *the* semantic differential, since reliability varies considerably between scales. Even that kind of reliability described earlier (p. 75) which is based on a global calculation depends ultimately on which scales are employed.

Can we throw any light on these between-scale variations in stability? Can we, for example, say in advance of an investigation which scales are likely to be the more reliable ones? This would clearly be of considerable practical value. We have been interested in the fact that some scales are easy to apply but others present greater difficulty. Subjects can readily make judgments on the scale *fair–unfair*, but they usually find that *fast–slow* is much more difficult to apply. It might be that these differences in ease of application are predictive of the test–retest reliability of the scales. We have investigated this possibility.

Experiment 3

This study allows us to make a comparison between an independently-obtained measure of the ease with which scales can be applied and the stability of responses to these scales. The stimulus person was again Mr. Harold Wilson, who at the time was the leader of the British Labour Party. After a group of 98 subjects had registered their conceptions of Wilson on a twelve-scale semantic differential form, they ranked the twelve scales on a separately prepared sheet for ease of applicability to the stimulus person. They were requested to make their judgments by moving in from extremes. In this way they first indicated the scale which was "most easy to apply" (ranked 1), then the "least easy" (ranked 12), then the "second most easy" (ranked 2), and so on. There was remarkable consistency in these responses, and the same overall ranking emerged from the responses of the male and female subjects. For example, *wise–foolish* was considered the scale most easy to apply, and *sweet–sour* was considered the most difficult one.

These overall rankings of ease of applicability were then related to the test–retest reliability of the scales. The stability coefficients were obtained from responses to Wilson of a further 75 subjects at about the same time. We investigated the relationship by means of the rank correlation, *rho*. The value of this correlation between ease-of-applicability ranks and the stability of scales was found to be $+0.55$ ($N=12$; $p<0.05$). But this value of *rho* was considerably depressed by the failure of a single scale, *large–small*, to fit the general pattern. This scale is a peculiar one in that responses to it may be either in terms of the physical size of the stimulus person or based on a more metaphorical usage of the scale. If we omit this scale from the calculations, the rank correlation between the two indices is $+0.83$ ($N=11$; $p<0.01$).

It appears then that we can predict the stability of semantic differential scales from the ease with which the scales can be applied to a particular stimulus person. If we are concerned with the selection of scales for inclusion in a form, this can pose something of a dilemma. The most reliable scales are likely to be the clearly defined ones (*wise–foolish*, *weak–strong*, etc.), but it often appears that useful information might be obtained from more subtle, metaphorical scales (*sweet–sour*, *hot–cold*, etc.). Yet if we set a fairly low minimum reliability coefficient we can reach a workable compromise. If we grant that a figure of 0.50 over 4 weeks is acceptably reliable, then we can select scales all of which are deemed reliable, but some of which yield information of a more allusive nature.

So far we have drawn attention to the fact that stability varies between scales, and indicated that these differences in stability are at least partly predictable. Scale stability will also vary somewhat between subjects. Di Vesta and Dick (1966), for example, showed that stability coefficients tend to be greater with increasing age of children. Does stability of scales also vary between concepts? It would be pleasing if stability were independent of the concept being judged, since in this case reliable scales could be selected by the user on the basis of stability data derived from other concepts. Let us now look into this question.

If stability were independent of the concept being judged, we should expect that the most reliable scales when applied to Concept A are also the most reliable scales when applied to Concept B; and so on. Information relevant to this is contained in Table 1 and Table 2. Both sets of data lead to the same conclusion; we shall refer at present to the coefficients shown in Table 1. If stability were not dependent on the stimulus person being judged, the most reliable scales for judgments of Wilson would be the most reliable scales for conceptions of the politicians Brown, Home and Heath. We would expect some agreement in the rank-order of reliability of the twelve scales over the four stimulus persons. A convenient measure of this agreement is the coefficient of concordance (W). W can vary from 0 to 1 and in the case of the figures in Table 1 its value is only 0·23. This is not statistically significant. The lack of agreement between rank orders of the scales which is represented by this value of W can be illustrated by the scale *true–false*. For Wilson this is the third most reliable scale, for Brown it is the twelfth, for Home it is the fifth, and for Heath it is the ninth. We have five other sets of data of the kind presented in Table 1, and in no case does W take on a significant value.

Once again we come up against the notion of concept-scale interaction. Not only does stability vary between scales; stability of a single scale varies between concepts, even between concepts within the limited category of British politicians. It follows that we cannot readily predict from coefficients obtained by the application of scales to Concepts A, B, C, etc., which of these scales will be most reliable when applied to Concept N. But although this appears to be a somewhat gloomy conclusion, it is only of importance in a minority of investigations. As suggested earlier, we are usually concerned with more gross limits of reliability, and providing the stability of a scale consistently exceeds, say, 0·50 over a long interval we shall probably not be interested in whether this coefficient is 0·65 or 0·60 when we apply the scale to another concept. However, we do need to take care not to try to predict stability across too wide a range of concepts. Studies have been made of semantic differential responses to concepts like Gloomy, Glowing, High, Nice etc. (e.g. Jenkins, Russell and Suci, 1958). Data about scale stability from concepts of this kind are probably quite inapplicable to specific substantive concepts like President Johnson, since the meaning of the scales and the ease with which they can be applied change so considerably between the two concept domains. A corollary of this conclusion is that we must be somewhat cautious about interpreting stability values derived from a combination of responses to a number of widely differing concepts (e.g. Norman, 1959); these values may tell us little about how reliable the scales will be when applied to a single concept.

To conclude this discussion of the stability of semantic differential responses over time it can be said that test–retest coefficients are usually acceptably high both with adults and children. It appears that increasing the permitted number of alternative responses by providing more scale points than the customary seven does not affect stability, at least with intelligent subjects. We can predict to some extent which scales will be most reliable in a particular context, but there is no doubt that stability varies both with scales and with concepts. It is meaningless to ask about the test–retest reliability of *the* semantic differential; one ought to enquire about the stability of the set of scales employed in a specified investigation. In short, since the semantic differential is a class of measuring instruments rather than itself being a single instrument, to ask about its test–retest reliability is to raise a more complex question than is usually the case. We have to evaluate the general technique by assessing the particular instruments which have been developed through it; in many cases the stability of these instruments can be shown to be quite acceptable.

Internal Consistency

Tests of internal consistency — the second type of reliability referred to above — are concerned with the consistency of a subject's responses on a single occasion. This is clearly distinct from stability, which is concerned with the reliability of a subject's responses over two or more occasions. Internal consistency is thus assessed from just one set of responses. Various procedures are available for this, the simplest of them being the split-half or odd–even correlation techniques.

If a test is assumed to be measuring a single attribute we can assess internal consistency by correlating subjects' scores on the first half of the test with their scores on the second half (the split-half method), or by correlating scores on the odd-numbered items with scores on the even-numbered items (the odd–even method). The higher a correlation of this kind, the more equivalent are the two parts of the test and the more confident we are that the instrument is discriminating among subjects along a single dimension.

Psychological tests are usually required to have high internal consistency, and we may wonder if this requirement applies to semantic differential forms. It clearly does not if each scale is supposed to be measuring a separate dimension; in this case we should not expect internal consistency of the form as a whole to be high. But as we have seen, the most satisfactory semantic differential instrument is one which contains scales pertaining to at least three important factors — Evaluation, Potency and Activity. Is it meaningful and appropriate to enquire about the internal consistency of the set of scales intended to measure a single factor? The answer to this question should of course be self-

D

evident, since it is implicit in the meaning of "factor" that the internal consistency of a set of scales with high loadings on a factor is high.

But in practice this kind of reliability may be somewhat lower than expected. We have already looked at the reasons for this in the section on factor analytic studies. The finding that the meaning of and inter-correlation between scales can vary between concepts implies that scales selected on the basis of previous results to represent one factor may in fact not be correlated to the anticipated degree. So the internal consistency of a set of scales intended to measure a single factor is a matter for empirical observation. It can depend upon the scales, the subjects, and the concepts involved in a particular investigation. Providing that the selection of scales has been judicious, in that evidence from related concepts has been used, it is of course unlikely that internal consistency will be low. Nonetheless actual evidence about internal consistency is rather scarce. We have therefore analysed the results of two experiments selected haphazardly from those reported later. Both involved indirect person perception and the factor consistency scores (corrected by the Spearman–Brown formula) are:

Evaluation	0·70 and 0·76
Potency	0·75 and 0·56
Activity	0·66 and 0·58

The scales involved were those in Table 1 (page 76), and had been selected from ones described in Osgood, Suci and Tannenbaum (1957). The consistency figures are not as high as would normally be required, and point again to the need for caution in interpreting factor scores.

A set of scales apparently representing a single factor may be internally consistent; but it is not logically necessary that this should be so. The question of internal consistency only arises of course if an investigation is concerned to measure separate factors. Many users of semantic differential scales make no claim to be assessing factor scores, and in these cases we do not require evidence of internal consistency. But it seems reasonable in other instances to request information about this characteristic.

Between-forms Reliability

It is not unusual for psychological tests to have more than one form. A number of allegedly parallel or equivalent forms of, say, an intelligence test might be developed. Naturally enough we need to know how well these forms correlate with each other before we can determine whether they are in fact parallel or equivalent. This kind of between-forms reliability may be assessed by correlating scores on the two versions administered either on separate occasions or when completed at one sitting. When the two forms are administered at one sitting we are in effect concerned with a special case of internal consistency measurement, as if we were correlating two halves of a test. If the two forms are completed at different times, we have an instance of internal consistency measurement which is also beset with some of the difficulties of stability measurement. Because of these similarities with the other two kinds of reliability already considered, we need not look into between-forms reliability in great detail.

If we have two twelve-scale semantic differential forms, both of which contain four scales with high loadings on the three major factors, we should expect the between-forms reliability of this instrument to be high. The crucial question here is how comparable are the factor loadings of the scales on the two forms (cf. Coyne and Holzman, 1966). We have already spent some time on this problem; it is clear that between-forms reliability of semantic differential instruments can be high; furthermore the reasons for a departure from an acceptable level are understood.

But there is one other aspect of this topic which deserves consideration. This concerns the comparability of forms which contain the same scales but which have them in different orders. Does the order in which the scales are presented matter? It is possible that responses to early scales in a form will induce a set to respond in a certain manner to later scales. If this were so, the order of presentation of scales would clearly be a crucial variable. Also involved here is the way in which the polar terms of each scale are arranged on a form. If the scales are laid out with all the positive terms on the left-hand side of the form, subjects may respond to each scale in a manner different from the way in which they respond to a randomly presented set. It is logically possible then for two forms of a set of scales to generate different response patterns even though identical scales make up the two forms.

Does this kind of difference occur in practice? In all our studies we have employed up to four different versions of the same instrument, and have varied the order and polarity of scales between versions. We have on many occasions investigated whether measured perceptions vary between these different versions, and are confident that the variations are so infrequent that we can attribute their occurrence to chance. It appears that serial order effects in responding to a set of scales do not occur in practice, at least when the order of scales is determined randomly.

However, it is in principle possible for an order effect to take place if there is a *systematic* bias in the sequence of scales on a form. Responses to earlier scales might influence responses to scales further down the page. For example, it might be the case that if a subject makes very similar responses to the first six scales on a form his seventh response will be partly determined by these previous responses. If such an influence were operative it could be of two kinds. Subjects might develop a habit or set to make their own judgments on a certain part of the page (i.e. irrespective of scale content) or they might develop a habit or set to respond at a certain point on all scales (i.e. irrespective of the part of the page). We have tried to demonstrate an order effect by taking an extreme situation in which these two kinds of response tendencies are encouraged.

Experiment 4

The stimulus person in this investigation was Mr. George Brown, the Deputy Leader of the Labour Party and a person well known to all the subjects. Judgments of Brown were recorded on two versions of an eight-scale semantic differential form. The same four scales appeared in positions 5 to 8 on both versions; these were selected with the knowledge from previous studies that average responses on a nine-point scale would approximate to 5. The first four scales to appear in the form were varied between the two versions. Version 1 comprised the scales *hard–soft*, *strong–weak*, *active–passive* and *rugged–delicate*. These scales were always in this order and arranged so that the positive term was always to the left of the page. Earlier investigations suggested that responses to Brown on these scales would score much higher than 5. The four scales in Version 2 (*profound–shallow*, *polite–blunt*, *wise–foolish*, *goodnatured–irritable* — presented in this order) were known to be dimensions on which Brown was judged rather negatively. Thus we know that subjects completing Version 1 would respond to the first four scales very positively and to the left of the page, and that subjects responding to the first four scales on Version 2 would make negative judgments down the right-hand side of the page. We were interested to see whether this extreme variation would result in differences in response patterns to the last four scales which were common to both versions and on which Brown was usually judged to be neutral. Version 1 was completed by 48 undergraduate subjects, and 47 others filled in version 2.

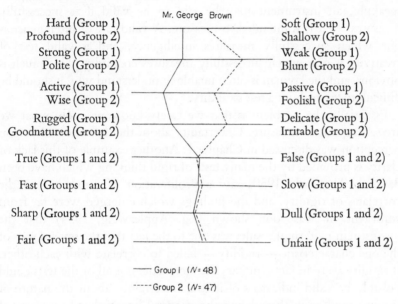

Figure 3   The influence of early responses upon later responses in conceptions of Mr. George Brown

The way in which these groups conceived Brown is shown in Figure 3. The mean responses of the two groups are both included in this diagram so that immediate comparison may be made. It is clear that we were unsuccessful in inducing a set which could distort responses on later scales despite the fairly massive manipulation. It is unlikely that such large systematic differences in scale patterning will occur in everyday use of semantic differential forms, and order of scales will not be of importance in actual employment of the instrument. Our previously mentioned failure to find differences between forms in which the order of scales was *randomly* varied gives further support to this conclusion. The between-forms reliability of a set of scales when the forms differ only in order and polarity of scales may be taken to be very high.

THE VALIDITY OF THE SEMANTIC DIFFERENTIAL

Although it is clearly important that a psychological measuring instrument be valid, it is often far from easy to assess validity. Roughly speaking, an instrument may be said to be valid if it successfully measures what it is intended to measure. A valid test of intelligence is one which successfully measures intelligence, and a valid test of creativity is one which successfully measures creativity. This much is obvious, and the layman is often unable to understand why it should be difficult to learn about a test's validity.

Essentially the problem is that we rarely know precisely what we are setting out to measure. Uncertainty about the definition of person perception was discussed in Chapter 1. Another example of this lack of clarity is provided by the many tests of rigid thinking which have been devized. The early 1950s saw a proliferation of research into the correlates of rigidity, and the findings which emerged were far from consistent. It was soon shown (e.g. Applezweig, 1954) that the inconsistent pattern of results was due to the fact that the several tests of the one characteristic — rigidity — failed to correlate with each other. If rigidity were in fact a unitary characteristic, not all of the tests could possibly be valid indicators of it. But uncertainty about the nature of rigidity resulted in there being these several uncorrelated measures of the one ill-defined concept. Many concepts employed by psychologists are of this kind; we cannot define them exactly and hence we do not know precisely what we want to measure. Since our main hope of specifying many such concepts often lies in precise measurement we often have to experiment with different measures, many of which turn out to be invalid.

What is it that we want to measure with the semantic differential? The instrument has been developed as an index of meaning or judgment.* Since we cannot yet precisely specify in a generally acceptable manner what we mean by "meaning" or "judgment", we cannot say *directly* whether the instrument successfully measures what we want it to measure. But there are several indirect ways in which validity can be assessed, and it is important to see how adequate the measure is according to these criteria. We shall look into this point in the present

* The term "judgment" is as usual employed here in the generic sense suggested in Chapter 1 to cover perception and conception.

section: our main interest is of course in the validity of the semantic differential as a measure of judgment of other people, and particular attention will be paid to this.

It is customary to distinguish between several kinds of validity. These are face validity, intrinsic validity, predictive validity, content validity, concurrent validity and construct validity. Although some are not wholly independent of others, we shall consider them separately in the hope that this will highlight the important features and difficulties of each.

Face Validity

This characteristic of an instrument is not really validity in the technical sense, but it is an interesting aspect of psychological tests which can often be important. Face validity is concerned with whether the instrument *appears* to be a good one to use. For strictly scientific purposes this is not important, but face validity is nevertheless often very desirable. When subjects do not know what we are measuring or when they are certain to be extremely cooperative, the appearance of the test is of little consequence. But when subjects or administrators need to be persuaded to make use of a test, then face validity can be crucial. If we want to measure people's judgments by calling on their homes (see Experiments 31 and 32), we are more likely to establish rapport if our measure appears to them to be interesting and appropriate. Similarly, if we have to persuade newspaper staffs to publish editions specifically for our investigations (see Experiments 30–33), we need to be able to show them a measuring instrument which appears to be a reasonable one to use.

So, although the importance of face validity has often been denied, in many practical situations it is a necessary characteristic of a test. There is no doubt that the semantic differential has a high degree of face validity. Obviously this cannot be measured quantitatively, but the experience of many investigators is that subjects take to it very readily and that it is thought to be a reasonable and attractive instrument.

Intrinsic Validity

This is a second characteristic which, despite its name, is not really a form of validity. Intrinsic validity is usually defined in terms of the square root of the test–retest reliability of an instrument. We have already discussed test–retest reliability in some detail, and it will suffice here to reiterate that this can be extremely high.

Predictive Validity

The predictive validity of a test is the effectiveness with which it predicts a future outcome and is usually measured in terms of the correlation between test score and an external criterion measure. The predictive validity of an intelligence test might be described in terms of the correlation between test scores and academic examination marks. Mechanical aptitude tests might be validated against on the job performance; and measures of group cohesiveness might be validated against the way groups actually behave. It is often difficult to distinguish between predictive validity and concurrent validity. We shall discuss this latter test characteristic shortly, and for the moment point out that predictive validity is concerned with behaviour that can occur only in the future. Although the criterion used to assess concurrent validity may in fact be measured in the future, it is in principle possible to make the measurement when the test measurement is taken. The distinction is a fine one.

When evaluating the predictive validity of the semantic differential we come up against a number of problems. First, responses to many kinds of concepts are not expected to be predictive of future behaviour and it would hardly be fruitful to try to validate a measure of the meaning of Afraid, Bodkin, Coarse, Devil and other similar concepts studied by Jenkins, Russell and Suci (1958). When we come to judgments of people, however, the question of predictive validity has more relevance: we should be able to predict from scale responses how a subject will behave towards the stimulus person. Yet it is frequently impossible to establish a situation in which the subject and stimulus person can interact in such a way that we can test the prediction. Another difficulty concerns the heterogeneity of the scales within a semantic differential form. On the basis of which responses do we make our prediction? Various possibilities are open. We could summate responses to all the scales, or take only specified dimensions, or select a number of apparently relevant scales. On the whole studies of individual scales seem preferable, but decisions about this will depend upon the aims of a particular study.

We meet difficulties of this kind when we try to assess the predictive validity of many psychological measuring instruments; these problems are not peculiar to the semantic differential and they should not deter us from trying to find out about its predictive validity. One kind of situation from which useful information might be drawn is the clinical setting. Osgood and Luria (1954) (see also Osgood, Suci and Tannenbaum, 1957, pp. 258–271) were able to make useful predictions in a case of triple personality, and Marks (1965, 1966) has drawn attention to some predictions which may be made about the behaviour of several categories of psychiatric patients from their responses to semantic differential scales.

It is likely that market research agencies hold jealously guarded details of predictive validity. Information about voting behaviour is more readily obtained, and Osgood, Suci and Tannenbaum (1957, pp. 142–3) report an interesting study of this. Three and one half months before the 1952 U.S. Presidential Election they compared the response of "undecided" voters with those of confirmed supporters of the two candidates. Responses to a number of political concepts (e.g. Price Controls, Labour Unionism, United Nations) were compared in an attempt to predict the eventual voting behaviour of eighteen "undecided" respondents from the similarity of their judgments to those of subjects whose minds were made up. In seventeen cases the predictions were correct, at least when only Evaluative and Potency scales were represented. Including an Activity scale among the predictor variables reduced the success with which predictions could be made.

The results of this study suggest that the semantic differential can have acceptable predictive validity. But it is important to notice that at this stage only *post hoc* predictions of voting behaviour can be validly made. If the predictions had been offered *before* polling day, the investigators would not have known which scales to use as predictors. And if all scales had been used (i.e. Activity scales as well as others), the predictions would not have been strikingly successful.

We have met with a similar difficulty in an analysis of data gathered by Blumler and his colleagues at the time of the 1964 British General Election. Blumler and McQuail (1968) conducted a valuable longitudinal study of two voting constituencies from which they drew representative samples of voters. Amongst the measures taken from these voters were semantic differential conceptions of the three party leaders — Douglas-Home, Grimond and Wilson. Data were obtained on several occasions during the election campaign and factors influencing attitudinal change were studied. We were particularly interested in whether the voting behaviour of "uncertain" respondents could be predicted from their semantic differential conceptions of the three leaders. We should not expect such accurate forecasting as in American studies since votes in Britain are cast for a party representative rather than for the leader of a party and since voters are in many cases choosing policies rather than individuals. A better test would be to predict voting behaviour from the way in which local candidates are perceived; this has yet to be studied.

Blumler and McQuail have kindly given us access to the data from "uncertain" voters obtained one month before the election. We have analysed these to test the predictive validity of the set of twelve scales employed. We shall first describe a *post hoc* analysis in terms of the three parties for which votes were cast. We looked at the responses made to the twelve scales before the election to see whether the group of "uncertain" subjects who eventually voted, for example, Conservative conceived the Conservative leader (Douglas-Home) more positively than they conceived the other leaders. We made twelve comparisons of these mean scale values with the mean responses to Wilson and twelve comparisons with responses to Grimond. If the measure here has predictive validity, we expect the group of respondents who later voted Conservative to judge Douglas-Home more positively than they judge the other two leaders. It was found that in 22 of the 24 cases this was so. Our *post hoc* predictions for the other party groups were similarly successful; we were correct on 23 out of 24 occasions for the group which eventually voted Liberal and on 17 out of 24 occasions for the group which eventually voted Labour. Clearly this *post hoc* group analysis is very encouraging.

But suppose now that, instead of being interested in the differences between groups of subjects, we had wanted to foretell which *individuals* would vote for each party. This is the kind of problem which faces public opinion investigators. Rather than study groups of "undecided" voters constituted according to their eventual decision, we should have had to look at each individual's responses to the three leaders and from these predict which way he would vote. We attempted to make this prediction by taking a total response value from each subject for each leader and using this as the basis for our forecast. Instead of looking at differences between groups on each of the twelve scales, we have summed responses to these scales and predicted from this total score how each individual would vote. Thus if a subject's total scores over the twelve scales were 49 for Douglas-Home, 73 for Grimond and 62 for Wilson, it was predicted that he would vote for the Liberal party since this party's leader was conceived most positively. The voting behaviour of 64 "undecided" subjects was predicted in this way, and our predictions were in fact correct on 40 occasions. However, this is barely significant ($p < 0.05$, one-tailed Sign Test). This level of ability to forecast individuals' behaviour is of little practical value, although these results and the group results described above do indicate that the semantic differential can predict behaviour with some degree of success.*

As we have suggested this is not a completely fair test of the instrument, since votes in British elections are not cast for the party leaders. Predictive validity might, however, be higher if investigators set up a self-correcting system, whereby the scales included on a form are continually modified on the basis of the success with which they have predicted voting behaviour in previous elections.

This brings us back to a point which we have often stressed. The semantic differential is a technique rather than an instrument which takes only one form. A study of validity allows us to say something about one form of a semantic differential; what we say will not necessarily apply to other forms. We can at this stage conclude that some well-constructed devices based on the technique have been shown to have predictive validity, and can surmise that other forms may be found to have yet higher validity. We shall return to this topic in the next section.

Content Validity

A test is said to have content validity when it covers a representative sample of the behaviour or characteristics which are being studied. Content validity is particularly important in the case of achievement tests. If we wish to use a test of, say, mathematical achievement we need to know whether the test samples all the aspects of this in which we are interested. If it does, then we can say that the test has adequate content validity.

It is usually argued that the content validity of measures of personality or attitude is of little importance, and that other types of validation are crucial. But the content validity of a semantic differential form is a

---

* Notice that we have dealt only with responses of "undecided" voters. Semantic differential judgments are very accurate predictors of the voting behaviour of persons whose minds are made up (see p. 97).

matter for careful inquiry. If we are interested in the meaning of a concept, we need to be satisfied that we are sampling all the important aspects of meaning. Similarly, if we are to measure whether the perceptions of a person generated by, say, two newspaper reports are different, we need to know whether we have included all the important dimensions of perception in our index.

Suppose that we have measured subjects' perceptions on a twelve-scale semantic differential form, and suppose that no differences between the two groups were observed on any of the twelve scales. Is it appropriate to conclude that the reports do not generate significantly different perceptions, or would another set of scales perhaps have yielded a difference? It is not at present possible to answer this question with assurance. The recurring observation that three major factors account for most of the variance in studies of a wide range of concepts suggests that these are indeed the primary dimensions of meaning. We have reviewed these findings above, and suggested that scales with a high loading on each of the factors should be included in any form. These scales, perhaps with a small number of others selected specifically for the particular investigation, ought to sample all the aspects of perception in which we could be interested. In other words, this procedure ought to ensure high content validity.

Yet it is immediately clear that this can only be partly true. We *could* be interested in those aspects of perception which we have specifically excluded from our purview. As was indicated at the beginning of this chapter we have given major emphasis to perceptual judgments about covert characteristics of people. We have thus set aside part of the content of perceptual judgments, and we cannot expect that as a measure of the *entire* perceptual process the semantic differential has high content validity.

However, as far as our restricted aims are concerned the evidence is such that we must at present believe that the Evaluative, Potency and Activity factors represent the major aspects of connotative meaning. So an adequate sample of the meaning of a concept ought to be gained by including scales to represent these factors. Even so there is some reason to question whether content validity is assured by this procedure. Let us return to our example of the two newspaper accounts of a person's behaviour. Suppose now that significant differences were found between the two groups on two of the twelve scales. Suppose also that these two scales were two of the four scales to represent the Potency factor. The kind of result is fairly common, and leads us once again to wonder about the value of organizing scales in terms of factors.

The reason for this concern is a doubt whether we can treat the factor as a single dimension if some scales which typify it yield significant differences between two reports whereas other scales for the same factor do not. We are left with the suspicion that if we had selected different scales to represent the Potency factor, the results might have been quite different. If different scales from the same factor yield different information, then how do we know whether we have sampled *all* the relevant aspects of perception; that is whether our measure has high content validity? This sampling problem is central to any discussion of validity. At the present time we cannot be absolutely sure that we have selected semantic differential scales to stand for each of the important aspects of perception. As a "best guess" we have already recommended the use of a standard set of scales based upon the three factors, but this "best guess" might well be improved upon in the future.

It is probably fair to say that as users of the semantic differential we are here being more introspective than is customary. This problem — to sample all the important aspects of the universe in which one is interested — faces the user of any sort of instrument, and it remains unsolved in the case of most if not all psychological indicators. The failure to solve this problem is of course not sufficient reason to reject an instrument as valueless, but it is a fair reminder that we may yet hope to increase our knowledge about the content validity of our measuring devices.

Concurrent Validity

If we are able to demonstrate an association between two measures, taken at approximately the same time, then we have evidence for the concurrent validity of each. For example, if we can show that subjects obtain similar results on two different intelligence tests then it seems quite likely that the two tests are measuring the same variable. There is of course a danger here: for it is possible to have a number of related measures while deceiving ourselves about the construct we are measuring. (Our tests might not be measuring intelligence at all but, say, a superior memory span.) For this reason predictive validity, where we can see with what success our measure forecasts some piece of criterion behaviour, is generally much more to be desired than is concurrent validity. However, as we have seen in the previous section, the semantic differential, being a measure of meaning or judgment, does not often lend itself to the prediction of behaviour, so that we frequently have to be satisfied with evidence of concurrent validity. Of course if we can establish such concurrent validity in conjunction with a measure whose predictive validity has been accepted, then we have indirect evidence that the semantic differential is itself a valid predictor.

Osgood, Suci and Tannenbaum (1957) have suggested that the Evaluative scales of the semantic differential may be used as a measure of attitudes. (See also Barclay and Thumin, 1963; Fishbein and Hunter, 1964; Fishbein and Raven, 1962; Tannenbaum, 1956.) This means that we can test the concurrent validity of a semantic differential form comprising such scales by comparing responses on these scales with responses on other forms of attitude scale. High levels of concurrent validity have in fact been reported in comparisons with Thurstone and Guttman scales and with Bogardus social distance scales (Osgood, Suci and Tannenbaum, 1957, pp. 193–4, 199; Proenza and Strickland, 1965). Attitude measurement in terms of latitudes of acceptance and rejection has been studied intensively by Sherif and his colleagues (e.g. Sherif and Hovland, 1961). The concurrent validity of semantic differential scales as indicators of attitude has been examined from this viewpoint by Diab (1965). He found close parallels between scale responses and subjects' latitudes of acceptance of attitude-relevant statements. There is no doubt that responses to evaluative scales provide a valid measure of at least part of an attitudinal complex. It does seem likely, however, that semantic differential evaluative responses alone are not satisfactory measures of attitudes in their entirety (e.g. Weksel and Hennes, 1965) and that we need to define "attitude" more broadly (e.g. Krech, Crutchfield and Ballachey, 1962, p. 139 ff.; Secord and Backman, 1964a, p. 97 ff.).

The semantic differential was originally devized not as a measure of attitudes but as an index of meaning. It is rather more difficult to establish concurrent validity in this sense, since other definitions of meaning (e.g. Creelman, 1966; Noble, 1952) are usually very different from that in terms of the semantic differential. However, it is possible to make an indirect test of validity. Kelly and Levy (1961), for instance, have studied the success with which comparisons between semantic differential profiles predict *differences* in the meaning of concepts. Their subjects were required to judge which of two profiles represented a particular concept; and the design of their study allowed them to relate the discriminability of concepts to the difference between semantic differential profiles. Kelly and Levy observed a clear positive relationship between these two quite separate measures. Grigg (1959) has also approached this question indirectly, and has reported expected differences between profiles of Self, Ideal Self and Neurotic. Terwilliger (1962) employed an index of ambiguity derived from information theory; he reports a successful test of predictions about ambiguity of meaning and patterns of semantic differential response. These and other studies provide substantial evidence that a semantic differential profile does reflect the meaning of a concept depicted by it.

Turning to the validity of the instrument as a measure of person perception, we find that several investigations are available. For example, it has often been found that judgments of politicians measured in terms of semantic differential responses are closely related to political belief. McGrath and McGrath (1961), Osgood, Suci and Tannenbaum (1957, p. 104 ff.) and Stricker (1963) have shown that this is the case in U.S.A.; and Blumler and McQuail (1968) and Gardiner (1965) have reported that profiles vary systematically between groups of English subjects holding different political beliefs. We too have found that conceptions of British politicians vary according to the political adherence of the perceiver. For example, in one investigation there were six out of a possible twelve significant differences in the judgments of Wilson made by Socialist and Conservative undergraduate groups. (Further findings relevant to political belief and judgment are discussed in Chapter 4.) This type of finding generates confidence in the validity of the instrument, though it is not altogether clear whether we are dealing here with predictive, concurrent or construct validity.

There is some evidence for the validity of the semantic differential as a measure of the way in which psychiatric patients perceive other people. In several studies Marks (1965) related patients' judgments of Myself, My Father and My Mother to psychiatrists' assessments of the way in which these people would be judged by the patients. He found that the correlations between the two measures typically exceeded 0·70. Hallworth (1965) has studied school-teachers' perceptions of their pupils. He reports close relationships between clusters of semantic differential scale responses and sets of personality ratings. For example, teachers' ratings of pupils' emotional stability, trustworthiness and persistence are closely related to their semantic differential judgments of the children on scales representing the Evaluative factor.

One interesting measure of person perception against which the concurrent validity of the semantic differential might be assessed is that based on Kelly's repertory grid technique (Bannister, 1962a, 1962b; Fransella and Adams, 1966; G. A. Kelly, 1955). This is essentially a sorting test from which the way in which persons (or other stimulus elements) are construed may be determined. A construct is measured in terms of a pair of adjectives similar to a semantic differential scale. There are two main forms of the test. In earlier applications of the technique subjects were required to use the constructs as dichotomous variables and to allot the stimulus elements to one or other pole (e.g. *good* or *bad*). It is now becoming more common (e.g. Bannister, 1963) to ask subjects to use the constructs as ordinal scales and to rank-order the stimulus elements (e.g. *most good* to *most bad*). In either case, responses are plotted in the form of a grid; the stimulus elements are presented along one axis and the constructs along the other. Evidence for the reliability and validity of the repertory grid test is steadily accumulating. Bannister and Fransella (1966), for example, reported stability co-efficients of up to 0·80 with an immediate retest, and Fransella (1965) observed similar consistency over a period of three weeks.

How far is the repertory grid technique similar to the use of the semantic differential? When the constructs to be used are provided by the administrator, the two procedures are of course much the same, and we should expect a close relationship between the two measures. Repertory grid measurement can, however, incorporate an interesting procedure which makes it more clearly distinct from orthodox semantic differential measurement. This procedure allows each subject to provide his own constructs. The latter are elicited by presenting the subject with groups of three stimulus elements and asking him to name some important way in which two of them are alike and thereby different from the third. For example, a subject might indicate that two people in a triad are intelligent but the third is stupid. It is assumed that this construct is a dimension which the subject commonly uses to perceive his interpersonal world.

Constructs elicited from the subject himself are usually referred to as "personal" constructs, whilst those provided by an investigator may be called "supplied" constructs. An important question is of course how closely a set of supplied constructs can parallel a set of personal constructs. It appears that the two kinds of constructs can yield very similar results (e.g. Fransella and Adams, 1966; Jaspars, 1963; Kieferle and

Sechrest, 1961; Tripodi and Bieri, 1963), but this will presumably depend upon the investigators and the subjects involved. Mitsos (1961) has looked into the value of eliciting personal scales from subjects for use in semantic differential measurement. He found that subjects made more extreme responses on personal scales but that the meaning of concepts measured in this way was not different from the meaning assessed on supplied scales.

In view of these similarities between semantic differential and repertory grid techniques, we should expect that the concurrent validity of the former in terms of the latter should be high. The relationship will of course depend upon the scales and constructs employed and a direct assessment of concurrent validity requires that the same materials be used for both techniques. We have not been able to locate much evidence on this point. Fransella (1965), however, noted that the measures yielded by the two techniques were uncorrelated. This is an unexpected finding, which might possibly be due to the use of only two subjects. Jaspars (1963) obtained information from 30 subjects and observed that the two measures were positively related. He cites correlations which range from $+0\cdot26$ to $+0\cdot78$. Further studies of this form of concurrent validity are clearly desirable.

Another instrument against which the concurrent validity of the semantic differential might be measured is the Adjective Check List (e.g. Gough and Heilbrun, 1965). We have devoted some time to studying the value of this device as a measure of person perception. The present form of the Adjective Check List (A.C.L.) consists of 300 adjectives presented in alphabetical order. It has been used as a self-rating personality measure and as an indicator of the way in which psychological counsellors and assessors perceive the personality attributes of another person. In either case responses are made by reading through the list and by checking the attributes which are considered to be applicable. Considerable analysis of A.C.L. responses has been carried out by the originators of the list, and twenty-four scales have been extracted from information gathered over a number of years. These scales represent clusters of personality attributes designated by titles like Defensiveness, Self-confidence, Personal adjustment, Endurance and Aggression.

The potential value of an instrument of this kind is immediately obvious. Students of person perception have commonly made use of check lists to measure subjects' impressions (e.g. Asch, 1946; Edwards,

1959; Hartshorne and May, 1930; Holmes and Berkowitz, 1961; Veness and Brierley, 1963). But the contents of a list often appear to have been selected arbitrarily or in order to test a restricted hypothesis, so that a set of responses cannot be taken as a valid indicator of person perception as a whole. And since the contents of lists vary between investigations it is not possible to compare results from a number of studies. It would be very helpful if a standard list were to be used, especially if the list were sufficiently long to tap a wide range of perceptual judgments and if research had indicated a meaningful set of clusters of items within it. The A.C.L. appears to fulfil the requirements of such a list, and we have consequently made some studies of its value and of how the results it yields are related to those from the semantic differential.

Experiment 5

This study was designed to assess the concurrent validity of the semantic differential measured against the A.C.L. The semantic differential scales were selected to yield information which would be useful in the analysis of another investigation (see Experiment 10), and they did not systematically represent a set of factors. The design required that subjects respond on these scales and on the A.C.L. Half the subjects in each of the two groups completed the A.C.L. first, and half completed the semantic differential first.

We used these instruments to measure subjects' indirect perception of a British politician, Mr. Harold Macmillan. Two narrative accounts of Macmillan's behaviour at a meeting were selected from national newspapers and half our subjects read each account. They then indicated their episodic perception of Macmillan's behaviour on both instruments. The narratives were used as part of a study of order effects in the perception of people: this aspect of the experiment is described in Chapter 6 (Experiment 28). We are here primarily concerned with the extent to which subjects' perceptions as recorded by the two different instruments were comparable.

For reasons that are discussed later in connection with Experiment 28, we predicted that subjects' perceptions of Macmillan would differ according to which narrative account of his behaviour they read. The point at issue here is whether these differences between perceptions based upon the two narratives would be the same for both the semantic differential and the A.C.L. If concurrent validity in this situation is high, we would expect a large difference between the groups on a particular semantic differential scale to be accompanied by a large difference between the groups on the relevant A.C.L. items. Group perceptions on semantic differential scales are represented in the usual manner, that is by an average numerical response which can potentially vary between 1 and 9. And group perceptions on A.C.L. items are represented by the number of subjects checking the items: each narrative group contained the same number of subjects — 48* — so we can make direct inter-group comparisons of responses to the A.C.L. items. It would be possible to compare responses on a single scale (e.g. *sociable*). But this would waste the additional information which the A.C.L. provides; since we used thirteen semantic differential scales we should only be looking at thirteen (or at best 26 if we could include both positive and negative items) of the 300 A.C.L. items. A more useful comparison is that between a single semantic differential scale and all the A.C.L. adjectives which have meanings similar to that scale. This is the procedure we adopted.

It was accordingly necessary to obtain a reliable measure of which A.C.L. items are synonymous with each semantic differential scale. For this purpose we obtained the assistance of ten judges, each of whom was a staff member of the Sheffield University Psychology Department. These judges were all unaware of the purpose of our study. They were requested to work through the A.C.L. twenty-six times, picking out on each occasion the items which were very similar in meaning to a polar term of one of the thirteen semantic differential scales. For example they looked for synonyms of *sociable* on one reading of the list, and for synonyms of *unsociable* at another time. There was of course some inter-judge variability, and we selected for analysis only those A.C.L. items chosen by seven or more of the ten judges. In this way we obtained a reliable set of synonyms for each of the twenty-six semantic differential terms.

The next step involved comparing responses to these synonyms with responses to the relevant semantic differential scales. We analysed both sets of responses in such a way that we could observe differences in perceptions based upon the two narratives. For example, analysis of the semantic differential data reveals that Macmillan is perceived to be more generous by readers of narrative 1 than by narrative 2 readers. Now, ten A.C.L. items were deemed to be synonymous with the polar

* Results from two subjects in one group were randomly discarded.

term *generous*. We counted how many of these items were checked more frequently by readers of narrative 1, how many were checked more frequently by readers of narrative 2, and how many were checked by the same number of subjects in each narrative group. We found in the case of *generous* that eight synonyms were checked more frequently by readers of narrative 1 and that one adjective fell into each of the two other categories. We next looked at the synonyms of the polar term at the opposite end of the semantic differential scale, that is synonyms of *ungenerous*. There were eight of these in the A.C.L. and in every case these were checked less frequently by the group exposed to narrative 1. By combining these two sets of information we were able to conclude that narrative 1 indicated Macmillan to be more generous than did narrative 2: in sixteen (i.e. 8 + 8) out of eighteen cases (89%) the items checked supported this conclusion. Thus as far as the scale *generous–ungenerous* is concerned the semantic differential results are supported by information from the A.C.L.

We analysed responses to all twenty-six sets of A.C.L. items in this way. The measure of difference between perceptions based on the two stories was in each case the percentage of items supporting the conclusion that narrative 1 generated a more positive perception. All these percentage measures of difference between A.C.L. perceptions of Macmillan's behaviour mediated by the two accounts were next compared with the differences between the mean semantic differential scale responses for the two groups. A strong association between the two kinds of measure is revealed by the observed rank correlation (*rho*) between these values of $+0 \cdot 82$ ($N = 13$). This indicates a very close similarity between the differences in perceptions of the two groups measured by the two indices, and is striking evidence of the concurrent validity of the two very different measures of person perception.*

Most psychological measuring instruments require that subjects respond within a framework defined by the investigator. The instruments to measure person perception with which we have so far dealt are of this kind. The semantic differential user specifies for his subjects a number of scales like *good–bad* and *fair–unfair*; constructs deployed in a

---

* In its customary form the A.C.L. is presented in a single order, and subjects are asked to give only positive responses (that an adjective *is* applicable). Its value may be increased by varying presentation order and by requesting negative responses as well as positive ones. An experiment leading to this conclusion has been reported in Warr and Knapper (1967).

repertory grid are determined either directly by the investigator or indirectly via elements which are initially chosen by the investigator; and the 300 items in the A.C.L. are those which Gough and his colleagues have found to be most useful. As indicated earlier in this chapter, one can often be fairly confident in using this kind of instrument that a relevant and a sufficiently varied set of indices has been chosen, but it is always possible that some dimensions customarily used by subjects have been forgotten. In spite of all our efforts we can never be certain that we have included measures of all the aspects of perception which subjects themselves deem to be important. Indeed it is unlikely that the individual perceiver himself is aware of all the dimensions he is using.

There have been a number of suggestions that subjects in investigations of person perception should be allowed to respond in an open-ended fashion (e.g. Bruner and Tagiuri, 1954; Hastorf, Richardson and Dornbusch, 1958; Shrauger and Altrocchi, 1964) and early work in the field (e.g. Asch, 1946) did in fact make some use of short descriptions by subjects of the stimulus person. A start has since been made towards an adequate systematization of free-response data (Beach and Wertheimer, 1961; Dornbusch and coworkers, 1965), and further progress in this area is likely.

One technique which may be valuable in determining the kind of perceptual judgments that subjects make when no response constraints are imposed by an investigator is multidimensional scaling (e.g. Messick, 1956a; Torgerson, 1952, 1958). Multidimensional scaling (M.D.S.) is a procedure which aims to identify the elementary dimensions which people use when they judge a set of stimuli. Subjects are not asked to respond on one or more specific scales, but are simply asked to indicate the degree of similarity between stimuli. It is usual to obtain similarity judgments (perhaps on a nine-point scale) between each pair of stimuli in the set being studied. Subjects are therefore required to make $N(N-1)/2$ judgments for any number, N, of stimuli.

The table of judgments is translated into a matrix of relative distances between all possible stimulus pairs, and this latter information is analysed to uncover the dimensions which were employed by subjects in their global judgments of similarity. The analysis involves converting the relative distances into absolute distances and factoring the implied matrix of scalar products. Variants of this procedure are described in detail by Kruskal (1964a, 1964b), Messick (1956a), Messick and Abelson (1956) and Torgerson (1958). The outcome of the set of operations is that the distances between stimuli are represented in a space, the dimensions of which correspond to the various ways the stimuli are perceived to differ. The points in the space represent the stimuli, and their projections on the dimensions are the scale values for the various attributes. In short, multidimensional scaling can tell us how many dimensions are needed to account most economically for subjects' responses and what value each stimulus has on each dimension. As with all factor analytic techniques, the dimensions have to be identified *post hoc*.

Application and validation of M.D.S. procedures have so far been largely concerned with physical stimuli. Much work has, for example, been carried out in the field of colour perception; and it is generally found that despite variations in technique the similarity judgments of normal subjects are analysable into the basic physical dimensions of colour — amplitude (i.e. intensity), frequency (i.e. hue) and complexity of wavelength (i.e. saturation) (e.g. Indow and Kanazawa, 1960). And if, for instance, only the amplitude and complexity of the colour stimuli are varied, then subjects will be found to judge the stimuli in terms of two dimensions — intensity and saturation (e.g. Indow and Shiose, 1956). Correlations between actual physical values and subjective scale values on any one dimension are found to be extremely high. Multidimensional scaling is clearly applicable to stimulus domains of many kinds. To date results have been reported from studies of capital letters (Künnapas, 1966), odours (Ekman and colleagues, 1964), attitude statements (e.g. Messick, 1956b) and the emotions communicated by facial expressions (Abelson and Sermat, 1962). Jackson and Messick (1963) have drawn attention to the importance of the technique in the study of person perception; and research into the perception of political figures (Messick, 1961) and of other groups in a competitive situation (Schroder, Driver and Streufert, 1967) has recently been reported.

Jackson, Messick and Solley (1957) have described an interesting attempt to isolate and identify the dimensions used in judgments of others. Twenty subjects were required to make similarity–difference judgments about each other. In this way the subjects (well acquainted with each other as members of a social fraternity) also served as stimulus persons. The judgments were analysed according to the M.D.S.

procedures described above and were found to yield three major factors. From other data gathered from subjects Jackson, Messick and Solley were able to tentatively identify the factors as friendship, studiousness and academic status. As they indicate, however, their interpretation of these dimensions of judgment might have been unsatisfactory since they had gathered only limited information about the individuals involved. And it is clear that the nature and number of dimensions employed will vary as a function of perceivers and of stimulus persons.

A major problem with this technique is to interpret the factor structure which emerges. Most investigators have attempted to relate the observed dimensions to denotative aspects of the stimulus range (e.g. amplitude of wavelength, academic status). But it is possible that subjects are in fact making judgments on the basis of less specific characteristics. It might in this case be found that the dimensions employed in perceiving others are similar to the factors customarily revealed in analyses of semantic differential responses. We have followed this line of thought to the stage of conducting an investigation in which subjects are required to register their conceptions of stimulus persons on semantic differential scales and also via global similar–different judgments. By carrying out an M.D.S. analysis of the latter judgments we can attempt to interpret the dimensions used here in terms of the connotative meaning of the stimulus persons.

Experiment 6

Aspects of this investigation have already been described on p. 70, where Experiment 1 is presented. Ninety-seven undergraduate students gave their judgments of eleven national leaders. They responded on a set of semantic differential scales, the factor structure of which was first assumed and later confirmed by analysis. But before these responses were made, subjects gave similar–different judgments of the type amenable to M.D.S. analysis. The major aim of the investigation was to compare the dimensions emerging from this analysis with the factors present in the set of semantic differential scales.

As described on p. 70 the semantic differential forms comprised scales representing the Evaluative, Potency and Activity factors. We wondered whether analogous dimensions would be revealed by the M.D.S. procedures. The first dimension extracted from a Torgerson (1958) analysis of the M.D.S. group data accounted for 60% of the variance, the second accounted for 17% and the third for 10%. These dimensions were rotated orthogonally before comparisons were made. Consider the first one. How can we determine whether this important dimension corresponds to the Evaluative factor which emerges so consistently from studies of semantic differential responses? A straightforward procedure is to compare the loadings *of each stimulus person* on this dimension with the average responses to them on the Evaluative semantic differential scales. If we are measuring the same construct, then there should be a strong association.

Rank correlations have been computed between loadings for each of the eleven stimulus persons on M.D.S. dimension 1 and their mean score on each semantic differential scale. This test makes it quite clear that the first dimension in the M.D.S. analysis is an Evaluative one. Scores on the Evaluative semantic differential scales (*good–bad, fair–unfair, true–false, kind–cruel* and *dangerous–safe*) correlate with loadings on the first dimension 0·96, 0·93, 0·91, 0·92 and 0·90 respectively. On the other hand the mean correlation between dimension 1 loadings and the other seven scales is only 0·48. Furthermore an interesting picture emerges of the *direction* of loadings on this first dimension. Stimulus persons can of course be positively or negatively loaded on the dimension. It should transpire that a zero loading corresponds to a mid-point semantic differential response (i.e. a score of 5), so that negative loadings are below 5 and positive loadings above 5. In the case of all the five Evaluative scales this is so. Not only is there an association between this first dimension and the Evaluative scales, but the two measures also have the same mid-point.

Splitting semantic differential scales into "Evaluative ones" and "others" is always somewhat arbitrary. It is possible to devise a more elegant test of the association between dimension 1 of the M.D.S. analysis and the Evaluative factor of the semantic differential. The extent to which each of the twelve semantic differential scales represents the first M.D.S. dimension is indicated by the correlation between mean judgments on the scale and stimulus person loadings on the dimension. We have already used this index in the results presented in the last paragraph. There should be an association between this correlation (the extent to which a scale represents dimension 1) and the factor loading (the extent to which a scale represents the Evaluative factor). In calculating this association we can concurrently use information about all twelve scales, since even scales from the Potency and

Activity factors have an Evaluative loading of some kind. The association turns out to be an extremely strong one ($rho = +0.92$), and emphasizes again that the first dimension present in the M.D.S. analysis of similar–different judgments is an Evaluative one. This is a very significant dimension, accounting for 60% of variance. We have here strong support for conclusions drawn from semantic differential studies about the role and nature of Evaluative judgments. (For another study of this kind see Warr, Schroder and Blackman, 1968.)

What of the other two semantic differential factors? Do these correspond to other dimensions in the multidimensional scaling analysis? We have carried out tests of the type described above in the case of the Activity and Potency factors, but no consistent pattern emerges. It appears then that the second and third dimensions present in the similar–different judgments are not analogous to the second and third factors in the semantic differential.* Other interpretations have to be placed upon these dimensions. This need not be attempted here. Instead we shall conclude that the results of Experiment 6, whilst not accounting for all factors in the semantic differential, lend further weight to the belief that its concurrent validity is high.

Construct Validity

Although this item "construct validity" was introduced only recently (American Psychological Association, 1954) the basic idea is not new. A measuring instrument or technique may be said to have construct validity if the existence of certain hypothetical explanatory constructs is supported by results obtained with it. For example, the construct "intelligence" has been discussed and refined to a point where we can make some predictions about it. We expect that children's intelligence will increase during their years at school, and indeed this is almost part of the meaning of the construct. A test of intelligence which failed to reveal an increase during this period would therefore be invalid. And conversely, a test which records the increase gains thereby in construct validity. Any examples of the successful use of an instrument to confirm an experimental hypothesis are evidence not only for the hypothesis but also for the construct validity of the instrument.

Construct validity is a more general notion than other forms of

* These data have also been analysed in terms of ethnocentrism and political belief of subjects. The result for subgroups were almost identical to those for the subjects as a whole.

validity, and there are accordingly more ways of assessing it. In fact, evidence about the other kinds of validity also contributes to a conclusion about the construct validity of a measuring device. From our understanding of the construct "intelligence" we expect that a test to measure intelligence will correlate highly with another test which aims to measure the same construct; hence to demonstrate *concurrent* validity is to provide information about construct validity. But just as construct validity is a more general notion, it is also a more loosely defined one. It is not usually clear, for example, at what point an adequate level of construct validity has been demonstrated. In the case of, say, predictive validity, evidence may be in the form of a fairly unambiguous correlation coefficient, but conclusions about construct validity may have to be drawn from several reports of how well investigators' expectations were borne out. Since one investigator's expectations may appear very improbable to another, and since it is not easy to decide when they are fulfilled, there is ample scope for argument.

One point is clear, however. Assessments of construct validity can only be made after the instrument has been used in research over quite a long period. Only if this condition is satisfied can there be sufficient evidence on which to base a conclusion. In the past ten years or so the semantic differential has been widely used and we ought now to be able to say something of its construct validity.

To investigate this characteristic of the semantic differential as a measure of *meaning* we need to look at how well expectations about the construct "meaning" are supported in studies using the instrument. The volume *The Measurement of Meaning* is a monument to the construct validity of the instrument, and very many investigations published since then constitute excellent testimonials. What of the construct validity of the semantic differential as a measure of *person perception*? We are continually being surprised how differences in person perception across conditions or across subject samples are revealed clearly by the instrument. Several cases of this kind are reviewed in later chapters. Similarly, results of the investigations of validity reported earlier suggest that construct validity is acceptable.

Many other workers present evidence for this conclusion. For example, Hallworth and Waite (1965) observed several anticipated differences between judgments by adolescent boys and girls, and Maclay and Ware (1961) recorded the variations they expected between groups from three different Indian cultures. Marks (1965) found that patients' semantic differential judgments of their father were in accordance with his hypothesis about their upbringing. Using the semantic differential to measure the way value systems are perceived has been found to be a fruitful approach to the study of "acculturation" of minority groups (Helper and Garfield, 1965), and the instrument also appears promising as a measure of situational anxiety (Alexander and Husek, 1962) and of aesthetic appreciation (Gray and Wheeler, 1967). In general then the construct validity of the semantic differential both as a measure of meaning and of several more limited notions may be taken to be adequate.

FACTORS AFFECTING THE USE OF SCALES

Each type of validity has so far been discussed separately. As we indicated earlier, this is to some extent artificial since the types are often closely related. There are in addition two general points about the validity of the semantic differential to be raised in this chapter. These are concerned with the optimal number of scale units and with the possibility that the context in which responses are made can influence the way in which a person is perceived. We shall look at these points in turn.

Number of Scale Units

At the beginning of this chapter we pointed out that most investigators have employed seven-point semantic differential scales, but that we have chosen to use sets of nine alternatives. At that stage we were concerned with the distribution of subjects' responses over the scale. It is also important to learn whether variations in scale length influence the way in which subjects respond in a more general sense: do scales of different lengths lead to different interpretations of subjects' judgments? One approach to this topic involves comparing the responses of matched groups of subjects who make judgments on scales of different lengths. We have carried out an experiment making use of this approach.

Experiment 7

In this investigation 106 undergraduate subjects registered their judgment of two concepts on ten-scale semantic differential forms. The concepts employed were Christmas and City of Sheffield. The order of presentation of concepts was counterbalanced, and subjects responded to one of them on seven-point scales and to the other on nine-point scales. Fifty-four subjects judged Christmas on seven-point scales and Sheffield on nine-point scales, whilst the other fifty-two subjects used nine-point scales for Christmas and seven-point scales for Sheffield. We were interested to see whether mean conceptions would differ according to the length of scale employed.

This was studied by converting the scale units so that they were equivalent and by comparing the equivalent scores from the two groups in each part of the investigation. For example, a score of 5 on a nine-point scale is equivalent to one of 4 on a seven-point scale, and it is possible to compare scores by means of a transposition based on this equivalence. It is clear from these comparisons that the mean judgments of the two groups are extremely similar. The average difference between mean responses to the ten scales was only 0·17 in the case of Sheffield and 0·36 in the case of Christmas. The difference between profiles may also be expressed in terms of the generalized distance statistic, D (see p. 59). D values were 0·23 and 1·32 respectively.

Experiment 7 dealt with non-person stimuli. We have also analysed the results of Experiment 2 in the manner described above to check whether scales of different lengths generate similar results in the case of judgments of people. It may be recalled that Experiment 2 (see p. 78) dealt with the relative stability of seven-point and nine-point scales in judgments of British politicians Heath and Wilson. We have also compared mean responses to the two types of scale on the two occasions on which measurements were taken. Once again we transposed the nine-point values to seven-point scales, and once again the resulting pairs of scores were almost identical. Details of the closeness of the profiles are given in Table 4.

It is clear from these studies that extremely similar profiles are

Table 4 Comparison of mean responses to seven-point and nine-point scales

Stimulus person	First measurement		Second measurement	
	Average mean difference	D	Average mean difference	D
Heath	0·21	0·27	0·23	0·29
Wilson	0·18	0·24	0·17	0·24

obtained from scales of seven and nine alternatives. And, as the results of Experiment 2 indicated, the longer scales are as reliable as the more customary seven-point ones. It is reasonable to suppose that the use of nine-point scales provides a more sensitive instrument than that available with seven-point dimensions. Tukey (1950) has noted that small numbers of scale units increase what are in effect "rounding errors", and Gulliksen (1958) has argued strongly for longer semantic differential scales than those in conventional use. There appear to be no strong arguments against these longer scales, at least with intelligent adult subjects (see p. 62), and we have accordingly incorporated nine alternatives into the semantic differential forms used in the experiments reported throughout this book. These have proved to be entirely satisfactory.

What about even longer scales? We might suggest that a scale of virtually unlimited alternatives would be very desirable if subjects could readily respond to it and if it met the other requirements dealt with in this chapter. A scale of this kind might be simply a straight line on which the mid-point alone was indicated. How would this compare with more orthodox scales?

Experiment 8

We have tried out undivided scales in a further investigation. The aims here were to see how well subjects could deal with scales of this type and to see how their judgments on them corresponded to those made by matched groups on orthodox divided scales. Subjects responded on the undivided scales by placing a check mark at the point on a line which represented their conception. The design of this experiment was the same as that of Experiment 7, and a further 117 undergraduate subjects took part. Fifty-nine of them registered their impression of World War One on ten divided scales and their conception of Examinations on the same scales presented without divisions; fifty-eight others responded to these two concepts on undivided and divided scales respectively. The results were transposed in the same manner as previously.

Once again there are no significant differences between the groups. The marked similarity between profiles is indicated by mean difference values of 0·19 for World War One and 0·20 for Examinations. (D-scores are 0·26 and 0·29.) There is no doubt that the undivided scales generate the same patterns of responses as do the customary scales. (See also Blumberg, De Soto and Kuethe, 1966.) In several ways the undivided scales are preferable: the importance of recall in immediate retests is minimized, and subjects are more free from what may seem to be artificial restrictions. The number of available responses is clearly greater, and this is intuitively an advantage. But the major objection to the use of undivided scales in large-scale research projects is that they are extremely laborious to score. The distance of each response from the negative end of the scale has to be measured, and this is very time-consuming. It is of course possible to take an approximate measure (to the nearest centimetre, say) but this yields a scale very similar to the orthodox divided ones. So, although the undivided scale has many virtues, we have preferred to use nine-point measurements. Perhaps undivided scales might be used more often in clinical and idiographic investigations where more emphasis is placed on individual judgments. Another possibility is the development of suitable automatic reading devices, possibly linked to a computer.

Order of Concepts

Earlier in this chapter we raised the question of the importance of scale sequence. It was concluded that the order in which scales are presented is unlikely to influence the way in which subjects will respond to those scales. A similar question concerns the order in which concepts are presented. In many investigations subjects are required to respond to a number of concepts and it is possible that previous concepts in a sequence will create a framework within which later ones will be judged.

This point is raised by Osgood, Suci and Tannenbaum (1957, p. 84), who stress that independence between the concepts judged on the same set of semantic differential scales is essential, since otherwise the indicated meaning of a concept would vary according to the other concepts amongst which it was placed. They refer briefly to an unpublished study by Aitken in which the context in which concepts were presented was systematically varied. Aitken failed to observe significant differences between the way in which subjects responded to each concept.

He studied a very varied set of concepts (e.g. Beauty, Steel, Electricity), and we deemed it advisable to conduct a similar experiment with the more restricted concept domain — people — in which we are particularly interested.

Experiment 9

In this investigation we required undergraduate subjects to indicate their conceptions of four people on a twelve-scale semantic differential form. As soon as a subject had responded to the first stimulus person, he responded to the second, third and fourth persons without pause. We employed two groups of 53 subjects, and manipulated the frame of reference by varying the first three stimulus persons. For one group these were persons likely to be perceived relatively positively

Table 5 Context effects in judgments of Douglas-Home

Scale	Group	Mean response to stimuli 1–3	Mean response to stimulus 4
1 True–false	1	3·67[b]	6·15
	2	7·18[b]	5·92
2 Wise–foolish	1	4·37[b]	5·36
	2	7·26[b]	5·39
3 Large–small	1	5·70[b]	4·08
	2	6·94[b]	4·11
4 Fair–unfair	1	3·22[b]	6·47
	2	7·04[b]	5·94
5 Sharp–dull	1	6·78[a]	4·81
	2	7·42[a]	4·57
6 Kind–cruel	1	2·77[b]	7·02[a]
	2	6·52[b]	6·26[a]
7 Tense–relaxed	1	7·01[b]	4·98
	2	4·66[b]	5·45
8 Strong–weak	1	7·26	4·17
	2	7·63	4·39
9 Bold–timid	1	7·50	4·38
	2	7·80	4·26
10 Emotional–unemotional	1	5·71	4·28
	2	5·87	4·45
11 Active–passive	1	7·77	5·15
	2	7·82	5·06
12 Rugged–delicate	1	6·92	3·19
	2	6·99	3·69

Stimuli: Group 1 (*N* = 53) 1–3 Stalin, Nasser, Hitler (random order); 4 Douglas-Home.
Group 2 (*N* = 53) 1–3 Churchill, Wilson, Kennedy (random order); 4 Douglas-Home.
[a] $p < 0.01$
[b] $p < 0.001$

(Churchill, Wilson, Kennedy — presented in random order), while for the other group the stimulus persons were Stalin, Nasser and Hitler. We were interested in whether responses to the fourth stimulus person, who was the same for both groups, would be affected by the radical differences between induced frames of reference. The fourth person was Sir Alec Douglas-Home who was at the time the British Prime Minister.

The results of this "sledgehammer" experiment are summarized in Table 5. We were unable to discriminate between the two groups' responses to the first three stimulus persons on all scales, and the seven top scales in the table are the ones of major interest. Despite the fact that the mean conceptions of these persons were extremely different in the case of these seven scales, conceptions of the fourth person were in general identical. This of course also applies to the five scales in which different frames of reference were not induced. These scales are numbers 8 to 12 in the table.

We are unable to explain the one anomalous finding — the different conceptions of Douglas-Home on the scale *kind–cruel*. It is nevertheless tempting to conclude that in day-to-day use of the scales (when variations in context of this magnitude are very unlikely), order-of-concept will not be a variable of great importance. Since we carried out this experiment Sommer (1965) has reported a similar study using a more varied set of concepts. He too finds that context is not an important variable. Ross (1965) has also reported an investigation in which he expected to be able to demonstrate context effects. He records "a strong confirmation of Osgood's view from a study designed to discredit it". All the published evidence suggests that the context in which concepts are judged on semantic differential scales is of little importance. Furthermore, we have made a practice of randomly varying the order in which concepts are presented in our investigations, and on every occasion when we have analysed results separately for groups according to serial position we have failed to observe significant differences. It appears that the validity of the instrument is not influenced by unwanted context effects.

CONCLUDING REMARKS

Let us now stand back and attempt to get a more general view of the ground covered in this chapter. We have dealt with a number of important methodological issues in much more detail than is customary, and we have posed several questions which are usually ignored in discussions of the adequacy of a measuring instrument. This may sometimes have resulted in our being able to give a less than satisfactory answer; but we firmly believe that questions of this kind ought to be asked of any instrument in common use.

We have been concerned to assess the adequacy of the semantic differential as a measure of person perception applicable in a variety of situations. It was acknowledged early in the chapter than an alternative approach is to derive separate instruments for differing situations and types of perceivers; we have, however, opted for the greater flexibility permitted by a more general instrument. The discussion has been mainly in terms of the semantic differential as a measure of dispositional judgments, but we have occasionally hinted that it might be used to study episodic perception. It has in fact been utilized in this capacity in several investigations reported below, and this dual role is a valuable aspect of the instrument. It is true that the semantic differential is employed mainly as a measure of covert characteristics, so that in using it we are leaving aside certain aspects of judgment which were identified in Chapter 1. But, granting this limitation, the instrument appears to be both reliable and valid as an index of person perception.

We have reviewed studies bearing upon this conclusion and have linked this review with accounts of several relevant studies of our own. However, there remains one formidable question brought up in many guises in the course of this chapter which we have not been able to answer entirely to our satisfaction. This concerns the decision about which scales should be included in a form. Behind this practical issue lurks an embarrassing theoretical uncertainty — how can we know whether we have measured "the whole of" the way a person is perceived? Our inability to satisfy ourselves on this issue is mainly due to the logical impossibility of specifying "the whole of" a concept like perception. In just the same way we cannot know whether our test measures "the whole of" intelligence, creativity or what-you-will. This is in fact the central difficulty in the measurement of validity. Since we cannot specify completely the concept in which we are interested (meaning, perception, intelligence, rigidity, cohesiveness, etc.), we can never really know whether we have a valid measure of it. We have to make do with second-best, indirect assessments of validity, and it is these which provide scope for the arguments rife amongst users of different tests.

E

Although we cannot know whether we have measured all aspects of the psychological process in which we are interested, we can still ask whether one indicator comes nearer to this ideal than another. In other words we can ask which of two measures is more valid, even though we cannot know when a measure is completely valid. But to ask this of two semantic differential forms is to raise a more difficult question than in the case of, say, two intelligence tests. This is because in the case of intelligence tests one can always apply criteria of internal consistency to a subject's responses and because one can reduce these responses to a single score (I.Q., perhaps, or a percentile value). One has, at least on the face of it, a unitary concept. But, as we have been at pains to show, this is not the case in the measurement of connotative meaning or perception. It is not clear what criteria of internal consistency to apply to semantic differential responses, and it is not fruitful to reduce a set of responses to a single score. On the other hand, by presenting a measure of meaning in terms of a relatively detailed profile, one does not conceal a possible failure to measure important aspects of meaning as an I.Q. score might disguise the omission of a relevant dimension of intelligence.

We have elaborated these points throughout this chapter and have on several occasions drawn attention to the fact that they arise from an uncertainty about how semantic differential scales are related to each other. The most appropriate way to reduce this uncertainty is by use of factor-analytic techniques, and it is for this reason that we have dealt at length with studies which have attempted to systematize the relationships between scales. The solution offered to the practical and theoretical problems of scale selection is in the nature of a "best guess" in the light of the evidence available at present. In general we prefer to utilize scales pertaining to each of the three major factors, although there are situations where additional scales relevant to a hypothesis may be included. And in all cases results should be analysed scale-by-scale rather than merely in terms of factor scores. We have justified these suggestions in the course of the chapter. In the series of experiments to be reported in later chapters they will be put into practice.

3
THE PROCESSING CENTRE

An important aspect of the perceptual system suggested in Chapter 1 is the way in which a perceiver processes the information which he has selected. We have argued that this involves the application of decision rules, either inference rules or combination rules. The present chapter is concerned with the functioning of these rules and with the properties of the processing centre as a whole.

Both kinds of decision rule may be conceptualized as prescriptions based upon expected relationships between characteristics. Consider the following inference rule applicable to a dispositional judgment "from *sincere* infer *reliable*". This is based upon the perceiver's expectancy that sincere people are also reliable. The expectancy may well be un-verbalized and it can of course be a probabilistic one, in that the perceiver may have a (possibly not conscious) estimate of likelihood that these two traits go together within other people. The measurement of these probabilistic expectancies will be treated in this chapter. A general point about the make-up of this and the following chapters is first called for.

It is fairly obvious that our judgments of other people which depend upon expected relationships between traits are very much the same in indirect and in direct perceptual situations. We might read in a newspaper article that a certain person is intelligent. The inferences we draw from this input are similar to inferences which follow if we directly observe that a person in our presence is intelligent. We shall be dealing here with activities which are common both to indirect and to direct perception. In later chapters we shall move on to consider separately those activities which are peculiar to each of the two types of perception.

CORRELATIONS BETWEEN PERSONAL CHARACTERISTICS

Early students of the way people are rated noted what appeared to be a constant error in perception. This resulted in spuriously high inter-correlations between ratings on certain traits. Thorndike (1920) argued that the problem arose from perceivers "suffusing ratings of special features with a halo belonging to the individual as a whole" (p. 25). He observed that some traits were seen to be intercorrelated to a greater degree than he felt should be the case. For example his analysis of the way army officers judged their subordinates revealed that rated intelligence was correlated with "physique" $+0.51$, with "leadership" $+0.58$ and with "character" $+0.64$. And teachers' ratings by their superiors yielded correlations between judged intelligence and "voice" of $+0.63$ and "ability to discipline" of $+0.80$. At about the same time Rugg (1921, 1922) — apparently without knowledge of Thorndike's paper — decided for just the same reasons that "the rating of character is nearly a chance event" (1922, p. 41). He concluded that personal judgments are practically valueless because a judge cannot avoid relating characteristics to each other in terms of his general attitude towards the stimulus person.

Somewhat later Newcomb (1931) drew attention to what he saw as a logical error which generated a very similar type of behaviour. He showed that when subjects rated the personality of others on a series of scales the intercorrelations between characteristics were typically higher than those resulting from direct observations of behaviour. He concluded that "the close relation between traits which is evident in the ratings may be presumed to spring from logical presuppositions in the minds of the raters, rather than from actual behaviors" (p. 288).

Newcomb gave greater emphasis to the *logical* nature of the association between responses, but Thorndike, Rugg and he were all concerned with the same phenomenon — that a judge "is unable to treat an individual as a compound of separate qualities and to assign a magnitude to each of these in independence of the others" (Thorndike,

1920, pp. 28–29). This tendency has since Thorndike's paper been termed "the halo effect". The title is not wholly appropriate since it suggests that characteristics are seen to be closely related only if they are favourable ones. To allow for the possibility of a negative halo effect Dudycha (1942) proposed that the expression "perseveration effect" was more suitable, but this suggestion has not been widely taken up.

These early articles (and several others published at about the same time) are particularly interesting because of their unanimous emphasis on the notion that this effect is an error. The tenor of the articles is that the propensity is an undesirable artefact, that it leads to false perceptions, and that it must be stamped out if judgments are to be at all valid. This now appears to be somewhat unrealistic. It is preferable to consider the tendency to believe that sets of characteristics go together within a stimulus person not as an "error" but as a necessary part of the process of person perception. Expectancies that certain traits are associated can be regarded as persisting components of a perceptual system, and specifically of the processing centre.

D. M. Johnson (1963) has provided evidence that they are permanent assumptions rather than transitory errors induced by a judging situation. He compared a situation in which a halo effect "error" would be maximized with one in which it would be minimal. His subjects made conceptual judgments about five stimulus persons on five nine-point scales. They made judgments on each of five successive days, responding on each day either to a single scale applied to the five stimuli or to a single stimulus on the five scales. The first condition was expected to minimize halo effect whereas the second is the judging situation which is typically said to bring about the effect. In fact the effect was displayed to an equal extent by both subject groups. It seems then that the tendency to assume that traits are associated is a strong one even in conditions where attempts have been made to minimize it.

The inference rules which perceivers employ have been studied in two different ways. Firstly the effects of presenting certain stimulus traits amongst others have been investigated, and in the second approach individual cue traits have been studied in isolation. We shall look at each method in turn.

The first technique was originally reported in a classic paper by Asch (1946). In this he described some ten experiments concerned with the way perceivers relate characteristics to each other (see also Asch, 1952, Chapter 8). This procedure was very simple: a series of characteristics was read out twice to subjects who were asked to indicate their impression of the person the traits were supposed to characterize. No other information about the stimulus person was provided, although it appears that this was assumed to be an adult male.* Subjects gave their impressions of the stimulus person in two ways. On the one hand they wrote a brief character sketch of the person, the modal length of which seems to have been about forty words. On the other hand they responded to a check list, usually of 18 items, by selecting the item from each pair of polar terms which was most in accordance with the impression they had formed. These pairs of items resemble semantic differential scales on which only two responses are possible. It is important to note, however, that the list could not be constructed according to the principles for representativeness outlined in the previous chapter; item selection was guided by "an informal sense of what was fitting or relevant" (p. 262). Some consequences of this will be discussed below.

That subjects make quite considerable inferences from very limited cues was evident from the type of impressions Asch's subjects reported. The written sketches often showed a good deal of imaginative embellishment of the stimulus information, and subjects apparently experienced no qualms about their willingness to go well beyond the material presented. In general the inferential nature of impression formation was clear from Asch's findings. But his experiments were designed to reveal something more specific about the actual basis on which these inferences are drawn. Knowledge about perceivers' inference rules was obtained by varying relatively minor aspects of the stimulus list. In his first experiment, for example, one group of subjects was exposed to the list *intelligent, skilful, industrious, warm, determined, practical, cautious*, whilst a second group was presented with the same first three and last three items with *cold* instead of *warm* in fourth place. By comparing the perceptual responses of the two groups of subjects it was possible to see what sorts of inferences derive from the cue trait *warmth*.

This trait appeared to be a very important one, since widespread differences were observed in the impressions formed by the two experimental groups. Varying only *warmth* in the list of seven traits produced very different impressions of the stimulus person's generosity,

---

* Incidentally, Asch's subjects were mostly women; this might be relevant when the relationship between his findings and those from later investigations is considered.

shrewdness, happiness, irritability, humour, sociability, popularity, ruthlessness, self-centredness and imaginativeness. Some of these inferences are of course due to similarities in the meanings of the terms employed, and as such are relatively trivial (though they do of course indicate the construct validity of Asch's measure). But other differences (in shrewdness and imaginativeness, for instance) do not derive from this type of semantic similarity and tell us something about judges' inference rules. By varying a number of aspects of this type of list, evidence became available about the kinds of inferences which are made from several cue traits. Asch used this technique to draw attention to a number of specific processes of cognitive organization which he believed lay behind the formation and change of impressions.

Many of his conclusions have aroused considerable interest. He argued for instance that certain traits were more central than others, in that judges thought them to be particularly important and in that more extreme and more frequent inferences were based on them.* The characteristic *warmth* was seen to be particularly central in this sense, whereas differences in *blunt–polite* were of much less importance. Another observation was that inferences from a cue trait are not made to all possible characteristics; the changes consequent upon variations in a cue trait are observed only in judgments of certain other attributes. Changing *warm* for *cold*, for example, did not affect judgments of the stimulus person's honesty, reliability or persistence. A third conclusion was about the context in which a cue trait was embedded. Inferences from a trait are partly dependent upon other attributes of the stimulus person. This was observed in experiments altering the other traits around the cue or varying the order in which the items were presented; Asch's procedure here points a way to the study of combination rules. A final, more general issue raised by Asch was the immediacy with which the inferences from traits are drawn and the way these inferences combine to create a rounded impression of the entire person. In Bartlett's (1932) terms, we might say that the perceiver exhibits a spontaneous, constructive "effort after meaning".

Later experiments based upon Asch's design have mainly aimed to extend the generality of his findings or to learn about specific aspects of his experimental situation. For example, Mensh and Wishner (1947) repeated two of his studies with subjects from another geographical

* In terms of the system employed in this book a central trait is an input which can call up a large number of decision rules.

region; and Boyle (1965) investigated the possibility that the two types of response elicited by Asch (the character sketch and the check list) might have interacted with each other. In both cases Asch's conclusions were in essence confirmed. Haire and Grunes (1950) presented rather more complex sets of material (for instance, that the stimulus person was "a factory worker"), and drew attention to a number of different ways in which perceivers organize relatively disparate information. Pepitone and Hayden (1955) also employed more complicated material than did Asch. They described the stimulus person as being a member of several social groupings, and introduced conflicting combinations of membership (for example "member of the New York Stock Exchange" and "member of the Finance Committee of the Communist party"). Subjects' impressions were in the form of written sketches, from which it was clearly seen that judges used a variety of devices to resolve the conflict. Most common were attempts to discount the discrepant material (e.g. "he is probably a Republican at heart").

Bruner and Tagiuri (1954) have reviewed the earlier studies of this type, and have raised a number of further pertinent questions about the way in which we organize our judgments of other people. They conceive of individuals' expectancies that certain traits go together within other people in terms of the subjects' "naive, implicit theories of personality". Following Bruner and Tagiuri's review and the paper by Cronbach (1955) it has become customary to describe the kinds of perceptual inferences revealed by Asch's experiments in terms of a subject's "implicit personality theory" — his expectancies (usually unverbalized and unclearly formulated) about the way in which characteristics are interrelated within other people. Sarbin, Taft, and Bailey (1960) have discussed this in terms of a perceiver's "postulate system". They emphasize that inferences are made by means of general statements postulated by the perceiver. Given the observation that a stimulus is sincere, a judge might utilize his postulate "sincerity is associated with reliability" to infer that the person is likely to be reliable.

The ideas of "implicit personality theory" and "postulate system" seem to be paralleled by our notion of a set of decision rules within a processing centre. A preference for any one of these terms will depend on the context in which discussion is taking place. We generally prefer to talk in terms of a set of single rules since it is these individually and in subgroups which we must study if we are to understand the operation of the whole. Furthermore, accepting the idea that object perception and person perception are essentially the same creates the need for a general term to describe the processing activities in both forms of judgment; "implicit personality theory" is suitable only for person perception. Nevertheless there are undoubtedly occasions when this term or "postulate system" seem to be more apposite than "a set of decision rules".

In the early 1950s the only available technique to investigate perceptual decision rules* was by means of Asch-type studies. To be sure, any investigation of impression formation yielded evidence for some type of inference process, but the nature of implicit personality theories themselves could only be determined by the more direct and yet more limited technique described here. This technique was not without its critics; Luchins (1948) for instance is particularly disapproving of Asch's claim to be able to observe with it subjects' formation of an impression of the *entire* person, since this is in effect logically impossible. And both Luchins and Asch himself draw attention to the artificiality of the experimental situation; we shall shortly collate the points relevant to this argument.

But firstly a particularly interesting comment by Wishner (1960) should be considered. He discussed the idea that traits differ in their centrality. *Warmth* had emerged from Asch's studies (and from others which we shall review in Chapter 4, pp. 231–238, as a very central characteristic, whereas *politeness* appeared to be peripheral. Wishner enquired how we could predict in advance of an investigation which traits are central and which are more peripheral. His basic hypothesis was that the composition of the check list on which impressions are measured is a crucial determinant of whether or not a cue trait is deemed to be central. If the check list happens to contain a lot of items which are in fact correlated with a cue trait, changing the cue trait will generate a very different series of responses to the check list items — so that the trait will be termed a central one. If on the other hand the items in the check list are *not* correlated with the cue trait, then this characteristic will appear from the results to be peripheral.

Wishner tested this possibility by analysing further the earlier results of Asch and of Mensch and Wishner. He predicted that

---

* It may be recalled that we use "decision rules" as a generic expression to cover both inference rules and combination rules. The former type of decision rule concerns a single input whereas the other deals with multiple inputs.

responses to check list items which are themselves significantly related to the dimension *warm–cold* will show greatest changes when this dimension is varied as part of an otherwise constant stimulus list. To check this prediction he used scales similar to semantic differential ones to measure the way a further group of subjects perceived their instructors. From this latter set of data he was able to derive estimates of the correlations between the traits studied in Asch's experiments, and specifically of the correlation between each trait and the dimension *warm–cold*. He then looked at the degree of association between these r values and the magnitude of the difference between perceptual responses made by the group of subjects exposed to *warm* and the group exposed to *cold* in the previous experiments. It emerged that *rho* between these two independently obtained measures was $+0.62$. Similar results were obtained from further investigations of the dimensions *intelligent–unintelligent, blunt–polite*, and *humane–ruthless*.

These findings provide clear evidence that the apparent centrality of a trait can depend on the nature of the items selected to measure subjects' impressions. If the items in a check list happen to correlate with the cue trait which is varied, then this trait will seem to be a central one. If they are unrelated, the cue trait will appear to be peripheral.* It does, however, seem that Wishner makes more of his results than is permissible, for he uses them to suggest that Asch's idea that traits differ in their centrality is merely an artefact of which response list happens to be used. But the point of Asch's discussion is that centrality is an attribute which exists in its own right — the particular importance of a trait which is not reducible to correlation coefficients (McCollough, 1961). That centrality may be measured by correlation coefficients is clear, and one value of Wishner's investigation is to bring this out, but we would agree with Asch that a trait can be central in the mind of a judge even when he is not actually making a judgment.

It seems then that Wishner's findings, important as they are, do not invalidate Asch's notion of centrality, nor his technique for measuring the kinds of inferences which subjects typically make when they form impressions of other people. Arguments which are potentially more damaging to the procedure have been raised by Asch himself (1946, p. 289) and by Luchins (1948). Some of these arguments seem to be

---

* This conclusion echoes the observation frequently made in Chapter 2 that the scales included in a measuring instrument must be representative of the relevant population of items.

misguided, and others we shall show from the results of later experiments to be unimportant.

It has, for example, been objected to the technique that our past experience of the stimulus person is usually of paramount importance in determining our impression of him, and that consequently in real life we are rarely confronted with the judging situation typical of Asch's experiments. In terms of the model suggested in Chapter 1, we often need to take account of stored stimulus person information. But in fact there are countless numbers of impressions formed each day from newspapers and films, from descriptions provided by others and from first meetings which cannot be influenced by past experience of the other person himself. There is unquestionably a difference between the impression we form of a stranger and the way we perceive close friends (see the study by Koltuv (1962) described on p. 132). Yet this does not invalidate Asch's findings; it merely indicates that they do not tell the whole story. The same assessment must be made of the arguments that there are likely to be different findings according to whether the stimulus person is a man or a woman, an adult or a child, and that the characteristics of the perceiver will influence his implicit personality theory.*

Apparently more cogent are the suggestions that Asch's technique neglects the social interaction between perceiver and perceived and that it takes no cognisance of the fact that we ourselves affect the person we are judging. This type of objection to many laboratory studies is quite common (see also Asch (1952) and Bruner and Tagiuri (1954)), and is apparently based on the assumption that what we have termed indirect perception without interaction never occurs. If in fact many of our perceptual judgments take place without face-to-face mutual influence (and this is surely true, as we have argued in Chapter 1), then these objections cannot apply to such judgments. It has also been argued against Asch's methodology that in real life we are not usually given descriptions of another person but rather have ourselves to decide whether he possesses certain cue traits. Yet there are of course many instances of indirect perception when this again is untrue; colleagues might describe another person in much the same way as Asch described his stimulus persons (cf. Kelley, 1950), and newspaper reporters certainly do this continually. Furthermore, similar phenomena to those reported by Asch have been observed in studies where the presence of

* Both these points are studied in Experiment 14.

cue traits is not signalled in the way he signalled it (e.g. Veness and Brierley, 1963).

The techniques devised by Asch and by other laboratory investigators have their limitations, but at worst they provide analogues of indirect perceptual situations and at best they can be relevant to a much wider range of conditions. Yet many investigators do seem to incorporate an unnecessary degree of artificiality into their designs. Luchins (1948, p. 319) has lamented the fact that "nowhere in Asch's report was there shown the relevancy of the experimental procedures to more natural judgments". Although we believe Asch's findings to be very relevant both to indirect and direct perception, we join Luchins in wondering whether the same effects would have been observed if Asch had not presented discrete pieces of information but had himself provided a fairly unified set of stimulus material. Would the same findings have been obtained if the seven stimulus traits had been presented as part of newspaper accounts with each trait individually inseparable from the general context? Experiments 10–13 were devized to look into this question.

Experiments 10 and 11

The first two studies of this series aimed to replicate Asch's experiments in much more natural situations. We wanted an arrangement which appeared to subjects to be quite genuine, but which allowed almost as much control of important variables as Asch achieved. In both cases we constructed typical indirect perceptual conditions, in which subjects formed impressions about a person described in a newspaper report.

Experiment 10 is concerned with inferences from the cue trait *warmth*. We composed two versions of a fictitious newspaper report about the manager of a football team. Both versions were built around the traits used in Asch's first experiment: *intelligent, skilful, industrious, warm, determined, practical, cautious*. The background material was intended to be fairly neutral or repetitive and served to link these characteristics in a natural way. The first version is reproduced below, where each characteristic or its equivalent is italicized. (This was of course not the case in the experimental situation.)

It is now six months since Norman Dixon became Rovers' seventh post-war manager. Time for a good hard look at the club and what it has achieved under Dixon's guidance.

Chairman of the Board Gus Williams believes that the club has never had a more *intelligent* manager. "Just look at the *skilful* way he's dealt with the club in these six months. He hasn't put a foot wrong." But Dixon is more than a skilful manager — he's also a very *hard-working* one. He's been in the football game for almost forty years — for the last twenty in the Cheshire League. As coach–manager for Winsford Town and Chelford he didn't spare any effort to maintain the success of his team.

Rovers' Captain, centre-half Andy Watson, feels the same way. "He's the most *warm-natured* manager I've known, but he certainly knows what he wants — and he'll get it. The main thing about Norman is that he's *determined* — determined to get the best out of the team, and determined for Rovers to do well."

There's no doubt that Norman Dixon is a very *practical* man. Whatever he's doing — whether it's thinking up a plan for the next match or setting out to sign up a new player — he's always very clear about the difficulties. Things haven't been easy for Rover's manager in these last few months and all the time he's had to act very *cautiously*. One slip and he could have pulled the whole club down with him.

Version 2 was the same as this in all respects, except that the second sentence of the third paragraph commenced "He can be a cold fish at times, but . . .". The reports were typewritten and were presented to subjects as having been taken from a newspaper. Fifty-three under-graduate subjects drawn from many departments of Sheffield University read version 1, and 52 matched subjects read version 2. After reading through the account once each subject gave his impression of the stimulus person (Norman Dixon) on 13 nine-point semantic differential scales.

These scales were not selected to measure "the whole of" subjects' perception of the stimulus person in the way outlined in Chapter 2. In addition to our aim of replicating Asch's findings under these new conditions, we had a second intention. We wanted to see if Wishner's (1960) index of trait centrality was equally powerful here. So we selected scales which appeared from his figures to embrace a wide range of associations with *warm–cold*. The scales which were employed are shown in Table 6. As usual we varied order and polarity of scales in several different versions of the semantic differential forms.

Table 6   Perceptions of Norman Dixon by subjects in the "warm" and "cold" groups
of Experiment 10

Scale	Group 1 (N=53)	Group 2 (N=52)	Probability value
1 Humane–ruthless	4·74	3·19	0·001
2 Goodlooking–unattractive	4·91	4·71	n.s.
3 Altruistic–self-centred	6·19	5·69	n.s.
4 Strong–weak	7·77	7·44	n.s.
5 Honest–dishonest	7·11	7·04	n.s.
6 Generous–ungenerous	6·36	5·44	0·05
7 Important–insignificant	6·81	7·06	n.s.
8 Reliable–unreliable	7·64	7·79	n.s.
9 Popular–unpopular	7·87	6·71	0·001
10 Sociable–unsociable	6·85	5·36	0·001
11 Goodnatured–irritable	6·49	4·88	0·001
12 Warm–cold	6·40	3·88	0·001
13 Happy–unhappy	5·91	5·92	n.s.

Our stimulus information was clearly more complex than that of Asch, and the appearance of the passage suggests that the cue trait would be of limited significance amongst the rest of the material. How important was it in fact, according to the responses made by the two groups of subjects? Mean values on each scale are set out in Table 6, and the significance of differences, assessed by *t*-tests, is indicated in the right-hand column of this table. Varying the single dimension in this setting clearly had a marked effect on subjects' perceptions: no less than five of the twelve judgments (excluding *warm–cold* itself) were significantly different across the groups. We must conclude that Asch's results were not limited to his somewhat artificial conditions but that they also obtain in a much more realistic experimental situation.

Can we draw the same conclusion about Wishner's analysis? We have processed the data in the manner outlined above, using first his estimates of the intercorrelations of each of the response traits with *warm–cold*. Wishner (1960, p. 100) reports that the rank correlation (*rho*) between these values and the magnitudes of the differences between the two experimental groups was +0·62. In the present case this value is +0·63. It is clear that once again the greater effects are found on scales related to the cue trait, and that the pattern of this relationship is very similar in both types of experimental situation. We were uncertain of the validity of using estimates of trait intercorrelations derived from Wishner's subject sample which was so different from ours, and accordingly obtained similar estimates from another experiment (Warr, 1966). As part of the latter investigation subjects rated an indirectly perceived stimulus person on the same set of scales and from their responses we recalculated the intertrait relationships. These values — obtained from judgments of this one person — correlated with Wishner's values +0·68, and the correlation between our estimate of trait relationships with *warm–cold* and the magnitude of the scale difference between groups was +0·70. Wishner's conclusions are upheld.

One of the satisfying aspects of Wishner's thesis is that it allows predictions about the importance of apparently peripheral traits to be made in any situation. He has reported a study (1960, p. 107) of the dimension *humane–ruthless* in which this serves as the cue trait amongst other characteristics, to which it is unrelated. He observed effects similar to those seen for *warm–cold* and other variables. Again we have studied how well his conclusion can be generalized to the more realistic situations which are our major concern.

In Experiment 11, which was of the same design as Experiment 10, we used Wishner's stimulus list. Two versions of a newspaper report were prepared, identical except for manipulation of the cue trait, and perceptual judgments were obtained on scales specially selected to vary in their degree of association with the cue trait. The connecting material in the reports was intended to be relatively neutral, but much more information was of course presented here than in the earlier studies. Version 1 is reproduced below with the stimulus traits italicized.

Mr. Alfred Wishlade, the new Chief Constable of Oldham, took up his duties at 9 a.m. yesterday. He has come here from Coventry where he was previously Deputy Chief Constable, and he earned for himself there a reputation for being *cautious* but extremely *scrupulous* in his dealings. His *good looks* fit in well with his well-known *humane* attitude to the law-breaker, and he already has an *impressive* record of crime detection.

He pointed out yesterday that he had yet to find his feet in Lancashire and he stressed the importance of pursuing a *flexible* policy. Mr. Wishlade already has a more than local renown through his *fearless* handling of the Teddy Boy riots in Birmingham in 1952 when, as an Inspector, he led a small police contingent of troubleshooters. His success then was attributed to the *dedicated seriousness* with which he approached the problem in hand. If he brings such qualities to Oldham he will no doubt make his presence felt in the town among both the law-breakers and the law-abiding.

The cue trait *humane* (*ruthless* in version 2) seems to be relatively unobtrusive. It was nevertheless of considerable importance in the determination of subjects' impressions. Results are summarized in Table 7, and judgments of Wishlade by the two groups of subjects were clearly very different. How were the scale differences related to their association with *humane–ruthless*? In Wishner's study $rho = +0.83$ (calculated from data in his Tables 7 and 8). If we use his estimates of intertrait correlations we find a corresponding value in this experiment of $+0.82$. Using measures of intertrait correlations obtained from responses by our own subjects (derived from Experiment 23) $rho = +0.84$. The same phenomena are clearly present in both cases. The rank correlation between our estimates of trait correlations with *humane–ruthless* and those of Wishner was $+0.80$.

We are satisfied that despite the apparent artificiality of Asch's experimental situation his conclusions are applicable to at least some

Table 7   Perceptions of Alfred Wishlade by subjects in the "humane" and "ruthless" groups of Experiment 11

Scale	Group 1 (N=45)	Group 2 (N=61)	Probability value
1 Kind–cruel	6·38	4·87	0·001
2 Active–inactive	8·24	8·15	n.s.
3 Altruistic–self-centred	6·36	5·24	0·02
4 Strong–weak	7·89	7·80	n.s.
5 Polite–blunt	5·04	3·43	0·001
6 Profound–shallow	6·67	6·26	n.s.
7 Humane–ruthless	6·67	3·54	0·001
8 Goodnatured–irritable	6·93	5·36	0·001
9 Important–insignificant	7·42	7·20	n.s.
10 Just–unjust	7·93	7·13	0·02
11 Direct–evasive	7·22	7·64	n.s.
12 Generous–ungenerous	6·60	5·31	0·001
13 Quick–slow	6·84	7·28	n.s.

instances of indirect person perception occurring in fairly normal situations. The same conclusion may be drawn about the usefulness of Wishner's approach to the measurement of inferences from cue trait. There is, however, one reservation to be made: the narratives employed in Experiments 10 and 11 were written with the intention that the additional material should be relatively uncomplicated and neutral. How far can our conclusions here be pushed? Do they hold in the case of longer, still more complex passages? Experiments 12 and 13 were intended to answer this question.

Experiments 12 and 13

These two investigations were replications of the previous two studies but with the addition of more detail to the narratives. In Experiment 12 we increased the length of the narrative about Dixon (used in Experiment 10) from approximately 250 words to 420 words. Details of his past career, other events in the club, and further comments about the team were included. The seven stimulus traits were included in the same way as previously; and the length and complexity of the narrative made the presence of the cue trait still less obvious. In a similar manner the length of the narrative used in Experiment 11 was doubled from its original 180 words by including many more details of the stimulus person's career and background. We used the same sets of semantic differential scales as previously, and the experimental procedure was unchanged. Ninety-nine subjects served in Experiment 12 and 98 in Experiment 13.

Let us consider first the results of Experiment 12. Varying *warm–cold* in the complicated narrative used here still led to clear differences in the inferences which subjects drew about other characteristics of the stimulus person. Apart from *warm–cold* itself, five significant differences between the two groups were observed. Furthermore, Wishner's analysis proved similarly useful in this situation. The rank correlation between his estimates of correlations with the cue trait and the magnitude of scale differences was found to be $+0.53$ (compared to $+0.62$ in his original study). Employing our own measure of intertrait relationships (derived from data from Experiment 17) we find that $rho = +0.75$.

Similar results were obtained from Experiment 13 in which *humane–ruthless* was varied. Although only two significant scale differences (apart from the cue trait itself) were observed, the *rho* values corresponding to those cited above were found to be $+0.80$ (using Wishner's estimates of association with the cue trait) and $+0.62$ (using our own estimates derived from Experiment 22). The correlations between our trait association estimates and those of Wishner were $+0.70$ and $+0.72$ for Experiments 12 and 13 respectively.

It appears then that the patterns of inference which are found when the stimulus material is of considerable complexity are very similar to those observed in the simplified situations employed by Asch, Wishner and others. Yet although the *pattern* of inference remains the same, it can be seen that the *potency* of a single cue trait diminishes as additional stimulus material is introduced. Although the average scale difference between the two groups in Experiment 10 was 0.82 it was only 0.51 in the more complicated context provided in Experiment 12; a similar drop from 0.97 to 0.60 occurred between the two investigations of *humane–ruthless*. Presumably the difference observed when *only* the seven traits are presented would be considerably greater than in either of these cases.

OTHER TECHNIQUES TO STUDY IMPLICIT PERSONALITY THEORIES

In all the experiments considered so far inferences between traits have been studied in terms of correlations between the responses of many subjects on several scales when applied to a single stimulus person. This stimulus person is typically assumed to be an adult male, to whom certain characteristics are attributed by the investigator. Koltuv (1962) has employed a different technique to measure the implicit personality theories of individual subjects. She required her subjects to indicate their judgments of each of forty different stimulus persons. Responses were on twelve seven-point scales which have some affinity with the semantic differential scales employed here. For each subject she was able to calculate the between-scale correlations deriving from the forty sets of judgments. The stimulus persons in her study were all real people, acquaintances of the subjects.

There are some difficulties attached to the representativeness of the sample of stimulus persons needed in this type of study. Indeed an interesting aspect of Koltuv's investigation was the demonstration of how inferences about traits are dependent upon the category of stimulus persons employed. Twenty of the stimuli were people with whom the subjects were very familiar, whereas the other twenty were less well known to them. The observed correlations between traits were significantly higher in the case of unfamiliar stimulus persons than in the case of the familiar ones. This provides further evidence that implicit personality theories — patterns of expected relationships — are most important when perceiving others about whom we have limited information; when we are familiar with the person we are judging, we rely more on our knowledge of him and less on our expectancies of people in general.

Koltuv's method of studying intertrait relationships is valuable, but it does require considerable effort on the part of the subject and of the investigator. A simpler technique for studying the inferences made by individual perceivers was pioneered by Bruner, Shapiro and Tagiuri (1958). They examined inference rules about single cue traits to see how these provided a basis for predicting combination rules. Cue traits were presented alone, without the contexts used in earlier studies, and the inferences made from them were studied in a very direct manner.

Suppose that we are interested in the cue trait *intelligence*. We could ask subjects how likely it is that intelligent people are aggressive, active, awkward and so on. Bruner, Shapiro and Tagiuri did this by requiring subjects to respond on a five-point scale to show how they judged this probability. One of the following categories had to be checked in the case of each response trait: very often are, tend to be, may or may not be, tend not to be, seldom are. This procedure can easily generate information about positive and negative inferences from various cue traits. The authors do not present details of the inferences from all the cue traits which they studied, nor do they apply more than an ordinal analysis. But it is clear that their subjects made several inferences which are by no means logically necessary ones. For example, more than half of the subjects indicated that the characteristic *intelligence* implies that a person is active, deliberate, enterprising, efficient, energetic, conscientious, honest, independent, reliable and responsible. We obviously have here a valuable index of inference rules about the input *intelligent*.

Further discussions of this type of index have been presented by Jackson (1962), Shapiro and Tagiuri (1958) and Uhr (1959). Warr and Sims (1965) have made use of six-point scales and have derived additional sets of measures; these are considered below. A sophisticated approach to the measurement and understanding of trait implication has been developed by Hays (1958); this is based upon probability or set theory. Subjects are required to make probability responses similar to those elicited by Bruner, Shapiro and Tagiuri, but this time on an eleven-point scale. Hays's model allows him to make predictions about the "weights" of individual characteristics and about the relative likelihood of sets of attributes occurring together. His 1958 paper is unfortunately a brief one, and relatively few details of his investigations are presented there.

Todd and Rappoport (1964) have, however, amplified Hays's account and have reported in some detail a study based upon his ideas. They raise the interesting question of how well the configurations of implicative relationships revealed by these more direct procedures deriving from the work of Bruner, Shapiro and Tagiuri correspond with those based on correlational techniques used by Koltuv and others. Their subjects responded in three different ways. They made judgments of the likelihood of occurrence of a trait in a person given that the person possesses another trait. These judgments, typical of those in other studies of inference rules referred to above, were analysed according to Hays's model. Subjects also indicated their judgments on seven-point scales, similar to semantic differential scales, of two sets of stimulus persons. One set comprised actual people known to subjects, and the other set was made up of hypothetical people similar to those studied elsewhere ("an intelligent person", etc.). These latter two classes of judgments were analysed in a manner similar to that used by Koltuv. A direct comparison of the correlational technique employed by Koltuv and the more direct method (employed by Bruner and associates) was thus possible.

The first part of Todd and Rappoport's analysis involved a comparison of the intertrait relationships revealed by the three sets of responses. The implicative associations between pairs of traits were found to be similar irrespective of subjects' task, in that correlations between the three sets of results all exceeded $+0.70$. The closest association was between the intertrait correlations obtained from judgments of real people and of hypothetical people; in this case the mean r was $+0.83$. When they turned to a comparison of the *structure* of the relationships revealed by the three procedures, however, Todd and Rappoport observed much less agreement. This second analysis was in terms of the factor or dimensional structure present in judges' responses. The two sets of correlational data were factor analysed, and subjects' other responses — about likelihood of association — were treated according to the Hays model. Very little overlap between the basic dimensions of cognitive structure present in the three sets of material was observed. This may be partly due to the fact that the factor structures were derived after axis rotation, whereas any form of rotation is difficult with the Hays model and was not attempted in this study. On the other hand the two factor analyses did not themselves result in similar factors even though each involved simple-structure rotation. It might in principle be possible to reduce the dissimilarity in cognitive structures derived from the models, but this was not Todd and Rappoport's intention.*

Looking generally at these studies of implicit personality theories it is clear that, despite uncertainty about the nature of appropriate models, several useful techniques to identify perceptual inference rules are available. Is it possible at this stage to select from them a preferred method? Although this would almost certainly be premature, one consideration does deserve mention. Investigators have either obtained judgments on several scales and then calculated intercorrelations between these judgments, or they have asked subjects to make "if . . . then . . ." judgments about attributes. Examples of the former method are provided by Wishner's and Koltuv's work, and the research by Bruner, Shapiro and Tagiuri exemplifies the second approach.

In Chapter 1 we conceptualized inference rules as being of the type "if A then X". It is fairly clear that there are instances when "if A then X" is valid whereas "if X then A" is not appropriate. For example, it has been noted (Warr and Sims, 1965) that *intelligence* (A) implies *dependability* (X) and *sincerity* (Y), whereas the reverse rules ("X implies A" and "Y implies A") seem rather unlikely. The correlational procedure described above takes no cognizance of this possibility, in that the $A:X$ relationship is necessarily the same as the $X:A$ relationship. For this reason (and on practical grounds) the more direct technique of Bruner and his colleagues which can obtain two values for an intertrait relationship $(A:X$ and $X:A)$ seems more likely to provide a true picture of inference rules as they are actually applied. Against this, however, Todd and Rappoport observed a close similarity in results from the two methods, and it may be that the frequency of variations in $A:X$ and

---

* These interpretations have benefitted from very helpful correspondence with F. J. Todd and H. C. Triandis.

X:A implicative relationships is so low that this point need not trouble us. Further comparative tests of the Todd and Rappoport type with special attention to this question seem desirable.

We turn now from these methodological questions to more substantive issues. Many questions about factors which influence decision rules have still to be tackled. Two major areas of interest concern differences between stimulus persons and between perceivers. Many of the experiments reviewed above used only one type of stimulus person — typically an adult male. How far are inference rules modified by inputs about certain other aspects of a stimulus person? Again, studies of individual differences in expected intertrait relationships are rare. We have postulated in Chapter 1 that the stable characteristics of the perceiver partly determine the nature of the decision rules he employs. Is there any evidence that this is so? In Experiment 14 we have looked into these questions. The investigation also aimed to provide more general information about the measurement and nature of implicit personality theories.

Experiment 14

Subjects' inferences from six different cue traits were studied by the method employed by Warr and Sims (1965). Responses were made on a six-point scale. (For example: People who are cynical: nearly always are, very often are, tend to be, tend not to be, seldom are, hardly ever are: ambitious, careless, cruel and so on.) The same twenty-five response traits were employed with each of the six cue traits. Approximately half of the response traits were expected to be favourably evaluated, and it was intended that they should represent a good sample of personal characteristics. Ninety-seven undergraduate subjects (52 male and 45 female) responded to the six cue traits, which were presented in randomized orders. We also employed six different orders of the response traits, so that in addition to a random order of presentation each cue trait was randomly associated with a different order of responding. (See Shapiro and Tagiuri (1958) and Uhr (1959) for a discussion of context influences.)

The cue traits also were selected to represent a wide range of personal characteristics. One characteristic with a high loading on each of six A.C.L. personality dimensions (Gough and Heilbrun, 1965; Chapter 2 of this volume) was chosen. The characteristics studied were *cynical, forceful, impulsive, practical, precise* and *reflective*. By measuring the inferences drawn from these different characteristics we hoped to be able to gain some fairly general knowledge of subjects' implicit personality theories.

We also studied several other questions. As well as responding to the class of "People" on these six cue traits, subjects were requested to make inferences about more restricted categories of individuals. The first task required subjects to make inferences relative to people in general. They were subsequently (thirty minutes later) asked for judgments about "Men" and about "Women". (Half the subjects responded first to "Men", and the remainder first to "Women".) Inferences were requested from three of the cue traits previously studied — *cynical*, *forceful* and *reflective*. After a further thirty minutes (spent on other experimental activities) we obtained information about inferences from the remaining cue traits relevant to two further person categories which were even more restricted — "Men Students" and "Bank Managers". Order of presentation was again varied.

Several other measurements were also taken. Subjects completed the Adjective Check List (A.C.L.) as a self description. We used this to relate several personality dimensions to subjects' implicit personality theories. And since the six cue traits are themselves embodied in the A.C.L. we were able to study differences between inferences from traits said to be possessed by subjects and from unchecked items. In addition, subjects indicated how they valued all of the characteristics studied. Responses here were also on a six-point scale (extremely desirable, very desirable, quite desirable, rather undesirable, very undesirable, extremely undesirable). These evaluations were measured in relation to each of the five classes of stimulus person investigated. Sequences of evaluative responses were randomized across stimulus classes as previously; they were in every case obtained half an hour after the earlier measures.

The evaluative judgments were required in order to test the hypothesis (Warr and Sims, 1965) that perceivers tend particularly to associate like-valued characteristics with each other, much as the notion of halo effect implies. Results pertaining to them will be withheld until later in this chapter. Similarly, we shall postpone discussion of the consequences of varying the stimulus classes until we have considered the inferences which subjects make about People.

As was anticipated from previous work, subjects had no difficulty in making the responses asked for, and a great deal of additional evidence

Table 8 Inferences drawn from the information that a stimulus person possesses a specified cue trait

Response trait	Cue trait					
	Cynical	Forceful	Impulsive	Practical	Precise	Reflective
Ambitious	+0·98	+2·54	+1·38	+1·06	+1·13	−0·06
Careless	−0·24	+0·26	+1·22	−1·78	−1·86	−1·20
Conceited	+1·05	+1·41	+0·24	−0·48	+0·09	−0·84
Conscientious	−0·11	+0·48	−0·76	+1·87	+1·61	+1·74
Cruel	+1·35	+0·91	−0·15	−0·91	+0·33	−1·57
Cynical		+0·95	−0·68	−0·84	+0·06	−0·23
Deceitful	+0·26	+0·07	−0·67	−1·22	−0·81	−1·36
Dependable	−0·42	−0·20	−1·18	+1·85	+1·69	+1·43
Discreet	−1·01	−1·09	−1·34	+0·62	+0·98	+1·42
Forceful	+0·75		+1·63	+0·81	+0·16	−0·93
Friendly	−1·13	+0·37	+1·53	+1·54	−0·05	+1·06
Helpful	−0·93	−0·01	+0·42	+1·67	+0·55	+1·32
High-spirited	−0·44	+1·47	+1·89	−0·03	−1·09	−1·46
Hypocritical	+0·63	+0·60	−0·29	−0·97	+0·07	−1·03
Impulsive	−0·26	+1·38		−1·22	−1·60	−1·79
Intelligent	+1·59	+1·15	+0·70	−0·99	+1·49	+1·75
Irritable	+1·20	+1·38	+1·36	−0·70	+0·39	−1·24
Lazy	+0·09	−1·73	−0·69	−1·75	−1·64	−0·06
Modest	−1·15	−1·50	−1·05	+0·51	+0·37	+1·53
Patient	−1·09	−1·62	−1·99	+1·17	−0·03	+1·84
Practical	−0·19	+0·75	−0·92		+1·85	+0·06
Precise	+0·60	+0·24	−1·21	+1·19		+1·00
Reflective	+0·59	−0·90	−1·74	−0·01	+1·01	
Sincere	−0·25	+0·20	+0·77	+1·31	+1·01	+1·80
Timid	−1·64	−2·40	−1·71	−0·90	−0·21	+0·77
Tolerant	−1·37	−1·44	−1·05	+0·63	−0·58	+1·71

about expected intertrait relationships was obtained. (As a warning to future students of this topic we should, however, mention that our conscientious randomization of presentation and response orders led to enormously complicated problems of tabulation and analysis.) Implication responses were scored from +3 ("nearly always are") to −3 ("hardly ever are"), and mean implication scores from each cue trait to each of the other attributes were calculated. In Table 8 we have set out these average values of inferences about People. Very many of them depart significantly from zero, but we have only computed significance in a sample of cases. Roughly speaking (and no greater accuracy is needed at the moment), a value of ± 0.50 is likely to be significant at $p < 0.05$ and one of ± 1.00 is certainly significant at $p < 0.001$.

The figures in Table 8 may be taken as statements of probabilistic inference rules. We can see evidence that subjects use rules like "from *cynical* infer *conceited* with a high degree of confidence" and "from *cynical* infer *hypocritical* with a lower degree of confidence". These inference rules will presumably be applied in perceptual and conceptual situations of all kinds. If it becomes clear in direct perception that a person is something of a cynic, we shall probably make use of inferences like those in Table 8 in forming our rounded, relatively coherent impression of him. In indirect perceptual situations use of these inference rules may be still more marked. In a relatively short newspaper account (similar to those used in the previous four experiments, for example), a reporter's indications that the stimulus person is forceful or that he is impulsive are likely to set up still stronger inferences, since the accompanying information is much more limited than it is in direct situations.*

Coupling the material in Table 8 with the data from studies referred to earlier we have quite a body of knowledge about the way subjects see traits to be related. What can we say by way of explanation of the implicit personality theories which are being revealed? There appear to be two quite different sorts of explanation which could be offered. On the one hand we might attempt to explain how people develop the inference rules which they employ, and on the other we might try to account for the way they are used at any point in time. The first type of explanation requires longitudinal information about the way implicit personality theories are generated. This knowledge, presumably based on developmental studies with children, has not yet been acquired, and we can but hope that it will soon be available. More feasible at this stage are attempts to understand the principles underlying the operations of the components of a perceptual system at a given moment. In terms of the schema outlined in Chapter 1 we need here to learn more about the way the processing centre operates. We have some information about inference rules, and we now require models of how they are applied. Some halting steps in this direction are made in the next section. After this we shall return to the other aspects of Experiment 14 which have yet to be examined.

* This point is taken up again on pp. 182 and 244.

A LOGICAL MODEL OF TRAIT IMPLICATION

In considering the nature of "implication" we can do a lot worse than turn to the work by logicians on this very topic. The development of formal logic has led to clear definitions of some types of implication and to a fairly complete understanding of the consequences of these definitions. We might employ the standard calculus of propositions as a model of trait implication to see whether definitions and their consequences become any clearer in our case.* Before making this attempt we have to spend a little time introducing the terms and symbols we shall employ. These are in fact very simple, and we shall try to avoid unnecessary detail. Readers interested in pursuing this topic can consult any of a large number of textbooks; relatively straightforward accounts are to be found in books by Ambrose and Lazerowitz (1962), Cooley (1942), Hughes and Londey (1965), Mourant (1963), Quine (1950) and other writers.

The propositional calculus is a set of interrelated expressions. The nature of these expressions is governed by rules about what is a "well-formed formula". Roughly speaking a well-formed formula contains variables and operators used in certain specified ways. The variables represent propositions (p, q, r, etc.) and the operators act on these variables. We shall at present only need to deal with a sample of the permissible operators. We have a single "monadic operator": $\sim$. This may be taken to mean "not" or "it is not the case that". In this way we might operate upon a variable, p, to produce the well-formed formula $\sim p$. This would be read as "not-p" or "it is not the case that p". The variable p can stand for any statement of the type "it is raining", "this is an elephant", "John is bored" and so on. In these examples $\sim p$ would represent the statement "it is not raining", "this is not an elephant", and "John is not bored".

In addition to the monadic operator, $\sim$, we shall use here three dyadic operators (or "connectives"). These are ., $\supset$ and $\equiv$. The first of these (.) stands for the connective "and". We might write $p \cdot q$ to indicate "p and q". We can of course write expressions of this kind to represent relations which are not true of necessity (i.e. "contingent" ones): $p \cdot q$ might stand for "it is raining and this is an elephant". On

* A fuller discussion of the value of model-building in psychology will be presented in Chapter 9 (p. 366 *et seq.*).

the other hand, some expressions of this kind might appear to be logically necessary (e.g. $p \cdot p$). Naturally, we can use . and $\sim$ together, to form expressions like $p \cdot \sim q$ or $\sim p \cdot q$. ("p and not-q" and "not-p and q" respectively).

The connective $\supset$ is the one with which we are most concerned. This represents a relationship referred to as "material implication". Material implication is not the same as logical entailment, but refers to a type of relationship defined in terms of the truth or falsity of the variable expressions it connects. More complete discussions of this point are presented in the texts referred to above. For our purposes we need to know that $p \supset q$ (read as "p implies q") is defined as $\sim(p \cdot \sim q)$. The brackets are used in a fairly commonsense way, so that $\sim(p \cdot \sim q)$ represents "it is not the case that both p and not-q". For example, this might stand for "it is not the case both that it is raining and Fred is not bored". In many cases a material implication relationship can be rephrased in terms of "if ... then ...", so that $p \supset q$ (which is by definition the same as $\sim(p \cdot \sim q)$) might also be read as "if p then q". For example, "if it is raining then Fred is bored".

This implicative relationship is the one we shall use as the basis of our model of inferences between traits, so we should perhaps say a little more about it. We shall take the variables p, q, r etc. to represent statements of the form "a person is intelligent" and "a person is ambitious". In practice it is simpler to employ the traits themselves as abbreviations of the full statement, and we shall usually make this abbreviation. If we have observed (for example, from experiments of the type described above) that *intelligence* (call this p) is seen to imply *ambition* (q) we might represent this by $p \supset q$ (read as "p implies q"). The cue trait *intelligence* might also have been found to imply *conscientiousness*. If we call the latter r, we can also write $p \supset r$ (read as "p implies r"). The propositional calculus might now be used to formalize possible relationships between q and r, $p \cdot q$ and r and so on. We shall look at some of these possibilities shortly.

It is important to notice that $p \supset q$ does not imply that $q \supset p$, nor that $\sim p \supset \sim q$ (read as "not-p implies not-q"). These limitations are implicit in the definition of $\supset$, and we shall not expand on the reasons for them at the moment. But $p \supset q$ ("p implies q") *does* imply $\sim q \supset \sim p$ ("not-q implies not-p"). By applying these aspects of the calculus to studies of implicit personality theory, several tests of the model are immediately available. For example, if being *intelligent* (p) implies being *ambitious* (q), being *ambitious* (q) need not imply being *intelligent* (p) and being *unintelligent* ($\sim p$) need not imply being *unambitious* ($\sim q$); but being *unambitious* ought to imply being *unintelligent* (i.e. $\sim q \supset \sim p$). Before passing on to other relationships let us summarize some of these equivalences implicit in the definition of $\supset$.

If this is the case	Then this is valid
$p \supset q$	$\sim(p \cdot \sim q)$
$p \supset q$	$\sim q \supset \sim p$
$\sim(p \supset q)$	$p \cdot \sim q$
$\sim p \supset q$	$\sim(\sim p \cdot \sim q)$
$p \supset \sim q$	$\sim(p \cdot q)$
If this is the case	Then this is not valid
$p \supset q$	$q \supset p$
$p \supset q$	$\sim p \supset \sim q$

The third connective with which we shall deal is known as material equivalence ($\equiv$). This is a stronger relationship than material implication ($\supset$), and is defined in terms of the latter. Thus $(p \equiv q) = \mathrm{df.}$ $(p \supset q) \cdot (q \supset p)$. This is read as "$p$ implies q, and q implies p", and it can be seen that $\equiv$ is a two-way implicative relationship. If we knew that *intelligence* (p) implied *ambition* (q) but that *ambition* did not imply *intelligence* we might take this to be a relationship of material implication. This is because although $p \supset q$ we cannot say that $q \supset p$. On the other hand, if *intelligence* (p) implies *ambition* (q) in our studies and if *ambition* implies *intelligence* (i.e. $p \supset q$ and $q \supset p$), then we could say that the relationship is one of material equivalence (i.e. $p \equiv q$). And we can derive a number of features of an equivalence ($\equiv$) relationship which do not hold for an implication ($\supset$) relationship. Some of these will be dealt with shortly.

We mentioned earlier that $p \supset q$ could often be read as "if p then q". This is a "conditional" expression in the same sense that $p \equiv q$ might be termed a "biconditional" expression. We can sometimes read $p \equiv q$ as "q if and only if p". These possibilities are related to the idea that "$p \supset q$" indicates that p is a *sufficient* condition for q, and that "$p \equiv q$" tells us that p is a *necessary and sufficient* condition for q.

Before looking in more detail into how the calculus can be applied to trait implication, we must make just one other comment. To be completely appropriate to statements like "if people are intelligent then they are ambitious" we should employ a more complex calculus known as the "lower (or restricted) predicate calculus" rather than the propositional calculus which we have introduced. So that we shall not frighten away yet more readers we shall not use the predicate calculus. Its virtue is that it includes "quantifiers" (e.g. "there is an x such that x has f" and "for all x, x has f"). But any well-formed formula in the propositional calculus has its more complex representation in the predicate calculus, so that we are not committing a grave error in our simplification.

Let us look then at some aspects of the propositional calculus and see how they might be relevant to studies of implicit personality theory. If a significant relationship is observed between traits then we can say that one trait implies the other, at least in the sense of $p \supset q$ ("p implies q", or "if p then q"). The data in Table 8 tell us, for example, that being *cynical* implies being *precise* $(+0\cdot60)$. But because *precise* does not imply *cynical* $(+0\cdot06)$ (i.e. $p \supset q$, but q does not $\supset p$), then the relationship is not one of material equivalence $(\equiv)$. In other words *cynical*$\supset$*precise*. On the other hand *cynical*$\supset$*forceful* $(+0\cdot75)$ and *forceful*$\supset$*cynical* $(+0\cdot95)$ so that we might say that *cynical*$\equiv$*forceful*. This is of course implicit in the definition of $p \equiv q$ as $(p \supset q) \cdot (q \supset p)$. We have therefore a way to decide whether a relationship between traits is one of $\supset$ or of $\equiv$. In both cases we can draw other relationships from this knowledge by using the propositional calculus, and sometimes we can point to different predictions which derive from the differences between $\supset$ and $\equiv$. Let us now look at some of these possibilities.

Consider firstly the effects of reversing or transposing the variables in an expression. We have earlier pointed out that $(p \supset q)$ does not imply that $(q \supset p)$. But on the other hand $(p \equiv q)$ does imply that $(q \equiv p)$ since $(p \supset q) \cdot (q \supset p)$ (i.e. the definition of $p \equiv q$) is the same as $(q \supset p) \cdot (p \supset q)$. This difference has interesting consequences as far as the negation of expressions are concerned. If $p \equiv q$, then $\sim p \equiv \sim q$ whereas this simple negative does not hold for $\supset$. Yet we know that if $p \supset q$, then $\sim q \supset \sim p$ (see above); and a similar relationship applies to $\equiv$ (i.e. if $p \equiv q$, then $\sim q \equiv \sim p$). We can now make several predictions from the model about the consequences of using negative cue traits. For example, we have seen from Table 8 that *cynical*$\supset$*precise*. It ought to be the case that not-*precise*$\supset$not-*cynical*, since if $p \supset q$ then $\sim q \supset \sim p$. On the other hand not-*cynical* need not imply not-*precise* (since $p \supset q$ does not imply $\sim p \supset \sim q$). From Table 8 we have also seen that *cynical*$\equiv$*forceful*. We can derive from the model that not-*forceful*≡not-*cynical*, and that not-*cynical*≡not-*forceful*. Many similar prospects are open.

Other interesting possibilities concern the combination of cue traits. If we observe that $p \supset r$ and that $q \supset r$, we should be able to observe that $(p \cdot q) \supset r$. (A similar relationship holds for ≡ in this case.) We can in this way look at how combination rules are fitted into the model. The nature of these rules is dealt with in a later section. The relation of transitivity is also relevant to studies of implicit personality theory. If we observe that $p \supset q$ and that $q \supset r$, we can derive from the model the equivalence $p \supset r$. Similarly if $p \equiv q$ and $q \equiv r$, then $p \equiv r$. This prediction can be tested by some of the results of Experiment 14. We used six different cue traits, and in addition to using these singly in the cue position employed each of them as a response trait to the other five characteristics. This means that we can study transitivity relationships. For instance, *cynical* $\supset$ *reflective* and *reflective* $\equiv$ *precise* (see Table 8). It should be the case that *cynical* $\supset$ *precise*, and this is in fact so. But there is a complicating factor here. We have so far spoken as though an implicative relationship were all-or-none, as though p always implied q or never implied q. In reality the inference rules which perceivers employ are of course probabilistic ones, varying in the present case from -3 to $+3$. To test predictions we therefore need to look at the trends apparent in these probabilistic values.

How can we do this to test the prediction that if $p \supset q$ and $q \supset r$ then $p \supset r$? We can take p and q as individual cue traits and r as all the other traits we have studied. If the two cue traits imply each other strongly, then we should find that the inferences from each of them to all the other traits (r) are very similar. In general terms, the stronger the relationship between p and q, the more similar should be the relationship between p and r and q and r. We can test this prediction by taking each of the six cue traits studied in Experiment 14 as p and q in turn, and can correlate the $p \supset q$ values with the similarity of the inferences from each of them to the other traits (treating these as r). The similarity of inferences to r can be measured in terms of the correlation between the figures in the columns of Table 8. We have made this calculation (using only those response traits which occur in all rows) and looked at the association between these 15 correlation values and the related $p \supset q$ figure. This association (*rho*) is $+0.76$ ($p < 0.01$).* The stronger the

* The value of *rho* is $+0.64$ ($p < 0.01$) if an average of $p \supset q$ and $q \supset p$ is taken as a measure of the closeness of a $p : q$ relationship.

relationship between p and q, the more similar are the $p \supset r$ and $q \supset r$ inferences.

This test provides satisfying support for part of the model. In this instance we have discarded the difference between $\supset$ and $\equiv$ in measuring the strength of a relationship. But there is another characteristic of transitivity relations which predicts different outcomes for $\equiv$ and $\supset$ relationships. If we know that $p \equiv r$ and that $q \equiv r$, then we can infer that $p \equiv q$. We cannot, however, infer that $p \supset q$ from a knowledge that $p \supset r$ and $q \supset r$. It will be recalled that we can identify potential $\equiv$ relationships from a set of data, since these are two-way implicative relationships (i.e. $(p \supset q) \cdot (q \supset p)$). In the results of Experiment 14 there are $\equiv$ relationships between *cynical* and *forceful*, *impulsive* and *forceful*, *practical* and *forceful* and between several other traits. We should be able to test the $[(p \equiv r) \cdot (q \equiv r)] \equiv (p \equiv q)$ formula with these values of p, q and r. We have tried this, with virtually no success. For example, although *impulsive* $\equiv$ *forceful* and *cynical* $\equiv$ *forceful* we find that *impulsive* $\supset$ not-*cynical*.

It appears then that the distinction between $\equiv$ and $\supset$ might not be applicable to the inferences people draw between personal characteristics. We are reluctant to abandon the idea until further negative tests have been conducted, but it might be that the basic model handles trait implication only in so far as relationships should be treated as being of material implication ($\supset$). In this case the $(p \supset q) \cdot (q \supset p)$ relations which occur would be treated in the same manner as the $(p \supset q)$ and the $(q \supset p)$ associations. Treating all the inferences drawn between personal characteristics as $\supset$ relationships does reduce the number of novel predictions from the model, but we are still left with an attractive framework within which to look at results from experimental studies. There is no doubt that we can use this model to formalize a wide-ranging set of possible relations between traits. At the present only a few of the predictions about observable relationships have been tested, but there is considerable scope for future examinations. Some relationships which should be observed if the model is valid are set out below. Several of the equivalences have been referred to already; justification for them can be found in the texts referred to at the beginning of this section.

If this is the case	Then this is valid
$p \supset q$	$\sim(p \cdot \sim q)$ (by definition)
$\sim(p \supset q)$	$p \cdot \sim q$
$\sim p \supset q$	$\sim(\sim p \cdot \sim q)$
$p \supset \sim q$	$\sim(p \cdot q)$
$p \supset q$	$\sim q \supset \sim p$
$p \supset \sim q$	$q \supset \sim p$
$p \supset q$	$(p \cdot r) \supset (q \cdot r)$
$(p \supset q) \cdot (q \supset r)$	$p \supset r$
$(p \supset q) \cdot (p \supset r)$	$p \supset (q \cdot r)$
$(p \supset r) \cdot (q \supset r)$	$(p \cdot q) \supset r$

A final equivalence to which attention should be drawn is $q \supset (p \supset q)$. This is one of two "paradoxes of material implication" — unlikely relationships which derive from the definition of this type of implication. The equivalence is unlikely within the framework of propositional logic since it has to be interpreted as "a true proposition is implied by any proposition". Within the framework of person perception it raises a very interesting question about intertrait relationships. It could be the case that inferences from a cue trait to another characteristic depend partly on the probability of occurrence of the latter. It could be the case that if people are generally believed to be ambitious (q), then other traits (p) are likely to be seen to imply ambition. Conversely, if a judge regards ambition as a fairly rare personal characteristic, then he may not see other traits as implying it. The results of experiments on trait inference could in this way be partly explained in terms of subjects' expectations about the frequency of occurrence of response traits. Data have yet to be gathered which test this possibility. For the moment it may be noted that it is an interesting novel development from the model outlined here.

THE PHENOMENA OF COJUDGMENT

We now have some knowledge of the nature of the inference rules within the processing centre. We can identify several rules of the type "from input A infer output X", and conversely we can point to certain outputs which are not relevant to some aspects of the stimulus information. There are some implicative relationships which are readily understandable — sometimes the related characteristics have a semantic or logical similarity — but we have not so far provided any more wide ranging principle to account for the pattern of inferences which perceivers typically make. One possibility here is the notion of cojudgment (Warr and Sims, 1965).

Cojudgment is the process by which attributes are clustered in relation to their affective tone. It is similar to the halo effect outlined at the beginning of this chapter, but is rather more amenable to study than the former. The difficulty with the halo effect is that, since it is defined in terms of a general impression affecting specific judgments, it cannot readily be measured. This is because it is logically impossible to obtain a valid index of *all* components and *all* interactions between these components of the general impression formed by individual perceivers.

Cojudgment is more amenable to operational definition. The term refers to the judgment that similarly evaluated attributes tend to be associated within other people. Cojudgment occurs when the possession of a desirable attribute is assumed to imply the possession of other desirable attributes or when the possession of an undesirable attribute is assumed to imply the possession of other undesirable attributes.

This process seems to involve at least three stages: (*a*) the perception of one or more attributes, (*b*) the evaluation of these attributes and (*c*) the assumption that the perceived attributes imply the presence of others which are similarly evaluated. These activities may of course occur in this or in a different sequence.

In Experiment 14 we not only measured assumptions about trait implication, but we also recorded subjects' evaluation of each of the traits used. The value placed upon a personal characteristic is likely to be an important factor in judgments about it (e.g. Edwards, 1953; 1957), and is probably part of its "functional significance" in the sense outlined by Hays (1958). Each subject in Experiment 14 indicated how he or she valued each of the traits employed there on a six-point scale which was scored from -3 to $+3$. This judgment was made in relation to "People" and to the other categories of stimulus person referred to earlier. We shall for the moment deal only with implications and evaluations about People.

By relating a subject's evaluation of a cue trait to his evaluation of each of the response traits we can assess his readiness to make cojudgments. Cojudgments are made when a positively evaluated cue trait is seen to imply other positively evaluated traits and when a negatively evaluated cue trait is seen to imply other negatively evaluated traits. We

F

can obtain an index of cojudgment for each subject in two ways. First we can multiply together the two evaluation scores (for cue trait and response trait) and multiply this product by the implication score. This will generate a positive value when cojudgment occurs and a negative value in other cases, and these values will be dependent on the extremity of evaluation and of implication scores. Some examples might help here:

Evaluation of cue trait	Implication score	Evaluation of response trait	Cojudgment score
+3	+1	+3	+ 9
+3	+1	−3	− 9
+2	+3	+2	+12
+2	+3	−2	−12
−1	−1	−1	− 1
−1	+1	−1	+ 1

A total cojudgment score can easily be obtained for each subject by summing the values in the right-hand column across all response traits. This technique is a precise one, but it could be influenced by differential response syles (in the sense used by Jackson and Messick (1958), Rorer (1965) and others). Variations in the tendency to use extreme response categories independent of their content would for instance affect this cojudgment measure to a marked extent. A simpler index of cojudgment which is not related to this sort of variable is in terms of a concordance rate — a measure of how *frequently* similarly evaluated traits are assumed to go together. We could calculate the total number of concordant pairs of responses made by a subject, assessing concordance in terms of evaluative responses. Eight possibilities are available here:

Evaluation of cue trait	Implication	Evaluation of response trait	Concordance
Positive	Positive	Positive	Yes
Positive	Positive	Negative	No
Positive	Negative	Positive	No
Positive	Negative	Negative	Yes
Negative	Positive	Negative	Yes
Negative	Positive	Positive	No
Negative	Negative	Negative	No
Negative	Negative	Positive	Yes

The total concordance score for each subject is available as a measure of cojudgment. Although this takes no account of the magnitude of evaluations or implications, it does in fact generate very similar results to those obtained with the more complex measure (Warr and Sims, 1965). But its simplicity makes it preferable, and we shall use it here as our measure of cojudgment.

Cojudgment measured in this way has some affinity with "tolerance of trait inconsistency" which has been studied by Steiner (1954) and Steiner and Johnson (1963). Steiner's technique, however, depends upon an externally derived average measure of evaluation which need not be closely related to evaluations of specific traits applied to specific stimuli by an individual subject. For this reason we prefer to use the type of cojudgment score outlined above.

In certain instances it is of course logically necessary that cojudgment occurs. These occasions arise when we study inferences between semantically-related characteristics. It would not be surprising to find that the cue trait *clever* implied *intelligent* and that these were both positively evaluated. If all the response traits in a list were as similar to *clever* in their meaning as is *intelligent* or were clearly opposite in meaning then a high cojudgment score would be generated, but this would be of no empirical concern. Cojudgment is interesting only when the attributes involved are semantically different.

This can present some difficulty if we wish to ascertain in an absolute sense whether a group of subjects is or is not making cojudgments. The problem arises from the fact that it is not always possible to determine the chance level of concordant responses. In Experiment 14 we used 25 response traits, and it might be assumed that the chance expectancy of concordant judgments is therefore 12·50. This assumption appears valid unless some response traits are very similar in meaning to a cue trait, in which case concordance is logically necessary. Can we demonstrate from the results of Experiment 14 that cojudgment occurs to a significant degree?

We have calculated the average total concordance scores around each of the six cue traits. These scores are presented in Table 9. It can be seen that the tendency to make cojudgments varies between cue traits, the total concordance score ranging from 19·48 for *practical* to 13·57 for *forceful*. If we take 12·50 as chance expectancy, all these values are significant, even the one for *forceful* which just exceeds the 5% level. It is possible to question this estimate of chance level in the way outlined in the last paragraph, and certainly in the case of *forceful* it appears incorrect. The response traits *ambitious* and *timid* seem sufficiently related (positively and negatively) to the cue trait *forceful* for their omission to be required. In this case we would have 23 response traits, a chance expectancy of 11·50 and a mean concordance rate of 11·57. But as far as the other attributes are concerned, we might conclude that cojudgment is in evidence to a significant degree.*

Table 9 Total concordance scores and mean evaluation scores for the six cue traits studied in Experiment 14

	Cue trait					
	Cynical	Forceful	Impulsive	Practical	Precise	Reflective
Total concordance score	15·48	13·57	13·65	19·48	15·34	17·02
Mean evaluation score	−1·00	+0·20	+0·22	+1·43	+0·89	+0·95

In practice, however, we are more interested in whether cojudgment varies between conditions and subjects than in its absolute level. In Experiment 14 the frequency of cojudgment is seen to vary between traits, and as the mean evaluation scores in Table 9 suggest, this may be a function of how extreme are the judges' evaluative responses. Later in this chapter we shall turn to differences in cojudgment between men and women and between judges of different personalities. For now it may be noted that people are on the whole likely to organize their implicit personality theories in a way which minimizes inconsistency in evaluative groupings. This appears to be a principle commonly employed in a processing centre of the type suggested in Chapter 1.

The principle might help to integrate results from a number of other studies. For example, certain aspects of the results of Edwards's (1959) investigation might be attributable to cojudgments by his subjects. Edwards was interested in the relationship between the social desirability of a personality characteristic and the probability that the characteristic will be attributed to other people. He observed that social desirability is a good predictor of whether an item will be attributed to

* The corresponding concordance rate around *intelligence* in an earlier study (Warr and Sims, 1965) was 17·50.

someone who is liked ($r=0.94$) but not of whether the item will be attributed to someone who is disliked ($r= -0.25$). Now, a person who is liked is a person who is perceived to possess attributes which are positively evaluated. Cojudgment by subjects would in this case result in the attribution of socially desirable characteristics to the person. But on this basis a positive relationship between desirability and probability of attribution is not to be expected in the case of a disliked person. This person is one with negatively evaluated characteristics, so that cojudgment here would result in a predominantly undesirable range of items being endorsed.

Some paradoxical aspects of findings by Secord and Berscheid (1963) might also be interpreted in terms of subjects' cojudgment. Their study used a procedure similar to that of Experiment 14 Implicative responses to each of eleven cue traits were obtained on three occasions. We are here concerned only with the first two sets of responses. On the first occasion the stimulus was identified only as "a person", and it was assumed that subjects took this to refer to a white person. Two days later the subjects responded again, but this time with the information that the stimulus person was a negro. Secord and Berscheid looked into the question of whether this difference in stimulus characterization influenced the inferences made from cue traits. They used traits half of which were shown by Katz and Braly (1935) to be associated with a negro stereotype and half of which were "non-stereotype" traits. In addition to these manipulations they also took measures of subjects' prejudice towards negroes.

Of relevance here are their observations that inferences from stereotype traits produce more stereotyping than do inferences from non-stereotype traits, but that the associations between cue traits and judged traits remain consistent whether the stimulus person is negro or white. Furthermore, and this may seem odd, there were no differences related to prejudice, so that prejudiced subjects did not infer more stereotype traits in the case of negroes than did unprejudiced perceivers. If we consider these results in terms of cojudgment, then the first finding concerning stereotyping seems likely to be due to subjects associating similarly evaluated traits within a stimulus person in the way they did in our studies. The second point — the consistency of inference despite changes in stimulus person — could be interpreted in terms of subjects evaluating the characteristics in a similar manner whether they are possessed by negroes or by whites. Lazy, dishonest and so on are likely to be evaluated similarly in both categories of stimulus person. The final aspect of the results described above — the failure to observe a difference in inference which is related to prejudice — could be due to there being no difference in evaluation of these traits by the two groups of subjects; the traits themselves have a fairly clear meaning and evaluative tone.

In short, these findings are predictable from the hypothesis that the major principle determining trait implication is cojudgment. Similar analyses could no doubt be made of other sets of results. All of these would of course only be speculative, but the prospect does point to one important recommendation. It would be valuable if in future studies of intertrait relationships, information were gathered about subjects' evaluations of the personal characteristics employed. Cojudgment undoubtedly occurs but the limits of its importance have yet to be determined.

FACTORS AFFECTING IMPLICIT PERSONALITY THEORY

In this section we shall look at what is known about the factors which influence an individual's implicit personality. It is obvious that one important variable affecting decision rules is the input — the cue trait in these studies. We have pointed out that the extent to which cojudgments are made partly depends upon which cue trait is being studied. Cojudgments are made around both positively and negatively evaluated attributes, but we do not yet know what aspects of the cue trait are relevant to this tendency. There is a hint in Table 9 that the more extremely evaluated cue traits give rise to more cojudgment, but it is too early to reach a firm conclusion.

Naturally enough the nature of the cue trait itself is a major factor determining the implications from that trait, and each cue implies its own set of characteristics. We have previously distinguished between traits in terms of whether they are central or peripheral, and the implication scores we have referred to could well be used as a convenient index of trait centrality. For this purpose we might use the average implication score, which is the algebraic average of inferences from a trait made by all subjects. In the case of *cynical*, for example, the average implication score is -0.05; for *reflective* it is $+0.23$. Unfortunately, however, this is not a valid measure of centrality since it is too dependent upon whether or not subjects all respond in the same direction. If all implication responses were positive, we could take this algebraic average as a measure of subjects' willingness to make inferences from a particular trait. But if one response amongst these positive ones were, say, − 3, the algebraic average would be reduced. And this would be despite the fact that the aberrant response was as extreme as is possible.

What is required as a measure of how well a trait generates inferences is a score which disregards the direction of these inferences. We can use a modulus sign to refer to a | implication | score (read as "modulus implication"). This is the *arithmetical* average of a set of implication scores, which indicates how readily subjects make inferences in either direction. The average | implication | score for responses − 3 and + 3 would be 3, whereas the average implication score of these two would be zero. The average | implication | score can yield a more satisfactory measure of centrality, and we can ask how the measure varies between the cue traits studied in Experiment 14. Rather surprisingly they do not vary in this respect, average | implication | values being 1·59, 1·66, 1·67, 1·65, 1·56 and 1·71 for the alphabetically-ordered attributes. These figures appear to be quite high, and it would be interesting to compare them with similar scores for other cue traits.*

A second question concerns the way implicit personality theories vary between stimulus persons. Do perceivers apply the same decision rules irrespective of the person being judged, or are these rules modified by the identity of the stimulus person, becoming in effect combination rules? We have so far described only those aspects of Experiment 14 which deal with "People", in other words with stimulus persons who are not specified. In studies already referred to, Koltuv (1962) found similar patterns of inference about familiar and unfamiliar stimuli (there were, however, differences in extremity), and Secord and Berscheid (1963) observed considerable consistency in associations between traits applied to negro or to white persons. Passini and

---

* Nidorf and Crockett (1965b) have investigated the validity of this kind of index of centrality. Their subjects gave written descriptions of a hypothetical stimulus person characterized by six attributes. They also made implication responses to each of these attributes taken as cue traits. Individual subjects' assessments of centrality of the six traits (in terms of what we have called total | implication | scores) were positively related to the amount of information they inferred from these traits when writing their free description of the hypothetical stimulus person.

Norman (1966) have looked at an extreme instance of this. Taking as their baseline the factorial structure of personality judgments made when judge and stimulus person are close acquaintances, they asked how this structure changes when the stimulus is totally unknown to the judge. They found that it remained essentially the same. It seems that the perceivers' implicit personality theories enter strongly into both forms of judgment and that they operate in essentially the same way. (See also Norman and Goldberg (1966).)

It may be recalled from the earlier description of Experiment 14 that all the cue traits examined there were applied to People, and that *cynical, forceful* and *reflective* were also studied in relation to Men and Women whilst the other three cue traits were related to Men Students and Bank Managers. We can now consider whether significant differences across stimulus persons emerged. Let us look first at differences between People, Men and Women. For each possible association between a cue trait and a response trait three comparisons of implication scores can be made. Since we studied 25 response traits, a total of 75 comparisons can be made for each category of stimulus persons. Rather to our surprise very few of these comparisons reveal a significant difference. For *cynical* and *reflective* there are only two significant differences, and for *forceful* there is but one. These rare discrepancies can clearly be blamed upon chance.

So far then there is no difference between the inference rules applied to different categories of people. But when we consider the rather different classes studied in relation to the cue traits *impulsive, practical* and *precise* a different picture emerges. When these chacteristics were attributed to People, Bank Managers and Men Students, quite different sets of decision rules were often brought into play. There are seventeen significant differences in implication scores for *impulsive*, thirteen for *practical* and six for *precise*. These differences seem to hinge upon the assumed nature of the stimulus persons.* For instance, *impulsive* implies *careless* in the case of People ($+1{\cdot}22$) and Men Students ($+1{\cdot}36$) but not in the case of Bank Managers ($+0{\cdot}40$); and *practical* implies *discreet* much more strongly for Bank Managers ($+1{\cdot}97$) than for People ($+0{\cdot}62$) or Men Students ($+0{\cdot}87$). In fact almost all the variations in inference rules were related to the somewhat atypical class of stimulus person Bank Managers. Implication scores for Men Students differed from others only in the case of response traits *intelligent* and *lazy*. For

* See the suggestion about the "paradox of material implication" on p. 146.

instance, although *impulsive* does imply *intelligent* for People ($+0.70$) and Bank Managers ($+0.98$) it does so more strongly for Men Students ($+1.27$). A similar pattern in reverse is found for the relationship between *impulsive* and *lazy* (-0.69, -0.92 and -0.05 respectively).

We may conclude that although inference rules are very stable across a wide range of stimulus categories there are certain sorts of stimulus to whom idiosyncratic rules are applied. Consistent with this conclusion are the results of Beilin's (1963) study using Asch's (1946) design outlined earlier in this chapter. He noted differences in the effects of manipulating a cue trait according to whether the stimulus person was identified as a Policeman or a Physicist, a Reporter or a Factory Worker.

What of the other measures we have taken in Experiment 14? How do these vary according to the nature of the stimulus person? As might be expected, evaluation scores are found to vary with stimulus person. There are significant differences on eleven of the twenty-six characteristics studied. A higher value is placed on being ambitious in the case of Men ($+1.35$) than in the case of Women ($+0.17$). To be careless is more negatively evaluated if one is a Bank Manager (-2.36) than if one is a Woman (-1.29). And being forceful is positively evaluated in a male stimulus person ($+0.72$) but negatively evaluated in Women (-0.52). These differences (and the many others observed) point to the need to take separate evaluation measures in studies of different categories of stimulus person. In fact of course it is partly the differences between trait evaluations when applied to different stimulus person classes that give rise to the variations in trait implications. Supporting evidence for this comes from the fact that only one of eighteen possible differences in cojudgment between stimulus categories was found to be significant. Thus the process of cojudgment functions as usual, but the change in evaluation of certain traits when applied to some classes of stimulus person results in a different pattern of implications.

So far we have noted differences in implicit personality theory which hinge upon the cue trait and the stimulus person. In the model of person perception sketched out in Chapter 1 some stable characteristics of the perceiver were assumed to influence the operation of the processing centre. We now turn to evidence bearing upon this assumption. We shall first review studies of the influence of the sex of the judge, and then consider particular personality attributes.

Shapiro and Tagiuri (1959) have reported an investigation of sex differences in trait implication. They studied four cue traits — *considerate, inconsiderate, intelligent* and *independent* — and analysed responses according to subjects' sex. The inferences which were drawn were found to be extremely similar for male and female perceivers. However, although the overall pattern of inferences was very similar, there were a few items on which significant differences occurred. Women for instance expected *intelligence* to imply *efficiency, responsibility* and *independence* more strongly than did men. Looking at the results of Shapiro and Tagiuri very generally we can observe that sex differences in inference rules were present in the case of some twelve percent of the characteristics studied.

A similar picture is present in the results of Experiment 14. Once again there are no differences between the overall mean implication scores of men and women for the six cue traits, but there are some differences in the specific inference rules applied. Considering for now only responses to People, there are four significant sex differences in mean implication scores (out of 25 comparisons) in the case of *cynical*, six for *forceful*, nine for *impulsive*, one for *practical*, four for *precise* and four for *reflective*. Although there are sex differences in implication scores in 19% of cases, these differences vary widely between cue traits. The input that a person is *impulsive* is clearly of different meaning to males and females (since there are nine significant differences) yet *practical* leads to very much the same set of inferences (only one significant difference).

It could be the case that these sex differences in inference rules are restricted to particular types of output, so that they are concentrated upon certain response traits. Inspection of the results of Experiment 14 suggests that this is not so. The twenty-eight significant differences are spread over twenty of the twenty-five response traits, no one trait being represented more than twice. In these circumstances we cannot make a very useful attempt to interpret these sex differences in terms of the output which is involved. For the moment we shall rest content to note that some *inputs* seem more liable to generate sex differences in inference rules than do others. Further work here is desirable.

Shapiro and Tagiuri stress that in their analysis women are more liable to make extreme inferences than are men. This tendency to make extreme responses (irrespective of direction) is assessed by the | implication | score, introduced on p. 153.* Since Shapiro and Tagiuri

---

* It may be recalled that this is conveniently read as "modulus implication".

helpfully present complete data from their investigation we have extracted from their figures those indices of | implication | and of implication which were discussed above. We expect from their interpretation that women will have a higher | implication | score in the case of a substantial majority of response traits. This expectation is borne out. Out of fifty-nine response traits women's | implication | scores exceed those of male judges on 40, 49, 36, and 38 occasions for cue traits *intelligent*, *considerate*, *independent* and *inconsiderate* respectively. This tendency is clearly a reliable one, and these values are respectively significant at the 1%, 1%, 5% and 2% levels according to a simple sign test. What about the results of Experiment 14? The pattern here is less clear. Although mean female | implication | responses to each of the six cue traits exceed male values, these differences do not reach significance. This could be partly due to the smaller numbers of response traits involved (less than half as many as Shapiro and Tagiuri's), and in view of the consistency of results across the 10 traits in these two studies we shall tentatively conclude that here is a meaningful difference between the inference rules used by the two sexes: women tend to generate higher | implication | scores than do men.

Turning to the mean implication scores calculated from Shapiro and Tagiuri's data, we find (as indeed the authors did in their somewhat different analysis) no significant overall differences and only isolated discrepancies in the case of a few specific response traits. On some of these occasions, males made more positive inferences and in the other cases the female subjects were more positive.

To this point we have seen from the two investigations that, although there are a few differences in inferences to specific response traits, the overall implication scores of men and women do not differ; but that there are significant differences in overall | implication | scores. We turn now to a third measure which is based upon implication responses. This is the overall average implication score from a cue trait, but now considered without regard to the sign of individual scores. We may ask whether there is a pattern in these values over the 59 response traits used by Shapiro and Tagiuri and the 25 response traits studied in Experiment 14.

For this analysis we first take the mean implication score to a response trait, discard the sign, and compute the average value for each cue trait across all response traits. A high overall score of this kind arises when members of a group of subjects agree to a large extent about the direction of an inference rule. The measure (which is of course independent of the other two scores discussed above) is in effect an index of how consistent a set of judges is as a group.

Applying this measure of response consistency to Shapiro and Tagiuri's figures we find that in the case of all the cue traits women as a group are more consistent than men. These differences are significant at the 1% level for *intelligent*, at the 2% level for *considerate*, at the 1% level for *independent* and at the 5% level for *inconsiderate*. Turning to our own data we observe that the female scores are significantly higher in the case of *forceful* ($p<0.001$), *impulsive* ($p<0.05$), *practical* ($p<0.001$) and *reflective* ($p<0.01$). Women also score more highly on the other two traits, but the differences in these cases do not reach significance.

We may now combine these interpretations and conclude that the male and female judges in these two studies vary in this respect: women tend to make more extreme implication responses overall (having higher | implication | scores) but these responses are more extreme in only a single direction rather than being *both* more positive *and* more negative in the case of one response trait. Furthermore the direction in which women's judgments are more extreme is not consistently one of positive or negative inference, since the overall implication scores of the two sexes do not differ.

In Experiment 14 we also obtained responses about less general stimulus categories than that of "People". It will be recalled that we studied judgments about Men and Women and about Men Students and Bank Managers. What about sex differences in relation to these more restricted categories? Analysis of implication and | implication | scores reveals the same pattern as for People, but in the case of overall implication scores regardless of sign the differences between male and female judges are no longer significant. They are, however, still in the same direction as for People. Until more evidence becomes available we must conclude that the sex difference in consistency of implication depends upon the category of stimulus studied: female perceivers' inference rules about People in general are more consistently applied than are males' but the rules about more specific stimulus categories do not differ in this respect.

Other between-sex comparisons of data from Experiment 14 may be made in terms of evaluative responses. Naturally enough there are several differences here. Women, for example, value impulsiveness more than do men ($+0.69$ versus -0.19), and ambitious Men are evaluated much more positively ($+1\cdot89$) by women judges than by men themselves ($+0\cdot88$). But these and other differences are fairly peripheral to our theme. A more central topic is cojudgment. We had the typically male suspicion that women are particularly likely to make cojudgments, and we tested this pleasing fantasy by analysing the cojudgment scores from Experiment 14 according to subjects' sex. Sad to relate no differences were found; mean scores were almost identical.

We may conclude from these studies that the sex of a perceiver does affect the inference rules incorporated in a perceptual processing centre, but that the differences do not range very widely. Some inferences from some inputs vary with the judge's sex, but the majority seem to be unaffected. There is no evidence that either sex makes consistently more positive or more negative inferences to other traits. Against this, however, we have seen that women are likely to make generally more extreme inferences (having higher overall | implication | scores), and that these differences in extremity are typically in a single direction. This direction varies between response traits. Sex differences are also present in the extent to which attributes are valued, but cojudgment does not vary with sex.

Let us now consider the influence of those stable characteristics concerned with aspects of personality. We have already drawn attention to a tendency to maximize consistency in the impression we form of others. Steiner (1954) and Steiner and Johnson (1963) have studied "tolerance of trait inconsistency", and have shown that this varies with the personality of the perceiver. In the first study Steiner observed subjects' propensities to reject the possibility that highly desirable and highly undesirable traits coexist within the same person. He found that this tendency was significantly more marked in persons scoring high on the California Ethnocentrism scale. A similar effect was noted in the 1963 paper, when a positive relationship with F-scale score was reported. High F-scale scorers were also shown to be loathe to alter their favourable impressions of an individual when they received moderately derogatory information about him.* The tendency to strive for consistency has also been investigated by Foulkes and Foulkes (1965), who noted its relationship to dogmatism. When high D-scale scorers were presented with clear reversals in information about a person they were more likely to achieve consistency than were low

---

* Other perceptual phenomena which vary as a function of F-scale score are described in the next chapter (see pp. 196–197).

scorers. But in this case the consistency was attained by one of the two methods — either by sticking to the original judgment, or by shifting completely from this to acceptance of the new material.

We have introduced the notion of cojudgment as a principle by which perceivers organize their inference rules, and see this notion as valuable in that idiosyncratic measures for each subject can be obtained. The tendency to cojudge has in an earlier study been shown to be positively related to F-scale score (Warr and Sims, 1965), and we may now ask whether it is associated with other personality characteristics. In Experiment 14 we obtained responses to Gough's Adjective Check List (see Chapter 2 p. 99). Subjects checked the items in this list in the orthodox manner as a personality measure, and we were accordingly able to relate scores on certain personality dimensions to differences in implicit personality theories. We have restricted our attention to three of the A.C.L. dimensions identified by Gough and Heilbrun (1965), namely Lability, Intraception and Order. In each case high and low scorers were isolated according to the procedures laid down by the originators of the list. The cojudgment behaviour of the top and bottom third of the sample was then compared.

As far as Lability (to do with "spontaneity, flexibility, need for change, rejection of convention and assertive individuality"*) is concerned, cojudgment is completely unaffected by differences in position on this dimension. But Intraception (the tendency "to engage in attempts to understand one's own behaviour or the behaviour of others"*) shows an interesting relationship to the willingness to make cojudgments. We had anticipated that high scorers on this dimension would make fewer cojudgments, but in fact they made significantly more concordant responses around the cue traits *practical* ($p<0.01$), *precise* ($p<0.01$) and *reflective* ($p<0.001$). There were no differences relative to the other cue traits. It may be that other comments by Gough and Heilbrun on the nature of intraception can help resolve this paradox. In examining the nature of the low scorer on this dimension they point out that he may "have talent, but he tends towards profligacy and intemperateness in its use. He is aggressive in manner, and quickly becomes bored or impatient with any situation where direct action is not possible. He is a doer, not a thinker".* The final dimension studied was Order; this is defined as the tendency "to place special emphasis on neatness, organization and planning in one's activities".* This

* These references are taken from the A.C.L. manual (Gough and Heilbrun, 1965).

personality characteristic clearly should be related to a propensity to cojudge, and our faith both in the A.C.L. and the notion of cojudgment was maintained by the finding that significant differences occurred in the case of all the six cue traits studied. In every instance high scorers on Order made many more cojudgments than their low-scoring counterparts.

We have also looked at how differences in these three personality variables are related to other aspects of implicit personality theories. None of the dimensions predict differences in average implication or average | implication | scores, although there are some differences in the way attributes are evaluated. There is a tendency for high scorers on Order to place more value on being *precise* and less on being *impulsive*, and for high scorers on Intraception to evaluate more positively the trait *reflective* and less positively *impulsive*. These differences are to be expected from the nature of the personality dimensions themselves, but since they represent only occasional significant differences amongst many comparisons it is not clear how much emphasis should be placed upon them.

As was mentioned earlier the cue traits studied in Experiment 14 were each selected to represent one A.C.L. dimension. This procedure was followed in the light of results obtained by Benedetti and Hill (1960). They reasoned that a perceiver's possession of a particular characteristic is likely to affect the inferences he makes from it. In a study employing Asch's design (see p. 119) they varied the characteristic *sociable–unsociable* amongst six constant traits and studied differences in the responses checked on a 20-item list. Measures had previously been taken of subjects' sociability, and they anticipated that the pattern of responding would vary with this perceiver characteristic. This expectancy was on the whole borne out, although the predicted differences were not obtained for all groups (probably because mean responses were too near the end of a continuum for variation to occur). In general the less sociable subjects made fewer unfavourable inferences from *unsociable* than did those scoring more highly. We had expected that a similar phenomenon would occur with the cue traits in Experiment 14 which were positive indicators of Lability, Intraception and Order, so that for example high-Order perceivers would make different inferences from *precise* from those of low-Order subjects. As reported in the last paragraph, this did not take place.

This could well be due to the fact that the single cue trait contributes in only small measure to a personality dimension on the A.C.L. A subject's response to, say, *precise* need not be predictive of his position on the dimension Order. A more direct test of whether possession of a single trait affects the inference rules about that trait involves comparing implication scores of subjects who checked the trait itself on their A.C.L. self-perceptions with the scores of subjects who did not check it. We have made this test for each of the six cue traits. To illustrate the procedure, consider the attribute *reflective*. Forty-three subjects had checked on the A.C.L. that they were reflective, whereas fifty-four had not checked it. We compared the mean implication scores around *reflective* for these two groups. And sure enough in the case of each category of stimulus person (People, Men and Women) the subjects who had checked *reflective* had a significantly larger average implication score around that trait. A similar result was obtained for *cynical*, *forceful* (with the exception of People), *impulsive* (with the exception of Men Students) and *precise* (except for Bank Managers). No differences were found in the case of *practical*. In general then, subjects who see themselves to possess a cue trait make inferences from it that are more consistent.

But we cannot conclude from these differences in implication scores that the traits differ in centrality according to whether a person possesses them. This is because a low mean implication score could be made up of a wide range of extremely positive and negative responses. As we have argued above, the | implication | score is a more suitable measure of centrality. How does this vary between those who possess and those who do not possess a cue trait? The short answer is that it does not. Mean | implication | scores are almost identical in all cases. Although then we can conclude that possessors of a cue trait tend as a group to be more uniform in their application of inference rules about this trait, we cannot conclude that possession increases its centrality in the sense of increasing its liability to generate strong inferences irrespective of their direction.

It may be noted in passing that in each case the group of subjects who checked a trait evaluated it more positively than those who left it unchecked. One might therefore wonder whether the differences in mean implication scores described here are partly dependent on differences in the way the traits are evaluated. We looked at this by splitting down *each* group (the possessors of a trait and the others) according to how they evaluated the trait. In every case the subgroup which evaluated the trait more highly had a higher mean implication score. Two factors are therefore involved in this phenomenon: possessing a trait and evaluating it positively. At this stage of the analysis we were dealing with small N's and large variances, and no estimate of the relative importance of these factors is possible. Studies specially designed to assess the relative contribution of each factor would be valuable.

COMBINATION RULES

Our discussion in this chapter of the processing centre has so far concentrated upon inference rules — those concerned with only a single input. We are able to say something about the nature of some rules of this kind and about a number of factors which influence their operation. Yet in practice inference rules are rarely applied by themselves. They concern only a single characteristic of a stimulus person, whereas the people we judge in real life have a multitude of characteristics. In these circumstances we use the other type of decision rule we have suggested — rules about a combination of inputs.

This practical truth does not imply that research into the more limited inference rules is a waste of time. Such research increases our repertoire of methods and concepts, and it provides us with substantive information of the kind presented above. Furthermore our conceptualization of person perception set out in Chapter 1 has explicitly assumed that combination rules and inference rules are in principle derivable from each other; from this standpoint we need to examine both single inputs and aggregates of these inputs.

Let us look at how combination rules might be related to inference rules. On what basis can we predict the consequences of combining input material? This is one of the most important questions facing psychologists of all orientations; it arises in studies of short-term memory, attitude change, sensory psychology, learning, verbal behaviour and of course perception. As far as judgments of others are concerned it is common to talk in terms of two possible approaches. One of these is characterized by labels like "configural", "clinical", "patterned", "intuitive", "non-linear" and so on, and the other viewpoint is variously referred to as "linear", "statistical", "actuarial" or "additive".*

* It is perhaps worth pointing to a terminological inconsistency in the literature here. "Additive" models are sometimes contrasted with "averaging" models and otherwise

How do these approaches differ? We shall first examine several kinds of linear models, and shall later move on to consider configural viewpoints. Within the framework of the present chapter we may phrase the central question thus: how can a combination rule about inputs A, B, C, D together be predicted from a knowledge of the several inference rules about A, B, C and D singly?* To answer this question we must obtain information about particular inference rules and also about the possible combination rules. As an example of the kind of method to be adopted, look first at the early study by Bruner, Shapiro and Tagiuri (1958). This investigation was not analysed to arbitrate between linear and configural models, and we cite it here as a neutral example. Bruner, Shapiro and Tagiuri used the technique discussed in relation to Experiment 14 to elicit probabilistic inference rules about cue traits *intelligent*, *considerate*, *independent* and *inconsiderate*. But in addition to mapping out expectancies based upon these single inputs they also elicited responses about double inputs (e.g. *intelligent and considerate*) and about some triple inputs (e.g. *intelligent, independent and considerate*). In many cases the combination rules were in a gross sense predictable from inference rules about single inputs. When the direction of the inference rules to an output characteristic was the same for two or three inputs taken individually, the combination rule was almost invariably in the same direction. In these cases a combined input also increased subjects' agreement about the nature of the ensuing output. However, when the direction of two inference rules differed (e.g. input A implied X; input B implied not-X), then predictability was reduced. In these cases it appeared that the inference rule about which there was greater agreement was the one which predominated.

When we turn to *linear models* themselves we can see that several possible modes of combination are available. Combination rules might for example be a simple *average* of inference rules, so that if A implied X very strongly and B implied X only very slightly, then we should

---

with "configural" ones. We should note that "additive" and "averaging" in the former comparison both refer to instances of linear combination, whereas the second comparison is at a higher level of generality contrasting the linear with the non-linear.

   * It is of course possible to invert this question, asking how inference rules may be predicted from combination rules. We should note that in both cases we are asking how an *investigator* can predict one from the other; there is no suggestion that the perceiver himself consciously builds up his combination rules from inference rules or breaks the former down for use as the latter.

expect that *AB* would imply *X* to a moderate degree. Or the combination rule might evolve *additively* from the inference rules. We should then anticipate that *AB* would imply *X* somewhat more strongly than this output was implied by input *A* or by input *B* alone. These two possibilities — averaging or additive models — are the linear formulations which have been most frequently investigated.

Studies by N. H. Anderson (e.g. 1962, 1965b) will serve as important examples of this line of research. He elicits relatively simple evaluative responses — how much a person is liked or disliked — and uses as stimulus material sets of adjectives which have previously been scaled singly in terms of their evaluative meaning. By placing together inputs of varying evaluation he can investigate the way individual items are combined. Anderson has contrasted averaging and additive linear models of input combination in order to see which best accounts for the final evaluation subjects place upon a set of material. For instance, he has compared evaluative responses to two very favourable stimuli presented together with responses to a combination of these two stimuli with two less favourable ones (Anderson, 1965b). According to the additive model the latter judgments should be more extreme than those to the pair of stimuli, whereas the averaging model predicts less extreme judgments for the four stimuli together. Anderson describes results which are clearly inconsistent with the additive model, in that the addition of the less favourable items leads to responses which also are less favourable. On the other hand if the adjectives which are placed together as a combined input are themselves of approximately the same value, then adding more material is found to generate more extreme responses (cf. Podell and Amster, 1966). Anderson reasons that this latter finding is nevertheless quite consistent with an averaging conception.

Another series of studies of these two forms of linear model, the averaging and the additive, has evolved around the "congruity principle" (Osgood and Tannenbaum, 1955). (See also Osgood, Suci and Tannenbaum, 1957, pp. 199–216.) This principle is essentially an averaging prescription, so that the outcome of combining two units of information is always a compromise between the values of the units taken singly. Work on the congruity principle has mainly involved study of semantic differential responses to concepts judged singly and when combined in an assertion (e.g. "Eisenhower is in favour of freedom of the press"). Not all of this work has concerned person perception, although the relevance of the congruity principle to this process is clear.

The principle has an immediate appeal to researchers in that it is a precisely-formulated and therefore readily-testable hypothesis. It does not, however, seem to be correct. Even the results of early studies of Osgood and his colleagues provided support which was far from convincing; predictions about the Evaluative factor were particularly inaccurate. L. R. Anderson and Fishbein (1965), Fishbein and Hunter (1964) and Triandis and Fishbein (1963) have modified the formula to emphasize a summating process, and they report more successful applications of the ensuing equation. Rokeach and Rothman (1965) have also taken exception to the congruity principle; their views will be examined shortly.

The additive linear approach has also been emphasized — in a quite different context — by Mahrer and Young (1961). They examined diagnostic judgments by clinicians. As inputs they provided brief comments about the behaviour and background of a patient. From each input they obtained clinicians' estimates of the probability that the patient belonged in specified diagnostic categories. These probability estimates are directly analogous to the inference rules studied in previous sections of this chapter. (See also Hoffman, 1960.) Mahrer and Young then enquired about combination rules by placing together two discrete inputs. They learned that the latter were in a general way additively predictable from the inference rules. For example, one input (A) in their study had a probability of being associated with paranoid schizophrenia of 0·69, and another (B) had a parallel probability of 0·45. When the two were combined to form input AB the probability of the patient being classified as a paranoid schizophrenic was seen to rise to 0·77.

We have so far looked at instances of research dealing with two kinds of linear model — the averaging and additive formulations. Although we have played this down to simplify discussion, it should be noted that they typically incorporate some kind of weighting factor. For example, it might be assumed that more extreme judgments take on greater importance in combination than do their less extreme partners. Evidence for this comes from a study by Podell and Podell (1963), where it was seen that judges actually behaved in this way. And Talbot (1967) has noted that subjects' own estimates of the importance of a scale in combination with others are paralleled by the extremity of the stimulus person's placement on that scale: if a stimulus is seen to be "extremely optimistic" then optimism is estimated to be much more important in a combined assessment than is this characteristic in stimulus persons who are rated neither optimistic nor pessimistic.

Another form of linear combination model is a *multiplicative* one. It is logically possible that rules about two single inputs join multiplicatively when they form combination rules. This does not seem likely in judgments of people, and direct empirical support for the possibility is not available. But several studies from another area have favoured a multiplicative model, and they may prove to have great bearing on person perception when research becomes concerned with the articulation of input dimensions (see pp. 200 and 370) and with refining models of the kind described above. Cliff (1959) investigated subjects' evaluative ratings of adjectives. He studied judgments of these alone, and also when they were qualified by "intensive" adverbs ("somewhat", "quite", "very"). The interesting finding emerged that the ratings of adverb-and-adjective were a multiplicative function of the two separate ratings. Howe (1962) pursued this idea to examine "probabilistic" adverbs ("possibly", "definitely"), and observed that derivations from Cliff's model fitted his results extremely well. He also placed together probabilistic and intensive adverbs in qualification of an adjective (e.g. "definitely somewhat evil"), and noted that judgments here were still predictable from a multiplicative model. (See also Howe, 1966.)

Let us move on now to *configural models* of combination. To see clearly how these differ from linear models we may first ask what it is that the linear approaches (additive, averaging or multiplicative) have in common. They all accept that the indices obtained from studies of inference rules can be applied elsewhere in combination without requiring amendments. In other words they all assume that the ratings, the evaluations, the probabilistic diagnoses or what-you-will which are obtained on one occasion remain valid and unchanged when the inputs are placed in the context of other material. In doing this the linear models explicitly deny that judges may respond to a configuration of material which can differ from the parts alone. What form could such a configuration take? The example used by Rokeach and Rothman (1965) is an apt one. They consider the individual inputs *father* and *irresponsible*, and suggest that *father* will typically be positively judged whereas *irresponsible* will take on a negative value. But the combined input (*irresponsible father*) will be more negatively evaluated than either of the two alone. They argue that within this configuration "over-assimilation" takes place, so that the combined input is quite different from the two components received separately.

Consider as a second example of configural judgment a possible way of interpreting MMPI and other test battery profiles. Clinicians usually prefer not to look at these as sets of separate scores, but rather to look for particularly deviant values and to imaginatively construct an interpretation of the profile around these aberrant tests. In this case the numerical values of each test may not be combined in any generalizable way (averaged for instance), but instead each is seen in relation to the configuration provided by several of the others.

Such a combinatorial process would certainly be a complex one. Some psychologists seem to view it as almost magical, and therefore as not possible. Their worry is that the configural approach may imply that combination rules can never be predicted from inference rules. Such an inherent unpredictability would render the approach valueless in an empirically-oriented psychology.

It is true that, if statements by supporters of configural models are cited in isolation, they may on quick reading seem to suggest that prediction is logically impossible. For example, Asch (1946, p. 286) has written: "The entire view possesses the formal properties of a structure, the form of which cannot be derived from the summation of the individual relations." And Rokeach and Rothman (1965, p. 131) have asserted that "the outcome of the cognitive interaction cannot be accurately predicted solely from a knowledge of the direction and intensity of the two stimuli considered separately." Opponents of the configural view may pick up this kind of statement as the basis of a strong objection. Thus Wishner (1960, p. 97) has noted: "It appears that an essential postulate of Asch's formulation is the unpredictability of the final impression from any prior knowledge of the denotations and connotations of elements of the stimulus list, individually or in interaction."

Yet this is surely a misinterpretation of the configural view. Asch has never supposed that impressions are in principle unpredictable; the point is that groups of input items, or indeed the complete group of these items, can combine together to generate a whole which alters the meaning of single pieces of information. (Consider again the example of *irresponsible father*, cited above.) Asch sees form perception as an analogue of person perception: a form percept is not a sum of parts in a linear sense, but is a unitary product or gestalt quality, which determines in quite specific and lawful ways the properties of the parts. The same process — although far more complex — is presumed to take place when we judge other people.*

What this means for research can most easily be grasped if we look first at configurations of only two separate inputs. We may conduct studies of the kind reported by, for instance, Anderson, but we should pay particular attention to the idiosyncratic relationship between the two members of a pair. Would this increase our ability to predict combination rules from inference rules? There is evidence from several sources that it might. Rokeach and Rothman (1965) have demonstrated empirically that clear predictions about combinations can be derived from a configural model. Furthermore they compared the success of these predictions with those from a linear model (the congruity principle), to the clear disadvantage of the latter. Their own model gives emphasis to the relations of relevance and importance which may exist between the members of a combined input, and they describe techniques to specify these relationships quantitatively. The relationship in meaning between items placed together has also been discussed by Willis (1960). He presents evidence that contrast effects occur when single inputs are combined, so that the current meaning of one input is idiosyncratically influenced by the nature of others in a set. Dustin and Baldwin (1966) have studied redundancy in pairs of stimulus characteristics. Redundancy was defined in terms of the extent to which the members of a pair imply each other. Their results suggest that combination rules are likely to be more extreme than inference rules, and that this effect is greater with pairs of cue traits that have low redundancy.†

It may be seen that research into configural models is quite feasible, and that these models allow for predictable relations between parts just as do their linear counterparts (cf. Hammond and Summers, 1965; Hoffman, 1960). Research strategy does, however, become massively

* We are greatly indebted to S. E. Asch for his helpful advice and comments on this issue.

† In considering the logical model of trait implication presented earlier we were able to show that the closer the implicative relationship between cue traits (i.e. the greater the redundancy in the set), the more similar are the inference rules about the traits (see p. 144). It is possible that the role of redundancy in combined inputs may be interpreted in terms of similarity in inference rules about each input.

complex as soon as we consider groups of more than two or three inputs. This is because the number of possible interactions between parts, groups of parts and the whole increases markedly with a larger number of items. Suppose that an impression is based upon interactions between inputs A, B, C, D and so on. If we treat the final outcome as an effect of separate dyadic interactions (between A and B, C and D, etc.), we run into a difficulty: when interaction has occurred between A and B, these are no longer present in their original form when they begin to interact with C, so that an additional entity needs also to be studied. And naturally we have larger groups of inputs to be evaluated as well (cf. Asch, 1968).

We need therefore to investigate all possible individual and grouped inputs; and from indices of all of these we might be successful in predicting the mode of combination. Viewed from this position it does seem that configurally-oriented research into double and triple inputs would be a sensible precursor to more ambitious studies of combination rules.

Yet all of this begs a question. We have still to show that configural combination models are superior to linear ones. As was noted above, Rokeach and Rothman (1965) found that they were, but in this kind of controversy more evidence is surely required. One investigator who has long been concerned with the issue as it touches clinical judgment is Meehl (e.g. Meehl, 1954, 1959, 1960; Meehl and Dahlstrom, 1960). Meehl has looked at the bases of diagnostic judgments about patients, typically employing as his material sets of test scores. On the whole it appears that clinicians may operate in a configural fashion, but that this non-linearity need not be considerable. "While our data do indicate that the clinician's judging behaviour with respect to the psychoticism variable is significantly configural, the *amount* of departure from a linear, additive model does not appear to be very great" (Meehl, 1960, p. 23). A similar conclusion might be drawn from the investigation by Hammond, Hursch and Todd (1964) of I.Q. judgments based upon Rorschach responses.

We are tempted to agree with Hammond and Summers (1965) that this configural–linear dichotomy is an unreal one. Some studies of linear models suggest that judgments are of that kind, and other research programmes lead to the conclusion that configural judgments are being made. There are clear *a priori* grounds — noted above — for expecting non-linearity in certain instances, but some combinations of input material may be sufficiently simple to be linear. A plausible conclusion is that both modes of combination can occur, and that the mode adopted will depend upon a number of factors (cf. Holt, 1958; Summers and Hammond, 1966). We might even anticipate that within the same judging situation combination of inputs can be both linear and configural. By making this assumption Gilberstadt and Duker (1965) and Meehl and Dahlstrom (1960) have successfully set down semi-statistical and semiclinical principles for interpreting test battery profiles.

The issue now becomes one of determining which factors are relevant to the linearity or non-linearity of combination rules. One clear possibility is the judge himself. We have pointed out (p. 155) that inference rules can depend upon the perceiver's stable characteristics, and similar individual differences in combination rules are to be expected. Several writers have suggested that modes of combination may vary from person to person (e.g. Kennedy and coworkers, 1966), and this is likely to be a fruitful research area. Secondly, the situation in which judgments are made may determine whether combination is linear or configural. For example, Schroder, Driver and Streufert (1966) have emphasized that simpler integrative procedures may be employed in times of stress.

A third factor relevant to which kind of combination rule is operative is the judgmental task itself. Part of the variability in research results arises from the range of different tasks which have been studied. It seems reasonable to assume that as additional positive information is received by a clinician making probabilistic diagnoses (see the study by Mahrer and Young described above), then the certainty of the inference will be increased. Yet additional favourable information need not operate in the same way to make a judge become progressively more attracted towards a stimulus person (see the studies by Anderson), nor need an associative link change scale values to a constant extent in the maintenance of congruity. On the other hand factors determining conforming behaviour (Mausner and Bloch, 1957) might combine to increase probability as they do in diagnostic situations.

As further examples of the wide range of investigations into this topic consider impressions of groups as a function of perceptions of individual members (e.g. Levy and Richter, 1963), or judgments about someone's attitudes based upon statements he has made (Weiss, 1963). Rimoldi (1956) has examined judgments of public figures, alone and in pairs. But his subjects indicated how "interested in knowing" the stimuli they were — a task rather different from the others described in this section. Combination of food preferences has been investigated by Gulliksen (1956). He examined evaluations of several foods in isolation and together. But his combined input was in size twice as large as his single inputs, since judges were explicitly told that the meal "beef and lamb" was twice as big as a meal of each alone. This seems to be different from studies of individual stimulus persons, but to have some similarity to studies of groups. We assume that some communalities will emerge, but for now we must be cautious in moving from one judgmental domain to another.

One final general point about combination rules should be made. Part of the difficulty in arbitrating between different formulations arises from the logic of model-testing. It is usually easy to see when a model is *inconsistent with* observed behaviour, but it is much more difficult to ascertain whether it adequately accounts for that behaviour. In effect we often cannot say how good a fit between model and reality is required for that model to be acceptable. Many of the studies mentioned in this chapter reveal fairly close parallels between observed and expected responses, but in most cases it would be unadvisable to conclude from the published findings that the model is thereby validated. What is needed is a greater number of studies which set up comparative tests of more than one model; in this way at least ordinal judgments of adequacy could be made.

RECAPITULATION

In this chapter we have looked at studies of the decision rules which make up the perceptual processing centre. Much of the work has dealt with inference rules (about a single input) and rather less with combination rules. Studies of inference rules have been reviewed, from early work by Asch (1946) to unpublished research of our own. Asch's technique and conclusions were scrutinized, and additional experiments reported which suggest that they are applicable to much more complex stimulus material than has previously been studied. Wishner's (1960) analysis of the judging process called up by Asch's material has also been shown relevant to this more complex material.

Other investigations into inference rules have been discussed, and developments of the work of Bruner, Shapiro and Tagiuri (1958) presented. Some additional forms of measurement have been tried out, and the notion of cojudgment introduced and applied. Analysis of data from Experiment 14 in terms of the nature of the stimulus person and of the perceiver has shed some light on factors which influence implicit personality theories, and we have drawn attention to differences in the extremity of inferences made by men and by women. In this chapter also we have developed a model of implicative relationships based upon the work of logicians and have described some preliminary tests of the model.

The final section has concerned combination rules themselves. We noted that formulations of the way inputs are combined may be primarily linear or primarily configural. Linear models emphasizing averaging, additive and multiplicative functions were described. We suggested that a configural approach is likely to be more fruitful, but argued that the mode of combination will vary with the judge, the situation, and the task.

4
INDIVIDUAL
DIFFERENCES IN
PERSON PERCEPTION

CHAPTER 3 has been concerned with some of the ways in which perceivers process the information they have selected from the material available to them. We placed greatest emphasis on processes common to most perceivers. In the present chapter we turn to some of the major differences between perceivers.

Inspection of Figure 1 on p. 20 reveals four components of our schematization of the perceptual process which are mainly concerned with variables specific to an individual perceiver. Apart from aspects of the processing centre — dealt with in the last chapter — we might be interested in the perceiver's store of information about the stimulus person, the perceiver's stable characteristics, and his current state. All these components in the first place affect which input is selected, but they also have links with the processing centre and ultimately with the various components of the output. In this chapter we shall consider how person perception is influenced by individual differences of these kinds. First to be examined are the effects of differences in stored stimulus person information, next the differences due to stable characteristics of the perceiver, and finally those due to his current state. We shall bring together findings from a wide variety of investigations and shall report a number of studies of our own.

STORED INFORMATION ABOUT THE
STIMULUS PERSON

We have already noted that a perceptual output carries with it certain expectancies. These expectancies may be seen to differ in their generality. They may concern an individual stimulus person (President Johnson or one's wife, for example), certain classes of stimulus person (such as women, Jews or dentists) or they may concern particular aspects of people in general (blond hair, spectacles or a southern accent for instance). The several levels of generality of expectancies are clearly levels which interact with each other, and it is usually difficult to disentangle for study one single kind. Roughly speaking, however, we may suggest that in the last chapter we have emphasized expectancies about classes of people and about aspects of people in general, and that the present section of this chapter is to deal with expectancies about individual stimuli. But many expectancies about classes of people and about people in general are related to a judge's value and habit systems. These may be viewed as parts of his stable characteristics, and we shall deal further with them when we return to that topic on p. 195.

We need firstly to reintroduce the notion of conception, which we defined in Chapter 1 as judgment made without the presence of a stimulus. The perceiver's store of information about a stimulus person (the component at the top right of Figure 1) contains vestiges of his perceptual experience relevant to this person. On the basis of this store — and without the stimulus person actually being present — the judge can form a conception of the stimulus person. A conceptual judgment may comprise any of the types of output described in the first chapter. The material giving rise to these conceptual outputs derived originally from perceptions, and entered the stimulus person store via the feedback loop shown in Figure 1. Conception may thus in its turn involve episodic judgments of overt fact ("he drank a lot at the party last night"), or of covert fact ("he enjoyed the party"). Or dispositional judgments may form the basis of a conception — judgments of overt characteristics ("he is agile") or of covert characteristics ("he is ambitious"). As was argued in the first chapter, each of these types of judgment generates expectancies about the stimulus person and his future behaviour. It is this relationship between conceptual expectancies and subsequent perception with which we are concerned in the present section.

Conceptions of a person may influence perceptual judgments of him in two major ways. Firstly they affect the dimensions we use in judging him. If we habitually view a person in terms of certain dimensions, we are likely to use these dimensions when next perceiving him. We may customarily view the Prime Minister in terms of dimensions which have political relevance, and probably have not thought of him in terms of a father or a husband. We are likely to bring to bear our habitually-employed dimensions when we next perceive him. The nature of these dimensions will in effect influence what we look for in perception. This point has been made by a number of writers. Bruner (1951, 1957) has discussed the "categories" which a person typically employs and how these lead him to expect to perceive behaviour relevant to these categories. G. A. Kelly (1955) has emphasized variations in the "constructs" employed in judging other people, while Harvey, Hunt and Schroder (1961) have developed their framework in terms of judges' "concepts". It is clear that the dimensions, categories, constructs or concepts which judges use to read their world constitute expectancies which influence their perception.

A second form of expectancy concerns the placement a stimulus is expected to have along a particular dimension. This is not a question of which dimensions a person uses, but rather how he places a stimulus along those dimensions which he does use. Conceptual expectancies of this kind derive from the fact that an essential part of a perceptual response is the attributive component, which is in fact just this type of placement (see p. 7). If a stimulus person is typically perceived or conceived as "very cheerful", the expectancies deriving from this judgment are likely to affect later judgments about the person.

Research on expectancy has taken many forms. Bruner and his colleagues have reported a number of studies of "perceptual readiness" and "hypothesis strength". Their work ranges from a finding that the perception of tachistoscopically presented nonsense syllables is affected by perceiver expectancies about English word sequences (Miller, Bruner and Postman, 1954) to a demonstration that perceivers fail to notice the inclusion of a bass viol in a briefly shown picture of a discus thrower (Bruner, Postman and John, 1949). Studies of a rather different kind have been described by Rosenthal (e.g. 1963, 1964). He has conducted a number of "meta-experiments" to investigate the way in which an experimenter's expectancy determines the results he obtains. By suggesting to different assistants that different experimental outcomes are likely he has consistently been able to obtain (through his assistants) discrepant sets of findings — in studies of rats and planaria as well as of humans. A typical finding is that perceivers' judgments of stimulus persons represented in photographs may vary according to the *experimenter's* expectancy. These studies show clearly the operation of expectancy in complex situations.

Of particular relevance to this section is Kelley's (1950) variant of Asch's (1946) approach to impression formation. Kelley generated expectancies about a directly perceived stimulus person by previously describing him as either "warm" or "cold". Perceivers' subsequent perceptions and the amount of their interaction with the stimulus person in a discussion group were influenced accordingly. This investigation is clearly of the second type of expectancy phenomenon — how expected placement along a dimension influences actual placement along that dimension. It is an unusual investigation in that it dealt with conceptual expectancies about a single individual rather than with those expectancies of greater generality (see p. 174) which are more often studied.

Kelley's study was of the relationship between expectancy and dispositional perception (as judged on personality traits), and it involved a direct perceptual situation. We have carried out several investigations of conceptual expectancy but our emphasis has been upon indirect episodic perceptual responses.* These studies were of the same design and may be collectively reviewed at this stage.

Experiment 15

As stimulus person for this experiment we used Mr. Edward Heath, who at the time was Secretary for Industry in the Conservative Government. He was well known to all our subjects although none had met him personally, having presumably formed their conceptions of the man over a fairly lengthy period of indirect perception via television, radio and the press.

The procedure differed from earlier studies in that we used a single instrument to measure both conceptions and perceptions of Heath. Both types of judgment were obtained (at different times) on twelve nine-point semantic differential scales. Conceptions were elicited by asking subjects to record their impressions of the stimulus on these scales, and perceptual responses were obtained a week later, immediately after exposure to a newspaper account of Heath's behaviour at a meeting.

The twelve scales, which are set out in Table 10, contain equal numbers of items representing the Evaluative, Potency and Activity

---

* It may be useful to treat this question as one of "perceptual constancy". We develop this idea in Chapter 8.

factors. Scale polarities and orders were as usual randomized on the experimental forms. Conceptual judgments were obtained from ninety-two undergraduate judges, who were one week later unexpectedly presented with a 300 word news item describing Heath's behaviour at a political meeting. Two different news items were used for reasons which will become apparent in Chapter 6. Each subject read carefully through his report, then, placing it aside,* filled in his semantic differential scales. On this occasion judges were asked for their perception of Heath's performance at the meeting. This request was elaborated to emphasize that subjects should give their impression of "Heath's behaviour, what he said and did at the meeting". In other words we were eliciting episodic judgments about Heath. None of the subjects reported any difficulty in carrying out this task.

To determine the relationship between conceptual expectancy and

Table 10   Product–moment correlations between conceptual expectancy and indirect perception of a politician (Heath) mediated by two narratives

Scale	Narrative 1 (N=46)		Narrative 2 (N=46)	
	r	p<	r	p<
True–false	+0·17	n.s.	+0·42	0·01
Wise–foolish	+0·68	0·001	+0·40	0·01
Sweet–sour	+0·40	0·01	+0·39	0·01
Fair–unfair	+0·35	0·02	+0·35	0·02
Strong–weak	+0·21	n.s.	+0·20	n.s.
Hard–soft	+0·24	n.s.	+0·26	n.s.
Large–small	+0·44	0·01	+0·36	0·02
Rugged–delicate	+0·60	0·001	+0·35	0·02
Sharp–dull	+0·37	0·02	+0·43	0·01
Hot–cold	+0·27	n.s.	+0·24	n.s.
Active–passive	+0·27	n.s.	+0·62	0·001
Fast–slow	+0·40	0·01	+0·61	0·001
Mean value	+0·37	0·001	+0·39	0·001

* We have carried out an experiment to determine whether the amount of exposure to a written narrative or news item has any effect on episodic perception. We compared mean semantic differential scale scores from subjects who read through a narrative once only and from subjects who were allowed unlimited perusal of the same narrative. There were no significant differences between scale means and in fact the profiles were startlingly similar for the two conditions.

subsequent perception we carried out a series of product–moment correlations between subjects' scores on each scale for their conception of Heath and their scale rating of Heath's behaviour. The results are presented in Table 10, which shows the value of r and the level of significance for each scale. The r values are presented separately for perceptions from each of the two news items. It can be seen that the mean values of r are very high and that 16 out of the 24 individual r values are significant at at least the 0·05 level of probability. (This means, for example, that if a subject conceives Heath as, say, a wise person, he subsequently tends to perceive Heath's behaviour as relatively wise, whereas others who receive the same stimulus input but have different conceptions perceive him differently.) The close association between conception and perception is especially noteworthy in view of the fact that the interval of a week between administration of the conception and perception scales would be expected to reduce the magnitude of the relationship. There is no doubt that indirect perception can be influenced materially by a person's previous conceptions; furthermore this effect holds good for perception via two different news items which (as will be shown in Chapter 6) give quite discrepant accounts of the stimulus person's behaviour.

Other studies of conceptual expectancy

Evidence for the relationship between perceivers' conceptions and their later episodic perceptions does not, however, derive from the results of only one experiment. Table 11 presents a summary of the results of five further experiments in which scale correlations were carried out by the same procedure as that described above. These experiments made use of a variety of stimulus persons, and of semantic differential scales. Although perception was indirect throughout, it was sometimes mediated by one narrative (Experiments 16 and 17) and sometimes by two narratives read in different orders (Experiments 26, 27 and 28 — details of which appear in Chapter 6). In spite of this variation in the properties of the communication channel and the measuring instrument, the picture revealed by the correlation data is a consistent one. Seventy-six out of a total of 124 correlations proved to be significant at the 0·05 level or beyond, and the overall mean value of r is $+0·32$, which is of course highly significant. The importance of conceptual expectancy in this type of person perception seems amply demonstrated.

G

Table 11 The relationship between conceptual expectancy and episodic perception —
summary of evidence from five investigations

Experiment number		Stimulus person	Number of correlations	Number of significant correlations (Mean $N=48$)	Mean value of r
	27	Heath	24	12	$+0{\cdot}28$
16	26	Wilson	48	26	$+0{\cdot}30$
17	28	Macmillan	52	38	$+0{\cdot}38$
Overall percentage of significant correlations and grand mean value of r				61%	$+0{\cdot}32$

Experiment 18

Although in these six experiments we made use of several different stimulus persons, all were in fact politicians. In order to be reasonably certain that subjects have formed fairly sophisticated conceptual expectancies, it is necessary to use stimulus persons who are well known to a wide range of perceivers: thus politicians are an obvious choice. In the present experiment we decided to use well-known stimuli of a rather different type; on this occasion we used not single stimulus persons but, instead, groups of people. Our groups were in fact soccer teams. The use of football teams permitted us to examine the importance to person perception of the event in which people are involved, the event in this case being a football match between our two stimulus groups. The significance attached to events in person perception has already been emphasized in the title of this volume and discussed in Chapter 1. Just as the context or situation in which an object is presented can affect its perception, so too can the event in which a stimulus person is participating have a crucial effect on the way that person is perceived: in Chapter 1 we have referred to this as present context information. Finally, in addition to making use of group stimuli perceived in the context of an event, the present experiment investigated both indirect perception via newspaper reports and direct perception of the event itself. We were thus able to compare the role played by conceptual expectancy in both direct and indirect person perception.

Hastorf and Cantril (1954) have shown how extremely partisan individuals can form quite different judgments of a sporting event. Their subjects were members of two colleges who perceived a football game between their respective teams. Judgments were made following exposure to a film of the game, and clear discrepancies were observed in the perceived fairness of the teams and in the number of infractions. In our study we hoped to develop the Hastorf–Cantril investigation in a number of ways: subjects were on the whole uncommitted to the stimulus teams, several aspects of their conceptual expectancies were assessed, our measure of perception was rather more complicated, and we looked at both direct and indirect perception.

Consider first that part of the experiment which concerned subjects' indirect judgment. Ninety-three undergraduate subjects of both sexes, none of whom had been recruited because of any special interest in football, gave conceptions of the Sheffield Wednesday and West Ham United teams on nine-point semantic differential scales. The scales were those used in Experiment 15 (see Table 10) with the exception of four which were replaced by scales more suitable for measuring judgments of teams rather than of individual people. The scales *good–bad* and *interesting–boring* from the Evaluative factor were substituted for *true–false* and *wise–foolish*; *bold–timid* (Potency factor) replaced *large–small*; and *tense–relaxed* (Activity) was included instead of *sharp–dull*. The usual procedures were adopted for randomization of scale order and polarities. About thirty minutes after the subjects had given their conceptions of the two teams, and during which time they were engaged on other tasks, they were asked to read a newspaper account of a game which took place between Sheffield Wednesday and West Ham United on March 6, 1965. (Two genuine news items were used, details of which are given in the description of Experiment 25 in Chapter 6.) Having read the report, subjects were asked to make judgments of the teams' performance in the match; they also gave their perceptions of the match itself.

Using the technique adopted in Experiments 15–17 and 26–28, product–moment correlations were calculated for each scale to determine the relationship between subjects' conceptions of the two teams and their subsequent indirect perceptions, based upon the news item. For both teams and regardless of which newspaper account was read (although once again the reports differed quite considerably) there were large numbers of significant correlations between conceptions and episodic perceptions. Overall, 21 out of 48 correlations were significant and the mean value of r was $+0\cdot27$. The relationship is not quite so highly positive as we found for politicians, but this is to be expected since many of our subjects, especially the women, would be relatively unfamiliar with the game of professional soccer and the teams used as stimuli; their responses are thus likely to be less reliable. Nevertheless we have convincing evidence that perceivers' conceptual expectancies have quite a large say in determining later perception even when the stimuli are perceived against the powerful background of a fairly complex event.

Will this effect still be present when the context is allowed to obtrude even more powerfully — when in fact the event itself is perceived directly? To answer this question we sent along a panel of 29 undergraduates to watch the football match in question, the same match that our other subjects perceived indirectly via one of the two newspaper reports.

The spectator panel was recruited to match the indirect perceivers as closely as possible and special care was taken that the panel did not comprise merely those students with a keen interest in football or an inclination to be entertained free of charge. In fact we were extremely successful in matching the two groups of subjects; this aspect of the study is described in Chapter 6 (p. 261). A few days prior to the game all members of the panel reported to the experimenters where they gave their conceptions of the Sheffield Wednesday and West Ham teams on the semantic differential scales described above. They were then given instructions about their attendance at the match itself and the subsequent recording of their perceptions. Within a few minutes of the end of the game, panel members gave their judgments of both the match and each of the two teams based upon what they had just observed.

In this case the correlations between conceptions and episodic perceptions of the two teams provide a very different picture of the association between conceptual expectancy and episodic judgment. The mean value of r is as low as $+0 \cdot 10$, and only one of the twenty-four correlations is significant. It is tempting to conclude that we have here a crucial difference between indirect and direct perception. In the former case (newspaper readers in this experiment) stimulus information is limited, and conceptions may exert a stronger influence on perceptual judgments than in direct perception where the stimulus information might overwhelm conceptions. This effect is consistent with findings from other studies. In Chapter 3 we noted that the inferences which subjects made from particular cue traits were greatest when only limited information about the stimulus person was provided. For example, as additional material was incorporated in Asch's (1946) stimulus list in Experiments 10 and 12, so did the importance of the cue trait diminish (see p. 132). In Koltuv's (1962) study of implicit personality theories (see p. 133) it was found that trait intercorrelations were lower when perceivers had more information about the stimulus person. Kelley (1950) noted that expectancies generated by "warm" and "cold" can be modified by particularly powerful stimulus person attributes, and it may be that these are more probable in direct perception. Projective techniques for diagnostic use make an assumption of the same kind. The idea of a measure like the Rorschach Test is to seriously limit the information from the stimulus so that judgments by the perceiver will be drawn mostly from his own characteristics.

It may be the case then that conceptions are typically of greater importance in indirect perception than in direct perception. The results of Experiment 18 bear this out * and suggest several lines of enquiry. For example, it would be interesting to see whether direct perceptions from subjects with more established impressions of the teams would be correlated rather more highly with their prior conceptions. Or increasing amounts of information might be provided about a stimulus. One could range from a sparse indirect description, through a fuller set of material (a film, perhaps) to a limited and then an unrestricted example of direct perception. A gradual reduction in the importance of conceptual expectancy would be predicted.

Experiments 19 and 20

We have emphasized that episodic perceptions of a stimulus person can only take place within the context of an event. In the last experiment the aspect of the event we concentrated upon was the activity (a game of football) in which our stimulus persons were engaging. There is a further aspect of events which is often extremely important when indirect perception takes place via the communication channel provided by the press. This concerns the topic about which a stimulus person is speaking. Many news items, especially those featuring public figures,

---

* They do not demonstrate it conclusively, since the time interval between conceptual and perceptual judgments was greater for the direct perception group. However, other studies suggest that this is unlikely to markedly affect the level of the association: Experiment 16 incorporated a week's interval, whereas only 30 minutes separated conception and perception in Experiment 26. Both investigations used Wilson as stimulus person, and very similar conception–perception correlations were obtained.

are reports of the content and the manner of delivery of speeches on various issues: indeed all the narrative accounts of political stimulus persons referred to so far in this volume have centred upon speeches made by politicians on topics of national interest. Our perceivers will have conceptions about these topics as well as about the stimulus persons.

The relationship between subjects' attitudes to a stimulus person, attitudes to the issue on which he expresses an opinion, and the resultant effect on attitude change is a topic which has interested many students of the communication process (see, for example, Heider, 1958; Kelman and Eagly, 1965; Osgood and Tannenbaum, 1955; and Tannenbaum, 1956). We are, however, less interested in investigating processes of attitude change than in seeing whether there is any relationship between subjects' conceptions of a speech topic and their subsequent perceptions of a stimulus person speaking on that topic. In the present experiments we took semantic differential measures of two topics, the Nationalization of Steel and Communism. By means of the correlation procedure used in the experiments already described we related these conceptions to subjects' later perceptions of a stimulus person's behaviour perceived indirectly through a news item. For each experiment we employed three narratives. In Experiment 19 subjects were presented with one of three news items containing a description of the then Liberal Party leader, Mr. Jo Grimond, addressing a meeting on the subject of steel nationalization. In Experiment 20 the three narratives described a speech by Senator Barry Goldwater in which he denounced Communism. Each of three narratives in both experiments presented the speaker's performance in a different light, but in all cases the speaker adopted the same line of argument in relation to the topic. (This contrasts with the situation in many of the experiments of other workers in which the speaker is made to take a number of different points of view with regard to an issue.) One reason for using different news reports was to investigate the generality of any correlation we might obtain: there is a further reason which will become apparent in Chapter 8 when another aspect of these experiments is discussed. For the moment let us say that there was a mean product–moment correlation of $+0.12$ for the six stories concerning the two stimulus persons. This figure is significant but it is not high and the magnitude of the correlation varies somewhat haphazardly between stories and between scales. On the whole there certainly is some evidence that subjects' expectancies about a topic can affect person perception, but the relationship is much less clearcut than that between stimulus person expectancies and perception. There is a need for more research on this question, using a wider range of speakers, topics, stimulus material and measuring scales.

We began this section by discussing the vital role of expectancy in perception, and the experiments described have shown how the expectancies which are a part of conception have a marked influence on the indirect perception of specific persons. We have noted, however, that conceptions about particular topics and persons are only one aspect of expectancy. In the remaining sections of this chapter we shall consider various characteristics of the perceiver which have a bearing upon other types of expectancy. First of all we shall examine how the perceiver's stable characteristics — his sex, personality, occupation, cultural background, political and religious beliefs, social class and so on — lead him to form expectancies about people in general and about various classes of stimulus persons. Finally we shall look at some aspects of the perceiver's current state which have an even closer bearing on his expectancies — those perceiver characteristics which concern perceptual set and motivation.

SEX DIFFERENCES

A great many investigators have mentioned the possibility of important sex differences in person perception. Some writers have indeed demonstrated quantitative or qualitative discrepancies between perceptions from male and female subjects; others have confined themselves to dark hints and warnings to researchers that the true explanation of their results may be inextricably linked with the question of sex. Most reviewers of current research pay pen service to the sex variable, among them G. W. Allport (1961), Bronfenbrenner, Harding and Gallwey (1958), V. B. Cline (1964), Shrauger and Altrocchi (1964), Taft (1955), Tagiuri (1968) and Wallach and Kogan (1959). This emphasis contrasts with the viewpoint commonly taken by students of object perception where relatively few differences have been noted between the performances of male and female subjects. The findings here have been described as "scattered . . . with only the most tentative and equivocal theoretical implications" (Bieri, Bradburn and Galinsky, 1958) although this may be because research in the area is as yet only at an exploratory stage (Anastasi, 1958).

All the more reason, then, for us to examine most closely the claims which have been freely made for the importance of sex differences in person perception. The relevant research has been conducted from several different points of view. The main areas of investigation have concerned the judging of emotion, the accuracy of person perception, self-perception and assumed similarity, inferences from descriptive traits, and various studies using free response techniques; let us look at these in turn.

As might have been expected, there is no shortage of findings relevant to that much-discussed topic, the recognition of emotional expression. The number of studies is paralleled by the variety of their conclusions. Buzby (1924), Jenness (1932), Levy and Schlosberg (1960), Vinacke (1949), and Weisgerber (1956) all report that women are very slightly superior to men at judging emotional expression from photographs, but Kanner (1931) found that men were superior. Hammes (1963) reported that female subjects make more extreme responses to photographically presented stimuli. Davitz (1964) and Gates (1923) failed to find any sex differences and Taft, in his 1955 review paper, reports some studies favouring men and some favouring women — but most (five in all) revealing no differences between male and female judges.

Accuracy of perception other than of emotion has been investigated by V. B. Cline (1955, 1964) who used motion films of stimulus persons in an interview situation. Judges were required to "postdict" how the stimulus persons behaved in everyday life and how they had rated themselves on an adjective check list. He found that women judges were slightly superior to men, but none of the differences were significant. Bronfenbrenner, Harding and Gallwey (1958) studied the accuracy of direct person perception and found no sex differences, although there were differences in the correlates of highly accurate perceivers according to sex (e.g. men sensitive to their own sex had different personalities to women sensitive to their own sex). Murstein (1966) found that women were slightly more accurate at perceiving hostility in women friends than were men when judging men friends. However, none of the differences reached significance and the pattern of relationship between perceiver hostility and perception was the same for both sexes. Many early studies of accuracy have been discredited on methodological grounds (see Chapter 1, p. 47), but in any case few of them revealed significant differences related to the sex of the judge (see Taft, 1955).

An interesting parable can be told about the work of Exline (1957, 1960). He observed (1957) that female subjects were more accurate than men in perceiving interpersonal preferences, and went on (1960) to look behind this sex difference. He reasoned that it may be because women score more highly on need for affiliation measures and that this need is related to sensitivity. Or perhaps women have a stronger norm of the importance of interpersonal awareness. To test these possibilities he replicated the earlier study, now taking the necessary additional measures. Sure enough, women had a stronger need for affiliation, but he observed no differences in norms of sensitivity. Unfortunately, however, the male subjects were now seen to be every bit as accurate as the females, so that his original hunch became quite inappropriate. Although sex differences in accuracy of person perception may sometimes be found, they are not always consistent.

There is evidence from a number of studies that accuracy of perception is linked with judges' propensities for assuming that others are similar to themselves. The concept of assumed similarity and its correlates has attracted a good deal of attention from students of person perception, but little of this has been directed at isolating differences between male and female perceivers. However, in a study by Kohn and Fiedler (1961) female subjects did tend to assume more similarity to a variety of stimulus persons than did male judges, and a comparable finding was obtained by Fiedler and Hoffmann (1962) using Dutch schoolchildren as subjects. In both these studies there was some indication that female subjects rated stimulus persons rather more favourably than did the male judges.

To obtain assumed similarity scores it is usually necessary for the subjects to rate themselves, and there has been some interest in the correlates of these self-perceptions. Sex differences in self-concepts have, however, generally been surprisingly few and far between (McDonald and Gynther, 1965; Wertheimer, 1960), and we may conclude from Wylie's (1961) review of previous work on sex differences in this area that the results at present are too inconsistent to permit unequivocal interpretation.

There are a number of investigations in which subjects are required to rate stimulus persons on descriptive traits, where there is no concern with the matter of perceptual accuracy or assumed similarity. Bieri (1962) for instance has stressed the importance of the stimulus person and the task, and he found that while males will accept more equivocal information in judging a man to be dominant, they require unequivocal information before they will judge him to be submissive. This suggests some relationship between perception and the judge's stereotype of the stimulus person's role. We would expect male/female differences in such circumstances, although Bieri's finding should be treated with some caution since his male and female subjects belonged to quite different occupational groups. Knapp and Ehlinger (1966) have studied episodic responses to a series of ambiguous silhouettes of a male and a female figure. Their results suggest that male judges are more apt to see the male stimulus in dominant roles, but that females are also likely to see their own sex as dominant. The basis of variations here again seems likely to lie in different generalized role conceptions. Men and women were observed to attribute different traits to photographs of women's faces in a study by Secord and Muthard (1955), but here the N for each group was only 10, and again there were some discrepancies in the occupations of the groups. Bayton, Austin and Burke (1965) investigated Negroes' judgments of how the "average Negro" or the "average white" would complete the Guilford–Zimmerman Temperament Survey. The only real sex difference to emerge was a tendency for male judges to believe that males were more friendly whilst female judges thought females were more friendly.

An interesting technique has been described by Moore (1966) in a study of sex differences in the perception of aggression. This involves very brief exposure (0·5 second) of pictures in a stereogram. Different pictures are presented to each eye and in a situation of binocular rivalry subjects' judgments of what they in fact see may be noted. Moore presented one picture with a content of violence (e.g. a man with a gun standing over a dead person) and one with a non-violent meaning (e.g. a farmer behind a plough). In this situation males perceived significantly more violence than females. This procedure may prove useful as a fairly direct measure of input selection.*

There has been increasing interest in recent years in allowing perceivers to give free-response descriptions of stimulus persons, rather than asking them for ratings on dimensions specified by the experimenter. It might be thought that such a procedure would reveal sex differences which would otherwise remain hidden. There is evidence that in a free-response situation women provide fuller and franker information about themselves and more information about others than do

* This idea is pursued further in Chapter 9 (see p. 360).

male subjects (Beach and Wertheimer, 1961; Sarason and Winkel, 1966). Women also tend to rate others more favourably (Sarason and Winkel, 1966) and, when possible, they seek out more information about the people they are judging than do men judges — although less information is sought about female stimulus persons regardless of the sex of the judge (Nidorf and Crockett, 1964). There is evidence that females make a greater number of inferences from information available, as opposed to the more straightforward description of stimulus persons favoured by male judges (Gollin, 1958; Sarbin, 1954). And when conflicting information was presented, the girl judges in Gollin's (1958) experiment made more attempt to rationalize it than did their boy counterparts.

Since one of the main purposes of the free-response type of experiment is that dimensions of description or judgment are specified by the judge and not by the experimenter it is of great interest to note whether male and female judges differ to any great extent in the way they categorize stimulus persons. In Nidorf and Crockett's (1964) study women used more categories and made finer distinctions than the men. (This ties in with Kohn and Fiedler's (1961) finding that women show more perceptual discrimination than men when rating stimulus persons well known to them.) Young men have been shown to use categories which emphasize physical appearance, occupation, values, abilities, motivation and interest, and boys to employ categories emphasizing aggression and non-conforming behaviour. Young women on the other hand emphasize the stimulus persons' social skills, and girls stress nurtural relationships, cooperativeness and happiness (Beach and Wertheimer, 1961; Campbell and Radke-Yarrow, 1956; Dornbusch and colleagues, 1965; Yarrow and Campbell, 1963).* Most of these examples of category usage by judges of different sexes seem to correspond well with what we would suppose to be the relevant roles of men, women, boys and girls in contemporary North American society. It appears likely that these role differences will be reflected in further observations of sex differences in category usage, but for the present we may note that Dornbusch and colleagues (1965) report that 11 of the 12 most-selected free-response categories were common to both male and female judges.

Before going on to our own results on sex differences in person

* It is still an open question whether these differences in category usage are reflected in differential expectancies of the kind noted earlier in the chapter (pp. 175–176).

perception, let us briefly recapitulate what has been said so far. What is the evidence for sex differences in person perception? From the studies at our disposal we may say that as far as the judgment of emotion and the accurate perception of self and others are concerned, the findings are equivocal; there is some indication that women assume more similarity than men. Most of the differences between male and female judges are found in experiments which allow subjects to give free descriptions of stimulus persons. From these studies we have some evidence that women tend to give fuller and more favourable descriptions, make more inferences, and may use different categories than do men. It should be emphasized, however, that the number of studies on which these very tentative conclusions are based is small and that significant differences in the field as a whole are rare and highly prized.

Bearing these reservations in mind let us proceed to a cautious examination of our own findings. We have already noted in Chapter 3 (pp. 155–159) that there are some scattered differences in the inference rules used by men and by women; a more stable finding reported there was the greater consistency in the application of rules by female subjects. This seems to fit in with the work reviewed above. In Chapter 8 we shall look at sex differences in perceptual constancy (which are not great), and we deal here with our main group of investigations. In all of these the subject panels have comprised approximately equal numbers of males and females. And in the great majority of the experiments we have analysed our results separately for male and female subjects. We thus have data concerning sex differences for over fifty different stimulus persons perceived in a wide variety of indirect situations. None of our experiments made use of judges' free responses and the dimensions of judgment were nearly always specified in the polar terms of the semantic differential. It is possible to compare mean scale scores for male and female subjects and if necessary to carry out t-test comparisons between them. We were able to make in all 1128 such comparisons and in 80 cases the differences proved significant at the 0·05 level of probability or beyond. The figure of 80 represents a percentage of the total of 7·1%, which echoes the comment made above in connection with our summary of previous work in this field: whatever sex differences there may be in person perception they are few and far between — at least when dimensions are specified.

Nevertheless we carried our analysis of these male/female mean score discrepancies a stage further, and looked at the pattern of differences in a number of ways. Most of these proved fruitless. The nature of the communication (e.g. photograph, news report, or both of these) was unrelated to the proportion of sex differences, and categorizing differences in terms of semantic differential factors was similarly unrewarding. We looked at average deviation scores from the neutral point, five, but again found no variations; and attempts to examine the data in terms of the sex of the stimulus person were not helpful, since the latter was almost always male.

One approach was however fruitful. Bearing in mind Fiedler's observation (noted above) that women tend to make more favourable responses than do men, we examined the proportion of the 1128 scales at our disposal on which women made more positive judgments. Overall this figure turned out to be 60% — well above the 50% expected by chance. So we looked at the data again in these terms. Analysis by type-of-communication and semantic differential factor grouping once more proved unrewarding, but one categorization of stimuli yielded a very interesting outcome.

This classification was in terms of whether or not the stimulus person was a nationally known personality. Many of our studies used as stimuli public figures like Wilson, Macmillan, Grimond and Goldwater, but several others were of people like Joseph Ladner, Henry Goodwin or Sir Joseph Edwards — stimuli who were either quite unknown or figments of our imagination. If we categorize stimuli on this basis, an interesting pattern of sex differences emerges. This pattern is shown in Table 12.

It can be seen that when the stimulus person is a well-known public figure (generally a politician) the mean scale scores of the female judges are more positive than the male scores just 51% of the time. This proportion is almost exactly what would be predicted from chance, and we can say that under these circumstances no sex differences are apparent. But when the stimulus person is unknown to the judges the picture is rather different: in 62% of cases female judges make more positive responses. Table 12 also includes a breakdown for the two stimulus person categories according to the type of communication. This variable apparently has little influence, except that the overall figure for unknown stimuli of 62% has been slightly deflated by the inclusion of perception from photographs alone (57%).

The final set of material in Table 12 comes from Experiment 18. These data concern judgments of the football game, and have been

Table 12 Summary of sex differences in person perception

		Number of comparisons	Number and percentage of instances that women make more positive judgments		Number and percentage of significant male/female differences	
Well-known stimulus persons (12 stimulus persons)	Perception from report alone (6 stimulus persons)	160	84	53%	11	7%
	Conception (6 stimulus persons)	152	75	49%	8	5%
	Totals and overall percentages	312	159	51%	19	6%
Unknown stimulus persons (41 stimulus persons)	Perception from photograph alone (12 stimulus persons)	240	137	57%	4	2%
	Perception from report and photograph (13 stimulus persons)	180	117	65%	16	9%
	Perception from report alone (16 stimulus persons)	324	209	65%	29	9%
	Totals and overall percentages	744	463	62%	49	7%
Football match	Perception of the game and two teams	72	61	85%	12	17%
Grand totals and percentages		1128	683	60%	80	7%

separated from the other two categories since the stimuli were some-what different. In fact, however, we had learned that subjects in this investigation (especially the women) knew very little about football and about the teams, and we might suggest that the stimuli in this investigation belong in effect to the category of "unknown" stimuli. Women judges here are more positive in 85% of cases, and this very high value is seemingly consistent with our interpretation of responses to the other 1056 scales.

Experiment 21

It appears then that women in general make more positive perceptual responses, but that this tendency is especially marked when they are not previously familiar with the persons being judged. When the stimuli are well-known public figures they are no more liable to make positive judgments than are men. Our evidence for this conclusion derives from a large range of stimuli and subjects and seems likely to be reliable, but the possibility does remain that our *post hoc* interpretation is somehow invalidated by differences in conditions, stimuli or judges which have escaped our notice. An experiment expressly designed to test the conclusion is desirable.

We have conducted such an experiment. The design of this investigation required indirect perceptual responses from two groups of subjects. Each group received the same communication, in which a single variable was, however, manipulated. This was the identity of the stimulus person — for one group a well-known individual and for the other group an unknown person. We constructed a 350-word account of the ceremonial opening of a sports centre and presented this to subjects as a typewritten copy of a newspaper report. Two versions were employed, exactly the same except that the stimulus person in one was identified as Mr. Harold Wilson and in the other was referred to as the Mayor of Swindon. Wilson is of course a member of the class of well-known stimulus persons referred to above, whereas it may reasonably be assumed that the Mayor of Swindon was quite unknown to our undergraduate subjects. Forty-six subjects (23 male and 23 female) served in each group. They made indirect episodic judgments on an eighteen-item semantic differential form. The larger-than-usual number of scales was employed in order to provide a more reliable measure of the dependent variable — the percentage of scales on which the mean female response was more positive than that of the male judges.

We expect this percentage figure to be smaller for Wilson than for the Mayor of Swindon if the argument developed above has any validity. The report about the unknown person in fact generated more positive female responses in twelve scales — 67%. This figure is very close to the values from the wide variety of studies cited in Table 12. What of the percentage figure for Wilson? This turned out to be only 28% (representing 5 scales on which women were more positive). It is clear that the identity of a stimulus person has a marked effect on differential responding by the two sexes.

The one respect in which the results of Experiment 21 do not quite tally with those summarized in Table 12 is that the figure of 28% more positive female responses in the case of Wilson is rather lower than the 50% we anticipated. It seems that this figure may be a somewhat unreliable one, since many of the differences on a scale were very small ones; a few more subjects may well have resulted in the alteration of some of the mean scores. This suggestion may be supported by the average difference between male and female values. For the Mayor of Swindon the average difference on the twelve scales where females were more positive was a considerable one — 0·48 — whereas it was much smaller in the case of the thirteen less positive responses to Wilson (0·29). In more general terms the D-score (see p. 59) between the male and female profiles was 2·34 for the Mayor of Swindon and 1·76 for Wilson.

This experimental test of the *post hoc* analysis of other data does then seem to support our interpretation. Female judges are liable to make more positive responses than men when the stimulus person is unknown. But in the case of well-known political figures this phenomenon is not present. This is of course a rather low-level generalization and we need to delve further into this topic before we can understand the issues involved. For example, our conclusions are based only on indirect perceptual situations. Will they be upheld in cases of *direct* perception? And it may be that our emphasis on political figures has biased our evidence about "well-known" people. Will similar findings emerge when non-political public figures are studied? Clearly there is once again scope for much more research.

PERSONALITY DIFFERENCES

No account of individual differences in person perception would be complete without some consideration of the role played by the personality of the perceiver. It is clear that personality factors are often of great importance in the field of object perception (see, for example, the reviews by G. W. Allport, 1961, and Anastasi, 1958); as far as person perception is concerned Jackson and Messick (1963) and other writers have stressed that close attention should be paid to the influence of the perceiver's personality on his judgments about others.

The area of personality differences is marked by a number of excellent reviews, notably the general overview by Tagiuri (1968), the exhaustive treatment given by Shrauger and Altrocchi (1964), and addenda to that paper by Altrocchi (1965a, 1965b). Indeed these and other writers have covered the ground so comprehensively that in the present section we shall be content merely to sketch in the main relevant findings, adding details where necessary of the occasional neglected paper and of work that has been published since the appearance of these reviews.* We shall follow other writers in treating "personality" very widely: the term will be used to refer to a broad band of relatively covert stable characteristics.

To begin our examination of the importance of personality variables we turn once again to findings about the accuracy of identification of emotional expression. Here we are well served by Tagiuri's (1968) chapter and the volume edited by Davitz (1964). Investigators have generally failed to demonstrate any personality correlates of accuracy in these episodic judgments although it seems widely agreed that there is a positive relationship between accuracy and verbal intelligence. Davitz (1964) also found that judges who displayed superior abstract-symbolic ability were better at identifying vocal expressions of emotion than were others. Apart from these studies of accuracy of emotional recognition are there any findings which relate aspects of person perception to specific perceiver personality characteristics? Examination

* The reader should note that in addition to the present discussion personality variables are mentioned at several other points throughout this volume. Accounts of the role of the perceiver's personality in the operation of implicit personality theories, in the formation of impressions from photographs and as related to constancy phenomena are given in Chapters 3, 7 and 8 respectively.

of the literature reveals a number of dimensions which appear to have a bearing upon the way people are perceived.

As might be expected there has been a good deal of interest in the relationship between various measures of authoritarianism and person perception. In the original formulation of this concept (Adorno and coworkers, 1950) it was explicitly assumed that authoritarian persons (scoring high on the F-scale) exhibited perceptual and emotional reactions to other people which were different to those of low F-scorers. Several studies of the accuracy of dispositional perception have indicated that variations in F-score are indeed related to differences in style of judgment. Some of these have revealed differences in the way subjects predict another's F-scale responses (Crockett and Meidinger, 1956; Rabinowitz, 1956; Scodel and Friedman, 1956; Scodel and Mussen, 1953; Simons, 1966), but differences in perception measured in other ways have also been found (Lipetz, 1960; Pederson, 1965; Rudin and Stagner, 1958; Schulberg, 1961). Newcomb's results (1961, Chapter 7) suggest that these differences may depend on how well judge and stimulus are acquainted with each other. In general it appears that "assumed similarity" is greater in high F-scorers — these people assume others to be like themselves to a greater extent than do low F-scorers.

Several interesting findings have emerged about the judgments made by high and low F-scorers of the power-related characteristics of other people. It is helpful (Wilkins and deCharms, 1962) to distinguish between "external power" (e.g. socio-economic status, education, positions of authority) and "internal power" (personal characteristics indicating confidence or forcefulness). Jones (1954) has noted that high F-scorers are not more sensitive to internal power characteristics of other people; in fact the *low* scorers seemed to be more aware of these attributes. Yet he did find that high scorers tended to make more *inferences about* power-related cues. This suggests that authoritarianism is not related to the *selection* of inputs about internal power but that it is related to differences in decision rules about these inputs (cf. Harvey and Beverly, 1961; Wright and Harvey, 1965). Roberts and Jessor (1958) concentrated upon external power — varying the age, education, income, or occupation aspects of a stimulus person. Again no differences between high and low F-scorers in power-related input selection were found. This study measured punitiveness towards the stimulus: although degree of authoritarianism was overall found to be unrelated to degree of punitiveness, there was an interaction with the external power of the stimulus. High *F*-scorers more than low *F*-scorers tended to respond with personal hostility to frustrating stimuli of low status, but they resorted to indirect or displaced hostility towards people of high external power. Low *F*-scorers seemed to respond in the same manner irrespective of the status of a stimulus.* Wilkins and deCharms (1962) varied both internal and external power in their investigation of judgments by high and low *F*-scorers. Once again, no differences in the perception of external power-related cues (i.e. in input selection) were observed, but again there were differences in the inferences drawn from the cues. Furthermore high *F*-scorers seemed to emphasize "external" factors and to make less use of "internal" cues; the opposite tendencies were noted in low *F*-scorers. Wilkins and deCharms also measured *evaluative* perceptual responses. It was found that high and low scorers did not differ in their acceptance of others, but rather in what they based their acceptance upon. Whereas low *F*-scorers are most influenced by internal power cues, high scorers emphasize external power-related characteristics.

A rather different measure of perceptual response is in terms of cojudgment (see Chapter 3, p. 146). Authoritarianism is found to be positively related to a willingness to make cojudgments (Warr and Sims, 1965). We have earlier (p. 159) reviewed studies by Steiner (1954) and Steiner and Johnson (1963) of how this aspect of personality influences the way disparate information about a stimulus is integrated. A consistent pattern of findings is emerging in this area. DeSoto, Kuethe and Wunderlich (1960) have noted an interesting example of complementary projection (see p. 224). They report that high *F*-scorers are more liable to attribute threatening characteristics to other people (indirectly perceived through photographs) than are low scorers. That this is related to a greater insecurity on the part of high *F*-scorers is suggested by the results of an investigation by Bossom and Maslow (1957). They found that the personality variable of emotional security was negatively associated with judgments that other people (again represented in photographs) were "cold". On the other hand Hammes (1963) has rather surprisingly reported that manifest anxiety is un-

---

* This consistency was not observed in studies by Epstein (1965) and Lipetz and Ossorio (1967). One possible explanation of their deviant results is that subjects were in situations of greater interpersonal stress. The increased stress may have required self-preservative reactions whose importance minimized the role of stimulus person status.

related to a tendency to judge others as dangerous or threatening.

Hostility or aggressiveness on the part of the perceiver is a facet of personality which has been studied in its own right. A perceiver's hostility has been shown to affect the impression he forms both of himself and of other people. Sarason and Winkel (1966) found subjects' behavioural hostility to be related to their self-ratings, and Murstein (1961, 1966), in two parallel studies making use of men and women judges, found that regardless of self-concept hostile persons were significantly less accurate at perceiving hostility in others. One type of hostility which has received particular attention over a number of years is anti-semitism. In general it seems that anti-semitic individuals tend to see semitic characteristics more readily in facial photographs (Allport and Kramer, 1946; Elliott and Wittenburg, 1955; Scodel and Austrin, 1957), and to rate strangers or neutral bystanders in conditions of stress or frustration rather more negatively than other perceivers (Berkowitz, 1961; Rule, 1966). Anti-negro prejudice has also been studied in relation to perceptual behaviour. An illustrative study is that of Secord, Bevan and Katz (1956). They obtained results which parallel those of Allport and Kramer, finding that anti-negro judges perceive individuals in photographs as more negroid than do unprejudiced subjects. DeFleur and Weske (1959) have analysed the way judges interpret two-person interactions in which one of the stimuli is a negro; they too report that responses vary with the perceiver's attitude towards negroes. Triandis and Davis (1965) and Triandis, Loh and Levin (1966) have classified these attitudes in a way which successfully predicts perceptual judgments.

An interesting approach to affective perceptual reactions involves the measurement of galvanic skin response. Vidulich and Krevanick (1966) have observed that GSR during perception can be strongly affected by the judge's characteristics. They measured this emotional response as subjects studied a series of photographs. Judges were identified as prejudiced or unprejudiced towards negroes, and the photographs were intended to be of three kinds. Some were "critical" scenes (with negroes or with negro–white interactions), others were "control" photographs (similar to the critical ones but involving only white people), and the third category comprised neutral material (landscapes or buildings). It was observed that the prejudiced judges gave significantly higher mean GSR's to the critical photographs, but that no differences occurred for the other two kinds of stimulus material. This finding parallels results by Rankin and Campbell (1955) in *direct* perceptual situations; they observed similar variations in GSR according to whether the experimenter was a negro or a white person.

This is an aspect of the more general question of how a perceiver's need and value systems influence his judgments. Many years ago Ansbacher (1937) and Stephens (1936) showed that personal interests can affect estimates of the size of objects. Bartlett (1932) noted that judgments of soldiers' faces differed according to group membership of perceivers, and many subsequent studies have indicated that values, motivational and need structures can influence the perception of other people (e.g. Fensterheim and Tresselt, 1953; Fiedler, Warrington and Blaisdell, 1952; Mueller, 1966; Phillipson and Hopkins, 1964; Postman, Bruner and McGinnies, 1948; M. D. Vernon, 1961). We must assume that these influences are both upon the input selector and upon the processing centre, but evidence about the selection of inputs is uncommon. Work in the general area of perceptual defence (reviewed by W. P. Brown (1961) and Natsoulas (1965)) does, however, suggest the operation of value systems upon selection. Paivio and Steeves (1963) have looked at the question directly. Their subjects listened to two tape-recordings simultaneously. The contents of the recordings were to do with different Allport–Lindzey values and one recording was played to each ear. It was found that subjects tended to recall more of the material pertaining to the value on which they scored more highly. Studies of this kind with immediate relevance to *person* perception are lacking.

Several investigations have been reported into differences between "repressors" and "sensitizers" (see Altrocchi, 1961; Gordon, 1957; Lazarus, Erikson and Fonda, 1951). A "repressor" is taken to be a person who cannot verbalize unpleasant or threatening aspects of his experience, who scores highly on defensiveness scales but who has little manifest anxiety. Sensitizers have typically been found to show more differentiation between stimulus persons. In related fields Foulkes and Foulkes (1965) have drawn attention to perceptual differences related to a judge's dogmatism, and work on other personality variables such as self-esteem and self-acceptance has been reviewed by Shrauger and Altrocchi (1964).

Intelligence is a further stable characteristic which has attracted the attention of students of person perception. Taft's (1955) review presents consistent evidence for a positive correlation between I.Q. and the ability to judge personal characteristics, and V. B. Cline's (1955) work echoes these findings. We have already noted the relationship between intelligence and recognition of emotion. Gollin (1958), who studied children's impressions of a young stimulus person, found that the more intelligent judges inferred more from the filmed presentation and were better able to account for conflicting information about the stimulus.

A perceiver characteristic which has aroused considerable interest in recent years is complexity–simplicity of cognitive structure. It appears to be logically necessary from the definition of this attribute that it influences person perception. A "complex" person is one who employs a wide variety of ways to process information about his world, whereas the cognitively "simple" individual makes use of a limited set of processing techniques. Several more precise definitions of complexity–simplicity have been suggested, and these differ somewhat between themselves. Important formulations have been suggested by Bieri (1955), Harvey, Hunt and Schroder (1961), Schroder, Driver and Streufert (1967) and Scott (1962, 1965, 1966). Vannoy (1965) has questioned whether different measures of the characteristic are inter-related, and results of his factor-analytic investigation suggest that there may be more than one kind of complexity.

This view is explicitly held by Harvey, Hunt and Schroder (1961) and Schroder, Driver and Streufert (1967). Within their framework complexity is seen to derive from two aspects of cognitive structure. This structure is assessed first in terms of the number of dimensions a person typically employs ("differentiation") and secondly in terms of the way these dimensions are interrelated (flexibility of "integration"). Complexity is a function of both differentiation and integration. This approach to cognitive complexity places major emphasis on integration, whereas Bieri's measures, for example, lay greater stress on differentiation.

Despite these methodological and theoretical discrepancies, it is already possible to draw some conclusions about the ways in which complexity–simplicity is related to the perception of social stimuli. Several studies have indicated that conflicting information is handled differently by judges varying in complexity (e.g. Bieri and colleagues, 1966; Crano and Schroder, 1967; Harvey, 1967; Harvey and Schroder, 1963; Ware and Harvey, 1967); this point is taken up again in Chapter 6. Scott (1963) has shown that less complex judges tend to attain greater consistency in their judgments of national groupings.

Bieri and colleagues (1966) summarize a number of investigations and note that more complex judges are more accurate in recognizing differences between themselves and others* and that they perceive more conflict in T.A.T. situations and seek more information related to the stimulus person's inner state. Schroder, Driver and Streufert (1967) describe a series of studies of information processing by groups of varying cognitive complexity. They show that groups of individuals with lower complexity scores tend to generate fewer alternative or conflicting perspectives in their interactions with others. Low scorers are also more likely to overgeneralize to other situations an impression of a person which is gained at one stage in an interaction. And they are more likely to react to interpersonal disagreement in a bifurcated manner, that is either by completely accepting or by completely isolating new information which becomes available.

Before finishing our discussion of specific perceiver personality attributes, it should be noted that we have concentrated upon perception by normal judges. There is evidence that maladjusted subjects can differ markedly from normals in the way they perceive other people (see Shrauger and Altrocchi, 1964). That perceptual distortion is a concomitant of many types of mental abnormality is well known, and relevant examples from the fields of object and person perception are provided in most text books of psychopathology (see, for example, Arieti, 1959; Ittelson and Kutash, 1961; also Chapter 1, p. 43).

Rather than talk in terms of specific personality traits, many investigators have concerned themselves with a rather grosser measure of the characteristics of a perceiver. We thus find that many studies make use of the perceiver's self-concept, relating this to various aspects of the way others are perceived. That the impression a perceiver has of himself will affect his judgments of others has been commented upon by many writers (for example, R. Brown, 1965; Simons, 1966), and a body of research has accumulated on the way this influence exerts itself. There is evidence for a relationship between self-concept and tolerance of trait inconsistency (Foulkes and Foulkes, 1965), and many studies have examined the perception of people similar to oneself. One point at issue is whether a person is attracted to someone he judges to be similar to himself, and another question concerns the association between real similarity and assumed similarity. This complex topic —

* See also Bieri (1955) and Leventhal (1957).

rather beyond the scope of the present discussion — has been ably reviewed by Lott and Lott (1965) and Tagiuri (1958b). Some experiments have involved ingenious manipulations of the self-concept, invariably resulting in changes in the subjects' judgments of others (Bramel, 1962, 1963; Secord, Backman and Eachus, 1964). These are essentially studies of projection, and up-to-date reviews of research on this topic have been provided by Altrocchi (1965a), Campbell and coworkers (1964) and Murstein (1959).

In our research programme we have not been primarily interested in differential perceptions by various classes of perceiver, and in fact we have made a conscious effort throughout the programme to use homogeneous student subject panels so that results from different experiments are as far as possible comparable. But it is clear from the preceding discussion that the between-subject variations which occurred are at least partly capable of being systematized in terms of judges' stable characteristics. We have from time to time taken self-concept and personality measures from our subjects, and have related these to their perceptual responses. This comparatively minor aspect of our programme will be briefly described here. The measures we took were of three kinds: the perceiver's self-concept via the semantic differential and via the Adjective Check List, and his expressed ethnocentrism.

Self-perceptions on the Semantic Differential

Our principal instrument for measuring judgment is the semantic differential and it would therefore seem sensible to make use of this device to investigate the relationship between perceptions of self and of another person. In a study of this question ninety-seven subjects gave their perceptions of themselves ("as you actually are, not as you would like to be") on eight semantic differential scales. Some minutes later they were presented with a short newspaper report concerning a stimulus person, Mrs. Crain, after which they rated her on twelve semantic differential scales, including the eight used for the self-perceptions.* This particular stimulus person was chosen especially because she appeared to be a fairly neutral and unexciting character, and because relatively little information about her was available in the report presented to the subjects. Under these circumstances it might have been expected that any influence of perceivers' self-perceptions

* The perceptions of Mrs. Crain were elicited as part of Experiment 35, which is described in Chapter 7.

upon other-perceptions would be likely to reveal itself. We tested this possibility by carrying out product–moment correlations between the scale ratings for self and for Mrs. Crain over the eight scales. The highest correlation we obtained was $+0.12$ and the mean value of r was $+0.07$ (for male subjects $+0.05$ and for females $+0.10$). None of these figures approach significance and it would seem fairly certain that, at least as far as this investigation is concerned, subjects' self-concepts had no projective influence upon the impression they formed of a fairly neutral stimulus person. It may be that greater similarity between perceiver and stimulus is required before an effect of this type can be observed.

Self-perceptions on the Adjective Check List

We did of course make use of only a very small sample of semantic differential scales to measure self-concept, and it is possible that a more comprehensive measure of the way a person regards himself would reveal some relationship that remained undetected in the investigation just described. Our next step was to combine another measuring instrument and experimental set-up.

The Gough Adjective Check List has been described in Chapter 2, and in Chapter 3 we discussed its use in studies of perceivers' decision rules. At present we are interested in relating an aspect of subjects' self-perceptions on the A.C.L. to their perceptions of a stimulus person described either as "humane" or as "ruthless". It may be recalled from our discussion of Experiment 13 in Chapter 3 that varying the descriptive trait humane–ruthless in a fairly complex narrative account led to widespread differences in perception of a stimulus person. Two groups of subjects were involved in this experiment, one reading a narrative containing *humane* the other reading a version with *ruthless*. In the present analysis we divided each of these groups according to their previous responses to the A.C.L. The list we used contained both *humane* and *ruthless* and we wondered whether subjects who checked this dimension as applicable to themselves would be most affected by changes in the dimension between the narratives. A total of 59 subjects had checked one of the adjectives in their self-descriptions, and of these thirty read version one of the narrative ("humane") and twenty-nine read version two ("ruthless"). Analysis of the responses of these 59 judges from the two experimental groups showed that the average difference between mean semantic differential scale scores for the two narratives was 0·55. If possession of a trait were important in this respect, the difference between the narrative subgroups who did *not* check the dimension on the A.C.L. should be smaller than this. It is in fact 0·71 — a difference which is far from significant, but which clearly does not support our hypothesis.

There is, however, a further way in which A.C.L. information can be used. It may be recalled from Chapter 3 that we analysed self-description responses in terms of three of the dimensions isolated by Gough and Heilbrun (1965). The dimensions studied were Lability, Order and Intraception. We selected one of the stimulus persons to whom these subjects had responded — Mr. Harold Macmillan (Experiment 17) — and looked at the differences in conceptual judgments between high and low scorers on the three dimensions. As far as Lability was concerned, scores on this attribute were quite unrelated to judgments, but in the case of the other two traits marked variations were present. Illustrative results — for the characteristic of Intraception — are presented in Table 13.

It can be seen that the mean scale ratings of those subjects who scored highly on Intraception are in every case more positive than those of the low scorers. Furthermore, there are seven out of a possible thirteen

Table 13 Conceptual judgments of Macmillan by subjects of high and low Intraception

Scale	High Intraception ($N=23$)	Low Intraception ($N=23$)	Significance of the difference ($p<$)
Generous–ungenerous	6·57	5·42	0·02
Happy–unhappy	5·78	4·04	0·01
Goodnatured–irritable	6·91	5·23	0·01
Sociable–unsociable	7·04	5·69	0·02
Reliable–unreliable	6·74	6·50	n.s.
Popular–unpopular	6·00	4·31	0·01
Warm–cold	6·44	4·31	0·001
Important–insignificant	6·22	5·35	n.s.
Humane–ruthless	6·65	5·85	n.s.
Goodlooking–unattractive	4·70	3·69	n.s.
Altruistic–self-centred	6·04	4·27	0·01
Strong–weak	5·48	5·39	n.s.
Honest–dishonest	6·87	6·12	n.s.

significant differences between high and low scorers. A similar picture emerges if we consider the conceptions of subjects with varying scores on the personality dimension labelled "Order": in this case the high scorers have more positive mean scale scores in twelve out of thirteen cases and there are six significant mean differences. We can advance no reason why subjects displaying more Order (the tendency "to place special emphasis on neatness, organization and planning in one's activities")* and Intraception (the tendency "to engage in attempts to understand one's own behaviour or the behaviour of others")* should rate the stimulus person more positively or why high scorers on Lability should fail to show such an effect. High scorers on Order are said by Gough to be more cautious, and might therefore be expected to judge someone as more neutral: however, there is no evidence from our results that they do so. There is nothing in Gough's definitions of Intraception and Order to suggest that the two dimensions overlap, but we should point out that almost half of our subjects scored high on both Intraception and Order or low on both these dimensions. Nevertheless there is clearly some evidence here for a personality determinant of perception, and we await with optimism the further attention to this important type of variable by investigators with the energy and appropriate orientation.

A Note on Ethnocentrism

Our final comment upon the importance of personality factors in person perception concerns the relation between perceiver ethno- centrism and judgments of others. Experiment 1 (p. 70) showed that the factor structure of subjects' conceptions of political stimulus persons was the same for judges displaying different degrees of ethnocentrism. Using the same data — semantic differential conceptions of eleven national leaders — we can see whether there are any differences in the mean scale responses to the leaders which can be related to the E-scores of the judges. We compared the mean scale scores for subject groups of high, medium and low ethnocentrism ($N=31$, 33 and 33 in each case). The number of significant differences between these groups' conceptions is not high. Only twenty-two out of a total of 396† comparisons (5·5%) are significant. We cannot place much emphasis on individual findings within this small total, but it is

* The quotations are from Gough and Heilbrun (1965).
† There are three levels of ethnocentrism, eleven stimulus persons and twelve scales.

noteworthy that the pattern of differences suggested again that it is the identity of the stimulus which largely mediates the importance of personality characteristics. For most stimulus persons no differences related to ethnocentrism were found, whereas in certain cases (e.g. Castro) differences occurred on over 20% of scales.

This theme — the interaction of stimulus, context and perceiver's stable characteristics — is one we shall emphasize in the next section. Although it is possible to point to differences in perceptual outputs which arise from the operation of the "stable characteristics" component of our schematic model, this component does not by any means affect *all* perceptual outputs.

OTHER STABLE CHARACTERISTICS

As further illustration of differences between individuals which can affect their judgments we shall devote some attention next to differences in cultural background, age, class, occupation, and political and religious belief. Each of these characteristics of a perceiver is fairly "stable" in the sense of this term employed in Chapter 1, and each can be shown to affect perception and conception. The characteristics are to some extent interrelated, and they may be associated with variables we have already considered.

Each one has been studied from a variety of standpoints. Consider for instance cultural differences in person perception. To examine this topic thoroughly we would need to consider the work of anthropologists, sociologists, philosophers, economists, and psychologists of many inclinations. A comprehensive review would obviously be impossible here. Instead we shall just look briefly at each characteristic in order to exemplify still further the wide range of stable characteristics which may determine perception and which need to be understood before a complete simulation of the process (see Chapter 9) is feasible.

With these limitations in mind we may start by asking what can be said about *cultural differences*. We shall treat the term "culture" relatively loosely and look at differences between different national groupings as well as at differences between environments within a single nation. It is clear that in a general way a judge's culture has some influence upon his perceptual responses. For example, Segall, Campbell and Herskovits (1966) have recorded cultural variations in object perception. Furthermore, interpretations of projective test stimuli are found to vary with differences in cultural background (Fisher and Fisher, 1960; Henry and Spiro, 1953). Frymier (1958) has developed what is in effect an aurally-presented projective test. This comprises ambiguous non-verbal sounds (a man yawning, blowing his nose, a pen writing and so on) and listeners are required to say what they are hearing. He reports interesting differences between responses of children of different cultures. Northern urban children in the U.S.A. perceive more human sounds and sounds of inanimate objects than their southern rural counterparts. The latter tend to emphasize animals and mechanical objects.

People of different cultures may use quite different category systems, so that very different aspects of the stimulus information are selected. American observers of a baseball game may select quite different inputs from those of uninitiated foreigners. Bagby (1957) showed this effect in a binocular rivalry situation of the type described previously.* Pictures were of a bullfight or a baseball game, and clear differences between Mexican and American subjects were recorded. Hanfmann and Getzels (1955) have observed variations in category usage between American and Russian judges of other people, and Wallace (1962) has emphasized how differences in kinship categories can determine perception.

Many investigators have noted cultural variations in the inferences drawn from particular stimuli (see, for example, Bruner and Perlmutter, 1957). A famous example is Bartlett's (1932) observation that visiting Africans judged London traffic policemen to be extremely friendly because this was their customary inference from the input of a raised arm. Again, the similarity between overt characteristics may be perceived quite differently by different culture-groups. Malinowski (1923-4a, 1923-4b) reported that Trobriand islanders do not see resemblances among maternal kinsmen but may exaggerate resemblances in the paternal line (see Segall, Campbell and Herskovits, 1966, Chapter 2).

The evaluative component of perceptual responses can also vary between groups from different cultural backgrounds. Lawlor (1955) has studied preferences for pictorial designs and reports striking cross-cultural differences. Investigations of the way people are judged also testify to this. The early work of Bogardus (1928; see also the Chapter in Newcomb and Hartley, 1947) mapped out the way that various

---

* See p. 188; also the work by Paivio and Steeves (1957) described on p. 199, and the discussion of this technique in Chapter 9 (p. 360).

culture-groups respond differentially to others, and more recent studies of the cultural bases of evaluative judgments have been reported by Lambert, Anisfeld and Yeni-Komshian (1965), and Triandis and Triandis (1960). J. G. Martin (1964) has emphasized that cultural standards can be more important than racial differences. He investigated the judged beauty of ten negro women represented photographically and obtained measures from white Americans, negro Americans and negro Africans. The responses of the negro Americans and the white Americans were very similar, whereas the negro Africans seemed to apply quite a different set of standards. Fong (1965) examined judgments about expressive behaviour made by Chinese and American subjects and he too observed that responses came to approximate to the modal perception in the host country.

It seems to be a logical truth that unless nations perceived each other differently wars could not occur, and there can be no dispute that cultural differences may affect perceptual judgments. A global conceptualization of aspects of this which has come to be known as the Whorfian hypothesis is that different language systems give rise to different sorts of perceptual process (Fishman, 1960; Whorf, 1940; see also the chapter in Newcomb and Hartley, 1947). Much evidence has been accumulated in support of this hypothesis. Yet although there is ample indication of judgmental variations across cultures, so too is there evidence for remarkable consistency. The identification of emotion appears to be largely unaffected by the cultural background of a perceiver, as do dispositional judgments based upon facial cues (Triandis, 1964b). Studies of children's perception of others which are described elsewhere in this chapter yield the same results in different cultures (Fiedler and Hoffman, 1962; Kohn and Fiedler, 1961). And we have referred in Chapter 2 to many demonstrations that the factor structure of connotative meaning is more or less invariant across cultural groups* (e.g. Osgood, 1962; Suci, 1960; Tanaka, 1962; Triandis and Osgood, 1958). If we are to make any generalization at this stage it is that cultural factors sometimes affect person perception but that they sometimes do not. Such a conclusion is not very useful, and work is clearly required to collate and systematize the intercultural similarities and differences. Much has recently been achieved in this area and valuable reviews have been provided by Anastasi (1958),

---

* This does not necessarily mean that the average responses to a concept are the same; often they are not (e.g. Maclay and Ware, 1961).

Dennis (1951), French (1963), Kluckholm (1954), Tajfel (1968) and Triandis (1964a).

Just as the limits of cultural influence on person perception have yet to be set, so too have the consequences of *age differences* still to be specified with any precision. It is manifest that older judges perceive people in a manner different to younger ones: not only do they often select different inputs but they may also draw different inferences. Yet the nature of these variations has not been studied at all intensively. Psychological aspects of aging have in general aroused considerable interest, and major handbooks on the topic (Birren, 1959; Birren and colleagues, 1963; Shock, 1963) deal at length with changes in the perception of *physical* stimuli. In contrast to this emphasis, no mention at all is made of person perception. There is ample scope here for systematic research programmes.

Some studies which may have relevance to the perception of people are available. For example, Talland (1959a, 1959b) has investigated the ability to switch between different perceptual sets as a function of age. Older judges (65 years and above) can formulate sets readily, but they cannot vary them as easily as can younger people.

Korchin and Basowitz (1956) have compared performances of old and young adults upon an ambiguous stimulus test. In their study thirteen pictures were presented in succession, the stimulus gradually changing from a cat to a dog. Throughout the series older judges altered their perception later in the sequence and tended to have longer reaction times. Further studies of aging which might have relevance to person perception have identified changes in self-concepts and personality characteristics as individuals grow older (e.g. Kuhlen, 1964; Perlin and Butler, 1963). These changes may well be reflected in differential judgments of others.

One study by Secord and Muthard (1955) has examined dispositional judgments by subjects varying in age from 18 to 49.* Male judges were required to give their impressions of female stimuli presented photographically, and a significant age effect was observed. Older persons judged the stimuli to be more temperamental, aggressive, easygoing, talkative and so on, tending on the whole to make more positive responses than subjects in the 18 to 21 age range. But apart from this study little attention appears to have been paid to age differences between adults in their judgments of each other.

* Comments on this investigation also appear on p. 188.

When we turn to variations among children we find that comparatively more work has been carried out. One aspect of person perception in very young children has aroused particular interest. This is the "smiling response". Even in their tenth week of life children may respond to faces by smiling, but this response is at first an indiscriminate reaction to all faces or simulated faces (e.g. Spitz and Wolf, 1946). Even fierce, supposedly frightening faces will elicit smiles, as will models with only the essential facial characteristics. This form of perceptual response becomes gradually more specific with increasing age as the child learns to discriminate between other people, and predictable variations between children from different environments have been demonstrated (Ambrose, 1961).

In conspicuous contrast to research with adults many of the investigations of person perception in children have dealt with judgments of *overt* characteristics. Several studies have dealt with young children's ability to recognize shapes, patterns, pictures, faces and so on when these are presented in an unaccustomed orientation (upside-down, for instance). Ghent (1960) reported that three- to four-year-old children had difficulty in identifying pictures of a boat, clown, horse or wagon when these are inverted, but that five- to seven-year-olds were quite capable of this. Other studies using patterns and pictures have been described by Ghent (1961), Ghent and Bernstein (1961) and Hunton (1955); and Brooks and Goldstein (1963) used as their stimuli photographs of faces of each child's friends. In all cases an increase in ability with age was noted.

Another group of experiments has examined the *amount* of stimulus material required for recognition of faces. Goldstein and Mackenberg (1966) studied the accuracy with which children could recognize classmates' pictures when only a part of the photographed face was visible. They showed that this ability clearly increased between ages four and ten, and that in general the upper part of the face provided the most information. To check whether accuracy in this task may have depended upon length of acquaintance or on evaluative judgments, Chance, Goldstein and Schicht (1967) repeated the investigation with appropriate modifications. Once again significant age effects were observed, but accuracy was unaffected by how long the children had known each other. The shortest time of acquaintance studied was in fact eight weeks, and it may be that this variable is in practice relevant when shorter periods are examined. In general it was seen that friends' faces were better identified than those of others, but this variable interacted with age in that friendship became progressively less important for older subjects.

Parallel investigations have dealt with the development of ability to make judgments about other fairly overt characteristics. Kogan, Stevens and Shelton (1961) have studied the way children rank photographs of stimulus persons according to their age. Even four-year-olds are very adept at this. Jahoda (1959) has examined judgments about social class membership. He has developed a pictorial test of the ability to discern class differences, and notes a steady increase in this ability between the ages of six and ten. The perception of class differences by *adolescents* has been studied by Ausubel and Shiff (1955) and Centers (1950). Similar investigations into the perception of racial differences have been made, and early work is reviewed by Clark and Clark (1947). They used dolls as their stimuli and reported increases in accuracy of identification from ages three to seven. But even the three-year-olds were correct in 77% of their judgments. Several other workers have looked into this issue, and broadly similar results have emerged from studies by Goodman (1952), Lambert and Taguchi (1956), Morland (1958), Springer (1950) and Stevenson and Stewart (1958). Techniques to measure children's perception of which role behaviour is appropriate to boys or to girls have been developed by Hartley and Hardesty (1964), and Gates's early study (Gates, 1923) drew attention to the way emotional recognition improves as children grow from three to fourteen.

Several of these investigations also recorded changes in the evaluative component of perceptual judgments. Ethnic prejudice for instance has been seen to develop relatively early. A study by Taylor and Thompson (1955) examined evaluative judgments of a different kind. Line drawings of faces served as stimuli, and distance between eyes, length of nose and so on were systematically varied. Judges were between seven and twenty-two years old, and changes in preference in the direction of typical adult judgments were observed with increasing age. Other studies have indicated that children perceive themselves and others progressively less favourably as they grow older. Fiedler and Hoffman (1962) and Kohn and Fiedler (1961) have elicited semantic differential judgments of several adult stimuli as well as self-perceptions, and report that with increasing age a child becomes more critical of himself and others. Against this, however, a developmental study of responses to the

H

Rosenzweig Picture-Frustration Test revealed a lower frequency of inwardly-directed blame in older children (Stoltz and Smith, 1959). Kagan (1956) has observed that ten-year-olds tend to see their same-sex parent as relatively more threatening than their other parent, whereas this differentiation does not occur in six-year-old judges. Children's selection of inputs with a content of violence has been examined by Moore (1966). He used a binocular rivalry situation (see p. 188) and observed a statistically significant linear increase with age in the amount of violence which is perceived.

The operation of the processing centre is also likely to be sensitive to the age of the perceiver. Gollin (1958) has reported changes in the kinds of inference drawn by children from eleven to sixteen years. And as far as accuracy of person perception is concerned, studies by Dymond, Hughes and Raabe (1952) and Burns and Cavey (1957) show significant increases from seven to eleven and three to six respectively.

Several investigations can be brought together in terms of their relevance to changes in cognitive structure with age, and especially in the structure used to process inputs about people. It is helpful to think of cognitive structure in terms of articulation, differentiation and integration (see pp. 200 and 370). "Differentiation" refers to the number of different dimensions a person has available to him, so that a differentiated perceptual structure is one made up of a lot of judgmental dimensions. "Integration" refers to the way these dimensions are combined; this is only partly dependent upon the number of dimensions available (differentiation) since dimensions may or may not be used in combination. And the third aspect of cognitive structure — "articulation" — is the fineness of discrimination along individual dimensions; a dichotomy (e.g. *old–young*) is an unarticulated scale, whereas *old–middleaged–young* and *very old–old–middleaged–young adult–teenager–child* are each more articulated.

It is of course to be expected that cognitive structure will increase in complexity during childhood. We anticipate that in general children's judgments of others will become more articulated, more differentiated and more integrated (cf. Harvey, Hunt and Schroder, 1961). The research by Fiedler referred to above (Fiedler and Hoffman, 1962; Kohn and Fiedler, 1961) is relevant to our anticipation, although it was not conducted within this theoretical framework. Their studies revealed differences in articulation between the ages of twelve and seventeen: older children were more sensitive to differences between stimulus persons on the semantic differential scales which the investigators provided. Signell (1966) has also reported that articulation in person perception increases between nine and sixteen. Her study was designed to examine differentiation and integration as well as articulation and she reports no variations in differentiation but possibly significant increases in integration.*

It appears from quite different investigations by Yarrow and Campbell (1963) and by Thorpe and Swartz (1965) that these variations in the integrative aspects of cognitive structure may be reliable ones. Yarrow and Campbell studied the types of categories which children employ in their judgments of others. Eight- to thirteen-year-old children were encouraged to talk freely about a close friend, and their responses were subsequently classified. No differences in category usage itself were found which could be related to age, and we may interpret this in terms of an absence of change in differentiation. But there were some significant variations in complexity and interconnectedness of response — in effect variations in what we have here called integration. In the other relevant study Thorpe and Swartz obtained responses to a projective test — the Holtzman inkblot technique — from subjects ranging from four to twenty-two years of age. They emphasize in their report that older judges generate more integrated impressions than younger ones in their "human content" responses.

We may conclude from these several research programmes that articulation and integration can be seen to increase during later childhood, but that differentiation remains unchanged. We might wonder whether the changes in differentiation which clearly take place in childhood have in fact already occurred in the earlier years.

Many other writers have dealt indirectly with the way children perceive other people. For example, much of Piaget's contribution (e.g. 1929, 1932) is in effect an account of changes in person perception as children grow older. But monographs purportedly dealing with "perception" typically fail to mention judgments of people. An illustrative case is Wohlwill's (1960) otherwise valuable review of the development of perceptual responses; this devotes no space at all to person perception.

* Signell's investigation also embraced conceptual judgments of nations. Although the main age difference in judgments of people was in articulation, this aspect of nation-judgments did not vary with age. Instead, the differences which emerged were towards greater differentiation and integration. She discusses this provocative finding in terms of different learning processes.

The varied studies summarized in this section cover a wide area, but are not yet in sufficient depth for many firm conclusions about person perception to be made.* It is often difficult to estimate the relative importance of parallel increases in intelligence and cognitive complexity, and perhaps one research approach would be to concentrate further upon this question. But one fact is clear: increasing age does not result in "across the board" changes in person perception. Only some aspects of the process change as a function of age, and only certain age ranges are relevant to even those aspects. This can readily be seen in studies which take semantic differential measurements of the way several concepts are judged at different ages (e.g. DiVesta, 1966; Donahoe, 1961; Maltz, 1963). Certain age changes are associated with changes in judgments of certain concepts on certain scales. This is of course far from surprising, but it does point to the question — which kinds of changes occur when? At present we know very little about this.

Another fairly stable characteristic of the perceiver which might enter into person perception is *political belief.* We expect, however, that this will be relevant to only a fairly circumscribed set of judgments — those pertinent to political personalities and systems. We have reviewed in Chapter 2 (pp. 91, 97) several studies of the validity of the semantic differential which concerned judgments by people of varying political leanings. It is clear that different affiliations give rise to different impressions of political persons and concepts. This was shown to be the case for conceptual judgments and for indirect perceptions mediated by written accounts: left-wing persons perceive politicians in a manner different from right-wing ones. (See also Warr, Schroder and Blackman, 1968.)

Jahoda (1954) has reported similar effects for photographically presented stimulus persons, and Berelson, Lazarsfeld and McPhee (1954) have observed that perceivers often judge the candidate of their choice to have views more near their own than is in fact the case. Cooper's (1955) subjects had to form judgments about written reports of a controversy involving a Republican politician. He observed that their evaluations were in accord with their assumptions about the political views of the writer; for example, Democrat subjects gave higher ratings to reports they thought came from Democrat writers than to those thought to emanate from Republicans.

* A recently-published volume by Lambert and Klineberg (1967) will unquestionably help here. We have unfortunately not been able to obtain a copy before closing this chapter.

Although political belief is a stable characteristic which we must take into account when interpreting person perception, it is, however, a characteristic which only mediates certain types of judgment. To take an extreme illustration, it is unlikely that a person's political outlook will influence his judgment of overt characteristics such as hair colour or height. Perhaps more surprisingly, however, we may also note that a judge's political belief does not affect his responses to *all* political figures. Although we found in Experiment 1 that Conservative and Labour supporters differed markedly in their conceptions of Wilson and Johnson (and incidentally of Castro), this personal characteristic was not related to differences in judgments about any of the other eight stimuli. Once again then, the stable characteristic is one which does mediate differences in perceptual outputs, but only outputs about a restricted range of stimuli. The present problem is to identify this range.

A major difficulty here is that political belief is of course associated with other perceiver characteristics. Eysenck (1954) has observed differences in "tough-mindedness" between people of different political outlooks,* and clear variations in E-scale and F-scale scores and in dogmatism have been recorded by Leventhal, Jacobs and Kudirka (1964), Rokeach (1960) and Warr, Faust and Harrison (1967). We cannot always be sure which independent variable we are discussing — political belief or a personality characteristic. The first of these is also related to other stable characteristics — notably socio-economic class and occupation.

What about differences in *social class*? There are very few investigations which examine this factor in judgments of the kind studied throughout this book, and we need to turn to related topics to find evidence with indirect bearing upon person perception. For example, there are apparently class differences in self-concept (Klausner, 1953; Wylie, 1961), and we might assume that these are related to differences in perception. Several studies of what is better termed *social* perception (see Chapter 1, p. 2) have indicated that the socio-economic class of a perceiver is related to his judgments of magnitude (Bruner and Goodman, 1947; Bruner and Postman, 1947). And it is also known that middle-class individuals use descriptive terms which differ from those employed by lower-class people (Schatzman and Strauss, 1955). This

* Some of Eysenck's conclusions have not passed without criticism. See the articles by Christie, Eysenck, and Rokeach and Hanley in *Psychological Bulletin*, 53 (1956).

suggests the possibility of a restricted form of the Whorfian hypothesis (see pp. 208, 385) — that linguistic differences exist between social classes within a society and that these differences are reflected in variations in the way experience is organized. Bernstein (e.g. 1962) has reported studies of this possibility which are on the whole in its favour, and Warren (1966) has noted some relevant class differences in conceptual judgments.

It is clear that a person's perception of the class structure of his society is dependent upon his own social standing. Lewis (1964) has observed that lower class judges are aware of fewer levels in the class structure than are their higher class counterparts. From their investigation of the perceived bases of class distinction Davis, Gardner and Gardner (1941) reported marked differences in outlook. For example, upper-class persons tend to emphasize time and permanence as the basis of social status, whereas lower-class judges place their major stress upon financial considerations. Jahoda (1959) observed that middle-class children were on the whole more able to identify class-related cues than were lower-class children.

Several workers have examined class differences in responding to projective tests. Stoltz and Smith (1959) pointed out that children from different classes made different interpretations of the Rosenzweig Picture-Frustration Test; lower-class judges tended to lay blame upon adult frustrators whereas higher-class children were more likely to blame themselves. Riessman and Miller (1958) have reviewed a number of studies of this kind in which adults responded to Rorschach and Thematic Apperception Tests. Prejudice is another topic which has been examined in terms of the social class of a judge. On the whole it appears that lower-class people are likely to exhibit more anti-negro prejudice (Simon, 1963) and that they score more highly on measures of ethnocentrism (Warr, Faust and Harrison, 1967). These differences will be reflected in some interclass differences in person perception.

A related characteristic — the judge's *occupation* — deserves mention at this point. Once again there are very few investigations concerned with the way this may be associated with person perception. Studies which have compared the perceptual processes of different occupational groups have usually treated this question as peripheral to their main aim. An example is the report by Zax, Cowen and Peter (1963) of judgments by nuns and female students. Rather more investigations have had the slightly scurrilous aim of comparing psychologists' accuracy in person perception with that of other occupations. An early instance was the study by Luft (1950), which revealed no significant differences in accuracy of clinical diagnosis between psychiatrists, clinical psychologists, social workers and physical scientists. V. B. Cline's results (1955) may have increased the professionals' self-respect, since he concluded that they were at least more successful than college students; Taft (1955) was not so sure.

The final stable perceiver characteristic to be considered in this section is *religious belief*. Books on psychological aspects of religion (e.g. Argyle, 1958; Clark, 1958; P. E. Johnson, 1959; Spinks, 1963) do not concern themselves at all with person perception, and this omission is perhaps a fair indication of the state of our knowledge in this area. A few isolated studies are, however, available. Bieri and Lobeck (1961) and McGrath (1962) have examined differences in self-concept between religious groups; and there are some documented accounts of how judgments may differ according to religious ideology (e.g. Robinson, 1965; Thomas, 1963). Long (1965) has provided evidence suggesting that Catholics tend to show a greater acceptance of other people than do Protestants. But even without this small number of research reports it is clear that religious belief and values may be associated with particular forms of judgment; anyone familiar with professional and social rivalry between religious groups in large cities can have no doubt about this.

Nevertheless we may once again note that this perceiver characteristic affects only specific types of judgment. Fiedler and Hoffman (1962) detected no differences in the way Calvinist and Catholic children conceive their parents and teachers, and there must be many a failure to discover religious differences in judgment which remains unpublished. What we need to know is what types of judgment are sensitive to differences in religious belief. Many input selection procedures and decision rules will be quite unaffected by this stable characteristic, whereas others will depend heavily on it. It does seem that the latter perceptual processes are those which are somehow relevant to the activities of a religious group to which the individual belongs or holds an attitude about. When we can measure relevance of this kind we shall be in a better position to set down the consequences for person perception of particular religious affiliations.

We have been especially interested in one facet of this general question. Suppose that we elicit judgments to which religious belief clearly is relevant. What dimensions of these judgments will be affected by this belief? As an illustration, consider judgments about a Catholic priest made by Catholic and Anglican perceivers. These judgments are in general likely to be influenced by the belief of the perceivers, but we may still ask which dimensions of judgment will reflect the differences in religious affiliation. If we use a set of semantic differential scales to measure perception, will the religion-linked differences occur on all scales, only on Evaluative ones, only on Potency ones, or according to some other principle? It is an elaboration of this question with which the following investigation is concerned.

Experiment 22

In this study we looked at differences attributable to the perceiver and at those attributable to the stimulus person. Three groups of undergraduate subjects were employed, a Catholic group ($N=48$) an Anglican group ($N=48$) and a group with heterogeneous outlooks ($N=79$). This last group comprised judges who admitted to no religious affiliation, and we shall somewhat imprecisely label it as a "neutral" group.

As in other experiments described in this book, we requested subjects to read through a written report and then to indicate their judgment of its central figure on semantic differential scales. In this case the report was a 350-word typewritten account, supposedly coming from an unspecified newspaper, and subjects were asked to make dispositional judgments (see p. 8) on the thirteen scales used in Experiments 11 and 13. The report concerned the position of a church official within a small community, and contained details of his opinions and attitudes as well as of his standing with local residents. We used two versions of this report, these differing only in that the stimulus was identified in one as a Roman Catholic priest and in the other as an Anglican parson.

The composition of subject groups was as follows:

		Perceivers			
		Catholic	Neutral	Anglican	Overall
Stimuli	Catholic	24	43	24	91
	Anglican	24	36	24	84
	Overall	48	79	48	175

It will be seen that in analysing the responses of these subjects we had available six sets of data for each of the thirteen semantic differential scales. The sets of responses *to each scale* were submitted to a two-way analysis of variance, so that for each of the thirteen scales we were able to examine the influence of the stimulus person, the influence of the perceiver, and the interaction between these two influences.

Consider first the role of the stimulus person. When we disregard the variations between perceivers, do we observe differences in the way the Catholic and Anglican stimuli are perceived? In none of the thirteen analyses of variance is the F-ratio pertaining to the stimulus statistically significant. Taking our subjects as a whole then, the two stimuli are not perceived differently.

What of the responses of the three subject groups, disregarding the differences in stimulus identity? In the case of four of the scales significant differences were observed. In three instances (*altruistic–self-centred, profound–shallow* and *generous–ungenerous*) the Anglican judges tended to perceive the stimulus (irrespective of his identity) more positively, and in the fourth case (*important–unimportant*) the neutral group gave the highest responses.

But of major interest is the interaction term in these analyses. We anticipate a perceivers-by-stimuli interaction, such that Anglican judges tend to perceive the Anglican stimulus relatively more positively than the Catholic stimulus and the Catholic judges tend to perceive the Catholic stimulus relatively more positively than the Anglican. Is this expectation borne out? The interaction F-ratio in five analyses is significant beyond the 0.05 level, and in a further two cases $p < 0.10$. There is clearly a very strong tendency for differential subjects-by-stimuli judgments to occur. Furthermore this effect is of the kind suggested above, rather than being for instance due to very deviant responses of the neutral group. Visual clarification of this is provided in Figure 4 (p. 220). We have there set out the overall mean responses to the seven scales on which a significant interaction effect was present. The scales involved are *altruistic–self-centred* ($p < 0.05$), *generous–ungenerous* ($p < 0.01$), *goodnatured–irritable* ($p < 0.05$), *humane–ruthless* ($p < 0.01$), *just–unjust* ($p < 0.10$), *kind–unkind* ($p < 0.05$) and *polite–blunt* ($p < 0.10$).

So it can be seen that the religious belief of a perceiver affects his perception of religion-linked stimuli. But the question raised in introducing this study requires us to take our analysis a step further. We wondered *which* perceptual dimensions are most likely to be subject to

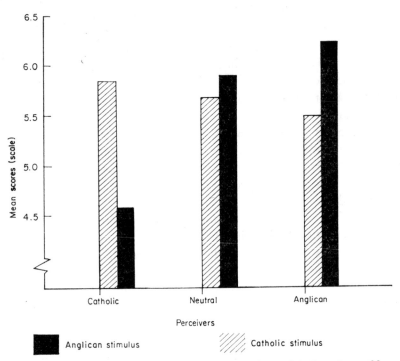

Figure 4   The interaction between perceivers and stimuli in Experiment 22

this kind of influence. At the back of our minds was the idea that religious affiliation is liable to influence mainly the evaluative component of person perception. It seemed possible that this perceiver characteristic does not operate upon the attribution of relatively non-evaluative properties such as activity, strength and shallowness. Support for this idea comes from inspection of the scales listed above which exhibited significant interaction effects: these all look to be evaluative dimensions, especially when contrasted with the six other scales (*active–passive, direct–evasive, important–unimportant, profound–shallow, quick–slow, strong–weak*). But to be certain of this we need to subject the responses to factor analysis and to relate the obtained factor loadings to interaction *F*-ratios from the analyses of variance.

The impressions of the 175 subjects have accordingly been analysed by the principal components method. Two significant components are present in these data, the first of which is clearly an Evaluative one.*

* Component loadings (rotated to a Varimax solution) are: *humane–ruthless*, 0·81; *kind–cruel*, 0·76; *goodnatured–irritable*, 0·69; *generous–ungenerous*, 0·69; *just–unjust*, 0·65;

If our expectation is correct, that religious belief influences mainly evaluative judgments, we should find that a scale's loading on this Evaluative factor is closely associated with the F-ratio of the interaction term in the previous analyses. The rank-correlation (rho) between these F-values and the Evaluative factor loadings (Varimax rotation)* is $+0.90$. The more a semantic differential scale is an evaluative one, the more likely is it to be subject to variations in responses depending upon the religious affiliation of the judge and of the stimulus person.

This is an interesting finding, and one which might have relevance to other stable characteristics of the perceiver. For instance, do differential perceptions based upon social class also exhibit this phenomenon? It is evident that many more investigations of this type are needed.

Recapitulation

In this section we have pointed to several relatively stable characteristics of a perceiver which may influence the way he forms impressions of other people. We have described investigations into the role of cultural background, the judge's age, and his political belief, social class, occupation and religious ideology. We have had difficulty in drawing conclusions about these factors, mainly because of the paucity of studies in the area.

The area is nevertheless an important one. An understanding of these perceiver characteristics is required before a complete explanation or adequate simulation of person perception may be attempted. The difficulty at present is that we cannot specify the sphere of influence of each factor. It is manifest that cultural differences or variations in political belief do not give rise to differences in all facets of person perception, but we do not yet know to which aspects of the process they are relevant. To learn about this we need to take more interest in studies which *fail* to find differences between perceivers; only when this is done will we be able to delimit the range of operation of each of the characteristics.

One original experiment has been presented in the section. In this we examined judgments of a stimulus which was clearly relevant to the perceiver characteristic under discussion. We were able to demonstrate

---

altruistic–self-centred, 0·52; *profound–shallow*, 0·38; *polite–blunt*, 0·29; *direct–evasive*, 0·28; *quick–slow*, 0·07; *strong–weak*, 0·07; *active–passive*, 0·04; *important–unimportant*, 0·04.

 * Without rotation this *rho* value is $+0.74$

clear subject-by-stimulus interaction effects, and furthermore to learn that these effects were mainly associated with the evaluative component of perception.

THE PERCEIVER'S CURRENT STATE

We turn now to another component of the perceptual system outlined in Chapter 1 which can mediate differences in the judgments made by different perceivers. The stable characteristics of a perceiver considered in the previous section may be contrasted with his transitory state at the time of perception. No doubt these two perceiver characteristics ultimately constitute a dimension rather than a dichotomy, and no doubt they mutually influence each other; but for purposes of analysis and exposition it is convenient to distinguish between them.

Under the heading "perceiver's current state" we wish to include all transitory influences with labels like set, *Einstellung*, *Aufgabe*, emotional state, goals, intentions, motivation and even expectancies which arise during a perceptual sequence. It appears preferable to group these notions on the basis of their impermanence and to contrast them with relatively stable attributes, rather than to try to separate "set" from "intention" or "motivation" as has sometimes been done.

One aspect of the perceiver's current state has been studied by Lundy (1956). He observed differences in direct person perception according to whether subjects were paying attention to themselves and their own behaviour or whether they were concentrating more upon other people in the group. Perceivers were less accurate when attending to themselves, and in this condition more projection was present in their judgments of others.

Several investigations have shown that the extent to which a perceiver is emotionally involved in a situation can affect the way he perceives that situation (Jones and Davis, 1965; Sherif and Sherif, 1967). Indeed this notion is behind much T-group training: it is clear that in general terms emotional involvement can crucially influence the way other members of a T-group are perceived (e.g. Bion, 1961; Bradford, Gibb and Benne, 1964). This phenomenon has been studied in a controlled investigation by Pepitone (1950). He examined high school children's judgments about members of an interviewing panel, and varied their involvement by leading some to believe that the panel had power to reward them whereas others were not made aware of this possibility. The reward in Pepitone's study was a ticket to an important basketball game, and post-manipulation measures showed clearly that for his subjects this was a very involving prospect. Members of the panel were judged differently by perceivers in the two conditions, and it was noted that perceptual distortions tended to be in a direction which made the potential reward seem more likely to those subjects in the involved group. One aspect of a study by Jones and coworkers (1959) also revealed differences related to the emotional involvement of a judge. Perceivers who were involved in a situation selected characteristics and made inferences which were different from those employed by subjects who were merely bystanders.

The motivational characteristics studied by McClelland and his colleagues are assumed to vary from situation to situation. For instance need for achievement (nAch) is not only treated as a fairly stable characteristic, but also as one which depends upon the present context (Atkinson, 1958; McClelland, 1961; McClelland and colleagues, 1953). Let us at this point look at the way these variables influence person perception, noting that they also shade into what we have termed "stable characteristics". As well as nAch we shall be concerned with need for affiliation (nAffil) and need for power (nPower).

It appears that these need structures may be validly and reliably measured by projective techniques, in particular the Thematic Apperception Test. They are therefore by definition reflected in characteristic ways of perceiving the social environment. It is logically necessary that high nAch subjects (according to the operational definition) make episodic judgments from pictures which are different to those of low scorers. But several studies have also been reported of other ways in which these variables influence person perception.

For example, Atkinson and Walker (1956) manipulated nAffil in an experimental setting. One group of subjects ("aroused") was required to respond to a number of sociometric rating tasks before taking part in an investigation of perception, whereas other subjects responded to the main task in neutral classroom conditions. The main task involved what was in effect a measure of input selection. Four images were simultaneously presented to subjects by means of a tachistoscope. Presentation was sufficiently brief for the stimuli not to be recognizable, but one of the four was in fact a face or group of faces. Subjects were asked to report which of the four pictures appeared to them to stand out most. Results showed that the "aroused" group selected more facial inputs than did the "neutral" group, suggesting that the perceiver's current level of nAffil can determine the social cues from the environment which he employs.

Berlew (1961) has been interested in whether accuracy of episodic person perception varies with the level of motivation. He wondered whether the Yerkes–Dodson principle is applicable to judgments of others. This principle suggests that moderate motivation is optimal for efficient performance of complex tasks so that there is a U-shaped relationship between motivation and efficiency.* Berlew measured motivation in terms of a combination of nAch, nAffil and nPower scores, and found that this relationship did indeed obtain. High and low scorers were both less accurate than perceivers with moderate motivation. Berlew and Williams (1964) have looked at this question using a single group of subjects in situations of different levels of motive-arousal. They observed that the same U-shaped relationship holds across situations.

A related facet of the perceiver's current state has been studied by Murray and by Feshbach and his colleagues. They have been interested in a judge's emotional state, particularly in the fact that a frightened person tends to distort his judgments of other persons. Murray (1933), in a delightful if not faultless experiment, observed that frightened 11-year-old girls (after two games of Murder) judged photographs of adults to be more malicious and threatening than after they had been in a "pleasure-invoking situation". He described this effect as "complementary projection" — judging that other people have characteristics which complement, or in a sense justify, one's own feelings. Complementary projection is distinguished from the more frequently noted "supplementary projection", in which one's own characteristics are attributed to a stimulus person.† Both types of projection were observed in older subjects by Feshbach and Singer (1957). They used electric shocks to generate fear, and recorded impressions of a person represented in a film. The anxious group of subjects attributed both more fear and more hostility to this stimulus person.

Emotional state can thus be seen to influence person perception. But

* This general issue has also been studied recently by Schroder, Driver and Streufert (1967).

† Notice that in the terms suggested in Chapter 1 (p. 8) these forms of projection may be both episodic (pertaining to a single episode of behaviour) or dispositional (relatively unrestricted judgments).

its influence may be specified more closely. In a later study Feshbach and Feshbach (1963) showed that the type of projection which accompanies emotional arousal depends to a great extent upon the stimulus person. Frightened boys tended to see other *boys* as more fearful (supplementary projection), whereas they were more likely to attribute malicious, fear-arousing characteristics to *adult* stimuli (complementary projection). Another factor mediating the importance of emotional state is whether the subject is in a position to express his emotion. Feshbach and Singer (1957) report tentative evidence that suppressing emotion leads to more projection, and Feshbach (1963) in a study of positive affect (happiness) observes this still more clearly. An interaction with the nature of the stimulus was once again observed in this latter study. Loeb and coworkers (1964) have carried out an analogous experiment with psychiatric patients; and they too noted that projection varied with both the state of the perceiver and the nature of the stimulus.

Another interesting set of investigations concerns perceiver sets which are less affective and more cognitive. Jones and Daugherty (1959), for example, have examined whether anticipated interaction with someone affects the way he is judged. Their subjects listened to tape-recordings of stimulus persons and then recorded their impressions. Some perceivers were told that they would have the opportunity to meet the person afterwards whereas others believed this to be impossible. Differences occurred in the judgments made by these two groups.

Zajonc (1960) has suggested that differences in perception may arise from different "tuning sets" — sets to transmit the impression to other people or to receive still more information. Cohen (1961) has looked at this question. He studied differences between "transmitters" and "receivers", and observed that subjects set to pass on their impressions to others developed significantly more simple, one-sided impressions from a list of adjectives containing discrepant material than did a group of receivers. Leventhal (1962) has also reported that this type of set can influence the way judges organize their perceptual outputs; in his study too the transmitters formed simpler impressions than the receivers.

Experiment 23

These investigations of "cognitive tuning" have manipulated

perceivers' set in terms of whether or not they are later to describe their *impressions* of a stimulus person. A related type of tuning set is an expectancy that one is to describe what *happened* in an event. Some perceivers (reporters or raconteurs, for example) who are later to describe a person's behaviour might perhaps perceive it differently from those who do not have to remember it. We have examined this question by presenting stimulus information which some judges knew they would subsequently have to recall.

Typewritten copies of a newspaper report about a local shopkeeper served as stimulus material. Indirect perceptions of this person were recorded on the thirteen semantic differential scales used in Experiment 10 (p. 128). Forty-seven undergraduate subjects were told before they read the report that they would be required to recall it before registering their impressions. Approximately one minute after the article had been read they wrote down the item as they recalled it. After this they gave their episodic impressions of the stimulus person. A further fifty-nine subjects gave their perceptions in the normal way, with no mention being made of recall. However, when they had completed their judgments of the stimulus person, they too were requested to recall the passage.

The semantic differential perceptions of the two groups were compared to see whether set to recall (and indeed recall itself) influenced subsequent judgments. We anticipated that the "recall group" would have been set to emphasize the salient points of the material and would in consequence give more extreme perceptual judgments. In fact, however, the average responses of the two groups were in every case almost identical, and our expectancy was clearly unsupported. This outcome may possibly be due to the nature of the stimulus material we used, which was not very complicated. Accuracy of recall was on the whole very high and it could be that material which is less easily assimilated would reveal the phenomenon.

This aspect of the design may also be responsible for a failure to obtain significant results in an extension of the study. A further sample of subjects later judged the stimulus person on the same scales as did these judges. But each of the latter perceivers read a different set of stimulus material — this being one of the recall protocols from the previous sample. We expected that these stimulus inputs would on the whole contain the essentials of the original material without their ramifications, so that the second set of perceptions would be similar to the first ones but rather less varied. In practice, however, both the means and the variances of the two groups of perceivers were almost the same.*

The results of this experiment warrant no further discussion here. But the study does point to an interesting line of research. Allport and Postman (1945) and Bartlett (1932) have described the systematic changes which occur when information, ideas or gossip are passed on from person to person. This area of study might benefit if measures of perceptual judgments were taken in addition to the more customary recall measures.

We turn now to the final group of studies to be considered in this section. These arise from Jones's discussion of "inferential sets". Jones and Thibaut (1958) and Jones and Davis (1965) emphasize that in interacting with other people the goals of an interaction determine the information we select and the inferences we draw. In the terms of Chapter 1 the goals of the interaction influence the perceiver's current state and thereby the input selector and the processing centre. Of particular note is the classification of interaction goals which Jones and Thibaut suggest. They argue that the goals which give rise to inferential sets may be of three kinds: "the facilitation of personal goal attainment, the deterministic analysis of personality, and the application of social sanctions" (p. 159). Let us look at these in turn.

The first goal — to satisfy one's own aims — is said to give rise to a "value-maintenance" set. This set induces the perceiver to select information relevant to what the other person can do for him and to draw inferences from this information which concern the stimulus person's duty or ability to help him. A value-maintenance set is likely to result in a perceiver emphasizing aspects of the other person which will assist or hinder his own personal goal attainment. The second goal — to understand another person — is rather different. This generates a "causal-genetic" set, in which the background, the characteristics and experiences of a stimulus became particularly salient and central. The final goal — to apply social sanctions — is said to lead to a "situation-matching" set. This set involves the perceiver in judging the appropriateness of the behaviour he is observing and in concentrating

* Rather optimistically we went on to correlate scale responses from parallel subjects in each sample. In this analysis the judgments of a subject were correlated with those of the subject who later read his recall protocol. The average correlation across the thirteen scales was $+0.02$.

upon the normative aspects of the other person's behaviour.

This categorization of inferential sets is an interesting one of obvious plausibility. To assess its validity we need to conduct experiments in which the stimulus material is constant and in which the set adopted by perceivers is manipulated. It should be possible to demonstrate that under these conditions judgments from constant stimulus material vary between the perceivers. Jones and deCharms (1957) have attempted this demonstration. They induced a value-maintenance set in members of some discussion groups by ensuring that the behaviour of a stimulus person was of personal relevance to them. This was achieved by making the possibility of reward dependent on the performance of the group as a whole and by ensuring that the stimulus person was seen to be responsible for the group's failure. The stimulus person in these conditions was seen as significantly less dependable than he was in a situation when a value-maintenance set had not been induced. In this latter situation an individual's reward was contingent upon his own behaviour (and not that of the group) so that the performance of the stimulus was of less personal relevance to the judges.

Jones and deCharms conclude that the inferences drawn from behaviour vary with the perceived relevance of that behaviour, and that a value maintenance set can be seen to depend upon the behaviour being relevant to one's own goals. However, they note that it is difficult to control behaviour to yield uniform stimulus material, and we may wonder whether their categorization of goals does not also apply to indirect perception in which no interaction takes place (and incidentally in which stimulus control is more feasible). Jones and Thibaut (1958) lay particular stress on the notion that inferential sets derive from the goals of an interaction, and seem to imply that their thesis is relevant only to direct perception on which interaction occurs. Yet it would appear to be an interpretative framework of wider reference, and we have studied it in a perceptual situation rather different from the ones they discuss.

Experiment 24

In this investigation we used a standard written account which was presented to two groups of perceivers — a procedure which allowed greater control of stimulus information than was achieved by Jones and deCharms. The narrative was of the case-study type and described a difficult situation which had arisen within an office. The account was in quite unsensational terms, and described how the chief clerk in an insurance agency — a hypothetical Mr. Cecil Martin — had recently been convicted of stealing a woman's handbag. He had been fined £20 but had been allowed to retain his job, and the female clerks in the office were alleged to be growing restless and anxious. The account was fairly detailed and described several aspects of Martin's background (in his thirties, single, well-qualified, etc.).

All the subjects in this investigation read the same account and later gave their dispositional perception of Martin. Impressions were recorded on a twelve-item semantic differential form which contained scales representing the three major factors. However, before making their judgments subjects were encouraged to think about the central problem in ways which were likely to induce particular sets. At an early stage in the investigation they were told that they would eventually have to answer a series of questions about the case. They were requested to read through the questions before turning to the narrative. Subjects next read the account itself and then answered the questions. Whilst answering these they were allowed to consult the narrative freely. Their final task was to indicate their perception of the stimulus person on the semantic differential scales.

Our independent variable was the group of questions posed. Two groups were used, each intended to induce a particular set. The situation-matching subjects were asked about the situation in the office and how this affected the behaviour and feelings of members of the company. They responded to nine multiple-choice questions ("Yes", "No" or "Don't Know") of the following kind:

Is the efficiency of the office likely to decline as a result of this series of events?
Is the trouble likely to blow over?
Are the newspaper reports of the case likely to result in business being taken from the company?
Are the clerks and typists likely to talk about Martin during working hours?

Subjects were also asked to put themselves in the place of Martin's manager and to consider what effect various courses of action would have. They were asked to underline which behaviours by the manager would be most appropriate. Illustrative alternatives are "ignore the problem", "ask Martin's colleagues to be sympathetic", "have a serious word with Martin", "promote Martin to a position elsewhere" and "dismiss Martin". In short, this version of the questionnaire was an attempt to force subjects to think for several minutes in a situation-matching way, so that they would reach some conclusions about how Martin's offence should be dealt with in his work environment.

The questions put to the causal-genetic subjects were very different. The "Yes", "No", "Don't know" items included:

Is Martin likely to be a heavy drinker?
Is he likely to have had a happy childhood?
Is he likely to be a heavy cigarette smoker?
Is it likely that his parents are wealthy?
Is he likely to enjoy gardening?

And the final item requested subjects to put themselves in Martin's place and to suggest why he stole the handbag. Possible answers available were "to obtain money", "to draw attention to himself", "for excitement", "he hates women" and several others of this kind. These questions were intended to encourage subjects to consider the reasons for Martin's behaviour and to develop some interpretative ideas about his background.

How did this manipulation affect the dispositional perceptions

Table 14 Indirect perception of Martin by judges with different set

Scale	Situation–matching set (N=48)	Causal–genetic set (N=49)	Significance of difference $p<$
True–false	5·46	5·41	n.s.
Good–bad	5·50	5·26	n.s.
Kind–cruel	5·46	5·67	n.s.
Fair–unfair	5·54	5·67	n.s.
Strong–weak	3·23	2·45	0·02
Hard–soft	3·67	3·22	n.s.
Bold–timid	3·06	2·37	0·02
Rugged–delicate	3·48	2·90	0·10
Dangerous–safe	5·53	4·42	0·02
Emotional–unemotional	6·31	6·29	n.s.
Active–passive	3·69	2·92	0·05
Fast–slow	4·31	3·61	0·05

generated by the narrative account? Average responses of the two groups are shown in Table 14, together with the two-tailed level of significance of differences between these means. The data in this table present a most intriguing picture. It is clear that the different sets generated very different impressions of the stimulus person. Subjects with a causal-genetic set judged Martin to be significantly less strong, bold, rugged, dangerous, active and fast. But this very marked influence of set does not extend to evaluative judgments: in the case of each evaluative scale the mean responses are extremely similar.

This phenomenon presents an interesting contrast with the findings from Experiment 22. On that occasion religious affiliation was seen to have major influence upon evaluative judgments and to leave other, attributive, responses relatively unaffected. Why should this difference occur? One possibility is that inferential sets are in themselves non-evaluative whereas stable characteristics such as religious outlook have a predominantly affective nature. This is likely to be less than completely true, and alternative interpretations are required. We may wonder whether the results of the present study arise from the relative detachment of our subjects: they were observing from outside the supposed network of interpersonal relationships and would be less involved than in the direct perceptual situations discussed by Jones and his colleagues.*

But whatever the explanation of this difference it is clear that the results of Experiment 24 lend support to the framework suggested by Jones and Thibaut (1958). In addition they indicate the relevance of this framework to indirect perceptual situations (see also Carlson, 1961). We may accept that inferential sets of the type described here are powerful sources of interjudge variability in person perception. They constitute further examples of the perceiver's current state which need to be accounted for in an explanation of this process.

ATTRACTION AND JUDGMENTS OF OTHERS

We have repeatedly emphasized that although certain characteristics of

---

* Experiment 24 has since been repeated with 73 Canadian university students as subjects. Once again there were clear differences between the groups, but it is interesting that judgments on the evaluative scales were now found to be most sensitive to the set manipulation. The causal-genetic group judged Martin to be significantly more good, kind and fair, as well as significantly less bold. The reasons for this between-sample variation have still to be explored.

the judge may be seen to affect person perception, these characteristics affect only a limited range of judgments. Although, for instance, we may conclude that the sex of a judge is a stable characteristic mediating the way people are perceived, this characteristic only influences *some* judgments about *some* people. The final aspect of the perceiver to be considered in this chapter is even more specific than most of those examined earlier. We turn now to the like–dislike relationship between a judge and a particular stimulus person.

Despite this type of specificity, attraction is in another sense very non-specific. It has an important role in the operation of all the components of the perceptual system we have postulated. Its presence in the output from this system is clear: we have suggested that all perceptual responses have three components — attributive, expectancy and affective components. These components interact with each other, so that, for example, the affective judgments (which are essentially like–dislike, approach–avoidance ones) exert influence upon other reactions. But the perceptual output feeds back to influence the judge's current state (see Figure 1, p. 20), which can depend heavily upon the attraction, disinterest or hostility which he feels towards the stimulus. In turn the perceiver's current state acts upon his input selector and his processing centre (through cojudgment for instance) to mediate subsequent judgments.

But attraction and other affective responses may also be important as an aspect of stored stimulus person information. We have pointed out that the information in store about a person (that which gives rise to conceptual judgments) has entered this store after it has passed through the perceptual system. The stored material in consequence has just the same three components — attributive, expectancy and affective aspects. When a judge utilizes stored material about a person, he may therefore be bringing to bear previous evaluations of the person. Furthermore, evaluative factors enter in a more general way into what we have termed the perceiver's stable characteristics. Religious and other affiliations, attitudes and values all have strongly affective aspects — directed towards classes of people rather than only towards individual stimuli (as are conceptions). As the earlier section has emphasized, these characteristics are often extremely important determinants of perception.

It can be seen that a like–dislike, approach–avoid, attraction–hostility factor is widely implicated in our scheme, and it would certainly appear to be a *sine qua non* of person perception. What evidence is there that this is in fact so?

Tagiuri (1958b, p. 317) has pointed out that factor analytic studies of mutual ratings by members of small groups concur in indicating the presence of three basic factors — initiative and influence, task competence and like–dislike. While the first two factors are not observed in every group, the last one is always present. Indeed it seems improbable that small informal groups can exist at all without at least a minimal degree of attraction between members (cf. Bonner, 1959; Cartwright and Zander, 1960). Homans (1961) has made sentiments of like and dislike cornerstones of his system to explain elementary social behaviour, and the conceptual framework of Thibaut and Kelley (1959) includes the general assumption that viable social relationships depend upon a satisfactory ratio of reward and cost — largely assessed in terms of like–dislike. R. Brown (1965) argues that the dimensions of status and solidarity can account for all social behaviour, and he treats liking, sympathy, trust, etc. as central aspects of solidarity. Foa (1961) and Leary (1957) have analysed studies of interpersonal relationships to conclude that two orthogonal axes — dominance–submission and love–hostility — can account for a wide range of earlier observations. Heider (1958) takes one feature of a "balanced" system to be a consistency in like–dislike relationships, and Newcomb (1961) has developed this notion in his intensive study of a student group. The enormous number of sociometric studies (e.g. Moreno, 1960) also testifies to the importance which has been attached to evaluative relationships as a basis of social behaviour.

Narrowing our interest down to person perception *per se*, there is much empirical evidence for the central importance of attraction. In Chapter 2 we reviewed the many factor analytic studies of semantic differential responses which reveal a major factor of evaluation. This factor typically accounts for most of the variance in subjects' judgments. And when more open-ended measurements are taken, as in Experiment 6 where we studied perceptual judgments by multidimensional scaling techniques, the major response dimension is again found to be a general evaluative one.* We have also shown that the structure of perceivers' implicit personality theories is strongly influenced by the way they evaluate personal characteristics, and that this structural principle gives rise to what may be termed cojudgment (see Chapter 3).

* This is also observed in a study by Warr, Schroder and Blackman (1968).

Many writers have indirectly stressed the importance of attraction in person perception when discussing the centrality of traits. The history of studies of the warm–cold dimension serves to exemplify this. It will be recalled from Chapter 3 (p. 123) that Asch (1946) argued for the centrality of this dimension in that changes along it generated wide differences in the way a person is perceived. Although Wishner (1960) pointed out limitations in Asch's analysis it seems likely (as we suggested in the previous chapter) that this dimension is indeed a very central one. The warm–cold dimension is of course heavily loaded on the evaluative factor, so that we are in effect approaching from yet another direction the conclusion that evaluative responses are essential components of person perception. Several additional investigations have indicated the marked influence of warm–cold judgments. Kelley (1950), for instance, manipulated these judgments by differential introductions of a stimulus person, and Veness and Brierley (1963) varied the perceived warmth of a speaker's voice. Hays' (1958) application of a model of implication, referred to in Chapter 3 (p. 134), showed that warmth was a central characteristic according to his definition of centrality, and Asch (1958) has extended his earlier analysis by considering the metaphorical usage of these terms. There have even been studies of the role of the dimension as an "irrelevant verbal stimulus". Cofer and Dunn (1952) asked subjects to rate photographs after they had learned a list of words. The list was varied so that for some subjects it included *warm* and for others it included *cold*. Rather surprisingly differences in indirect perception were observed according to which of these two terms was in the list.*

It can be seen that investigators of many different orientations have been led to the same conclusion — that our impressions of other people are very much dependent upon whether we find them attractive or unattractive. Some workers wish to go beyond this position to assert that the like–dislike aspect is more important than any other facet of the process.

So far, however, we have talked in general terms; can we now say anything more specific about studies of the influence of evaluation upon person perception? Firstly we shall briefly examine the relation between attraction and social interaction, and then we shall consider in more detail the effect of personal evaluation upon the *perception* of

---

* This rather extreme indication of the emphasis placed upon the warm–cold dimension was, however, not supported in a replication attempt by Kjeldergaard and Jenkins (1958).

others. In reviewing the relevant studies it should be borne in mind that the causal relationship is not a simple one-way one, and that a fairly complex matrix of causal influence will be required to completely account for the phenomena.

Conforming behaviour in groups has repeatedly been shown to be influenced by the way other group members are evaluated. Conformity is typically found to be related to liking (e.g. Berkowitz, 1954, 1957; Schachter and coauthors, 1951). Studies of attitude change (which is, on analogy with the two types of perception described in this book, in effect "indirect conformity") reveal the same pattern (e.g. Aronson and Golden, 1962). Furthermore, people communicate more with others they like, and the performance of cohesive groups — those in which the members are strongly attracted to each other — tends to be better than that of others (see Lott and Lott, 1965). Patterns of attraction and perceived attraction have also been shown to be one basis of changes in group composition and structure over time (e.g. Backman and Secord, 1962; Secord and Backman, 1964b).

Clearly then the extent to which group members are attracted to each other in part determines their relationships one to another. And it is axiomatic that different interpersonal relationships are accompanied by different perceptual inputs and hence by outputs which are likely to differ. In general terms then attraction mediates social relationships which in turn mediate person perception; but can we say anything more direct about the way differences in liking generate particular differences in the judgments made about others?

From our knowledge of cojudgment we can point out that the attribution of certain desirable traits to another person will lead to the inference that he possesses additional desirable characteristics. Some factors influencing this process have been discussed in Chapter 3. Another concomitant of liking is the perception of similarity. Fiedler, Warrington and Blaisdell (1952) showed that subjects perceive others whom they like most to be similar to themselves; and this conclusion has since been supported in a number of later studies. (See Lott and Lott (1965) for a review of these.) Furthermore there is a tendency for perceivers to incorporate congruent relationships in their judgments of liking — they assume that their own evaluative judgments are reciprocated in other people, so that if A likes B he will assume that B likes him. A considerable amount of work in diverse situations has been reported (e.g. Tagiuri, 1958b; Tagiuri, Blake and Bruner, 1953;

Tagiuri, Bruner and Blake, 1958), and a number of interesting generalizations about congruency now seem possible. This topic will be discussed further in the next chapter (p. 250).

We have argued so far in this section that a generalized like–dislike reaction is central to person perception and that this reaction can be shown to have several consequences for behaviour and for other aspects of the way persons are judged. Within this framework the *determinants* of attraction now become relevant. It is clear that if we can learn about some of the factors giving rise to evaluative responses we shall learn something further about the antecedents of perceptual judgment itself. This is our aim, but in order to fulfil it we should need here to involve ourselves in discussions of a wide range of topics which are in fact covered in other reports. So a brief summary of the determinants of attraction will suffice.

Several personal traits seem to be generally appreciated by others: self-acceptance, sensitivity, relevant ability, and several personality and attitudinal characteristics have all been shown to generate favourable responses. Variables of a more "situational" type which also increase attractiveness are physical proximity, cooperative relationships, acceptance by others, external threats and several status factors. All these objects of study are relevant to person perception in that they influence it through like–dislike reactions. Valuable reviews of their nature and influence on attractiveness have been provided by Lott and Lott (1965) and by Mann (1959).

Although we have so far mainly considered positive evaluations — attraction, liking and so on — it should of course be borne in mind that similar effects on person perception accompany negative responses. Disliking or feeling hostile towards another person goes along with attributing to him certain types of characteristics and with expecting him to behave in certain ways. These phenomena are frequently similar to those accompanying attraction. Thus there is general agreement on the differences between characteristics attributed to liked and to disliked persons, and the phenomena seem essentially the same in both cases (Pastore, 1960). Expectancies related to liking and disliking appear to operate according to a similar pattern and have been studied by Berkowitz (1960b, 1960c) and others. Furthermore, just as there are similarities in the *consequences* of attraction and of disliking, so are there similarities in their determinants. Personal characteristics have been isolated which give rise to rejection (e.g. Kidd, 1951) and situational factors like physical proximity are known to lead also to negative evaluations (Warr, 1965). Comprehensive accounts of work on fairly strong negative reactions — aggression and hostility — have been provided by Berkowitz (1962), Buss (1961) and Pepitone (1964).

One complex aspect of evaluative judgments has recently aroused considerable interest. This concerns the nature of changes in perception when information about the stimulus person is increased. The impressions we form of a stimulus person are presumably liable to change as we receive more information about him. But how far do our early perceptions — particularly our evaluative reactions — determine the way we select and employ later information? Several studies of order effects in impression formation have been reported, and these will be reviewed in Chapter 6 (see p. 264). Of particular relevance here are investigations into the way later information about a person is integrated with early judgments of like–dislike. Some predictions about this have recently been derived from cognitive dissonance theory. For example, Davis and Jones (1960) studied the consequences of dissonance between perceivers' evaluation of a stimulus person and his later behaviour. And Walster and colleagues (1966) and Walster and Prestholdt (1966) have studied changes in evaluation of a person as additional discrepant information is introduced. This type of study holds promise for increasing our understanding of the way the evaluative, the attributive and the expectancy components of person perception interact with each other.

In summary of this section we can note that the like–dislike relationship to a stimulus person is a most potent influence on the way he will be perceived. The relationship appears to be important at all stages of the perceptual system we have proposed, and empirical evidence for its primacy is readily obtained. We have drawn attention to work on the antecedents of attraction and have pointed to some of the consequences which differences in judgments of attraction can have for perception. This factor is clearly one which can lead to different perceivers making quite different judgments.

One final aspect concerns people's habitual emphasis on evaluative tone as an organizing principle. Casual observation suggests that perceivers vary in the emphasis they give to their global like–dislike evaluation: whereas some people treat this as quite detached from their judgments about a stimulus person, other people tend to make all their judgments dependent upon it. The latter group are very much more likely to select inputs and to apply decision rules which arise from their like–dislike feelings about the person. We have noted in Chapter 3 that cojudgment varies with *F*-scale score. Other investigators have observed that perceivers of low cognitive complexity are more prone than others to categorize people on the basis of their evaluative reactions to them (Campbell, 1960 cited in Crockett, 1965; Supnick, 1964 also cited in Crockett, 1965). Scott (1963) has obtained similar results in a study of conceptions of nations: the tendency to form balanced groups of nations — either all liked or all disliked — was clearly related to the complexity of the judge. The importance of evaluative tone as a basis of person perception is no doubt universal, but studies of variations in its importance may yield fruitful insights into the process.

SUMMARY

In this chapter we have dealt with several individual differences between perceivers. We have related this discussion to the schematic perceptual system outlined in Chapter 1, so that our main emphasis has been on the components labelled "perceiver's stable characteristics" and "perceiver's current state". But we have also examined "stored stimulus person information". This stored information is specific to a stimulus person and has already been processed by the system. It therefore consists of expectancies as well as attributive and affective judgments. The role of expectancies about a particular individual was the first question dealt with in this chapter.

It is not surprising that these conceptual expectancies influence person perception, but previous research on this topic is rare. Other investigators have examined expectancies about *classes* of stimuli rather than about individual persons. In contrast the studies described early in the chapter stressed the association between conceptions and perceptions of individual stimulus persons. The question was also raised whether conceptions of the topic of a speech influence perceptions of a speaker.

Variations between perceptual judgments have frequently been imputed to sex differences. The second section of this chapter reviewed evidence bearing upon this issue, and the collated results led to the conclusion that sex differences in person perception were in fact far from widespread. Personality influences upon perception were next considered. Although there is no reliable evidence that the judge's personality is related to his accuracy, there are clear suggestions that several personality characteristics have some influence upon the types of judgments he makes. Other stable characteristics such as age, socio-economic status, cultural background, political and religious belief, and occupation were also examined. Once again it was shown that these factors could be of importance in certain situations, and there is no doubt that their influence needs to be accounted for in a comprehensive attempt at explanation.

Several aspects of the perceiver's current state have also been considered. It was clear that a standard set of stimulus information may be judged quite differently by subjects in varying emotional states or with varying cognitive sets. The role of motivation and of emotional involvement, arousal and suppression was first examined, after which we turned our attention to what have been termed tuning sets and inferential sets. In each case evidence for their operation was reviewed. In the final section of the chapter the paramount importance in person perception of a global evaluative response was emphasized. It was shown that a like–dislike reaction is present in any perceptual process, and factors affecting the nature of this reaction and some consequences of it were explored.

Throughout the chapter we have had no difficulty in producing evidence that the nature of the perceiver himself influences the judgments he makes. Any complete model or explanation of person perception must account for a wide range of individual differences. But it is easy to exaggerate the importance of these differences. Most stable characteristics do not have a continuing, ubiquitous influence on the way we judge other people. We have noted that intelligence may effect judgmental accuracy, but it is probably unrelated to judgments on, say, Potency scales; many differences in cultural background or in socio-economic status will be quite unrelated to the majority of perceptual judgments, and personality factors are found to determine only relatively isolated sets of judgments. In a similar manner, the current state of the perceiver — his level of anxiety or his cognitive set for instance — will have bearing upon only certain perceptual phenomena.

Dimensions of difference between perceivers *are* important, but they only apply to a limited set of perceptual responses. *Some* judgments about *some* stimuli are influenced by *some* perceiver characteristics; the problem now is to specify the nature of these limitations. To do this it is essential to look at research which fails to reveal interindividual differences as carefully as we examine that which does reveal judgmental variations. There is at present a tendency to value only those studies which obtain significant differences between judges. This is too narrow a view, for unless we can determine those perceiver characteristics which are *unimportant* in a particular situation we cannot specify the limits of those which do matter. This is an area in which negative results really are as interesting as positive ones.*

Nevertheless we have been able to discuss many topics of which our understanding has increased considerably during the last few years. For instance we have a fairly clear idea about how F-scale score is relevant to certain judgments about certain types of stimulus, about how a judge's fearfulness may lead to projection which is predictably either complementary or supplementary, and about how attitudinal complexes may influence evaluative judgments about only some classes of stimuli. It does seem on the whole that most differences between perceivers are important to judgment only in certain conditions and when certain kinds of stimuli are involved. To rephrase the present problem, we have to recognize and study the possible interactions between the nature of the judge, the nature of his response and the nature of the stimulus. Several examples of interaction effects have been noted throughout this chapter, and many more should be anticipated.

* Only when the investigator's hypothesis is a plausible one, of course. An elaborate study which showed that the stable characteristic, colour of the perceiver's eyes, was unrelated to judgments of other people's height is of little value. But one which revealed that anxiety does not influence judgments about an authority figure in an ego-relevant setting might be very important.

5

THE DIRECT PERCEPTION OF PEOPLE

In Chapter 1 (pp. 1–51) we introduced the terms "direct" and "indirect" perception, the two forms of judgment being distinguished in terms of the presence or absence of an intervening communication. In this way perception mediated by a newspaper report, a film or photograph, a television broadcast, telephone conversation or letter is indirect perception whereas judgments of others at meetings, in interviews, lectures and games are direct judgments. We pointed out that psychologists have given major emphasis to direct perceptual situations, and we argued that the process of indirect perception is sufficiently important to warrant more detailed attention than it has previously received. The two chapters which follow this one emphasize factors which are peculiar to indirect person perception. At the same time, we cannot overlook those which are specifically relevant to direct perception, and they are discussed in the present chapter. All three chapters concern themselves with the differences and similarities between the two types of judgment.

The schematic diagram of perception laid out in Figure 1 (p. 20) is assumed to be a valid representation of both direct and indirect perception. Certainly those components of the diagram which we have already examined in the previous two chapters would seem to hold good for both types of perceptual judgment. Such components include the processing centre (Chapter 3), the perceiver's stable characteristics and current state, his stored information about and affective reactions to the stimulus person (Chapter 4). All these factors have an important bearing upon the final judgment whether or not an intervening communication is involved in the process. Furthermore, if we turn aside from our own findings, there are several experiments on person perception where direct and indirect situations have yielded comparable outcomes. For example, Pepitone (1964) has reported parallel studies using face-to-face judgments (direct perception) and transcripts of interviews (indirect perception). Miller, Banks and Ogawa (1962, 1963) have described interesting investigations of monkeys' ability to judge affective expression. Here similar findings emerged from situations in which the animals perceived each other directly and those in which perception was indirect, through a television transmission.

The similarities between direct and indirect perceptual judgments (of both objects and people) are easy to find, yet there *are* important differences, and at this point we shall attempt to identify some of them. A major difficulty in discussing this question is that the types of perception within each category vary so widely. The criterion of an intervening communication is a very broad one, so that to discuss as one group perceptions mediated by a telephone system, a newspaper, a film or a radio broadcast is somewhat misleading. It was with just this difficulty in mind that we presented a more detailed system of classification of the two types of perception in Chapter 1. This classification system (Figure 2, p. 30) is in terms not only of an intervening communication, but also in terms of whether interaction between judge and stimulus occurs and whether the behaviour giving rise to the judgment is present or past. Although in principle this three-way division generates eight categories of perception, some of these are logically impossible (interacting with someone in the past for instance), so that five types of judgment are in practice available. In discussing differences between direct and indirect perception it will be helpful to employ this system of classification.

JUDGMENTS WITHOUT INTERPERSONAL INTERACTION

Let us look first at the perceptual situations where no interaction takes place: categories two, four and five of Figure 2. Category five is of course unique in that it alone is concerned with the perception of an event which occurs in the past. This distinguishes the perception involved in a very special way from any judgments which are possible in direct perception. Moreover we should note that this type of indirect perception, involving recorded television and radio material, films, and all written and printed media, is by far the most common type of indirect perception. However, leaving aside this special characteristic of category five, we can point to a number of important differences between direct and indirect perception when no interaction takes place.

The major variation concerns the impoverished nature of the input in indirect perception. Although in every perceptual situation the input is controlled to some extent by the stimulus himself, an important additional control is exerted over the input to indirect perception. This influence usually comes from an agent other than the stimulus or the perceiver. A newspaper account, for example, provides the reader with a set of stimulus material which is very largely determined by the reporter and subeditors, and the information presented in a radio broadcast is largely chosen by the commentator and producer. But this restriction of stimulus information is not only the result of selection by human intermediaries. It is also necessitated by the nature of the communication channel, so that certain sorts of input are not possible in certain indirect perceptual situations. For example, cues from bodily and facial movements are not usually available to a perceiver judging on the basis of a radio interview, and vocal inputs cannot occur in perception via photographs or written reports.

If we acknowledge that the stimulus information is typically less varied and complex in indirect perception, then we should ask what are the consequences of this. It would appear that, since less information is available, the importance or salience of what *is* presented is correspondingly greater. Perception in category two (direct judgments without interaction) can be based upon a wide range of inputs. Imagine, for example, being in the audience at a large public meeting; as you witness just one statement from the platform speaker you receive literally thousands of inputs concerning the semantic content of what has been said, the speaker's intonation, his appearance, gestures and facial expression, the reaction of the audience and of the chairman of the meeting, even the draped flag at the back of the hall. Contrast this with reading an account of the same meeting in an evening newspaper (category five). Even supposing this particular statement had been quoted verbatim, a large part of the total input available to the direct perceiver has now been lost. Instead, we are subject to the stringencies

I

of the communication channel and its agent, the reporter of the meeting, which will almost inevitably lead to impoverishment of input.* But that same statement by the speaker (which in the direct situation may be swamped and lost in relation to the total input) is now given added salience by the preselection process which is the mark of indirect perception.

This increased salience of each unit of stimulus information in the indirect situation means that factors affecting person perception may be differentially important in direct and indirect perception. For example, a central trait (see pp. 121 and 123) which in indirect perception is particularly important may be much less significant amongst the thousands of other inputs available in direct perception. Spectacles influence personal judgments more in indirect than in direct perception (Thornton, 1944). Furthermore, some aspects of the perceiver himself may in consequence be more important in indirect perception. In so far as less stimulus material is available to generate a rounded self-consistent judgment, the indirect perceiver might make more use of his own conceptions, value systems, etc. This notion is one familiar to students of projective tests; the rationale behind these forms of measurement is that if the stimulus is fairly indeterminate, then responses must be mainly based upon factors internal to the perceiver. In a similar manner conceptual expectancies about a stimulus are more important in indirect perception than in direct perception (see Chapter 4, p. 182). It also seems likely that false impressions can be generated more easily in the case of indirect perception. Careful and skilful selection within the channel can often result in considerable variation and distortion of perception. This type of skilled manipulation is in fact the hallmark of the successful film producer, newspaper reporter, photographer, raconteur and propagandist.

Related to this is a difference in the types of input which are available in the two forms of perception. We have already alluded to differences in the variety and range of inputs, but in addition to these we may note that in many instances of indirect perception, the *form* of the information is dissimilar to that in direct situations. Apart from the obvious differences between typewritten inputs (in a newspaper or book) and the vocal and visual information available in direct perception, a more

---

* Almost inevitably, but of course not always. If the direct observer was particularly insensitive and the reporter experienced and "perceptive", then it is possible that the same observer reading the report later would actually enrich his input.

subtle distinction is worthy of note. Often in indirect perception, the stimulus information has been preprocessed into dispositional judgments. For instance, judgments in category five (indirect perception of past behaviour, no interaction) are often based upon information which is provided as an *output* of the perceptual system of an intermediary. A reporter may describe a stimulus person as "wealthy and successful", or a raconteur may describe the subject of his story as "a very humorous person"; and indirect perception will very likely be partially based upon these dispositional inputs. In direct perception such inputs are less probable, since a stimulus person does not usually provide this information in such an abbreviated form; more generally we have to derive it ourselves from his behaviour. So, in this respect too, direct perception is a more complex operation than is its indirect counterpart.

Up to this point we have concentrated upon direct and indirect judgments which do not involve interaction between perceiver and stimulus. We have noted that the major difference between the two forms of perception is in the restricted stimulus information available in indirect perception. Such restriction is necessitated by the type of communication medium involved and is usually under the control of an intermediary. Several implications of this have been examined. For instance, there are discrepancies in information salience, false impressions are more easily generated in indirect perception, and reliance upon the perceiver's stored information and upon preprocessed stimulus material is also more probable in this type of situation. In addition, several communication variables are peculiar to indirect judgments. The operation of some of these is considered in Chapters 6 and 7.

JUDGMENTS BASED UPON INTERACTION

What are the consequences of introducing interpersonal interaction into a perceptual situation? The two perceptual categories so far omitted from this discussion are categories one and three of Figure 2, which respectively embrace direct and indirect judgments made in interaction with the stimulus. Examples of perceptual category one include conversations, meetings, interviews, parties and games; and comparable indirect situations involve telephone conversations, radio communications and television interviews when the participants are in different studios. It is true that whether or not perception is direct the consequences of this type of interaction are similar. But it is also clear that in direct perception interpersonal interaction is both enriched and more frequent. The range of inputs available in a telephone conversation is obviously limited, and even in a two-way television link-up, person perception is likely to be based upon much less information than if the interaction were a direct face-to-face confrontation. Thus although we should be aware that interaction can take place in indirect perceptual situations, we should also be clear that any discussion of the effects of such interaction will mainly be concerned with direct perception. With this in mind we proceed to such a discussion.

It is of course logically necessary that interpersonal interaction depends upon judgments made about each other by the persons who are interacting.* Interesting discussions of the interconnection of person perception and interaction have been presented by Hastorf, Richardson and Dornbusch (1958), Heider (1958), Newcomb (1958, 1961), Tagiuri (1958b, 1968) and others (see Chapter 1, p. 5); more general examinations which give greater emphasis to the process of interaction have been made by Argyle (1967), Homans (1961), Newcomb, Turner and Converse (1965), and Thibaut and Kelley (1959). The ways in which interaction sequences may be classified according to their significance for person perception have been considered by Jones and Thibaut (1958) and Sarbin, Taft and Bailey (1960).

The analysis by Sarbin, Taft and Bailey (1960, pp. 216–223) is based upon the extent to which information is transmitted reciprocally between members of an interaction. They distinguish between three classes of interaction: non-reciprocal, symmetrically reciprocal and asymmetrically reciprocal. Several subclasses are suggested, so that "non-reciprocal interaction" includes not only what we have termed indirect perception without interaction, but also two categories which more clearly involve some two-way transaction between people. For example, "parallel behaviour" may occur when two people are talking with little attention to each other. Another suggested type of non-reciprocal interaction is that of actors in rituals and ceremonials who interact in that they take their cues from each other but who nevertheless are preprogrammed to respond in certain specified ways.

A symmetrically reciprocal interaction is said to occur when the behaviour of each person occurs in response to that of the other. This very common social relationship is distinguished from asymmetrical

---

* Asch (1952, p. 163) has referred to the "mutually shared field" of interacting individuals.

reciprocity, where one person initiates most of the communications and the other(s) mainly have to respond. An asymmetrically reciprocal interaction is exemplified by clinical, selection and other types of interview, and symmetrical reciprocity is to be observed widely in meetings, discussions and in other less formal social situations.

A systematization which is almost the same as the scheme presented by Sarbin, Taft and Bailey has been put forward by Jones and Thibaut (1958). Both groups of writers imply that the type of perceptual judgment made will vary with the nature of the interaction. Roughly speaking, the more contingent the perceiver's behaviour is upon the behaviour of the stimulus, the more the perceiver tends to make episodic or dispositional judgments about him. But this generalization has to be modified to take account of the goals of any interaction. In this way, an interviewer's behaviour may not be greatly contingent upon that of the interviewee, yet he has to make detailed assessments of the other person.

It is with this in mind that Jones and Thibaut (1958) proposed an additional classification of interaction situations. This classification is in terms of the personal goal which is mediated by an interaction with another person. Three types of goals are proposed, and it is suggested that each gives rise to a different perceptual set within a perceiver. These goals are (a) the facilitation of personal goal attainment, giving rise to a "value-maintenance" set, (b) the deterministic analysis of the personality of the other person, giving rise to a "causal-genetic" set, and (c) the application of social sanctions, which gives rise to a "situation matching" set. We have already examined this categorization of perceptual sets in Chapter 4 (pp. 227–231), at which stage we concluded that it was a useful and plausible scheme. Experiments cited there provided empirical support for the idea that the individual's goals in an interaction influence his set and hence his judgments about other people. We went a little further than Jones and Thibaut, however, and noted that their categorization was also pertinent to indirect situations in which no interaction takes place.

But although this aspect of the perceiver's current state influences perception whether or not interaction takes place, it does seem in general that certain aspects of the perceiver and of the situation will assume greater importance when he interacts with the stimulus. The goals of a perceiver, operating in conjunction with the context of an interaction, will be of particular salience in direct perception (Jones and

Davis, 1965). Here the relationship between the perceiver and the stimulus person is usually more well defined than in indirect perception: hence we can expect more perceptual judgments to be made. This seems especially likely when we bear in mind that in the direct situation, the perceiver–stimulus relationship can change rapidly from moment to moment, and different expectancies are likely to succeed one another quite quickly.

Irrespective of the degree to which an interaction is reciprocal, persons who are talking together have to work in some synchrony with each other. This means that — quite apart from major goals of personal assessment discussed above — each person is set to interpret the behaviour of the other and to predict his future actions so that he may be ready with an appropriate response. This type of perceptual set would seem to be generally more important in direct situations than in indirect ones, and it has a number of interesting corollaries. For example, it suggests that episodic judgments are more important in situations where there is interaction. And that these judgments will emphasize the moment-to-moment *intentions* of the stimulus person. For instance, if you are arguing with a stranger at a bar, you may be less concerned with fairly general aspects of his personality than with how he will react to your next statement and whether he intends to punch you on the nose; you will also very likely be considering your own next reaction. In interaction with someone we often have to respond quickly and appropriately on the basis of necessarily incomplete episodic judgments of what the other intends to do. These supposed intentions will often seem to concern ourself, so that our judgments will often be in terms of the degree to which our aims intermesh with those of the other person. This process is of course rather more rare in the perceptual situations examined earlier in the chapter — those which specifically exclude interaction.

In short, we are more involved in self-perceptions and in episodic judgments of the stimulus person when interpersonal interaction characterizes the perceptual situation. And we do not make these judgments by remaining passive and awaiting the next piece of material, as we do when we are reading newspapers, watching films and so on. Instead the perceiver himself effects changes in his environment so that he can to some extent control those aspects of the stimulus person which are presented. The *judge* continually needs information about the current state and the stable characteristics of the *stimulus*, and he solicits this information by asking questions, trying out certain behaviours and generally testing expectancies which he has developed.

The perceiver's expectancies therefore appear to be most important in perceptual categories which involve interaction. These expectancies will derive partly from dispositional judgments ("he has an aggressive personality"), but they also depend to a large extent upon episodic judgments ("he's looking pugnacious", "he's shouting", "his eyes are gleaming"). They are likely to concern the stimulus person's potential to affect the perceiver himself ("he's about to attack me"). And of course the perceiver's *behaviour* is also influenced by these expectancies, so that he works in support of or in opposition to the stimulus person's supposed aims. This process is made more complex by the fact that the perceiver's behaviour is also a function of his judgments of what the *stimulus person expects* him to do. Person A perceives person B partly in terms of his expectancies about B and partly in terms of his judgments of B's expectancies about him (A). The ramifications of this are widespread. Suppose, for instance, that A judges that B expects him (A) to emit behaviour x, but that in fact, he emits another behaviour which is not in accord with this supposed expectancy. Person A might now assume that B is "surprised" or "confused", and he might behave in a manner appropriate to reduce (or even to increase) this supposed confusion. It may, however, be the case that in reality B had not anticipated that A would emit x in the first place, so that A's sequence of behaviour (arising from his episodic judgment about B's expectancies) is interpreted in a manner quite dissimilar to the way A judges B to be interpreting it. The possible matrices of expectancy, intention and judgment are so disturbingly complex that we are still a long way from devizing procedures to study and to measure them. At present we largely have to make do with relatively "arm-chair" theorizing, such as the particularly vivid discussions by Goffman (1956).

Set and expectancy then are aspects of the perceiver's current state which seem to be of particular salience in direct situations. We might also be interested in looking at the emotional state of the perceiver: one such state which appears to be more potent in direct perception is anxiety or tension on the part of the perceiver. On the whole such tension is obviously more likely to occur in direct perceptual situations. Paivio (1965) has recently reviewed work on anxiety induced by the presence of other people, and the large variety of studies of the dynamics of interaction testifies to the widespread existence of social anxiety. The ways in which a perceiver's anxiety or fearfulness can affect his judgments have been reviewed in the previous chapter (p. 224), and we are now suggesting that these processes are more prevalent when interaction of some kind occurs. Furthermore the degree of anxiety has been shown to vary according to the nature of the interaction. Studies of stuttering have indicated that when a person's goal is to make a good impression he is more prone to stutter (Blood-stein, 1949), and that if a person has difficulty in predicting another's response (in asymmetrically reciprocal situations perhaps) he will also be more likely to stutter (Fransella, 1965). We can see here a potential interplay between a perceiver's emotional state, his perception of the stimulus person and the way he interacts with the stimulus person.

The manner in which interaction and affective responses are associated is a topic which has received great research attention. Interpersonal evaluations are a necessary part of interaction, and it seems likely that the affective component of judgment is of greater importance here than in perceptual situations which do not involve inter-action. It can be shown that if person A judges that B disapproves of him, changes in A's self-perception in that context will ensue (Jones, 1962). (Presumably A's behaviour towards B will also be altered, so that in turn B will make different judgments of A.) In more general terms we can see that the affective relationship between people will markedly influence their interaction (Secord and Backman, 1961, 1965). This is especially true in *informal* situations when the conclusion or continuation of an interaction will greatly depend upon whether or not the individuals are attracted to each other.

Of particular interest here are studies of assumed similarity. It is well known that persons who are liked are perceived to be similar to oneself. Fiedler, Warrington and Blaisdell (1952) showed this to be the case with a Q-sort of personality items and Fiedler (1954) and Backman and Secord (1962) have since reported similar findings in other situations. One aspect of assumed similarity has received extensive treatment from Tagiuri and his colleagues. They have been interested in "perceptual–affective congruency" (Tagiuri, Bruner and Blake, 1958) — the degree to which people assume that others have feelings similar to their own (see also Tagiuri, 1958b; Tagiuri, Blake and Bruner, 1953). Studies in this area have revealed that group members have a very marked predilection to assume that others' feelings for them are congruent with their feelings for the others. If person A likes

B, he will perceive that *B* likes him, and a similar pattern of *dislike* relationships is also liable to develop.

Furthermore perceivers are found to make congruent judgments about the relationships between other people, so that if *A* perceives that *B* likes *C* he will assume that *C* likes *B*. It appears that in this way members will exaggerate the consistency of affective relationships within any interaction sequence. DeSoto and Kuethe (1959) have shown this to be the case in a rather different type of investigation. Instead of asking subjects for their judgments about particular other people, they enquired about how probable certain interpersonal relationships were in general thought to be. Measures were taken of the probability of such relationships as liking, trusting, confiding in, hating, dominating and so on, and the estimates of likelihood that were observed were in line with Tagiuri's findings. In addition DeSoto and Kuethe pointed out several differences between positive and negative relationships in terms of their transitivity. For example, although "likes" and "trusts" were seen to be symmetrical and transitive, "dislikes" and "hates" were symmetrical but intransitive.

Affective relationships and assumed affective relationships enter into person perception in all these different ways. Many of the studies cited above have used indirect techniques to gain insight into what goes on in a face-to-face situation, but some of the effects just noted have in fact been shown to result from actual interpersonal interaction. Bieri (1953) demonstrated experimentally that subjects who interact with each other come to assume greater similarity between themselves. And Backman and Secord (1962) and Triandis (1959b) have observed this kind of phenomenon in ongoing real-life situations — a sorority and a factory respectively.

Interpersonal interaction is also likely to influence the effects of like–dislike reactions in another way. This has to do with the obvious fact that interactions are behaviour sequences of some length. It is known that perceivers will misjudge negative evaluations of themselves (Harvey, Kelley and Shapiro, 1957; Harvey, 1962; Harvey and Clapp, 1965) and we might assume that a single negative evaluation in the course of an indirectly presented set of stimulus material (a written report, say) will be readily distorted. On the other hand a judge who is interacting with a disapproving stimulus person over a longer period of time might well accumulate a *series* of negative evaluations so that eventually distortion will be impracticable. In so far as interactions between people may reflect relatively long-term relationships, it seems likely that the nature and influence of affective reactions will become more clear-cut than in judgmental situations which do not contain interpersonal interaction.

The role of like–dislike relationships in person perception was strongly emphasized in the previous chapter. The discussion there dealt with various aspects of attraction and hostility which were held to be relevant to all forms of perception. However, it seems that these affective relationships are particularly salient when interaction is taking place, and it may be suggested that our conclusions are on the whole more applicable to these situations than to those in which perceivers judge each other without interaction.

We turn now to a rather different point. It is noteworthy that some cues are available in direct perception which are not present in indirect perception and that the reverse is also the case. Several cues specific to indirect perception are examined in Chapter 7, and at this stage we shall look at those which occur only in direct perceptual situations. An obvious example is tactual stimulation, in the form of hand-shakes, back-slaps, hugs, kisses and so on. This type of input may be quite common even in some quite formal interactions, and it constitutes a source of information which clearly is not available to indirect perceivers.

A form of input which has received more systematic research attention concerns the way people in interaction *look at each other*; inputs of this type are of course precluded from indirect perception. Eye-contact plays an important part in ensuring interpersonal synchronization, in that people adjust the position of their gaze to signal conversational behaviour.* For example, speakers look up at the end of their comments and typically look away at the start of long utterances (Kendon, 1966), and listeners look at another person much more than do speakers (e.g. Exline, Gray and Schuette, 1965; Nielsen, 1962). Feedback about the consequences of our actions can often be obtained by observing the visual reactions of the other person. Eye-contact is more probable when people like each other and when they are cooperating rather than competing; individual differences have been studied and it appears that women are more likely to look at each other's eyes than are men. Evidence for these generalizations and for several others has been summarized in reports by Argyle and Dean

* Witness the difficulty of conversing with someone who is wearing dark sunglasses.

(1965), by Exline (1963) and by Exline and Winters (1965). This type of stimulus input to person perception is a particularly interesting one, and methodological innovations described in the papers just referred to* suggest that progress in understanding it will be rapid.

Other aspects of non-verbal communication have been emphasized in recent publications. For example, studies have been reported of judgments based upon bodily position, gestural behaviour and facial expression. Some of these types of input may of course occur in indirect perceptual situations, but on the whole it is true to say that they are of particular relevance to direct perception. Ekman (1957, 1964, 1965a, 1965b) has reported a series of observations of differential communication by head and body cues, and has looked into the accuracy of judgments mediated by these cues. And Rosenfeld (1966) has noted differences in postural–gestural behaviour related to the goals of a stimulus person. There have been very many studies of person perception based upon facial characteristics but since these have typically involved *indirect* judgments (employing photographs as stimulus material) they are examined collectively in Chapter 7 (pp. 296–318).

RECAPITULATION

In this chapter we have given emphasis to some aspects of judging others which are especially important in direct perception. This topic was treated in two parts: first we compared direct and indirect perception when no interpersonal interaction takes place, and in the final portion of the chapter we examined the consequences which arise from the introduction of interaction into the perceptual situation.

In nearly all cases the stimulus information available to a judge in indirect perception is less than that present in direct perception. We have pointed out that this discrepancy gives rise to differences in the judgmental process, so that certain stimulus cues and certain aspects of the perceiver are more salient in indirect perception.

Interaction between perceiver and stimulus may be classified according to reciprocity and on the basis of participants' goals. We have described some categorizations and have pointed out ways in which interaction may shape perception. In general it appears that in judging someone with whom we are interacting our current state and the

* See also Gibson and Pick (1963) for a rather different approach to the same question.

present context is of paramount importance. Both these factors will vary rapidly and will often be characterized by more anxiety than is usual in indirect situations without interaction. Perceptual expectancies and attraction between people are also of greater consequence, and some features of these were noted. Finally we drew attention to some types of stimulus information which may be present only in direct judgments.

This chapter has been mainly a conjectural one. We have not been able to adduce new evidence in support of our discussion, and have not presented any studies directly comparing the two sorts of judgment. One such investigation is reported in the next chapter (Experiment 25; see also Chapter 4, p. 182), and others are desirable. It is clear, however, that direct perception is characterized by complex phenomena which are not observed in indirect situations, and that these phenomena need to be isolated and studied. In the same way those processes peculiar to indirect perception need to be examined. The next two chapters attempt this examination.

6

THE COMMUNICATION VARIABLE IN INDIRECT PERCEPTION

IN several respects this chapter complements the previous one in that we shall emphasize one kind of judgment. We turn now to *indirect* person perception. But we shall look at this process in rather more detail than was attempted when we examined direct perception, and in addition the present chapter contains the results of several experimental investigations of our own. In the first part we shall raise some general issues concerned with the nature of the process, and with the accuracy of indirect perception; later in the chapter we describe some studies of how judgment is affected by the order of presentation of information.

We have noted in Chapter 1 and Chapter 5 that indirect perception may be of several types. Let us concentrate here upon the most common variety — indirect perception of past behaviour (perceptual category five in Figure 2). Naturally enough there can be no inter-personal interaction in these cases; and the medium of communication may be a description of the stimulus person by a third party, a news-paper report, a book, a photograph, a film or a recorded television or radio broadcast. The inputs to the perceptual system in this sort of judging situation are of an interesting type, in that we are here likely to get information which is *preprocessed*, usually into dispositional judgments (see p. 8). Information about a stimulus person might well be provided by someone else (a newspaper reporter for instance), and in this case it must be based upon an output from *his* perceptual system.*
The reporter may provide as stimulus information straight statements of

---

* That this can reduce the accuracy of indirect perception is clear. Other examples of the increased possibility of distortion in indirect judgment have been noted on p. 244.

fact ("repetitive outputs" in the language of Chapter 9, p. 372), episodic judgments about the behaviour of the person in a particular situation, or judgments of a dispositional kind. In direct perception it is not often that we are presented with dispositional information, except in the unusual case where the stimulus person himself tells us directly about a dispositional characteristic he possesses (for example, he might tell us he was very clever or arrogant, or both). On the other hand in the type of indirect perception we are considering the perceiver is frequently presented with an input comprising information of this kind. It should be noted, however, that such an input is very likely to be the *output* of a dispositional judgment made by a third party on a previous occasion.

In direct perception we examine the object or person concerned and form an impression of it or him which is based upon our own observations. In indirect perception we do not examine the person or object in the true sense. Instead we are seeing or hearing the channel itself — we may be looking at a television or cinema screen, listening to sounds from a loudspeaker or reading a report in a magazine or newspaper. In all these instances the presence of the communication channel implies some sort of editing and control over and above that exercised by the stimulus and perceiver themselves. In the case of the newspaper, usually for reasons of space, this editing is of a fairly comprehensive nature, so that a politician's speech may be reported in such a way that the actual words he used never appear at all in the report. In other cases, in a television relay of the speech for example, the communication presents something very close to the original. It is important to bear in mind, however, that what the viewer sees and hears is not exactly the same as that which is seen by an observer in the hall where the speech is being delivered. The producer of the programme must edit his camera shots, which means that we shall not be able to see the whole of the speaker and the whole of his surroundings all of the time. It is also unlikely that the speech will be relayed in its entirety: selection is again taking place. The same processes of editing, selection and control apply to a greater or lesser extent to all examples of indirect perception.

This does not necessarily mean that less information is received in indirect perception than in direct perception. The television presentation of an event might be structured by an announcer whose commentary includes details intended to tie together shifts from camera to camera; the commentator might provide background material or generate expectancies not possessed by a person perceiving the event directly. An interesting discussion of the point has been presented by Lang and Lang (1960).

It will be clear that many of the experiments reported in Chapters 2, 3 and 4 have concerned indirect perception. The communication medium in which we have been most interested is the newspaper, and many of our studies have employed material which originally appeared in the national press. One aim in using this type of authentic stimulus material is to get close to indirect perceptual situations as they exist in real life. There is a need for such studies to parallel the more controlled investigations in which realism is of limited importance. In Chapter 3 we described some attempts at parallel investigations (Experiments 10–13) where Asch's and Wishner's materials were used in the guise of newspaper reports. And many studies of the relation between conception and perception described in Chapter 4 used communications of considerable complexity which were culled from leading newspapers. It cannot be disputed that this form of perceptual input is one which in our everyday lives gives rise to a tremendous number of judgments of other persons; for example, most people in the Western world read at least one paper every day (U.N.E.S.C.O., 1964; Williams, 1959).

But studies of indirect judgments mediated by newspaper reports are of interest for another reason. This pertains to the accuracy of the press. The topic of newspaper accuracy has generally been dealt with in terms rather foreign to the approach offered in this book. For example, many investigations have concentrated upon the comparison procedures of content analysis. These have repeatedly shown that different newspapers devote very varied amounts of space to particular forms of material (e.g. Abu-Lughod, 1962; International Press Institute, 1953; Warr and Knapper, 1965). Discrepancies are particularly marked when comparisons are made between newspapers of different nations (Kayser, 1953; Schramm, 1959), and the question may be raised — what is the "right" amount of space to devote to each type of material to give an accurate representation of the world's events? Alternatively there have been studies of accuracy in more molecular terms, in which the treatment accorded in different papers to specific events is investigated (His Majesty's Stationery Office, 1949; Williams, 1962). It is not hard to find different information about an event appearing in different papers, or indeed in different editions of the same paper.

Studies of the accuracy of newspaper reporting have not so far looked at the information which is actually *received*. Instead investigators have tended to make a decision about what is transmitted and then assumed that this decision corresponds to the perceptual judgments of the readers. In studying newspaper communications within the framework of indirect perception we have been able to look at the accuracy of communications in terms of the judgments based upon them. If, for instance, two reports of one event generate different impressions, then there is a sense in which one or both is inaccurate. This approach to the study of accuracy and its implications will be considered below when we discuss a set of comparisons between indirect judgments of a single event.

FORMING IMPRESSIONS FROM NEWSPAPER REPORTS

In several experiments described in Chapter 4 we utilized two communications. These studies (Experiments 15–17) related subjects' conceptions of a person to their episodic perception of his behaviour as represented in a report. We were able to show a similar relationship between conception and perception even though the reports appeared to have differing contents. However, these apparent differences in communication content do not necessarily show that the reports in fact generated different impressions. We can check on this point by comparing mean perceptions of the stimulus person from the readers of each report.

The relevant investigations have already been described in Chapter 4 and need here only a brief resumé. Our interest at this stage is in showing that the reports we used did indeed generate significantly different impressions. This is important, first to show that the role of conceptual judgments (reviewed in Chapter 4, pp. 174–185) is the same despite differing perceptual judgments, and secondly to show that reports drawn from the national press do indeed generate quite different perceptions of the same event.

Consider first the results of one experiment which had as its stimulus person Mr. Harold Wilson (Experiment 16). Here we used two narratives which had appeared as reports in national newspapers. Narrative 1 came from the *Daily Telegraph* of October 2 1963 and narrative 2 from the *Daily Mail* of the same day. Both were accounts of a speech made by Wilson to a meeting of the British Labour Party, then in opposition to the Government. They contained similar factual information but appeared to give rather different emphasis to this information: narrative 1 concentrated upon the accomplished delivery of the speech, whereas the second version devoted more attention to the reactions of his audience. Subjects were assigned haphazardly to a narrative (50 to version 1 and 44 to version 2)* and after reading it through once (see the footnote to p. 178) recorded their episodic perceptions of Wilson's behaviour at the meeting. The usual form of nine-point semantic differential scales was used, the scales being selected to cover the three major factors. The scales were also used in Experiment 15 (see Table 10, p. 178) and elsewhere.

The fact that indirect perception of Wilson's behaviour at this event differed according to which narrative account was read is clear from a comparison of the judgments made by the two groups. No less than seven significant differences were present in the twelve scales employed.† We can now be confident about the generality of the conception–perception association discussed in Chapter 4. In that chapter a similar relationship between these two forms of judgment was noted for *both* narratives in the course of several experiments. It can now be seen that in the case of Experiment 16 the two narratives certainly did generate differing impressions. However, although the communication itself is a powerful determinant of indirect perception, subjects' conceptions nevertheless appear to exert a fairly constant influence over and above this determinant.

The same conclusion holds for the other studies of conception reported in Chapter 4. The narratives in both Experiment 15 and Experiment 17 clearly gave rise to very different impressions of the same event. Three significant differences in scale score were observed in the first of these studies where we compared judgment from reports in the *Daily Telegraph* and in the *Yorkshire Post*, and nine differences were obtained in Experiment 17 which made use of descriptions of Mr. Macmillan's behaviour appearing in the *Daily Telegraph* and *The Guardian*.‡ A further point about Experiment 17 was the use of the A.C.L. as a measure of episodic person perception in addition to the

---

* There were in fact no differences between the groups' conceptions of Wilson.

† These figures are in fact presented in detail in Table 17 (p. 271). The two left-hand columns of this table refer to the two narratives described here.

‡ See Table 18 (p. 272) and Table 19 (p. 273) for details of these results.

semantic differential. We have already reported (p. 102) an extremely close correspondence between the results obtained with the two measures. Pertinent here is the observation that there were significant differences between perceptions based upon the two narratives on rather more than one third of the 300 A.C.L. items.

It is indisputable that the communication is an important influence upon the judgment of an event perceived indirectly. And it does not require much familiarity with day to day reporting in the press for one to be aware that different accounts of the same event can vary markedly among newspapers, in a variety of ways and no doubt for a variety of reasons. It is likely that these reports will differ in the accuracy with which they transmit impressions of the event, and it is these various transmitted impressions (or episodic perceptual judgments) that we have been measuring and comparing. Discrepancies between judgments based on different reports indicate inaccuracy — but of course we cannot so far say which of the reports is the more inaccurate. To do this we need some externally derived criterion against which to compare the impression obtained from each communication. In the next experiment we describe our attempts to provide such a criterion and to make the relevant comparisons with regard to accuracy.

Experiment 25

The criterion we used for this investigation took the form of subjects' *direct* perceptions of a football match.* It was against the yardstick of these direct judgments that we compared indirect perceptions of the same game made via two newspaper reports. To provide a situation which was as realistic as possible our newspaper reports were not only genuine, but they were also presented to subjects within the pages of the papers themselves.

We recruited a panel of paid volunteers (16 male and 13 female undergraduates) and sent them to see a fairly typical association football match between two teams placed reasonably high in Division 1. The game was between Sheffield Wednesday and West Ham United and took place on Sheffield's ground. After the match the spectator panel recorded their episodic judgments of the match and of the two participating teams and these perceptions were later compared with similar judgments made indirectly via newspaper accounts. These indirect perceptions came from a further 93 undergraduate volunteers

---

* For a discussion of certain aspects of this study see Experiment 18, p. 180.

(51 male, 42 female) who read one of two newspaper reports of the match under experimental conditions. Of the 93 subjects none had been members of the panel and only 5 had attended the football match in question. Care was taken to recruit some members of the spectator panel who were not ardent football supporters, so that our panel should be matched as closely as possible to the more randomly selected subjects who were later to read the reports. The matching of subject groups is dealt with more fully in the discussion of the results below.

Roughly half of our 93 subjects read a report from the *Sunday Express* (Manchester edition) of March 7 1965; the other half read a report from the *Sheffield Telegraph* of March 8. Genuine copies of both newspapers were used in the experiment. The reports were both positioned prominently on the back pages of the newspapers; they each were accompanied by (different) photographs, but were not of equal length (*Sheffield Telegraph* 450 words, *Sunday Express* 300 words) or emphasis. The *Sunday Express* report was unenthusiastic about the match and about the performance of both teams, as was indicated by the headline *Fastest way to drive out fans*. The report in the *Sheffield Telegraph* appeared to give rather a more favourable impression of the match and of the Sheffield Wednesday team in particular, its headline being *Vic's goal sparks off new look*.

A semantic differential form comprising twelve nine-point scales from each of the three factors described earlier was used to measure subjects' perceptions of the two teams and of the match. The scales used are listed in Table 15 below. We also obtained from subjects information about how often they attended football matches and how keenly they supported each of the teams. We have already described (Experiment 18, p. 182) how conceptual judgments of the two teams were taken from all subjects and how these correlated more highly with indirect perception than with direct perception.

For comparisons between the spectator panel and the two sets of newspaper readers to be valid it is necessary to show that the composition of the three groups was similar. Several indices are available for assessing this similarity. The frequency of attendance at football matches was almost exactly the same for the groups, and they all supported the two teams to a similar extent.* The conceptions of the teams recorded before exposure to the stimulus information were also

---

* There were clear sex differences in these measures, but since the sex ratio was identical in the groups this does not affect the success with which they were matched.

Table 15 Mean perceptions of the match of Sheffield Wednesday and of West Ham United, by the panel and the two newspaper groups

	Scale	Sunday Express group (N=44)	Sheffield Telegraph group (N=49)	Panel (N=29)	Significance of difference between Sunday Express and Sheffield Telegraph subject groups
Sheffield Wednesday	Good–bad	3·73	5·31	5·83	0·001
	Interesting–boring	3·41	4·93	5·38	0·002
	Sweet–sour	4·16	4·33	5·35	n.s.
	Fair–unfair	5·25	5·49	5·38	n.s.
	Strong–weak	4·55	5·91	6·59	0·001
	Hard–soft	5·39	6·27	6·41	0·02
	Bold–timid	4·43	5·60	6·48	0·01
	Rugged–delicate	5·84	6·53	6·45	n.s.
	Tense–relaxed	5·52	6·33	5·17	0·05
	Hot–cold	4·57	5·20	5·76	n.s.
	Active–passive	5·11	6·38	6·90	0·001
	Fast–slow	3·89	5·62	5·79	0·001
West Ham United	Good–bad	3·77	5·02	5·21	0·01
	Interesting–boring	3·57	4·86	5·31	0·01
	Sweet–sour	4·27	4·45	5·10	n.s.
	Fair–unfair	5·30	5·67	6·76	n.s.
	Strong–weak	4·23	5·84	4·69	0·001
	Hard–soft	5·14	6·31	4·86	0·002
	Bold–timid	4·68	5·84	4·93	0·01
	Rugged–delicate	5·50	6·47	4·79	0·01
	Tense–relaxed	5·48	5·96	4·72	n.s.
	Hot–cold	4·55	5·20	4·62	n.s.
	Active–passive	5·14	5·65	6·07	n.s.
	Fast–slow	4·27	5·49	5·28	0·01
The match	Good–bad	2·63	4·67	5·45	0·001
	Interesting–boring	2·54	4·54	6·00	0·001
	Sweet–sour	4·02	4·31	4·90	n.s.
	Fair–unfair	5·23	5·38	6·10	n.s.
	Strong–weak	3·79	5·44	5·72	0·001
	Hard–soft	4·51	6·29	5·86	0·001
	Bold–timid	4·14	5·54	5·62	0·001
	Rugged–delicate	5·15	6·77	5·97	0·001
	Tense–relaxed	5·14	6·40	5·21	0·001
	Hot–cold	3·81	4·90	5·14	0·01
	Active–passive	4·12	5·56	5·86	0·002
	Fast–slow	3·21	5·02	5·66	0·001

very similar; of 72 possible comparisons only four yielded significant differences. We may be satisfied that the subject groups in the experiment were adequately matched. How similar were their perceptions of the event?

The mean responses of the two groups of indirect perceivers and of the spectator panel are shown in Table 15. It is evident that the impressions based on the two newspaper reports are very different: in fact the numbers of significant mean scale score differences for profiles of Sheffield Wednesday, West Ham United and the Match are 8, 7 and 10 respectively, making a total of 25 significant differences out of a possible 36. Once again the role of the communication is shown to be crucial in the formation of indirect perceptions of one event.

What about the direct perception from the spectator panel? In many instances this departs markedly from the perceptions based upon the newspaper reports. A summary indication of these differences is provided by D-scores (see p. 59). In Table 16 the D-scores between reader and panel profiles are presented. These provide a rough-and-ready indication of which newspaper report generated the impression closer to the direct perception of the subjects who were actually present. If we take the perception of the spectator panel to be an accurate impression of the event — in that these perceivers had access to all the observable information about it — then we can make some assessment of the accuracy of the reports.

Table 16 D-scores between mean profiles of the panel and the two groups of readers

	Sunday Express readers with panel	Sheffield Telegraph readers with panel
Sheffield Wednesday	5·28	2·18
West Ham United	3·35	3·29
The match	6·38	2·55

Table 16 shows large differences between the D-scores for the profiles of Sheffield Wednesday and of the Match according to which newspaper account the subjects read. The D-scores between the two newspaper groups for the profiles of West Ham United were found to be almost identical. On the whole the report generating an impression

of the match and team which coincided most closely with the perceptions of the spectator panel was from the *Sheffield Telegraph*. Can we
say that the report of the match appearing in this newspaper is more
accurate than the report from the *Sunday Express*? Some reservations
appear necessary before this conclusion can be accepted. First, the
perceptions recorded from subjects are partly dependent upon the
nature of the subject group. It is clear from results presented in Chapter
4 that conceptions of the teams affect the perceptions which will be
formed, so that differently composed reader and panel groups might
have judged the match differently. This *might* have influenced our
accuracy measure. If so, we have to conclude that "accuracy" will vary
from one group to another, and we therefore should strive for a
representative sample of readers or of football spectators to provide our
criterion. Against this, however, is the fact that the groups employed
were adequately matched, so that some confidence in the conclusion
seems warranted.

It may be noted that in this experiment we were attempting to
measure the most elusive aspect of accuracy — the connotative
meaning of the event to our subjects. Such a facet of accuracy is the one
most likely to vary according to the subjects involved. There would be
less variability between subject groups over the more overt aspects of
the event such as the number of goals scored, the goal scorers, playing
conditions and so on. We cannot be entirely happy with the use of
D-scores as our measure for reasons suggested in Chapter 1 (p. 60); but
since we are here dealing with the accuracy of a communication and
not with the accuracy of a perceiver several of the arguments do not
apply. It seems that — given the limitations noted above — fruitful
studies of communication accuracy in indirect perception could be
developed from the ideas outlined here.

READING MORE THAN ONE REPORT
— PRIMACY AND RECENCY EFFECTS

The experiments reviewed above have involved fairly complex
communications. In terms of the framework suggested in Chapter 1,
the inputs which we have studied have been multiple ones. And the
outputs from these multiple inputs have been shown to differ
markedly, despite the fact that the pairs of communications employed
supposedly represented the same event. What outputs would ensue if

we now combined the two multiple inputs, that is if subjects were asked to read *both* communications about an event? This situation is more typical of everyday indirect perception, since inputs about interesting events commonly arise from more than one source.

By combining pairs of narratives about an event we can investigate the relative power of each input and also the order effects which might take place when narratives are read sequentially. Here we shall describe four experiments, the first three of which make use of the narratives concerning Wilson, Heath and Macmillan that were originally used in Experiments 15, 16 and 17. The effects of combining these pairs of narratives will be examined in the light of recent work on primacy and recency effects in personal impression formation. The fourth experiment is similar to the first three, but makes use of specially prepared narratives counterbalanced rather more carefully than is possible for genuine newspaper communications.

Previous Research on Order Effects

As long ago as 1925 Lund investigated the effect of order of presentation with two conflicting communications about a controversial issue (Lund, 1925). He was concerned with the study of procedures of persuasion, and on the basis of his results he postulated a law of primacy, i.e. that the communication presented first will have the greater influence in changing opinion. Later, in 1957, Hovland and his colleagues devoted a whole book to studies of the order of presentation in persuasion (Hovland, 1957; see also Hovland, 1958). A great deal of work reported there is concerned with attitude change. For instance, Hovland and Mandell begin the volume by reporting an unsuccessful replication of Lund's original experiment, in which they were unable to find evidence for either primacy or recency effects upon attitudes to a variety of topics. More relevant to our present interests, however, are the chapters by Luchins (Luchins, 1957), who investigated the influence of order of stimulus material on impression formation. His subjects were presented with two short but conflicting paragraphs describing the behaviour of a hypothetical person, "Jim", one paragraph seeming to imply that Jim was an extravert, the other that he was an introvert. Subject groups received the paragraphs in different orders and then filled in a questionnaire concerning Jim and his likely behaviour in a variety of different situations. Over a number of experiments Luchins found a consistent primacy effect which he attributed to the influence

of *Einstellung* or set. He regarded the *Einstellung* as the same phenomenon which apparently operated in problem-solving tasks. Here the
set which is induced by early items can cause a similar, but now
inappropriate, pattern of responses to different items later in the series.
Luchins's explanation was apparently substantiated by some further
experiments in which the *Einstellung* was minimized by warning
subjects beforehand of possible primacy effects, or by interpolating a
simple task between the reading of the two paragraphs. By these means
the primacy effect was considerably reduced and in some cases a recency
effect took its place.

A different approach which uses less complex stimulus material is
found in the work initiated by N. H. Anderson. He uses sets of discrete
dispositional characteristics of the type often mentioned earlier in this
book. Subjects respond on a single evaluative scale, and the list of
stimulus items are made up according to their predetermined position
on this scale. Attributes rated "high" (that is, favourably) on the scale
include terms like *kind, creative* and *brilliant,* and "low" attributes
include *shallow, opinionated* and *unattractive.* By combining sets of "high"
adjectives with "low" ones in the description of a person, and by
studying perceptual responses to these combinations made on the single
evaluative scale, Anderson can see the effects of changes in the order of
presentation of characteristics.

Let us look for a moment in more detail at Anderson's approach.
Suppose that two groups of subjects are exposed to the same six
adjectives to describe a stimulus person and that three of the adjectives
are known to be high (*H*) and three of them to be low (*L*) on the
evaluative scale. One group might be presented with the terms in the
order *HHHLLL* and the other group might receive the same list in the
sequence *LLLHHH.* Subjects respond on the general evaluative scale
after exposure to a list, and a comparison of the scale scores for the
different combination group provides information about the importance of order of presentation in determining impressions of the
stimulus person. The following schematic presentation of a typical
finding illustrates this.

	Stimulus material	Perceptual response
Group 1	*HHHLLL*	*H*
Group 2	*LLLHHH*	*L*

If a set of three *H* adjectives followed by three *L* adjectives results in evaluations which are significantly higher than those based on *L–H* sets, we have evidence for a relatively greater importance of the earlier items in one or both of the lists — i.e. for a primacy effect. Anderson has observed primacy effects in this kind of situation fairly consistently.

How could such an effect be explained? Asch (1946) had himself noted similar effects, and he put forward a "directed impression" hypothesis, which states that the first adjective of a set changes the meaning of the others. This idea has much in common with Luchins's notion of *Einstellung*. Anderson rejects this hypothesis on the basis of his finding (Anderson and Barrios, 1961) that a primacy effect does not obtain when sets of only two adjectives (one *H* and one *L*) are presented. (See also Podell and Podell, 1963.) Further evidence against the "directed impression" hypothesis is claimed by Anderson and Norman (1964) as a result of experiments in which they presented subjects with lists of foods, newspaper headlines and typical life events as well as adjectives describing persons, and then asked for relevant evaluations. Primacy effects were found for headlines and for foods, and the latter are cited by the authors as evidence against Asch's explanation. It is unrealistic, they claim, to expect the meaning of "turnip" to vary according to whether it is presented before or after "sherbet".

If the primacy effect is not due to the impression from the first attribute directing the impressions made by the latter attributes, then perhaps the effect is due to subjects paying less attention to later adjectives. With this in mind Anderson and Hubert (1963) made one group of subjects attend to all adjectives equally by requiring recall of the list as well as a final evaluative response. They found a primacy effect when recall was not required, but interpolated recall reduced this effect and in one condition caused a recency effect. Stewart (1965) also found a recency effect when he ensured equal attention throughout the set by eliciting a cumulative response after each adjective, although the subjects in his control condition showed a primacy effect.

It does therefore seem that shifts of attention might be implicated in the commonly observed primacy effect. Anderson (1965a; 1965b) has incorporated this idea into a weighted average model, according to which changes in attention represent one of the factors which can alter the weights attached to adjectives. Other factors include a gross inconsistency within a set, or instructions to discount certain terms in making a judgment (Anderson and Jacobson, 1965).

A rather different approach to the study of primacy and recency

effects has been adopted by Mayo and Crockett (1964). They followed
up an observation made by Luchins (1957) that there are wide differences between individuals as far as the importance of presentation order
is concerned. The stable perceiver characteristic to which they turned
was one aspect of cognitive complexity (see pp. 200 and 212). Measures
were obtained from Kelly's Repertory Grid Test (see p. 98) of cognitive
differentiation, and these values were related to judges' impressions of a
stimulus person, "Joe". Two blocks of tape-recorded communications
about Joe, of high or low valence, were presented to subjects in one of
two orders, HL or LH. After each communication judges rated Joe by
free description, on a Conflict Situations Questionnaire and on an
Adjective Check List. Recency effects were found for the subjects of low
cognitive complexity while the high complexity judges had far more
ambivalent final impressions of the stimulus person. This accords with
Mayo and Crockett's prediction that persons of high cognitive
complexity would be better able to reconcile disparate information.
The relationship between a subject's high cognitive complexity and his
ability to integrate opposing perceptual inputs has been further
confirmed in a later experiment by Nidorf and Crockett (1965a); and
associated studies have been described by Harvey and Schroder (1963),
Leventhal and Singer (1964), Meltzer, Crockett and Rosenkrantz
(1966) and Rosenkrantz and Crockett (1965).*

A related stable characteristic of the perceiver which appears also to
mediate the importance of serial order is dogmatism. Foulkes and
Foulkes (1965) have presented results which suggest that if high
D-scorers alter their impression to accommodate disparate inputs
occurring later the shifts will be extreme ones, providing much greater
evidence for recency effects than do the less marked changes of low
D-scorers. Another relevant perceiver characteristic has been noted by
Luchins and Luchins (1965). They observed that subjects' ideas about
a "normal" degree of extraversion might determine their attribution of
this characteristic to "Jim".

It is clear from the studies reviewed in this section that in some
circumstances, especially when relatively simple material is used, serial
order effects may be observed. We wonder whether similar effects may
take place when complex communications of the kind typically
involved in real-life indirect perception are involved. With this in
mind, four further investigations have been conducted.

* Additional references are cited on p. 200.

Experiments 26, 27 and 28

The first three of these experiments made use of narratives about Wilson, Heath and Macmillan which figured in Experiments 16, 15 and 17 respectively. In the present studies subjects were required to read *both* narratives about the stimulus person, and we compared the judgments which were made on the basis of this combined input. As indicated earlier in the chapter, the narratives taken singly led to significantly different impressions. These perceptions, already recorded as part of the earlier experiments, served as part of the data analysed here. In addition, groups of 94, 92 and 98 undergraduate subjects read the two narratives together in Experiments 26, 27 and 28 respectively. Responses were on the same semantic differential scales as those used previously, and were made immediately after both reports had been read.

At the start of an experimental session, which involved several other tasks, subjects were asked for their conceptions of the relevant politician (Wilson, Heath or Macmillan, as the case might be). Later in the session they were assigned to one of two groups in roughly equal proportions. (For the exact N of each group see the appropriate tables below.) These two groups corresponded to the different orders of presentation of the narratives: the first group received narrative 1 followed by narrative 2, and the second group the same two narratives in reverse order. Subjects were asked to read the first narrative presented to them, place it aside, read the second narrative, place this aside, and then report their impression of the behaviour of the politician concerned on the semantic differential form.

To summarize the design of these three experiments, we had in effect four groups of subjects in each experiment. Each group recorded their episodic judgment of the stimulus person's behaviour on the same set of semantic differential scales. The four groups read one or two narratives as follows:

Group	Narrative
1	1
2	2
3	1 then 2
4	2 then 1

Methods of Measuring Order Effects

Various methods have been used to assess the effects of primacy and recency in impression formation and attitude change experiments. Lund's technique involved measuring a subject's prior attitude to the issue in question, his attitude after being exposed to the first communication and, finally, his attitude after being exposed to both the first and second communications (Lund, 1925). In his studies these measures are available for two groups receiving the communications in a different order. Lund inserted the several measures into a simple formula to obtain an indication of the importance of serial position. We cannot readily apply this kind of formula, since we are more concerned with measuring subjects' perceptions of a stimulus person's behaviour and this cannot be judged in isolation from a specific situation. Thus it would be unrealistic to attempt to elicit prior perceptions of, say, Wilson's behaviour without providing any account of this behaviour.

We have therefore turned our attention to another more common technique for measuring order effects. This technique, used by Luchins (1957), N. H. Anderson (e.g. 1962), Mayo and Crockett (1964) and others, derives from their use of the design which we outlined earlier. Stimulus material is scored on some dimension (e.g. extraversion/introversion; general desirability) before subjects are presented with two sets of material — *HL* or *LH*. If judgments based upon a pair of communications in which the one of high valence (or of extraversion) came first yield a higher (or more extraverted) rating of the stimulus person than judgments based upon a pair in which the communication of low valence (or introversion) came first, then a primacy effect is assumed to have been present in at least one of the pairs of communications. The procedure may be roughly summarized as follows:

(a) If *HL* minus *LH* is positive, then a primacy effect obtains in at least one of the pairs of communications.

(b) If *HL* minus *LH* is negative, then a recency effect obtains in at least one of the pairs of communications.

We have tried to apply this kind of measure to the results of the present set of experiments; the relevant findings are outlined below.

Order Effects and the Difference Score Measure

Table 17 Episodic judgments of Wilson's behaviour by subjects who had read narrative 1 alone, narrative 2 alone, narratives 1 then 2, and narratives 2 then 1 [a]

Scale	Narrative 1 ($N=50$)	Narrative 2 ($N=44$)	Narrative 1 followed by narrative 2 ($N=55$)	Narrative 2 followed by narrative 1 ($N=42$)	Difference scores ($HL-LH$)
True–false	4·62	5·23	5·60	4·79	−0·81
Wise–foolish	4·92	5·34	6·07	5·31	−0·76
Sweet–sour	4·50*	5·16*	4·98	4·62	−0·36
Fair–unfair	5·38	5·68	5·87	5·45	−0·42
Strong–weak	6·04*	7·14*	7·22	6·93	−0·29
Hard–soft	6·48	6·21	6·76	6·52	0·24
Large–small	5·46*	6·41*	6·44	6·57	0·13
Rugged–delicate	6·20*	6·80*	6·56	6·83	0·27
Sharp–dull	6·42	6·77	6·93	6·67	−0·26
Hot–cold	4·14*	6·23*	5·16	4·93	−0·23
Active–passive	6·70*	7·52*	7·38	7·33	−0·05
Fast–slow	5·61*	6·61*	6·29	6·76	0·47
Mean difference score					−0·17

[a] Significant mean differences between perceptions of behaviour based on narrative 1 (alone) and those based on narrative 2 (alone) — $p<0.05$ — are indicated by asterisks.

Let us look first at Experiment 26 which is concerned with newspaper reports about Mr. Harold Wilson. The first two columns of Table 17 show the assessment of Wilson's behaviour by groups of subjects who had read only one of the narratives. On the basis of these mean scores a particular narrative can be said to be of high or low valence. In fact on all scales except *hard–soft* narrative 2 is shown to be the more positive. Column three shows the perceptions based upon the two narratives when narrative 1 preceded narrative 2, and column four the mean perceptions for the order narrative 2–narrative 1. The last column shows the result of calculating the simple difference scores for each scale: using the valence scores provided by columns one and two for each scale the mean perceptions for the *LH* order were subtracted from the *HL* order means. The mean difference score across all the scales is − 0·17, and this is shown at the foot of the last column. The figure indicates a non-significant recency effect (Wilcoxon matched-pairs signed rank test). Some of the differences between mean perceptions based on narrative 1 alone, and on narrative 2 alone are very slight, so that it is perhaps unfair to term one narrative H and the other L in these cases. Consequently some of the valency scores are rather arbitrary. Significant differences between narratives 1 and 2 are indicated on the table by asterisks and, if the difference scores are calculated for these scales only, an even smaller recency effect is found. So there are no consistent order effects revealed by this form of measurement. It should be noted in passing that there are no differences between the groups' conceptions of Wilson, which were measured well before the perceptual judgments were elicited.

Table 18 The effects of presentation order on perceptions of Heath's behaviour[a]

Scale	Narrative 1 (N=46)	Narrative 2 (N=46)	Narrative 1 followed by narrative 2 (N=50)	Narrative 2 followed by narrative 1 (N=48)	Difference scores (HL − LH)
True–false	5·74	5·52	5·96	6·04	− 0·08
Wise–foolish	6·20*	4·89*	5·88	5·85	0·03
Sweet–sour	5·00	4·50	4·38	4·52	− 0·14
Fair–unfair	6·13*	5·13*	5·90	5·98	− 0·08
Strong–weak	7·11	6·89	7·18	6·98	0·20
Hard–soft	6·83	6·54	7·00	7·19	− 0·19
Large–small	6·22	6·00	6·26	6·15	0·11
Rugged–delicate	6·59	6·41	6·52	6·46	0·06
Sharp–dull	6·13	5·76	6·58	6·29	0·29
Hot–cold	5·24	4·59	5·02	5·17	− 0·15
Active–passive	6·98	6·59	6·70	7·27	− 0·57
Fast–slow	6·13*	5·28*	5·98	5·88	0·10
Mean difference score					− 0·04

[a] Significant mean differences between perceptions of behaviour based on narrative 1 (alone) and those based on narrative 2 (alone) — $p < 0.05$ — are indicated by asterisks.

Table 18 presents the same information for Heath (Experiment 27), and in this case there is virtually no effect whatsoever according to the mean difference score. Once again we may note that there were no significant differences between the four groups' *conceptions* of the stimulus person.

The mean difference score for the Macmillan data (Experiment 28), shown in Table 19, again fails to reveal an order effect. On this occasion there were two significant differences (scales *warm–cold* and *good-looking–unattractive*) between the conceptions of the politician obtained from the two-narrative groups, but if the scores on these two scales are ignored in the calculations the result is hardly affected.

Table 19 The effects of presentation order on perceptions of Macmillan's behaviour[a]

Scale	Narrative 1 (N=48)	Narrative 2 (N=50)	Narrative 1 followed by narrative 2 (N=49)	Narrative 2 followed by narrative 1 (N=46)	Difference scores (HL – LH)
Generous–ungenerous	5·52*	4·32*	4·51	5·11	−0·60
Happy–unhappy	4·50	4·34	4·55	4·98	−0·43
Good natured–irritable	5·75*	4·00*	5·14	5·57	−0·43
Sociable–unsociable	5·88*	4·58*	5·65	5·91	−0·26
Reliable–unreliable	5·71	5·04	5·47	5·17	0·30
Popular–unpopular	4·40*	5·20*	4·86	4·96	0·10
Warm–cold	5·27*	4·16*	5·25	5·48	−0·23
Important–insignificant	4·44*	6·30*	4·45†	5·33†	0·88
Humane–ruthless	5·94*	3·62*	5·02	5·35	−0·33
Good-looking–unattractive	4·69	4·62	4·47	4·26	0·21
Altruistic–self-centred	5·13*	4·18*	5·14	4·54	0·60
Strong–weak	4·02*	6·14*	4·94	4·70	−0·24
Honest–dishonest	5·85	5·38	5·29	5·06	0·23
Mean difference score					−0·02

[a] Significant differences between narrative 1 and narrative 2 — $p < 0.05$ — are indicated by asterisks. A significant difference between 1–2 and 2–1 is indicated by a dagger.

Order Effects and Multiple Correlation Analysis

It is evident from the results presented above that the difference scores do not reveal any significant effect related to order of presentation. This conclusion might perhaps have been predicted from an examination of the mean scores of the two-narrative groups, shown in columns three and four of Tables 17, 18 and 19. Over the three stimulus persons there is in fact only one significant difference between the groups receiving the narratives in different orders.

But it could be said that this is an unsatisfactory way of measuring order effects in the case of these data. There are at least two major difficulties. One, alluded to above, is that because the differences between single narratives are sometimes very small we cannot always easily and meaningfully determine on which scales a narrative is H or L in the sense used by Anderson and others. This means that our comparisons could rest on a very weak foundation. A second problem concerns the validity of summing over scales as a technique for reaching an overall conclusion. Not only are we summing unlike quantities in that the differences between the two narratives when read singly vary considerably between scales, but it is also likely that we are throwing away useful information in deriving this composite score. We felt that a different form of analysis was required which would be more sensitive to these difficulties.

A statistic was needed which would provide information about the relative importance of each of the two stories in generating the impression based upon the pair of narratives read sequentially. One statistic of this kind is derived from calculations involved in the computation of the multiple correlation coefficient, R. Just as the simple product–moment correlation, r, gives us information about how well we can predict one variable from the other, R indicates how well one variable can be predicted from the combination of several others. In this case we could use R to see how well the perception of a stimulus person's behaviour based upon two reports could be predicted from the perceptions generated by each of the two narratives read singly. We have information about each of these perceptions on 12 scales (13 in the case of Macmillan) and we would be able to obtain multiple correlations between the mean values presented in the earlier tables.* This procedure is of course only legitimate if the subjects registering each perception are well matched. We have already presented evidence that this is so.

The multiple correlation values for the three stimulus persons are presented in the right-hand columns of Table 20. In the case of Wilson and Heath at least, the R values are very high. This means that we can account for an extremely large part of the variance in perceptions based on two narratives read together (represented by R^2 in each case) in terms of the scale perceptions derived from reading each of the narratives singly. For example, consider the data from Experiment 26 where the stimulus person was Wilson. The multiple correlation

---

* In retrospect we can see advantages in using a rather larger number of scales in studies of this design.

Table 20 Order effects in terms of multiple correlation values and beta coefficients for the Wilson, Heath and Macmillan narratives

Stimulus person	Beta coefficients				Multiple R	
	Narrative 1 before narrative 2 1st story presented	Narrative 1 before narrative 2 2nd story presented	Narrative 2 before narrative 1 1st story presented	Narrative 2 before narrative 1 2nd story presented	Narrative 1 before narrative 2	Narrative 2 before narrative 1
Wilson	0·71	0·27	0·51	0·54	0·94	0·97
Heath	0·59	0·35	0·40	0·60	0·95	0·97
Macmillan	0·76	0·24	0·19	0·67	0·65	0·61

between perceptions based on the two stories read singly and the two read sequentially in the order 1–2 is 0·94. This means that 88% (i.e. R^2) of whatever causes the variation in the twelve scale values based upon the two narratives read sequentially can be attributed to variations in scale perceptions of each of the stories read singly.

But R has an additional use here. The proportion of the variance indicated by an R^2 value can be split into the fractions contributed by each of the two single variables. We can by this means get an idea of the relative importance of the two individual narratives in generating the cumulative effect when read sequentially. The relevant equation for the present number of variables is $R^2 = \text{beta }_{12\cdot3}\, r_{12} + \text{beta }_{13\cdot2}\, r_{13}$. From this one can isolate the contribution made by each narrative to the variance in the set of responses to the two narratives read together. The measure of the contribution made by each narrative (i.e. the beta $\times r$ values) may be translated into standard scores, so that differences between individual variances are controlled, and the final index is known as a β coefficient. The basis and nature of the calculations involved have been described by Garrett (1959, p. 418). The two members of a pair of β coefficients may be compared in order to learn which single story is of greater importance in determining the overall impression generated by the sequential reading of two narratives.

Consider now the β coefficients in Table 20. Subjects' perceptions of Wilson based upon sequential reading of the two narratives in the order 1–2 are clearly more determined by the content of narrative 1 than by the content of narrative 2 (β coefficients of 0·71 and 0·27 respectively). But there is no difference between the importance of the two narratives when the pair is read sequentially in the reverse order. Similar discrepancies are found for the other experiments, and at first sight the β coefficients in Table 20 do not fall into a straightforward pattern.

However, on further inspection it is possible to make some sense of them. The following simple model can account for the variations in a most economic manner. Let us assume two possible kinds of mechanism which may be at work in determining a judgment based upon a pair of narratives: the influence of the narrative itself, and the influence of the serial position of each narrative. The marked influence of a particular narrative would be revealed if it contributed much more than the other to the combined perception irrespective of its serial position. This kind of influence would be indicated by a much larger coefficient for this narrative in whatever position it is presented. If there were no clear discrepancy of this kind we should conclude that neither narrative was exerting a disproportionate influence. If we have evidence for a narrative influence we shall describe this by saying that mechanism N is operating.

What of the second mechanism in our simple model — the influence of serial position? This may take three forms. The first narrative presented may have a predominant effect; this is in fact an order effect which indicates primacy and we shall here refer to it as mechanism OP. Or the second narrative presented may have a predominant effect; this is a recency effect and we shall refer to it as mechanism OR. And, finally, when there is no order effect, or when order effects cancel out we shall refer to mechanism OE ("order equal").

If we can show that perceptions based on two narratives together are heavily dependent on the narratives when read singly, then we can ask whether one or both of these two mechanisms is at work. In the case of Wilson and Heath the R values are very high, and we can be confident that virtually all of the combined perception is due to one or both of the mechanisms we have referred to. In the Macmillan experiment (Experiment 28) the R values are only barely significant and some extraneous factor we have not measured is influencing subjects' perceptions. So we shall give greater emphasis to the interpretation of the former experiments.

Let us now examine the coefficients in Table 20 in terms of our model. A straightforward procedure to decide which mechanisms are operative is to compare the narrative 1 columns (columns 1 and 4) with the narrative 2 columns (2 and 3) and to compare the position 1 columns (1 and 3) with the position 2 columns (2 and 4). A rough-and-ready way to do this is to total or average the values in columns 1 and 4 and compare these with a similar figure from columns 2 and 3, in order to decide whether mechanism N is operative; and to make a similar comparison of columns 1 and 3 and 2 and 4 to see which form of the second mechanism (order) is present. This summation or averaging of β coefficients is unlikely to be mathematically acceptable, and we only recommend it as an economical way to grasp the relationships between the values in Table 20.

The picture which emerges from the table when these procedures are applied is as follows. For Wilson narrative 1 has a greater effect than narrative 2, but position 1 also has an advantage over position 2 (mechanisms N and OP); for Heath narrative 1 has more influence than narrative 2 (mechanism N) but this time the slight order effects cancel out (mechanism OE); in the case of Macmillan the relevant mechanisms are again N and OE.

The important point to note is that mechanism N is present in the results for all three experiments: in other words the influence of a particular story is very evident. As far as Heath and Macmillan are concerned the order effects, if any, are overwhelmed by this influence of a particular narrative. In the Wilson experiment a primacy effect (OP) does appear to exist, but again it seems to have been interfered with to a great extent by the predominant influence of narrative 1.

This all-pervading influence of the communication was in some ways not unexpected, especially in view of the rather complicated material presented to subjects. However, our findings were not in complete harmony with those of other investigators in the field who had by and large found no difficulty in obtaining order effects of one sort or another. At this stage therefore we shall postpone a full discussion of our findings, and shall instead present the results of a fourth experiment to investigate order effects. In this study we attempted to counterbalance the influence of narrative content.

Experiment 29

In order to provide realistic stimulus material we have made use of genuine newspaper reports in all the experiments reported so far in this chapter. It seemed, however, that our very desire for authenticity was working against us in that a possible order effect (primacy for the Wilson experiment) was being interfered with by the all-too-interesting content of our narratives. We therefore devized a compromise experiment in which the material used was still fairly complex and still had the appearance of being from a genuine newspaper, but this time a firmer control was kept over the story content. Thus any order effects that were present would be able to assert themselves more easily.

Two reports were prepared about a hypothetical boundary dispute between the City of Norwich and the County of Norfolk. The reports, which purported to come from two genuine local newspapers, were concerned with a speech made on the boundary issue by a hypothetical "Sir Joseph Edwards". The reports were almost equal in length and both agreed about the factual content of the speech. They differed, however, in the impression they gave of Sir Joseph's performance and of his reception by the audience. More specifically, the adjectives chosen to describe Sir Joseph and his behaviour differed radically between the two stories, narrative 1 employing positive adjectives and narrative 2 negative adjectives. The text of the two stories is given below.

Narrative One

Sir Joseph Edwards put up a *powerful* performance at Norwich last night when he spoke on the local by-law amendment which seeks to bring to an end a ten-year boundary dispute between the City and the Norfolk County Council. In a *sober* and *positive* speech which lasted for almost forty minutes he outlined the long and complicated history of the disagreement, pointing out that the case for each party in the dispute was now so familiar to all that any further discussion was pointless. The time had now come for a decision one way or another. Each side had its supporters and detractors, but Sir Joseph made no secret of his *solid* support for the City's position: he felt, he said, that the exchange of land between the City and the County was the most satisfactory way of dealing with the problem. He claimed he had always been quite *flexible* in listening to views from outside the town — when at this point several voices from the floor cried out in protest he dealt with the interruptions in a *lively* fashion. In the past Sir Joseph has often been known for his ability to cast a *sharp* eye into some of the more dusty corners of local politics, even if his mode of expressing his views has tended to be rather *impetuous*. Judging by his reception last night it seems as if he is going to be *successful* in bringing another weary wrangle to a timely end.

Norwich Mercury

Narrative Two

The row over the boundary dispute between Norfolk County Council and the City of Norwich was not helped by Sir Joseph Edwards' *colourless* speech in Norwich last night in which he revealed his *shallow* understanding of the conflict. Sir Joseph's aim, in so far as any aim could be perceived from what he said, is to end the complex wrangling which has gone on for the past ten years without any concrete results having been achieved. He believes that a solution can be found by adopting the City's proposed by-law amendment which will allow for the exchange of land between both parties. As Sir Joseph said, the details of the exchange are well known; it is, however, doubtful whether a speech as *tame* and *timid* as this will do much to allay the fears of the County. Those who oppose the City on this issue recalled Sir Joseph's promises when he was elected to the Council and accused him of a *disreputable* "about-face": there were some cries of "*ungrateful*" from the audience. Sir Joseph received the heckling *quietly* and *calmly* enough, but the rest of what he had to say was interrupted by a barrage of shouted questions. As the meeting reached its conclusion Sir Joseph looked understandably *pessimistic* about the future of the Norwich plan. If, in spite of the objections, Sir Joseph and his supporters have their way, a sad precedent will have been created.

Eastern Daily Press

The relevant adjectives, of opposite polarity for each narrative, are indicated above by italics. The adjectives were selected from ones previously used in work with the semantic differential to be representative of the three major factors. The Evaluative factor was represented by *sober*, *positive* and *successful* (in narrative 1) and by *disreputable*, *ungrateful* and *pessimistic* (narrative 2); the Potency factor was present in *powerful*, *solid* and *sharp* (narrative 1) and *shallow*, *tame* and *timid* (narrative 2); finally *flexible*, *lively*, *impetuous* (narrative 1) and *colourless*, *quiet(ly)* and *calm* (narrative 2) were all from the Activity factor.

It was hoped to create narratives which would generate clearly different perceptions and which would at the same time be of a fairly balanced content so that one was not more influential than the other irrespective of its serial position. We shall indicate how far our aims met with success in a later section; for the moment attention should be drawn to the need to include other linking material which varied between the narratives. It was extremely difficult to produce realistic communications based on the chosen adjectives without introducing some material into one story which was not present in the other.

No direct measure was taken of whether or not subjects regarded the stories as authentic but at one stage a subject asked to be excused from participation in the experiment on the grounds that he lived in

Norwich and "knew all the details of the dispute"! The narratives were prepared in the usual typewritten format, with no headings or sub-headings, but with the name of the supposed paper at the foot of the sheet. The relevant adjectives were of course not italicized in the version given to subjects.

Twelve-scale semantic differential forms were used to measure subjects' episodic perceptions of Sir Joseph's behaviour. The forms comprised four scales from each of the three factors, but none of the scales used coincided with the adjectives embedded in the two narratives. Scale polarities and orders were randomized in the usual manner. In Table 21, however, the positive adjective is shown first and scales of each factor are shown in blocks in the order: Evaluation, Potency and Activity.

Two groups of 40 undergraduate subjects each (approximately equal numbers of either sex) read and indicated their impressions based upon either narrative 1 or narrative 2; two different subject groups of 49 and 48 undergraduates did the same for *both* narratives for the two different orders of presentation. The instructions were as for Experiments 26,

Table 21 The effects of presentation order in perceptions of Sir Joseph Edwards[a]

Scale	Narrative 1 (N=40)	Narrative 2 (N=40)	Narrative 1 followed by narrative 2 (N=49)	Narrative 2 followed by narrative 1 (N=48)	Difference scores (HL − LH)
True–false	5·95*	4·95*	5·54	5·60	−0·06
Good–bad	6·28*	4·95*	5·54	5·73	−0·19
Kind–cruel	5·33	5·95	5·18	5·52	0·34
Fair–unfair	5·95	5·35	5·51	6·04	−0·53
Strong–weak	7·60*	3·35*	5·46	5·35	0·11
Hard–soft	6·68*	3·10*	5·46	5·04	0·42
Bold–timid	7·85*	2·90*	5·84	5·50	0·34
Rugged–delicate	7·03*	3·95*	5·32	5·19	0·13
Dangerous–safe	5·30*	4·24*	4·67†	3·77†	0·90
Emotional–unemotional	5·30*	3·48*	4·63†	3·75†	0·88
Active–passive	7·73*	3·68*	5·90	6·00	−0·10
Fast–slow	6·20*	3·30*	4·78	4·60	0·18
Mean difference score					0·20

[a] Significant differences between narrative 1 and narrative 2 — $p < 0.05$ — are indicated by asterisks. And significant differences between 1–2 and 2–1 are indicated by daggers.

27 and 28 and subjects were asked to give their perception of Sir Joseph Edwards's behaviour at the meeting, based upon what he had said and done.

Table 21, which is in the same form as Tables 17, 18 and 19 shows the mean perceptions of Sir Joseph's behaviour based on the individual narratives (columns one and two) and on two narratives read sequentially (columns three and four). Asterisks indicate significant differences between means for the perceptions based on one narrative alone. For these it is evident that we were successful in providing stories which differed considerably in the impression they gave of the stimulus person's behaviour, as measured by the relevant scale dimensions. Although there are more significant differences (two) between columns three and four than in the previous experiments, this number is still rather surprisingly low. The difference scores, which are shown in column five, were calculated in the same way as for the Wilson, Heath and Macmillan experiments. The mean difference score of $+0.20$ is the largest obtained but the slight primacy effect it indicates is not quite statistically significant.

The data for Experiment 29 were also subjected to analysis by multiple regression techniques and the relevant information is summarized in Table 22.

Inspection of Table 22 shows that the multiple correlation values are high, indicating that perceptions based on the combined narratives can be interpreted in terms of the perceptions based upon the individual stories. Application to the coefficients of the simple model suggested earlier shows that mechanisms N and OP appear to be at work: i.e. there is evidence that narrative 1 has a greater effect than narrative 2, but the first position also has greater influence on perception. These data for Sir Joseph Edwards present a very similar picture to the comparable figures for Wilson: a primacy effect appears to be present, but it is largely overshadowed by the story content itself. The implications of this finding, especially in view of the careful attempt which has been made to counterbalance the stories, will be discussed below in conjunction with the other findings on order effects.

Order Effects and Story Content: A General Discussion of Experiments 26, 27, 28 and 29 and their Implications

The work reviewed in this chapter leads clearly to the conclusion that order effects in person perception can be generated, but that these

Table 22 Order effects in terms of multiple correlation values and beta coefficients for the Sir Joseph Edwards narratives

| Stimulus person | Beta coefficients | | | | Multiple R | |
	Narrative 1 before narrative 2 1st story presented	Narrative 1 before narrative 2 2nd story presented	Narrative 2 before narrative 1 1st story presented	Narrative 2 before narrative 1 2nd story presented	Narrative 1 before narrative 2	Narrative 2 before narrative 1
Sir Joseph Edwards	1·10	0·63	0·95	1·04	0·90	0·92

effects vary from one investigation to another. It seems unwise to ask whether "primacy" or "recency" is the rule; rather we should enquire into the conditions which generate recency, those which lead to primacy and those in which no serial phenomena are measurable.

It appears that recency effects occur most readily under some rather special circumstances: when another task is interpolated between the communications (Luchins, 1957), when a cumulative response to stimuli is required (Luchins, 1958; Mayo and Crockett, 1964; Stewart, 1965), or when concomitant recall of the stimulus material is requested (Anderson and Hubert, 1963). Such conditions were not present in the four experiments we have just described and we are therefore not surprised that our own investigations failed to reveal any evidence for a recency effect.

Primacy effects have been demonstrated in a rather larger number of investigations. It is interesting, however, that these effects are most clear-cut when the stimulus material has been extremely simple, usually a short list of adjectives (e.g. Asch, 1946), and when the subjects' responses have been made on a single dimension (e.g. Anderson and Barrios, 1961). Where the material has been more complex the primacy effects have sometimes been reduced or even eliminated altogether. Thus Anderson and Norman (1964) failed to demonstrate the effects when using life events as stimulus material, and Rosenkrantz and Crockett (1965) found no primacy effect when using tape-recorded anecdotes about a stimulus person. Gollin (1954) noted no order effects in his study of indirect perception mediated by motion pictures. It would seem likely that when fairly complicated stimulus material is used, the communications themselves interfere to a marked extent with whatever order effects might otherwise be present. This influence of the communication has been mentioned by Rosenkrantz and Crockett (1965) and by Luchins and Luchins (1965). Our own experiments made use of stimulus material that was not only complex, but was (in three cases at least) authentic in the sense that it comprised genuine newspaper reports. We might expect this material to have a considerable influence on subjects' judgments and to interfere with the effects of presentation order. The multiple regression data of Table 20 seem to amply confirm that this is the case. Although there is some limited evidence for a primacy effect, the influence of the communications themselves is always extremely marked. Even an attempt to counterbalance this influence by providing equally weighted stories revealed only a slight primacy effect, and failed to eradicate the action of the communication (Table 22).

It is helpful to look at this question in the light of the discussion of combination rules presented in Chapter 3 (pp. 163–172). We contrasted at that point linear and configural models of combination, and suggested that each may be valid in certain situations. The core of a configural model is the idea that parts of a set of material (or indeed the set as a whole) may take on particular importance relative to the rest so that they influence the meaning of component individual inputs. As we suggested in Chapter 3, this implies that studies of the combination of inputs need to encompass the relationships between inputs making up the total stimulus array. If one item is somehow more important than the other to a judge, it will naturally take priority in the combined input. Yet this same item may be the junior partner in another combination of items.

In a more molar sense we may say that the two narratives of the pairs we have studied in this chapter each constitute single inputs. We expect then that one may take priority over the other in the eyes of our subjects, so that their combined influence may not be mechanically predictable in terms of a general principle of primacy or recency. If narrative A takes priority over narrative B and is read first, then we shall observe primacy. But if narrative A is read before narrative C, primacy will not obtain if C is somehow prepotent over A.

We should perhaps rephrase the research question as follows: what is there about one input in relation to another which ensures its prepotence in a combined stimulus array? If the material is very simple, it may be that being received first is the important characteristic. If the material has to be recalled it may be that coming last is what counts. But in many cases where complex stimulus material is studied the answer is far from obvious.

Consider again the narratives employed in Experiments 26, 27, 28 and 29. From Tables 20 and 22 it can be seen that narrative 1 is the more influential story in each case. It is not true, however, that narrative 1 is always the more positive or favourable narrative, as can be seen by consulting columns one and two of Tables 17, 18 and 19 and 21.* Nor does the calculation of deviation scores for the narratives provide any

* Studies reported as this book goes to press do suggest that the sequence in which positive and negative information is received is a variable of some importance. See Briscoe, Woodyard and Shaw (1967); Richey, McLelland and Shimkunas (1967).

clue to the prepotency of narrative 1 in the combined perceptions. The deviation scores, which are the mean of all subjects' deviations from the scale centre (5) for all scales, are almost identical in the case of each pair of narratives. Another possible explanation could be in terms of how unanimous certain readers are about the impression given by a particular report: if a story induced more agreement in the way the stimulus person was judged then we might expect this story to be more influential. This sort of agreement between perceivers could be measured in terms of the variance in the responses to each semantic differential scale. An examination of the relevant standard deviations, however, reveals no systematic differences between the narratives.

We attempted to obtain an overall measure of the impact of our narratives by counting the number of apparently central traits (in the sense of the term described in Chapter 3) referred to in each narrative, but this proved quite meaningless, mainly because the newspaper stories we used contained hardly any direct description of the stimulus person. Instead they tended to concentrate more on describing his behaviour and what he said. As something of a last resort, we went to the trouble of applying Flesch's readability formulae (e.g. Chall, 1958) to the stories, but once again the results were negative.

We are consequently still uncertain why one narrative may exert greater influence than another when the two are read in sequence. The beta coefficients described earlier do, however, seem to provide a way of identifying the prepotent member; and perhaps research should next concentrate upon obtaining measures from judges themselves of comparative "vividness", "interestingness" and so on, to see what characteristics of this kind are associated with prepotency in combined inputs. This approach would parallel the recent trend in studies of inference and combination rules (see the investigation by Rokeach and Rothman (1965) described on p. 169). Another line of enquiry would be to start with stories of the "Sir Joseph Edwards" type and work backwards — simplifying the narratives until the counterbalancing was really effective and order effects outweighed narrative effects.

As we noted above, the work with simple stimulus material has provided models to account for the effects of order of presentation, notably the directed impression or *Einstellung* model and the weighted average model (embracing changes in attention and the discounting of some material). Various tests of these models which use more complicated stimulus material may be suggested. For example, subjects could be told previously that they were to get two conflicting communications, or they could be warned about possible order effects, both of which — according to Luchins' evidence — should wipe out any primacy effects. Alternatively subjects could be asked to make a private or public judgment between readings of the two reports, which should induce recency effects; a time interval or interpolated task between the two reports should produce the same result. Equal attention to both narratives could be ensured (assuming that it does not take place anyway) by requiring recall at the end of the experiment.

To test the weighted average model by using more complex material would, however, be difficult, for if any of the effects postulated by Anderson are taking place they may well be doing so *within each narrative*. Thus a person may attend to one part of a news account but not another, he may discount one sentence but accept the next. This seems especially likely since in real life communications rarely contain *all* favourable or *all* unfavourable material: they are a mixture of both. On the other hand, persons may typically discount material coming from certain sources (a particular television channel or daily newspaper, for instance) and studies might be made of the role of perceived reliability of source and discounting effects in presentation order experiments.

Despite these difficulties more research with complex material is surely desirable, if only to check on the validity of generalizations so readily drawn by some commentators on this issue. We have grave doubts whether studies of small numbers of traits (indispensable to scientific progress though they unquestionably are) can tell students of the mass media much about the best way to transmit their information. As a final warning to those overeager to generalize to real-life communication situations, let us note some results of a study by Bossart and Di Vesta (1966). Their stimulus material was complex — a 900-word narrative about a fictitious group of people, the Meblus. And one of their results was a slight but significant primacy effect for evaluative judgments. These researchers did what few other investigators have done and took follow-up measures after an interval of two weeks. By then the primacy effect had quite dissipated. Public relations officers and party political managers please note.

We might attempt a summary of research to date in this way. Serial order effects in person perception may take place. Sometimes they are of primacy and sometimes they are of recency. But on many occasions perception is unaffected by order *per se*, and some characteristics of the items in relation to the total configuration are responsible for one input being more salient than the others. And even when order is seen to matter, we have no evidence that its influence will be maintained beyond the experimental situation.

7
VARIATIONS
WITHIN A
COMMUNICATION

As the experiments already reported have amply demonstrated, the impressions we form about people and events can be markedly affected by the particular communication which mediates indirect perception. In Chapter 6 we treated the communication variable in a rather molar fashion, being in general more concerned with a narrative as a whole than with specific aspects of it. We adopt now a somewhat more molecular approach in the hope that we might learn something about which aspects of a communication are particularly important in determining judgments based upon it. Particular emphasis will once again be given to newspaper communications, and we shall consider the role of five kinds of input. The influence of newspaper headlines will first be examined, after which visual material such as the photographs accompanying an article will be studied. Subsequent sections will deal with typography and newspaper layout and with the identity of the paper in which a communication is transmitted.

THE INFLUENCE OF HEADLINES UPON PERCEPTION

Very few newspaper items appear without headlines and any visitor to a newspaper office knows that considerable effort and money is expended in composing headlines of appropriate length and content. It might well be thought that the headline is a vital constituent of any news item, and a brief glance at the relevant research literature is sufficient to provide a fund of quotations to this effect. We find it stated that headlines provide "a brief and attractive manner of presenting the reader with a sample of the paper's offerings" (Tannenbaum,

1953), and that they "create the picture of the world-scene that the public carries in mind for an entire day" (Winship and Allport, 1943). Allport and Lepkin (1943) go so far as to suggest that "a headline, if striking enough, may even help to establish the tone of one's work and reflections for the day".

Many popular critics (e.g. Liebling, 1961, p. 188; Williams, 1962), while discussing the inaccuracy of the press, have specifically drawn attention to differences between headlines; and the Report of the Royal Commission on the Press (His Majesty's Stationery Office, 1949) devotes a considerable portion of its main appendix to an account of the indirect judgments likely to follow from different headlines. Journalism textbooks have usually given a generous amount of space to this question. One such work (Evans, 1961) points out that although "headlines should reflect the tone of the story . . . opinions may differ between newspapers about what is the more important feature of a story. The headlines will reflect this". There follow six pages of instruction for would-be headline writers.

Is there any direct evidence for the frequently claimed influence of the headline? We can demonstrate that a larger headline is more likely to be read, and — more important — that a larger headline is likely to lead to more of the accompanying item being read (Knapper and Warr, 1965). But what about the actual *content* of headlines? Emig (1928) found in a questionnaire investigation that 51% of respondents claimed to base their opinions on "reading or skimming the headlines", 31% on reading news stories and 38% on reading both headlines and stories. This seems to show that newspaper readers certainly believe themselves to be influenced by headline content. Kingsbury and Hart (1934) observed that bias was present in headlines concerning a wide number of vital public issues, but they produced no evidence to show whether this bias affects interpretation. The study by Allport and Lepkin (1943) to investigate the effects of headlines on war-time morale made use of 126 "good-news" and "bad-news" headlines taken from a sample of the American press. The headlines were presented individually on cards in standard type face and subjects were asked to rate them on an eleven-point scale according to how they were made to feel about active participation in the war effort. It was shown that all headlines concerning the war tended to stimulate an expressed intention to participate more actively in the war effort, but that the "bad-news" headlines were significantly more influential than the "good-news" headlines.

A serious fault of the Allport and Lepkin experiment is that the reading situation was quite unrealistic so that no conclusions can be drawn about the effect of headlines relative to the news item as a whole. This shortcoming was remedied in an experiment by Tannenbaum (1953) in which he made use of what appeared to be a genuine newspaper front page. Tannenbaum's experiment was intended to test two hypotheses: (1) that the same news story presented with different headlines gives rise to different impressions, and (2) that this headline effect is in inverse proportion to the amount of the story read. The experiment involved the insertion of two test stories on the front page of a student newspaper. One story concerned a murder trial, and the other was about a scheme to accelerate the college teaching programme. The stories were both written in a neutral vein, but each was in turn assigned one of three different headlines, specially prepared to induce a different judgment about the topic of the item. Thus the "murder trial" story, for example, appeared with three different headlines — a "guilty" headline (i.e. suggesting the defendant's guilt), an "innocent" headline and a "neutral" headline. Some 400 subjects read each version of the mock newspaper and were asked whether they believed the defendant to be guilty or innocent; similar questions about the "college acceleration" story were posed. Subjects also indicated how much of the relevant news items they had read. On the "trial" story the results showed a significant association ($p<0\cdot05$) between the particular headline read and the reader's conclusion about the defendant's guilt; no headline effect was found for the "acceleration" story. For both items Tannenbaum found a highly significant negative correlation between the amount of a narrative read and the influence of the headline.

It would appear from this study that headlines can indeed influence indirect perception, but that their influence is conditional upon other factors. We have been sufficiently interested in the results to replicate Tannenbaum's investigation with quite different material. However, instead of measuring readers' judgments in terms of only a rather limited question we have obtained more general perceptual responses of the kind studied throughout this book. In addition we have specifically looked at the possibility that headline effects of the type reported by Tannenbaum derive entirely from the impressions of readers who have read only part of an item. Although this is indeterminate in Tannenbaum's published data, it is possible that the headline influence observed over all subjects in his "trial" story is in fact almost entirely due to a large effect obtained from the subgroups who read only part of the story (possibly the headline *only* or the head-line and the first few lines).

Experiment 30

Subjects were given apparently authentic copies of a provincial morning paper. These were the same as an original issue except that they contained a story about a fictitious stimulus person. This item was specially written by the paper's editor and was loosely based upon an actual event which had been described in the paper some time pre-viously. It concerned a dispute over the colour of a barn roof between a farmer and the local planning board, and was written in a fairly neutral vein with both the board's and the farmer's position being stated quite fully. The content of the story appeared in identical form in all the newspapers, but there were two different versions of the headline. In one set of papers this read *Black roof row just red tape says angry farmer*, whereas the second version was headed *Black roof eyesore must go says planning board*. The aim of this alteration was to observe whether giving further emphasis to the farmer's behaviour (in the first headline) would generate measurable effects. The experimental story was of single column width and appeared in a fairly prominent position on the top right-hand side of the newspaper's front page.

Two groups of undergraduate students from Sheffield University in roughly equal proportions of men and women served as subjects for the investigation. Forty-eight subjects were given version one of the newspaper, and fifty others received version two. Their attention was not directed specifically at the experimental story. Instead they were asked to read any items on the front page which interested them.* After five minutes the papers were collected and subjects were asked to give their (dispositional) impression of the farmer in the "black roof dispute" story. Some subjects — those who had not read the item — were of course unable to make judgments about him. Responses were on the twelve nine-point semantic differential scales used in Experiments 26 and 27 (see, for instance, Table 17 on p. 271). These scales embrace the three major factors discussed in Chapter 2; and as usual scale order and

* Tannenbaum's subjects were asked to read six items including the two experimental ones.

polarity were varied between several versions of the instrument. In addition to these indirect perceptual judgments, subjects also provided two other pieces of information. On the reverse of the semantic differential form they first indicated on an eleven-point scale how reasonable they thought the farmer's position to be. Secondly they noted down how much of the story they had read; responses here were "none", "headline", "all" (the complete item and headline) or "part" (more than the headline but not the complete item).

Out of a total of 98 subjects reading the two versions of the newspaper thirty-three did not read the experimental story at all, and a further 13 read only the headline and subsequently gave neutral judgments of the stimulus person (responding on the fifth position of each scale). Of the remaining 52 subjects, twenty-two reported that they had read all of the story (thirteen from the version one group; nine from the other group), and thirty had read part of it (nine and twenty-one from the version one and version two groups respectively). Several comparisons of the dispositional judgments by these four subgroups are possible.

We first compared perceptual responses of *all* the subjects who had read some or all of each version. Despite differences in the headlines average responses were almost identical in this analysis. Similarly, no differences were noted in a comparison of judgments made by the subjects who had read all of the story. On the other hand, when the profiles of the groups who had read only part of the story were examined, two significant differences were observed — on the scales *strong–weak* and *active–passive* ($p < 0.05$). A comparison between the ratings of how reasonable subjects thought the farmer's position to be revealed no significant differences. These results broadly support those of Tannenbaum. They also suggest that even when no differences are present across *all* subjects, some headline effect may occur in the case of those who read only a portion of the story. This latter effect could be the factor giving rise to observed differences across *all* subjects in Tannenbaum's study.

In summary, the evidence reported so far suggests that headlines are of little importance in the case of perceivers who read most or all of the item below them. Yet we may question the generality of this conclusion. Subjects in both Tannenbaum's and our own investigations were rather more intelligent and sophisticated than the reading population as a whole. It is possible that these subjects discounted the input provided by the headlines and that headlines appear in consequence to be less important than they really are. To test this possibility we need to investigate the behaviour of a less biased sample of readers.

Experiment 31

We have accordingly obtained data from two samples of readers who are broadly representative of the general population. These samples were selected and the data gathered by a market research agency of national repute. Members of each sample ($N=99$ and 107) were interviewed individually in their homes and each respondent read through an article in a national daily paper to which the interviewer drew his or her attention. After reading this article subjects gave their dispositional judgments of the person it described on a twelve-scale semantic differential form. The scales employed had been used in Experiment 1, and are listed on p. 70.

The story concerned a soldier who had been found guilty of unlawful wounding. One version of it was the article which appeared in the centre page of the published edition of the paper, and the other version was prepared specially for this investigation. The story itself was unchanged between versions, and differences were present only in the headlines. The original version was headed *Soldier's fighting instinct led to brawl*, and in version two this was amended to *Man fined £40*. The latter heading is clearly less evocative; it was suggested by the paper's Night Editor as being quite appropriate to the item.

In requiring subjects to read all the story before giving their judgment we wanted to learn whether headline effects might be present even in this condition when less sophisticated subjects than previously studied were employed. In fact one significant difference between median scale scores was observed (*dangerous–safe*, $p < 0.01$). This result, whilst clearly not conclusive, does suggest that headlines can affect impression formation by the average reader even when he reads right through to the end of an item. This effect seems to be more likely in real-life situations than in studies using only sophisticated groups of subjects.

One interesting question is whether readers remember headlines so well that a headline effect may show itself after an interval although it is not present in judgments made immediately after the item is read. It is possible that headlines serve as economically coded abbreviations of a story so that they are more readily retained by readers than is the more complex, redundant material which follows them. In this case the subsequent material could determine judgments made immediately after reading but the headlines might become more salient as time passes. We have not tested this possibility in a rigorous way, but have obtained some results which suggest that it is unlikely. In a further investigation we used a genuine news item concerning the English water-speed record holder, Donald Campbell. The item first appeared in a provincial daily paper with the headline *Doubts over Campbell's fitness for speed bid*. In addition to the original papers the study also employed specially prepared copies in which the item was preceded by *Campbell shrugs off doubts on his fitness*. The design of the investigation was similar to that described above except that our measures were multiple-choice questions about the content of the item and that we required subjects to recall the headline. Although readers were found to have retained most of the information in the article, no differences were observed between the versions. However, very few subjects could recall the headline, and it appeared that they had largely ignored this.

These investigations barely scratch the surface of this complex topic. They do, however, suggest a number of generalizations to be tested in a coordinated research programme. It seems that headlines can most readily influence indirect perceptions when only a part of the item is read. In these cases the headline content clearly has a proportionately greater importance. Yet the role of headlines when all the item is read may be greater if the readers are less sophisticated than the usual student subject. Although there is no evidence that headline content is more easily retained than item content, this may in fact be so for particularly striking headlines. In these cases of course headline influence is likely to be more marked. In short the effect on perception of headlines *in themselves* is probably much smaller than is commonly assumed. Their influence is in interaction with the item they precede. If this item is informative and if subjects read it, it will be more important than the headline; conversely if the headline is more salient than the item it will naturally be a more important determinant of perception. As in most other areas of study we have to moderate statements about a single variable by considerations of additional ones: it is the combined input which matters more than one single input.

PERSON PERCEPTION THROUGH PHOTOGRAPHS

Another communication variable — and one with greater relevance outside the newspaper page — is that of illustration, or more specifically the content of photographs. The importance of illustrative material in newspapers is revealed by content analyses, such as that by Warr and Knapper (1965) which showed that for the two largest British national dailies 29% and 22% respectively of the total non-advertisement space was devoted to pictorial matter in the course of a typical week. The majority of this pictorial material comprised news photographs. There is also considerable evidence (e.g. McLean and Hazard, 1953) for reader interest in newspaper pictures; and Woodburn (1947), quoting the results of one hundred readership studies, reports that "three times as many men and four times as many women read the average one-column picture as read the average news story". High on the list of preferences come pictures of *people* in the news.

A more interesting aspect of this phenomenon is the impressions that are conveyed to the reader by the use of photographs. Many commentators seem to believe that pictures of people have a unique capacity for communicating something of the characteristics of their subjects. This point is made by Girvin (1947), and in the International Press Institute's manual for journalists (Evans, 1961) the picture editor is recommended to ask of a photograph: "Does it arouse my emotions of fear, sympathy? . . . Does it show the *happy* victor, the *bragging* dictator, the *crestfallen* criminal?" (original italics). It would certainly seem that newspaper photographs are commonly believed to be capable of communicating or creating particularly vivid episodic or dispositional impressions.

Psychologists have long been interested in studying judgments based upon photographs of people — but their studies have mostly been from a less practical standpoint. The use of photographic stimuli has often been largely incidental to the main aim of discovering something about the role of visual cues in the *direct* perception of people (cf. Chapter 1, p. 26). Nonetheless the relevant studies have provided us with a fund of information concerning indirect person perception. A common approach has been to try and link various physical characteristics of people with their personalities. There have been several attempts to relate gross physical structure to basic personality, notably by Kretschmer (1936), Rees and Eysenck (1945) and Sheldon (1940). In most cases considerable use was made of photographs and drawings of stimulus persons. However, the greatest interest has centred not upon general physique but rather upon the cues provided by a person's face — again often perceived indirectly via a photograph.

There is good reason to think that physiognomy is an especially important purveyor of information. Munn (1961, p. 570) quotes the results of an investigation in which the eye movements of 98 women were photographed as they looked at a male stimulus person: 32% of the total fixation time was upon the man's face. And Wallace (1941), who was able to vary the bodily proportions of a two-dimensional schematized stimulus person, showed that such variations had little effect on personality judgments when the face was kept constant. Ekman (1965a, 1965b) and Ekman and Friesen (1967) have noted that facial cues may communicate information about emotional experience which is different from that communicated by body cues. There is no doubt that we all frequently take physiognomic cues to be a guide to the thoughts, feelings and personality of others. Novelists, poets and playwrights commonly refer to facial expression in these terms, and films and television make great use of close-up shots of the face; employers still often ask for a photograph to be attached to application forms. There is even an instrument to measure personality (the Szondi Test — see Deri, 1949; Szondi, 1952) which requires subjects to judge photographs of faces. This is based upon the assumptions that aspects of personality are expressed in faces and that it is possible to infer personality dimensions from a photograph. Although we may regard as naive early studies, such as that by Lombroso and Ferrero (1896) who commented upon and provided examples of the supposed "criminal face" of prostitutes and malefactors, there is now an abundance of evidence to show that people will readily make episodic or dispositional judgments of all kinds from photographs of faces.

Not only are people ready to make these inferences, but there is also a considerable measure of agreement about the inferences made. Such agreement is commented upon by Secord (1958), who quotes as evidence a number of his own studies of the way personality traits are inferred from photographs. Subjects have been found to agree by and large on the attribution of intelligence to facial portraits (see, for example, Brunswik, 1956; Gaskill, Fenton and Porter, 1927; and

Pintner, 1918). And in the straightforward judgment of the "pretti-ness" of young women's faces Iliffe (1960) found considerable agree-ment among 4355 judges of different ages, sex, occupation and geographical location. Brooks and Hochberg (1960), using schematic drawings of babies in which eye height was systematically varied, found that judges consistently agreed on the resultant "cuteness" of the face.

Tomkins and McCarter (1964) have commented in detail on inter-judge consensus about the emotions represented in facial photographs. Their stimulus materials were posed expressions of enjoyment, interest, surprise, fear, anger, disgust, shame, distress and neutrality. Among the results of their study was the finding that judges overwhelmingly agreed on their judgment of which emotion was being experienced by the stimulus person. And particularly noteworthy was the observation that this agreement persisted even when judgments were *incorrect*. Tomkins and McCarter term these error consistencies "common confusions", and report, for example, that people concur in mistaking surprise for interest, distress for shame, anger for disgust and so on.

So the general agreement which exists among judges need not indi-cate that their impressions are accurate. Certainly as far as dispositional judgments are concerned investigators who have compared the inferences made from faces with some external criterion of the relevant trait have nearly always found large discrepancies. Thus Brunswik (1956) found hardly any relationship between measured I.Q. and intelligence as judged from photographs,* and only a small correlation between an external criterion of likeability (based upon the stimulus persons' own judgments of each other) and likeability ratings by observers who had only photographs on which to base their judgments. And Sappenfield (1965) demonstrated that although there is a large measure of intersubject agreement when judging facial photographs for masculinity–femininity, such judgments are greatly inaccurate. Viteles and Smith (1932) found that attempts to predict vocational aptitude from photographs were most unsuccessful, and in a rather unusual experiment which involved judging stimulus persons appearing live on a stage, Cleeton and Knight (1924) found that the dispositional judg-ments made had little validity.

Applying the model suggested in Chapter 1 we may draw attention to several sources of variation in judgments from photographs. Consider first the perceiver's stable characteristics and his current state.

* Earlier studies, for example by L. D. Anderson (1921), had obtained similar results.

Relevant work on these components of the perceptual system has been reported by Chambers (1961) and Levy and Dugan (1960). There has also been interest in the way dispositional judgments by normal subjects differ from judgments made by the mentally ill (e.g. Bannister, 1962b; Izard, 1959; Izard, Randall and Cherry, 1963). And Fensterheim and Tresselt (1953) found that subjects who were asked to attribute traits reflecting Spranger values to a series of photographs and then rank the photos in order of preference liked best those faces which they considered reflected values similar to their own. Bevan, Secord and Richards (1956) tested the hypothesis that a stimulus person with whom a perceiver identifies himself will be judged as having a more similar physiognomy than a "rejected" stimulus person. Secord (1958), although mainly concerned with the consensus among perceivers, also draws attention to several similar sources of variation among judges of facial expression: these include the perceiver's unique past experience of other people, his cultural prejudice (against negroes, for example), his age, sex and general state of motivation. We have already examined a number of these variables in Chapter 4.

Present context information (see Chapter 1, p. 17) is also found to be important in judgments based upon visual inputs. Frijda (1958) and M. G. Cline (1956) have presented line drawings of faces in pairs: the interpretation of the expression of one of the pair was found to vary according to the perceived expression of the other. Levy (1960) has reported similar phenomena in dispositional judgments based upon photographs. Razran (1950) showed that adding an ethnic label to a photograph caused a shift in judgments of the faces in a direction determined by established stereotypes of the ethnic groups to which the stimulus persons apparently belonged. Earlier the same author had shown that a person's name may be a contributing variable in the impression obtained from a photograph of his face (Razran, 1938). And it was even shown by Maslow and Mintz (1956) that impressions from photographs could be affected by the aesthetic appeal of the room where the judging took place.

When we talk of physiognomic cues or of facial expression we are using very general terms which embrace a number of aspects of the face, and it should be noted that not all investigators have examined the same variables. Secord (1958) isolated three aspects of the face which have, either singly or in combination, interested psychologists: these are the basic structure of the face (length of nose, height of brow, etc.), the "fixed" expression of the face (e.g. the relatively permanent anxious look to be found on some faces) and the temporary expression of the face, as when we smile or frown. Examination of the research literature shows that the greatest number of studies has been concerned with the perception of a person's temporary facial expression, particularly in so far as this provides a clue to his emotional state. Among the many people who have used photographs or posed and unposed pictures to investigate episodic judgments of emotion are Felecky (1914), Fernberger (1928), Gates (1923), Kanner (1931), Landis (1929) and Triandis and Lambert (1958). Many more studies have been reviewed by Davitz (1964), Honkavaara (1961), Schlosberg (1954), Woodworth (1938) and others. On the whole it appears that we can judge emotions from facial stimuli fairly well, but again it is interesting that knowledge of the relevant situation or background considerably aids the accuracy of judgment (see Munn, 1940; Sherman, 1927a, 1927b). Some investigators have attempted to break down the temporary facial expression into its various components to see if some are more important than others in the expression of emotion. Results often tend to be somewhat contradictory so that while Buzby (1924) found that the upper part of the face, the eye and brow, were more important than the mouth in accurately conveying an emotional state, Dunlap (1927) found that the mouth muscles were more important than the eye muscles. Frois-Wittman (1930) concluded, however, that the whole expression was more important than any individual muscle movement.

Surprisingly few studies have been concerned with either permanent or temporary expressions other than as a clue to emotion, although Thornton (1943) did demonstrate that persons shown in photographs to be smiling were judged as more honest. Instead it is in connection with the so-called basic structure of the face that there has been the greatest interest in isolating the most salient features and relating them to inferences about specific personality traits. We have already referred to the study by Brooks and Hochberg on the effect of eye height on the perceived "cuteness" of babies: these writers found that a position in the middle of the face was judged most favourably. Using a similar type of schematized face Winkler (1951) investigated the role of the shape, height and angle of incline of the mouth, and Kremenak (1950), in a study of the eye region, found that the eyebrows had a greater expression value than the shape of the eyes. Brunswik and Reiter

(1937) varied a number of facial features using simple line drawings as stimulus material. They found that "medium-ness" seemed to be of crucial importance, e.g. when judges were asked to judge intelligence a high or medium forehead, medium nose and medium mouth appeared to connote high intelligence — and anything deviating too widely from the norm was perceived as being accompanied by a reduction in the characteristic. The generality of these findings is suggested by the studies of Rohrachter (1952), Samuels (1939) and White and Landis (1930), who used photographs matched to the original line drawings. Stritch and Secord (1956) have investigated the possibility of studying the combined effects of groups of facial cues; this problem is clearly a complex one.

One rather paradoxical aspect of the face's basic structure is how easily it can be altered, not by anything as drastic as surgery, but simply by the addition of a moustache or beard, by changing the hairstyle (see Seiller-Tarbuk, 1951), by the wearing of spectacles or by the addition of makeup. Lipstick has been found to be important in determining judgments of women by men in direct perceptual situations (McKeachie, 1952); and taking together results from studies by Brunswik (1939) and Thornton (1943, 1944) we may conclude that spectacles generally increase the perceived intelligence of stimulus persons. In the latter case the effect is much greater when perception is indirect. This gives rise to the interesting possibility that inputs about facial characteristics might be especially important in indirect person perception — when fewer additional cues are available.*

The three aspects of the face described by Secord are of value in that they provide a useful way of classifying physiognomic cues. In our experiments, however, we have not generally studied any one of these aspects in isolation. This is partly because of the methodological difficulties of singling out for investigation just one set of facial cues, but a more important reason concerns a further factor in the photograph judging situation which we believe to be particularly crucial. This factor has to do with the communication channel itself: for whenever we see a person's face indirectly (usually photographed or filmed) then a further set of *communication* variables is able to affect the perceptual process, and any of the three aspects of the face discussed above could be overridden by the camera angle, the lighting effects used, etc. Our main interest in perception through photographs is

* See also p. 244.

therefore not for what they reveal of the "real" person they picture, but instead for the reason that photographs are an important channel of indirect person perception. Rather than studying the accuracy of judgments mediated by photographs, we have concentrated upon the process whereby such judgments are made.

The first aim of our investigations was to see whether a photograph could alter the impression generated by a news item which it accompanied, and whether different accompanying photographs could produce correspondingly different impressions from the same news item. Experiments 32 and 33 deal with these questions. From this point we proceeded to ask what aspects of the photographic presentation might influence perception, and Experiment 34 deals with one such aspect, the angle from which the photograph is taken. In Experiment 35 some of the findings of the previous experiment are tested in the more realistic setting of the newspaper page, when again the photographs are accompanied by news items. Finally, in Experiment 36 we examine the relative roles of verbal and visual information in indirect person perception through newspapers.

Experiment 32

If a photograph is added to a news item description of a person, is the resultant impression gained by readers of this combination likely to differ from the impression formed by readers of the text alone? It is this question that the present experiment was designed to study.

The stimulus material consisted of two versions of a short 170-word news item concerning a Women's Royal Army Corps lieutenant named Anne Brown. The story, headlined *One woman with a thousand men*, told of the posting of Miss Brown as Assistant Adjutant to a Royal Corps of Signals unit, and was accompanied by a small $3'' \times 1\frac{1}{2}''$ full-face picture of a smiling girl in uniform. The report and photograph were both perfectly genuine and the item appeared on a centre page in the normal edition of a national morning newspaper. A second version of this newspaper was prepared especially for the purposes of this experiment in which Miss Brown's photograph did not appear, and suitable filler material was provided beneath the item so that the page contained no blank spaces. The headline, type face and text of the item were otherwise identical in both versions.

The semantic differential forms used for measuring dispositional judgments of Anne Brown were identical to those used in Experiment

31, containing a total of twelve scales from the three factors. The subjects were also common to both experiments and had been selected to be representative of the British population as a whole across age, sex and socio-economic background. A total of 99 subjects saw the version of the newspaper containing the story and photograph, and 107 subjects received the version without the photograph. The method of eliciting responses from subjects and all other aspects of procedure were exactly as for Experiment 31: subjects were individually given a copy of the entire newspaper and the relevant article was drawn to their attention. After reading through the item once they gave their impression of the stimulus person on the semantic differential form.

When the median scores for the twelve semantic differential scales are compared there are two significant differences between the two versions, on the scales *emotional–unemotional* ($p < 0.05$) and *kind–cruel* ($p < 0.05$). Those subjects who had read the news item with the photograph perceived Anne Brown as significantly kinder and less emotional than did the readers who had received the text alone. The finding that the addition of a fairly unexciting photograph could in this way change the perception generated by a minor news item seemed to be important enough to warrant a more ambitious repetition of the experiment.

Experiment 33

Results from the previous study demonstrated that adding a genuine photograph to an authentic news item was able to change the way in which a representative sample of the population perceived the person described. Experiment 33 made use of stimulus material that was subject to greater experimental manipulation in order to test the generality of the previous finding and to see whether the *type* of photographic accompaniment used could also affect perception.

A fictitious 300-word news report was prepared by a journalist as being a typical item of local interest. The report, headlined *One man holds up a road*, described how the construction of a new road was being prevented by the refusal of a resident (the stimulus person) to quit his home which lay in its path. The opinions of the stimulus person and his actions to prevent eviction were outlined. The reporter had taken care to avoid biasing the report in favour of or against the stimulus person. Special copies of a local daily paper were prepared for the experiment in which the fictitious story was "planted" on the front page of an otherwise genuine edition, and there is no reason to suppose that the subjects believed the newspaper and the articles in it were other than genuine. Three different versions of the newspaper were prepared and in each the relevant communication was in a different form. The first version of the communication comprised the text of the item and a headline, but in the other two versions the report and headline were accompanied by a 6″ × 3½″ photograph of the subject of the story. In version two the picture showed a well-dressed smiling man, while version three illustrated a man frowning from under a cloth cap. The photographs were of two unknown individuals and had been selected from the newspaper files as suitable by the paper's chief photographer. In all cases the communication occupied the same central position on the paper's front page, and all the reports and headlines were identical in content and appearance.

Subjects' dispositional perceptions of the stimulus person were measured by twelve nine-point semantic differential scales. These scales appear in Table 23, grouped in terms of factors. One hundred and seventeen subjects, all undergraduate students from Sheffield University, took part in the experiment. They were randomly assigned to groups each of which received one of the three versions of the communication. Each subject was handed a copy of the newspaper and his attention drawn to the front page article. Instructions for reading

Table 23   Mean perceptions mediated by three versions of a communication

	Version 1 (N=39)	Version 2 (N=37)	Version 3 (N=41)
True–false	6·46	6·84	6·63
Wise–foolish	4·05	4·05	3·63
Sweet–sour	4·85	4·49	4·66
Fair–unfair	4·69	4·24	4·12
Strong–weak	6·77	6·65	7·10
Hard–soft	5·49	5·70	6·24
Large–small	4·41	3·65	4·54
Rugged–delicate	6·10	5·78	7·32
Sharp–dull	5·46	6·00	5·56
Hot–cold	5·69	5·46	5·46
Active–passive	5·31	5·76	5·73
Fast–slow	4·05	4·19	3·93

through the report and for completing the semantic differential scales were standard. Subjects' attention was not specifically drawn to the accompanying photograph.

Table 23 gives the mean responses to each scale for the groups of subjects reading the three versions of the report. Several significant differences are present. That adding a photograph to a news item can change the perception generated is shown by the application of t-tests to the means of versions one and three; this reveals significant differences for the scales *hard–soft* ($p<0.05$) and *rugged–delicate* ($p<0.01$). Although there are no statistically significant differences for the other photograph/no photograph comparison (version one with version two) we may say that the findings from this experiment give some support to the conclusion of Experiment 32 — that the addition of a photograph to a report can change perceptions based upon it. A comparison of the perceptions mediated by versions two and three shows a further two significant differences for the scales *large–small* ($p<0.05$) and *rugged–delicate* ($p<0.001$). The reports in both these versions were of course accompanied by photographs of the stimulus person, so that these scale differences indicate that not only can the addition of a photograph change perception through a news item, but that the resultant perception depends to some extent upon the nature of the picture chosen.

If we examine the results of this experiment in terms of the three scale factor groupings, the interesting finding emerges that all the significant differences occur within the Potency factor. This result is of course not general to all studies of perception involving photographs, but as far as the photographs used in Experiment 33 are concerned traits within the Potency factor seem to be particularly important for judges. It would be interesting to attempt to relate the characteristics of these photographs to the perceptions they elicit, and we make some further suggestions as to how this could be done later in the present chapter.

Experiment 34

Much of the work reviewed above has indicated that the facial *expression* adopted by the stimulus person in a photograph is an input from which important inferences are drawn. There have, however, been very few instances of experimenters manipulating the communication channel itself, and changing the nature of the photograph while keeping the subject's expression constant. This is perhaps rather surprising in view of the fact that one of the skills of the portrait photographer is commonly held to be his ability to project the sitter's "personality" into his photograph, and textbooks of photography are full of advice on how this may be achieved by techniques of lighting and camera angle. Fosdick and Tannenbaum (1964), in an experiment in which 16 news photographers were told to photograph sculptures to connote different degrees of Evaluation, Potency and Activity, reported agreement for a number of stylistic devices used by the photographers. Among the stylistic elements found to be important were camera angle, light contrast and print density. Unfortunately Fosdick and Tannenbaum did not measure whether the connotations attempted by the photographers were in fact successfully communicated to perceivers of the photographs they produced. There is an earlier study by the same authors (Tannenbaum and Fosdick, 1960) in which it was shown that a lighting angle of 45° from the side could have a significantly favourable effect on subjects' perceptions of the photograph compared with photographs employing other lighting angles. The effect was not found for all models, however.

The present experiment was intended to examine a communication variable that was similar to but simpler than lighting angle. Our own independent variable was the angle from which the stimulus person was photographed — front view or side view. Eight stimulus persons were used for this experiment, all of whom were photographed from the front (full-face) and side (profile) under similar conditions of lighting, background, etc. The facial expressions were of course constant. The persons, all of whom were unknown to the subjects, were specially chosen to cover a fairly wide range of age and social background. The males comprised a youth, two men in middle age, and one who was elderly; there was one teenage girl, two women in their middle twenties and a woman over sixty. Occupations were diverse and included typist, design engineer, storekeeper and housewife.

Sixteen different transparencies (8 front view, 8 side view), each showing the head and shoulders of one of the stimulus persons, were prepared from the photographs. These were projected in turn on a screen according to a design which ensured that groups of subjects saw the eight different stimulus persons without seeing two views of any one person. Order of presentation of the photographs was varied between subject groups to counteract any possible order effects; each of the sixteen photographs was seen by a total of either 59 or 47 male and female undergraduate subjects. After each photograph had been exposed for 45 seconds subjects gave their perceptions of the stimulus person on the twelve semantic differential scales used in Experiment 29 (see Table 21, p. 281).

Mean scale scores were obtained for each pair of photographs and the first important aspect of the results is that the scale means represented a wide range of values (from 2·98 to 7·55) and were not generally clustered around the mid-point five. This again shows that subjects were quite prepared to make inferences about a fairly large number of personality traits on the basis of the very limited information yielded by a 45-second exposure to a photograph. This intriguing finding is very much in line with other investigators' reports of the inferences made from facial cues.

A second, more central aspect of the results concerns the different perceptions generated by the front-view and side-view photographs. When t-test comparisons were made for each stimulus person between the mean scale scores for the two angles of photography they revealed that out of a total of 96 possible comparisons 19 were significantly different at the 0·05 level or beyond. The number of significant t values for any one stimulus person ranged from nought to six, but in the case of only two stimulus persons (one male, one female) no significant differences were observed. There are then enough such differences distributed among the eight faces photographed to indicate that angle of photography can indeed be an important determinant in the impression generated by facial cues.

The next step is to see whether the differences in perceptions based upon front-view or side-view follow any pattern. For example, does either viewpoint consistently generate more favourable impressions? The answer to this question is no, as far as our results are concerned: the mean value for all side-view ratings is 5·25, while the front-view mean is 5·08. Then does either viewpoint generate more extreme impressions, ones that deviate more from the neutral rating, five? Comparison of mean deviation scores for the front-view versus the side-view photographs shows that once again the answer is no. If there are no systematic differences between the two viewpoints can we say why some faces generate more differences than others? At a fairly gross level, there are certainly no differences which appear to be linked with either the age or the sex or the stimulus persons. Nor does an examination of the photograph which generated most differences (six) provide much help: it shows a plumpish woman in her middle twenties. Although it is tempting to examine features of the two photographs of this face and attempt to isolate those cues known to relate to various traits, following the work of earlier investigators (e.g. Secord, 1958), such *post-hoc* rationalizing could be misleading. Instead future experiments are required in which photographs could be taken from different angles in order to deliberately isolate the effects of certain important traits; for example, a hooked nose, believed to connote unfavourable impressions, would be emphasized in a profile as opposed to a full-face photograph. This would of course require preselection of stimulus persons on the basis of their possession of certain key facial traits. Finally in connection with this experiment, the results reveal that the differences noted between front- and side-view portraits were not confined to particular semantic differential scales or factors: in fact there were only three scales on which no differences occurred (*kind– cruel, fair–unfair*, and *emotional–unemotional*). As usual the semantic differential form employed was specially constructed to contain scales representing the three main factors.

Experiment 34 has demonstrated that a fairly straightforward communication variable such as the angle of photography can have an important effect on the perceptions of a stimulus person. As far as the simple variable of front-view or side-view photography is concerned, just what sort of effect takes place seems to depend largely on the particular stimulus person, and much further research (as suggested above) is needed before we will be in a position to predict whether a given face can create a more favourable impression by a profile or full-face portrait.

Experiment 35

Would this factor of camera angle be so vital when the photograph forms part of a newspaper communication and is combined with written matter? Experiment 35 was designed to put this question to the empirical test; it was also intended as a corollary to Experiment 33. In this earlier experiment we had in some respects maximized the possibility of obtaining a different perception based on the different newspaper versions, for we had made use of photographs of two different people.

The present experiment on the other hand used just one stimulus person photographed from the front and from the side: in fact the photographs were those which had generated most differences (six) due to camera angle in Experiment 34. On this occasion, however, the photographs were accompanied by a news report which apparently pertained to the stimulus person. The report itself was genuine and had appeared in a national morning newspaper. It was 250 words in length, with the headline *Wife falls from Atlantic liner — she is rescued after 80 minutes in sea*; there was a description of an accident at sea concerning an estranged wife, with some brief details of her personality and the reasons for her visit to England. The item was accompanied by a 4″ × 6″ photograph of the wife, with the simple caption: *Mrs. Cecilia Crain*. For the experiment, however, special copies were made of the item in which the original photograph was replaced by one of the two photographs selected from Experiment 34. The prepared photographs were those used in the previous experiment; they were each head and shoulder portraits of a plumpish young woman whose expression was neutral. One picture was a profile and one full-face. Transparencies were prepared of the items in which everything except the picture was exactly as it had appeared in the original newspaper. To the best of our knowledge all subjects who saw the projected transparencies believed the report and accompanying photograph to be genuine; the original item had appeared some months previously and no subjects recalled having seen it before.

Subjects (in groups of about a dozen) were allowed to see the transparency until everyone had finished reading through the item once slowly. The subject groups comprised undergraduates in roughly equal numbers of both sexes; fifty-six subjects saw the version with the front-view photograph and forty-one subjects the version with the side-view photograph. As soon as they had read the item subjects gave their dispositional perception of Mrs. Crain on semantic differential scales similar to those used for Experiment 34.

Mean scale scores were calculated for the two groups of subjects and *t*-test comparisons reveal that there are two significant differences between mean profiles of the stimulus person based on the two versions of the report. The version accompanied by the full-face portrait generates an impression that she is significantly more passive and more timid than she would appear to be to readers of the side-view version. For both these scales significant differences were present in Experiment 34: the direction of the differences is also the same, although the values of *t* are smaller for the present experiment. These results appear to indicate that the effect of the two different photographs, though still present, has been somewhat reduced by their inclusion in a news item. Conversely we may say that when the same standard text is combined with one of two different photographs of the same person to form a news item, impressions of the stimulus person formed from the combined communication are likely to be influenced to a certain extent according to which photograph is used. It should be remembered in connection with this experiment that no deliberate attempt was made to prepare two photographs which gave alternately favourable and unfavourable impressions of the stimulus person: on the contrary the situation was as controlled as possible with even facial expression held constant, and the only changing variable was the relatively simple one of front-view or side-view. Nevertheless two photographs varied along this dimension were able to affect indirect person perception in a fairly complex situation.

Experiment 36

We have not concerned ourselves here with any more detailed investigations of how particular aspects of photographs might determine indirect person perception. Instead we have devoted some attention to a problem which we believe equally relevant to an understanding of the communication variables in impression formation; this concerns the relative importance of verbal or written material and of visual material.

"One picture is worth a thousand words" is an adage to be found on the lips of many engaged in communication and education. But there is scant scientific evidence to confirm or deny such a precise ratio. There has been some investigation of the word-association responses of children to differing pictorial and verbal stimuli (e.g. Bourisseau, Davis and Yamamoto, 1965) and in a field more relevant to our own present interests Langfeld (1918) showed that captions could have an effect on the perception of emotions from photographs, and Secord, Bevan and Dukes (1953) investigated the relative importance for impression formation of occupational labels and facial cues as revealed in photographs. Mehling (1959) inquired into the effect on attitude of combining news and photographs and reported that "photographs with words were more effective than words alone in changing evaluative judgments toward both the source and the concept about which the source made an assertion". Similar studies of attitude change have been reported by Brinkman (1963) and W. F. Kelly (1963). Although the findings of the latter author were rather equivocal, Brinkman, whose stimulus material comprised editorials and political cartoons, produced results which were consistent with those of Mehling.

As far as our own investigations are concerned, in both Experiments 33 and 35 it was evident that some interaction was taking place between the verbal and visual components of the communication. We felt that more information about the nature of this interaction would be of value and we set out to measure the relative importance of verbal and visual information in a fairly precisely controlled manner. The present experiment therefore made use of three different communications about a stimulus person: (a) a narrative report in the form of a "pen-portrait" of the person, (b) a photograph of the person, and (c) a combination of both the narrative and the photograph. Hereafter (a) is referred to as a verbal communication, (b) as a visual communication, and (c) as a verbal-and-visual communication.

Four different stimulus persons were used for the experiment and the information about each one came from a different day's edition of the same national newspaper. All the communications came from the paper's "gossip column" and were essentially similar in content and style: each presented information about a (different) girl in her late teens. The verbal content of each report centred upon the activities, interests and opinions of the stimulus person. For example one report described a nineteen year old debutante from Northern Ireland who had had a skiing accident while on holiday in Switzerland. The report briefly sketched this young lady's career to date (as a ballet dancer and art student), her interests (painting) and pointed out that she did not intend to be deterred by the mishap. All four verbal communications were of about the same length (roughly 150 words), and each was accompanied by a short headline and similarly sized (approximately 4" × 6") photograph of the particular young lady. For each of the four stimulus persons three sets of information were prepared upon transparencies, and presentation to subjects was by projection on to a screen. The written description alone (report and headline) constituted the verbal communication (Ve); the photograph alone constituted the visual communication (Vi); and the item as it originally appeared in the newspaper constituted the verbal-and-visual communication (Ve+ Vi).

Two hundred and thirty undergraduate subjects (115 males and 115 females) from several departments of Sheffield University took part in

Table 24   The assignment of three communications to the four groups of subjects; communications about the four stimulus persons are either verbal (Ve) visual (Vi) or a combination of both types (Ve + Vi)

Group	N	SP_1	SP_2	SP_3	SP_4
1	60	Ve + Vi	Vi	Ve	
2	58		Ve + Vi	Vi	Ve
3	58	Ve		Ve + Vi	Vi
4	54	Vi	Ve		Ve + Vi

the experiment and were randomly assigned to one of four groups in such a way that the numbers of male and female subjects in each group were the same. Each group was presented with three different kinds of information about three different stimulus persons: Table 24 shows how the communications were assigned to the four groups. It was emphasized to subjects that the three communications to which they were to be exposed related to three separate individuals. Each communication was then displayed for sixty seconds after which subjects indicated their dispositional perception of the stimulus person on the twelve semantic differential scales used for Experiment 33 (see Table 23, p. 304).

When the mean scale scores for each stimulus person are compared, significant differences are found to be present on a number of dimensions: thus each stimulus person was on the whole perceived as being different from the other three. Furthermore it is again evident from an examination of the mean scale scores that subjects were able to form quite definite impressions of the stimulus persons on the basis of the limited information available to them — whatever form that information took. Since these observations are peripheral to the main purpose of this experiment no supporting statistical evidence is presented; however, we would of course expect these findings on the basis of the work reviewed earlier in this chapter. Another interesting side finding that is worthy of mention is that there were hardly any significant differences between means for male and female subjects (4 out of a possible 144); the relevance of this finding has been considered in more detail in Chapter 4 (pp. 185–194).

Of greater interest here are the comparisons between the means for the various conditions of presentation of the communications. Experiments 32 and 33 showed that the addition of a photograph to a purely verbal news item can result in a different perception of the stimulus person being generated. This finding is supported by a comparison of Ve and the Ve+ Vi perceptions for the present experiments. A series of *t*-tests reveals significantly different responses for a number of scales. For the first stimulus person (SP_1) the significant differences are on the scales *wise–foolish* ($p<0.02$) and *large–small* ($p<0.02$); for SP_2 the differences are significant for *sweet–sour* ($p<0.001$) and *large–small* ($p<0.01$); for SP_3 four differences are significant, namely *wise–foolish* ($p<0.02$), *large–small* ($p<0.001$), *rugged–delicate* ($p<0.01$) and *active–passive* ($p<0.01$). Only on the scale *large–small* is there a significant difference for SP_4. It is clear that in the case of the four sets of communication used in this experiment, the addition of a photograph of the stimulus person leads to the formation of impressions which are significantly different in some important respects from those generated by the written report alone. The difference on the scale *large–small* is to be expected since judgment of size is presumably based mainly on visual information, but quite different and sometimes surprising dimensions are also affected: a case in point is the scale *wise–foolish*. Once again there is some evidence that although the effect of adding visual information is common to a number of stimulus persons, the magnitude of the effect depends partly on the nature of the stimulus person herself. However, we should mention that the communications used here were selected quite haphazardly from a large number of similar items appearing in the same newspaper — no effort was made to choose reports in which the photograph seemed inappropriate to the text. Thus we feel our findings have considerable relevance to the day-to-day communication taking place via the mass media.

Taking the mean scale scores for the three presentation conditions it is of course possible to make comparisons between Vi and Ve+ Vi and others between Ve and Vi, but that significant differences will be present is almost self-evident from the above discussion. The differences between perceptions mediated by Ve and by Vi are not immediately relevant to us here, but as a method of investigating the judgments made in person perception it might be of interest to study the contents of a verbal communication which generate the same perception as that generated by a photograph. The relationship between Ve and Vi presented singly and the combined Ve+ Vi presentation condition is of major importance and will be considered in detail below.

The discussion so far has centred upon comparisons between individual scale scores. It is possible, however, to analyse in more general terms the information transmitted by the different communications. One technique which appears to be fruitful in this connection involves the use of correlational data. By correlating the twelve mean scale scores generated by the verbal communication (Ve) with the twelve mean scores for the verbal-and-visual communication (Ve+Vi) it is possible in the case of any of the stimulus persons to assess the overall importance of adding visual information. An example may perhaps clarify this argument. Suppose that in the case of SP_1 the Ve means were found to correlate perfectly with the Ve+Vi means. This $+1.00$ correlation would indicate that one set of scale means was completely predictable from the other. An event or value which is completely predictable in terms of another cannot be held to add any information to the situation as it stands (see Attneave, 1959). Thus we would interpret a correlation of $+1.00$ between Ve and Ve+Vi to mean that combining Ve and Vi (to form Ve+Vi) adds no further information to Ve. The more it is possible to predict Ve+Vi from Ve (i.e. the higher the correlation) the less information is transmitted by the addition of Vi to Ve (see also Warr and Knapper, 1966a).

Table 25 Relationships between the mean perceptions mediated by different communications about the four stimulus persons

	$r_{Ve.Ve+Vi}$	$r_{Vi.Ve+Vi}$	$r_{Ve.Vi}$
SP_1	$+0.81$	$+0.78$	$+0.76$
SP_2	$+0.80$	$+0.33$	-0.03
SP_3	$+0.85$	$+0.80$	$+0.77$
SP_4	$+0.92$	$+0.76$	$+0.70$

Table 25 shows the relevant values of r for the four stimulus persons: of particular interest are the values for SP_2. This is the only stimulus person for which the correlation between the verbal and visual material is low ($r_{Ve.Vi}=0.03$) meaning that in this case the picture when seen alone was perceived very differently from the report alone. Given this fact, however, if the influence of the verbal material alone and the visual material alone on combined communication were equal then we would expect the values of $r_{Ve.Ve+Vi}$ and $r_{Vi.Ve+Vi}$ to be similar and fairly low. In fact these values are not similar, $r_{Ve.Ve+Vi}$ having the high value of 0.80 and $r_{Vi.Ve+Vi}$ the low value of 0.33. This suggests that the verbal material is accounting for more of the variance than the visual material, that it is a more important determinant of the combined perception than the photograph, and that perhaps the report is in some way providing a frame of reference which alters the meaning of the photograph. This effect would not be revealed very clearly for any of the other stimulus persons since the correlation between perceptions of the verbal material and those of the visual material are fairly high. However, it is interesting to note that the $r_{Ve \cdot Ve+Vi}$ values are in all cases greater than the $r_{Vi \cdot Ve+Vi}$ values, suggesting that the verbal material is generally a more important determinant of perception than the visual material when these two aspects of the communication are combined. We examined the relative importance of verbal and visual information in more detail by the application of the multiple correlation techniques first described in Chapter 6 (see p. 273).

Multiple correlation coefficients (R values) were calculated for each stimulus person between the two sets of mean perceptions based upon Ve and upon Vi alone and the mean perceptions based upon Ve+Vi. These values of $R_{Ve+Vi (Ve, Vi)}$ were high: 0·85, 0·86, 0·88, and 0·93 respectively for the four stimulus persons indicating (in the manner described in the previous chapter) that the proportion of the variance of Ve+Vi attributable to the joint action of Ve and Vi is in all cases high. (This proportion is found by squaring R so that in the case of SP_1, for example, $R=0·84$ and $R^2=0·72$.)

Table 26 The relative importance of verbal and visual material expressed in terms of beta coefficients

	Beta coefficient	
	Ve	Vi
SP_1	0·53	0·37
SP_2	0·78	0·31
SP_3	0·59	0·34
SP_4	0·75	0·23

We are here less interested in the values of R^2 than in the relative magnitude of the β coefficients, which, it will be recalled, are derived from R^2 and which express in terms of standard scores the relative contribution made to the value of Ve+Vi by Ve and by Vi. The β coefficients are shown in Table 26. It can be seen that in all instances Ve is of greater importance than Vi in determining Ve+Vi: the ratios of Ve to Vi are 1·43 to 1, 2·5 to 1, 1·74 to 1, and 3·26 to 1 for SP_1 to SP_4 respectively. It is therefore clear that, as we had suspected from the values of r, the verbal content has a greater influence than the visual content in determining the perceptions generated by the combined communication. It will no doubt be noted that the ratios listed above vary quite markedly in size and it would be interesting to determine those characteristics of the communication which affect the relative importance of Ve and Vi when measured in this way. What, for instance, makes the report of SP_4 particularly prepotent in relation to the photograph? Is this due to a particularly powerful story or an especially insipid photograph? Evidence concerning order effects from Chapter 6 suggest the former interpretation. Our attempts there to provide an explanation for this prepotency were far from fruitful, however, and we can only reiterate our earlier plea for more research on the topic.

Concluding Remarks on the Effects of Visual Material

The present section has described the results of five experiments concerned with the role of photographs in indirect person perception, and discussed the contribution of many more studies to our understanding of person perception mediated by visual cues. A major interest here has been in the consequences of combining verbal and visual material within a single communication. We have noted that, when a written report and a photograph are placed together in a newspaper item, the verbal material tends to be more important than the visual in generating impressions of the stimulus person. This observation should be placed against the backcloth of previous comments on combination rules (Chapter 3, pp. 163–172) and sequential stimulus inputs (Chapter 6, pp. 282–288). We have noted there several different views about the nature of input combination, and we have emphasized that a configural approach often appears to be the most fruitful. It is clear that the meaning of a particular input can be changed by the nature of other inputs occurring at the same time. In the present instance, we expect that the meaning of a photograph can be altered by an accompanying report (and of course that a report can be altered by a concomitant photograph).

In the studies described above the verbal material assumed greater importance in this interaction than did the visual input. But we take it that the relative importance of the two types of information will vary with the content of each. Some of the factors relevant to the content of verbal information are dealt with elsewhere in this chapter (e.g. the effect of adding different headlines to a report) and in this volume (e.g. the effect of inserting "warm" or "cold" into a narrative description). As far as visual information is concerned we have dealt in this section with just one important aspect of the content of photographs: this concerns the structure and expression of the face. Facial cues are undoubtedly important factors, but there are also many similar factors, relevant to both direct and indirect perception, which have received scant attention from psychologists. If we assess a man's personality from his face, might we not take into consideration his physique, bearing, and gestures, as well as the clothes he wears? The latter at least have interested some psychologists (the most famous discussion is probably that by Flügel, 1950), but empirical studies in this area are surprisingly rare. There is some experimental evidence, however, that clothing influences perception of status (Douty, 1962; Hoult, 1951; Thibaut and Riecken, 1955), as well as personal impressions of others (Douty, 1962; Stone, 1959). Clothing effects are perhaps epitomized by the findings of the much-quoted investigation by Lefkowitz, Blake and Mouton (1955); these authors showed that a well-dressed stooge could cause a higher degree of traffic signal violations than could the same person when shabbily dressed.

We have already commented on background and context effects in the perception of people (see pp. 36 and 299): that these are important in indirect as well as direct perception has been shown, for example, by Munn (1940) with reference to the judging of emotions. A mere glance at many of the pictures to be found in the daily press will reveal what a powerful potential influence could be the background against which the stimulus person is photographed. When we consider media other than newspapers a whole host of further variables intrude, such as, for example, the movements of the face and body, and of course the voice. Motion film has in fact been used to investigate emotion (e.g. Hochberg, 1964) and other expressive behaviour (see Carmichael, Roberts and Wessel, 1937; Estes, 1938), and research to link together judgments based upon still and moving pictures would be worthwhile at this stage.

Any visual cues can be interpreted only within the context in which they are presented, and context effects are likely to be of vital importance in determining a judgment. A newspaper *report* might be considered as providing the context in which a news photograph is perceived, and we have seen that when a photograph and report are combined verbal information (the context in this sense) is likely to be more important than visual information. We have mainly been concerned with context effects in *indirect* perception, but it is worth considering whether the generalizations we have made in this connection would also hold good when person perception is *direct*. In the case of direct face-to-face interaction we suspect that visual information will be rather less important than it is in indirect perception. For, when we interact with a person, other cues (bearing, voice, the person's manner and what he says, for example) are likely to provide a particularly powerful context within which to judge straightforward "appearance" as it would be seen in a photograph (see Chapter 5, p. 244).

The fact that verbal material is probably relatively more important than visual information when the two types are presented in combination should not, however, detract from the clearly demonstrated finding that photographs play an important part in determining the impressions we form of people. Experiments 32 and 33 both showed how the effect of a communication could be considerably modified by the addition of a photograph. We also know that fairly trivial communication variables — such as the angle of photography studied in Experiment 34 — can be of great importance, even when the photographs are incorporated in a newspaper item (Experiment 35). We still do not know, however, how a communication like this interacts with those aspects of the face itself — general structure, expression, grooming for instance — which have been shown to be themselves determinants of the impression formed.

Although we now have a fairly clear understanding of the operation of the individual variables considered in this section, we still know very little of the way in which these relevant factors interact with each other to determine perception. Even in the case of indirect perception, which is in principle less complex than the direct perceptual process, there is still a great need for further research before we can gain a grasp of the interdependence of stimulus and context variables and of those aspects of the perceiver which were noted in Chapter 4. The formulations and techniques set out in this section may perhaps add more strength to our arm.

TYPOGRAPHY AND PAGE MAKEUP

News not only has to be written and illustrated, but it has also to be presented to the readers, and a considerable amount of care and effort is expended by newspaper staffs to provide suitably typography and layout for the news items of the day. Journalism textbooks (see for example Dodge and Viner, 1963; Evans, 1961) usually devote lengthy sections to the discussion of typeface and page makeup, the principal aim being to obtain a readership for an item commensurate with its "news value" as interpreted by the newspaper staff. How much is in fact known about the effects on item readership of different typographies and positions on the newspaper page? These communication variables may emerge as important factors in indirect person perception mediated by the press.

Typography has been studied experimentally by a number of researchers, many of whom have concentrated on the legibility of various typefaces (see Burt, 1959; English, 1944; Murphy, 1962; Nuckols, 1965; Poulton, 1967; Powers, 1962; Tinker and Paterson, 1943; and Wiggins, 1964). Using speed of reading as the main measurement criterion, the work of these investigators has shown that readability of print can be affected by the choice of typeface, its boldness, size, leading and spacing, line length and width of margin. There has been considerable interest in the effects on reading speed of newspaper columns with unjustified right-hand margins, and Powers (1962) produced the interesting finding that unjustified type (which is of course cheaper to set up) can be read more quickly than justified type.

Implicit in much of the work on legibility is the notion that high readability results in a greater degree of item readership, but of course it does not necessarily follow that a typeface which is highly legible will attract more readers — the reader may not be able to judge legibility with any accuracy. Huistendahl was aware of this paradox, and in his studies (1964, 1965) considered only reader *estimates* of reading speed and typeface attractiveness. Tinker and Paterson (1942) provided some evidence that readers did in fact place high aesthetic value on typefaces they judged to be most legible. Readers do not always know what is "best" for them, however, for although they have been shown to prefer justified type with column rules (Ruthenbeck, 1965) it is known that such devices do nothing to increase legibility (see again Powers, 1962).

Different typefaces may attract readers for reasons other than legibility and R. O. Martin (1963) was interested in the non-verbal aesthetic appeal of different types. Many investigators have studied the connotations of various typefaces, particularly in so far as these connotations interact with other aspects of the news item, such as its verbal content. Haskins (1958) reported that readers believed different typefaces were suitable for different sorts of editorial material, and Sherrill (1963) found that subjects thought that a given typeface was better suited to one message source than to another. Davis and Smith (1933) studied the determinants of what they called "feeling tone" in typefaces. If different types connote different impressions then the question arises as to whether the connotations derived by readers correspond to those intended by the people responsible for choosing a particular typeface. Brinton (1958) and Tannenbaum, Jacobson and Norris (1964) have investigated whether typeface connotations are the same for encoder and decoder. The answer seems to be that on the whole they are, although judgments of typefaces by professional encoders tend to be more extreme and more consistent.

In contrast to the great interest in newspaper typography there have been few studies of an item's page position which have any general applicability to communication in the press. There have of course been many extensive investigations of "best positions" for display advertisements in both newspapers and magazines (see for example Burton, 1955) but only very occasionally does one come across a study of page position effects relevant to news stories — such as the isolated investigation by Murphy (1957) which was carried out within the rather specialized field of agricultural journalism.

Experiment 37

Although a study of the interactions between typographic connotations and readers' indirect judgments of stimulus persons seemed a fascinating possibility, we felt that it was perhaps premature to assume that such typeface effects could be of great importance in indirect perception. Hardly any of the studies of typography referred to above considered typeface within the context of the newspaper page: instead the different type versions were typically presented to subjects on specially printed cards often containing a minimum of verbal material. We, on the other hand, were chiefly interested in whether or not changing a news item's typography could influence readership when the item was embedded in a newspaper page with the surrounding material held constant. To look at "readership" here is in a gross sense to look at input selection (see p. 17). The first part of the present experiment was designed to examine this, using the typographic variable of plain face or bold face, one of the most common alternatives open to the subeditor specifying the setting of a particular story. The second part of the experiment was intended to shed some light on the importance to selection of the position an item occupies on the newspaper page.

The material used in the experiment consisted of "stone-proofs" of an inside page of a provincial morning daily paper. These had the appearance of a genuine newspaper page, except that they were printed on one side only. There were three versions of the page, the first being identical to a page which had appeared in a normal edition of the paper. The second version was the same as version one except that the body of a short single-column item headlined *The Vicar's Tanner Poem* appeared in a bold typeface instead of the plain face of the first version. The typeface used for this item was in fact 7 point Scotsman Royal (Bold for version two). On the third version, the *Vicar's Tanner Poem* item was moved from the central page position it had occupied in the first two versions to the right-hand periphery of the page. The type-setting of the item was as in version two. The position of a second item was also varied between versions one and two and version three. This item, also single column and several paragraphs in length, was headlined *Sporting Cavalcade*, and appeared at the bottom right of the page in the first two versions and in a central position on version three: the type-setting was the same for all versions of this item.* Although we discussed the form of all these variations with members of the newspaper staff beforehand, it should be stressed that all the items used were quite authentic, and the setting up of the pages was done throughout by the usual stone-sub under customary working conditions.

The subjects were 117 undergraduates divided into two groups of 29 and one of 59, corresponding to the three versions of the newspaper page. In subgroups of about ten people, subjects were each handed a copy of the page and invited to read it "in a perfectly natural way". It was explained that they should read the paper as if they had picked it

---

* Illustrations of the pages employed in this investigation are presented in Knapper and Warr (1965).

up under normal circumstances, and should read only those items that interested them, ignoring those which did not. It was stressed that the page was a perfectly genuine offprint from a local newspaper and that subjects would not be required to recall the contents of the page. The subjects were asked to fold over the paper as soon as they had read all they wished and then individually consult one of a number of investigators who asked them to indicate on a measured-up version of the same news-sheet how much of every item on the page they had read. These indices of input selection were entered by investigators on to specially prepared forms and the total number of headlines seen and the total number of column inches read for each item for each version of the page was later calculated. In the analysis presented below these figures have been translated into percentages to allow for variations in the sizes of items.

On each version of the page there was a total of twenty news items, seventeen of which remained constant over the four versions. The position of two items was varied in the manner already described and the layout of a third was changed slightly for reasons which need not concern us here. In addition there were two advertisements which will be ignored in this discussion.

Versions one and two were exactly the same apart from the fact that the *Vicar's Tanner Poem* item was printed in a plain typeface in version one and a bold face in version two. Comparison of the readership of this item between the two versions should therefore reveal the effect on input selection of this typeface change. In fact an examination of average proportion of the item which was read reveals that in each case the proportion was exactly the same: 63.51%. It should be pointed out of course that although there is no effect of altering the typeface in this case, it would obviously be necessary to carry out a more comprehensive study embracing a larger number of news items and different sorts of typeface alterations before any more general conclusions could be drawn about the effect of change of typeface on news item readership.

Before analysing the effect of changing the position of an item, it is necessary to show that readership of the constant news items does not vary between the different page versions. Application of the median test confirmed that in the case of the seventeen constant items there are no differences approaching statistical significance in the proportion of an item read. As far as the number of subjects who read the headlines is concerned, there was a significant difference in the case of only one comparison.

Table 27 Mean percentage of subjects reading headlines, and mean proportion of story read for the two items whose page positions were varied

News item	Version 1 and version 2 ($N=58$)		Version 3 ($N=59$)	
	Headline	Story	Headline	Story
Vicar's Tanner Poem	93·10%	63·51%[a]	83·05%	39·75%[a]
Sporting Cavalcade	53·45%[b]	11·38%	74·58%[b]	19·66%

[a] [b] Significant differences

And what of the two items whose page position was varied? The relevant findings are summarized in Table 27. In the case of the *Vicar's Tanner Poem* there is a significant difference between the mean proportion of the story read in versions one and two and the proportion read in version three (median test, $p<0·01$). There are, however, no significant differences in the proportions of subjects who read the headlines over the different versions. In the case of the second item, *Sporting Cavalcade*, exactly the reverse holds good: while there are no significant differences between the proportions of the story read between the first two versions and version three, there is a significant difference ($p<0·05$) between the proportion of subjects who read the headlines in versions one and two and the proportion who read the headline in the last version. An examination of the page positions and subject matter of these two items suggests a probable explanation for these apparently contradictory findings.

On versions one and two the *Vicar's Tanner Poem* item occupies a position in the centre of the page, and it is on these versions that subjects read most of the item: when the item is moved away from the page centre (version three) a significantly smaller amount of it is read, as is shown by the means in Table 27. The proportion of subjects selecting the headline of this item is, however, very high throughout the three page versions. Even when the item was positioned on the page periphery more than eight out of ten readers read the headline — so many in fact that it is not possible to increase this proportion to a significant extent with the present number of subjects. Furthermore the heading *Vicar's Tanner Poem* is a rather unusual one, and the item itself sufficiently interesting to induce fairly large numbers of subjects to continue reading it. Not so the item *Sporting Cavalcade*, which contains material of a fairly commonplace local interest. Here the proportion of people reading the item's headline is significantly greater in version three (where the item is in the page centre), but there are few subjects who carry on to read the text of the item — too few in fact to provide a significant decrease when the item appears in the less favourable position of the first two versions.

What do these results suggest about the influence of page position on input selection in indirect perception? It seems that if an item occupies a central position on a newspaper page its headline is more likely to be read than if the same item is positioned at the edge of the page. Selection of headlines *is* affected by item location. But this does not guarantee that people will read a higher proportion of the item. The amount of a story which is read depends more upon the intrinsic importance of the item itself than on its position. These conclusions are reminiscent of our interpretation of the role of headlines in determining perception (p. 295). Headlines need to be viewed as part of a configuration embracing the item they precede; in a similar way the influence of page position on input selection is partly dependent upon the stimulus material itself.

Generalizations about input selection and perceptual reactions in indirect judgment are slowly emerging. These generalizations are needed both by theoretically-oriented psychologists and by communicators of more practical bent; it is to be hoped that increased empirical attention will be paid to these areas so that the generalizations may become both better supported and more detailed.

NEWSPAPERS AS A COMMUNICATION SOURCE

The previous section has been concerned with readership (i.e. input selection) rather than with the impressions formed from news items. Whether or not a news item is read is obviously an important factor influencing indirect perception, but probably of more general interest is the way our indirect perceptions can be influenced, given that we *have* in fact selected a particular news item. Earlier in this chapter we considered the effects of two fairly obvious communication variables present in the newspaper reading situation. We now come to what seems perhaps a more unlikely variable — this concerns how our perceptions of a news item can be influenced by the conception we have of the newspaper in which it appears.

The fact that readers tend to form quite detailed impressions of newspapers has interested a number of students of the mass media (e.g., Tannenbaum and McLeod, 1963). It has been common to make comparisons between readers' conceptions of various newspapers and their image of an "ideal newspaper" — often for commercial and advertising purposes (e.g., Deutschmann and Kiel, 1960). Special semantic differential scales have been developed to measure conceptions of newspapers (Lyle, 1960) and at least one investigator has examined newspapers in terms of personality theory (Gardiner, 1968). Whether or not we talk in terms of conceptions or personalities it is certain that we form impressions of newspapers based upon our perceptions of the paper's content, appearance, style of reporting, etc., and that these impressions differ from paper to paper.

Psychologists have for some time been interested in the way our attitudes towards a communication source may affect our interpretation of the message itself. Their investigations have mainly concerned attitude change. It is clear that communications from sources held in high esteem (for reasons of prestige, expertise, trustworthiness, impartiality, etc.) are regarded as more fair and more credible than communications from other sources; furthermore these same communications are more likely to induce opinion change in line with the persuasive content of the communication (Hovland and Weiss, 1951; Kelman and Hovland, 1953; Manis, 1961). Other studies of this topic have for example indicated that subjects who learn that T. S. Eliot approves of a poem are likely to increase their previous rankings of it (Aronson, Turner and Carlsmith, 1963) and that the credibility of an advertisement is related to the reputation of the magazine in which it appears (Fuchs, 1964; Lucas and Britt, 1950). Believing that a source is biassed — either negatively or positively — can cause the material communicated to be largely discounted (Pepitone, 1964). Investigations of this type are well reviewed and interpreted by Cohen, 1964; Hovland, Janis and Kelley, 1953; Klapper, 1960; and Sherif, Sherif and Nebergall, 1965.

Newspapers generally constitute a *channel* of communication in that they transmit information from other sources. Yet they frequently also serve as sources themselves, since what they transmit is often not attributed to its original encoder. We have already noted that readers can have quite clear conceptions of a paper and that conceptions differ from paper to paper. We may now wonder whether differences in the way newspapers are conceived influence the manner in which messages attributed to them are received. Of particular interest here is whether the indirect perception of people and events is partly determined by the identity of the source of a communication — in this case of the newspaper. To investigate this question we need to attribute the same communication to different newspaper sources and to look at the indirect perceptual responses mediated by each source. The following experiment is of this design.

Experiment 38

Two genuine news items were used in the investigation. One concerned a single individual and the second described a complex event. The individual stimulus person was Cardinal Mindszenty of Hungary and the communication about him originally appeared in the *Daily Mirror*. The event was a London play, "Portrait of Murder", and the report about this was taken from *The Guardian*. The 320-word item on Cardinal Mindszenty described how the Primate had quarrelled with the Government of Hungary and had been incarcerated in the American Embassy in Budapest for the past seven years; the tone of the article was mildly critical of the Cardinal's present refusal to accept safe conduct out of the country. The review of "Portrait of Murder" was 250 words long and unenthusiastic about the play, the plot and acting of which were briefly described. It was expected that subjects would have very little knowledge of either the play or the Cardinal, and in addition to our selection of these little-known stimuli the experiment took place over a year after the items had originally appeared in the press. Two versions of each story were prepared in typewritten form, without headlines, bylines or subheadings. At the top of the item appeared in normal type "Reprinted from [name of paper]" followed by the actual date of issue. On the first versions of each item the genuine newspaper title appeared (*Daily Mirror* or *The Guardian*). On the second versions of the two items the name of another newspaper was substituted: these latter newspapers were genuine and as well known to the subjects as the authentic papers. They were specially chosen, however, to provide a contrast with the type of newspaper represented by the originals. Thus the Cardinal Mindszenty item was attributed to the *Daily Telegraph* (a so-called "quality"* newspaper as opposed to the *Daily Mirror* which is a "popular"*) and the "Portrait of Murder" item to the *Daily Express* (a "popular" newspaper in contrast to the "quality" paper, *The Guardian*). As far as we know none of the subjects was aware of the deception.

Measurement was by twelve-scale semantic differential forms. In the case of the item about Cardinal Mindszenty the form used was the same as that employed in Experiment 29 (see Table 21, p. 281). The scales used for "Portrait of Murder" were basically selected from the three factors, but included some scales which seem particularly appropriate to the judgment of plays (e.g., well acted–badly acted). In addition a measure of the style of writing of each item was taken on scales representing the three factors and based upon the recommendations of Tannenbaum and McLeod (1963).

A total of 117 undergraduate subjects took part in the experiment, all subjects reading both communications. The different versions of each story were read by roughly equal numbers of subjects. Stories were presented without special comment from the experimenter, they were read through once, after which subjects judged the topic of the news item (Cardinal Mindszenty or the play "Portrait of Murder") and the style of writing of the item. The order in which subjects made their four judgments was randomized, except that the pair of judgments about an item always followed that item.

Comparisons of perceptual responses between versions of the two stories for both news items reveal no significant difference. In other words we were unable to demonstrate any effect of newspaper title upon readers' perceptions of the subject of a news item. However, comparisons between versions for the mean style ratings reveal a total of five significant differences over the two news items. The style of the "quality" *Daily Telegraph* was rated significantly more true ($p < 0.05$) and more sour ($p < 0.002$) than that of the "popular" *Daily Mirror*. And the "quality" newspaper *The Guardian* was rated significantly more fair ($p < 0.05$), more responsible ($p < 0.05$) and more accurate ($p < 0.01$) than the "popular" paper the *Daily Express*. We emphasize again that the reports were identical in each case.

This latter finding indicates that subjects' conceptions of a newspaper source do influence their perception of its content. But we have not

---

* The terms are taken from the *Report of the Royal Commission on the Press 1947–1949*, p. 8.

been able to show a similar effect upon readers' perception of the stimulus person or event described. Whether or not these effects occur is still an open question, and the possibility that they take place in other circumstances cannot be ruled out. The stimulus person and stimulus event in this experiment were chosen in the hope that subjects would not have clearly defined conceptions of them. It could be that with more controversial or well-known stimuli about which the paper was known to have strong views an effect would be observed. In these cases conceptions of the stimulus and of the source might interact to generate an observable effect. Evidence about the operation of the congruity principle (see p. 165) has largely arisen from less complex situations than that studied here (e.g., Osgood and Tannenbaum, 1955; Tannenbaum, 1956; Tannenbaum and Gengel, 1966; Tannenbaum, Macaulay and Norris, 1966), and the principle may perhaps be found to apply to source and topic conceptions of the kind investigated in this experiment.

CONCLUDING REMARKS

The present chapter has dealt with some of the more obvious communication variables within the newspaper page which can affect our perception of a stimulus person or event. We have investigated the importance of headlines, photographs, layout and typography and of the particular paper in which an item appears. Although these are probably the variables most likely to be important in determining reader perceptions, they are by no means the only communication variables we could have studied. Tannenbaum (1955) talks about the "indexing process" in communication ("a single . . . stimulus element or a stimulus complex that may serve to predispose a particular interpretation or meaning of the total stimulus pattern"). Such influence, he claims, may be in terms of attracting attention to the message or of helping to decode the message. Possible indices suggested by Tannenbaum include captions to pictures and colour (of advertisements), in addition to the variables we ourselves have already discussed. There have been investigations of the effects on communication and comprehension of different kinds of graphs (Parker, 1963), statistical tables (Feliciano, 1962), the verb-voice of newspaper articles (Maurer, 1963), bylines (the correspondent's name) (Greenberg and Tannenbaum, 1961) and even incorrect grammar in messages (Sencer, 1965).

The number of communication variables it is possible to study is clearly immense, and it should of course be remembered that we have considered only one of the mass media — the press. Communication via radio, film or television involves yet further complex variables concerned with sound, motion, lighting, etc. Any study of input selection or outputs from indirect person perception must pay close attention to the different sorts of communication variables and the interactions between them. So far we have some knowledge of the individual variables themselves; of the interactions we know very little.

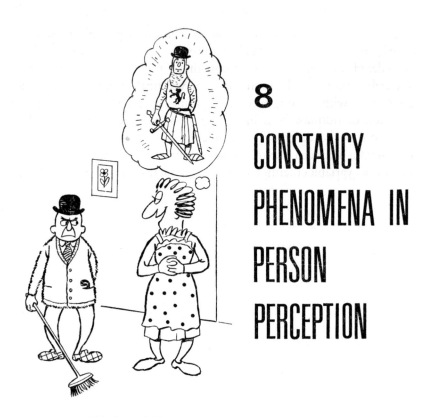

8
CONSTANCY PHENOMENA IN PERSON PERCEPTION

THE NATURE OF CONSTANCY

In Chapter 1 (pp. 31–45) we drew attention to several aspects of object perception which have been extensively studied by experimental psychologists. We looked at the similarities between object perception and person perception and set up the working hypothesis that the two processes are essentially the same. By this we meant that they will both eventually prove to be explicable in terms of the same higher-order laws. A set of laws sufficient to explain either object perception or person perception is of course not yet available, and our understanding of these activities is still at the stage of fairly low-level generalizations. Some of these generalizations about the way we perceive objects were considered in Chapter 1 and corresponding generalizations about person perception were also suggested at that point. In this chapter we discuss one facet of perception in greater detail. Evidence will be presented that very similar processes are at work when we perceive either objects or the behaviour of people.

The particular aspect we examine here is perceptual constancy. It is well known that if a person is asked to judge the size of a familiar object which is some distance away from him, his judgment will not usually conform to the size of the image projected on his retina. Instead the object will be seen as larger than the size of the retinal image would suggest — in fact more like its "actual" size.

Similarly, an object does not appear to shrink or expand as we move around it; we adjust our perception so that its size remains fairly constant despite considerable changes in the image it projects. This process of adjustment is usually referred to as size constancy. Analogous adjustments give rise to brightness constancy: a piece of white chalk appears white despite variations in level of illumination which "ought to" result in changes in its whiteness. And further visual constancies may be isolated by which perceived colour and shape vary less than do the relevant stimuli impinging upon the sense organs. Nor are constancy phenomena in object perception restricted to visual judgments; comparable processes are at work in auditory judgments and in judgments of value (cf. Brunswik, 1956, p. 70 ff.; Postman and Tolman, 1959).

The importance of these constancy effects lies in the resulting stability of our perceptual world. Despite fairly large changes in stimuli reaching the sense organs the characteristics of objects are experienced as remaining approximately constant. A considerable economy is introduced into the perceptual system by this tendency to alter our episodic judgments so as to minimize the effects of changes in the external environment. It is tempting to believe that a similar economy occurs in the perception of people.

This point has been raised by Brunswik (1934; 1956), Cantril (1957), Heider (1958) and Icheiser (1949). Heider (p. 28) suggests that just as there is a size, shape or colour constancy, so there might be a "wish constancy". By this he means that we can recognize a wish as being the same whether it is expressed explicitly or implied indirectly through a piece of behaviour. In the same way it seems plausible that a person might be seen to have the same characteristics despite the fact that he behaves rather differently in different situations. We shall develop this idea in some detail in the next few pages, and shall describe experiments which study one aspect of constancy in the perception of people.

In doing this it will be useful to have clearly before us an instance of the laboratory investigation of constancy in object perception. We can then see how close is the correspondence between these two types of constancy phenomena. An early investigation by Thouless (1931a, 1931b) will adequately serve as an example. Thouless studied constancy effects in the way subjects perceive the shape of objects and his methods are very similar to those adopted by later workers. In one experiment he exposed a circular disc and asked for subjects' judgments of the shape of the disc. They made these estimates by selecting a matching disc from a series of circular and elliptical ones which they had been given. When the stimulus disc was directly in front of them and in a vertical plane, the perceptual judgment was of course straightforward. But Thouless also rotated the disc away from the subject by turning it on a horizontal axis through its centre. In this way the circle made to incline at say, 45° appeared elliptical to the subject, and his task was more complicated. Thouless found that judgments of shape represented a compromise between the stimulus shape (an ellipse) and the real shape (the circle). Subjects did not see the shape they "ought to" have seen if they were perceiving only on the basis of retinal stimulation; instead they exhibited a "phenomenal regression to the real object" — the phenomenal or apparent shape was inbetween the stimulus shape and the real shape. This same regression phenomenon has been termed by Brunswik (e.g. 1928) a "perceptual compromise".

How could we set up a parallel laboratory investigation of constancy in person perception? Since we are mainly concerned with judgments of covert characteristics (see Chapter 1, p. 3) we are spared the necessity of studying judgments of overt fact which might entail the rotation of portly stimulus persons about their middles. Instead we should need to look at the kinds of judgments we have studied in earlier experiments and present information about the person in a particular context which is at variance with our subjects' knowledge of the "real" person. In this way we should have measures of the stimulus (analogous to the shape of the ellipse in Thouless's experiment) and of the "real" person (analogous to the circular shape of the disc), and we could see whether subjects' estimates (similar to those of apparent or phenomenal shape) were a compromise between these two values. Several commonly-used formulae are available to provide an index of constancy in object perception and it would obviously be of great value if we could make use of them in studies of the perception of people.

Degree of constancy is often assessed by means of a Brunswik ratio

(Brunswik, 1928) or a Thouless ratio (Thouless, 1931a). The Brunswik ratio is of the form $(P - S)/(R - S)$, where P is the phenomenal or apparent shape, S is the stimulus shape and R is the real shape of an object. The Thouless ratio is the same as this except that the logarithm of each value is placed in the formula. In both cases a higher ratio indicates greater constancy — more regression towards the real object. But it is unfortunately obvious that we cannot make use of these formulae to study person perception, since we cannot obtain a single objective measure of each of the terms. We cannot obtain one straight-forward measure of S in the way we can measure the shape of an ellipse, nor can we directly measure R, the "real" person.

If the *only* method to investigate constancy were by means of this type of ratio, we should be unable to study the phenomenon in person perception. However, we need not be dependent on this form of measurement. Indeed it is surprising how popular it has remained; Woodworth and Schlosberg (1954, p. 436) have expressed disapproval of the technique, and severe methodological and statistical criticisms have been levelled at it by Brunswik himself (1940), Epstein and Park (1963) and Koffka (1935, pp. 226-7). A promising alternative approach is to measure constancy in terms of correlation coefficients. Brunswik (1940, 1944, 1956) has reported studies each of which involved a large number of stimuli. In these investigations he calculated constancy values in terms of the correlations between real, projected and perceived sizes across the range of objects. The disadvantage here is that a lot of stimuli are required, and a more economic correlational procedure is available which is particularly suited to measuring constancy in person perception. This is to use only one stimulus person and to calculate correlations across subjects.

Suppose that we were to record each subject's judgment of the "real" person. In this way we would have as many values of R (analogous to the "real shape") as we have subjects, and we could then correlate these values of R with values of P derived from observing behaviour in a particular situation. The higher the correlation coefficient, the greater would be the degree of perceptual constancy.

We have of course obtained many measurements of this kind in Experiments 15 to 17 and 26 to 28 which were described in Chapters 4 and 6. In these investigations we obtained semantic differential measures of subjects' conceptions of a stimulus person. These con-ceptual judgments — equivalent to judgments of the "real" person —

were related to the subjects' subsequent episodic perception of the person's behaviour. In Chapter 4 we summarized data from a large number of cases where conceptual judgments were clearly related to the way the stimulus person's behaviour was perceived. A total of 148 constancy values of this type are available from the experiments reviewed in that chapter. The average correlation between conception and episodic perception (i.e. the degree of constancy) is found to be $+0.34$. This is statistically very significant, and although it accounts for only a relatively small proportion of the variance, no doubt when measurement unreliability has been allowed for (cf. Block, 1963) the true correlation is rather higher. We can therefore be confident that subjects do exhibit constancy in judging others in situations of the kind we have studied. But this is an extremely general conclusion based upon correlation coefficients which vary from -0.10 to $+0.68$. Can we discover why they differ from situation to situation?

It may be that generalizations which have been established about constancy in object perception are also applicable to person perception, and that some of these could help us to make sense of the differences in the data we have already accumulated. Let us here consider a number of these generalizations — first in fairly comprehensive terms and afterwards to see whether they are of use in interpreting the results in a more specific manner.

SOME GENERALIZATIONS ABOUT CONSTANCY

A number of the differences in object perception constancy are attributable to variations between perceivers. The tendency to make constancy judgments is an individual perceiver characteristic which is consistent over time and over tasks. Thouless (1938) has observed high test–retest reliability coefficients and Sheehan (1938) and others have found positive intercorrelations between behaviour in different constancy tasks. Several stable characteristics of the perceiver (see Figure 1, p. 20) which influence constancy have been isolated. It is clear for example that subjects' intelligence is negatively related to constancy in object perception (e.g. Leibowitz and coworkers, 1959; Thouless, 1932). Similarly constancy is found to be greater with relatively unsophisticated subjects who do not deliberate much over their judgments (e.g. Gottheil and Bitterman, 1951; Thouless, 1932).

Systematic variations in constancy with age are also observable (e.g. Brunswik, 1956, pp. 22, 82–86; Thouless, 1932). The perceiver's current state is another factor which affects constancy in object perception. Subjects who are instructed to make fairly immediate judgments exhibit more constancy than those adopting a critical approach (see Brunswik, 1956, p. 97), and perceivers to whom the stimulus is exposed only briefly are similarly prone to a high degree of constancy.

These generalizations about individual differences do not go very far towards accounting for the constancy figures available from our earlier experiments on person perception. Here the subject groups were fairly homogeneous and the data were analysed without heed to variations between perceivers. Our subjects were on the whole both intelligent and sophisticated so that we would predict even greater constancy effects with a more representative sample of perceivers. However, it would be both feasible and probably rewarding to test out in the field of person perception those generalizations concerning the current state and stable characteristics of perceivers which have been found to be of particular pertinence to constancy phenomena in the perception of objects.

Generalizations about present stimulus information and present context information can likewise be tested in studies of person perception. Many cues about the nature of an object are available from context stimuli. For example, differences in texture and in reflection are indicators of depth and slant. It is significant that as these cues about the nature of the object are impoverished, so is constancy minimized (e.g. Epstein and Park, 1963; Holway and Boring, 1941; Leibowitz and Bourne, 1956; Nelson and Bartley, 1956). An analogous hypothesis about person perception suggests itself. Just as we can reduce the information available about, for instance, angle of tilt in a shape constancy experiment, so we can limit subjects' knowledge in a study of person perception. This might be achieved by altering the degree to which we specify the identity of the stimulus person (for example, a perceptual situation in which the stimulus person was described as "an important politician" instead of "Mr. Wilson" would effectively limit the number of contextual cues available to perceivers). From the generalization that perceptual constancy is greatest when the nature of the "real" object is clear we can draw another hypothesis about person perception. Since the better our acquaintance with a person the clearer is the nature of the "real object" (i.e. the more detailed is our conception), so the degree of constancy should be positively related to knowledge of the stimulus person (members of the family rather than casual acquaintances for example). This possibility has yet to be tested.

Looking back to our paradigm study of shape constancy described earlier (p. 332) we might expect that a straightforward relationship between degree of constancy and angle of tilt will be observed. It is reasonable to suppose that as the angle of tilt from the vertical is increased, so does amount of constancy decrease. This is predictable from the fact that more cues about the nature of the object are available when the disc approaches the vertical plane than when it nears the horizontal. Several tests of this hypothesis have been made, and the results are far from consistent. Epstein and Park (1963) have reviewed the relevant investigations and have drawn attention to a number of methodological and quantitative difficulties. There is undoubtedly some evidence for the hypothesis, but there are also results which fail to support it.

Are there any grounds for accepting a similar hypothesis about constancy in person perception?

Here we might expect that the amount of constancy will decrease as the discrepancy between the information presented and the "real" person increases. Consider the experiments on indirect perception described in Chapter 4. In these we first elicited from subjects their conceptions of the stimulus person: these semantic differential measures provide our index of the "real" person. We then presented our subjects with one of two sets of information relevant to the stimulus person, on the basis of which they gave their perception of him. Now it is quite possible that one of the pair of narrative reports is more "discrepant" than the other in that it provides information which is more at odds with subjects' conceptions of the stimulus person. (Incidentally, the experiments were not designed with this in mind.) We should of course predict that the amount of constancy exhibited by the perceivers who read the more discrepant report would be less than that shown by the other group. We have carried out a *post hoc* analysis of our data to see if this hypothesis is supported.

As a global measure of constancy we have used the average correlation over all scales between conceptions and episodic perceptions. The measurement of discrepancy is, however, rather more difficult. We do not have conveniently objective measures of discrepancy corresponding to measures of tilt, but we can nevertheless obtain a rough idea of which narrative is the "more tilted" by making use of the average values of responses to each semantic differential scale. We could compare conceptual judgments of the "real person" with the perceptual judgments based upon one of two narratives. This would provide an index of discrepancy for each narrative. We can be fairly confident that such an index does reflect the information content of the report, for the results of the experiments described in Chapter 6 (for instance, pp. 258–260) indicate quite clearly that narrative content is reflected closely in readers' semantic differential responses. If we sum the differences between conceptions and perceptions over all the scales for which we have responses we can obtain a satisfactory measure of discrepancy. The measure is analogous to a measure of the difference between the "real" object (e.g. a circle) and the "comparison" object (e.g. an ellipse) in an experiment on shape constancy.

Going back to our original hypothesis we would predict that subjects who read the less discrepant narrative will exhibit more constancy. The smaller the differences between the mean values of conception and episodic perception, the greater will be the correlation between individual conceptual and perceptual responses. Stated this way, the prediction might appear to be tautologous. It might seem that similar mean values are necessarily reflected in high correlations between individual responses in the two situations. This is in fact not so. There is nothing in the nature of a product–moment correlation which relates its magnitude to the similarity between mean values of the two variables. This can readily be demonstrated by drawing examples from the results of experiments described in Chapter 6. A zero correlation or a very high correlation can be found both when the means of the two measures are very similar and when they are very different. The figures below show this.

Experiment and subject group	Scale	Discrepancy	Correlation between conception and episodic perception
Experiment 27, group 4	Rugged–delicate	1·19	+0·07
Experiment 26, group 4	Sweet–sour	0·03	+0·06
Experiment 28, group 1	Popular–unpopular	1·59	+0·66
Experiment 28, group 1	Humane–ruthless	0·06	+0·57

Thus there is no logical necessity inherent in the prediction. The null hypothesis that discrepancy and constancy values are unrelated is one which is open to refutation by observation rather than by statistical artefact. Nevertheless, to dispel any lingering doubts on this point we have tested the prediction that there is a negative relationship between these two values by using data from two matched groups of subjects. So to arrive at our discrepancy value we have compared subjects' episodic perceptions of the stimulus person not with their own conceptions of that person, but with the conceptions provided by a matched group. The procedure may be described schematically in this way: matched groups A and B have been studied, the discrepancy score deriving from a comparison of A's conception and B's episodic judgment, and the constancy score deriving from the two sets of responses by B. In this way our measure of discrepancy is drawn from figures different from those on which our measure of constancy is based, so that we cannot be studying a statistically necessary relationship.

We are fortunate in already having all the information we need, including conceptions from two matched groups, in a number of previous experiments. A measure of discrepancy between the "real" person and the "comparison" person can in each case be obtained by relating the average conceptual responses of one group to the average episodic perceptual responses of the other group. In this way it is a fairly straightforward matter to decide which of two narrative accounts is the more discrepant. Our prediction requires that subjects' perception based on the more discrepant narrative will exhibit less constancy. Data from the earlier experiments which pertain to this prediction are shown in Table 28.

We have indicated there which of the two narratives or which sequence of two narratives is the less discrepant. A measure of constancy is provided by the average correlation between the conception of the "real" person and the episodic perception of the "comparison" person, calculated across all the scales in an experiment. The overall average constancy measures of $+0.37$ and $+0.30$ are therefore each based upon 74 correlation coefficients.

These figures lend some support to our hypothesis. There is a tendency for subjects to exhibit greater constancy when their episodic perception is based on less discrepant information. But the data do not constitute a very adequate test. In several cases the two narratives in a pair contained information which differed from the "real" person by

Table 28 The relationship between constancy and a narrative's discrepancy from subjects' conceptions

Experiment	Less discrepant narrative(s)	Average degree of constancy	
		Less discrepant narrative	More discrepant narrative
15	1	+0·37	+0·39
16	1	+0·35	+0·29
17	1	+0·43	+0·31
26	1/2	+0·31	+0·26
27	1/2	+0·32	+0·23
28	1/2	+0·42	+0·34
Overall		+0·37	+0·30

very similar amounts. In Experiment 27, for instance, the average discrepancy score across all scales for the 1/2 group was 0·55 and for the 2/1 group 0·57. And the average difference *over all studies* between the discrepancy scores of the two narratives in a pair was only 0·12. With differences in an independent variable which are as small as this, tests of differences in a dependent variable are clearly unsatisfactory.

At the same time the results are at least encouraging. The hypothesis might be supported in an experiment where greater control of the independent variable — discrepancy — is exerted. After having developed viable measures of this characteristic and of constancy in person perception we felt that it would be useful to continue this line of research by carrying out such an experiment.

Experiment 39

Since we needed to control the information to which subjects were exposed, we constructed narratives especially for this experiment. Three narratives were employed, each of which described the behaviour of the same stimulus person at the same meeting. As far as possible the factual content of the reports was unchanged, but we attempted to manipulate the impression which each report would generate.

Once again the narratives described the behaviour of a speaker at a political meeting. This time the speaker was Mr. Jo Grimond, then leader of the British Liberal Party, and the accounts contained details of a speech in which he outlined several aspects of Liberal policy. The

M

main theme of his talk was said to be a dislike for the Socialist party's plan to nationalize the steel industry. All the issues raised were topical ones, and no subject doubted that the reports were genuine.

Version 1 of the report was designed so that subjects would make fairly neutral perceptual responses. Versions 2 and 3, although containing the same details of Grimond's behaviour, differed from the first version in that they were likely to generate respectively very positive or very negative responses. The style of each report can be gauged from the first few sentences. These are reproduced below.

Version 1

The Liberal party leader Mr. Grimond, speaking at a rally in Nottingham yesterday, spoke out against the Labour Government's plans to nationalize the steel industry. A large number of party supporters had travelled in from all over the Midlands for this, the first large-scale meeting since the general election.

They were clearly expecting great things of their leader, and Mr. Grimond did his best not to disappoint them. But his reception was fairly mild compared to the ovations he has been used to of late, and there seemed to be some frustration that he had no policy proposals which would enhance the party's reputation with the electorate.

Version 2

The Liberal Party leader, Mr. Grimond, yesterday returned clearly refreshed from his holiday abroad. He celebrated his return by launching a spirited attack on the Socialists' plans to nationalize the steel industry.

Mr. Grimond was speaking at a Liberal Party rally in Nottingham. Supporters of the party had poured in from all parts of the country to attend the meeting. They will doubtless return home today encouraged by the fighting speech made by their leader.

Version 3

The Liberal Party leader Mr. Grimond, speaking at a rally in Nottingham yesterday launched a biting if ineffective attack on the Labour Government's plans to nationalize the steel industry. A large number of party supporters had travelled in from all over the

Midlands for this, the first large-scale Liberal meeting since the general election.

They were clearly expecting great things of their leader, but in fact most of them went away bitterly disappointed. There was a complete absence of the enthusiastic ovations Mr. Grimond had been used to of late; instead he was greeted by applause that was embarrassingly polite, and even a few derisory jeers.

Each version was approximately 300 words long, with the headline "Grimond slams nationalization plans". The reports were typewritten on single sheets of paper, and were described to subjects as being excerpts from a newspaper account. Each subject was of course aware of the existence of only one report.

The procedure was similar to that employed in earlier experiments. Subjects' conception of Grimond and their episodic perception of his behaviour based upon one of the reports were obtained at different times. Two hundred and twenty-three undergraduate subjects took part in the investigation, 59, 117 and 47 of whom read versions 1, 2 and 3 respectively. A ten-item semantic differential scale was used (see Table 29 below). This was specially devised to be applicable to a number of political concepts as well as to persons. In the present case we were also interested in subjects' judgments about the main topic of Mr. Grimond's speech — the nationalization of steel — and these were also measured. This aspect of the study has been described in Chapter 4 (p. 184).

Subjects were assigned haphazardly to the different narratives. (Indeed the imbalance in subject numbers shows that this was carried out rather *too* haphazardly.) A study of groups' conceptual responses on each of the ten scales demonstrated that we had successfully matched them. Only one of the thirty intergroup comparisons revealed a significant difference.

Subjects' conceptions of Grimond were on the whole fairly neutral. For this reason version 1 was expected to contain information consistent with judgments of the "real" person. Versions 2 and 3 were expected to contain much more discrepant information. In addition version 2 was intended to generate a positively discrepant impression whilst version 3 was intended to yield negatively discrepant perceptions.

How successful were we in these manipulations of our independent variables? First, the episodic judgments based upon the three reports were very significantly different. Of the thirty possible differences between mean scale scores twenty-six were significant, often at well beyond the 0·001 level. And inspection of these responses leaves no doubt that version 1 was indeed a neutral one whilst versions 2 and 3 were positive and negative respectively. Secondly, the intended variations in discrepancy were assessed. We calculated average discrepancy scores for the three versions, using the matched group technique outlined above. Since we had available three groups in this experiment, we arbitrarily selected one of the other two as a matching group. Discrepancy scores for Group 1 were based on Group 3 conceptual responses, Group 2 on Group 1 responses and Group 3 on Group 2 responses. The average discrepancy between the "real" person and the "comparison" person across the ten scales was 0·73 for version 1, 1·78 for version 2, and 2·73 for version 3.

Our independent variable manipulations were clearly satisfactory. In this experiment we have a much greater difference between the discrepancy scores of the different narratives than we had in the experiments summarized in Table 28. Whereas the average difference between the discrepancy scores of a pair of narratives in the earlier experiments was only 0·12, all the average differences between narratives in this experiment exceed 0·90. Furthermore, versions 2 and 3 of this experiment clearly contain information which is very much more discrepant than that contained in any of the narratives we have studied previously. The average discrepancy score in the previous experiments was only 0·59, which is similar to the smallest figure in this investigation — the figure for version 1.

Our successful manipulation of discrepancy scores allows us to make two specific derivations from the hypothesis. The first — and major — prediction is that subjects' perceptions based on version 1 will exhibit more constancy than those based on versions 2 and 3. And secondly, we can predict from the hypothesis and from the earlier studies that constancy in subjects reading these two latter versions will be less than we found previously (since the discrepancy scores are so large), but that the constancy exhibited by readers of version 1 will approximate the level of constancy in the earlier experiments (since the average discrepancy scores are similar). These predictions are tested by the results presented in Table 29.

The first prediction is adequately confirmed. The average correlation

Table 29   Measures of constancy exhibited by three groups of subjects in Experiment 39

	Version 1 (N=59)	Version 2 (N=117)	Version 3 (N=47)
Average discrepancy score	0·73	1·78	2·73
Pleasant–unpleasant	+0·34	+0·07	+0·19
Exciting–dull	+0·26	−0·02	+0·10
Fresh–stale	+0·25	+0·14	−0·03
Valuable–worthless	+0·47	+0·14	+0·01
Fair–unfair	+0·57	+0·04	+0·32
Interesting–boring	+0·37	+0·06	+0·18
Tense–relaxed	−0·02	+0·15	0·00
Bold–timid	+0·23	+0·14	+0·42
Loud–soft	+0·23	+0·05	+0·25
Colourful–colourless	+0·36	+0·14	+0·22
Average correlation	+0·31	+0·09	+0·17

between conceptual responses and episodic perception is very much higher for subjects exposed to version 1 than for other subjects. A Wilcoxon matched-pairs signed-ranks test applied to the version 1 values and the average values of the other versions indicates that this difference is significant at the 0·01 level. The degree of constancy shown by subjects in groups 2 and 3 is very much lower than in any of the earlier experiments. Indeed it is effectively zero, which presumably accounts for the failure to find a significant difference between the correlations arising from these two versions. Finally, there is a very close correspondence between the average degree of constancy exhibited by subjects in group 1 (+0·31) and the average degree found in earlier experiments (+0·34, see p. 334); this is consistent with the similarity between the discrepancy scores for the narratives employed.

The results of Experiment 39 appear to provide substantial support for the hypothesis. Looking back at the procedure used to study shape constancy which was considered earlier, we can describe the present experiment and results in terms of this analogy — constancy is very great when the comparison object is similar to the "real" object, that is when the circular disc is not tilted far from the frontal-parallel plane (version 1), but as the angle of tilt away from or towards the subject is increased (versions 2 and 3) so does constancy decline.

But suppose the "real" object were not a circle but an ellipse. Would increasing the discrepancy between this and the comparison object yield the same changes in degree of constancy? Or, rephrasing this in terms of indirect person perception, would results similar to those of Experiment 39 be found if the "real" person was not one who is judged in a fairly neutral manner? Subjects' conceptions of Grimond are fairly neutral ones, so that by increasing the discrepancy of the information contained in our narratives 2 and 3 we were at the same time generating perceptions of his behaviour which were more extreme than those based on version 1. We may wonder whether the conditions of this experiment constitute a special case. The hypothesis is undoubtedly supported, but we have only adduced evidence about the case when the "real" person is a fairly neutral one. It could be that the differences in degree of constancy are due to versions 2 and 3 containing material which generates more extreme responses rather than being due to differences in discrepancy alone. Evidence bearing on the other case would be valuable — when the "real" person is conceived in a fairly extreme manner so that the discrepant reports are those which present more neutral information.

Experiment 40

We have conducted a further experiment to investigate this other possibility. Instead of studying the way in which the behaviour of a fairly neutral stimulus person is viewed, we selected a person about whom judgments were likely to be rather extreme. Reports were prepared of the performance of Senator Barry Goldwater addressing a Republican convention in July 1964. These reports were fictitious but were based upon real events, and no subject expressed doubts about their authenticity.

The design of this experiment was the same as that of the previous study. Three groups of undergraduate subjects were employed, each of which was presented with a report entitled "Goldwater nominated for President" allegedly drawn from the *Washington Daily Post*. The crucial difference from Experiment 39 was that the report which was intended to contain the least discrepant information was in the present case the most extremely worded one. This extremely worded report (version 1) was read by 39 subjects. Version 2 (read by 34 subjects) was rather less extreme and the third version ($N=33$) was designed to generate fairly neutral perceptions of Goldwater's behaviour. We would therefore expect both these versions to generate more discrepant impressions.

Comparison of the three groups' conceptual responses showed that we had allocated subjects in an unbiassed way. We used the same ten semantic differential scales as previously, and only two of the thirty possible comparisons of mean values yielded significant differences; these both arose from a single group's atypical responses to one scale. What about our manipulation of the extremity and the discrepancy of information content? We calculated discrepancy scores in the same way as previously: a relatively high score again indicates a more discrepant narrative. But we also need to know how the impression each narrative was intended to create was in fact perceived by our subjects. For example, did the "neutral" version really generate less extreme perceptions of Goldwater's behaviour than the more extremely worded narratives. The *extremity* of subjects' views about this behaviour was checked in terms of average polarity scores for each narrative. A polarity score is simply the extent to which the responses of (in this case) a group deviate from the neutral point. That we were successful in varying discrepancy and polarity scores in opposite directions is clear from these summary figures:

	Version 1	Version 2	Version 3
Mean discrepancy score	0·39	0·88	1·91
Mean polarity score	2·41	1·47	0·51

So we have shown that the three versions differed in the extent to which they represented Goldwater's behaviour as unusual. Version 3 contains much discrepant information, whilst version 1 is a description of behaviour fairly close to subjects' conceptions of the "real" Goldwater. At the same time it is clear that the least discrepant narrative (version 1) is in fact an extremely worded one, having the highest polarity score. As discrepancy increases across the three narratives, so does polarity decline. Naturally enough, the three versions were sufficiently different to generate varying perceptions of Goldwater's behaviour. Of the thirty comparisons of mean episodic judgment based on the three narratives, no less than twenty yielded statistically significant differences.

The hypothesis implies that subjects who read version 1 will exhibit

Table 30 Measures of constancy exhibited by three groups of subjects in Experiment 40

	Version 1 (N=39)	Version 2 (N=34)	Version 3 (N=33)
Average discrepancy score	0·39	0·88	1·91
Pleasant–unpleasant	+0·69	+0·36	+0·20
Exciting–dull	+0·40	0·00	−0·17
Fresh–stale	+0·31	+0·06	+0·26
Valuable–worthless	+0·40	+0·30	+0·51
Fair–unfair	+0·27	+0·19	+0·33
Interesting–boring	+0·66	+0·37	+0·21
Tense–relaxed	+0·47	+0·17	+0·18
Bold–timid	+0·41	+0·56	+0·09
Loud–soft	+0·44	+0·52	+0·38
Colourful–colourless	+0·17	+0·35	−0·01
Average correlation	+0·42	+0·29	+0·20

greatest constancy. If this is in fact the case we shall be able to conclude that the inverse relationship between discrepancy and constancy observed in Experiment 39 is not an artefact arising from the positive association between discrepancy and polarity obtained in that study. The results set out in Table 30 give clear support to this derivation. The subjects whose perception of Goldwater's behaviour is mediated by version 1 exhibit significantly more constancy than those who were exposed to the other versions. The overall constancy value (+0·42) for this narrative is higher than in the earlier study, and it is interesting that the discrepancy score is similarly lower than previously.

FURTHER COMMENTS ON CONSTANCY IN PERSON PERCEPTION

These investigations strongly suggest that our generalization is valid: constancy is less when the information presented about a stimulus person is markedly discrepant from perceivers' conceptions of the person. Evidence in support of the generalization comes from the *post hoc* analysis of experiments reported in earlier chapters and from the more satisfactory tests constituted by Experiments 38 and 39. We can tie together the results of all these studies by looking at the relationship across them all between discrepancy and constancy. Data are now available from eighteen different narratives, and the rank correlation between the two variables across these eighteen sets of data is -0.52 ($p < 0.025$). As we have already noted, several of the results are unreliable, and this figure might be higher if all the experiments had been designed to test the hypothesis. Alternatively the possibility could be tested that the relationship is not a linear one; it might be that constancy is high with both non-discrepant and *extremely* discrepant information, so that there is in fact a U-shaped relationship between constancy and information discrepancy.

Our emphasis in this chapter has been on the analogy between object perception and person perception, but we should not miss the opportunity to draw attention here to parallels in the study of attitude change. Attitudes' resistance to change is a form of constancy of cognitive structure, so that greater change represents less constancy. Within this framework we may ask about the relationship between amount of attitude change and the extent to which the position advocated in a communication is discrepant from the subject's own standpoint. This issue has been approached by a number of investigators. Goldberg (1954), Hovland and Pritzker (1957), Zimbardo (1960) and others have indicated that attitude change is a linear function of communication discrepancy, whereas Carlson (1956) and Insko, Murashima and Saiyadain (1966) have reported a curvilinear relationship.

Koslin, Stoops and Loh (1967) point out several methodological problems (such as ensuring that a sufficient range of discrepancies is sampled), which they apparently overcome in an investigation lending clear support to the hypothesis of curvilinearity: change first increases and then declines as a function of increasing communication discrepancy. Transposing this we may say that constancy in attitude structure first declines and then increases with increasing discrepancy. Constancy in the perception of persons and objects may turn out to be of this kind; perhaps narratives of still greater discrepancy need to be introduced into experiments like those described in the last section.

We have already (pp. 334–335) drawn attention to other generalizations about object perception which may be tested in studies of person perception using the techniques and indices suggested above. Certain stable characteristics of the perceiver are particularly easy to work with, and we have reanalysed some of the results of the experiments discussed in this chapter to investigate them. The sex of a perceiver has already been shown to influence some aspects of person perception (see Chapter 3, pp. 155–159; and Chapter 4, pp. 185–194), and we may wonder whether it is related to the tendency to exhibit constancy. To investigate this possibility we have arbitrarily selected six of the eighteen available sets of data (involving in all sixty-six semantic differential scales) and have reanalysed them in terms of subjects' sex. The average constancy value for male perceivers is $+0.32$ and for females the figure is $+0.31$. Clearly there are no significant differences here, at least as far as this class of stimulus person is concerned. A stable perceiver characteristic which seems more likely to be predictive of constancy is ethnocentrism. Scores on an ethnocentrism scale are available for subjects in Experiment 38, and we have recalculated the data from this study in terms of E-score. Once again there are no differences between groups.

A final more general point about constancy may be noted. It appears that social psychologists' use of the term is slightly less specific than the way it is employed by experimental psychologists in their studies of object perception. Discussions by the former of constancy in person perception are mainly to do with the fact that we assume *consistency* in the behaviour and characteristics of others and of ourselves (see for example Cantril (1957), Heider (1958), and Kilpatrick and Cantril (1961)). We have described this notion of constancy in terms of episodic and dispositional judgments (see Chapter 1, p. 9). Both forms of judgment are economic reformulations of a complex set of inputs and both carry with them expectations that the stimulus will continue to behave in certain ways and will continue to be of a certain type. Constancy of this kind is readily observed in almost all studies of perception.

But the phenomenon has been approached by experimental psychologists along certain specific methodological roads. In a sense the relevant investigations in the field of object perception have assumed the existence of constancy and have aimed to delineate the way in which the phenomenon is affected by other variables, whilst social psychologists have been more concerned to draw attention to the phenomenon itself. The discussion in this chapter has attempted to apply the insights and understanding of experimental psychology to the study of person perception: we assumed consistency of judgment at the outset, and have studied some of the factors affecting this consistency. The parallels between the perception of objects and of people have in this way been highlighted.

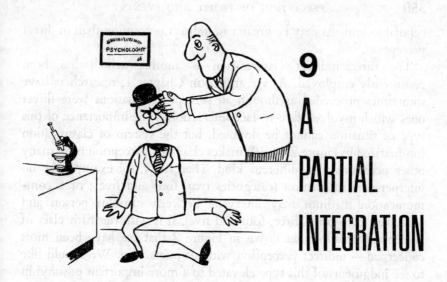

9
A
PARTIAL
INTEGRATION

In our opening chapter we made a number of distinctions between operations in person perception and between ways of viewing this process. These distinctions have been retained in later chapters in a way which we hope is useful. The classification of judgments as either episodic or dispositional is for example central to our approach. Episodic judgments concern only single episodes of behaviour, whereas dispositional perceptions have less restricted validity. Differences between these two forms of judgment and the relationships between them have been noted on several occasions throughout the book. We have, for example, pointed out that some studies of perceptual accuracy deal with the validity of episodic judgments (recognition of emotional expression, perhaps), whereas others require dispositional impressions (assessment of someone's personality, for instance). We have observed some logical differences between these, and have wondered about their relative importance in differing situations. The studies of perceptual constancy described in Chapter 8 are instances of research procedures which derive directly from this straightforward but neglected distinction.

Another distinction which is often overlooked is that between conception and perception. Judgments in the absence of a stimulus have been labelled "conceptions", and the way these contribute to perceptual impressions has been examined at several points in the book. In discussing this contribution we have observed that the role of conceptual judgments may be greater in indirect perception than in direct perception.

The direct–indirect classification is another which has been consistently employed. As we argued in Chapter 1, researchers have sometimes proceeded as though all perceptual situations were direct ones which involved face-to-face interactions. The importance of this type of situation cannot be doubted, but the system of classification summarized in Figure 2 (p. 30) makes clear that perception is on many other occasions of a different kind. There may, for example, be no interpersonal interaction (categories two, four and five); or a communication medium may intervene between stimulus person and perceiver (categories three, four and five). It is with the fifth class of perceptual situations set down in Figure 2 that we have been most concerned — indirect perception without interaction. We should like to see judgments of this type elevated to a more important position in psychology, for it is clear that a very high proportion of our day-to-day judgments derive from information which has been received indirectly.

We have also been eager in our research programme to come close to day-to-day judgments as they are actually made. Many investigations into person perception require subjects to operate with somewhat artificial situations and to make judgments which are narrowly circumscribed. We are completely in accord with the controlled laboratory approach as one research strategy, and indeed this is the approach adopted in many of our own studies. (Consider, for instance, the methodological investigations in Chapter 2, or the studies of inference rules in Chapter 3.) But it must be emphasized that there are no scientific canons which oblige the psychologist to direct his attention only to behaviour of a limited, laboratory-based kind. We have been concerned to translate some of the interesting findings from relatively artificial situations into more realistic (and less controlled) settings. In this way the conclusions drawn by Asch and Wishner from their studies of very limited stimulus inputs have been checked against more complex descriptive material in Experiments 10 to 13. And we have devoted much time to investigating the role of communication channel variables in perception based upon the mass media (Chapter 7). This issue is surely of great importance, but we have learned that it is not one which has been of much interest to psychologists in their empirical endeavours. The discussion of serial-order phenomena in Chapter 6 is a further example of the need to provide a broader framework within which to view some findings from controlled laboratory experiments. Several studies of primacy and recency — whilst unquestionably important in themselves — do not fit easily into real-life settings.

Another notion which we have stressed (in Chapters 1 and 8, for instance) is the essential similarity between person perception and object perception. The working hypothesis has been set up that these two processes will in due course turn out to be subsumed under the one set of general principles. We are of course far from that happy state at the present time, and the evidence we have presented has merely served as beginning support for the idea. Yet even if this working hypothesis proves to be untenable, there is one clear fact to stress: students of object perception and person perception can derive both conceptual and methodological benefit from each other's work. On several occasions in the preceding chapters we have tried to point out issues on which more interaction between experimental and social psychologists is desirable.

DIAGRAMMATIC REPRESENTATION OF PERSON PERCEPTION

Our working hypothesis about object perception and the judgment of people requires that the schema we have set out in Figure 1 applies to both processes. We should not lose sight of this fact, even though Figure 1 is framed around a terminology more conveniently employed for the perception of people. It may be recalled that the suggested schema is of an information-processing system with ten components. (That each component may be subdivided is of course clear.) Three of the components are aspects of the input; these have been labelled "present stimulus person information", "present context information" and "stored stimulus person information". As well as components representing the more stable and the more transitory states of the perceiver the system contains two major transformation subsystems — the input selector and the processing centre. And the output from the system (which feeds back into earlier components) is seen as having three aspects — expectancy responses, attributive responses and affective responses.

We have detailed the operation of these components in the course of the book. For example, Chapter 3 concentrates upon the processing centre, and Chapter 4 on the perceiver's stable characteristics and his current state. It would be possible to review at this point what has been said about each component in the earlier chapters. But this would be tedious, and in any case we have liberally sprinkled summaries and reviews throughout those chapters. Instead we shall here note a few variables and approaches which did not comfortably fit into our previous discussions, and shall attempt to tie some kind of a knot in a few of the loose ends we have left. After this we shall move into a more detailed perspective of the whole schema; the possibility that it may be modelled as a set of computer programmes will be examined.

But first let us look in general terms at the value of setting down a schema like that in Figure 1. We may wonder whether a representation at such a high level of generality provides any new information. Since it is couched in very general terms, does it tell us anything we did not previously know? The answer to this will of course partly depend upon the relevant sophistication of the person who views the diagram, but the important point here is that the question is to some extent an inappropriate one. For Figure 1 is only in a subordinate sense a representation of facts or a description of reality. It is much more a statement of hypothesised relationships between assumed components.

This brings us back to the suggestion made in Chapter 1 (p. 23) that the best way to *define* complex processes such as perception is not to seek simple semantic equivalents but rather to picture in some detail what it is that people are thought to do when they perceive. And although we have a rough idea what happens in perception it is just these details which are lacking. So as a definition Figure 1 is merely an aggregate of assumptions, and we can assess its definitional validity only by following through and testing these assumptions.

What are the assumptions underlying Figure 1 and how can they in fact be tested? We are inclined to take a rather pragmatic line on this. The assumptions behind Figure 1 are of this type: "it seems helpful to group factors x, y, z under the heading M, and to treat M as being in interaction with N and O in certain ways". In this manner, for example, we have separated an "input selector" from the "processing centre", and we have drawn out a component to be called "stored stimulus person information". The assumptions behind our representation of the perceptual process are thus about the best ways to group judgmental variables and about the way the ensuing groups of variables might interact with each other.

How then can we test these assumptions? Mainly it seems in terms of whether or not they "work". And the "work" to be done by Figure 1 is of two kinds. Firstly we hope that the schema provides a framework for discussions of person perception into which the results of previous studies can be fitted. The large majority of research reports deals (quite legitimately) with only specific aspects of the process, and attempt to integrate all the varied sets of data into a single frame are relatively uncommon. Figure 1 is valuable therefore in so far as it provides a setting for discussing and interrelating the work of investigators of differing orientations. To us it seems to do this job well, but there is little doubt that improvements will ultimately be required.

The value of the schema derives also from another application — as a spur to new conceptualizations and research designs. It should make clear possible deficiencies in the distribution of research efforts and suggest new avenues of investigation. Throughout the book we have noted many issues which are unresolved and which need further research attention, and we shall not list these again. Instead we shall briefly look at aspects of each component with which we have not previously dealt and which should be mentioned for the sake of completeness. At this point also we shall emphasize some research possibilities which have not been adequately treated in previous chapters.

COMPONENTS OF THE INFORMATION PROCESSING SYSTEM

In this section each component will be examined in turn, following roughly the sequence in which the subsystems are presented in Figure 1 (p. 20). We should emphasize again that this is not a summary of previous discussions. Instead it is an attempt to encompass material which is pertinent to each component but which appeared to be tangential to the relatively goal-directed discussions of earlier chapters.

Present Stimulus Person Information

That some information about the stimulus must be received at the time of judgment is clearly a necessary condition for perception. It follows that all the studies of person perception which we have detailed have involved some kind of present stimulus information. This may have been a single dispositional characteristic, a set of such characteristics, a complex verbal passage, a line drawing, a still photograph, a photograph with written caption, a film, or a sequence of behaviour in interaction with the judge. The investigator's aim may have been primarily to examine the action upon a fixed stimulus input of some other variables (personality or current emotional state for example), or he may have been more interested in the role of particular stimulus dimensions in their own right.

Our previous discussions have not usually concerned this latter question. We have noted the salience of certain kinds of input — warm–cold cues, verbal rather than visual information, religion-related characteristics, for example — but there have been many research programmes which we have so far been unable to annotate. Vocal characteristics as timbre, inflection and stress have, for example, aroused much interest as sources of information for judgment. Kramer (1963, 1964) has reviewed the literature dealing with these aspects of perceptual input and has demonstrated that there is considerable interjudge consistency in the way they are interpreted. There is also ample evidence that cues derived from the voice are in fact employed by perceivers as they judge other people. Kastenbaum (cited in Gollin, 1958) and Veness and Brierley (1963) have shown how the general warmth of a voice is regularly detected and utilized. And W. E. Lambert and his associates have detailed the role of language and dialect variations in impression formation (Anisfeld and Lambert, 1964; Lambert, Anisfeld and Yeni-Komshian, 1965; Lambert and colleagues, 1960).

What of the accuracy of judgments from vocal inputs? Early studies suggested that this might be at a high level. Cantril and Allport (1935) were, for instance, able to show that age and several personality characteristics could be correctly inferred from a speaker's voice. But later work has tended to more gloomy conclusions, and it appears that in many instances accuracy is not as high as might have been anticipated. There are several possible reasons for this observation,* and the area does still seem in need of serious objective study.

A related kind of information about a stimulus person is his hand-writing. This variable is peculiar to indirect perception and it has of course been extensively studied. Although we may question the design

---

* For example, data from differing judgmental tasks need to be viewed less globally for a more valid conclusion to be drawn. And, on a quite different level, speakers may well vary their verbal behaviour between situations (Goldman-Eisler, 1954). Other problems to do with accuracy have been raised in the first chapter (pp. 47–49).

and interpretation of many early investigations, it appears on the whole that different people make very similar judgments from handwriting and that this can indeed reflect the stable and current characteristics of a stimulus. A wide perspective on early research is provided in a set of papers edited by W. Johnson (1944). Eysenck's (1945) results speak for the validity of personality judgments made by a professional graphologist, and correlational studies of handwriting characteristics and personality measures have been described by Talmadge (1958). He demonstrated the reliability of handwriting measures and suggested that observed low but significant relationships with personality were sufficiently promising to warrant further investigation. Doob (1958) reached a similar conclusion about grammatical style; and Thorndike (1948) has explored the basis of differences in punctuation habits.

These inputs may well influence person perception, though their influence is of course a limited one. An investigation with direct bearing upon this has been reported by Carlson (1960). He varied the familiarity of words appearing in a written article and examined the effect of this manipulation upon impression formation. His undergraduate subjects were more favourably disposed towards the author of the article containing the unfamiliar words than towards the stimulus who wrote in simpler terms.

The correlates of constriction and expansiveness in subjects' doodles have been studied by Wallach and Ruthellen (1960). They report that expansiveness is related to personality in an interesting way: graphic designs are predictable from an interaction of introversion–extraversion and anxiety. From studies of this type it is but a short step to the many varieties of psychological test, responses to which are of course an important form of input to person perception in certain specialized situations. It would be unwise for us to attempt here a review of the test materials which are available and the interpretations which are typically placed upon particular judgmental inputs. Of the many relevant books four may, however, be noted as having an approach emphasizing perceptual activities. These are by G. W. Allport (1961), Bieri and colleagues (1966), Meehl (1954) and P. E. Vernon (1964).

Several other facets of the component "present stimulus person information" have received close attention. The way facial characteristics may determine judgment was examined in Chapter 7. At that point too we mentioned studies of inferences deriving from clothing. Despite many years of research, there are still many unresolved issues in these two fields. Another sort of stimulus input which is becoming more amenable to measurement is bodily posture, and we have also cited studies of this in Chapter 6 as well as at the end of Chapter 5. Related variables like style of walking, footsteps, hand movements and mannerisms are all inputs which may warrant more serious investigation.

Students of person perception have naturally been concerned with many other inputs. Kogan and Shelton (1960) have varied age and occupation in an attempt to assess their relative importance in different contexts, Iverson and Reuder (1965) have examined the effects of stimulus self-deprecation, while studies by Gergen and Jones (1963) and Jones and coworkers (1959) have looked at what might loosely be termed the stimulus person's responsibility for his actions. Complex aspects of status and power have been stressed in several investigations (see p. 196), and other interesting work has concerned that crucial set of input variables which is indicative of another person's intentions towards ourselves or other people (e.g. Jones and Davis, 1965; Pepitone, 1958; Pepitone and Sherberg, 1957; Strickland, 1958; Thibaut and Riecken, 1955). With inputs as complex as this, investigators perforce become involved with the second component of our schema — present context information. Let us now note briefly some characteristics of context.

Present Context Information

This term has been used to refer primarily to the social or physical environment in which the *stimulus person* is located. The environment of the stimulus is of course often that of the judge as well, so that "context" is typically in relation to both members of a perceptual episode. But in indirect perception these two persons are necessarily separated, so that in some studies we might have to examine two different contexts. It seems likely that in most cases the judge's context is less important to indirect perception than information about the stimulus person's surroundings, and unless it has been otherwise indicated we have used "present context information" to describe the environment of the stimulus.

It is clear that context can markedly influence person perception, and experimental demonstrations of its role were noted in Chapter 1 and Chapter 7. But although this fact is an obvious one, it should nevertheless be emphasized. For it is the potentially vital context effects which are typically excluded from many controlled studies of interpersonal judgment. Since people are usually perceived as agents in a sequence of events we need to try to set up controlled situations in which the context effects of physical and interpersonal events are both present and measurable (cf. Heider, 1967; Jones and Davis, 1965).

That judgments are partly determined by context is implicit in the framework developed by psychophysicists. Bieri and colleagues (1966) and Sherif and Hovland (1961) have worked to apply generalizations about the role of judgmental anchors and about assimilation and contrast effects to social judgment. Other research in this area has been reported by Holmes and Berkowitz (1961), Levy (1960, 1961) and Manis (1967).

What about the social context of the perceiver (rather than of the stimulus)? Hundreds of studies of social conformity bear witness to the importance in perception of the judgments made by people around us. Interestingly enough though, few of these deal specifically with the perception of people. Several research possibilities are open here. For example we might set up the context of the stimulus to be in opposition to the context of the perceiver. In both cases other people could provide the context, and the stimulus person and his environment might be presented to judges on film. Variables determining relative importance could then be sought.

Stored Stimulus Person Information

In many judgments we do not have prior acquaintance with a stimulus, so that we have no information about him in store. But if a perceptual encounter is other than very brief, then material is soon in our memory and is able to influence later perceptions. The stored material may be judgments of either an episodic or a dispositional kind, and we have easily shown in Chapters 4 and 8 that it can act upon later inputs to modify a perceptual output. We need say little more at this stage.

But it should be stressed for one last time that in our discussions of this component we are referring to a very circumscribed set of memory material. This material concerns the stimulus himself, and not the notions which are part of a judge's wider attitudes and expectancies. In this way we treat "he is a colonel" as part of the stored stimulus person information, whereas our memories about the habitual reactions to colonels in general are seen as part of our stable characteristics, and decision rules from the input *colonel* are part of the processing centre. We can justify this differentiation of stored ideas only on the pragmatic basis suggested on p. 352, and for now shall conclude that abstracting a separate "stored stimulus person information" component seems to assist conceptualization and research.

The dynamic, variable nature of stored stimulus person information should not be overlooked. Not only is the material we have in store about a person continually changing as we receive more information, but in addition forgetting is always taking place. And the material brought out of store is itself moulded and changed in an "effort after meaning" as we "reconstruct" the person himself (Bartlett, 1932). The material in store is not simply retained in its pristine state ready for recall, but rather a few central impressions are available as an "organized setting" within which we construct our idea of the whole person. Bartlett has himself argued persuasively that affective reactions are particularly salient in this regard, and that remembering is largely a matter of generating a rounded judgment about these reactions.

In this light we would wish to say that remembering is the same as making a conceptual judgment. These seem to be the same active process in which material being drawn from store becomes more self-consistent and meaningful. And both involve continuous transformations in that the output (or what is recalled) feeds back again into store from where it may be retrieved and altered again. The inputs to a conception come from the stored stimulus person information component, and these are operated upon by the input selector, the perceiver's current state and stable characteristics, and the processing centre. We have looked at these operations in previous chapters, and they appear to be the ones described in rather different terms by Bartlett in his discussions of remembering. Bartlett was not interested to describe the process in terms of several interacting components of an information-processing system, and it may be that this development could increase the predictive power of his theoretical formulation. For example, to implicate the input selector in conceptual judgments is to say that this component is also at work in remembering where it picks out information to be transformed later in the system. These several operations may be amenable to separate examination.

Separating a stored stimulus person information component as we have done also brings out the similarities between remembering and perception. Perception begins when information becomes available from the other two input components of the system, and this information is thought to be handled in just the same way as is information from store. But a major difference between conception and perception (which we have noted in Chapter 4) is that the input to conceptual judgments is simpler than that to perception, since this material has already passed through the system on its way into the stored stimulus person information component.

We take it then that to make a conceptual judgment about a person is to recall something about him. And that conception and perception are essentially the same. These notions are brought out clearly by the organization of Figure 1. They seem to be sufficiently interesting to justify on pragmatic grounds (p. 352) the isolation of a set of activities under the separate heading "stored stimulus person information".

The Input Selector

This fourth component is assumed to select only certain aspects of the present or stored stimulus person information or of the present context information. By this filtering procedure a judge can reduce to manageable proportions the vast array of material he might in principle process. There can be no dispute that some form of selection takes place, but the role of the input selector has not been investigated in much detail by students of person perception. We ourselves have gradually come to see it as especially important in the process, and it has in our successive revisions of Figure 1 taken on an increasingly major function. This seems to be an occasion where the diagrammatic approach has pinpointed the need for much more research in a specific area.

How then could we learn more about the input selector? To do this we need to concentrate more on *overt* characteristics of the stimulus. Episodic judgments of overt fact or dispositional judgments of overt characteristics (see p. 9) must be studied more intensively, since these are relatively pure assessments of input selection. It should then be possible to derive relationships between judgments about overt variables and judgments about covert ones. In a sense of course this is what several investigators have been doing, but one change of emphasis is suggested. Investigators typically assume that the input material they provide — often about overt characteristics — is all admitted into the perceptual system and that nothing else is so admitted. In looking for the covert judgments which follow information about overt characteristics, research workers have specified the overt information which is to be used and have assumed that this represents what is actually selected (cf. Lee and Tucker, 1962). A different emphasis would be to measure judgments about overt characteristics as well as those about covert characteristics. We could then look for relationships between the two sets of variables, both of which have by this procedure been observed instead of postulated.

One fairly direct measure of input selection which has recently received increasing attention derives from the use of a stereoscope. This device simultaneously presents different stimulus material to each eye so that an investigator can determine how a judge resolves the binocular rivalry conflict. Stereoscopes have long been used to study squares, circles, colours and so on, but Engel (1956) showed that stereoscopic judgments of faces yielded interesting results. Judges might see one facial input as dominant, so that the other is effectively invisible; or they might attempt (often successfully) to combine the two inputs.* Engel (1958) and Hastorf and Myro (1959) followed up these findings, and the technique has also been used by Bagby (1957) and Moore (1966). These latter studies have been described in Chapter 4 (pp. 207 and 212). Pettigrew, Allport and Barnett (1958) studied stereoscopic judgments by members of different races in South Africa. As stimuli they used faces of people from four racial groups and their judges were also drawn from these same groups. Identification of race was seen clearly to depend both upon the input material and upon the perceiver. Engel (1961) and Ittelson and Slack (1958) have provided summary reviews of studies employing binocular rivalry techniques, and an understanding of the input selector might perhaps be built up from the foundations they have laid.†

Another lead we might follow in trying to determine the way this component operates was provided many years ago by Allport and Vernon (1933). These investigators set out to identify consistencies in the way people express themselves. Their interest was not so much in

---

* It is interesting that Engel (1958) found "combined" judgments to be aesthetically preferable to single ones. This parallels studies of quite a different orientation reviewed in Chapter 7 (p. 301), which found "mediumness' to be particularly important in facial characteristics.

† Notice that stimulus material for this kind of investigation may also be presented aurally. A start on this procedure has been made by Paivio and Steeves (1958). The sophisticated methodology employed by experimental psychologists studying "selective listening" (e.g. Broadbent, 1958) may prove useful to social psychologists looking at input selection in person perception.

perception as in determining dimensions of difference in self-expression — the ways in which people differ in their characteristic ways of behaving. With this in mind Allport and Vernon looked at styles of talking, writing, walking, sitting, gesturing, laughing, frowning and so on, and were able to demonstrate that people are self-consistent in their numerous modes of expression. (See also G. W. Allport, 1961, Chapter 19.)

This kind of study holds clear promise for students of perception. What it in effect does is reveal the structure of stimulus material which perceivers are *in principle* able to use. Once we have specified the relevant dimensions of people as stimuli, then we can apply our classification of *possible* inputs to particular judgmental situations, observing which of the dimensions each perceiver is in fact using. Surprisingly little attention has been paid to this question, and what we can say about the kinds of cues available is largely guesswork. We need to set up "dictionaries of the environment" which tell us what dimensions are available; these can then be employed to see the "vocabulary" which a perceiver can use. Knowing the "words" a person employs is to know the inputs he is selecting, and just as people vary in their real language utilization so too will they employ different "words" in their perceptual activities. As well as having different vocabularies, perceivers will also vary in their "definitions" of the words available to them; to know about the "definition" of a "word" is to know about the decision rules which are called up by a perceptual input.

The Perceiver's Stable Characteristics and Current State

We have indicated that the perceiver's stable characteristics and his current state influence the input selector by inserting links between these components in Figure 1. That some people characteristically select certain cues and that present goals affect input selection is clear. But it is difficult to observe these phenomena directly since the measures taken are usually outputs from the perceptual system and have been transformed in the processing centre. More studies like that by Atkinson and Walker (1956) (see p. 223) which take tachistoscopic measurements seem to be desirable.

The emphasis here is on thresholds in person perception, and it may also be possible to approach threshold measurement from a different direction. The more willing a judge is to accept a characteristic in others the lower is his threshold for that characteristic. So we could look at how readily the characteristic is inferred from a variety of cue traits. This could be done by measures of inference rules like those described in Chapter 3, and emphasis would now shift to the response traits. The more a particular response trait is judged to be implied by a range of cue traits the lower is the subject's threshold for that trait. This index of input selection might now be related to stable and transitory perceiver characteristics. For instance, a person who sees himself to have a particular characteristic may have a lower threshold for that characteristic in others.*

It is not necessary at this point to review studies of how perceiver variables can influence the processing centre and thereby the outputs from a perceptual system. This question has been considered in detail in Chapters 3 and 4. We should only reiterate that these influences are sufficiently varied to suggest that decision rules will differ between persons and within the same person at different times. We know something about these differences, and we have concluded that although they may be considerable they are not "across the board".

For example sex differences in person perception undoubtedly occur but they are present only in some aspects of some judgments about some stimuli. The limits of the differences have still to be set. The difficulty here is that studies which *fail to reveal* individual differences do not get published. Until we can review research on both sides of the boundary — indicating differences and indicating no differences — we cannot map out the location of that boundary. It does seem that we should emphasize studies which fail to reveal systematic inter-subject variation as much as we attend to those which yield the more highly-prized values of p (cf. Bakan, 1966).

The Processing Centre

Chapter 3 has been exclusively concerned with the nature and measurement of decision rules and we shall not trouble to retread the ground covered there. Our approach has been molecular in the sense that we have looked for the simplest input–output transformation (termed an inference rule) and at how this may be assessed. The idea has been that we need to know about inference rules before we can understand the principles underlying the more complex combination rules.

---

* It may be noted that this procedure provides a much purer measure of input selection than the technique described on p. 162. That technique was aimed at locating differences in perceptual *output* which are associated with certain aspects of self-perception.

We have assumed that combination rules are predictable from inference rules, but it should again be emphasized that we do not see this as a simple mechanically-operating conjunction. We closed Chapter 3 with the suggestion that in many cases the mode of combination is configural. This implies that research emphasis has to be given to relationships within and between subgroups and between subgroups and the whole input array. On the other hand combination may sometimes be linear, and inter- and intrajudge variations are to be expected. It has been argued that the question "Is combination linear or configural?" is out-dated, and that we need now to answer a somewhat different query: under what conditions does each style of combination occur?

In studying the processing centre we need also to address ourselves to questions of overall organization. It is clear that there must be general principles guiding the transformation activities of the centre which allow it to develop coherent, consistent, patterned perspectives on a stimulus person. Cojudgment has been suggested as one such principle, but more complex guidelines are probably also in use. In general terms we might assume that the available set of decision rules can vary from person to person, but that each judge's set (his implicit personality theory) is as a whole organized around some systematic assumptions. Studies of decision rules which are more global in approach than those we have reviewed are clearly desirable.

The Output Components

We have included in our schema of person perception three output components — expectancy, attributive and affective responses. These were introduced at some length in Chapter 1, and we need not present them again. But the relationship between the three kinds of response does warrant brief recapitulation. We observed that attributive responses may be of two kinds — episodic or dispositional — but that both kinds carried with them expectancy components. To attribute a temporary or permanent characteristic to someone is to expect him to behave in certain ways. And we have argued strongly that all judgmental activity involves an affective reaction, which is of course interwoven with the attributive and expectancy responses. We take it then that the three output components are very closely in league with each other. In a sense of course they are a single phenomenon — "the judgment" — but it is useful to separate them on pragmatic grounds of the type suggested on p. 352.

How well are these output components understood? Research has typically concentrated on attributive responses, and an extensive body of knowledge about these has been built up. We do, however, know relatively little about episodic attributive judgments, and further attention to these would not go amiss. And the problem of selecting for study a sample of attributive dimensions which represents the population of such dimensions for each judge has not really been solved. We return to this in the final section of the chapter.

In so far as expectancies are contained within attributive judgments, understanding of them might be assumed to parallel knowledge of the attributive component. But this assumption would not be wholly valid (cf. Feldman, 1966; Triandis, 1964a). To know that a judge attributes characteristic X to a stimulus is not to know with certainty the kinds of anticipations he might develop. This is for at least two reasons. Firstly, expectancies will derive from a *configuration* of attributive responses. We are back again to the problem that the meaning of X may depend upon whether it accompanies Y or Z. A second basis of uncertainty about expectancy reactions is that they can vary between judges. One inferred characteristic may generate several different anticipations in a group of perceivers. This process is effectively the same as that by which an *input* is transformed into an output; attributed characteristics are outputs which recirculate to serve again as inputs. We have incorporated this notion in the feedback loops around the sides of Figure 1.

What of the affective component? Our main emphasis has been on fairly gross evaluative aspects and we have concluded that evaluation enters into every judgment of another person (see pp. 231–238) .Yet there is no doubt that the basis of this universal reaction will vary from situation to situation. Although it is true that a perceiver will spontaneously place a value on a politician making a speech as he will on his partner at a dance, the bases of these evaluations will naturally be quite different. We need to attune our research to the recognition that different types of evaluation enter into different types of interpersonal judgment.

These variations seem to be of two kinds. Firstly we may evaluate a stimulus person in terms of a particular role. Judgments may be of "goodness" as a golfer, a club member, a professor, an administrator, a father and so on. These evaluative responses can no doubt combine to generate an overall impression of a stimulus person, but there are clearly occasions when they are kept separate from each other. On these occasions — seemingly very frequent — we are not making global, overall affective judgments about a person, but are more concerned with only certain aspects of his characteristics and behaviour.

The second way in which affective reactions may be less than completely general is more clearly to do with the perceiver. This arises from the obvious fact that there are different kinds of affective response. What has been called "positive evaluation" may be manifested in love, respect, amusement, curiosity, confidence and in several other ways. Negative evaluation may be fear, jealousy, distrust, anger, contempt, irritation and so on. We do not know much about how these several kinds of affective response are interrelated. Neither do we know how they vary between direct and indirect perception or how they depend upon whether or not interpersonal interaction occurs. To look at these topics we might consider using GSR recordings (see p. 198), possibly in association with verbal responses. But whatever research strategy is adopted, affective reactions — general or specific — should not be neglected for the more readily-measured attributive aspects of judgment.

The System in Operation

The perceptual system we have been discussing is of course much more complicated than we have been able to suggest in words. Within each of the components are myriad subunits which we hardly understand. The perceiver's stable characteristics for example comprise all aspects of his personality and attitudes as well as memories which are not specific to one individual. How these are developed and how they work together during perception is still largely a mystery.

Although we have talked as though the system begins operation when information enters from one of the top boxes, this too is clearly an oversimplification. Information is continually passing through the components at times when we are making neither perceptual nor conceptual judgments. There is some motivational and cognitive structure which for example instructs the input selector to seek out people as well as to attend to only certain aspects of them. Furthermore many of the system's activities are not conscious ones. We have sometimes talked as though a judge was aware of the expectancies he derives from a certain attributive response. This is of course rarely so (although, as we observed in Chapter 1, *disconfirmation* of an expectancy soon brings it into consciousness). We have not been able to do justice to the continuous to-and-fro sequence of operations which takes place during a long exposure to a stimulus person. During a conversation for instance early judgments may feed back to influence later ones, the perceiver's current state may alter in several ways, the present context information and stored stimulus person information components may change radically, and a number of expectancies may be translated into reality.

That we have been less than adequate in treating these complexities must be acknowledged. To learn more about them we have adopted an approach that picks out the essential features of person perception as an information-processing activity and which concentrates first upon these features. This approach does make it easier to discuss and investigate the process, but it inevitably leads to an apparently simplistic treatment. This is of course regrettable, but we hope that it is only temporary.

How could we increase our ability to conceptualize the dynamic interaction which takes place within the system? It would be of tremendous benefit if we could build a working model which allowed us to see what was occurring during a sequence of activities. This might be like the cut-away replicas of jet engines or nuclear reactors which serve to enlighten many a puzzled schoolboy. Such a replica of person perception is not for this century, but recent technological advances do suggest one way for us to learn about how the components of a perceptual system operate together over time. It is to the possibility of a working model that we now turn.

THE SIMULATION OF PERSON PERCEPTION

In recent years there has been a surge of interest in ways of simulating complex processes. Economic developments, weather conditions, industrial activities, international relationships have all been subject to the creative attention of the model-maker (e.g., Guetzkow, 1962). Within the narrow confines of psychology simulation has also become popular: we now have models which simulate aspects of learning, concept formation, problem solving, decision making, perception, and even of social interaction.

A model may be a mechanical, mathematical or simply a verbal structure. Strictly speaking it is not the same as an explanation, although it can fulfil many of the functions of an explanation. It is an interrelated set of propositions or functions which is found to apply to an explanatory system. The model could originally be developed quite apart from the set of facts in which we are interested. Thus we might have an interrelated set of propositions about hydraulic actions, and might later find that this model applies to what we know and believe about instincts. Or we might have an interrelated set of propositions about probability theory which is later found to apply to learning. A third example is the model of implicative relationships developed by logicians which in Chapter 3 we related to the way inferences are drawn in person perception.

Models of this kind have an existence in their own right, and are not specifically devized to account for a particular collection of facts.* Explanations on the other hand involve conscious attempts to account for specific sets of facts; and explanations are developed and expressed in terms relative to these facts. The relationship between a model and an explanation is analogous to the connection between two pieces of material joined by a zip fastener. After starting to connect the two pieces we increase the breadth of contact by zipping them together. Similarly after finding that part of a model fits the facts we try to increase the breadth of the contact between the model and the explanation of those facts. The logical structure of the model is isomorphic with that of the explanatory system, but the model may be expressed in terms very different from those needed to explain facts.

If models do not themselves constitute explanations, what then is their value? They have a number of advantages, not least of which is the way they require their formulator to think clearly about his topic. In developing a model one has to think very carefully through the process being dealt with, and clarification and possibly insight will ensue. In more general terms, we noted at the end of the preceding section that models can often act as a sort of "visual aid". Tinbergen's (1951) hydraulic model of instincts or Broadbent's (1957) drainpipe model of attention are instances of this; and in a less obvious way so are mathematical or graphical models of individual or group structures (Harary, Norman and Cartwright, 1965). Models are also valuable as devices by which we relate together previously unrelated facts or through which we make predictions about reality.

---

* This does not mean that models are always constructed without any intention of using them as aids to understanding. We might well devize or develop a model in the hope that this will aid later interpretation. But many models are translated from fields which are quite separate.

To varying degrees these characteristics of a model are also possessed by the isomorphic explanatory system. But there is one practical feature of models of complex processes which is not common to explanations. We can effectively carry out experiments with the model itself. We could see what happens when a mechanical learning model is placed in certain conditions; or we could try out various types of production schedules on our model of an industrial organization. This modern version of "armchair theorizing" is extremely stimulating and valuable, and it is particularly convenient if the model has been developed as a computer programme. In this case unusually complex predictions about the operation of a large set of variables can be studied very economically. Computer simulation has all the characteristics and advantages of other models, but it possesses this great practical virtue to an outstanding degree.

Computers have recently become more accessible to psychologists, and rapid advances in computer technology have been accompanied by attempts to simulate psychological processes (e.g. Borko, 1962; Feigenbaum and Feldman, 1963). These have often been concerned with relatively microscopic treatments of object perception — the recognition of visually presented patterns for instance (Uhr, 1966) — but more global discussions of perception (Gyr and coworkers, 1966), of brain functioning (e.g., George, 1962) and of personality simulation (Messick and Tomkins, 1963) are also available. Simulation of person perception has not yet been attempted, and this is an attractive possibility. Within the framework suggested in this book it is apparently feasible.

In developing a computer simulation of perception we do not in fact design a computer which perceives. The term "computer simulation" is a little misleading in that it is by means of a computer *programme* that one simulates an activity. In simulating person perception in this style we need then to write a programme which will operate upon a set of data in a manner which is isomorphic with the way in which a perceiver deals with his perceptual data. The programme constitutes the model. This possibly clarifies the meaning of our earlier suggestion that models are not the same as explanations. We do not *explain* person perception by reading out the computer programme. But we do have a set of propositions in the programme which correspond to those making up the explanatory system.

Let us see how we might begin to programme person perception. We shall discuss some of the preliminary analyses which take place before programming commences, but shall not get as far as translating these analyses into language acceptable to a computer. We shall not be able to end this section with a finished model, but we shall be forced to look at the components of our system as interacting features rather than as relatively isolated units. In this way we shall have to come to terms with at least some of the dynamic aspects of the process. As computer simulation develops beyond the point we shall reach here, researchers will have no option but to work with an interactive system. The present section might set the stage for that desirable development.*

The Input

As we have indicated, the input to a perceptual system is of three types — present stimulus person information, present context information, and stored stimulus person information. To programme *all* instances of person perception we need to isolate all possible inputs of these three types. We need to be able to specify every unit of information which enters the system.

This is clearly a hopeless task at present, mainly because in many areas we do not know what types of input information are important. Still, we can make a start by limiting our attention to a manipulable set of characteristics. Suppose for the moment that we are concerned only with present stimulus person information, and that we are not dealing with the other two types of input. Suppose for instance that we are studying an experimental situation similar to that devised by Asch (1946), in which lists of stimulus characteristics are read out to subjects who have to make perceptual responses (see pp. 119–120). We might in this case be concerned with only three stimulus characteristics; to assume this will keep our discussion within practical bounds.

To programme the output from these characteristics we need first to decide what values each one can take. There are basically two types of stimulus characteristics — categorical and dimensional ones. Categorical variables take on values representing qualitatively different categories (English, French; employed, unemployed; schizophrenic, manic-depressive), whereas dimensional variables vary quantitatively along scales which are at least ordinal ones. Dimensional characteristics can vary from a baseline at one end of the scale (age for example increases from zero), or from a central baseline (as the personality characteristics

---

* Since completing this chapter we have continued working to develop the ideas set out here. Computer simulation of person perception does appear to be practicable.

like extraversion–introversion do). In programming the consequences of each input we need first to decide what sort of variable we are concerned with. In fact dimensional characteristics *can* be viewed as categorical ones in some cases (we might treat age as taking on two values for instance — young and old). This clearly is not always satisfactory (cf. Attneave, 1962; Restle, 1961), but it will serve to make our examination more simple. Let us then assume that the three input variables with which we are to deal are categorical ones taking on only two values.

In taking these decisions we have made simplifying assumptions about what may be termed the differentiation and the articulation of input information (cf. Bieri and colleagues, 1966). "Differentiation" refers to the number of independent characteristics which we can identify in a stimulus person (or object), and "articulation" denotes the number of values each input can take on (see also p. 212). We have treated stimulus persons in a very undifferentiated way by assuming they can vary in only three characteristics, and we have shown but little articulation by allowing these three characteristics to take on only two values. In practice we should have to make many more differentiations and articulations, but to start illustrating a computer programme development we shall avoid these complications.

It might appear that with three inputs each of which takes on one of two values we shall need to consider eight different consequences. If we call our input variables A, B and C and label their values as 0 or 1, we have this table of possibilities.

	Input		
	A	B	C
	1	1	1
	1	1	0
	1	0	0
Value	1	0	1
	0	1	0
	0	1	1
	0	0	1
	0	0	0

Unfortunately this omits consideration of the input selector in the system. It may be the case that one or more inputs are not selected: the perceiver might not notice it or he might discount it. Certainly this facility has to be incorporated in our model.* We need then to add another 18 possibilities. Thus:

	One input selected			Two inputs selected					
	A	B	C	A	B	C	A	B	C
	1	–	–	1	0	–	1	–	0
	0	–	–	1	1	–	1	–	1
Value				0	1	–	0	–	1
	–	1	–	0	0	–	0	–	0
	–	0	–						
				–	1	0			
	–	–	1	–	1	1			
	–	–	0	–	0	1			
				–	0	0			

Twenty-six input states are so far possible for three dichotomous variables. In real life of course we are processing much more complicated material. If we were dealing with eight variables which could take on eight values, and if all eight variables were always selected, no less than 16,777,216 discriminations (8^8) would be possible. By allowing for configural combinations and for perceiver variations yet to be considered, this number would be at least tripled. And yet we *do* operate on this scale. In the similar, yet apparently more simple, matter of colour perception more than $7\frac{1}{2}$ million different discriminations are possible (Brown and Lenneberg, 1954). Our three dichotomous variables are but a small beginning to a complete simulation.

Nevertheless, these generate considerable complexity. For we must also discuss the order in which inputs are selected. It seems possible that serial order effects can occur in person perception (see Chapter 6), and these should be incorporated in our model. Order of presentation is even more important when considerably more than three inputs are available. If the perceiver has only a limited time in which to make a judgment (as he often has), then he will probably not be able to take in all the available information. Order of selection is therefore crucial to his perceptual output, since those inputs with low priority might remain unselected and thus irrelevant. Our simulation of person

* The way in which we might programme the role of perceiver characteristics in input selection is considered below on p. 375.

N

perception must make allowance for varying presentation orders. As far as our three dichotomous variables are concerned, complete allowance for this raises the number of possible inputs to 78.* It is a straightforward logical matter to handle this increased number, but since our aim here is illustrative rather than substantive we shall drop the facility to treat each serial order from our putative computer simulation. We shall merely note that a comprehensive model needs to account for this aspect of information intake, and shall instead deal only with the twenty-six possible inputs set out above.

The Processing Centre and Output

The next two components of the perceptual system summarized in Figure 1 deal with the perceiver's stable and transitory states. These will be examined presently, but first we shall look at the processing centre. Our model needs to incorporate certain decision rules about each of the twenty-six possible inputs. We have distinguished between an inference rule and a combination rule, meaning that the former deals with one input in isolation and that a combination rule is about inferences from an aggregate of inputs. Consider first the inference rules which have to be built into the processing centre.

These must firstly comprise repetitive rules — from input $A1$ infer output $A1$. By this means we can ensure that part of the perceptual output is unprocessed, being the same as the input. We assume that repetitive inferences are made from all inputs, so that the input *warm* for instance implies the output *warm*. But the more interesting rules concern inferences to other characteristics. These may give rise to episodic judgments (about current characteristics) or to dispositional judgments (of a less restricted application). Once again we shall simplify our discussion by discarding an aspect of what has to be modelled; for now we shall omit consideration of episodic judgments and shall restrict our attention to dispositional ones. What must we know in order to devize appropriate inference rules which generate this latter type of judgment?

Firstly we need to be aware how many output characteristics are relevant to a particular input. Input A may be capable of generating inferences to, say 30 other characteristics, whilst input B may allow

* When only one variable is selected order is irrelevant, so that we still have six alternative inputs; when two variables are selected we have two orders for each of the twelve inputs listed above; and selecting all variables in the six possible orders gives rise to forty-eight inputs.

inferences to only 3 other characteristics. Inputs which imply a lot of characteristics are sometimes termed "central traits" (see Chapter 3, pp. 121 and 123) whereas others are more peripheral. We need to be able to specify the degree of centrality of any input by stipulating the number and nature of inferences derivable from it. This task is a gigantic one, and not at present possible. Let us restrict our inference rules to a single inference from each input state. Suppose then that input A calls up a set of inference rules leading to an output X, and that B and C generate inferences leading to outputs Y and Z respectively. Suppose also that when input A takes on the value of 0 or 1 (written as $A0$ or $A1$) the inference rules require that outputs $X0$ and $X1$ are generated. Similarly, $B0$ and $B1$ imply $Y0$ and $Y1$, and $C0$ and $C1$ imply $Z0$ and $Z1$.* In short, we shall also treat the three possible outputs as dichotomous ones.

When the three input variables in our model occur singly (i.e. A or B or C), then we have six input states. We must therefore build in six inference rules (which apply only to single inputs) about X, Y and Z. In addition we need the six repetitive inference rules about A, B and C which we considered above, so that twelve single outputs are required. So far so good. We turn now to the combination rules which have to be incorporated in the processing centre. These tell us about inferences from combinations of two or three input variables.

It might seem that if we have determined the inference rules (that is, the rules about single inputs), then we can easily specify the rules about combinations of inputs. For example, if we have built in two inference rules $A1 \rightarrow X1$ and $B0 \rightarrow Y0$, then we might be able to build in a compound rule $A1, B0 \rightarrow X1, Y0$. Unfortunately, there is evidence that combination rules often have a more subtle nature than this. We have shown in Chapter 3 (pp. 167–172) that inputs may interact in a rather complex manner, so that their overall composition has to be taken into account as well as their individual states. Consider a specific example: in our model we have so far stipulated these inference rules

$$A1 \rightarrow X1 \qquad B1 \rightarrow Y1 \qquad C1 \rightarrow Z1$$
$$A0 \rightarrow X0 \qquad B0 \rightarrow Y0 \qquad C0 \rightarrow Z0$$

We might therefore attempt to write this type of combination rule

$$A1, B1 \rightarrow X1, Y1 \qquad A0, B1 \rightarrow X0, Y1$$

* Notice that probabilistic inferences (see p. 22) can be accommodated within this framework. For example $Z0$ might represent "probably threatening" and $Z1$ "definitely threatening".

Yet it could be the case that the change in value of A (from 1 to 0) influences the rule about B. Suppose that input A was the sex of the stimulus person, and input B was whether or not the stimulus person smoked a pipe. The input *pipe-smoker* ($B1$) will generate different inferences according to whether it is coupled with *male* ($A1$) or *female* ($A0$).

This suggests that combination rules need to be devized according to the relationship between the inputs involved. For example we need to assess the degree of independence between inputs A and B before writing the combination rules. If A and B are wholly independent, then we can probably write combination rules which *are* simply combinations of the single inference rules. As the inputs become less independent, so up to a point do we have to increase the subtlety of our combination rules.

We have so far assumed that the inference rules from one input deal only with a single output ($A \to X$, $B \to Y$, $C \to Z$). An interesting case arises when a particular output may be inferred from several different inputs. For example output X may derive from an inference rule about input A or from a rule about input B. Such a set of rules would be of this type:

$$A1 \to X1 \qquad B1 \to Y1 \qquad C1 \to Z1$$
$$A0 \to X0 \qquad B0 \to Y0 \qquad C0 \to Z0$$
$$\qquad\qquad B1 \to X1$$
$$\qquad\qquad B0 \to X0$$

These state the single inferences we have already discussed, but in addition tell us that $B \to X$ in the same way as $A \to X$. What effect does the addition have on combination rules — about A, B for instance? The compound input $A1$, $B1$ now implies the output $X1$, $X1$. Is $X1$, $X1$ different to $X1$ alone? This can be viewed in at least two ways: we might point out that we have increased the *redundancy* of our inputs, or that we have increased the *salience* of characteristic X. In either case we have to make allowances in our model.

We have frequently emphasized the importance of this issue, but even at this stage of the book we cannot draw any firm conclusions about the manner in which combination rules are derived. We hope that the value of understanding inference rules has been brought out by the examples in the preceding pages; discussions of combination rules are most meaningful within a context which encompasses the more simple rules. And just as the actual values placed into the inference rules of our model will have to be derived from empirical observation (as in Experiment 14), so will combination rules have to be determined by systematic research programmes. In Chapter 3 we have set down suggestions about possible investigations into this issue.

At some point we shall have to derive combination rules to fit into the model. For the present we shall assume that inputs A, B and C are independent and that each implies only one output (X, Y and Z respectively). In this case we need to write twenty combination rules in addition to the six inference rules. These twenty combination rules correspond to the twenty inputs of more than one variable listed on pp. 370 and 371, and could be straightforward compounds of the inference rules suggested above. In addition we need to build into the model the twenty repetitive combination rules (e.g. $A1$, $B1 \rightarrow A1$, $B1$) of the kind already considered in relation to the six inference rules. All of this means that we need to provide 52 inference and combination rules to deal with three dichotomous variables which are assumed to be independent in themselves and in their implications, and each of which is allowed to imply only a single output.

The Perceiver

Up to this point we have ignored the components of our system which represent the perceiver. We need to allow for differences in the perceiver's stable characteristics (age, personality, sex and so on) and in his current state ("nervous", "interested", "elated", etc.). These components can influence both the input selector and the processing centre, and the influences need at some stage to be built into the model.

We shall, however, not trouble further in this example with the perceiver's current state and shall restrict our attention to his stable characteristics. Ideally we need to be able to specify all the relevant perceiver characteristics and the way they act upon the input selector and the processing centre. In practice of course we cannot do this, although as Chapter 4 has indicated we already can build in some of the important variables. We shall here assume that three dichotomous perceiver characteristics are possible — P, Q and R with values 0 or 1 in each case; and that all perceivers have the three characteristics in some value.

How can these stable characteristics of the perceiver affect the selection of inputs? We assume that they operate in association with the input variables themselves. A certain sort of perceiver will select information about certain variables if this is available. Thus, characteristic $P1$ might ensure selection of input A, whereas A might not be selected if characteristic $P0$ is at work. Or particularly salient input variables might be selected by all perceivers. Our simple example has minimized salience differences by assuming that A, B and C are independent (though this ultimately depends on the nature of the variables themselves of course), and we have assumed that any number of the three inputs can be selected. So let us partly allow for this in the rules about input selection. A suitable set is presented below. This is of course arbitrary, and could be replaced with others. Suggested rules are:

$P1$: Select A	$Q1$: Select B	$R1$: Select C
$P0$: Do not select A	$Q0$: Select B	$R0$: Do not select C

Since we have stipulated that perceivers have all three characteristics, these rules imply that input B will always be selected. On the other hand, selection of the other inputs depends upon the perceiver's characteristics. These rules have a number of interesting consequences. Somewhat paradoxically they reduce the complexity of the model. The alternative inputs now depend upon perceiver characteristics in this manner:

Perceiver			Inputs selected		
$P1$	$Q1$	$R1$	A	B	C
$P1$	$Q1$	$R0$	A	B	
$P1$	$Q0$	$R0$	A	B	
$P1$	$Q0$	$R1$	A	B	C
$P0$	$Q1$	$R1$		B	C
$P0$	$Q1$	$R0$		B	
$P0$	$Q0$	$R0$		B	
$P0$	$Q0$	$R1$		B	C

In the case of only two perceiver types ($P0$, $Q1$, $R0$ and $P0$, $Q0$, $R0$) will B *alone* be selected, and all three inputs will also be selected by only two perceiver types ($P1$, $Q1$, $R1$ and $P1$, $Q0$, $R1$). The other four types of perceiver will select two inputs — either A, B or B, C. Since the input variables have been treated as dichotomous ones, the total number of possible inputs for all perceivers is now only eighteen.*

* This figure comprises two single inputs ($B0$, $B1$), four double inputs each for A, B and for B, C and the eight possible triple inputs.

What we have in effect done by introducing this perceiver influence on the selector is to reduce the number of legitimate inputs by cutting out some of those shown on pp. 370 and 371.

The rules illustrated here seem to be meaningful ones. Perceiver characteristic Q might be the judge's sex, and input variable B might be the stimulus person's sex. What we have stipulated in this case is that all perceivers, irrespective of their sex, select information about the sex of a stimulus person. On the other hand the other two inputs (social class and religious belief, perhaps) are only selected by persons who are attuned to these aspects of a person. Now let us see how the three perceiver characteristics might affect the decision rules which make up the processing centre.

Consider first the inference rules — those concerned with a single input. Input B is the only one which can be selected on its own, and we have already stipulated that B implies only output Y ($B0 \rightarrow Y0$, and $B1 \rightarrow Y1$). We may now add a limitation, that the nature of the inference from $B1$ and $B0$ depends upon the perceiver. (Not all inference rules will depend upon perceiver characteristics; we cite this merely as an example.) As the table on p. 376 shows, characteristics P and R always have the value 0 when B is selected by itself. They are thus irrelevant to inference rules from B, and Q is the only perceiver characteristic which can affect these rules.

We might suggest this type of interaction between input and perceiver characteristics:

Perceiver characteristic*	Input*	Inference*
Q1	B1	Y0
Q0	B1	Y0
Q1	B0	Y1
Q0	B0	Y0

Since B is the only input that can occur in isolation, our computer programme now seems to need only four inference rules. In fact we can reduce these to a simple rule in our programme: $Q1, B0 \rightarrow Y1$; otherwise $B \rightarrow Y0$. The value of such a simplified form of instruction is obvious.

* As an example of this possibility take Q as the sex of the perceiver, B as the sex of the stimulus person, and Y as judgment of aggressiveness. Q1 and B1 might be "male", Q0 and B0 "female", Y0 "aggressive" and Y1 "not aggressive".

The combination rules (for more than a single input) are also simplified by the introduction of restrictions based upon the stable characteristics of the perceiver. Since input B is assumed to be selected by all perceivers, there are now only two forms of double input about which combination rules are required — AB and BC. But our assumptions about input selection (summarized in the table on p. 376) mean that perceiver characteristics P and R can only have one value for these inputs and thus cannot influence the decision rules; for input AB, $P=1$ and $R=0$, and for input BC, $P=0$ and $R=1$. Consequently the perceiver characteristic Q (representing for example the judge's sex) is the only one to operate upon a double input. How does it do this? Since a double input (AB or BC in this case) can take on four possible values (e.g. $A1, B1$; $A1, B0$; $A0, B1$; $A0, B0$), the *maximum* number of combination rules for AB and BC which allows for an interaction between input and perceiver is eight in each case. We might suggest that for male perceivers $A0, B1 \rightarrow X0, Y0$; $A1, B1 \rightarrow X1, Y0$ and so on, but that these rules differ for female perceivers. In practice the differences are likely to be fewer than the maximum of eight. A similar principle applies to a triple input, since perceiver characteristics P and R are also irrelevant to this, both always having the value 1 when three input items are selected (see p. 376). The *maximum* number of combination rules for a triple input is therefore sixteen (eight for $Q=0$ and eight for $Q=1$).

The maximum number of combination rules to be built into our programme overall is now seen to be thirty-two. In practice we should not need to programme these individually, but could save space in the same way as the number of inference rules was reduced. We could write "if . . . then . . ., otherwise . . .," instructions, the exact nature of which would depend on the set of rules we have to process.* It does seem then that we can accommodate all the inputs and the stable perceiver characteristics allowed for in a very simple programme. Apart from the small number of decision rules, we have also stipulated that repetitive inferences are always drawn ($A1 \rightarrow A1$; $A1, B0 \rightarrow A1, B0$, and so on). These can be neatly incorporated into a computer simulation without taking up space by simply requiring each input to be immediately printed out.

* An illustrative instruction might be: *If* the perceiver has characteristic Q1 and the input is $A1, B0$ *then* infer $X1, Y1$; *otherwise* (whatever the perceiver characteristic) infer $X1, Y0$ from $A1, B0$ and from $A1, B1$.

Conclusions

This rather detailed discussion has tried to show that despite the tremendous complexity of person perception aspects of the process are quite amenable to simulation. We have built several very severe restrictions into our scheme, but once a workable model has been achieved these can surely be gradually relaxed.

The limiting assumptions we have made can be summarized here. We have dealt only with dispositional judgments, and even so we have omitted consideration of their affective aspects. We have left aside context information, stored stimulus person information, variations in order of input, and the perceiver's current state. We have allowed only stimulus persons of low differentiation and articulation by incorporating only three dichotomous input variables; and we have assumed that although input variables can be combined they are in meaning independent of each other, and that each implies only a single output variable. These output variables have also been regarded as dichotomous. Only three two-value perceiver characteristics have been admitted to the model, and these have been made to operate in a very simple manner.

In a more realistic scheme these assumptions would be made less restrictive. Such a scheme appears to be possible at present, and would be valuable for the reasons suggested at the beginning of this section. Simulations are vehicles of clearer reasoning in that the nature and consequences of assumptions need to be thought through; they generate predictions in the same manner as do explanatory systems; and their explicit formulation of procedures and outcomes makes it possible to test out possibilities by manipulating the model to generate very specific conceptualizations.

A further advantage of this detailed model-making is apparent from the arguments in the last few pages. We need to have very precise information about how people actually do judge others for us to insert the necessary values into the model. We need for instance to have extremely specific information about sex differences if we are to incorporate sex as a perceiver variable. This means that a developing simulation will direct research in a most purposeful manner. In parallel with model-construction, observable facts will have to be assembled to provide flesh for the logical skeleton which the model provides. The model will not only bring up research questions, but it will also force the investigator to try to answer them. Since many of these empirical questions are very circumscribed, it is quite possible that without external pressures of the kind induced by a model no research worker would trouble to resolve them.

To simulate aspects of person perception is therefore both feasible and valuable. Computer simulation is particularly attractive. A computer has logical tastes which are very hard to satisfy, so that this sort of simulation carries with it tests of how precisely the model is formulated. If a programme simulating a process is acted upon by a computer, one can conclude that *logically* the scheme is feasible. Tests of one's logical competence are less readily available in other sorts of model-making. A second advantage of computer simulation is rather different. This lies in the fact that one can ask the computer to utilize rules which save the programmer enumerating all the possible outcomes of a decision. In models of person perception the number of relevant outcomes can be very great. But the computer can scan these without the programmer having to work his own way through them. This facility is clearly very time-saving. A related point concerns the use of "heuristic methods" in computer programming. It is customary to distinguish between heuristic programmes and "algorithms". An algorithmic programme is one which will deal with all possibilities and therefore guarantees a solution. Although this is very convenient, it is so expensive of time and storage space that it is often not practical. An algorithmic programme to simulate games of chess would have to consider all the sequences of outcomes from each possible move before it took a decision.* This is much too complicated and lengthy to be worthwhile. In a similar way the algorithm to open a combination lock is to try out all the combinations; sales of this type of lock testify to its impracticality.

It is probable that algorithmic programmes will be equally impractical in simulating person perception. The number of possibilities soon becomes too large. What we shall almost certainly have to devize are heuristic programmes. These are in effect "rules of thumb" which *may* turn out to offer the best principles. A heuristic programme simulating chess players might include the notion that outcomes which threaten one's own queen need not be pursued, or the principle that

* Shannon estimates that there are something like 10^{120} games to be explored, with less than 10^{16} microseconds available in a century to explore them. See the paper by Newell, Shaw and Simon, pp. 39–70 in Feigenbaum and Feldman (1963).

only a certain set of opening moves needs to be considered. These heuristics may pay off, but the pay-off is not guaranteed. Their value lies in the way they simplify the process. It is clear that people use heuristic methods continually in their everyday activities, and that a programme to simulate person perception could well employ them. If the simulation turned out to be a good one, we should have acquired useful insights into the way people do in practice perceive others. A heuristic which works may well correspond to the sort of "rule of thumb" which people in fact use. Model-makers who work with computer programmes are more able to build in heuristic procedures than those who rely on other media; this advantage is likely to prove very important as techniques of heuristic programming develop (cf. Sass and Wilkinson, 1965).

One final point about computer simulation of person perception: it is of course possible to commence one's programme at stages other than the input stage. We began by considering the nature of the input and worked through to the output. We might alternatively start at the output and work backwards. In effect this would treat the perceptual process as one of solving problems — "Is the stimulus person cheerful?", "Is he intelligent?", "Is he wearing brown shoes?" This is certainly how we sometimes work in judging others (cf. Moore, 1958), and to write a programme of this kind would have tremendous practical advantages. This is because we should then be dealing with a process which is logically the same as that programmed by workers with very different interests. The classic Logic Theory Machine of Newell, Simon and Shaw is a heuristic problem-solving programme which works backwards, as is Gelernter's Geometry-Theorem Proving Machine. (Reports of these programmes are conveniently located in the set of readings edited by Feigenbaum and Feldman, 1963.) And work on simulating concept formation would also become very relevant (Hovland, 1960; Hovland and Hunt, 1960; Hunt, 1962; see also Feigenbaum and Feldman, 1963). It might therefore prove economical to build upon these programmes when we start to simulate the perception of others.

To recapitulate this section: we have attempted a detailed illustration of how person perception might be simulated by means of computer programmes. We see this form of simulation as valuable for several reasons. First it forces a research worker to examine the components of the perceptual system in interaction and to keep before him the process as a whole. Secondly it ensures greater clarity and persistence of thought than is usually managed. Thirdly it directs research activities in an economic way, and fourthly, it can handle processes in a much more complex manner than is otherwise possible. In addition to these considerations a computer model will be accompanied by an iso-morphic explanatory system; and explanation is our business.

THOUGHTS ON FUTURE RESEARCH

A book of this kind ought to provide some pointers to possibly fruitful research approaches. But we have eschewed a "suggestions for future research" section which might by convention be printed about here. Research ideas are best presented alongside the substantive discussions of each topic, and this is what we have tried to do. Profitable techniques and areas of investigation have been noted on many of the preceding pages, and we shall not try here to bring all of these together in one place.

Instead we shall look generally at the kinds of questions that ought to be asked by investigators studying person perception. What kinds of questions should our experiments be designed to answer? How can these questions be sharpened? What should we ask our judges to do? A series of broad issues of this type will be raised in this concluding section.

Let us first consider the question: how many sets of variables should we try to study in one investigation? This is a query of some topical concern, since students of person perception (in parallel with researchers in other fields) are starting to move away from the single variable type of study. It is becoming more common to investigate several factors at once, often in experiments much more complex than would have been possible ten years ago. In general terms it can be seen that in studies of person perception experimental variations may be in the stimulus person, in the perceiver and in the type of response which is elicited. Whereas earlier studies typically looked at one of these groups of factors, some more recent investigations have varied two or three at once.

A few examples are in order. Feshbach and Feshbach (1963) have varied together the perceiver's current state (fear) and the stimulus person (adult or child) (see p. 225). The perceiver's sex is often investigated in relation to several other variables. Bayton, Austin and

Burke (1965), for instance, used two types of stimulus ("the average negro" and "the average white") and ten conceptual response categories. They observed a difference in the pattern of judgments of the two stimuli which depended upon the sex of the perceiver (see p. 188). This interaction was also clear in Experiment 21 (p. 193). Differences in men's and women's perceptions were mediated by the extent to which the stimulus person was familiar or unfamiliar. A more complicated illustration of a study encompassing several factors is provided by Experiment 22 (p. 218). In that investigation we observed how the religious affiliation of a perceiver and of a stimulus person had an interactive effect which depended upon the kind of judgments which were being made.

It is hard to deny the value of experiments which deal with several groups of variables in this way (cf. Cattell, 1966). On a rather base level we should note that they can provide complex results which are more likely to interest students and colleagues than are findings from many single-variable studies. More important is the point that we have less difficulty generalizing to real-life situations. Since these situations are characterized by the simultaneous operation of several factors, an investigation which looks at a number of these at once is manifestly closer to day-to-day activities than a study which examines only a single variable. A third virtue of studying several groups of influences at once is simply that we may by this means learn more. Not only will we be able to examine more than one main effect, but we shall also be able to ponder the many intriguing interaction effects which are turned up.

In general then studies of several groups of variables at once are surely desirable. But they are not without their difficulties, and it would be foolish to advocate that all studies of person perception should henceforth be of this kind. No-one to our knowledge has advocated this, but there are signs that a multiple-variable band-wagon is getting up speed and that researchers who are not on it may be left behind in the rush to the journals. This would be unfortunate. Let us consider why simple research designs to study a single variable are still needed.

Firstly, there are considerable practical problems attached to the manipulation of several variables at once. For a start, a lot of subjects are required. Suppose we want to manipulate three groups of variables in one experiment (perhaps the stimulus person, the kind of perceptual response, and the perceiver), and that we only look at two values of each variable. This requires eight groups of subjects, and it is desirable to have about thirty subjects in each group. Many investigators have difficulty in locating the required number of judges, and yet they could make a considerable contribution in a less ambitious manipulation. Similarly, it would be a pity if researchers felt impelled to look at the number of variables and then compromised by using only a small number of subjects. This can lead to interaction effects which are statistically significant and theoretically provocative, but which are in fact grossly unreliable.

Again, the analysis of data from complex designs of this type is usually practicable only when relatively sophisticated computers and programmes are available. Hand-analyses are of course possible, but it seems unnecessary to require investigators who do not have suitable facilities to spend weeks calculating interaction F values when they could be more fruitfully engaged on simpler studies of single variables. This leads to our third (and most significant) argument against a universal indulgence in studies of more than one variable.

There are many fields where we simply do not know enough about how a single factor operates. It is unwise to attempt multiple-variable studies until each of the variables is at least partly understood. In Chapter 7 we reviewed many investigations of communication variables in indirect perception. It was clear that the role of headlines, type-face and pictorial matter is almost unknown. Many single-variable studies are needed before more comprehensive designs can be contemplated.

It appears that multiple-variable investigations of person perception are to be encouraged, but only in certain instances. The investigator needs to be confident of his facilities and his subjects, and he needs to be working with issues which already have been broached. In these circumstances progress is very likely. But valuable results will also derive from less ambitious projects where single variables are studied intensively and where statistical operations need not be advanced ones. Studies of this kind should not be neglected for the sake of increased "sophistication" in areas where the simple design is still the appropriate one.

We turn now to a somewhat different point. In Chapter 1 the parallels between object perception and person perception were stressed. We argued there that experimental psychologists and social psychologists could learn a lot from each other, and we have repeatedly advocated greater mutual concern with problems conventionally assigned to one of these two groups. Similarly the clinical psychologist is much involved in person perception, and his work is probably more intimately related to that of the social psychologist than is usually acknowledged. We have from time to time attempted to bring together research results from the two fields, but have no doubt that greater concentration on this by persons more qualified than ourselves would bring rewards. These would flow partly from a recognition that researchers in one area have been asking questions about peripheral issues or in an inappropriate way; or it might be that the questions which so bewilder one group have already been answered by investigators in the other field.

Just as experimental and clinical psychologists can assist us in asking questions about person perception, so too are those people professionally concerned with communications and the mass media likely to help in this endeavour. The interests of this group are interwoven with those of students of person perception, and yet each group at present views the topic of their mutual interest in a quite different way. Not only is perceptual research relevant to experts in mass communications, but in addition they themselves can help this research by sharing their conceptualizations and by asking questions which to them are the important ones.

There is another specialist whose contribution to research on interpersonal judgment could be enormous. This is the philosopher. His interest in judgmental problems seems to be of two kinds. Firstly, philosophical analysis can bring to bear on most issues conceptual tools which are quite unknown to the psychologist. An illustration of the benefits which this form of application can yield is provided by Fishman's (1960) delightful essay on the Whorfian hypothesis (see p. 216). Similar philosophical attention to some of the confusions in the field of person perception would not go amiss. But in addition to this general potential of philosophical work, a second more specific advantage to students of person perception is clear.

The judgments about stimulus persons which we have studied are analogous to statements about people with which some philosophers are much concerned. That branch of philosophy which is sometimes known as "the philosophy of mind" deals almost exclusively with the meaning of statements about a person. Illustrative titles of books in this area are *The Concept of Mind* (Ryle, 1949) and *The Concept of a*

Person (Ayer, 1963). The statements about "minds" and "persons" with which philosophers work and the perceptual responses about people with which we have dealt seem to have quite a lot in common. Although it would be very unconventional, a research grant employing a psychologist and a philosopher together might produce quite a breakthrough.

The final topic we shall examine is the measurement of person perception. This has already been broached on many of the earlier pages, but here we shall look at it from a slightly different angle. We shall be interested in the general question: what is it that we want our subjects to tell us? In our own research we have mainly wanted them to tell us where they place a stimulus person along each of several bipolar scales. We used the semantic differential, and a case for the employment of this instrument has been presented in Chapter 2. Attention was there drawn to its many practical virtues, but at the same time we noted that some of these virtues could themselves be construed as deficiencies. In using the semantic differential we were certainly asking our subjects important questions, and yet there are respects in which the questions were not completely appropriate ones.

For example, the semantic differential specifies in advance the scales on which responses are to be made. The advantages of this are clear, and we have discussed them in Chapter 2. But it could be argued that we are placing undesirable restrictions upon our judges. The work on factor structure and scale intercorrelation does suggest that the semantic differential will be less unsatisfactory in this respect than many other indices, but it is still possible that a perceiver might infer characteristics which are unrepresented in the scales we provide.

We also pointed out in Chapter 2 the benefits of having an instrument which can be applied generally to differing judgmental tasks. Our research has exploited this universality and we have been able to derive comparable results from many different situations. But we might in other projects be particularly interested in the differences between situations and stimuli, and it is likely that we should then want quite different sets of indicators (see p. 53). Despite our faith in the semantic differential we have no doubt that there is a need for other measures of person perception.

What kinds of index are likely to become important to psychologists investigating the process? Consider first a class of open-ended devices which has lately received much psychometric attention. It is possible to ask judges to make paired-comparison judgments without specifying the dimensions which are to be used. Typically a judge would be required to estimate "similarity" between members of a pair, and all possible pairs of stimulus persons in a set would be judged. Statistical transformations may then be applied to recover the judgmental dimensions present in a subject's responses. By these transformations we can determine (a) the number of dimensions needed to reproduce the original similarity judgments with minimal error, (b) the "scores" of each stimulus on each dimension, and (c) the relative importance of each of the dimensions which have been indicated. We still have to determine by *post hoc* interpretation the best label to attach to each dimension.

Several procedures to achieve these valuable indices have been developed. They are collectively viewed as multidimensional scaling analyses, and we have assayed a somewhat fuller account of the central notions on pp. 103–105. Experiment 6 employed multidimensional scaling as a methodological tool, and there is no doubt of its value (see also Messnick and Kogan, 1966; Pederson, 1965; Robinson and Hefner, 1967; Walters and Jackson, 1966). We have moved on to employ the procedures in studies of international judgment,* and have found that they can generate very satisfying patterns of results. Research of this kind into the dimensions of judgments based upon facial or gestural information would be valuable. Similarly we might look at the possible relationships between inputs in studies of combination rules by applying paired comparison techniques to sets of cue traits.

All this would be to the good. But one important limitation of present multidimensional scaling models should be emphasized. Those techniques which are currently available are based upon the assumption that each stimulus must fall on each judgmental dimension. That is to say that the analysis of paired-comparison data cannot take account of instances when an idiosyncratic judgment of similarity is made. If a subject is in fact viewing the stimulus array in terms of dimensions A, B and C and judges all pairs in the light of A, B and C, then all is well. But if he makes one or two judgments on the basis of characteristic D, this will not be revealed. Furthermore if he changes his standard of judgment consistently for all pairs which include stimulus i, this idiosyncrasy (despite its consistency) cannot be picked up. It is to be hoped that the

* These investigations were completed, after this book went to press. They are reported in Warr, Schroder and Blackman (1968).

mathematical underpinnings of multidimensional scaling will prove to be adjustable in this respect. For now, however, we must conclude that multidimensional scaling is a very valuable tool but only in shedding light on the general, non-specific dimensions of judgment.

We need to use another form of measure (possibly in conjunction with multidimensional scaling) which allows judges to apply different scales to different stimuli. To this end we might allow subjects to respond verbally in terms of their own choosing. Several studies have recently been reported in which judges have described other people as they wish and in which the investigator has subsequently classified their descriptions (see pp. 103 and 188). It is sometimes difficult to categorize successfully the wide range of material which this procedure generates, but to include free-response measures in a larger battery of tests will probably prove to be essential. It will allow investigators to pick up the idiosyncratic response which might be very important to a judge, but which conventional generalized instruments cannot possibly tap.

An example from a study of international judgment (Warr, Schroder and Blackman, 1968) might make this clearer. As well as paired-comparison responses for multidimensional scaling, semantic differential judgments and other output measures, we have asked each judge to list the five aspects of each government which to him are most important. The intersubject variability here is tremendous, and each judge himself may apply quite different dimensions to different stimuli. In this way a respondent may observe that the British government "wants to join the common market". Few other judges are concerned with this attribute, and the judge in question naturally does not apply the notion to other governments such as that of U.S.A. and U.S.S.R. This response (which in ancillary indices is rated by the subject as particularly important) would remain unobserved if we had relied on more standardized measurement procedures. In a similar way most studies of person perception fail to detect many dimensions of judgment which are applied to only a small range of stimuli.

It appears then that measurement in investigations of person perception should become more individual-oriented. We need to move towards procedures which allow subjects to respond on dimensions which they themselves select and which are as articulated as they want them to be. We should ask our judges to tell us what they want to tell us, rather than always asking them what we think we want to know.

This is not to say that *all* studies should be of this kind, for valuable information can be obtained through generalized measures of the type we have described. But parallel studies which emphasize and try to render manageable the idiosyncratic responses that judges so readily make cannot fail to advance our knowledge.

As a final possibility let us consider a technique which in a sense is the extreme instance of individual-oriented, let-the-subject-tell-us-what-he-wants-to design. This possibility is to carry out studies which examine intensively the introspective reports of a person who is making judgments. We might present stimulus information in the form of, say, a photograph and request that a judge verbalize what is going through his mind. The pitfalls in this approach have been emphasized repeatedly over the past sixty years, but it nevertheless appears to have more value than is conventionally acknowledged. By training judges and adopting many of the methods of Külpe, Titchener, Wundt and their contemporaries we might derive fresh insight into what really does go on in person perception.

This may seem to be a retrograde suggestion, rather out of place at the end of a book which has emphasized rigorous measurement endeavours. But we do not wish to cast aside these endeavours for the sake of complete reliance on introspection. The point is that psychologists need more than precise and reliable measures if they are to increase their understanding. As a means of developing hypotheses and new concepts we could try some systematic, controlled studies of introspection. After all, where else do good ideas come from?

REFERENCES

Abelson, R. P. and Sermat, V. (1962). Multidimensional scaling of facial expressions. *Journal of Experimental Psychology*, **63**, 546–554.

Abu-Lughod, I. (1962). International news in the Arabic Press. *Public Opinion Quarterly*, **26**, 600–612.

Adorno, T. W., Frenkel-Brunswik, E., Levinson, D. J. and Sanford, R. N. (1950). *The Authoritarian Personality*, Harper, New York.

Alexander, S. and Husek, T. R. (1962). The anxiety differential: initial steps in the development of a measure of situational anxiety. *Educational and Psychological Measurement*, **22**, 325–348.

Allport, F. H. (1955). *Theories of Perception and the Concept of Structure*, Wiley, New York.

Allport, F. H. and Lepkin, M. (1943). Building war morale with news-headlines. *Public Opinion Quarterly*, **7**, 211–221.

Allport, G. W. (1961). *Pattern and Growth in Personality*, Holt, Rinehart and Winston, New York.

Allport, G. W. and Kramer, B. M. (1946). Some roots of prejudice. *Journal of Psychology*, **22**, 9–39.

Allport, G. W. and Postman, L. J. (1945). The basic psychology of rumor. *Transactions of the New York Academy of Sciences, Series II*, **8**, 61–81.

Allport, G. W. and Vernon, P. E. (1933). *Studies in Expressive Movement*, Macmillan, New York.

Altrocchi, J. (1961). Interpersonal perceptions of repressors and sensitizers and component analysis of assumed dissimilarity scores. *Journal of Abnormal and Social Psychology*, **62**, 528–534.

Altrocchi, J. (1965a). Addendum I to Shrauger and Altrocchi's (1964) review; prepared for a seminar in Personality and Person Perception, Duke University, North Carolina.

Altrocchi, J. (1965b). Addendum II to Shrauger and Altrocchi's (1964) review; prepared for a seminar in Personality and Person Perception, Duke University, North Carolina.

Ambrose, A. and Lazerowitz, M. (1962). *Fundamentals of Symbolic Logic*, Holt, Rinehart and Winston, New York.

Ambrose, J. A. (1961). The development of the smiling response in early infancy. In B. M. Foss (Ed.), *Determinants of Infant Behaviour*, Vol. 1. Methuen, London.

American Psychological Association. (1954). *Technical Recommendations for Psychological Tests and Diagnostic Techniques*. American Psychological Association, Washington.

Anastasi, A. (1958). *Differential Psychology*, Macmillan, New York.

Anderson, L. D. (1921). Estimating intelligence by means of printed photographs. *Journal of Applied Psychology*, **5**, 152–155.

Anderson, L. R. and Fishbein, M. (1965). Prediction of attitude from the number, strength, and evaluative aspect of beliefs about the attitude object: a comparison of summation and congruity theories. *Journal of Personality and Social Psychology*, **2**, 437–443.

Anderson, N. H. (1961). Scales and statistics: parametric and nonparametric. *Psychological Bulletin*, **58**, 305–316.

Anderson, N. H. (1962). Application of an additive model to impression formation. *Science*, **138**, 817–818.

Anderson, N. H. (1965a). Primacy effects in personality impression formation using a generalized order effect paradigm. *Journal of Personality and Social Psychology*, **2**, 1–9.

Anderson, N. H. (1965b). Averaging versus adding as a stimulus-combination rule in impression formation. *Journal of Experimental Psychology*, **70**, 394–400.

Anderson, N. H. and Barrios, A. A. (1961). Primacy effects in personality impression formation. *Journal of Abnormal and Social Psychology*, **63**, 346–350.

Anderson, N. H. and Hubert, S. (1963). Effects of concomitant recall on order effects in personality impression formation. *Journal of Verbal Learning and Verbal Behavior*, **2**, 379–391.

Anderson, N. H. and Jacobson, A. (1965). Effect of stimulus inconsistency and discounting instructions in personality impression formation. *Journal of Personality and Social Psychology*, **2**, 531–539.

Anderson, N. H. and Lampel, A. K. (1965). Effect of context on ratings of personality traits. *Psychonomic Science*, **3**, 433–434.

Anderson, N. H. and Norman, A. (1964). Order effects in impression formation in four classes of stimuli. *Journal of Abnormal and Social Psychology*, **69**, 467–471.

Angyal, A. F. (1948). The diagnosis of neurotic traits by means of a new perceptual test. *Journal of Psychology*, **25**, 105–135.

Anisfeld, E. and Lambert, W. E. (1964). Evaluational reactions of bilingual and monolingual children to spoken languages. *Journal of Abnormal and Social Psychology*, **69**, 89–97.

Ansbacher, H. (1937). Perception of number as affected by the monetary value of the objects. *Archives of Psychology*, No. 215.

Applezweig, D. G. (1954). Some determinants of behavioral rigidity. *Journal of Abnormal and Social Psychology*, **49**, 224–228.

Argyle, M. (1957). *The Scientific Study of Social Behaviour*, Methuen, London.

Argyle, M. (1958). *Religious Behaviour*, Routledge and Kegan Paul, London.

Argyle, M. (1967). *The Psychology of Interpersonal Relations*, Penguin, Harmondsworth, England.

Argyle, M. and Dean, J. (1965). Eye-contact, distance and affiliation. *Sociometry*, **28**, 289–304.

Arieti, S. (1959). *American Handbook of Psychiatry*, Basic Books, New York.

Aronson, E. and Golden, B. W. (1962). The effect of relevant and irrelevant aspects of communicator credibility on opinion change. *Journal of Personality*, **30**, 135–146.

Aronson, E., Turner, E. and Carlsmith, J. M. (1963). Communicator credibility and communicator discrepancy as determinants of opinion change. *Journal of Abnormal and Social Psychology*, **67**, 31–37.

Arthur, A. Z. (1966). Response bias in the semantic differential. *British Journal of Social and Clinical Psychology*, **5**, 103–107.

Asch, S. E. (1946). Forming impressions of personality. *Journal of Abnormal and Social Psychology*, **41**, 258–290.

Asch, S. E. (1952). *Social Psychology*, Prentice-Hall, Englewood Cliffs.

Asch, S. E. (1958). The metaphor: a psychological enquiry. In R. Tagiuri and L. Petrullo (Eds.), *Person Perception and Interpersonal Behavior*. Stanford University Press, Stanford.

Asch, S. E. (1968). Gestalt psychology. In D. Sills (Ed.), *International Encyclopedia of the Social Sciences*, Vol. 6. Macmillan, New York.

Atkinson, J. W. (Ed.) (1958). *Motives in Fantasy, Action and Society*, Van Nostrand, Princeton.

Atkinson, J. W. and Walker, E. L. (1956). The affiliation motive and perceptual sensitivity to faces. *Journal of Abnormal and Social Psychology*, **53**, 38–41.

Attneave, F. (1954). Some informational aspects of visual perception. *Psychological Review*, **61**, 183–193.

Attneave, F. (1959). *Applications of Information Theory to Psychology*, Henry Holt, New York.

Attneave, F. (1962). Perception and related areas. In S. Koch (Ed.), *Psychology: A Study of a Science*, Vol. 4, McGraw-Hill, New York.

Ausubel, D. P. and Shiff, H. M. (1955). Some intrapersonal and interpersonal determinants of individual differences in sociempathic ability among adolescents. *Journal of Social Psychology*, **41**, 39–56.

Ayer, A. J. (1963). *The Concept of a Person*, Macmillan, London.

Backman, C. W. and Secord, P. F. (1962). Liking, selective interaction and misperception in congruent interpersonal relations. *Sociometry*, **25**, 321–335.

Bagby, J. A. (1957). A cross-cultural study of perceptual predominance in binocular rivalry. *Journal of Abnormal and Social Psychology*, **54**, 331–334.

Bakan, D. (1966). The test of significance in psychological research. *Psychological Bulletin*, **66**, 423–437.

Baker, B. O., Hardyck, C. D. and Petrinovich, L. F. (1966). Weak measurements vs. strong statistics: an empirical critique of S. S. Stevens' proscriptions on statistics. *Educational and Psychological Measurement*, **26**, 291–309.

Bannister, D. (1962a). Personal construct theory: a summary and experimental paradigm. *Acta Psychologica*, **20**, 104–120.

Bannister, D. (1962b). The nature and measurement of schizophrenic thought disorder. *Journal of Mental Science*, **108**, 825–842.

Bannister, D. (1963). The genesis of schizophrenic thought disorder: a serial invalidation hypothesis. *British Journal of Psychiatry*, **109**, 680–686.

Bannister, D. and Fransella, F. (1966). A grid test of schizophrenic thought disorder. *British Journal of Social and Clinical Psychology*, **5**, 95–102.

Barclay, A. and Thumin, F. J. (1963). A modified semantic differential approach to attitudinal assessment. *Journal of Clinical Psychology*, **19**, 376–378.

Bartlett, F. C. (1932). *Remembering*, Cambridge University Press, Cambridge.

Bayton, J. A., Austin, L. J. and Burke, K. R. (1965). Negro perception of negro and white personality traits. *Journal of Personality and Social Psychology*, **1**, 250–253.

Beach, F. A. (1951). Body chemistry and perception. In R. R. Blake and G. V. Ramsey (Eds.), *Perception: An Approach to Personality*. Ronald Press, New York.

Beach, L. and Wertheimer, M. (1961). A free response approach to the study of person cognition. *Journal of Abnormal and Social Psychology*, **62**, 367–374.

Beardslee, D. C. and Wertheimer, M. (Eds.) (1958). *Readings in Perception*, Van Nostrand, Princeton.

Beilin, H. (1963). Impression formation under varied set and stimulus-trait conditions. *Journal of Social Psychology*, **60**, 39–55.

Bender, I. E. and Hastorf, A. H. (1950). The perception of persons: forecasting another person's responses to three personality scales. *Journal of Abnormal and Social Psychology*, **45**, 556–561.

Benedetti, D. T. and Hill, J. G. (1960). A determiner of the centrality of a trait in impression formation. *Journal of Abnormal and Social Psychology*, **60**, 278–280.

Berelson, B., Lazarsfeld, P. F. and McPhee, W. N. (1954). *Voting*, University of Chicago Press, Chicago.

Berkowitz, L. (1954). Group standards, cohesiveness and productivity. *Human Relations*, **7**, 509–519.

Berkowitz, L. (1957). Liking for the group and the perceived merit of the group's behavior. *Journal of Abnormal and Social Psychology*, **54**, 353–357.

Berkowitz, L. (1960a). The judgmental process in personality functioning. *Psychological Review*, **67**, 130–142.

Berkowitz, L. (1960b). Some factors affecting the reduction of overt hostility. *Journal of Abnormal and Social Psychology*, **60**, 14–21.

Berkowitz, L. (1960c). Repeated frustrations and expectations in hostility arousal. *Journal of Abnormal and Social Psychology*, **60**, 422–429.

Berkowitz, L. (1961). Anti-Semitism, judgmental processes, and displacement of hostility. *Journal of Abnormal and Social Psychology*, **62**, 210–215.

Berkowitz, L. (1962). *Aggression: A Social Psychological Analysis*, McGraw-Hill, New York.

Berlew, D. E. (1961). Interpersonal sensitivity and motive strength. *Journal of Abnormal and Social Psychology*, **63**, 390–394.

Berlew, D. E. and Williams, A. F. (1964). Interpersonal sensitivity under motive arousing conditions. *Journal of Abnormal and Social Psychology*, **68**, 150–159.

Bernstein, B. (1962). Social class, linguistic codes, and grammatical elements. *Language and Speech*, **5**, 221–240.

Bevan, W., Secord, P. F. and Richards, J. M. (1956). Personalities in faces: V. Personal identification and the judgment of facial characteristics. *Journal of Social Psychology*, **44**, 289–291.

Bieri, J. (1953). Changes in interpersonal perceptions following social interaction. *Journal of Abnormal and Social Psychology*, **48**, 61–66.

Bieri, J. (1955). Cognitive complexity–simplicity and predictive behavior. *Journal of Abnormal and Social Psychology*, **51**, 263–268.

Bieri, J. (1962). Analyzing stimulus information in social judgments. In S. Messick and J. Ross (Eds.), *Measurement in Personality and Cognition*. Wiley, New York.

Bieri, J. and Blacker, E. (1956). The generality of cognitive complexity in the perception of people and inkblots. *Journal of Abnormal and Social Psychology*, **53**, 112–117.

Bieri, J. and Lobeck, R. (1961). Self-concept differences in relation to identification, religion, and social class. *Journal of Abnormal and Social Psychology*, **62**, 94–98.

Bieri, J., Atkins, A. L., Briar, S., Leaman, R. L., Miller, H. and Tripodi, T. (1966). *Clinical and Social Judgment: The Discrimination of Behavioral Information*. Wiley, New York.

Bieri, J., Bradburn, W. M. and Galinsky, M. D. (1958). Sex differences in perceptual behavior. *Journal of Personality*, **26**, 1–12.

Bion, W. R. (1961). *Experiences in Groups*, Tavistock, London.

Birren, J. E. (Ed.) (1959). *Handbook of Aging and the Individual*, University of Chicago Press, Chicago.

Birren, J. E., Butler, R. N., Greenhouse, S. W., Sokoloff, L. and Yarrow, M. R. (Eds.) (1963). *Human Aging*, U.S. Department of Health, Education and Welfare, Washington.

Block, J. (1963). The equivalence of measures and the correction for attenuation, *Psychological Bulletin*, **60**, 152–156.

Bloodstein, O. N. (1949). Conditions under which stuttering is reduced or absent: a review of the literature. *Journal of Speech and Hearing Disorders*, **14**, 295–302.

Blumberg, H. H., DeSoto, C. B. and Kuethe, J. L. (1966). Evaluation of rating scale formats. *Personnel Psychology*, **19**, 243–259.

Blumler, J. G. and McQuail, D. (1968). *Election Television in the 1960s*. In preparation.

Bogardus, E. S. (1928). *Immigration and Race Attitudes*, Heath, Boston.

Boneau, C. A. (1960). The effects of violations of assumptions underlying the *t*-test. *Psychological Bulletin*, **57**, 49–64.

Bonner, H. (1959). *Group Dynamics: Principles and Applications*, Ronald Press, New, York.

Borko, H. (Ed.) (1962). *Computer Applications in the Behavioral Sciences*, Prentice-Hall, Englewood Cliffs.

Bossart, P. and Di Vesta, F. J. (1966). Effects of context, frequency and order of presentation of evaluative assertions on impression formation. *Journal of Personality and Social Psychology*, **4**, 538–544.

Bossom, J. and Maslow, A. H. (1957). Security of judges as a factor in impressions of warmth in others. *Journal of Abnormal and Social Psychology*, **55**, 147–148.

Bourisseau, W., Davis, O. L. and Yamamoto, K. (1965). Sense-impression responses to differing pictorial and verbal stimuli. *Audio-visual Communication Review*, **13**, 249–258.

Boyle, D. G. (1965). The role played by the character sketch in Asch's experiment on forming impressions of personality. *British Journal of Social and Clinical Psychology*, **4**, 14–16.

Bradford, L. P., Gibb, J. R. and Benne, K. D. (Eds.) (1964). *T-Group Theory and Laboratory Method*, Wiley, New York.

Bramel, D. (1962). A dissonance theory approach to defensive projection. *Journal of Abnormal and Social Psychology*, **64**, 121–129.

Bramel, D. (1963). Selection of a target for defensive projection. *Journal of Abnormal and Social Psychology*, **66**, 318–324.

Brinkman, P. D. (1963). The differential functions of editorials and editorial cartoons in achieving opinion change. Unpublished dissertation, Indiana University.

Brinton, J. E. (1958). Measurement of aesthetic qualities of type-faces. Report presented to the Association for Education in Journalism, University of Missouri.

Briscoe, M. E., Woodyard, H. D. and Shaw, M. E. (1967). Personality impression change as a function of the favorableness of first impressions. *Journal of Personality*, **35**, 343–357.

Broadbent, D. E. (1957). A mechanical model for human attention and immediate, memory. *Psychological Review*, **64**, 205–215.

Broadbent, D. E. (1958). *Perception and Communication*, Pergamon Press, London.

Bronfenbrenner, U., Harding, J. and Gallwey, M. (1958). The measurement of skill in social perception. In D. C. McClelland, A. L. Baldwin, U. Bronfenbrenner and F. L. Strodtbeck (Eds.), *Talent and Society*, Van Nostrand, Princeton.

Brooks, R. M. and Goldstein, A. G. (1963). Recognition by children of inverted photographs of faces. *Child Development*, **34**, 1033–1040.

Brooks, V. and Hochberg, J. (1960). A psychophysical study of "cuteness". *Perceptual and Motor Skills*, **11**, 205.

Brown, R. (1965). *Social Psychology*, The Free Press, New York.

Brown, R. W. and Lenneberg, E. H. (1954). A study in language and cognition. *Journal of Abnormal and Social Psychology*, **49**, 454–462.

Brown, W. P. (1961). Conceptions of perceptual defense. *British Journal of Psychology Monograph Supplements*, No. 35.

Bruner, J. S. (1951). Personality dynamics and the process of perceiving. In R. R. Blake and G. V. Ramsey (Eds.), *Perception: An Approach to Personality*. Ronald Press, New York.

Bruner, J. S. (1957). On perceptual readiness. *Psychological Review*, **64**, 123–152.

Bruner, J. S. (1958). Social psychology and perception. In E. E. Maccoby, T. M. Newcomb and E. L. Hartley (Eds.), *Readings in Social Psychology*, 3rd ed. Holt, New York.

Bruner, J. S. and Goodman, C. C. (1947). Value and need as organizing factors in perception. *Journal of Abnormal and Social Psychology*, **42**, 33–44.

Bruner, J. S. and Perlmutter, H. V. (1957). Compatriot and foreigner: a study of impression formation in three countries. *Journal of Abnormal and Social Psychology*, **55**, 253–260.

Bruner, J. S. and Postman, L. (1947). Tension and tension release as organizing factors in perception. *Journal of Personality*, **15**, 300–308.

Bruner, J. S. and Postman, L. (1948). An approach to social perception. In W. Dennis (Ed.), *Current Trends in Social Psychology*. University of Pittsburgh Press, Pittsburgh.

Bruner, J. S. and Tagiuri, R. (1954). The perception of people. In G. Lindzey (Ed.), *Handbook of Social Psychology*. Addison-Wesley, Reading, Massachusetts.

Bruner, J. S., Goodnow, J. L. and Austin, G. A. (1956). *A Study of Thinking*, Wiley, New York.

Bruner, J. S., Postman, L. and John, W. (1949). *Normalization of Incongruity*, Research memorandum, Harvard University.

Bruner, J. S., Shapiro, D. and Tagiuri, R. (1958). The meaning of traits in isolation and in combination. In R. Tagiuri and L. Petrullo (Eds.), *Person Perception and Interpersonal Behavior*. Stanford University Press, Stanford.

Brunswik, E. (1928). Zur Entwicklung der Albedowahrnehmung. *Zeitschrift für Psychologie*, **109**, 40–115.

Brunswik, E. (1934). *Wahrnehmung und Gegenstandswelt*, Deuticke, Leipzig and Vienna.

Brunswik, E. (1939). Perceptual characteristics of schematized human figures. *Psychological Bulletin*, **36**, 553.

Brunswik, E. (1940). Thing constancy as measured by correlation coefficients. *Psychological Review*, **47**, 69–78.

Brunswik, E. (1944). Distal focussing of perception: size-constancy in a representative sample of situations. *Psychological Monographs*, **56**, No. 1, Whole No. 254.

Brunswik, E. (1956). *Perception and the Representative Design of Psychological Experiments*, University of California Press, Berkeley.

Brunswik, E. and Reiter, L. (1937). Eindrucks-Charactere schematisierter Gesichter. *Zeitschrift für Psychologie*, **142**, 67–134.

Burke, C. J. (1963). Measurement scales and statistical models. In M. H. Marx (Ed.) *Theories in Contemporary Psychology*. Macmillan, New York.

Burns, N. and Cavey, L. (1957). Age differences in empathic ability among children. *Canadian Journal of Psychology*, **11**, 227–230.

Burt, C. (1959). *A Psychological Study of Typography*, Cambridge University Press, Cambridge.

Burton, P. W. (1955). *Principles of Advertising*, Prentice-Hall, New York.

Buss, A. H. (1961). *The Psychology of Aggression*, Wiley, New York.

Buzby, D. E. (1924). The interpretation of facial expression. *American Journal of Psychology*, **35**, 602–604.

Campbell, D. T. (1955). An error in some demonstrations of the superior social perceptiveness of leaders. *Journal of Abnormal and Social Psychology*, **51**, 694–695.

Campbell, D. T., Miller, N., Lubetsky, J. and O'Connell, E. J. (1964). Varieties of projection in trait attribution. *Psychological Monographs*, **78**, No. 15, Whole No. 592.

Campbell, J. D. and Radke-Yarrow, M. J. (1956). Interpersonal perception and behavior in children. *American Psychologist*, **11**, 416.

Cantril, H. (1957). Perception and interpersonal relations. *American Journal of Psychiatry*, **113**, 119–127.

Cantril, H. and Allport, G. W. (1935). *The Psychology of Radio*, Harper, New York.

Carlson, E. R. (1956). Attitude change through modification of attitude structure. *Journal of Abnormal and Social Psychology*, **52**, 256–261.

Carlson, E. R. (1960). Word familiarity as a factor in forming impressions. *Psychological Reports*, **7**, 18.

Carlson, E. R. (1961). Motivation and set in acquiring information about persons. *Journal of Personality*, **29**, 285–293.

Carmichael, L., Roberts, S. O. and Wessel, N. Y. (1937). A study of the judgment of manual expressions as presented in still and motion pictures. *Journal of Social Psychology*, **8**, 115–142.

Cartwright, D. and Zander, A. (1960). *Group Dynamics: Research and Theory*, Row, Peterson, Evanston, Illinois.

Cattell, R. B. (Ed.) (1966). *Handbook of Multivariate Experimental Psychology*, Rand McNally, Chicago.

Centers, R. (1950). Social class identification of American youth. *Journal of Personality*, **18**, 290–302.

Chall, J. S. (1958). *Readability: An Appraisal of Research and Application*, Ohio State University Press, Columbus.

Chambers, J. L. (1961). Trait judgment of photographs and adjustment of college students. *Journal of Consulting Psychology*, **25**, 433–435.

Chance, J., Goldstein, A. G. and Schicht, W. (1967). Effects of acquaintance and friendship on children's recognition of classmates' faces. *Psychonomic Science*, **7**, 223–224.

Chowdry, K. and Newcomb, T. M. (1952). The relative abilities of leaders and non-leaders to estimate opinions of their own groups. *Journal of Abnormal and Social Psychology*, **47**, 51–57.

Clark, W. H. (1958). *The Psychology of Religion*, Macmillan, New York.

Clark, K. B. and Clark, M. P. (1947). Racial identification and preference in Negro children. In T. M. Newcomb and E. L. Hartley (Eds.), *Readings in Social Psychology*. Holt, New York.

Cleeton, G. U. and Knight, F. B. (1924). Validity of character judgments based on external criteria. *Journal of Applied Psychology*, **8**, 215–231.

Cliff, N. (1959). Adverbs as multipliers. *Psychological Review*, **66**, 27–44.

Cline, M. G. (1956). The influence of social context on the perception of faces. *Journal of Personality*, **25**, 142–158.

Cline, V. B. (1955). Ability to judge personality assessed with a stress interview and sound-film technique. *Journal of Abnormal and Social Psychology*, **50**, 183–187.

Cline, V. B. (1964). Interpersonal perception. In B. A. Maher (Ed.), *Progress in Experimental Personality Research*, Vol. I. Academic Press, New York.

Cline, V. B. and Richards, J. M. (1960). Accuracy of interpersonal perception — a general trait? *Journal of Abnormal and Social Psychology*, **60**, 1–7.

Cofer, C. N. and Dunn, J. T. (1952). Personality ratings as influenced by verbal stimuli. *Journal of Personality*, **21**, 223–227.

Cohen, A. R. (1961). Cognitive tuning as a factor affecting impression formation. *Journal of Personality*, **29**, 235–245.

Cohen, A. R. (1964). *Attitude Change and Social Influence*, Basic Books, New York.

Cooley, J. C. (1942). *A Primer of Formal Logic*, Macmillan, London.

Cooper, J. B. (1955). Perceptual organization as a function of politically-oriented communication. *Journal of Social Psychology*, **41**, 319–324.

Coyne, L. and Holzman, P. S. (1966). Three equivalent forms of a semantic differential inventory. *Educational and Psychological Measurement*, **26**, 665–674.

Crano, W. D. and Schroder, H. M. (1967). Complexity of attitude structure and processes of conflict reduction. *Journal of Personality and Social Psychology*, **5**, 110–114.

Creelman, M. B. (1966). *The Experimental Investigation of Meaning*, Springer, New York.

Crockett, W. H. (1965). Cognitive complexity and impression formation. In B. A. Maher (Ed.), *Progress in Experimental Personality Research*, Vol. II. Academic Press, New York.

Crockett, W. H. and Meidinger, T. (1956). Authoritarianism and interpersonal perception. *Journal of Abnormal and Social Psychology*, **53**, 378–380.

Cronbach, L. J. (1955). Processes affecting scores on "understanding others" and "assumed similarity". *Psychological Bulletin*, **52**, 177–193.

Cronbach, L. J. (1958). Proposals leading to analytic treatment of social perception scores. In R. Tagiuri and L. Petrullo (Eds.), *Person Perception and Interpersonal Behavior*. Stanford University Press, Stanford.

Cronbach, L. J. and Gleser, G. C. (1953). Assessing similarity between profiles. *Psychological Bulletin*, **50**, 456–474.

Crow, W. J. and Hammond, K. R. (1957). The generality of accuracy and response sets in interpersonal perception. *Journal of Abnormal and Social Psychology*, **54**, 384–390.

Davis, A., Gardner, B. B. and Gardner, M. R. (1941). *Deep South: A Social Anthropological Study of Caste and Class*. University of Chicago Press, Chicago.

Davis, D. R. and Cullen, J. H. (1958). Disorganization of perception in neurosis and psychosis. *American Journal of Psychology*, **71**, 229–237.

Davis, K. E. and Jones, E. E. (1960). Changes in interpersonal perception as a means of reducing cognitive dissonance. *Journal of Abnormal and Social Psychology*, **61**, 402–410.

Davis, R. C. and Smith H. J. (1933). Determinants of feeling tone in type faces. *Journal of Applied Psychology*, **17**, 742–764.

Davitz, J. R. (Ed.) (1964). *The Communication of Emotional Meaning*, McGraw-Hill, New York.

DeFleur, M. L. and Weske, F. R. (1959). The interpretation of interracial situations: an experiment in social perception. *Social Forces*, **38**, 17–23.

DeSoto, C. B. and Kuethe, J. L. (1959). Subjective probabilities of interpersonal relationships. *Journal of Abnormal and Social Psychology*, **59**, 290–294.

DeSoto, C., Kuethe, J. L. and Wunderlich, R. (1960). Social perception and self-perception of high and low authoritarians. *Journal of Social Psychology*, **52**, 149–155.

Dennis, W. (1951). Cultural and developmental factors in perception. In R. R. Blake and G. V. Ramsey (Eds.), *Perception: An Approach to Personality*. Ronald Press, New York.

Deri, S. (1949). *Introduction to the Szondi Test*, Grune and Stratton, New York.

Deutschmann, P. J. and Kiel, D. (1960). *A Factor Analytic Study of Attitudes Towards the Mass Media*, Scripps-Howard Research, Cincinnati.

Diab, L. N. (1965). Studies in social attitudes: III. Attitude assessment through the semantic differential technique. *Journal of Social Psychology*, **67**, 303–314.

Di Vesta, F. J. (1966). A developmental study of the semantic structures of children. *Journal of Verbal Learning and Verbal Behavior*, **5**, 249–259.

Di Vesta, F. J. and Dick, W. (1966). Test-retest reliability of children's ratings on the semantic differential. *Educational and Psychological Measurement*, **26**, 605–616.

Dodge, J. and Viner, G. (Eds.) (1963). *The Practice of Journalism*, Heinemann, London.

Donahoe, J. W. (1961). Changes in meaning as a function of age. *Journal of Genetic Psychology*, **99**, 23–28.

Doob, L. W. (1958). Behavior and grammatical style. *Journal of Abnormal and Social Psychology*, **56**, 398–401.

Dornbusch, S. M., Hastorf, A. H., Richardson, S. A., Muzzy, R. E. and Vreeland, R. S. (1965). The perceiver and the perceived: their relative influence on the categories of interpersonal cognition. *Journal of Personality and Social Psychology*, **1**, 434–440.

Douty, H. I. (1962). The influence of clothing on perceptions of persons in single contact situations. Unpublished dissertation, Florida State University.

Dudycha, G. J. (1942). A note on the "halo effect" in ratings. *Journal of Social Psychology*, **15**, 331–333.

Dunlap, K. (1927). The role of eye-muscles and mouth-muscles in the expression of the emotions. *Genetic Psychology Monographs*, **2**, 197–233.

Dustin, D. S. and Baldwin, P. M. (1966). Redundancy in impression formation. *Journal of Personality and Social Psychology*, **3**, 500–506.

Dymond, R. F. (1949). A scale for the measurement of empathic ability. *Journal of Consulting Psychology*, **13**, 128–133.

Dymond, R. F. (1950). Personality and empathy. *Journal of Consulting Psychology*, **14**, 343–350.

Dymond, R. F., Hughes, A. S. and Raabe, V. L. (1952). Measurable changes in empathy with age. *Journal of Consulting Psychology*, **16**, 202–206.

Edwards, A. L. (1953). The relationship between the judged desirability of a trait and the probability that the trait will be endorsed. *Journal of Applied Psychology*, **37**, 90–93.

Edwards, A. L. (1957). Social desirability and probability of endorsement of items on the interpersonal check list. *Journal of Abnormal and Social Psychology*, **55**, 394–396.

Edwards, A. L. (1959). Social desirability and the description of others. *Journal of Abnormal and Social Psychology*, **59**, 434–436.

Ekman, P. (1957). A methodological discussion of non-verbal behavior. *Journal of Psychology*, **43**, 141–149.

Ekman, G., Engen, T., Künnapas, T. and Lindman, R. (1964). A quantitative principle of qualitative similarity. *Journal of Experimental Psychology*, **68**, 530–536.

Ekman, P. (1964). Body position, facial expression, and verbal behavior during interviews. *Journal of Abnormal and Social Psychology*, **68**, 295–301.

Ekman, P. (1965a). Differential communication of affect by head and body cues. *Journal of Personality and Social Psychology*, **2**, 726–735.

Ekman, P. (1965b). Communication through non-verbal behavior: a source of information about an interpersonal relationship. In S. S. Tomkins and C. I. Izard (Eds.), *Affect, Cognition and Personality*. Springer, New York.

Ekman, P. and Friesen, W. V. (1967). Head and body cues in the judgment of emotion: a reformulation. *Perceptual and Motor Skills*, **24**, 711–724.

Elliott, D. N. and Wittenburg, B. H. (1955). Accuracy of identification of Jewish and non-Jewish photographs. *Journal of Abnormal and Social Psychology*, **51**, 339–341.

Elliott, L. L. and Tannenbaum, P. H. (1963). Factor structure of semantic differential responses to visual forms and prediction of factor scores from structural characteristics of the stimulus shapes. *American Journal of Psychology*, **76**, 589–597.

Emig, E. (1928). The connotation of newspaper headlines. *Journalism Quarterly*, **4**, 53–59.

Engel, E. (1956). The role of content in binocular resolution. *American Journal of Psychology*, **69**, 87–91.

Engel, E. (1958). Binocular fusion of dissimilar figures. *Journal of Psychology*, **46**, 53–57.

Engel, E. (1961). Binocular methods in psychological research. In F. P. Kilpatrick (Ed.), *Explorations in Transactional Psychology*. New York University Press, New York.

English, E. (1944). A study of the readability of four newspaper headline types. *Journalism Quarterly*, **21**, 217–219.

Epstein, R. (1965). Authoritarianism, displaced aggression, and social status of the target. *Journal of Personality and Social Psychology*, **2**, 585–589.

Epstein, W. and Park, J. N. (1963). Shape constancy: functional relationships and theoretical formulations. *Psychological Bulletin*, **60**, 265–288.

Estes, S. G. (1938). Judging personality from expressive behavior. *Journal of Abnormal and Social Psychology*, **33**, 217–236.

Evans, H. (Ed.) (1961). *The Active Newsroom. IPI Manual on Techniques of News Editing, Sub-editing and Photo-editing*, International Press Institute, Zurich.

Exline, R. (1957). Group climate as a factor in the relevance and accuracy of social perception. *Journal of Abnormal and Social Psychology*, **55**, 382–388.

Exline, R. (1960). Effects of sex, norms and affiliation motive on accuracy of perception of interpersonal preferences. *Journal of Personality*, **28**, 397–412.

Exline, R. V. (1963). Explorations in the process of person perception: visual interaction in relation to competition, sex, and need for affiliation. *Journal of Personality*, **31**, 1–20.

Exline, R. V. and Winters, L. C. (1965). Affective relations and mutual glances in dyads. In S. S. Tomkins and C. I. Izard (Eds.), *Affect, Cognition and Personality*. Springer, New York.

Exline, R. V., Gray, D. and Schuette, D. (1965). Visual behavior in a dyad as affected by interview content and sex of respondent. *Journal of Personality and Social Psychology*, **1**, 201–209.

Eysenck, H. J. (1945). Graphological analysis and psychiatry: an experimental study. *British Journal of Psychology*, **35**, 70–81.

Eysenck, H. J. (1954). *The Psychology of Politics*, Routledge and Kegan Paul, London.

Eysenck, H. J. (1966). Personality and experimental psychology. *Bulletin of the British Psychological Society*, **19**, No. 62, 1–28.

Feigenbaum, E. A. and Feldman, J. (Eds.) (1963). *Computers and Thought*, McGraw-Hill, New York.

Feleky, A. M. (1914). The expression of the emotions. *Psychological Review*, **21**, 33–41.

Feliciano, G. D. (1962). The relative effectiveness of seven methods for presenting statistical information to a general audience. Unpublished dissertation, University of Wisconsin.

Feldman, S. (Ed.) (1966). *Cognitive Consistency*, Academic Press, New York.

Fensterheim, H. and Tresselt, M. E. (1953). The influence of value systems on the perception of people. *Journal of Abnormal and Social Psychology*, **48**, 93–98.

Fernberger, S. W. (1928). False suggestion and the Piderit model. *American Journal of Psychology*, **40**, 562–568.

Feshbach, S. (1963). The effects of emotional restraint upon the projection of positive affect. *Journal of Personality*, **31**, 471–481.

Feshbach, S. and Feshbach, N. (1963). Influence of the stimulus object upon the complementary and supplementary projection of fear. *Journal of Abnormal and Social Psychology*, **66**, 498–502.

Feshbach, S. and Singer, R. (1957). The effects of fear arousal and suppression of fear upon social perception. *Journal of Abnormal and Social Psychology*, **55**, 283–288.

Fiedler, F. E. (1954). Assumed similarity measures as predictors of team effectiveness. *Journal of Abnormal and Social Psychology*, **49**, 381–388.

Fiedler, F. E. (1958). *Leader Attitudes and Group Effectiveness*, University of Illinois Press, Urbana.

Fiedler, F. E. (1964). A contingency model of leadership effectiveness. In L. Berkowitz (Ed.), *Advances in Experimental Social Psychology*, Vol. I. Academic Press, New York.

Fiedler, F. E. and Hoffman, E. L. (1962). Age, sex and religious background as determinants of interpersonal perception among Dutch children: a cross-cultural validation. *Acta Psychologica*, **20**, 185–195.

Fiedler, F. E., Warrington, W. G. and Blaisdell, F. J. (1952). Unconscious attitudes as correlates of sociometric choice in a social group. *Journal of Abnormal and Social Psychology*, **47**, 790–796.

Fishbein, M. (Ed.) (1967). *Readings in Attitude Theory and Measurement*, Wiley, New York.

Fishbein, M. and Hunter, R. (1964). Summation versus balance in attitude organization and change. *Journal of Abnormal and Social Psychology*, **69**, 505–510.

Fishbein, M. and Raven, B. H. (1962). The AB scales: an operational definition of belief and attitude. *Human Relations*, **15**, 35–44.

Fisher, R. and Fisher, R. L. (1960). A projective test analysis of ethnic subculture themes in families. *Journal of Projective Techniques*, **24**, 366–369.

Fishman, J. A. (1960). A systematization of the Whorfian hypothesis. *Behavioral Science*, **5**, 323–339.

Flügel, J. C. (1950). *The Psychology of Clothes*, Hogarth Press, London.

Foa, U. G. (1961). Convergences in the analysis of the structure of interpersonal behavior. *Psychological Review*, **68**, 341–353.

Fong, S. L. M. (1965). Cultural influences in the perception of people. *British Journal of Social and Clinical Psychology*, **4**, 110–113.

Form, W. H. and Sauer, W. L. (1960). Organized labor's image of community power structure. *Social Forces*, **38**, 332–341.

Fosdick, J. A. and Tannenbaum, P. H. (1964). The encoder's intent and use of stylistic elements in photographs. *Journalism Quarterly*, **41**, 175–182.

Foulkes, D. and Foulkes, S. H. (1965). Self-concept, dogmatism and tolerance of trait inconsistency. *Journal of Personality and Social Psychology*, **2**, 104–110.

Fransella, F. (1965). The effects of imposed rhythm and certain aspects of personality on the speech of stutterers. Unpublished dissertation, University of London.

Fransella, F. and Adams, B. (1966). An illustration of the use of repertory grid technique in a clinical setting. *British Journal of Social and Clinical Psychology*, **5**, 51–62.

French, D. (1963). The relationship of anthropology to studies in perception and cognition. In S. Koch (Ed.), *Psychology: A Study of a Science*, Vol. 6. McGraw-Hill, New York.

Friedman, C. J. and Gladden, J. W. (1964). Objective measurement of social role concepts via the semantic differential. *Psychological Reports*, **14**, 239–247.

Frijda, N. H. (1958). Facial expression and situational cues. *Journal of Abnormal and Social Psychology*, **57**, 149–155.

Frois-Wittman, J. (1930). The judgment of facial expression. *Journal of Experimental Psychology*, **13**, 113–151.

Frymier, J. R. (1958). Relationship of aural perceptions to cultural situations. *Perceptual and Motor Skills*, **8**, 67–70.

Fuchs, D. A. (1964). Two source effects in magazine advertizing. Unpublished dissertation, Stanford University.

Gage, N. L. and Cronbach, L. J. (1955). Conceptual and methodological problems in interpersonal perception. *Psychological Review*, **62**, 411–422.

Gage, N. L. and Exline, R. V. (1953). Social perception and effectiveness in discussion groups. *Human Relations*, **6**, 381–396.

Gage, N. L., Leavitt, G. S. and Stone, G. C. (1956). The intermediary key in the analysis of interpersonal perception. *Psychological Bulletin*, **53**, 258–266.

Gardiner, H. W. (1965). The 1964 British and American elections: a semantic differential assessment of political concepts. *Bulletin of the British Psychological Society*, **18**, 3A.

Gardiner, H. W. (1968). *Newspapers as Personalities: A Psychological Study of the British National Daily Press*, Pergamon Press, Oxford.

Gardner, R. W., Holzman, P. S., Klein, G. S., Linton, H. B. and Spence, D. P. (1959). Cognitive control: a study of individual consistencies in cognitive behavior. *Psychological Issues*, **1**, No. 4.

Garrett, H. E. (1959). *Statistics in Psychology and Education*. Longmans Green, New York.

Gaskill, P. C., Fenton, N. and Porter, J. P. (1927). Judging the intelligence of boys from their photographs. *Journal of Applied Psychology*, **11**, 394–403.

Gates, G. S. (1923). An experimental study of the growth of social perception. *Journal of Educational Psychology*, **14**, 449–461.

Gemelli, A. and Cappellini, A. (1958). The influence of the subject's attitude in perception. *Acta Psychologica*, **14**, 12–23.

George, F. H. (1962). *The Brain as a Computer*, Pergamon Press, Oxford.

Gergen, K. J. and Jones, E. E. (1963). Mental illness, predictability, and affective consequences as stimulus factors in person perception. *Journal of Abnormal and Social Psychology*, **67**, 95–104.

Ghent, L. (1960). Recognition by children of realistic figures in various orientations. *Canadian Journal of Psychology*, **14**, 249–256.

Ghent, L. (1961). Form and its orientations: a child's eye view. *American Journal of Psychology*, **74**, 177–190.

Ghent, L. and Bernstein, L. (1961). Influence of the orientation of geometric forms on their recognition by children. *Perceptual and Motor Skills*, **12**, 95–101.

Ghiselli, E. E. (1964). *Theory of Psychological Measurement*, McGraw-Hill, New York.

Gilberstadt, H. and Duker, J. (1965). *A Handbook for Clinical and Actuarial MMPI Interpretations*, Saunders, Philadelphia.

Gibson, J. J. and Pick, A. D. (1963). Perception of another person's looking behavior. *American Journal of Psychology*, **76**, 386–394.

Girvin, R. E. (1947). Photography as social documentation. *Journalism Quarterly*, **24**, 207–220.

Goffman, E. (1956). *The Presentation of Self in Everyday Life*, Social Sciences Research Centre, Edinburgh.

Goldberg, S. C. (1954). Three situational determinants of conformity to social norms. *Journal of Abnormal and Social Psychology*, **49**, 325–329.

Goldman-Eisler, F. (1954). A study of individual differences and of interaction in the behaviour of some aspects of language in interviews. *Journal of Mental Science*, **100**, 177–197.

Goldstein, A. G. and Mackenberg, E. J. (1966). Recognition of human faces from isolated facial features: a developmental study. *Psychonomic Science*, **6**, 149–150.

Gollin, E. S. (1954). Forming impressions of personality. *Journal of Personality*, **23**, 65–76.

Gollin, E. S. (1958). Organizational characteristics of social judgment: a developmental investigation. *Journal of Personality*, **26**, 139–154.

Goodman, M. E. (1952). *Race Awareness in Young Children*, Addison-Wesley, Reading, Massachusetts.

Gordon, J. E. (1957). Interpersonal predictions of repressors and sensitizers. *Journal of Personality*, **25**, 686–698.

Gottheil, E. and Bitterman, M. E. (1951). The measurement of shape constancy. *American Journal of Psychology*, **64**, 406–408.

Gough, H. G. and Heilbrun, A. B. (1965). *The Adjective Check List Manual*, Consulting Psychologists Press, Palo Alto.

Gray, P. H. and Wheeler, G. E. (1967). The semantic differential as an instrument to examine the recent folksong movement. *Journal of Social Psychology*, **72**, 241–247.

Greenberg, B. S. and Tannenbaum, P. H. (1961). Effects of bylines on attitude change. *Journalism Quarterly*, **38**, 535–537.

Grigg, A. E. (1959). A validity study of the semantic differential technique. *Journal of Clinical Psychology*, **15**, 179–181.

Guetzkow, H. (Ed.) (1962). *Simulation in Social Science*, Prentice-Hall, Englewood Cliffs.

Guilford, J. P. (1965). *Fundamental Statistics in Psychology and Education*, 4th ed., McGraw-Hill, New York.

Gulliksen, H. (1956). Measurement of subjective values. *Psychometrika*, **21**, 229–244.

Gulliksen, H. (1958). How to make meaning more meaningful. *Contemporary Psychology*, **3**, 115–119.

Gunderson, E. K. E. and Nelson, P. D. (1963). Adaptation of small groups to extreme environments. *Aerospace Medicine*, **34**, 1111–1115.

Gyr, J. W., Brown, J. S., Willey, R. and Zivian, A. (1966). Computer simulation and psychological theories of perception. *Psychological Bulletin*, **65**, 174–192.

Haire, M. and Grunes, W. F. (1950). Perceptual defenses: processes protecting an organized perception of another personality. *Human Relations*, **3**, 403–412.

Hallworth, H. J. (1965). Dimensions of personality and meaning. *British Journal of Social and Clinical Psychology*, **4**, 161–168.

Hallworth, H. J. and Waite, G. (1965). A comparative study of value judgments among adolescent boys and girls. *Bulletin of the British Psychological Society*, **18**, 59, 3A.

o

Hamilton, V. (1960). Imperception of phi: some further determinants. *British Journal of Psychology*, **51**, 257–266.

Hammes, J. A. (1963). Judgment of emotional facial expressions as a function of manifest anxiety and sex. *Perceptual and Motor Skills*, **17**, 601–602.

Hammond, K. R. and Summers, D. A. (1965). Cognitive dependence on linear and non-linear cues. *Psychological Review*, **72**, 215–224.

Hammond, K. R., Hursch, C. J. and Todd, F. J. (1964). Analyzing the components of clinical inference. *Psychological Review*, **71**, 438–456.

Hammond, K. R., Wilkins, M. M. and Todd, F. J. (1966). A research paradigm for the study of interpersonal learning. *Psychological Bulletin*, **65**, 221–232.

Hanfmann, E. and Getzels, J. W. (1955). Interpersonal attitudes of former Soviet citizens as studied by a semi-projective method. *Psychological Monographs*, **69**, No. 4, Whole No. 389.

Harary, F., Norman, R. Z. and Cartwright, D. (1965). *Structural Models*, Wiley, New York.

Harrison, R. and Lubin, B. (1965). Personal style, group composition and learning. *Journal of Applied Behavioral Science*, **1**, 286–301.

Hartley, R. E. and Hardesty, F. P. (1964). Children's perceptions of sex roles in child-hood. *Journal of Genetic Psychology*, **105**, 43–51.

Hartshorne, H. and May, M. A. (1930). *Studies in the Nature of Character: III. Studies in the Organization of Character*, Macmillan, New York.

Harvey, O. J. (1962). Personality factors in resolution of conceptual incongruities. *Sociometry*, **25**, 336–352.

Harvey, O. J. (1967). Conceptual systems and attitude change. In C. W. Sherif and M. Sherif (Eds.), *Attitude, Ego-Involvement and Change*. Wiley, New York.

Harvey, O. J. and Beverly, G. D. (1961). Some personality correlates of concept change through role playing. *Journal of Abnormal and Social Psychology*, **63**, 125–130.

Harvey, O. J. and Clapp, W. F. (1965). Hope, expectancy and reactions to the unexpected. *Journal of Personality and Social Psychology*, **2**, 45–52.

Harvey, O. J. and Schroder, H. M. (1963). Cognitive aspects of self and motivation. In O. J. Harvey (Ed.), *Motivation and Social Interaction: Cognitive Determinants*. Ronald Press, New York.

Harvey, O. J., Hunt, D. E. and Schroder, H. M. (1961). *Conceptual Systems and Personality Organization*, Wiley, New York.

Harvey, O. J., Kelley, H. H. and Shapiro, M. M. (1957). Reactions to unfavorable evaluations of the self made by other persons. *Journal of Personality*, **25**, 398–411.

Haskins, J. B. (1958). Testing suitability of typefaces for editorial subject-matter. *Journalism Quarterly*, **35**, 186–194.

Hastorf, A. H. and Bender, I. E. (1952). A caution respecting the measurement of empathic ability. *Journal of Abnormal and Social Psychology*, **47**, 574–576.

Hastorf, A. H. and Myro, G. (1959). The effect of meaning on binocular rivalry. *American Journal of Psychology*, **72**, 393–400.

Hastorf, A. H., Bender, I. E. and Weintraub, D. J. (1955). The influence of response patterns on the "refined empathy score". *Journal of Abnormal and Social Psychology*, **51**, 341–343.

Hastorf, A. H., Richardson, S. A. and Dornbusch, S. M. (1958). The problem of relevance in the study of person perception. In R. Tagiuri and L. Petrullo (Eds.), *Person Perception and Interpersonal Behavior*. Stanford University Press, Stanford.

Hatch, R. S. (1962). *An Evaluation of a Forced Choice Differential Accuracy Approach to the Measurement of Supervisory Empathy*, Prentice-Hall, Englewood Cliffs.

Hays, W. L. (1958). An approach to the study of trait implication and trait similarity. In R. Tagiuri and L. Petrullo (Eds.), *Person Perception and Interpersonal Behavior*. Stanford University Press, Stanford.

Heider, F. (1944). Social perception and phenomenal causality. *Psychological Review*, 51, 358–374.

Heider, F. (1958). *The Psychology of Interpersonal Relations*, Wiley, New York.

Heider, F. (1967). On social cognition. *American Psychologist*, 22, 25–31.

Heider, F. and Simmel, M. (1944). An experimental study of apparent behavior. *American Journal of Psychology*, 57, 243–259.

Helper, M. M. and Garfield, S. L. (1965). Use of the semantic differential to study acculturation in American Indian adolescents. *Journal of Personality and Social Psychology*, 2, 817–822.

Helson, H. (1948). Adaptation level as a basis for a quantitative theory of frames of reference. *Psychological Review*, 55, 297–313.

Helson, H. (1959). Adaptation level theory. In Koch, D. (Ed.), *Psychology: A Study of a Science*, Vol. 1. McGraw-Hill, New York.

Helson, H. (1964). *Adaptation-level Theory*, Harper and Row, New York.

Henry, J. and Spiro, M. E. (1953). Psychological techniques: Projective tests in field work. In A. L. Kroeber (Ed.), *Anthropology Today*. University of Chicago Press, Chicago.

Hastorf, A. H. and Cantril, H. (1954). They saw a game. *Journal of Abnormal and Social Psychology*, 49, 129–134.

His Majesty's Stationery Office (1949). *Report of the Royal Commission on the Press 1947–1949*, H.M.S.O., London.

Hochberg, J. E. (1964). *Perception*, Prentice-Hall, Englewood Cliffs.

Hochberg, J. E. and McAlister, E. (1953). A quantitative approach to figural "goodness". *Journal of Experimental Psychology*, 46, 361–364.

Hoffman, P. J. (1960). The paramorphic representation of clinical judgment. *Psychological Bulletin*, 57, 116–131.

Holmes, D. and Berkowitz, L. (1961). Some contrast effects in social perception. *Journal of Abnormal and Social Psychology*, 62, 150–152.

Holt, R. (1958). Clinical and statistical prediction. *Journal of Abnormal and Social Psychology*, 56, 1–12.

Holway, A. H. and Boring, E. G. (1941). Determinants of apparent visual size with distance variant. *American Journal of Psychology*, 54, 21–37.

Homans, G. C. (1961). *Social Behavior: Its Elementary Forms*, New York. Harcourt, Brace and World.

Honkavaara, S. (1961). *The Psychology of Expression: Dimensions in Human Perception* (British Journal of Psychology Monograph Supplement No. 32), Cambridge University Press, Cambridge.

Horn, J. L. (1961). Significance tests for use with r_p and related profile statistics. *Educational and Psychological Measurement*, 21, 363–370.

Hoult, T. F. (1951). Clothing as a factor in the social status rating of men. Unpublished dissertation, University of Southern California.

Hovland, C. I. (Ed.) (1957). *The Order of Presentation in Persuasion*, Yale University Press, New Haven.

Hovland, C. I. (1958). The role of primacy and recency in persuasive communication. In E. E. Maccoby, T. M. Newcomb and E. L. Hartley (Eds.), *Readings in Social Psychology*, 3rd ed. Holt, New York.

Hovland, C. I. (1960). Computer simulation of thinking. *American Psychologist*, **15**, 687–693.

Hovland, C. I. and Hunt, E. B. (1960). The computer simulation of concept attainment. *Behavioral Science*, **5**, 265–267.

Hovland, C. I. and Pritzker, H. A. (1957). Extent of opinion change as a function of amount of change advocated. *Journal of Abnormal and Social Psychology*, **54**, 257–261.

Hovland, C. I. and Weiss, W. (1951). The influence of source credibility on communication effectiveness. *Public Opinion Quarterly*, **15**, 635–650.

Hovland, C. I., Janis, I. L. and Kelley, H. H. (1953). *Communication and Persuasion*, Yale University Press, New Haven.

Howe, E. S. (1962). Probabilistic adverbial qualifications of adjectives. *Journal of Verbal Learning and Verbal Behavior*, **1**, 225–242.

Howe, E. S. (1966). Verb tense, negatives, and other determinants of the intensity of evaluative meaning. *Journal of Verbal Learning and Verbal Behavior*, **5**, 147–155.

Hughes, G. E. and Londey, D. G. (1965). *The Elements of Formal Logic*, Methuen, London.

Hvistendahl, J. K. (1964). Reader estimates of reading time and attractiveness of type in six different forms. Communications Research Report No. 2. South Dakota State College, Brookings.

Hvistendahl, J. K. (1965). The effect of typographic variants on reader estimates of attractiveness and reading speed of magazine pages. Communications Research Report No. 3. South Dakota State College, Brookings.

Hunt, E. B. (1962). *Concept Formation: An Information Processing Problem*, Wiley, New York.

Hunton, V. D. (1955). The recognition of inverted pictures by children. *Journal of Genetic Psychology*, **86**, 281–288.

Icheiser, G. (1949). Misunderstandings in human relations. *American Journal of Sociology*, **55**, 2, Part 2.

Iliffe, A. H. (1960). A study of preferences in feminine beauty. *British Journal of Psychology*, **51**, 267–273.

Indow, T. and Kanazawa, K. (1960). Multidimensional mapping of Munsell colors varying in hue, chroma, and value. *Journal of Experimental Psychology*, **59**, 330–336.

Indow, T. and Shiose, T. (1956). An application of the method of multidimensional scaling to perception of similarity or difference in colors. *Japanese Psychological Research*, **3**, 45–64.

Insko, C. A., Murashima, F. and Saiyadain, M. (1966). Communicator discrepancy, stimulus ambiguity and influence. *Journal of Personality*, **34**, 262–274.

International Press Institute (1953). *The Flow of News*, I.P.I., Zurich.

Ittelson, W. H. (1960). *Visual Space Perception*, Springer, New York.

Ittelson, W. H. and Kutash, S. B. (Eds.) (1961). *Perceptual Changes in Psychopathology,* Rutgers University Press, New Brunswick.

Ittelson, W. H. and Slack, C. W. (1958). The perception of persons as visual objects. In R. Tagiuri and L. Petrullo (Eds.), *Person Perception and Interpersonal Behavior.* Stanford University Press, Stanford.

Iverson, M. A. and Reuder, M. E. (1965). Personality impressions of selfpunitive and extrapunitive stimulus persons. *Journal of Social Psychology,* **65,** 67–83.

Izard, C. E. (1959). Paranoid schizophrenic and normal subjects' perceptions of photographs of human faces. *Journal of Consulting Psychology,* **23,** 119–124.

Izard, C. E., Randall, D. H. and Cherry, E. S. (1963). The picture description test: a preliminary report. Office of Naval Research Technical Report.

Jackson, D. N. (1962). The measurement of perceived personality trait relationships. In N. F. Washburne (Ed.), *Decisions, Values and Groups,* Vol. 2. Pergamon Press, Oxford.

Jackson, D. N. and Messick, S. (1958). Content and style in personality assessment. *Psychological Bulletin,* **55,** 243–252.

Jackson, D. N. and Messick, S. (1963). Individual differences in social perception. *British Journal of Social and Clinical Psychology,* **2,** 1–10.

Jackson, D. N., Messick, S. J. and Solley, C. M. (1957). A multidimensional scaling approach to the perception of personality. *Journal of Psychology,* **44,** 311–318.

Jahoda, G. (1954). Political attitudes and judgments of other people. *Journal of Abnormal and Social Psychology,* **49,** 330–334.

Jahoda, G. (1959). Development of the perception of social differences in children from six to ten. *British Journal of Psychology,* **50,** 159–175.

Jahoda, G. (1966). Impressions of nationalities — An alternative to the "stereotype" approach. *British Journal of Social and Clinical Psychology,* **5,** 1–16.

Jansen, M. J. and Smolenaars, A. J. (1967). A short report on an interculturally standardized semantic differential. *Acta Psychologica,* **26,** 209–215.

Jaspars, J. M. F. (1963). Individual cognitive structures. Paper read at the 17th International Congress of Psychology, Washington.

Jenkin, N. (1958). Size constancy as a function of personal adjustment and disposition. *Journal of Abnormal and Social Psychology,* **57,** 334–338.

Jenkins, J. J., Russell, W. A. and Suci, G. J. (1958). An atlas of semantic profiles for 360 words. *American Journal of Psychology,* **71,** 688–699.

Jenness, A. (1932). The recognition of facial expressions of emotion. *Psychological Bulletin,* **29,** 324–350.

Johansson, G., Dureman, I. and Sälde, H. (1955). Motion perception and personality. *Acta Psychologica,* **11,** 289–296.

Johnson, D. M. (1963). Reanalysis of experimental halo effects. *Journal of Applied Psychology,* **47,** 46–47.

Johnson, P. E. (1959). *Psychology of Religion,* Abingdon Press, New York.

Johnson, W. (Ed.) (1944). Studies in language behavior. *Psychological Monographs,* **56,** No. 2, Whole No. 255.

Jones, E. E. (1954). Authoritarianism and first impressions. *Journal of Personality,* **23,** 106–127.

Jones, E. E. (1962). Some determinants of reactions to being approved or disapproved as a person. In S. Messick and J. Ross (Eds.), *Measurement in Personality and Cognition*. Wiley, New York.

Jones, E. E. and Daugherty, B. N. (1959). Political orientation and the perceptual effects of an anticipated interaction. *Journal of Abnormal and Social Psychology*, **59**, 340–349.

Jones, E. E. and Davis, K. E. (1965). From acts to dispositions: the attribution process in person perception. In L. Berkowitz (Ed.), *Advances in Experimental Social Psychology*, Vol. 2. Academic Press, New York.

Jones, E. E. and deCharms, R. (1957). Changes in social perception as a function of the personal relevance of behavior. *Sociometry*, **20**, 75–85.

Jones, E. E. and Thibaut, J. W. (1958). Interaction goals as bases of inference in interpersonal perception. In R. Tagiuri and L. Petrullo (Eds.), *Person Perception and Interpersonal Behavior*. Stanford University Press, Stanford.

Jones, E. E., Davis, K. E. and Gergen, K. J. (1961). Role playing variations and their informational value for person perception. *Journal of Abnormal and Social Psychology*, **63**, 302–310.

Jones, E. E., Hester, S. L., Farina, A. and Davis, K. E. (1959). Reactions to unfavorable personal evaluations as a function of the evaluator's perceived adjustment. *Journal of Abnormal and Social Psychology*, **59**, 363–370.

Kagan, J. (1956). The child's perception of the parent. *Journal of Abnormal and Social Psychology*, **53**, 257–258.

Kanner, L. (1931). Judging emotions from facial expressions. *Psychological Monographs*, **41**, No. 3, Whole No. 186.

Katz, D. and Braly, K. W. (1935). Racial prejudice and racial stereotypes. *Journal of Abnormal and Social Psychology*, **30**, 175–193.

Kayser, J. (1953). *One Week's News: Comparative Study of 17 Major Dailies for a Seven-day Period*, U.N.E.S.C.O., Paris.

Kelley, H. H. (1950). The warm–cold variable in first impressions of persons. *Journal of Personality*, **18**, 431–439.

Kelly, G. A. (1955). *The Psychology of Personal Constructs*, Norton, New York.

Kelly, W. F. (1963). Effectiveness of news photographs in attitude formation. Unpublished dissertation, University of California, Los Angeles.

Kelly, J. A. and Levy, L. H. (1961). The discriminability of concepts differentiated by means of the semantic differential. *Educational and Psychological Measurement*, **21**, 53–58.

Kelman, H. C. and Eagly, A. H. (1965). Attitude toward the communicator, perception of communication content, and attitude change. *Journal of Personality and Social Psychology*, **1**, 63–78.

Kelman, H. C. and Hovland, C. I. (1953). "Reinstatement" of the communicator in delayed measurement of opinion change. *Journal of Abnormal and Social Psychology*, **48**, 327–335.

Kendon, A. (1966). Gaze direction as a signal in social performance. *Bulletin of the British Psychological Society*, **18**, No. 59, 12A.

Kennedy, J. L., Koslin, B. L., Schroder, H. M., Blackman, S., Ramsey, J. O. and Helm, C. E. (1966). Cognitive patterning of complex stimuli: a symposium. *Journal of General Psychology*, **74**, 25–49.

Kidd, J. W. (1951). An analysis of social rejection in a college men's residence hall. *Sociometry*, **14**, 225–234.

Kieferle, D. A. and Sechrest, L. (1961). Effects of alterations in personal constructs. *Journal of Psychological Studies*, **12**, 173–178.

Kilpatrick, F. P. and Cantril, H. (1961). The constancies in social perception. In F. P. Kilpatrick (Ed.), *Explorations in Transactional Psychology*. New York University Press, New York.

Kingsbury, S. M., Hart, H. and Associates. (1934). Measuring the ethics of American newspapers: IV. The headline index of newspaper bias. *Journalism Quarterly*, **11**, 179–199.

Kjeldergaard, P. M. and Jenkins, J. J. (1958). Personality ratings as influenced by verbal stimuli — some negative findings. *Journal of Personality*, **26**, 51–60.

Klapper, J. T. (1960). *The Effects of Mass Communication*, The Free Press, Glencoe.

Klausner, S. J. (1953). Social class and self-concept. *Journal of Social Psychology*, **38**, 201–205.

Klein, G. S. (1951). The personal world through perception. In R. R. Blake and G. V. Ramsey (Eds.), *Perception: An Approach to Personality*. Ronald Press, New York.

Kluckholm, C. (1954). Culture and behavior. In G. Lindzey (Ed.), *Handbook of Social Psychology*. Addison-Wesley, Reading, Massachusetts.

Knapp, R. H. and Ehlinger, H. (1966). Sex differences in the incidence of responses to the dyadic silhouette test. *Journal of Social Psychology*, **68**, 57–63.

Knapper, C. and Warr, P. B. (1965). The effect of position and layout on the readership of news items. *Gazette*, **11**, 323–328.

Koffka, K. (1935). *Principles of Gestalt Psychology*, Harcourt Brace, New York.

Kogan, N. and Shelton, F. C. (1960). Differential cue value of age and occupation in impression formation. *Psychological Reports*, **7**, 203–216.

Kogan, N., Stevens, J. W. and Shelton, F. C. (1961). Age differences: a developmental study of discriminability and affective response. *Journal of Abnormal and Social Psychology*, **62**, 221–230.

Kohn, A. R. and Fiedler, F. E. (1961). Age and sex differences in the perception of persons. *Sociometry*, **24**, 157–164.

Koltuv, B. B. (1962). Some characteristics of intrajudge trait intercorrelations. *Psychological Monographs*, **76**, No. 33, Whole No. 552.

Komorita, S. S. and Bass, A. R. (1967). Attitude differentiation and evaluative scales of the semantic differential. *Journal of Personality and Social Psychology*, **6**, 241–244.

Korchin, S. J. and Basowitz, H. (1956). The judgment of ambiguous stimuli as an index of cognitive functioning in aging. *Journal of Personality*, **25**, 81–95.

Koslin, B. L., Stoops, J. W. and Loh, W. D. (1967). Source characteristics and communication discrepancy as determinants of attitude change and conformity. *Journal of Experimental Social Psychology*, **3**, 230–242.

Kramer, E. (1963). Judgments of personal characteristics and emotions from nonverbal properties of speech. *Psychological Bulletin*, **60**, 408–420.

Kramer, E. (1964). Personality stereotypes in voice: a reconsideration of the data. *Journal of Social Psychology*, **62**, 247–251.

Krech, D., Crutchfield, R. S. and Ballachey, E. L. (1962). *Individual in Society*, McGraw-Hill, New York.

Kremenak, M. (1950). Der Eindruckswert der Augengegend auf Grund schematischer Darstellungen. Unpublished dissertation, University of Vienna.

Kretschmer, E. (1936). *Physique and Character*, 2nd ed., Kegan Paul, Trench, Trubner, London.

Krieger, M. H. (1964). A control for social desirability in a semantic differential. *British Journal of Social and Clinical Psychology*, **3**, 94–103.

Kruskal, J. B. (1964a). Multidimensional scaling by optimizing goodness of fit to a nonmetric hypothesis. *Psychometrika*, **28**, 1–27.

Kruskal, J. B. (1964b). Nonmetric multidimensional scaling: a numerical method. *Psychometrika*, **29**, 115–129.

Kuhlen, R. G. (1964). Personality change with age. In P. Worchel and D. Byrne (Eds.), *Personality Change*. Wiley, New York.

Künnapas, T. (1966). Visual perception of capital letters. *Scandinavian Journal of Psychology*, **7**, 189–196.

Lambert, W. E. and Klineberg, O. (1967). *Children's Views of Foreign Peoples: A Cross-national Study*, Appleton-Century-Crofts, New York.

Lambert, W. E. and Taguchi, Y. (1956). Ethnic cleavage among young children. *Journal of Abnormal and Social Psychology*, **53**, 380–382.

Lambert, W. E., Anisfeld, M. and Yeni-Komshian, G. (1965). Evaluational reactions of Jewish and Arab adolescents to dialect and language variations. *Journal of Personality and Social Psychology*, **2**, 84–90.

Lambert, W. E., Hodgson, R. C., Gardner, R. C. and Fillenbaum, S. (1960). Evaluational reactions to spoken languages. *Journal of Abnormal and Social Psychology*, **60**, 44–51.

Lambert, W. W. and Lambert, W. E. (1964). *Social Psychology*, Prentice-Hall, Englewood Cliffs.

Landis, C. (1929). The interpretation of facial expression in emotion. *Journal of General Psychology*, **2**, 59–72.

Lang, K. and Lang, G. E. (1960). The unique perspective of television and its effect. In W. Schramm (Ed.), *Mass Communications*. University of Illinois Press, Urbana.

Langfeld, H. S. (1918). The judgment of emotions from facial expressions. *Journal of Abnormal and Social Psychology*, **13**, 172–184.

Lawlor, M. (1955). Cultural influences on preference for designs. *Journal of Abnormal and Social Psychology*, **61**, 690–692.

Lazarus, R. S., Erikson, C. W. and Fonda, C. P. (1951). Personality dynamics and auditory perceptual recognition. *Journal of Personality*, **19**, 471–482.

Leary, T. (1957). *Interpersonal Diagnosis of Personality*, Ronald Press, New York.

Lee, J. C. and Tucker, R. B. (1962). An investigation of clinical judgment: a study in method. *Journal of Abnormal and Social Psychology*, **64**, 272–280.

Lefkowitz, M., Blake, R. R. and Mouton, J. S. (1955). Status factors in pedestrian violation of traffic signals. *Journal of Abnormal and Social Psychology*, **51**, 704–706.

Leibowitz, H. and Bourne, L. E. (1956). Time and intensity as determiners of perceived shape. *Journal of Experimental Psychology*, **51**, 277–281.

Leibowitz, H., Waskow, I., Leoffler, N. and Glaser F. (1959). Intelligence level as a variable in the perception of shape. *Quarterly Journal of Experimental Psychology*, **11**, 108–113.

Leventhal, H. (1957). Cognitive processes and interpersonal prediction. *Journal of Abnormal and Social Psychology*, **55**, 176–180.

Leventhal, H. (1962). The effects of set and discrepancy on impression change. *Journal of Personality*, **30**, 1–15.

Leventhal, H. and Sharp, E. (1965). Facial expressions as indicators of distress. In S. S. Tomkins and C. E. Izard (Eds.), *Affect, Cognition and Personality*. Springer, New York.

Leventhal, H. and Singer, D. L. (1964). Cognitive complexity, impression formation and impression change. *Journal of Personality*, **32**, 210–226.

Leventhal, H., Jacobs, R. L. and Kudirka, N. Z. (1964). Authoritarianism, ideology and political candidate choice. *Journal of Abnormal and Social Psychology*, **69**, 539–549.

Levy, L. H. (1960). Context effects in social perception. *Journal of Abnormal and Social Psychology*, **61**, 295–297.

Levy, L. H. (1961). Adaptation, anchoring and dissipation in social perception. *Journal of Personality*, **29**, 94–104.

Levy, L. H. and Dugan, R. D. (1960). A constant error approach to the study of dimensions of social perception. *Journal of Abnormal and Social Psychology*, **61**, 21–24.

Levy, L. H. and Richter, M. L. (1963). Impressions of groups as a function of the stimulus values of individual members. *Journal of Abnormal and Social Psychology*, **67**, 349–354.

Levy, N. and Schlosberg, H. (1960). Woodworth scale values of the Lightfoot pictures of facial expression. *Journal of Experimental Psychology*, **60**, 121–125.

Lewis, L. S. (1964). Class and the perception of class. *Social Forces*, **42**, 336–340.

Liebling, A. J. (1961). *The Press*, Ballantine Books, New York.

Light, C. S., Zax, M. and Gardiner, D. H. (1965). Relationship of age, sex, and intelligence level to extreme response style. *Journal of Personality and Social Psychology*, **2**, 907–909.

Lindzey, G. and Rogolsky, S. (1950). Prejudice and identification of minority group membership. *Journal of Abnormal and Social Psychology*, **45**, 37–53.

Lipetz, M. E. (1960). Effects of information on the assessment of attitudes by authoritarians and nonauthoritarians. *Journal of Abnormal and Social Psychology*, **60**, 95–99.

Lipetz, M. E. and Ossorio, P. G. (1967). Authoritarianism, aggression and status. *Journal of Personality and Social Psychology*, **5**, 468–472.

Loeb, A., Feshbach, S., Beck, A. T. and Wolf, A. (1964). Some effects of reward upon the social perception and motivation of psychiatric patients varying in depression. *Journal of Abnormal and Social Psychology*, **68**, 609–616.

Lombroso, C. and Ferrero, G. (1896). *La Femme Criminelle et la Prostituée*. Germer Baillière, Paris.

Long, B. H. (1965). Catholic-Protestant differences in acceptance of others. *Sociology and Social Research*, **49**, 166–172.

Lord, F. M. (1953). On the statistical treatment of football numbers. *American Psychologist*, **8**, 750–751.

Lott, A. J. and Lott, B. E. (1965). Group cohesiveness as interpersonal attraction. *Psychological Bulletin*, **64**, 259–309.

Lucas, D. B. and Britt, S. H. (1950). *Advertising Psychology and Research*, McGraw-Hill, New York.

Luchins, A. S. (1948). Forming impressions of personality: A critique. *Journal of Abnormal and Social Psychology*, **43**, 318–325.

Luchins, A. S. (1957). Chapters 4 and 5 in C. I. Hovland (Ed.), *The Order of Presentation in Persuasion*. Yale University Press, New Haven.

Luchins, A. S. (1958). Definitiveness of impression and primacy-recency in communications. *Journal of Social Psychology*, **48**, 275–290.

Luchins, A. S. and Luchins, E. H. (1965). Anchorage and ordering effects of information on personality impression. *Journal of Social Psychology*, **66**, 1–14.

Luft, J. (1950). Implicit hypotheses and clinical prediction. *Journal of Abnormal and Social Psychology*, **45**, 756–759.

Lund, F. H. (1925). The psychology of belief. IV: The law of primacy in persuasion. *Journal of Abnormal and Social Psychology*, **20**, 183–191.

Lundy, R. M. (1956). Assimilative projection and accuracy of prediction in interpersonal perceptions. *Journal of Abnormal and Social Psychology*, **52**, 33–38.

Lyle, J. (1960). Semantic differential scales for newspaper research. *Journalism Quarterly*, **37**, 559–562.

McCollough, C. (1961). Forming and acting on impressions. *Journal of Psychology*, **52**, 63–75.

McClelland, D. C. (1961). *The Achieving Society*, Van Nostrand, Princeton.

McClelland, D. C., Atkinson, J. W., Clark, R. A. and Lowell, E. L. (1953). *The Achievement Motive*, Appleton-Century-Crofts, New York.

McDonald, R. L. and Gynther, M. D. (1965). Relationship of self and ideal-self descriptions with sex, race, and class in Southern adolescents. *Journal of Personality and Social Psychology*, **1**, 85–88.

McGrath, J. E. (1962). Value-orientations, personal adjustment, and social behavior of members of three American religious groups. Technical Report No. 15. University of Illinois Group Effectiveness Research Laboratory, Urbana.

McGrath, J. and McGrath, M. (1962). Effects of partisanship on perceptions of political figures. *Public Opinion Quarterly*, **26**, 236–248.

McHugh, R. B. (1963). Comment on "Scales and statistics: parametric and nonparametric". *Psychological Bulletin*, **60**, 350–355.

McKeachie, W. J. (1952). Lipstick as a determiner of first impressions of personality. *Journal of Social Psychology*, **36**, 241–244.

McKellar, P. (1963). Three aspects of the psychology of originality in human thinking. *British Journal of Aesthetics*, **3**, 129–147.

Maclay, H. and Ware, E. E. (1961). Cross-cultural use of the semantic differential. *Behavioral Science*, **6**, 185–190.

McLean, M. S. and Hazard, W. R. (1953). Women's interest in pictures: the Badger village study. *Journalism Quarterly*, **30**, 139–162.

Mahrer, A. R. and Young, H. H. (1961). The combination of psychodiagnostic cues. *Journal of Personality*, **29**, 428–448.

Malinowski, B. (1923–24a). The psychology of sex and the foundations of kinship in primitive societies. *Psyche*, **4**, 98–129.

Malinowski, B. (1923–24b). Psychoanalysis and anthropology. *Psyche*, **4**, 293–333.

Maltz, H. E. (1963). Ontogenetic change in the meaning of concepts as measured by the semantic differential. *Child Development*, **34**, 667–674.

Manis, M. (1961). The interpretation of opinion statements as a function of recipient attitude and source prestige. *Journal of Abnormal and Social Psychology*, **63**, 82–86.

Manis, M. (1967). Context effects in communication. *Journal of Personality and Social Psychology*, **5**, 326–334.

Mann, R. D. (1959). A review of the relationships between personality and performance in small groups. *Psychological Bulletin*, **56**, 241–270.

Marks, I. M. (1965). *Patterns of Meaning in Psychiatric Patients* (Maudsley Monograph No. 13), Oxford University Press, Oxford.

Marks, I. M. (1966). Semantic differential uses in psychiatric patients. *British Journal of Psychiatry*, **112**, 945–951.

Martin, J. G. (1964). Racial ethnocentrism and judgment of beauty. *Journal of Social Psychology*, **63**, 59–63.

Martin, R. O. (1963). The nonverbal language of typographic layout: an experimental study of consumer preferences for various arrangements of type and abstract elements in typographic layouts. Unpublished dissertation, Syracuse University.

Maslow, A. H. and Mintz, M. L. (1956). Effects of esthetic surroundings: 1. Initial short-term effects of three esthetic conditions upon perceiving "energy" and "well-being" in faces. *Journal of Psychology*, **41**, 247–254.

Maurer, L. L. (1963). The effects of verb voice on connotative meaning and retention of material presented in four newspaper articles. Unpublished dissertation, University of Wisconsin.

Mausner, B. and Bloch, B. L. (1957). A study of the additivity of variables affecting social interaction. *Journal of Abnormal and Social Psychology*, **54**, 250–256.

Mayo, C. W. and Crockett, W. H. (1964). Cognitive complexity and primacy-recency effects in impression formation. *Journal of Abnormal and Social Psychology*, **68**, 335–338.

Meehl, P. E. (1954). *Clinical Versus Statistical Prediction: A Theoretical Analysis and Review of the Evidence*, University of Minnesota Press, Minneapolis.

Meehl, P. E. (1959). A comparison of clinicians with five statistical methods of identifying psychotic MMPI profiles. *Journal of Counselling Psychology*, **6**, 102–109.

Meehl, P. E. (1960). The cognitive activity of the clinician. *American Psychologist*, **15**, 19–27.

Meehl, P. E. and Dahlstrom, W. G. (1960). Objective configural rules for discriminating psychotic from neurotic MMPI profiles. *Journal of Consulting Psychology*, **24**, 375–387.

Mehling, R. (1959). Attitude changing effect of news and photo combinations. *Journalism Quarterly*, **36**, 189–198.

Meltzer, B., Crockett, W. H. and Rosenkrantz, P. S. (1966). Cognitive complexity, value congruity and the integration of potentially incompatible information in impressions of others. *Journal of Personality and Social Psychology*, **4**, 338–343.

Mensh, I. N. and Wishner, J. (1947). Asch on "Forming impressions of personality": Further evidence. *Journal of Personality*, **16**, 188–191.

Messick, S. J. (1956a). Some recent theoretical developments in multidimensional scaling. *Educational and Psychological Measurement*, **16**, 82–100.

Messick, S. J. (1956b). The perception of social attitudes. *Journal of Abnormal and Social Psychology*, **52**, 57–66.

Messick, S. J. (1957). Metric properties of the semantic differential. *Educational and Psychological Measurement*, **17**, 200–206.

Messick, S. J. (1961). The perceived structure of political relationships. *Sociometry*, **24**, 270–278.

Messick, S. J. and Abelson, R. P. (1956). The additive constant problem in multi-dimensional scaling. *Psychometrika*, **21**, 1–15.

Messick, S. and Kogan, N. (1966). Personality consistencies in judgment: dimensions of role constructs. *Multivariate Behavioral Research*, **1**, 165–175.

Messick, S. J. and Tomkins, S. S. (Eds.) (1963). *Computer Simulation of Personality*, Wiley, New York.

Miller, G. A. (1951). *Language and Communication*, McGraw-Hill, New York.

Miller, R. E., Banks, J. H. and Ogawa, N. (1962). Communication of affect in "co-operative conditioning" of rhesus monkeys. *Journal of Abnormal and Social Psychology*, **64**, 343–348.

Miller, R. E., Banks, J. H. and Ogawa, N. (1963). Role of facial expression in "co-operative avoidance conditioning" in monkeys. *Journal of Abnormal and Social Psychology*, **67**, 24–30.

Miller, G. A., Bruner, J. S. and Postman, L. (1954). Familiarity of letter sequences and tachistoscopic identification. *Journal of General Psychology*, **50**, 129–139.

Miron, M. S. (1961a). The influence of instruction modification upon test-retest reliabilities of the semantic differential. *Educational and Psychological Measurement*, **21**, 883–893.

Miron, M. S. (1961b). A cross-linguistic investigation of phonetic symbolism. *Journal of Abnormal and Social Psychology*, **62**, 623–630.

Miron, M. S. and Osgood, C. E. (1966). Language behavior: the multivariate structure of qualification. In R. B. Cattell (Ed.), *Handbook of Multivariate Experimental Psychology*. Rand McNally, Chicago.

Mitchell, R. A. (1965). The 1964 general election, cognitive dissonance and the semantic differential. Unpublished dissertation, University of Sheffield.

Mitsos, S. B. (1961). Personal constructs and the semantic differential. *Journal of Abnormal and Social Psychology*, **62**, 433–434.

Mogar, R. E. (1960). Three versions of the F-scale and performance on the semantic differential. *Journal of Abnormal and Social Psychology*, **60**, 262–265.

Moore, M. (1966). Aggression themes in a binocular rivalry situation. *Journal of Personality and Social Psychology*, **3**, 685–688.

Moore, O. K. (1958). Problem solving and the perception of persons. In R. Tagiuri and L. Petrullo (Eds.), *Person Perception and Interpersonal Behavior*. Stanford University Press, Stanford.

Moreno, J. L. (Ed.) (1960). *The Sociometry Reader*, The Free Press, New York.

Morland, J. K. (1958). Racial recognition by nursery school children in Lynchburg, Virginia. *Social Forces*, **37**, 132–137.

Mourant, J. A. (1963). *Formal Logic*, Macmillan, New York.

Mueller, W. J. (1966). Need structure and the projection of traits onto parents. *Journal of Personality and Social Psychology*, **3**, 63–72.

Munn, N. L. (1940). The effect of knowledge of the situation upon judgment of emotion from facial expressions. *Journal of Abnormal and Social Psychology*, **35**, 324–338.

Munn, N. L. (1961). *Psychology: The Fundamentals of Human Adjustment*, Harrap, London.

Murphy, D. R. (1957). Page position and readership in a farm magazine. *Journalism Quarterly*, **34**, 499–500.

Murphy, D. R. (1962). *What Farmers Read and Like*, Iowa State University Press, Ames.

Murray, H. A. (1933). The effect of fear upon estimates of the maliciousness of other personalities. *Journal of Social Psychology*, **4**, 310–329.

Murstein, B. I. (1959). The concept of projection: a review. *Psychological Bulletin*, **56**, 353–371.

Murstein, B. I. (1961). The effect of amount of possession of the trait of hostility on accuracy of perception of hostility in others. *Journal of Abnormal and Social Psychology*, **62**, 216–220.

Murstein, B. I. (1966). Possession of hostility and accuracy of perception of it in others: a cross-sex replication. *Journal of Projective Techniques*, **30**, 46–50.

Nagle, B. F. (1954). Productivity, employee attitude and supervisor sensitivity. *Personnel Psychology*, **7**, 219–233.

Natsoulas, T. (1965). Converging operations for perceptual defense. *Psychological Bulletin*, **64**, 393–401.

Nelson, T. M. and Bartley, S. H. (1956). The perception of form in an unstructured field. *Journal of General Psychology*, **54**, 57–63.

Neuringer, C. (1963). Effect of intellectual level and neuropsychiatric status on the diversity and intensity of semantic differential ratings. *Journal of Consulting Psychology*, **27**, 280.

Newcomb, T. M. (1931). An experiment designed to test the validity of a rating technique. *Journal of Educational Psychology*, **22**, 279–289.

Newcomb, T. M. (1958). The cognition of persons as cognizers. In R. Tagiuri and L. Petrullo (Eds.), *Person Perception and Interpersonal Behavior*. Stanford University Press, Stanford.

Newcomb, T. M. (1961). *The Acquaintance Process*, Holt, Rinehart and Winston, New York.

Newcomb, T. M. and Hartley, E. L. (1947). *Readings in Social Psychology*, Holt, New York.

Newcomb, T. M., Turner, R. H. and Converse, P. E. (1965). *Social Psychology: The Study of Human Interaction*, Holt, New York.

Nidorf, L. J. and Crockett, W. H. (1964). Some factors affecting the amount of information sought about others. *Journal of Abnormal and Social Psychology*, **69**, 98–101.

Nidorf, L. J. and Crockett, W. H. (1965a). Cognitive complexity and the integration of conflicting information in written impressions. *Journal of Social Psychology*, **66**, 165–169.

Nidorf, L. J. and Crockett, W. H. (1965b). Measuring the connotations of personality traits: a validation study. *Journal of Social Psychology*, **66**, 307–309.

Nielson, G. (1962). *Studies in Self-confrontation*, Monksgaard, Copenhagen.

Noble, C. E. (1952). An analysis of meaning. *Psychological Review*, **59**, 421–430.

Norman, W. T. (1959). Stability characteristics of the semantic differential. *American Journal of Psychology*, **72**, 581–584.

Norman, W. T. and Goldberg, L. R. (1966). Raters, ratees and randomness in personality structure. *Journal of Personality and Social Psychology*, **4**, 681–691.

Notcutt, B. and Silva, A. L. M. (1951). Knowledge of other people. *Journal of Abnormal and Social Psychology*, **46**, 30–37.

Nuckols, J. W. (1965). An analysis of the comparative reading times for 11-pica and 15-pica copy. Unpublished dissertation, South Dakota State University.

Osgood, C. E. (1952). The nature and measurement of meaning. *Psychological Bulletin*, **49**, 197–237.

Osgood, C. E. (1953). *Method and Theory in Experimental Psychology*, Oxford University Press, New York.

Osgood, C. E. (1962). Studies on the generality of affective meaning systems. *American Psychologist*, **17**, 10–28.

Osgood, C. E. and Luria, Z. (1954). A blind analysis of a case of multiple personality using the semantic differential. *Journal of Abnormal and Social Psychology*, **49**, 579–591.

Osgood, C. E. and Sebeok, T. A. (Eds.) (1965). *Psycholinguistics: a Survey of Theory and Research Problems*, Indiana University Press, Bloomington.

Osgood, C. E. and Stagner, R. (1941). Analysis of a prestige frame of reference by a gradient technique. *Journal of Applied Psychology*, **25**, 275–290.

Osgood, C. E. and Suci, G. J. (1952). A measure of relation determined by both mean difference and profile information. *Psychological Bulletin*, **49**, 251–262.

Osgood, C. E. and Tannenbaum, P. H. (1955). The principle of congruity in the prediction of attitude change. *Psychological Bulletin*, **62**, 42–55.

Osgood, C. E., Suci, G. J. and Tannenbaum, P. H. (1957). *The Measurement of Meaning*, University of Illinois Press, Urbana.

Paivio, A. (1965). Personality and audience influence. In B. A. Maher (Ed.), *Progress in Experimental Personality Research*, Vol. 2. Academic Press, New York.

Paivio, A. and Steeves, R. (1963). Personal values and selective perception of speech. *Perceptual and Motor Skills*, **17**, 459–464.

Passini, F. T. and Norman, W. T. (1966). A universal conception of personality structure? *Journal of Personality and Social Psychology*, **4**, 44–49.

Peak, H. (1958). Psychological structure and person perception. In R. Tagiuri and L. Petrullo (Eds.), *Person Perception and Interpersonal Behavior*. Stanford University Press, Stanford.

Parker, J. H. (1963). Influence of type of graph and other variables on the comprehension of trend information. Unpublished dissertation, University of Wisconsin.

Pastore, N. (1960). Attributed characteristics of liked and disliked persons. *Journal of Social Psychology*, **52**, 157–163.

Pederson, D. M. (1965). The measurement of individual differences in perceived personality-trait relationships and their relation to certain determinants. *Journal of Social Psychology*, **65**, 233–258.

Pepitone, A. (1950). Motivational effects in social perception. *Human Relations*, **3**, 57–76.

Pepitone, A. (1958). Attributions of causality, social attitudes and cognitive matching processes. In R. Tagiuri and L. Petrullo (Eds.), *Person Perception and Interpersonal Behavior*. Stanford University Press, Stanford.

Pepitone, A. (1964). *Attraction and Hostility*, Atherton Press, New York.

Pepitone, A. and Hayden, R. (1955). Some evidence for conflict resolution in impression formation. *Journal of Abnormal and Social Psychology*, **51**, 302–307.

Pepitone, A. and Sherberg, J. (1957). Cognitive factors in interpersonal attraction. *Journal of Personality*, **25**, 757–766.

Perlin, S. and Butler, R. N. (1963). Psychiatric aspects of adaptation to the aging experience. In J. E. Birren, R. N. Butler, S. W. Greenhouse, L. Sokoloff and M. R. Yarrow (Eds.), *Human Aging*. U.S. Department of Health, Education and Welfare, Washington.

Pettigrew, T. F., Allport, G. W. and Barnett, E. O. (1958). Binocular resolution and perception of race in South Africa. *British Journal of Psychology*, **49**, 265–278.

Phillipson, H. and Hopkins, J. (1964). Personality: an approach to the study of perception. *British Journal of Medical Psychology*, **37**, 1–15.

Piaget, J. (1929). *The Child's Conception of the World*, Harcourt Brace, New York.

Piaget, J. (1932). *The Moral Judgment of the Child*, Kegan Paul, Trench, Trubner, London.

Pintner, R. (1918). Intelligence as estimated from photographs. *Psychological Review*, **25**, 286–296.

Podell, H. A. and Podell, J. E. (1963). Quantitative connotations of a concept. *Journal of Abnormal and Social Psychology*, **67**, 509–513.

Podell, J. E. and Amster, H. (1966). Evaluative concept of a person as a function of the number of stimulus traits. *Journal of Personality and Social Psychology*, **4**, 333–336.

Postman, L. and Tolman, E. C. (1959). Brunswik's probabilistic functionalism. In S. Koch (Ed.), *Psychology: A Study of a Science*, Vol. 1. McGraw-Hill, New York.

Postman, L., Bruner, J. S. and McGinnies, E. (1948). Personal values as selective factors in perception. *Journal of Abnormal and Social Psychology*, **43**, 142–154.

Poulton, E. C. (1967). Searching for newspaper headlines printed in capitals or lower-case letters. *Journal of Applied Psychology*, **51**, 417–425.

Powers, S. P. (1962). The effect of three typesetting styles on the speed of reading newspaper content. Unpublished dissertation, University of Florida.

Proenza, L. and Strickland, B. R. (1965). A study of prejudice in Negro and white college students. *Journal of Social Psychology*, **67**, 273–281.

Quine, W. V. O. (1950). *Methods of Logic*, Henry Holt, New York.

Rabinowitz, W. (1956). A note on the social perception of authoritarians and non-authoritarians. *Journal of Abnormal and Social Psychology*, **53**, 384–386.

Rankin, R. E. and Campbell, D. T. (1955). Galvanic skin response to Negro and white experimenters. *Journal of Abnorma and Social Psychology*, **51**, 30–33.

Razran, G. H. S. (1938). Conditioning away social bias by the luncheon technique. *Psychological Bulletin*, **35**, 693.

Razran, G. (1950). Ethnic dislikes and stereotypes: a laboratory study. *Journal of Abnormal and Social Psychology*, **45**, 7–27.

Rees, L. and Eysenck, H. J. (1945). A factorial study of some morphological and psychological aspects of human constitution. *Journal of Mental Science*, **91**, 8–21.

Reichenbach, H. (1938). *Experience and Prediction*, University of Chicago Press, Chicago.

Restle, F. (1961). *Psychology of Judgment and Choice*, Wiley, New York.

Richey, M. H., McLelland, L. and Shimkunas, A. M. (1967). Relative influence of positive and negative information in impression formation and persistence. *Journal of Personality and Social Psychology*, **6**, 322–327.

Riessman, F. and Miller, S. M. (1958). Social class and projective tests. *Journal of Projective Techniques*, **22**, 432–439.

Rimoldi, H. J. A. (1956). Prediction of scale values for combined stimuli. *British Journal of Statistical Psychology*, **9**, 29–40.

Roberts, A. H. and Jessor, R. (1958). Authoritarianism, punitiveness and perceived social status. *Journal of Abnormal and Social Psychology*, **56**, 311–314.

Robinson, J. P. and Hefner, R. (1967). Multidimensional differences in public and academic perceptions of nations. *Journal of Personality and Social Psychology*, **7**, 251–259.

Robinson, M. P. (1965). The "lumen vitae" religious projective pictures, presented as a group test on lantern slides. In A. Godin (Ed.), *Child and Adult before God*. Loyola University Press, Chicago.

Rohracher, H. (1952). *Kleine Charakterkunde*, Urban and Schwarzenberg, Vienna.

Rokeach, M. (1960). *The Open and Closed Mind*, Basic Books, New York.

Rokeach, M. and Rothman, G. (1965). The principle of belief congruence and the congruity principle as models of cognitive interaction. *Psychological Review*, **72**, 128–142.

Rommetweit, R. (1960). *Selectivity, Intuition and Halo Effects in Social Perception*, Oslo University Press, Oslo.

Rorer, L. G. (1965). The great response-style myth. *Psychological Bulletin*, **63**, 125–156.

Rosenberg, M. J., Hovland, C. I., McGuire, W. J., Abelson, R. P. and Brehm, J. W. (1960). *Attitude Organization and Change*, Yale University Press, New Haven.

Rosenfeld, H. M. (1966). Instrumental affiliative functions of facial and gestural expressions. *Journal of Personality and Social Psychology*, **4**, 65–72.

Rosenkrantz, P. S. and Crockett, W. H. (1965). Some factors influencing the assimilation of disparate information in impression formation. *Journal of Personality and Social Psychology*, **2**, 397–402.

Rosenthal, R. (1963). On the social psychology of the psychological experiment: the experimenter's hypothesis as unintended determinant of experimental results. *American Scientist*, **51**, 268–283.

Rosenthal, R. (1964). The effect of the experimenter on the results of psychological research. In B. A. Maher (Ed.), *Progress in Experimental Personality Research*, Vol. 1. Academic Press, New York.

Ross, J. (1965). Change in the use of the semantic differential with a change in context. *Journal of Verbal Learning and Verbal Behavior*, **4**, 148–151.

Rudin, S. A. and Stagner, R. (1958). Figure-ground phenomena in the perception of physical and social stimuli. *Journal of Psychology*, **45**, 213–225.

Rugg, H. (1921). Is the rating of human character predictable? *Journal of Educational Psychology*, **12**, 425–438, 485–501.

Rugg, H. (1922). Is the rating of human character predictable? *Journal of Educational Psychology*, **13**, 30–42, 81–93.

Rule, B. G. (1966). Anti-Semitism, stress, and judgments of strangers. *Journal of Personality and Social Psychology*, **3**, 132–134.

Ruthenbeck, K. E. (1965). An inquiry into the acceptability of unjustified type composition and omission of column rules to newspaper readers. Unpublished dissertation, South Dakota State University.

Ryle, G. (1949). *The Concept of Mind*, Hutchinson, London.

Samuels, M. (1939). Judgments of faces. *Character and Personality*, **8**, 18–27.

Sappenfield, B. R. (1965). Test of a Szondi assumption by means of M-F photographs. *Journal of Personality*, **33**, 409–417.

Sarason, I. G. and Winkel, G. H. (1966). Individual differences among subjects and experimenters and subjects' self-descriptions. *Journal of Personality and Social Psychology*, **3**, 448–457.

Sarbin, T. (1954). Role theory. In G. Lindzey (Ed.), *Handbook of Social Psychology*. Addison-Wesley, Reading, Massachusetts.

Sarbin, T. R., Taft, R. and Bailey, D. E. (1960). *Clinical Inference and Cognitive Theory*, Holt, Rinehart and Winston, New York.

Sass, M. A. and Wilkinson, W. D. (Eds.) (1965). *Computer Augmentation of Human Reasoning*. Spartan Books, Washington.

Saugstad, P. (1966). Effect of food deprivation on perception-cognition. *Psychological Bulletin*, **65**, 80–90.

Schachter, S., Ellertson, N., McBride, D. and Gregory, D. (1951). An experimental study of cohesiveness and productivity. *Human Relations*, **4**, 229–238.

Schatzman, L. and Strauss, A. (1955). Social class and modes of communication. *American Journal of Sociology*, **60**, 329–338.

Schlosberg, H. (1954). Three dimensions of emotion. *Psychological Review*, **61**, 81–88.

Schroder, H. M., Driver, M. J. and Streufert, S. (1967). *Human Information Processing: Individuals and Groups Functioning in Complex Social Situations*, Holt, Rinehart and Winston, New York.

Schulberg, H. C. (1961). Authoritarianism, tendency to agree and interpersonal perception. *Journal of Abnormal and Social Psychology*, **63**, 101–108.

Scodel, A. and Austrin, H. (1957). The perception of Jewish photographs by non-Jews and Jews. *Journal of Abnormal and Social Psychology*, **54**, 278–280.

Scodel, A. and Friedman, M. (1956). Additional observations on the social perceptions of authoritarians and nonauthoritarians. *Journal of Abnormal and Social Psychology*, **52**, 92–95.

Scodel, A. and Mussen, P. (1953). Social perceptions of authoritarians and non-authoritarians. *Journal of Abnormal and Social Psychology*, **48**, 181–184.

Scott, W. A. (1962). Cognitive complexity and cognitive flexibility. *Sociometry*, **25**, 405–414.

Scott, W. A. (1963). Cognitive complexity and cognitive balance. *Sociometry*, **26**, 66–74.

Scott, W. A. (1965). Psychological and social correlates of international images. In H. C. Kelman (Ed.), *International Behavior: A Social-psychological Analysis*, Holt, Rinehart and Winston, New York.

Scott, W. A. (1966). Measures of cognitive complexity. *Multivariate Behavioral Research*, **1**, 391–395.

Schramm, W. (1959). *One Day in the World's Press: Fourteen Great Newspapers on a Day of Crisis*, Stanford University Press, Stanford.

Secord, P. F. (1958). Facial features and inference processes in interpersonal perception. In R. Tagiuri and L. Petrullo (Eds.), *Person Perception and Interpersonal Behavior*. Stanford University Press, Stanford.

Secord, P. F. and Backman, C. W. (1961). Personality theory and the problem of stability and change in individual behavior: an interpersonal approach. *Psychological Review*, **68**, 21–32.

Secord, P. F. and Backman, C. W. (1964a). *Social Psychology*. McGraw-Hill, New York.

Secord, P. F. and Backman, C. W. (1964b). Interpersonal congruency, perceived similarity and friendship. *Sociometry*, **27**, 115–127.

Secord, P. F. and Backman, C. W. (1965). An interpersonal approach to personality. In B. H. Maher (Ed.), *Progress in Experimental Personality Research*, Vol. 2. Academic Press, New York.

Secord, P. F. and Berscheid, E. S. (1963). Stereotyping and the generality of implicit personality theory. *Journal of Personality*, **31**, 65–78.

Secord, P. F. and Muthard, J. E. (1955). Personalities in faces: II. Individual differences in the perception of women's faces. *Journal of Abnormal and Social Psychology*, **50**, 238–242.

Secord, P. F., Backman, C. W. and Eachus, H. T. (1964). Effects of imbalance in the self-concept on the perception of persons. *Journal of Abnormal and Social Psychology*, **68**, 442–446.

Secord, P. F., Bevan, W. and Dukes, W. F. (1953). Occupational and physiognomic stereotypes in the perception of photographs. *Journal of Social Psychology*, **37** 261–270.

Secord, P. F., Bevan, W. and Katz, B. (1956). The Negro stereotype and perceptual accentuation. *Journal of Abnormal and Social Psychology*, **53**, 78–83.

Seeleman, V. (1940). The influence of attitude upon the remembering of pictorial material. *Archives of Psychology*, No. 258.

Segall, M. H., Campbell, D. T. and Herskovits, M. J. (1966). *The Influence of Culture on Visual Perception*, Bobbs-Merrill, Indianapolis.

Seiller-Tarbuk, L. (1951). Die Eindruckswirkung der Gesichts – und Hauptbehaarung. Unpublished dissertation, University of Vienna.

Sencer, R. A. (1965). An investigation of the effects of incorrect grammar on attitude and comprehension of written English messages. Unpublished dissertation, Michigan State University.

Shapiro, D. and Tagiuri, R. (1958). Some effects of response context on trait inferences. *Journal of Personality*, **26**, 42–50.

Shapiro, D. and Tagiuri, R. (1959). Sex differences in inferring personality traits. *Journal of Psychology*, **47**, 127–136.

Sheldon, W. H. (1940). *The Varieties of Human Physique*, Harper, New York.

Sherif, C. W., Sherif, M. and Nebergall, R. E. (1965). *Attitude and Attitude Change: The Social Judgment–Involvement Approach*, Saunders, Philadelphia.

Sherif, C. W. and Sherif, M. (Eds.) (1967). *Attitude, Ego-Involvement and Change*, Wiley, New York.

Sherif, M., Harvey, O. J., White, B. J., Hood, W. R. and Sherif, C. W. (1961). *Intergroup Conflict and Cooperation: The Robbers' Cave Experiment*, University of Oklahoma, Norman.

Sherif, M. and Hovland, C. I. (1961). *Social Judgment*, Yale University Press, New Haven.

Sherman, M. (1927a). The differentiation of emotional responses in infants. I. Judgments of emotional responses from motion picture views and from actual observation. *Journal of Comparative Psychology*, **7**, 265–284.

Sherman, M. (1927b). The differentiation of emotional responses in infants. II. The ability of observers to judge the emotional characteristics of the crying of infants and of the voice of an adult. *Journal of Comparative Psychology*, **7**, 335–351.

Sherrill, P. N. (1963). Effects of typeface suitability on message source recognition: an experiment in communication behavior. Unpublished dissertation, Stanford University.

Shock, N. W. (1963). *A Classified Bibliography of Gerontology and Geriatrics: Supplement Two 1956–1961*. Stanford University Press, Stanford.

Sheehan, M. R. (1938). A study of individual consistency in phenomenal constancy. *Archives of Psychology*, No. 222.

Shrauger, S. and Altrocchi, J. (1964). The personality of the perceiver as a factor in person perception. *Psychological Bulletin*, **62**, 289–308.

Siegel, S. (1956). *Nonparametric Statistics for the Behavioral Sciences*, McGraw-Hill, New York.

Signell, K. A. (1966). Cognitive complexity in person perception and nation perception: a developmental approach. *Journal of Personality*, **34**, 517–537.

Simon, W. B. (1963). Race relations and class structures. *Journal of Social Psychology*, **60**, 187–193.

Simons, H. W. (1966). Authoritarianism and social perceptiveness. *Journal of Social Psychology*, **68**, 291–297.

Smith, A. J., Jaffe, J. and Livingston, D. G. (1955). Consonance of interpersonal perception and individual effectiveness. *Human Relations*, **8**, 385–397.

Smith, H. C. (1966). *Sensitivity to People*, McGraw-Hill, New York.

Solley, C. M. and Murphy, G. (1960). *Development of the Perceptual World*, Basic Books, New York.

Sommer, R. (1965). Anchor-effects and the semantic differential. *American Journal of Psychology*, **78**, 317–318.

Spinks, G. S. (1963). *Psychology and Religion: An Introduction to Contemporary Views*, Methuen, London.

Spitz, R. A. and Wolf, K. M. (1946). The smiling response: a contribution to the ontogenesis of social relations. *Genetic Psychology Monographs*, **34**, 57–125.

Springer, D. V. (1950). Awareness of racial differences by pre-school children in Hawaii. *Genetic Psychology Monographs*, **41**, 215–270.

Stagner, R. and Osgood, C. E. (1941). An experimental analysis of a nationalistic frame of reference. *Journal of Social Psychology*, **14**, 389–401.

Stagner, R. and Osgood, C. E. (1946). Impact of war on a nationalistic frame of reference: I. Changes in general approval and qualitative patterning of certain stereotypes. *Journal of Social Psychology*, **24**, 187–215.

Steiner, I. D. (1954). Ethnocentrism and "tolerance of trait inconsistency". *Journal of Abnormal and Social Psychology*, **49**, 349–354.

Steiner, I. D. (1955). Interpersonal behavior as influenced by accuracy of social perception. *Psychological Review*, **62**, 268–274.

Steiner, I. D. (1959). Human interaction and interpersonal perception. *Sociometry*, **22**, 230–235.

Steiner, I. D. and Dodge, J. S. (1957). A comparison of two techniques employed in the study of interpersonal perception. *Sociometry*, **20**, 1–7.

Steiner, I. D. and Johnson, H. H. (1963). Authoritarianism and "tolerance of trait inconsistency". *Journal of Abnormal and Social Psychology*, **67**, 388–391.

Stephens, J. M. (1936). The perception of small differences as affected by self-interest. *American Journal of Psychology*, **58**, 480–484.

Stevenson, H. W. and Stewart, E. C. (1958). A developmental study of racial awareness in young children. *Child Development*, **29**, 399–409.

Stewart, R. H. (1965). Effect of continuous responding on the order effect in personality impression formation. *Journal of Personality and Social Psychology*, **1**, 161–165.

Stoltz, R. E. and Smith, M. D. (1959). Some effects of socioeconomic, age, and sex factors on children's responses to the Rosenzweig Picture-Frustration study. *Journal of Clinical Psychology*, **15**, 200–203.

Stone, G. P. (1959). Clothing and social relations: a study of appearance in the context of community life. Unpublished dissertation, University of Chicago.

Stricker, G. (1963). The use of the semantic differential to predict voting behavior. *Journal of Social Psychology*, **59**, 159–167.

Strickland, L. H. (1958). Surveillance and trust. *Journal of Personality*, **26**, 200–215.

Stritch, T. M. and Secord, P. F. (1956). Personality in faces: VI. Interaction effects in the perception of faces. *Journal of Personality*, **24**, 270–284.

Suci, G. J. (1960). A comparison of semantic structures in American Southwest culture groups. *Journal of Abnormal and Social Psychology*, **61**, 25–30.

Summers, D. A. and Hammond, K. R. (1966). Inference behavior in multiple-cue tasks involving both linear and nonlinear relations. *Journal of Experimental Psychology*, **71**, 751–757.

Szondi, L. (1952). *Experimental Diagnostics of Drives*, Grune and Stratton, New York.

Taft, R. (1955). The ability to judge people. *Psychological Bulletin*, **52**, 1–23.

Taft, R. (1960). Judgment and judging in person cognition. In H. P. David and J. C. Brengelmann (Eds.), *Perspectives in Personality Research*. Crosby Lockwood, London.

Tagiuri, R. (1958a). Introduction to R. Tagiuri and L. Petrullo (Eds.), *Person Perception and Interpersonal Behavior*. Stanford University Press, Stanford.

Tagiuri, R. (1958b). Social preference and its perception. In R. Tagiuri and L. Petrullo (Eds.), *Person Perception and Interpersonal Behavior*. Stanford University Press, Stanford.

Tagiuri, R. (1960). Movement as a cue in person perception. In H. P. David and J. C. Brengelmann (Eds.), *Perspectives in Personality Research*. Crosby Lockwood, London.

Tagiuri, R. (1968). Person perception. In G. Lindzey and E. Aronson (Eds.), *Handbook of Social Psychology*, 2nd ed. Addison-Wesley, Cambridge, Massachusetts.

Tagiuri, R. and Petrullo, L. (Eds.) (1958). *Person Perception and Interpersonal Behavior*, Stanford University Press, Stanford.

Tagiuri, R., Blake, R. R. and Bruner, J. S. (1953). Some determinants of the perception of positive and negative feelings in others. *Journal of Abnormal and Social Psychology*, **48**, 585–592.

Tagiuri, R., Bruner, J. S. and Blake, R. R. (1958). On the relation between feelings and perception of feelings among members of small groups. In E. E. Maccoby, T. M. Newcomb and E. L. Hartley (Eds.), *Readings in Social Psychology*, 3rd ed. Holt, New York.

Tajfel, H. (1967). Social and cultural factors in perception. In G. Lindzey and E. Aronson (Eds.), *Handbook of Social Psychology*, 2nd ed. Addison-Wesley, Cambridge, Massachusetts.

Tajfel, H. and Wilkes, A. L. (1964). Salience of attributes and commitment to extreme judgments in the perception of people. *British Journal of Social and Clinical Psychology*, **3**, 40–49.

Talbot, G. T. (1967). Cognitive style and interpersonal judgment: a comparison of two models. Unpublished dissertation, Princeton University.

Talland, G. A. (1959a). Age and the effect of anticipatory set on accuracy of perception. *Journal of Gerontology*, **14**, 202–207.

Talland, G. A. (1959b). Facilitation of accurate perception by anticipatory sets: the progressive effects of aging. *Gerontologia*, **3**, 339–350.

Talmadge, M. (1958). Expressive graphic movements and their relationship to temperament factors. *Psychological Monographs*, **72**, No. 16, Whole No. 469.

Tanaka, Y. (1962). A cross-cultural study of national stereotypes held by American and Japanese college graduate subjects. *Japanese Psychological Research*, **4**, 65–78.

Tanaka, Y. and Osgood, C. E. (1965). Cross-culture, cross-concept, and cross-subject generality of affective meaning systems. *Journal of Personality and Social Psychology*, 2, 143–153.

Tanaka, Y., Oyama, T. and Osgood, C. E. (1963). A cross-culture and cross-concept study of the generality of semantic spaces. *Journal of Verbal Learning and Verbal Behavior*, **2**, 392–405.

Tannenbaum, P. H. (1953). The effect of headlines on the interpretation of news stories. *Journalism Quarterly*, **30**, 189–197.

Tannenbaum, P. H. (1955). The indexing process in communication. *Public Opinion Quarterly*, **19**, 292–302.

Tannenbaum, P. H. (1956). Initial attitude towards source and concept as factors in attitude change through communication. *Public Opinion Quarterly*, **20**, 413–425.

Tannenbaum, P. H. and Fosdick, J. A. (1960). The effect of lighting angle on the judgment of photographed subjects. *Audio-Visual Communication Review*, **8**, 253–262.

Tannenbaum, P. H. and Gengel, R. W. (1966). Generalization of attitude change though congruity principle relationships. *Journal of Personality and Social Psychology*, **3**, 299–304.

Tannenbaum, P. H. and McLeod, J. M. (1963). Public images of mass media institutions. In *Paul J. Deutschmann Memorial Papers in Mass Communication Research.* Scripps-Howard Research, Cincinnati.

Tannenbaum, P. H., Jacobson, H. K. and Norris, E. L. (1964). An experimental investigation of typeface connotations. *Journalism Quarterly*, **41**, 65–73.

Tannenbaum, P. H., Macaulay, J. R. and Norris, E. L. (1966). Principle of congruity and reduction of persuasion. *Journal of Personality and Social Psychology*, **3**, 233–238.

Taylor, C. and Thompson, G. G. (1955). Age trends in preferences for certain facial proportions. *Child Development*, **26**, 97–102.

Terwilliger, R. F. (1962). Free association patterns as a factor relating to semantic differential responses. *Journal of Abnormal and Social Psychology*, **65**, 87–94.

Thomas, J. L. (1963). *Religion and the American People*, Newman Press, Westminster, Maryland.

Thibaut, J. W. and Kelley, H. H. (1959). *The Social Psychology of Groups*, Wiley, New York.

Thibaut, J. W. and Riecken, H. W. (1955). Some determinants and consequences of the perception of social causality. *Journal of Personality*, **24**, 113–133.

Thorndike, E. L. (1920). A constant error in psychological rating. *Journal of Applied Psychology*, **4**, 25–29.

Thorndike, E. L. (1948). The psychology of punctuation. *American Journal of Psychology*, **61**, 222–228.

Thornton, G. R. (1943). The effect upon judgments of personality traits of varying a single factor in a photograph. *Journal of Social Psychology*, **18**, 127–148.

Thornton, G. R. (1944). The effect of wearing glasses upon judgments of personality traits of persons seen briefly. *Journal of Applied Psychology*, **28**, 203–207.

Thorpe, J. S. and Swartz, J. D. (1965). Level of perceptual development as reflected in responses to the Holtzman inkblot technique. *Journal of Projective Techniques*, **29**, 380–386.

Thouless, R. H. (1931a). Phenomenal regression to the "real" object, Part 1. *British Journal of Psychology*, **21**, 339–359.

Thouless, R. H. (1931b). Phenomenal regression to the "real" object, Part 2. *British Journal of Psychology*, **22**, 1–30.

Thouless, R. H. (1932). Individual differences in phenomenal regression. *British Journal of Psychology*, **22**, 216–241.

Thouless, R. H. (1938). Factor analysis in problems of perception. In H. Piéron and I. Meyerson (Eds.), *Eleventh International Congress of Psychology*. Alcan, Paris.

Thurstone, L. L. (1944). *A Factorial Study of Perception*. University of Chicago Press, Chicago.

Tinbergen, N. (1951). *The Study of Instinct*, Clarendon Press, Oxford.

Tinker, M. A. and Paterson, D. G. (1942). Reader preferences and typography. *Journal of Applied Psychology*, **26**, 38–40.

Tinker, M. A. and Paterson, D. G. (1943). Differences among newspaper body types in readability. *Journalism Quarterly*, **20**, 152–155.

Todd, F. J. and Rappoport, L. (1964). A cognitive structure approach to person perception: a comparison of two models. *Journal of Abnormal and Social Psychology*, **68**, 469–478.

Tomkins, S. S. and McCarter, R. (1964). What and where are the primary affects? Some evidence for a theory. *Perceptual and Motor Skills*, **18**, 119–158.

Torgerson, W. S. (1952). Multidimensional scaling: I. Theory and method. *Psychometrika*, **17**, 401–419.

Torgerson, W. S. (1958). *Theory and Methods of Scaling*, Wiley, New York.

Triandis, H. C. (1959a). Categories of thought of managers, clerks and workers about jobs and people in industry. *Journal of Applied Psychology*, **43**, 338–344.

Triandis, H. C. (1959b). Cognitive similarity and interpersonal communication in industry. *Journal of Applied Psychology*, **43**, 321–326.

Triandis, H. C. (1960). A comparative factorial analysis of job semantic structures of managers and workers. *Journal of Applied Psychology*, **44**, 297–302.

Triandis, H. C. (1964a). Exploratory factor analyses of the behavioral component of social attitudes. *Journal of Abnormal and Social Psychology*, **68**, 420–430.

Triandis, H. C. (1964b). Cultural influences upon cognitive processes. In L. Berkowitz (Ed.), *Advances in Experimental Social Psychology*, Vol. 1. Academic Press, New York.

Triandis, H. C. and Davis, E. E. (1965). Race and belief as determinants of behavioral intentions. *Journal of Personality and Social Psychology*, **2**, 715–725.

Triandis, H. C. and Fishbein, M. (1963). Cognitive interaction in person perception. *Journal of Abnormal and Social Psychology*, **67**, 446–453.

Triandis, H. C. and Lambert, W. W. (1958). A restatement and test of Schlosberg's theory of emotion with two kinds of subjects from Greece. *Journal of Abnormal and Social Psychology*, **56**, 321–328.

Triandis, H. C. and Osgood, C. E. (1958). A comparative factorial analysis of semantic structures in monolingual Greek and American college students. *Journal of Abnormal and Social Psychology*, **57**, 187–196.

Triandis, H. C. and Triandis, L. M. (1960). Race, social class, religion, and nationality as determinants of social distance. *Journal of Abnormal and Social Psychology*, **61**, 110–118.

Triandis, H. C., Loh, W. D. and Levin, L. A. (1966). Race, status, quality of spoken English, and opinions about civil rights as determinants of interpersonal attitudes. *Journal of Personality and Social Psychology*, **3**, 468–472.

Tripodi, T. and Bieri, J. (1963). Cognitive complexity as a function of own and provided constructs. *Psychological Reports*, **13**, 26.

Tukey, J. W. (1950). Discussion of the symposium: statistics for the clinician. *Journal of Clinical Psychology*, **6**, 61–74.

Ulrich, L. and Trumbo, D. (1965). The selection interview since 1949. *Psychological Bulletin*, **63**, 100–116.

Underwood, B. J. and Schulz, R. W. (1960). *Meaningfulness and Verbal Learning*, Lippincott, Chicago.

Uhr, L. (1959). Some further effects of response context on trait inferences. *Journal of Psychology*, **48**, 79–85.

Uhr, L. (Ed.) (1966). *Pattern Recognition*, Wiley, New York.

U.N.E.S.C.O. (1964). *World Communications: Press, Radio, Television, Film,* U.N.E.S.C.O., Paris.

Vannoy, J. S. (1965). Generality of cognitive complexity-simplicity as a personality construct. *Journal of Personality and Social Psychology,* **2,** 385–396.

Veness, T. and Brierley, D. W. (1963). Forming impressions of personality: two experiments. *British Journal of Social and Clinical Psychology,* **2,** 11–19.

Vernon, M. D. (1961). The relation of perception to personality factors. *British Journal of Psychology,* **52,** 205–217.

Vernon, M. D. (1962). *The Psychology of Perception,* Penguin Books, Harmondsworth, England.

Vernon, P. E. (1936). The matching method applied to investigations of personality. *Psychological Bulletin,* **33,** 149–177.

Vernon, P. E. (1964). *Personality Assessment: A Critical Survey,* Methuen, London.

Vidulich, R. N. and Krevanick, F. W. (1966). Racial attitudes and emotional response to visual representations of the Negro. *Journal of Social Psychology,* **68,** 85–93.

Vinacke, W. E. (1949). The judgment of facial expressions by three national-racial groups in Hawaii: I. Caucasian faces. *Journal of Personality,* **17,** 407–429.

Viteles, M. S. and Smith, K. R. (1932). The prediction of vocational aptitude and success from photographs. *Journal of Experimental Psychology,* **15,** 615–629.

Wallace, A. F. C. (1962). Culture and cognition. *Science,* **135,** 351–357.

Wallace, R. P. (1941). Apparent personality traits from photographs varied in bodily proportions. *Psychological Bulletin,* **38,** 744–745.

Wallach, M. A. and Kogan, N. (1959). Sex differences in judgment processes. *Journal of Personality,* **27,** 555–564.

Wallach, M. A. and Ruthellen, C. G. (1960). Personality functions of graphic constriction and expansiveness. *Journal of Personality,* **28,** 73–88.

Walster, E. and Prestholdt, P. (1966). The effect of misjudging another: overcompensation or dissonance reduction? *Journal of Experimental Social Psychology,* **2,** 85–97.

Walster, E., Walster, B., Abrahams, D. and Brown, Z. (1966). The effect on liking of underrating or overrating another. *Journal of Experimental Social Psychology,* **2,** 70–84.

Walters, H. and Jackson, D. N. (1966). Group and individual regularities in trait inference: a multidimensional scaling analysis. *Multivariate Behavioral Research,* **1,** 145–163.

Ware, E. E. (1958). Relationships of intelligence and sex to diversity of individual semantic meaning spaces. Unpublished dissertation, University of Illinois.

Ware, R. and Harvey, O. J. (1967). A cognitive determinant of impression formation. *Journal of Personality and Social Psychology,* **5,** 38–44.

Warr, P. B. (1965). Proximity as a determinant of positive and negative sociometric choice. *British Journal of Social and Clinical Psychology,* **4,** 104–109.

Warr, P. B. (1968). A serial position effect in the preparation of abstracts. *Language and Speech,* **8,** 228–236.

Warr, P. B. and Knapper, C. (1965). A content analysis of the English national daily press. *Gazette,* **11,** 139–147.

Warr, P. B. and Knapper, C. (1966a). The relative importance of verbal and visual information in indirect person perception. *British Journal of Social and Clinical Psychology,* **5,** 118–127.

Warr, P. B. and Knapper, C. (1966b). The role of expectancy and communication content in indirect person perception. *British Journal of Social and Clinical Psychology*, **5**, 244–253.

Warr, P. B. and Knapper, C. (1967). Negative responses and serial position effects on the adjective check list. *Journal of Social Psychology*, **73**, 191–197.

Warr, P. B. and Sims, A. (1965). A study of cojudgment processes. *Journal of Personality*, **33**, 598–604.

Warr, P. B., Faust, J. and Harrison, G. J. (1967). A British ethnocentrism scale. *British Journal of Social and Clinical Psychology*, **6**, 267–277.

Warr, P. B., Schroder, H. M. and Blackman, S. (1968). The Structure of Political Judgment. *British Journal of Social and Clinical Psychology*. In Press.

Warren, N. (1966). Social class and construct systems: an example of the cognitive structure of two social class groups. *British Journal of Social and Clinical Psychology*, **5**, 254–263.

Weckowicz, T. E. and Witney, G. (1960). The Müller-Lyer illusion in schizophrenic patients. *Journal of Mental Science*, **106**, 1002–1007.

Wedell, C. and Smith, K. U. (1951). Consistency of interview methods in appraisal of attitudes. *Journal of Applied Psychology*, **35**, 392–396.

Weisgerber, C. A. (1956). Accuracy in judging emotional expressions as related to college entrance test scores. *Journal of Social Psychology*, **44**, 233–239.

Weiss, W. (1963). Scale judgments of triplets of opinion statements. *Journal of Abnormal and Social Psychology*, **66**, 471–479.

Weksel, W. and Hennes, J. D. (1965). Attitude intensity and the semantic differential. *Journal of Personality and Social Psychology*, **2**, 91–94.

Wells, W. D. and Smith, G. (1960). Four semantic rating scales compared. *Journal of Applied Psychology*, **44**, 393–397.

Wertheimer, M. (1960). Values in person cognition. In D. Willner (Ed.), *Decisions, Values and Groups*. Pergamon Press, Oxford.

White, R. K. and Landis, C. (1930). Perception of silhouettes. *American Journal of Psychology*, **42**, 431–435.

Whorf, B. L. (1940). Science and linguistics. *Technology Review*, **44**, 229–248.

Wiggins, R. H. (1964). The effects of lower-case alphabet, length of line, and spacing on speed of reading of 8-point Regal type. Unpublished dissertation, University of Iowa.

Williams, F. (1959). *Dangerous Estate — the Anatomy of Newspapers*, Arrow Books, London.

Williams, R. (1962). *Britain in the Sixties: Communications*, Penguin Books, Harmondsworth, England.

Willis, R. H. (1960). Stimulus pooling and social perception. *Journal of Abnormal and Social Psychology*, **60**, 365–373.

Wilkins, E. J. and deCharms, R. (1962). Authoritarianism and response to power cues. *Journal of Personality*, **30**, 439–457.

Winkler, M. (1951). Der Ausdruckswert der Mundgegend auf Grund schematischer Darstellungen. Unpublished dissertation, University of Vienna.

Winship, E. C. and Allport, G. W. (1943). Do rosy headlines sell newspapers? *Public Opinion Quarterly*, **7**, 205–210.

Wishner, J. (1960). Reanalysis of "Impressions of personality". *Psychological Review*, **67**, 96–112.

Witkin, H. A., Lewis, H. B., Hertzman, M., Machover, K., Meissner, P. B. and Wapner, S. (1954). *Personality through Perception*, Harper, New York.

Wohlwill, J. W. (1960). Developmental studies of perception. *Psychological Bulletin*, **57**, 249–288.

Woodburn, B. W. (1947). Reader interest in newspaper pictures. *Journalism Quarterly*, **24**, 197–201.

Woodworth, R. S. (1938). *Experimental Psychology*, Holt, New York.

Woodworth, R. S. and Schlosberg, H. (1954). *Experimental Psychology*, Holt, New York.

Wright, J. M. and Harvey, O. J. (1965). Attitude change as a function of authoritarianism and punitiveness. *Journal of Personality and Social Psychology*, **1**, 177–181.

Wylie, R. (1961). *The Self Concept*, University of Nebraska Press, Lincoln.

Yarrow, M. R. and Campbell, J. D. (1963). Person perception in children. *Merrill-Palmer Quarterly*, **9**, 57–72.

Zajonc, R. B. (1960). The process of cognitive tuning in communication. *Journal of Abnormal and Social Psychology*, **61**, 159–167.

Zax, M., Cowen, E. L. and Peter, M. (1963). A comparative study of novice nuns and college females using the response set approach. *Journal of Abnormal and Social Psychology*, **66**, 369–375.

Zax, M., Gardiner, D. H. and Lowy, D. G. (1964). Extreme response tendency as a function of emotional adjustment. *Journal of Abnormal and Social Psychology*, **69**, 654–657.

Zimbardo, P. G. (1960). Involvement and communication discrepancy as determinants of opinion conformity. *Journal of Abnormal and Social Psychology*, **60**, 86–94.

AUTHOR INDEX

Abelson, R. P.   104
Abu-Lughod, I.   257
Adams, B.   98
Adorno, T. W.   196
Alexander, S.   109
Allport, F. H.   32
Allport, G. W.   21, 32, 49, 185, 195, 198, 290, 354, 355, 360, 361
Altrocchi, J.   103, 185, 195, 199, 201, 202
Ambrose, A.   140
Ambrose, J. A.   210
Amster, H.   165
Anastasi, A.   185, 195, 208
Anderson, L. D.   298
Anderson, L. R.   166
Anderson, N. H.   37, 61, 63, 165, 171, 267, 270, 284
Angyal, A. F.   93
Anisfeld, E.   208, 354
Ansbacher, H.   199
Appelezweig, D. G.   88
Argyle, M.   32, 217, 246, 252
Arieti, S.   201
Aronson, E.   235, 325
Asch, S. E.   5, 26, 33, 34, 99, 103, 119, 120, 121, 122, 123, 124, 125, 126, 130, 155, 161, 168, 170, 172, 177, 183, 187, 234, 246, 267, 284, 369
Atkinson, J. W.   223, 361
Attneave, F.   41, 314, 370
Austin, G. A.   7
Austin, L. J.   188, 382
Austrin, H.   198
Ausubel, D. P.   211
Ayer, A. J.   28, 386

Backman, C. W.   3, 96, 202, 235, 250, 251
Bagby, J. A.   207, 360
Bailey, D. E.   8, 15, 32, 122, 246, 247
Bakan, D.   362
Baker, B. O.   63
Baldwin, P. M.   169
Ballachey, E. L.   32, 96
Banks, J. H.   242
Bannister, D.   98, 299
Barclay, A.   96
Barnett, E. O.   360
Barrios, A. A.   267, 284
Bartlett, F. C.   4, 121, 199, 207, 227, 358
Bartley, S. H.   335
Basowitz, H.   209
Bass, A. R.   64
Bayton, J. A.   188, 382
Beach, F. A.   38
Beach, L.   103, 189
Beardslee, D. C.   34
Beilin, H.   155
Bender, I. E.   47
Benedetti, D. T.   161
Benne, K. D.   222
Berelson, B.   214
Berkowitz, L.   18, 36, 37, 100, 198, 235, 236, 237, 357
Berlew, D. E.   224
Bernstein, B.   210, 216
Berscheid, E. S.   151, 153
Bevan, W.   39, 198, 299, 310
Beverley, G. D.   196
Bieri, J.   6, 8, 43, 99, 185, 187, 200, 201, 216, 251, 355, 357, 370
Bion, W. R.   222
Birren, J. E.   209

429

Bitterman, M. E. 334

Blackman, S. 107, 214, 233, 387, 388

Blaisdell, F. J. 199, 235, 250

Blake, R. R. 235, 236, 250, 317

Bloch, B. L. 171

Block, J. 334

Bloodstein, O. 250

Blumberg, H. H. 112

Blumler, J. G. 91, 92, 97

Bogardus, E. S. 207

Boneau, C. A. 63

Bonner, H. 233

Boring, E. G. 335

Borko, H. 368

Bossart, P. 287

Bossom, J. 197

Bourisseau, W. 310

Bourne, L. E. 335

Boyle, D. G. 122

Bradburn, W. M. 185

Bradford, L. P. 222

Braly, K. W. 151

Bramel, D. 202

Brierley, D. W. 100, 126, 234, 354

Brinkman, P. D. 311

Brinton, J. E. 320

Briscoe, M. E. 285

Britt, S. H. 325

Broadbent, D. E. 360, 367

Bronfenbrenner, U. 47, 185, 186

Brooks, R. M. 210

Brooks, V. 298

Brown, J. S. 368

Brown, R. 2, 13, 201, 233

Brown, R. W. 371

Brown, W. P. 199

Bruner, J. S. 7, 11, 13, 19, 24, 26, 32, 35, 103, 122, 125, 133, 134, 135, 164, 172, 176, 199, 207, 215, 235, 236, 250

Brunswik, E. 3, 9, 22, 32, 36, 39, 40, 43, 297, 298, 300, 301, 331, 332, 333, 335

Burke, C. J. 63

Burke, K. R. 188, 383

Burns, N. 212

Burt, C. 319

Burton, P. W. 320

Buss, A. H. 237

Butler, R. N. 209

Buzby, D. E. 186, 300

Campbell, D. T. 41, 47, 198, 202, 206, 207

Campbell, J. D. 189, 212

Cantril, H. 180, 331, 348, 354

Cappellini, A. 43

Carlsmith, J. M. 325

Carlson, E. R. 231, 347, 355

Carmichael, L. 317

Cartwright, D. 233, 367

Cattell, R. B. 383

Cavey, L. 212

Centers, R. 211

Chall, J. S. 286

Chambers, J. L. 299

Chance, J. 210

Cherry, E. S. 299

Chowdhry, K. 47

Clapp, W. F. 251

Clark, K. B. 211

Clark, M. P. 211

Clark, W. H. 217

Cleeton, G. U. 298

Cliff, N. 41, 167

Cline, M. G. 18, 36, 299

Cline, V. B. 47, 48, 185, 186, 199, 217

Cofer, C. N. 234

Cohen, A. R. 225, 325

Converse, P. E. 246

Cooley, J. C. 140

Cooper, J. B. 214

Cowen, E. L. 216

Coyne, L. 85

Crano, W. D. 200

Creelman, M. B. 96

Crockett, W. H. 47, 153, 189, 196, 238, 268, 270, 284

Cronbach, L. J. 47, 48, 59, 60, 122

Crow, W. J. 47

Crutchfield, R. S. 32, 96

Cullen, J. H. 43

Dahlstrom, W. G. 170, 171
Daugherty, B. N. 225
Davis, A. 216
Davis, D. R. 43
Davis, K. E. 14, 15, 198, 222, 227, 237, 248, 356, 357
Davis, O. L. 310
Davis, R. C. 320
Davitz, J. R. 46, 186, 195, 300
Dean, J. 252
deCharms, R. 196, 197, 228
De Fleur, M. L. 198
Dennis, W. 41, 209
Deri, S. 297
DeSoto, C. B. 112, 197, 251
Dunlap, K. 300
Deutschmann, P. J. 325
Diab, L. N. 96
Dick, W. 78, 79, 81
Di Vesta, F. J. 66, 78, 79, 81, 214, 287
Dodge, J. 319
Donahoe, J. W. 58, 214
Doob, L. W. 355
Dornbusch, S. M. 53, 103, 189, 246
Douty, H. I. 317
Driver, M. J. 5, 104, 171, 200, 201, 224
Dudycha, G. J. 119
Dugan, R. D. 299
Duker, J. 171
Dukes, W. F. 310
Dunn, J. T. 234
Dureman, I. 43
Dustin, D. S. 169
Dymond, R. F. 47, 49, 212

Eachus, H. T. 202
Eagly, A. H. 184
Edwards, A. L. 99, 147, 150
Ehlinger, H. 188
Ekman, G. 104
Ekman, P. 253, 297
Elliott, D. N. 198
Elliott, L. L. 65
Engel, E. 360
English, E. 319
Epstein, R. 197

Epstein, W. 333, 335, 336
Erikson, C. W. 199
Estes, S. G. 317
Evans, H. 290, 296, 319
Exline, R. V. 5, 187, 252, 253
Eysenck, H. J. 43, 214, 215, 297, 355

Faust, J. 215, 216
Feigenbaum, E. A. 368, 380, 381
Feldman, J. 368, 380, 381
Feldman, S. 24, 364
Feleky, A. M. 300
Feliciano, G. D. 328
Fensterheio, H. 39, 199, 299
Fenton, N. 297
Fernberger, S. W. 300
Ferrero, G. 297
Feshbach, N. 225, 382
Feshbach, S. 224, 225, 382
Fiedler, F. E. 49, 57, 187, 189, 191, 199, 208, 211, 212, 217, 235, 250
Fishbein, M. 24, 96, 166
Fisher, R. 207
Fisher, R. L. 207
Fishman, J. A. 208
Flügel, J. C. 317
Foa, U. G. 233
Fonda, C. P. 199
Fong, S. L. M. 208
Form, W. H. 5
Fosdick, J. A. 306
Foulkes, D. 159, 199, 201, 268
Foulkes, S. H. 159, 199, 201, 268
Fransella, F. 98, 99, 250
French, D. 209
Friedman, C. J. 57
Friedman, M. 196
Friesen, W. V. 297
Frijda, N. H. 299
Frois-Wittman, J. 300
Frymier, J. R. 207
Fuchs, D. A. 325

Gage, N. L. 5, 47
Galinsky, M. D. 185
Gallwey, M. 185, 186

Gardiner, D. H.   62
Gardiner, H. W.   97, 325
Gardner, B. B.   216
Gardner, M. R.   216
Gardner, R. W.   43
Garfield, S. L.   109
Gaskill, P. C.   297
Gates, G. S.   186, 211, 300
Gemelli, A.   43
Gengel, R. W.   328
George, F. H.   368
Gergen, K. J.   14, 356
Getzels, J. W.   207
Ghent, L.   210
Ghiselli, E. E.   61
Gibb, J. R.   222
Gibson, J. J.   253
Gilberstadt, H.   171
Girvin, R. E.   296
Gladden, J. W.   57
Gleser, G. C.   59
Goffman, E.   15, 249
Goldberg, S. C.   154, 347
Golden, B. W.   235
Goldman-Eisler, F.   354
Goldstein, A. G.   210
Gollin, E. S.   41, 189, 200, 212, 284, 354
Goodman, M. E.   211, 215
Goodnow, J. L.   7
Gordon, J. E.   199
Gottheil, E.   334
Gough, H. G.   99, 103, 136, 160, 204, 205
Gray, D.   252
Gray, P. H.   109
Greenberg, B. S.   328
Grunes, W. F.   122
Guetzkow, H.   366
Guilford, J. P.   62
Gulliksen, H.   111, 172
Gunderson, E. K. E.   39
Gynther, M. D.   187
Gyr, J. W.   368

Haire, M.   122
Hallworth, H. J.   97, 108

Hamilton, V.   43
Hammes, J. A.   186, 197
Hammond, K. R.   5, 169, 170, 171
Hanfmann, E.   207
Harary, F.   367
Hardesty, F. P.   211
Harding, J.   185, 186
Hardyck, C. D.   63
Harrison, G. J.   215, 216
Harrison, R.   53
Hart, H.   290
Hartley, E. L.   207, 208, 211
Hartshorne, H.   100
Harvey, O. J.   176, 196, 200, 212, 251, 268
Haskins, J. B.   320
Hastorf, A. H.   47, 48, 103, 180, 246, 360
Hatch, R. S.   47
Hayden, R.   122
Hays, W. L.   134, 135, 147, 234
Hazard, W. R.   296
Hefner, R.   387
Heider, F.   15, 17, 32, 36, 37, 39, 41, 184, 233, 246, 331, 348, 357
Heilbrun, A. B.   99, 136, 160, 204, 205
Helper, M. M.   109
Helson, H.   8, 37
Hennes, J. D.   96
Henry, J.   207
Herskovits, M. J.   41, 206, 207
Hill, J. G.   161
H.M.S.O.   257, 327
Hochberg, J. E.   32, 34, 41, 298, 317
Hoffman, E. L.   187, 208, 211, 212, 217
Hoffman, P. J.   166, 169
Holmes, D.   18, 36, 100, 357
Holt, R.   171
Holway, A. H.   335
Holzman, P. S.   85
Homans, G. C.   233, 246
Honkavaara, S.   46, 300
Hopkins, J.   199
Horn, J. L.   60
Hovland, C. I.   8, 96, 265, 325, 347, 356, 381

Hoult, T. F. 317
Howe, E. S. 167
Hubert, S. 267, 284
Hughes, A. S. 212
Hughes, G. E. 140
Hvistendahl, J. K. 319
Hunt, E. B. 381
Hunt, D. E. 176, 200, 212
Hunter, R. 96, 166
Hunton, V. D. 210
Hursch, C. J. 170
Husek, T. R. 109

Icheiser, G. 36, 39, 331
Iliffe, A. H. 298
Indow, T. 104
Insko, C. A. 347
International Press Institute 257
Ittelson, W. H. 3, 32, 201, 360
Iverson, M. A. 356
Izard, C. E. 299

Jackson, D. N. 35, 60, 104, 105, 133, 148, 195, 387
Jacobs, R. L. 215
Jacobson, A. 267, 320
Jaffe, J. 5
Jahoda, G. 5, 211, 214, 216
Janis, I. L. 325
Jansen, M. J. 57
Jaspars, J. M. F. 98, 99
Jenkin, N. 43
Jenkins, J. J. 61, 64, 67, 82, 90, 234
Jenness, A. 186
Jessor, R. 196
Johansson, G. 43
John, W. 176
Johnson, D. M. 119
Johnson, H. H. 149, 159, 197
Johnson, P. E. 217
Johnson, W. 355
Jones, E. E. 14, 15, 42, 196, 222, 223, 225, 227, 228, 235, 237, 246, 247, 250, 356, 357

Kagan, J. 212
Kanazawa, K. 104

Kanner, L. 186, 300
Katz, B. 39, 198
Katz, D. 151
Kayser, J. 257
Kelley, H. H. 125, 177, 183, 233, 234, 246, 251, 325
Kelly, G. A. 13, 24, 98, 176
Kelly, J. A. 96
Kelly, W. F. 311
Kelman, H. C. 184, 325
Kendon, A. 252
Kennedy, J. L. 171
Kidd, J. W. 236
Kieferle, D. A. 98
Kiel, D. 325
Kilpatrick, F. P. 348
Kingsbury, S. M. 290
Kjeldergaard, P. M. 234
Klapper, J. J. 325
Klausner, S. J. 215
Klein, G. S. 43
Klineberg, O. 214
Kluckholm, C. 209
Knapp, R. H. 188
Knapper, C. 27, 102, 257, 290, 296, 314, 320
Knight, F. B. 298
Koffka, K. 333
Kogan, N. 185, 211, 356, 387
Kohn, A. R. 187, 189, 208, 211, 212
Koltuv, B. B. 125, 132, 133, 134, 135, 153, 183
Komorita, S. S. 64
Korchin, S. J. 209
Koslin, B. L. 347
Kramer, B. M. 198
Kramer, E. 354
Krech, D. 32, 96
Kremenak, M. 300
Kretschmer, E. 297
Krevanich, F. W. 198
Krieger, M. H. 64
Kruskal, J. B. 104
Kudirka, N. Z. 215
Kuethe, J. L. 112, 197, 251
Kuhlen, R. G. 209

Künnapas, T. 104
Kutash, S. B. 201

Lambert, W. E. 26, 38, 208, 211, 214, 354
Lambert, W. W. 26, 300
Lampel, A. K. 37
Landis, C. 300, 301
Lang, G. E. 257
Lang, K. 257
Langfeld, H. S. 310
Lawlor, M. 207
Lazarsfeld, P. F. 214
Lazarus, R. S. 199
Lazerowitz, M. 140
Leary, T. 233
Lee, J. C. 360
Lefkowitz, M. 317
Leibowitz, H. 334, 335
Lenneberg, E. H. 371
Lepkin, M. 290
Leventhal, H. 48, 201, 215, 225, 268
Levin, L. A. 198
Levy, L. H. 5, 36, 37, 96, 171, 186, 299, 357
Lewis, L. S. 216
Liebling, A. J. 290
Lindzey, G. 39
Lipetz, M. E. 196, 197
Livingston, D. G. 5
Lobeck, R. 217
Loeb, A. 225
Loh, W. D. 198, 347
Lombroso, C. 297
Londey, D. G. 140
Long, B. H. 217
Lord, F. M. 61
Lott, A. J. 202, 235, 236
Lott, B. E. 202, 235, 236
Lowy, D. G. 62
Lubin, B. 53
Lucas, D. B. 325
Luchins, A. S. 26, 37, 123, 124, 126, 265, 268, 270, 284
Luchins, E. H. 268, 284
Luft, J. 217

Lund, F. H. 265, 270
Lundy, R. M. 222
Luria, Z. 91
Lyle, J. 325

McAlister, E. 41
McCarter, R. 298
Macaulay, J. R. 328
McClelland, D. C. 223
McCollough, C. 124
McDonald, R. L. 187
McGinnies, E. 199
McGrath, J. E. 97, 217
McGrath, M. 97
McHugh, R. B. 63
McKeachie, W. J. 301
McKellar, P. 27
Mackenberg, E. J. 210
Maclay, H. 108, 208
McLean, M. S. 296
McLelland, L. 285
McLeod, J. M. 325, 327
McPhee, W. N. 214
McQuail, D. 91, 92, 97
Mahrer, A. R. 166, 171
Malinowski, B. 207
Maltz, H. E. 58, 214
Manis, M. 325, 357
Mann, R. D. 236
Marks, I. M. 91, 97, 108
Martin, J. G. 208
Martin, R. O. 320
Maslow, A. H. 197, 299
Maurer, L. L. 328
Mausner, B. 171
May, M. A. 100
Mayo, C. W. 268, 270, 284
Meehl, P. E. 170, 171, 355
Mehling, R. 310
Meidinger, T. 196
Meltzer, B. 268
Mensh, I. N. 121, 123
Messick, S. J. 61, 103, 104, 105, 148, 195, 368, 387
Miller, G. A. 32, 176
Miller, R. E. 242

Miller, S. M.   216
Mintz, M. L.   299
Miron, M. S.   59, 65, 66
Mitchell, R. A.   62, 77, 80
Mitsos, S. B.   99
Mogar, R. E.   62
Moore, M.   188, 212, 360
Moore, O. K.   381
Moreno, J. L.   233
Morland, J. K.   211
Mourant, J. A.   140
Mouton, J. S.   317
Mueller, W. J.   69, 199
Munn, N. L.   18, 36, 297, 300, 317
Murashima, F.   347
Murphy, D. R.   319, 320
Murphy, G.   41
Murray, H. A.   224
Murstein, B. I.   186, 198, 202
Mussen, P.   196
Muthard, J. E.   188, 209
Myro, G.   360

Nagle, B. F.   47
Natsoulas, T.   199
Nebergall, R. E.   325
Nelson, P. D.   39
Nelson, T. M.   335
Neuringer, C.   62
Newcomb, T. M.   ¡45, 118, 196, 207, 208, 233, 246
Nidorf, L. J.   153, 189, 268
Nielsen, G.   252
Noble, C. E.   96
Norman, A.   257, 284
Norman, R. Z.   367
Norman, W. T.   64, 67, 78, 79, 82, 154
Norris, E. L.   320, 328
Notcutt, B.   47
Nuckols, J. W.   319

Ogawa, N.   242
Osgood, C. E.   6, 32, 34, 55, 56, 57, 58, 59, 61, 64, 65, 66, 67, 68, 69, 70, 71, 75, 78, 84, 91, 96, 97, 112, 165, 166, 184, 208, 328

Ossorio, P. G.   197
Oyama, T.   64, 65, 69

Paivio, A.   199, 207, 249, 360
Park, J. N.   333, 335, 336
Parker, J. H.   328
Passini, F. T.   153
Pastore, N.   236
Paterson, D. G.   319
Peak, H.   36
Pederson, D. M.   196, 387
Pepitone, A.   15, 122, 222, 223, 237, 242, 322, 356
Perlin, S.   209
Perlmutter, H. V.   207
Peter, M.   216
Petrinovitch, L. F.   63
Petrullo, L.   3, 49
Pettigrew, T. F.   360
Phillipson, H.   199
Piaget, J.   213
Pick, A. D.   253
Pintner, R.   298
Podell, H. A.   166, 267
Podell, J. E.   165, 166, 267
Porter, J. P.   297
Postman, L.   22, 32, 176, 199, 215, 227, 331
Poulton, E. C.   319
Powers, S. P.   319
Prestholdt, P.   237
Pritzker, H. A.   347

Quine, W. V. O.   140

Raabe, V. L.   212
Rabinowitz, W.   196
Radke-Yarrow, M. J.   189
Randall, D. H.   299
Rankin, R. E.   198
Rappoport, L.   134, 135, 136
Raven, B. H.   96
Razran, G.   38, 299
Rees, L.   297
Reichenbach, H.   22
Reiter, L.   300

P

Restle, F. 370
Reuder, M. E. 356
Richards, J. M. 299
Richardson, S. A. 103, 246
Richey, M. H. 285
Richter, M. L. 5, 171
Riecken, H. W. 41, 317, 356
Riessman, F. 216
Rimoldi, H. J. A. 171
Roberts, A.H. 196
Roberts, S. O. 317
Robinson, J. P. 387
Robinson, M. P. 217
Rogolsky, S. 39
Rohracher, H. 301
Rokeach, M. 166, 167, 168, 169, 170, 215, 286
Rommetweit, R. 32
Rosenberg, M. J. 24
Rosenfeld, H. M. 253
Rosenkrantz, P. S. 268, 284
Rosenthal, R. 176
Ross, J. 114
Rothman, G. 166, 167, 168, 169, 170, 286
Royal Commission on the Press 290, 327
Rudin, S. A. 36, 196
Rugg, H. 118
Rule, B. G. 198
Russell, W. A. 61, 64, 67, 82, 90
Ruthellen, C. G. 355
Ruthenbeck, K. E. 319
Ryle, G. 8, 11, 14, 385

Saiyadain, M. 347
Sälde, H. 43
Samuels, M. 301
Sappenfield, B. R. 298
Sarason, I. G. 189, 198
Sarbin, T. R. 8, 15, 22, 32, 122, 189, 246, 247
Sass, M. A. 381
Sauer, W. L. 5
Saugstad, P. 38
Schachter, S. 235
Schatzman, L. 215

Schicht, W. 210
Schlosberg, H. 34, 186, 300, 337
Schroder, H. M. 5, 104, 107, 171, 176, 200, 201, 212, 214, 224, 233, 268, 387, 388
Schuette, D. 252
Schulberg, H. C. 196
Schulz, R. W. 66
Scodel, A. 47, 196, 198
Scott, W. A. 238
Sebeok, T. A. 6, 32
Sechrest, L. 99
Secord, P. F. 3, 39, 96, 151, 153, 188, 198, 202, 209, 235, 250, 251, 297, 299, 301, 308, 310
Seeleman, V. 39
Segall, M. H. 41, 206, 207
Seiller-Tarbuk, L. 301
Sencer, R. A. 328
Sermat, V. 104
Shapiro, D. 35, 133, 134, 135, 136, 138, 155, 156, 157, 158, 164, 172, 251
Shaw, M. E. 285
Sheldon, W. H. 297
Shelton, F. C. 211, 356
Sherberg, J. 356
Sherif, C. W. 222, 325
Sherif, M. 5, 8, 96, 222, 325, 356
Sherman, M. 18, 36, 300
Sherrill, P. N. 320
Shiff, H. M. 211
Shimkunas, A. M. 285
Shock, N. W. 209
Shrauger, S. 103, 185, 195, 201
Siegel, S. 60
Signell, K. A. 213
Silva, A. L. M. 47
Simmel, M. 36, 37, 41
Simon, W. B. 216
Simons, H. W. 196, 201
Sims, A. 133, 135, 136, 137, 147, 149, 150, 160, 197
Singer, R. 224, 225, 268
Slack, C. W. 3, 32, 360
Smith, A. J. 5

Smith, G. 58
Smith, H. C. 47
Smith, H. J. 320
Smith, K. R. 298
Smith, M. D. 212, 216
Smolenaars, A. J. 57
Solley, C. M. 41, 104, 105
Sommer, R. 114
Spinks, G. S. 217
Spiro, M. E. 207
Spitz, R. A. 210
Springer, D. V. 211
Stagner, R. 36, 56, 75, 196
Steeves, R. 199, 207, 360
Steiner, I. D. 5, 48, 149, 159, 197
Stephens, J. M. 199
Stevens, J. W. 211
Stevenson, H. W. 211
Stewart, R. H. 211, 267, 284
Stoltz, R. E. 212, 216
Stone, G. P. 317
Stoops, J. W. 347
Strauss, A. 215
Streufert, S. 5, 104, 171, 200, 201, 224
Stricker, G. 97
Strickland, L. H. 41, 356
Stritch, T. M. 301
Suci, G. J. 56, 58, 59, 61, 64, 66, 67, 68, 75, 78, 82, 84, 90, 91, 96, 97, 112, 165, 208
Summers, D. A. 169, 170, 171
Supnick, L. E. 238
Swartz, J. D. 213
Szondi, L. 297

Taft, R. 5, 8, 15, 22, 32, 42, 45, 122, 185, 186, 199, 217, 246, 247
Tagiuri, R. 3, 5, 17, 26, 32, 35, 36, 41, 43, 44, 45, 46, 47, 49, 103, 122, 125, 133, 134, 135, 136, 155, 156, 157, 158, 164, 172, 185, 195, 202, 233, 235, 236, 246, 250, 251
Taguchi, Y. 211
Tajfel, H. 32, 40, 209
Talbot, G. T. 166
Talland, G. A. 209

Talmadge, M. 355
Tanaka, Y. 5, 57, 64, 65, 69, 208
Tannenbaum, P. H. 56, 58, 59, 61, 64, 65, 66, 67, 68, 75, 78, 84, 91, 96, 97, 112, 165, 184, 289, 290, 306, 320, 325, 327, 328
Taylor, C. 211
Thibaut, J. W. 41, 42, 227, 228, 231, 233, 246, 247, 317, 336
Thomas, J. L. 217
Thomson, G. G. 211
Thorndike, E. L. 118, 119, 355
Thornton, G. R. 244, 300, 301
Thorpe, J. S. 213
Thouless, R. H. 40, 43, 332, 333, 334, 335
Thumin, F. J. 96
Thurstone, L. L. 43
Tinbergen, N. 39, 367
Tinker, M. A. 319
Todd, F. J. 5, 134, 135, 136, 170
Tolman, E. C. 22, 331
Tomkins, S. S. 298, 368
Torgerson, W. S. 103, 104, 105
Tresselt, M. E. 39, 199, 299
Triandis, H. C. 53, 57, 67, 135, 166, 198, 208, 209, 251, 300, 364
Triandis, L. M. 208
Tripodi, T. 99
Tucker, R. B. 360
Tukey, J. W. 111
Turner, E. 325
Turner, R. H. 246

Uhr, L. 133, 136, 368
Ulrich, L. 47
Underwood, B. J. 66
U.N.E.S.C.O. 257

Vannoy, J. S. 200
Veness, T. 100, 126, 234, 354
Vernon, M. D. 34, 199
Vernon, P. E. 32, 41, 355, 360, 361
Vidulich, R. N. 198
Vinacke, W. E. 186
Viner, G. 319

Viteles, M. S.   298

Waite, G.   108
Walker, E. L.   223, 361
Wallace, A. F. C.   207, 297
Wallach, M. A.   185, 355
Walster, E.   237
Walters, H.   387
Ware, E. E.   66
Ware, R.   200, 208
Warr, P. B.   27, 102, 107, 129, 133, 135, 136, 137, 147, 149, 150, 160, 197, 214, 215, 216, 233, 237, 257, 290, 296, 314, 320, 387, 388
Warren, N.   216
Warrington, W. G.   199, 235, 250
Weckowicz, T. E.   43
Wedell, C.   47
Weisgerber, C. A.   186
Weiss, W.   171, 325
Weksel, W.   96
Wells, W. D.   58
Wertheimer, M.   34, 103, 187, 189
Weske, F. R.   198
Wessel, N. Y.   317
Wheeler, G. E.   109
White, R. K.   301
Whorf, B. L.   208
Wiggins, R. H.   319
Wilkes, A. L.   39, 40
Wilkins, E. J.   196, 197
Wilkins, M. M.   5
Wilkinson, W. D.   381
Willey, R.   368

Williams, A. F.   224
Williams, F.   257
Williams, R.   257, 290
Willis, R. H.   169
Winkel, G. H.   189, 198
Winkler, M.   300
Winship, E. C.   290
Winters, L. C.   252
Wishner, J.   33, 121, 123, 124, 127, 128, 129, 130, 132, 135, 168, 172, 234
Witkin, H. A.   43
Witney, G.   43
Wittenburg, B. H.   198
Wohlwill, J. W.   41, 213
Wolf, K. M.   210
Woodburn, B. W.   296
Woodworth, R. S.   34, 46, 300, 333
Woodyard, H. D.   285
Wright, J. M.   196
Wunderlich, R.   197
Wylie, R.   187, 215

Yamamoto, K.   310
Yarrow, M. R.   189, 212
Yeni-Komshian, G.   208, 354
Young, H. H.   166, 171

Zajonc, R. B.   225
Zander, A.   233
Zax, M.   62
Zimbardo, P. G.   347
Zivian, A.   368

SUBJECT INDEX

Accuracy in perception, 12, 46–49, 186–187, 201, 210, 211, 222, 224, 253, 298, 349, 354–355
and the press, 257, 258–264, 290
methodological difficulties concerning, 186, 355
Achievement need, 223–224
Adjective Check List (Gough's), 99–103, 136, 137, 160–162, 203–206, 260
Adolescents, 211
Affective component, 6, 7, 8, 15–16, 18, 19, 68, 105–107, 198, 207–208, 211, 231, 232, 250–252, 363–365, *see also* Attraction, Emotional state of perceiver
Affiliation need, 187, 223–224
Age, 18, 209–214, 299, 354, 356
Aggression, perception of, 188, 189, 198
Algorithmic methods in computer programming, 380
Ames distorted room, 37
Anti-semitism, 198
Anxiety, 109, 197, 224–225, 249, 382
Appearance, physical, 189, 317
Aptitude, vocational, 298
Articulation, 212–214, 370
Artificiality and realism in person perception research, 26–27, 123, 126, 130, 278, 280–281, 284, 287–288, 291, 350, 384
Assumed similarity, 48, 49, 187–188, 201, 235, 250–251
and authoritarianism, 196
Attitude change, 235, 265, 270, 310, 325–326, 347–348
Attitudes and person perception, 3–5, 18, 24, 96, 118, 184, 198, 232, *see also* Perceiver characteristics, Values, etc.
Attraction, 44–45, 202, 231–238, *see also* Affective component
Attributive component, 7–13, 14, 15, 15–16, 68, 176, 232, 363–364
Authoritarianism, 197–198, 215
and cojudgment, 160, 197
and projection, 197
Awareness, interpersonal, 187

Binocular rivalry, 188, 212, 360
Bodily characteristics, 41, 189, 243, 253, 296, 297, 356

Camera angle and lighting in photographs, 306–310
Captions to photographs, 310
Categorization 7–8, *see also* Attributive component
Causality, mechanical, 41–42
social, 41–42
Centrality of traits, 121–122, 123–124, 152, 153, 162, 234, 244, 286, 373, *see also* Implicit personality theory, Warm-cold variable, Humane-ruthless variable
Channel of communication, 6, 27, 28, 29, 183, 191, 241, 242, 245, Ch. 6, Ch. 7, 350
selection and control in, 243–245, 256–257, *see also* Indirect perception
Children, 41, 66, 82, 97, 108, 200, 208, 210–213, 215, 218, 222, 225, 310
Classification, *see* Categorization
Class, social, 18, 19, 211, 215–216, 221

439

Clinical diagnosis, 91, 97, 166, 168, 170, 171–172, 183, 217, 355–356

Clothes, 317, 355

Cognitive complexity, 200, 201, 212–214, 237–238, 268

Cognitive dissonance, 237

Cojudgment, 146–152, 159, 160, 232, 233, 235, 238, 363
　and authoritarianism, 197
　and sex factors, 158

Combination rules, 21–22, 41, 123, 133, 144, 153, 163–173, 286, 316 362–363, 373–375, 378, 387
　configural models for, 163, 164, 167–173, 285
　congruity principle in, 165
　linear models for, 164–167, 169–171, 285

Communication medium, see Channel of communication, Indirect perception

Communication theory, 6

Computer simulation, 368–380

Concealed figures, 35

Conception and perception, 4, 24, 175–185, 214, 244, 257, 258, 259, 325, 326, 327–328, 333, 336–346, 349, 358–359, see also Recall and perception, Stored information about stimulus person

Conforming behaviour, 235, 357

Congruency, 44–45, 236, 250

Congruity principle, 165, 328

Connotative meaning, see Meaning, Semantic differential

Constancy phenomena, 12, 39, 43, Ch. 8, 349

Content analysis of newspapers, 257, 296

Context information, in object perception, 36, 335
　in person perception, 17, 36, 121–122, 180–181, 224, 299, 317–318, 335, 356–357, 359

Covert distal variables, 3, 11–13, 13, 14, 32, 54, 55, 91, 115, 360

Cultural factors, 41, 56, 66, 108, 187, 206–208, 360

Current state of the perceiver, 11, 19, 38, 174, 222–231, 232, 238–239, 298, 335, 355, 361–362

Decision rules, see Combination rules, Inference rules

Defence, perceptual, 199

Definition of person perception, 2, 23, 351–352

Denotative meaning, see Meaning

Development of person perception, see Age, Adolescents, Children

Diagnosis, clinical, 91, 97, 166, 167, 170, 171, 183, 355–356

Differences, individual, 42–43, Ch. 4, 362, see also Perceiver characteristics, Habits, Sex factors, Values, etc.

Differentiation, 199–200, 212–214, 268, 370

Direct perception, 15, 26–31, 177, 180, 182–183, 187, 198, 222, 231, Ch. 5, 260, 263, 296, 318, 350

Dispositional judgments, 8–9, 10–13, 14, 15, 18, 29, 32, 46, 48, 53, 115, 175, 196, 208, 224, 245, 247, 249, 255, 256, 298–299, 349, 372

Distal variables, see Covert distal variables, Overt distal variables

Dogmatism, 199, 215, 268
　and implicit personality theory, 160

Dominance-submissiveness, 188

Doodles, 354

Editing, see Channel of communication, selection and control in

Effort after meaning, 121, 358, see also Recall and perception

Einstellung, 19, 266–267, 286, see also Set, mental

Emotion-judging, 18, 46, 47, 105, 208, 241, 297, 298, 299–301, 310, 317, 349
　personality differences in, 195
　sex differences in, 185

Emotional state of perceiver, 222–224, 249, *see also* Affective component

Empathy test, 46

Episodic judgments, 8–11, 12, 13, 14–15, 29, 32, 46, 48, 53, 115, 175, 183, 188, 195, 224, 246, 248, 258, 337, 338, 341, 349

Errors, logical, 118–119

E-scale, *see* Ethnocentrism

Ethnic labels, 299

Ethnocentrism, and implicit personality theory, 159–160
  and perceptual constancy, 348
  and person perception, 205, 215, 216
  and semantic differential responses, 71–72

Evaluative tone, 237–238, *see also* Affective component, Attraction, Cojudgment

Events, perception of, 12, 179–183, 258, 259–264, 357

Expectancy component, 6, 7, 8, 13–15, 16, 18, 35, 38, 68, 174–185, 222, 232, 236, 249, 348, 363–365, *see also* Conception and perception, Sets

Extreme scale responding, 64, 153, 156–158

Eye-contact, 252–253

Eye-movements, 297

Facial expression, 209, 210, 211, 243, 253, 296–309, 317, 355, 387

Femininity, 298

Field dependence, 43

Figural after effect, 37

Figure-ground phenomena, 35–36

Films as stimulus material, 186, 224, 284, 297, 317

Football, 180–182, 191, 260–264

Form perception, 168–169

Free-response techniques, 103, 268, 386–388
  and sex differences, 188–190

F-scale, *see* Authoritarianism

Galvanic skin response, 198, 365

Gestalt phenomena, 34–35, *see also* Combination rules

Gestures, 253, 317, 356, 387

Goals, 221, 250, 253
  interaction, 227–231, 247–248, *see also* Intentions of stimulus person, Roles

Grammatical style, 355

Graphology, 355

Habits and person perception, 19, 175, *see also* Attitudes and person perception, Perceiver characteristics, Values, etc

Halo effect, 118–119, 137, 147, *see also* Cojudgment

Handwriting, 354

Headlines in newspapers, 289–295, 384
  and accuracy, 289
  readability of, 323–324

Heuristic methods in computer programming, 380–381

Hostility, 186, 197, 198–199, 224, 232, 237

Humane-ruthless dimension, 129–130, 131, 203

Illusions, perceptual, 33–34, 36, 43

Implicit personality theory, 122, 123, 125, 132–139, 153–162, 183, 233
  and implication scores, 147–148, 152–153, 156–157, 162–163
  and personality factors, 137, 159–163
  and sex factors, 155–159
  as a function of stimulus person, 153–155, 158
  logical model of, 140–145, *see also* Cojudgment, Combination rules, Inference rules

Indirect perception, 26–31, 125, 177, 179, 181, 182, 183, 184, 190, 214, 228, 234, 241–245, 248, 251, 252, 253, Ch. 6, Ch. 7, 336, 344, 350, 354–356 selection and control in, 27–29, 256, 243–244, *see also* Channel of communication

Individual differences in perception, 42–43, 154–162, Ch. 4, 362, *see also* Perceiver characteristics, Habits, Sex factors, Values, etc.

Inference, perceptual, 7, 9, 10, 11, 13, 15, 41–42, Ch. 3, 183, 189, 196, 207, 209, 212, 227–228, 297, 306 probabilistic, 22, 139, 373

Inference rules, 17–22, 41, 119–121, 132–139, 143, 146, 153, 154, 155, 156, 157, 158, 159, 160, 161, 163, 164, 165, 166, 167, 168, 169, 171, 286, 350, 361, 362–363, 372–375, 377, *see also* Cojudgment, Combination rules

Inferential sets, 227–231, 247–248

Information theory, 6–7

Input selection, 17, 18, 19, 22, 188, 196, 197, 199, 207, 208, 211–212, 217, 223, 227, 232, 324, 358–362, 365, 370–372, 375–378

Inputs, perceptual, 6, 7, 13, 15, 16, 20, 21, 44, 152, 156, 164, 165, 166, 167, 168, 169, 178, 235, 243–245, 246, 253, 255, 256, 264, 269, 285–286, 289, 295, 316, 348, 354–355, 364, 369–376

Insecurity, 197

Instantiation, 9–10, *see also* Attributive component

Integrative flexibility, 200–201, 212–214, *see also* Combination rules

Intelligence, 195, 199, 214, 297, 298, 301, 335

Intentions of stimulus person, 15, 222, 248, 249, 356, *see also* Goals, Roles

Interaction goals, 227–231, 247–248

Interaction, in object perception, 31–32, 43
  in person perception, 26–27, 28, 29–30, 43–44, 125, 198, 225, 227, 228, 234, 235, 242, 245–253,
318, 352, *see also* Direct perception, Goals, interaction

Interests, 39, 188, 199

Intergroup relationships, 5, 233

Interpersonal relations, 5, 233, 235, 251

Interviews, 47, 222, 245, 247

Intraception, and implicit personality theory, 160–161
  and person perception, 204–205

Introspection, 388–389

Lability, and implicit personality theory, 160–161
  and person perception, 204

Language systems, 208–209, 216

Legibility of type, 319–320, 323–324

Levellers, 43

Logical model of trait implication, 140–146

Masculinity, 298

Meaning, connotative, 54–55, 105, 264
  denotative, 54, 105, *see* Semantic differential

Measurement, in person perception, 23–24, 39, Ch. 2, 386
  methodological difficulties in, 47–49
  of implicit personality theory, 117–136
  of order effects, 270–273

Memory, *see* Conception and perception, Recall and perception, Stored information about stimulus person

Mental illness, 43, 97, 201, 225, 299

Mental set, 19, 38, 222, 225–231, 249, 266, *see also* Expectancy component in person perception

Meta-experiments, 176

Models, 140–146, 366–382

Motivation and person perception, 38, 189, 199, 222, 224, 299, *see also* Current state of the perceiver

Movie films, 186–187, 224, 284, 297, 317

Multi-dimensional scaling, 104–107, 233, 387–388

Multiple-variable studies of person perception, 382–384

Need for achievement, 223–224
Need for affiliation, 187, 223–224
Need-systems, *see* Attitudes, Values
Negroes, as perceivers, 188, 208
  as stimulus persons, 151, 188, 198, 208, 382
Newspaper reports as stimulus material, 125, 126, 128, 177–179, 180–184, 218, 219, 226, 243, 256, 257–287, Ch. 7, 341, 344, *see also* Accuracy in perception and the press, Headlines in newspapers, Typography
Newspapers, accuracy of, 259–264
  as a communication source, 324–328
  content analysis of, 257, 296
  headlines, 289–295, 332–333
  impressions of, 324–328
  order effects in, 265–287

Object perception, and its relation to person perception, 2, 8, 23, 31–45, 46, 186, 195, 206, 330, 351, 384
  constancy in, 330–336, 343, 347, 348
  sex factors in, 186
Occupations and person perception, 122, 188, 189, 215, 216, 356
Open-ended responding, *see* Free response techniques
'Order', and implicit personality theory, 160–161
  and person perception, 205
Order effects, in newspapers, 264–288
  serial, 237, 350, 371–372
Outputs, perceptual, 6, 7, 13, 16, 17, 21, 23, 120, 174, 206, 225, 232, 235, 255–256, 358, 363–365, 372, 374
Overt distal variables, 2, 9–13, 13, 14, 32, 54, 210–211, 332, 359–360

Parametric and non-parametric statistics, 60–63
Perceiver characteristics, *see* Current state of the perceiver, Personality, Sets, Stable characteristics of the perceiver, etc.
Perseveration effect, *see* Halo effect

Personality, 3, 12, 18, 236, 297, 355
  and implicit personality theory, 137, 159–162
  and object perception, 43, 195
  of the perceiver in person perception, 195–206
Persuasion, order of presentation in, 265–266
Photographs, as stimulus material, 26, 46, 186, 188, 191, 197, 198, 208, 210, 211, 214, 234, 243, 297, 318
  camera angle and lighting in, 306, 310
  captions to, 310, 328
  compared with verbal material, 204–207, 210, 211, 316, 318, *see also* Bodily characteristics, Facial expression, etc.
Physiognomy, *see* Facial expression
Political beliefs and person perception, 91–93, 97–98, 214–215
Politicians as stimulus persons, 179, 182, 184, 191–194, 215, 259, 269, 340–346
Postulate system, 122, *see also* Implicit personality theory
Power, 'internal' and 'external', 196, 197
  need for, 223–224
Prejudice, 151, 198, 211, 216, 299
Present context information, *see* Context information
Primacy and recency, 237, 264–288, 350, 371–372
Processing centre, 13, 16, 19, 21–22, Ch. 3, 174, 199, 227, 232, 361, 362–363, 372–375, *see also* Combination rules, Inference rules
Projection, 48, 197, 202, 222, 225
Projective tests, 201, 207, 216, 223, 244
Proximal variables, 3
Punctuation habits, 355

Radio as a communication channel, 243, 245
Readability formula, 286

Readiness, perceptual, 176, *see also* Conception and perception, Current state of the perceiver, Expectancy component in person perception, Sets, inferential

Realism, *see* Artificiality and realism in person perception research

Recall and perception, 5, 225, 227, 267, 284, 358, 359, *see also* Conception and perception, Stored information about stimulus person

Redundancy in stimulus array, 41, 169–170, 374

Reliability of measures, 74–87

Religious affiliation and person perception, 18, 67, 217–219, 231, 232

Remembering, *see* Recall and perception

Repertory grid technique, 98–99, 103, 268

Repressors, 199

Roles, 14, 188, 189–190, 211, Ch. 5, 364, *see also* Goals, Intentions of stimulus person

Rules, combination, *see* Combination rules

Rules, inference, *see* Inference rules

Scaling, *see* Multi-dimensional scaling, Semantic differential

Schizophrenia, paranoid, 166, *see also* Mental illness

Schoolteachers as perceivers, 97, 118

Selection of stimulus material, *see* Input selection

Self-concept, 198, 201, 205, 210, 211, 215, 217, *see also* Assumed similarity, Projection

Self-deprecation, 356

Self-descriptions, 46–47

Self-esteem, 199

Self-expression, 360

Semantic differential, 55, 56–116, 202–203, 214, 386

and the generalised distance score, 59–60, 72

concept order and, 112–114

concept-scale interaction in, 65, 68–71, 82

context effects in, 112–114

factor structure of, 63–74, 84–85, 94, 106–107, 116, 233, 386

labelling of response scales on, 57–58

number of scale units on, 57–58, 62, 77, 78–79, 109–110

parametric statistics used with, 60–62

prediction with, 89–93

reliability of, 58–59, 75–86

scale order in, 85–86

scale sampling for, 65–66

scale selection for, 67–70, 94–96, 115–116

speed of response with, 58–59

use of undivided scales on, 110–112

validity of, 55, 58–59, 88–109

Sensitizers, 199

Serial order effects, 237, 265–288, 350, 371–372

Sets, inferential, 228–231, 247

mental, 19, 38, 222, 225–231, 249, 266, *see also* Conception and perception, Current state of the perceiver, Expectancy component in person perception

Set theory, 134, 163

Sex factors, in implicit personality theory, 155–159

in object perception, 185

in perceptual constancy, 347

in person perception, 186–194, 252, 299, 362, 383

Sharpeners, 43

Similarity between perceiver and perceived, 44, 45, 48, *see also* Assumed similarity

Simulation of person perception, 366–382

Smiling response, 210

Soccer, 180–183, 191, 260–264

Social class, 18, 19, 211, 215–216, 221

Social desirability, 150

Social perception, 2–3, 215

Sociometry, 223, 233

Spectacles as a cue, 244

Speech topic, 183, 184

Spew hypothesis, 66

Stable characteristics of the perceiver, 11, 18–19, 155, 159, 174, 175, 223, 231, 232, 238–240, 268, 298, 334, 347, 355, 361–362, 365, 375–378, *see also* Age factors in person perception, Personality, Set, etc.

Stereoscope, 188, 360

Stereotyping, 151, 188, 299

Stored information about stimulus person, 5, 17–18, 24, 125, 174–175, 232, 347–359, *see also* Conception and perception, Recall and perception

Stuttering, 250

Style, grammatical, 355

Subject-matter store, *see* Stored information about stimulus person

T-groups, 53–222

Tape-recordings as stimulus material, 199, 225, 268, 284

Telephone as a communication channel, 245

Television as a communication channel, 242, 245, 256, 287, 297

Tests, projective, 201, 207, 216–217, 223, 244

psychological, 355–356

Thresholds, 361–362

Topic of speech, 182–184

Trait centrality, *see* Centrality of traits

Tuning sets, 225–226, *see also* Sets, inferential

Typography, and page makeup in newspapers, 319–324

legibility of, 319

Validity of measures, 88–109

Values, 39, 108, 175, 189, 199, 232, 244, 299

Verbal material compared with visual material, 302–305, 309, 311–317 318

Visual stimulus material, *see* Bodily characteristics, Facial expression, Gestures, Photographs, etc.

Visual interaction, 252–253

Vocal cues, 354

Vocational aptitude, 298

Voting behaviour, 91–93, 97

Warm-cold variable, 33–34, 120–121, 123–124, 126–129, 131, 177, 182, 234, *see also* Centrality of traits

Weber's law, 40

Whorfian hypothesis, 208, 216, 385